The Adi Granth

Or the holy scriptures of the Sikhs

Ernest Trumpp

Alpha Editions

This edition published in 2019

ISBN : 9789353898847

Design and Setting By
Alpha Editions
email - alphaedis@gmail.com

THE

ĀDI GRANTH,

OR

THE HOLY SCRIPTURES OF THE SIKHS,

TRANSLATED FROM

THE ORIGINAL GURMUKHĪ,

WITH INTRODUCTORY ESSAYS,

BY

DR. ERNEST TRUMPP,

PROFESSOR REGIUS OF ORIENTAL LANGUAGES AT THE UNIVERSITY OF MUNICH,
MEMBER OF THE ROYAL BAVARIAN ACADEMY OF SCIENCES.

PRINTED BY ORDER OF THE SECRETARY OF STATE FOR INDIA IN COUNCIL.

LONDON:
WM. H. ALLEN & CO., 13, WATERLOO PLACE, PALL MALL, S.W.
AND
N. TRÜBNER & CO., 57 AND 59, LUDGATE HILL, E.C.

1877.

PREFACE.

In offering this volume to the learned public, I think it right to premise a few words on the way and the peculiar circumstances under which the translation of the Sikh Granth has been made.

The work was entrusted to me by the India Office authorities towards the end of the year 1869, in the expectation that the translation could be made at home. But after I had fairly taken up the task, I soon perceived, that in spite of my knowledge of the modern North-Indian vernaculars, which I had formerly acquired in the country itself, and of Sanskrit and Prākrit, it was next to impossible to make a trustworthy translation of such a difficult book, as the Sikh Granth proved to be, without native assistance. There existed neither a grammar of the old Hinduī dialects nor a dictionary, and though I was able to make out many obscure words by dint of careful comparison with the modern idioms and the Prākrit, yet there remained a considerable residuum of words and grammatical forms to which I could get no clue, being destitute of all literary means.

When I reported this circumstance to the India Office, considerable difficulties arose, as the original plan had to be changed; but it was finally arranged that I should go myself to the Panjāb, in order to work first the Granth through with the aid of some Sikh Granthīs. I started therefore for India towards the close of the year 1870, in the expectation, that all difficulties would be easily surmounted there. But after I had succeeded in engaging two Sikh Granthīs at Lahore, I was not a little surprised, when they declared to me, that the Granth could not be translated in the literal grammatical way I desired. I soon convinced myself, that though they professed to understand the Granth, they had no knowledge either of the old grammatical forms or of the obsolete words; they could only give me some traditional explanations, which frequently proved wrong, as I found them contradicted by other passages, and now and then they could give me no explanation whatever; they had not even a clear insight into the real doctrines of the Granth. Other persons, who were recommended to me for their learning, I found equally ignorant. I went even to lay a number of difficult passages before some Granthīs at Amritsar, but was likewise sorely disappointed. Finally I gave up all hope of finding what I wanted, as I clearly saw, that the Sikhs, in consequence of their former warlike manner of life and the troublous times, had lost all learning; whereas the Brāhmaṇs, who alone would have had the necessary erudition to lend me a helping hand, never had deigned to pay any attention to the Granth, owing to the animosity which formerly existed between the Sikhs and the Hindū community.

Thus I was again thrown upon my own resources, and had to find out the way through this labyrinth for myself. But though the explanations of the Sikh Granthīs were in so many cases insufficient or futile, they were still of great use to me, as they indirectly helped me to find out the right track.

I was sure in my own mind that, as the language of the Granth had become already obsolete to a great extent, some attempts at some sort of lexicography must have been made in the preceding times, and I inquired therefore carefully after commentaries on the Granth. At first I was positively told that there was no such thing in existence; but in progress of time I succeeded in detecting three commentaries, two of which explained in a rough way a number of obsolete Hinduī and dēshī (provincial) words, and the other a number of Arabic and Persian words, which were received into the Granth in a very mutilated form. These commentaries, though very deficient, proved very useful to me, and I therefore got them copied, as their owners would not part with them.

I first attempted to write down the translation as I read on with the Granthīs; but I soon found that this would not do, as I frequently perceived that I had been misled by them. Nothing therefore remained to me, but to read first the whole Granth through, in order to make myself conversant with its contents and its style. As I went on, I noted down all grammatical forms and obsolete words I met with, and thus I gradually drew up a grammar and a dictionary, so that I could refer to every passage again, whenever I found it necessary for the sake of comparison.

After I had gone through the Granth in this wearisome way and prepared my tools, I returned to Europe in the spring of the year 1872, and began to write down the translation for the press. I had thus to do the work twice, but I saw, under the disadvantages under which I had been labouring, no other way open, if I wished to lay down a solid foundation and to give a translation which should be of any scientific value.

That in many passages, even after all the trouble I have taken, my translation may partly prove deficient, I fully allow, and in a first attempt on such a vast field, which has hitherto hardly been touched, this will appear natural enough to any man, who is conversant with the peculiar difficulties of such an undertaking.

The Sikh Granth is a very big volume, but as I have noted on p. cxxi, l. 3, and on p. cxxii, l. 4, incoherent and shallow in the extreme, and couched at the same time in dark and perplexing language, in order to cover these defects. It is for us Occidentals a most painful and almost stupefying task, to read only a single Rāg, and I doubt if any ordinary reader will have the patience to proceed to the second Rāg, after he shall have perused the first. It would therefore be a mere waste of paper to add also the minor Rāgs, which only repeat, in endless variations, what has been already said in the great Rāgs over and over again, without adding the least to our knowledge.

A number of introductory essays has been added to this translation, which, I trust, will not be unwelcome to the learned public, as they will serve to clear up all those points which may be of interest to science regarding the Sikh reformatory movement.

I have spent seven years on the elaboration of this volume, the task proving infinitely more arduous than I had ever imagined, and though I can hardly expect that the Granth will attract many readers, the less so, as Sikhism is a waning religion, that will soon belong to history, yet I venture to hope, that my labours will not be in vain. The Sikh Granth, which will always keep its place in the history of religion, lies now open before us, and we know authentically what their Gurus taught.

But the chief importance of the Sikh Granth lies in the linguistic line, as being the treasury of the old Hinduī dialects, and I hope that the day will not be far distant when these hitherto hidden treasures will be made available for the furtherance of modern Indian philology by being embodied in a grammar of the mediaeval Hinduī dialects.

As hitherto nothing of the Sikh Granth has been published, I have added in the Appendix the original text of the Japjī, which may serve as a specimen of the language, and at the same time as a criterion for the translation.

For this translation of the Granth, as well as for its publication, the public is indebted to Her Majesty's Government for India, which, in due consideration of the importance of the work, planned its execution and defrayed its expenses.

The English reader will no doubt detect in this volume many an expression that will appear to him more or less unidiomatic. For all such shortcomings I must beg his pardon, which he will surely grant, when he hears that English is not my mother-tongue, and that I was therefore often at a loss how to translate such abstruse philosophical matters clearly and correctly into an idiom which, since I no longer hear it spoken, is gradually receding from my memory.

ERNEST TRUMPP.

MUNICH, 23*rd January*, 1877.

TABLE OF CONTENTS.

INTRODUCTORY ESSAYS.

PAGE

PREFATORY REMARKS . . . . i–vii

I. THE LIFE OF BÂBÂ NĀNAK.

JANAM-SĀKHĪ OF BĀBĀ NĀNAK (A.) . . . . vii–xlv

JANAM-SĀKHĪ OF BĀBĀ NĀNAK (B.) . . . . . . xlvi–lxxvi

II. SKETCH OF THE LIFE OF THE OTHER SIKH GURUS.

2. GURU ANGAD . . . . lxxvii–lxxviii

3. GURU AMAR-DĀS . . . . lxxviii–lxxix

4. GURU RĀM-DĀS . . . . lxxix–lxxx

5. GURU ARJUN . . . . lxxx–lxxxii

6. GURU HAR-GŌVIND . . . . lxxxii–lxxxv

7. GURU HAR-RĀI lxxxv

8. GURU HAR-KISAN . . . . lxxxv–lxxxvi

9. GURU TĒG-BAHĀDUR . . . . lxxxvi–lxxxix

10. GURU GŌVIND SINGH . . . . lxxxix–xcvi

III. SKETCH OF THE RELIGION OF THE SIKHS . . . . xcvii–cxviii

IV. ON THE COMPOSITION OF THE GRANTH . . . . cxix–cxxi

V. ON THE LANGUAGE AND THE METRES USED IN THE GRANTH . . . . cxxii–cxxxviii

TRANSLATION OF THE ĀDI GRANTH.

	PAGE
Japjī	1–13
Sō Daru	14–16
Sō Purkhu	16–18
Sōhilā	18–21
RĀG SIRĪ RĀG	
Sabds.	
Nānak, I.–XXXIII.	21–40
Amar-dās, XXXIV.–LXIV.	40–57
Rām-dās, LXV.–LXX.	57–60
Arjun, LXXI.–C.	60–74
Astpadīs.	
Nānak, I.–XVII.	74–89
Amar-dās, XVIII.–XXV.	89–96
Arjun, XXVI.–XXVII.	96–98
Nānak, Jōgī andare	99–101
Arjun, Pai pāe	101–102
Nānak, Pahare	103–105
Rām-dās, Pahare	105–106
Arjun, Pahare	106
Čhants.	
Nānak, I.	107–108
Arjun, II.–III.	108–111
Rām-dās, Vaṇjārā	111–112
Vārs, I.–XXI.	113–125
Speech of the Bhagats.	
1. Kabīr, I.–III.	126
2. Trilōčan, I.–V.	126–127
3. Kabīr, I.–IV.	127–128
4. Bēṇī, I.–V.	128–130
5. Ravidās, I.–III.	130
RĀG MĀJHU.	
Sabds.	
Rām-dās, I.–VII.	131–134
Arjun, VIII.–L.	134–152
Astpadīs.	
Nānak, I.	152–153
Amar-dās, II.–XXXIII.	153–180
Rām-dās, XXXIV.	180–181
Arjun, XXXV.–XXXIX.	181–185
Arjun, Bārah māhā	185–188
Arjun, Din raiṇi	189
Vārs, I.–XXVII.	190–211
RĀG GAUṚĪ.	
Sabds.	
Nānak, I.–XX.	212–221
Amar-dās, XXI.–XXXVIII.	222–230
Rām-dās, XXXIX.–LXX.	231–246
Arjun, LXXI.–CCXLII.	246–314
Tēg-bahādur, CCXLIII.–CCLI.	314–316
Astpadīs.	
Nānak, I.–XVIII.	317–331
Amar-dās, XIX.–XXVII.	331–337
Rām-dās, XXVIII.–XXIX.	337–338
Arjun, XXX.–XLIV.	339–349
Čhants.	
Nānak, I.–II.	349–350
Amar-dās, III.–VII.	350–354
Arjun, VIII.–XI.	355–358
Bāvanakhrī, by Arjun, I.–LV.	358–377
Sukhmanī, by Arjun, I.–XXIV.	378–424
Thitīs, by Arjun, I.–XVII.	424–430
Vārs.	
Rām-dās, I.–XXXIII.	430–450
Arjun, XXXIV.–LIV.	450–458
Speech of the Bhagats.	
1. Kabīr, I.–LXXIV.	458–481
Bāvanakhrī, by Kabīr, 1–45	481–485
Thitīs, by Kabīr, 1–16	486–487
Vārs of Kabīr, 1–8	488
2. Nāmdēv	489
3. Ravidās	489–491
RĀG ASA.	
Sō dar, by Nānak	492–493
Sabds.	
Nānak, I.–XXXIX.	493–509
Amar-dās, XL.–LII.	509–516
Rām-dās, LIII.–LXVII.	516–521
Arjun, LXVIII.–CCXXX.	521–576
Tēg-bahādur, CCXXXI.	576
Astpadīs.	
Nānak, I.–XXII.	577–591
Amar-dās, XXIII.–XXXVII.	592–600

	PAGE
Arǰun, XXXVIII.-XLII.	600–602
The Paṭī, by Nānak	602–604
The Paṭī, by Amar-dās	604–605
Čhants.	
Nānak, I.-V.	606–609
Amar-dās, VI.-VII.	610–612
Rām-das, VIII.-XXI.	612–623
Arǰun, XXII.-XXXV.	623–634
Vārs.	
Nānak, I.-XX.	635–650
Angad, XXI.-XXIV.	650–652
Speech of the Bhagats.	
1. Kabīr, I.-XXXVII.	652–665
2. Nāmdēv, I.-V.	665–666
3. Ravidās, I.-VI.	666–668
4. Dhannā, I.-III.	668–669
5. Shēkh Farīd, I.-II.	669–670
SLŌKS OF KABĪR, 1-243	671–685
SLŌKS OF SHĒKH FARĪD, 1-130	685–694
SAVĀĪE OF THE BHAṬṬS.	
Savāīē on Nānak, by the Bhaṭṭ Kalasu, I.-X.	694–696
Savāīē on Angad, by the Bhaṭṭ Kalasahār, I.-V., by the Bhaṭṭ Kalu, VI.-X.	697–699
Savāīē on Amar-dās, by the Bhaṭṭ Kalhu, I.-IX., by the Bhaṭṭ Jālap, X.-XIV., by the Bhaṭṭ Kīratu, XV.-XVIII., by the Bhaṭṭ Bhikā, XIX. XX., by the Bhaṭṭ Salh, XXI., by the Bhaṭṭ Bhalhau, XXII.	700–705
SLŌKS OF TĒG-BAHĀDUR, 1-56	706–708
ONE ḌŌHRĀ OF GŌVIND SINGH	708

APPENDIX.

Original Text of the Japjī 709–715

ERRATA.

PAGE

xlviii, n. 5, Dēvānagarī, *read:* Dēvanāgarī.

lxxx, n. 1, *add at the end:* Cf. p. cxvi, note 3.

xciv, n. 1, l. 2, ਕਿਨ, *read:* ਰਿਨ.

xcv, l. 5 from below, *add after* ਆਂਖ: ਤਰੇ.

xcv, l. 4 from below, ਅਨੇਕ, *read:* ਏਕ.

xcv, l. 2 from below, ਮੈਂ, *read:* ਭੈਂ.

civ, n. 1, l. 4, अहकार, *read:* अहंकार.

cxxii, l. 11 from below, ਨਤਰੇ, *read:* ਨ ਤਰੇ.

cxxiii, l. 5 from below, ਰੁਹਭਤੀ, *read:* ਰੁਰਭਤੀ.

cxxxiii, l. 2 from below, ccxxi, *read:* cxxi.

37, n. 4, l. 1, ਪਰਿ, *read:* ਪਂਰਿ.

70, n. 1, l. 2, महत्तचादि, *read:* महत्तत्वादि.

93, n. 1, l. 4, Magar, *read:* Magahar or Mag-har (Cf. p. 463, n. 1).

98, n. 3, l. 1, Alokh, *read:* Alakh.

99, n. 2, l. 1, ਮਿਤੇ, *read:* ਮਿਠੇ.

159, n. 5, l. 1, ਭਿਲਾਉ, *read:* ਭਿਲਾਊ.

175, n. 1, l. 1, ਭੇਲਿ, *read:* ਭੇਲਿ.

210, n. 2, l. 1, Brahman, *read:* Brāhmaṇ.

210, n. 5, l. 1, Bhagavad-Gīta, *read:* Bhagavad-Gītā.

225, n. 2, l. 1, ਮਨ, *read:* ਭਨ.

PAGE

264, n. 3, l. 1, ਘਾਲੁ, *read:* ਘਾਲੁ.

305, n. 2, l. 1, ਭੀਠੀ, *read:* ਭੀਠੀ.

311, n. 1, l. 1, ਆਢੁ, *read:* ਆਰੁ.

319, n. 3, l. 1, ੲਰੰਗਾਰੁ, *read:* ਏਰੰਗਾਰੁ.

323, text, l. 24, Harīchand, *read:* Harīčand.

323, n. 5, l. 1, Harīchand, *read:* Harīcand.

323, n. 5, l. 2, Vishvāmitra, *read:* Višvāmitra.

324, n. 1, l. 1, Hiraṇyakashipu, *read:* Hiraṇyakašipu.

335, n. 1, l. 1, ਵਠਤੈ, *read:* ਵਰਤੈ.

338, n. 1, l. 1, ਮੁਲਾਇ, *read:* ਮੁਲਾਇ.

442, n. 1, l. 2, ਮੇਲਲਾ, *read:* ਮੇਵਲਾ.

460, n. 2, l. 1, ਭਰਵਰ, *read:* ਮਰਵਰ.

631, n. 2, l. 1, ਗਗਣੁ, *read:* ਤਗਣੁ.

657, n. 3, l. 1, ਪਹਿਤਿ, *read:* ਪਹਿਤਿ.

663, n. 1, l. 1, *insert* "which all MSS. exhibit" *after* ਪਵਨ.

663, n. 4, l. 1, ਭੰਡੀ, *read:* ਭੰੜੀ.

668, n. 4, l. 1, ਸਭਾਉ, *read:* ਸਮਾਉ.

677, n. 1, l. 1, ਮੁਠੀ, *read:* ਮੂਠੀ.

691, n. 3, l. 2, ਡੀਂਝ, *read:* ੜੀਂਝ.

INTRODUCTORY ESSAYS.

I.

THE LIFE OF NĀNAK ACCORDING TO THE JANAM-SĀKHĪS.

PREFATORY REMARKS.

When I was working my way through the Granth at Lahore, I felt naturally desirous to obtain some details of the life of Nānak, the founder of the religious system of the Sikhs, whose words, as preserved in the Sikh Granth, were so often dark and unintelligible to me, in order to get thereby a clearer insight into his maxims and his way of thinking. I found that different accounts of the life of Nānak were current among the Sikhs, called *Janam-patrīs* or *Janam-sākhīs*.[1] I compared different copies, and found that they agreed on the whole, but deviated in minor points, one or other story being either added or left out. During my stay at Lahore (1870–72) a Janam-sākhī was lithographed with not unfair and in some cases very bold woodcuts. By comparing this copy with the current manuscripts I found that everything, which appeared to throw a dubious or unfavourable light on Nānak, had been left out, whereas other things, which spoke of his deification, had been interpolated. More close research soon convinced me that the usual Sikh tradition concerning Nānak could by no means be trusted; I had reason enough to assume that the formation of myths about their first Guru had already progressed very far, notwithstanding that his life falls altogether within the period of historical light, as among the rubbish of miraculous and often absurd stories I could detect very few historical facts which deserved credit. The man, as I had him before me in his own words and sayings, as contained in the Granth, would by no means agree with what the miraculous stories had made of him.

Without mentioning my suspicions to the Sikh Granthīs, who would have considered every such doubt on the deity of Nānak as a heinous crime, to be atoned for only by endless transmigrations, I made diligent inquiries as to the existence of older and more trustworthy traditions

[1] ਜਨਮਪਤ੍ਰੀ, literally a leaf of paper, on which the birth of a child, the year, the lunar date, and the configuration of the planets at the moment of birth, are set down. Usually a horoscope, founded on those circumstances, is added. The Janam-patrī is drawn up by the family Brāhmaṇ, and serves in India as a birth-certificate. ਜਨਮਸਾਖੀ signifies *evidence or story of the birth* (*or life*) *of a person*. The words are frequently interchanged, though Janam-sākhī usually implies *episode or story* of the life of a person.

regarding the life of Nānak. I applied to different persons, who, I had heard, were in possession of old Gurmukhī manuscripts, in order to get Janam-sākhīs of Nānak, but all my efforts proved in vain, none but the usual compilations being forthcoming.

After my return to Europe in 1872, some manuscripts of the Granth were forwarded to me from the India Office Library, for the prosecution of my labours, and to these some other Gurmukhī manuscripts were added, in the expectation that the one or the other might prove useful in my researches. In looking them over, I found an old manuscript, partly destroyed by white ants, the early characters of which, resembling those of the old copy of the Granth, preserved at Kartārpur, and signed by Guru Arjun himself, at once caught my eye. On the first leaf it contained in Sanskrit letters the short title, **नानक का ग्रन्थ जनमसाखी का**, *A book of Nānak, referring to his birth* (*or life*). The copy had been presented to the Library of the East India House, according to the entry on the first leaf, by the famous H. T. Colebrooke, without his being aware, as it appears, of the contents of the book. As soon as I commenced to read the book, I observed with great pleasure, that this was a description of the life of Nānak quite different from all the others I had hitherto seen. As the characters, so also was the idiom, in which it was composed, old and in many words and expressions agreeing with the diction of Guru Arjun.

After a lengthened examination and comparison of this manuscript with the later Janam-sākhīs, I am satisfied that this is the fountain, from which all the others have drawn largely: for the stories, as far as they are common to both relations, very frequently agree verbally, with the only difference, that the later Janam-sākhīs have substituted more modern forms for old words, which with the progress of time had become unintelligible. This old Janam-sākhī, as hinted already, belongs, according to all external and internal marks, to the latter end of the time of Guru Arjun or to that of his immediate successor. The Granth, which Guru Arjun compiled of the writings of his four predecessors and the old famous Bhagats, as well as of his own numerous poetical effusions, is cited throughout, without any paraphrase, whereas the later Janam-sākhīs have deemed it already necessary to add to every quotation from the Granth a paraphrase in the modern idiom.

We are enabled now, by the discovery of this old Janam-sākhī, which is now-a-days, as it appears, quite unknown to the Sikhs themselves, to distinguish the older tradition regarding Nānak from the later one, and to fix, with some degree of verisimility, the real facts of his life. There is no lack, even in this old relation, of many wonderful stories, as indeed might be expected from Indians, owing to their wild, uncurbed phantasy and the low standard of education among the masses of the population; but compared with the later Janam-sākhīs, which enter into the minutest details, in order to satisfy curiosity, and which have no sense but for the miraculous, however absurd, it is relatively sober.

We subjoin here a brief summary of the life of Nānak according to this oldest authority, in order to contrast it with the narrations of the later compilers.

Nānak was born in the Samvat year 1526, in the month of Vaisākh (= A.D. 1469, April–May), in a village, called Talvaṇḍī on the banks of the Rāvī (the Hydraotes of the Greeks), not far above Lahore.[1] His father's name was Kālū, by caste a Khatrī, of the Vēdī family or clan, a plain

[1] Talvaṇḍī, the birthplace of Nānak, is situated in the Zilā (ضلع, in Panjābī pronounced **ਜਿਲਾ**) of Lahore (Panjābī **ਲਾਹੌਰ**), in the Collectorate (**ਤਸੀਲ** = تحصيل) of Sarakpur. The place is now called Nānakāṇā (**ਨਾਨਕਾਣਾ**); it has a Gur-dvār and is a place of pilgrimage for the Sikhs. Malcolm (Sketch of the Sikhs, p. 7, note 7) is mistaken, in placing the village on the banks of the Biās (Panjābī **ਬਿਆਸਾ**), called now Raipur. There is in the Jalandhar Duāb a place called Tilvaṇḍī, near Sultānpur, not far from the confluence of the Biās and Satluj (thus this river is pronounced in Panjābī), but it is not the birthplace of Nānak.

farmer, who held also the office of ਪਟਵਾਰੀ paṭvārī (a valuer of the produce of the fields) in the service of the feudal Lord of the village.[1]

At his birth the whole Hindū pantheon appeared and announced that a great Bhagat (saint) was born to save the world.

Of his childhood nothing particular is mentioned, except that he did not play like other boys of his age, but was always occupied in his meditations on the Supreme Lord.

At the age of seven his father took him to a Hindū school to learn to read and write. He is said to have surprised the Hindū schoolmaster by his superior knowledge, the pupil commencing at once to instruct the master, when the latter gave him a wooden slate, on which the letters of the alphabet were written. In proof of this, thirty-four verses from the Granth are quoted, inscribed the "*wooden slate*" (ਪਟੀ, paṭṭī), which Nānak is supposed to have uttered on that occasion, but, no doubt, the story was invented in order to account for the verses, as is evident from other cases of the kind.

The further development of Nānak's character is not touched upon, apparently because at that time nothing was known about it. One story only is inserted, which tells how Nānak, whilst grazing his father's buffaloes, allowed them to break into a cultivated field and destroy the crop. When the owner of the field sued Nānak's father for damages, Nānak denied his guilt, and when the field was inspected, it was found uninjured.

The marriage of Nānak, as well as that of his sister Nānakī with Jairām, which to the later compilers have offered such an exuberant field, is totally omitted here. It is only briefly remarked that by the order of God two sons were born in the house of Nānak, Lakhmī-dās and Sirī-čand, but that Nānak continued to lead a recluse life.

Then follows a miraculous story that one day Nānak laid himself down under a tree and fell asleep. By chance Rāe Bulār came there and saw that while the shadows of the other trees had travelled round, that of the tree under which Nānak slept remained stationary. This circumstance induced Rāe Bulār to impress on Kālū, who bore ill-will towards his son on account of his dreaming propensities, that Nānak was a great man and that the father was exalted by him; but these words made no impression on Kālū's mind, who slightingly answered, that the things of God only God knew. The later Janam-sākhīs have embellished and enlarged this story by adding another miracle, that a large black snake expanded its hood over Nānak in order to protect him from the glowing rays of the sun.

Then it is stated expressly, that Nānak always kept company with Faqīrs and was averse to any earnest labour or calling, which greatly alarmed his family, who would not recognize his divine calling, and especially his worldly-minded father Kālū, whom the narrators seem to take a secret pleasure in describing as a miser. His family at last considered him a *lunatic* and began to mourn this calamity.[2] At the instigation of the relatives a physician was called, but he could do nothing, Nānak showing himself the cleverer of the two.

It is very significant, that this whole circumstance is carefully passed over in the later Janam-sākhīs, as every other point which throws an unfavourable or doubtful light on Nānak.

At last his parents sent Nānak to Sultānpur, to his brother-in-law Jairām, who held an appointment in the commissariat of Navāb Daulat Khān. They probably despaired of bringing him into an orderly course of life at home; but according to the original text, he was sent by the

[1] Talvaṇḍī is mentioned as the property of Rāe Bhōe; the Lord in Nānak's time was Rāe Bulār, a Musalmān Rājput of the Bhaṭṭī family, a descendant of Rāe Bhōe.

[2] The original text (p. 26) runs thus: ਤਧਿ ਸਾਰਾ ਪਰਵਾਰੁ ਸਭੁ ਕੁਟੰਬੁ ਵੇਰੀਆ ਦਾ ਲਾਗਾ ਝੂਰਣਿ ਆਖਣ ਲਗੇ ਜੋ ਵਡਾ ਹੈਫੁ ਹੋਆ ਜੋ ਕਾਲੂ ਦਾ ਪੁਤੁ ਦਿਵਾਨਾ ਹੋਆ.

order of God. By the good services of his brother-in-law, Nānak also was appointed to the commissariat, and he conducted himself to general satisfaction. His wife and two children he left behind at Talvaṇḍī, his domestic life being by no means happy, owing, it appears, to his own fault, as nothing is reported prejudicial to his wife. At Sultānpur he was joined by a certain Mardānā, by profession a begging musician of the Musalmān persuasion. After his daily work he spent his nights with Mardānā in praising God, Mardānā playing the rebeck, whilst he himself improvised verses to the tunes.

One morning he went to the canal to bathe. Whilst bathing, angels seized him and carried him to the divine presence. Here he received the prophetic initiation, a cup of nectar being presented to him with the injunction to proclaim the name of Hari on earth. After this he was brought back again to the canal, whence he returned home. He was received with amazement: for his servant, to whom he had handed over his clothes when entering the water, had run home on Nānak's disappearance, and spread the news that he was drowned. On hearing this intelligence, even the Khān himself is said to have ridden to the spot and to have given orders to the fishermen to search with their nets for the corpse of Nānak, but they had been unable to find it.

After this accident, which somehow seems to be based on a historical fact, Nānak divided all he had among the poor, left his house, and turned Faqīr, Mardānā accompanying him. The Khān endeavoured to retain a faithful servant, but Nānak stood firm in his resolution.

The later compilations have given to this story quite a different turn. According to them Nānak goes to Sultānpur by the advice of Rāe Bulār, who can bear no longer Kālū's disrespectful treatment of his wonderful son. At Sultānpur he is appointed to the commissariat. But he gives alms so abundantly, that Jairām considers it advisable to report it to Kālū, who, in consequence of this news, comes to Sultānpur, and sharply enjoins on his son a more parsimonious conduct. At Nānak's request his accounts are examined by Jairām, but a considerable surplus appears in his favour. In order to accustom Nānak to economy, his marriage is planned by Jairām at Kālū's request, and this is described in full detail. But notwithstanding his married state Nānak continues his former habits of giving lavish alms, which leads to domestic quarrels and the interference of his parents-in-law. This is very graphically described, the later compilers here apparently feeling very sure of the ground under their feet.

To the story of the bath in the canal, which could not quite be set aside, a different turn is given. Nānak's initiation into the Guruship is not mentioned (though this is the very turning-point of the whole story), as according to these later compilations *Nānak has entered the world as Avatār, as the Formless one himself.* It is therefore related, that one of the Gōvind-faqīrs advised him to bathe in the river daily, in order to cure himself of a liver-complaint. One day Nānak, whilst taking a bath, was lost in the river. On this the rumour was spread that Nānak had been guilty of embezzlement. When he reappeared after three days (it is not even hinted where he was during those three days), the Khān ordered an inquiry to be made into his accounts, but it turned out that 760 Rupees were due to him, which Nānak would not accept, but taking his discharge retired into the wilderness, leaving his wife and children behind.

As it appears, Nānak stayed at first in the vicinity of Sultānpur. His first saying, which made some noise amongst the people, was: "*There is no Hindū and no Musalmān,*" but this brought upon him again the charge of madness. At the instigation of the Kāzī the Navāb Daulat Khān summoned him to his presence in order to interrogate him about this new doctrine. It was just the time of noonday-prayer and the Khān invited Nānak to accompany him to the mosque. The Kāzī said prayers, but Nānak, instead of listening devoutly, began to laugh. Prayers being over the Kāzī complained of the irreverent conduct of Nānak. Being called to account by the Khān he replied, that he laughed, because the prayers of the Kāzī were nugatory. Being asked for a nearer explanation he continued, that the Kāzī had left a foal in his courtyard, in which there was an open well; and that whilst saying prayers his thoughts were always wandering back to the foal, lest it should fall into the well. On this the Kāzī fell down at Nānak's feet and confessed that it was true. Nānak rose at once in the estimation of all, and the Khān dismissed him graciously. He now commenced wandering about the country, accompanied by Mardānā, the musician.

Up to this point both relations agree, at least in substance, though the later compilations, out of love for the miraculous, strive hard to exaggerate everything into the supernatural. But with the commencement of the wanderings of Nānak nearly all points in common cease and the old and the later tradition diverge in such a manner that they cannot be reconciled. This proves sufficiently, either that very little was known about them or that very little could be said about them, as the old Janam-sākhī testifies. The later tradition, which pretends to have a knowledge of all the details of the life of Nānak, was therefore compelled to put forth as voucher for its sundry tales and stories Bhāī Bālā, who is said to have been the constant companion of Nānak from his youth up, whereas our old Janam-sākhī does not even once mention Bhāī Bālā, though at every new wandering of Nānak it gives the names of his companions. If Bhāī Bālā had been the constant companion of Nānak and a sort of mentor to him, as he appears now in the current Janam-sākhīs, it would be quite incomprehensible, why never a single allusion should have been made to him in the old tradition.

We will now briefly sum up here, what the old Janam-sākhī has to say about the further life of Nānak.

His *first* wandering is said to have been to the *east.* There he came to a certain Shēkh Sajan, who had built a temple for Hindūs and a mosque for Muhammadans. He received all who came to him, with ostensible friendliness, but murdered them, whilst sleeping, and plundered their goods. Nānak got quickly at the bottom of his rascality and convinced him of his sinful life, which brought him to repentance.

At Dillī he is said to have vivified a dead elephant. But when the then emperor, who had heard of this miracle, called on Nānak to kill the elephant and to vivify it in his presence, he prudently declined.

Also Ṭhags, with whom he fell in on his way, he brought to repentance by his firm and intrepid conduct.

Other adventures, which he is narrated to have experienced, are so childish and nonsensical, that it is not worth while mentioning them.

At the capture of Sayyidpur he is reported to have been taken prisoner by the troops of Bābar, but by a miracle he attracted the attention of Bābar, who released him with the other prisoners. As Bābar conquered the Panjāb in 1524, a personal meeting of Nānak with Bābar is not impossible, but it is not very probable. For Nānak speaks in the Granth several times of the great calamities which at that time befell various cities of the Panjāb; Bābar also is mentioned by him, but no allusion whatever is made to his having come into personal contact with Bābar.

The meetings and verbal contests with other Faqīrs and Shēkhs, which are described at full length, are in themselves very probable, but in other respects of no importance, except that they give some hints to the mental development of Nānak. After some lengthened wanderings Nānak retraced his steps to his home at Talvaṇḍī.

His unquiet spirit gave him no rest at home and he soon commenced his *second* wandering, which was directed to the *south.* The incidents of this period also are of little consequence. That on this excursion he should have come to *Ceylon* (Singhala dvīpa), as is reported, is in the highest degree unlikely. The whole story is so mixed up with the miraculous, that it bears the stamp of fable on its front. It is based on altogether erroneous suppositions, the king and the inhabitants of Ceylon being represented as common Hindūs, the Sikh author being quite unaware of the fact that the popular religious belief there was Buddhism. That Nānak founded there a "Sangat" (congregation), the order of whose divine service even is detailed, contradicts all history, and is an invention of later times, when Sikhism had commenced to spread to the south. From this tour Nānak is said to have returned to Talvauḍī and to have spent some time at home.

His *third* wandering he directed to the *north*, where he is reported to have visited Kashmīr, which is not improbable.

On this tour he is said to have eaten the poisonous fruits and blossoms of the Akk-tree in a dried state. Nothing remarkable is mentioned on this tour, except that he had a long conversation with a Kashmīrī Paṇḍit, which ended in the Paṇḍit's becoming a disciple of Nānak. His visit to mount Sumēru, where he is reported to have had a long discussion with Mahādēv and the chief Jōgīs, belongs of course to the realm of fiction.

His *fourth* wandering he is said to have directed to the *west*, going on a pilgrimage to *Mekkah*. On arriving at Mekkah, he laid himself down, and by chance stretched his feet towards the Ka'bah. The Kāzī Ruknu-ddīn, on observing this, reproached Nānak with irreverence towards the house of God. Nānak replied: "Put my feet in that direction, where the house of God is not." The Kāzī turned the feet of Nānak, but wherever he turned them, thither the Ka'bah also turned. On account of this miracle the Kāzī kissed the feet of Nānak and had a long conversation with him, in which he was, of course, out-argued by Nānak. This hajǰ of Nānak is a favourite theme with the Sikhs and a whole book has been written about it called ਮਕੇ ਦੀ ਗੋਸਟਿ *The Conversation of Mekkah*, which is eagerly read by them. Owing to their credulity and utter want of geographical and historical knowledge, no doubt of the reality of this hajǰ seems to have occurred to them, though it is as clear as daylight, that the whole story is an invention from beginning to end.

His *fifth* wandering Nānak is said to have made to *Gōrakh-haṭarī*, a place not yet discovered by geographers. Of this expedition nothing is reported except a conversation with the eighty-four Siddhs,[1] who belong likewise to the realm of phantasy.

Nānak closed his life at Kartārpur in the Jalandhar Duāb, in the bosom of his family, with whom he seems to have become reconciled towards the close of his earthly career, though all the Janam-sākhīs observe a deep silence on this point and only mention the bare fact. When he felt his death approaching, he nominated, to the great disappointment of his two sons, his devoted servant and disciple Lahaṇā (or Angad) his successor in the Guruship. He died in the Samvat year 1595, on the tenth of the light half of the month of Asū (A.D. 1538, about the 10th of October).[2]

This is the sum of all that can be gathered from this oldest source as to the life of Nānak. It is a biography containing very little to attract our interest and, *mutatis mutandis*, applicable to nearly every Hindū Faqīr. If more could have been said of Nānak, we might be sure, that his devoted disciples, who revered in him the saviour of the world, would not have passed it over in silence. The writers of the later Janam-sākhīs, to whom this picture of Nānak appeared too scanty and mean, did their best to embellish it with all sorts of wonderful tales and stories, but in comparison with this older tradition they cannot be held in any account.

[1] Siddha, *i.e.* a perfect Jōgī, of whom generally eighty-four are enumerated, but their names are nowhere stated; they are popularly considered as a kind of demi-gods.

[2] This is the date given by the old Janam-sākhī; the later compilations give the year 1539; see the translation.

We append here a literal translation of the old Janam-sākhī marked **A**. Of the current Janam-sākhīs, which differ from each other merely in minor points, we give only those parts, which are of interest for the sake of comparison. This later compilation is marked **B**.[1]

A.

JANAM-SĀKHĪ OF BĀBĀ NĀNAK.

By the favour of the true Guru!

The holy true Guru came to save the world; in the Kali-yug Bābā Nānak was born, the supreme Brahm's own devotee.

By the favour of the true Guru!

In Sambat, 1526, Bābā Nānak was born in the month of Vaisākh;[2] in a moonlight night at an early hour, while yet about a watch of the night was remaining, he was born. Unbeaten sounds were produced at the gate of the Lord. The thirty-three crores of gods paid homage (to the child Nānak). The sixty-four Jōginīs, the fifty-two heroes, the six ascetics, the eighty-four Siddhs, the nine Nāths, paid homage,[3] "because a great devotee has come to save the world; to him homage should be paid!"

At that time Kālū, a Khatrī by caste, a Vēdī (by clan), was living at Talvaṇḍī, a village of Rāe Bhōe, the Bhaṭṭī; there (Nānak) was born.

When he became big, he began to play with the boys,[4] but the views of the boys and his were different. In his spirit he was occupied with the Lord.

When Bābā (Nānak) was five years old, he began to talk of the Shāstras and of the Vēdas; whatever he says, that he (also) understands; everybody received comfort from him. The Hindūs say, that some form of a god has become incarnate and the Musalmāns say, that some holy man of God has been born.

[1] I used for this purpose a Gurmukhī MS. belonging to myself, a MS. belonging to the India Office Library, marked $\frac{495}{2885}$ Bibliotheca Leydeniana, and a lithographed copy, published at Lahore (1871) with the title: ਜਨਮਸਾਖੀ ਬਾਬੇ ਨਾਨਕਜੀਦੀ ਹਸਬ ਫੁਰਮਾਇਸ਼ ਹਾਫਜ਼ ਕੁਤਬ ਦੀਨ ਲਾਹੌਰ ਛਾਪੇਖਾਨੇ ਮੁਰਤਜ਼ਵੀ ਦਿਹਲੀ ਹਾਫਜ਼ ਅਜ਼ੀਜ਼ ਦੀਨ ਦੇ ਅਪਰਾਰ. This book, containing many bold woodcuts, is utterly spoiled in the latter half by the maliciousness of the scribe, the letters being purposely so disfigured, that they can no longer be read without the help of a manuscript. Large extracts are also contained in the ਸਿਖਾਂ ਦੇ ਰਾਜ ਦੀ ਵਿਥਿਆ, published at Ludihāṇā by the American Mission Press, 1868.

[2] Both Janam-sākhīs agree as to the year, but not as to the month; for according to B (2), he was born in the month of Katak (middle of October—the middle of November). The month Vaisākh is middle of April—middle of May; his birth took therefore place either in May or November of 1469 A.D.

[3] Compare B (2). [4] See B (3).

When the Bābā was seven years old, Kālū said: "O Nānak, read!"[1] Then he brought Guru Nānak to the schoolmaster. Kālū said: "O schoolmaster, teach this one to read!" The schoolmaster wrote a slate and gave it to him, containing the thirty-five letters (of the Gurmukhī alphabet); the slate (is contained) in the Rāg Āsā, Mahalā I.[2] The first word he read was: "By the favour of the holy true Guru!"

[Now follows a quotation of thirty-four verses from the Rāg Āsā, but without any translation or paraphrase being added to it. After some conversation between the schoolmaster and Nānak on the subject of these verses the story continues.]

The Paṇḍit became astonished and paid reverence (to him), "because this is a perfect one." "What comes into thy mind, that do!" Then the Guru Bābā went home and sat down. It was the order of the Lord, that he did no work whatever. When he sits down, he remains seated; when he goes to sleep, he remains asleep. He associates with Faqīrs. His father Kālū became astonished, what would become of him.[3]

. . . . (two leaves being lost). Nothing of the field of this one is spoiled.[4] Then the Bhaṭṭī said: "Sir, my field indeed is laid waste; I am robbed, my field is spoiled. Procure me justice, if not, I go to the Turks." Guru Nānak answered: "O Dīvān, health (to (thee)! if one blade be spoiled or cut off, then answer must be made for it; but send thou thy own man and look!" Then Rāe Bulār sent his own footmen. . . . . . . (a lacuna in the MS.) Not one blade was destroyed. Then the Bābā made a Sabd;[5] it is written in the Rāg Sūhī, Mahalā I.[6] [four verses follow without a paraphrase]. Then Rāe Bulār called that Bhaṭṭī a liar. Nānak and Kālū both went home.

Then came the order of the Lord, that in the house of Guru Nānak two sons should be born, Lakhmī-dās and Sirī-čand. But Nānak's retirement from the world was not given up; Guru Nānak going to trees remained (there) retired from the world (MS. p. 21).

Then one day the Bābā Guru Nānak went and fell asleep in a garden.[7] The day went down again and he did not rise. At that time Rāe Bulār, the Bhaṭṭī chief, was occupied in this business (of his chieftainship, *i.e.* measuring land). Coming and coming when he entered the garden, some one had fallen asleep under a tree. But when he looked on, he saw, that the shade of the other trees had gone, and that the shade of this tree was remaining. Rāe Bulār said: "Awaken him!" When he was raised, it was found, that it was the son of Kālū. Then Rāe Bulār said: "Friends, we have seen a wonderful thing, and look also at this, it is not empty!"[8] Then Rāe Bulār went home and sent for Kālū, and said to him: "Kālū, don't be saying to this thy son: 'Fie upon thee, die!' he is a great man, my town is a sacrifice to him. Kālū, thou hast become exalted and I also am exalted, in whose town this one has been born." Kālū said: "The things of God even God knows," and went home.

Guru Nānak kept company with Faqīrs, with any one (else) he did not converse. The whole family was grieved thereby, and said: "He has become mad." Then came the mother of Guru Nānak

[1] See B (3).

[2] Mahálā I. designates the writings of Nānak, Mahálā II. those of Angad, etc. Every piece is thus marked in the Granth. The paṭṭī (or wooden slate) is found in the Rāg Āsā (Lahore lithographed edition of the Granth), p. 477 *sqq*.

[3] Compare B (3), at the end.

[4] See B. (4), where the same story is related.

[5] The Čaupadā and Dupadā are called by one common name मघर, Sabd.

[6] See Rāg Sūhī, Sabd, Mah. I. v. 7.

[7] See B (5).

[8] That is: it forebodes something important.

and said to him: "Son, it does not behove thee, to sit with Faqīrs, thou hast a house and family, daughters[1] and sons, do some work! leave off making continually good words! the people laugh at us, that the son of Kālū has become mad." Such words his mother spake, but they made no impression whatever on the heart of Nānak.

He went away again and fell down. As he had fallen, so he passed four days. When she had ceased rubbing him,[2] the wife of the Bābā came to her mother-in-law and said: "O mother-in-law, how canst thou sit down, whose son has fallen? It is now the fourth day, he does neither eat nor drink." Then his mother came and said: "Son, it does not become thee to fall down; eat and drink something and look after thy fields and crops! be a little attentive to thy work! thy whole family is grieved. And, son, what does not please thee, that do not, we will not say anything to thee: why hast thou gone away again?" Then Kālū heard of it and came. He said: "Son, what are we commanding thee? but to do work is good. Though the sons of Khatrīs have money, yet they do (some) work. Son, our field out there stands ripe (for the sickle) and (that) it may not be wasted, how, if thou wouldst be standing in it? then the people will say: 'the son of Kālū has become a good son.' The field is with its owners, O son!" Then Guru Nānak said: "O father, a private field is ploughed by us, that we take care of. The plough is carried over it by us, seed is sown, a hedge made round it; day and night we stand and protect it. O father, we do not take care of our own field, what knowledge have we of another's (field)?" Then Kālū became astonished and said: "Look, people, what this one is saying!" Then Kālū said: "When hast thou cultivated a private field? Give up such foolish talk; but if it please thee, I will give thee at the next harvest a new field under cultivation, it will be seen, how thou wilt make it ripen and eat!" Guru Nānak answered: "Father, we have now cultivated a field and it has grown up well, it looks quite well." Kālū said: "Son, I have not seen any field of thine, what dost thou say?" Then Guru Nānak answered: "Father, this field has been cultivated by us, of which thou wilt hear." Then Bābā Nānak recited one Sabd, in the Rāg Sōraṭhi it is contained, Mahalā I.[3] [now follows the Sabd with one Rahāu]. Then the Bābā said again: "O father: our field is sown, as thou hast heard. Our field is sown and stands and has grown up. We have so much reliance on this field, that the whole government tax will fall off, it will make no further demand. Sons and daughters will become happy, and the poor, brothers and relatives, all will be profited thereby. The Lord, for whom I have done farming work, gives me much assistance; for that day, when there is union with him, I am much rejoicing. Whatever I ask, that he is giving me. Father, such a great Lord I have sought and found. Traffic, service, shop, all has been entrusted by him (to me)." Then Kālū became astonished and said: "Such a Lord, O son, we have never seen nor heard of." Nānak answered: "O father, by whom my Lord has been seen, by them he is praised." Then Guru Nānak recited one Sabd in the Rāg Āsā, Mahalā I.[4] [now follows one Sabd, consisting of four verses]. Then Kālū said: "Give up these things and walk after the manner of other people; it is nothing to live without a calling." Then Bābā Nānak remained silent. Kālū rose and went after his work. He said: "This work is beyond our strength, but may not the field

[1] It appears hence, that Nānak had also daughters, not only two sons, as stated by the later Janam-sākhīs.

[2] The original is: ਜਾਂ ਮਲਿ ਚੁਕੀ; ਮਲਲਾ, to rub (a person in a swoon). Had Nānak epileptic fits? In B. (6) this is more represented under the head of idleness, Nānak is called there a ਮਲਖਟੂ, an idler. In the Lahore lithographed edition of the now current Janam-sākhī it is related (p. 387), that Nānak assumed the behaviour of a *madman*, in order to drive the people away (ਦਿਵਾਨਾ ਤਉਰ ਪਕੜਿਆ). Something seems to have been the matter with him, as is now and then hinted at.

[3] See, Sōraṭhi, Sabd II. (1), Mah. I.

[4] See, Āsā, Čaupadā I., Mah. I.

outside be damaged!" Then came his mother and began to give him instruction: "O son, forget for four days the name! stand up, put on clothes and go about in the lanes and streets, that the people may be reassured (of thy health) and that every one may say: 'The son of Kālū has become well (again).'" Then the Bābā recited a Sabd [now follows a Sabd, consisting of four verses].[1]

Then his mother rose and went away and gave information (as to his state) in the family. The whole family and clan of the Vēdīs began to grieve and to say, that a great calamity had happened, that the son of Kālū had become mad.

Then Bābā Nānak did neither eat nor drink for three months. The whole clan of the Vēdīs became dispirited. All began to say: "Kālū, how canst thou sit down quietly, whose son has fallen (sick)? Call some physician and give him some medicine, thy son will become well, then what is the outlay of some Rupees?" Kālū rose and called a physician. When the physician had come, he took the arm of Nānak to feel his pulse. Nānak pulled away his arm and standing on his legs he rose and said: "O physician, what art thou doing?" The physician answered: "I look after the disease, that may be in thy spirit." The Bābā laughed and uttered a Slōk [now follow four verses].[2] The Bābā made also a Sabd on the subject of the physician in the Rāg Mālār [there follow four verses].[3]

The physician being afraid stood in the shop and said: "Brother, don't be anxious, this is removing the pain." Then the Bābā uttered a Sabd, in the Rāg Gauṛī, Mahalā I. [there follow six verses].[4]

Then came the order of the Lord, that Guru Nānak went away (from home). The brother-in-law of Bābā Nānak was Jairām, who was the steward of the Nabāb Daulat Khān.[5] Jairām had heard that Nānak was distracted in his mind and did no work whatever. He wrote a letter that Nānak should come to him. Guru Nānak read this letter and said: "May it be so, I will join Jairām." The people of the house said, that it would be good, if he would go, perhaps his mind would become settled there. The Bābā rose and went to Sultānpur. The wife of the Bābā began to weep and said: "Thou wast never kissing me before, thou art now going abroad, how wilt thou come (again)?" The Bābā said: "O silly one, what were we doing here? and what shall we do there? I am of no use to thee." She rose and addressed again this petition to him: "When thou wast sitting in the house, then I had, in my view, the sovereignty of the whole world. O dear, this world is of no use to me whatever." Then the Guru became tender and said: "Do not be anxious: every day the sovereignty shall be thine." She said: "Sir, I shall not remain behind, take me with thee." The Bābā answered: "It is (the order) of the Lord, that I am going. If I shall gain some livelihood there, I shall call thee there. Mind thou my order." Then she kept silence. Guru Nānak then took leave from his relatives and friends and went to Sultānpur. He arrived there and met with Jairām. Jairām was very happy and said: "Brother Nānak, it is very good." Then Jairām went to the court and made this petition to Daulat Khān: "Nabāb, health! one brother-in-law of mine has come; he wishes to meet the Nabāb." Daulat Khān said: "Go and bring him!" Jairām went and brought Guru Nānak; he put some present (before the Nabāb) at meeting with him. The Khān was much pleased and said: "What is the name of this one?" Jairām said: "Sir, his name is Nānak." The Khān rejoined: "He seems to be a good and honest man, entrust my work to him!" Nānak became happy and smiled. The Khān gave him a dress of honour, and Guru Nānak and Jairām then went home. They com-

[1] The place, where this Sabd is to be found, is not indicated.

[2] The place, where the Slōk occurs, is not indicated.

[3] To be found in Malār, Sabd 7, Mah. I., but the verses are given there in a different order.

[4] See Gauṛī, Sabd 17, Mah. I.

[5] See this story enlarged in B. (11).

menced their work; they did their work in such a way, that everybody was pleased with it. All the people said: "Well, well, this is some good man; every one praised (him) before the Khān." The Khān was very much pleased. Whatever salary Guru Nānak got, of that he ate (= spent) something, the rest he gave away for God's sake. By night he sang always praise (to God). Afterwards Mardānā, the Ḍūm,[1] came from Talvaṇḍī and remained with the Bābā. To others, who came afterwards, he procured an interview with the Khān and a stipend, all got their bread by the favour of Guru Nānak. All were pleased and when the Bābā's food was prepared, they all came and sat down. By night continually praise was said (by Nānak), and when as yet a watch of the night[2] was remaining, the Bābā went to the river to bathe. When it became dawn of day, he put on his clothes, applied the Tilak (to his forehead), and having taken the account-book in the office he sat down to write.

One day the order of the Lord was made, that the river was going continually. He went therefore there, taking one servant with him. Stripping off his clothes, he entrusted them to the servant and began to bathe. As he was doing so, according to the order of the Lord, servants (= angels) took him away to the threshold of the Lord. The servants said: "Sir, Nānak is present." Then he (Nānak) obtained a sight of the true court (of God); the Lord was kind (to him). Meanwhile that servant (of Nānak) was standing by his clothes. Standing and standing he (finally) returned (home) and said, that Nānak had gone into the river, but had not come out again. He went to the Khān and said: "Khān, health! Nānak has gone into the river, but no more come out." The Khān mounted his horse and came out to the bank of the river. He called fishermen and made them throw a net (into the river). The fishermen searching became tired, but did not find him. The Khān was very much grieved, he mounted again his horse and said: "Nānak was a good steward," and returned home. It was the order of the Lord, that Nānak, the devotee, was present (at the threshold). Then a cup of nectar was filled and given him by the order (of the Lord). The command was given: "Nānak, this nectar is a cup of my name, drink it!" Then Guru Nānak made salutation and drank it. The Lord was kind and said: "Nānak, I am with thee, I have made thee exalted and who will take thy name, they will all be made exalted by me. Having gone mutter my name and make also other people mutter it! Remain uncontaminated from the world! Remain in the name, (in giving) alms, in performing ablutions, in worship and remembering (me)![3] I have given thee my own name, do this work (I told thee)!"

Then Guru Nānak made salutation and stood up. Then the order of the Lord came: "Nānak, of what kind is the greatness of my name?" The Bābā answered, whilst a sound (of music) was made without instruments being beaten, as it is written in Sirī Rāg, Mahalā I. [there follow four verses].[4]

Then again a voice came: "Nānak, my order has come into thy sight, praise thou my order! what is done by any one (but me)? and at my gate what hast thou heard? (what) are the musical instruments playing?" The Bābā answered: (and a sound arose), as written in the Rāgu Āsā, Japu, Mahalā I. [there follows a Slōk].[5] Then came again the order: "Nānak, on whom thy (favourable) look is, on him is also mine; on whom thy benevolence is, on him is also mine.

[1] ਡੂਮੁ, a caste of Musalmāns, who are professional drummers and musicians.

[2] ਪਹਰੁ, a watch, equal to three hours.

[3] The words are important as containing the duties inculcated to the Sikhs; they are: ਨਾਮੁ ਦਾਨ ਇਸਨਾਨੁ ਸੇਵਾ ਸਿਮਰਨੁ.

[4] See Sirī Rāg, Sabd 2, Mah. I.

[5] This Slōk is now not found in the Rāg Āsā, but is the first line in the Japjī; it is the well-known ਆਦਿ ਸਚੁ, etc.

My name is: the Supreme Brahm, the Supreme Lord; and thy name is: the Guru, the Supreme Lord."[1] Then Nānak fell on his feet. A dress of honour was given to him; a sound and voice arose, it was the Rāg Dhanāsarī, the Ārtī [there follow four verses].[2]

Then order was given to those ministers, that they should bring Nānak back to that very ferry; so they brought him there on the third day and went off. He came out from the river. When the people saw him, they said: "Friends, this one had fallen into the river, whence has he come?" Nānak entered his house; giving away everything he removed his abode far off. Many people assembled, the Khān also came and said: "Nānak: what has happened to thee?" The people said: "Sir, this one had fallen into the river, he has been hurt in the river." Then the Khān answered: "Friends, this is a great pity." He was much grieved, rose and went away.

At that time there was on the body of Guru Nānak only a Langōṭī,[3] he kept no other piece (of clothing). He went and sat down with Faqīrs. Mardānā, the Ḍūm, also went and sat down with him. Guru Nānak continued in silence for one day. The following day he rose and said: "There is no Hindū and there is no Musalmān." The people went and said to the Khān, that Nānak was saying: "There is no Hindū and no Musalmān." The Khān said: "Don't think of it, he is a Faqīr." One Kāzī was sitting near; he said: "Khān, this is wonderful, that he is saying: there is no Hindū and no Musalmān." The Khān said to a man, that he should call him, saying: "Nānak, the Khān is calling thee." Guru Nānak said (to that man): "What have I to do with thy Khān?" The people then said: "He has run mad and is a lunatic." Guru Nānak said to Mardānā: "Play the rebeck!" Mardānā played it, it was the Rāg Mārū and the Bābā uttered the Sabd, Mahalā I. [there follow four verses].[4] Then the Bābā was silent. When he said anything, then he said this very word, "that there was no Hindū and no Musalmān." The Kāzī said then: "O Khān, is it good, that he says: 'There is no Hindū and no Musalmān'?" Then the Khān said: "Go and fetch him!" Then footmen (of the Khān) went and said: "Sir, the Khān is calling you. The Khān says: 'For God's sake, give me an interview! I wish to see thee.'" Then Guru Nānak rose and went, saying: "Now, my Lord has called me, I shall go." He went, having placed a club[5] on his neck. He came and met with the Khān. The Khān said: "Nānak, for God's sake, take off the club from thy neck! gird thy waist! thou art a good Faqīr." Then Guru Nānak took off the club from his neck and girded his waist. The Khān said: "Nānak, it is a misfortune to me, that a steward like thou becomes a Faqīr." Then he seated Nānak at his side and said: "Kāzī, if thou wilt ask anything, ask now, otherwise this one will not utter again a word." The Kāzī becoming friendly, smiled and said: "Nānak, thou, who art saying: 'there is no Hindū and no Musalmān,' what dost thou mean by it?" Nānak uttered a Slōk in the Rāg Mājh [there follow four verses].[6]

When Nānak had uttered this Slōk, the Kāzī became amazed. The Khān then said: "O Kāzī, it has proved a failure to question him!"

The time of the afternoon prayer had come.[7] All arose and went to say their prayers, and the Bābā also went with them. The Kāzī stood in front of them all and began to pray. Then the Bābā looking towards the Kāzī laughed. The Kāzī saw that Nānak was laughing. After the prayer was finished, the Kāzī said: "Khān, health! hast thou seen, that the Hindū, looking to-

[1] In the Granth the (human) Guru is frequently identified with the Supreme Lord, which this story tries to explain and to account for. The words of the original are: ਅਰੁ ਤੇਰਾ ਨਾਉ ਗੁਰੁ ਪਰਮੇਸਰੁ.

[2] Granth, Lahore lithographed edition, p. 732.

[3] A piece of cloth, wrapt round the waist, passing between the legs and tucked behind, serving instead of trousers.

[4] Rāg Mārū, Sabd 7, Mah. I.

[5] ਮੁਤਗ੍ਰਾ = Sansk. मुद्गर, a club or large stick.

[6] See Mājh, Vār VIII., Slōk I.

[7] See B, Sākhī 17.

wards the Musalmāns, was laughing? thou, who art saying, that Nānak is a good man." The Khān said: "Nānak, what does the Kāzī say (against thee)?" The Bābā answered: "O Khān, what have I to care for the Kāzī? The prayer of the Kāzī however has not been accepted (by God), therefore have I laughed." The Kāzī said: "He is making subterfuges, let him manifest my fault." The Bābā rejoined: "Khān, when this one was standing praying, his mind was not fixed (on God). His mare had been delivered of a she-foal and he had come (to prayer) having loosened the foal. In the enclosure is a well and this one said (in his heart): 'May it not be, that the foal will fall into the well!' his mind had wandered there." Then the Kāzī came and fell down at his feet and said: "Wonderful, wonderful, on this one is the favour of God!" Then the Kāzī believed. Nānak uttered a Slōk:

> He is a Musalmān, who clears away his own self, who is sincere, patient, of pure words.
> Who does not touch what is standing, who does not eat what is fallen down:
> That Musalmān will go to paradise, (says) Nānak.

When the Bābā had uttered this Slōk, then the Sayyids, the sons of the Shēkhs, the Kāzī, the Muftī, the Khān, the chiefs and leaders were amazed. The Khān said: "Kāzī, Nānak has arrived at the truth, to ask him more has proved a failure." Wherever the Bābā looked, there all were saluting him. Then the Bābā uttered a Sabd, in Sirī Rāg, Mahalā I.[1] [there follow four verses]. After the Bābā had recited this Sabd, the Khān came and fell down at his feet. Then the people, Hindūs and Musalmāns, began to say to the Khān, that God was speaking in Nānak. The Khān said: "O Nānak, (my) dominion, property, authority and revenue, all is thine." Nānak answered: "God will reward thee. I cannot remain now here. Dominion, property and household-goods are thine, we forsake (all) and go." Having gone he sat down among the Faqīrs. Then the Faqīrs rose, joined their hands and stood before him; they began to praise him and to say: "Nānak has become (our) true daily bread and is coloured in the dye of the True one." Nānak said then: "Mardānā, play the rebeck!" Mardānā played the rebeck, the Rāg Tilang was made. The Bābā uttered the Sabd, Mahalā I. [there follow four verses].[2] Then the Faqīrs came, kissed his foot and shook his hand. The Bābā was much pleased with the Faqīrs and showed much kindness to them. The Khān also came; Hindūs and Musalmāns, everybody stood before him saluting him. Then they took leave from the Guru. When the Khān came home, he saw that the rooms of his treasury were filled. (At this) the Bābā was much pleased.

Taking Mardānā with him he wandered about; they did not enter any village, they did not stop in any jungle nor on any river. Now and then, when Mardānā was hungry, the Bābā said: "Mardānā, thou art hungry?" Then Mardānā answered: "Yes, thou knowest all." Nānak said: "Mardānā, go straight on to the village, there in front is the Khatrī Upal, go to his house and stand there silently; there they will give thee food. O Mardānā, to thee, who art going with me, some Hindū, some Musalmān, whoever will come and follow me, will fall down at thy feet, they will bring and put before thee exquisite food; some will bring Rupees and Paisās (copper coins); some will bring fine calicos; no one will ask anything, whence thou hast come and whose servant thou art. Whoever will come and follow me, he will say: 'I will bring and lay down all my property.' They will say: 'We have become exalted, that this interview has been given (to us), that the Bābā has been pleased.'"

One day Mardānā was sent to a town; in (thus) sending him much worship was paid to him. When he went, the whole town came and fell down at his feet. He made up a bundle of copper coins and clothes and brought it. The Bābā laughed. Mardānā brought the clothes and the copper coins to the Bābā. Then the Bābā said: "Mardānā, what hast thou brought?" Mardānā answered: "Sir, true king, alms in thy name; the whole town rose to thy service. O King! I

[1] See Sirī Rāg, Sabd 27, Mah. I.

[2] See Rāgu Tilang, Sabd 3, Mah. I.

said that I would bring these things and clothes to the Bābā." The Guru answered: "Mardānā, thou hast done quite well, but these things are of no use whatever to me." Mardānā said: "O king, what shall I do?" The Bābā answered: "Throw them away!" Then Mardānā threw all the things away, the whole bundle he scattered about there. After that Mardānā said: "O king, if one is willing to give alms in thy name and puts it into the mouth of a disciple, does his love in any way reach thee? And this thought is also in my heart, that thou art not touching anything nor putting into thy mouth, with what dost thou satiate thyself?" The Guru Bābā answered: "Mardānā, play the rebeck!" Mardānā played the rebeck and the Rāgu Gauṛī Dīpakī was made, Mahalā I. The Bābā uttered the Sabd [there follow four verses]. Then Mardānā being moved (thereby) paid worship (to him).

Then they departed thence. Wandering about they came to the house of Shēkh Sajan. His house was on the road; he had built there an idol-house and a mosque. If a Hindū came, he gave him a place (to stay in), and if a Musalmān came, he paid attention to him. When the night came on, he used to say: "Go to sleep!" Taking them in, he threw them into a well and killed them. And when it became morning, he took a staff and rosary into his hands, spread out a carpet to pray on and sat down.

When the Bābā and Mardānā came, he did much service to them and said to his people: "In this one's hem is much wealth, but it is concealed; on whose face there is such a splendour, he is not empty. It is all a story that he is a Faqīr." When night had set in he said: "Rise and go to sleep!" Then the Bābā said: "O Sajan, having recited one Sabd (song) to the service of God, we will go to sleep." Shēkh Sajan replied: "Well, be it so, Sir! recite it, the night is fast passing." Then the Bābā said: "Mardānā, play the rebeck!" Mardānā played the rebeck; the Rāg Sūhī was made. Nānak uttered the Sabd, Mahalā I. [there follow six verses].[1] (Then Shēkh Sajan said): "I am a sacrifice to the interview (with thee)." His mind returned to him; when he reflected, he found that all his sins were discovered. He rose and fell down at the feet (of Nānak), he kissed them and said: "Sir, pardon my sins!" The Bābā replied: "Shēkh Sajan, at the threshold of God the sins are pardoned by two words." Shēkh Sajan humbly said, "Sir, say those words by which sins are forgiven." Then Guru Nānak became compassionate and said: "Tell the truth, that murders have been perpetrated by thee!" Then Shēkh Sajan began to tell the truth. He said, "Yes, many sins have been committed by me." Then said Guru Nānak: "Whatever remains of their[2] property, that bring! Shēkh Sajan obeyed the order and brought it. It was given away in the name of God (as alms). He (Shēkh Sajan) began to mutter: "O Guru, Guru!" and relied on the name.—Say: vāh Guru!

Then he went on from thence on the road and came to Pāṇīpath. In Pāṇīpath was a Pīr, named Shēkh Saraf; his disciple was Shēkh Vaṭīhar. He had come to fill the water-jug of that Pīr with water. The Bābā and Mardānā were both seated further on. When he came, he saluted them and said: "Peace be to thee, O Darvēsh!" Guru Nānak replied: "To thee be peace, O hand-servant of the Pīr!" Shēkh Vaṭīhar became astonished and said: "Till this day no one has answered my salutation. But let it be so, I will go and inform my Pīr of it." He came and said: "O Pīr, health! having heard the voice of a Darvēsh I have become astonished." The Pīr replied: "Tell, that I may see, what sort of a man he is." Then Shēkh Vaṭīhar said: "May the Pīr live in health! I had gone to fill the jug: he was sitting in front (of me), in going I saluted him and said: 'Peace be to thee, O Darvēsh!' Then he replied: 'To thee be peace, O hand-servant of the Pīr!'" The Pīr said: "Son, who said to thee, 'to thee be peace,' his sight has been seen (by me). Show me, where that man was seen (by thee)." Then Shēkh Saraf having taken his

[1] See Rāg Sūhī, Sabd 3, Mah. I.

[2] The property of the murdered persons.

disciple Vaṭīhar with him, came to Guru Nānak and said [there follow a number of questions on the part of the Shēkh, to which Nānak answers in long verses]. The Shēkh kissed his hands and feet and went to his house. The Bābā and Mardānā continued their wanderings and they came thus to Dillī.

At that time Sultān Ibrahīm Bēg was King of Dillī.[1] Having come there he remained there during the night. Among the elephant-drivers much service was rendered to him (Nānak). At that time there had fallen down dead an elephant. The people were beating their breasts (in token of grief) and weeping. The Bābā asked: "Why are you weeping?" They answered: "We are weeping for an elephant." The Bābā said: "Whose was the elephant?" The elephant-driver replied: "It was the elephant of the King, it belonged to the one God."[2] The Bābā said then: "Why do you then weep?" They answered: "Sir, it was our livelihood." The Bābā replied: "Take up another occupation!" They said: "Our work had been prosperous, our family was happy and had its sustenance (from it)." The Bābā showed then compassion and said: "This elephant lives, don't be weeping!" They said: "Sir, how shall the dead one live?" The Bābā said: "Go and move your hands upon its face, say: 'vāh Guru!'" They obeyed his order and moved their hands (upon its face). Then the elephant rose and stood. This matter was reported to the King. Sultān Ibrahīm Bēg sent for the elephant. Having mounted he came to see it, having come he sat down and said: "O Darvēsh, hast thou vivified this elephant?" The Bābā replied: "The destroyer and vivifier is God, and the prayer of the Faqīrs is for the mercy of God." The King said again: "Kill it and show it!" Then the Bābā uttered this Slōk:

> He kills and vivifies.
> O Nānak, besides the One there is none other!

Then the elephant died. The King said again: "Make it alive!" The Bābā answered: "Your majesty, the iron being heated in the fire becomes red, but it does not remain a moment on the hand, and (red-hot) coals remain but for a short time. So the Faqīrs become red in God and take upon themselves a complete devotion to God, but their devotion gives way (again)." The King understood this and was much pleased. He said then: "Agree to something!" The Bābā answered with the Slōk:

> Nānak is hungry after God, for other things he does not care.
> Our search is for the sight (of God), for other things we do not search at all.

The King understood this, rose and went. The Bābā continued wandering about.

First (Nānak) passed his retired life in the *east*. There in his retirement Mardānā, the rebeck-player, was with him. At that time he practised wind-eating. The attire of the Bābā was one mango-coloured raiment, and one white raiment; on his feet he had one pair of shoes and one pair of slippers. Over his neck a shirt,[3] on his head a Kalandar's hat, a necklace of bones, on his forehead a Tilak (mark) of saffron.

Then he met on the road Shēkh Bajīd[4] Sayyid, who was going along being mounted on a pālkī (a kind of sedan-chair); with his wooden-frame (on which he was riding) were six bearers. He alighted under a tree and they (the bearers) commenced to pull and to fan him. Then Mardānā

[1] The MS. writes the name ਬ੍ਰਹਮੁ ਬੇਗ, instead of Ibrahīm Bēg. Ibrahīm Lōḍī was King of Dillī from 1517–1526, and fell in battle against Bābar.

[2] The original is: ਇਕੋ ਖੁਦਾਇ ਦਾ ਥਾ, rather a curious expression.

[3] The ਖਫਨੀ (كَفْنِي) is a kind of woollen shirt without sleeves, worn by Faqīrs.

[4] Very likely بَايَزِيد.

said: "Is God one?" The Bābā replied: "O Mardānā, God is one." Then said Mardānā: "O King, whose creation are those and whose creation is he, who has come mounted on a pālkī? Those are running on their feet and with naked bodies have brought him on their shoulders, and this one, who is seated, they fan." Nānak answered with the Slōk:

> The ascetics, who in a former birth have borne the sting of cold,
> Were then worn out; now, O Nānak, they adorn their body.

The Bābā went on saying: "O Mardānā, from austerity comes dominion and from dominion hell. Whoever is born from the womb of a mother, he comes naked (into the world). (There is) pleasure and pain (in this world) and last the account, when he departs." Then Mardānā fell down at his feet.

Departing thence they came to Benares. Having arrived there they sat down in a square.[1] At that time there was at Benares a Paṇḍit, called Čatur-dās, who had come to make his ablutions. He saluted him (*i.e.* Nānak) and having seen his (Faqīr's) garb he sat down and said: "O devotee, thou hast no Sāligrām![2] thou hast no necklace of Tulsī (holy basil)! thou hast no rosary! thou hast no mark (on the forehead) of white clay! and thou callest thyself a devotee! What devotion hast thou taken up?" The Bābā said: "Mardānā, play the rebeck!" Mardānā played the rebeck and the Rāg Basant was made. The Bābā uttered the Sabd, Mahalā I. [there follows one verse].[3] The Paṇḍit rejoined: "This truly is collecting barren soil, O devotee, but what is that thing, by means of which the world is gained and the Lord is obtained (also)?" The Bābā uttered then the second Pauṛī [there follows one verse]. The Paṇḍit asked again: "The earth indeed is dug up, but without watering it how shall it become green? and how shall the gardener consider it his own?" Then the Bābā uttered the third Pauṛī. Then the Paṇḍit Čatur-dās said: "Sir, thou art a perfect devotee of the Lord, my understanding, being overcome by the senses, is dull like a white heron." Then the Bābā uttered the fourth Pauṛī. The Paṇḍit went on saying: "Sir, thou art a worshipper of the Lord, but make also this city holy! Say something in its praise!" Then Guru Nānak asked: "What is its excellency?" The Paṇḍit answered: "Sir, its excellency is science, by reading which prosperity is accruing, and where thou sittest down, there the world will respect thee; by taking this advice thou wilt become great." Then the Bābā uttered a Sabd in the Rāg Basant, Mahalā I. [there follow four verses and one Rahāu].[4] The Paṇḍit Čatur-dās said again: "We, who are instructing the world, and we, who are reading (ourselves), is the name of the Lord also necessary to us?" Then Guru Nānak asked: "Sir, what are you reading and what are you teaching the world, your disciples?" The Paṇḍit answered: Sir, the words of the Supreme Brahm I make the world read with the first wooden slate."[5] Then the Bābā said in the Rāg Rāmkalī, Ōākār, Mahalā I. [there follows one verse and one Rahāu]. After that the fifty-four Pauṛīs (following were uttered) and the Ōākār made (thus). Then the Paṇḍit came and fell down at his feet and became a relier on the name; he began to mutter: "O Guru, Guru!"[6]

The Bābā departed thence and came to Nānak-matā.[7] That Banyā-tree had become dry since

[1] ਚਉਰਾ is a square court (in a temple, monastery, etc.) or an open square of the town, where markets are held.

[2] सालिग्राम, an ammonite-stone, found in the river गंडकी and worshipped as sacred to Vishṇu. It is usually written शालिग्राम.

[3] See Rāg Basant, Sabd 9, Mah. I.

[4] See Rāg Basant, Sabd 11, Mah. I.

[5] The sense is: with the first wooden slate, I write for them, I make them read, etc.

[6] Compare with this relation the story in the Sikhā̃ dē rāǰ dī vithiā, p. 289, where it is nearly literally contained, only those words and phrases being left out, which were unintelligible to the later reviser.

[7] According to what follows, this appears to have been the name of a Banyā̃-tree.

many years. A small smoking fire was kindled there (by Nānak) and it became green again. The Jōgīs saw this, came and sat down there. Then the Jōgīs asked: "O young man, whose disciple art thou? from whom hast thou got thy initiation?" The Guru Bābā replied with the Sabd in the Rāg Sūhī, Mahalā I. [there follow four verses].[1] The Jōgīs then said: "O young man, become a Jōgī and take the garb of (our) denomination!" The Bābā answered with a Sabd, Rāg Sūhī, Mahalā I. [there follow four verses].[2] Then the Jōgīs paid him reverence, (saying): "This is a great man, by whose sitting (under it) the Banyā-tree, the Faqīrs' cooking-place, has become green!"

The Guru Bābā started thence. They came to some goods-stores of grain-merchants and sat down at the door of the chief (of them). In his house a son had been born and the people were coming to congratulate him. Some one came and applied red lac-dye,[3] another gave a hundred thousand blessings. Mardānā being seated looked at the spectacle. When the day had declined, he rose and went; in the house no notice was taken of him. Mardānā, who had become excessively hungry, said: "O King, this one has taken no notice whatever of us; in his house a son has been born to-day, he has now risen and gone with his own pomp. But if thou wilt order me, I will go into his house, he is giving a present to the begging people on the occasion of the birth of a son, I may also bring away something." The Bābā laughed and said: "O Mardānā, in this one's house no son has been born, into his house a debtor has come. Be silent, this night I shall remain, to-morrow I shall rise and go. But if it be thy mind, then go (to the house), but do not pronounce a blessing, stand there silently!" Mardānā answered: "Well, Sir, I will go and see." He went and stood there silently; nobody took any notice of him. He rose and came back. Then the Bābā said: "Mardānā, play the rebeck!" Mardānā played the rebeck, the Rāg Sirī Rāg was sung, and the Guru Bābā uttered the Sabd, Mahalā I. [there follow four verses].[4] When it became morning, that baby died. Then weeping and beating their breasts they came out (from the house). Mardānā said: "Sir, what has happened to this man? Yesterday they were applying red lac-dye and laughing and sporting!" To this the Bābā answered with this Slōk:

> From which mouths congratulations and Lakhs of blessings are given:
> Those mouths are again beaten in grief, mind and body suffer agony.
> Some have died, some are buried, some are floated away in the river.
> The congratulation is gone, but thou, O Nānak, praise the True one!

Then the Bābā and Mardānā departed thence. On the road they fell in with an enclosed field of pulse. The watchman (of the field) began to parch half-ripe pulse-stalks (for them). It came into the mind of Mardānā: "If the Bābā would go, I would take two or three stalks." The Bābā smiled and sat down. The watchman brought the parched pulse-stalks and put them down (before Nānak) and Nānak gave them to Mardānā. Then it came into the mind of that boy: "I should fetch something from the house to put into the mouth of the Faqīrs." He rose and went. The Bābā asked (him, why he went). He said: "I will fetch something from the house to put into thy mouth." Then Nānak made this Slōk:—

> Thy mattrass and coverlet is a bed of straw;
> Love is thy sweetmeats.
> Nānak is much satiated with thy virtues, O Sultān!

He got then a kingdom for offering as alms a handful of pulse.

[1] See Rāg Sūhī, Sabd 9, Mah. I.
[2] Rāg Sūhī, Sabd 8, Mah. I.
[3] अलता (or अलिता) *s.m.* a kind of cloth, half-cotton and half-silk (Sansk. अलक्त). It signifies also red lac-dye, to stain the feet with (at festivities). The latter is meant here.
[4] Sirī Rāg, Pahirē 1, Mah. I. (p. 84).

The Bābā departed thence and went on. Then said Mardānā: "Sir, where shall the rainy season be spent?" The Bābā answered: "Well, if some village be met with, there a stay will be made." Having gone above one Kōs from the city they sat down in a village. In that village one Khatrī was attached (to Nānak). He came one day to have an interview, and after having had the interview he came continually to do service. One day he made the vow, that without having had an interview he would not take any draught of water. One of his neighbouring shopkeepers asked: "Brother, why art thou continually going, to what rendezvous art thou going?" That disciple replied: "Brother, some pious man has come, I go to meet him." That one said: "Sir, let me also have an interview with him!" One day that one also came with him; (but) coming and coming he attached himself to a slave-girl. Thence they were always going together from home, but that one went to the whore's house, and the other, who had been coming before, went to do service to the Guru, the Lord. One day that one said: "O brother, I go to do a bad work and thou art going to render service to the holy man. To-day let us make an agreement between ourselves, that we will see, what will accrue to me and what will happen to thee. If thou wilt come first, sit down here, and if I should come first, I will sit down here. To-day we will go together away." When that one went, he found the slave-girl not at home. Being vexed he rose and came to the (appointed) place and sat down there. In his stray thoughts he began to dig up the ground; when he looked on, it was a gold coin.[1] Then having drawn out his knife he began to dig (more). When he looked, they were charcoals, a whole jar full. The other, after he had fallen down at the foot of the Guru, went away. Outside the door a thorn pierced his foot. Having bound up his foot with a cloth he came (to the appointed place), with one shoe drawn off and one being put on. That one asked: "O brother, why hast thou drawn off one of thy shoes?" He replied: "O brother, a thorn has pierced my foot." That one said: "O brother, to-day I have found a gold muhar and thee a thorn has pierced; we must ask about this matter. For thou goest to do service to the Guru and I go to commit sin." Then both came and told the whole truth. The Guru said: "Be silent!" They replied: "Sir, may an explanation be given (to us)!" Then the Guru said: "The jar of charcoals were gold muhars; it is what he has sown in his former birth. He had given one muhar to a holy man, these his alms had become muhars. But in proportion as he ran after wickedness, the muhars became charcoals. And in thy destiny an impaling-stake was written. In proportion as thou wast coming to do service (to me), the impaling-stake decreased, of the impaling-stake became a thorn, as the result of service rendered (to me)."' Then they rose and fell down at his feet and became devotees of the name; they began to mutter: "Guru, Guru!" Then the Bābā recited a Sabd, in Rāg Māṛū, Mahalā I. [there follow four verses].[2]

Then they departed thence. On the road they fell in with Ṭhags.[3] Having seen the (travellers) they said: "In whose face there is such a lustre, he is not empty, in his purse there is much money, but it is concealed. They surrounded the Bābā and stood before him, but with seeing his sight they became weak (= discouraged) within. The Guru asked them: "Who are you?" They answered: "We are Ṭhags, we have come for thy jewels." Then the Bābā said: "Well! Having done one work you may kill (me). Where that smoke is coming into sight, thither come a little further on! There you may kill and brand me!" The Ṭhags said: "Where is the fire, where? we will kill and remove him!" Then said some Ṭhags: "We have killed many men, but laughing none has said: 'kill me!' where is he going in hope?" Then two Ṭhags

[1] ਮੁਹਰਿ *s.f.* a gold coin or muhar (= أَشْرَفي), worth about one £1 11*s.* 8*d.*

[2] Rāg Māṛū, Sabd 3, Mah. I.

[3] ਠਗ, a robber, who inveigles his victim and kills him; literally: a cheat.

ran towards the fire. When they came there, a funeral pile was burning and the troops[1] of Rāma and the troops of Yama were standing and quarrelling. The Ṭhags asked: "Who are you and why are you quarrelling?" Those answered: "We are the troops of Yama, having received the order of the Lord we are going to take this creature (here) to the pot-hell.[2] But after us these troops of Rāma have come and have snatched him away from us. Ask them, why they have torn him away from us." The Ṭhags asked then: "Why have you snatched him away from these?" The troops of Rāma answered: "The Guru, the Lord, whom you have come to kill, by his favourable look the smoking fire of this one's funeral pile has been applied, (having been) a sacrifice to him he has (now) reached paradise." The Ṭhags hearing this ran back and said: "By whose favourable look one has become entirely emancipated, when the fire was applied (to his pyre), him we have come to kill." Then they came and fell down at his feet. The others asked and were told the matter; then they also came and fell down at his feet. Joining their hands (in supplication) they stood before him and began to beseech (him) and said: "Sir, make us attached to the name! Destroy thou our sins! we have perpetrated very horrible sins." Then Guru Nānak became moved with compassion and said: "Your sins will then be extinguished, when you abandon this occupation and take to agriculture; and whatever (stolen) thing rests with you, that give away in the name of the Lord (as alms)! Seek the favour of ascetics and devotees!" They obeyed his order; whatever thing they had, they brought and put down before him. They began to mutter: "Guru, Guru!" Their life was adjusted.[3] Then the Bābā recited a Sabd, in the Srī Rāg, Mahalā I. [there follow four verses].[4] The Guru was much pleased and departed thence. Say: vāh Guru!

Then they came to the country of Kauṛū.[5] One day Mardānā became hungry; he rose and went. He came to the door of a woman and stood there. She called him and asked him if he wished to eat. Then she bound him with a thread, made him a ram and seated him. Having bound him she went for water. The Bābā came then and having seen (him) he (Mardānā) began to bleat (like a sheep). When she came back with her water-jar, Guru Nānak asked her and said: "My man has come here." She answered: "No one has come here, look (yourself)!" Then the Bābā uttered (this) Slōk:

> The female traffickers in barren soil ask musk from the bramble.
> Without (good) works, O Nānak, how will they meet with their Lord?

On this the jar on her head remained fixed, it did not go off, as a punishment for her falsehood; she went about with it. Then Nūr Shāhi heard that such a (great) conjurer had come, that the jar did not go off. She gave the order that no female conjurer in the town should remain behind. Then, wherever there was a conjurer, they all came with their skill. One came mounted on a tree, another came mounted on a deer-skin, another on the moon, another on a wall, another brought with her a tiger, another came beating a drum. Having come they commenced to practise their jugglery, binding threads. Then the Bābā saw Mardānā bound; Mardānā began to mew. The Bābā laughed and said: "Mardānā, say: 'vāh Guru!' bow thy head and bring the rebeck!" Then Mardānā bowed his head and the thread broke and fell off his neck. He brought the rebeck. Then the Guru said: "Play the rebeck, O Mardānā!" Mardānā played it and the Sabd in the Rāgu Vaḍhans, Mahalā I. was sung [there follow four verses].[6] Then no answer whatever was

[1] ਗਣ, troops of inferior deities.
[2] ਕੁੰਭੀ ਨਰਕੁ, name of a hell, in which people are boiled as in a pot.
[3] ਜਨਮੁ ਸਵਾਰਿਆ, their life was adjusted, *i.e.* they gained the object of their life, or: were emancipated.
[4] Sirī Rāg, Sabd 4, Mah. I.
[5] Cf. Sākhī 25 (Lahore edit.). There the name of the country is written ਕਾਵਰੂ, Kāvarū or ਕਾਰੂ, Kārū.
[6] Vaḍhans, Sabd 2, Mah. I.

made. Intelligence reached Nūr Shāhī that no mantra nor charm was availing. Nūr Shāhi was the head of all conjurers; she came with her best disciples mounted on an apparatus of paper, and began to apply her mantras and charms. Then Nānak recited the Sabd, in the Rāg Sūhī, Mahalā I. [there follow four verses].[1] The Bābā having said: "Vāh, vāh!"[2] rose. Nūr Shāhi also became tired of practising her mantras and spells, they took no effect whatever. She said: "I have done wrong," and remained silent from shame. Drums also were standing near, they began to dance and to sing. Then the Bābā said: "Mardānā, play the rebeck!" Mardānā played the rebeck, the Rāg Srī Rāg was made, Mahalā I., the Bābā uttered the Sabd [there follow four verses and a Slōk].[3] After the Guru had said this Slōk, Nūr Shāhi said (within herself): "I will delude him with the Māyā (= wealth)." She brought things of many kinds: pearls, jewels, gold, silver, coral, camphor, clothes; whatever good things there were, she brought and put them down before him. She began to beseech him, that he should desire something. The Guru replied: "Mardānā, play the rebeck!" Mardānā did so and the Rāg Tilang was made, Mahalā I. [there follow four verses].[4]

After this she fell down at the feet of the Guru. Having put a veil over her cheeks she stood before him and commenced to say: "How shall our salvation be brought about and how will the water-jar go off from the head of this one?" The Guru answered: "Having said: 'vāh Guru!' you will make the water-jar go off from her head and your salvation also will be effected; mutter: 'Guru, Guru!'" Then she came and fell down at his feet; she became a votary of the name. Say: vāh Guru!

Then the Bābā departed thence. Going about he came to a desert and sat down. Then by the order of the Lord the Kali-yuga came to frighten him,[5] having assumed a visible form. A storm arose and the trees began to fly about. Mardānā got very much afraid and said: "O King, thou hast brought me into the desert and killed me; even grave and shroud I must forego." Guru Nānak said: "Mardānā, don't become troubled!" Mardānā answered: "Up to this day I have now lived, but such a calamity I have not seen, for what has happened here to us!" Then a form of fire was shown;[6] a smoke arose from the four sides and in the four quarters a fire was made. Then Mardānā covering his face fell down and said: "Sir, I am waiting." Then a form of water was made (by the Kali-yuga); he came having gathered clouds. Water began to rain, but it fell at some distance from the Guru. Then the Guru said: "Mardānā, disclose thy face, rise and sit down! play the rebeck!" "Mardānā rose, sat down and played the rebeck." The Rāg Mārū was made. The Bābā uttered the Sabd, Mahalā I. [there follow four verses].[7] Then assuming the form of a Daitya he (the Kali-yuga) came near. The top of his head he had raised up to heaven. In proportion as he approached, he decreased in size. Joining his hands he stood and said: "Sir, take something from me! walk in my word!" The Guru Bābā asked him: "What hast thou?" Kali-yuga answered: "I have everything. If thou order me, I will build thee a palace of pearls and stud it with gems and rubies, I will besmear it with sandal-powder and aloe-wood." Then the Guru recited a Sabd (as written) in the Rāg Sirī Rāg, Mahalā I. [there follow three verses].[8] The Kali-yuga said: "Take something from me! thou mayest become a Sultān, thou mayest exercise sovereignty." Then the Guru recited the fourth Pauṛī [there follows the fourth verse]. Then the Kali-yuga walked round (Nānak) in adoration, came and fell down at

[1] Sūhī, Kučajī 1 (p. 840).

[2] Vāh, vāh = bravo! bravo!

[3] These lines are not found among the Sabds of Nānak.

[4] Tilang, Sabd 4, Mah. I.

[5] Cf. Sākhī 26 (Lahore ed.).

[6] *i.e.* by the Kali-yuga.

[7] The quotation is wrong; in the Granth these verses are ascribed to Guru Arjun; see Mārū, Sabd 1, Mah. V. (p. 1108).

[8] Sirī Rāg, Sabd 1, Mah. I.

his feet and said: "Sir, how may my salvation be effected?" Guru Nānak answered: "If among a crore some one will become my disciple, his sacrifice (= devotion to me) will become thy salvation." The Kali-yuga then fell down at his feet and was dismissed by the Bābā. Say: vāh Guru!

The Guru and Mardānā continued their wanderings; they came to a city of ants.[1] When they looked about, trees and shrubs, all appeared black, the whole ground also. When Mardānā saw this, he was much frightened and said: "Sir, let us depart hence! such a great black thing I have never seen, go away from this black thing!" The Guru Bābā replied: "Mardānā: (here) is their realm, though some one (*i.e.* ant) may go to a hundred jungles. If some young one of an animal is born, they eat it, and if eggs be laid by some snake, they eat them also, but none will come near thee." Then said Mardānā: "Sir, has ever any one come here?" The Guru answered: "Mardānā, one day one Rājā had come up here. Having formed a host of fifty-two complete armies he had marched out against some Rājā and come to this country. One ant went and met him and said: 'O Rājā, remain here and do not march on! And if thou art marching, then march according to my will.' The Rājā asked: 'What is thy will?' The ant replied: 'O Rājā, my will is this, that having eaten my bread thou shouldst go.' The Rājā said: 'I am the Rājā of fifty-two complete armies, how should I eat thy bread?' The ant replied: 'If not, thou wilt go after a battle.' The Rājā said: 'Well, let it be so!' O Mardānā, the Rājā taking his fifty-two complete armies began to fight with the ants. The chief of the ants gave the order to the ants: 'Go and fetch poison!' Having filled their mouth with poison from the Piyāl-tree they brought it; every one died, to whom they applied it. O Mardānā, the whole host of fifty-two complete armies died with (= by) the order of the Lord; the Rājā alone remained alive. Then that ant went and said: 'O Rājā, hear my word, now thou wilt accept my bread.' The Rājā joining his hands stood (as a suppliant) and said: 'Well, may it be so!' Then that ant gave the order to the (other) ants: 'Go and bring nectar!' In the nether region there are seven pools of nectar and seven pools of poison. The ants went, filled their mouth with nectar and brought it. To whom they applied it, he rose and stood; so the host of fifty-two complete armies rose and stood with the order of the Lord. Then the Rājā having risen went to eat bread with his fifty-two complete armies. When the bread was given (them), it was cold, and when the grass was given to the horses, it was soaked, and when the corn was given, it was chopped. The Rājā asked: 'Why is such bread given and soaked grass and chopped corn?' The ant answered: 'O Rājā, some time ago a Rājā had come, for him I had prepared bread; what was left by him, that I have served out to thy army, and the corn, and grass, that was left by his horses, was given to thy horses.' When the Rājā on going away looked about, full magazines stood there. The pride of the Rājā was humbled and he said: 'Such are the habits of the Rājās.' Then the Rājā returned to his house." The Bābā uttered this Slōk:

> Lions, hawks, falcons and birds of prey he makes eat grass.
> Who eat grass, them he makes eat flesh, such is his habit.
> In rivers he shows heaps of sand and on dry land he makes bottomless pools.
> Having killed the creatures he vivifies them, (if) he bestows his look and favour on the creatures.
> He establishes an ant and gives it dominion and an army he reduces to ashes.
> Nānak (says): as it pleases the True one, so he gives a morsel.

Then Mardānā fell down at his feet. Say: vāh Guru!

They departed thence and having come to a village they sat down there. In that village no

[1] Cf. Lahore edit., Sākhī 27.

one gave them a place to stay in, they began to rail (at them). Then the Guru Bābā uttered this Slōk:

> When I keep silence, they say, in this man there is no understanding.
> When I speak, they say, he rattles much away.
> When I sit down, they say, he is seated on a bed of straw, he has laid down.
> When I rise and go, they say, he is gone having thrown ashes on his head.
> When I bow down, they say, he performs worship continually bowing down.
> There is no abuse and no taunt, by which I may cut off their false accusation.
> (But) here and there, (says) Nānak, the true Guru (= God) preserves (my) honour.

He did not remain there twenty-four minutes. Mardānā said then: "Sir, what order has been given (by God) regarding these people?" The Bābā answered: "Mardānā, this town will be thriving." Then they went to another town. There much attention was paid to them, they remained there a night. Early in the morning they rose and started. Then the Guru said: "This town will be ruined, it will become a place where eight roads meet."[1] Mardānā said: "I see a fine justice at thy gate; where thou dost not get a place to sit on, that (town) is made thriving (by thee), and by whom much attention and service is rendered to thee, their town is ruined." The Guru Bābā replied: "O Mardānā, when the people of that city will go to another town, then others also will be spoiled, and when the people of this town will go to another town, they will also save them and give them good advice." Mardānā answered: "Sir, if it please thee, procure also salvation to that town!" Then the Bābā recited a Sabd, in the Rag Malār, Mahalā I. [there follow four verses].[2]

Then they went again to the country of Āsā.[3] There was Shēkh Farīd, who lived in a jungle, to which the Bābā went. Shēkh Farīd said: "Allah, Allah, O Darvēsh!" The Guru Bābā answered: "Allah, O Farīd, is my aim.[4] Come, Shēkh Farīd, Allah, Allah is always my aim." Then taking his hand he sat down. Shēkh Farīd looking at the face of the Bābā said, entering into a conversation with him:

> Desire either dominion or desire Allah!
> Do not put thy feet on two boats, lest thou drown thy goods!

The Guru Bābā answered with the Slōk:

> Put thy feet on two boats, ship thy goods in two:
> One boat may be sunk, one may pass across.
> (They require) neither water nor a boat,
> They are not sunk nor do they pass away:
> The goods, the true wealth, are naturally contained (in God).

Then Shēkh Farīd recited this Slōk:

> O Farīd, who art enamoured with (this) witch, the world is a false distinction.
> O Nānak, whilst looking on with the eyes the field is wasted.

[1] The sense is: it will be totally trodden under foot.

[2] Rāg Malār, Sabd 1, Mah. I.

[3] Cf. Lahore ed., Sākhī 28. It is not known exactly, if Āsā is a real or only a fancy name. Farīd, a Muhammadan Pīr, lived not far from Lahore, lower down the Rāvī. There are still many followers of Farīd in the Panjāb. A great portion of his poetical compositions has been incorporated in the Granth. Farīd is not mentioned by De Tassy in his "Histoire de la littérature Hindouī et Hindūstānī."

[4] The original is: ਅਲਹ ਫਕੀਰ ਜੁਹਦੀ, literally: Allah is my effort, I am striving for him (ਜੁਹਦੀ = Arab. جُهْدِي or جَهْدِي). There is no doubt that Nānak picked up some little Arabic as well as Persian by his frequent intercourse with Muhammadan Faqīrs.

The Guru Bābā answered with the Slōk:

> Love to the witch comes, springing up by itself, by itself.
> O Nānak, the field is not wasted, if its guardian be attentive.

Then the Shēkh recited this Slōk:

> O Farīd, the body has lost its strength, the heart is broken, no strength whatever is left.
> The beloved has become (my) physician, he applies remedies and medicines (to me).

The Guru Bābā answered with the Slōk:

> Verify in thy own person the true friend, to talk with the mouth is senseless.
> Perceive him in the heart, my friend is not far from thee.

Then the Shēkh uttered a Sabd (as written) in the Rāg Sūhī [there follow three verses].[1]
The Guru Bābā answered with the Sabd in the Rāg Sūhī, Mahalā I. [there follow five verses].[2]
Then Farīd uttered a Sabd, in the Rāg Āsā [there follow three verses].[3]
The Bābā answered with a Sabd in the Rāg Sūhī, Mahalā I. [there follows one verse].[4]

The Bābā and Shēkh Farīd remained together one night in the jungle. Then came one servant of God there. Having seen (them) he rose and went home, filled a bowl with milk and brought it towards the close of the night, after having thrown four Ashrafīs into it. The Shēkh took his portion (of the milk) and left the portion of the Guru. Then Shēkh Farīd uttered this Slōk:

> Those who wake obtain gifts from the Lord.
> At the commencement of the night there is the blossom, at the end of the night also the fruit.

The Bābā answered with the Slōk:

> The gifts are the Lord's, what can he be prevailed upon?
> Some, though waking, do not obtain (them), some, who are asleep, he makes rise and meets (with them).

Then the Bābā said: "Shēkh Farīd, move thy hand in this milk and see what it is." When Shēkh Farīd looked, there were four Ashrafīs; he dropped the bowl and went away. Then the Guru Bābā recited a Sabd, in the Rāg Tukhārī, Mahalā I. [there follow five verses].[5] Then the Bābā and Shēkh Farīd started thence. Then that man came and saw that the bowl was lying on the ground. When he lifted it up, it was of gold, and filled with Ashrafīs. He began to regret it and said: "Those were wealthy Faqīrs; if it had come into my mind, I would have put in religion: so I have brought money and have got money." He took the bowl and went home.

Then the Guru Bābā and Shēkh Farīd came to the country of Āsā. At that time the Rājā of the country of Āsā, whose name was Samundar,[6] had died. His skull did not burn (when his corpse was burnt), though they made different efforts. Thereupon the astrologers were asked, who said: "This one has once told a falsehood, therefore his soul has come into trouble." The people of the country of Āsā were speaking the truth, by day they were sowing and by night they were cutting (the corn). The people of Āsā began to lament. The astrologers said: "He will then become emancipated, when the feet of a saint touch (him)." The road to the country of Āsā was therefore shut up, only one gate was left, that if by chance a Faqīr should come, he would be carried along from that gate. At that time Bābā Nānak and Shēkh Farīd arrived there. When

[1] Rāg Sūhī, Farīd, 2.
[2] Rāg Sūhī, Sabd 4, Mah. I.
[3] Rāg Āsā, Shēkh Farīd, 1.
[4] Apparently a misquotation, for the verse is not found there.
[5] Rāg Tukhārī, Chant, Bārahamātrā 2, Mah. I. (p. 1234).
[6] In the Lahore edition and in MS. (B.) the name is given as: Syām Samundar.

they had come near, Guru Nānak said: "Shēkh Farīd, put thy foot (on it)." Shēkh Farīd replied: "What is my power, that I should put forth my foot?" Then the Bābā put his foot (on it) and the skull burst; he was emancipated. Then all the people of the country of Āsā came and fell down at (their) feet. The Bābā recited a Sabd, in the Rāg Mārū, Mahalā I. [there follow four verses].[1] Then the people brought bread. Who offered bread to Shēkh Farīd, to him he said: "I have already eaten bread and also bound some up in the hem of my garment." Then the people of the Āsā country said: "O servant of God, art thou some untruthful man of that country, in which Shēkh Farīd lives, who has a loaf of bread made of wood and if one offers him bread, says: 'I have eaten already and also bound some up in the hem of my garment.'" Then Farīd threw down the bread of wood and said: "For telling once a lie the Rājā has got such a great punishment (what will then be my state)?"[2] The Bābā was pleased at this. When Shēkh Farīd took leave, the Bābā said: "Shēkh Farīd, truly God is in thee, but take thou a Pīr (spiritual leader)." Shēkh Farīd answered: "Well, it may be." When Shēkh Farīd departed, they embraced each other. The Guru Bābā recited then a Sabd, in the Rāg Srī Rāg, Mahalā I. [there follow four verses].[3] The Bābā remained some days (longer) in the Āsā country and the whole country began to mutter: "Guru, Guru!" and became devotees of the name. In the Āsā country there is (still) a Manjī.[4] The Bābā was much pleased with the Āsā country. Say: vāh Guru!

Then the Bābā came to the country of Bisīār. There they gave him no place to sit on. Wherever they go and stand, there the people apply cow-dung,[5] seeing them gone. Then he came to Jhaṇḍā, the carpenter, who took him to his house. This one was drinking after he had washed his feet. Whilst he was drinking, the Guru came into sight. He became an Udāsī (Faqīr) and began to wander about with (Nānak).

By the favour of the holy true Guru! The writing of the Jugāvalī[6] (comes now). At that time he (*i.e.* the Guru) was sitting on the sea-shore; he practised wind-eating; with him was Jhaṇḍā, the carpenter, of the Bisīār country. He got the Jugāvalī, with Jhaṇḍā it was finished.

At that time it was read with astonishment. [There follows the Jugāvalī.][7]

Nānak was pleased and discharged Jhaṇḍā, the carpenter, to the Bisīār country. Then the Bābā and Mardānā departed thence. Going along they came into a great desert, where they did not meet with anybody. Mardānā, who had become very hungry, said: "Out of attachment to thee I became thy musician and was eating the morsels, I begged from the country; this also is now denied to me. We have fallen into a great jungle; if God ever will draw us out, we shall come out of it. Now if some lion will roar and fall on (us), he will kill us." The Bābā replied: "O Mardānā, none will come near thee, but be thou prudent!" He said: "Sir, how shall I be prudent? I have fallen into a desert." The Bābā replied: "O Mardānā, we are not in a desert, we are in a village, wherever the name comes into our mind." There the Bābā uttered the Sabd, in the Rāg Āsā, Mahalā I. [there follow four verses].[8] Then the Bābā said: "O Mardānā, keep (this) Sabd in (thy) mind, except by thee (these) words are not understood." Then the Bābā said: "Mardānā, play

[1] Rāg Mārū, Sabd 2, Mah. I.

[2] This I have supplied from the Lahore edition, as it is missing in the original.

[3] Sirī Rāg, Sabd 10, Mah. I.

[4] ਮੰਜੀ, properly a small couch or stool, bedecked with silk clothes, on which the Granth is placed and adored by the people.

[5] As if the place had been polluted.

[6] ਜੁਗਾਵਲੀ, the row of Yugas.

[7] All the other Janam-sākhīs do not mention this. It is apparently an old interpolation, as it has nothing whatever to do with the narrative of Nānak's wanderings.

[8] Rāg Āsā, Sabd 33, Mah. I.

the rebeck!" Mardānā replied: "My body is pierced by hunger, I cannot play this rebeck." The Bābā said: "Mardānā, follow me, we will go to some village." Mardānā replied: "I cannot go even to a village, my body is pierced by hunger; I am Mardānā." The Bābā said then: "O Mardānā, I shall not let thee die, be sensible!" Mardānā replied: "Sir, how shall I be sensible, I am Mardānā, my life is done for." The Bābā said then: "Mardānā, eat the fruit of this tree till thou art satiated, but put none into the hem of thy garment!" Mardānā answered: "Well, Sir!" and began to eat. He liked the flavour of the fruit and said: "If possible I will eat all, perhaps they may never come to hand." Some of them he also bound up in the hem of his garment, saying (to himself): "If I become hungry again, I will eat them." When Mardānā became hungry again, he said: "I will eat some of the (fruits)." When he put it into his mouth, he fell down at that very time. The Bābā said: "What is the matter, Mardānā?" He replied: "Thou hadst said, O King, that I should eat to my satiety, but I should bind none into the hem of my garment. I said to myself that I would also bind some into the hem of my garment, perhaps they might not come to hand again. These I have put into my mouth; this is the matter that happened." The Bābā said: "Thou hast done wrong, that thou didst put them into thy mouth, these are poisonous fruits, but having pronounced a word over them they were made nectar-fruits. Then the Bābā put his foot on his head and he became quite well again, rose and sat down. Then Mardānā said: "A fine thing is the attachment to thee and serving thee! I am a Ḍūm and desire to eat by asking and begging; thou art a great man free from pleasure and pain, thou dost not eat nor drink anything nor dost thou enter any village, how shall I remain with thee? give me leave to go!" The Bābā said: "Mardānā, I am much pleased with thee, why dost thou ask leave from me?" Mardānā replied: "It is all very well, that thou art pleased with me, but discharge me, I will go home." The Bābā replied: "Mardānā, by all means remain!" Mardānā said: "I will remain, if thou stillest my hunger; what thy food is, that should be mine, make it also my food! If thou do this, then I will remain with thee. If thou makest this promise, that thou wilt also think of my business, then I will remain with thee, if thou wilt not do it, then give me leave." The Guru Bābā replied: "Go, Mardānā! thou hast been exalted in this and that world." Then Mardānā sprang up and fell down at his feet. By the Guru Bābā so many things were imparted (to him); with the raising up of his head he got the thorough knowledge of the Shāstras and Vēdas. Then Mardānā commenced (again) to wander about with the Bābā.

Twelve[1] years, after he had become an Udāsī, he (= Nānak) came to Talvaṇḍī and sat down outside, two Kōs from it, in a desert. Stopping there for twenty-four minutes, Mardānā begged and said: "If order be given to me, I will go home and inquire after my house (= wife), and see how my people are, if somebody is still alive or not." The Bābā laughed and said: "Mardānā, thy people will die, how wilt thou hold fast the world? But if it be thy mind, then go; having met with them come again, but come quickly! Go also to the house of Kālū, but do not take our name." Mardānā having fallen down at his feet went and came to Talvaṇḍī and entered his house. Then many people assembled; every one who came, fell down at his feet and all people said: "It is Mardānā, the Ḍūm, but he is the shade of Nānak. He is no (more) that, he has become greater than the world." All who come fall down at his feet. Mardānā having seen his family went to the yard in front of the house of Kālū and sat down. Then the mother of the Bābā rose and fell on his neck and began to weep. Having wept she said: "Mardānā, from whence? hast thou also information about Nānak?" Then all the people of the yard gathered together and began to ask. Mardānā said: "My dear, when the Bābā was at Sultānpur, I was with him as Ḍūm; since that time I know nothing of him." Having sat there for twenty-four minutes Mardānā rose and

[1] Compare: Sikhā̃ dē rāǰ dī vithiā, p. 291.

went. The mother of the Bābā said then: "My dear, that this one has so quickly risen and departed from the yard, that has its reason." She stood up, took some clothes and some sweetmeats and went after Mardānā, with whom she met and said: "Mardānā, bring me to Nānak!" Mardānā remained silent. They went on above two Kōs to the place where the Bābā was sitting. When the Bābā saw that his mother and Mardānā had come, he came and fell down at her feet. His mother began to weep and kissed his head and said: "I am a sacrifice, I am a sacrifice, my son, for thee I am a sacrifice. I am a sacrifice for that place, where thou art wandering about. I have been made happy by thee, that thou hast shown me thy face." The Bābā seeing the love of his mother became soft and began to weep. Having wept he laughed and said: "Mardānā, play the rebeck!" Mardānā played the rebeck and the Bābā made the Sabd, in the Rāg Vaḍhans, Mahalā I. [there follow four verses].[1] Then his mother put the clothes and sweetmeats before him and said, "Son, eat!" The Bābā answered: "O mother, I am satiated." His mother said: "Son, with what food art thou satiated?" The holy Guru Bābā said: "Mardānā, play the rebeck!" Mardānā played it and the Bābā made the Sabd, in the Sirī Rāg, Mahalā I. [there follows one verse and one Rahāu].[2] His mother said again: "Take this patched quilt off thy neck and put on new clothes!" Then the Bābā recited the second Pauṛī [there follows one verse with a Rahāu]. His father Kālū also heard this news, he mounted a horse and came. When he had come, the Bābā fell down at his feet and paid reverence to him. Then Kālū began to weep and said: "Nānak, mount the horse and come to our house." Then the Guru replied: "O father, horses are of no use to me." He recited the third Pauṛī [there follows one verse with a Rahāu]. Kālū said again: "Go once to (our) house, we have built a new house, see it, thou hast returned after a long time. There is thy family, meet with it, and if it shall please thee, thou mayst go again." Then the Bābā uttered the fourth Pauṛī [there follows one verse with a Rahāu]. Kālū went on to say: "O son, thy soul has become embittered by some matter, tell it me! if thou tell me, I will procure thee another marriage; I will get up a good company for thee at the wedding-procession, with splendour I will get thy marriage solemnized." The Bābā uttered a Sabd in the Rāg Sūhī, Čhant, Mahalā I. [there follow four verses].[3] Then the Bābā said: "O father and mother, that one is the all-arranging Supreme Being; the union, that is made by him, is good." His mother said then: "O son, rise and go! give up this perverse talk, what union may be made again, by which we shall again meet?" The Bābā made then the Sabd, in Rāgū Mārū, Mahalā I. [there follow four verses].[4] After this the Bābā said: "O father and mother, we, who have come, shall come (again) at some fit opportunity. But mind now the order: I am an Udāsī." His mother replied: "O son, how shall this give contentment to my heart, as thou hast come after having led a retired life for many years?" The Bābā said: "O mother, mind my word, thou wilt obtain contentment." Then his mother kept silence. The holy Guru Bābā departed then from that place.

Having seen the Rāvī and the Čanāu (Chenāb) he went into the wilderness and came to the country of Paṭaṇ.[5] Three Kōs from the country of Paṭaṇ was a desert, thither he went and sat down, Mardānā being with him. The Pīr of Paṭaṇ had been Shēkh Farīd; on his throne sat (now) Shēkh Briham. One of his disciples had come early in the morning to collect wood, whose name was Shēkh Kamāl; he had gone out to collect fuel for the kitchen of the Pīr. He saw that near an Akk-tree both the Bābā and Mardānā were sitting. Mardānā played then the rebeck and began to sing a Sabd; he gave a Slōk in the Rāg Āsā. Shēkh Briham had had a conversation with the Bābā (before).

[1] Rāg Vaḍhans, Sabd 1, Mah. I.
[2] Sirī Rāg, Sabd 7, Mah. I.
[3] Rāg Sūhī, Čhant 4, Mah. I.
[4] Rāg Mārū, Sabd 1, Mah. I.
[5] Compare the Lahore edition, Sākhī 83.

Slōk.

Thou thyself art the wooden tablet, thou thyself art the pen, thou art also the writing upon it.
Why should the One be called another, O Nānak?

When Kamāl heard this Slōk, he left his wood and came near and said: "Sir, tell this Rabābī (player of the rebeck), that he should repeat this verse." Mardānā was told to do so and repeated it. Kamāl learnt it; he took the wood he had collected, made his salām and returned to Paṭaṇ. Having thrown down the wood he went to his Pīr, made his salām and said: "Pīr, health to thee! a beloved man of God has fallen in with me." The Pīr said: "Kamāl, where did he meet with thee?" Kamāl answered: "O Pīr, health to thee! I had gone to gather fuel; a Rabābī is with him and his name is Nānak; he recites his own Slōks." The Pīr said: "Son, hast thou learnt some verse?" Kamāl replied: "O Pīr, health to thee! One verse I also have committed to memory." He says: 'Thou thyself art the wooden tablet, thou thyself art the pen, thou art also the writing upon it. Why should the One be called another, O Nānak?'" The Pīr said: "O son, hast thou somewhat understood the meaning of this verse or not?" Kamāl answered: "Pīr, health to thee! to thee all is manifest." Then the Pīr said: "O son, by whom this verse has been spoken, his sight I have seen (already), he is a Faqīr of God, bring me also to him! words of God are spoken by him." Then Shēkh Briham ascended a sedan-chair and went taking Kamāl with him; he went along above three Kōs; when he looked, the Bābā was sitting there. Shēkh Birāham[1] went and standing said: "Nānak, peace be on thee!" The Guru Bābā answered: "And on thee be peace! O Pīr, health to thee, come! God has been merciful to us, that I have got a sight of thee." Then having kissed the hands mutually they sat down. The Pīr asked then: "O Nānak, having heard one verse of thine, I have become astonished. I said: 'By whom this verse has been spoken, his sight I have seen.'" Nānak replied: "Sir, a favour has been bestowed on me, that I have obtained a sight of you." The Pīr said: "Nānak, give me an explanation of this verse. Thou sayst: 'There is one, O Nānak, why another?' But there is one Lord and two definitions. What shall I accept, and what shall I reject? Thou sayst: 'There is only One,' but the Hindūs say that the truth is with them, and the Musalmāns say that the truth is with them. Say, who is right and who is wrong?" Bābā Nānak answered: "Sir, there is one Lord and one definition, accept the One and reject another (God)."

Slōk.

Why should another be served, who is born and dies?
Remember the One, O Nānak, who is contained in water and earth!

When the Bābā had given this Slōk, the Pīr said:

Tear the silk petticoat and make a flag of it,[2] put on a small blanket!
Put on those clothes, in which the bridegroom is obtained.

The Guru Bābā gave the answer:

Tear any petticoat, put on any blanket—.
Sitting in the house the bridegroom is obtained, if thou keep thy mind firm (on him).
In the house is the woman, her beloved abroad, she grieves continually remembering him.
He meets with her without delay, if she make a sincere desire (for him).

[1] The name is written differently: Briham, Biraham, and Birāham, as here. Very likely it is corrupted from Ibrāhīm.

[2] The Faqīrs are in the habit of erecting a flag in front of their dwellings.

When Nānak had given this answer, the Pīr said:

Slōk.

I have been young and he did not sport (with me).
Having grown up I departed.
The woman has sunk into the grave weeping: "I have not met with my Lord."

The Bābā answered:

Slōk.

The woman is foolish, thin, black, of an impure heart.
If she had virtues, she would constantly enjoy her beloved.
O Nānak, by her vices she is confounded.

The Pīr asked again:

Slōk.

What is that word, what those virtues, what that gem and charm:
What is that, I should get into my power, O sister, by which the beloved one may come into my power?

The Bābā answered with the Slōk:

Bowing is the word, parting with the virtue, the tongue the gems and charm:
These three, O sister, get into thy power, by which the beloved one will come into thy power.
Who serves the beloved one, his the beloved one becomes.
Nānak (says): who gives up all her companions, with her the beloved one will be.

When Nānak had given this answer, the Pīr said: "Nānak, I want one knife, give me that knife, by which man becomes slaughtered. With the common knife they slaughter animals, and when it passes over the neck of man, he will be slaughtered. Give me that knife, by which egotism becomes slaughtered." The Bābā answered: "O Pīr, take it!"

Slōk.

The knife of truth consider altogether as true!
Its working is inestimable.
Apply it to the whetstone of truth and hide it;
Put it into a sheath of virtues!
Who is slaughtered by this becomes a Shēkh.
Behold, covetousness, the blood, has flowed out.
If, being slaughtered, thou cling to truth:
Thou wilt be absorbed in the sight (of God) at the gate, (says) Nānak.

When the Bābā had given him this knife, the head of the Pīr turned round and he said: "Well, well done! thou art the beloved of God, God has bestowed a great favour (on thee)." Then the Pīr said again: "O Nānak, let me hear one Vār[1] of God! Our intention is this: a Vār cannot be made without two and thou art saying, he is only one. Let me see, whom thou wilt make the partner of God!" The Bābā said: "Mardānā, play the rebeck!" Mardānā played it, and the Rāg Āsā was sung, the Guru gave the Slōk in the Vār of Āsā, Mahalā I. [there follow three Slōks and one Pauṛī].[2] Nine Pauṛīs were made on this topic. Then the Pīr rose and stood erect. He came and kissed his hands, saying: "Nānak, thou hast obtained God, between thee and God there is no difference, but be thou merciful, that God may also come and remain with me." The

[1] ਵਾਰ, a song of praise.

[2] Āsā, Vār I. (p. 511). The second Slōk is noted down in the Granth as being of Angad, whereas it is here quoted as being made by Nānak.

Bābā answered: "Shēkh Briham, God will accomplish thy trip."[1] The Pīr said: "Sir, give me your word!" The Bābā replied: "Go, you have my word." The Shēkh rose then and stood, and the Bābā took leave of him.

The Bābā also rose, and passing through Dipālpur, Kačhanpur, Kāsūr and Paṭī, he came to Gōidawāl and stopped there, but nobody allowed him to stay there. There was one Faqīr there, to his hovel he went. That Faqīr was leprous. The Bābā having gone there stood and said: "O Faqīr, allow me to remain here during the night!" The Faqīr said: "Animals are destroyed, who come near me, but it is the favour of God that a human shape has come again into my sight." He remained there. The Faqīr began to lament. The Bābā uttered then a Sabd, in the Rāg Dhanāsarī, Mahalā I. [there follow four verses].[2] The Guru became compassionate and said: "Mardānā, play the rebeck!" He did so, and the Rāg Gauṛī was made, the Bābā recited the Sabd, Mahalā I. [there follow ten verses].[3] Then in consequence of the interview (with the Guru) the leprosy was removed and his body was healed. He came and fell down at (Nānak's) feet and became a votary of the name; he began to mutter: "Guru, Guru!"

Then the Bābā started thence; he came through Sultānpur, Vairōwāl, Jalālābād to Kiṛīā, a Paṭhān town; there he made Paṭhān people his disciples. Those Paṭhān people moving along began to sound drums and said: "Courage, Shāh Nānak!" Then the order was given to Mardānā: "Play the rebeck!" He did so and the Rāg Tilang was made; the Bābā uttered the Sabd, Mahalā I. [there follow ten verses].[4] Then the Paṭhān people becoming brave began to shout: "Courage, Shāh Nānak!"

Then the Guru departed thence; he came again through Vaṭālā and Saidpur to Sanḍeālī. In the houses of the Paṭhāns weddings were solemnized and with the Bābā were also some Faqīrs, who were hungry and empty. Having gone there the Bābā sat down, but nobody took any notice of them, though the Faqīrs were sorely depressed by hunger. The Bābā rose and stood, he took the Faqīrs and Mardānā with him, went and begged,[5] but no one responded to the demand. The Bābā became very angry and said: "Mardānā, play the rebeck!" He did so, and the Rāg Tilang was made, the Bābā uttering in anger the Sabd, Mahalā I. [there follow four verses].[6] When the Guru had recited this Sabd a Brāhmaṇ came with a basket of fruits and met with them saying: "O kind one, may the Sabd of wrath, that has been uttered, be revoked!" The Bābā answered: "Sir, now it is too late to revoke it, it is spoken; but thou, who hast come and met us, art pardoned. Twelve Kōs from here is a pond, thither bring thy family, do not remain here; if thou shalt remain here, thou wilt be killed." The Brāhmaṇ took his family and went away twelve Kōs and sat down in a desert. When by the power (of God) it had become morning, Mīr Bābar, the King, marched on and struck Saidpur[7] and all the villages round about, Hindūs and Musalmāns were promiscuously cut down, the houses sacked and pulled down. Such a slaughter came on the Paṭhāns by the Sabd of the Bābā. It was the wrath of a great man. God minds the words of Faqīrs, as he is minded by the Faqīrs; God being adored by the Faqīrs hears their word. What-

[1] The sense is: God will bring thee safely through (this life).

[2] Dhanāsarī, Sabd 5, Mah. I.

[3] This is again a misquotation, for in the Granth these verses are ascribed to Guru Rām Dās (fourth Guru); see: Gauṛī pūrbī, Karahalē, I. (p. 258; Transl. p. 337).

[4] Rāg Tilang, Rāisā, I. (p. 799).

[5] It is denied by the Sikhs, that Nānak ever begged, but the text here says plainly: ਜਾਇ ਸੁਆਲੁ ਪਾਇਆ. It is also expressly stated, that he begged on his *second* tour; see p. xxxiv.

[6] Rāg Tilang, Sabd 5, Mah. I.

[7] Cf. Transl. p. 509.

ever comes into the mind of the Faqīrs, that he does. But who are these Faqīrs? Who are given to kindness and love, who ask little, who walk in sincerity and patience, who have subdued their body and soul and who do not make forethought; who are careful and tender-hearted and upright, they are Darvēshes of God, they are Faqīrs. This also this married servant (of God) desires to be. Who among the four castes puts on the garb of Faqīrship, be he a Hindū or Musalmān, a thief, fornicator or highwayman, he ought to be served and his (former) works should not be taken into account.

The Bābā and Mardānā were thrown into the prison of Saidpur (at the capture of the place); then they came into the hands of Mīr Khān, the Mugal. Mīr Khān, the Mugal, gave the order, that these slaves should be carried away. The Bābā got a bundle on his head and for Mardānā a horse was seized. The Bābā uttered then a Sabd, in Rāg Mārū, Mahalā I. [there follow four verses].[1] Mardānā said: "Sir, what is the matter regarding these (women), who are standing on their feet and go along weeping?" The Bābā replied: "Mardānā, play the rebeck!" Mardānā said: "Sir, in my hand is a horse." The Bābā said: "Say: vāh Guru! and let the horse go from thy hand." Mardānā let the horse go and played the rebeck, the Rāg Tilang was made, the Bābā uttering the Sabd, Mahalā I. [there follow twenty-two verses].[2] When the Bābā had recited these Sabds, Mīr Khān, the Mugal, came. When he looked, he saw that the bundle on the head (of Nānak) was going on supported by a hand and that the horse was walking behind (Mardānā). He reported this to Sultān Bābar and said: "A Faqīr, who has been taken prisoner, on his head a bundle is going; with him is a Ḍūm, behind whom a horse is walking; he is playing a rebeck and worshipping God." The King replied: "A town, in which there are such Faqīrs, should not have been struck." Then the Mīr said: "See to bestow favour on them!" Then having gone above two Kōs the tents were pitched. There mills were put before them and they were told to grind the corn of the government. The Paṭhān, Khatrī, and Brāhmaṇ women were all seated together and mills put before them, before the Bābā too a mill was put, but it turned by itself, the Bābā sat and filled in a handful (when the corn was ground). Then the King came there and the Bābā recited a Sabd, in the Rāg Āsā, Mahalā I. [there follow seven verses].[3] The King began then to ask miracles; at that time the Sabd was made in the Rāg Tilang, Mahalā I. [there follow four verses].[4] When the Bābā had recited this Sabd, the King Bābar came on and kissed his feet, saying: "In the face of this Faqīr God is coming into sight."[5] Then all the people, Hindūs as well as Musalmāns, began to make salām (to Nānak). The King said, "O Darvēsh, accept of something!" The Guru Bābā replied: "I do not want anything, but release the prisoners of Saidpur and what has been taken from them restore to them!" King Bābar gave the order that they should release the prisoners and restore their property to them. All the prisoners of Saidpur were set at liberty, but they would not go without the Bābā; so the Bābā returned with them on the third day to Saidpur. When he arrived there, he saw that a promiscuous slaughter had been made. The Bābā said then: "O Mardānā, what has happened here!" Mardānā replied: "O King, what was thy will, that has happened." The Bābā said: "Play the rebeck!" Mardānā did so, and the Rāg Āsā was made, the Bābā uttering the Sabd [there follow seven verses].[6] When

[1] Mārū, Sabd 6, Mah. I.

[2] This is a misquotation; in the Granth these verses are ascribed to Guru Rām Dās (Mah. IV.); see Tilang, Sabd I, Mah. IV. (p. 800).

[3] This is properly an Aṣṭpadī; see Rāg Āsā, Aṣṭpadī XI., Mah. I. (p. 460).

[4] These verses are not to be found in the Rāg Tilang.

[5] Mulisin Fānī says in the Dābistān (II., 249), that there was a report that Nānak had called the Mugals into the country. This is by no means countenanced by the Sikh tradition.

[6] Āsā, Aṣṭpadī XII., Mah. I.

Bābar marched away, the Bābā recited the Sabd in the Rāg Sōraṭhi, Mahalā I. [there follow four verses].[1] When the Bābā came to Saidpur, the Hindūs and the Musalmāns commenced to bury and to burn the dead ones; in every house they began to weep and to beat their breasts and to lament. The Guru fell into a trance; at that time the Sabd was made in Rāg Āsā [there follow ten verses].[2] One day Mardānā said: "Sir, why has this (town) been alike destroyed and why have so many been killed?" The Guru Bābā replied: "Mardānā, go and sleep under that tree, when thou wilt rise, I will give thee an answer." Mardānā went and slept there. One drop of grease had fallen on his breast when eating bread. As soon as he was (therefore) fallen asleep, ants came and fell on him. When one ant bit the sleeper, he bruised them all with his hand and threw them away. The Bābā said: "What hast thou done, O Mardānā?" Mardānā answered: "For the sake of one, who has bitten me, all have been killed." The Bābā laughed and said: "In this very wise they have been killed for the sake of one." Then Mardānā came and fell down at his feet. Many people of Saidpur became votaries of the name.

At that time Jhāṛū, the distiller, was in prison; he wrote (to Nānak); he was a Kharaṛ[3] of Khānpur, but by visiting the society (of the pious) he put his trust in God and became an Udāsī.

The Bābā started thence. Passing through Pasrūr he came to the small fort of Miyā̃ Miṭhā,[4] and at a distance of a little more than half a Kōs he went into a garden and sat down there. Miā̃ Miṭhā was informed of it and said amongst his disciples: "Nānak is an excellent Faqīr, but when he will meet with us, we will skim him off, as the cream is skimmed off the milk." The Bābā said: "Mardānā, what does Miā̃ Miṭhā say?" Mardānā answered: "Sir, he is thy musical instrument, as he is caused to sound, so he sounds." Then the Guru Bābā said: "Mardānā, when Miā̃ Miṭhā will meet us, we will so squeeze him, as the juice is squeezed out of a lemon." Then Miā̃ Miṭhā rose and said: "Go on, friends, we will have an interview with Nānak." His disciples said: "Thou hadst before said, 'When Nānak will meet with us, we will so skim him off, as the cream is skimmed off the milk.'" Miā Miṭhā̃ said: "Rise, an answer has come (to me): 'as the juice is squeezed out of a lemon, so, when Miā̃ Miṭhā will meet (with me), I will squeeze him out. The milk is nothing when the cream is taken off, and the lemon when squeezed out will be a refuse.'" Then Miā̃ Miṭhā came to the interview; haviug saluted he sat down.

Miā̃ Miṭhā said then:

Slōk.

> The first is the name of God, the second the prophet:
> O Nānak, if thou read the Kalima,[5] thou wilt be accepted at the threshold.

The Bābā answered:

> The first is the name of God, the prophet is the cowkeeper at the gate.
> O Shēkh, if thou make a right aim, thou wilt be accepted at the threshold.

The Bābā added: "O Shēkh Miṭhā, at that gate there is no place for two; whoever remains there, he remains there having become one (with God)." Then Shēkh Miṭhā said: "O Nānak, how will the lamp burn without oil?"

Slōk.

> Him, who cannot be deceived, fraud does not deceive, the dagger does not inflict one wound (on him).
> The mind of this covetous one palpitates; how should the lamp burn without oil?

[1] These verses are not to be found in the Rāg Sōraṭhī.

[2] Āsā, Asṭpadī XII., Mah. I. (p. 461).

[3] Name of a savage tribe of the Rachnā Duāb.

[4] Compare: Sikhā̃ dē rāǰ dī vithiā, pp. 257, sqq.

[5] The Moslem confession of faith.

The Bābā answered :

Slōk.

(1). The book of the Kur'ān should be performed, the wick of fear should be applied to this body.
Understanding of truth should be brought and kindled :
Thus the lamp burns without oil ; make light, thus the Lord is met with.
(2). To this body adhere (different) tempers.
Comfort is obtained by performing service (to God).
All the world is coming and going.
(3). (If) in the world service (to God) be performed,
Then at the threshold a seat is obtained.
Nānak says : the arm will be leisurely swung (there).[1]

Then Shēkh Mit̤hā said : "Sir, what is that Kur'ān, by reading which one may become approved of? and what is that book, by acting up to which one may become accepted? and what is that Darvēsh-ship, by which one may become worthy of the gate (of God)? and what is that fasting, by which the heart remains fixed and does not move? and what is that prayer, by the performing of which a favourable glance (of God) falls (on one)?

The Bābā answered and said : "Mardānā, play the rebeck!" Mardānā did so, and the Bābā made the Sabd in the Rāg Mārū, Mahalā I. [there follow fifteen verses].[2] Then Shēkh Mit̤hā said : "Thou hast praised the one name, what is this one name?" The Bābā answered : "O Shēkh Mit̤hā, has any one attained to an estimate of the one name?" Shēkh Mit̤hā said : "For kindness' sake show it to me!" The Bābā seized the arm of Shēkh Mit̤hā, led him to a corner and said : "Shēkh Mit̤hā, the one name of God was void." Then the Bābā said : "Allah!" and with saying this the other became ashes. Seeing this Shēkh Mit̤hā became astonished; when he looked on, there was a handful of ashes there. Then came again a voice : "Allah!" and with this he rose and stood erect. Thereupon Shēkh Mit̤hā came on and kissed his feet. Then the Bābā said in a state of ecstasy : "On those, who are present, favour is bestowed, to those, who are not present, he is incompassionate. Faith is a friend, the faithless one is an infidel; arrogance is wrath, wrath is unlawful. Sensuality is the devil; conceit is infidelity; the mouth of him, who slanders one behind one's back, is black; he, who is without faith, is impure; the tender-hearted one is pure. Wisdom is mildness; who is without greediness, is a saint; the dishonest one is not honourable; the ungrateful one is shameless. Truth is paradise, falsehood is hell; clemency is an oath; force is oppression; justice is the Kur'ān; praise (of God) ablution; the cry (to prayer) discrimination;[3] theft is covetousness; adultery is impurity; leading the life of a Faqīr is patience; impatience is deceit. The way is the Pīr; who has no Pīr, is going astray. Honesty is a friend, the dishonest one is worthless. The sword becomes men, justice the kings. Who knows and makes known so many things, he is called wise, (says) Nānak." Then the Bābā took leave of Miā̃ Mit̤hā and departed thence. Say : vāh Guru!

Going along the bank of the river Rāvī he came to Lāhaur. In the Lāhaur Pargana (district) was a man, who owned a Crōre (of Rupees), named Dunī Čand, a Dhupur̤ Khatr̤ī, the Srādh of whose father was then performed. When he heard, that Nānak, the ascetic, had come, he went and paid reverence to the Bābā and took him with him. The Guru went and sat down (in his house). Then the performance of that matter (*i.e.* the Srādh) was taken up. He (Dunī Čand)

[1] An idiomatic expression for a comfortable life without cares.

[2] This is a misquotation, the verses being ascribed in the Granth to Guru Arjun (fifth Guru). See Mārū, Sōlahē, V. Mah., 12.

[3] The original is ਬਾਂਗ ਬਲੇਕ ਹੈ ; ਬਲੇਕ is in itself senseless ; it is very likely a slip of the pen instead of ਬਿਬੇਕ.

gave orders: milk, coagulated milk, fuel, grain was kept ready and the Brāhmaṇs ate; he went also to call the Bābā. The Bābā asked: "What has happened in thy house?" He answered: "It is the Srādh of my father, in his name the Brāhmaṇs eat." The Bābā said: "To-day it is the third day to thy father (since he has died) and he has eaten nothing[1] and thou art saying, that thou art feeding one hundred men." Dunī Čand humbly replied and said: "Sir, where is he?" The Bābā said: "He has fallen into a wood near a village, five Kōs from here the birth of a wolf takes place. But go thou and bring (him) food and don't be afraid! With thy going his human intellect will return (to him); he will eat the food and will speak too." Dunī Čand brought the food there and put it before (the wolf, in which his father's ghost was). Then he asked: "O father, how hast thou come into this birth?" He replied: "Without the perfect Guru I have come into this birth. I was the disciple of a religious man,[2] who had allowed me to eat the flesh of fish. With me were profligate companions (and thus) the lust also seized me, my desire went also that way. When the time of my death came, I became distressed; in punishment thereof I have come into this birth." Then that one rose and went away and this one ran off. Dunī Čand came back and fell down at the feet (of Nānak), and took the Guru Bābā to his house. Upon its door seven flags were fastened, of which every one was worth one Lakh (of Rupees). The Bābā asked: "Whose flags are these?" Dunī Čand answered: "Sir, these flags are mine." Then the Bābā gave him a needle and said: "Keep it as a deposit of mine, we shall demand it again in the other world." Dunī Čand brought the needle to his wife and said: "Keep this needle, which the Guru gave (me) and said: 'We shall demand it in the other world.'" His wife replied: "Will this needle go on with thee to the Lord?" Dunī Čand said: "What is to be done?" His wife replied: "Go, give it back to him." Dunī Čand brought the needle back to the Bābā and said: "This needle cannot go with me to the other world, take it back!" The Guru Bābā replied: "How wilt thou bring these flags there, as thou art not able to bring a needle there?" Dunī Čand rose and bowed his head and said: "Sir, tell me that word, by which they may arrive there." The Guru replied: "Give in the name of the Lord! put (food) into the mouth of ascetics and uninvited guests, thus (the flags) will arrive there with thee." Then Dunī Čand gave away (as alms) the flags of seven Lakhs (of Rupees) and removed them. He obeyed the order. The order of the Guru is this, whoever will obey it, will be saved. Then Dunī Čand became a votary of the name and began to mutter: "Guru, Guru!" The Bābā said then: "Mardānā, play the rebeck!" Mardānā did so, and the Vār of Rāg Āsā was made, fifteen Pauṛīs on the subject of Dunī Čand.

After that the Bābā went to his house and remained some days in Talvaṇḍī. One day a Brāhmaṇ came, who was strict in the observance of the prescribed religious duties; he was hungry and having come in he pronounced a blessing. The Bābā was just sitting at his meal and said: "Come, O Misr, the meal is ready!" The Paṇḍit replied: "I shall not eat this food, I shall eat that which I have prepared myself. When I shall dig up the ground a cubit long and make a Čaukā[3] and when I shall dig up the ground a span long, I will make a hearth, and having washed the fuel, I will lay it upon it;—of what kind is the ground of this cooking-place?—I will not eat." The Bābā said: "Give to this Paṇḍit a new cooking-place." A new cooking-place was given him. The Paṇḍit went out and began to make a Čaukā and to dig up the ground; wherever he dug, there bones came forth. He went about digging for four watches (= twelve hours). When he had become quite exhausted by hunger, he said (within himself):

[1] The sense is: Thou hast made no offering to his manes.

[2] ਆਚਾਰੀ, properly: strict in observing the prescribed religious duties.

[3] The ਚਉਕਾ (*m.*) is a small place, defined by lines and smeared with cow-dung, in which Hindūs cook their food.

"I will go to the Bābā." He came, fell down at his feet and said: "May that food be given to me, I am dead of hunger." The Guru said: "That time of meal is passed, but go and say: 'vāh Guru!' dig up the ground, make a cooking-place and eat!" Then the Bābā uttered a Sabd in the Rāg Basant, Mahalā I. [there follow four verses].[1]

One day the Guru gave the order, that in the last watch of the night the praises (of God) should be sung. One boy of seven years rose from his house and came (too), and stood behind the Guru. When the recital of the Ārtī[2] was made, he rose and went. One day the Bābā said: "Keep to-day the boy back." When he went away, after having bowed his head, the society held him back and placed him before the Guru. The Guru asked him saying: "Why art thou coming here and rising at this time? Till now it is for thee the time of eating, playing and sleeping." That boy replied: "Sir, one day my mother said to me: 'O my son, kindle a fire!' I set to kindle it. When I had put on the wood, the fire first seized the small pieces and afterwards the larger ones. At this I became afraid, lest I might (also) depart (this world) whilst little; in growing big we may meet or not meet (with God), like the pieces of wood. Therefore I said: 'I will mutter the Guru!'" The assembly hearing this became astonished, and the Bābā also was much pleased. The boy fell down at his feet. At that time the Bābā uttered the Sabd in the Rāg Sirī Rāg, Mahalā I. [there follow four verses].[3]

By the favour of the true Guru!

Then the Bābā started from his house and passed the *second time* a retired life in the *Dakhan* (*south*). He got his livelihood by filling his begging vessel with morsels;[4] on his feet he had sandals of wood, in his hand a staff, on his head rolls of rope; on his forehead as Tilak the paint of a point. With him were Saidō and Sīhō of the Ghēhō Jaṭ tribe. The Bābā went to the country of Dhanāsarī and remained some days there. At night-time Saidō and Sīhō of the Ghēhō tribe both went to the river to perform worship. They went when yet one watch of the night was remaining, and thought in their heart that what the Guru had got from the Khavājah,[5] he had got in that very place. One night they went and saw a man coming towards them, in whose hand was a fish. That man asked: "Who are you?" Saidō and Sīhō said: "We are the disciples of Guru Nānak." That man asked (further): "What for are you come here?" Saidō replied: "We are always going here in the last watch of the night to worship the Khavājah, because our Guru has obtained (something)[6] from the Khavājah." Then Saidō asked: "Sir, who are you and where will you go?" That man answered: "I am the Khavājah and am continually going to the Guru; I go at this time to pay worship to him. To-day I bring him a fish as an offering." Then Saidō and Sīhō came and fell down at his feet and said: "We are saying that the Guru has got it from you, and you are saying that you are always going to perform service (to the Guru), and that you bring to-day an offering to the Guru." Then Khavājah Khiḍir said: "O ye men of the Lord, I am the water and that Guru is the wind. I have many times been produced from him and many times I have been absorbed in him." Both disciples, Saidō and Sīhō of the Ghēhō tribe, went then and fell down at the feet of the Guru. The Guru asked: "Why

[1] Rāg Basant, Sabd 3, Mah. I.

[2] The ਆਰਤੀ is here the piece of poetry sung at the oblation of the Ārtī.

[3] It is a misquotation, the verses being ascribed in the Granth to Guru Arjun; see Sirī Rāg, Sabd 4, Mah. V.

[4] The begging of Bābā Nānak is here most plainly asserted. *Cf.* p. xxix. note 5.

[5] ਖੋਆਜਾ or ਖੋਆਜਾ ਖਿਦਿਰਿ (خواجه خضر), according to Muslim tradition the prophet Elias. In Sindh and the lower Panjāb Khavājah Khiḍir is worshipped also by the Hindūs as the river god Indus, under the more common name of *Jindā Pīr*.

[6] It is not mentioned, what the Guru had or was supposed to have obtained.

have you come to-day at this (early) time? you have come before the day has risen." Saidō the Ghēhō told him, how they had met with the Khavājah. Then the Bābā uttered the Slōk in the Jap [there follows one verse].[1] The Guru Bābā remained after that some days in the country of Dhanāsarī; many people there became votaries of the name and began to mutter: "Guru, Guru!"

There was a cloister of Jainas there, the people of which performed much worship. When they heard that the Guru was come, they collected their disciples and came with them; they spread out their beds outside the door and sat on them. They then sent word to the Guru, that he should come out to them. When Guru Bābā came out, the head Jaina asked him: "Thou, who art eating grain new and full, and who art eating split vetches and drinking cold and unstrained water, and callest thyself a Guru, what authority hast thou got, that thou art always killing living creatures?" The Bābā recited (in answer) a Pauṛī of a Vār in the Rāg Mājh [there follows a Pauṛī] and (two) Slōks.[2]

When the Guru Bābā had said these Slōks, the head Jaina came and fell down at his feet; he became a votary of the name and began to mutter: "Guru, Guru!" At that time in a state of ecstasy this whole Vār of the Rāg Mājh was made in the country of Dhanāsarī, and written down by Saidō, the Ghēhō; the whole is to be read. In the country of Dhanāsarī many became votaries of the name; there is also a Manjī there. Say: vāh Guru!

The Bābā departed thence and wandered along. There was a Rākshasa of the Dhanāsarī country, who was eating men. The Bābā passed there, Saidō and Sīhō being with him. The Rākshasa came up to them, having seen that the iron boiler was put on. He seized the Bābā and carried him away, who seeing this laughed. Saidō and Sīhō began to weep and said: "He will also throw our bodies into the boiler." The Bābā sat down in the heated boiler and fell into a state of ecstasy. At that time the Sabd was made in the Rāg Mārū, Mahalā I. [there follow four verses].[3] The Rākshasa kept on heating the boiler, but the boiler did not become hot, it became cold. Then he came and fell down at his feet and said: "Sir, effect my salvation!" Then Sīhō gave him the Pāhul;[4] he became a votary of the name and was emancipated (saved).

The Bābā went on, wandering about. Further on, on the sea-shore, Makhdūm Bahāvadīn[5] was sitting on a carpet and playing. The Guru went up to him. Then Makhdūm Bahāvadīn having seen him saluted him and said: "Peace be on thee, O Darvēsh!" The Bābā answered and said: "On thee be peace, O Makhdūm Bahāvadīn, the Ḳuraishī!" Then having kissed his hand he sat down. Makhdūm Bahāvadīn said: "O Darvēsh Nānak, come let us make a trip on the sea." The Bābā said: "Makhdūm Bahāvadīn, hast thou seen anything in making this voyage?" Makhdūm Bahāvadīn replied: "O Nānak, one day a tower came into sight." The Bābā said: "Go and bring information about it!" Makhdūm Bahāvadīn replied: "I promise to do it, Sir!" Makhdūm Bahāvadīn threw his prayer-carpet into the ocean and sporting, sporting he went out (into the sea). He saw there one tower and went there. As he went on, he saw twenty men seated there. He went to them, saluted them and shook hands with them and sat down. When night had set in, twenty dishes of food came down from heaven; the Faqīrs ate the food. Four

[1] See the last Slōk of the Japjī.

[2] The Pauṛī is in Mājh Vār XXV., but in the Granth ascribed to Guru Amar Dās (third Guru); the following two Slōks are in Vār XXVI. and also in the Granth attributed to Bābā Nānak.

[3] These verses are not to be found among the Sabds of Rāg Mārū.

[4] The Pāhul (now pronounced Pāhuḷ) is the initiatory rite of the Sikhs, which is here carried back as far as the time of Bābā Nānak, which is by no means probable, as it is never mentioned in the Granth. The more ancient rite of the Pāhul consisted simply in the drinking of some sherbet with two other disciples and uttering: "Vāh Guru!"

[5] Bahāu-ddīn, the famous Musalmān Saint of Multān.

watches (of the night) they worshipped God. At daybreak those twenty men went away. Makhdūm Bahāvadīn remained that day there. When the day had risen one watch (= three hours), one boat came along, and it began also to sink. Makhdūm lifted up his hands before God, that this boat should not sink whilst he stood there. The boat ceased to sink. When night had set in, those men came back and remained together during the night, but no food came down from the sky. The Faqīrs went on remembering God during the night. When it became morning, those men went again away. Makhdūm Bahāvadīn remained also that day there. When the second day had set in, that tower began to fall in. Then Makhdūm joining his hands begged that the tower, whilst he was sitting there, should not fall in, and it ceased to fall. When night had set in, those men also came; they sat together during the night, but no food came down from heaven. Then those friends said: "Who is the unfortunate man, who has thrown an obstacle into the way of God's works?" They began to reflect and to inquire among themselves. Then said Makhdūm Bahāvadīn: "I have preserved the boat and the tower." Those men asked: "O Darvēsh, what is thy name?" Makhdūm Bahāvadīn answered: "My name is Makhdūm Bahāvadīn, the Pīr." Those men said: "O Darvēsh, here is no place for Pīrs and Kings;[1] the Pīrs and Kings are lustrous in the world and are the gate and foundation of the way of God; the head of Pīrs and Kings is high."

Makhdūm Bahāvadīn having said: "Peace be on you!" took up his prayer-carpet and put it on the sea and sat thereon. But the carpet did not go, the four watches of the day he remained sitting on the ocean. When the day began to sink, those men also came. When they saw that he was sitting on the ocean, those men asked: "O Darvēsh, why art thou sitting here?" Makhdūm Bahāvadīn replied: "My prayer-carpet does not go." Those disciples then said: "Write the name of the true Guru Nānak (on it), that thy carpet may go!" He wrote then (the name of) the true Guru Nānak and the carpet of Makhdūm Bahāvadīn went along and he came back to the Bābā. Having made his salutation he sat down. The Bābā asked: "What hast thou seen, O Makhdūm Bahāvadīn?" He replied: "Sir, thou knowest all; I have come back as a sacrifice to thy slaves." The Bābā said: "O Makhdūm Bahāvadīn, works are a carcass, it is forbidden to the devotees to sit down there." Makhdūm Bahāvadin came then and kissed (his, the Bābā's) feet. At that time the Sabd was made in the Rāg Sirī Rāg, Mahalā I. [there follow eight verses].[2] Then Makhdūm Bahāvadīn flung away the prayer-carpet from his hands; he was ordered, that he should go and take a Pīr. Makhdūm Bahāvadīn said: "Sir, whom shall I make my Pīr?" The Bābā gave the answer: "Whom Shēkh Farīd has made (his Pīr)." Makhdūm Bahāvadīn made his salutation, shook hands and was dismissed by the Bābā. The Bābā also departed thence. He went along on the road of the ocean;[3] further on Mačhind and Gōrakhnāth were sitting.[4] When Mačhind saw (him), he said: "O Gōrakhnāth, who is coming here on the ocean?" Gōrakhnāth answered: "Sir, this is Nānak." The Bābā made his appearance; having said: "Adēs, adēs (salutation)!" he sat down. Mačhind asked and said: "O Nānak, what did the ocean of the world appear (to thee)? In which wise is the ocean crossed?" The Bābā uttered a Sabd in the

[1] Great Faqīrs are also called *Kings*; thus Nānak is usually called Nānak Shāh by the Muhammadans.

[2] These verses are not to be found among the Sabds of Sirī Rāg.

[3] That is to say: he went along on the sea-shore, but on the ocean.

[4] Mačhind (properly Mačhēndra) and Gōrakh are Jōgīs (both have therefore the title of nāth), Gōrakhnāth being the son of Mačhēndra and grandson of Ādināth, according to Price's Hindī and Hindūstānī Selections, vol. i. p. 141. In later times Gōrakhnāth was considered the founder of the Jōgī sect, though without reason. At any rate Mačhind and Gōrakhnāth were not contemporaries of Nānak, as Gōrakhnāth was, according to all accounts, a contemporary of Kabīr. It need therefore hardly be mentioned that this whole story is an invention of the Sikhs, who consider Mačhind as a fabulous being, half-man and half-fish.

Rāg Rāmkalī, Mahalā I. [there follow four verses with two Rahāus].[1] At that time the Sabd was also made [there follow four verses].[1] Mačhind said further: "O Nānak, practise the Yōga, that thou mayst become free from vacillation and cross in comfort the water of existence." The Guru recited a Sabd in the Rāg Rāmkalī, Mahalā I. [there follow four verses].[2] Then Gōrakhnāth humbly said: "O Guru: thy Pīrship (spiritual guidance) is (my) prayer; from the beginning, from the beginning of the Yugas it has gone on." The Bābā replied: "Whom wilt thou make (thy) Guru, O Gōrakhnāth?" Gōrakhnāth said: "Who is such a Guru, that he may put his hand on thy head? that is thy Guru, who may be born from thy body." The Bābā replied: "Very well." Then the Bābā departed and went along. The conversation with Mačhind is finished, it was written by Saidō of the Ghēhō Jaṭ tribe. Say: vāh Guru!

Then mention was made of Singhala-dīpa (Ceylon). They went and stood on the bottomless ocean. The Bābā said: "How shall this bottomless ocean be crossed and passed?" His disciples Saidō and Sīhō humbly said: "Sir, by thy order the mountains will cross." The Bābā said: "Keep on reading this Slōk: the true name is the creator, the Supreme Spirit, without fear, without enmity, of timeless form, unproduced from a womb. By the favour of the holy true Guru!" Then the Bābā said: "In whose disciple's mouth this Slōk will be and who will continue reading it, and as many people after him will hear it, they will all cross the water of existence." At this the disciples fell down at his feet and said: "Sir, whom thou pleasest, him thou makest cross." Then they went across the ocean (to Ceylon). In Singhala-dīpa they went to the Rājā Siv-nābhi and took up their abode in his garden on the other side of the ocean. At that time the garden of the Rājā Siv-nābhi, which was worth nine Lakhs, was dried up; it became green again, what bore flowers, got flowers, what bore leaves, got leaves. When Maghōr, the gardener, saw that the garden, which had been dried up for years, had become green, he went and informed the Rājā Siv-nābhi of it, saying: "Sir, come out! with the sitting down in it of a Faqīr the garden has become green!" The Rājā Siv-nābhi sent slave-girls of exquisite beauty, who, having arrived there, began to dance. They sang many Rāgs and made many sports, but the Bābā did not say anything, he remained sunk in meditation. Afterwards the Rājā Siv-nābhi came (himself). Having come he began to ask and said: "Sir, what is thy name? what is thy caste? art thou a Jōgī? Be so kind as to come to my palace!" The Bābā recited a Sabd in the Rāg Mārū, Mahalā I.[3] [there follow four verses]. Then the Rājā Siv-nābhi asked: "Sir, art thou Gōrakhnāth?" The Bābā recited then the fifth Pauṛī [there follows one verse]. When the Bābā had concluded (this verse), the Rājā came and fell down at his feet, humbly begging and saying: "Sir, be so kind as to come to my house." The Bābā replied: "I do not go on foot." Rājā Siv-nābhi said: "Sir, all is given to thee. If it be thy wish, mount a horse or an elephant! or mount also a travelling-throne!" The Bābā replied: "We will ride on men." The King said: "Sir, there are also many men (at thy disposal), mount!" The Bābā replied: "Your honour, if there be such a man, who is a Rājā (or) a prince, and if there be the Rājā of the city, on his back I will mount." The Rājā said: "O King, I am thy creature, the Rājā am I, mount!" The Bābā mounted on the back of the Rājā. The people (seeing this) began to say, that the Rājā had run mad. When he (the Bābā) had come, he sat down. The Rāṇī Čandkalā and the Rājā Siv-nābhi joined their hands (in supplication) and stood before him, humbly saying: "Do you wish to eat, Sir?" The Bābā answered: "I am keeping a fast." The Rājā said: "Sir, how may we bestow any benefit (on you)?" The Guru answered: "If there would be some flesh of man, I would eat it." The Rājā Siv-nābhi

[1] Rāmkalī, Sabd 3, 4, Mah. I.

[2] Rāmkalī, Sabd 5, Mah. I.

[3] These verses are not to be found among the Sabds of Rāg Mārū.

said: "Sir, many men also are a sacrifice for you." The Bābā replied: "Your honour, if there would be such a man, a son in the house of the Rājā, a prince of twelve years, his flesh I would eat." On this the Rājā and the Rāṇī became thoughtful; then the Rājā said: "O Lord, perhaps there is a son in the house of some Rājā." The Rāṇī said then: "How shall I give him up by thy order?" A fight ensued with her; when she was overcome, she gave her son up. The Rāṇī said then: "Your honour, there is a son in our house, look at his janam-patrī!" When the janam-patrī was examined, it was found, that he was twelve years old." The Rājā said then: "O son, thy body is required for the Guru! what is thy desire?" The boy replied: "O father, what benefit is derived from this, that my body should be required for the Guru?" The Rājā said: "As this one has been married seven days, his wife also should be asked." Then the Rāṇī and the Rājā went and sat down at the side of their daughter-in-law. The Rājā said: "O daughter, the body of thy husband is required for the Guru, what is thy pleasure?" The girl replied: "O father, this one's body is required for the Guru, and my widowhood is sacrificed to the Guru, what other benefit is derived from this?" Then the four came to the Guru and stood before him. The Rājā Siv-nābhi said: "Sir, here is the boy!" The Bābā replied: "Your honour, thus he is of no use to me. The mother should seize his arms and his wife should seize his feet and thou shouldst take a knife into thy hand and slaughter him, then he will be of use to me." The Rājā Siv-nābhi obeyed the order of the Guru; taking a knife into his hand he slaughtered his son. Having boiled (the flesh) he brought it and put it before him. Then the Bābā said: "You three, closing the eyes and saying: 'Vāh Guru!' put (it)[1] into your mouth!" The Rājā and the Rāṇī and the Rājā's daughter-in-law closed their eyes and said: "Vāh Guru!" When they put it into their mouth, the four were sitting there, but when they opened their eyes, the Guru Bābā was not there. The Rājā became distressed and went to the wilderness; he stood on his feet bare-headed and wandered about saying: "Guru, Guru!" Then after twelve months he (the Guru) came and gave him an interview and applied him to his feet; the regeneration and dying of the Rājā Siv-nābhi was cut off, he became a disciple. Saidō the Jaṭ, of the Ghēhō tribe, gave him the Pāhul by the order (of the Guru); all the people of Singhala-dīpa became disciples, they began to mutter: "Guru, Guru!" the whole region was pardoned after the Rājā Siv-nābhi.[2]

The evening service of the society of Singhala-dīpa.

When night sets in, then all assemble together and sit down in the Dharmsālā. Then one disciple goes for the food of the night. In the morning they all go and eat together. In whose disciple's house the meal takes place, into his kitchen twenty-one maunds of salt are brought.

At that time the secret devotional service was made manifest. By the favour of the holy true Guru is written the Prān-sangalī[3] (viz.): the story of the empty palace;[4] meditation on the Formless one; the recital of the secret devotional service by the Bābā, the consideration of the vital breath and the body. At that time the Bābā was wind-eating. It was made beyond the ocean in Singhala-dīpa, in the country of the Rājā Siv-nābhi; at that time the disciples Saidō and Sīhō were with him, when the Prān-sangalī was made. First part: Rāgu Āsā, Mahalā I. [there follow twenty-one verses].[5] At that time the Prān-sangalī was made, the knowledge of the soul is

[1] It is not stated, what they should put into their mouth, very likely, purposely.

[2] The story of Rājā Siv-nābhi is also contained in the later Janam-Sākhīs, but totally changed; see Lahore edition, p. 120. It was thought too offensive, as it borders on madness.

[3] Literally: the chain of the breath. The Prān-sangalī formerly formed a part of the Sikh devotional service, but is now unknown amongst them (at least in the Panjāb).

[4] The words of the original are: ਸੁੰਨ ਮਹਲ ਕੀ ਕਥਾ.

[5] I cannot find these verses in the Rāg Āsā; they were, as it appears, not received into the collection of the Granth, if they are not altogether fictitious.

(therein) discussed, but none could take it, it was (therefore) left there. By Saidō the Ghēhō he caused it to be written, having made him wash his feet near the small shop of Gōrakh. Near the little shop of Gōrakh is a square, in that he (the Guru) began to remain separated (from the world). But the secret devotional service was not made manifest, it was given to the Rājā Siv-nābhi. The word was pronounced (by the Guru): if one man shall come from Jambu-dīpa (India), for him it should be written.

The Guru departed thence. He came to the house of a carpenter and remained there during the night. This man performed much service to him and laid out a couch for him. The Bābā slept (on it) during the night; in the morning he seized with his hand the wood of the hut and smashed the couch with a side-post. When he came out, Saidō the disciple humbly said: "Sir, in the whole town nobody was giving us a place, but this carpenter gave us a place. His things also have been ruined; he had one hut and a couch, this also thou hast pulled down and gone away. What is the matter concerning him?" The Bābā replied: "O Saidō, his love (to me) has been accepted. When that (carpenter) came to his house, those four feet (of the couch) were buried in the ground, but beneath them were four pots of money; of the hovel a palace was raised, and of the low couch fine bedsteads were made." Then Saidō and Sīhō fell down at his feet.

The Bābā went then to his house (*i.e.* home to Talvaṇḍī), and remained some days at home. Then he set out again and began to pass his *third* retired life in the *northern* region. In this (third) retired life he was eating the fruits and blossoms of the Akk-tree,[1] but in a dried state. On his feet he had a skin and on his head also, his whole body was wrapped up. On his forehead he had a Tilak of saffron. At that time were with him Hasū, the blacksmith, and Sīhā, the calico-printer. The Bābā went to Kashmīr and remained some days there; many people became votaries of the name. At that time there was in Kashmīr a Panḍit, Brahm-dās; he heard that a Faqīr had come. With him (*i.e.* the Panḍit) went two camels (laden) with the Purāṇas, and on his neck he had an idol. Having come he said: "Rām, Rām!" and sat down. Having seen the garb (of the Bābā) he said: "Thou art a Sādh, why hast thou put on skins? and why hast thou twisted round ropes? why hast thou given up the (prescribed) works? and why art thou touching meat and fish?" The Bābā replied with the Vār in the Rāg Malār, Mahalā I. [there follow two Vārs].[2] Then the Panḍit Brahm-dās came and fell down at his feet and said: "Sir, when this thing was not, where was then the Lord?" The Bābā recited the Sabds in the Rāg Mārū, Mahalā I. [there follow sixteen verses].[3] Then the Panḍit Brahm-dās came and fell down at his feet; he flung away the stone (idol) from his neck and became a votary of the name, he began to perform service (to it). But the desire did not leave his mind, whatever service he performed, that he did naturally sighing; it came into his mind, that he was performing this service also before. The sacrifice of his egotism was (therefore) not acceptable. One day the Guru Bābā said: "Go and take a Guru!" The Panḍit replied: "Sir, whom shall I make my Guru?" The Guru Bābā said: "Go, in the wilderness is a house, there four Faqīrs are sitting, they will point him out to thee." Brahm-dās started off; having gone there he made obeisance to them. Those disciples having paused for twenty-four minutes said: "Thy Guru is in that mansion." The Panḍit came back and made his obeisance. A woman dressed in crimson clothes stood before him, and taking her slipper beat him badly. Weeping he went back (to those disciples). Those disciples asked him: "Hast thou met with the Guru?" He related to them the accident that had happened to him. Then said those disciples: "O brother, that was the Māyā, whom thou

[1] Which are considered very poisonous.

[2] Of these Vārs the first Slōk is ascribed in the Granth to Amar Dās. See Malār, Vār 1, 2 (p. 1414).

[3] Rāg Mārū, Sōlahē, 15, Mah. I.

wast desiring." Then he came and fell down at the feet of the Guru Bābā; he drove away the two camels with the Purāṇas and began to mutter: "Guru, Guru!" he became the dust of the feet of the society. (This) true story was written by Hasū, the blacksmith, and Sīhā̃, the calico-printer.

The Bābā departed thence. Having passed a Lakh and a quarter of mountains he ascended Sumēru, where the residence of Mahādēv (Shiva) was. There Mahādēv, Gōrakhnāth, Bhartharī, Gōpī-čand and Čarpaṭ were sitting. The Bābā went up to them, made his salutation and sat down. The Siddhs gave him then a small round box and said to him: "O child of the Kali-yug, go, fill it (with water) and bring it!" The Bābā went to fill the box; when he put it into the water, diamonds and pearls began to fall into it. The Guru Bābā beat the box with earth, so that it broke into pieces. He joined then the pieces again together and recited the Slōk:

> He breaks, fashions and adorns:
> O Nānak, without the True one there is none other.

Then the strength of the mantras went off; he put the box into the water and got water (in it); having filled it he brought it back to the Siddhs. All the Siddhs drank of the water, but the water was not exhausted. Mahādēv asked then: "Art thou a householder or a lonely man?" The Bābā replied: "What are the characteristic signs of a lonely man and of a householder?" [there follows a number of verses about the state of a householder, about loneliness and Bairāg (indifference to the world)]. Then said Bhartharī: "O Nānak, become thou a Jōgī, who continues to live for ever!" The Bābā replied: "What is the form of the Jōg?" Bhartharī said: "The form of the Jōg is the earring, the patched quilt, the wallet, the staff (and) the horn, the sound of which is emitted in the universe." The Bābā recited the Sabd in the Rāg Āsā, Mahalā I. [there follow four verses].[1] Then the Siddhs said: "Nānak, go thou to the mountain (Kailāsa?), there is an assembly there, a meeting of the Siddhs takes place there." The Bābā replied: "How many days' journey is it to the mountain?" The Siddhs said: "The mountain is distant three days' journey; we are going there with the pace of the wind." The Bābā said: "Go ye, I shall come slowly." The Siddhs started and after them the Bābā too; he went there in one moment on the flight of his desire. Having come there he sat down under a Ficus Indica, afterwards the Siddhs also came; when they looked about, he was (already) sitting there. The Siddhs asked: "When has this one come?" The forerunner of the Siddhs said: "To-day it is the third day, that this one has come." The Siddhs became astonished at this. When the time of the cup came, the flagon went round; they brought it also to the Bābā, who asked: "What is this?" The Siddhs answered: "This is the cup of the Siddhs, drink thou?" The Bābā said: "What does it contain?" The Siddhs answered: "It contains raw sugar and the blossoms of the Dhāvā-tree." The Bābā recited then a Sabd in the Rāg Āsā, Mahalā I. [there follow four verses].[2] Then the Siddhs said: "Ādēs, ādēs! (salutation, salutation!)" but the Bābā said: "Ādēs to the primeval divine male!" He started thence.

His *fourth* retired life was passed in the *west*. On his feet he had shoes of leather and trousers of leather; on his neck he had a necklace of bones, on his forehead a Tilak of a dot, his clothes were blue. He played amongst children; (thus) playing he went on a Hajj. One Hājī fell in with him and they remained together during the night. The Hājī asked him and said: "O Darvēsh, thou hast no cup, no staff, no skin, no sack, art thou a Hindū or a Musalmān?" The Bābā recited a Sabd, in the Rāg Tilang, Mahalā I. [there follow four verses].[3] The Hājī said again: "Sir, we are living in this world, what will be our state?" The Bābā recited the Sabd in the

[1] Rāg Āsā, Sabd 37, Mah. I.

[2] Āsā, Sabd 38, Mah. I.

[3] Tilang, Sabd 2, Mah. I.

Rāg Tilang, Mahalā I. [there follow four verses].[1] Then they went on travelling to Mekka. As they went along the road, a cloud went along with them over their heads. When the Hājī saw this, he said: "A cloud is over me." He began to say: "No Hindū has ever gone to Mekka, do thou not go with me! either go before or behind me!" The Bābā replied: "Well, let it be so! go thou ahead!" So he went ahead. When he looked again, there was no Bābā nor a cloud. Then the Hājī began to beat his hands (in grief) and said: "I have had a sight of God." But as he could no longer stop (him), he got alarmed.

The Bābā entered Mekka. It had been written before in books, that one Nānak, a Darvēsh, would come, then water would be produced in the wells of Mekka. When the Bābā had entered Mekka he lay down to sleep, stretching his feet towards Mekka. It was the time of evening prayer. The Kāzī Rukn Dīn came to make his prayers; when he had beheld (Nānak) he said: "O servant of God, why dost thou stretch out thy feet in the direction of the house of God and towards the Ka'bā?" The Bābā replied: "Where the house of God and the Ka'bā is not, drag my feet to that direction!" The Kāzī Rukn Dīn turned the feet of the Bābā round, but in whatever direction he turned the feet of the Bābā, to that direction the face of the Miḥrāb[2] was also turning. The Kāzī Rukn Dīn became astonished and kissed his feet saying: "O Darvēsh, what is thy name?" The Bābā recited the Sabd in the Rāg Tilang, Mahalā I. [there follow four verses].[3] When the Bābā had concluded, the Kāzī Rukn Dīn made his salām and said: "Vāh, vāh (wonderful, wonderful!), to-day I have obtained a sight of a Faqīr of God." He went then to the Pīr Patalīā and said: "Nānak, the Darvēsh, has come." The Pīr Patalīā came to have an interview with him; he saluted him and having shaken hands with him he sat down; they began then to speak the praises of God. Then the Kāzī Rukn Dīn asked and said: "Sir, those who are reading the thirty letters, will they get some advantage from it or not?" The Bābā said: "By the favour of the true Guru!" The conversation that was held on the subject mentioned by Rukn Dīn is (written) in the Rāg Tilang,[4] Mahalā I. The speech was made by the Bābā; Shēkh Rukn Dīn was the Kāzī of Mekka. The Bābā said: [there follow thirty verses]. Then the Kāzī Rukn Dīn said: "O Darvēsh Nānak, the Hindūs and Musalmāns, who are reading the Vēda and the book (*i.e.* the Kur'ān), will they obtain God or not?" The Bābā answered with the Sabd in the Rāg Tilang, Mahalā I. [there follow four verses].[5] Then the Kāzī Rukn Dīn said: "Sir, those who are not reading these (the Vēda and the Kur'ān) and are practising bad works, who never keep fasts nor say their prayers, and who are drinking wine or drinking Bhang[6] and beer,[7] what will be their state at the day of resurrection?" The Bābā uttered this Slōk:

His worship (= the Prophet) has said in his decision and in the book:
Dogs, who watch well at night-time are better than not-praying men.
The wretches, who do not wake and remain asleep after the call (to prayer),
In their bone is uncleanness; though men, they are like women.
Who do not obey the Sunnat and divine commandment nor the order of the book:

[1] This is again a misquotation, the verses being attributed in the Granth to Guru Arjun. The order of the verses also is inverted; see Tilang, Sabd 1, Mah. V.

[2] مِحْراب the arched niche in a mosque, the front of which is always directed towards Mekka.

[3] These verses are not to be found among the Sabds of Tilang.

[4] Nothing of this kind is found in the Rāg Tilang.

[5] These verses are attributed in the Granth to Kabīr! See Tilang, Kabīr, I.

[6] Bhang, an intoxicating potion, made from hemp-leaves.

[7] The word is घेजा, Pers. بوزه.

They are burnt in hell, like roasted meat put on a spit.
Great misery will befall them, who are drinking Bhang and wine.
A pig is interdicted from liquor and beer, nor is it Bhang-drinking.
Who walk according to the advice of their lust, they will suffer great pain:
At the day of the resurrection there will be a clamour and noise.
At that day the mountains will fly about as when cotton is carded,
O Kāzī, none other will sit (there), God himself will stand.
According to justice all will be decided, the tablet is handed over at the gate.
Just inquiries are made there, by whom sins were committed,
They are bound and thrown into hell, with a layer (of earth) on their neck and with a black face.
The doers of good works will be unconcerned at that day.
Those will be rescued, O Nānak, whose shelter his worship (the Prophet) is.[1]

Then Pīr Pataliā said: "Sir, we are living in the world, how will God be obtained?" The Bābā replied with the Sabd in the Rāg Tilang, Mahalā I. [there follow four verses]. When the Bābā had uttered this Sabd, the Kāzī Rukn Dīn and the Pīr Pataliā came and kissed his hands and his feet and with their saying: "Vāh Guru!" water was produced in the well. The Bābā was pleased and departed thence; he came home again.[2]

His *fifth* retired life. The Bābā went to Gōrakh-haṭaṛī. There he was seen by the Siddhs, who asked: "What Khatrī art thou?" The Bābā replied: "My name is Nānak." The eighty-four Siddhs, making their (different) postures, were sitting there. Then the Siddhs said: "O devotee, say some praise (of God)!" The Bābā answered: The conversation with the Siddhs (is written) in the Rāg Rāmkalī, Mahalā I. [there follow five verses].[3] The Siddhs gave him then a cup of five Seers (= ten pounds). The Bābā put it on the ground; at this the Siddhs became puffed up and said: "See something or show something!" The Bābā replied: "Well, let it be so; if you will do something, I will look." Then the Siddhs began to show their power; some one made fly (in the air) a deer-skin, another caused a stone to move about, another gave forth fire, another caused a wall to run about. The Bābā came into a state of ecstasy; at that time he made this Slōk:

If I put on fire and make a house of snow and cause the best food to be made.
If I turn all pains into water and drink it and drive the earth about.
If I put the sky on scales and weigh it and put afterwards a Ṭank[4] into (the scales).
If I increase so much, that I be not contained (in any place), if I lead all about by a nose-ring.
If I ascertain all the power there is and also tell it:—
As great as the Lord is, so great are his gifts, in giving he does his pleasure.
O Nānak, on whom his favourable look his, (he gets) the greatness of the true name.
O Nānak, the faces of the workers of miracles (will be) black; greatness is in the true name.

Then the Siddhs said: "Ādēs (salutation!)" but the Bābā said: "To the primeval divine male

[1] This last verse looks very suspicious, and very unlike Nānak, though his name is inserted. It contains a plain confession of the Islām and the intercession of Muhammad, which Nānak nowhere else has made.

[2] I need hardly mention here, that this whole story is without any foundation whatever, though a very big ਗੋਸਟਿ (conversation) is made up under the title: ਮੱਕੇ ਦੀ ਗੋਸਟਿ, which is in my possession.

[3] Rāg Rāmkalī, Siddh Gōsṭī 1, Mah. I. (p. 1039).

[4] A ṭank is equal to four māsās. The sense of this phrase is: to weigh most accurately, which is done by putting a ṭank into one of the scales, in order to make it sink.

(be) salutation!" At that time the word was spoken (as written) in the Rāg Gauṛī, Astpadī, Mahalā I. [there follows one Astpadī].[1] The Siddhs said then: "Ādēs, ādēs!" the Bābā (however) said: "To the primeval divine male (be) salutation!"

After that the Guru Bābā went home. One day the order of the Lord was made (manifest), that one disciple of good caste in Khaḍūr was muttering: "Guru, Guru!" and that the whole of Khaḍūr was minding the (goddess) Durgā, and that all were teazing that disciple, who remained in the quarter of the Tihaṇās, and that his worshipper was Lahaṇā. One day that disciple was sitting and repeating his jap (muttering). Guru Angad heard it and asked, whose this word was. That disciple replied: "Guru Nānak's." Guru Angad came together with that disciple and fell down at the feet (of the Bābā), and as soon as he had seen his sight, he tore away the jingling balls from his hands and feet and threw them away; he began to mutter: "Guru, Guru!" and came to serve him; he scoured the pots and swung the fan. One day Guru Angad went towards the close of night; when he looked about, he saw a woman dressed in crimson clothes sitting and pulling (the fan). Guru Angad humbly said: "O King, who was that?" The Bābā replied: "O Angad, that was Durgā; every eighth day she is coming to do service to the Guru." Then Guru Angad fell down at his feet. One day by the order of the Lord the foot of the Bābā was shaking. When Guru Angad looked on, several (living) creatures were taking leave of his feet.[2]

One day Guru Angad had got clothes from the town and put on a suit. The Guru Bābā gave him the order to bring grass. Guru Angad brought grass from the pools, but all his clothes became sullied by mud. When the mother (the wife of Nānak) saw this, she began to be angry with the Bābā and said: "This one also is driven away (by thee) by worldly business; he is another's son, who has brought (the grass) having sullied his clothes with spots and mud." The Bābā laughed and said: "O mother, this is not mud, this is sandal-wood perfume of this and that world." The mother remained silent at this. Then the Bābā went and slept; when it was dinner-time, a slave-girl began to awaken him. She licked the feet of the Bābā with her tongue, and at the moment of licking them she saw that the Bābā was standing in the ocean; a boat of disciples was with him, which he was pushing on and pulling out. Then the mother also came and said: "Is Nānak awake?" The slave-girl said: "Nānak is not here, O mother, he is standing in the ocean." The mother began to beat the slave-girl and said: "Also this one commences to make drolleries." Then the Bābā awoke and the mother said: "O child, this slave-girl also commences to make drolleries, she says, that Nānak is standing in the ocean." The Bābā replied: "O mother, do not care for what a mad slave-girl talks." The slave-girl became then mad, but as a reward for the sight (she had had), she was received into the society (of the disciples).[3] Many people became at that time votaries of the name.

Then by the order (of the Lord) Gōrakhnāth came to the Bābā and said: "A wide diffusion (of thy name) is made." The Bābā replied: "O Gōrakhnāth, if any one will belong to us, you will see yourself." Then the Bābā went out of the house and many people, votaries of the name, followed him. By the order (of the Lord) copper coins were laid on the ground; many people took the copper coins, rose and went away. When they went further on, Rupees were laid on the ground; many people taking the Rupees went away. When they went further on, gold muhars were laid down. Whoever had remained with him took the gold muhars and went away. Two disciples remained as yet with him. When they went further on, there was a funeral pyre, upon which four lamps were burning; a sheet was spread over it, (under which) a dead one was

[1] Not to be found among the Astpadīs of the Rāg Gauṛī.

[2] The words of the original run thus: ਜਬ ਗੁਰੂ ਅੰਗਦ ਦੇਖੈ ਤਾ ਕਈ ਜੀਅ ਪੈਰਾ ਨਾਲਿ ਵਿਦਾ ਹੋਦੇ ਹੈਨਿ. I have translated them literally, but their sense is not quite clear to me.

[3] A wonderful example of Sikh credulity!

lying, but a stench was coming (from him). The Bābā said: "Is there any one who will eat this one?" The other disciple, who was (with him), turned away his face and spit out, and having spit out walked away. Guru Angad alone came on, and having received a promise stood there and said: "O Sir, from which side shall I apply my mouth?" It was said: "From the side of the feet the mouth should be applied." When Guru Angad lifted up the sheet, Guru Nānak was lying there asleep. Then Gōrakh pronounced the word: "O Nānak, he is thy Guru, who will be produced from thy body." Then his name was changed from Lahaṇā to Guru Angad. Gōrakhnāth departed and Nānak returned to his house. Then the people began to repent very much (of what they had done). Those who had taken the copper coins said: "If we had gone further on, we would have brought Rupees," and those, who had taken the Rupees, said: "If we had gone further on, we would have got gold muhars." Then the Bābā uttered the Sabd in the Rāg Sirī Rāg, Mahalā I. [there follow four verses].[1]

Then one day the order of the Lord came, that Makhdūm Bahāva-dīn, the Pīr of Multān, went to the mosque on a day of a festival, and many disciples of his and people came with him to pray. The word of Makhdūm Bahāva-dīn was then fulfilled; he began to shed tears and to weep. His disciples asked: "May the Pīr live in health, why art thou weeping?" Makhdūm Bahāva-dīn replied: "O servants of God, this word must not be told." The disciples said: "May the Pīr live in health, be so kind as to tell us!" Then Makhdūm Bahāva-dīn said: "From to-day the faith of none will remain firm, all will become infidels." The disciples said: "May the Pīr live in health, be so kind as to expound us this." Makhdūm Bahāva-dīn replied: "O friends, when a Hindū will come into paradise, then there will be light in paradise. Then as many as be intelligent, the faith of all these does not remain firm." The disciples began to say: "May the Pīr live in health! the learned people say, that for a Hindū paradise is not decreed." Then Makhdūm Bahāva-dīn said: "Who among you is well read and intelligent, him bring to me!" They brought a learned man. Makhdūm Bahāva-dīn wrote then a Slōk and gave it to him (to the purport): "We have packed up, give us some notice." And orally he added: "The name of that Darvēsh is Nānak, he is living in Talvaṇḍī; when he asks for this, give it to him." That man went to Talvaṇḍī; above two Kōs from it he sat down and said: "If it be true, he will send for me." The Bābā sent then one disciple to him and said: "In that garden is a man, who has come from Multān, he is a man of Makhdūm Bahāva-dīn, call him and bring him here." He brought him to the Guru; having come he (*i.e.* the messenger) kissed his feet. The Guru asked for the paper Makhdūm Bahāva-dīn had written, and read it. Makhdūm Bahāva-dīn had written: "We have packed up, give us some notice." The Bābā wrote a Slōk above that Slōk:

> Who is filled up, he will pack up . . . .[2]
> O Nānak, their faces are bright, who depart having done what is right.

Then the Bābā wrote him in plain prose: "Depart thou, we also shall come forty days after." At that time the Sabd was made in the Rāg Sirī Rāg, Mahalā I. [there follow five verses].[3] Then that man went to Multān. Makhdūm Bahāva-dīn had gone out with his disciples, when that messenger brought him the letter; having seen it he began to weep. His disciples asked: "Sir, why do you weep?" He replied: "O friends, I had written: if you go, we will go together, we will go to the threshold of God. He has written me: go thou first, we also shall come forty days after. O friends, I am anxious about those forty days, because I shall have to remain forty days in darkness; O friends, on account of those forty days I am weeping, for how will they be passed? If he would go, we would go with comfortable light." When the departure (death) of Makhdūm Bahāva-dīn had taken place, tranquillity entered the heart of his disciples and of the people.

[1] Sirī Rāg, Sabd 3, Mah. I. [2] The paper is torn here. [3] Sirī Rāg, Sabd 24, Mah. I.

Then the Bābā came to the bank of the Rāvī; he put five Paisā before Guru Angad and fell down at his feet;[1] this became known then among his retinue. Then among all the society the intelligence was spread, that the Guru Bābā was in the house of Čānaṇ; the society came to see him, Hindūs and Musalmāns also came. Then Guru Angad with joined hands stood before him; the Bābā said: "Ask something!" Guru Angad said: "O King, if it please thee, may that, which was broken off from the society, be again applied to (its) skirt!"[2] The answer was given to Guru Angad: "For thy sake all are pardoned." Then Guru Angad fell down at his feet. At that time the Sabd was made in the Rāg Mājh, Mahalā I. [there follow four verses].[3] Then the Bābā went to a Sarīh-tree and sat down under it; the Sarīh-tree had become dry and became now green again, leaves and blossoms came forth; then Guru Angad fell down at his feet. Then the mother (the wife of Nānak) began to weep; brothers, relations, all the retainers began to weep. At that time the Sabd was made in the Rāg Vaḍhans, Mahalā I. [there follow four verses].[4] Then the society began to sing funeral songs; the Bābā fell into a trance. At that time the order was given and the Rāg Tukhārī was made. The Bābā uttered the Bārah māhā; it was night, towards dawn of day, at the time of his departure. The Rāg Tukhārī, Barah māhā, Mahalā I. [there follow seventeen verses].[5] Then his sons said: "O father, what will be our state?" The Guru answered: "Not even the dogs of the Guru are in want, you will get plenty of clothes and bread, and if you will mutter: 'Guru, Guru!' the end of your existence will be obtained." Then the Hindūs and Musalmāns, who were votaries of the name, began to say, the Musalmāns: "We shall bury him," and the Hindūs: "We shall burn him." Then the Bābā said: "Put ye flowers on both sides, on the right side put those of the Hindūs and on the left those of the Musalmāns. If the flowers of the Hindūs will remain green to-morrow, then they shall burn me; and if the flowers of the Musalmāns will remain green, then they shall bury me." Then the Bābā ordered the society, that they should recite the praises (of God); the society began to recite the praises, (as written) in the Rāg Gauṛī pūrbī, Mahalā I. [there follow four verses];[6] Rāg Āsā, Mahalā I. [there follow two verses];[7] then from Dhanāsarī Rāg [there follows one verse];[8] then the Slōk was read: "The wind is the Guru," etc. When (this) Slōk was read . . . . . having taken up (his feet?) he fell asleep . . . . .[9] When they lifted up the sheet, there was nothing at all. The flowers of both parties had remained green. The Hindūs took theirs and went and the Musalmāns took theirs and went. The whole society fell on their knees. Say: vāh Guru! In the Samvat year 1595, the tenth day of the light half of the month of Asū, Bābā Nānak was absorbed (= died) in Kartārpur.[10]

It was said: vāh Guru, vāh Guru, vāh Guru, vāh Guru! The Sakhī is finished.

[1] This was the initiation or appointment to the Guruship; afterwards, as it appears from the later Janam-Sākhīs, a cocoa-nut also was placed before the successor; see p. xlviii, l. 15.

[2] The sense is: may those, who were excluded from the society (of the disciples), be again restored!

[3] A misquotation, the verses being ascribed in the Granth to Guru Arjun; see Rāg Mājh, Sabd 18, Mah. V. (p. 113).

[4] Vaḍhans, Alāhaṇīā̃, 1, Mah. I.

[5] Rāg Tukhārī, Bārah māhā, 1, Mah. I.

[6] Gauṛī pūrbī dīpakī 1, (20), Mah. I. (p. 175).

[7] Āsā, Sabd 30, Mah. I.

[8] The MS. is torn here and only a few words remain.

[9] The leaf here is tattered.

[10] Anno Domini 1538.

B.

THE JANAM-SĀKHĪ OF BĀBĀ NANAK.

(*Enlarged recompilation of* **A.**)

The Janam-patrī of Bābā Nānak was written in the Samvat year fifteen hundred and eighty-two,[1] on the fifth day of the light half of the month of Vaisākh. The book was written by Paiṛā, a Mōkhā,[2] a Khatrī of Sultānpur. Guru[3] Angad caused it to be written, and Paiṛā wrote it according to the oral dictation of Bālā, a Sandhū Jaṭ.[4]

Bhāī[5] Bālā had come from Talvaṇḍī (the jagīr) of Rāe Bhōe, the Bhaṭṭī,[6] and had looked out for Gurū Angad.

Two months and seventeen days were spent in writing (this book). Wherever he had wandered about with Guru Nānak, that Bhāī Bālā dictated with facility.

Gurū Angad was much pleased with Bhāī Bālā; (for) Bhāī Bālā had wandered about with Mardānā, the rabābī, in the company of Nānak; also at the time, when Nānak was employed in the commissariat, Bhāī Bālā was with him.

---

(1).

How the Janam-Patrī of Nānak was obtained.

One day the thought came into Gurū Angad's mind: "My Guru Nānak was perfect, between him and the Supreme Lord there was no difference whatever. I should like to know,[7] in which wise my Guru was born." This thought was occupying his mind. Meanwhile in the latter half of the month of Katak Bālā, the Sandhū Jaṭ, came to see Guru Angad. Guru Angad was keeping himself concealed. Bālā, the Sandhū, had this desire, that if the Guru would come forth, he would have an interview with him. Then Bhāī Bālā heard that Guru Nānak had appointed (as

[1] *i.e.* A.D. 1525. If Angad was born in 1561 Sambat, he was then twenty-one years of age.

[2] मोखा was the name of his गोत्र or clan; by caste he was a Khatrī.

[3] The word Guru is written differently: गुठ, gur, गुठु, guru and गुठू Gurū.

[4] Bālā, as will be seen, is here represented as the constant companion of Nānak; the old Janam-Sākhī never mentions his name. He was a Jaṭ (जटेटा) of the Sandhū clan; Cust made him a Sindhī!

[5] Bhāī is an honorary title for saintly Sikhs, literally: brother.

[6] Rāe Bhōe, a Musalmān Rajput, was formerly the jagīrdār of Talvaṇḍī, the birth-place of Nānak, after whom the place was named; see p. iii, note 1.

[7] The original is: देखां, I should like to see.

his successor) one Khatrī, by name Angad, a Trihuṇ Khatrī,[1] but that it was not known in which place he kept himself concealed. But he heard further the news, that he was sitting at Khanḍūr, a village of the Khaharā-Jaṭs. Having heard this, Bālā came to see Gurū Angad.[2] He searched for the Guru and found him. He saw that Guru Angad was twisting vāṇ.[3] Bhāī Bālā, the Sandhū, went and bowed his head before him. Gurū Angad said: "Come, brother! true is the creator;[4] come, sit down!" Gurū Angad left off twisting vāṇ and began to ask Bhāī Bālā: "O brother disciple, from whence hast thou come? why didst thou come? and who art thou?" Then Bālā, the Sandhū, joining his hands in supplication, said: "Guru, I am a Jaṭ; my clan is Sandhū and my name is Bālā. My birth-place is Talvanḍī, (the village of) Rāe Bhōe, the Bhaṭṭī; I am come for the sake of an interview with the Gurū." Gurū Angad asked further: "Bhāī Bālā, whose disciple art thou?" Bhāī Bālā said: "Guru, I am the disciple of Guru Nānak; with me Gurū Nānak, the son of Kālū, the Vēdī, had met." Gurū Angad asked further: "Bhāī Bālā, hadst thou seen Gurū Nānak?" Bhāī Bālā said: "Guru Nānak was three years older than I, I was following Guru Nānak and going about with him. But at that time I had not this faith, that he is a perfect and great Guru; I was with him in the capacity of a servant." When Bhāī Bālā had said this, Guru Angad wept and did not stop his tears in any way. Thus that night passed. When it had become morning, Guru Angad said: "Call Bhāī Bālā." Bhāī Bālā came and bowed his head. Guru Angad asked Bhāī Bālā: "Bhāī Bālā, is it known to thee, how the birth of Guru Nānak did take place?" Bhāī Bālā answered: "Sir, that I do not know. But so much I heard from the mouth of the people, that Hari Dayāl the Brāhmaṇ says, that in these auspicious moments, in the twenty-seven lunar mansions and at the full moon of Katak, not any such one was born into the world. In the house of Kālū, the Vēdī, a great *Avatār* is born. So much I had heard. I had also heard that Mahatā[5] Kālū caused a Janam-patrī[6] to be written." Guru Angad said: "Bhāī Bālā, how could this Janam-patrī be procured?" Bhāī Bālā answered: "The Guru knows it;[7] but by searching it may come to hand." Guru Angad said: "Bhāī Bālā, is there any such one, by whom a trace of the Janam-patrī may be procured?" Bālā said: "Let it be searched, Sir!" Guru Angad said: "Bhāī Bālā, thou art an inhabitant of that place, by thee a trace of it may be procured. Search and get it from any one."

Bhāī Bālā, the Sandhū, said: "Sir! Mahatā Kālū, the Vēdī, has a brother, it is Mahatā Lālū, the Vēdī, from him it may be searched." Guru Angad answered: "Bhāī Bālā, you must search for it." Then Bhāī Bālā said: "Give me one of your own men; he and I will go and say to Mahatā Lālū, the Vēdī: 'Bhāī Lālū, thou hast become very old, Guru Angad has shown thee much benevolence: search after the Janam-patrī of Guru Nānak and give it (to us)! We have inquired and found Guru Angad: between Guru Nānak and Angad there is no difference whatever.'" Then Angad said: "Bhāī Bālā, what the society (of the disciples) says, that is

[1] Angad was a Khatrī, of the Trihuṇ clan. His former name was Lahaṇā. According to the Janam-Sākhī it was changed by Nānak to Angad: ਜੋ ਮੇਰੇ ਅੰਗ ਤੇ ਉਤਪੇਤ ਹੋਇਆ ਹੈ. Compare also p. xliv, l. 6.

[2] The lithographed Lahore copy inserts here: ਜੋ ਕੁਛ ਸਰਤ ਆਹੀ ਸੋ ਭੇਟ ਲੈ ਆਇਆ: he brought a present, as his circumstances would permit him, significant for the later Sikh times.

[3] ਵਾਣੁ, coarse twine made of munj. This occupation of Angad was afterwards considered as unbecoming a Guru and therefore left out in the Lahore lithographed copy.

[4] ਸਤ ਕਰਤਾਰ was the old form of Sikh salutation.

[5] ਮਹਤਾ is an honorary title given to Khatrī merchants, corresponding to *master*.

[6] About the ਜਨਮ ਪਤ੍ਰੀ, see the remarks, p. i, note 1. The first marriage and the birth of the first child is also frequently added. I have seen and examined many of this kind.

[7] *i.e.* I do not know it, you know it better.

true." Guru Angad was much pleased with Bhāī Bālā. "Well, Bhāī Bālā, take some disciple and go!" Bhāī Bālā said: "O Guru, whom thou sendest, him I take with me." Then Guru Angad called Lālā, the Punnū. He was a disciple, a Jaṭ. Guru Angad said: "Bhāī Lālā Punnū, thou art a disciple, thou art attending to the Guru, go thou with Bhāī Bālā to Talvaṇḍī, bring the Janam-patrī of Guru Nānak." Lālā, the Punnū, said: "Blessed is our lot, that we shall see the Janam-patrī of Guru Nānak, we shall consider it as if we had had an interview with Guru Nānak." Guru Angad said: "Bhāī Lālā, may the creator come into thy mind!"[1]

Bhāī Bālā, the Sandhū, and Lālā, the Punnū, came to Talvaṇḍī, (the village of) Rāe Bhōe, the Bhaṭṭī. Having arrived there they met Mahatā Lālū. They said: "Bhāī Lālū, give us the Janam-patrī of Guru Nānak! Guru Angad asks for it." Bhāī Lālū answered: "It is not with me." Bhāī Bālā said: "Thou art the brother of Mahatā Kālū, search thou in the house." Lālū, the Vēdī, rejoined: "Bhāī Bālā, thou art the friend of Guru Nānak, speak the truth: is Angad Guru or Sirī Čand?"[2] He told them also something else. Bhāī Bālā said: "Bhāī Lālū, Angad has become Guru, before whom Guru Nānak put five paisās and a cocoa-nut and bowed his head.[3] What competition is there against him? We have sought and found him. To his honour, Sirī Čand, as being his son, due reverence will be paid." Then Bhāī Lālū said: "Bhāī Bālā, look, I am searching. My brother's wife has departed and my brother Kālū also." They began to search in the house. Searching and searching they found on the fifth day the Janam-patrī and Bhāī Lālū gave it into the hand of Bālā, and Bālā put it into the hand of Lālā, the Punnū. Then Bhāī Lālā said to Bhāī Bālā: "Bhāī Bālā, go thou also with me! much honour will be paid to thee." Bhāī Bālā answered: "Well, brother, go on!"

When Bhāī Lālā and Bālā went away, Lālū, the Vēdī, said: "Ye take away the Janam-patrī of Guru Nānak, but take also with you some offering of mine!" Bālā said: "Well, brother Lālū, whatever comes into thy mind, that is good." Bhāī Lālū gave five paisās and a cocoa-nut and said: "Put my offering before Guru Angad, bow the head and say: 'O Guru, if ever his honour Sirī Čand should take offence (at this), you must render me assistance.'"[4] On this Bhāī Bālā said: "O Lālū, there is no ground for fear."

Bhāī Lālā and Bālā took the Janam-patrī and brought it to Khanḍūr, (a village of) the Khaharā Jaṭs, and put it before Guru Angad. Guru Angad was very much pleased and said: "Bhāī Bālā, may the creator come into thy mind! to-day thou hast procured us an interview with Nānak." Having taken it into his hands Guru Angad kissed it and put it on his eyes and on his head. When he looks at it, he sees that the letters are shāstrī.[5] Guru Angad reflected: "May there be such a disciple, who is read in both kinds of letters?" Mahimā, a Khaharā-Jaṭ, in whose house Guru Angad was staying, said: "Guru, in Sultānpur is Paiṛā, a Mōkhā Khatrī, he reads both letters." Guru Angad then said: "Bhāī Mahimā, he should be brought." Mahimā

[1] This is a Sikh blessing.

[2] ਸਿਰੀ ਚੰਦ, name of the eldest son of Nānak, as in the later Janam-Sākhīs he is always mentioned first; in the old Janam-Sākhī Lakhmī-dās is on the contrary mentioned first; see p. viii, l. 22.

[3] This rite of investiture with the Guruship, practised also by the following Gurus, when nominating their successor, differs somewhat from that mentioned on p. xlv, l. i. But from what follows, it may be concluded that it was the common way of doing homage to a superior.

[4] The passage runs thus in the original: ਜੇ ਗੁਰੂਜੀ ਕਦੀ ਸਿਰੀ ਚੰਦ ਹੋਰੀ ਬੁਰਾ ਮੰਨਣ ਤਾਂ ਤੁਸਾਂ ਖਸਮਾਣਾ ਕਰਣਾ. This passage, being very significant as to the violent character of Sirī Čand, was in the Lahore lithographed copy changed in the following way: ਜੇ ਕਦੇ ਸਿਰੀ ਚੰਦ ਹੋਰੀ ਬੁਰੀ ਮੰਨਣਾ ਤਾਂ ਤੁਸਾਂ ਗੁਸਾ ਨ ਕਰਣਾ: if ever Sirī Čand should take offence (at this), you must not be angry (with him)! (sic!)

[5] *i.e.* Dēvānagarī. This notice is very important, as it shows that the so-called Gurmukhī letters were in use before the Sikh Gurus, and not invented by them.

answered: "Well, Sir, I will bring him, at my bidding he will quickly come." Mahimā went to Sultānpur and brought Paiṛā, the Mōkhā. Having come, Paiṛā, the Mōkhā, bowed his head and Guru Angad showed him the Janam-patrī. He read it off quite fluently. Guru Angad was much pleased and said: "Paiṛā, put this for us into Gurmukhī letters!" Paiṛā answered: "Well, Sir! procure good paper, I will write it." The Guru procured paper, ink and pen, and gave them to him. Paiṛā wrote and Guru Angad caused it to be written.

Say, O brother: vāh. Gurūjī!—The narrative is continued.

(2).

Circumstances of the birth of Nānak.

The Janam-patrī of Guru Nānak is written.[1]

In Sambat 1526, the fifteenth of the light half of the month of Katak, Nānak was born at Talvanḍī, (a village) of Rāe Bhōe, the Bhaṭṭī. He was born in the house of Kālū, a Vēdī Khatrī by caste. In the Kali-yug the name of Bābā Nānak was given to him. He founded his own sect (or way). Whilst one watch and a half of the night were remaining, in the moonlight night an unbeaten sound was produced at the gate of Bābā Nānak. The thirty-three crores of gods, the eighty-four Siddhs,[2] the nine Nāths,[3] the sixty-four Jōginīs,[4] the fifty-two Vīras,[5] the six Jatīs,[6] paid homage to him (saying): "The incorporeal Supreme Spirit has come to save the world; to him homage should be paid, who has come as an Avatār!" At midnight and twenty-four minutes he was born in the house of Kālū, the Vēdī.[7] The family priest of Kālū the Vēdī was the Brāhmaṇ Hari Diyāl. Early in the morning Kālū went to the house of Hari Diyāl and said: "Panḍit, do me a favour!" The Panḍit said: "Mahatā Kālū, why hast thou come at such a time?" Kālū rejoined: "A male child has been born. Do me the favour and set down his Janam-patrī." Hari Diyāl said: "Well, Mahatā Kālū, having performed (religious) service and worship I will come. Meanwhile go thou." Kālū came again to his house. The Panḍit came afterwards, after the day had risen for five Ghaṛīs.[8] Having come he called out: "Mahatā Kālū, I have come." Kālū led him in; he had spread out cushions and seated the Panḍit upon them. Being seated the Panḍit said: "Mahatā Kālū, bring paper (and) saffron,[9] and let me hear also the sound, the child emitted, when it was born; tell me the time when it was born." Kālū said: "I know about the birth, that it was midnight and twenty-four minutes when it was born, but about the sound I know nothing." On this the Panḍit said: "Ask from within; ask the midwife Daulat."[10] Kālū called the midwife Daulat out. She came out saying: "Why have you called me out?" Kālū said: "The Panḍit is asking, thou knowest it, tell it." The midwife answered: "Panḍit, what do you ask?" The Panḍit said: "What sound did the child emit when it was born?" The midwife answered: "O Panḍit, how many children were born

[1] It is quite evident that what follows cannot be the original Janam-patrī of Nānak. The headings we have added.

[2] Perfect Jōgīs.

[3] The nine Nāths of the Jōgīs.

[4] The ਜੋਗਿਣੀ (योगिनी) are a sort of female fiends attendant upon Durgā.

[5] It is not known exactly, who are meant by the fifty-two Vīras. They are perhaps a sort of deified heroes.

[6] The ਜਤੀ (यति) are ascetics; who these six are is not known. The Jainas worship seven Jatīs.

[7] In the Lahore lithographed copy the words from: "In the Kali-yug" to here are left out.

[8] A Ghaṛī is twenty-four minutes, five Ghaṛīs therefore = two hours' time.

[9] ਕੇਸਰ or saffron is used, to blot out any letter, that may be written by mistake.

[10] As far as may be concluded from the name, a Musalmān midwife.

under my hands! but such a child and in such a manner was never born. The voice he emitted was such, as if some very wise one would laughingly join (us). I am quite out of my wits about this child." The Paṇḍit said: "Hear, Kālū: the child is born when the twenty-seven lunar mansions were full. If he were born before midnight, he would become a great merchant; this one is born in the following watch, the night declining (already). This night was a very momentous point of time, on his head an umbrella[1] will needs be turned. I am very much surprised, I will see what sort of umbrella will be turned (over him)." The Paṇḍit was sunk in deep reflection and said: "Kālū, let me see the child." Kālū asked for the child from within, from his wife. But the wife of Kālū said: "I shall not give it, the days are chilly." The Paṇḍit said: "It will do him no harm, you may rely on my word." Then Kālū brought him out in his clout on his hands and sat down with him before the Paṇḍit. The Paṇḍit was versed in divine knowledge. Having seen him he stood up, joined both his hands and worshipped him. The Paṇḍit said: "Kālū, take him away." Kālū brought the child to the inner room, and having returned said: "Come (again) and point out some name for it; for in what auspicious moments is it born!" The Paṇḍit said: "Kālū, I will determine on a name and give it him." The Paṇḍit reflected for thirteen days. When thirteen days had passed, a coat was put (on the child) and the name given: Nānak the Formless one.[2] Then Kālū said: "O Paṇḍit, this name should not have been given, this name is common to Hindūs and Turks." The Paṇḍit said again: "This is a man, in whom is a great Avatār; he has come to thy house; such a great Avatār has never been before. There has been Srī Rām Čand and there has been Srī Krisn, the Lord; those the Hindūs worship, but this one both Hindūs and Turks will worship; his name will be current on earth and in heaven. Wood and grass will say: "Nānak, Nānak!"[3] The ocean will grant him access, he will mentally recite the Formless (Supreme) one. And he will be much given to ablutions and the creature he will consider as a creature. Without the Supreme Lord he will acknowledge none else. O Kālū, this will be my grief that I shall not see his dignity (he will attain to). What do I know how long my life will be?"

When Nānak had become five years old, he used to lose everything which he took from the house. Kālū went to reproach the Paṇḍit: "Well, Paṇḍit, a (fine) umbrella is turned (over him)!" The Paṇḍit said to Kālū: "Now thou reproachest me, but that time will come, when thou with a straight face wilt not utter a word."[4]

(3).

Nānak sent to school.

When Nānak became big, he commenced to play with boys, but his view did not agree with that of the boys; he studied with himself over the Formless one.

When he had become seven years of age he began to talk of the Shāstras and the Vēdas. Whatever he talks, that he understands. Every one puts reliance on him. The Hindūs begin to say: "Some form of a god has been born." The Musalmāns say: "Some holy man of God is born."

Then Kālū said: "O boy Nānak, learn now to read."

[1] ਛਤ੍ਰ, an umbrella, the sign of royalty.

[2] In A. this name ਨਿਰੰਕਾਰੀ, the Formless one, is not even hinted at.

[3] ਹੋਇ ਜਾਵੈਗਾ is here used in the sense of: *to be done* = *to be said*, not in the sense now common: *to become.*

[4] This whole passage is simply left out in the Lahore lithographed copy, as derogatory to Nānak, for whom it only has praise.

Kālū went to the (village) schoolmaster and said:[1] "O schoolmaster, look out for an auspicious moment, for we will send the boy to school." The schoolmaster answered: "Now the time is good." Then Kālū asked from his wife for a two-pice piece, betel-nut and rice, and brought it and handed Nānak over to the schoolmaster for the purpose of reading. Kālū said: "O schoolmaster, teach Nānak to read!" The schoolmaster said; "Well, that shall be done, Sir!" Then the schoolmaster wrote him a wooden slate and gave it him.[2] Nānak read one day. On the following day he remained silent. The schoolmaster said: "Nānak, why remainest thou silent? why dost thou not read?" Nānak answered: "O schoolmaster, hast thou read anything, which thou mayst let me read?" The schoolmaster said: "I have read everything." Then Nānak rejoined: "O schoolmaster, by reading these words nooses are laid (on men); that which we must read, is all wind." Then Nānak uttered a Sabd in the Sirī Rāg, Mahalā I.

[Now follow four Paurīs with a lengthy paraphrase[3] from Sirī Rāg, Sabd 6, Mahalā I.]

The Paṇḍit became astonished and paid reverence (to Nānak) as to a perfect man.[4] "What comes into thy mind, that do!"

Then Nānak came home and sat down, he did no work. When he sat down, he remained seated. He associated with Faqīrs. His father Kālū became astonished, that Nānak went on in this manner.

(4).

Nānak grazes his father's buffaloes and spoils a corn-field, which is miraculously restored.

When Nānak had become nine years old, the (brahmanical) cord was placed (on him). He learnt also to read some Turkish.[5] He did not disclose the thoughts of his mind to any one.

His father Kālū then said: "O son Nānak, take the buffaloes which are in my house and pasture them!" Nānak took the buffaloes and went out (to the pasture-ground); having grazed them he brought them back at night to the house. The following day he went out again. Having left the buffaloes, he fell asleep at the border of a field sown with wheat. The buffaloes went and fell upon the wheat and browsed it and the wheat was spoiled. The owner of the wheat came and said: "Brother, why hast thou laid waste my field? give answer for this devastation!" Nānak answered: "Nothing of what is thine has been wasted, O brother! What is it, if some buffalo has pilfered from it? God will put a blessing on this (field)." But that man did not desist, he began to quarrel with Nānak. Then Nānak and the Bhaṭṭī proprietor came to Rāe Bulār,

[1] This story is also contained in the Sikhā̃ dē rāj̃ dī vithiā (Ludihāṇā, 1868), p. 201, but rather altered. The extracts from the Janam-Sākhī, which this book contains, are taken from more modern sources, and the explanations added are of little or no value whatever.

[2] The Hindūs in the Panjāb write on small wooden slates painted black, with a colour made of white earth. When the slate is written over, the letters are washed off with water. The boys, whilst imitating the letters, pronounce them aloud, which causes a considerable din.

[3] Whenever the Granth is quoted in the later times, a translation, or rather a paraphrase, is always added to it, which proves sufficiently, that at that time the Sikhs no longer understood the idiom of the Granth. These paraphrases are usually very indifferent and frequently misinterpret the original text completely, or simply pass over what was unintelligible to them.

[4] The Lahore lithographed copy has here significantly: ਤੂ ਪਰਮੇਸੁਰੁ ਹੈ, thou art the Supreme Lord.

[5] Under ਤੇਰਕੀ, Turkish, very likely *Persian* is to be understood, the official language of those days. This is also corroborated by the fact, that some *Persian* verses of Nānak are found in the Granth, though his knowledge of Persian must have been very deficient. To this very likely alludes the notice in the Siyar-ul-muta'aχχirīn (Briggs' translation, vol. i. p. 110), that some Sayyid Husain, who had no children of his own, charged himself with his education and introduced him to the knowledge of the most esteemed writings of the Islām. In the Lahore lithographed copy this is (no doubt intentionally) left out.

the headman of Talvaṇḍī, by tribe a Bhaṭṭī. Then the headman said: "Call Kālū!" Aside people had said that Nānak was mad and that he should send for Kālū. They brought Kālū. Then Rāe Bulār said to Kālū, that he was not warning this his son, who was laying waste the fields of others. "Well, though considering him mad, thou hast let him alone. Go now and make amends for the devastation done to others! If not, thou wilt have to answer before the Turkish authorities." Kālū said: "Sir, what shall I do? this one is verily mad." Then the Rāe said: "I have forgiven this trespass to thee, Kālū, but go and make amends for the damage." Nānak spoke then: "Sir, nothing of the property of this one has been damaged, he speaks a falsehood." The owner of the field rejoined: "Sir, my whole field has been laid waste; I have been plundered. Grant me justice, if not, I go to the Turks." Nānak answered: "Sir, not one blade has been spoiled and cut off! Send thou thy own men, they shall see and report." Then Rāe Bulār sent his own footmen. When those footmen having gone see, what do they see? not one blade of the field was spoiled. The footmen come and report: "Sir, nothing at all is wasted." Then Rāe Bulār called the owner of the field a liar. Nānak and Kālū both went home.[1]

(5).

A black serpent expands its hood over Nānak when resting under a tree.

When Bābā Nānak was nine years of age, he had gone out (one day) to graze the buffaloes. They were the days of (the month of) Vaisākh (April–May), at the time of noon he came and rested under a tree and made also his buffaloes stand (there). As soon as he had taken to rest, a black snake came and sat at his head expanding its hood (over him). They were the days of measuring (the fields under cultivation). Rāe Bulār having measured wheat was going home; when he looked on, a boy had fallen asleep (there) and a black snake sat at his head, expanding its hood (over him). Rāe Bulār stopped; when he looks on, what does he see? that the shade of the other trees is gone and that the shade of that tree, under which the boy was sleeping, had remained there. He reflected in his mind: if that boy really lives, then he is some prophet, and if he has drunk the breath of the snake, he is dead. Afterwards some people came there. Rāe Bulār said to them: "Look, who this boy is, who lies there?" When they looked on, what did they see? that it was Nānak, the son of Kālū, the Paṭvārī,[2] who was lying there. They said to Rāe Bulār: "O Rāe, the son of Kālū, thy Paṭvārī, is lying there." Rāe Bulār said: "Look, that ye raise him up." They raised the sleeper and Nānak stood up and sat down. When he looked about, he saw, that Rāe Bulār stood at his head. Nānak joining his hands saluted him. The Rāe dismounted from his horse, embraced Nānak and kissed his head, and showed him much politeness. Rāe Bulār said: "Look, friends, a wonderful thing has been seen (already) and to-day also see! This one is not empty, on him is some mercy of God." The people were astonished (saying): "O brother, Rāe Bulār has become very kind to this boy." Having gone home he called Kālū and said to him: "O Kālū, the son of thy house Nānak do not consider as thy son, he is a devotee of the Supreme Lord. Do not say to this (thy) son: 'Be cursed, die!' he is a great person, my town is a sacrifice to him.[3] Kālū, thou also hast been exalted, in whose house thy son Nānak has been born." Kālū said: "The thing of God God knows," and went home.

[1] This whole story is left out in the Lahore lithographed copy, as it was felt that this duplicity did not redound to the honour of Nānak. It is also missing in a MS. copy of the India Office Library, No. 2885, which is nearly identical with the Lahore lithographed edition of the Janam-Sākhī.

[2] ਪਟਵਾਰੀ, land steward; his business is to keep the land-accounts of the village.

[3] The words: Do not say to this thy son—to the end of the sentence, are left out in the Lahore lithographed copy (likewise in the MS. No. 2885) as being too disrespectful. The answer of Kālū also is given differently: ਭਲਾ ਗਾਇਜੀ ਬਹੁਤ ਭਲਾ.

(6).

Nānak refuses to do any work; the attempt to cure him from his supposed madness fails.

But Nānak kept company with Faqīrs, he spoke with nobody else. His whole family was grieved and distressed thereby, they said: "Nānak has become mad." Then his mother came to Nānak and said: "It will not do for thee to sit with Faqīrs, give up these perpetual foolish words! The people laugh at us, that the son of Kālū has become an idler." When his mother had said these words to Nānak, he did not mind them at all, he lay down again, he did not speak with any one, as he lay down, so he remained for four or five days. His mother came again and said to him: "O son, how does it behove thee to lie down? rise, eat and drink something! Look after the fields! all thy family is grieved. And, O son, if anything do not please thee, then don't do it, we say nothing to you; why art thou so thoughtful?" Then information was given to Kālū; Kālū said: "O son, what were we telling thee? it is good to do work. If the sons of Khatrīs have money, do they no work? O son, it is good to do (some) work! Our field out there stands ripe, if thou wouldst go and stand in it, it would not be wasted. Then every one will say: 'Well done, well done, the son of Kālū has become a good son!' O son, the field is with (its) owners!" Nānak answered: "By us a private field has been ploughed, of that we are taking care. The plough has been carried (over it), the proper time for sowing the ground has come; the eight watches we were standing there. O father, we take care of our own field,[1] how shall we have knowledge of another's field?" Kālū became astonished and said: "Look, people, what this one is saying!" Then said Kālū: "When hast thou ploughed a private field? Give up (these) silly words, and if it be thy pleasure, I will give thee at the next harvest a private ploughed field, I will see, how thou wilt make it ripen!" Then Nānak said: "O father, the field has now been ploughed by us and it has grown up well, it looks quite well." Then Kālū said again: "O son, we have seen no cultivated field of thine at all, how shall I know, what thou art saying?" Nānak answered: "O father, that field has been cultivated by us, thou thyself wilt hear." Then Nānak uttered a Sabd in the Rāg Sōraṭhi (Sabd 2, 1, Mah. I.). [Kālū said again: "O Nānak, sit thou in the shop, our field is the shop." Then the second Pauṛī was said. Then Kālū said again: "O son, if thou wilt not sit in the shop, take thou horses and traffic with them! Thy spirit is melancholy. Do (some) business and see also foreign countries! we shall say, that he is gone for (some) business and that he will come now." Then the third Pauṛī was said. Then Kālū said again: "O Nānak, thou art gone from us, but go and do some service, perhaps thy spirit will come to rest therein, we have given up thy gaining (anything). O son, if thou wilt become an Udāsī, then all people will say to us, that the son of Kālū has become a Faqīr and the people will reproach us." Then the fourth Pauṛī was said.][2] Then Nānak said: "O father, our field is sown, thou hast heard how. O father, our field has sprung up well, we have so much confidence in this field, that the whole government tax will fall off, sons, daughters and the whole family will eat to their satiety and will be happy; the debt of the Lord will be removed, and the poor, brothers and relatives, all will be profited by it. The Lord, whose husbandry I have carried on, gives me much assistance; for that day I rejoice much.[3] Whatever I ask, that he gives me. O father, I have found out a great Lord, traffic and shop, all has been entrusted (by him to me)." Then Kālū

[1] The negation which A. has, is left out here, very likely purposely.

[2] The words in brackets are an addition. It is easily perceived, that they do not agree with the context, but rather interrupt it. All the additions made by the second compiler will thus be pointed out by brackets.

[3] The text is here so much shortened, that the words are no longer intelligible, whereas they are quite plain in the first compilation.

became astonished and said: "We have not at all seen (or) heard of thy Lord." The Bābā said: "By whom my Lord has been seen, by them he is praised." The Gurū Bābā uttered one Sabd in the Rāg Āsā (Čaupadā 1, Mah. I.). Then Kālū said again: "Give up these things, walk after the manner of the people, it is nothing to live without a business." Then Nānak remained silent, Kālū rose and went home and took to his work; he said: "This work is beyond our strength, but may not the field outside be damaged!" Then all the family of the Vēdīs began to grieve, they said: "It is a great pity, that the son of Kālū has become mad." Nānak remained silent; three months he lay down and ate and drank nothing. The whole family of the Vēdīs became dispirited and all began to say to Kālū: "How dost thou sit down (quietly), whose son remains lying down? Call thou some physician and get medicine for him! The people will say, that Kālu, on account of the money, does not get his son cured. (This is) much money, if (thy) son become well." Then Kālū stood up and went and brought a physician. The physician came and began to seize the arm of the Bābā. The Bābā drew away his arm, lifted up his leg, stood up and sat down. He began to say: "O physician, what art thou doing?" The physician said: "I am looking after the disease, that may be in thy spirit." The Bābā laughed and made the Sabd [there follow four verses]. On the subject of the physician he made also another Sabd, in the Rāg Malār [there follow two verses]. Say, O brother: vāh Gurūjī![1]

(7).

Nānak sows a field and neglects it thoroughly. His father expostulates with him.

[When the Bābā had become twelve years of age, then Kālū said, after he had reflected in his mind: "Nānak has read, but he should (now) be put into some business." Then Kālū said to Nānak: "Son, apply thyself to some business!" Nānak answered: "Well, father, if you tell me anything, I will do it." Kālū said: "Son, in such and such a place sow thou a field!" "Well, father, I am sowing." Kālū gave to Nānak one maund and a quarter of seed, Nānak took it, went and cast it. The field sprang up, but who protects it? Any one's cattle, any one's ass, any one's filly, any one's horse eat it away, Nānak removes none (of them). Kālū went and saw that his field had sprung up well. Becoming angry (that the field had been wasted) he began to reproach him (*i.e.* Nānak), and said: "A fine son has in thee been born in my house to cause destruction!" and going away he began to say to the Paṇḍit Hari Dayāl: "A fine umbrella is turned about in my house; such are thy Vēdas and Purāṇas! my field, that had sprung up, is wasted by him!" The Paṇḍit Hari Dayāl said: "Thou hast no information whatever, thou art luckless! thou hast no profit whatever from Nānak, other people will be profited by Nānak and how many will be liberated (by him)! having heard the words of Nānak they will do them. Nānak will become famous among Hindūs and Musalmāns. The people having heard and read the Vēdas (and) the book (= the Kur'ān) will do (them). The four Vēdas, the eighteen Purāṇas, the six Shāstras and the Bhāgavad-(Gītā) and as many Gītās as there are, all will suddenly come out of the mouth of Nānak without having read (them) (as) from the invisible (world). Hear, Kālū, be not alarmed about him! It is weighty to say of him, what cannot be said of a corporeal being, that Nānak appears to me even as the Formless one (the Supreme Being). Between him and the Formless one there is no difference whatever." Then Kālū remained silent.

When Nānak was fifteen years of age, Kālū said to him: "What sort of a man art thou,

[1] Here the second compiler breaks off suddenly without carrying the story to the end, which is also rather abruptly finished in the first compilation. It is very significant that this whole Sākhī is left out in the Lahore edition, as it was considered rather derogatory to Nānak.

who wast born in my house? In the time of old age my name is drowned by thee. I have no more any hope. First Nānakī was born and then thou. I had hoped that my name would remain after me, and thou hast been born such a man! Whilst I live my name is drowned by thee." Nānak remained silent. Then Kālū said again: "I am gradually worn out and die and thou givest me no answer!"

When Nānak had become seventeen years of age, Kālū said to Nānak: "Son, I have become anxious about thee, think of something!" Nānak answered: "Well, father, pardon me now! Whatever thou wilt tell me concerning the field, that I will do."]

(8).

Nānak is sent on a trading trip and spends his money on Faqīrs. He is beaten by his father and protected by Rāe Bulār.

[Then Kālū said: "Take twenty Rupees and go and bring four or five things! Bring salt and turmeric and some other things, that I shall point out to thee; and if thou wilt make this time a good traffic, then I will give thee again many Rupees." Nānak answered: "Well, father, thou wilt see thyself, what a good traffic I shall make." Kālū gave him the twenty Rupees and (sent) one servant with him.[1] They set out; when they had gone twelve Kōs, he saw that an assembly of Sādhs was sitting there, and how was it? Except a strip of cloth between the legs, they had no kind of clothes on. Among them was a Mahant; him Nānak asked: "Sir, are you not in possession of clothes or are clothes not pleasant to your body?" The Mahant said: "How, brother, why dost thou ask? what object hast thou?" Then Bālā, the Jaṭ, who was as servant with him, said: "Hear, Nānak, thou hast come for the purpose of traffic, go and take up that traffic, that Kālū has told thee." Nānak said: "Hear, brother Bālā, my father has said, that I should make good traffic. Shall I make a good traffic or a bad one, tell me thy advice." Bālā answered: "Kālū has sent thee for good traffic." Then Nānak said: "Bālā, this is good traffic and that is bad traffic." Bālā replied: "Sir, know thou (thyself), thou art the son, he is the father." Then Nānak asked these Sādhs: "Why have you not given me an answer?" The Mahant said: "O boy, we are Nirbāṇīs,[2] to us abstinence from clothes is necessary." Nānak said: "You will also not be eating?" The Mahant replied: "O lad, when the Lord sends, then we are eating, otherwise we remain silent; for this reason we are dwelling in the jungle; having become Sanyāsīs we no longer dwell in a village, in a village there is hope (of getting something)." Then Nānak said: "Hear, O Mahant, what is thy name?" The Mahant mentioned his name: "(my) garb (is that of a) Nirbāṇī, (my) name: the dust of the saints." Nānak became very happy and said: "Hear, brother Bālā, I cannot give up this traffic." Bālā said: "Hear, Nānak, Kālū will be angry with me, see thou to it!" Nānak replied: "This is a good traffic, there is no loss in it, but on the contrary an increase." Bālā said: "You must know it." Then Nānak took the twenty Rupees from Bālā and put them before the Mahant. The Mahant said: "How, O lad? these are of no use to us, and they are given thee by thy father for the sake of traffic; what dost thou mean by giving them to Faqīrs?" Nānak replied: "Hear, O Mahant! my father had said to me: 'If thou come having made good traffic, then it is good.' This is good traffic, every other traffic is bad."

[1] The lithographed Lahore edition adds here: ਨਫਰ ਨਾਲ ਬਾਲਾ ਆਹਾ: the servant with (him) was Bālā, whereas the MS. (No. 2885), which otherwise agrees verbatim with the Lahore edition, does not mention the name here, but further on.

[2] ਨਿਰਬਾਣੀ, an order of Faqīrs, who pretend to be freed from every want and to be emancipated whilst as yet in the body.

The Mahant said: "Hear, O lad, what is thy name? who art thou?" Nānak replied: "Hear, O Mahant, my name is Nānak Nirankārī (the Formless one), I am the son of Kālū, a Khatrī of the Vēdī tribe." Then said that Mahant: "Hear, O lad, what is this? Nirankārī and the son of a Khatrī?" Nānak replied: "In the Dvāpara yuga we had performed devotion to the Formless one, the devotion was complete, but desire entered us; therefore our birth took place in a low house. Then our birth took place in the house of an oilman; on account of that desire we were again born in the house of a Khatrī. At that time also we were incorporeal and now also we are incorporeal."[1] Then the Mahant said: "O lad Nānak, ask thou something!" Nānak replied: "What shall I ask? the One Formless one I desire, I desire nothing else." Then the Mahant said again: "O lad, thou thyself art the Formless one, what shall we give to thee? But do (one) work, take these Rupees and bind them in thy bundle and bring provisions for these, that the Atīts (Faqīrs) may eat, money is of no use to us." Then Nānak took Bālā with him and went to the town, he took provisions and fuel and raw pots and brought them and put them before the Mahant. Then the Mahant said: "Nānak Nirankārī, thou art indeed the Formless one. The Atīts had passed seven days in fasting; now go thou!" Then Nānak bowed his head, rose and went. After (that) an Atīt asked the Mahant: "Sir, why didst thou send him away, he had done service to thee." The Mahant replied: "Hear, O Atīt, he was himself the Formless one, he had come to inquire after us, we had to take from him our provisions, but service we had not to exact from him; his splendour could not be borne by us, therefore we gave him leave."

When Nānak had gone above one Kōs, he began to ask Bālā: "Brother Bālā, what has been done by us?" Bhāī Bālā said: "Hear, O Nānak, by me none (*i.e.* Rupees) have been eaten (= spent), thou didst demand them and I gave them to thee." Then Nānak said: "Bālā, we did not make the mistake." Bālā replied: "If I made the mistake, thou must know, if I did not make the mistake, then thou must know. As thou wast inexperienced, so was I inexperienced; Kālū knows (this) or thou must know it." Having come there (*i.e.* home) Nānak did not enter his house and Bālā went to his own house. Kālū was informed, that Bālā, the servant (of Nānak), had entered his house and that Nānak had not come. Kālū became alarmed and went to the house of Bālā and called him out. Bālā came out of the house and Kālū asked: "Bālā, where is Nānak and where are the Rupees?" Bālā said: "Mahatā Kālū, in going along Nānak has given the twenty Rupees away to feed Faqīrs." Kālū said again: "I, who had sent thee with him, what for did I send thee with him? that you should feed Faqīrs?" "Mahatā Kālū, thou hadst said to Nānak: 'make a good traffic!' He said: 'Hear, Bālā, we must make a good traffic;' by him the good traffic has been made, thou mayst cry or not." Then Kālū said: "Show me to a certainty where he is!" Bālā took Kālū and came with him to the pond. Having come there Kālū seized Nānak and began to ask: "Where are those twenty Rupees?" Nānak did not say anything. Kālū became angry and gave Nānak two slaps on his left cheek and on his right cheek he gave him (two) with his right hand.[2] Nānak shed tears, but said nothing, the water ran down his cheeks. One man went to Rāc Bulār and said: "Kālū, the Paṭvārī, has given his son a severe beating. Nānakī, the daughter of Kālū, has fallen for the

[1] The MS. No. 2885 has the words: In the Dvāpara yuga we had performed devotion to the Formless one, the devotion had become complete; then also we were incorporeal and now also we are incorporeal. About the different births nothing is said. The Lahore edition has (intentionally) left out this whole passage.

[2] The MS. No. 2885 gives this passage more clearly: ਕਾਲੂ ਗੁਸਾ ਖਾਇ ਕਰਿ ਨਾਨਕ ਨੂੰ ਦੁਇ ਤਮਾਚੇ ਸਜੇ ਹਥ ਦੇ ਖਬੀ ਗਲ੍ਹ ਤੇ ਅਤੇ ਦੁਇ ਤਮਾਚੇ ਖਬੇ ਹਥ ਦੇ ਸਜੀ ਗਲ੍ਹ ਤੇ, *i.e.* Kālū having become angry struck Nānak two slaps with the right hand on the left cheek and two slaps with the left hand on the right cheek. (The verb (ਮਾਰੇ) is dropped.) In the Lahore edition this whole passage, which all Janam-Sākhīs have, is intentionally left out, it only says that Kālū became very angry.

sake of Nānak at the feet of Kālū (saying): 'O father, forgive him this fault for my sake!'" Nānakī had released Nānak, when a man of Rāe Bulār came (and said): "Go, Kālū, the Rāe is calling thee, and bring also Nānak with thee!" Kālū said: "Sir, what shall I bring? this my son has quite upset me, what shall I do?" That servant of Rāe Bulār said: "Go, brother, go there!" That servant brought both to Rāe Bulār. The Rāe was sitting in anger; when he saw Nānak, he wept. The Rāe rose and embraced Nānak, he took him and kissed his head. When he looked at his face, what did he see? that the water was running down his cheeks! Then the Rāe said: "Hear, Kālū, I had told thee, don't call Nānak bad, and (yet) thou hast beaten him to-day. My word has made no impression on thee, thou hast had no love to God nor affection to thy son, that there is only one son in thy house; Kālū, thou art a great fiend! Kālū, Nānak is not (held) worthy in thy house. What shall I do, as this one has no knowlege of himself?" Kālū replied: "Sir, I had given him twenty Rupees; there is no traffic and no Rupees (more), what shall I do? You are quarrelling with me. I had sent (also) a servant with Nānak; that one began to say, that he has fed Faqīrs." Rāe Bulār asked the servant Bālā: "Where has Nānak thrown away the twenty Rupees?" Bālā told before the Rāe the whole thing that had happened. Then the Rāe said: "Till now I never called thee bad, but now I call thee so, because thou, uproarious, unhappy man, hast beaten so much Nānak for the sake of twenty Rupees. Go, Umēdā, bring from within from the Rāṇī twenty Rupees and put them into the hand of the uproarious Kālū! What shall I do, as he (Nānak) will not eat in my house, otherwise I would keep him in my own house, he is not to be kept in thy house; to-day or to-morrow we were entrusting him to somebody." Meanwhile Umēdā brought the Rupees from the Rāṇī Khōkhar and put them before Rāe Bulār. The Rāe taking them into his hand began to give them to Kālū, but Kālū would not take them and said: "Sir, the Rupees are thine and I also am thine and Nānak also is thine. I am not at all grieving about the Rupees, I am grieving about his conduct." The Rāe replied: "He is acting well, Kālū, take the Rupees! As long as the steps of Nānak are here, so long we will serve him." Then said Umēdā, the Vazīr of the Rāe: "Kālū, take the Rupees! it is not good to disobey the word of the Rāe. Rāe Bulār must be obeyed, otherwise he will take it amiss." Then Kālū took the twenty Rupees. Kālū having taken the Rupees became astonished. The people of Talvaṇḍī, the Khatrīs and the Brāhmaṇs and the Jaṭ families, they all began to be angry (and said): "Art thou a Khatrī? Thy birth is rather like that of Čaṇḍāl, that thou hast thus beaten thy son. And thou hast taken twenty Rupees from the Rāe!" Then the next morning Kālū went again to the Rāe and fell down at his feet and said: "I have no place whatever, don't beat me; take back again these twenty Rupees!" The Rāe replied: "These twenty Rupees we have not given to thee, I had to give them to Nānak, to him they are given, how should they be again taken from thee?" Kālū answered: "Sir, where were Rupees with Nānak, that they were borrowed by thee from him?" The Rāe replied: "Kālū, thou dost not know it; as much wealth and property there is in this world, the Lord of all that is Nānak, what he gave, that we were eating and drinking."]

(9).

Jairām's betrothal with Nānakī and subsequent marriage.

[When Nānak was eighteen years of age, they were the days of Čēt and Vaisākh, the Paltā Jairām had come for the sake of measuring (the corn-fields), (for) he was an Āmil. Before (him) the daughter of Kālū, Nānakī, was drawing water from a well; the sight of Jairām, the Paltā, fell on her, she was very beautiful. Jairām seeing her fell in love with her and said to the Rāe: "O Rāe, whose is this girl?" The Rāe replied: "O brother, this girl belongs to Kālū, the Paṭvārī." Jairām asked further: "O Rāe, Kālū the Paṭvārī, what sort of people are they?" Rāe Bulār said: "O brother, they are Khatrīs, of the Vēdī clan." Jairām said: "O Rāe, if her betrothal has not been made somewhere else, bring about my betrothal with her." The Rāe replied: "O brother, if between them and you intermarriages take place, I will speak about it, but if not, how can I speak about it?" With Jairām was a Brāhmaṇ cook, but very intelligent. Him Jairām asked: "Sir, between us and the Vēdīs do betrothals take place or not?" Nidhā, the Brāhmaṇ, replied: "O brother, they are taking place." The Rāe called then Kālū and asked: "Kālū, do betrothals take place between him and you or not?" Kālū answered: "They are taking place." The Rāe said further: "Kālū, thy daughter has become big, betroth her with Jairām!" Kālū replied: "O Rāe, those who have a daughter, do not speak themselves, those speak, with whom something is wrong. I am thy servant, whatever is in my power I shall be ready to do." The Rāe said: "She is our daughter, don't trouble yourself about it!" Jairām called again on the Rāe: "O Rāe, what news about the betrothal?" The Rāe answered: "The asking in marriage of others' daughters is not a law, but a matter of submission and entreaty. Call thou him and speak with him, what will have to be said on our part, that we shall also say. Jairām replied: "How shall I speak? you are Rājās, you understand it." The Rāe said: "Do not speak thyself, let it be told by the Brāhmaṇ." Jairām replied: "Well, Sir, the Brāhmaṇ may go." Jairām called the Brāhmaṇ and said: "Sir, go to Kālū, the Vēdī's house, for the sake of betrothal." The Brāhmaṇ answered: "O Rāe, let us both, you and I, be together and speak to Kālū!" On Saturday, when one watch and a half of the day was yet remaining, the Brāhmaṇ said to Kālū: "Look, Mahatā Kālū, thou art a good Khatrī and Jairām also is a great man; it is a good union, consent to a betrothal!" Kālū replied: "Art thou speaking, O Brāhmaṇ, or is Jairām speaking?" The Brāhmaṇ replied: "O Mahatā, how should Jairām speak? he has sent me." Then said the Rāe: "Kālū, the Brāhmaṇ speaks truth, how should Jairām speak? What the Brāhmaṇ says, that he says." Then said Kālū: "Well, O Rāe, thy word is on my head; what you do, that is acceptable to my seven generations!"

The betrothal of Jairām and Nānakī took place. In the coming (month of) Manghar the work was done.[1] Jairām took the Ḍōlī (with his wife) to his house (at Sultānpur). Afterwards Kālū began to send Nānak,[2] but Nānak did not go. Kālū said: "Go and bring thy sister." Then the Rāe called Nānak, comforted him and said: "Go for this time and bring thy sister, after we shall entrust you (to them) there." Nānak went and as it was some journey, he took Bālā, the Sandhū, with him, as he had an affection for Bālā. Having gone there he began to ask leave for his sister. Then Jairām said: "Nānak, remain thou also here, I am not sending (thee and Nānakī)." Nānakī said then to Jairām: "Send me this time, that the father Kālū and the mother, both may be pleased and Nānak also may be pleased, he will say: 'I have not come back empty.' Then don't send me again! I stand in awe of Nānak. When a dream comes to me, whatever comes forth out of his mouth (in the dream), that is taking place; for this reason I tell you this." Jairām said: "Well, go, when wilt thou come again?" Nānakī said: "When thou wilt come to do the government work, then take me with thee, I am not coming by myself." Nānak took Nānakī with him and they went home and joined

[1] The words of the original are: ਆਵਦੇ ਮੰਘਰਿ ਕਾਜੁ ਹੋਆ; they allude briefly to the wedding which took place in Manghar. But the Lahore edition is not content with this brief allusion; it gives a description of the marriage procession, and that much money and sweetmeats were distributed. That this is quite a recent addition is proved by the MS. 2885, which contains nothing of this kind, but agrees here quite with our text.

[2] *i.e.* to Sultānpur, to look after his sister.

(their people). When [the season of Vaisākh came again, the measuring (of the corn-fields) commenced. Jairām came to Talvaṇḍī, and having measured there he was on the point of bringing back his wife. Rāe Bulār heard of it, he showed Jairām much attention and entreaty; Jairām was much pleased with the Rāe, he said also to the Rāe: "O Rāe, I am very much pleased with you, may boldly some service be ordered to me!" The Rāe said: "O brother, thy father-in-law is very foul-tongued and Nānak thy brother-in-law is a perfect Sādh. We were saying this, that you should keep him with you." Jairām replied: "O Rāe, what is better than this? He shall go with me." Then the Rāe said: "O brother, it will not do, that he go with you, after two months we will send him; you must bring about his betrothal there somewhere" (*i.e.* with somebody). Jairām replied: "Well, Rāe, what Rām will do, that is good." Jairām took his wife and went home.]

(10).

Nānak gives away his drinking vessel and ring to an Atīt. Arrangements for his departure to Sultānpur.

[When Nānak had become twenty years of age, one day an Atīt (Faqīr) came and sat outside of the town. There also Nānak went with pleasure and sat down. In Nānak's hand was a drinking vessel (Lōṭā) and on one hand a ring of gold. The Atīt said: "Who art thou? what is thy name?" Nānak replied: "My name is Nānak Nirankārī, I am a Vēdī Khatrī." Then the Atīt said again: "Whose are we?" Nānak replied: "You are the Nirankār's." Then the Atīt said: "You are a Nirankārī [1] and I am a Nirankārī, between thee and me what difference is there?" Nānak replied: "None whatever." Then the Atīt said: "Give me this drinking vessel and ring!" Nānak took off the ring from his hand and put (it and) the drinking vessel before the Atīt. Then the Atīt said: "They have come to hand, let them remain with me." Nānak said: "O God, when the spittle is thrown out of the mouth, it is not again taken up." The Atīt replied: "O Nānak, thou art really the Nirankārī (Formless one) and we are the copy." Nānak went then to his own house and the Atīt took the drinking vessel and the ring and went off. Kālū asked Nānak: "Where is the drinking vessel and the ring?" Nānak remained silent and did not speak. Kālū having become angry said: "Go, leave my house! I do not hold thee back!" Rāe Bulār heard this and called Kālū: "O Kālū, what has happened again?" "Sir, I am (your) dust: the ring and the drinking vessel he has thrown away somewhere; it is not known what he has done." The Rāe then said to Kālū: "Let him be sent to Jairām; here thou art annoyed and he also is grieved; whatever happens there, that happens." The Rāe wrote a letter to Nānakī and Jairām and wrote a good deal: "We have entrusted Nānak to thee; whatever will be done on thy part, that should be done without delay." Jairām also wrote a letter: "Nānak, come and join us." When Nānak had read this letter, he said: "I will join Jairām." The people of the house said: "If Nānak go, it is good."]

(11).

Nānak arrives at Sultānpur and enters the Commissariat.

On the third of the light half of the month Manghar, in Sambat 1540,[2] Nānak went to Jairām; he came on the fifth day from Talvaṇḍī to Sultānpur. On the seventh of the light half of Manghar, he met with Nānakī, his sister. Nanakī on seeing Nānak fell down at his feet. Nānak said: "O sister, thou art older (than I), I on the contrary will fall at thy feet, or shouldst

[1] Here Nirankārī has the sense: *of the Formless one.*

[2] The Lahore edition has Sambat 1544, against all MS. authority.

thou fall at my feet?"[1] Nānakī replied: "O brother, thou art speaking the truth, but though thou mayst be a man, thou appearest to me as my Supreme Lord." Jairām was not at home. The Bēbē[2] put down a stool (for Nānak) and began to ask: "O brother, art thou very happy?" Nānak replied: "O Bēbē, I am always happy." He was (still) sitting when Jairām afterwards came home. When he looked about, Nānak was sitting in front. When Nānak saw that his brother-in-law Jairām had come, he rose and ran to fall down at his feet. Jairām was a very intelligent man; he seized the hands of Nānak and did not allow him to apply them to his feet, he himself put his hand on the feet of Nānak. Then Guru Nānak said: "O brother-in-law, why is this inverted custom made by thee?" Jairām replied: "O Nānak, you know, that we were brothers-in-law, and (now) I consider thee as the Supreme Lord. It has been my good luck, that you have come to me; you have given me your sight, and I have been exalted thereby. Don't you do anything, sit down and live with ease!" Guru Nānak replied: "O brother-in-law, if there would be some business (for me), it would be a good thing." Jairām said: "Well, brother, as this (thought) has arisen in your mind, it is good. Have you read some Turkish?" Guru Nānak replied: "We have read some Hindī." Jairām said: "Brother Nānak, will you take the Commissariat?" Guru Nānak replied: "O brother-in-law, whose is the Commissariat?" Jairām said: "It belongs to the Navāb Daulat Khān Lōdī, it is a great commissariat; if it be possible, then take it!" Gurū Nānak replied: "Well, brother-in-law, the Formless one will bring it to an issue!" The Bēbē Nānakī said again: "Thou art the form of the Supreme Lord, as the morsel is, so eat it in sitting down, do thou not fall into these troubles! thou dost not come up to these troubles, thou art a Faqīr." Gurū Nānak replied: "If one eats his bread in doing (some) work, it becomes pure, and the Turks are saying: 'What is eaten lawfully, that is good.'" Then Bēbē Nānakī said: "Well, brother, as thou art thinking and liking, so it is right." Then Bēbē Nānakī said further to Jairām: "Sir, are you acquainted with his circumstances or not?" Jairām replied: "O servant of the Supreme Lord, I am acquainted." Then Bēbē Nānakī continued to say: "Where shall his betrothal be made? if he conceive an affection for the married state, then business will be done by him." Jairām replied: "I will see about it. If he will give himself to business, then some Khatrī also will give the hand to a betrothal; do not be hasty! Keep the Lord in thy mind!" Bēbē Nānakī replied: "Sir, I am not cleverer than thou, but I had to tell you this." On the fourteenth of the light half of the (month of) Manghar the Commissariat was given (to Nānak) by Jairām. Say, O brother: vāh Gurū-jī!

(12).

Nānak in the Commissariat; visited by his father. His accounts are examined by Jairām and found correct.

[One thousand Rupees in cash were given (to him by Jairām).[3] Bālā, the Sandhū, said: "O Gurū (Angad), I also was with him. I said: 'O brother Nānak, thou hast taken one thousand Rupees and the Commissariat, give me leave to go.' Then Gurū Nānak said: 'O

[1] This story is also to be found in the Panjābī Grammar (edited by the American Missionaries, Ludihāṇā) p. 97 *sqq.*, but the text is not given correctly; they print *e.g.* ਪਰ ਲਾਗਾ instead of ਪਰਿ ਲਾਗਾ, as if ਪਰ and ਪਰਿ were the same, whereas the latter is the Locative and written so in the MSS.

[2] ਬੇਬੇ the same as بیبی, *bībī*, a lady, used also in addressing a sister, out of respect or endearment; generally ਜੀ is added to ਬੇਬੇ, to enhance the respect.

[3] It is not quite clear, by whom the Rupees were given to Nānak, if by Jairām, as head-steward, or by Navāb Daulat Khān; the original only says: ਇਕ ਹਜਾਰ ਰੁਪਈਆ ਨਕਦੁ ਦਿਵਾਇਆ.

brother Bālā, thou hast made an unsolid friendship (with me), whilst living thou art leaving me?' I replied: 'Sir, thou wast the son of a Khatrī and didst thy own business, I will now also do my own work.' Then Gurū Nānak said: 'O brother Bālā, we shall pass (here) some days, this profession must be done by us, what our business is, that we shall do; behold thou the amusement (show) of the Formless one! what feats the Formless one is doing! remain thou with us, live (with me)!' Then I replied: 'Well, Nānak, as you like, what you will say, that I will do.' Then I also began to do work with Nānak. When in this work two years[1] had passed, Mahatā Kālū came to get information (about it), and met with Gurū Nānak. Gurū Nānak rose and fell down at the feet of Kālū. Mahatā Kālū kissed his head and pressed him to his neck and comforted him. He began to ask: 'O son, two years have now passed, since thou wast sent here, what is gained, what eaten?' Nānak replied: 'Father, much has been eaten (spent), much has been gained, but no Damṛī[2] remains with us.' Then Mahatā Kālū began to quarrel with me (*i.e.* Bālā). Gurū Nānak made me a sign, and so I did not speak. Kālū began to say: 'I had thought, Nānak is now employed in business, what of my property he had (formerly) squandered, that he will now have gained and will restore to me.' He talked in such a way, as it was usual with Kālū. He met then with Nānakī and Jairām and began to say: 'What have you done? are you looking after him? you have not looked after his business nor have you made an effort for his betrothal, you have done nothing at all.' Bēbē Nānakī replied: 'Since he has come here, he has squandered nothing of thine, you are not thankful, that he is happy and has taken to his work, one day he will make profit; and we have also some information concerning a betrothal, to-day or to-morrow it will take place in some direction; we have lost nothing in it, what must we look out? O father, if (the betrothal) is in any direction being brought about on your part, then do so! As it is painful to us, so it is still more painful to you.' Kālū said: 'O daughter Nānakī, if it will be done by me, then what is it necessary to me (to ask you)? And, daughter, if you make (it, *i.e.* the betrothal), it must be made in the house of a good Khatrī; an indifferent one must not be made.' Jairām said then: 'We must not make entreaties, O Mahatā! There is a Khatrī Mūlā, of the Čōṇā family, in (the village of) Pakhō, the Radhāvā,[3] in his house is a daughter; he also is called a good man and is Paṭvārī of the Radhāvā. He is making the betrothal (of his daughter) for the sake of religious merit;[4] there we have looked out for a betrothal; what is pleasing to the Lord, that will take place. O Mahatā, compose your mind, Rām will make (all) right.' Kālū said then: 'The shame is common to the sons and to the sons-in-law. I was saying in my mind: the happiness of Bēbē Nānakī I have seen with my eyes, now it is my wish, that whilst living I see the happiness of Nānak; then my mind will be composed.' Then Jairām said: 'O Mahatā, remain thou here, and the mother-lady we will also call and bring here.' Kālū replied: 'O son Jairām, it is hard for me to remain here, as I am occupied there.' Jairām said: 'O Mahatā, thou art in the place of Parmānand,[5] thou art my father.' Then Kālū said: 'Jairām, when the betrothal of Nānak takes place, then give me information; keep my son Nānak under your eyes, lest he waste any money.'

"Then Bēbē Nānakī said: 'O father, you are not thankful. You were daily crying: "to-day

[1] All MSS. read: ਦੁਇ ਵਰੇ, two years, but in the Lahore edition this is changed (apparently without any authority, for in the Panjābī Gram. p. 99, and in the Sikhā̃ dē rāǰ dī vithiā, p. 211, we find also ਦੁਇ ਵਰਹੇ) to: ਮਹੀਨੇ ਦੇ ਗੁਜਰੇ (p. 29), two months.

[2] ਦਮੜੀ, the eighth part of a Paisā.

[3] Thus the name is written in the MSS. Radhāvā (also pronounced Randhāvā, as I was told) is the proper name of a tribe of Jaṭs. ਪਖੇ ਦੇ ਰਧਾਵੇ signifies therefore literally: in Pakhō, the Radhāvā's (village being left out). See p. lxiv, l. 25.

[4] That is to say: without taking any money for her.

[5] Parmānand is said to have been the father of Jairām.

this is wasted (by him);" now he does not waste thine own. And, O father, when he is feeding the Faqīrs, then our heart is trembling; if there is no deficiency in the money of the Government, and if we remain unabashed on the part of the Government, it is all right. And, O father, when he is rendering account, some surplus comes out; he is some form of the Formless one.' Then Jairām said: 'O Mahatā, for this reason we cannot say anything to him.' Kālū replied: 'O son Jairām, if you render again account and if some surplus comes out, you would do well to take it to yourself, to him a Lakh (of Rupees) and a straw is the same. And call thou Bālā and admonish him, I am also telling it him.' Jairām sent a man and called Bālā; he said to him: 'Bhāī Bālā, thou art the special friend of Nānak, we were thinking of thee thus, that as Nānak is, so art thou; take thou care of Nānak, that he do not waste his money on any stranger.' Kālū said then: 'It is a shame, that (my) son and Bālā remain together.' What Jairām said I did not take amiss, but that which Kālū said. I answered to Kālū: 'Mahatā Kālū, may not some suspicion be in thy mind, that Bālā is remaining with Nānak and will make some extravagance! In my opinion Ghī also is a bad thing, and some other greediness is a bad thing: to us, who were remaining with Nānak, Nānak appears as the Supreme Lord. Mahatā Kālū, thou art hungry after money and I have a craving after this one. What he (Nānak) does, that he does. We make further no apology; if thou art hungry after money, then remain thou with him, whatever comes into his hand that take!' Then said Jairām: 'O Mahatā, Bhāī Bālā speaks the truth: Nānak is not a man, he appears as something else. Well, Mahatā, depart thou now! when the betrothal has taken place, at that very time the affair (*i.e.* the marriage) must be done by us quickly, love will then spring up to his wife and then he will comprehend himself (what he has to do).' Then Kālū went home.

"When one month had passed, some good man brought Jairām this information about Nānak: 'Hear, Jairām, thy brother-in-law is a steward and is squandering the money of the Government, thou dost not take care of him; dost thou not know, how the temper of the Paṭhāns is?' Jairām became sorry, he went home and took Nānakī aside. He began to say: 'Hear, O beloved of the Lord, a certain man said to-day to me: "Jairām, thy brother-in-law is a steward, he is squandering the money, thou dost not admonish him; dost thou know the temper of the Paṭhāns or not?" What shall I do now, wife? What you say, that I will do.' Nānakī replied: 'What comes into thy mind, that do, what can I say, I must also walk according to thy word.' Jairām said: 'Give me some advice, O wife, I will do it.' Nānakī replied: 'Sir, has no faith yet come to you? You will think, that I am taking the side of my brother. Whatever be the Māyā of the world, that all goes out of the hands of Nānak. But well, Sir, it is in thy mind, do this work: take thou once an account; if the account has turned out full, be it in excess or be it not in excess, but be it not deficient, then thou wilt not again be bewildered by the word of any one.' Jairām replied: 'Well, wife, I do not take it, if thou hast faith (in him), what should I do?' Nānakī said: 'Sir, don't let it go now, I will call my brother.' Jairām replied: 'Well, wife, as you like.' Nānakī sent the slave-girl Tulsā and called Nānak. The slave-girl Tulsā went and made her salām. Nānak said: 'O Tulsā, why hast thou come to-day?' Tulsā replied: 'Sir, my lady told me: "Go to my brother and tell him, that he should give me his sight;" therefore I have come.' Nānak said: 'Go, Tulsā, I am coming.' Afterwards Gurū Nānak asked Bhāī Bālā: 'Why has the Bēbē called me?' I said: 'She may have called you on account of anything.' Gurū Nānak rejoined: 'Bhāī Bālā, my heart gives me witness, that some tale-bearing has been made about me.' Bālā said: 'Sir, what tale-bearing can any one make about thee? what art thou doing?' Then Gurū Nānak said: 'Bhāī Bālā, bring a plate of sweetmeats.' I brought it. Nānak put all the sweetmeats into his lap, they were one Seer and a half (= three pounds). Nānak took them and came to Nānakī. Bēbē Nānakī was standing. 'Come brother,' she said, and put a stool for him. Nānak sat on the stool, I also was with him.

Nānak asked: 'O Bēbē, why have I been called?' She replied: 'O brother, many days have passed since I have seen you, I had a longing to see you, then I sent for you.' Gurū Nānak said: 'Bēbē-jī, I doubt it; tell me why you have called me!' Then the Bēbē replied: 'O brother, all is known to thee, but it cannot be told.' Nānak said: 'I know in my own mind, that somebody has made a tale-bearing about me, therefore say I also, that account should be taken from me.' The Bēbē Nānakī comforted him, but Gurū Nānak said: 'No, this is a matter of account, here no regard is had to any one.' Then the Bēbē said: 'Well, brother.'

"In Samvat 1543,[1] on the fifteenth of the light half of the month of Manghar, the account was made; the account of three months was given. One hundred and thirty-five Rupees remained due to Nānak after (deducting) eating, drinking, taking and giving. Then Nānak said to Jairām: 'Well, brother-in-law, we have become justified in thy sight: take this Commissariat and give it to some one else! ours is the Formless one, the creator!'[2] Then Jairām fell at his feet and Bēbē Nānakī began to weep and to say: 'First beat me and then go!' Nānak said: 'O brother-in-law: now the account has turned out full, but if it would be less or more, then how? you would bring me into difficulties.' Jairām replied: 'O brother, formerly I knew something, but now faith has come to me on both sides; pardon me for this fault! I have erred very much!' . . . .[3]

"Nānak went to the Commissariat and sat down there; all the workmen began to congratulate him, Hindūs and Musalmāns were happy."]

(13).

Nānak's betrothal. He has to give account and comes out with a surplus.

[In Samvat 1544, on the fifth of the light half of (the month of) Manghar, the betrothal of Nānak took place in the house of Mūlā, the Čōṇā, in Pakhō, the Radhāvā's (village). Jairām and Bēbē Nānakī gave notice to Mahatā Kālū and to the lady mother[4] and congratulated; they called them (saying): "If you come, the marriage expenses will be made." Kālū having heard this was very happy and likewise the lady mother. Who had brought this information, his mouth was filled with sugar-candy and Khīr,[5] which the mother prepared with her own hands. Having filled his mouth she began to say: "I am a sacrifice to thy mouth, which has given me the information of the congratulation of Nānak." Then all the females of the Vēdīs came by night and sat down to sing; they began to say: "One Nānak, a good man, has been produced in our family; as his betrothal has lawfully taken place, our family is rendered spotless by him." And the lady mother sent congratulation to her father's house in the Mānjhā.[6] Rāmā Jhangaṛ[7] was the father of the lady and Bhirāī was her mother; they were the maternal grandfather and grandmother of Nānak and the father and mother-in-law of Kālū. She sent word to them: "Come and go to Sultānpur, we will make fine expenses (in the marriage)." Bhirāī, the grandmother, and Rāmā, the grandfather, and Kisnā, the grandmother's brother, these three having heard this, were happy and came thence to Talvaṇḍī and met Kālū. Having met him they rose and went from Talvaṇḍī with Kālū and Lālū, the Vēdī, and the mother lady, six men were ready. Two servants were with Rāmā, three servants and one Mardānā, the Ḍūm[8] of the house, in all four men were with Kālū, so that all together there were twelve men. When they

[1] All the MSS. have the year 1543, only the Lahore edition has changed it to 1544.

[2] The MS. No. 2885 reads: ਅਸਾੜਾ ਕਾਰ ਹੈ ਕਰਤਾਰ ਹੈ, our work is (to say and to testify): the creator is!

[3] We break off here, as the lengthened speeches and mutual compliments are quite irrelevant.

[4] The words are: ਅਸਾ ਧੀਧੀ.

[5] ਖੀਰ is rice boiled in milk.

[6] ਮਾਂਝਾ, the Mānjhā is the central part of the Bārī Duāb.

[7] ਝੰਗੜ is the family name, properly Rāmā of the Jhangaṛ family.

[8] About ਡੂਮ, see p. xi, note 1. Though Musalmāns, they are also attached to Hindū houses.

were on the point of starting, they went to Rāe Bulār to take leave of him. Kālū went and stood before the Rāe; the Rāe asked: "How, Kālū?" Kālū said: "The betrothal of Nānak, thy slave, has taken place, we are going to make the marriage expenses in Pakhō, the Radhāvā's (village), may leave be given to us!" The Rāe replied: "Kālū, it is good, but is Nānak careful?" Kālū said: "O Rāe, he has given me ground for apprehension." "No, Kālū, I spoke on account of something else, thy temper is harsh, but he is a Sādh, do not quarrel with him!" "This is not my intention, O Rāe! and, O Rāe, you have been made equal to the Supreme Lord, speak you with kindness!" The Rāe said: "Go, Kālū, may God do you good, may he accomplish the work! We also love him, but, Kālū, kiss the head of Nānak as being mine, go, the Lord protect you!"

Kālū mounted a cart and started; on the fifth day they arrived at Sultānpur, on Thursday. They entered the house of Parmānand, the Paltā, and congratulations began to be made. Nānak obtained information, that the mother and the father, the father's younger brother, the maternal grandfather and grandmother and uncle (on the mother's side) and also Mardānā, the Ḍūm, had come. He rose and ran and fell down at the feet of Kālū. Kālū lifted him up, and kissed his head. Nānak said: "O father, is the Rāe pleased?" Kālū replied: "O son, it is good, that thou didst remind me, the Rāe had said, that I should kiss thy head." Then Nānak fell down at the feet of his mother lady; his mother kissed his head and pressed him to her neck. Then Nānak fell down at the feet of his uncle Lālū. Lālū took him to his neck, kissed his face and said: "O son, thou hast made our family spotless here and the future the Lord knows." Then Nānak fell down at the feet of his grandfather Rāmā. Rāmā took him to his neck and did not let him go. Then the grandmother Bhirāī said: "Let him go from thy neck!" Rāmā replied to Bhirāī: "When my desire will be fulfilled, then I will let him go." . . . .

In Samvat 1544, on the seventh of the light half of the month of Māgh, they started from Sultānpur, having reflected on a good moment and day. Nidhā, the Brāhmaṇ, was sent in advance to the village of Pakhō, the Radhāvā. The grandson of Pakhō, the Radhāvā, was Hitā, his Paṭvārī was Mūlā, the Čōṇā. Nidhā, the Brāhmaṇ, went and gave information to Mūlā: "O Mahatā Mūlā, be happy!" Mūlā replied: "Reverence to thee, O Pāndhā! Come! whence hast thou come?" Nidhā said: "I have come from Sultānpur." Mūlā said then: "Why hast thou come?" Nidhā replied: "O brother, Jairām and Parmānand, the Paltā, have sent me." Mūlā said: "Why hast thou been sent?" Nidhā replied: "Kālū, the father-in-law, has come from Talvaṇḍī for the sake of making the marriage expenses. And Jairām had said to me: 'Go thou and bring information to Mahatā Mūlā.;' therefore have I come." Mūlā replied: "May they come on my head!"

On Sunday, the tenth, after a watch of the day had risen (= passed), they arrived. Mūlā had made some preparations (of food) and put down (for them). Parmānand, the Paltā, went and gave the wedding presents with his own hands. In taking and giving congratulations the custom was well observed from the side of both parties. Then Kālū, the Vēdī, said to Parmānand: "O brother, ask thou for the appointment of the marriage day!" Parmānand was an intelligent man, he took Mūlā and sat aside with him. The matter was accomplished. "Look, O Mahatā, the lad is a young man, and it is heard that the girl also is grown up: give thou a day for the marriage, the Vēdīs have come from Talvaṇḍī, and the Jhangaṛs, the relatives of the mother of the lad, have come from the Mānjhā." Mūlā answered: "O brother, be of good cheer! give me one year's delay, then having ascertained a good time for the marriage I will send you word." Having said this he dismissed them in a good manner with honour. They re-entered Sultānpur with great joy. Congratulations began to be made; Bēbē Nānakī called her companions and they sat down to sing. On the fourth day they took leave.

Then Mardānā, the Ḍūm, said: "O Nānak, give me some marriage present of thy own." Nānak replied: "O Mardānā, what wilt thou take? We have some business with thee."

Mardānā said: "Sir, give me some good thing!" Nānak replied: "Of a good thing thou wilt earn grief." Mardānā said: "If thou wilt give me a good thing, how shall I be grieved?" Nānak replied: "O Mardānā, thou art a Mirāsī,[1] thou art pleased with money and clothes, and the future thing (the other world) thou dost not know." Mardānā said: "O Nānak, if you know a good thing, give us that!" Nānak replied: "We have given to thee the skill of the strings, this (art) is necessary for us." Then Mardānā rose and stood and paid reverence. Then Nānak took off his coat from his neck, gave it to him and put it on his neck, saying: "O Mardānā, mind my word!" Mardānā said: "Sir, command me!" "Mardānā, thou art the Mirāsī of the Vēdīs, thou must not beg from others!" Mardānā replied: "Well, Sir, I agree to this, but you must take care of me!" Nānak said: "Hear, O Mardānā, the creator takes care of all."

Then all the families took leave and departed, after having met with joy and comfort. Nānak's conduct was the same as of old; if one came (to beg), he did not send away any one empty. Rumours were spread among the people that Nānak will be ruined to-day or to-morrow. The people came and informed Nānakī and Jairām. Nānakī said to Jairām: "You must look out, (else) you may be led astray by the talk of the people." Jairām was pondering within, but he did not let out any breath. Then one day Nānak said himself to Jairām: "O brother-in-law, account should be given to the Government, many days have passed (now)." Jairām went to the Navāb and said: "O Navāb, health! The steward Nānak says: 'If the Navāb would take account, it would be well.'" Navāb Daulat Khān said: "Jairām, call thy brother-in-law, the steward." Jairām sent the Brāhmaṇ Nidhā and called him (saying): "Nānak, bring the ledger and give account." Nānak was much pleased and brought the ledger. The people were filling the ears of the Navāb (saying): "Navāb, health! The steward is squandering the money of the Navāb."[2] Having come (Nānak) saluted the Navāb. The Navāb asked: "O steward, what is thy name?" Nānak replied: "My name is Nānak Nirankārī." The Navāb said to Jairām: "Jairām, I have understood nothing, what did the steward say?" Jairām satisfied the Navāb in Persian: "You say, (he is) incomparable, countless, without a sample, to whom this quality is applied, his servant I am." The Navāb laughed and said: "Jairām, is Nānak married?" Jairām replied: "Sir, he is not married." Then the Navāb said: "I understand now, if he will be married, such talk will not be conceived (by him)." Then the Navāb said: "Nānak, I have heard that thou art squandering my money; dost thou not know that I am Daulat Khān Lōdī?" Nānak replied: "Navāb, health! May account be taken! Whatever comes out for the Navāb, that will now be paid and you may take it, and what will come out for (this) poor one, that you may give him or not give him, as you please." The Navāb said: "Jairām, in what manner does the steward speak?" Jairām replied: "Navāb, health! The steward is truthful, he is not guilty of a crime." The Navāb said then: "Call Jādō Rāe Navī Sindā!" Jādō Rāe Navī Sindā came and saluted. The Navāb said: "O Jādō Rāe, account should be taken from Nānak in a good manner!" Jādō Rāe answered: "Navāb, health!" He began to make the account; the account lasted five days and five nights. Jādō Rāe Navī Sindā raised many difficulties, but with the Lord and with truth nothing could be brought against (him); three hundred and twenty-one Rupees came out as surplus for Nānak from the side of the Navāb. Jairām was happy, he came and paid reverence to the Navāb. The Navāb

[1] ਮਿਰਾਸੀ, a singer generally in India (ميراثي, an adjective formed from مراثي, Pl. of مرثية); they are Musalmāns and attach themselves also to Hindū families, from which they get some allowance.

[2] It is clearly seen from these words that the reason for giving account was very different from that stated above, where Nānak is said to have asked it himself.

said: "How is it, Jairām, is the account made up?" Jairām replied: "Health, O Navāb! it is made up." The Navāb said: "How has it turned out?" Jairām replied: "Health, O Navāb, call Jādō Rāe!" Jādō Rāe was called; having come he paid reverence to the Navāb. The Navāb said: "Has the account been taken? and how has it turned out?" Jādō Rāe replied: "Navāb, health! three hundred and twenty-one Rupees have come out as surplus to Nānak." The Navāb said: "What, ours or his?" Jādō Rāe replied: "Of Nānak, they are due to Nānak on the part of the Government." Then the Navāb said: "The people were saying that Nānak is squandering the money." Then Jairām said: "O Navāb, health! the people are bearing much spite." The Navāb said: "Call the treasurer Bhavānī-dās!" The treasurer was called, came and saluted. The Navāb said: "Bhavānī-dās, the money that is due to Nānak, give him now! and give him three thousand Rupees in addition." Bhavānī-dās replied: "Very well, health, O Nānak!" Bhavānī-dās gave him the three hundred and twenty-one Rupees and three thousand Rupees in addition. Nānak took the bags and came home; some of them he took to his shop, but the most of them he placed with his sister. Afterwards Jairām came very happy. Nānakī asked: "How did the account turn out?" Jairām said: "O beloved of God, I am quite astonished. I was thinking that Nānak was openly squandering the money, and now, that the account is being made, comes out on the contrary a surplus for him." Nānakī said: "What surplus has to-day come out?" Jairām replied: "A surplus of three hundred and twenty-one Rupees after eating, drinking and giving away."]

(14).

Marriage of Nānak, which turns out unhappy.

[In Samvat 1545, for the seventh of the light half of (the month of) Hāṛ, the marriage day was written. Nānakī made congratulations in the house and by the hand of the Brāhmaṇ Nidhā a letter was sent, sprinkled with saffron. Sweetmeats and Cardamom seeds and five Rupees in cash were sent to Talvaṇḍī to the house of Kālū. In the house of Kālū, the Vēdī, they commenced to rejoice and to make congratulations. Kālū sent a man to his father-in-law's family in the Mānjhā; there also congratulations were made; they began to divide fruits (among their friends). Kālū went to Rāe Bulār: "O Rāe, be blessed!" The Rāe said: "Kālū, what (is the matter)?" Kālū replied: "The day fixed for the marriage of thy slave[1] Nānak has come (to us)." The Rāe said: "Kālū, don't call Nānak again our slave, we shall be grieved thereby." Kālū replied: "Well, Sir, politeness becomes us." . . . . .[2]

Who went to the wedding? Kālū, Lālū, Parasrām, the son of Lālū, Nandlāl, Indrasain, Phirandā, Jagatrāe, Lōlčand, Jagsītmall, Jadmall; all the Vēdīs were ready. When the first day of (the month of) Bhādō had risen, seven days passed, then they started from Talvaṇḍī. From the Mānjhā came Rāmā, the maternal grandfather, and Kisnā, the (maternal) uncle, and two other companions with them. When they had arrived at Sultānpur, the beginning was made in the house of Parmānand and Jairām, the Paltā. When yet five days remained for the appointed day of the marriage, they started from Sultānpur. Having come to the twenty-second resting-place,[3] they stopped and alighted in a garden. Parmānand, the Paltā, the father of Jairām, sent the Brāhmaṇ Nidhā, (saying to him): "Go and inform Mūlā, (that) the marriage company of the Vēdīs has come, let it be known to you." Nidhā went and informed Mūlā, the Čōṇā, he gave him a benediction and said: "O patron, be happy!" Mūlā said: "O Paṇḍit, reverence

[1] The Lahore edition has struck out the word ਗੁਲਾਮ, which all MSS. have, and substituted in its place ਪੁਤ੍ਰ, son.

[2] We drop here some other complimentary words.

[3] ਮਾਜਾ *s.m.* rest, resting-place.

(to thee)!" Nidhā said: "O patron, the marriage company of the Vēdīs has alighted in a garden, in order to inform you Bhāī Parmānand has sent me." Mūlā replied: "It is well." Then Mūlā went and assembled his own brothers and relatives; he went to Hitā, the Radhāvā, and said: "O Čaudharī,[1] the marriage company of the Vēdīs has come." Hitā, the Radhāvā, said: "O son Ajitā, go with Mūlā; whatever Mūlā says, give that supply! Whatever vessels, clothes, people, he may desire, that give, and remain thou thyself also with him! My body, O Mūlā, is old, else I would be myself with thee." "Well, Čaudharī, what your order is, that is yourself." "Mūlā, good people have come to thy house, have an eye on (thy) honour, and restrain thy tongue, this is what I have to say. I have heard that Kālū, the Paṭvārī of the Bhaṭṭīs, is foul-tongued, and thou also hast a sharp tongue. But well, among them Parmānand and Jairām are called good men, therefore from thy own part politeness must be shown (to them)." Mūlā replied: "Well, Čaudharī, you are our refuge and asylum and the Lord also is our support." "Well, Mūlā, go, mind my order." Then Mūlā having assembled the head men of the caste sent excellent food; Ajitā, the Randhāvā, was with them, much honour and politeness was shown (to them). At night the marriage company (of the Vēdīs) rose and entered (the village) with fine music, inside much honour was shown (to them). When one watch and a quarter of the night had passed, the (four) circuits (round the marriage fire) took place. "This, which I am telling, O Guru, I have seen with my own eyes, I was present and speak as an eye-witness." Guru Angad having heard some words became happy and began to weep in love. "When the time of the circuits (round the fire) came, Nānak said: 'Bhāī Bālā, remain thou with me.' O Guru, whatever was Nānak's secret expense, that was with me. I said: 'Well, Sir, I will remain with you.' O Guru, it was a good enjoyment. Three days the marriage company remained, on the fourth day it took leave. Having taken the Ḍōlī (with the young wife) they came to Sultānpur. Kālū and Lālū said, that the lad and his wife should go to their own house and Nānak said: 'I will remain here.' Nānakī and Jairām said, they should remain here, for who would attend to the business of the commissariat? Then Kālū said: 'O daughter Nānakī, thy mother sits (at home) full of expectation, she also is longing for comfort.' This contention was going on, when Mūlā came. When Mūlā heard of it, he said, that the lad and the girl should remain here, they should not be sent to Talvaṇḍī. This strife was going on for several days, then Parmānand said: 'Mūlā,[2] this is now the first time, the mother of the lad is also full of expectation and desire, let them go to their own house, then having returned they shall remain here, the business of the commissariat is here.'

"Nānakī and the mother, the Čōṇī,[3] and all the other marriage company that had come from Talvaṇḍī, went with the Ḍōlī of the mother, the Čōṇī; Nānak (also) went to Talvaṇḍī and left the commissariat to me.

"Nānak returned again to Sultānpur and took the mother, the Čōṇī, to her father Mūlā's house, then he went to the commissariat and sat down there and commenced his work. As the custom of Gurū Nānak was, so it continued to be. He showed little affection to his wife and the mother, the Čōṇī, became (in consequence thereof) angry, the conduct of the Guru did not please her, the Guru did not apply her to his mouth (*i.e.* he did not kiss her). Two months passed and he did not enter the house.

[1] ਚਉਧਰੀ, the head officer of a village.

[2] In other MSS. he is also called ਮੂਲ ਚੰਦ Mūlčand, čand being an epithet frequently added to the names of Khatrīs.

[3] ਮਾਤਾ ਚੋਣੀ, the mother, the Čōṇī, *i.e.* Nānak's wife. As soon as a girl is married, her proper name is dropped and she is only called by the name of her family. Nānak's wife was of the Čōṇā family and she is therefore only called by that name; her maiden name was Sulakhaṇī (ਸੁਲਖਣੀ); see p. lxviii, l. 5.

"When Mūlā came to see his daughter, she said to him: 'O father, where hast thou given me away? This one is feeding the people and does not at all care for his house.' Mūlā went to Jairām, made a great row and said: 'Having obtained my daughter thou hast drowned her!' And to Nānak he said: 'O thou, whence hast thou been born?' But Nānak did not speak at all. The name of the mother, the Čōṇī, was Sulakhaṇī, and because she came to the house of the Guru, she was called the mother, the Čōṇī. They made continually altercations and months on months passed in squabbles. The name of the mother-in-law of Nānak was Čandōrāṇī. Čandōrāṇī came to her daughter and the daughter began to weep before her mother. Čandōrāṇī became very angry and went to Bēbē Nānakī and began to quarrel with her. She said: 'How so? You begin to govern thus, that you ruin other people's daughters? You have no fear of God, thou dost not admonish thy brother, thou dost not consider thy sister-in-law as one (with thee), thou dost not look after thy sister-in-law! Neither does thy husband admonish his brother-in-law, tell me, what you have in your mind?' Bēbē Nānakī replied: 'Hear, O aunt, how shall I admonish my brother? My brother is no thief, nor adulterer, nor gambler, he is not committing any wickedness, this is (all), that he is giving alms to the naked and hungry; with what one earns oneself, one may do what one pleases. Then you may reproach him, when your daughter remains hungry or naked.' . . . . . Čandōrāṇī remained silent, she could not say anything. She came back to her daughter and said: 'O daughter, thy sister-in-law has put me quite to shame, I could not give her any answer; O daughter, behave thou also a little humbly.' Sulakhaṇī replied: 'O mother, I am not hungry nor naked, jewels, clothes, food, all this I have.' 'But daughter, if thou hast all this, why art thou giving a bad name to the son of a Khatrī?' She said: 'O mother, what shall I do? He is not applying me to his mouth, he does not speak to me face to face, what shall I do, to whom shall I speak?' Čandōrāṇī went then again to Bēbē Nānakī and commenced to say: 'O daughter, I have much admonished thy sister-in-law; she admits, that she is not hungry nor naked, but she says that he does not speak to her face to face, nor apply her to his mouth: what shall I do?' Bēbē Nānakī replied: 'O aunt, the manner of my sister-in-law is rough, ... but she herself will become discreet.' 'Well, daughter Nānakī, there is no question of any want, but consider thou thyself: what is the custom of the women, that also is desired.' Bēbē Nānakī replied: 'Thou art right, the Lord will make it well; comfort her and admonish her also, that she should walk according to his word, that she should be gentle and give up roughness. Thou also knowest, O aunt, that I am taking care of my brother and I do not consider Nānak as my brother, I consider Nānak as the Lord; put thou true faith in him! We are so afraid of Nānak, that we dare not say a word to him, for Nānak is a Faqīr.' Čandōrāṇī went then home."]

(15).

Nānak's two sons are born. He quits the commissariat.

Gurū Nānak carried on the commissariat and satisfied everybody, he commenced also to come to his own house. When he had become thirty-two years of age, a son was born in the house of the Gurū, the turning pin of the world; the name of Sirī Čand was given to him. When Sirī Cand was four years of age, Lakhmī-dās, the gentleman, was in the womb.

The Gurū was sitting in the commissariat, when one day a man of the Gōvind people[1]

[1] The expression is: ਇਕੁ ਗੋਵਿੰਦ ਲੋਕੁ; the verb referring to it is throughout kept in the Sing., so that it cannot be translated by: some people of Gōvind. ਇਕੁ ਗੋਵਿੰਦ ਲੋਕ stands therefore for ਇਕੁ ਗੋਵਿੰਦ ਲੋਕਾਂ ਦਾ, ਲੋਕ being in Panjābī also used in the sense of "*man*" (Sing.). The Gōvind lōk were a sect of Faqīrs. See: Sikhā̃ dē rāǰ dī vithiā, p. 268.

appeared to him in a Turkish garb. Guru Nānak said: "Sir, sit down." Then that Gōvind man sat down and said: "O servant of God, what pain hast thou?" Nānak replied: "Sir, I have no pain whatever." The Gōvind man continued to say: "Why has thy colour become yellow?" Nānak replied: "Sir, I am the son of a Khatrī, without bathing I do not eat. Four watches pass while I am sitting (in the commissariat); when two Gha̤rīs (= forty-eight minutes) of the day are as yet remaining, then, having bathed, I put a morsel into my mouth." The Gōvind man answered to Nānak: "O brother, all is present with thee: rise thou early in the morning, dip in the canal and sit then in the commissariat after having put some Ghī, molasses and some raw grains of corn into thy mouth, then thy liver will remain green, it will not wither away." Nānak took up this custom. When six months had (thus) passed, Nānak dived in the canal and was lost. After his servant had waited (for some time) he rose and came and informed the Navāb. The fishermen began to search for him, but became tired of it; they threw in also a large net, but did not get him. Then in the commissariat and in the public office the noise was made, that Nānak, the Vēdī, had been lost. Some said this, some that. Some said: "He has squandered the money of the Government, for he was feeding the Faqīrs." Three days and nights he was lost. On the third day Nānak came out of the canal. When he had come out, the noise arose that Nānak is sitting among the Faqīrs. The people said: "A demon has seized Nānak, the steward. Daulat Khān Lōdī seized Jairām and said: "Nānak, thy brother-in-law, was my steward, answer thou for my money." Jairām went to Nānak and said: "Nānak, Daulat Khān the Navāb demands account, go and give it!" Nānak rose and went with him and gave the account, 760 Rupees came out as surplus to Nānak. Daulat Khān was informed that 760 Rupees came out as due to Nānak on the part of the Government. Daulat Khān said again: "O Nānak, sit down in the commissariat, what is thy own bill, settle that and take it and go on with the business of the commissariat." Nānak replied: "O Navāb, this money is of no use to me, this money belongs to God, feed the Faqīrs with this money." Nānak got discharged and did not enter his house, he remained outside. Mūlā, his father-in-law, burnt and became hot like coals.

On the third month (after) Lakhmī-dāṣ was born in the house of Guru Nānak. Mūlā, the Čōṇā, his father-in-law, was a votary of the Paṇḍit Sāmā; he went to him and wept: "Look, Sir, Nānak is neither doing any business nor does he go anywhere; I am very much afflicted."

(17).[1]

Mūlā, his father-in-law, complains against Nānak and declares him mad. Nānak proves that he is in his senses. The prayers in the mosque.

Then Mūlā the Čōṇā went to the Navāb and complained. The Navāb Daulat Khān said: "O Yār Khān, who is this man, of whom does he complain?" Yār Khān asked Mūlā: "Who art thou and of whom dost thou complain?" Mūlā answered: "Sir, I am the father-in-law of Nānak, the steward, and I complain of Nānak." Yār Khān told it to the Navāb. The Navāb said: "Bring him here!" Yār Khān brought Mūlā and the Navāb asked him: "Why art thou complaining of Nānak?" Mūlā said: "Navāb, health! The 760 Rupees, which came out as due to Nānak, should go to the wife of Nānak." The Navāb said: "O Mūlā, Nānak is saying, that they should be given to the Faqīrs." Mūlā answered: "Navāb, health! Nānak has become mad." The Navāb said: "These have a just claim. Apply to Nānak a Mullā! If he has not become mad, then give the money to the Faqīrs!" Then the Mullā commenced

[1] In the sixteenth Sakhī it is related that the admonitions of the Paṇḍit Sāmā made no impression on Nānak.

to make incantations to Nānak, but Nānak remained absorbed (in thought). When the smell of the burnt roll of candlewick went into the nose of Nānak, he said:

Slōk.

Whose field is wasted, what need have they of a threshing-floor?
O Nānak, woe to their life, who write and sell the name!

The Mullā said further: "Who art thou? tell me thy name!" Then Nānak uttered a Sabd in the Rāg Mārū, Mahalā I. [there follow four verses].[1] The Mullā became comforted and began to praise (him). Having come the Mullā said to the Navāb: "Navāb, health! Nānak is not mad, with him some saint has met, he is in his senses." The Navāb said then: "Call Jairām!" Jairām was called. The Navāb said: "Jairām, what shall be done? We cannot keep the money of Nānak, and Nānak has said that it should be given to the Faqīrs. His father-in-law complains against him (saying): 'We know, that Nānak has become mad,' and the Mullā says that Nānak is in his senses. Speak thou! what thou sayest, that we will do.'" Jairām was very much afraid of Nānak, he remained therefore silent. The Navāb said again: "Jairām, why dost thou not give an answer?" Jairām replied: "Navāb, health! The Navāb understands everything (better than I); what shall I answer?" The Navāb said: "Jairām, (his) wife has also a right." Jairām replied: "Nānak is also present, he is not gone far off." Then the Navāb said: "Call Nānak!" A man went to call Nānak, but Nānak did not come. The man returned and said to the Navāb: "Sir, he does not come." The Navāb Daulat Khān became angry and said: "Seize and bring him!" The man went again and said: "O Nānak, the Navāb has become very angry." Then Nānak rose and came and stood before the Navāb, he made his salām (to him). The Navāb got angry and said: "Nānak, why didst thou not come?" Nānak replied: "Hear, O Navāb! when I was thy servant, I came to thee, now I am not thy servant, now I have become the servant of God." The Navāb said then: "If thou hast become such a one, then go with me and say prayers! it is Friday to-day." Nānak said: "Go, Sir!" The Navāb, the Kāzī, Nānak and many innumerable people went together and stood in the great mosque. As many people as were in the mosque, they all began to say in their place, that Nānak has to-day come over to this side, and among all the respectable Hindūs in Sultānpur a noise was made. Jairām was much grieved and went home. When Nānakī saw that her lord was much grieved, she rose and said: "What is the matter to-day, that thou hast come so grieved?" Jairām replied: "Hear, O servant of God, what thy brother Nānak has done! he is gone with the Navāb to the great mosque to say prayers! and in the whole town, among Hindūs and Musalmāns, a noise is made, that to-day Nānak is coming over to this side; why should I not be grieved?" Nānakī said: "Compose thy mind, rise and eat food! do not be in anxiety about Nānak! Nānak, my brother, is under his (*i.e.* God's) strong protection, no one is able to look towards Nānak with a bad eye; rise thou and eat with joy!" Whilst they were talking thus, a noise arose. Jairām had left Nidhā, the Brāhmaṇ, as a spy; he came and congratulated Jairām, (saying): "O patron, comfort and joy set in! no apprehension is to be made!" Jairām and Nānakī began to ask Nidhā: "Tell, Nidhā, how has it happened?" Nidha said: "I was not within (the mosque), but I have heard it from the mouth of the Turks, that the Navāb made his prayer and that Nānak remained standing. When the Navāb had finished his prayer, he began to say to Nānak: 'O Nānak, thou hadst come to make prayers, why didst thou not say them?' Nānak replied: 'With whom shall I make prayers?' The Navāb said: 'Thou shouldst have made them with us.' Nānak replied: 'Thou hadst gone to Kandahār in order to buy horses, with

[1] See Rāg Mārū, Mah. I. Sabd 7.

whom shall I pray?' Daulat Khān said: 'O Nānak, thou art telling so much falsehood, I am standing here.' Nānak replied: 'Hear, O Khān, thy body was standing here, and he who was saying the prayers had gone to Kandahār to buy horses.' Then the Kāzī said: 'Navāb, health! how much falsehood is the Hindū telling!' The Navāb replied: 'O Kāzī, Nānak is truthful. At the time of bowing down my spirit had gone to Kandahār for the sake of horses.' Again the Kāzī made a calumny (saying): 'Hear, O Khān! we surely had not gone, he should have said prayers with us!' Then the Navāb said: 'Nānak thou shouldst have prayed with the Kāzī!' Nānak replied: 'O Navāb, the Kāzī had gone to his house to take care of a colt, "perhaps my colt may be falling into the pit."'"

Then both believed.[1] "So, O brother, I have heard." Nānakī said again: "O Misr, where hast thou left Nānak?" Nidhā replied: "I have left him there." Jairām began to quarrel with Nidhā: "If thou hadst stood there for one hour, Nānak would have come out and thou wouldst have met with him." Nidhā replied: "Sir, he was in the mosque, and all the people that were there, returned to their houses, but he did not come into my sight, who knows where he is gone?" Nānakī comforted Jairām: "Be thou not anxious at all, Nānak is coming now." In the meanwhile Nānak came to Jairām's house. The slave-girl Tulsā cried from below: "Mistress, your brother has come!" Jairām became very happy and began to ask Nānak: "O brother Nānak, how did the mentioned affair happen? tell thy own story, what is heard from thy own mouth, that is genuine information." Nānak said: "O brother-in-law! Daulat Khān and the Kāzī began to say their prayers, we remained standing by. When he (the Khān) had finished his prayers, he began to say: 'O Nānak, hast thou come to say prayers or to stand here, thou hast not said prayers.' We replied:

> The forehead he knocks on the ground, the heart rises to heaven,
> Daulat Khān, the Paṭhān, buying horses in Kandahār.

The Navāb said: 'I have not understood it, what didst thou say?' I said again: 'Thou hadst gone to Kandahār to buy horses, how should I have made prayers?' The Kāzī said then; 'Look, O Khān, how much falsehood the Hindū is telling!' The Khān replied: 'O Kāzī, the Hindū is truthful. At the time, we were making the bows (in prayers), our heart had gone to Kandahār for the sake of horses.' Then the Kāzī said: 'We indeed had not gone anywhere, he should have said (prayers) with us.' I replied to the Kāzī: 'In (thy) courtyard a pit was dug, while bowing down on the ground (thy) spirit was with (thy) colt.' The Navāb said: 'O Nānak, why art thou saying this?' I replied: 'The mare of the Kāzī had brought forth a colt, and in his courtyard is a pit; when the Kāzī made his bowings, his spirit was dwelling on the colt, "perhaps the colt may fall into the pit and die."' This I said; then Daulat Khān laughed: 'Now, Kāzī, what does Nānak say? speak the truth!' The Kāzī began to say: 'O Khān, the matter is indeed so.' Then the Navāb said to the Kāzī: 'Nānak is a perfect Faqīr.[2] Now not a word can be said against him.' The Navāb said further: 'Hear, Nānak, thy money I cannot keep and thy father-in-law has brought a complaint against thee, that it is the right of (thy) wife, and thou hadst said, that I should give it to the Faqīrs, say now, to whom shall I give the money?' I replied to the Navāb: 'I have told thee, know thou, (what is further to be done)!' The Navāb said: 'Hear, Nānak; the one half of thy money we will give to thy wife and the other half to the Faqīrs, give thou it with thy own hands!' I replied: 'We know nothing at all, know thou!' This word we have spoken, whether it please thee, O brother-

[1] Here the Lahore edition adds (against all the other MSS.): Both fell at his feet and said: "Sir, thou thyself art indeed God."

[2] The Lahore edition has here again: ਨਾਨਕ ਤੇ ਆਪ ਖੁਦਾ ਹੈ, Nānak indeed is himself God.

in-law, or displease thee!" Jairām said: "What is done by thee, that is done." Then Nānak and Jairām took their food, and having eaten they sat down. Afterwards Mūlā and Čandōrāṇī came in. Before Mūlā and Sāmā, the Paṇḍit, had been quarrelling. Now Čandōrānī, the mother-in-law, came; having seen Nānak she pealed like thunder and began to say: "Hear, Nānak, for this purpose thou hast married, that having increased the family thou leavest it and runnest away?" So she went on chatting. . . . Mūlā did not again give up his daughter. Lakhmī-dās was as yet on the haunch (*i.e.* a baby) and Sirī Čand was four years and three-quarters old.

(18).

Nānak leaves his family, which is broken up.

[Nānak then went away from Sultānpur and remained outside (of it in the jungle); he did not come (any longer) to the house of his wife. Čandōrāṇī and Mūlā did not give up their daughter; prating on he (*i.e.* Mūlā) made much altercation. At last the matter was settled thus. Bēbē Nānakī said: "Well, aunt, Sirī Cand shall remain with me, and my sister-in-law and Lakhmī-dās you take with you. If there should be any question about property and if my sister-in-law should become excited about anything, we will make a present of it to her; we cannot struggle with the Lord." Then Čandōrāṇī and Mūlā took their daughter and grandson with them. . . . .[1]]

(84).

Nānak returns to Talvaṇḍī.

Then Gurū Nānak and Bālā came to Talvaṇḍī; his uncle Lālū met with him and said: "My brother Kālū is departed and my lady sister-in-law is also departed, thou art my arm, remain now with me! what thou sayst, that I will do!" Gurū Nānak replied: "O uncle Lālū, we also must go, we cannot remain." Then uncle Lālū said again: "Well, Sir, what thou wilt say, that we must mind." Gurū Nānak remained there fifteen days.

(85).

Nānak joins his wife at Pakhō. Questions about the succession in the Guruship.

Then Gurū Nānak and Bālā came to (the village) of Pakhō, the Radhāvā, and began to remain there.[2] One day the mother, the Čōṇī, said: "Bhāī Bālā, let now the ascetic stop (here), he has wandered enough about." Bālā replied: "Well, madam!" Bhāī Bālā said then to Gurū Nānak: "Sir! give me now leave!" Gurū Nānak replied: "Bhāī Bālā, where we remain, there remain thou also!" Bālā said: "Sir, going and remaining depends on the Lord, but, Sir, who will be after thee (thy successor)?" Gurū Nānak replied: "Bhāī Bālā, afterwards Lahaṇā, the Khatrī, the son of Phērū, the Tihaṇ Khatrī, will meet with us, he will remain after me (as Guru)." Bālā asked again: "O Gurū, will he also be a good man?" Gurū Nānak replied: "Bhāī Bālā, he will be like me." Bālā asked again: "Sir, what about his honour Sirī Čand?" The Gurū replied: "Bhāī Bālā, he will not be in want of bread and clothes, they will follow him, but that thing (*i.e.* the Guruship) belongs to Lahaṇā." Then Bālā took leave and went to Talvaṇḍī.

[1] We break off here and give the conclusion of the life of Nānak. The intermediate wanderings of Nānak, as related here, have very little in common with the original compilation and are full of wonderful stories, which bear the stamp of invention on their front. We pass them over as irrelevant to our object in view.

[2] The home of Nānak's wife, where she had been staying in the house of her parents since her separation from her husband.

(86).

Bālā presses Angad to tell him how he became Nānak's disciple and successor.

Then Bālā said: "Hear, O Gurū (Angad)! between Gurū Nānak and thee there is no difference whatever! and till here I have information about the Gurū; what I have seen with my own eyes, that I have dictated. Of what follows I have no knowledge." Then Gurū Angad said: "Bhāī Bālā, thou hast given us a sight of Gurū Nānak, the creator is merciful to thee." Bālā replied: "Sir, thou hast taken from me the whole account, give me now, Sir, thy own story, how did it happen with thee?" Guru Angad replied: "Take my account, O Bhāī Bālā! thus it happened with us. We had gone to Kāngṛā with the family (wife) to worship the Dēvī. We had heard before, that one Nānak, a Vēdī Khatrī, had become an ascetic and was staying there. We said: 'As we have come here, we will also have an interview with him.' We went out and had an interview with him and every hair of us became cool. The Gurū asked us: 'How, brother, what is thy name? whence art thou, O brother disciple?' I answered: 'O Gurū, there is a village of the jungle, there we dwell and my name is Lahaṇā.' Then the Gurū said: 'Who art thou?' We replied: 'O Gurū, we are a Tihaṇ[1] Khatrī and have come on a pilgrimage to the Dēvī.' The Guru said then: 'Well, brother, go and having worshipped the Dēvī come (again)!' We replied: 'Sir, now our going is stopped, if crores of Dēvīs be put together, they will not come up (= be equal) to your sight. For which sake we were going there, that business has been accomplished here.' The Guru said: 'Hear, O brother Lahaṇā, what will be due to you on our part, that you will take.' Then, brother Bālā, whilst I looked out for my own opportunity, all the bonds of my body broke, and when I moved away, my breath became stopped. The Gurū said then: 'Brother Lahaṇā, go now to thy own house and take thy wife with thee!' I did not go.[2] Thus, O brother Bālā, it happened with me." Then Bālā replied: "Sir, between Gurū Nānak and thee there is no difference whatever. Gurū Nānak did not hide anything from me, what defect hast thou seen in me, that thou hidest (things) from me?" Gurū Angad said: "Bhāī Bālā, show to me, that I have hidden anything from thee?" Bālā replied: "Sir, manifest that, why Gurū Nānak has given thee the name of Angad?" Gurū Angad understood in his mind that this was a perfect man, and that it was not good to hide anything from him, as he had stayed with Gurū Nānak.

Gurū Angad said then: "One day I had brought a bundle of grass from without (*i.e.* the jungle) for the cow. The mother, the Čōṇī, was sitting at the side of Gurū Nānak, and having seen on my clothes splashings of mud she said to Gurū Nānak: 'Fear a little God, O ascetic, this one is also the son of a Khatrī!' Gurū Nānak replied: 'Hear, O daughter of Mūlā! these are not splashings of mud, they are Kungū[3] of the threshold (of God).' Bhāī Bālā, thus my name Angad was given to me."

Bālā said: "Sir, having become Guru you keep (things) back from the disciples! Rather say, that you are not a Sikh!" Then Guru Angad answered: "Bhāī Bālā, one day the mother, the Čōṇī, brought her two sons to Gurū Nānak and sat down. She began to say: 'Though thou hast sons of thy own, thou art throwing this thing into other houses.[4] It is not becoming to thee, that thou givest it to the sons of strangers, whereas thou hast sons of thy own.' A mouse fell into the sight of Nānak, which was dead. Guru Nānak said: 'O son Sirī Čand, this mouse is dead, it is not good that it should lie here; touch it with the toe of thy foot, that it may be

[1] ਤਿਹਣੁ or ਤ੍ਰਿਹਣੁ is the name of the clan.

[2] The Lahore edition interpolates here an apparition of the Dēvī to Lahaṇā, professing to be herself the servant of Nānak. The story is apparently newly made up, as all the other MSS. do not contain it.

[3] ਕੁੰਗੂ *m.* a fine powder composition of red colour, rubbed by women on the forehead.

[4] The Guruship is meant here by the thing (ਵਸਤੁ).

removed to some distance!' But Sirī Čand answered: 'I have seen many such conjurers, who putting down a wing let fly off a pigeon, and who from skins make cats.'[1] Upon this Guru Nānak remained silent. When an hour had passed, I came. Then Guru Nānak said: 'O child Angad, a dead mouse is lying here, touch it with the toe of thy foot and throw it to some distance.' I touched it with the toe of my foot and it fell down in some direction. Then Nānak said: 'O daughter of Mūlā! this is the son of a stranger and this one is my own son, what shall I do? To whom the creator gives it, he takes it' (*i.e.* the Guruship). Then, Bhāī Bālā, my name became Angad."

Bālā said: "Sir, another doubt has come to me: is there in me some great vice that you are putting a screen before me every twenty-four minutes?" Guru Angad answered: "Hear, Bhāī Bālā![2] One day I and Bhāī Būṛā were with Nānak, it was midnight. Guru Nānak said: 'Bhāī Būṛā, what time of the night is it?' Būṛā looked, came and said: 'Sir, it is midnight.' Guru Nānak said: 'Bhāī Būṛā, I know it is not midnight, it is a watch of the night.'[3] Būṛā went again out and looked; it was midnight. Būṛā said (therefore) again: 'Sir, it is midnight.' Guru Nānak said the third time: 'Būṛā, it is not midnight, it is a watch of the night.' Būṛā said the third time: 'Sir, it is midnight, it is not a watch of the night.' Guru Nānak then said: 'Bhāī Būṛā, remain seated!' Then Guru Nānak said again: 'Son Angad, see thou, how much of the night it is?' I went out to see; it was midnight. Having come in I said: 'Sir, it is midnight.' Guru Nānak said again: 'Son Angad, it is a watch of the night, go and see!' Then I understood in my mind, that it was (indeed) midnight, but that the Guru's view was different. I came and said: 'O Guru, a watch of the night is remaining, but there was a defect in my eyes.' Then Guru Nānak became much pleased and said: 'Son Angad, bow thy head before the creator!' I bowed my head, but Būṛā became displeased in his mind. Then Guru Nānak said: 'Bhāī Būṛā, bow thy head before Angad!' But Būṛā became much displeased. Then Guru Nānak said: 'Būṛā, don't be displeased! this is the order of the creator.' Thus, Bhāī Bālā, it happened with us."

Upon this Bālā said: "Why are you continually keeping the secret from me?" Guru Angad answered: "Bhāī Bālā, the mouth is middling and the greatness unfathomable, it cannot be told, it must be kept in the heart. But as thou dost not leave off, it must be told." Bālā said: "Sir, let it be told!" Then Guru Angad said: "The discipleship is difficult and all is the creator's; but this is the conduct of the world. But, Bhāī Bālā, this story has not been written.[4]

"One day my daughter was going about and fell into the sight of Guru Nānak. He said: 'Son Angad, having dressed thy daughter bring her to me.' I dressed and brought her to him. Guru Nānak said: 'Son, go thou, sit outside!' I went and sat down on the threshold. Guru Nānak and my daughter sat down on the bedstead, then the rail of the bedstead broke. Guru Nānak was sitting in his composure of mind.[5] I said then (to myself): 'In the Guru's composure of mind discomposure must take place.' I seized then that rail and sat down. Thus, Bhāī Bālā, it happened with us, if you will accept it or not." Bālā said: "O Guru! true, true, true!" Then Guru Angad said: "Bhāī Bālā, this story, that has been heard, must be taken as

[1] The Madārīs (followers of the Musalmān Pīr Madār) are such jugglers. They put down a wing of a pigeon, read a mantra over it and a pigeon flies off, etc.

[2] This story is left out in the Lahore lithographed edition.

[3] That is: it is the last watch of the night.

[4] This story, which throws a good deal of light on the reason of the intimacy of Nānak and Angad, is naturally left out in the Lahore lithographed copy, being too discreditable to the character of Nānak.

[5] The MS. $\frac{495}{2885}$ reads here: ਗੁਰੂ ਨਾਨਕ ਆਪਣੇ ਖਿਆਲ ਵਿਚਿ ਆਹਾ, Gurū Nānak was in his own thought.

true, and, Bhāī Bālā, thou must consider Guru Nānak as true. And if one will consider him as true, his vices and sins, as many as they may be, will, by taking his words as true, be washed away. And if one will do the words of Guru Nānak, he will arrive there, where Guru Nānak is." . . .[1]

"One time there was in a certain town a pool full of black mud. When rain was falling, all the filth of the town was collected there. The Guru having gone near it threw a cup into it. At that time both sons of the Guru were with him and I (*i.e.* Angad) also was with him. The Guru looked first towards Sirī Čand and said: 'Son, take the cup out from the pool!' Sirī Čand answered: 'Where one must go, there one may go, some others will take it out with pleasure and not give it up.' Then the Guru looked towards Lakhmī-dās and said: 'Son, take out the cup from the pool!' He answered in the same manner as Sirī Čand had done. Then the Guru looked towards me. I did not let the Guru speak, but jumped with my clothes into the pool and brought the cup out. Though my clothes were full of mud, I felt very happy."

(89).

Death of Nānak.

As it was the Bābā Guru's habit to remain in Kartārpur (towards his end), so he remained. At the time of praising (the Lord) praise was made, towards the end of the night ablution was made and recitation and austerity practised, the Lord was magnified; then crowds (of disciples) come and cooking goes on. In the mind of Guru Bābā Nānak dwelled this thought: "When will that time come, in which I shall see the Lotus-foot of the Lord?" When some days had passed, the month of Asū came. Then Guru Nānak became very joyful and happy. On the seventh of Asū it happened, that songs of joy were sung and the praise of the Lord was made. Bābā Nānak fell into deep reflection. After that he said to his attendants: "I think, that to-day my absorption will take place; smear a place with cow-dung, throw Kusa-grass upon it and make things ready." His attendants began to weep; Guru Nānak comforted them. Then his attendants began to collect the (necessary) things and a man went to call Lakhmī-dās and Sirī Čand, (saying): "You are called for." Lakhmī-dās and Sirī Čand did not come, they began to say: "Why should we go, as he is in good health?" The mother, the Čōṇī, went by her own disposition to the Guru. When Guru Nānak saw that her hands were sullied with Dāl, he said: "How, O Čōṇī? If thou hast anything to say, say it! And why are thy hands sullied?" When the mother saw that the Guru was in the state of absorption, she said: "To-morrow is a Srādh, it is the date of thy father; if it please thee, we will go and make the Srādh." The mother, the Čōṇī, having become very humble, begged of him. Then Guru Nānak said: "Well, be it so, O Čōṇī! make the Srādh! Remaining (as yet) the eighth and ninth, we shall be absorbed on the tenth." Having seen the submissiveness of the mother, the Čōṇī, the Guru became merciful and said: "Prepare the things for the Srādh!" Then the mother in token of sacrifice clung to the feet of the Bābā. The Guru Bābā then gave the order: "Give up to-day preparing the things for (my) absorption!" This word was noised about among the people, that the Guru Bābā will be absorbed on the tenth. On the eighth the Srādh of his father was performed, on the ninth the whole family of the Guru Bābā assembled.[2] Then Lakhmī-

[1] Here both the Manuscripts, which we have hitherto followed, break off, after some conversation between Angad and Bhāī Bālā on the former Bhagats and why Kabīr alone reached the presence of the Supreme Lord. The death of Nānak is not mentioned by them and we are therefore restricted to the Lahore lithographed copy alone, which relates some more stories of Angad's blind obedience to the commands of Guru Nānak and of the disobedience of his sons.

[2] We leave out the story, that all Prophets, Pīrs, Saints, etc., came to take leave of Nānak, as it is not worth mentioning.

dās and Sirī Čand besought him much, saying: "Sir, the Guruship you have given to Lahaṇā, what is our support?" The Guru answered: "Children, you will have plenty of food and clothes." Then Lakhmī-dās and Sirī Čand said: "Food and clothes we shall have, but nobody will mind us." The Guru answered: "Children, don't be anxious! The dogs of Gurus and Pīrs are minded, you also will be minded. But the greatness of the name is with Angad." When they had heard this order of the Guru Bābā, Lakhmī-dās and Sirī Čand and all the family and the disciples fell down at his feet.

When two watches and a half of the night were remaining, the Guru Bābā fell into deep meditation. All the things (for cremation) were prepared. Then the Lord appeared to him and in the true region a cry of victory arose. When the Bābā had given up his meditation, he began to say: "I am a sacrifice, have mercy on me the lowest sinner! Blessed be the Lord!" Then the Lord, having become merciful, said: "I have pardoned thy way (*i.e.* thy religious system and the followers of it), before and after, whoever will take thy name, he shall become emancipated." Then with the order of the Lord the Guru Bābā was absorbed in Samvat 1596, on the tenth day of the dark half of the month of Asū. The Mahājans (*i.e.* Khatrīs) and the people of Gōvind[1] began to perform the duties of the world (*i.e.* to prepare for cremation) and put Guru Nānak on the funeral pile. There were also Paṭhāns, who were disciples of the Guru. They said: "We also will have a sight of him." The Mahājans said: "Khāns, now it is not your time." They answered: "Bābā Nānak is our Pīr, we will have his sight." The Mahājans said: "To-day is not the time to see him, go away!" The Paṭhāns came on with might and began to say: "Bābā Nānak is our Pīr, we will do with him as it is customary to Pīrs, we will bring him to the grave-yard." The Mahājans had, on account of the Turks, drawn sheets round about (the corpse). Then one disciple said: "Ye brethren, Hindūs and Musalmāns, what for are you quarrelling? The Guru Bābā is not here indeed, he has departed to the true region." When he went and looked, there was nothing on the funeral pile; the quarrel of both parties ceased.

(90).

Impression made by the death of Nānak.

All the retinue, the attendants, the Mahājans and the people of Gōvind began to say: "Rām! Rām!" They praised Guru Nānak, (saying): "Vāh, vāh! Guru Nānak has been the visible Supreme Lord! but by our own lot we have not been able to worship him in any way." They began to repent and having seen the sport of the Guru Bābā they were confused with fear. The Musalmāns began to take the name of God, (saying): "Vāh, vāh God! Guru Bābā Nānak has been a great man, of a great spirit, he was the image of God himself." They set to praise God. Hindūs and Musalmāns, having seen this, were astonished. The family and attendants of Guru Bābā Nānak set fire to the funeral pile and performed the funeral ceremonies, (saying): "The Guru Bābā Nānak is bodily gone to Paradise!"

Slōk.

How shall I, the sinful worm, utter thy praises?
The speaker art thou thyself, thou thyself singest thy praises.
Who sings, reads, hears and writes (them) with an attentive mind:
Him surely Hari unites (with himself).
I am a musician, begging at (thy) door: may by thy favour the name be given to me!
Give (me) the name, (the bestowing of) gifts and ablution, that I may become fully satiated!
The musician has by silent repetition (of the name) obtained comfort, meditating on the lotus-foot.
O Nānak, it is the prayer of (thy) slave: keep me in thy asylum!

[1] See about the ਗੋਵਿੰਦ ਲੋਕ, p. lxviii, note 1.

II.

SKETCH OF THE LIFE OF THE OTHER SIKH GURUS.

2.—GURU ANGAD (A.D. 1538–1552).

THE disciples (Sikhs, सिख) of Nānak would no doubt have soon dispersed, and gradually disappeared, as well as the disciples of many other Gurus before Nānak, if he had not taken care to appoint a successor before his death. The disciple, on whom his choice fell, was *Lahaṇā*,[1] who had joined Nānak not long before his death. None of his early disciples seems to have remained with Nānak, and we may fairly conclude that there was not one amongst them who had attained to any degree of learning. The way, in which Nānak used the disciples who attached themselves to his person, was not very conducive to impart to them any considerable knowledge; they were in fact little more than his menial servants (see p. xliii, l. 18 *sqq.*). No Brāhmaṇ of any note or learning had, as it appears, joined him, and the mass of the disciples were ignorant Jaṭs, who, on an average, could neither read nor write.

What Nānak looked chiefly for in his successor, were not scientific accomplishments, or a cultivated mind, but *blind obedience to the commands of the Guru.* The stories, which are told in the Janam-sākhīs, of the total "*sacrificium intellectus*" of Lahaṇā, are therefore very significant (*cf.* p. xliv, l. 1 *sqq.*; p. lxxiv, l. 9 *sqq.*).

Lahaṇā became first acquainted with Nānak at Kāngṛā, whither he had gone to worship the Dēvī. He heard there, that Nānak, a great Faqīr, was staying there, and after the first interview he attached himself firmly to him and no more left him. This is the relation of the later Janam-sākhīs, whereas the old Janam-sākhī states that Angad became acquainted with Nānak by the medium of another disciple of the village of Khaḍūr (see p. xliii, l. 3 *sqq.*), which seems far more probable.

The later Sikh tradition states, that Nānak changed the name of Lahaṇā into that of Angad when conferring on him the Guruship, *as being a part of himself*,[2] but the old tradition knows nothing of this neither does the panegyric of Angad in the Granth allude to any such change of name, which, if it had been known at those times, would certainly not have been passed over in silence. The Bhaṭṭ Kīratu (Transl. p. 703, V. xv.), on the contrary, gives him both names ("Then Angad Lahaṇā becoming manifest," etc.), from which it would appear, that he bore both names at the same time. I need hardly remark, that the explanation, which the Sikhs give of the signification of the name of Angad, is altogether fanciful, for अङ्गद् is an old Hindū proper name and signifies literally: *giving* (one's) *limbs or body.*

Angad settled down at the village of Khaḍūr, on the banks of the Biāsā, which was very probably his native place. He gained his subsistence by his own handiwork (see p. xlvii, l. 4) and led the life of a recluse. He was altogether unlettered and could himself neither read nor write, as may be fairly concluded from p. xlviii, l. 4 from below. The later tradition, which makes him the inventor of the Gurmukhī letters (see Sikhā̃ dē rāj dī vithiā, p. 20, l. 13 *sqq.*), is therefore without any foundation.

[1] (Also written: Lahiṇā), a Tihuṇ (=Trihuṇ, Tēhuṇ) Khatrī (p. xlvii, l. 1).

[2] See p. xlvii, note 1.

The few verses of Angad, which are contained in the Granth (marked Mahállā II.[1]), are but a poor repetition of the words of Nānak and shallow in the extreme. Being fully aware of the importance of the "*successio episcoporum*" to the Sikh community, he nominated before his death (4th March, 1552) his devoted servant *Amar-dās* his successor, deeming, like Bābā Nānak, neither of his sons worthy of the Guruship.

3.—GURU AMAR-DĀS (A.D. 1552–1574).

Guru Amar-dās was a Khatrī of the Bhállā[2] clan, born in the village Vāsarkī (ਵਾਸਰਕੀ) in the district of Amritsar. The story goes, that he went in his youth on a pilgrimage to Harduār. There a thirsty Paṇḍit drank water from his hands; after he had quenched his thirst, he asked Amar-dās, who he was and whence he had come? Amar-dās answered, that he was a Bhallā Khatrī from the Panjāb, from a village called Vāsarkī. The Paṇḍit asked him further who his Guru was? When Amar-dās answered, that he had not taken any Guru, the Paṇḍit felt vexed and said: "Alas! I have committed a great sin, that I have drunk water from this man who has got no Guru! I am a great transgressor, that at the time of being thirsty I did not (first) reflect! how will my transgression now be done away?" On hearing this Amar-dās felt much ashamed in his mind; he fell down at the feet of the Paṇḍit and said: "Mahārāj, pardon now my fault, as soon as I shall come home, I shall take a Guru."

When he had come home, he began to look out for a Guru. One day he heard, that in the vicinity, in the village of Khaḍūr, there was a perfect Guru, Bābā Angad, and that he, who would take his instruction, would cross over (the world of existence), and that in him all qualities, that are required in a Guru, as steadiness, contentment, forbearance, mercy, devotion, etc., are to be found..

Thereupon Amar-dās went to Khaḍūr, seized the feet of Guru Angad and said: "O Lord, having heard your name I have come to you for the sake of my own salvation; give me mercifully the name of the Guru!" Guru Angad received him kindly and he remained with him, serving him with heart and body.

It is related that Amar-dās was so conscientious in the service of the Guru, that he did not eat any bread from the store-room of the Guru, but got his subsistence by carrying round on his back a bundle of salt and oil and selling it to the people.

He was performing to Angad all sorts of menial services, as Angad had done to Nānak. Thus he used to bring daily for the sake of the ablutions of the Guru a large metallic jar of water from the river of Gōvindvāḷ, which was about two Kōs distant; out of reverence for his Guru he is said to have made the way from Khaḍūr to Gōvindvāḷ in walking backwards, lest he should turn his back on his Guru. One night, when he was carrying water from the river, he is said to have slipped and to have fallen into a weaver's hole. When the weaver asked his wife who it

[1] All the Sikh Gurus call themselves "Nānak" in order to designate themselves as the legitimate successors of Nānak. For the sake of distinction between them ਮਹਲਾ ਪਹਿਲਾ (mahállā pahilā, *first court*), ਮਹਲਾ ਦੂਜਾ (mahállā dūjā, second court), etc., is added to their respective compositions in the Granth (see p. lxxxi); otherwise they are also mentioned by the name of ਪਹਿਲੀ ਪਾਤਸਾਹੀ, *first reign*, etc., as the Sikhs soon commenced to look on their Gurus as their sovereigns (thence the address: ਸਚ ਪਾਤਸਾਹ, O true king!). In later times, when Nānak was gradually looked upon as an *Avatār*, every succeeding Guru was considered as an incarnation of Bābā Nānak. In the Granth itself no allusion of this kind is found, only the Bhaṭṭs, whose panegyrics are added at the end of the Granth and who know no bounds in their flattery, commence praising Nānak as Avatār.

[2] In the Granth written ਭਲਾ bhálā, as no letter is doubled in the writing of the Granth.

was, she answered: "Who will fall at this time? it must be that unfortunate, homeless Amarū."[1] Amar-dās rose and returned to the river and having filled his jar he brought it to the Guru. Angad heard from somebody, that the people were calling Amar-dās "the homeless one" (ਨਥਾਵਾਂ). Being fully satisfied of his sincerity and devotion, he took him to his neck and said: "Amarū is not homeless, but from this day the Lord has made him the home of the homeless and the asylum of those, who have no asylum; who will follow him, will obtain great happiness." On that very day Angad put five Paisās and a cocoa-nut before him, bowed his head before him and said to all the societies (of the saints): "Now I am entrusting the throne of the Guruship to Amar-dās, bow ye all your heads before him! he is a perfect Guru, the Lord has received him to-day; who will be on his side, he will also be pleasing to the Lord."

After the death of Guru Angad, Amar-dās took up his residence at Gōvindvāḷ. He was a humble, patient and pious man, round whom many disciples assembled. Though unlettered, like his master, who could teach him only the few simple tenets he had heard himself from Nānak, he composed many verses, which were incorporated in the Granth (Mahállā III.), and which are conspicuous for simplicity and clearness.

The offerings of his numerous disciples enabled him to build a great walled well (ਬਾਉਲੀ) at Gōvindvāḷ, in which eighty-four steps led down to the water. The Sikhs believe, that whoever sits down on those eighty-four steps one by one and makes ablution and reads the Japǰī to the end, gets free from the eighty-four Lakhs of forms of existence and enters paradise. A great Mēlā is still held every year round that well.

Guru Amar-dās died the 14th of May in the year 1574, having appointed in the usual way Rām-dās as his successor in the Guruship.

4.—GURU RĀM-DĀS (A.D. 1574–1581).

Rām-dās was a Khaṭrī of the Sōḍhī clan (ਸੋਢੀ) and a native of the village Gurūčakk (ਗੁਰੂਚਕ).[2] He had come in early youth to the house of his grand-parents at Gōvindvāḷ and remained there. His grand-parents were very poor and he sustained them and himself by selling boiled grain (ਘੁੰਗਣੀਆਂ).

It is said, that one day he sat near the door of Bābā Amar-dās selling boiled grain, when Amar-dās by chance called his family-priest and said to him: "Misr, our little daughter has now become of ripe age, go and look out in some good house (for a suitable partner), that we may betroth her." When the family-priest had gone, the wife of the Guru said: "For my daughter a lad must be sought of the same age, as the lad there is, who is selling boiled grain, the girl being of about the same age." At the same time Guru Amar-dās said in his own mind: "Our girl is now this lad's, for it is the religious observance of the Khatrīs, that the thought, which first comes into the mind, must be performed." Having considered this he called that lad and asked: "My dear boy, who art thou?" He answered: "I am a Sōḍhī Khatrī." When Amar-dās had heard this he thanked God and said: "Blessed be thou, Lord, that thou hast preserved the honour of my word: for if this lad would be no Khatrī, my caste-fellows would reproach me for giving him my daughter."[3] At that very time he put into the hem of the lad the betrothal-presents and a few days after the wedding took place and Rām-dās took his wife to his native village Gurūčakk.

[1] ਅਮਰੂ is a diminutive form of ਅਮਰ.

[2] The word ਗੁਰੂ was very likely added more recently, when Guru Rām-dās had taken up his abode there. The real name was therefore only ਚਕ.

[3] This passage is very significant as to the observance of caste by the earlier Sikh Gurus.

Guru Amar-dās was particularly fond of his daughter (whose name was Mōhanī), so that passing his son Mōhan, he entrusted the Guruship to his son-in-law Rām-dās, who was a pious and peaceful man. He was eager in collecting disciples and great crowds used to flock to his residence at Gurūčakk.

His income from the voluntary offerings of his disciples must have been considerable: for it enabled him to restore magnificently an old tank which he called *Amritsar* (the nectar-tank), in the midst of which he built a place of worship, to which he gave the name of *Harmandar* (ਹਰਮੰਦਰ, temple of Hari). The new town, which soon sprang up round this tank, was first called *Rām-dās-pur* (city of Rām-dās), afterwards the name of Amritsar was extended to the whole town and the old name Gurūčakk fell into oblivion.

This was of the greatest importance for the firm establishment of Sikhism, for the Sikhs obtained thereby a fixed central place of worship, where the disciples annually assembled round their Guru and performed their ablutions in the nectar-tank. Rām-dās, though without any scientific education, gave himself much to literary work. He composed a great many verses, in which he expounded his doctrines, and though no originality of thought is to be found in them, they belong to the better compositions of the Granth (Mahállā IV.). He spent his days in peace and rest, as under his Guruship the organization of the Sikh community had not yet progressed so far as to arouse the suspicion and alarm of the Muhammadan Government. He died on the 3rd of March, 1581, having nominated his son *Arjun* (Arjun-mall)[1] his successor in the Guruship. From Rām-dās the succession remained *hereditary* in the family, which added greatly to increase the wealth and the authority of the Gurus, as the Sikhs were thereby gradually accustomed to look on their Gurus as their actual sovereigns.

5.—GURU ARJUN (A.D. 1581–1606).

Up to Guru Arjun the Sikhs were a community neither very numerous nor much taken notice of, their Gurus leading the life of Faqīrs and being averse to outward show and pomp, though Amar-dās, and more so Rām-dās, had already considerable means at their disposal from the voluntary offerings of their disciples.

This state was changed considerably under Guru Arjun, who was an enterprising and active man, and the first Guru *who meddled with politics.* After the Sikhs had obtained under the Guruship of his father Rām-dās a visible sacred place, which served them as a rallying point, Guru Arjun's first object was, to give them also a *sacred code,* in order to unite them more closely by one common religious tie and to separate them from the mass of the Hindūs. He collected therefore the verses of the preceding Gurus, to which he added his own very numerous (but carelessly written) compositions, and in order to prove that the tenets of the Sikh Gurus were already entertained and proclaimed by the earlier popular saints (Bhagats), he inserted considerable extracts from their writings as *loci probantes* at the end of nearly every Rāg. This miscellaneous collection he called *Granth* (or *Granth sāhib,* ਗ੍ਰੰਥ ਸਾਹਿਬ), *i.e. the book,* and it was thenceforth held sacred as the Bible of the Sikhs, supplanting gradually the authority of the Vēdas and Purāṇas, which the unlettered people had never been able to read, whereas the Granth was composed in their mother-tongue and intelligible to the vulgar.

The story goes, that the disciples assembled one day round Guru Arjun and said, that by hearing the verses which Guru Nānak had uttered, tranquillity came to the mind and desire

[1] It is not quite clear if Rām-dās had two or three sons. It is certain that Bhārat-mall was the brother of Arjun, which is confirmed by the Dābistān (II. p. 273), where it is mentioned, that Bhārat followed after his brother Arjun-mall, though the Sikhs themselves disavow the succession of Bhārat.

for worship was increased, but that by the numerous verses which were uttered by other Sōfīs,[1] and to which the name of Bābā Nānak was (also) given, pride and worldly wisdom were springing up in the hearts of men; it was therefore necessary to put a sign on the words of Nānak, that people might be able to distinguish them from the words of others.

Hearing this, Guru Arjun collected all the words of Nānak from different places, and having also collected the verses of the other Gurus and the words of other Bhagats, which were not contrary to the words of Nānak, he gave them to the writer Bhāī Gur-dās, that he should write them in one place (*i.e.* book) with *Gurmukhī characters.* And because Angad and the other Gurus had put down in their words the name of Nānak, he thought that it would be difficult for the disciples to distinguish their several speeches; where therefore the word of Nānak is, he put down the sign: ਮਹਲਾ ਪਹਿਲਾ, and where the words of the second reign were, there he wrote ਮਹਲਾ ਦੂਜਾ, and in this wise ਮਹਲਾ ਤੀਜਾ and ਮਹਲਾ ਚੋਥਾ, and his own words he marked ਮਹਲਾ ਪੰਜਵਾਂ; in this way he distinguished the words of the several Gurus. Similarly he marked also the speeches of the Bhagats by putting down their names. When all the speeches were made up into one volume, Arjun gave out the order to all disciples, that they should mind whatever was written in it, and reject everything else, though it bore the name of Nānak.

It is said, that Arjun left a few blank pages in the volume, predicting that the verses of the *ninth* reign would be written upon them and that before that no Guru would utter a speech (that was to be written),—a prophecy *ex eventu.*

Another measure, which Arjun set a-going, was likewise of the greatest importance for the organization of the Sikh community.

We have mentioned already, that the Gurus had no fixed income, but what was voluntarily offered to them by their disciples. Arjun saw clearly enough, that for his aspiring schemes and the extension of his spiritual authority, he required considerable sums, which should be forthcoming with some regularity. He reduced therefore the voluntary offerings of his disciples to a kind of tax, which he levied by deputies,[2] whom he nominated in the several districts, and who forwarded whatever they had collected annually to the Guru. In this wise the Guru was on the one hand enabled to hold a court and to keep always a strong band of adherents round his body, and to extend his authority by the not inconsiderable sums he had at his command, wherever he found an opportunity, and on the other hand the Sikhs were thereby gradually accustomed to a kind of government of their own, and began to feel themselves as a firmly organized and strong party within the state.[3] This institution of deputies of the Guru, though very useful in a political and financial point of view, led soon to very hard oppression, so that the last Guru was compelled to give way to the continual complaints of his adherents and to abolish it.

Guru Arjun was the first Sikh Guru who laid aside the garb of a Faqīr and kept an establishment like a grandee; he engaged also in trade in a grand style, as he either loved money or was much in want of it, though the Sikh tradition is now quite silent about such transactions of their Gurus. Under Arjun, who had apparently a great talent for organization, the Sikh

[1] In the Sikhā̃ dē rāǰ dī vithiā, p. 29, l. 2 from below, ਸੋਢੀਆਂ is found, which is a misprint for ਸੋਫੀਆਂ Sōfīs (or Sūfīs). For the first Sōḍhī Guru was Rām-dās, who cannot be meant here, and of other Sōḍhī poets tradition is altogether silent.

[2] These deputies were called ਮਸੰਦ, *masand*, a corruption of the Arabic-Persian مَسْنَد (or more properly مُسْنَد), a support on which one leans, or a person to lean upon, used in the sense of "*deputy*" in the Indo-Persian idiom.

[3] See the remarks of Muḥsin Fānī in the Dābistān, II. p. 271, who very well perceived the purport of this measure.

community increased very considerably and spread fast over the Panjāb; but in proportion as the Sikhs began to draw public attention on themselves, the suspicion of the Muhammadan Government was roused, and Guru Arjun was the first who fell a victim to it.

There are different accounts of the causes of the death of Arjun.[1] The common Sikh tradition is, that Arjun had a son named Har-gōvind. When he had attained to the years of discretion, a barber and Brāhmaṇ came and brought about his betrothal with the daughter of Čandū-sāh, who was a servant (finance administrator) of the Emperor of Dillī. Čandū-sāh heard from the people, that in the house, where his daughter had been betrothed, they lived after the manner of Faqīrs and were eating offerings. He got very angry with the Brāhmaṇ and the barber and turned them out of his house. When Arjun heard of this, he sent word to Čandū-sāh, that the betrothal was given up on his part, he could betroth his daughter somewhere else. Čandū-sāh became greatly ashamed at this breaking off of the match and from that day was a bitter enemy of the Guru. He calumniated him to the Emperor, and Guru Arjun was several times summoned to Lahore, where he suffered severe treatment. One day this wretch suggested to the Emperor, that he should sew Arjun up in a raw cow-hide, which the Hindūs abhor most, and burn him. When the cow-hide was brought before him, he begged to be allowed to take first a bath in the Rāvī. The Emperor granted this request; Arjun jumped into the Rāvī, and was lost in it; the people searched much for his corpse, but could not find it. Guru Arjun died in the year 1606, having nominated his young son Har-gōvind his successor in the Guruship.

This account of the cause of the death of Guru Arjun is very unsatisfactory. It is easily perceived that the real charge which was brought against the Guru, is passed over in silence by the Sikh tradition, even if we admit that Čandū-sāh was actuated by private enmity for the reasons stated above. Fortunately the Dābistān (II. p. 272) throws some light on this dark point. There we learn, that the Emperor Nūru-ddīn Jahāngīr called to his court (when at Lahore) Arjun-mall, on account of his having offered prayers for the King's son Khusrau, who had rebelled against his father. Khusrau having been taken, the King ordered the imprisonment of Arjun-mall, and wanted to extort a large sum of money from him. The Guru was helpless; they kept him prisoner in the sandy country of Lahore until he died from the heat of the sun and ill treatment. This happened in 1606.

From this it appears that Arjun was arraigned on the charge that he had joined (with his adherents) in the rebellion of Khusrau. Whichever way he died, his death was ascribed to the bigotry and cruelty of the Muhammadan Government, and his disciples were burning to revenge it. The death of Guru Arjun is therefore the great turning-point in the development of the Sikh community, as from that time the struggle commenced, which changed the whole character of this reformatory religious movement.

6.—GURU HAR-GŌVIND (A.D. 1606–1638).

After the death of Guru Arjun, some troubles arose in the Sikh community, as the uncle of the youthful Har-gōvind, Pirthī-mall,[2] claimed for himself the succession in the Guruship. Pirthī-

[1] Malcolm (Sketch of the Sikhs, p. 32) gives a different story, that a Hindū zealot, Danī-čand, a Khatrī, whose writings Arjun refused to admit into the Granth, caused his death by prevailing upon the Muhammadan Governor of the province to imprison Arjun. The whole story looks very unlikely and I have hitherto not been able to trace it in any Sikh tradition that has come under my observation.

[2] It is very likely that ਪਿਰਥੀ ਮੱਲ is identical with ਭਾਰਤ ਮੱਲ (see the Dābistān, II. p. 273) and ਪੀਰਮੱਲ. His progeny, called ਪੀਰਮੱਲੀਏ, and his disciples, called contemptuously ਮੀਣੇ (ਮੀਣਾ *m.* an ox with the horns bending down the face), were at a later time excommunicated by Guru Gōvind Singh.

mall seems to have been of an intriguing disposition; he is said to have gone to Čandū-sāh to Dillī, in order to get the Guruship by his assistance, but becoming obnoxious to the Sikhs by his intrigues, he was soon deserted and Har-gōvind was acknowledged as the rightful successor to his father.

In order to revenge the death of his father he for the first time armed his followers and took bloody revenge of Čandū-sāh and the Muhammadans whom he considered concerned in his death.

The Sikh accounts agree by no means on this point and are full of confusion, as they apparently try to smooth over many uneven things and to conceal the real facts of the life of their Guru.[1] According to one relation it was Čandū-sāh, instigated by Pirthī-mall, who told the astrologers of the King, that they should frighten the King by telling him that for one month and a quarter there was great danger for him; if he would call Guru Har-gōvind from the Panjāb, all would go well. On this the King (or Emperor) sent men to bring him from Amritsar; when he arrived, the King told him that he should for his sake sit forty days in prison and perform worship. Others say, that the King sent him for forty days to the fort of Guāliar to perform devotion there. When the forty days were over, a Sikh, named Bidhī-čand, who was staying with the Guru, gave himself the appearance of a physician, met the King and said, that Har-gōvind, whom he kept in prison for the sake of his own comfort, was a great saint, he should speedily set him at liberty, for those, who had caused his imprisonment, were his enemies. The King called Har-gōvind, acknowledged his fault and asked the Guru to forgive it. Har-gōvind had a priceless pearl, which he offered as a present to the King. When the King had seen its splendour, he was much pleased and said: "If one other like it could be found, it would be very well." The Guru answered, that on the neck of his father Arjun there was a necklace containing more than one hundred and eight of such pearls, but they were now in the possession of his Dīvān Čandū-sāh. When the King heard this, he was astonished, and asked how Čandū-sāh got them from his father? The eyes of the Guru were filled with tears; he told the King the whole story and added, that when his father under the hard treatment of Čandū-sāh had died at Lahore,[2] he took the whole necklace from him. The King became very angry, and when he had ascertained the full truth also from other people, he seized Čandū-sāh and handed him over to the Guru, to revenge himself on him as he pleased. He took him with himself to Amritsar and began to punish him. It is said, that they bound a rope round his feet and dragged him through the bāzār of Amritsar and Lahore. As he had seated Arjun on heated frying-pans and hot sands, so did Har-gōvind to him, till he at last died being dragged about in the bāzār.

All this appears very improbable, as it is far more likely that he revenged himself without any reference to authority. We know from the Dābistān, that Har-gōvind was a man of a warlike spirit and addicted to hunting; he always kept a strong band of armed followers round his person and he is said to have had eight hundred horses in his stable. He built the town of Har-gōvind-pur on the banks of the Biāsā, to serve him, in case of necessity, as a firm retreat. His warlike inclinations prompted him also to enter the service of the Emperor Jahāngīr, but his irregular conduct involved him in many difficulties. It is expressly stated in the Dābistān (II. p. 274), that

[1] The history of the later Sikh Gurūs from Har-Gōvind to Gōvind Singh is involved in a great deal of obscurity, as the Sikh accounts are so frequently contradictory and dictated by prejudice or hatred against the Muhammadans. This part of their history requires as yet a careful, critical sifting, as the Sikhs themselves have no idea of historical truth.

[2] From this tradition it would follow, that Arjun had really died of ill treatment, as the Dābistān reports, and not by drowning in the Rāvī. This is also more or less confirmed by Arjun's tomb, erected at Lahore; for if Arjun's corpse had not been found, how could a tomb have been erected over it?

he appropriated to himself the pay due to the soldiers in advance, in consequence of which and on account of the mulct imposed upon his father Arjun, the Emperor Jahāngīr sent him to the fort of Guāliar, where he remained imprisoned for twelve years. At last the Emperor released him, being moved by pity. The Sikh tradition is quite silent on this point; and his imprisonment at Guāliar, which it restricts to forty days, is ascribed to quite different reasons, as we have seen above.

After the death of Jahāngīr (1628) Har-gōvind entered the service of the Emperor Shāh-jahān, but he seems soon to have left his service and to have taken up a reckless course of life again. Shāh-Jahān sent troops against him, who took Rāmdāspur and plundered the Guru's property. Thence he fled to Kartārpur, where he soon had a serious encounter with the Paṭhān Pāindah Khān.[1] According to the Sikh tradition Pāindah Khān was living with the Guru in his tent (he is even said to have been his foster brother). One day a Sikh brought a sword, a hawk and a beautiful dress as presents to the Guru, which he bestowed on Pāindah Khān, who gave them again away to his son-in-law. When the Guru heard this, he became angry with Pāindah Khān and expostulated with him about it. Pāindah Khān denied it at first, but was convicted, whereupon he was beaten by some Sikhs present and turned out of the tent.

Pāindah Khān got the ear of the Mugul authorities, and as he was considered a fit instrument to strike a blow at the dreaded Guru, troops were entrusted to him, with whom he besieged Har-gōvind at Kartārpur. A severe struggle ensued, in which the Imperial troops were vanquished and Pāindah Khān himself slain by the Guru.

Encouraged by this victory he moved to Bhagvāṛā in the vicinity of Lahore. He seized some horses belonging to the Emperor, but being pursued he fled to the hills. He took up his abode at Kīratpur (near Anandpur), in the house of his eldest son Gur-dittā, who was living there with Bābā Buḍhā,[2] and some time after, having given the throne of the Guruship to his grandson Har-rāi, he died there A.D. 1638, the 10th of March.[3]

Guru Har-gōvind has given quite a different appearance to the Sikh community. The peaceful Faqīrs were changed into soldiers and the Guru's camp resounded with the din of war; the rosary was laid aside and the sword buckled on. As the Guru's expeditions were nearly always directed against the Muhammadans and the extortionate provincial authorities, we need not wonder, that his popularity fast increased with the ill-treated Hindū rural population; every fugitive or oppressed man took refuge in his camp, where he was sure to be welcomed without being much troubled about religion, and the charms of a vagrant life and the hope of booty attracted numbers of warlike Jaṭs, who willingly acknowledged him as their Guru, the more so as he allowed his followers to eat all kinds of flesh, that of the cow excepted. The home of the Sikhs was now the camp, where the heterogeneous elements, by close contact, and stimulated by the same hopes and fears, soon welded together into a new community. The expeditions and fights however were as yet on a small scale and partook more of a local character, and were therefore hardly ever noticed by the authorities, who were either too shortsighted and indolent or too powerless to stop effectually the concourse of such a turbulent and dangerous crowd.

[1] In Gurmukhī written ਪੈਂਡੇਖਾਂ.

[2] ਬਾਬਾ ਬੁਢਾ, a notorious freebooter in the Panjāb, who had become a disciple of Har-gōvind. He got therefore the honorary title of ਬਾਬਾ (father Buḍhā).

[3] There is a great diversity about the date of Har-gōvind's death. The year given is that commonly recorded by the Sikhs. In the Dābistān the year 1645 is mentioned, corresponding to the Hijrah 1055. Muhsin Fānī says (II. 281), that he saw Har-gōvind in the year of the Hijrah 1053 (= 1643) at Kīratpur. We do not know how to reconcile these two dates, which differ by seven years. Perhaps there is a mistake in the Arabic ciphers of the Dābistān.

That a Guru like Har-gōvind had no time nor taste for meditation and the composition of religious poetry need hardly be remarked; not a single verse of his is therefore to be found in the Granth.

7.—GURU HAR-RĀI (A.D. 1638–1660).

Har-gōvind had five sons, Gur-dittā, Aṭall, Tēg-bahādur, Aṇī-rāi and Sūrat-mall. Tēg-bahādur was from youth up of a contemplative mind and did not care for anything; like a madman he is said to have observed deep silence;[1] the four other brothers were worldly-minded and continually quarrelling amongst themselves about the succession in the Guruship. Their father was therefore greatly perplexed to whom he should give the throne of the Guruship and could not make up his mind. They say, that one day at Kīratpur the little son of Gur-dittā came to his grandfather and seated himself on his lap; when the Guru began to fondle him, Har-rāi took off the turban of his grandfather and put it on his own head. The Guru, who was not much pleased with his own sons, on seeing this rejoiced, and thought within himself that he would give the throne to this boy; by doing so the mouths of all the brothers would be shut and a stop put to their mutual jealousy. Having reflected on this he called together the society (of the disciples), put a cocoa-nut and five Paisās before Har-rāi and bowed his head before him, saying: "brother Sikhs, the Lord himself has put the turban of the Guruship on the head of this boy, now no one has anything more to say about it; whoever is my disciple, he shall consider Har-rāi as his Guru, he will become a great, perfect saint." The society was much pleased with this decision of the Guru, they bowed their heads before Har-rāi, and also the four brothers (*i.e.* the sons of the Guru) remained silent,[2] as none of them had the power to wrest the Guruship from him. Har-rāi was, according to all accounts, a wise and sensible man, and of a more peaceful disposition of mind than his grandfather had been.

When Dārā Shikōh, the brother of Aurang-zēb, came to the Panjāb in order to make war against his brother, he sought the alliance of Guru Har-rāi, who joined him with his Sikhs. But when Dārā had been beaten and killed, the Guru prudently withdrew from the scene of war and retreated to Kīratpur, sending at the same time his eldest son Rām-rāi with an apology to Aurang-zēb, who received him kindly, but retained him as a hostage at his court, thereby securing the peace of the Panjāb. This whole incident of the joining of the Guru in the rebellion of Prince Dārā is totally passed over by the Sikh tradition, neither is the mission of Rām-rāi to the court of Dillī mentioned.

Har-rāi seems to have had neither inclination nor calling for poetry; no single verse of his is therefore found in the Granth. He died in peace and tranquillity at Kīratpur A.D. 1660,[3] having nominated his younger son Har-kisan his successor in the Guruship.

8.—GURU HAR-KISAN (A.D. 1660–1664).

Guru Har-rāi had two sons, Rām-rāi and Har-kisan. It is said that the Guru was displeased with his eldest son, because he made disciples of his own and worked miracles. When he had therefore one day gone away to visit his own disciples, Har-rāi declared his younger son his successor in the Guruship before all the societies (of the disciples). When Rām-rāi heard of this,

[1] The Sikhā̃ dē rāǰ dī vithiā (p. 39) says of him: ਸੁਦਾਈਆਂ ਵਾਂਙੂ ਚੁਪਚਾਪ ਰਹਿੰਦਾ ਸਾ.

[2] Some say, that Gur-dittā had died already before his father; but this is by no means certain. He died at Kīratpur, where a splendid tomb was built to him.

[3] The date of his death differs considerably. Some give the year 1661, some 1663, and some 1664.

he was much vexed; he said before the Sikhs, that Har-kisan was still a minor, on whom the small-pox had not yet broken out, if he should get through the small-pox, then he might take the Guruship.

According to one tradition (as given in the Sikhā̃ dē rāj̃ dī vithiā, p. 43) Guru Har-kisan was summoned to the court of Dillī in the following way. Aurang-zēb one day asked his courtiers, who amongst the Faqīrs of Bābā Nānak was now the best? They answered, that now a young lad, by name Har-kisan, was reported to be their leader, who already in his youth was a perfect Faqīr. Thereupon the Emperor ordered that they should quickly bring him to Dillī, as he wished to see him. One Khatrī, who was a Dīvān (minister) of the Emperor and one of the disciples of the Guru, offered himself to bring Har-kisan. He went to Kīratpur and communicated to the Guru the wish of the Emperor, who set out with the messenger and with many disciples in a Pālkī for Dillī. Here the matter is represented as if Aurang-zēb desired to see the Guru out of curiosity, whereas we know from other sources, that this was by no means the case.

Rām-rāi, the elder brother of Har-kisan, was detained as hostage at the court of Aurang-zēb, and was apparently not on a good footing with his father, and therefore was passed over. When Rām-rāi heard of the death of his father and that his younger brother had been installed as Guru, he complained to the Emperor and asked for his decision. Aurang-zēb was very glad to have an opportunity of interfering, and summoned the young Har-kisan to his court, who reluctantly obeyed.

Whilst staying at Dillī, Har-kisan was attacked by the small-pox, so that he was unable to appear at court. When the Guru became very weak, the disciples asked him whom they should acknowledge as Guru after him? It is said, that after some reflection he put five Paisās and a cocoa-nut on the ground, and having bowed his head said to the disciples: "Go, your Guru is in the village of Bakāḷā (ਬਕਾਲਾ), near Anandpur." He died in 1664. No verse of his is contained in the Granth.

In the disturbances which followed the death of Har-kisan, Rām-rāi was disavowed by all parties. He went therefore to the hills and settled at Dehrādūṇ (ਦੇਹਰਾਦੂਣ),[1] where he started a sect of his own, and collected many disciples. He still lived in the times of Guru Gōvind Singh and frequently quarrelled with him. He taught his disciples not to bow the head before any one but himself, and not to worship any god or goddess but himself. His disciples were called "Rām-rāīē" (ਰਾਮਰਾਈਏ), and were afterwards excommunicated by Guru Gōvind Singh.

It is reported that Rām-rāī, for the sake of one of his disciples, underwent in a deep cave a very severe course of austerities (ਜੋਗ ਅਭਿਆਸ); when the breath had risen to the tenth gate, the disciples, who were near him, knew that the Guru had died, and they burnt his body after the manner of the Hindūs. They erected there a tomb (ਸਮਾਧ) and called it ਰਾਮਰਾਇ ਦਾ ਦੇਹਰਾ; hence that hilly country received the name of Dēhrādūṇ; there every year a great Mēlā is held, where many holy personages assemble.

9.—GURU TĒG-BAHĀDUR (A.D. 1664–1675).

After the death of Har-kisan, dissensions arose among the Sikhs as to the succession in the Guruship. A company of disciples went to Bakāḷā, in order to pay their reverence to Tēg-bahādur as their Guru. But Tēg-bahādur at first refused to accept the Guruship: for the Sōḍhīs thereabout had set up a Guru of their own, and Rām-rāi also was raising claims to the succession.

[1] ਦੇਹਰਾ signifies *a shrine* and ਦੂਣ (*s.f.*) *a valley between two mountains*, literally therefore: *the shrine-valley*.

At last Tēg-bahādur was prevailed upon, chiefly by the entreaties of his mother, to take upon himself the burden of the Guruship, and he was soon generally acknowledged as the head of the community.

Tēg-bahādur left then Bakāḷā, where he had lived in seclusion, and removed to Mākhōvāḷ (माखेवाल), which is near Kīratpur, on the banks of the Satluj; this place was afterwards called Anandpur, as being the residence of the Guru.

Some time after he left this place and went, as the story goes, on a pilgrimage to Paṭṇā with his wife and kindred, where he stayed for about five or six years, and where Gōvind Singh was born and also received his first education from the Paṇḍits of that place, which deeply tinged his mind with the Hindū superstitions. Very likely Tēg-bahādur no longer felt safe in the Panjāb, where the spies of Aurang-zēb kept a watchful eye on the proceedings of the Sikhs, and he resolved therefore to leave the Panjāb altogether, and to settle under the garb of a Hindū pilgrim in some populous place, where he could remain concealed or unnoticed. On the following events of the life of Guru Tēg-bahādur the accounts differ very widely, as the Sikh tradition is endeavouring to conceal or do away with everything that could throw an unfavourable light on him. According to the Sikh tradition, Guru Tēg-bahādur was a saint, who, even after his accession to the Guruship, remained an Udāsī (*i.e.* indifferent to the world) and was totally taken up with meditation and devotion.

He removed from Paṭṇā again to Anandpur on account of some enmity with the people, the reasons of which are not stated.

He is said to have been very fond of wandering about in the jungles with some disciples.[1] On one of these wanderings he is said to have come to Hindūstān. When he arrived at Āgrā he stopped in a garden, and sent his signet-ring and a shawl to the bāzār to dispose of them and to buy some provisions. The confectioner, to whom these things were offered for sale, took fright, lest they should be stolen goods, and brought them to the Kutvāl. The Kutvāl, having taken the signet-ring, went to Tēg-bahādur into the garden and began to interrogate him, who he was and whence he had come? When he had ascertained that it was Tēg-bahādur, he sent a message to Aurang-zēb at Dillī, that Guru Tēg-bahādur had by chance fallen into his hands, and asked for orders regarding him. The Emperor Aurang-zēb was making all efforts to bring the whole world to the Musalmān faith, and he had in those days imprisoned many Brāhmaṇs, as he hoped, that if these first became Musalmāns, the other people would readily follow their example. When the Emperor heard that Guru Tēg-bahādur had been seized, he was very glad, because he had heard much of the Nānak-panthīs and wished to meet with them. He sent therefore orders to Āgrā, that he should be quickly sent to Dillī.

When the Guru had come to Dillī, the Emperor had many disputations with him, and tried all means to bring him over to the Musalmān faith. Tēg-bahādur, who was not a learned man nor conversant with disputations, gave no answer, and when the Emperor desired to see miracles from him, he remained silent. At last he was thrown into prison with three disciples, and told that he would not be set at liberty till he would embrace the Musalmān religion. When the Guru remained firm, they began to torture him. He managed to send a letter to his son Gōvind at Anandpur, informing him of his hopeless state. Gōvind answered him with a consolatory Dōhrā, but could do nothing for him.[2] When no more any hope was left for the Guru, two Sikhs fled and only one remained with him. Despairing of life, and being weary of the cruel treatment he had to suffer, he ordered the Sikh to cut off his head. He refused at first to

[1] What is concealed under these harmless words we shall see hereafter.

[2] See Translation of the Granth, p. 708.

commit such a crime, but when the Guru pressed him hard, he at last struck off his head with a sword. Tēg-bahādur died A.D. 1675.

When Gōvind heard of the death of his father, he sent his sweepers (ਚੂਹੜਾ čūhṛā)[1] to Dillī to bring the corpse of the deceased to Anandpur. They entered the jail under the pretext of sweeping there, and brought away the corpse on a cart laden with grass. The body was burnt at Anandpur and a great shrine erected there; the head, which had remained at Dillī, some Sikhs burnt there, and erected a tomb which was called Sīs-ganj (ਸੀਸਗੰਜ, head-stack).

According to this tradition[2] of the Sikhs, as it is essentially contained in the Sikhā̃ dē rāǰ dī vithiā, p. 47, *sqq.*, Guru Tēg-bahādur appears quite as an innocent man, who suffered severely at the hands of the bigoted Aurang-zēb, and who, in order to avoid a contumelious death, with which he had been threatened, got his head cut off by one of his disciples. To this view his compositions, which are contained in the Granth and which bear the stamp of a rather melancholy and world-renouncing character, seem to have contributed greatly, and it is not to be overlooked, that as to his sanctity and renunciation of worldly desires, those very verses are appealed to in the foregoing tradition. We need therefore not wonder if Tēg-bahādur, after the troubles and turmoils of the times were somewhat forgotten, appeared to the later Sikhs in this light.

But we must not rashly conclude from the words of Tēg-bahādur, as far as they have been handed down to posterity, that he was altogether a quiet, world-renouncing Faqīr, who did not meddle in worldly affairs or the politics of those days; for the moral views of the Sikhs of those times were already so thoroughly confused and their hatred against the Muhammadans so great, that they considered rebellion against the established government and plundering the property of the Muhammadans quite as lawful acts.

The reasons alleged in the Sikh tradition for the persecution and death of their ninth Guru appear very defective and improbable, though the bigotry of the Emperor Aurang-zēb is conceded on all hands and may not have been altogether strange to it. Some hint as to the real cause of the destruction of Tēg-bahādur is given by the Sairu-lmuta'aχχirīn (Briggs's translation, vol. i. pp. 112, 113), where it is stated, that he was taken prisoner on account of his predatory proceedings and executed as a rebel against the Government.

The Sākhīs,[3] which Sirdār Attar Singh, chief of Bhaḍour,—who with an enlightened mind follows up the history and religion of his nation,—has lately published, throw a very significant light on the wanderings of Tēg-bahādur and their real character, and tend to confirm the charges brought against him by Muhammadan writers. As these Sākhīs reproduce the Sikh tradition, we have the less reason to question their trustworthiness. According to them the Guru appears by no means as a harmless, spiritual instructor, but riding at the front of well-armed disciples, who,

[1] Their descendants are said to be the ਮਜਬੀ ਸਿਖ (Majbī Sikh), as those sweepers were received into the Khālsā by Guru Gōvind Singh for their daring courage. ਮਜਬੀ is a corruption from the Arabic مَذْهَبِي (regular, due Sikhs).

[2] The traditions about the imprisonment and death of Tēg-bahādur differ very much and are frequently contradictory. Some ascribe his persecutions and consequent death to the inveterate hatred of Rām-rāi (see M'Gregor, History of the Sikhs, vol. i. p. 66; Malcolm, Sketch of the Sikhs, p. 39), some solely to the bigotry of Aurang-zēb. Cunningham (History of the Sikhs, pp. 61, 62) comes nearer the truth, as he consulted also a Muhammadan authority. The Sikh reports must be taken with great precaution and critical discernment.

[3] Their title is: The Travels of Guru Tegh Bahādur and Guru Gōbind Singh. Translated from the Original Gurmukhī by Sirdar Attar Singh, Chief of Bhadour. January, 1876. Lahore, Indian Public Opinion Press. It would have been very useful if the translator had also added some critical apparatus about the probable time of the composition of these Sākhīs. They cannot be very old, as the British territory thereabout is already mentioned (p. ii).

if not willingly provided, levied contributions on the Zamīndārs and the inhabitants of the villages through which they passed, and made predatory incursions on the Muhammadan population. The Guru had not only a strong band of Sikhs with him, but he engaged also some rural clans to enter his service, promising them, that he would pay them handsomely and put them in the way of obtaining booty (Sākhī 44). It is also stated, that the Muhammadan soldiers were at the heels of the Guru, trying to capture him (Sākhī 50). That it was dangerous to receive the Guru, we see from the same Sākhī, where one Rūpā Khatrī, in whose house the Guru wanted to put up, says: "Sir, I cannot entertain you at my house, for the Emperor will destroy me and my family." From this it may be safely concluded, that the Guru was outlawed at that time.[1] We can therefore easily understand, why the Kutvāl of Āgrā seized Tēg-bahādur, when he fell into his hands. The Muhammadan reports, which ascribe his capture and execution to political reasons, deserve therefore full credit, the Sikh tradition itself confirming by these Sākhīs the charges brought against him.

10.—GURU GŌVIND SINGH (A.D. 1675–1708).

Tēg-bahādur was succeeded by his son Gōvind Singh, who was only fifteen years old when his father died. As he was surrounded on all sides by dangers, he retreated to the mountains, where he kept himself concealed, being occupied with hunting and archery, in which latter art he became a great adept. He studied also Persian and read a good deal of Hindī, but never attempted the study of Sanskrit, though he occasionally tried to imitate it in his compositions, which on the whole are very difficult and intricate.[2]

[1] We must remark here, that in these Sākhīs no distinct line is drawn between the wanderings of Guru Tēg-bahādur and those of Guru Gōvind Singh, so that it remains uncertain, where the first end and where the second commence. As I have not the original text at my disposal, I cannot say, if this is owing to some fault of the text or to some oversight of the translator. This great defect seems at any rate not to have struck him, as he makes no remark about it. It is certain that the Sākhīs from 51 refer to Guru Gōvind Singh, the fight at Mukt-sar having taken place under him. In Sākhī 56 it is also stated that the Guru was only thirty-five years old, which could only be said of Gōvind Singh.

[2] Gōvind Singh describes his youth briefly in the following verses of the Vičitr nāṭak:

ਮੁਰ ਪਿਤ ਪੂਰਬ ਕੀਯਸਿ ਪਯਾਨਾ ॥ ਭਾਂਤਿ ਭਾਂਤਿ ਕੇ ਤੀਰਥਿ ਨਾਨਾ ॥ ਜਬਹੀ ਜਾਤਿ ਤ੍ਰਿਬੇਣੀ ਭਏ ॥ ਪੁੰਨ ਦਾਨ ਦਿਨ ਕਰਤ ਬਿਤਏ ॥ v. 280.	"My father had travelled to the east, To different kinds of Tīrthas. When going along he was at Tribēṇī, The days passed in bestowing alms.
ਤਹੀ ਪ੍ਰਕਾਸ ਹਮਾਰਾ ਭਯੋ ॥ ਪਟਨਾ ਸਹਰ ਬਿਖੈ ਭਵ ਲਯੋ ॥ ਮਦ੍ਰ ਦੇਸ ਹਮ ਕੋ ਲੇ ਆਏ ॥ ਭਾਂਤਿ ਭਾਂਤਿ ਦਾਈਅਨ ਦੁਲਰਾਏ ॥ v. 281.	"There I was manifested. I took birth in the city of Paṭnā. He took me (then) to Madra-dēs, (Where) I was fondled by various nurses.
ਕੀਨੀ ਅਨਕ ਭਾਂਤਿ ਤਨ ਰਛਾ ॥ ਦੀਨੀ ਭਾਂਤਿ ਭਾਤਿ ਕੀ ਸਿਛਾ ॥ ਜਬ ਹਮ ਧਰਮ ਕਰਮ ਮੋ ਆਏ ॥ ਦੇਵ ਲੋਕ ਤਬ ਪਿਤਾ ਸਿਧਾਏ ॥ v. 282.	"My body was preserved in various ways. I received instruction of various kinds. When I had come to years of discretion, My father went to heaven."

By ਮਦ੍ਰ ਦੇਸ the Panjāb is meant. The verses following describe his hunting expeditions and after his accession to the Guruship his wars with the hill Rājās.

When he had attained to years of manhood, he stood publicly up as Guru, and commenced to collect the dispersed and intimidated members of the Sikh community. During his retreat he had matured his plans; his aim was to wreak bloody revenge on the murderers of his father, to subvert totally the Muhammadan power, and to found a new empire upon its ruins.

As his mind was deeply tinged, owing to his early education by Hindū Paṇḍits, with the superstitious notions of the Hindūs, he resolved, before embarking on his great enterprise, to secure to himself the aid of the goddess Durgā, who was his special object of worship. After he had procured some Paṇḍits from Benares, he went with them to the hill of the Naiṇā-dēvī (ਨੈਣਾਦੇਵੀ), which is about six Kōs distant from Anandpur. There he began to practise the severest austerities according to the directions of the Paṇḍits. When he had gone through the course of thess austerities, the Brāhmaṇs began to offer up his burnt offerings, throwing hundreds of maunds of Ghī, raw sugar and molasses into the fire.

When the burnt offering (ਹੋਮ) was completed, the Paṇḍits told the Guru, that he should now, in order to make a powerful offering, cut off the head of his own son and put it before the goddess. Gōvind Singh had four sons,[1] but when he asked their mothers to give him one, they flatly refused it. The Guru asked the Paṇḍits, what was now to be done? and when they answered, that the head of some one else would do, five (others say twenty-five) disciples offered their heads, one of which was cut off and offered to the goddess, and thus the burnt offering made complete. The story goes, that thereupon the Dēvī appeared and said: "Go, thy sect will prosper in the world" (ਜਾਹ ਤੇਰਾ ਪੰਥ ਜਗਤ ਵਿਖੇ ਤੁਰ ਪਵੇਗਾ).[2]

When the Guru had returned from the hills to Anandpur, he assembled the societies of the disciples, and told them that he required the head of a disciple; he, who loved his Guru, should give it. Most of them were terror-struck and fled; but five out of them rose and offered resolutely their heads. Their names (which have been carefully recorded, whereas the name of the poor victim offered to the Naiṇā-dēvī is not mentioned) were: Dharm Singh, Sukkhā Singh, Dayā Singh, Himmat Singh and Muhkam Singh. These five he took into a room, and told them that, as he had found them true, he would give them the Pāhuḷ of the true religion (ਸਚੇ ਧਰਮ ਦੀ ਪਾਹੁਲ). He made them bathe and seated them side by side; he dissolved purified sugar[3] in water and stirred it with a two-edged dagger, and having recited over it some verses, which are written in the ਅਕਾਲ ਉਸਤਤ,[4] he made them drink some of this sherbet, some part of it he peured on their head

[1] The names of the four sons of Gōvind Singh are: Jōrāvar Singh, Fatē Singh, Jujhār Singh and Jīt Singh.

[2] There can hardly be any doubt that this bloody human sacrifice was really offered, as all reports agree on this point. The Sikhs, who felt very much the atrocity of such an act, would never have ascribed anything of this kind to their Guru, if it had not really taken place. At the same time we may learn from this fact, that the Brāhmaṇs, even as late as the seventeenth century, did not scruple to offer up a human sacrifice.

[3] ਪਤਾਸਾ (Sindhī पताशो), purified sugar; also some kind of sweetmeats made of it.

[4] The ਅਕਾਲ ਉਸਤਤ (the praise of the Timeless one) follows immedlately after the Japjī in Gōvind's Granth. It commences with the words:

ਅਕਾਲ ਪੁਰਖ ਦੀ ਰਛਾ ਹਮ ਨੈ ॥	"The protection of the timeless divine male is to us.
ਸ੍ਰਬ ਲੋਹ ਦੀ ਰਛਿਆ ਹਮ ਨੈ ॥	The protection of all iron is to us.
ਸਰਬ ਕਾਲਜੀ ਦੀ ਰਛਿਆ ਹਮ ਨੈ ॥	The protection of the All-time is to us.
ਸਰਬ ਲੋਹਜੀ ਦੀ ਰਛਿਆ ਹਮ ਨੈ ॥	The protection of the All-iron is to us."

ਨੈ is an old Hindī Dative Affix. ਸਰਬ ਕਾਲਜੀ, the All-time (*i.e.* he who comprehends all time) and ਸਰਬ ਲੋਹਜੀ, the All-iron (*i.e.* he who is all iron), are epithets for the Supreme Being.

and the rest he sprinkled on their body; then patting them with his hand he cried with a loud voice: "Say, the Khālsā of the Vāh-Guru! victory of (= to) the holy Vāh-Guru!" (ਵਾਹਗੁਰੂਜੀ ਕਾ ਖਾਲਸਾ ਸਿਰੀ ਵਾਹਗੁਰੂਜੀ ਕੀ ਫਤੇ). After he had given the Pāhuḷ[1] to these five in this manner, he took it likewise from them, and in this way all the rest of his disciples were initiated, to whom he gave the name of the *Khālsā*,[2] adding to the name of each of them the epithet of *Singh* (lion). Then he gave the order, that whoever desired to be his disciple, he must always have five things with him which all commence with the letter Kakkā (*i.e.* K), viz.: *the hair* (ਕੇਸ, which must not be cut), a *comb* (ਕੰਘਾ), a *knife* (ਕਰਦ), a *sword* (ਕਿਰਪਾਲ), and *breeches reaching to the knee* (ਕੱਛ), otherwise he would not consider him as his disciple. In order to separate his Sikhs totally from the Hindūs and to form them into a distinct body, which as such should also be known by outward signs, he issued many other regulations, which are called ਰਹਿਤਨਾਮਾ (book of conduct). As he had perceived, that the Hindūs had become an easy prey to the Muhammadan invaders by their division into castes, which nursed a rancorous feeling and did not allow the lower orders to bear arms, he abolished the caste altogether, in order to put all on a footing of equality, and received people of all castes into the Khālsā. But this offended the pride and prejudices of the higher castes to such a degree, that a great many of his disciples left him and would no longer acknowledge him as their Guru; the Khālsā consisted therefore chiefly of men of the lower orders, especially of Jaṭs, whereas the disciples, who did not acknowledge the authority of Guru Gōvind Singh on account of his inovations, simply called themselves *Sikhs*, without adding to their names the title of *Singh*.[3] He tried also to infuse his own spirit into the Ādi Granth, which was already generally received as the holy book of the Sikh community, as he slightingly remarked that the Ādī Granth, such as it was, only instilled into the minds of the Sikhs a spirit of meekness and humbleness. He therefore sent men to Kartārpur, where the official volume, signed by the hand of Guru Arjun himself, was preserved, to bring it to him, in order to make additions to it; but the Sōḍhīs, to whom the volume was entrusted, refused to give it away, as they did not acknowledge Gōvind Singh as Guru.[4] They sent him word, that he should make a new Granth, if he was able to do so. This message incensed Gōvind Singh, and he resolved forthwith to make a Granth of his own for his followers, which should rouse their military valour and inflame them to deeds of courage. He set to work, and composed a big heavy Granth and when it was completed (Sambat 1753 = A.D. 1696), he called it *the Granth of the tenth reign* (ਦਸਵੀਂ ਪਾਦਸਾਹੀ ਕਾ ਗ੍ਰੰਥ).[5]

[1] The Pāhuḷ was no new invention of Gōvind Singh, as frequently asserted, but only the renovation of an old Sikh rite (see p. xxxv, note 4), which in those troublous times seems to have fallen into disuse. His object was to put the Sikh community on a new and firmer basis by administering the Pāhuḷ to all his disciples. The sherbet drunk at the ceremony of the Pāhuḷ the Sikhs call ਅਮ੍ਰਿਤ (nectar).

[2] ਖਾਲਸਾ, the name of the new Sikh commonwealth, is derived from the Arabic خَالِصَة. It signifies: *one's own, pure property;* thence: *the Guru's (or God's) own, special property.* This is the most appropriate explanation, in spite of the Sikh saying: ਖਾਲਸਾ ਨਾਮੁ ਖਲਾਸਿਆਂ ਕਾ ਘਰਨ ਸਰਮ ਕਾ ਪਿੰਜਰਾ ਛੋੜਿ ਗਏ.

[3] Among this latter class were also the Nānak pōtrā, the descendants of Bābā Nānak, some of whom visited me at Lahore. This class of Sikhs differ very little from the Hindūs, as they are equally particular as to caste (especially as regards intermarriages) and do not refrain from smoking, as the Gōvind Singhīs do. As far as I could perceive, the stricter Sikhs are now fast decreasing in number, since they no longer enjoy any public privileges.

[4] These Sōḍhīs were the ਧੀਰਮਲੀਏ, the descendants of Dhīr-mall. See p. lxxxii, note 2.

[5] Only a small portion of it was composed by Gōvind Singh himself, by far the greater portion of it was made up by his court poets. The idiom of it is the older Hindī, but couched in very difficult and frequently obscure language.

Gōvind Singh knew very well, that he could not accomplish his schemes with an undisciplined crowd; his great aim was therefore to exercise his Sikhs in the use of arms. When this point was reached to some degree, an opportunity for trying their valour was not long wanting, though Gōvind Singh assures us, that war was made upon him without a cause.[1] According to tradition the war broke out on account of an elephant, which the hill Rājās demanded from Guru Gōvind Singh, and which he refused to give up. The hill Rājās marched with a considerable force on Anandpur and some severe battles were fought, in one of which, near the town of Čamkaur (ਚਮਕੌਰ), the two eldest sons of Gōvind Singh were killed; but the Rājās were at last successively repulsed and compelled to flee to the hills. When the Rājās perceived, that they could effect nothing against Gōvind Singh, they addressed the Emperor and asked for assistance, which was readily granted. In union with the Imperial troops they again attacked Anandpur and besieged it. When Gōvind Singh saw the danger of his position, he left his troops there and fled with those five Sikhs (whose names have been mentioned above) and his two youngest sons to the town of Māčhūvāṛā (ਮਾਛੂਵਾੜਾ), where he concealed himself for some time in the house of a Sikh. When the Imperial troops followed him also there, he managed his escape with those five Sikhs by disguising himself and putting on the dress of a Musalmān, and reached safely Mālvā; but his two sons he was compelled to leave behind at that place. They were betrayed into the hands of the Imperial troops, who brought them to Sirhind (in Panjābī ਸਰੰਦ). Vazīr Khān, the Governor of Sirhind, informed the Emperor Aurang-zēb of it, and asked for orders regarding them. He was ordered to put them to death. He put the poor children under the foundation of a wall, closed the place up and buried them thus alive. It is said that the weeping of the children was heard for some days.

The Guru was meantime pursued by the Imperial forces, but as they could follow him in the sandy deserts only slowly, owing to the want of water and provisions, he found time to collect again a body of Sikhs round his person. When the troops at last came up with him and brought him to action at a place called afterwards Mukt-sar (ਮੁਕਤਸਰ), he was defeated with his small band; but as the Imperialists were under the impression that the Guru had been slain, they desisted from further persecution, as they were nearly dying of thirst.[2] Thus Gōvind Singh found some rest; he built on the battle-field a large tank, which he called ਮੁਕਤਸਰ (the tank of emancipation), as he asserted that many had there been emancipated. He settled in a village of Mālvā and remained peaceful, only bent on making disciples, in which he is said to have been very successful.[3] He built there a large residence for himself, which he called *Damdamā* (ਦਮਦਮਾ). This place became the Benares of the Sikhs, and many resort thither, as a residence at Damdamā is considered a very meritorious act. A saying of Gōvind Singh is current among the Sikhs, that whoever would dwell at Damdamā, he would become wise, be he ever so great a fool. The study of the Granth is much in vogue there and the Gurmukhī writers of Damdamā are considered the best.

[1] Vičitr nāṭak, v. 285: ਲੋਹ ਪਗਾ ਤਬ ਮੇ ਬਿਨ ਕਾਜਾ. It is very remarkable, that Gōvind Singh passes here in complete silence the reason, or reasons, which led to these sanguinary conflicts with the hill Rājās, which he describes in such glowing colours (if he does not too much exaggerate the importance of these fights, which is by no means certain).

[2] This fight is recorded in Sākhī 53 (Attar Singh's edition). There it is stated, that forty Sikhs fell and obtained the crown of martyrdom and that 250 Muhammadans were killed. It is openly conceded, that the Imperial forces remained masters of the battle-field. During the fight the Guru had retired to a hillock and after the departure of the Muhammadans he came down from that hillock to the battle-field and wiped the faces of his wounded followers.

[3] It is said that Gōvind gained 120,000 disciples.

Some time after the Guru left his retreat at Damdamā and went to Sirhind, where his two youngest sons had been buried alive. The Sikhs with him were so exasperated, that they wanted to burn down the town and to destroy it utterly. But Gōvind prudently damped their rash zeal, as he feared that such an act would bring down upon him new persecutions. He only ordered his disciples, that whoever passed through Sirhind on his way to the Gangā should dig up two bricks and throw them into the Jamnā, and on his way back he should likewise dig up two bricks and throw them into the Satluj, otherwise his ablution in the Gangā would be of no use to him. They built there a great shrine, which the Sikhs still visit. From Sirhind the Guru went to Anandpur, his old haunt, and settled there again, as he seems not to have been molested towards the close of the reign of Aurang-zēb. Some say, that he was summoned to the court of Aurang-zēb; but this is doubtful, at any rate he never obeyed the summons. It is equally doubtful if the Zafar-nāmā, in which Guru Gōvind Singh exposed the wrongs he and his predecessors experienced at the hands of the Mugul Emperors and their Governors, ever was presented to Aurang-zēb.

When Aurang-zēb died (in 1707), Gōvind Singh rejoiced much at being now freed from his bitterest enemy. His son Bahādur Shāh had to contend with his younger brother Āzim for the crown; both brothers assembled large armies, and in the bloody battle near Āgrā Āzim was beaten and killed with two of his sons. According to a Sikh tradition Gōvind Singh joined Bahādur Shāh with his followers and assisted him in this war.[1] This appears very probable and would account for the otherwise hardly comprehensible turn in the Guru's life, that of entering the service of the Emperor Bahādur Shāh, who entrusted him with a military command in the Ḍekhan. When this war of succession was over and Bahādur Shāh firmly seated on the throne of Dillī, the Guru is said to have visited the Emperor at Dillī and to have been graciously received by him. From Dillī he returned to Anandpur and was implicated again in a short predatory warfare with the petty hill chiefs, whom he routed.

About this time the abrogation of the institution of the so-called Masands or hereditary deputies of the Guru took place. The Masands had become a regular plague to the Sikhs, extorting money in every possible way and ill treating the poor people more than ever the Government tax-gatherers had done. This gives some significant hints as to how the Sikh Gurus were ever enabled to keep such large bands of armed men and to wage such an obstinate and persevering struggle against the Government. In the times of Guru Gōvind Singh the oppression of the Sikhs by his deputed collectors must have been beyond endurance, so that they at last resolved to bring the matter before their dreaded Guru in the form of a play. The passage in the Sikhā̃ dē rāǰ dī vithiā, pp. 70, 71, is very instructive as to the overbearing conduct of the Masands of the Guru. The Guru took the hint to heart, and as he perceived that the institution had become thoroughly hateful and unbearable to his disciples, he resolved to abolish it altogether. He punished the Masands severely and excommunicated them.[2]

[1] Thus it is stated in the Sikhā̃ dē rāǰ dī vithiā, p. 68: ਆਖਦੇ ਹਨ ਕਿ ਉਸ ਜੰਗ ਵਿਚ ਗੁਰੂ ਗੋਵਿੰਦ ਸਿੰਘ ਨੈ ਬੀ ਆਪਣੀ ਫੌਜ ਭੇਜਕੇ ਬਹਾਦੁਰ ਸ਼ਾਹ ਦੀ ਕੁਛ ਮੱਦਤ ਕੀਤੀ, though the high pretensions of the Sikh tradition, that Bahādur Shāh vanquished his brothers and ascended the throne by means of the Sikh host (ਬਲਕਿ ਸਿੱਖਾਂ ਦੀ ਫੌਜ ਦੇ ਸਬਬਹੀ ਬਹਾਦੁਰ ਸ਼ਾਹ ਆਪਣੇ ਭਰਾਵਾਂ ਤੇ ਫਤੇ ਪਾਕੇ ਤਖਤ ਪੁਰ ਬੈਠਾ) are by no means countenanced by history.

[2] The Guru cannot have been so ignorant of the proceedings of his Masands as he pretended to be; for he must have known that such large sums of money, as he was continually demanding and spending on his troops, were not forthcoming willingly, especially from a poor population. It must surprise every one, that the Mugul Government did not stop this secret tax-gathering of the Sikh Gurus, as we can hardly assume that the authorities were kept in ignorance of it.

After Gōvind Singh had settled his affairs at home, he marched for the Dekhan, where he had been appointed to the command of five thousand horse.[1] On the march there he fell in with a Paṭhān, who was the grandson of that Pāindah Khān with whom Guru Har-gōvind had fought. The Guru showed to this man great affection, and engaged him in his service and took him with him.[2] One day the Guru began to mock at him; when he perceived that the Paṭhān paid no heed to his taunts, he began to put him to shame, saying: "If the son (and) grandson, whose father (and) grandfather have been killed by somebody, goes to him in order to get his subsistence from him, say, what shameless man must he be?" The Paṭhān answered: "If a man remains with the enemy of his father (and) grandfather and gets his subsistence from him, he must be a very shameless, nose-cut person." The Guru continued: "If a Paṭhān remain with the enemy of his father (and) grandfather, what dost thou consider him?" He answered: "I do not consider him a Paṭhān, but a weaver."[3] The Guru said further: "If thou wouldst meet with the enemy of thy father (and) grandfather and a weapon would be in thy hand, say, what wouldst thou do?" He answered: "I would not let him live." The Paṭhān wondered why the Guru asked him such things and reflected on it. He recollected that Gōvind Singh was descended from Har-Gōvind, with whom the battle of Kartārpur was fought; he felt ashamed in his mind and resolved to take his revenge at a given opportunity. One day a Sikh brought to the Guru from abroad a very beautiful dagger. The Guru seeing its brightness and its edge was much pleased with it and kept it always with him. One day he asked the Paṭhān by how many thrusts of this dagger a man might be killed? He answered, that one thrust of it was enough. The Guru went on to say: "Well, if he, by whom thy father and grandfather may have been killed, would come before thee and this dagger were in thy hand, what wouldst thou do with him?" The Paṭhān on hearing this got very angry in his heart, but could say nothing. Shortly after the Guru fell asleep and all his door-keepers went to their own tent. The Paṭhān, who had remained sitting near him, took gently the dagger out of the hand of the Guru and thrust it into his belly. When he thought that he was dead, he rose and fled. The Guru, who was not dead, on seeing the wounds of the dagger, cried out: "O brother Sikhs, I am dead!" All the Sikhs assembled together and running in the four directions they seized that Paṭhān and brought him back to the Guru. It is said, that the Guru praised the bravery of the Paṭhān and set him free, telling the Sikhs, who were overcome by grief on seeing the wounds of the Guru, that they should not be sorrowful, for this was ordered so by the Lord; the Paṭhān had not struck him (treacherously), but he had himself provoked him to kill him by putting him to shame.[4]

[1] The Sikhs are now loath to concede this appointment of Gōvind Singh. In the Sikhā̃ dē rāǰ dī vithiā it is only said: ਇਕ ਦਿਨ ਗੋਵਿੰਦ ਸਿੰਘ ਪੂਰਬ ਦੇਸ ਦੇ ਸੈਲ ਨੂੰ ਗਿਆ: one day Gōvind Singh went on a journey to the south. Gōvind Singh can have been only a short time in the Dekhan, others extend his stay there. The chronology of these events requires a careful research, which can only be carried out at the hands of more trustworthy materials, which have as yet to be searched for.

[2] There is a Sākhī in the "*Sākhī Book of the description of Guru Govind Singh's religion and doctrine,*" translated into English by Sirdār Attar Singh, chief of Bhadour, Benares (printed at the Medical Hall Press), 1873, which gives some more details about the story in question (see Sākhī 98, p. 198 *sqq.*). It is stated there, that the grandson of Pāindah Khān saluted the Guru in a Darbār held by him, having been sent by his mother, who considered the Guru as a prophet. The Guru presented him with five gold Muhars and ordered him to come every day to his house to play with him at chess. For this service he received five Rupees per diem.

[3] The ਜੁਲਾਹ, or weaver, is considered in India a coward.

[4] Cunningham gives a somewhat different story, p. 79, following MacGregor in this point (vol. i. p. 99). Malcolm, who is here very brief, seems to have had the same tradition before him, which we have given more in detail, following the Sikhā̃ dē rāǰ dī vithiā, p. 76 *sqq.* In this book however a great chronological blunder

The wounds were sown up and healed again, but it seems that the Guru was bent on dying, One day he bent his bow with great force and by so doing the stitches of the wounds were broken and the blood began to flow. The surgeon bound up his wounds again, but the Guru obtained no rest. He mounted a Pālkī and travelled towards the south. When he had arrived at a town named Nadēṛ (ਨਦੇੜ),[1] the Guru became greatly exhausted by his wounds. He said to his Sikhs, that he saw that he would not live any longer, they should therefore stop in this place. When they were staying there for some days and his pain was not relieved, he said to his disciples, that they should give some alms, as medicines were no more of any use to him. The Sikhs brought together a great quantity of food of various kinds and feasted Brāhmaṇs and Saints and distributed in alms ornaments and clothes. The Guru felt that his dissolution was near at hand, and ordered his Sikhs to keep ready wood (for cremation) and a shroud. Having done so they all joined their hands and asked: "O true Guru, whom will you seat, for the sake of our welfare, on the throne of the Guruship?" He answered: "As the nine Kings before me were at the time of their death seating another Guru on their throne, so shall I now not do; I have entrusted the whole society (of the disciples) to the bosom of the timeless, divine male. After me you shall everywhere mind the book of the Granth-sāhib as your Guru; whatever you shall ask it, it will show to you. Whoever be my disciple, he shall consider the Granth as the form of the Guru, and whichever disciple wishes to have an interview with me, he shall make for one Rupee and a quarter, or for as much as he is able, Kaṛāh parsād;[2] then opening the book and bowing his head he will obtain a reward equal to an interview with me." Having given them some other directions the Guru soon after became senseless. Meantime the disciples heaped up a pyre of sandal-wood and kept every other thing ready. One hour before he expired he said to the disciples: "Bathe me and put on me new clothes and give me all my weapons; when my breath departs, do not take off these clothes, but burn me with them and with all my weapons!"[3] He then sat himself down upon the funeral pyre, and having meditated on the Supreme Lord, he uttered with his mouth and with love the following Savaiyā:

> Since I seized thy feet, I brought nothing else under (my) eye.
> O merciful Rām, the Purāṇās and the Qur'ān teach various systems, I did not mind one (of them).
> The Smriti, the Shāstras and the Vēdas, all teach many modifications, I did not recognize one (of them).
> O disposer of happiness, bestow mercy (on me)! I did not say "I," all I recognized as "Thee."[4]

is committed, it being stated, that Nādir Shāh sent his own physician from Dillī to look after the wounds of Gōvind Singh. Nādir Shāh invaded India in 1738, whereas Gōvind Singh died in 1708. In the Sākhī quoted it is stated, that Lakhā Singh ran after the boy and cut off his head.

[1] Nadēṛ is a town in the valley of the Godavery.

[2] ਕੜਾਹ ਪਰਸਾਦ, the offering up of ਕੜਾਹ (a kind of sweetmeat, made of flour, ghī and sugar) to a holy person (as, for instance, the Guru), and then distributing it among the worshippers.

[3] This is confirmed by the Sākhī quoted: see p. 201.

[4] The original is (Sikhā̃ dē rāǰ dī vithiā, p. 81):

ਸਵੈਯਾ

ਪਾਇ ਗਹੇ ਤੁਮਰੇ ਜਬ ਤੇ ਤਬ ਤੇ ਕਛੁ ਆਂਖ ਨਹੀਂ ਆਨ੍ਯੋ ।
ਰਾਮ ਰਹੀਮ ਪੁਰਾਨ ਕੁਰਾਨ ਅਨੇਕ ਕਹੈ ਮਤ ਅਨੇਕ ਨ ਮਾਨ੍ਯੋ ।
ਸਿਮ੍ਰਿਤ ਸਾਸਤਰ ਬੇਦ ਸਭੀ ਬਹੁ ਭੇਦ ਕਹੈ ਹਮ ਏਕ ਨ ਜਾਨ੍ਯੋ ।
ਸ੍ਰੀਅਸਪਾਨ ਕ੍ਰਿਪਾ ਤੁਮਰੀ ਕਰ ਮੈਂ ਨ ਕਹ੍ਯੋ ਸਭ ਤੋਹਿ ਪਛਾਨ੍ਯੋ ।

ਸ੍ਰੀਅਸਪਾਨ = Sansk. श्रेयस्पाणि, he who holds happiness in his hands, an epithet of Viṣhṇu.

Having uttered these verses he closed his eyes and expired A.D. 1708. All the Sikhs and saints, who from many parts were assembled there, raised the shout of Jaikār (Victory!) and sang a beautiful song and the eyes of many people were filled with tears on account of the separation of the Guru. Beautiful edifices were erected there, and in the midst of them all the shrine of the Guru, and round this some Dharm-sālās, in which the Granth-sāhib was deposited. To the town of Nadēṛ they gave the name of Abčal-nagar.[1] They put up many swords, shields, spears and steel discuses in that shrine, and the Sikh people, who go there on pilgrimage, worship those weapons, as they believe that they belonged to Guru Gōvind Singh.

The object of his life Gōvind Singh could not carry out, though he tried to secure it even by a human sacrifice, and he died broken-hearted and weary of life far from the scenes of his exploits; but he has contributed a good share to the destruction of the Muhammadan power in India by his bloody struggles, inuring his Sikhs to a continual warfare, and moulding them by his new ordinances into a distinct nation of fanatical soldiers, the Khālsā. A body containing such elements could not remain quiet; their course was prescribed to them, and they had indeed no other choice but to conquer or to be conquered. We need therefore not wonder that the Sikhs, though repeatedly repulsed, soon succeeded in erecting their own sway on the ruins of the declining Muhammadan Empire.

[1] ਅਬਚਲ ਨਗਰ, the immovable city; ਅਬਚਲ = ਅਬਿਚਲ, Sansk. अविचल. MacGregor (vol. i. p. 101) states that the Sikhs call it Aphullanuggur, a strange mistranscription; Cunningham, History of the Sikhs, p. 394, writes it similarly Upchullunuggur.

III.

SKETCH OF THE RELIGION OF THE SIKHS.

THE religious system of the Sikhs has been touched already by different writers, but in such general terms, that but little can be gathered from them. Even H. H. Wilson, in his "Sketch of the Religious Sects of the Hindūs," has very cautiously handled this matter, and contented himself with offering a few short, though pertinent, remarks about it. All these authors had not read the Granth themselves, but received the information they gave from second hand; it is therefore partly defective, partly labouring under mistakes.

Nānak himself was not a speculative philosopher, who built up a concise system on scientific principles; he had not received a regular school-training, and uttered therefore his thoughts in a loose way, which are now scattered through the Granth, and must first be patiently searched out and collected into a whole, before we can form an idea of his tenets.

Nānak himself was by no means an independent thinker, neither had he any idea of starting a new religious sect: he followed in all essential points the common Hindū philosophy of those days,[1] and especially his predecessor *Kabīr*, who was at that time already a popular man in India, and whose writings, which were composed in the vulgar tongue, were accessible to the unlearned masses. This obligation, which Nānak and the following Sikh Gurus owe to Kabīr, is acknowledged by the reception of a great portion of the verses of Kabīr into the Sikh Granth itself. That also the writings of other famous Bhagats were known to and used by the Sikh Gurus, is sufficiently attested by the Granth, into which they were partly incorporated and thereby saved from oblivion.

The doctrines once uttered by Bābā Nānak were taken up by the following Sikh Gurus without any perceptible deviation; and after the volume of the Granth had been collected by Guru Arjun, they were never called into question, the Granth being held sacred as an immediate divine revelation.

The tenth Guru, Gōvind Singh, relapsed in many points again into Hindūism, he being a special votary of Durgā; but notwithstanding this he always asserted the unity of the Supreme, and the innovations he introduced were not so much touching the doctrine as the practical course of life.

We need therefore in the following sketch of the Sikh religion not anxiously distinguish between the words of Bābā Nānak and those of the following Gurus, as none of them excelled by any originality of thought, every succeeding Guru being content to expatiate on the few ideas handed down to him by his predecessors.

The chief point in Nānak's doctrine was the *unity of the Supreme Being*, though the Hindū

[1] Particularly the system laid down in the Bhagavad-gītā, which was very popular among the Bhagats.

mind was already more or less familiarized with this idea, it having been asserted long before Nānak by most of the Hindū philosophical systems and popularized by the Bhagats, especially the ingenious Kabīr.

That the Supreme is One and that there is no other, is frequently inculcated. Thus says Nānak:

> "Whom shall I call the second? there is none.
> In all is that One Spotless one (= the Supreme).[1]

That on this point there is full concord between Hindūs and Musalmāns, is openly conceded. Nānak says:

> "Know, that there are two ways (*i.e.* of Hindūs and Musalmāns), but only one Lord."[2]

The same is also conceded with reference to the Hindū sects of those days, which, though wearing different garbs, acknowledge the One Supreme. Nānak says of them:

> "There are six houses, six Gurus, six (methods of) instruction.
> The Guru of the Gurus is One, the garbs many."[3]

This Supreme Being is (according to the nomenclature of the Vaiṣhṇava sect, to which nearly all the Bhagats belonged) called by different names, such as: *Brahm, the Supreme Brahm, Paramēsur* (the Supreme Lord), and especially *Hari, Rām, Gōvind.*

This Being is alone really existing (ਸਚੁ or ਸਤਿ), uncreated (ਅਜੂਨੀਸੈਭੰ), endless (ਅਨੰਤ), timeless (ਅਕਾਲੁ), eternal (ਅਵਿਗਤ); it contains in itself all qualities and is at the same time without qualities.[4] It is therefore inaccessible (ਅਗੰਮ, ਅਗੋਚਰ), invisible, incomprehensible (even to the gods) and indescribable—qualities which are frequently dwelt upon in the Granth.[5]

It is the ground or root (ਮੂਲੁ) of all things, the source, from which all have sprung, the primary cause (ਕਾਰਨਕਰਨ); in this sense it is called the *creator* (ਕਰਤਾ or ਕਰਤਾਰ). But we must not misunderstand this appellation, for no creation out of nothing is thereby intended. When the Absolute Being is styled the creator, the *expansion* of the same into a *plurality of forms* is thereby meant; creation is therefore in some places plainly called ਪਸਾਰਾ, expansion. Arjun says (Transl. p. 400, 6): "He himself is One and he himself is many;" and p. 421, 5: "From that Lord all the creation (has sprung). If it pleases him, he makes an expansion. If it pleases him, he is of one form

[1] Gaurī, Mah. I., Asṭp. V., Pause (Transl. p. 320):

ਦੂਜਾ ਕਉਣੁ ਕਹਾ ਨਹੀ ਕੋਈ ॥
ਸਭ ਮਹਿ ਏਕੁ ਨਿਰੰਜਨੁ ਸੋਈ ॥

Other passages, see Transl. p. 17, *vv.* 5; 2; p. 414, 8.

[2] Gaurī, Mah. I., Asṭp. V., 8 (Transl. p. 321):

ਰਾਹ ਦੋਵੈ ਖਸਮੁ ਏਕੋ ਜਾਣੁ ॥

See also Transl. p. 482, 5.

[3] Āsā, Mah. I., Sabd XXX., 1 (Transl. p. 505).

[4] Mājh, Mah. V., XXI., 3 (Transl. p. 143):

ਤੂੰ ਨਿਰਗੁਣੁ ਸਰਗੁਣੁ ਸੁਖ ਦਾਤਾ ॥

See also Transl. p. 416, XXI., Slōk.

[5] See Transl. p. 431, III., Pauṛī; p. 457, XX., Pauṛī; p. 493, I., 1, 2.

(only)."[1] Everywhere and in all things and beings the One is diffused, he is filling all places. Thus says Nāmdēv (Transl. p. 665, II., 4):

> "Here is Bīṭhal, there is Bīṭhal, without Bīṭhal the world is not.
> In every place, says Nāmā, in all thou art fully contained."[2]

Yea the whole universe and all things therein are identified with the Supreme. Nāmdēv says (Transl. p. 665, Pause, 2):

> "All is Gōvind, all is Gōvind, without Gōvind there is no other.
> As in one string there are seven thousand beads, (so) is that Lord lengthwise and crosswise.
> A wave of water, froth and bubble do not become separate from the water.
> This world is the sport of the Supreme Brahm, playing about he does not become another."[3]

All the finite created beings have therefore no separate existence apart from the Absolute, they are only its various forms and appearances, its frolics. Nānak says (Transl. p. 329, XVI., 5): "In all living creatures the One sports," and (p. 652, XXIV., Slōk I.): "By himself the vessels are formed, he himself also fills them." All creatures are therefore alike with the only difference that the Absolute becomes self-conscious in man. Kabīr says (Transl. p. 682, 204):

> Kabīr in saying: "thou, thou," has become "thou," "I" has not remained in me.
> When my own self, (which is) another's, has been effaced, (then) where I look, there (art) "thou."[4]

It is owing to the Māyā (deception), which the Absolute has spread out over the whole universe, that the creatures are led to consider themselves as individual beings, distinct from the Supreme, and fall thereby into the error of *egotism* (ਹੰਕਾਰੁ, the idea of individual existence) and *duality*. Nānak says (Japjī, 27, Transl. p. 10): "By whom a Māyā of various colours, kinds and sorts is produced." And Kabīr says (Transl. p. 127):

> "One is wonderful, hear, O Paṇḍit! now nothing can be said;
> By whom the Gods, Gaṇas and Gandharvas are deluded, (by whom) a rope is applied to the three worlds."

[1] The original is:

ਤਿਸੁ ਪ੍ਰਭ ਤੇ ਸਗਲੀ ਉਤਪਤਿ ॥
ਤਿਸੁ ਭਾਵੈ ਤਾ ਕਰੈ ਬਿਸਤਾਰੁ ॥
ਤਿਸੁ ਭਾਵੈ ਤਾ ਏਕੰਕਾਰੁ ॥

Similar is the expression, Gauṛī, Sukhmanī XXII., Slōk (Transl. p. 418):

ਨਾਨਕ ਏਕੋ ਪਸਰਿਆ ਦੂਜਾ ਕਹ ਦ੍ਰਿਸਟਾਰ ॥

[2] There are a great many passages of this kind in the Granth; compare Transl. p. 133, VII., 2.

[3] The same idea is also boldly expressed by Ravidās (Transl. p. 130, I.):

ਤੋਹੀ ਮੋਹੀ ਮੋਹੀ ਤੋਹੀ ਅੰਤਰੁ ਕੈਸਾ ॥
ਕਨਕ ਕਟਿਕ ਜਲ ਤਰੰਗ ਜੈਸਾ ॥

> "Between thee and me, me and thee, what is the difference?
> Like gold and the bracelet (made of it), like water and a wave."

We now prefer this rendering of the first line. *Cf.* also Transl. p. 116, VII., Pauṛī.

[4] The original is:

ਕਬੀਰ ਤੂੰ ਤੂੰ ਕਰਤਾ ਤੂੰ ਹੂਆ ਮੁਝ ਮਹਿ ਰਹਾ ਨ ਹੂੰ ॥
ਜਬ ਆਪਾ ਪਰ ਕਾ ਮਿਟਿ ਗਇਆ ਜਤ ਦੇਖਉ ਤਤ ਤੂੰ ॥

The world is therefore in fact nothing but a *play* or *sport* (ਖੇਲ) of the Absolute Being,[1] which is expanding or contracting itself, as it pleases; Hari establishes and disestablishes, vivifies and destroys *ad libitum*. An infinite number of worlds is stated to be produced by him, which, like a plaything, appear and disappear. Thus says Rām-dās:

> "By thyself all the creation is produced, by thyself, having created, the whole is caused to disappear (again)."[2]

No teleological principle whatever is assigned for the production or destruction of the created beings; they are cosmogonic revolutions, which could not be accounted for and were therefore referred to a sporting propensity of the Absolute. We need hardly remark, that this whole definition and description of the Supreme is altogether *pantheistic*. The Hindū way of thinking comprehends in the Absolute both *spirit and matter*, as the creation of material bodies out of nothing is totally incomprehensible to the Hindū mind; to him the material essence is therefore co-eternal with the spirit (ਪੁਰਖੁ). The matter put in the Absolute is however not the gross, sensible matter (ਬਿਖਿਆ = विषय), but purely *atomic* (ਸੂਖਮ = सूक्ष्म), which by the expansion of the Absolute receives the grosser, sensible form by the conjunction of infinite atoms. God is therefore the absolute vital substance, the all-filling world-soul (ਜਗਜੀਵਨ), as he is frequently called.

We can distinguish in the Granth a grosser and a finer kind of Pantheism. The grosser Pantheism identifies all things with the Absolute, the universe in its various forms being considered the expansion of it;[3] the finer Pantheism on the other hand distinguishes between the Absolute and the finite beings and borders frequently on Theism. Though God is producing all things out of himself and is filling all, yet he remains *distinct from the creatures* and is not contaminated by the Māyā,[4] as a lotus in a pond of water remains distinct from the water surrounding it. The

[1] See: Transl. p. 17, II., 2.

[2] The original is (Sō Purkhu, Mah. IV., I., 5, Transl. p. 17):

ਤੁਧੁ ਆਪੇ ਸ੍ਰਿਸਟਿ ਸਭ ਉਪਾਈ ਜੀ ਤੁਧੁ ਆਪੇ ਸਿਰਜਿ ਸਭ ਗੋਈ ॥

As to the innumerability of the worlds, see Transl. p. 6, *v.* 19; p. 397, *v.* 7, where Arjun says: "Many times the expanse of the world was spread out. Many crores (of worlds) of many kinds were made. From the Lord they emanated and in the Lord they are absorbed."

[3] This kind of Pantheism, which, according to the expressions used, borders occasionally on Materialism, is chiefly represented by the Bhagats Nāmdēv and Ravidās. See p. xcix, note 3.

[4] Kabīr says (Transl. p. 474, LII., 2):

> "Whose body the universe is, he is not in it, the creator is not in it.
> Who is putting (the things) together, he is always aloof from them."

And Arjun says (Transl. p. 148, XXXV., 2):

> "In every body he dwells near.
> The donor of the living beings is always distinct (from them)."

Cf. also Transl. p. 151, XLI., 3, with note 2. In order to understand the words of Kabīr and Arjun more fully, we must compare what is said of the Supreme Being in the Bhagavad-gītā, Chap. XIII., Shlōk 14 *sqq.*

> "It is existing both apart from and within existing things, it is animate and also inanimate.
> It cannot be recognized on account of its subtilty, and it exists both far and near.
> Not distributed among beings and yet existing as if distributed."

And in Chap. XIII., Shlōk 12, it is said:

> "It is called the Supreme Brahm, without beginning, neither existent nor non-existent."

The sense of this line is, that it has and has not a real existence, *i.e.* that it is spirit and matter.

Supreme is in its essence ਜੋਤਿ (light, the all-energizing vital power), which, though diffused into all creatures, remains distinct from them; the material bodies are dissolved again into atoms, whereas the emanated light is re-absorbed into the fountain of light. In this finer shade of Pantheism creation assumes the form of *emanation* from the Supreme (as in the system of the Sūfīs); the atomic matter is either likewise considered co-eternal with the Absolute and immanent in it, becoming moulded into various, distinct forms by the energizing vigour of the absolute ਜੋਤਿ; or the reality of matter is more or less denied (as by the Sūfīs, who call it the عَدَم, τὸ μὴ ὄν), so that the divine ਜੋਤਿ is the only real essence in all; this last view borders on Idealism.

That an Absolute Being, thus defined, cannot be a self-conscious spirit, endowed with a free will and acting according to teleological principles, seems never to have struck their minds. For after the strongest pantheistic expressions, the Supreme is again addressed as a self-conscious personality, who governs all things and takes care of all creatures and with whom man endeavours to enter into personal relations. Contradictory sentences of this kind we find a great many in the Granth.[1]

To this personification of the Supreme it is owing, that *intellectual* and *moral* qualities are frequently ascribed to him, though, strictly speaking, there is no room for them in this system. He is called very wise (ਸੁਜਾਣੁ, ਸੁਰਤੀ), acquainted with the secrets of the hearts or the inward governor (ਅੰਤਰਜਾਮੀ), not deceivable (ਅਛਲ), etc., kind to his devotees (ਭਗਤਵਛਲ), merciful, just, etc. In other places qualities are again attributed to him, which are contradictory to each other, and which clearly show that they are to be taken in a pantheistic sense. Thus says Nānak (Transl. p. 35, XXV., 1):

> "He himself is enjoying pleasure, he himself is the pleasure, he himself is amusing (others) with pleasure.
> He himself is the petticoat (= the woman), he himself is the husband of the bed."[2]

We should be wrong in assuming that Nānak forbade the worship of other gods on the ground of the unity of the Supreme. Far from doing so, he took over the whole Hindū Pantheon, with all its mythological background, with the only difference that the whole was subordinated to the Supreme Brahm. The position of the popular gods was thereby, though not openly attacked, naturally lowered, and their service must needs appear less important, yea even useless for the attainment of the highest object of mankind. The folly of idolatry is occasionally ridiculed in the Granth, especially by Kabīr. He says (Transl. p. 657, I., 1-3):

> "The female gardener breaks off leaves, in the leaves, in the leaves (there is) life.
> The stone, for the sake of which she breaks off the leaves, is lifeless.
> A stone is shaped by the hammer and formed into an image, giving it a breast and feet.
> If this image be true, then it will eat the hammerer."

And, Transl. p. 678 (*v.* 136), he says:

> "Kabīr (says): a stone is made the Lord, the whole world worships it.
> Who remains in reliance on this, is drowned in the black stream."

It is a mistake, if Nānak is represented as having endeavoured to unite the Hindū and Muhammadan idea about God. Nānak remained a thorough Hindū, according to all his views, and if he had communionship with Musalmāns and many of these even became his disciples, it was owing to the fact that Sūfism, which all these Muhammadans were professing, was in reality nothing but

[1] See such addresses to the Supreme, Transl. p. 143, XXI., and p. 144, XXIV., XXV.

[2] In a similar sense Arjun says (Transl. p. 143, XXI., 3):

> "Thou art perfectly composed, sensual and given to pleasure."

a Pantheism, derived directly from Hindū sources, and only outwardly adapted to the forms of the Islām. Hindū and Muslim Pantheists could well unite together, as they entertained essentially the same ideas about the Supreme;[1] the Hindū mythology was not pressed on the Musalmāns, as the Hindū philosophers themselves laid no particular stress upon it—the belief in the minor gods, the transient manifestations of the Supreme, being with them a matter of choice. On these grounds tolerance between Hindūs and Turks is often advocated in the Granth and intolerance on the part of the Turks rebuked.[2]

Our next question is: *What is the relation of man to the Supreme?*

The human soul is represented as being light (ਜੋਤਿ) from light, *a scintilla aminae divinae*, which has emanated from the Absolute and is by itself *immortal*.[3]

According to the popular belief of the Hindūs, which is occasionally alluded to in the Granth, four Lakhs of souls have once for all emanated from the fountain of light, their number neither increasing nor decreasing.[4] The human souls form only a small part of the creation, which is limited to eighty-four Lakhs of forms of existence, viz.: nine Lakhs of aquatic animals (ਜਲਚਰ), seventeen Lakhs of immovable creatures (ਅਸਥਾਵਰ = स्थावर, such as trees, etc.), eleven Lakhs of creeping animals (ਕਿਰਮ = कृमि), ten Lakhs of feathered animals (ਪਖੀ), twenty-three Lakhs of quadrupeds (ਚੇਪਾਇਆ), and four Lakhs of men (ਮਨੁਖ).

It is the aim and object of the individual soul as a divine spark to be reunited with the fountain of light, from which it has emanated, and to be re-absorbed in it. As long as it has not reached this goal, it is unhappy, being separated from its source, the Supreme. Why the soul has emanated and what for, is nowhere stated in the Granth; we must therefore look also on this process as a sport of the Absolute (ਖੇਲ). But the return of the individual soul to the eternal fountain of light is cut off in consequence of works practised whilst in the body, and by its impurity, contracted by second love (ਦੂਜਾ ਭਾਉ) or duality (ਦੁਬਿਧਾ = द्विविध), which subject the soul to metempsychosis, the coming and going (ਆਵਾਗਵਨੁ).

This leads us to the question: if the individual soul is light, how did it happen, that it fell into *impurity* or *sin*?

That the world is actually under the dominion of sin, Nānak could and would not deny; he declared himself, that the object of his mission was, to show to mankind the way, by which it could be saved from this state of misery.

According to the pantheistic premises, as stated above, sin cannot be the free, deliberate act

[1] Kabīr says (Rāg Āsā, XIII., 4, Transl. p. 657):

ਕਹਤ ਕਬੀਰ ਰਾਮ ਗੁਨ ਗਾਵਉ ॥
ਹਿੰਦੂ ਤੁਰਕ ਦੋਊ ਸਮਝਾਵਉ ॥

[2] See a passage of this kind in Rāg Āsā, Kabīr VIII., 2 (Transl. p. 655), where he wittingly says:

ਸਕਤਿ ਸਨੇਹੁ ਕਰਿ ਸੁੰਨਤਿ ਕਰੀਐ ਮੈ ਨ ਬਦਉਗਾ ਭਾਈ ॥
ਜਉ ਰੇ ਖੁਦਾਇ ਮੋਹਿ ਤੁਰਕੁ ਕਰੈਗਾ ਆਪਨਹੀ ਕਟਿਜਾਈ ॥

[3] Arjun says, Sirī Rāg, Mah. V., Sabd XIV., 1 (Transl. p. 66):

ਮਨੁ ਤਨੁ ਧਨੁ ਜਿਨਿ ਪ੍ਰਭਿ ਦੀਆ ਰਖਿਆ ਸਹਜਿ ਸਵਾਰਿ ॥
ਸਰਬ ਕਲਾ ਕਰਿ ਥਾਪਿਆ ਅੰਤਰਿ ਜੋਤਿ ਅਪਾਰ ॥

[4] Compare with this what the Bhagavad-gītā says, Chap. XV., Shlōk 7:

ममैवांशो जीवलोके जीवभूतः सनातनः ।
मनः षष्ठानीन्द्रियाणि प्रकृतिस्थानि कर्षति ॥

"An eternal portion of me only having become endowed with life in the world of life, attracts the mind and the five senses, which belong to nature."

of man; it must have on the contrary its origin in the Absolute Being itself, as all creatures are said to be subject to an *absolute destiny* (ਲੇਖੁ, ਭਾਗੁ, ਕਿਰਤੁ). This is plainly taught in the Granth. Ravidās says (Transl. p. 666, I., 3):

"As far as living creatures are, they are subject to destiny."

On the forehead of every man his lot is written from the beginning, which cannot be effaced, though one try to do so. Nānak says (Gauṛī, Mah. I., Sabd X., 1, Transl., p. 217):

"The lot has fallen, none effaces it.
What do I know, what will happen in future?
What has pleased him, that has come to pass.
None other is acting (but he)." [1]

Thero are consequently numbers of passages in the Granth which pointedly deny the *liberum arbitrium* in man; man comes and goes according to the pleasure of Hari; he acts, speaks, etc. as he is caused to do. Arjun says (Transl. p. 398, *v.* 5):

"The power of this one is not in this one's hand.
The cause of causes is the Lord of all.
The creature is helpless and must obey.
What pleases to that one, that will be."

Very pointed is the expression of Arjun (Transl. p. 399, XI., 7), that man like a mimic shows many appearances, and that the Lord makes him dance as it pleases him. Man is naturally impelled to actions by the three qualities (ਤ੍ਰੈਗੁਣ), which penetrate every created being, even the gods themselves. These three qualities are the ਸਤੋ (सत्त्व, the quality of goodness), the ਰਜੋ (रजस्, the quality of passion) and the ਤਮੋ (तमस्, the quality of darkness); they are innate in every body, but not in equipoise, the one or the other being predominant. The actions of all men are consequently determined by the quality that has a ruling influence on them.

To this must be added, that the Supreme has spread the Māyā (deception) over the whole universe, the gods not excepted, by which the created beings are deluded into egotism and duality.[2] The wise and the fool, the good and the bad, are therefore alike, they cannot be considered responsible for what they think, say or do, as they are acting under influences and impulses which are not under their control.[3] This is now and then keenly felt and acknowledged. Thus Arjun (Transl. p. 418, *v.* 7) asks:

"When by himself the form of the world is created,
And laid out in the three qualities:
Then religious demerit and merit, what is it?"

The original is:

ਕਿਰਤੁ ਪਇਆ ਨਹ ਮੇਟੈ ਕੋਇ ।
ਕਿਆ ਜਾਣਾ ਕਿਆ ਆਗੈ ਹੋਇ ।
ਜੋ ਤਿਸੁ ਭਾਣਾ ਸੋਈ ਹੂਆ ।
ਅਵਰੁ ਨ ਕਰਣੈਵਾਲਾ ਦੂਆ ॥

[2] The Brāhmaṇ Trilōčan says (see Transl. p. 127, II.):

ਮਾਇਆ ਮੂਠਾ ਚੇਤਸਿ ਨਾਹੀ ਜਨਮੁ ਗਵਾਇਓ ਆਲਸੀਆ ॥

[3] Amar-dās says plainly:

ਜਿਸੁ ਆਪੇ ਭੁਲਾਏ ਸੁ ਕਿਥੈ ਹਥੁ ਪਾਏ ।
ਪੂਰਬਿ ਲਿਖਿਆ ਮੇਟਣਾ ਨ ਜਾਏ ॥

See Transl. p. 154, II., 3. Folly and error, produced in man by the Māyā, is directly ascribed to a divine causality. See Transl. p. 126, Kabīr I., Pause; p. 494, III., 3.

And Ravidās boldly asks (Transl. p. 130, I., Pause):

"If I would not commit sins, O Endless one!
How would be thy name 'purifier of the sinners'?"

With reference to the delusion of the Māyā, Kabīr says (Transl. p. 470, XXXIX.) openly:

Pause.

"Hari, the deceiver, has practised deceit on the world.
In separation from Hari how shall I live, O my mother?
(2). Say, who is a man, who is a woman?
Reflect on this truth in thy body!
(3). Kabīr says: my mind is reconciled with the deceiver.
The deceit is gone, the deceiver is known (by me)."

Under the influence of the three qualities and the delusion of the Māyā man commits acts,[1] which subject the soul to transmigration.

According to common Hindū notions every action carries with itself its fruit or reward. If one, under the influence of the quality of *goodness*, has done here meritorious acts (ਪੁੰਨ, पुण्य), he is after his death admitted into heaven or paradise, where he is allowed to enjoy the fruits of his works, till they are exhausted; then he is turned back again into a womb and born on earth in a high caste and in a pious family, to commence anew the old course, which may end, according to his actions, to his advantage or disadvantage. If he has acted under the impulse of the quality of *passion*, he is reborn after his death in the house of worldly-minded men. But if he has acted under the influence of the quality of *darkness* and heaped up demerits, he is variously punished by Yama (or Dharm-rāi), and then born in the body of some animal,[2] or even thrown into hell (ਨਰਕ); when his punishment there is over, he is then born in some vile animal body and has to go through various transmigrations, till he be born again in a low human womb.[3] There is a great latitude in these popular views concerning future rewards and punishments, and we find many allusions to them in the Granth, partly couched in melancholy, partly in jocose terms.

Every soul is supposed to have migrated through the eighty-four Lakhs of forms of existence,

[1] I find it nowhere stated in the Granth, if the soul itself is considered *inactive*, as in the system of the theistic Sāṅkhyā (and the Bhagavad-gītā), where the three qualities are represented as exercising their influence through the medium of matter, which transmits the good or bad impressions to the seat of sensibility (मनस्); this again forwards them to consciousness (अहकार), and this to the intellect (बुद्धि), which conveys them to the soul, who takes cognizance of them.

[2] Kabīr says (*v.* 108, Transl. p. 676):

ਹਰਿ ਕਾ ਸਿਮਰਨੁ ਛਾਡਿਕੈ ਅਹੋਈ ਰਾਖੈ ਨਾਰਿ ।
ਗਦਹੀ ਹੋਇਕੈ ਅਉਤਰੈ ਭਾਰੁ ਸਹੈ ਮਨ ਚਾਰਿ ॥

"Having given up the remembrance of Hari the woman keeps the Ahōī(-fast).
Having become a jenny-ass she is born again and carries a load of four maunds."

[3] Ravidās says (Āsā, I., 2, Transl. p. 666):

ਤ੍ਰਿਗਦ ਜੋਨਿ ਅਚੇਤ ਸੰਭਵ ਪੁੰਨ ਪਾਪ ਅਸੋਚ ।
ਮਾਨੁਖਾ ਅਵਤਾਰ ਦੁਲਭ ਤਿਹੀ ਸੰਗਤਿ ਪੋਚ ॥

"The thoughtless one is produced in the womb of a reptile, (he who is) indifferent to religious merit (or) demerit.
The human birth is hard to obtain, in that (human) society also he is low."

before it reached the human birth;[1] the human birth is therefore considered so valuable, as final emancipation can only be worked out in it.

No man is thus able to work out his final emancipation, as even in the best case, when he is under the influence of the quality of goodness accumulating meritorious works, which hold out to him future rewards, the Māyā sticks to him, who deludes him into the error of duality, and so long as he is not freed from this error of duality, he cannot reach the gate of salvation (ਮੋਖ ਦੁਆਰੁ),[2] as only light, purified from all earthly desires, can be re-absorbed in the eternal light.

We need hardly remark, that this whole system is contradictory to itself; for on the one hand it is asserted, that the lot of every man is written from the beginning on his forehead, that he acts under the influence of the three qualities, and is in addition deluded by the Māyā into error, and on the other hand he is made accountable for his works and rewarded or punished accordingly, and after all subject to the trouble of transmigrations.

The Hindū mind was not unaware of these contradictions, but transmigration was considered necessary in order to account for the different lot of man in this world, which they were at a loss how to account for otherwise. Why are some high, honoured, rich, happy, etc., and why are others low, poor, crippled, etc., and this so frequently without any apparent merit or fault of their own? The only answer, which the pantheistic philosophers could give, that this was all the sport of the Supreme,[3] could not satisfy the popular mind, which instinctively felt that there must be some causal connexion between the actions of man and the evil in this world. It was therefore supposed that the lot of man in this present life depended on actions done by him in a former birth, though he had no longer any remembrance of them. The philosophers had to reckon with this popular idea, and took it up, though unconnected with their system and contradictory to it.

The transmigration of the soul, which has in India so firmly and universally laid hold of the popular mind, appears to the Hindū (and so likewise to the Sikh) the greatest of evils, and the question, which occupies all the thoughts of his mind, is, how to be freed from it? His aim is not heaven nor paradise,[4] for he is not allowed to remain there for ever; his aim is, as held out to him by the Bhagats and their followers, the Sikh Gurus, the *total dissolution of individual existence*

[1] Kabīr says (Gauṛī, XIX., Transl. p. 480):

ਲਖ ਚੋਰਾਸੀਹ ਜੀਅ ਜੋਨਿ ਮਹਿ ਭ੍ਰਮਤ ਨੰਦੁ ਬਹੁ ਥਾਕੋ ਰੇ ।

"Wandering about in the womb of the eighty-four Lakhs of creatures Nand became much worn out, O dear!"

[2] The Māyā produces spiritual blindness or infatuation (ਮੋਹ), the consequence of which is regeneration. Nānak says (Āsā, Mah. I., Sabd XXIII., 4, Transl. p. 503):

ਇਤੁ ਮੋਹਿ ਫਿਰਿ ਜੂਨੀ ਪਾਹਿ । ਮੋਹੇ ਲਾਗਾ ਜਮਪੁਰਿ ਜਾਹਿ ॥

"In this spiritual blindness one falls again into the womb.
Who clings to spiritual blindness goes to the city of Yama."

[3] This answer is frequently given in the Granth. Compare Japjī 17, 18, Transl. p. 6; Transl. p. 509, V.

[4] Nānak says (Āsā, Mah. I., Sabd XXXVIII., 3, Transl. p. 509):

ਗੁਰ ਕੀ ਸਾਖੀ ਅੰਮ੍ਰਿਤ ਬਾਣੀ ਪੀਵਤਹੀ ਪਰਵਾਣੁ ਭਇਆ ॥
ਦਰ ਦਰਸਨ ਕਾ ਪ੍ਰੀਤਮੁ ਹੋਵੈ ਮੁਕਤਿ ਬੈਕੁੰਠੈ ਕਰੈ ਕਿਆ ॥

"The discourse of the Guru is a nectar-speech, who drinks it becomes acceptable.
Who is very fond of the sight of the gate (of God) becomes emancipated, what shall he do in paradise?"

by the re-absorption of the soul in the fountain of light.[1] His aim is, in one word, the *Nirbāṇ* (निर्वाण), the total cessation of individual consciousness and reunion with the Vacuum (ਸੁੰਨ, शून्य).

If there could be any doubt on the pantheistic character of the tenets of the Sikh Gurus regarding the Supreme, it would be dissolved by their doctrine of the Nirbāṇ. Where no personal God is taught or believed in, man cannot aspire to a final personal communion with him, his aim can only be absorption in the Absolute Substance, *i.e.* individual annihilation. We find therefore no allusion to the joys of a future life in the Granth, as heaven or paradise, though supposed to exist, is not considered a desirable object. The immortality of the soul is only taught so far as the doctrine of transmigration requires it; but when the soul has reached its highest object, it is no more mentioned, because it no longer exists as individual soul.[2]

The Nirbāṇ, as is well known, was the grand object which Buddha in his preaching held out to the poor people. From his atheistic point of view he could look out for nothing else; personal existence, with all the concomitant evils of this life, which are not counterbalanced by corresponding pleasures, necessarily appeared to him as the greatest evil. His whole aim was therefore to counteract the troubles and pain of this existence by a stoical indifference to pleasure and pain, and to stop individual consciousness to its utmost limit in order to escape at the point of death from the dreaded transmigration, which he also, even on his atheistic ground, had not ventured to reject. Buddhism is therefore in reality, like Sikhism, nothing but unrestricted Pessimism, unable to hold out to man any solace, except that of annihilation.

In progress of time Buddhism has been expelled from India, but the restored Brahmanism with its confused cosmological legends and gorgeous mythology of the Purāṇas was equally unable to satisfy the thinking minds. It is therefore very remarkable, that Buddhism in its highest object, the Nirbāṇ, soon emerges again in the popular teachings of the mediaeval reformatory movements. Nāmdēv, Trilōčan, Kabīr, Ravidās, etc., and after these Nānak, take upon themselves to show the way to the Nirbāṇ, as Buddha in his time had promised, and find eager listeners; the difference is only in the *means* which these Bhagats propose, for obtaining the desired end.

In the Kali-yuga, announces Nānak, as well as the popular saints before him, *is the name of Hari the only means of obtaining final emancipation* (ਮੁਕਤਿ).[3]

[1] Kabīr exemplifies this process by the words:

"A drop is mixed with a drop.
A drop cannot be separated from a drop."

See Transl. p. 484, *v.* 29. Compare also the next following verse.

[2] Kabīr expresses this very forcibly (Gauṛī, Kabīr XXI., 1, Transl. p. 481):

ਜਬ ਹਮ ਹੋਤੇ ਤਬ ਤੁਮ ਨਾਹੀ ॥ ਅਬ ਤੁਮ ਹਹੁ ਹਮ ਨਾਹੀ ॥
ਅਬ ਹਮ ਤੁਮ ਏਕ ਭਏ ਹਹਿ ਏਕੈ ਦੇਖਤ ਮਨੁ ਪਤੀਆਹੀ ॥

"When I was, thou (wast) not. Now art thou and I am not.
Now I and thou have become One, my mind is assured seeing One (only)."

[3] Amar-dās says (Gauṛī, Asṭp. I., 7, 8, Transl. p. 331):

ਜੁਗ ਚਾਰੇ ਨਾਮੁ ਉਤਮੁ ਸਬਦੁ ਬੀਚਾਰਿ ॥
ਕਲਿ ਮਹਿ ਗੁਰਮੁਖਿ ਉਤਰਸਿ ਪਾਰਿ ॥
ਸਾਚਾ ਮਰੈ ਨ ਆਵੈ ਜਾਇ ॥
ਨਾਨਕ ਗੁਰਮੁਖਿ ਰਹੈ ਸਮਾਇ ॥

"In the four Yugas the name is the highest (thing); having reflected on the word (of the Guru),
The disciple will cross over (the water of existence) in the Kali-yug.
(When) the true (disciple) dies, he does not come nor go (again).
Nānak (says): the disciple remains absorbed (in the Supreme)."

There are innumerable passages of this kind in the Granth.

Austerities (ਤਪ), renunciation of the world and its pleasures (ਬੈਰਾਗ), bathing at holy watering-places (ਤੀਰਥ), the giving of alms (ਦਾਨ), are not denied to be meritorious acts; but they are by no means sufficient for gaining complete emancipation,[1] as they are not powerful enough to clear away egotism.[2] This can only the name of Hari effect, which washes away in a miraculous manner all the filth of sins,[3] liberates from all further transmigrations and reunites with Hari. The name of Hari is the universal medicine for mankind;[4] whoever mutters it, is saved in a moment.

This muttering of the name of Hari (ਜਪੁ) seems to be a very easy way of salvation; the Sikh Gurus however took good care, lest it should be made too easy, so that they themselves might be considered more or less superfluous guides. They taught therefore, that nobody was able to take the name of Hari by himself; any attempt of this kind was loudly declaimed against and severely condemned.[5] The name of Hari can only be obtained from the *true Guru* (ਸਤ ਗੁਰੁ), who alone can bestow the right initiation and communicate the mantra of the name of Hari.[6]

The Guru on his part again gives the name of Hari only to those on whose forehead this lot is written from the beginning.[7] We meet here again with the *decretum aeternum;* salvation by the name is by no means universal, but restricted to the elect;[8] they are chosen, not according to their meritorious works, but according to the pleasure of Hari, the leading principles of which

[1] Nānak says (Japjī, 21, Transl. p. 7):

"Tīrthas, austerity, mercy, gifts given: if one obtain (their merit), it is the honour of a sesam-seed."

[2] Nānak says (Sirī Rāg, Asṭp. XIV., 4, Transl. p. 86):

"Though I give (in charity) castles of gold and present many excellent horses and elephants.
Though I give land and many cows, yet (there is) egotism within (me)."

[3] Nānak says (Japǰī, 20, Transl. p. 7):

ਭਰੀਐ ਹਥ ਪੈਰੁ ਤਨੁ ਦੇਹ ॥ ਪਾਣੀ ਧੋਤੈ ਉਤਰਸੁ ਖੇਹ ॥
ਮੂਤ ਪਲੀਤੀ ਕਪੜੁ ਹੋਇ ॥ ਦੇ ਸਾਬੂਣੁ ਲਈਐ ਓਹੁ ਧੋਇ ॥
ਭਰੀਐ ਮਤਿ ਪਾਪਾ ਕੈ ਸੰਗਿ ॥ ਓਹੁ ਧੋਪੈ ਨਾਵੈ ਕੈ ਰੰਗਿ ॥

"If hand, foot, body, trunk become defiled: By washing with water the dust will be removed.
If the cloth be polluted by urine: By applying soap it will be washed.
If the intellect be defiled with sins: It is washed by the dye of the name."

[4] See Gauṛī, Sukhmanī IX., 5, Transl. p. 394.

[5] Nānak says (Gauṛī, Mah. I., Asṭp. XII., 5, Transl. p. 326):

ਬਿਨੁ ਦਮ ਕੇ ਸਉਦਾ ਨਹੀ ਹਾਟ ॥ ਬਿਨੁ ਬੋਹਿਥ ਸਾਗਰ ਨਹੀ ਵਾਟ ॥
ਬਿਨੁ ਗੁਰੁ ਸੇਵੇ ਘਾਟੇ ਘਾਟਿ ॥ *Cf.* Transl. p. 337, XXVIII., 4.

[6] See Gauṛī, Mah. I., Asṭp. XV., 4, Transl. p. 328.

[7] Arjun says (Gauṛī, Mah. V., Sukhmanī IX., 5, Transl. p. 394):

"The praising of the Beautiful one and the singing of (his) excellences
Is not obtained by any skill nor by any religious practice.
Nānak (says): he obtains it, to whom it is decreed by destiny itself."

It is nowhere hinted at, how the Guru knows, or finds out, to whom this lot has been decreed. The meeting of the disciple with the Guru, or *vice versâ*, of the Guru with the disciple, is therefore ascribed to a providential act of the Supreme, so that the disciple has in this very fact the badge of his salvation. Nānak says (Āsā, Mah. I., Sabd XVIII., 4, Transl. p. 501):

ਨਦਰਿ ਕਰੇ ਤਾ ਸਤਿ ਗੁਰੁ ਮਿਲੈ ॥ ਪ੍ਰਣਵਤਿ ਨਾਨਕੁ ਭਵ ਜਲੁ ਤਰੈ ॥

[8] Amar-dās says (Māǰh, Mah. III., Asṭp. I., 1, Transl. p. 153):

ਕਰਮੁ ਹੋਵੈ ਸਤਿ ਗੁਰ ਮਿਲਾਏ ॥

"(Whose) destiny it is, (him) the true Guru unites (with Hari)."

are nowhere hinted at, so that also the emancipation of the elect necessarily falls under the category of "*sport.*" This is occasionally expressed in very decisive terms. Thus says Arjun (Transl. p. 397, XI., 2): "If it please the Lord, man obtains salvation. If it please the Lord, he makes a stone cross. If it please the Lord, he rescues a sinner. He himself acts, he himself reflects. The inward governor sports and expands. What pleases him, that work he causes to be done."

But on the other hand it was felt that such a doctrine, if strictly carried out, would naturally render men thoroughly indifferent to their salvation, if nothing depended on their own exertion. We find it therefore stated in other passages of the Granth, that those, who are seeking the Lord, obtain him in their own heart; that with those, who are thirsting for the sight of the Lord, he will meet;[1] the people are frequently exhorted to come to the true Guru (Transl. p. 464, XVIII., 2) and to receive meekly his instruction, which necessarily presupposes in them a free decision for good or evil. The disciple is even warned not to come to the Guru for the sake of food,[2] as a mere bodily intercourse with the Guru will not save him (see Transl. p. 495, IV., 2–4).

We might naturally expect that Nānak would bring forward some proof that he himself really was the true Guru, sent and confirmed by the Supreme Lord. In the old Janam-Sākhī there is a tradition to this purport, that Nānak was called to the threshold of God and solemnly installed as Guru (see p. xi); but in the Granth itself we find no trace of it and Nānak never alludes to anything of this kind. It is everywhere presupposed as self-evident that he is the true Guru, and he never takes the slightest pains to prove it. The following Gurus in their turn appeal to Nānak, that he had instituted a successive initiation into the Guruship, and dispense therefore with every proof.

The Granth is full of the praise of the Guru, who in every way is extolled and magnified.[3] The Guru is the only infallible guide to complete emancipation (Transl. p. 95, VII., 1); he is the *mediator* (ਵਿਚੋਲਾ) between Hari and mankind, without whom nobody can become acceptable at the divine threshold; he is the boat (ਬੋਹਿਥੁ), that carries men over the water of existence (ਭਵ ਜਲ);[4] yea, he is the very fulness of Hari himself.[5]

The disciple has therefore to submit to the direction of the Guru unconditionally; mind and body he has to surrender to him, for his salvation depends entirely on the favour and mercy of the Guru, who freely disposes of the treasures of Hari. Bābā Nānak says (Transl. p. 209, XXV., Pauṛī): "If the true Guru become merciful, then (one's) wish is fulfilled. If the true Guru become merciful, the nine treasures are obtained. If the true Guru become merciful, then one is absorbed in the True one." Whatever the Guru does, is approved by Hari; whom the Guru unites with Hari, he remains united with him. The Guru is even possessed of a magic power: like as the philosopher's stone (ਪਾਰਸ) turns everything, that it is touching, into gold, so the Guru

[1] See Transl. p. 396, 6.

[2] The Gurus used to keep up a large cooking establishment to feed their disciples, no small attraction for a lazy hungry population. This was already the practice at the time of Bābā Nānak; see p. lxxv, l. 17. *Cf.* Transl. p. 699, VII.; p. 704, III.

[3] See a passage of this kind, Transl. p. 377, LV., last Slōk.

[4] Nānak says (Sirī Rāg, Mah. I., Sabd IX., 3, Transl. p. 26):

ਗੁਰੁ ਪਉੜੀ ਬੇੜੀ ਗੁਰੂ ਗੁਰੁ ਤੁਲਹਾ ਹਰਿ ਨਾਉ ॥
ਗੁਰੁ ਸਰੁ ਸਾਗਰੁ ਬੋਹਿਥੋ ਗੁਰੁ ਤੀਰਥੁ ਦਰੀਆਉ ॥
ਜੇ ਤਿਸੁ ਭਾਵੈ ਊਜਲੀ ਸਤ ਸਰਿ ਨਾਵਣ ਜਾਉ ॥

[5] Arjun says (Sirī Rāg, Mah. V., Sahd IX., 4, Transl. p. 64):

ਪਾਰ ਬ੍ਰਹਮੁ ਪ੍ਰਭੁ ਏਕੁ ਹੈ ਦੂਜਾ ਨਾਹੀ ਕੋਇ ॥
ਗੁਰਿ ਪੂਰੈ ਪੂਰਾ ਭਇਆ ਜਪਿ ਨਾਨਕ ਸਚਾ ਸੋਇ ॥

totally changes all, who come into contact with him. The saving power of the Guru is so extensive, that not only the greatest sinners are purified by him, but also his disciples become in their turn (apparently by some magical process)[1] the means of salvation to their respective families. This is taught in numberless passages of the Granth (see Transl. p. 43, V., 3; p. 390, 5).

That, which the Guru teaches the disciple for the sake of effecting his final emancipation, is, if we may trust the Granth, contained in a few meagre sentences.

The Guru gives the name of Hari to the disciple, which he is enjoined to mutter continually. He is required to repeat and sing the qualities (ਗੁਣ) of Hari, to meditate on them continually and never to forget them one moment from his mind. Then he is taught to clear away his own "I" and to consider himself identical with Brahm. This is the highest degree of knowledge, which is often alluded to, but nowhere more fully detailed. The Guru strives hard to surround himself with some mysterious halo, but in reality he has nothing to teach the disciple but the pantheistic sentence: "*Sō ham*," *i.e.* I am that, I am identical with the Supreme.[2] This knowledge and its effects are frequently described in glowing colours; the disciple gets thereby uncontaminated from the world and remains without any blemish, becomes purer than pure; darkness is dispelled and light diffused in his mind; he looks on all things as the same, pleasure and pain, friend and enemy; he is patient towards all, kind to all, he stops his running mind, destroys his egotism, in fact he is the Supreme Lord himself.[3]

To a disciple, who has reached this fourth[4] or highest step of the soul, religious works are no longer obligatory, as he is free from the Māyā and duality, and whatever he does, he must do with an indifferent mind, without any desire for future rewards.[5] The disciple must overcome all his desires and wishes, which are not directed on Hari, so completely, that he becomes totally *hopeless* (ਨਿਰਾਸ) in the world, that he dies, whilst living, being merged in meditation on Hari; thus he becomes emancipated whilst being as yet in the body, and when he dies, he does not come again.[6]

From the foregoing remarks it is plain enough, that in a religion, where the highest object

[1] Amar-dās (Sirī Rāg, Mah. III., Sabd III., 4, Transl. p. 42) says expressly:

ਪਾਰਸਿ ਪਰਸਿਐ ਪਾਰਸੁ ਹੋਇ ਜੋਤੀ ਜੋਤਿ ਸਮਾਇ ॥

[2] Nānak says (Sirī Rāg, Astp. XI., 8, Transl. p. 84):

ਬਿਨੁ ਗੁਰ ਪ੍ਰੀਤਿ ਨ ਊਪਜੈ ਹਉਮੈ ਮੈਲੁ ਨ ਜਾਇ ॥
ਸੋਹੰ ਆਪੁ ਪਛਾਣੀਐ ਸਬਦੁ ਭੇਦਿ ਪਤੀਆਇ ॥
ਗੁਰਮੁਖਿ ਆਪੁ ਪਛਾਣੀਐ ਅਵਰ ਕਿ ਕਰੇ ਕਰਾਇ ॥

[3] See Transl. p. 391, VIII., Astp. 1–6; p. 263, XXXIII., XXXIV.

[4] See about this fourth step (ਚਉਥੀ ਪਉੜੀ, ਚਉਥਾ ਪਦੁ or ਤੁਰੀਆ), Transl. p. 157, note 3; p. 522, II., 2, where a popular description of the four steps is given.

[5] Arjun says (Gauṛī, Sukhmanī, IX., Astp. 2, Transl. p. 393):

ਬੈਸਨੋ ਸੋ ਜਿਸੁ ਊਪਰਿ ਸੁਪ੍ਰਸੰਨ ॥ ਬਿਸਨ ਕੀ ਮਾਇਆ ਤੇ ਹੋਇ ਭਿੰਨ ॥
ਕਰਮ ਕਰਤ ਹੋਵੈ ਨਿਹਕਰਮ ॥ ਤਿਸੁ ਬੈਸਨੋ ਕਾ ਨਿਰਮਲ ਧਰਮ ॥
ਕਾਹੂ ਫਲ ਕੀ ਇਛਾ ਨਹੀ ਬਾਛੈ ॥ ਕੇਵਲ ਭਗਤਿ ਕੀਰਤਨ ਸੰਗਿ ਰਾਚੈ ॥

[6] Amar-dās says (Gauṛī, Mah. III., Astp. I., 8, Transl. p. 331):

ਸਾਚਾ ਮਰੈ ਨ ਆਵੈ ਜਾਇ ॥ ਨਾਨਕ ਗੁਰਮੁਖਿ ਰਹੈ ਸਮਾਇ ॥

Ibidem Astp. VII. 3, Transl. p. 335:

ਜੀਵਨਮੁਕਤੁ ਗੁਰਮੁਖਿ ਕੋ ਹੋਈ ॥ ਪਰਮ ਪਦਾਰਥੁ ਪਾਵੈ ਸੋਈ ॥
ਤ੍ਰੈਗੁਣ ਮੇਟੇ ਨਿਰਮਲੁ ਹੋਈ ॥ ਸਹਜੇ ਸਾਚਿ ਮਿਲੈ ਪ੍ਰਭੁ ਸੋਈ ॥

of life is the extinction of individual existence, there can be no room for a system of moral duties; we need therefore hardly point out, how wrong the statement of some authors is, that Sikhism is a *moralizing Deism.*

We have already noticed that the chief duty of the disciple is blind obedience to his Guru, and in the second place service to the saints. This latter point is considered quite essential to salvation and therefore frequently enjoined; the disciple should become the dust of the feet of the pious (ਸਾਧੁ), he should wash their feet and drink the water used in so doing; he should offer up his life to the pious and become their sacrifice. The society of the saints is the greatest blessing; for in their society all filth is removed, true knowledge of Brahm is obtained and the jewel of the name found, so that the gate of Hari (*i.e.* final emancipation) is naturally reached.[1] The other duties are summed up in the triad: ਨਾਮ, ਦਾਨ, ਇਸਨਾਨ, *i.e.* remembering the name, giving alms and practising ablutions; but the two latter duties, as in fact all, except the muttering of the name, are no longer required, when the highest step, the knowledge of Brahm, is obtained. Other duties are occasionally inculcated, as far as they tend towards the burning of egotism and the removal of duality, such as abstaining from falsehood and slander, not looking on another's wife, purifying the heart from the five vices, ਕਾਮ (lust), ਕ੍ਰੋਧ (wrath), ਲੋਭ (greediness), ਮੋਹ (infatuation or spiritual blindness) and ਅਹੰਕਾਰ (egotism).[2]

Charity to animal life is frequently inculcated in the Granth on pantheistic grounds (all creatures being considered alike), and in consequence abstinence from animal food;[3] but this injunction, which went right against the habits of the Jaṭ population of the Panjāb, was never observed and therefore silently dropped afterwards; only the killing of the cow was in later times interdicted as sacrilegious, though in the Granth itself no trace of a peculiar sanctity of the cow is to be found.

Remarkable it is, but quite in accordance with the pantheistic principles of the system, that prayer to the Supreme is hardly ever mentioned in the Granth,[4] whereas prayer to the Guru is frequently enjoined.[5]

The high position, which the Guru claimed for himself, naturally led to a *deification* of the same, and though Nānak spoke modestly of himself and confessed himself unlearned and the lowest of sinners,[6]

[1] Compare Gauṛī, Mah. V., Sukhmanī, XV., 6, Transl. p. 406, and VII., 1–8, Transl. p. 389.

[2] See Gauṛī, Mah. V., Sukhmanī, IX., 1, Transl. p. 393.

[3] Kabīr says (Transl. p. 682, *v.* 199):

ਕਬੀਰ ਜੀਅ ਜੁ ਮਾਰਹਿ ਜੋਰੁ ਕਰਿ ਕਹਤੇ ਹਹਿ ਜੁ ਹਲਾਲੁ ॥
ਦਫਤਰੁ ਦਈ ਜਬ ਕਾਢਿਹੈ ਹੋਇਗਾ ਕਉਨੁ ਹਵਾਲੁ ॥

[4] And even when prayer to the Supreme is mentioned, no object or contents of it are detailed, so that it seems to be a mere accommodation to popular notions. Arjun says (Transl. p. 387, V. 8):

ਕਰਉ ਬੇਨਤੀ ਪਾਰਬ੍ਰਹਮੁ ਸਭੁ ਜਾਨੈ ॥ ਅਪਨਾ ਕੀਆ ਆਪਹਿ ਮਾਨੈ ॥

And Transl. p. 502, XXI., 2:

ਸਚਾ ਅਰਜੁ ਸਚੀ ਅਰਦਾਸਿ ॥ ਮਹਲੀ ਖਸਮੁ ਸੁਣੇ ਸਾਬਾਸਿ ॥
ਸਚੈ ਤਖਤਿ ਬੁਲਾਵੈ ਸੋਇ ॥ ਦੇਇ ਵਡਿਆਈ ਕਰੇ ਸੁ ਹੋਇ ॥

[5] Nānak says (Sirī Rāg, Mah. I., Asṭp. IV., 5, Transl. p. 77):

ਸਤਿ ਗੁਰ ਅਗੈ ਅਰਦਾਸਿ ਕਰਿ ਸਾਜਨੁ ਦੇਇ ਮਿਲਾਇ ॥
ਸਾਜਨਿ ਮਿਲਿਐ ਸੁਖੁ ਪਾਇਆ ਜਮ ਦੂਤ ਮੁਏ ਬਿਖੁ ਖਾਇ ॥

[6] Nānak says humbly of himself (Āsā, Mah. I., Sabd XXIX., 2, Transl. p. 505):

ਨਾ ਹਉ ਜਤੀ ਸਤੀ ਨਹੀ ਪੜਿਆ ਮੂਰਖ ਮੁਗਧਾ ਜਨਮੁ ਭਇਆ ॥
ਪ੍ਰਣਵਤਿ ਨਾਨਕ ਤਿਨ ਕੀ ਸਰਣਾ ਜਿਨ ਤੂੰ ਨਾਹੀ ਵਿਸਾਰਿਆ ॥

It is incomprehensible, how the later tradition, in the face of confessions of this kind, could deem Nānak to be an Avatār.

the following Gurus soon commenced, owing to the abject flattery of their adherents, to identify the Guru with the Supreme himself.[1] The consequence was such a deification of man as has hardly ever been heard of elsewhere. Life, property and honour were sacrificed to the Guru in a way, which is often revolting to our moral feelings. It was therefore a very fortunate event for the more free and moral development of the Sikh community, that, with the tenth Guru Gōvind Singh, the Guruship was altogether abolished.

With precepts of this kind the disciples of Nānak would have sunk into a state of dull apathy to the world around them, or they would have led a contemplative life in monasteries, as the Buddhists did, if Nānak, cautioned by his many disputes and contentions with the Jōgīs, and convinced by practical experience of the wickedness and hypocrisy of the erratic Faqīrs, had not enjoined to them, to remain in their secular occupation and not to leave the world. It is owing to this sound principle, that the Sikhs have not become a narrow-minded sect of Faqīrs, but that they developed themselves by degrees into a political commonwealth.

Nānak and his followers taught, that the state of a householder (ਗ੍ਰਿਸਤੀ) was equally acceptable to Hari as retirement from the world,[2] and that secular business was no obstacle to the attainment of final emancipation. Salvation does not depend on outward circumstances, neither on the performance of austerities,[3] but on the inward state of the mind, which even amongst the daily business of life may remain absorbed in meditation on Hari (this kind of devotion is called ਰਾਜਜੋਗ or ਰਾਜਨਜੋਗ). The evil practices of the mendicant Faqīrs as well as the rogueries of the Brāhmaṇs are therefore frequently exposed in the Granth and severely censured. By such pious tricks transmigration cannot be overcome, but the soul gets on the contrary still more sullied and depraved.

The institution of *caste* was not directly assailed by Nānak, though he and the other Bhagats did not put any stress upon it. He expresses his mind on this point very clearly by saying (Transl. p. 494, III., Pause): "Thou (O God) acknowledgest the light (that is in him) and dost not ask after (his) caste. For in the other world there is no caste" (*cf.* also Transl. p. 114, III., Slōk I.). Kabīr even occasionally ridicules it, as well as the Brāhmaṇ and the Mullā. Emancipation is not confined to the higher castes, but made accessible to all men, even to the Čaṇḍāl.[4] Different stories are therefore cited in the Granth, that even the lowest men attained to salvation by muttering the name.[5] Nānak received all men as his disciples without any regard to caste, recognizing in

[1] Guru Arjun, who oversteps all bounds in the praise of the Guru, says for instance (Sirī Rāg, Mah. V., Sabd XXIX., 2, Transl. p. 73):

ਗੁਰੁ ਸਮਰਥੁ ਅਪਾਰ ਗੁਰੁ ਵਡਭਾਗੀ ਦਰਸਨੁ ਹੋਇ ॥
ਗੁਰੁ ਅਗੋਚਰੁ ਨਿਰਮਲਾ ਗੁਰ ਜੇਵਡੁ ਅਵਰੁ ਨ ਕੋਇ ॥
ਗੁਰੁ ਕਰਤਾ ਗੁਰੁ ਕਰਣਹਾਰੁ ਗੁਰਮੁਖਿ ਸਾਚੀ ਸੋਇ ॥

That really the Guru (not the Supreme) is meant by these words, is clearly seen from *v.* 3, where he says:

ਗੁਰੁ ਦਾਤਾ ਹਰਿ ਨਾਮੁ ਦੇਇ ਉਧਰੈ ਸਭੁ ਸੰਸਾਰੁ ॥

[2] Arjun says (Āsā, Mah. V., Sabd CLVII., 2, Transl. p. 573):

ਥਿਰ ਥਿਰ ਚਿਤ ਥਿਰ ਹਾਂ ॥ ਬਨੁ ਗ੍ਰਿਹੁ ਸਮਸਰਿ ਹਾਂ ॥
ਅੰਤਰਿ ਏਕ ਪਿਰ ਹਾਂ ॥ ਬਾਹਰਿ ਅਨੇਕ ਧਰਿਹਾਂ ॥
ਰਾਜਨਜੋਗ ਕਰਿਹਾਂ ॥ ਗੁਰ ਸਿਉ ਨੇਤ ਪਿਆਨਿ ਹਾਂ ॥

[3] Kabīr ridicules occasionally outward austerities; he says (Transl. p. 664, IV., 2):

ਜਲ ਕੈ ਮਜਨਿ ਜੇ ਗਤਿ ਹੋਵੈ ਨਿਤ ਨਿਤ ਮੇਂਡੁਕ ਨਾਵਹਿ ॥
ਜੈਸੇ ਮੇਂਡੁਕ ਤੈਸੇ ਓਇ ਨਰ ਫਿਰਿ ਫਿਰਿ ਜੋਨੀ ਆਵਹਿ ॥

[4] See Transl. p. 430, XVII., Pauṛī.

[5] See Transl. p. 489, Nāmdēv.

all the dignity of the human birth, and laid thus the foundation of a popular religion, and it was quite in accordance with these principles, that Guru Gōvind Singh finally abolished caste altogether in the Khālsā, though the deeply-rooted prejudices of the higher castes refused to submit to it.

The dignity of the Brāhmaṇs as family priests, etc., was likewise left untouched, and of nearly all the Gurus it is reported, that they had their family priests, though the teaching of the Brāhmaṇs, as well as the authority of the Vēdas and Purāṇas, is often reproved.[1] It was the last Guru, Gōvind Singh, who positively prohibited the employment of Brāhmaṇs in any capacity, and introduced a new ritual partly taken from the Granth, and partly from his own compositions.

From the foregoing sketch of the Sikh religion, as laid down in the Granth, we must well distinguish the popular notions of the masses. The vulgar are nowhere given to lofty metaphysical speculations; their ideas are concrete and adapted to their every-day wants. Pantheism has never been the religion of a whole nation, or of any large body of men, not even in India, the home of Pantheism. In spite of all the definitions of the Granth, the common people constructed for themselves a God such as they required for their outward and inward wants. The teaching of the Granth gradually disaccustomed them from idolatry and the worship of the inferior deities, and impressed them with the idea of One Supreme Lord, whom however they could not realize under the abstract notion of an Absolute Substance, but only as a personal, self-conscious Supreme Being, who created all and governs and disposes all according to his will. It is not improbable, that the Islām had a great share in working silently these changes, which are directly opposed to the teaching of their Gurus. The mass of the Sikh population is now at all events thoroughly imbued with these deistic notions and even educated Sikhs were quite astonished, when I proved to them the contrary from the Granth. I met only a very few devotees, who, being fairly read in the Granth, knew about "the secret."

Guru Gōvind Singh did not and could not essentially change the teaching of his predecessors. He describes the Supreme Being nearly in the same terms in his Jāpjī, as the Ādi Granth does, though he was personally addicted to the worship of the goddess Durgā; he made the worship of the One Supreme obligatory, though the adoration of the minor deities, as we are taught by his own Granth, was by no means rejected.[2]

The changes and additions he made in Sikhism concerned chiefly the ceremonial and social duties of his adherents; as he received men of all castes and creeds into the Khālsā and endeavoured

[1] Nānak says (Āsā, Mah. I., Sabd XXI., 4, Transl. p. 502):

ਪੰਡਿਤ ਪੜਹਿ ਵਖਾਣਹਿ ਵੇਦੁ ॥ ਅੰਤਰਿ ਵਸਤੁ ਨ ਜਾਣੈ ਭੇਦੁ ॥
ਗੁਰ ਬਿਨੁ ਸੋਝੀ ਬੂਝ ਨ ਹੋਇ ॥ ਸਾਚਾ ਰਵਿ ਰਹਿਆ ਪ੍ਰਭੁ ਸੋਇ ॥

[2] The Rahit-nāmās go in this respect much farther, condemning all other worship but that of the One Supreme. The Rahit-nāmā of Prahlād-rāi says, *v.* 13:

ਅਕਾਲ ਪੁਰਖ ਕੋ ਛਾਡਿਕੈ ਭਜੈ ਦੇਵ ਕੋ ਅਉਰ ॥
ਜਨਮ ਜਨਮ ਭਰਮਤ ਫਿਰੈ ਲਹੈ ਨ ਸੁਖ ਕੀ ਠਉਰ ॥

The worship of idols is also positively forbidden in the Rahit-nāmās; see Prahlād-rāi, *v.* 14:

ਪਾਹਨ ਕੀ ਪੂਜਾ ਕਰੈ ਸਿਖ ਬਿਨ ਨਿਵਾਵੈ ਸੀਸ ॥
ਸੋ ਸਾਕਤ ਨਿਗੁਰਾ ਸਦਾ ਸ੍ਰਾਪਿਆ ਸ੍ਰੀ ਜਗਦੀਸ ॥

"Who adores a stone and bows his head to any one but a Sikh:
He is a Sākat (and) without a Guru, he is always cursed by the Lord of the world."

to weld them into one religious and political body, he set up a number of new ordinances binding on all. These injunctions are laid down in a number of so-called *Rahit-nāmās* or books of conduct,[1] which all pretend to be dictated by the Guru himself, but none of which appear to be genuine, as they vary very greatly, and were, as may be easily proved, all composed after the death of the Guru, some of them even as late as the end of the last century. They cannot therefore be adduced as a direct testimony of what Gōvind Singh himself ordained and introduced into the Khālsā, but only as an evidence of the later development of Sikhism.

The initiatory rite into the Khālsā is the Pāhuḷ, which has already been described (p. xc). It is generally administered by five Sikhs and not before the attainment of years of discretion; its administration is considered very meritorious, and by instructing a disciple in the doctrines of the Guru, one will get final emancipation even whilst living.[2]

Every Sikh is enjoined to read the Granth for his devotion, especially the Japjī of Nānak and the Jāpjī of Gōvind Singh; these two he should always read when taking his meals.[3] In the morning he is to repeat some portion of the Granth, and when beginning any work he is to say an Ardās (ਅਰਦਾਸਿ, prayer, supplication).[4] In the evening, when taking his food, he is to read the Rahirās (ਰਹਿਰਾਸਿ, supplication),[5] consisting of selections from the Ādi Granth (see Transl. p. 14, Sō daru, note 1), to which in later times also some portions from the Granth of Gōvind Singh were added. As these religious duties took up a great deal of time, they were seldom observed by the vulgar, and are now generally neglected. They content themselves with uttering the ground-mantra (ਪਰਮ ਬੀਜ): ਸਤਿ ਅਕਾਲ ਸ੍ਰੀ ਗੁਰੂ.

[1] Two of these Rahit-nāmās have lately been published in an English translation by Sirdār Attar Singh of Bhadouṛ; but it is a pity that he has not given the Gurmukhī text also. The translation is very free and gives only the sense generally, not verbally. Fortunately I brought the original text of the Rahit-nāmā of Prahlād-rāi with me, so that I am enabled, for the sake of accuracy, to quote it, where it may seem necessary. The title of Sirdār Attar Singh's publication is: "The Rayhit Nama of Pralad Rai, or the excellent conversation of the Daswan Padsha, and Nand Lal's Rayhit Nama, or rules for the guidance of the Sikhs in religious matters." Lahore, printed at the Albert Press, 1876.

[2] Prahlād-rāi says, *v.* 28:

ਸਿਖ ਕੋ ਸਿਖ ਜੋ ਅਮ੍ਰਿਤ ਦੀਨਾ ॥ ਕੋਟ ਅਸਮੇਧ ਜਗ ਫਲ ਲੀਨਾ ॥
ਜੋ ਗੁਰ ਕੀ ਬਾਣੀ ਸਿਖ ਲਾਵੈ ॥ ਜੀਵਨ ਮੁਕਤਿ ਪਦਾਰਥ ਪਾਵੈ ॥

[3] Prahlād-rāi, *v.* 10:

ਬਿਨ ਜਪ ਜਾਪ ਜਪੇ ਬਿਨਾ ਜੋ ਜੇਵੈ ਪ੍ਰਸਾਦਿ ॥ ਸੋ ਬਿਸਟਾ ਕਾ ਕ੍ਰਿਮ ਹੋਇ ਜਨਮ ਗਵਾਇਓ ਬਾਦਿ ॥

This injunction would presuppose, that every Sikh should be able to read, but this was never the case and no means whatever were taken to secure this end.

[4] According to a note of Sirdār Attar Singh to Nand Lāl's Rahit-nāmā, p. 5, the Sikhs read as Ardās the first verses from Gōvind Singh's story of Bhagavatī, called ਚੰਡੀ ਕੀ ਵਾਰ, the first lines of which run thus: "The goddess Bhagavatī was first worshipped by Guru Nānak; then by Gurus Angad, Amar-dās and Rām-dās, and to them she was propitious. Then followed Gurus Arjun, Har-rāi, Har-gōvind and Tēg-bahādur, and they also rose to the highest honours. Guru Gōvind Singh was also assisted by her."

[5] ਰਹਿਰਾਸਿ (thus it is written in the Granth, see Rāg Āsā, Mah. IV., IV., Pause, Transl. p. 15) signifies *prayer, supplication;* its derivation is not known. It is frequently now spelt ਰਹੁਰਾਸਿ, hence the transcription of Sirdār Attar Singh "Row Rass." He details in the Rahit-nāmā of Nand Lāl, p. 4, note *, the component parts of the Ardās as now in use among the Sikhs. In reference to the morning and evening prayer the following verse is contained in Prahlād-rāi's Rahit-nāmā (*v.* 12):

ਪ੍ਰਾਤਕਾਲ ਗੁਰ ਗੀਤ ਨ ਗਾਵੈ ॥ ਰਹਿਰਾਸ ਬਿਨਾ ਪ੍ਰਸਾਦ ਜੋ ਖਾਵੈ ॥
ਬਾਹਰਮੁਖੀ ਸਿਖ ਤਿਹ ਜਾਨੋ ॥ ਸਭ ਵਰਤਨ ਤਿਸ ਭਿਖਿਆ ਮਾਨੋ ॥

Temples, shrines and burning places are not to be worshipped, nor are other religions to be praised.[1] The Vēdas, Shāstras, Purāṇas and the Qur'ān are not to be minded, neither the Panḍit nor the Mullā. All Hindū and Musalmān rites are to be discontinued; the Hindū ceremonies at the time of birth, marriage and death should not be observed; no Shrādh should be performed, and if it be performed, the words of the Granth should be used. No Tilak should be applied to the forehead, nor should the sacred cord (ਜਨੇਊ) nor a rosary (ਮਾਲਾ) be worn; circumcision should not be practised.

A Sikh is never to wear a cap (ਟੋਪੀ), nor to shave his head or beard, nor to wear red clothes.[2] He should bathe in cold water, comb his hair twice every day and bind his turban after adjusting the tresses; he is never to take off his turban whilst taking his food. He is to clean his teeth every day with a tooth-stick. He should always wear breeches (ਕਛ, the Hindū Dhōtī being a forbidden article), and have steel about his person, especially a sword.

The use of tobacco in any shape is prohibited.[3] Gambling, especially the play of Čaupaṛ (ਚਉਪੜ, a kind of chess), and visiting prostitutes, deserve severe punishment.

A Sikh should never buy meat from a butcher, but eat only the flesh of such animals whose head was severed by a Sikh with one stroke of the sword; this kind of slaughtering animals is called ਝਟਕਾ. Beef is not even so much as mentioned in the Rahit-nāmās, as its use was altogether considered abominable. To eat of the leavings of the meal of another entails the pain of death.

Especial attention is paid to the making and distributing of the Kaṛāh Prasād (ਕੜਾਹ ਪ੍ਰਸਾਦ), which in some way resembles the Communion Service of Christians, the Kaṛāh Prasād being consecrated to the Guru and in his name given to eat to the assembled votaries. It should be made of equal quantities of ghī, flour and sugar. The cooking-place should first be swept clean and then plastered with cow-dung; the cooking utensils should likewise be well washed. The Sikh, who prepares the Prasād, should enter the cooking-place after bathing and purifying himself, and only utter: vāh Guru! He should fill a new jar with water, drawn from a well with an iron bucket, and place it at his side. When the Kaṛāh Prasād is ready, it should be put on a stand, and the people should sit round it praying (*i.e.* saying: vāh Guru!). It should be distributed to all in equal portions.[4]

The disciple is strictly to obey the orders of the Guru and never to forsake him; apostacy is visited with the severest punishments; he is also to minister to his brother Sikhs.[5] He is to pay taxes, if demanded by the Guru;[6] the withholding of the customary offerings of the tenth

[1] Prahlād-rāi says, *v.* 20:

ਮੜ੍ਹੀ ਗੋਰ ਦੇਵਲ ਜੋ ਮਾਨੈ ॥ ਪਰਪੰਚਨ ਕੇ ਉਚ ਬਖਾਨੈ ॥
ਸੋ ਮਾਰਗ ਸਿਖ ਗੁਰੂ ਕਾ ਨਾਹੀ ॥ ਫਾਸਿ ਪਰਿਓ ਜਮ ਫੰਦਨ ਮਾਹੀ ॥

[2] The custom of wearing blue clothes (in remembrance of Gōvind Singh making his escape in blue clothes) soon fell into disuse; only the Akālīs preserved this custom. See p. cxviii, note 2.

[3] Prahlād-rāi says, *v.* 9:

ਸੂਹੇ ਅੰਬਰ ਪਹਿਨ ਕਰਿ ਮੁਖ ਨਾਸੇ ਨਸਵਾਰ ॥ ਲਏ ਤਾੜਨਾ ਸੀਸ ਪਰ ਸੁਟੀਏ ਨਰਕ ਮੰਝਾਰ ॥

[4] The Kaṛāh Prasād and its preparation is described in Nand Lāl's Rahit-nāmā, p. i, 8.

[5] Prahlād-rāi says, *v.* 8:

ਮੇਰੇ ਹੁਕਮ ਮਾਨੇ ਨਹੀ ਕਰੇ ਨ ਸਿਖ ਕੀ ਸੇਵ ॥ ਸੋ ਧੀਰਜ ਮਲੇਛ ਕੇ ਪ੍ਰਗਟਿ ਪਛਾਨੇ ਭੇਵ ॥

[6] Prahlād-rāi says, *v.* 7:

ਹੁਕਮ ਦੇਖ ਕਾਰ ਨਹੀ ਗਾਧੈ ॥ ਗੋਲਕ ਗੋਪ ਮਿਥਿਆ ਮੁਖ ਭਾਖੈ ॥
ਕਾੜ ਭੇਟ ਸੁਖ ਮੰਨਤ ਚੁਰਾਵੈ ॥ ਐਸਾ ਸਿਖ ਗੁਰੂ ਨਹੀ ਭਾਵੈ ॥

"Who, having seen the order (of the Guru), does not pay taxes. Who, having hid the money-box (in which the

part of his income, the defrauding of the Khālsā and others deputed by the Guru, is severely censured. He should consider only the precepts of the Guru as true and all others as false.[1] The Granth is to be minded like the Guru, and the Khālsā like the Guru, as it is the visible body of the Guru, (and in consequence) the visible body of the Timeless one.[2] The persons, to whom the Guru gives authority (or a Hukm-nāmā), should be equally obeyed, and those, who set themselves up as rivals with them, should be burnt with their families.[3]

With regard to his family the Sikh is enjoined to dispose suitably of his daughter (or sister) and not to take any money for her hand.[4] The killing of daughters is strictly forbidden.

Among the moral duties truthfulness and kindness to the poor are especially inculcated; falsehood, dealing fraudulently, stealing, slandering and fornication, are branded as deadly sins. A Sikh should earnestly strive to subdue the five passions: lust (ਕਾਮ), wrath (ਕ੍ਰੋਧ), greediness (ਲੋਭ), infatuation (ਮੋਹ), and pride (ਹੰਕਾਰ).

The injunctions regarding the intercourse with people of other creeds evince already a narrow-minded bigotry and a deep fanatical hatred.

A Sikh is not even to salute one, who is not a Sikh, otherwise he is an apostate and accursed by God. Who bows his head to one, who wears a cap (*i.e.* a Muhammadan) or shaves his head (*i.e.* a Hindū), is doubtless worthy of hell.[5] He is not even to place a piece of cloth or anything belonging to a Muhammadan on his head, otherwise he will suffer many deaths.[6] A true Sikh should always be engaged in war with the Muhammadans and slay them, fighting them face to face; it is his duty to destroy the enemies of his faith,[7] and to help in the diffusion of the

money, set aside for the Guru, is put), talks falsehood with his mouth. Who, acknowledging the vow of an offering of taxes, steals (them); such a disciple is not pleasing to the Guru." Compare also Nand Lāl's Rahit-nāmā, p. 3, 24.

[1] The Rahit-nāmā of Nand Lāl (p. 6, 46) has the further injunction: "Do not listen to any calumny respecting the Guru, and he who speaks ill of the Guru, must be killed with a sword." In this way the infallibility of the Guru could easily be kept up.

[2] Prahlād-rāi says, *v.* 21:

ਗੁਰੂ ਖਾਲਸਾ ਮਾਨਿਐ ਪ੍ਰਗਟਿ ਗੁਰੂ ਕੀ ਦੇਹਿ ॥
ਜੋ ਸੋ ਕੋ ਮਿਲਬੋ ਚਹੈ ਖੋਜ ਇਨ੍ਹ ਮਹਿ ਲੇਹਿ ॥

"The Khālsā should be minded as the Guru, it is the manifest body of the Guru.
Who desires to meet with me, he having searched finds me in them."

And in *v.* 24 he says:

ਅਕਾਲ ਪੁਰਖ ਕੀ ਮੂਰਤਿ ਏਹਾ ॥ ਪ੍ਰਗਟਿ ਅਕਾਲ ਖਾਲਸਾ ਦੇਹਾ ॥

"This one is the shape of the timeless divine male. The Khālsā is the visible body of the Timeless one."

[3] Prahlād-rāi says, *v.* 15:

ਕਰੀ ਥਾਪਨਾ ਜਾਸ ਕੀ ਸੋਊ ਆਨੇ ਹਾਥ ॥ ਤਿਨ ਕੀ ਸਮਸਰਿ ਜੋ ਕਰੈ ਜਰਿ ਜਾਵੈ ਕੁਲ ਸਾਥ ॥

[4] See Nand Lāl's Rahit-nāmā, p. 3, 16, 17.

[5] Prahlād-rāi says, *v.* 20:

ਟੋਪੀ ਦੇਖ ਨਿਵਾਵੈ ਸੀਸੁ ॥ ਸੋ ਸਿਖ ਨਰਕੀ ਬਿਸਵੇਬੀਸੁ ॥

[6] See Nand Lāl's Rahit-nāmā, p. 2, 9.

[7] These duties are frequently inculcated. See Nand Lāl's Rahit-nāma, p. 7, 62, 64; p. 9, 73, 77, 79.

Sikh religion.[1] No confidence whatever should be placed in Jōgīs (who are contemptuously called ਕਾਨ ਫਟਾ, ear-cropt) and Turks.[2]

Towards the Sikh sectarians the same implacable hatred is evinced. A true Sikh should abstain from all intercourse with the following people, who are accursed (excommunicated) by the Guru: (1) the Mīṇē (ਮੀਣੇ), the progeny of Pirthīmall;[3] (2) the Dhīrmalliē (ਧੀਰਮੱਲੀਏ), the progeny of Dhīrmall (see p. lxxxii, note); (3) the Rāmrāīe (ਰਾਮਰਾਈਏ), the disciples of Rām-rāi, the son of Guru Har-rāi (see p. lxxvi, l. 27 *sqq.*); (4) the Masands, the former deputies of the Guru (see p. xciii, last line and note 2); (5) the head-plucked ones (ਸਿਰਗੁੰਮ, *i.e.* the Jainas, who are now called in the Panjāb ਸਰਾਵਗੀ or ਨਾਸਤਿਕ, atheists). To these are added as equally heinous (6) those who kill their daughters (ਕੁੜੀਮਾਰ).[4]

There are some other injunctions of minor importance, which are hardly worth mentioning, such as: not to blow out a lamp with the mouth; not to extinguish fire with water, from which one has been drinking; not to remain naked from the waist downwards at night; not to bathe without a ਕਛ (or breeches); not to distribute food without being fully dressed, etc.

We see from these minute ordinances, that the Sikh reformatory movement soon ended again in a new bondage, which was quite as tiresome as that which they had thrown off. By precepts of this kind the Sikhs, the majority of whom consisted of rude and ignorant Jaṭs, could morally but little be improved, as no provision whatever was made to raise them to a higher standard of education and culture, Guru Gōvind Singh being only intent on rendering them subservient to his will and on kindling their martial valour and hatred against the Muhammadans. We need therefore not be surprised, that they soon surpassed their fellow-countrymen in all sorts of vices and debauchery, to which they added a rapacious and overbearing conduct, so that they became a regular scourge to the country, after they had succeeded in overthrowing the Muhammadan power. They could easily destroy by their martial fury an old weak establishment, but were not able to erect a new solid fabric upon its ruins, as they had not in themselves the necessary moral and intellectual capacities.

In conclusion we have to notice some denominations, which sprang up in the bosom of the Sikh community.

(1). *The Udāsīs.* This body was founded by Sirī Čand, the eldest son of Nānak. There are four subdivisions amongst them, who only differ from each other by some outward signs. They no more marry, after they have given up their household (ਗਿਰਿਸਤ) and turned Udāsīs (*i.e.* indifferent

[1] See Nand Lāl's Rahit-nāmā, p. 9, 80. The spreading of Sikhism by force of arms is here clearly enjoined. No wonder therefore, if the Sikhs became gradually more fanatical than the Muhammadans.

[2] Prahlād-rāi says, *v.* 22:

ਕਾਨ ਫਟੇ ਅਰ ਤੁਰਕ ਕਾ ਕਰੇ ਨਾ ਭੂਲ ਬਿਸਾਹਿ ॥ ਜੋ ਸਿਖ ਸੋਂ ਹਿਤ ਨਾ ਕਰੈ ਪਰੈ ਨਰਕ ਮੈ ਜਾਇ ॥

"He should by no means put any confidence in an ear-cropt one and in a Turk.
Who does not entertain love with a Sikh, goes to hell."

[3] We have stated p. lxxx, note 1, that it was not quite clear, if Rām-dās had two or three sons. But from the Sikhā̃ dē rāǰ dī vithiā, p. 57, l. 15 *sqq.*, and a note of Sirdār Attar Singh to his translation of the Rahit-nāmā of Prahlād-rāi, p. 1, we find that he had three sons. The name of the eldest son was Pirthīmall, that of the second Arjun, and that of the third Dhīrmall. The Mīṇē are therefore not the disciples of Dhīrmall, as supposed on p. lxxxii, note 2, but the descendants of Pirthīmall, who had tried to poison his younger brother Arjun, on whom the Guruship had been conferred, and who was therefore called by his father ਮੀਣਾ ਚੋਰ, a contemptible thief.

[4] Prahlād-rāi says, *v.* 18:

ਕੁੜੀਮਾਰ ਮਸੰਦ ਕਾ ਮੀਣੇ ਕਾ ਪ੍ਰਸਾਦਿ ॥ ਲਏ ਜੋ ਇਨ ਤੇ ਹਾਥ ਕਾ ਜਨਮ ਗੁਵਾਵੈ ਬਾਦਿ ॥

to the world); they are therefore a society of monks, though they do not live together in monasteries. Some of them do not cut their hair, like the regular Sikhs, some have short-cut hair (ਘਾਵਰੀਆਂ), some wear long tufted hair (ਜਟਾਉ), and some shave head and face. They practise the Hindū rites concerning birth, death,[1] marriage and Shrādh, as all the old Sikhs did. They wear clothes dyed with red ochre (ਗਿਰਮਟੀ) and apply to their forehead a high Tilak. Their sacred book is the Ādi Granth, whereas they reject the Granth of Gōvind Singh. Formerly they were very strict in their religious duties and led an ascetic life, subsisting on coarse bread, baked on live coals (ਅਧੂਕਰੀ), which they begged. As they obstinately advocated a mode of life, which was irreconcilable with secular occupations, and as they refused to submit to the authority of the established Gurus, Guru Amar-dās eliminated them from the Sikh community and they were thence no longer acknowledged as Sikhs, though they themselves never gave up this claim. The Udāsīs have set up a Guruship of their own, and after the death of a Guru some disciple, whom the Guru has elected, assumes the spiritual authority; they address each other by the title of ਭਾਈ (brother). Their devotional service is very simple; in the morning and evening they play a violin or a rebeck and sing a song of praise (ਕੀਰਤਨ) to the Supreme Lord, which is mostly taken from the Granth, imitating in this way the simple worship of Bābā Nānak.

The Udāsīs were always a small body, as their principles found no favour with the population. Now-a-days they have much deviated from their former ascetic habits and have for the greater part taken to secular occupations, differing only by some outward tokens from other people. Some of them bore a hole through their privities and insert a large ring of iron or brass to prevent them from fornication (ਬਿਭਚਾਰ).

(2). *The Suthrē* (Sing. ਸੁਥਰਾ, pure). Their founder is said to have been a Brāhmaṇ, named Sūčā (ਸੁਚਾ); they took their origin under Guru Har-rāi.[2] This body, which is still to be found in nearly every town of the Panjāb, has greatly degenerated; they are notorious for their drunkenness and debauchery, so that they have become a by-word in the Panjāb, being just the contrary of what their name implies. It is stated, that they obtained from one of the former Emperors a written order, that every shopkeeper should give them one Paisā as alms; they wander therefore continually about the Bāzārs, begging and clashing together two staves (ਡੰਡਾ). On their head and neck they wear a rope of black wool and keep two staves in their hand; to their forehead they apply a Tilak of black colour. They perform the usual Hindū rites, make Shrādhs and erect tombs over the ashes of a burnt corpse of a member of their order; the bones they collect and throw into the Gangā. With meditation and worship they do not trouble themselves very much; they recite the verses of Nānak, which they partly learn by heart, and sing some praises in honour of the Dēvī. They visit the Dēhrās (shrines) of the ten Gurus and make offerings there. They all add the title of "Shāh" (literally *King*) to their names, as Ravīl-shāh, etc. They have a Guruship of their own and receive novices (ਚੇਲਾ), but there is no order nor regular discipline among them; now mostly profligates and vagabonds join them. They are a public nuisance, like so many other mendicant orders, and disavowed by the Sikhs.

(3). *The Divānē Sādh* (ਦਿਵਾਨੇ ਸਾਧ, the mad saints). They keep their hair uncut, like the Sikhs, and wear on their neck a necklace of shells (ਸੰਖ ਦੀ ਮਾਲਾ) and on their turban a very large feather (ਕਲਗਾ); they consist for the greater part of Jaṭs and tanners (ਚਮਾਰ). Their devotional service consists in muttering the true name (ਸਤ ਨਾਮ). Most of them are married, but some few remain also unmarried. In their other habits they are like the Sikhs and acknowledge the Ādi Granth as their sacred book.

[1] They burn their dead, but always erect a tomb (ਸਮਾਧ) over their ashes, like the Jōgīs and Sanyāsīs.

[2] Wilson, Religious Sects of the Hindūs, p. 177, states, that they look up to Tēg-bahādur as their founder. What authority he had for this statement is not mentioned by him.

(4). *The Nirmalē Sādhū* (the pure saints). These people were originally strict Sikhs and followed exclusively the Granth and the regulations of Gōvind Singh; they stood in high esteem with the Sikh community and exercised great influence on the people. Formerly they used to wear white clothes and dwelt at Amritsar, Mukt-sar and other places, which are sacred to the Sikhs (as Damdamā, etc.), but in the course of time they gradually relapsed into Hindūism by applying their mind to the Shāstras and especially the Vēdānta. In consequence of this internal change of mind their outward habits also underwent some changes; they deposed their white robes and adopted the common garb of the Hindū Faqīrs, consisting of reddish-yellow clothes. They also now visit the holy watering-places on the Gangā and Jamnā and conform to nearly all the Hindū rites. At the time of birth and death they perform the Vēdic ceremonies and burn their dead, but do not use the Hindū mantras at weddings. They are now in a state of transition and deeply tinged with Hindū notions, so that they can no longer be considered as regular Sikhs. They live mostly together in separate societies under a Guru and choose celibacy; there is some learning cultivated among them and even Sanskrit studies are to some extent attended to. They do not beg, but live on the offerings of the people; they receive men of all castes into their society, as within the brotherhood no caste is acknowledged. They have a large establishment at Amritsar, where they are much respected by the people for the purity of their morals.[1]

(5). *The Akālīs* (the worshippers of the ਅਕਾਲ, or Timeless Being). This body is said to have been instituted by Guru Gōvind Singh himself. They were the zealots among the Sikhs, who watched over the purity of their religion and withstood firmly the innovations,[2] which the Bairāgī Bandā, who after the death of Gōvind Singh assumed the leadership among the Sikhs in the Panjāb, endeavoured to introduce into Sikhism. They wear blue chequered clothes and bangles or bracelets of steel round their wrists and frequently also a discus of steel on their turban. They established themselves in great numbers at Amritsar, where they assumed the direction of the religious ceremonies and acted the parts of defenders of the faith in the days of Sikh independency, as they assumed the right of convoking a Gur-matā (a national council, literally: the Guru's advice) and directing its consultations. Thus they became a formidable body, which was dreaded even by the Sikh chiefs, as they were always ripe for a fanatical outbreak. They lived on the offerings of the people, which they often extorted by force. As they were in fact more a political than a religious body, their influence ceased with the destruction of the Sikh community, and now-a-days they are hardly taken notice of; they are gradually dwindling away like Sikhism itself, in whose bosom of late even an atheistic or materialistic sect has sprung up, that of the *Gulāb-dāsīs*, who deny every creation and the existence of any Supreme Being. The old tough Hindūism has therefore every prospect of outliving also this reformatory movement, which was impeded in its course and eventually rendered baneful by being made subservient to political interests.

[1] One Nirmalā Sādhū of the Amritsar establishment, Ātmā Singh, was for a considerable time my instructor.

[2] These innovations did not concern the doctrinal parts, but only some outward forms and customs of Sikhism. He endeavoured to induce the Sikhs to abandon their blue dress, to abstain from drinking liquors and Bhang (to which even Gōvind Singh had been addicted) and from eating flesh. He tried also to make them exclaim: ਧਰਮ ਦੀ ਫਤੇ (victory to religion!), ਦਰਸਨ ਦੀ ਫਤੇ (victory to the (Sikh) system!), instead of the exclamation ordered by Guru Gōvind Singh: ਵਾਹ ਗੁਰੂਜੀ ਦੀ ਫਤੇ (bravo, victory to the Guru!), ਵਾਹ ਖਾਲਸਾਜੀ ਦੀ ਫਤੇ (bravo, victory to the Khālsā!). As the bigoted Bandā insisted on these innovations, many Sikhs, especially the Akālīs, who refused to comply with them, were put to death. After the defeat and cruel execution of Bandā all these innovations were put aside again, except the blue dress, which only the fanatical Akālīs retained.

IV.

ON THE COMPOSITION OF THE GRANTH.

The Ādi Granth in its present state was collected by Guru Arjun, as stated on p. lxxxi; after Arjun the verses of Tēg-bahādur were added and one single Dōhrā of his son, Guru Gōvind Singh, in answer to some Dōhrās of his father. We have no further information, how the writings of the predecessors of Arjun had been collected and preserved, and we must wholly depend for their authenticity on the testimony of Arjun himself.

Besides the writings of the Sikh Gurus, considerable extracts from the writings of famous Bhagats were also inserted in the Granth; the works of Kabīr are still extant in India, as they were preserved by his disciples, the Kabīr-panthīs, who have a considerable establishment at Benares, but hitherto few selections only have been published of them, though they are far superior in form as well as in originality of thought to the versifications of the Sikh Gurus. The writings of the other Bhagats seem to be lost, as I was never able, in spite of manifold researches, to detect a trace of them; perhaps one piece or another may yet be found in progress of time.

Nearly all the panegyrics of the Bhaṭṭs were composed for the occasion and are abject flatteries, without any intrinsic value whatever; they were apparently all added by Guru Arjun himself.

The authors of the Granth are therefore the following:

(A). *Sikh Gurus.*—(1). Bābā Nānak (Mah. I.). (2). Angad (Mah. II.). (3). Amar-dās (Mah. III.). (4). Rām-dās (Mah. IV.). (5). Arjun (Mah. V.). (6). Tēg-bahādur (Mah. IX.). (7). Gōvind Singh (Mah. X.; only one Dōhrā. See Transl. p. 708).[1]

(B). *Bhagats.*—(1). Bēṇī.[2] (2). Bhīkan.[2] (3). Dhannā.[3] (4). Farīd (Shēkh).[4] (5). Jaidēv.[5] (6). Kabīr.[6] (7). Nāmdēv.[7] (8). Pīpā.[8] (9). Rāmānand.[9] (10). Ravidās.[10] (11). Sadhnā.[11] (12). Saiṇu.[12] (13). Sūrdās.[13] (14). Trilōčan.[14]

[1] In many copies Mah. X. is not added to this Dohrā, though good copies testify to it.

[2] About Bēṇī (ਬੇਣੀ) and Bhīkan (ਭੀਖਣ) no particulars are known.

[3] Dhannā (ਧੰਨਾ) is said to have been a cultivator (Jaṭ). See Transl. p. 668, note 2. He became a disciple of Rāmānand. See Price, Hindī Selections, p. 124. [4] About Shēkh Farīd see Transl. p. 685, note 4.

[5] Jaidēv (ਜੈਦੇਵ) = Sansk. जयदेव, the well-known author of the Gīta-gōvinda.

[6] See about Kabīr, Transl. p. 126, note 1; p. 93, note 1.

[7] Nāmdēv (ਨਾਮਦੇਵ, frequently only ਨਾਮਾ) was a calico-printer (ਛੀਂਬਾ), a famous Bhagat, who is considered the first Marāṭhī writer; his verses are therefore particularly interesting in a linguistic point of view. See about him Transl. p. 93, note 1.

[8] Pīpā, Rāǰā of the fort of Gangaraun (गंगरौन गढ़ का राजा), as he is styled by the Bhakta-mālā (see Price, Hindī Selections, p. 87), was first a votary of the Dēvī, but became afterwards a disciple of Rāmānand.

[9] Rāmānand (about A.D. 1400), a disciple of Rāmānuj. Twelve disciples of Rāmānand are mentioned, among them Kabīr, Ravidās, Pīpā, Dhannā, etc. Rāmānand received men of all castes as his disciples, and declared that the knowledge of Brahm made a man free from all social bonds.

[10] See about Ravidās, Transl. p. 130, note 3.

[11] Sadhnā was a butcher (ਕਸਾਈ). Nothing particular is known about him, if we abstract from the two wonderful stories related about him in the Bhakta-mālā.

[12] Saiṇu is said to have been a barber (ਨਾਉ). He is also enumerated among the twelve disciples of Rāmānand, whom he himself quotes (Rāg Dhanāsarī, Saiṇu).

[13] Sūrdās, a Brāhmaṇ, was first an Amīn (commissioner) of the Emperor, but squandered the money of the district treasury on saints. He fled then to the forest of Vrindāvan and became himself a Bhagat.

[14] About Trilōčan see Transl. p. 126, note 4; p. cxxiii.

(C). *Bhaṭṭs.*—(1). Bhalhau. (2). Bhikā. (3). Dās (Dāsu). (4). Gangā. (5). Haribans. (6). Jalan. (7). Jālap. (8). Kal (Kalu, Kalhu). (9). Kalasu. (10). Kalasahār. (11). Kīratu. (12). Mathurā. (13). Nal. (14). Raḍ. (15). Sal (Salh).

The Bhaṭṭ Kalasu eulogized Bābā Nānak; Kalasahār and Kalu: Guru Angad; Kalu, Jālap, Kīratu, Bhikā, Sal and Bhalhau: Guru Amar-dās; Kalu, Kalasahār, Nal, Raḍ, Dāsu, Jalan, Gangā, Mathurā, Kīratu and Sal: Guru Rāmdās; Kalu, Kalasahār, Mathurā and Haribans: Guru Arjun. Thence it would appear, that the Bhaṭṭ Kalasu lived towards the close of the life of Nānak or under Guru Angad; Jālap, Bhikā and Bhalhau under Guru Amar-dās; Kīratu, Nal, Raḍ, Dāsu, Jalan, Gangā and Sal under Guru Rām-dās; and Kalu, Kalasahār, Mathurā and Haribans under Guru Arjun. The panegyric of Angad was composed under Guru Arjun, very likely to fill up the gap.

The Granth itself consists of the following portions:

I. *The Jap (or Japǰī)*, an introductory chapter, by Nānak.

II. *The Sō daru*, consisting of extracts from Rāg Āsā and Rāg Gūǰrī, used by the Sikhs as evening prayer (ਰਹਿਰਾਸ) together with:

III. *Sō purkhu*, consisting of extracts from Rāg Āsā.

IV. *Sōhilā*, consisting of extracts from the Rāgs Gauṛī, Āsā, and Dhanāsarī, used as a prayer before retiring to rest.

These pieces were intended for devotional purposes and therefore put at the beginning of the Granth. Then follow:

V. *The Rāgs*, which form the body of the Granth.

(1). Sirī Rāg (ਸਿਰੀ ਰਾਗੁ).
(2). Rāg Māǰh (ਰਾਗੁ ਮਾਝ).
(3). Rāg Gauṛī (ਰਾਗੁ ਗਉੜੀ).
(4). Rāg Āsā (ਰਾਗੁ ਆਸਾ).
(5). Rāg Gūǰrī (ਰਾਗੁ ਗੂਜਰੀ).
(6). Rāg Dēvgandhārī (ਰਾਗੁ ਦੇਵਗੰਧਾਰੀ).
(7). Rāg Bihāgṛā (ਰਾਗੁ ਬਿਹਾਗੜਾ).
(8). Rāg Vaḍhansu (ਰਾਗੁ ਵਡਹੰਸੁ).
(9). Rāg Sōraṭhi (ਰਾਗੁ ਸੋਰਠਿ).
(10). Rāg Dhanāsarī (ਰਾਗੁ ਧਨਾਸਰੀ).
(11). Rāg Jaitsirī (ਰਾਗੁ ਜੈਤਸਿਰੀ).
(12). Rāg Ṭōḍī (ਰਾਗੁ ਟੋਡੀ)
(13). Rāg Bairāṛī (ਰਾਗੁ ਬੈਰਾੜੀ).
(14). Rāg Tilang (ਰਾਗੁ ਤਿਲੰਗ).
(15). Rāg Sūhī (ਰਾਗੁ ਸੂਹੀ).
(16). Rāg Bilāvalu (ਰਾਗੁ ਬਿਲਾਵਲੁ).
(17). Rāg Gauḍ (ਰਾਗੁ ਗੋਡ).
(18). Rāg Rāmkalī (ਰਾਗੁ ਰਾਮਕਲੀ).
(19). Rāg Naṭnārāin (ਰਾਗੁ ਨਟਨਾਰਾਇਨ).
(20). Rāg Mālīgauṛā (ਰਾਗੁ ਮਾਲੀਗਉੜਾ).
(21). Rāg Mārū (ਰਾਗੁ ਮਾਰੂ).
(22). Rāg Tukhārī (ਰਾਗੁ ਤੁਖਾਰੀ).
(23). Rāg Kēdārā (ਰਾਗੁ ਕੇਦਾਰਾ).
(24). Rāg Bhairau (ਰਾਗੁ ਭੈਰਉ).
(25). Rāg Basantu (ਰਾਗੁ ਬਸੰਤੁ).
(26). Rāg Sārang (ਰਾਗੁ ਸਾਰੰਗ).
(27). Rāg Malār (ਰਾਗੁ ਮਲਾਰ).
(28). Rāg Kānaṛā (ਰਾਗੁ ਕਾਨੜਾ).
(29). Rāg Kaliāṇ (ਰਾਗੁ ਕਲਿਆਨ).
(30). Rāg Prabhātā (ਰਾਗੁ ਪ੍ਰਭਾਤਾ).
(31). Rāg J̌aiǰāvantī (ਰਾਗੁ ਜੈਜਾਵੰਤੀ).[1]

The verses of the different Gurus have been distributed into these fore-mentioned Rāgs, apparently without any leading principle, as hardly any verse is internally connected with another. The name of the Rāg is therefore a mere superscription, without any reference to its contents. At the conclusion of a Rāg frequently some sayings of one or more Bhagats are added, which seem to have been selected in the same arbitrary way as chance might offer them. No system nor order is therefore to be looked for in any of the Rāgs. In the first four Rāgs the most important matter was

[1] There were originally only thirty Rāgs; the last, Rāg J̌aiǰāvantī, was composed by Tēg-bahādur, and contains only four verses.

collected and they are therefore also comparatively of the largest compass; the following minor Rāgs seem to be a second gathering or gleaning, as materials offered themselves, no attention being paid to the contents, but only to the bulky size of the Granth. By thus jumbling together whatever came to hand, without any judicious selection, the Granth has become an extremely incoherent and wearisome book, the few thoughts and ideas, that it contains, being repeated in endless variations, which are for the greatest part nothing but a mere jingling of words.

VI. The so-called *Bhōg* or conclusion of the Granth. This portion contains:

(1). Some Slōks (four in number) by Nānak, and (sixty-seven) by Arjun.[1]
(2). Three small pieces by Arjun (ਗਾਥਾ, ਫੁਨਹੇ and ਚਉਬੋਲੇ).
(3). Slōks of Kabīr.
(4). Slōks of Shēkh Farīd.
(5). Savayyē (Savāīē) of Arjun.
(6). Savayyē of the Bhaṭṭs (or Bhāṭs):
  (*a*). Panegyric of Guru Bābā Nānak.
  (*b*). Panegyric of Guru Angad.
  (*c*). Panegyric of Guru Amar-dās.
  (*d*). Panegyric of Guru Rām-dās.
  (*e*). Panegyric of Guru Arjun.
(7). Slōks in excess of the Vārs, by Nānak.
(8). Slōks by Amar-dās.
(9). Slōks by Rām-dās.
(10). Slōks by Arjun.
(11). Slōks by Tēg-bahādur.
(12). A piece called Mundāvaṇī (ਮੁੰਦਾਵਣੀ) by Arjun, consisting of two Slōks.[2]
(13). Rāg-mālā (an enumeration of the Rāgs with the Rāgiṇīs) by an unknown author.

[1] They are called in the Granth ਸਲੋਕ ਸਹਸਕ੍ਰਿਤੀ, whence some rashly concluded, that they were really Sanskrit Shlōks. But this is a great mistake. Neither Nānak nor Arjun understood anything of Sanskrit, and these verses are therefore composed in the usual Panjābī of those days. What is meant by ਸਹਸਕ੍ਰਿਤੀ, see p. cxxxiii, *Remark.*

[2] Some copies of the Granth insert before or after the Mundāvaṇī some Slōks of Nānak (Mah. I., which Cunningham, p. 371, strangely interprets by: "Hymn of the first woman or slave"); a Ratan-mālā (or rosary of gems) belonging to the Rāg Rāmkalī, by Nānak; and a short story (in prose) of Rāh-mukām Siv-nābh, Rājā (of Ceylon), by an unknown author.

V

ON THE LANGUAGE AND THE METRES USED IN THE GRANTH.

From the foregoing survey of the various contributors to the Granth it may be easily inferred, that the idiom of the Granth is not the same throughout; it varies considerably according to the time or the province in which the author lived. Though the Granth, as regards its contents, is perhaps the most shallow and empty book that exists, in proportion to its size, it is, on the other hand, in a linguistic point of view, of the greatest interest to us, as it is a real treasury of the old Hinduī dialects, specimens of which have been preserved therein which are not to be found anywhere else. The Granth contains sufficient materials, which will enable us to investigate those old and now obsolete dialects, from which the modern idioms have had their origin, so that the gap, which hitherto existed between the older Prākrit dialects and the modern languages of the Ārian stock, may, by a careful comparative study of the same, be fairly filled up. It is to be regretted, that the oldest and therefore most interesting specimens of the language of mediaeval India are comparatively few in number.

Very likely the oldest writer in the collection of the Granth is *Nāmdēv*, who is also considered the oldest Marāṭhī poet; he lived about the fourteenth century of our era, though we have no materials at hand, by which we might be enabled to fix his time more accurately. We know from the Bhakta-mālā, that he was a native of the Dekhan and lived in the town of Panḍharpur (in the Bhakta-mālā written पंडरपुर and पंडुरपुर), being the illegitimate child of a daughter of Vāmdēv and by profession a calico-printer (not a tailor, as Molesworth will have it). The peculiarities of the modern Marāṭhī are already visible in his compositions, though not in such a degree as in the verses cited by Molesworth in his Marāṭhī-English Dictionary, Introduction, p. xxvi, so that the suspicion arises, that either the verses of Nāmdēv, as far as received into the Granth, were adapted to the Hinduī, or that the verses cited by Molesworth were adapted to the modern Marāṭhī. In order to illustrate his style and its peculiar grammatical features, we subjoin here a few lines taken from Rāg Gauṛī (Transl. p. 489):

ਦੇਵਾ ਪਾਹਨ ਤਾਰੀਅਲੇ ॥ ਰਾਮ ਕਹਤ ਜਨ ਕਸ ਨਤਰੇ ॥ ਰਹਾਉ ॥
ਤਾਰੀ ਲੇ ਗਨਿਕਾ ਬਿਨੁ ਰੂਪ ਕੁਬਿਜਾ ਬਿਆਧਿ ਅਜਾਮਲੁ ਤਾਰੀਅਲੇ ॥
ਚਰਨ ਬਧਿਕ ਜਨ ਤੇਊ ਮੁਕਤਿ ਭਏ ॥ ਹਉ ਬਲਿ ਬਲਿ ਜਨ ਰਾਮ ਕਹੇ ॥ ੧

Pause.

"By God stones are caused to swim. How should not men by the order of Rām cross?

(1). Seizing the raft the whore, the hump-backed woman without beauty, the hunter and Ajāmal were brought across.

The man who struck the feet (of Krishṇa) became emancipated. I am a sacrifice to the man, (who) utters: Rām!"

We have perhaps in देवा the inflectional *ā* of Marāṭhī nouns of the first declension, but the Instrumental case-affix ने is not yet added (nor is it in Hinduī), the Formative as such serving as Instrumental, the same as in Sindhī. ਕਸ is the Marāṭhī कसा, how? In ਤਰੀਅਲੇ we have a participle past passive, formed by the affix *ī-alē*, the conjunctive vowel *i* of the modern Marāṭhī being lengthened to ī, and at the same time a short *a*-sound added = तारिले; but by the side of such formations we find also the regular Hinduī form of the participle past, like ਭਏ. The pronoun of the first person singular is ਹਉ, hañ, and not मी, as now in Marāṭhī. Nearly all the postpositions are still wanting, so that pieces of this kind are extremely difficult to translate.

About the same time lived the Brāhmaṇ *Trilōcan*, who was likewise an inhabitant of the Dekhan, as may be safely concluded from the peculiarities of his style, which resembles very closely that of Nāmdēv. We subjoin here a sample of the same taken from the Sirī Rāg (Transl. p. 127, III. IV.):

ਬਿਖਮ ਘੋਰ ਪੰਥਿ ਚਾਲਣਾ ਪ੍ਰਾਣੀ ਰਵਿ ਸਸਿ ਤਹ ਨ ਪ੍ਰਵੇਸੰ ॥
ਮਾਇਆ ਮੋਹੁ ਤਬ ਬਿਸਰਿ ਗਇਆ ਜਾਂ ਤਜੀਅਲੇ ਸੰਸਾਰੰ ॥ ੩
ਆਜੁ ਮੇਰੈ ਮਨਿ ਪ੍ਰਗਟ ਭਇਆ ਹੈ ਪੇਖੀਅਲੇ ਧਰਮਰਾਉ ॥
ਤਹ ਕਰ ਦਲ ਕਰਨਿ ਮਹਾਬਲੀ ਤਿਨ ਆਗਲੜੈ ਮੈ ਰਹਣੁ ਨ ਜਾਇ ॥ ੪

(3). On a difficult, terrible road thou must go, O man, (whither) sun and moon do not penetrate.
The infatuation of the Māyā is then forgotten (by thee), when thou hast left behind the world.
(4). To-day he has become manifest in my mind, Dharm-rāu has been seen.
His very strong hands break in pieces (men), before him I cannot abide.

We meet here likewise with the forms ਤਜੀਅਲੇ, ਪੇਖੀਅਲੇ by the side of ਭਇਆ, which we have noticed in Nāmdēv.

Jaidēv (Jayadēva), though the time in which he lived has hitherto not yet been fixed with certainty, belongs in all likelihood also to the fourteenth century. Wilson, who enumerates him with the disciples of Rāmānand, is apparently mistaken, as the Bhakta-mālā nowhere states that Jaidēv was a disciple of Rāmānand, which it certainly would have done if any tradition to this purport had been current among the Vaishṇavas. But we consider it equally wrong, if Lassen (Gīta-gōvinda, Prolegomena, p. iv.) is inclined to date back the Gīta-gōvinda to the twelfth century of our era (about 1150); against such a supposition his own Prākrit verses, as preserved in the Granth, speak too strongly, which decidedly bear the stamp of a later age. Only the following piece of Jaidēv, which is a curious mixture of Sanskrit and the vulgar tongue, is contained in the Granth (Rāg Gūjrī, Srī Jaidēv):

ਪਰਮਾਦਿ ਪੁਰਖੁ ਮਨੋਪਿਮੰ ਸਤਿ ਆਦਿ ਭਾਵ ਰਤੰ ॥
ਪਰਮਦ ਭੁਤੰ ਪਰਕ੍ਰਿਤਿ ਪਰੰ ਜਦਿ ਚਿੰਤਿ ਸਰਬਗਤੰ ॥ ੧
ਕੇਵਲ ਰਾਮ ਨਾਮ ਮਨੋਰਮੰ ॥ ਬਦਿ ਅਮ੍ਰਿਤ ਤਤਮਇਅੰ ॥
ਨ ਦਨੋਤਿ ਜ ਸਮਰਣੇ ਨ ਜਨਮ ਜਰਾਧਿ ਮਰਣ ਭਇਅੰ ॥ ਰਹਾਉ ॥
ਇਛਸਿ ਜਮਾਦਿ ਪਰਾਭਯੰ ਜਸੁ ਸ੍ਵਸਤਿ ਸੁਕ੍ਰਿਤ ਕ੍ਰਿਤੰ ॥
ਭਵ ਭੂਤ ਭਾਵ ਸਮਬ੍ਯਿਅੰ ਪਰਮ ਪ੍ਰਸੰਨ ਮਿਦੰ ॥ ੨
ਲੋਭਾਦਿ ਦ੍ਰਿਸਟਿ ਪਰਗ੍ਰਿਹੰ ਜ ਦਿਬਿਧਿ ਆਚਰਣੰ ॥
ਤਜਿ ਸਕਲ ਦੁਹਕ੍ਰਿਤ ਦੁਰਮਤੀ ਭਜੁ ਚਕ੍ਰਧਰ ਸਰਣੰ ॥ ੩
ਹਰਿ ਭਗਤ ਨਿਜ ਨਿਹਕੇਵਲਾ ਰਿਦ ਕਰਮਣਾ ਬਚਸਾ ॥
ਜੋਗੇਨ ਕਿੰ ਜਗੇਨ ਕਿੰ ਦਾਨੇਨ ਕਿੰ ਤਪਸਾ ॥ ੪
ਗੋਬਿੰਦ ਗੋਬਿੰਦੇਤਿ ਜਪਿ ਨਰ ਸਕਲ ਸਿਧਿ ਪਦੰ ॥
ਜੈਦੇਵ ਆਇਉ ਤਸ ਸਫੁਟੰ ਭਵ ਭੂਤ ਸਰਬ ਗਤੰ ॥ ੫

(1). The primeval Spirit (is) incomparable,[1] first, steeped in love.
Joyful,[2] far from nature, though in thought penetrating all.

Pause.

Only the name of Rām is beautiful. Utter (the name) consisting of the essence of nectar!
By the remembrance of which[3] there is no burning[4] (in the heart), neither fear of birth, the trouble of old age (and) death.
(2). (If) thou desirest the discomfiture[5] of Yama and the others, (know): fame (and) welfare (are to) the doer of meritorious works.
In the present, past and future time he is equally continuing,[6] he is extremely propitious and tender.
(3). Greediness and the other (vices), looking upon another's wife (and) what (is) twofold conduct (= duality).
Having given up all bad works flee to the asylum of the discus-holder, O foolish one!
(4). Devotion to Hari (must be) (in one's) heart only; what is the use of works (and) words? of Yōg, of sacrifice, of alms and austerity?
(5). Mutter: "Gōvind, Gōvind," O man! this is the step to every perfection.
Jaidēv (says): the coming[7] of that (man) is fruitful,[8] all (his) regeneration is gone.

Of *Rāmānand* also, who lived towards the end of the fourteenth or the beginning of the fifteenth century, one piece only is contained in the Granth. It is found in the Rāg Basant and runs thus:

ਕਤ ਜਾਈਐ ਰੇ ਘਰਿ ਲਾਗੋ ਰੰਗੁ ॥ ਮੇਰਾ ਚਿਤ ਨ ਚਲੈ ਮਨੁ ਭਇਓ ਪੰਗੁ ॥ ਰਹਾਉ ॥
ਏਕ ਦਿਵਸ ਮਨ ਭਈ ਉਮੰਗੁ ॥ ਘਸਿ ਚੰਦਨ ਚੋਆ ਬਹੁ ਸੁਗੰਧੁ ॥
ਪੂਜਨ ਚਾਲੀ ਬ੍ਰਹਮ ਠਾਇ ॥ ਸੋ ਬ੍ਰਹਮ ਬਤਾਇਓ ਗੁਰ ਮਨਹੀ ਮਾਹਿ ॥ ੧
ਜਹ ਜਾਈਐ ਤਹ ਜਲ ਪਖਾਨ ॥ ਤੂ ਪੁਰਿ ਰਹਿਓ ਹੈ ਸਭ ਸਮਾਨ ॥
ਬੇਦ ਪੁਰਾਨ ਸਭ ਦੇਖੇ ਜੋਇ ॥ ਊਹਾ ਤਉ ਜਾਈਐ ਜਉ ਈਹਾ ਨ ਹੋਇ ॥ ੨
ਸਤਿ ਗੁਰ ਮੈ ਬਲਿਹਾਰੀ ਤੋਰ ॥ ਜਿਨਿ ਸਕਲ ਬਿਕਲ ਭ੍ਰਮ ਕਾਟੇ ਮੋਰ ॥
ਰਾਮਾਨੰਦ ਸੁਆਮੀ ਰਮਤ ਬ੍ਰਹਮ ॥ ਗੁਰ ਕਾ ਸਬਦੁ ਕਾਟੈ ਕੋਟਿ ਕਰਮ ॥ ੩

Pause.

Where shall it be gone, Sir? colour is applied to (my) house (= body).
My reasoning faculty does not move, my mind has become lame.

[1] All the MSS. read: ਮਨੋਪਿਮੰ, but there must be some mistake or another in this word; very likely it is miswritten for: ਅਨੋਪਿਮੰ (Sansk. अनुपम, *u* changing with *o*, and *a* with *i*, as in many other instances).

[2] ਪਰਮਦ ਭੁਤ, being excessive joy; ਭੁਤ is shortened from भूत.

[3] ਜ must here (as in *v.* 3) be separated from ਸਮਰਲਾ; it is the Prākrit relative neuter ਜ, but the Anusvāra is very frequently not written in the Granth.

[4] ਦਨੋਤਿ, instead of ਦੁਨੋਤਿ, from the Sansk. root दु, दुनोति, intransitively used here.

[5] ਪਰਾਭਯ, discomfiture = Sansk. पराभव, *v* being frequently exchanged for the semi-vowel *y*.

[6] ਸਮਬ੍ਯਿਅੰ (sam-abyã) = Sansk. सम and अव्यय, in later Hinduī अबै.

[7] ਆਇਓ (= ਆਇਆ), the participle past used as a substantive: the coming.

[8] ਸਫੁਟ = Sansk. स्फुट, blown, budded (like a flower) = fruitful, bearing its fruit. It is an idiomatic expression: "the destiny of a man buds," *i.e.* it comes to its fulfilment.

(1). One day excessive joy has sprung up (in my) mind,
Having rubbed very fragrant sandal-perfume[1] (on my body).
The Brahm, (which) I go[2] to worship,[3]
That Brahm was shown (to me) by the Guru (as being) in (my) very mind.
(2). Where one goes,[4] there (in) water (and) stone
Thou art remaining brimful, being contained in all.
All the Vēdas (and) Purāṇas I have searched through.[5]
One should go there, if he is not here, (they say).
(3). O true Guru, I am thy sacrifice,
By whom all my restless[6] errors were cut off.
The Lord of Rāmānand, Brahm, is sporting (in all).
The word of the Guru cuts off crores of works.

The idiom of Rāmānand is already that of the old Hinduī and in no particular differing from the style of Kabīr and his co-disciples, who in their numerous writings have delivered to us the language spoken in those days in the valley of the Ganges.

Nānak and his successors in the Guruship were all Panjābīs, but it is remarkable, that their idiom does not differ so much from the Hinduī of those days in a grammatical point of view, as the modern Panjābī does from the Hindī.[7] But we must not rashly conclude from this fact, that the Panjābī of those days was essentially the same as the Hinduī, and that the peculiar grammatical forms of the Panjābī were developed in a later period, for such an assumption is disproved by the old Janam-Sākhī of Bābā Nānak, which is written in the regular Panjābī, a dialect which differs considerably from the Hinduī, as it uses pronominal suffixes and other grammatical forms, which are quite unknown in Hinduī and only to be found in the cognate Sindhī, to which it approaches far more than to the Hinduī. It is therefore almost certain, that Nānak and his successors employed in their writings purposely the Hinduī idiom, following the example of Kabīr and the other Bhagats, who had raised the Hinduī to a kind of standard for religious compositions, and by employing which they could make themselves understood to nearly all the devotees of India, whereas the proper

[1] ਚੋਆ (or ਚੋਵਾ), a perfume, made of sandal-wood, therefore generally: ਚੰਦਨ ਚੋਆ.

[2] ਚਾਲੀ, first person of the present tense: I go or use to go; the older form of the verb is ਚਾਲਣਾ, later ਚਲਣਾ.

[3] ਪੂਜਨ ਬ੍ਰਹਮ ਠਾਇ. ਠਾਇ is an old Hinduī Dative-postfix (shortened from स्थानि), identical with the modern तईं or ताईं.

[4] ਜਾਈਐ, the old Prākrit passive, which is still in frequent use in the old Hinduī.

[5] ਜੋਇ, participle past conjunctive of ਜੋਇਣਾ (Hindī जोहना), to look out for.

[6] ਬਿਕਲ, Sansk. विकल; in Hinduī ਬਿਕਲ has the sense of "uneasy, restless" (not of "imperfect, deficient," as in Sanskrit).

[7] In order to prevent any mistake as to the nomenclature, we add here, that we understand by the *old Hinduī* the idiom of the old Bhagats, such as Kabīr and his contemporaries; by *Hinduī* the later Hinduī of the times of Gōvind Singh and thereabout, as this idiom differs already in many essential points from the old Hinduī. By *Hindī* we mean the modern idiom since the beginning of our century and as spoken at present. There is of course no essential difference between *Hinduī* and *Hindī* as regards the signification of the two adjectives, "*hinduī*" being derived from "*hindū*," a Hindū, and "*hindī*" from the Arabic noun "*hind*," India, but the two adjectives are very convenient to designate different periods of the development of the language of the Hindūs in Hindūstān proper. Where we do not find it necessary to distinguish between the older and later Hinduī, we comprehend the language of both periods under the general term *Hinduī*, in contradistinction to the modern *Hindī*.

Panjābī was only intelligible to the people of the Panjāb. The idiom of the Sikh Gurus however is not the pure Hinduī, but a sort of mixture of both dialects, as they frequently introduce provincialisms, which give a peculiar colouring to their diction, but at the same time bring it nearer home to the understanding of their countrymen. The Granth of Gōvind Singh is composed in pure Hinduī, as he received his early education in Hindūstān, but it has thereby become nearly unintelligible to the Sikhs of the Panjāb, to whom it must be translated, if anything is to be explained to them from it.

It would exceed the limits of these remarks, were we to enter more fully into the peculiarities of the idiom of the Granth, which can only be treated in a grammatical analysis of the same. A few hints, which in a great measure also refer to the old Hinduī, may suffice here. The general impression, which we receive from the study of the Granth, is, that the grammatical forms of the language are not yet firmly fixed, but are rather in a state of transition, the genius of the language apparently endeavouring to build up a new structure out of the ruins of the Prākrit, which had gone to pieces. We find therefore a number of forms promiscuously employed, as usage had not yet decided for a few select ones. This is manifest not only in the inflexion of the nouns, for which a new way had to be found out, the old Prākrit terminations having almost totally been lost in the progress of time, but also in that of the verbs.

As regards the declensional process of the nouns, most of them have still a vocalic termination (*u*, *ō*, *i*), which is very closely to be attended to, as the right understanding of a sentence frequently depends on the vocalic termination of the noun or nouns. In later MSS. the final vowels are frequently dropped, as the copyists had no longer a right understanding of their grammatical relation, or carelessly exchanged, so that a sentence becomes easily confused thereby. This is especially the case with the Locative singular, which ends in *i* (if the noun in the Nominative terminate in *u*), and the Ablative singular, which may likewise end in *i* (in the modern Panjābī in *ī*), where the final vowel in inferior copies is not seldom either dropped altogether or confounded with "*u*," which represents the Nominative. The Nominative plural is variously formed and in like manner the Formative singular and plural, the details of which we must forego here.

The case-affixes and postpositions[1] are manifold, as may be expected at the time of the reconstruction of a shattered language. In the *Genitive* we find the affixes ਹਿ *hi* and ਅਸਿ *asi*, which are peculiar to the old Hinduī, and the inflected affixes ਕਾ *kā*, ਕੇਰਾ *kērā*, ਚਾ *čā*, ਜਾ *ǰā*, ਰਾ *rā* (also ੜਾ *ṛā*), the Panjābī ਦਾ *dā*, and even the Sindhī ਸੰਦਾ *sandā*. In the *Dative* the postpositions ਕਉ *kau*, ਕੋ *kō*, ਕੂ *kū* (*kū̃*), ਕਹੁ *kahu*, ਕਹ *kah*, ਕੈ *kai*,[2] ਖੇ *khē* (as in Sindhī), ਠਾਇ *ṭhāi*, ਥਾਨਿ *thāni*, ਥੈ *thai;* special Panjābī forms are ਨਉ *nau*, ਨੂ *nū* (*nū̃*), ਨੋ *nō;* the Genitive case-affix ਹਿ *hi* is, as in Prākrit, also used for the Dative, and peculiar to the old Hinduī. The *Accusative* is either identical with the Nominative or expressed by the Dative case-signs. In the *Ablative* we find the affixes ਹਿ *hi*, ਹੂ *hū*, ਹੁ *hu*, ਓ *ō*, ਔ *au*, ਇ *i*, ਈ *ī*, and the postpositions ਕਿਅਹੁ *kiahu*, ਦੂ *dū*, ਥਾਵਹੁ *thāvahu*, ਥੋ *thō* (= *thō̃*), ਤੈ *tai*, ਸੋ *sō* (= *sō̃*), etc. In the *Locative singular* we meet with the affix *i*, in the

[1] Case-affixes we call those remnants of the old Prākrit case-terminations, which are still usually connected with the noun itself; postpositions we call those adverbial nouns, which are now employed to make up for the cases and which are still written separately. To the affixes we must also add ਕਾ *kā* and its derivatives, though they are now always written as separate words, as they are originally an affix (Sansk. कृ) and inflected (for they turn the noun, which they follow, properly into an adjective). Under "case-signs" we comprehend both affixes and postpositions.

[2] That the Hindī and Hindūstānī *kē* (के کے) is really a Dative-postposition, is sufficiently borne out by the Hinduī; some disputed points in Hindūstānī grammar are to be settled accordingly, irrespectively of the decisions of the Maulavīs, who have no idea of the old Hinduī.

Locative plural with the affix *ī* (now pronounced ī̃), or the Locative is expressed by means of postpositions, as: मै *mai*, माहि *māhi*, विचि *viči*, etc. The *Instrumental* is generally expressed by the *Formative* (without a case-sign) or by the affix "*i*," which outwardly coincides with the Ablative. But the postpositions and the case-signs generally are as yet very sparingly used, the noun is usually put in the Formative, and the reader has to find out for himself its grammatical connexion; in many sentences not a single case-sign is to be met with, so that the translation can only be made according to conjecture. This unsettled state of the language often occasions very great perplexities.

The verb is as yet very little developed. Generally three tenses only are in use: the Present (in the later Hinduī the Present indefinite and in Hindī the Subjunctive),[1] the Preterite, and the Future. Of the Imperfect I have found only a few curious forms; the Perfect and Pluperfect, which very seldom occur, are compound tenses.

The Present tense offers a great variety of personal terminations, many of which coincide, the Anusvāra being generally dropped in the writing of the Granth, so that the person can in many instances only be found out by the context. The Future offers two forms, one of which is made up by the terminations सा, सहि, सी, etc., corresponding to the Prākrit terminations स्सामि, स्ससि, स्सदि, etc., and the other of which is a compound tense, as now used in Hindī and Hindūstānī (see my Sindhī Grammar, p. 291, annotation).

The Preterite is made up either by means of the participle past alone or by personal terminations added to it (as in Sindhī).

There is still a regular *passive* voice for the Present, Imperative, Future, and partly also for the Preterite, which has been lost already (with a few exceptions) in the later Hinduī, which shows the first attempts to make up for it by having recourse to a composition.

There is not only a participle present active, formed by the terminations "*antō*," "*ant*," "*atu*," "*at*," "*tā*" or "*dā*," but also a participle present passive, formed by the termination "*īatu*," "*īat*." The participle past offers still the older form "*iā*" (*iō iau*); many are also directly taken over from the Prākrit without any further assimilation. To this must be added, that pronominal suffixes are not unfrequently connected with the verb, especially in the Preterite, more rarely so with the noun. In Sindhī this is still very common and quite a peculiar feature of this idiom, but in the later Hinduī only a few traces of it are to be met with, and in Hindī and Hindūstānī it is altogether unknown.

From these few remarks it may be inferred, that the idiom of the Granth is well worth a closer investigation, as we shall thereby get a clearer insight into the formation of the modern North-Indian vernaculars, the peculiarities of which cannot be fully laid open without going back to the source from which they have sprung, and which has fortunately been preserved to us in the Granth.

The whole Granth is written in verses, as the Hindūs have very little taste for prose-compositions. The artificial measures of Sanskrit poetry are all discarded; the metres that are used in the Granth, are either old *Prākrit* metres or later inventions, perhaps of the poets themselves. There are two leading principles in Hinduī poetry, viz.: the verses are measured by *quantity* only, *i.e.* by the

[1] This mood (though originally the Present tense) is in our modern Hindī and Hindūstānī grammars generally called the *Aorist*, which is quite an inappropriate appellation. In native Hindūstānī grammars it is designated by مُضارع, as it in some way corresponds to the Arabic مُضارع, which De Sacy translated by *Aorist*. Thence it was applied also to the Hindī and Hindūstānī. But it was quite lost sight of that the technical terms of Arabic grammar cannot be properly applied to the Hindūstānī verb, which in its conjugation is totally different from the Arabic verb; and if the Maulavīs term this tense or rather mood (as it is now) مُضارع, the Arabic not offering a more suitable appellation, we at any rate must not render it by "*Aorist*," as this term conveys a different meaning altogether.

the number of moras (not by number of syllables or fixed feet), and they must *rhyme* together; the metres are therefore all so-called *mātrā čhandas* (regulated by quantity), as they are intended for singing[1] or a rhythmical recitation. The greatest attention is paid to the rhyme, as in our modern poetry; and if the poet cannot command it readily, the last word is tortured into it and thereby frequently so disfigured, that its original form is hardly recognisable.

It cannot be our object here to give a full description of all the metres employed in the Granth, as this would carry us beyond the limits of a preliminary discourse; we must content ourselves with laying down here the general rules and giving a survey of the most common metres, which will enable the student to find out by scanning those fancy metres of some poets, to which no name has been given in the Granth, as very likely no name was known for them, whereas the usual metres are always indicated by their appropriate names. The Sikhs themselves seem now to have lost all knowledge of the metrical laws of the Granth, for I never met a person who could give me the least clue to them, and the learned Brāhmaṇs disdain to read the Granth.

The length of the syllables is determined by allotting to a short syllable one mātrā or kalā, *i.e.* mora, and to a long syllable two mātrās. A syllable is long either by nature (as *ā, ī, ū, ē, ō, ai, au*) or by position (when a naturally short vowel is followed either by a double or a conjunct consonant); but if the second part of a conjunct consonant be a semi-vowel, a *k̤, p̤, b* or *h*, the preceding vowel may remain short, if the metre requires it. On the other hand, a single consonant may be *doubled*, in order to gain a long syllable; this is especially the case, if it be originally doubled in Prākrit; for instance तिसु tisu may also be pronounced tissu (Prākrit तिस्स). To this circumstance especial attention must be paid, as the doubling of a consonant is never indicated in the writing of the Granth, not even in such cases where in common pronunciation it is still doubled.

A diphthong may again be severed into two short syllables, as *ai* = a-i, *au* = a-u, wherever required by the metre. A naturally long vowel may be pronounced *short*; this is especially the case with *ē* and *ō*, which may be considered as *anceps*, as in Prākrit; even the diphthongs *ai* and *au* may be rendered short under the pressure of the metre. On the other hand, the poets take the liberty of lengthening a short vowel, whenever necessary for the sake of the metre, not only at the end of a verse or hemistich, but also in the midst of a verse, though this is comparatively seldom the case. Two vowels may be contracted into one, especially *i* with a following vowel, *i* being changed in this case into the semi-vowel *y*, as *iu* = *yu*; even a short and a long vowel may be contracted, as *aī* to *ai* (short or long, as the metre may require it).

Another point, which must well be attended to, is, that the pronunciation of the Hinduī differs greatly in poetry from that usual in prose. In prose the consonants are now frequently mute, and so always a final consonant containing short *a*; but in scanning a verse, no vowel is, as a rule, to be passed over; even a conjunct consonant must now and then be separated into its constituent parts (by the insertion of *i* or *a*), in order to gain the necessary number of mātrās.

1.—THE DŌHĀ (OR DŌHRĀ)[2] AND SŌRAṬṬHĀ.

The Dōhrā, which is comparatively little used in the Granth, is a distich, the two verses of which rhyme at the end. Each verse consists of twenty-four mātrās, which are distributed into feet (गण) of 6 + 4 + 3 and 6 + 4 + 1 mātrās respectively, there being a caesura at the end of every

[1] In the Granth the key-note (घरु) is therefore generally added, as the verses of the Granth are still sung in the public worship of the Sikhs, especially in the Har-mandar at Amritsar, accompanied by stringed musical instruments.

[2] Sanskrit द्विपथा, Prākrit दोहा; dōharā (usually now pronounced dōhrā) is the diminutive of it. The Dōhā is an old Prākrit metre, as it is already found in Kālidāsa's Vikramōrvašī (edited by Bollensen, St. Petersburg, 1846), p. 55 and p. 373.

first hemistich. The syllables of a whole Dōhrā may therefore be from forty-eight short ones to twenty-three long and two short ones, the final mātrā of each verse being always short. We subjoin here two Dōhrās of Tēg-bahādur (Transl. p. 708), in order to show their scansion.

ਬਲ ਛੁਟਕਿਓ ਬੰਧਨ ਪਰੇ ਕਛੂ ਨ ਹੋਤ ਉਪਾਇ ॥
bălă čhŭṭkiō | bandănă | parē || kăčhū nă hō|tă ŭpā|ĭ ||

ਕਹੁ ਨਾਨਕ ਅਬ ਓਟ ਹਰਿ ਗਜ ਜਿਉ ਹੋਹੁ ਸਹਾਇ ॥
kăhŭ nānăkă | ăbă ō|ṭă hărĭ || găjă jiŭ hō|hŭ săhā|ĭ || *v.* 53.

ਸੰਗਿ ਸਖਾ ਸਭਿ ਤਜਿ ਗਏ ਕੋਊ ਨ ਨਿਬਹਿਓ ਸਾਥ ॥
sangĭ săkhā | săbhĭ tăjĭ | găē || kōū nă nĭb|hyō sā|thă ||

ਕਹੁ ਨਾਨਕ ਇਹ ਬਿਪਤਿ ਮੈ ਟੇਕ ਏਕ ਰਘੁ ਨਾਥ ॥
kăhŭ nānăkă | ĭhă bĭpă|tĭ maī || ṭēkă ēkă | răghŭ nā|thă || *v.* 54.

The Sōraṭṭhā is the reverse of the Dōhrā, the smaller half preceding the longer one; it is very seldom met with in the Granth.

2.—THE DUPADĀ.[1]

The Dupadā is of very frequent occurrence in the Granth; it consists usually of a distich of two verses, which rhyme at the end, each verse containing thirty-four mātrās, and being divided by a caesura into two equal hemistichs. The verse is distributed into feet of $2 \times 6 + 4 + 5 + 2$ Kalās, the last syllable always being long. We subjoin an example taken from Rāg Gauṛī, Mah. V., Sabd 115, 2 (Transl. p. 291):

ਦੀਨਾ ਨਾਥ ਅਨਾਥ ਕਰੁਣਾ ਮੈ ਸਾਜਨ ਮੀਤ ਪਿਤਾ ਮਹਿਤਰੀਆ ॥
dīnā nā|thă ănā|thă kărŭṇā | maī || sājănă mī|tă pĭtā | măhĭtărī|ā || $17 + 17 = 34$ K.

ਚਰਨ ਕਵਲ ਹਿਰਦੈ ਗਹਿ ਨਾਨਕਾ ਭੈ ਸਾਗਰ ਸੰਤ ਪਾਰਿ ਉਤਰੀਆ ॥
čărănă kăvălă | hĭrdaī | găhĭ nānă|kā || bhaī sāgără | săntă pā|rĭ ŭtărī|ā || $17 + 17 = 34$ K.
68 K.

The Dupadā presents many varieties. One kind consists of only one verse, the two hemistichs of which rhyme together, and are also written as separate verses and counted as such. In this case the verse is scanned by $6 + 4 + 5 + 2 \parallel 6 + 4 + 4 + 2 = 33$ Kalās, or by $6 + 4 + 3 + 2 \parallel 6 + 4 + 4 + 2 = 31$ Kalās, the last syllable always being long. Now and then we meet with Dupadās, which alternately contain 34, 33 and 31 Kalās. Usually a Rahāu also is added, scanned in the same way, but counted as a separate verse. We subjoin here an example, taken from Rāg Gauṛī, Mah. V., Sabd 114 (Transl. p. 291):

ਰਾਮ ਕੋ ਬਲੁ ਪੂਰਨ ਭਾਈ ॥ ਤਾਤੇ ਬ੍ਰਿਥਾ ਨ ਬਿਆਪੈ ਕਾਈ ॥ ਰਹਾਉ ॥
rāmă kō bă|lŭ pūră|nă bhā|ī || tātĕ brĭthā | nă bĭā|paī kā|ī ||
$6 + 4 + 3 + 2 \parallel 6 + 4 + 4 + 2 = 15 + 16 = 31$ K.

[1] Sanskrit द्विपदा. Colebrooke, Miscellaneous Essays, ed. Cowell, vol. ii. p. 85, note 1, states, that the Dwipadikā has in each verse twenty-eight mātrās; but such a metre is not to be found in the Granth.

ਜੋ ਜੋ ਚਿਤਵੈ ਦਾਸੁ ਹਰਿ ਮਾਈ ॥ ਸੋ ਸੋ ਕਰਤਾ ਆਪਿ ਕਰਾਈ ॥ ੧

jŏ jŏ čĭtă|vai dā|sŭ hărĭ mā|ī || sō sō kar|tā ā|pĭ kărā|ī ||
6 + 4 + 5 + 2 || 6 + 4 + 4 + 2 = 17 + 16 = 33 K.

ਨਿੰਦਕ ਕੀ ਪ੍ਰਭ ਪਤਿ ਗਵਾਈ ॥ ਨਾਨਕ ਹਰਿ ਗੁਣ ਨਿਰਭਉ ਗਾਈ ॥ ੨

nindăkă kī | prăbhă pătĭ | găvā|ī || nānăkă hărĭ | gŭṇă nĭr|bhăŭ gā|ī ||
6 + 4 + 3 + 2 || 6 + 4 + 4 + 2 = 15 + 16 = 31 K.

3.—THE TIPADĀ (OR TRIPADĀ).

The Tipadā is essentially the same as the Dupadā. It consists, as a rule, of a stanza of three distichs, to which generally a Rahāu is added; the rhyme generally varies in every distich. There is a considerable variety in the scansion, some distichs being scanned by 6 + 5 + 4 + 2 and 6 + 5 + 4 + 2 = 17 + 17 or 34 Kalās, others by 6 + 5 + 4 + 1 and 6 + 5 + 4 + 1 = 16 + 16 or 32 Kalās, the last syllable in this case being short. We subjoin a Tipadā of Kabīr, taken from Rāg Gauṛī, Kabīr 19 (Transl. p. 464):

ਕੰਚਨ ਸਿਉ ਪਾਈਐ ਨਹੀ ਤੋਲਿ ॥ ਮਨੁ ਦੇ ਰਾਮੁ ਲੀਆ ਹੈ ਮੋਲਿ ॥ ੧

kănčănă syŭ pā|īai nă|hī tō|lĭ || mănŭ dē rā|mŭ līā | hai mō|lĭ ||
16 + 16 = 32 K.

ਅਬ ਮੋਹਿ ਰਾਮੁ ਅਪੁਨਾ ਕਰਿ ਜਾਨਿਆ ॥ ਸਹਜਿ ਸੁਭਾਇ ਮੇਰਾ ਮਨੁ ਮਾਨਿਆ ॥ ਰਹਾਉ ॥

ăbă mōhĭ rā|mŭ ăpŭnā | kărĭ jān|yā || săhăjĭ sŭbhā|ĭ mērā | mănŭ mān|yā ||
17 + 17 = 34 K.

ਬ੍ਰਹਮੈ ਕਥਿ ਕਥਿ ਅੰਤੁ ਨ ਪਾਇਆ ॥ ਰਾਮ ਭਗਤਿ ਬੈਠੇ ਘਰਿ ਆਇਆ ॥ ੨

brăhămai kăthĭ | kăthĭ antŭ | nă pāĭ|ā || rāmă bhăgătĭ | baiṭhē ghă|rĭ āĭ|ā ||
17 + 17 = 34 K.

ਕਹੁ ਕਬੀਰ ਚੰਚਲ ਮਤਿ ਤਿਆਗੀ ॥ ਕੇਵਲ ਰਾਮ ਭਗਤਿ ਨਿਜ ਭਾਗੀ ॥ ੩

kăhŭ kăbīră | čănčălă mă|tĭ tĭā|gī || kēvălă rā|mă bhăgătī | nĭjă bhā|gī ||
17 + 17 = 34 K.

4.—THE ČAUPADĀ.

The Čaupadā is in very frequent use in Hinduī poetry, the greatest part of the Granth being composed in this metre. In the Rāmāyan of Tulsī-dās the Čaupadā is usually a stanza of four tetrastichs, each of which consists of two distichs, the two verses of each distich again always rhyming at the end. Each verse contains sixteen mātrās, the distich therefore thirty-two. There is a caesura in each verse after the sixth, seventh, eighth, ninth or tenth mora; the last syllable of a verse is generally long, but it may be also short.[1] We subjoin here a tetrastich from Tulsī-dās (Hinduī edition of Tulsī-dās Rāmāyan, Medical Hall Press, Benares, 1869), p. 329, last Čaupaī:

[1] Colebrooke states, *l. c.* p. 85, that each verse (*i.e.* distich) contains thirty moments (seven times 4 + 2) and terminated by a long syllable. This is wrong, as shown by the example quoted from Tulsī-dās, the Rāmāyan of whom he seems not to have examined himself.

आये भरत संग सब लोगा ॥ कृसतनु स्रीरघु बीर बियोगा ॥

āyē bhărătă | sāngă săbă lōgā || krĭsătănŭ srī răghŭ | bīră bĭyōgā ||

16 + 16 = 32 K.

बामदेव बसिष्ठ मुनि नायक ॥ देखे प्रभु महि धरि धनु सायक ॥

bāmădēvă băsĭṣhṭhă | mŭnĭ nāyăkă || dēkhē prăbhŭ măhĭ dhărĭ | dhănŭ sāyăkă ||

16 + 16 = 32 K.

In the Granth also the Čaupadā consists, as a rule, of four tetrastichs, each containing two distichs of thirty-two mātrās severally, one or two Rahāus, consisting of one distich, being usually added to the stanza. We subjoin an example taken from Rāg Gauṛī, Mah. III., 1 (Transl. p. 222):

ਗੁਰਿ ਮਿਲਿਐ ਹਰਿ ਮੇਲਾ ਹੋਈ ॥ ਆਪੇ ਮੇਲਿ ਮਿਲਾਵੈ ਸੋਈ ॥

gŭrĭ mĭlĭaī | hărĭ mēlā hōī || āpē mēlĭ | mĭlāvaī sōī || 16 + 16.

ਮੇਰਾ ਪ੍ਰਭੁ ਸਭ ਬਿਧਿ ਆਪੇ ਜਾਣੈ ॥ ਹੁਕਮੇ ਮੇਲੇ ਸਬਦਿ ਪਛਾਣੈ ॥ ੧

mērā prăbhŭ săbhă bĭdhĭ | āpē ǰāṇaī || hŭkămē mēlē | săbdĭ păčhāṇaī || 16 + 16.

ਸਤਿ ਗੁਰ ਕੈ ਭਇ ਭ੍ਰਮੁ ਭਉ ਜਾਇ ॥ ਭੈ ਰਾਚੈ ਸਚ ਰੰਗਿ ਸਮਾਇ ॥ ਰਹਾਉ ॥

sătĭ gŭră kaī bhăĭ | bhrămŭ bhău ǰāī || bhaĭ rāǰaī săčă | răngĭ sămāī || 16 + 16.

ਗੁਰਿ ਮਿਲਿਐ ਹਰਿ ਮਨਿ ਵਸੈ ਸੁਭਾਇ ॥ ਮੇਰਾ ਪ੍ਰਭੁ ਭਾਰਾ ਕੀਮਤਿ ਨਹੀ ਪਾਇ ॥

gŭrĭ mĭlĭaī | hărĭ mănĭ văsaī sŭbhāī || mērā prăbhŭ bhārā | kīmătĭ năhī pāĭ || 16 + 16.

ਸਬਦਿ ਸਲਾਹੈ ਅੰਤੁ ਨ ਪਾਰਾਵਾਰੁ ॥ ਮੇਰਾ ਪ੍ਰਭੁ ਬਖਸੇ ਬਖਸਣਹਾਰੁ ॥ ੨

săbdĭ sălāhaī | ăntŭ nă pārāvārŭ || mērā prăbhŭ băkhsē | băkhsăṇăhārŭ || 16 + 16 K.

But there are also many Čaupadās in the Granth consisting only of one distich and a half or even of one distich with one or two Rahāus added. In this case all the three verses of the tetrastich must have the same rhyme. *E.g.* Rāg Gauṛī, Mah. V., I. (Transl. p. 246):

ਕਿਨ ਬਿਧਿ ਕੁਸਲ ਹੋਤੁ ਮੇਰਾ ਭਾਈ ॥ ਕਿਉ ਪਾਈਐ ਹਰਿ ਰਾਮ ਸਹਾਈ ॥ ਰਹਾਉ ॥

kĭnă bĭdhĭ kŭsălă | hōtŭ mērā bhāī || kyŭ pāīaī | hărĭ rāmă săhāī || 16 + 16 K.

ਕੁਸਲ ਨ ਗ੍ਰਿਹਿ ਮੇਰੀ ਸਭ ਮਾਇਆ ॥ ਊਚੇ ਮੰਦਰ ਸੁੰਦਰ ਛਾਇਆ ॥

kŭsălă nă grĭhĭ | mērī săbhă māĭā || ūčē măndără | sŭndără čhāĭā || 16 + 16 K.

ਝੂਠੇ ਲਾਲਚਿ ਜਨਮੁ ਗਵਾਇਆ ॥ ੧

ǰhūṭhē lālăčĭ | ǰănămŭ găvāĭā || 16 K.

Example of a tetrastich consisting only of one distich, Rāg Gauṛī, Mah. V., XXIX. (Transl. p. 261):

ਜੋ ਪਰਾਇਓ ਸੋਈ ਅਪਨਾ ॥ ਜੋ ਤਜਿ ਛੋਡਨ ਤਿਸੁ ਸਿਉ ਮਨੁ ਰਚਨਾ ॥ ੧

ǰō părāĭō | sōī ăpănā || ǰō tăǰĭ čhōḍănă | tĭsŭ syŭ mănŭ răčănā || 16 + 16 K.

5.—THE PANǰPADĀ.

The Panǰpadā occurs but rarely in the Granth. It consists commonly of five distichs, each of which has its own rhyme; one or two Rahāus may be added to them. Occasionally the stanza contains also six distichs with one or two Rahāus in addition. There is a great variety of the Panǰpadā, as nearly every distich differs from the other in the number of the mātrās; the distichs are scanned by 15 + 15, 16 + 16, 17 + 17, or even 20 + 20 Kalās, there being a caesura in every verse after the seventh, eighth, ninth or tenth mora.

As examples may serve, Rāg Āsā, Mah. I., XXIII., a Panǰpadā consisting of six distichs with a Rahāu after the first distich (Transl. p. 503):

ਮੋਹੁ ਕੁਟੰਬੁ ਮੋਹੁ ਸਭ ਕਾਰ ॥ ਮੋਹੁ ਤੁਮ ਤਜਹੁ ਸਗਲ ਵੇਕਾਰ ॥ ੧
mōhŭ kuṭambŭ | mōhŭ sabhă kāră || mōhŭ tumă tajăhŭ | sagală vēkāră || 15 + 15 = 30 K.

ਮੋਹੁ ਅਰੁ ਭਰਮੁ ਤਜਹੁ ਤੁਮ ਬੀਰ ॥ ਸਾਚੁ ਨਾਮੁ ਰਿਦੈ ਰਵੈ ਸਰੀਰ ॥ ਰਹਾਉ ॥
mōhŭ ărŭ bharămŭ | tajăhŭ tumă bīră || sācŭ nāmŭ ridai | ravai sarīră || 16 + 16 = 32 K.

ਗੁਰ ਦੀਖਿਆ ਲੇ ਜਪੁ ਤਪੁ ਕਮਾਹਿ ॥ ਨਾਮੋਹੁ ਤੂਟੈ ਨਾ ਥਾਇ ਪਾਹਿ ॥ ੫
gură dīkhiā lē | japŭ tapŭ kamāhĭ || nāmōhŭ tūṭai | nā thāĭ pāhĭ || 16 + 16 = 32 K.

Panǰpadā of Kabīr, Rāg Gauṛī, XV. (Transl. p. 462):

ਜਿਉ ਜਲ ਛੋਡਿ ਬਾਹਰਿ ਭਇਓ ਮੀਨਾ ॥ ਪੂਰਬ ਜਨਮ ਹਉ ਤਪ ਕਾ ਹੀਨਾ ॥ ੧
jyŭ jală čhōḍĭ bāharĭ | bhaïō mīnā || pūrabă janamă hau | tapă kā hīnā || 17 + 17 = 34 K.

Panǰpadā of Kabīr, Rāg Gauṛī, L. (Transl. p. 474):

ਪੇਵਕੜੈ ਦਿਨ ਚਾਰਿ ਹੈ ਸਾਹੁਰੜੈ ਜਾਣਾ ॥ ਅੰਧਾ ਲੋਕੁ ਨ ਜਾਣਈ ਮੂਰਖ ਏਆਣਾ ॥ ੧
pēvakaṛai dină čārĭ hai | sāhuraṛai jāṇā || andhā lōkŭ nă jāṇaī | mūrakhă ēāṇā || 20 + 20 = 40 K.

6.—THE ASṬPADĪ.[1]

The Asṭpadī, which is very extensively employed in the Granth, is a stanza consisting usually of eight, and occasionally of more distichs, the two verses of each distich rhyming together at the end. There are also Asṭpadīs, the strophes of which consist of two distichs or of three verses severally, in which latter case all the three verses must have the same end-rhyme. The single verses are scanned by 26 or 24 moras, with a caesura after the thirteenth mora, so that a distich contains either 50 or 48 Kalās. To every Asṭpadī one or two Rahāus may be added, which are never counted.

E.g. Asṭpadī, consisting of distichs, Sirī Rāg, Mah. III., II. (Transl. p. 90):

ਹਉ ਮੈ ਕਰਮ ਕਮਾਵਦੇ ਜਮ ਡੰਡੁ ਲਗੈ ਤਿਨ ਆਇ ॥
hau mai karmă kamāvadē | jamă ḍanḍŭ lagai tină āĭ || 13 + 13 = 26 K.

ਜਿ ਸਤਿ ਗੁਰੁ ਸੇਵਨਿ ਸੇ ਉਬਰੇ । ਹਰਿ ਸੇਤੀ ਲਿਵ ਲਾਇ ॥ ੧
jĭ satĭ gurŭ sēvanĭ sē ubărē | harĭ sētī livă lāĭ || 13 + 11 = 24 K.
50 K.

ਮਨ ਰੇ ਗੁਰਮੁਖਿ ਨਾਮੁ ਧਿਆਇ ॥
mană rē gurmukhĭ nāmŭ dhiāĭ || 13 K.

ਧੁਰਿ ਪੂਰਬਿ ਕਰਤੈ ਲਿਖਿਆ ਤਿਨਾ ਗੁਰਮਤਿ ਨਾਮਿ ਸਮਾਇ ॥ ਰਹਾਉ ॥
dhurĭ pūrabĭ kartai likhiā | tinā gurmatĭ nāmĭ samāĭ || 13 + 13 = 26 K.

ਵਿਣੁ ਸਤਿ ਗੁਰ ਪਰਤੀਤਿ ਨ ਆਵਈ ਨਾਮਿ ਨ ਲਾਗੋ ਭਾਉ ॥
viṇŭ satĭ gură pratītĭ nă āvaī | nāmĭ nă lāgō bhāŭ || 13 + 11 = 24 K.

ਸੁਪਨੈ ਸੁਖੁ ਨ ਪਾਵਈ ਦੁਖ ਮਹਿ ਸਵੈ ਸਮਾਇ ॥ ੨
supănai sukkhŭ nă pāvaī | dukhă mahĭ savai samāĭ || 13 + 11 = 24 K.
48 K.

[1] The Čhapaī is not to be found in the Granth, but is much employed by Gōvind Singh.

Asṭpadī consisting of two distichs severally, Sirī Rāg, Mah. V., I., 1 (Transl. p. 96):

ਜਾ ਕਉ ਮੁਸਕਲੁ ਅਤਿ ਬਣੈ ਢੋਈ ਕੋਇ ਨ ਦੇਇ ॥
jā kau muskǎlǎ ǎtǐ bǎṇai | ḍhōī kōǐ nǎ dēī || 13 + 11 = 24 K.

ਲਾਗੂ ਹੋਏ ਦੁਸਮਨਾ ਸਾਕ ਭਿ ਭਜਿ ਖਲੇ ॥
lāgū hōē dusmǎnā | sākǎ bhǐ bhǎjjǐ khǎllē || 13 + 11 = 24 K.

ਸਭੋ ਭਜੈ ਆਸਰਾ ਚੁਕੈ ਸਭੁ ਆਸਰਾਉ ॥
sabbhō bhǎjjai āsǎrā | čǔkai sǎbhǔ āsǎrāu || 13 + 11 = 24 K.

ਚਿਤਿ ਆਵੈ ਓਸੁ ਪਾਰਬ੍ਰਹਮੁ ਲਗੈ ਨ ਤਤੀ ਵਾਉ ॥
čǐtǐ āvai ōsǔ pārbrǎhǎmǔ | lǎgai nǎ tattī vāu || 13 + 11 = 24 K.

96 K.

7.—THE SLŌK.

The Slōk used in the Granth is not to be confounded with the epic Sanskrit Shlōk consisting of 16 + 16 syllables, the word Slōk being taken in the Granth in the more general sense of a stanza. The Slōk of the Granth consists usually of one distich, but also of a triplet, or two or three distichs, which rhyme at the end, there being a caesura in each verse after the twelfth mora; the whole verse is scanned by 12 + 10 = 22 moras.

E.g. Slōk of Kabīr I. (Transl. p. 671):

ਕਬੀਰ ਮੇਰੀ ਸਿਮਰਨੀ ਰਸਨਾ ਊਪਰਿ ਰਾਮੁ ॥
kǎbīrǎ mērī sǐmǎrǎnī | rasnā ūpǎrǐ rāmǔ || 12 + 10 = 22 K.

ਆਦਿ ਜੁਗਾਦੀ ਸਗਲ ਭਗਤ ਤਾ ਕੋ ਸੁਖੁ ਬਿਸ੍ਰਾਮੁ ॥
ādǐ jǔgādī sǎgǎlǎ bhǎgtǎ | tā kō sǔkhǔ bǐsrāmǔ || 12 + 10 = 22 K.

44 K.

Japjī, Slōk at the end of it (Transl. p. 13):

ਪਵਣੁ ਗੁਰੂ ਪਾਣੀ ਪਿਤਾ ਮਾਤਾ ਧਰਤਿ ਮਹਤੁ ॥
pavǎṇǔ gǔrū pāṇī pǐtā | mātā dhǎrtǐ mǎhǎtǔ || 12 + 10 = 22 K.

ਦਿਵਸੁ ਰਾਤਿ ਦੁਇ ਦਾਈ ਦਾਇਆ ਖੇਲੈ ਸਗਲ ਜਗਤੁ ॥
dǐvǎsǔ rātǐ duǐ dāī dāyā | khēlai sǎgǎlǎ jǎgǎtǔ || 12 + 10 = 22 K.

ਚੰਗਿਆਈਆ ਬੁਰਿਆਈਆ ਵਾਚੈ ਧਰਮੁ ਹਦੂਰਿ ॥
čǎngyāīā buryāīā | vāčai dhǎrmǔ hǎdūrǐ || 12 + 10 = 22 K.

ਕਰਮੀ ਆਪੋ ਆਪਣੀ ਕੇ ਨੇੜੈ ਕੇ ਦੂਰਿ ॥
kǎrǎmī āpō āpṇī | kē nēṛai kē dūrǐ || 12 + 10 = 22 K.

ਜਿਨੀ ਨਾਮੁ ਧਿਆਇਆ ਗਏ ਮਸਕਤਿ ਘਾਲਿ ॥
jǐnī nāmǔ dhǐāiā | gǎē sǎmǎkǎtǐ ghālǐ || 12 + 10 = 22 K.

ਨਾਨਕ ਤੇ ਮੁਖ ਉਜਲੇ ਕੇਤੀ ਛੁਟੀ ਨਾਲਿ ॥
nānǎkǎ tē mǔkhǎ ǔjǎlē | kētī čhǔṭī nālǐ || 12 + 10 = 22 K.

132 K.

Remark. In the Bhōg of the Granth (see p. ccxxi) there are some Slōks by Nānak and Arjun called ਸਲੋਕ ਸਹਸਕ੍ਰਿਤੀ. As they are neither Sanskrit Shlōks nor composed in the Shlōka metre, the question is, what is meant by ਸਲੋਕ ਸਹਸਕ੍ਰਿਤੀ? The easiest solution would be to understand by it the *Sanskriti metre*, which is much used in Prākrit. In Prākrit poetry the Sanskriti is a stanza consisting of four verses, which together contain the number of 96 moras, each verse averaging between 18 and 28 moras. Very likely by the word ਸਹਸਕ੍ਰਿਤੀ a variation of this metre is intended, as those Slōks in the Granth do not contain the same number of moras.

The Slōk of Mah. I. is scanned by $2 \times 5 + 5 + 4 = 28$ Kalās, as:

ਪੜ੍ਹਿ ਪੁਸਤਕ ਸੰਧਿਆ ਬਾਦੰ ॥ ਸਿਲ ਪੂਜਸਿ ਬਗੁਲ ਸਮਾਧੰ ॥

paṛi pusta|ka sandhiā | bādam || sila pūja|si bagula sa|mādham || 14 + 14 = 28 K.

ਮੁਖਿ ਝੂਠੁ ਬਿਭੂਖਨ ਸਾਰੰ ॥ ਤ੍ਰੈਪਾਲ ਤਿਹਾਲ ਬਿਚਾਰੰ ॥

mukhi jhūṭhu | bibhūkana | sāram || traipāla | tihāla bi|čāram || 14 + 14 = 28 K.

The whole first Slōk contains five verses of this kind and consequently $5 \times 28 = 140$ Kalās.

The ਸਲੋਕ ਸਹਸਕ੍ਰਿਤੀ of Mah. V. are scanned in a different way, as shown by the first Slōk, which runs thus:

ਕਤੰਚ ਮਾਤਾ ਕਤੰਚ ਪਿਤਾ ਕਤੰਚ ਬਨਿਤਾ ਬਿਨੋਦ ਸੁਤਹ ॥

katanča | mātā | katanča | pitā || katanča | banitā | binōda | sutaha || 4 + 4 + 4 + 3 = 15, 4 + 4 + 4 + 3 = 15 } = 30 K.

ਕਤੰਚ ਭ੍ਰਾਤ ਮੀਤ ਹਿਤ ਬੰਧਵ ਕਤੰਚ ਮੋਹੁ ਕੁਟੰਬ ਤੇ ॥

katanča | bhrāta | mīta hi|ta bandhava || katanča | mōhu ku|ṭamba tē || 4 + 3 + 4 + 4 = 15, 4 + 4 + 4 = 12 } = 27 K.

ਕਤੰਚ ਚਪਲ ਮੋਹਨੀ ਰੂਪੰ ਪੇਖੰਤੇ ਤਿਆਗੰ ਕਰੋਤਿ ॥

katanča | čapala | mōhanī | rūpam || pēkhantē | tyāgam | karōti || 4 + 3 + 4 + 4 = 15, 4 + 4 + 4 = 12 } = 27 K.

ਰਹੰਤ ਸੰਗ ਭਗਵਾਨ ਸਿਮਰਣੁ ਨਾਨਕ ਲਬਧ੍ਯੰ ਅਚੁਤ ਤਨਹ ॥

rahanta | sanga | bhagvāna | simaraṇu || nānaka | labdhyam | accuta | tanaha || 4 + 3 + 4 + 4 = 15, 4 + 4 + 4 + 3 = 15 } = 30 K.

114 K.

In this Slōk the first and fourth, and the second and third verse rhyme together, and have also the same number of moras. Whatever be therefore understood by ਸਲੋਕ ਸਹਸਕ੍ਰਿਤੀ, so much is evident, that they have no uniform metre, as the Slōks also vary considerably in the number of verses.

8.—THE ḌAKHAṆĀ.

The Ḍakhaṇā is a couplet of two verses, which rhyme at the end, each verse being divided by a caesura into two hemistichs after the twelfth mora, the whole verse containing $12 + 10 = 22$ Kalās, which may be distributed into Gaṇas of $5 + 4 + 3 \,||\, 3 + 4 + 3$. As regards the number of moras, the Ḍakhaṇā therefore coincides with the Slōk (see sub. 7), the only difference being, that the Ḍakhaṇā is always restricted to one couplet. In the Granth the Ḍakhaṇā is always found in connexion with the so-called Čhant (see the next following metre), which it usually precedes.

We subjoin two Ḍakhaṇās, from Sirī Rāg, Čhant I., 1, 2, Mah. V. (Transl. p. 109):

ਹਠ ਮਝਾਹੂ ਮਾ ਪਿਰੀ ਪਸੇ ਕਿਉ ਦੀਦਾਰੁ ॥

haṭha majhāhu mā pirī | pasē kiu dīdāru || 12 + 10 = 22 K.

ਸੰਤ ਸਰਣਾਈ ਲਭਣੇ ਨਾਨਕ ਪ੍ਰਾਣ ਅਧਾਰੁ ॥

santa saraṇāī labhaṇē | nānaka prāṇa adhāru || 12 + 10 = 22 K.

44 K.

ਧੂੜੀ ਮਜਨੁ ਸਾਧ ਖੇ ਸਾਈ ਥੀਏ ਕ੍ਰਿਪਾਲੁ ॥
dhūṛī măjănŭ sādhă khē | sāī thīē kripālŭ || 12 + 10 = 22 K.

ਲਧੇ ਹਭੇ ਥੋਕੜੇ ਨਾਨਕ ਹਰਿ ਧਨੁ ਮਾਲੁ ॥
laddhē habbhē thōkăṛē | nānăkă hărĭ dhănŭ mālŭ || 12 + 10 = 22 K.
44 K.

9.—THE ČHANT.

Čhant (ਛੰਤ) is in the Granth the name of a stanza, which consists of three couplets, each couplet having its own rhyme. Each verse of the couplet contains 28 moras, being scanned by 8 + 8 + 8 + 4, with a caesura after the sixteenth mora, the whole couplet therefore 28 + 28 = 56 moras. *E.g.* Sirī Rāg, Čhant, Mah. V., I. (III.) (Transl. p. 109):

ਚਰਨ ਕਮਲ ਸਿਉ ਪ੍ਰੀਤਿ[1] ਰੀਤਿ ਸੰਤਨ ਮਨਿ ਆਵਏ ਜੀਉ ॥
čărănă kămălă sĭŭ | pirīti rīti || santănă mănĭ ā|văē jĭŭ || 28 K.

ਦੁਤੀਆ ਭਾਉ ਬਿਪਰੀਤਿ ਅਨੀਤਿ ਦਾਸਾ ਨਹ ਭਾਵਏ ਜੀਉ ॥
dŭtīā bhāu | bĭprīti ănīti || dāsā năhă bhā|văē jĭŭ || 28 K. — 56 K.

ਦਾਸਾ ਨਹ ਭਾਵਏ ਬਿਨੁ ਦਰਸਾਵਏ ਇਕ ਖਿਨੁ ਧੀਰਜੁ ਕਿਉ ਕਰੈ ॥
dāsā năhă bhāvăē | bĭnŭ dărsāvăē || ĭkă khĭnŭ dhīrăjŭ | kĭŭ kărai || 28 K.

ਨਾਮ ਬਿਹੂਨਾ ਤਨੁ ਮਨੁ ਹੀਨਾ ਜਲ ਬਿਨੁ ਮਛੁਲੀ ਜਿਉ ਮਰੈ ॥
nāmă bĭhūnā | tănŭ mănŭ hīnā || jălă bĭnŭ măčhŭlī | jĭŭ mărai || 28 K. — 56 K.

ਮਿਲੁ ਮੇਰੈ ਪਿਆਰੇ ਪ੍ਰਾਨ ਅਧਾਰੇ ਗੁਣ ਸਾਧ ਸੰਗਿ ਮਿਲਿ ਗਾਵਏ ॥
mĭlŭ mērai pĭārē | prānă ădhārē || gŭṇă sādhă sangĭ mĭlĭ | gāvăē || 28 K.

ਨਾਨਕ ਕੇ ਸੁਆਮੀ ਧਾਰਿ ਅਨੁਗ੍ਰਹੁ ਮਨਿ ਤਨਿ ਅੰਕਿ ਸਮਾਵਏ ॥
nānăkă kē sŭā|mī dhārĭ ănŭgrahŭ || mănĭ tănĭ ankĭ să|māvăē || 28 K. — 56 K.

168 K.

10.—THE PAUṚĪ.

The Pauṛī (ਪਉੜੀ) is on an average a stanza of five verses (though it may also contain more or less) which all rhyme together at the end, and are divided by a caesura into two hemistichs. In the Granth the Pauṛī usually follows after one or two Slōks and constitutes in connexion with the Slōk or Slōks the so-called *Vār*, which is therefore a mixed stanza. The verses of the Pauṛī are therefore, as a rule, scanned in the same way as the Slōk, viz. by 12 + 10 moras, which may, as in the Dakhaṇā, be distributed into Gaṇas of 5 + 4 + 3 || 3 + 4 + 3.

We subjoin a Pauṛī taken from Sirī Rāg, Vār I., Mah. III. (Transl. p. 113):

ਹਰਿ ਇਕੋ ਕਰਤਾ ਇਕੁ ਇਕੋ ਦੀਬਾਣੁ ਹਰਿ ॥
hărĭ ikkō kartā ikkŭ || ikkō dībāṇŭ hărĭ || 12 + 10 = 22 K.

ਹਰਿ ਇਕਸੈ ਦਾਹੈ ਅਮਰੁ ॥ ਇਕੋ ਹਰਿ ਚਿਤਿ ਧਰਿ ॥
hărĭ ikkăsai dāhai ămărŭ || ikkō hărĭ čittĭ dhărĭ || 12 + 10 = 22 K.

[1] Though the word is written here ਪ੍ਰੀਤਿ, it must be read piriti, for the sake of the metre.

ਹਰਿ ਤਿਸੁ ਬਿਨੁ ਕੋਈ ਨਾਹਿ ਡਰੁ ਭ੍ਰਮੁ ਭਉ ਦੂਰਿ ਕਰਿ ॥
hărĭ tĭsŭ bĭnŭ kōĭ nāhĭ || ḍărŭ bhrămŭ bhaŭ dūrĭ kărĭ || $12 + 10 = 22$ K.

ਹਰਿ ਤਿਸੈ ਨੋ ਸਾਲਾਹਿ ਜਿ ਤੁਧੁ ਰਖੈ ਬਾਹਰਿ ਘਰਿ ॥
hărĭ tĭsaī nō sālāhĭ jĭ || tŭdhŭ răkhaī bāhărĭ ghărĭ || $12 + 10 = 22$ K.

ਹਰਿ ਜਿਸ ਨੋ ਹੋਇ ਦਇਆਲੁ ਸੋ ਹਰਿ ਜਪਿ ਭਉ ਬਿਖਮੁ ਤਰਿ ॥
hărĭ jĭsă nō hōĭ dăyālŭ sō || hărĭ jăpĭ bhaŭ bĭkhămŭ tărĭ || $12 + 10 = 22$ K.
110 K.

But the metre of the Pauṛī may also differ from that of the Slōk, as in fact any metre may be optionally employed as well in the Slōk as in the Pauṛī, so that the appellation of Slōk and Pauṛī is quite indefinite and by no means implies a fixed or uniform metre. The safest thing is always to trace the metre by scanning. We subjoin here an example of a Slōk and Pauṛī taken from Rāg Gauṛī, Bāvanakhrī, Mah. V., XXXV. (Transl. p. 370), in order to prove this. The Slōk is scanned by 25 moras, distributed into Gaṇas of $4 + 6 + 6 \parallel 6 + 3$ Kalās, whereas the Pauṛī is scanned by 32 moras, distributed into Gaṇas of $2 \times 6 + 6 + 4$ Kalās. In the Pauṛī the hemistichs are occasionally written separately (as verses) and rhyme then together, the end-rhyme being in this case dispensed with.

Slōk.

ਨਾਨਕ ਨਾਮੁ ਨਾਮੁ ਜਪੁ ਜਪਿਆ ਅੰਤਰਿ ਬਾਹਰਿ ਰੰਗਿ ॥
nānăkă | nāmŭ nāmŭ | jăpŭ jăpĭā || ăntărĭ bāhărĭ rangĭ || $4 + 6 + 6 \parallel 6 + 3 = 25$ K.

ਗੁਰਿ ਪੂਰੈ ਉਪਦੇਸਿਆ ਨਰਕੁ ਨਾਹਿ ਸਾਧ ਸੰਗਿ ॥
gŭrĭ pūr|aĭ ŭpădē|sĭā nărăkŭ || nāhĭ sādhă | săngĭ || $4 + 6 + 6 \parallel 6 + 3 = 25$ K.
50 K.

Pauṛī.

ਨੰਨਾ ਨਰਕਿ ਪਰਹਿ ਤੇ ਨਾਹੀ ॥ ਜਾ ਕੈ ਮਨਿ ਤਨਿ ਨਾਮ ਬਸਾਹੀ ॥
nannā nără|kĭ părăhĭ tē | nāhī || jā kaĭ mănĭ | tănĭ nāmă bă|sāhī || $2 \times 6 + 6 + 4 = 32$ K.

ਨਾਮੁ ਨਿਧਾਨੁ ਗੁਰਮੁਖਿ ਜੋ ਜਪਤੇ ॥ ਬਿਖੁ ਮਾਇਆ ਮਹਿ ਨਾ ਓਇ ਖਪਤੇ ॥
nāmŭ nĭdhā|nŭ gŭrmŭkhĭ jō | jăpătē || bĭkhŭ māyā | măhĭ nā ōĭ | khăpătē || $2 \times 6 + 6 + 4 = 32$ K.

ਨੰਨਾਕਾਰੁ ਨ ਹੋਤਾ ਤਾ ਕਹੁ ॥ ਨਾਮੁ ਮੰਤ੍ਰੁ ਗੁਰਿ ਦੀਨੋ ਜਾ ਕਹੁ ॥
nannākā|rŭ nă hōtā | tā kăhŭ || nāmŭ mantră | gŭrĭ dīnō | jā kăhŭ || $2 \times 6 + 6 + 4 = 32$ K

ਨਿਧ ਨਿਧਾਨ ਹਰਿ ਅੰਮ੍ਰਿਤ ਪੂਰੇ ॥ ਤਹ ਬਾਜੇ ਨਾਨਕ ਅਨਹਦ ਤੂਰੇ ॥
nĭdhă nĭdhānă | hărĭ ămrĭtă | pūrē || tăhă bājē | nānăkă ănhădă | tūrē || $2 \times 6 + 6 + 4 = 32$ K.
128 K.

11.—THE SAVAYYĀ (OR SAVĀĪĀ).

The Savayyā is a stanza of different length, as it may contain one, two or three couplets, now and then even more. On an average the single verse is scanned by $2 \times 8 + 8 + 8 + 8$ or 32 moras, the caesura dividing the same into two equal hemistichs; but there are also verses of $8 + 8 \parallel 8 + 6$, $8 + 8 \parallel 8 + 5$ and $8 + 8 \parallel 8 + 4$ moras. We meet also with verses consisting only of $8 + 8 + 8$

or 8 + 8 + 4 moras; in this case the verse is not divided by a caesura. The couplets composing the Savayyā have either one common or each their own end-rhyme, occasionally also the hemistichs rhyme together, especially when the stanza consists only of one couplet.

An example of a regular Savayyā is the stanza quoted on page xcv, which we will transcribe here in order to show its scansion.

pāi gahē tumārē | jabba tē tabba ‖ tē kacchu ākha | tarē [1] nahī ānyō ‖ 8 + 8 ‖ 8 + 8 = 32 K.
rāma rahīmā [2] purāna kurāna ‖ anēka kahē mata | ēka [3] na mānyō ‖ 8 + 8 ‖ 8 + 8 = 32 K.
simrita sāstara | vēda sabhē bahu ‖ bhēda kahē hama | ēka na jānyō ‖ 8 + 8 ‖ 8 + 8 = 32 K.
sirī aspāna [4] | kripā tumarī kara ‖ maĩ na kahyō sabha | tōhi pachānyō ‖ 8 + 8 ‖ 8 + 8 = 32 K.
128 K.

We insert here a Savayyā consisting of two couplets, each verse of which contains 8 + 8 ‖ 8 + 6 and 8 + 8 ‖ 8 + 5 moras respectively. Savāīē referring to Mah. I. (Transl. p. 694):

ਗਾਵਉ ਗੁਨ ਪਰਮ ਗੁਰੂ ਸੁਖ ਸਾਗਰ ਦੁਰਤ ਨਿਵਾਰਣ ਸਬਦ ਸਰੇ ॥
gāvau guna parama | gurū sukha sāgara ‖ durta nivārana | sabda sarē ‖ 8 + 8 ‖ 8 + 6 = 30 K.
ਗਾਵਹਿ ਗੰਭੀਰ ਧੀਰ ਮਤਿ ਸਾਗਰ ਜੋਗੀ ਜੰਗਮ ਧਿਆਨੁ ਧਰੇ ॥
gāvahi gambhīra | dhīra mati sāgara ‖ jōgī jangama | dhyānu dharē ‖ 8 + 8 ‖ 8 + 6 = 30 K.
ਗਾਵਹਿ ਇੰਦ੍ਰਾਦਿ ਭਗਤ ਪ੍ਰਹਿਲਾਦਿਕ ਆਤਮ ਰਸੁ ਜਿਨਿ ਜਾਣਿਓ ॥
gāvahi indrādi | bhagata prahilādi‖ka ātma rasu jini | jāniō ‖ 8 + 8 ‖ 8 + 5 = 29 K.
ਕਬਿ ਕਲਸੁ ਜਸੁ ਗਾਵਉ ਗੁਰ ਨਾਨਕ ਰਾਜ ਜੋਗੁ ਜਿਨਿ ਮਾਣਿਓ ॥
kabi kalasu jasu gā|vau gura nānaka ‖ rāja jōgu jini | māniō ‖ 8 + 8 ‖ 8 + 5 = 29 K.
118 K.

12.—THE GĀTHĀ.

The Gāthā, of which only a small piece (of 24 stanzas by Arjun) is to be found in the Granth, is not the usual Āryā metre, consisting of 7½ feet respectively and containing 30 + 27 = 57 Kalās, but comprehends a number of the many varieties of that metre, which have come into use in the later Prākrit and are destitute of the end-rhyme, for which they substitute an internal rhyme after the twelfth mora, though not always. Each stanza must therefore be scanned by itself, in order to determine the exact metre. We subjoin here as examples the first two Gāthās.

The first Gāthā is a couplet scanned by 29 + 29 = 58 Kalās and called *Vigīti*, as:

ਕਰਪੂਰ ਪੁਹਪ ਸੁਗੰਧਾ ਪਰਸ ਮਾਨੁਖ੍ਯ ਦੇਹੰ ਮਲੀਣੰ ॥
karpūra | puhapa su|gandhā ‖ parsa | mānukhya | dēham | malīnam ‖ 12 + 17 = 29 K.
ਮਜਾ ਰੁਧਿਰ ਦੁਰਗੰਧਾ ਨਾਨਕ ਅਥਿ ਗਰਬੇਣ ਅਗਾਨਣੋ ॥ ੧
majjā | rudhira dur|gandhā ‖ nānaka | atthi | garbēna | agyānanō ‖ 12 + 17 = 29 K.
58 K.[5]

[1] In the text on p. xcv ਤਰੇ has fallen out.

[2] The original has only ਰਹੀਮ, but the metre requires ਰਹੀਮਾ, which is also justified by the grammar, as it is the Vocative.

[3] In the text there is a misprint on p. xcv, as ਏਕ must be read instead of ਅਨੇਕ.

[4] Though written in the original ਸ੍ਰੀਅਸਪਾਨ, an *i* must here be inserted in the conjunct consonant *sr*, in order to get the necessary number of moras.

[5] As regards the distribution of the feet there are always 4 + 4 + 4 in the first Pada, in the second Pada we have 3 + 5 + 4 + 5, but in the fourth Pada 4 + 3 + 5 + 5.

The second Gāthā is a couplet scanned by 27 + 29 and called *Čandrikā*, as:

ਪਰਭਾਣੋ ਪਰਜੰਤਿ ਆਕਾਸਹ ਦੀਪ ਲੋਅ ਸਿ ਖੰਡਣਹ ॥

prăm̄āṇ̄ō | prăjănti | āk̄āsăhă || dīpă | lōă sĭ | kh̄andăṇăhă || 15 + 12 = 27 K.

ਗਛੇਣ ਨੈਣ ਭਾਰੇਣ ਨਾਨਕ ਬਿਨਾ ਸਾਧੂ ਨ ਸਿਧੵਤੇ ॥

gačh̄ēṇă | n̄aiṇă | bh̄ār̄ēṇă || n̄ānăkă | bĭnā | s̄ādhū nă | s̄idhyătē || 12 + 17 = 29 K.

56 K.

The name of the metre is always added in the Granth, where it is a conventional metre, as stated already; where it is not added, it is more or less a fancy metre of the poet. Such stanzas are designated by the Sikhs by the general appellation of "*Pauṛī.*"

TRANSLATION OF THE ADI GRANTH.

OM!

The true name is the creator, the Spirit without fear, without enmity, having a timeless form, not produced from the womb.[1]

By the favour of the Guru!

JAPU.[2]

At the beginning is the True one, at the beginning of the Yug is the True one.[3]
The True one is, O Nānak! and the True one also will be.

1.

By meditation (and) meditation it (*i.e.* the knowledge of the True one) is not effected, though I meditate a hundred thousand times.

By silence (and) silence it is not effected, though I keep on a continual absorption of mind.

The hunger of the hungry does not cease, though I bind together the load of (all) the worlds.[4]

There may be acquired a thousand, a hundred thousand dexterities, not one goes with (at the time of death).

How does one become[5] a man of truth (knowing the True one), how is the embankment of falsehood broken?

He who walks[6] in his (*i.e.* God's) order and pleasure, O Nānak! (and) with (whom) it is (thus) written.

[1] ਅਜੂਨੀ, free from the womb (the same as ਅਜੋਨੀ), ਸੈਭੰ = संभव, birth, production. Other forms are: ਸੈਭੂ, ਸੈਭੋ, ਸੈਭਵਿਆਉ.

[2] The Japu is composed by Bābā Nānak himself. The Sikh tradition runs thus: ਗੁਰੂ ਨਾਨਕਜੀ ਦੀ ਗੋਸਟਿ ਸਿਧਾਂ ਨਾਲ ਹੋਈ ਹੈ ਸੁਮੇਰ ਪਰਬਤ ਤੇ ਜਪੁਜੀ ਦੀ ਚਰਚਾ ਉਥੇ ਹੋਈ ਹੈ. Guru Nānak had a conversation with the Siddhs (Jōgīs) on the mountain Sumēru; there the discourse of the Japu-jī was made. The Japu-jī is composed in so-called ਪਉੜੀ (ladder), verses of unequal length, within which the rhyme may vary.

[3] Manī Singh comments on this: ਆਦਿ ਜਗਤ ਨ ਥਾ ਤਉ ਭੀ ਬ੍ਰਹਮ ਸਤ ਥਾ ਜਉ ਜਗਤ ਹੂਆ ਤਉ ਭੀ ਬ੍ਰਹਮ ਸਤ ਥਾ: when there was as yet no beginning of the world, Brahm was true (existing); when the world was made, then also Brahm was true.

[4] ਪੁਰੀਆਂ, etc. There are said to be fourteen cities, seven celestial and seven sub-terrestrial ones = the whole universe. ਗੰਢਣਾ = ਗਢਣਾ, *v.a.* to bind together (into a bundle).

[5] ਹੋਈਐ is a passive form, properly: it is become, not as the Sikhs now explain it: we become.

[6] ਚਲਣਾ is a verbal adjective, walking.

2.

By (his) order are made the forms (of all things), his order (however) cannot be told.

By his order are made the living beings, by his order greatness is obtained.

By his order are the high and the low, by his order pain and pleasure are set down.

By his order some are pardoned, some are by his order always caused to wander about (in transmigration).

Every one is under (within) his order, exempt from his order is no one.

O Nānak! if one understand his order, he will not speak in self-conceit.

3.

One sings his (*i.e.* God's) power, if one has power (so to do). Another sings (his) liberality, if he knows (his) sign.[1]

One sings his beautiful qualities and greatnesses.—Another sings a difficult thought of science.

One sings: having made the body he reduces it to ashes. Another sings: having taken life he gives it again.

One sings: he is known (manifest), (but) seen afar off. Another sings: being present he sees in the presence.

There is no end of sayings and tellings. The story, story is told by crores, crores, crores.[2]

He (*i.e.* God) goes on giving, they taking become tired. For ages and ages they go on eating.

The Lord goes on executing his order. O Nānak! he expands unconcerned.

4.

True is the Lord, of a true name, in language his love is infinite.[3]

If they speak and ask, he gives, he gives, the Liberal bestows gifts.

What shall again be placed before (him), by means of which his court may be seen?

What speech shall be uttered by the mouth, which having heard he may bestow love?

Reflect at early dawn on the greatness of the true name!

From the destiny comes clothing, from his (favourable) look the gate of salvation.

Thus, O Nānak! it is known, that he himself is true in all (things).[4]

5.

He cannot be established, he is not made. He himself is the Supreme Being.[5]

[1] ਨੀਸਾਣੁ *s.m.* explained in the commentary by ਲੇਖੁ, lot, destiny. The sense is apparently, that God may be known from the gifts he is bestowing. But ਨੀਸਾਣੁ may also be referred to the Sansk. निशाण = निशामन, *perception*: "If he knows the perception (of it), if he is able to perceive it" (*i.e.* the ਦਾਤਿ).

[2] The sense is: God is praised in various ways by innumerable people.

[3] An old Sikh commentary gives the following explanation of this dark passage: ਹੋਰ ਨਾਉ ਪਰਮੇਸੁਰ ਜੀ ਕੇ ਸਭ ਉਸਤਤਿ ਸਿਫਤਿ ਭਾਖਿਆ ਹੋਨਿ ਜਿਉ ਜਿਉ ਅੰਦਰਿ ਭਾਉ ਵਸਦਾ ਹੈ ਤਿਉ ਤਿਉ ਸਲਾਹਿ ਲੈਲੈ ਉਠਦੇ ਹੈਂ, "All the other names of God are uttered in praise; as inside (in the heart) love dwells, so they praise him."

[4] Explained by the commentator: ਸਭੁ ਕਰੇ ਕਰਾਏ ਆਪਿ ਆਪਿ "He himself does and causes to be done all."

[5] ਨਿਰੰਜਨ (निरञ्जन), an epithet of the Supreme Being, free from any stain or contact with the Māyā; pure, light.

By whom he is worshipped, by him honour is obtained. O Nānak, if the abode of virtues [1] be praised.

If he be praised, heard, if love (to him) be kept in the mind. He [2] puts away his pain and brings comfort to his house.

From the mouth of the Guru [3] (=God) is the sound, from the mouth of the Guru is the Vēda, in the mouth of the Guru it is contained (or absorbed).

The Guru is Īsar (Shiva), the Guru is Gōrakh (Vishṇu), Brahmā, the Guru is the mother Pārbatī.

If I would know, would I not tell? the story cannot be told.

O Guru! let me know the One! That the one liberal patron of all living beings may not be forgotten by me! [4]

6.

I bathe at a Tīrtha, if I please him; without pleasing him, what shall I do with bathing?

As much as I see created, what is obtained without destiny,[5] that I may take it?

In (thy) advice are gems, jewels and rubies, if I hear the instruction of the one Guru.

O Guru! let me know the One, that the one liberal patron of all living beings may not be forgotten by me!

7.

If (one's) life last the four periods (of the world), or become tenfold more. If he be known in the nine regions (of the earth), and every one go with (him).

If having got a good name he obtain renown and fame in the world. If his (God's) merciful sight do not come upon him, none will ask a word about him.

Having made him a worm amongst worms (in hell) he puts the sin on the sinner.[6]

O Nānak! he who is void of qualities (=God) bestows favour, he grants favour to the virtuous.

Such a one is not seen, who may bestow some favour on him (God).

8.

By having heard (his name) the Siddhs,[7] Pīrs, Gods and Nāths [8] (have been made). By having heard the earth, the white (Bull),[9] the sky.

By having heard the (seven) insular continents, the (seven) Lōkas, the (seven) Pātālas. By having heard, death cannot affect (them).

O Nānak! (his) worshippers are always happy. By having heard, pain and sins are annihilated.

[1] ਗੁਣੀ ਨਿਧਾਨੁ, "the abode of virtues or of (all) the qualities" is a frequent epithet of the Supreme Being.

[2] *i.e.* the ਸੇਵਕ or worshipper.

[3] ਗੁਰੁ (or ਗੁਰੂ) has in the Granth two meanings; it may denote God, the Supreme Being (ਵਾਹੁ ਗੁਰੂ), or the Guru (who is always considered as an Avatār or incarnation of the Deity).

[4] Said to be the petition of Angad.

[5] ਵਿਣੁ ਕਰਮਾਂ, without destiny. ਕਰਮ in the plural denotes the works of a former birth, and is therefore equivalent to *destiny* (the state of a man in this life depending on the works of a former birth).

[6] The explanation of Manī Singh: ਕੀਟਾਂ ਅੰਦਰਿ ਕੀਟ ਕਰੀਐਗਾ ਦੋਸਾਵਾਲੇ ਜੋ ਪਾਪੀ ਹੈਨ ਸੋ ਭੀ ਇਸ ਨੂੰ ਦੋਸ ਦੇਵਨਗੇ "He will be made a worm amongst worms, also the sinners will blame him," is false, the subject being the same (God).

[7] About the Siddhas or perfect ones, see Wilson's Vishṇu Purāṇa, p. 227. In the Granth Siddh denotes also a Jōgī who has attained to supernatural power.

[8] ਨਾਥ, *i.e.* the nine Nāths or great Gurus of the Jōgīs.

[9] Manī Singh says: ਧਉਲ ਧਰਤੀ ਦੇ ਭਾਰ ਨੂੰ ਉਠਾਇ ਖਲੋਤਾ ਹੈ "The white bull stands, having lifted up the load of the earth." (धवल = वृषश्रेष्ठ).

9.

By having heard (his name) Īsar (Shiva), Brahmā and Indra (have been made). By having heard, they praise with their mouth the mantra.[1]

By having heard, the skill of Jōg (and in) their body the secret (of God).[2]

By having heard, the Shāstras, the Smriti and the Vēdas (are obtained).

O Nānak! (his) worshippers are always happy. By having heard, pain and sins are annihilated.

10.

By having heard (his name), truth, contentment and (divine) knowledge (is obtained). By having heard, the (merit of the) bathing of the sixty-eight Tīrthas.

By having heard and reading, reading (the name) they obtain honour (at the threshold of God). By having heard meditation comes naturally to them.

O Nānak! (his) worshippers are always happy. By having heard, pain and sins are annihilated.

11.

By having heard, the songs (stories) of the Avatārs[3] (have been made). By having heard, (they have become) Shēkhs, Pīrs and Kings.

By having heard, the blind find the road. By having heard, the unfordable (water or river) (becomes) fordable.[4]

O Nānak! (his) worshippers are always happy. By having heard, pain and sins are annihilated.

12.

The state of him, by whom (the name) is minded,[5] cannot be told. If one tells it, he repents of it afterwards.

There is no paper, pen nor writer (to describe it). Sitting they reflect (on him, by whom the name) is minded.

Such is the name of the Supreme Being. If one mind it, he knows it in his heart.

13.

If one mind (the name), understanding and wisdom is obtained in the heart. If he mind (it), the knowledge of the whole world.

If he mind (it), he is not struck in the face. If he mind (it), he does not go with Yama.

Such is the name of the Supreme Being. If one mind it, he knows it in his heart.

14.

If he mind (it), he is not hindered on the road. If he mind (it), he becomes manifest with honour.[6]

[1] ਮੁਖਿ ਸਲਾਹਨ ਮੰਤ "They sing or recite (in his praise) the mantra," *i.e* the गायत्री.

[2] Manī Singh says: ਤਨ ਵਿਚ ਉਨਾਂ ਨੂੰ ਪਰਮੇਸਰ ਦਾ ਭੇਦ ਆਇਆ ਹੈ "into their body the secret of God has come."

[3] ਸਰਗੁਣ = Hindī सरगुण (Sansk. सर्वगुण), possessing all qualities, an epithet for an Avatār. ਗਾਹ *m.* Sansk. गाथ, a song.

[4] ਅਸਗਾਹ *adj.* unfordable (Sansk. अ + सगाध).

[5] ਮੰਨੇ ਕੀ ਗਤਿ, a very short expression. It must be thus constructed: ਨਾਉ ਕੇ ਮੰਨੇ ਕੀ ਗਤਿ, the state of the name being minded.

[6] *i.e.* at the threshold of God.

If he mind (it), he does not anxiously go his way.[1] If he mind (it), he has connexion with piety.
Such is the name of the Supreme Being. If one mind it, he knows it in his heart.

15.

If he mind (it), he obtains the gate of salvation. If he mind (it), he brings about the salvation of his families.

If he mind (it), he is saved, and saves the disciples of (his) Guru. If he mind it, O Nānak! he does not wander about in begging.

Such is the name of the Supreme Being. If one mind it, he knows it in his heart.

16.

The saints (or pious) are chosen, the saints are foremost. The saints obtain honour at the threshold (of God).[2]

The Guru is the one object of meditation to the saints. The saints are lustrous at the gate of the King.

If one tell (it), he may reflect. There is no counting of the works of the Creator.

The Dhaul (white bull) is Dharm (religious and civil law), the son of Dayā (mercy), by whom the rule of contentment is fixed.[3]

If one understand this, he becomes truthful (knowing the truth).

How much is the load upon the Dhaul? There is another earth and beyond another, another. Upon him what load is there and under him what power?

The (different) kinds of living beings, the names of the colours; the destiny of all, (in which) the pen (of God) has moved on.

If one know to write this account, how much will be the written account?

How much is (his = God's) power, his beautiful forms? how much his bountifulness? who knows the food (he is bestowing)?

The expansion (of the universe) is made from one ṭank.[4] From this Lakhs of rivers have been made.

[1] ਮਗੁ ਨ ਚਲੈ ਪੰਥੁ. The Sikhs explain it in different ways. Manī Singh is altogether silent on this point; but another old commentary says: ਆਗੇ ਪੈਂਡੇ ਬੀਚ ਇਕ ਮਗੁ ਪੰਥੁ ਜੋ ਹੈ ਸੋ ਖਰਾ ਕਠਨ ਹੈ ਉਸਿ ਉਪਰਿ ਚੜ੍ਹਿ ਨਾਹੀ ਸਕੀਦਾ "On the journey onwards there is a very heavy (difficult) road, on which one cannot ascend." But this is rather a Musalmān idea. ਮਗੁ signifies also (in Sansk. ਮਘ) "anxious," and this seems to be required by the context.

[2] The commentaries explain the word ਪੰਚ in different ways (understanding by it the *five elements*, etc.). But it is certain, from other passages of the Granth, that ਪੰਚ signifies a holy, pious man.

[3] It is not quite clear what is meant by this. Manī Singh says: ਧੌਲ ਜੋ ਹੈ ਧਰਮ ਹੈ ਦਇਆ ਕਾ ਪੁਤ੍ਰ ਹੈ ਈਸਰ ਸੰਤੋਖ ਉਪਰ ਸੂਤ ਥਾਪਿਆ ਹੈ ਜਲ ਧਰਤੀ ਥੋਂ ਦਸੂਣਾ ਹੈ ਧਰਤੀ ਨੂੰ ਨਾਹੀ ਗਾਲ ਸਕਦਾ ਹੈ ਜੋ ਕੋਈ ਸੰਤੋਖ ਕਰਦਾ ਹੈ ਸਚਿਆਰ ਉਹੋ ਹੈ "The Dhaul is Dharm, the son of Dayā, Īsar has fixed the rule (line) on contentment. The water is tenfold more than the earth, but it cannot dissolve the earth. He who is content is truthful." The sense seems to be: The earth is supported, not by a white bull, but by a fixed law and the mercy of God, who has ascribed to all limits and bounds.

[4] This word (ਕਵਾਉ) is explained differently. Manī Singh says, it signifies ਓਅੰਕਾਰ (Om); another old commentator says, that ਕਵਾਉ is equal to ਟੰਕ = four māsās: ਏਕ ਮਾਸਾ ਪਉਣ ਏਕ ਮਾਸਾ ਪਾਣੀ ਏਕ ਮਾਸਾ ਅਗਨਿ ਏਕ ਮਾਸਾ ਧਰਤੀ ਏਹ ਚਾਰ ਮਾਸੇ ਕੀਏ ਤਿਸ ਕਾ ਏਕ ਟੰਕ ਕਵਾਉ ਹੋਆ "One māsā of wind, one māsā of water, one māsā of fire, one māsā of earth, these four māsās were made; a Kavāu is one ṭank of it." This best suits the context.

What is (thy) power? what (thy) thought? I cannot be sacrificed (to it) one time (*i.e.* I cannot come up to it).

What is pleasing to thee, that is a good work. Thou, O Formless![1] art always in safety.

17.

(There are) innumerable (silent) repetitions (of the name of God), innumerable reverences.
Innumerable worships, innumerable austerities.
Recitations of innumerable books and of the Vēda with the mouth.
Innumerable jōgs (of those, who) remain secluded in their heart.
Innumerable devotees, reflecting on the comprehension of his qualities.
Innumerable truthful ones, innumerable bountiful ones.
Innumerable heroes, eating iron in the face.[2]
Innumerable apply continual meditation in silence.
What is (thy) power? what (thy) thought? I cannot be sacrificed (to it) one time.
What is pleasing to thee, that is a good work. Thou art always in safety, O Formless!

18.

(There are) innumerable fools, stark-blind ones. Innumerable thieves, living on the wages of iniquity.
Innumerable rulers,[3] who commit tyranny. Innumerable cut-throats, who commit murder.
Innumerable sinners, who commit sin. Innumerable liars, who wander about in falsehood.
Innumerable barbarians, who eat dirt. Innumerable calumniators, who put a load on (their) heads.
Nānak expresses a low thought.
I cannot be sacrificed one time (*i.e.* I cannot reach thee).
What is pleasing to thee, that is a good work. Thou art always in safety, O Formless!

19.

(There are) innumerable names,[4] innumerable places. (There are) innumerable, inaccessible, inaccessible worlds.

Innumerable speak (his praise), bending the head downwards.[5]

Of letters (consists) the name, of letters the praise (of the name). Of letters (divine) knowledge, songs, the metrical recitals of (his) qualities.

Of letters (consists) writing, speaking, voice.

In letters is the description of destiny.[6] By whom these (letters) have been written, upon him it (*i.e.* destiny) is not.

[1] Explained by the commentator: ਰੂਪ ਰੰਗ ਤੇ ਰਹਿਤ ਹੈ "Thou art free from form and colour."

[2] ਮੁਹਿ ਭਖ ਸਾਰ is inverted, for the sake of the rhyme, instead of ਸਾਰ ਭਖ "iron-eating in the face," an idiomatic expression for—exposing one's face bravely to the iron (in battle).

[3] ਅਮਰ is explained by ਰਾਜੇ rājās; it may be = أمير (its broken plur. is أمرا). But it may also be translated: Innumerable give orders of violence.

[4] Names, *i.e.* of created beings or things.

[5] ਸਿਰਿਭਾਰੁ is adjective, bending the head downwards (and the feet upwards), as some Faqīrs do. An old commentator (without name) says: ਸਿਰਤਲਵਾਏ ਹੋਇਕੇ ਜਸੁ ਕਰਦੇ ਹੈਨ "With the head downwards they praise him."

[6] ਸੰਜੋਗ *conjunction*, instead of ਸੰਜੋਗ ਵਿਜੋਗ *conjunction* and *separation* (of the beings) = destiny.

As he commands, so, so it falls. As much as is created, so much is the name (of it).[1]
Without a name there is no place.
What is (thy) power? what (thy) thought? I cannot be sacrificed one time.
What is pleasing to thee, that is a good work. Thou art always in safety, O Formless!

20.

If hand, foot, body and trunk become defiled. By washing with water the dust will be removed.
If the cloth be polluted by urine. By applying soap it will be washed.
If the intellect be defiled with sins. It is washed in the dye of the name (of God).
There is no rehearsal of meritorious (or) sinful deeds.[2] Having done a deed, (man) puts it down in writing[3] and takes it with him (to Yama).
He himself having sown will himself eat (the fruit). O Nānak! by order (man) comes and goes.[4]

21.

Tīrthas, austerity, mercy, gifts given: if one obtain (their merit), it is the honour of a sesam-seed.
If (the name of God) be heard, minded and loved in the heart: he bathes inwardly (as) at a Tīrtha.
All virtues are thine, I have none. Without virtues being practised worship is not made.
Be blessed! is the speech of the Brahman. He is pleasing to the True one, (who has) always a desire in (his) heart.[5]

What is that season, what the time, what the lunar date, what the week-day? What those seasons, what the month, in which the forms have been created?

The time is not found out by the Paṇḍits, though it be written out of a Purāṇ. The time is not found out by the Kāzīs, though they write out a document from the Korān.

The lunar date, the week-day, the Jōgī does not know; the season, the month, nobody (knows).

When the creator makes the creations, he himself (only) knows. How shall I tell (him)? how shall I praise (him)? how shall I describe (him)? how shall I know (him)?

O Nānak! from the saying of (others)[6] every one says (it), one is more clever than the other.

Great is the Lord, of a great name, by whom creation is made. O Nānak! if one thinks (anything is made) by himself, he, having gone onwards (to the other world) will not be honoured.[7]

[1] The sense is: every created thing has its name and thereby its own destiny. God alone is ਅਲੇਖੁ, *i.e.* not subject to destiny.

[2] ਪੁੰਨ, religious merit by good actions; ਪੁੰਨੀ is the Gen. Plur.

[3] The Sikh tradition is, that every man writes down (unknowingly) all his acts and deeds, and will present the tablet of them to Dharm-rājā (Yama) when dying.

[4] He comes and goes, *i.e.* man is subjected to transmigration by reason of his former (bad) works.

[5] The Sikh commentaries do not know what to make of these words. The sense seems to be this:—The Brahman, when asking for a gift, says ਸੁਅਸਤਿ (स्वस्ति), Blessed! As men give gifts willingly when thus addressed by a Brahman, so God is also pleased when there is always desire in the heart to praise him and to ask from him. The following verses are not logically connected with the preceding. Nānak is in the habit of rambling from one thought to another without any attention to logical coherence.

[6] ਆਖਣਿ ਆਖੈ; ਆਖਣਿ must here be taken as the Ablative Sing. The Sikh commentators, who are all totally unacquainted with the grammar of the old Hinduī, pass all such words in deep silence, without giving the least hint.

[7] Explained thus by the old commentator: ਜੇ ਕੋਈ ਜਾਣੈ ਜੋ ਤਿਲਕਭਰ ਭੀ ਮੈ ਥੋ ਹੋਇਆ ਹੈ ਸੋ ਦਰਗਾਹ ਕਰਤੇ ਕੀ ਸੋਭਾ ਨਾ ਪਾਵੈ "If one thinks, that as much as a sesam-seed is made by me, he will not obtain honour at the threshold of the creator."

22.

There are Lakhs of nether regions in the nether regions, (Lakhs) of heavens in the heavens. Having sought the end, the end, they have become tired, the Vēdas say one word.

The books (of the Musalmāns) say: (there are) eighteen thousand (worlds), one single hair out of the hairs of a horse.[1]

If there would be an account (of the works of God), it would be written, (but) the account is destroyed (*i.e.* impossible). O Nānak! he is called great, he himself knows his own self.

23.

That I may praise (him), so much understanding I have not obtained. Rivers and brooks fall into the ocean, (but the ocean) is not known[2] (by them).

Kings and Sultāns with rings, with houses, wealth and property, do not become equal to an ant, if from its mind he (God) is not forgotten.[3]

24.

There is no end of his praises, in saying (them) there is no end.

There is no end of his works, in (his) giving there is no end.

There is no end in seeing (his works), no end in hearing (them).

No end is known, what counsel is in (his) mind. No end is known, what his form is. No end nor limit is known.

On account of (not getting) his end, how many lament! His bounds cannot be obtained. This end nobody knows. If much be said, much (more) is (to be said).

Great is the Lord, high his place. Higher than high is his name.

If one be so high, he may know this high one.

So great a one, as he himself is, he himself (only) knows.

O Nānak! by his favourable look and by destiny the gift (of knowing his name is obtained).

25.

His great benevolence cannot be written. He is a great giver, there is not a bit of greediness (in him).

Some warriors ask boundless (things). Some have no consideration nor thought (to ask anything).

Some are consumed and broken down by passion. Some having taken (his gifts) deny it.

Some fools go on eating. Some are always afflicted by pain and hunger.

This also is thy gift, O bountiful! Imprisonment (and) release is made by (thy) decree. The other (things) no one can tell.

If one having eaten (his gifts) falls into reviling. He will know, how much he will be struck in the face.[4]

[1] The Sikhs are in great trouble about the explanation of these words, and give all possible comments. But the sense is apparently: the eighteen thousand worlds, which the Musalmāns assert to have been created, are just as much as a single hair out of the hairs of a horse; *i.e.* there are innumerable other worlds. ਧਾਤੁ, *s.m.* signifies—*a constituent part of anything*; here, a single hair out of those which constitute the hairs of a horse.

[2] ਨ ਜਾਣੀਅਹਿ "is not known"—must be referred to ਸਮੁੰਦ. The other ਸਮੁੰਦ is an adjective (समुद्र), *having a sealing-ring*, the sign of royalty or power. But the whole verse is without any apparent logical connexion and the Sikh commentators are totally bewildered about it.

[3] The sense is: if by an ant (a low creature or man) God is not forgotten, wealthy kings will not be equal to it.

[4] ਜੇਤੀਆਂ supply ਚੋਟਾਂ, blows.

He himself knows, himself having given (the gift).

This also some, some say. On whom he bestows his praise and laud: he, O Nānak! is king of kings.

26.

Invaluable are his qualities, invaluable the occupation (with them). Invaluable those occupied (with them), invaluable the store-rooms.[1]

Invaluable (those who) come (to them), invaluable (those who) take away (*i.e.* stores from them). Invaluable (those who) please (him), invaluable (those who) are absorbed (in him).

Invaluable (his) justice, invaluable his court (of justice).

Invaluable (his) balance, invaluable (his) measure.[2] Invaluable (his) bountifulness, invaluable the perception (of it).[3]

Invaluable (his) work, invaluable (his) command.

Any thing more invaluable than invaluable cannot be told.

They go on telling (them),[4] telling (them) in devotion. They tell them who read the Vēdas and the Purāṇas.

The learned men tell and explain them. The Brahmās and Indras tell them.

The Gōpīs and Gōvind (Krishṇa) tell them. Īsar (Shiva) and the Siddhs tell them.

As many as are made Buddhas (sages), tell them. The Dēvas and Dānavas (demons, enemies of the Dēvas) tell them.

The Gods and Naras[5] and Munis tell them, having worshipped. Some tell (and some) begin to tell them. Some having told, told them, rise and go off.

So many creatures are made and others (still) he makes. Yet nobody, nobody is able to tell (his qualities).

As great as he pleases, so great he becomes (by self-expansion). O Nānak! that True one (=God) knows it.

If some contentious man tell (it): he is written down as a fool above fools.[6]

27.

What is that gate, what that house, in which sitting he supports all?[7]

There are many innumerable musical instruments and souuds; how many are the players?

How many Rāgs with the Rāgiṇīs are sung and how many are the singers?

To thee sing wind, water, fire, at (thy) door sings Dharm-rājā.

The Čitraguptas sing (to thee), who write down continually, know and weigh the religious deeds.

(To thee) sings Īsar (Shiva), Brahmā, the Dēvī; having always remembered (thee) they obtain honour.

At thy gate sings Indra with the gods sitting on Indra's throne.

[1] ਵਾਪਾਰੀਆ a trader occupied in any business. These are the pious disciples, who are called in the Granth ਨਾਮ ਦੇ ਵਾਪਾਰੀਏ; the ਭੰਡਾਰ, or store-houses, are the ਸਾਧੁ, or saints, from whom the name may be obtained.

[2] ਪਰਵਾਣੁ signifies here "measure" and is the same as परिमाण, as proved by other passages of the Granth.

[3] Compare v. 3.

[4] ਆਖਣਾ "to tell," *i.e.* the qualities or the praises of the name, the greatness of the name.

[5] Naras, a kind of centaurs, with the limbs of horses and human bodies.—Wilson, Vishṇu Purāṇa, p. 42.

[6] The Sikh commentaries have totally misunderstood the whole verse.

[7] It may also be translated by the second person, "thou supportest," as concluded from Sōdar (after the Jap-jī), where ਸੋ ਦਰੁ ਤੇਰਾ is found.

(To thee) sing the Siddhs (Jōgīs) in their deep meditations,[1] the Sādhs (devotees) sing (to thee) having reflected.

(To thee) sing the truthful and contented, (to thee) sing the hardy heroes. (To thee) sing the Paṇḍits and Rakhīsars (great abstinent men), who read continually with the Vēdas (in their hands).

(To thee) sing the fascinating women, who enchant the mind in the heavens, in the mortal world[2] and in the nether regions.[3]

(To thee) sing the gems, produced by thee, with the sixty-eight Tīrthas.

(To thee) sing the heroes very powerful in battle, (to thee) sing the four mines.[4]

(To thee) sing the (nine) regions, the countries, the worlds,[5] which are made and preserved by thee.

Those sing to thee, who please thee; thy worshippers, steeped (in thee) are full of happiness. Many others, who sing (to thee), do not come to my mind; what can Nānak reflect (judge)?

He, he is always the real Lord, true, of a true name. He is and will be, he will not be destroyed, by whom creation is made.

By whom a Māyā (illusive world) of various colours, kinds and sorts is produced. Having made (it), he sees, his own work is, as his greatness is.

What is pleasing to him, that he will do, no order can be given (to him).

He is King, Lord of Kings; Nānak (says): the order (pleasure) of the Lord abides (firmly).

28.

(Who) makes contentment the earring, shame the vessel (bowl) and wallet, (who applies to his body) ashes of meditation. (Who makes) death his patched quilt, his body a virgin, the use of the staff faith.[6]

He is an Āīpanthī,[7] (joining) all assemblies; by the heart being overcome the world is overcome.

Salutation to him, salutation! Who is first, spotless,[8] without beginning, immortal (not killed), having the same dress through all ages.

[1] The difference of ਧਿਆਨ and ਸਮਾਧਿ is thus stated by Patanjali: "Restraint of the body, retention of the mind and meditation exclusively confined to one object, is *dhyān*; the idea of identification with the object of such meditation, so as if devoid of individual nature, is *samādhi.*"—Vish. Pur. p. 637, note 21.

[2] ਮਛੁ "the mortal world" (instead of ਮਾਤ, Sansk. मर्त्त्य), commonly called the ਮਾਤ ਲੋਕ (मर्त्त्यलोक), "the world of mortals."

[3] "The fascinating women in heaven and on earth are the Apsarasas, who are of two kinds, ਲਉਕਿਕ (*laukik*), worldly, who are said to be thirty-four in number, and ਦਇਵਿਕ (*daivik*), ten in number."—Vish. Pur. p. 150, note 21. "In the regions of Pātāla, the lovely daughters of the Daityas and Dānavas wander about, fascinating the most austere."—Vish. Pur. p. 204.

[4] The four mines are: ਅੰਡਜ (what is born or produced from an egg); ਜੇਰਜ (what is born from a fœtus, ਜੇਰ = Sansk. जरायु); ਉਤਭੁਜ (produced by growing out, as plants, trees and some lower animals, Sansk. उद्भिज्ज); ਸੇਤਜ (Sansk. स्वेदज), produced from sweat (as lice, etc.).

[5] ਵਰਭੰਡਾ, *s.m.* = ਬਰਭੰਡ, Brahma-egg, globe, world; *m* is first changed to *b* and then aspirated by the influence of the preceding *r*.

[6] ਜੁਗਤਿ ਡੰਡਾ signifies here: *use of the staff*, Sansk. दण्डयुक्ति; all the Sikh explanations are wrong. The sense is: he uses faith for the same purposes as he uses his staff.

[7] Amongst the twelve divisions of the Jōgīs there is one called *Āīpanthīs*, of whom Manī Singh says: ਸਭਨਾਂ ਨਾਲ ਨਿਰਵੈਰ ਹੋਇ ਵਰਤਦੇ ਹਨ "They live without enmity with all men."

[8] ਅਨੀਲੁ "not blue," an epithet of the water = spotless, and thence water generally. But here its original signification must be kept fast: *spotless*. The explanation of the old commentary: ਅਨੀਲੁ ਕਵਨ ਕਹੀਐ ਪਾਣੀ "what is called anīlu"? "water," is therefore wrong.

29.

(His) food (is divine) knowledge, mercy the cook, in every body sounds (his conch's) sound.[1]

He himself is the Lord of Lords, whose are all the increases and perfections, to the others the enjoyment.[2]

Union and separation, both works he sets agoing, (his divine) allotment comes into account.

Salutation to him, salutation! Who is first, spotless, without beginning, immortal, having the same dress through all ages.

30.

There is one Māyā,[3] who was delivered of "setting agoing," her three servants are chosen. One is the creator of the world, one the storekeeper, one keeps the court of justice.[4]

As it is pleasing to him, so he sets agoing, as his order is. He sees, but into their sight he does not come, he is very wonderful.

Salutation to him, salutation! Who is first, spotless, without beginning, having the same dress through all ages.

31.

His seat are the worlds, his storehouses the worlds. Whatever is put down by him (in them), (is put down) once (and for ever). Having made (all things) the creator sees (them). O Nānak! the work of the True one is true (*i.e.* real and lasting).

Salutation to him, salutation! Who is first, spotless, without beginning, immortal, having the same dress through all ages.

32.

If from one tongue a Lakh be made, if (from) a Lakh twenty Lakhs (of tongues) be made. If Lakhs, Lakhs of times the one name of the Lord of the world be uttered.

Are on this way the steps of fellowship ascended becoming twenty-one (twentieths)?[5] Having heard the words (of the birds) the worms became emulous of the sky (*i.e.* of flying).

O Nānak! by (his) favourable glance he is obtained, false is the idle boasting of the false ones.

1 Very likely an allusion to the vital breath.—ਨਾਦ signifies also in Hindī and Panjābī the conch itself, not only its sound.

2 ਰਿਧਿ ਸਿਧਿ may generally signify: prosperity and success; here not the perfections, which are obtained by the practice of the Jōg, of which eight are enumerated (see Wilson's Vish. Pur. p. 45, note 5), elsewhere eighteen; see Gūjrī V. *mah*. 1, 4.

3 ਮਾਈ = Māyā. In the Bhāgavata Purāṇa the divine will, contemplating its expansion into manifoldness, is made to denote a female deity, coequal and coeternal with the First Cause, whose name is Māyā. By her the Lord made the universe. This (originally poetical) personification of the divine will is also adopted here.—See Vish. Pur. p. 21, note 1.

4 ਸੰਸਾਰੀ, the *worldly* or *creator of the world*, is Brahmā; the ਭੰਡਾਰੀ, or storekeeper, is Vishṇu (the preserver), and the judge, Shiva (the destroyer).

5 We have preferred to give the whole sentence as interrogative. Whom Nānak impugns here is not known. ਪਤਿ ਪਵੜੀਆਂ, the steps of fellowship are said to mean ਮੁਕਤਿ, final emancipation; ਪਤਿ = पंक्ति. ਵੀਹ ਵਿਸਵੇ, "twenty twentieths" is a Panjābī expression implying *the whole, certainty*. One above it means absolute truth, and it is therefore explained by the commentators by ਉਤਮੁ ਪਦੁ, the highest degree or ਤੁਰੀਅ (तुरीय), the fourth state of the soul, as absolute identity with the Supreme Being, by abstraction from without.

33.

In uttering (the name) there is no power, in silence there is no power. There is no power in begging, in giving there is no power.

There is no power in living, in dying there is no power. There is no power in dominion and wealth, (by it is) uproar in the mind.

There is no power in intelligence, divine knowledge and reflection. There is no power in cleverness, (by which) the world may be liberated.

In whose hand the power (of liberation) is, he, having created, sees. O Nānak! no one is high or low.[1]

34.

There (are) nights, seasons, lunar dates, week-days (made by him). Wind, water, fire, the nether region.

In the midst of it the earth is placed as a Dharmsālā (Karavān-serai). On it (the earth) are different kinds of living beings and of practices.

Their names are many and endless. (Their) actions, actions[2] are taken into consideration (by God).

He himself is true and true is his darbār. There obtain honour the pious and the chosen.

(According to his) glance (and their) work, the sign (=lot of the creatures) is put down. The raw ones obtain ripeness there. O Nānak! after one has gone (there), the place is seen.

35.

This is the practice of the Dharm-Khanḍ[3] (region of justice, as told in the last verse). Tell now the works of Giān-Khanḍ (the region of divine knowledge).

(There are) many winds, waters, fires, many Kāns (Krishṇas) and Mahēs (Shivas). Many Brahmās, (by whom) creation is formed, and dresses (disguises) of forms and colours.

Many regions of works,[4] many Mērus, many Dhruvas and instructions (of Nārada).[5]

Many Indras, many moons, suns, many orbs and regions.

Many Siddhs, many Buddhs and Nāths (Jōgīs), many disguises of the Dēvī. Many Dēvas, many Dānavas, many Munis, many gems and oceans.

Many mines, many voices,[6] many Lords and kings. Many Vēdas, many worshippers; O Nānak! there is no end of the account.

36.

In Giān-Khanḍ divine knowledge is very strong. There are sounds (of music), pastimes, pleasures and joys.

The character (sign) of Sharm-Khanḍ (the region of happiness[7]) is beauty. There is shaped a very incomparable form (shape).

Its words cannot be told. If one tell them he afterwards repents of it.

There is formed discernment, intelligence and wisdom in the mind. There is formed the knowledge of the Gods and Siddhs.

[1] We have deviated from the common explanations of the Sikhs, which are mostly ludicrous and pass in silence whatever offers particular difficulties.

[2] ਕਰਮੀ is the Formative Plur. dependent on ਵੀਚਾਰੁ.

[3] The Sikhs identify ਧਰਮਖੰਡ with Brahmā-lōka.

[4] The ਕਰਮ ਭੂਮਿ is on this world, according to the Purāṇas; Vish. Purāṇa, p. 212.

[5] His name the Sikh commentators expressly add. On his instruction see Vish. Purāṇa, p. 117.

[6] ਖਾਣੀ, the four mines (of production); ਬਾਣੀ signifies the (four) stages of voice from the stirring of the breath unto articulate utterance.

[7] ਸਰਮ, the Sansk. शर्म (n.) joy, happiness (not the Pers. شَرم).

37.

The character of the region of works (Karm-Khanḍ) is power. There is none else.

There are heroes very powerful in battle. In them Rām (God) remains quite brimful (or filling them).

There Sītā[1] is cool (happy) in greatness. Their beauties cannot be told.

They do not die nor are they deceived. In whose heart Rām dwells.

There dwell some communities of Bhagats (devotees). They are joyful, (for) that True one is in their heart.

In Sač-Khanḍ[2] dwells the Supreme Being (the formless). Having created he sees it and is happy by the sight.[3]

There are regions, orbs and wŏrlds. If one would enumerate them, there is no end of the account. There are worlds and worlds and forms. As his order is, so is the work (done).

He sees and expands, having reflected.

O Nānak! the telling (of it) is hard iron.

38.

Continence is the work-shop,[4] patience the goldsmith. Understanding the anvil, the Vēda the tool. Fear the bellows, the heat of austerities the fire. The vessel is love, in this melt Amrita (nectar). (Then) the sabd is formed[5] in the true mint.[6] This is the work of those, on whom his look and the destiny is (fixed).

O Nānak! the looker on is happy by the sight.

One Slōk.

Wind[7] is the Gurū, water the father, the great earth the mother. Day and night, the two are female and male-nurse; the whole world sports.

Dharm-rājā rehearses the good and bad works in the presence (of God). By their own actions some are near and some are afar off (from God).

By whom the name (of God) has been meditated upon, they are gone (to the other world) having cast off their labour.

O Nānak! their faces are bright, and with them (after them) how many people are saved (liberated)![8]

(End of the Jap-jī).

[1] Sītā, the wife of Rāma. ਸੀਤੇ, cool, refreshed, happy, an allusion to her name Sītā.

[2] The ਸਚ ਖੰਡ corresponds to the सत्यलोक, the habitation of Brahmā.

[3] The Sikh commentaries explain ਨਦਰਿ ਨਿਹਾਲ by: ਜਿਸ ਕਉ ਨਦਰਿ ਕਰਿ ਦੇਖਤਾ ਹੈ ਸੋ ਨਿਹਾਲ ਹੋਤਾ ਹੈ "whom he looks at, he becomes happy;" but there is no indication of the change of the subject.

[4] ਪਹਾਰਾ is the workshop of a goldsmith.

[5] ਸਬਦੁ, the sabd or word of the Guru, the instruction of the Guru concentrated in the name of God. ਘੜੀਐ may also be translated as Imperative or Jussive: should be formed.

[6] ਸਚੀ ਟਕਸਾਲ, the true mint is explained by: ਸਤ ਸੰਗਤਿ, the assembly of the true or pious; in this assembly the true instruction is obtained, as shown by the following verse: for those, on whom his look and mercy is, are the ਸਾਧ Sādhs.

[7] With reference to the wind or breath being the Guru (of all) the Sikhs relate: when Brahmā created the human body, all the limbs, etc., quarrelled, which should be the most important; then Brahmā decided that breath was the greatest, without which the whole body could not live.

[8] ਕੇਤੀ ਛੁਟੀ ਨਾਲਿ, supply: ਕੇਤੀ ਸਰਿਸਟਿ, how much creation or people, a common omission in the Granth.

Om! By the favour of the true Guru.

SŌ DARU.[1]

Rāg Āsā; mahalā I.[2]

I.

What is that thy gate, what thy house, where sitting thou supportest all? Thy musical instruments and sounds are many and innumerable, many are thy musicians.

Many Rāgs of thine with the Rāginīs are sung, many are thy singers. To thee sing wind, water, fire, to thee sings Dharm-rājā at thy gate.

To thee sing the Čitraguptas, who write down continually, know and weigh the religious deeds. To thee sing Īsar, Brahmā, the Dēvī, having always remembered thee they obtain honour.

At (thy) gate sings Indra with the Gods sitting on Indra's seat. To thee sing the Siddhs in their deep meditations, to thee sing the Sādhs (saints) having reflected.

To thee sing the chaste, the truthful, the contented, to thee sing the hardy heroes. To thee sing the Panḍits and Rakhīsars, who read continually with the Vēdas (in their hands).

To thee sing the fascinating women, who enchant the mind in heaven, on earth and in the nether region. To thee sing the gems, created by thee, with the sixty-eight Tīrthas.

To thee sing the heroes very powerful in battle, to thee sing the four mines. To thee sing the regions, the countries (orbs), the worlds, which are made and preserved by thee.

Those sing to thee, who please thee; thy worshippers, steeped (in thy love) are full of happiness. Many others, who sing to thee, do not come to my mind; what can Nānak judge?

He, he is always the true Lord, true, of a true name. He is and will be, he will not cease to be, by whom creation is made.

By whom a Māyā of various colours, kinds and sorts is produced. Having made it he sees, his own work is as his greatness is.

What is pleasing to him, that he will do, his order cannot be reversed. He is King, Lord of Kings; Nānak (says): the order of the Lord abides.[3]

Āsā; mahalā I.

II.

(1). Having heard (it) every one calls him great. How great he is, has it been seen?

His value cannot be obtained nor told. The expounders (of it) remain absorbed in thee![4]

1. *Pause.*

O my great Lord, O deep and profound one! O abode of qualities! Nobody knows, how much and great thy attire is!

(2). All intelligent ones have met and worked up their intelligence. All valuers have met and put down his value.

[1] Sō dar, the words, with which the following Sabd begins. They are taken from Rāg Āsā and inserted here, because they are used for evening prayer by the Sikhs. We find them already in the Jap-jī (with some few alterations), v. 27.

[2] Mahálā (= mahállā) always denotes the *authorship of a piece*, as mahálā páhilā, the first quarter = Bābā Nānak; mahalā dūjā = Angad, etc.

[3] These and the like verses, without a fixed number of lines, are called by the Sikhs *sabds* (words).

[4] This is a Čaupadā (a verse consisting of four couplets).

By the men endowed with divine knowledge and the Gurus of the Gurus.[1] Not a bit can his greatness be told.

(3). All truths, all austerities, all good actions. The greatnesses of the Siddhs (Jōgīs).

Without thee perfections have been obtained by none. By destiny they are obtained and not prevented.

(4). What is the helpless praiser (of thy name)? With praises thy store-rooms are filled.

To whom thou givest, what means has he (to refuse it)? O Nānak! the True one is upholding (him).

Āsā; mahalā I.

III.

(1). If I praise (the name), I live; if it be forgotten, I die. Praising the true name is difficult.

If one has hunger after the true name. He removes his pain by that hunger.[2]

1. *Pause.*

Why is he forgotten, O my mother? True is the Lord, of a true name.

(2). Having told a little of the greatness of the name, they have become tired, its value was not found. If all having met begin to tell it: it does not become greater nor smaller.

(3). He does not die nor become sorrowful. He keeps on giving and does not take food (himself). This is his quality, there is no other. Nor has there been another, nor will there be another.

(4). As great as thou thyself art, so great is thy gift. By whom day and night has been made.

Those, who forget the Lord, are low caste people. O Nānak! without the name they are low (mean) people.[3]

Rāgu Gūjrī; mahalā IV.[4]

IV.

(1). O people of Hari, O true men of the true Guru, make supplication to (=near) the Guru!

We low worms are in the asylum of the true Guru; mercifully manifest (to us) the name!

1. *Pause.*

O my friend, O Gur-dēv! manifest to me the name of Rām! The name taught by the Guru is my soul's friend, the glory of Hari is my prayer (*i.e.* I desire).

(2). Very great are the fortunes of the people of Hari, who have faith in Hari, Hari, thirst after Hari.

If the name of Hari, Hari is obtained, they are satiated, having joined the society (of the saints) they manifest his qualities (*i.e.* praise him).

(3). By whom the taste (flavour) of the name of Hari, Hari has not been obtained, they are luckless with Yama.

Those, who have not come into the asylum of the true Guru and into the society (of the saints), in curse (misery[5]) they have lived, in curse they will live.

(4). By which people of Hari the society of the true Guru is obtained, on their forehead from the beginning (this) decree was written.

Blessed, blessed is the society of the saints, (in) which the taste of Hari has been obtained! the pious people, O Nānak![6] having met, disclose the name.

[1] ਗੁਰਗੁਰਹਾਈ, the Instrum. Plur.

[2] Literally: It is gone (by him) having eaten his pain by that hunger.

[3] ਸਨਾਤਿ is the Arab. صناعت, art, trade; equal to low-born people.

[4] The fourth mahalā is *Gurū Rāmdās*.

[5] ध्रिग = धिक् (*r* is an addition in old Hinduī), fie! for shame! but in Hinduī it has also the meaning of *curse, misery*.

[6] All the Sikh Gurūs call themselves Nānak, because they consider themselves as incarnations of Bābā Nānak, as will be seen in the course of the Granth.

Rāgu Gūjrī; mahalā V.[1]

V.

(1). Why, O my heart, excogitatest thou an effort, in the completion of which Hari is engaged? In rock and stone are beings produced, their daily food is placed before them.

1. *Pause.*

O my Mādhava, he who falls in with the society of the saints, is saved. By the favour of the Guru the highest degree is obtained, dry wood is (made) green.

(2). Mother, father, (household) people, son, wife—none is in the protection (support) of the other.[2]

On every head the Lord provides the daily food; why, O my heart, hast thou been afraid?

(3) Flying, flying a hundred kōs it (*i.e.* the crane) comes, behind it its young ones are left.

Who feeds them, who nourishes them? he (God) in his mind has remembered them.[3]

(4). All the (nine) treasures, the eighteen perfections[4] the Lord has put on the palm of his hand. O humble Nānak! though one become always a sacrifice, a sacrifice, a sacrifice, there is no end nor limit of thine (found).

SŌ PURKHU.

Rāgu Āsā; mahalā IV.

Om! by the favour of the true Guru!

I.

(1). That Supreme Being is Hari, Hari is the Supreme Being, unattainable, unattainable, infinite.

All meditate, all meditate on thee, O Hari, O true creator!

All creatures are thine, thou art the provider of the creatures.

O saints! meditate on Hari, who causes to forget all pains!

Hari himself is the Lord, he himself is the worshipper, what is, O Nānak! the helpless being?

(2). Thou, O Hari! the one Supreme Being, art unintermittingly contained in every body.

Some are donors, some are beggars, all are thy wonderful shows.

Thou thyself art the donor, thou thyself the enjoyer, without thee I do not know another, Sir!

Thou art the Supreme Brahm,[5] endless, endless, what can I tell and explain thy qualities?

Who serve, who serve thee, Sir, their sacrifice is humble Nānak.

(3). Who meditate on thee, O Hari! who meditate on thee, O Hari! those people live comfortably in the world.

Those have become liberated, those have become liberated, by whom Hari has been meditated upon, the noose of Yama has broken away from them.

[1] Mahalā V. = Arjun.

[2] ਧਰਿਆ = ਧਰਿ, *s.f.* protection, prop, support; ਆ is meaningless, and only added to make up the rhyme; similarly ਪਾਰਾਵਾਰਿਆ instead of ਪਾਰਾਵਾਰ. Arjun's poetry is distinguished by such violence; he often spoils the words at the end of a verse so, that they are hardly recognizable.

[3] ਕਰਿਆ might, in Arjun's poetry, also be taken for ਕਰਿ; then the translation would run thus: having remembered them in his mind.

[4] ਨਿਧਾਨ and ਸਿਧਾਨ = ਨਿਧਨ ਸਿਧਨ ਨੂੰ (Accus. Plur.). We find in the Granth also eighteen siddhis mentioned.

[5] ਪਾਰਬ੍ਰਹਮ, Sansk. ब्रह्मपार, the farthest limit of Brahmā, beyond Brahmā, whom Brahmā even cannot reach; or perhaps more simply = परब्रह्म, the Supreme Brahm.

By whom the fearless, by whom the fearless Hari has been meditated upon, all their fear will go, Sir![1]

By whom my Hari is worshipped, they will be absorbed in the form of Hari, Hari.

Those are blessed, those are blessed, by whom Hari is meditated upon, humble Nānak will be their sacrifice.

(4). With thy worship, with thy worship (thy) store-houses are filled, O endless, endless one!

Thy worshippers, thy worshippers praise thee, O manifold, manifold, endless Hari!

They offer to thee manifold, manifold adoration, Sir! they practise to thee austerities, they mutter (thy name), O endless one!

They read many different, different Smritis and Shāstras of thine,[2] they practise the Kriyā and the six works.[3]

Those are Bhagats, those are good Bhagats, who please my Lord Hari.

(5). Thou art the first Being (male), boundless,[4] the creator, like thee there is no other.

Thou art in all ages the (only) one; always, always thou art One, thou art that immoveable creator.

What is pleasing to thyself, that exists; what thou thyself dost, that is made.

By thyself all the creation is produced; by thyself all (the creation) is made and caused to disappear.

Humble Nānak sings the praises of the creator, who knows all.

Āsā; mahalā IV.

II.

1. *Pause.*

Thou art the creator, true, my Lord.

What is pleasing to thee, that will be done; what thou givest, that I obtain.

(1). All is thine, thou art meditated upon by all.

On whom thou bestowest mercy, he obtains the gem of (thy) name.

By the disciple of the Guru it is obtained, by the self-willed it is lost.[5]

By thyself (one) is separated (from thee), by thyself one is united (with thee).

(2). Thou art the ocean, all is in thee.

Without thee there is none other.

The living creatures are thy sport.

Having fallen in with separation, they are separated, with union—there is union.[6]

(3). Whom thou lettest know, that man knows (them).

He always tells and explains the qualities of Hari.

[1] ਗਵਾਸੀ may be pause instead of ਗਵਸੀ, will go, or causal: he will remove.

[2] ਤੇਰੇ might also be translated: to thee, instead of being taken for an adjective.

[3] ਕਿਰਿਆ = Sansk. क्रिया may be taken generally as a holy action (as sacrifice) or specially as *obsequies.* The six works or duties are now: ਸਿਖਾ (Sansk. शिखा), ਸੂਤ, ਧੋਤੀ, ਜਨੇਊ, ਮਾਲਾ, ਤਿਲਕ, *i.e.* the lock of hair on the crown of the head, the toothpick, the Dhōtī, the Brahmanical thread, the rosary and tilak; these are binding on the Khatrī (cf. Sirī Rāg, Asṭp. 26, 5).

[4] ਅਪਰੰਪਰ = Hindī अपरंपार, Sansk. अपारपार, the limit of that which is illimitable, an epithet of Vishṇu; identical with ਅਪਰਪਾਰ, which is also found in the Granth.

[5] ਗੁਰਮੁਖਿ, he who turns his face towards the Gurū, a disciple of the Gurū, and ਮਨਮੁਖਿ, he who turns his face towards his own mind, self-willed, not attending to the Gurū's instruction.

[6] ਮਿਲਣਾ, to fall in with, is constructed with the *Locative* (ਵਿਜੋਗਿ); ਸੰਜੋਗੀ is likewise the Locative, but with lengthened final ī (ਸੰਜੋਗਿ ਮਿਲਿ). But ਸੰਜੋਗੀ may also be taken as an adjective, *united*; then the construction would be: ਸੰਜੋਗੀ ਨੂੰ ਮੇਲੁ ਹੈ. Where all case-signs are left out, the construction is more or less a mere conjecture. The sense, however, is plain: when thou separatest them (from thee, by transmigration), they are separated; when thou unitest them, they are united (absorbed in thee).

By whom Hari is worshipped, he obtains comfort.
He is easily (naturally) absorbed in the name of Hari.
(4). Thou thyself art the creator, all is made by thee.
Without thee there is no other one.
Thou, having created, created, seest and knowest it.
O humble Nānak! the disciple of the Guru will become manifest (at the threshold).

Āsā; mahalā I.

III.

(1). In that pond his dwellings are made; water and fire are made by him.

In mud, which is spiritual blinduess, the foot does not (=cannot) go; we looked, they were submersed in it.[1]

1. *Pause.*

O heart, O foolish heart! dost thou not think of the One?
By Hari being forgotten thy virtues are wasted.
(2). I am not chaste, nor truthful, nor read, foolish and ignorant I am born.
Nānak says: I am in the asylum of those, by whom thou art not forgotten.

Āsā; mahalā V.

IV.

(1). The body of man has been received (by thee), this is thy opportunity to be united with Gōvind.
Other works are of no use to thee. Join the society of the Sādhs (saints)! Adore only the name!

1. *Pause.*

Acquire the means of crossing the waters of existence!
Thy birth (life) goes for nothing in the enjoyment of the Māyā.

(2). Repetition (of the name), austerity, continence, religious works have not been practised (by me), O King Hari!

Nānak says: I have done mean actions! Keep the honour of him, who has fallen on thy asylum!

SŌHILĀ.[2]

Rāgu Gauṛī Dīpakī; mahalā I.

Om! By the favour of the true Guru!

I.

(1). In which house praise is said and the creator thought of.
In that house sing a song of praise and remember the creator!

1. *Pause.*

Sing thou a song of praise of my fearless one!
I am a sacrifice to that song of praise, by which always comfort is obtained.

[1] This verse is generally misunderstood by the Sikhs. First, the text of nearly all the MSS. is wrong; they write: ਪੰਕਜ ਮੋਹ, but it must be written ਪੰਕ ਜੁ ਮੋਹ. ਪੰਕਜ does not signify, as the Sikhs will have it, *mud*, this is ਪੰਕ. If we write ਪੰਕ ਜੁ ਮੋਹ, the sense is quite plain. The first line alludes to Vishṇu sleeping on the ocean (Vish. Pur. p. 634). Nānak says: he, in whom is ਮੋਹੁ, cannot approach him, he is drowned in the mud.

[2] ਸੋਹਿਲਾ *m.* is a song of praise, generally sung at marriages (in honour of the bride and bridegroom), but also in honour of God. The Sōhilā is now used as a prayer, which is said before retiring to rest at night.

(2). Day by day the creatures are supported, the giver will see (to their support).
The value of thy gifts is not obtained (found out); what is the estimate of that donor?
(3). The year and day for the wedding is written, having met apply oil (to the bride and bridegroom)!
Give, O friend! a blessing, by which[1] union with the Lord may be effected!
(4). To every house (comes) this invitatory letter, these calls are always made.
If the caller be remembered, those days, O Nānak! will come.

Rāgu Āsā; mahalā I.

II.

(1). There are six houses, six Gurūs, six doctrines.[2]
The Gurū of the Gurūs is one, the dresses different.[3]

1. *Pause.*

O father![4] in which house praise is said to the creator.
That house keep, it is thy greatness.
(2). Of seconds, minutes, gharīs, watches,[5] lunar dates, week-days, a month is made up.
The sun is the same, the seasons many. O Nānak! many are the dresses of the creator.

Rāgu Dhanāsarī; mahalā I.

III.

(1). The dish is made of the sky,[6] the sun and moon are made the lamps, the orbs of stars are, so to say, the pearls.

The wind is incense-grinding, the wind swings the fly-brush, the whole blooming wood is the flames (of the lamps).

1. *Pause.*

What an illumination is made![7] In the region of existence (world) there is no (such) illumination (made) to thee. The kettle-drum sounds an unbeaten sound.[8]

(2). Thousands are thy eyes, and (yet) thou hast no eye; thousands are thy forms, and (yet) thou hast not one.

Thousands are thy pure feet, and (yet) not one foot is without odour; thousands are thy odours, thus walkest thou, O enchanting one!

[1] ਜਿਉ is here the Ablative, *by which.* ਅਸੀਸੜੀਆ (dim.) may be Sing. or Plur.

[2] The six religious (and philosophical) systems of the Hindūs are: (1) Vēdānta, (2) Sānkhya, (3) Yōga, (4) Mīmānsā, (5) Nyāya, (6) Vaišēṣika.

[3] ਵੇਸ is the dress worn by the devotees (or faqīrs) of the different sects.

[4] ਬਾਬਾ is an endearing address to a junior (even to a girl).

[5] ਵਿਸੁਆ, a twentieth part of time; ਚਸਾ corresponds more to our minute. The ਘੜੀ (घटिका) has only twenty-four minutes. The whole day and night is divided into eight watches (ਪਹਰ, Sansk. प्रहर), each consisting of three hours (or about eight gharīs).

[6] ਮੈ = Sansk. मय, made of, consisting of (elsewhere written ਮਇ).

[7] ਆਰਤੀ (Sansk. आरात्रिक), a religious ceremony. A platter (ਥਾਲੁ) containing lamps (ਦੀਪਕ), incense (ਧੂਪੁ) and flowers (and, as it seems, even pearls) is moved circularly round the head of the image, accompanied with the beating of the kettle-drum (and with ringing of bells).

[8] ਅਨਹਤਾ ਸਬਦ, an unbeaten sound, *i.e.* a sound not produced by beating, an expression which will be frequently met with in the Granth, and which has reference to the practice of the Jōg, as will be explained in its proper place. The explanation of the Sikhs, that ਅਨਹਤਾ means "endless," is wrong and a mere guess.

(3). In all (creatures) is light, he is the light. From his light, light is made in all.

By the testimony of the Guru the light becomes manifest. What is pleasing to him, that becomes an Ārtī (illumination).

(4). (My) mind is longing after the nectar of the lotus of the foot of Hari, daily I am thirsting after it.

Give water of mercy to the deer Nānak, by which dwelling may be made in thy name.[1]

Rāgu Gaurī Pūrbī; mahalā IV.

IV.

(1). With lust and wrath the town is much filled; a Sādhū having come breaks (them) to pieces.[2]

The Guru being obtained by an original decree (of God) causes in the heart devotion to Hari to be excited in the country.[3]

1. *Pause.*

Make to the Sādhū joining of hands,[4] it is a great religious merit.

Make (to him) prostration,[5] it is a great religious merit.

(2). By the Sākats[6] the relish of the enjoyment of Hari is not known; in their heart is the thorn of selfishness.

As, as they walk, they are pierced, they are pained, they suffer death, on their head is punishment.

(3). The people of Hari are absorbed in the name of Hari, Hari; the pain of birth and the fear of death are broken.

The eternal Supreme Being, the Lord is obtained (by them), great is their splendour in the world and universe.

(4). We poor and wretched, O Lord! are thine; O Hari! protect, protect us! thou art very great.

To humble Nānak the name is support and defence; even in the name of Hari is the pith of comfort.

Rāgu Gaurī Pūrbī; mahalā V.

V.

(1). I make supplications, hear, O my friend! it is (here) the time to render service to the saints.

Here (in this world) having obtained the gain of Hari, depart! in the world to come (further on) thy dwelling (will be) easy.

[1] The words must be thus separated: ਹੋਇ ਜਾ ਤੇ, etc., by which (water of mercy) I may dwell in thy name.

[2] ਖੰਡਲ ਖੰਡਾਹੇ, he causes (them, *i.e.* ਕਾਮ ਕਰੋਧ) to be broken to pieces.

[3] ਭਗਤਿ ਹਰਿ ਲਿਵ ਮੰਡਲ ਮੰਡਾਹੇ, the construction of these words is difficult; the subject is the Guru, who causes to be excited (ਮੰਡਾਹੇ = ਮੰਡਾਹਿ or ਮੰਡਾਏ) ਲਿਵ ਭਗਤਿ devotion in the heart (= hearty devotion) in the country (ਮੰਡਲ must be taken as Locative).

[4] ਅੰਜੁਲੀ (Sansk. अञ्जलि), joining the palms of the hands and lifting them up to the forehead in token of reverential salutation.

[5] ਡੰਡਉਤ, *s.f.* prostration, in which the hands are placed on the ground and the breast brought almost in contact with the earth (Sansk. दण्डवत् प्रणाम).

[6] ਸਾਕਤ (Sansk. शाक्त), the designation of a sect, who worship the female principle according to the ritual of the Tantras. There are two chief divisions of them, *Dakṣiṇācārī* and *Vāmăčārī*, or right and left hand ritualists. The worship of the first is public, addressed to the goddesses, especially to forms of *Durgā*, as *Bhavānī* and *Pārvatī*. The worship of the latter, addressed to Tāntrika impersonations of *Durgā*, as *Dēvī*, *Kālī*, *Syāmā*, or a woman representing the शक्ति, is private and said to be celebrated with impure practices.

1. *Pause.*

The (fixed) limit of days and nights decreases, O! O heart! by joining the Guru thy business is adjusted.

(2). This world is in the abnormal state of doubt; he who knows Brahm is saved.

Whom he having awakened makes drink this juice, by him the inexpressible story is known.

(3). For which (object) you are come, that buy ye; the indwelling of Hari in the heart is by means of the Guru.

(If) in your own house (his) residence (is), you will easily obtain comfort, there will not be again a turn of transmigration.

(4). O heart-knowing Supreme Being, O disposer of the destiny! make full the heart's faith!

Thy slave Nānak asks this comfort: make me the dust of the saints!

Om! By the favour of the true Guru!

THE RĀG SIRĪ RĀG.

Mahalā I.; *Ghar* I.[1]

(*Čaupadās.*)[2]

I.

(1). A mansion of pearls may then be raised, with gems indeed it may be studded.

With musk, kungū,[3] aloe-wood and sandal-wood having plastered it he (*i.e.* the builder) may be delighted.[4]

Having seen (it) likely[5] it (*i e.* the name) is forgotten, thy name does not come into (his) mind.

1. *Pause.*

Without Hari life is consumed.

I have asked my own Guru and seen, that there is no other place (but Hari).

(2). The ground may indeed be studded with diamonds and rubies, on the bedstead rubies may be set.

An enchanting woman, with jewels on her face, may glitter and make shows in merriment.

Having seen (her) likely it is forgotten, thy name does not come into (his) mind.

(3). I may become a Siddh, I may employ miraculous power, I may say to prosperity: Come!

I may sit down concealed (or) manifest, thy people may pay reverence (to me).

Having seen (this) likely thy name does not come into (my) mind, it is forgotten.

(4). I may become a Sultān, and having assembled an army I may put my foot on the throne.

I may obtain command and sit down; O Nānak! all is wind!

Having seen (this) likely thy name does not come into (my) mind, it is forgotten.

[1] ਘਰੁ signifies, according to the unanimous testimony of the Sikhs, *a musical note or key*, according to which these verses are to be played and sung. But the exact knowledge of it seems to be lost; for in spite of many inquiries, I have never been able to get an accurate description of it.

[2] This word ਚਉਪਦਾ is missing in some MSS.; the verses are in reality Tripadās. The Sikhs call the Dupadās, Tripadās and Čaupadās generally *sabd.*

[3] ਕੁੰਗੂ, *s.m.* is a very fine composition, of a red colour, made of āmlā (Sansk. आमलक), which women apply to their foreheads.

[4] No person is mentioned; it may therefore be applied to the first or third person singular.

[5] ਮਤੁ is not to be confounded with ਮਤਿ (lest); ਮਤੁ is the Sansk. मे मतम् *according to my opinion*; we have therefore translated it with *likely*.

Sirī Rāg; mahalā I.

II.[1]

(1). (If my) life (be) crores, crores, if wind-drinking (be my) nouriture.[2]

If (dwelling) in a cave I do not see neither moon nor sun, (if) I have no place for dreaming (and) sleeping.

Yet thy value is not found out (by me), how great shall I call thy name?

1. *Pause.*

True is the Formless in his own place.

Having heard, heard the word (one) tells it; if it pleases (to any), he longs (for it).[3]

(2). (If) I be killed and cut (in pieces) repeatedly, (if) I be ground on the grinding stone.[4]

(If) I be burned with fire, (if) I be reduced to ashes (mixed with ashes).

Yet thy value is not found out (by me), how great shall I call thy name?

(3). (If) having become a bird I roam about and go to a hundred heavens.

(If) I do not come into the sight of any one, nor do drink and eat anything.

Yet thy value is not found out (by me), how great shall I call thy name?

(4). O Nānak! if having read, read a paper consisting of a hundred thousand maunds consideration (an idea of him)[5] be made.

(If) the ink do not run short, (if) the wind move the pen.

Yet thy value is not found out; how great shall I call thy name?

Sirī Rāg; mahalā I.

III.

(1). According to destiny one speaks,[6] according to destiny one eats.

According to destiny a way is made, according to destiny one hears and sees.

According to destiny the breath is taken; what shall I go to ask a learned man?

1. *Pause.*

O father, the creation of Māyā is deception.

By the blind one the name is forgotten; he has neither this nor that (world).

(2). What lives, dies; being born[7] it is here (in this world) eaten up by death.

Where having sat down one is informed, there none has gone with.[8]

As many weepers as there are, they all bind together a bundle of rice-straw.[9]

[1] On the occasion when these verses are said to have been uttered by Nānak, see Sikhā̃ dē rāj di vithiā, p. 260.

[2] ਅਪਿਆਉ explained by ਭੋਜਨ; it is the Sansk. आप्याय, satiety; food.

[3] This line is very intricate, as no subject whatever is indicated. The commentary says: ਜੇਹੀ ਕਿਸੇ ਨੂੰ ਚਾਹਣੀ ਹੈ ਤੇਹੀ ਤਮਾ ਲਾਉਂਦਾ ਹੈ, as one has desire, so he covets (it).

[4] ਪਾਇ, lengthened instead of ਪਇ, having fallen (on the grinding-stone).

[5] ਭਾਉ is here identical with ਭਾਵਨਾ, idea, consideration.

[6] ਬੋਲਣੁ ਬੋਲਣਾ = ਬੋਲਣੁ ਬੋਲਦਾ (similarly ਆਖਣੁ ਆਖਣਾ); the subject is, as usual, not mentioned.

[7] ਜਾਇਐ from ਜਾਉਣਾ = Sindhī जापणु, to be born.

[8] ਜਿਥੈ ਬਹਿ ਸਮਝਾਈਐ where one, having sat down, is informed; of what, is not mentioned. Very likely it should be supplied: of one's good and bad actions, for ਸਮਝਾਉਣਾ has this secondary signfication: to correct, to put right.

[9] To bind up a bundle of rice-straw = to do a useless business. Weeping after a dead person is a useless thing.

(3). (Though) every one says very much and no one says little.
(His) value is not obtained by any one, by saying he does not become great.
Thou alone art the true Lord; of other creatures (there are) many worlds.
(4). Who are low-born amongst the low, who are the lowest of the low.
In their society and community is Nānak; what emulation (have I) with the great?
Where the low ones are cared for, there is pardon by thy (merciful) look.

Sirī Rāg; mahalā I.

IV.[1]

(1). Covetousness is a dog, falsehood a sweeper, food obtained by cheating carrion.
Another's defamation (is stirring up) another's dirt, tale-bearing fire, wrath a Čanḍāl.[2]
Enjoyments, praising myself, these are my works, O creator!

1. *Pause.*

O father! may (such things) be spoken, by which honour is obtained.

Those who do excellent works, are called excellent at the gate (of God), those who do low works, sit outside and weep.

(2). (There is) the enjoyment of gold, the enjoyment of silver, the enjoyment of a fascinating woman (and) of the scent of sandal-wood.

(There is) the enjoyment of a horse, the enjoyment of a bed, the enjoyment of a palace; sweet is the enjoyment of meat.

So many are the enjoyments of the body; how shall the name dwell in (this) body?
(3). That speech is acceptable, by which speech honour is obtained.
He who speaks insipid things, comes to grief; hear, O foolish ignorant heart!
Those, who please him, are good; what will the others say?

(4). They have understanding, they have honour, they have wealth in their lap, in whose heart he (God) is contained.

What for praising them? is any one (else) beautiful?
O Nānak! without (his) glance they are not fond of giving nor of the name.

Sirī Rāg; mahalā I.

V.

(1). A ball of intoxication, of falsehood is given by the giver.[3]
The intoxicated forget death, they enjoy themselves four days.
The True one is found by those Sōfīs, who keep fast his court.

1. *Pause.*

O Nānak! know the True one as true!
By whose service comfort is obtained and (one) goes to thy threshold with honour.
(2). He is outwardly true liquor of molasses,[4] in whom the true name is.

[1] The following verses Nānak is said to have uttered in conversation with the Panḍits of Benāres.—See Sikhā̃ dē rāǰ di vithiā, p. 298.

[2] The way in which the Sikh Panḍits explain the Granth may be seen from the Sikhā̃ dē rāǰ di vithiā, p. 299, where the following explanation is given: ਪਰਾਈ ਨਿੰਦਾ ਵਿਸਟਾ ਹੈ, ਕ੍ਰੋਧ ਅਗਨ ਚੰਡਾਲ ਦੇ ਸਮਾਨ ਹੈ "another's defamation is dirt, wrath is fire, it is like a Čanḍāl." The Panḍit in question did not understand the meaning of ਮੁਖ ਸੁਧੀ, and he therefore simply left them out.

[3] The giver here is God, who deludes by his Māyā.

[4] A strong liquor is distilled from ਗੁੜ, or molasses.

I sacrifice myself for those, who hear and explain (it).

Then the heart is known as drunk, when it obtains a place in the palace (of God).

(3). When the name is the water (to bathe in), good actions (and) truth the scent of sandal-wood on the body.

Then the face becomes bright; the gifts of the one giver are Lakhs.

Pain is ordered from the part of him, with whom comfort rests.

(4). Why is he forgotten from the mind, whose the life of the creatures is?

Without him all is impure, whatever there is of clothing and food.

All other words are false; what is pleasing to thee, that is acceptable.

Sirī Rāg; mahalā I.

VI.

(1). Having burnt the love (of the world) rub it and make it ink; make understanding the best paper.

Make love the pen, make the mind the writer; having asked the Guru, write the decision.

Write the name, write (its) praise, write that which has no end nor limit.

1. *Pause.*

O father! know to write this account!

Where account will be asked, there will be made the true sign (or signature).

(2). Where greatness will be obtained, always pleasure and delight.

(There) from their face marks will issue, in whose heart the true name is.

If it does accrue[1] by destiny, then it is obtained, not by prattle of words.

(3). Some come, some rise and go, to whom the name of chieftain is given.

Some are born as beggars, some have great courts.

Having gone onwards (to the other world) it will be known, that without the name there is change of form.[2]

(4). Out of thy fear dread is very great; being consumed, being consumed, the body becomes tattered.

Those who had the name of Sultān and Khān, have been seen becoming ashes.

O Nānak! when one has risen and departed, all false love breaks down.

Sirī Rāg; mahalā I.

VII.

(1). All juices are sweet by minding (the name), (all are) seasoned by hearing (it).

The acid (juices) will go off by uttering (the name) with the mouth, by the sound[3] they are made spices.

On whom he looks in mercy, to him the thirty-six kinds of food[4] are one substance.[5]

1. *Pause.*

O father! other food is a poor pleasure.

By the eating of which the body is pained and disorder rules in the mind.

(2). Red clothing is a red heart;[6] whiteness (of clothes), truthfulness and donation.

[1] The words ਕਰਮਿ ਮਿਲੈ ਤਾ ਪਾਈਐ must thus be constructed: ਜੇ ਮਿਲੈ ਕਰਮਿ ਤਾ ਪਾਈਐ.

[2] ਵੇਕਾਰ, change of form, etc., implies here transmigration. He who is not imbued in the name, will be subject to a course of transmigration.

[3] The ਨਾਦ, sound, denotes here ਓਅੰਕਾਰ, uttering Ōm!

[4] ਅਮ੍ਰਿਤ means here food.

[5] On the occasion when these verses are said to have been uttered, see Sikhā̃ dē rāǰ dī vithiā, p. 293.

[6] ਰਤਾ has a double meaning: red, and steeped in love (to God); the latter is here understood.

Blueness and blackness (of clothes), wicked actions; putting on clothes, meditation on the feet (of Hari).

The waistband is made of contentment, wealth and youth is thy name.

Pause.

O father! other clothing is a poor pleasure.

By the putting on of which the body is pained and disorder rules in the mind.

(3). To have a knowledge of a horse's saddle, of a golden back-strap,[1] this is thy way.

Quiver, arrow, bow, sword-belt are the constituent parts of virtue (with thee).

A musical instrument, a spear, appearing publicly with honour, (this) is thy business, O my caste![2]

Pause.

O father! other[3] mounting is a poor pleasure.

By which mounting the body is pained and disorder rules in the mind.

(4). (My) house and mansion is the delight in (thy) name, thy (merciful) look my family.

That is (thy) order, which will please thee, (though there be) other very boundless talk.

O Nānak! the true kiug does not ask nor deliberate.

Pause.

O father! other sleeping is a poor pleasure.

By which sleep the body is pained and disorder rules in the mind.

Sirī Rāg; mahalā I.

VIII.

(1). A body (besmeared) with kungū, adorned with jewels, perfume of aloë-wood, the breath (kept fast) in the body.

The mark of the sixty-eight Tīrthas in the face—in this there is display of little wisdom.

In that is wisdom: praising the true name, the abode of (all) excellences.

Pause.

O father! other wisdom, other and other:

If it be practised a hundred times, it is the false effort of the false ones.

(2). He (=one) may apply himself to worship, he may be called a Pīr, the whole world may flock to him.

He may make his own name famous, he may be counted amongst the Siddhs.

When his (honour) does not fall into account (before God), all (his) worship is (but) a wretched thing.

(3). Those who are established by the true Guru,[4] nobody can efface.

Within them is the abode of the name, by the name they will become manifest.

(By whom) the name is worshipped, the name is minded, they are always unbroken[5] and true.

(4). When dust is mingled with dust, what will become of the soul?

[1] ਸਾਖਤਿ (Pers. ساخت) is the Sindhī शाखत, a back-strap of a horse, merely put on for ornament's sake.

[2] Nānak is said to have uttered these verses on being asked by his father Kālū to mount a horse and to go home.—See Sikhā̃ dē rāj etc., p. 294.

[3] The word ਹੋਰ, other, does not quite agree with the preceding verse, and seems to be a mere repetition without any reference to the context. The sense is: this and all such other mounting.

[4] The Sikhs always now refer the words ਸਤਿ ਗੁਰੁ to their Guru, as an incarnation of the Deity.

[5] ਅਖੰਡ, unbroken, not subject to death (जिस का नाश न हो).

All clevernesses are burnt (with the body); it rises and goes weeping.
O Nānak! the name being forgotten what will become (of it) when having gone[1] to the gate (of God)?

Sirī Rāg; mahalā I.

IX.

(1). The virtues of the virtuous woman are spread (abroad), the vicious woman pines.
If the fascinating woman longs for her husband, there is no meeting (with him), the friend (=husband) is hard-hearted.
There is no boat nor buoy, he is not obtained, the friend is far off.

Pause.

My perfect Lord is motionless on his throne.
If he makes the disciple[2] perfect, the True and Unweighable one is obtained.
(2). The palace of my Lord Hari is beautiful; in it are gems and rubies.
His castle of pearls, pure diamonds and gold, is delightful.
Without a ladder how shall I ascend to (his) castle?
I am happy by the meditation on Hari (my) Guru.
(3). The Guru[3] is the ladder, the Guru is the boat, the Guru is the buoy, the name of Hari.
The Guru is the pond, the sea, the boat, the Guru is the Tīrtha and the sea.
If she pleases him, she is bright, she goes to bathe in the true tank.
(4). He is called brimful,[4] dwelling on a full throne.
(Dwelling) in a full, beautiful place, he fulfils the hope of the hopeless.
O Nānak! if he is found full, how shall his qualities diminish?

Sirī Rāg; mahalā I.

X.

(1). Come, sister, cling to my neck, (cling) to my breast, O dear companion!
Having joined (me) tell (me) stories about thy powerful sweetheart (husband).
In the true Lord are all virtues, in us are all vices.

Pause.

O creator! every one is in thy power.
One word should be considered: when thou art, what are the others?
(2). Go ask the woman beloved by her husband: by what cleverness is he enjoyed by you?
"Easily with contentment she is adorned, who speaks sweetly.
The sweet friend is then met with, when I hear the word (instruction) of the Guru."
(3). How many are thy powers, how great is thy donation?
How many are thy living creatures, who praise thee day and night?
How many are thy forms and colours, how many the high-born and the outcasts?
(4). If the True one is found, comfort[5] springs up (in the heart); the true ones are absorbed into the True one.

[1] ਗਇਆ must be read ਗਇਆਂ (in having gone), but in all such cases the Anusvāra is never placed.

[2] As the word ਗੁਰੁ signifies also God, ਗੁਰਮੁਖਿ may denote a man who turns his face towards God, a seeker of God.

[3] The Guru is here the Gurdēv (the incarnate Guru). This is shown by the whole context.

[4] ਪੂਰਾ, full, denotes in reference to God: all-filling, all-pervading and perfect in himself.

[5] ਸਚੁ signifies here *comfort, joy*.

If attention is made, honour springs up; by the words of the Guru he (=one) eats up his fear.
O Nānak! the true king himself unites (him with himself).

Sirī Rāg; mahalā I.

XI.

(1). It has come to a good issue,[1] that I have been saved, (that) egotism has died away from (my) house (=body).
The messengers (of Yama) render service again, (because I have) faith in the true Guru.
He who abandons his own volitions[2] is an idle talker; the True one (alone) is without concern.

Pause.

O heart! if the True one is found, fear departs.
How shall (one) become without dread and fear?
The disciple is absorbed by means of the word (of the Guru).
(2). How much utterance (of the name) is made (and yet) in uttering no end is reached!
How many are the beggars! he alone is the bountiful.
By the indwelling in the heart of him, whose the life of the creatures is, comfort is obtained.
(3). The world is a dream, (in which) a play is made; for a moment he (God) makes her play the play.
United (by God), those who are alike, meet together, separated (by God) they rise and go.
What has pleased him, that is done, anything else cannot be done.
(4). By the disciple the thing[3] (*i.e.* the name of Hari) is purchased, (this is) true trade-stock, true capital.
By whom the true (stock) is sold, praise to that perfect Guru!
O Nānak! he will recognize (know) the thing, who traffics in truth.

Sirī Rāg; mahalā I.

XII.

(1). A metal is again joined to a metal, he who praises is absorbed into the object of praise.
Apply (to thyself) deep red,[4] thick, true colour!
The True one is found by the contented, having uttered "Hari" with one mind.

Pause.

O brother, (become) the dust of the holy people!
In the assembly of the saints the Guru (=God) is obtained, (final) liberation and the cow of all things.[5]
(2). High and beautiful is (his) place, above is the palace of Murāri.[6]
By true (=good) works the gate of the house and palace of the beloved is obtained.
The mind of the disciple is instructed having reflected on the Supreme Spirit.[7]

[1] ਭਲੀ ਸਰੀ ਜਿ, *i.e.* ਭਲੀ ਗਲ ਸਰੀ ਜੇ, literally: a good thing has been effected, that.

[2] ਕਲਪ ਤਿਆਗੀ must here be taken in the sense of: he who says or pretends, that he is abandoning his volitions or designs.

[3] ਵਸਤੁ, as often used in the Granth, signifies *the thing κατ' ἐξοχήν*, *i.e.* the name of Hari.

[4] ਲਾਲੁ ਗੁਲਾਲੁ; both are adjectives (for ਗੁਲਾਲੁ is also used as adjective) signifying "red."

[5] ਪਦਾਰਥ ਧੇਨੁ is identical with ਕਾਮ ਧੇਨੁ, the cow that grants all wishes. ਪਦਾਰਥ signifies in Hinduī also: all things.

[6] मुरारि (मुरारि), the enemy of Mura (a Daitya), name of Vishṇu or Krishṇa = God.

[7] ਆਤਮਰਾਮ (the same as ਪਰਮਾਤਮਾ), Sansk. आत्माराम, the Supreme Spirit. It denotes the world-soul (enjoying itself), identified with Vishṇu or Hari.

(3). If the threefold work[1] be practised, there arises hope and anxiety.

How shall without the Guru the triad[2] cease to be? by being united with the self-existing,[3] comfort arises.

(By whom) in his own house his (God's) palace is recognized to be, he washes off his dirt (sin), if he (God) looks (on him) in mercy.

(4). Without the Guru the dirt does not go off; without Hari how is there perfume in the house?

(By whom) the one word (*i.e.* the name) is reflected upon, he gives up (all) other hope.

O Nānak! (by whom) he (*i.e.* Hari) is seen and pointed out (to me), (for him) I always sacrifice myself.

Sirī Rāg; mahalā I.

XIII.

(1). Woe to the life of the unfavoured woman, she is ruined by second love.[4]

Like a wall impregnated with saltpetre day and night falls and tumbles down (so she goes to ruin).

Without the word (=name) no comfort arises, without the beloved pain does not go.

Pause.

O handsome young woman! what is decoration without the beloved?

At the gate thou obtainest no entrance to the house, at the threshold the false one is wretched.

(2). He himself the wise one is not mistaken, he is a true, great husbandman.

First having brought the soil in order he sows the seed of the name (in it).[5]

The nine treasures are produced (from) the one name, (according to) destiny the sign (=lot) falls.

(3). The wise one, who does not know the Guru, what is his wisdom and good conduct?

By the blind the name is forgotten, in the self-willed is great mistiness.[6]

His coming and going does not cease; having died he is born (again) and becomes wretched.

(4). Sandal-wood has been bought, kungū and red lead for the parting-line of the hair.

Very much perfume,[7] camphor with betel-leaves.

If the woman does not please the sweetheart,[8] all (this) apparatus is useless.

(5). The enjoyment of all pleasures is useless, all ornaments are an abnormal thing.

As long as she is not perforated[9] by the word (of the Guru), how shall she receive honour at the gate of the Guru?

O Nānak! those favoured women are blessed, who are in love with their husband.[10]

[1] ਤ੍ਰਿਬਿਧਿ ਕਰਮ is संचित (what is collected, heaped up), प्रारब्ध (what has been commenced), and क्रियमाण (what is being done).

[2] ਤ੍ਰਿਕੁਟੀ (formed from the Sansk. त्रिकूट, having three heads or horns), *triad*, the three qualities ਸਤੋ (सत = सत्त्व, the true nature, the quality of goodness), ਰਜੋ (रज = रजस्, passion), and ਤਮੋ (तम = तमस्, darkness), inherent in all that is created.

[3] ਸਹਜੁ, the same as स्वाभाविक, self-existing, an attribute of the Supreme Being; but it may also be translated by: *composure (of mind); composure (of mind) being obtained.*

[4] ਦੂਜਾ ਭਾਉ, second love (other than the love of God) = worldly love; *duality.*

[5] ਦਾਣੁ is here, for the sake of the rhyme, = ਦਾਣਾ, grain, seed.

[6] ਅੰਧ ਗੁਬਾਰ, a frequent expression in the Granth: deep darkness or mistiness (غُبار).

[7] ਚੋਆ ਚੰਦਨ, name of a perfume, ਚੋਆ (Amaranthus oleaceus) and ਚੰਦਨ, sandal-wood ground together to a paste.

[8] ਜੇ ਧਨ ਕੰਤਿ ਨ ਭਾਵਈ; ਕੰਤਿ is here neither Ablative nor Locative, but stands for ਕੰਤਹਿ (Dative).

[9] ਭੇਦਣਾ, *v.a.* To perforate, to split; in the passive: to be perforated = to be thoroughly imbued in.

[10] ਸਹੁ is a Sindhī word (सड़), and signifies properly: bridegroom.

Sirī Rāg; mahalā I.

XIV.

(1). Empty and frightful is the body, when the soul (or life) departs from it.
The burning fire is extinguished, not any smoke has issued from it.[1]
The five (elements)[2] have wept, filled with pain, they are destroyed by second love.

Pause.

O fool! mutter Hari, remembering his qualities.
Egotism and selfishness is captivating, the whole (world) is ruined by egotism.

(2). By whom the name is forgotten, having stuck to another business:
They, by giving themselves to duality,[3] are consumed and dead; in their heart is the fire of thirst.
Those are saved, who are preserved by the Guru, the others are cheated and deceived by their (worldly) business.[4]

(3). Dead is friendship, love is gone, enmity and opposition is dead.
(Worldly) business is stopped, egotism is dead, selfishness and wrath is absorbed.
It is owing to destiny that the True one is obtained; the disciple is always suppressing (his senses).

(4). By true work the True one is found, by the wisdom of the Guru he falls into the skirt (of the disciple).
That man is not born (again) nor does he die, he does not come nor go.
O Nānak! he who is foremost at the gate, he will go dressed to the threshold (of God).[5]

Sirī Rāg; mahalā I.

XV.

(1). The body being burnt has become earth, the mind by the infatuation of the Māya (like) dross.
The (old) vices have again clung to it, the cruel ones sound (again) the trumpet.
Without the word (of the Guru) he (or the mind) is brought into error, duality sinks the boat's load.

Pause.

O mind! be attentive to the word and cross (thereby) over!
By whom the name proceeding from the mouth of the Guru is not understood, he, having died, is born (again), he comes and goes.

(2). That is called a pure body, in which the true name is.
(Such a) body is steeped in true fear (of God), the tongue has a true taste.
(If) it (*i.e.* the body) is looked upon with a true glance (of mercy), it will not get into distress again.

[1] ਭਾਹਿ ਬਲੰਦੀ; life is compared to a burning fire, which is extinguished without leaving any trace of its existence.

[2] The five are here the elements (तत्त्व), viz.: पृथ्वी (earth), जल (water), अग्नि (fire), वायु (breath), आकाश (ether), of which the body is composed according to Hindū notion. The Sikhs refer the five to ਕਾਮ (lust), ਕ੍ਰੋਧ (wrath), ਲੋਭ (covetousness), ਮੋਹ (infatuation), ਹੰਕਾਰ (selfishness).

[3] ਦੁਬਿਧਾ has in the Granth not the sense of *doubt*, but retains its original meaning: *duality*, twofoldness (Sansk. द्वैविध्य), like ਦੂਜਾ ਭਾਉ.

[4] ਹੋਰਿ ਮੁਠੀ ਧੰਧੈ ਠਗਿ must be constructed thus: ਹੋਰਿ ਠਗਿ ਮੁਠੀ ਧੰਧੈ; ਮੁਠੀ is fem. (supply ਲੋਇ), ਠਗਿ is part. past conj.

[5] ਦਰਿ ਪਰਧਾਨ foremost at the gate (of the Guru), *i.e.* quite given to the attention and service of the Guru. ਪੈਧਾ, dressed, *i.e.* in a dress of honour (خلعت).

(3). From the True one wind (air) has proceeded, from the wind water has been engendered.
From water the three worlds have been made, into every body light is infused.[1]
The pure does not become defiled; by him, who is steeped in the word, honour is obtained.
(4). This mind is contented in the True one, (if) he (God) casts upon it a look of mercy.
The five beings[2] are steeped in true fear, there is true light in the mind.
O Nānak! the vices are forgotten; those who are protected by the Guru (obtain) honour.

Sirī Rāg; mahalā I.

XVI.

(1). O Nānak! on the boat of the True one there is crossing over by means of reflection on the Guru.[3]
Some come, some go, quite full of selfishness.
The intoxicated with obstinacy of mind are drowned, the disciple that True one is bringing across.

Pause.

How shall it be crossed without the Guru, (how) shall comfort be obtained?
As it is pleasing (to thee), so keep me, I have none other.
(2). If I look before me, there is a conflagration of the jungle,[4] on my back there are green sprouts.
By whom it is produced, by him it is destroyed, in every body (vessel) the True one is brimful.
He himself (also) unites to union[5] (with himself), to his true palace and presence (he conveys).
(3). At every breath I remember thee, I never forget thee.
As, as the Lord dwells in the mind, (so, so) the disciple drinks nectar.
Mind and body are thine, thou art the Lord, having removed pride thou indwellest.
(4). By whom this world is produced, having made the forms (beings) of the three worlds.
(His) light is known by the disciple, (whereas) the self-willed is bewildered in mistiness.
The light (which is) unintermittingly in every body, he comprehends, who bears in mind the wisdom of the Guru.[6]
(5). The disciples, by whom it (*i.e.* the light) is known, are applauded.
They are united with the True one, they manifest the qualities of the True one.
O Nānak! by the name they are contented, their soul and body is with the Lord.

Sirī Rāg; mahalā I.

XVII.

(1). Hear, O heart! O beloved friend! be united (with the Supreme Being), this is the time.
As long as there is there the breath of youth, give (him) this body!
Without virtue it is of no use, the body decaying is reduced to ashes again.

[1] This is not quite in accordance with the cosmogonies of the Purāṇas; see Vishṇu Purāṇa, p. 16, note 25.

[2] ਪੰਚ ਭੂਤ, the five beings (not elements), *i.e.* ਕਾਮ, ਕ੍ਰੋਧ, ਲੋਭ, ਮੋਹ, ਹੰਕਾਰ, which are personified.

[3] ਤਰਣਾ, to cross (the ocean of existence); the crossing is made possible by reflection or meditation (ਵਿਚਾਰਣਾ) on the Guru, who is the mediator of salvation.

[4] ਡਉ, *s.m.* a burning of the jungle, ਡਉ ਜਲੈ, literally: a conflagration of the jungle is burning.

[5] ਮੇਲਿ ਮਿਲਾਉਲਾ is a frequent expression in the Granth; ਮੇਲਿ is the Locative of ਮੇਲੁ, union, so that ਮੇਲਿ ਮਿਲਾਉਲਾ literally signifies: to unite in or to union (with himself); from the Supreme Being all emanates and into it all is again reunited.

[6] ਬੁਝੈ ਗੁਰਮਤਿ ਸਾਰੁ; these words are very comprehensive; ਸਾਰੁ is = ਸਾਰੇ (from ਸਾਰਣਾ), to keep in mind, to think or reflect upon (Sindhi: सारणु, Sansk. सारण).

Pause.

O my heart! having obtained (this) profit go to thy house!

(If) by the disciple the name is praised, the fire of egotism is removed.

(2). (If) having heard, heard a literary composition be made,[1] (if) having written and read a load, one understand it.

His thirst is day and night very great, (as there is in him) the disease and abnormal state of egotism.

He (*i.e.* God) is without concern, unweighable, (but) the wisdom of the Guru calculates his (God's) value.[2]

(3). (If) I acquire lakhs of clevernesses, friendship and intimacy with lakhs (of people).

Without the society of the saint[3] I am not satiated, without the name I have pain and affliction.

Having muttered Hari in the heart, (final) emancipation is obtained, the disciple recognizes his own self.

(4). Body and heart is sold to the Guru, the heart is given with the head.

By the disciple the three worlds are searched through, searching and looking about.

He, who is united to union (with God) by the true Guru, he, O Nānak! is with the Lord.

Sirī Rāg; mahalā I.

XVIII.

(1). There is no anxiety about death, no hope of life.

Thou takest care of all creatures, thou countest their breath and morsel.

Within the disciple thou dwellest, as it pleases (thee), so thou determinest.[4]

Pause.

O heart! muttering Rām, the mind is soothed.

In the heart grudge is burnt and extinguished, by the disciple divine knowledge is obtained.

(2). (If) the state of the heart be known, if the Guru be joined, fear ceases.

From which house, when being dead, one must depart, in that, whilst living, kill thyself and die!

From the unbeaten, beautiful sound he (*i.e.* Hari) is obtained, by means of reflection on the Guru.[5]

(3). If the unbeaten sound is obtained, egotism is annihilated.

For him, who serves his own true Guru, I always sacrifice myself.

Standing at the threshold (of God) he is dressed (with a dress of honour), in whose mouth the name of Hari dwells.

(4). Where I see, there he is diffused, there is union of Shiva and of his Shaktis.[6]

[1] ਗੰਢਣੁ ਗੰਢਣਾ; ਗੰਢਣੁ (= Sansk. ग्रन्थन), binding together, making a ਗ੍ਰੰਥ (literary composition).

[2] ਸਾਰੁ is here a verb, ਸਾਰਣਾ, to compute, to calculate. As regards the verbal forms, I must refer to my Grammar to the Granth, which I intend to publish, as it would carry me too far to explain in notes all the different grammatical forms.

[3] ਸਾਧ, when used in the singular, often denotes the Guru.

[4] ਨਿਰਜਾਸਣਾ is traditionally explained by the Sikhs = ਨਿਰਣਾ ਕਰਣਾ, to judge, to determine. Its etymology is obscure (perhaps identical with the Hindī निर्जोषण, निर्जोष = निश्चय).

[5] ਅਨਹਦ is the same as ਅਨਹਤਾ, unbeaten. The sound not produced by beating (a drum, etc.) is said to be produced in the ਦਸਵਾਂ ਦੁਆਰ or tenth gate (of the human body), *i.e.* the vault of the head, where the vital breath, by the practice of Jōg, is concentrated, and where that sound is believed to be produced thereby. ਅਨਹਦ ਘਾਲੀ is the same as ਅਨਹਦ ਸਬਦੁ.

[6] About the Shaktis of Mahādēva or Shiva, see Vishṇu Purāṇa, p. 51, note 4. Rudra (=Shiva) is with his energies an agent in creation.

In three qualities[1] the body is bound up; he who has come into the world is a sport.

By separation (from God) they are separated in pain, the self-willed do not obtain union (with God).

(5). If the mind retired from the world dwell in its (own) house (body), if it be imbued with true fear (of God).

It enjoys the great delight of divine knowledge, it will not again become hungry.

O Nānak! kill this (thy) mind and be united (to God), there will not be again pain.

Sirī Rāg; mahalā I.

XIX.

(1). This mind is foolish and covetous, given to and allured by covetousness.

The Sāktā (worshipper of the Shakti) is not affected by the word (of the Guru), in foolishness he is coming and going.

If a Sādh (holy man) meet with the true Guru, the abode of qualities (*i.e.* the Supreme Being) is obtained (by him).

Pause.

O (my) mind! give up egotism and pride!

Having served Hari, the Guru, the ocean, thou wilt obtain honour at the threshold.

(2). Having muttered the name of Rām day and night, the disciple knows the wealth of Hari.

All comforts are in the enjoyment of the taste of Hari; in the assembly of the saints divine knowledge is obtained.

(By whom) always, day and night, the Lord Hari is worshipped, (to him) the name is given by the true Guru.

(3). By the dog falsehood is practised; by reviling the Guru he is wasted and consumed.

Erring he wanders about, he has much pain; Yama having killed (him), makes him a threshing-floor.[2]

The self-willed obtains no comfort, the disciple (obtains) comfort and splendour.[3]

(4). Here (in this world) business is pushed on, (but) the writ of the True one is authoritative.

He is the friend (of) Hari who serves the Guru; by the agency of the Guru he is foremost.

O Nānak! who does not forget the name, he (is) conspicuous[4] by (this) true work.

Sirī Rāg; mahalā I.

XX.

(1). If but a little the beloved be forgotten, there is great sickness in the mind (produced).

How shall honour at the threshold be obtained, when Hari does not dwell in the mind?

By meeting with the Guru comfort is obtained, the fire dies, the (three) qualities are absorbed.[5]

Pause.

O mind, day and night remember the qualities of Hari!

Those men are rare in the world, by whom the name is not a single moment forgotten.

[1] The three qualities are ਸਤੋ, ਰਜੋ, ਤਮੋ.

[2] *i.e.* He beats him hard like a threshing-floor.

[3] ਸੁਭਾਨੁ = Sansk. सु + भानु, splendour, lustre.

[4] ਨੀਸਾਣੁ may here be translated by "conspicuous" (literally, a flag); true work (Sansk. सत् कर्म) = not forgetting the name—is that which has a real value or merit. By not forgetting the name, a man becomes honoured at the threshold of Hari. But ਨੀਸਾਣੁ may also be taken = ਨੀਸਾਣੈ, he attends to, is intent on (with the Locative) true work.

[5] ਗੁਣ ਸਮਾਹਿ. ਸਮਾਹਿ is here verb (ਸਮਾਉਣਾ = ਸੰਮਾਉਣਾ, to be absorbed) and not postposition (*in*).

(2). (If) light be united with the source of light, there is conjunction of the intelligence with the principle of intelligence.[1]

By the destruction of egotism they are gone, there are no (longer) doubt and grief.

In which disciple's mind Hari dwells, his union (with Hari) the Guru brings about.

(3). If I make (my) body (like that) of a fascinating woman, the enjoyer will enjoy (it).

With that love should not be made, that appears as transitory.

That Lord is the husband of the bed, he dallies (with) the disciple (as with) a beloved woman.

(4). Having removed the four fires[2] by throwing the water of Hari (upon them), die, O disciple!

Within (thee) the lotus is (then) opened, filled with nectar thou wilt be satiated.

O Nānak! having made the true Guru (thy) friend, thou wilt attain the True one, having gone to the threshold (of God).

Sirī Rāg; mahalā I.

XXI.

(1). O beloved, mutter Hari, Hari! having taken the wisdom (=instruction) of the Guru say: Hari!

O mind, if the touchstone be applied to the True one, if he be weighed by a full weight:

His value is not obtained by any one, O heart! he is a priceless[3] gem.

Pause.

O brother, the diamond of Hari is in the Guru!

In the true assembly[4] the true Guru is obtained by praising (Hari) day and night by means of the word (of the Guru).[5]

(2). The true stock-in-trade (or goods), wealth and capital is obtained from the Guru's revelation.

As fire dies by water being poured upon it, thus thirst (is extinguished) by the slave of slaves.[6]

The executioner[7] of Yama does not touch (the disciple), thus he crosses the water of existence and will cause (others) to cross.

(3). To the disciple falsehood is not pleasing; to him, who is attached to truth, truth is pleasing.

To the Sāktā (=impious) truth does not please, falsehood is allotted to the false one.

By the Guru being joined (with them) they (=the true ones) are steeped in truth, the true ones are absorbed in the True one.

(4). In the heart is a gem, a ruby; the name is a jewel, the best thing,[8] a diamond.

The true stock and wealth is the name; in every body is the profound and deep (Supreme Being).

O Nānak! by the disciple the diamond is obtained, if Hari bestow mercy on him.

[1] The Supreme Being is ਜੋਤੀ (ਜੋਤੀ ਸਰੂਪੀ), self-resplendent or the source of light, which is the principle of life in rational beings. In consequence of the ਜੋਤਿ (light) being infused into the created spirits, there is ਸੁਰਤਿ, *intelligence*, in them. The Supreme Being is therefore ਸੁਰਤੀ, intelligent, or the principle of intelligence, from which the ਸੁਰਤਿ of the (rational) beings has emnnated.

[2] The four fires or heats are said to be: ਹਿੰਸਾ, ਮੋਹ, ਕ੍ਰੋਧ, ਲੋਭ.

[3] ਮੋਲਿ ਅਮੋਲਿ, such like compounds are very frequent in the Granth, signifying literally: *priceless in price.*

[4] ਸਤ ਸੰਗਤਿ, the true assembly or the assembly of the true disciples or saints.

[5] ਸਬਦਿ ਸਲਾਹਣਾ, to praise Hari by means of the ਸਬਦ or word of the Guru.

[6] ਦਾਸਨਿ ਦਾਸੁ, the slave of slaves (servus servorum), i.e. *the Guru.* This phrase is of frequent occurrence in the Granth.

[7] ਜੰਦਾਰ, which the Sikhs traditionally explain by *messenger* (ਦੂਤ), is the same as ਜੰਦਾਲ = ਚੰਡਾਲ, a Čaṇḍāl = executioner.

[8] ਪਦਾਰਥੁ, like ਵਸਤੁ, the thing, the real thing or substance = the best thing or including all things.

Sirī Rāg; mahalā I.

XXII.

(1). By wandering about the fire (of the heart) is not extinguished, if one wander from country to country.

From his heart the dirt (=sin) does not go off, wretched is his life, wretched his (faqīr's) dress.

Devotion is not brought about by anything, except by the instruction of the true Guru.

Pause.

O heart, attending to the Guru, remove the fire!

If the word of the Guru dwells in the mind, the thirst of egotism dies away.

(2). O mind! it (*i.e.* the name) is a priceless gem, from the name of Rām honour is obtained.[1]

Having joined the assembly of the true ones Hari is obtained by the disciple, having applied his devotion[2] to Hari.

When his own self is gone, comfort is obtained, (as) water mixing with water is absorbed (in it).

(3). By whom the name of Hari, Hari is not kept in his thoughts, he comes and goes vicious.

By whom the true Guru, the Spirit,[3] has not been joined, he pines in the water of existence and causes (others) to pine.

This gem, O soul! which is priceless, goes thus for a kauḍī (cowrie).

(4). Those are perfect and wise men, by whom, being desirous[4] for, the true Guru is found.

Having met with the Guru the water of existence is crossed (by them), at the threshold they are manifest[5] (present) with honour.

O Nānak! they will have bright faces, (in whom) contemplation springs up (and) attention (to the) word (of the Guru).[6]

Sirī Rāg; mahalā I.

XXIII.

(1). Make traffic, O trader! take with care a stock of goods.

Such a thing should be bought, with which one gets through (the water of existence).

In the other world is a very knowing banker, he will look after the thing.[7]

[1] ਪਾਵਣਾ (प्रापण) is also *neuter*, to be received, to come to hand.

[2] ਲਿਵ *s.f.* (Sindhī लंउं *s.f.*), Sansk. लय, the entering into a thing, absorption in = deep meditation or intense devotion to.

[3] The true Guru is often called in the Granth ਪੁਰਖੁ (पुरुष). पुरुष is called in the Vishṇu-Purāṇa Vishṇu (who is identified with Brahma), पुरुष (spirit, individuality) being the first form of the Supreme. See Vishṇu Purāṇa, p. 9. The true Guru is considered as an Avatār of the Supreme Being, and therefore the attribute of ਪੁਰਖੁ is conferred on him too. Bābā Nānak is considered by the Sikhs as an Avatār (incarnation) of the Supreme (Vishṇu), who became again incarnate in the nine following Gurus; for this reason they all call themselves Nānak.

[4] ਰਸਿ is adjective (रसिन्), having a taste for, longing for, or having a right understanding for the matter.

[5] ਪਰਵਾਣੁ has here the sense of प्रत्यच, manifest, present, as used already by Tulsī Dās (and written by him परमान).

[6] No Sikh, how much soever I inquired, could explain me this verse. The sense is: those have (or will have) bright faces in whom contemplation (ਧੁਨਿ) and attention (ਨੀਸਾਣੁ) of the word springs up. ਸਬਦ, sound, word, is nearly always the word of the Guru.

[7] The ਵਣਜਾਰਾ, or trafficker (retail dealer) takes his ਵਖਰ stock of goods (or ਰਾਸਿ capital) from the ਸਾਹ (साधु), wholesale merchant or banker, to whom he is accountable.

Pause.

O brother, say Rām! attentively.

Having taken the praise of Hari as thy stock of goods go, if the Lord sees it, he puts confidence in it.

(2). Who have no capital of truth, how shall they obtain comfort?

By carrying on a base traffic heart and body become base.

Like a deer caught in a snare he has much pain and weeps always.

(3). The base ones (like base coins) are not received at the treasury, they do not obtain the sight of Hari the Guru.

The base ones have neither caste nor fellowship, by baseness nobody prospers.

The base practise baseness; having come (into this world) they lose their honour when having gone.

(4). O Nānak! the heart should be instructed by the word of the Guru (and in) the praise (of Hari).

Those who are steeped in the love of the name of Rām, have no burden nor doubt.

In muttering Hari is the greatest profit, the fearless Hari (dwells then) in the heart.

Sirī Rāg; mahalā I.

II. *Ghar.*

XXIV.

(1). Wealth, youth and a flower are guests for four days.

Like the leaf of a lotus,[1] after having brought forth flowers, is withering away.

Pause.

Enjoy pleasure, when youth is fresh (blooming), O beloved!

The few days (of youth) are (soon) over and the coat (=body) has become old.

(2). My merry friends have departed and are fallen asleep in the grave-yard.[2]

I also shall go sad and weep with a feeble voice.

(3). Thou hearest not at all the intelligence with thy ears, O woman!

Forthwith thou wilt come to thy father-in-law's house, thou wilt not be continually in thy father's house.

O Nānak! know, she who has fallen asleep in her father's house out of season, has lost the bundle of her virtues and is gone off, having bound together vices.

Sirī Rāg; mahalā I.

II. *Ghar.*

XXV.

(1). He himself is enjoying pleasure,[3] he himself is the pleasure, he himself is amusing (others) (with pleasure).

He himself is the petticoat (=woman), he himself is the husband of the bed.

Pause.

Given to pleasure is my Lord, brimful he is contained (everywhere).

(2). He himself is the fisher and the fish, he himself is the water and the net.

[1] ਪਬਣਿ, Sindhi पब॒णि, Sansk. पद्मिनी, the lotus plant, (not the flower) Nelumbium speciosum.

[2] ਜੀਰਾਣਿ is explained by the Sikhs = ਕਬਰਾਂ (in the graves), but the proper sense of the word is grave-yard. ਜੀਰਾਣੁ = Sansk. जीर्ण, decayed, the last syllable being originally hāṇ = āṇ, *i.e.* स्थान, place, the place of the decayed.

[3] ਰਸੀਆ, ਰਸੁ, ਰਾਵਣਾ, refers chiefly to sensual pleasure. ਰਾਵਣਾ is the causal of ਰਵਣਾ (= ਰਮਣਾ, रमना), and signifies either *to amuse, to divert*, or to cause (others) to dally with.

He himself is the bait[1] of the net, he himself is within (it) the greediness (of the fish).
(3). My beloved himself is in many ways playful, O my (female) friend!
He continually dallies (with) the favoured woman; behold! this is my state.
(4). Nānak bows with supplication: thou art the lake, thou art the gander.
Thou art the crane,[2] thou art the white lotus, thou thyself seest (thy) opening.[3]

Sirī Rāg; mahalā I.

III. *Ghar.*

XXVI.

(1). Make this body the earth, (good) works the seed, the bow-holder[4] will pour water (upon it).

(Make) the mind the husbandman, cause Hari to spring up (as a sprout) in the heart, thus thou wilt obtain the state of final emancipation.

Pause.

Why art thou proud, O fool! of the Māyā (illusive wealth)?

Thy father, son, all thy wives, thy mother, will at the end not be thy companions.

(2). He who pulls out (from his heart) the abnormal state of sensuality and the wicked ones,[5] becomes meditating on the Supreme Spirit, after having given them up.

Then silent repetition (of the name), austerity and continence is made, when they (*i.e.* the wicked) are checked, the lotus opens in the hermitage (*i.e.* secluded heart).

(3). (Who) subdues the twenty-seven fold body,[6] (who) in the three stations[7] remembers continually death.

He recognizes in the ten and eighteen[8] the Infinite; Nānak says: thus he is in one (continual) absorption (of thought).

Sirī Rāg; mahalā I.

III. *Ghar.*

XXVII.

(1). Make works the earth, the name the seed, give continually the water of truth.

Having become a husbandman, grow faith; paradise and hell is thus (obtained) by the fool (and) wise.[9]

[1] ਮਣਕੜਾ *s.m.* diminutive of ਮਣਕ (= माणक), a plant (Arum Indicum), the root of which is sometimes eaten and used as a bait for fish.

[2] ਕਉਲੁ (Sansk. कमल) must here be translated by *crane*, for the sake of contrast. ਕਵੀਆ, Sansk. कविका, is the white lotus, that opens at night-time.

[3] ਵਿਗਸੁ instead of ਵਿਗਾਸ (Sansk. विकास), the opening of the lotus (at night-time).

[4] ਸਾਰਿੰਗਪਾਣੀ, in whose hand is a bow, an epithet of Vishṇu.

[5] ਦੂਸਟ, the wicked are ਕਾਮ, ਕ੍ਰੋਧ, ਲੋਭ, ਮੋਹ, ਹੰਕਾਰ.

[6] ਤੀਸ ਸਪਤਾਹਰੋ, the twenty-seven fold, *i.e.* body. The body is said to consist of twenty-five parts, of ਆਤਮਾ and of ਸਨ = twenty-seven.

[7] ਖੇਤ੍ਰ *s.m.* station = ਅਵਸਥਾ, *i.e.* जाग्रत्, स्वप्न, सुषुप्ति, waking, dream and deep sleep; a fourth (तुरीय) is also counted, the absorption of the soul in Brahma.

[8] The ten are said to be the four Vēdas and the six Shāstras; the eighteen are the eighteen Purāṇas.

[9] The words are so elliptic, that they are hardly intelligible. The sense is: thus paradise is obtained by the wise and hell by the fool.

Pause.

Likely thou wilt think, that it (*i.e.* paradise) is obtained by (mere) words.

By the conceit of wealth, by the beauty of the body, in this wise the (human) birth is lost.

(2). Vice is on the body (like) mud, this mind is a frog, who does not get any information respecting the lotus.

The black bee is the teacher, who continually talks; how shall it (*i.e.* the mind) understand, when he (the black bee) does not make it understand?

(3). Speaking and hearing is (like) the voice of the wind (*i.e.* useless), this mind is attached to the Māyā.

The (merciful) glance of the Lord is heart-pleasing to them, by whom he is considered as One and meditated upon.

(4). (By whom) the thirty (days of fasting) and the five (prayers daily) have been kept, he, having made the name his companion, goes off, having frustrated the design of Satan.

Nānak says: it must be departed, what for is property and wealth amassed?

Sirī Rāg; mahalā I.

IV. *Ghar.*

XXVIII.

(1). He is the Lord, by whom the world is made budding, (by whom) the world is made green.

By whom the water and earth have been fixed; blessed is the creator.

Pause.

Thou must die, O Mullā! thou must die! remain in the fear of the creator![1]

(2). Then thou art a Mullā, then thou art a Kāzī, if thou knowest the name of God.

None, though he be very learned, will remain, it is gone onwards.[2]

(3). He is a Kāzī, by whom his own self is abandoned and the one name is made his support.

He is and will be, he will not be destroyed, true is the creator.

(4). Five times he prays, he reads the book of the Qorān.

Nānak says: when the grave calls, drinking and eating is stopped.

Sirī Rāg; mahalā I.

IV. *Ghar.*

XXIX.

(1). There is one dog (and) two bitches with (me).

Bewildered they always bark early in the morning.

Falsehood is a knife, stolen (goods) carrion.

I remain in the form of a bowman,[3] O creator!

Pause.

I have no road of honour,[4] nor do I practise good works.

I am ugly and remain in an unclean form.

[1] ਭੀ at the beginning of a sentence and in connexion with au imperative, is an exhortatory particle, like the Sanskrit अपि.

[2] ਪਾਇ ਭਰਣਾ, to carry the foot = to go on, to quicken one's step.

[3] ਧਾਣਕ, armed with a bow; a caste of low people, who are armed with a bow and live by hunting.

[4] ਪਤਿ ਕੀ ਪਦਿ, road of honour, *i.e.* I do not walk honourably.

Only thy name saves the world.
This is my hope, this my support.
(2). With my mouth I utter calumny day and night.
I look at another's wife and am of low occupation.[1]
Lust and wrath dwell in my body, I am a Čanḍal.
O creator! I remain in the form of a bowman.
(3). Ensnared (caught) is my understanding by an elegant dress.
I am a cheater, I cheat the country.
I am very clever, great is my weight.[2]
I remain in the form of a bowman, O creator!
(4). I am ungrateful, I live on the wages of iniquity.
How shall I, wicked thief, show my face?
The humble Nānak expresses his thought.
I remain in the form of a bowman, O creator!

Sirī Rāg; mahalā I.

IV. *Ghar.*

XXX.

1. There is one (and the same) understanding in as many creatures as there are.
Without understanding none is created.
As their understanding is, so is their way.
The account is one and the same, (in consequence of which) they come and go.[3]

Pause.

Why, O soul! practisest thou cleverness?
He (*i.e.* God) takes and gives, there is no remissness (on his part).[4]
(2). Thine are the creatures and thou belongest to the creatures.
To whom (else) shall they come and weep, O Lord?
As thou art the Lord, they come (to thee) and weep.
Thou art theirs and they are thine.
(3). We contradict, we contradict.
Thou weighest (us) within thy sight.
Who (does) good works, he has full understanding.
Without good works it (*i.e.* the understanding) decreases in the heart.
(4). Nānak bows (= says): what sort of a man will get divine knowledge?
He who knows his own self, will comprehend (God).
Who reflects by the favour of the Guru:
That sage is acceptable at the threshold (of God).

[1] Occupied with or in a low business, or a low-caste man.

[2] It is difficult to say what is exactly meant by ਬਹੁਤਾ ਭਾਰੁ, as there is no hint to what it is to be referred. Very likely the sense is: my weight (ਭਾਰੁ may have this meaning) is great, which I, as a clever man, have or exercise.

[3] ਲੇਖਾ is the final account taken and asked at the threshold of God, according to which they come and go, *i.e.* are subjected to transmigration.

[4] ਢਿਲ ਪਾਈ = ਢਿਲ ਪਵੇ.

Śirī Rāg; mahalā I.

IV. *Ghar.*

XXXI.

(1). Thou art the ocean, wise and clear-sighted, how shall I, the little fish, obtain (thy) end?
Wherever I see, there art thou, if I go out from thee, I burst and die.

Pause.

I do not know the fisher nor do I know the net.
When pain overtakes me, I remember thee.
(2). Thou, O-beloved! art known as brimful, I am far off. Whatever I do, that is in thy presence.
Thou seest, I do not acknowledge (it). Neither thy work nor thy name.
(3). As much as thou givest, so much I eat. I have no other door, to which door shall I go?
Nānak makes one supplication: soul and body, all is with thee.
(4). He himself is near, he himself is far, he himself is in the midst.
He himself sees and hears, he himself by his power makes the world.
That order, O Nānak! which is pleasing to him, is authoritative.

Sirī Rāg; mahalā I.

IV. *Ghar.*

XXXII.

(1). Why is the creature conceited in its mind?
The gift is in the hand of the giver.
As he pleases, so he gives or does not give.
What is effected by the word of the creature?

Pause.

Who himself is true, to him pleases truth.
Who is blind and ignorant, (to him pleases) nonsensical talk.
(2). Whose the trees are, (his is) the garden.
As their kind (species) is, so is their name.
According to the nature of the blossom the fruit is defined (set down).
Having sown himself he himself will eat it.
(3). A wall is raw, (if) the clay in it be raw.[1]
If the intellect is unsalted, the flavour is insipid.
O Nānak! the simple-minded are put right (*i.e.* succeed).
Without the name there is no commendation (at the threshold of God).

Sirī Rāg; mahalā I.

V. *Ghar.*

XXXIII.

(1). The fraudless (man) fraud does not deceive, nor can a dagger wound him.
As the Lord keeps him, so he remains, (but) the soul of this greedy man is agitated.

[1] ਕਚੀ ਕੰਧ, ਕਚਾ ਗਾਜੁ (= ਗਜੁ), the wall is raw, not good, firm, if the clay from which it is made be raw, *i.e.* bad, sandy.

Pause.

How shall the lamp burn without oil?
(2). If the Purāṇas are highly appreciated, if the wick of fear is applied to this body.
The understanding of truth is unawares[1] kindled.

Pause.

This is the oil, thus the lamp burns.
Make a light, the Lord then meets (with thee).
(3). In this body sticks a Banyā̃.[2]
Comfort is obtained, if worship (of God) be made.
The whole world is coming and going.
(4). (If) in the world worship (of God) be practised:
Then a seat at the threshold will be obtained.
Nanāk says: the arm will be swung.[3]

Sirī Rāg; mahalā III. (*Amardās.*)

I. *Ghar.*

Om! By the favour of the true Guru.

I. XXXIV.[4]

(1). I serve my own true Guru with one mind, with one thought and love.
The true Guru is the heart's desire and Tīrtha of him, whom he instructs.
He obtains the boon, for which his heart has been anxious; the fruit he wishes, he gets.
If the name be reflected upon, if the name be asked, he is easily absorbed in the name.

Pause.

O my mind! taste the juice of Hari and thy thirst will cease.
The disciples, by whom it has been tasted, remain easily absorbed.
(2). By whom the true Guru has been served, they have obtained the treasure of the name.
In their heart the love of Hari dwells, in their mind conceit has ceased.
The lotus of the heart has opened, meditation is easily brought about.
The pure heart is delighted with Hari and at the threshold honour is obtained.
(3). Those who serve their own true Guru are rare in the world.
By whom egotism and selfishness are destroyed and Hari is kept in the breast.
Who have love to the name, for them I sacrifice myself.
Those are happy in the four periods (of the world), in whom the inexhaustible, endless name is.
(4). By meeting with the Guru the name is obtained, spiritual blindness and (worldly) thirst cease.
With Hari their heart is delighted, in their house they are solitary.[5]

[1] ਅਜਾਣਿ is = अज्ञ, without knowing, unawares.

[2] Banyā̃, a Hindū retail-dealer. The Banyā̃s are rather notorious for their greediness and unscrupulousness.

[3] ਬਾਹ ਲੁਡਾਈਐ, the arm will be swung. In India people who walk about happy and without concern usually swing their arms in walking.

[4] The Sabds (Dupadās and Čaupadās) are counted in one continual number, but at the same time the verses of the different mahalās (or Gurus) are counted separately. The first number indicates therefore the number of verses belonging to the several mahalās, the second the totality of Sabds etc., in a Rāg.

[5] The sense is: they retire from the world and worldly pursuits.

I shall sacrifice myself for those, who have obtained the taste of Hari.

O Nānak! by his (merciful) look the true name is obtained, the vessel of virtues.[1]

Sirī Rāg; mahalā III.

II. XXXV.

(1). Who having put on many dresses[2] deceives (others), practising in his mind and heart hypocrisy.

He does not obtain the palace of Hari, after his death he enters into ordure.

Pause.

O my mind! the disciple, who (dwells) solitary in his own house.

He practises true abstinence and will become manifest (=honoured).

(2). By whom his mind is overcome by means of the word (instruction) of the Guru, he obtains the state of final emancipation in his house.

By whom the name of Hari is reflected upon, him he (*i.e.* Hari) brings to the communion of the true assembly.

(3). If (one) enjoy a lakh of women, if he exercise dominion over the nine regions (of the earth).

Without the true Guru he does not obtain comfort, again and again he falls into the womb.[3]

(4). By whom the necklace of Hari is put on their neck, having directed their thought on the feet of the Guru.

Behind them follows increase and success, they have not a bit of covetousness.

(5). What pleases to the Lord, that is done, anything else cannot be done.

Humble Nānak lives by taking the name; O Hari, give (it to me) according to thy inherent good disposition!

Sirī Rāg; mahalā III.

I. *Ghar.*

III. XXXVI.

(1). Whose the government is, his is every body.

By performing the work of a disciple the True one becomes manifest in the heart.

Within whom the True one dwells, he has true knowledge of the True one.

Those who are united with the True one, are not separated (from him), they dwell in their own house.[4]

Pause.

O my beloved, without Hari I have none other!

The true Guru is the true (real) Lord, union (with Hari) is made by the pure word (instruction of the Guru).

(2). Who by the word (of the Guru) is united (with Hari), he remains united, whom he (Hari) unites himself.

In a second love no one is united, again and again he comes and goes.

In all the One dwells, the One is contained (in them).

[1] ਗੁਣ ਤਾਸੁ, a frequent attribute of the name, about the same as ਗੁਣੀ ਨਿਧਾਨ; ਤਾਸ is the Arabic طاس (cup); in Panjābī it denotes a *large metallic plate* or *vessel*. ਗੁਣ ਤਾਸੁ may be translated by *the vessel of virtues*, or the vessel (receptacle) of (all) qualities.

[2] ਭੇਖ, the dress of a faqīr. This verse is spoken against the deceitful faqīrs.

[3] ਜੋਨੀ ਪਵਣਾ, to fall into the womb, *i.e.* to be born again in the course of transmigration.

[4] The meaning is: when united with the Lord they dwell in their own house solitary (retired from the world), and do not wander about like faqīrs. Or "house" may be taken as the *inner man*.

That disciple, to whom he himself (=Hari) is merciful, is absorbed in the name.

(3). Having read, having read an astrological treatise, the Paṇḍits reflect (on it).

Their understanding and intellect are led astray, they do not understand, in their heart is the passion of covetousness.

They wander about in the eighty-four lakhs[1] (of transmigrations), wandering and wandering they become wretched.

What is written before must be done, nobody is erasing it.

(4). The service of the true Guru is difficult; the head should be given after having abandoned one's own self.

If he falls in with the word (of the Guru), he is united with Hari; all (his) worship is recompensed.

By touching the philosopher's stone he becomes a philosopher's stone, light is absorbed in the luminous (Supreme Being).

To whom it is decreed before, with them the true Guru will fall in.

(5). O heart, do not say: (I am) hungry, hungry, do thou not utter a cry!

By whom the eighty-four lakhs (of forms of existence) are created, he gives support to every one.

The fearless is always merciful, he remembers all.

O Nānak! if it (=truth) be understood by the disciple, he will obtain the gate of salvation.

Sirī Rāg; mahalā III.

IV. XXXVII.

(1). By whom, having heard, it (*i.e.* the name) is minded, they dwell in their own house.

Having praised the true Hari by means of the instruction of the Guru, the vessel of virtues is obtained.

Those who are steeped in the word (of the Guru) are pure, I shall always be their sacrifice.

In whose heart Hari dwells, in their body he is manifest.

Pause.

O my mind, meditate on the pure Hari, Hari!

On whose forehead it is written from the beginning, those disciples constantly meditate on him.

(2). O ye holy men of Hari, behold and look! he dwells near brimful.

By whom he is recognized by means of the instruction of the Guru, those see him always in their presence.

He always dwells in the heart of the virtuous, from the vicious he is far.

The fleshly-minded are without virtues, without the name they pine and die.

(3). By whom the word (instruction) of the Guru is heard and minded, they meditate in their mind on that Hari.

By being attached daily to devotion, mind and body become pure.

False is the colour of the safflower, it passes away and they weep in pain.

In whose heart the name is shining, he will always, always be firmly established.

(4). Having obtained the boon of human birth he does not think of the name of Hari nor meditate (on it).

After his foot has slipped, he cannot remain (here), in the other world he does not obtain a place.

That time does not come to hand (again) at the end, having gone, he regrets it.

On whom he (Hari) looks (in mercy), he is saved, having constantly directed his thoughts on Hari.

[1] There are eighty-four lakhs of forms of existence (जोनि = योनि), through which transmigration runs: nine lakhs of जलचर (moving in the water), twenty-seven lakhs of स्थावर (stationary, like trees, etc.), eleven lakhs of कृमि (worms, etc.), ten lakhs of पची (birds), twenty-three lakhs of चौपाय (quadrupeds), four lakhs of मनुष्य (men).

(5). They look at all things, (but) the fleshly-minded get no understanding.

The worship of those disciples is acceptable, whose heart is pure.

They sing the qualities of Hari, they always repeat: Hari! having sung the qualities of Hari, they are absorbed (in him).

O Nānak! their speech is always true, who remain meditating on the name.

Sirī Rāg; mahalā III.

V. XXXVIII.

(1). By whom with one mind the name is meditated upon, having reflected by means of the instruction of the Guru.

Their faces are always bright in that true court (of God).

Those always, always drink nectar, who are attached to the true name.

Pause.

O brother, to the disciple honour will always be given!

If Hari, Hari is always meditated upon (by him), he washes off the filth of egotism.

(2). The fleshly-minded do not know the name, without the name honour is lost.

They have not tasted the relish of the name, they cling to another love.

Worms of ordure fall upon ordure, they are absorbed in ordure.

(3). His human birth is fruitful, who walks in the love of the true Guru.

He saves his own family, blessed is the mother who has given birth to him.

The name of Hari, Hari is meditated upon (by him), upon whom he bestows his mercy and pleasure.

(4). By which disciples the name is meditated upon, having removed from within their own self.

Those are pure from inside and outside, the true ones are absorbed in the True one.

Those have become acceptable, who meditate on Hari by the instruction[1] of the Guru.

Sirī Rāg; mahalā III.

VI. XXXIX.

(1). To the devotees of Hari, Hari is wealth and capital, having asked the Guru they carry on traffic.

They praise continually the name of Hari, the name of Hari is (their) trading stock and support.

By the perfect Guru the name of Hari is established (in them), the devotees of Hari have an inexhaustible storehouse.

Pause.

O brother, admonish this heart (of thine)!

Why does this (thy) heart indulge in laziness? O disciple, read (repeat) the name!

(2). The devotee of Hari has love to Hari, if he reflect attending to the Guru.

By hypocrisy devotion is not made, the word duality is wretched.

That man, though united (by the Guru with the Supreme Spirit) does not blend (with him), in whose heart is the thought of difference.[2]

(3). He is called a worshipper of Hari, who keeps Hari in the breast.

Soul and body he entrusts and puts before (Hari), having destroyed egotism[3] from within.

Blessed and acceptable is that disciple who is never discomfited.

[1] ਜਿਨ ਗੁਰਮਤੀ ਹਰਿ ਧਿਆਇ signifies literally: in whose contemplation Hari is by means of the —.

[2] ਬਿਬੇਕ, separation, discrimination, here identical with ਦੁਬਿਧਾ, duality. The sense is: a man who still considers himself different, apart from the Supreme Spirit, cannot be united with him.

[3] Egotism = the idea of individual existence as distinct from the Supreme Being.

(4). If he (Hari) is found by destiny, then he is obtained; without destiny he cannot be obtained.
Eighty-four lakhs are longing for him; whom he unites, he is united with Hari.
O Nānak! by the disciple Hari is obtained, by being always absorbed in the name of Hari.

Sirī Rāg; mahalā III.

VII. XL.

(1). The name of Hari is an ocean of comfort, by the disciple it is obtained.
By whom daily the name is meditated upon, he is easily absorbed in the name.
His heart is in love with the true Hari, his tongue sings the qualities of Hari.

Pause.

O brother, the world is pained by second love!
He who has come to the asylum of the Guru obtains comfort, having daily meditated on the name.
(2). To the true one dirt does not stick, a pure mind meditates on Hari.
If by the disciple the word (of the Guru) is known, he is absorbed in the immortal name of Hari.
By the Guru divine knowledge is kindled very bright, ignorance and darkness pass away.
(3). The fleshly-minded are filthy, filled with dirt, (in them) is the thirst and passion of egotism.
Without the word the dirt does not go off, they die and are born (again) and become wretched.
They cling to imposture[1] and have neither this nor that side.
(4). The disciple practises silent repetition of the name, austerity and continence; his love is (directed) to the name of Hari.
By the disciple the one name of the creator is always meditated upon.
O Nānak! the name is meditated upon (by him), (which) is the support of all creatures.

Sirī Rāg; mahalā III.

VIII. XLI.

(1). The fleshly-minded is filled with spiritual blindness, indifference to the world and loneliness he does not practise.

He does not know the word (of the Guru), he is always in pain, at the threshold of Hari he loses his honour.

By the disciple egotism is parted with, by being attached to the name comfort is obtained (by him).

Pause.

O my mind, day and night (my) hope has been fulfilled continually!
Who having served the true Guru burns his spiritual ignorance, he is lonely in his (own) house.
(2). The disciple practises (good) works, indifference to the world and joy in Hari springs up (in him).
Day and night he performs devotion, having annihilated egotism he is free from care.
By great luck the true assembly is obtained, Hari is obtained and (thereby) easily joy.
(3). That man is a saint and indifferent to the world, that man establishes the name in his heart.
Within whom lurks no darkness, who thoroughly removes from within his own self.
The treasure of the name is shown (to him) by the true Guru, by drinking the juice of Hari he is satiated.

[1] पाउ़ठघात्ती, deceit, imposture, compounded of पउ़ठा, *s.f.* roguery (Sansk. धूर्त्तता, by inversion of the first syllable धतुरा), and بَازِي, play, playing with roguery, practising imposition on people by empty pretences or some hocus pocus. They cling to imposture (as knavish faqīrs are wont to do) and lose thus this and that world, are deprived of both.

(4). By whomsoever is obtained the society of the pious by a perfect destiny, he is indifferent to the world.

The fleshly-minded wanders about, he does not know the true Guru, egotism clings to his heart.

O Nānak! those who are steeped in the word (of the Guru) and dyed in the name of Hari, are without fear, what can happen (to them)?

Sirī Rāg; mahalā III.

IX. XLII.

(1). In the house the wares are laid out, all the thing is within.

If every moment the name be remembered, some disciple will obtain it.

The treasure of the name is inexhaustible, by a great destiny it is obtained.

Pause.

O my heart, give up calumny, egotism and conceit!

O disciple, meditate thou always with one mind on Hari!

(2). The faces of the disciples, who reflect on the word of the Guru, are bright.

Here (in this world) and there (that world) they obtain comfort, having muttered, muttered in their heart: Murāri!

In their (own) house the palace (of Hari) is found (by them), by reflecting on the word of the Guru.

(3). The foreheads of those, who turn away their face from the true Guru, (will be) black.

Daily they earn pain, they are perpetually looked out for by the vile men[1] of Yamā.

(Even) in a dream they have no comfort, they are consumed by much anxiety.

(4). The donor of all is one, he himself gives presents.

Nothing can be said, he gives to whom he pleases.

O Nānak! by the disciple he (=Hari) is obtained, he himself knows him.

Sirī Rāg; mahalā III.

X. XLIII.

(1). If the true Lord be served, the True one gives greatness.

(In whose) heart he dwells by the favour of the Guru, he removes egotism.

This running mind he will save, when he himself looks down upon it (in mercy).

Pause.

O brother, O disciple, meditate on the name of Hari!

(In whose) heart the treasure of the name always dwells, he receives a place in the palaces (of Hari).

(2). Soul and body of the fleshly-minded is blind, he has no place nor site.

In many births he wanders about like a crow in an empty house.

By means of the instruction of the Guru there is light in the heart, by the word (of the Guru) the name of Hari is obtained.

(3). The world endowed with the three qualities is blind, the infatuation of the Māyā is darkness.

The greedy worship for the sake of food, reading the Vēdas they raise a cry.

Amongst worldly pursuits they are consumed and dead, they have neither this nor that side.

(4). By the infatuation of the Māyā is forgotten the father and preserver of the world.

[1] ਜਾਲਾ is here derived from the Sansk. जाल्म, a low, vile man; ਜਮ ਜਾਲੇ quite corresponds to ਜਮ ਜੰਦਾਰ, cf. Sirī Rāg, Sabd 21, 2. The words may, however, also be translated: they are always overcome by the net of Yama.

Without the Guru it (*i.e.* the world) is thoughtless, the whole (creation) is (therefore) bound by (Yama) the death.

The followers of the Guru are saved, having remembered the true name.

Sirī Rāg; mahalā III.

XI. XLIV.

(1). (In) the three qualities is the infatuation of the Māyā, the disciple obtains the fourth degree.[1]

He is united by him (with himself) in mercy, the name of Hari comes and dwells in his heart.

In whose bag there is religious merit, them he unites with the assembly of the pious.

Pause.

O brother! keep fast the true instruction of the true Guru!

(Who) is acquiring the thoroughly True one, (him) he (*i.e.* Hari) unites (with himself) by the word (of the Guru).

(2). By whom the name is known, for them I sacrifice myself.

Having given up my own self, I sit down at (their) feet and walk according to their will.

(Who) obtains the gain of Hari, the name of Hari, he is naturally absorbed in the name.

(3). Without the Guru the palace (of Hari) is not obtained, the name is not gotten.

Seek such a true Guru, from whom that True one may be obtained.

He who kills the demons,[2] lives in comfort, what is pleasing to him, that is done.

(4). As the true Guru is looked upon, so will be the happiness.[3]

If a man have faith (in the Guru), he will have no doubt whatever.

O Nānak! there is one light and two forms (shapes), by the word (of the Guru) union (between the two) is effected.

Sirī Rāg; mahalā III.

XII. XLV.

(1). Having abandoned the nectar they are greedy of worldly objects, they perform a false worship.

They forsake their own religion, they do not understand, their (life) is daily spent in pain.

The fleshly-minded are blind, they do not think, they are dead, being drowned without water.

Pause.

O my heart, flee always to the asylum of Hari!

If the word of the Guru dwells within, Hari is not forgotten.

(2). This body is a puppet of the Māyā, within which wicked egotism is put.

The fleshly-minded comes and goes, is born and dies (again), his honour is lost.

By serving the true Guru, comfort is always obtained, by the Luminous one light is united (with himself).

(3). The service of the true Guru is full of comfort, the fruit, that (one) wishes, he obtains.

By chastity, truthfulness and austerity his body is pure, he makes Hari Hari dwell in his heart.

He remains always in joy, day and night, meeting with the beloved he obtains comfort.

(4). I sacrifice myself for those, who have come to the asylum of the true Guru.

At the true gate there is true greatness (obtained), they are easily absorbed in the True one.

O Nānak! by his (merciful) look he is obtained, the disciple he unites to union (with himself).

[1] ਚਉਥਾ ਪਦੁ = ਤੁਰੀਯ, the fourth or mystic state of the soul, in which it is united with the Supreme Spirit or Brahm by intense meditation and abstraction from all objects of the senses.

[2] The ਅਸੁਰ are ਕਾਮ, ਕ੍ਰੋਧ, ਲੋਭ, ਮੋਹ, ਹੰਕਾਰ, according to Sikh interpretation.

[3] The happiness of a man depends on what he takes the Guru for.

Sirī Rāg; mahalā III.

XIII. XLVI.

(1). The works, which the fleshly-minded practise, are like ornaments on the body of an unfavoured woman.

The husband of the bed does not come, continually she is wretched.

The palace of the beloved she does not obtain, his household is not seen (by her).

Pause.

O brother, meditate with one mind on the name!

He who keeps company with the society of the pious, obtains comfort by silently repeating the name of Rām.

(2). That (fem.) disciple is always a favoured woman, by whom the beloved is kept in the breast.

She speaks sweetly, she walks humbly, her husband dallies with her on the bed.

Those favoured women are beautiful, who have infinite love to the Guru.

(3). By a perfect destiny the true Guru is found, when the destiny is rising.

From within pain and error is cut off and comfort is obtained.

She who walks according to the pleasure of the Guru, will not find any pain.

(4). In the decree of the Guru is nectar, which one may easily obtain.

Those who have got it, have drunk it, having removed egotism from within.

O Nānak! if the name is meditated upon by the disciple, union is effected with the True one.

Sirī Rāg; mahalā III.

XIV. XLVII.

(1). When she knows her own beloved, she puts body and soul before him (as an offering).

She does those works, which the favoured women do.

There is (thereby) easily union (or meeting) with the True one, the True one gives (her) greatness.

Pause.

O brother, without the Guru devotion cannot be made.

Without the Guru devotion is not obtained, though every one desire it.

(2). On account of another love (than God's) the sum of the eighty-four lakhs (of births) is allotted to the fascinating woman.

Without the Guru she gets no sleep, in pain she passes the night.

Without the word (of the Guru) the beloved is not obtained, she wastes her lifetime uselessly.

(3). In egotism she goes about in the world, (but) there is no wealth nor prosperity on her side.

Every blind one, that does not think of the name, is bound by Yama, the death.

When the true Guru is found, wealth is obtained, having remembered the name of Hari in the heart.

(4). Those who are attached to the name are pure by the inherent nature of the Guru.[1]

(Their) heart and body are dyed with colour, their tongue tastes sweet juice.

O Nānak! that colour does not go off, which Hari has applied in the beginning.[2]

Sirī Rāg; mahalā III.

XV. XLVIII.

(1). (If) he (Hari) bestows mercy on the disciple, then devotion is made (by him), without the Guru devotion cannot be made.

[1] The Guru being the ਪਾਰਸੁ or touchstone.

[2] In the beginning (ਧੁਰਿ loc.) when the destiny of every being was fixed.

He himself unites (with himself); he, who understands (the truth), becomes pure.

Hari is true, true is his word, by the word (of the Guru) union (with Hari) is effected.

Pause.

O brother! why is he, who is destitute of devotion, come into the world?

(By whom) the service of the perfect Guru is not made, he has uselessly wasted his human birth.

(2). He himself is the life of the world, the giver of comfort, he himself by his gift unites (with himself).

What are these helpless creatures, what shall one say and tell (to him)?

He himself gives greatness to the disciple, he himself causes (him) to do service.

(3). Having seen his family he is bewildered with infatuation, at the time of departing it does not go with (him).

Serving the true Guru the abode of virtues (or qualities = God) is obtained; his value[1] is not to be found out.

The Lord Hari is my companion and friend, the Lord will be my companion at the end.

(4). (One) may say in his own mind and thought and get it said (by others),[2] (but) without the Guru self does not go.

Hari is the donor, propitious to his devotees,[3] having bestowed mercy he dwells[4] in (their) heart.

O Nānak! he gives beauty and understanding, the Lord himself gives greatness to the disciple.

Sirī Rāg; mahalā III.

XVI. XLIX.

(1). Blessed is the mother, who has borne (the disciple), blessed and foremost is (his) father.

Having served the true Guru, comfort is obtained (by the disciple), from within conceit is gone.

Standing at the gate (of the Guru) the holy people serve (him), they obtain the abode of (all) qualities.

Pause.

O my mind, turning with the face towards the Guru meditate on that Hari!

If the word of the Guru dwells in the mind, soul and body become pure.

(2). Having bestowed mercy he has come to the house, he himself has come and joined (it).

By whom he is praised by means of the word of the Guru, they are easily coloured.

The true ones are absorbed in the True one, they remain united (with him) and are not separated (again).

(3). Whatever is to be done, that he has done, anything else cannot be done.

Those who are separated long times, he has united (with himself), having put them down in the account-book of the true Guru.

He himself will cause the work to be done, anything else cannot be done.

(4). Having given up the passion of egotism, soul and body is dyed with colour (love).

Day and night the name of the fearless, formless, is contained in the heart.

O Nānak! by himself they are united (with himself) by means of the perfect, infinite word (of the Guru).

[1] Construct ਤਿਸ ਦੀ ਕੀਮ = ਤਿਸ ਗੁਣ ਨਿਧਾਨ ਦੀ ਕੀਮ ਨ ਪਾਈ.

[2] He may say—that his own self is gone and he may get it said by others, *i.e.* it may be attested by others. But forms like ਕਹੈ ਕਹਾਏ bear in the Granth also the sense of an *intensive* verb: *he may well say.*

[3] ਭਗਤਿ ਵਛਲੁ (भक्तवत्सल), kind to the devotees, a frequent attribute of Hari in the Granth.

[4] ਵਸਾਈ stands here instead of ਵਸਈ, *a* beiog lengthened for the sake of the rhyme.

Sirī Rāg; mahalā III.

XVII. L.

(1). Gōvind is the abode of (all) qualities, his end cannot be attained.

By talking and chatting he is not obtained, (he is obtained) if egotism departs from within.

By meeting with the true Guru he (*i.e.* the disciple) is always steeped in the fear of God, he himself (*i.e.* God) comes and dwells in the heart.

Pause.

O brother! some disciple understands (the truth).

Those who do works without understanding (the truth), lose the blessing of their human birth.

(2). Those have obtained the relish (of the name) who have tasted it, without having tasted it they go astray in error.

The true name is nectar, which cannot be described at all.

He who drinks it has become acceptable, being absorbed in the perfect word (of the Guru).

(3) If he himself gives, then it is received, nothing else can be done.

In the hand of the giver is the gift, which he bestows by the medium of the Guru.

As it is made by him, so it has been (made); as he does the works, (so they are).

(4). The name is chastity, truthfulness, and abstinence; without the name one does not become pure.

By a perfect destiny the name dwells in the heart, by means of the word (of the Guru) union is effected.

O Nānak! he who abides in the love (of Hari), easily obtains the qualities of Hari.

Sirī Rāg; mahalā III.

XVIII. LI.

(1). If (one) subdue his body and practise upturned austerity,[1] egotism does not depart from within.

If he practise very spiritual[2] works, he will never obtain the name.

If he, living, die by means of the word of the Guru, the name of Hari comes and dwells in the heart.

Pause.

Hear, O my heart, flee to the asylum of the true Guru!

By the favour of the Guru one is freed from the world, he crosses the water of existence by means of the word of the Guru.

(2). In the whole (creation) the three qualities are inherent, second love (duality) and (consequent) disorder.[3]

The Paṇḍit reads, (but) is bound by the fetter of spiritual ignorance; he does not understand out of love to the visible world.

By meeting with the true Guru the triad (the three qualities) goes off, on the fourth station is the gate of salvation.

(3). From the Guru the (right) way is obtained, the dimness of spiritual ignorance ceases.

[1] ਉਰਧ ਤਪ, austerity practised by lifting up the arms or standing on the head and lifting the feet upwards, etc. It is often mentioned in the Granth.

[2] ਅਧਿਆਤਮ (=अध्यात्म or अध्यात्मिक), very spiritual, affectedly spiritual.

[3] ਤ੍ਰੈਗੁਣ ਸਭਾ ਧਾਤੁ ਹੈ should be constructed; ਸਭਾ (*i.e.* ਸ੍ਰਿਸਟਿ, creation) ਸੈ ਤ੍ਰੈਗੁਣ ਧਾਤੁ ਹੈ, in all (the creation) the three qualities are the constituent element: ਦੂਜਾ ਭਾਉ ਵਿਕਾਰੁ must also be taken as Nominatives.

If (one) die by means of the word (of the Guru), he is saved, he obtains the gate of salvation.
By the favour of the Guru he remains united (with God); true is the name of the creator.
(4). This mind is very strong, it does not give up in any (way) its scheme.
It inflicts pain (upon itself) by another love and is much punished.
O Nānak! those who cling to the name are saved, having removed egotism by the word (of the Guru).

Sirī Rāg; mahalā III.

XIX. LII.

(1). If he bestow mercy, the Guru is obtained, who establishes the name of Hari (in the heart).
Without the Guru he is not obtained by any one, he wastes uselessly his human birth.
By doing self-willed works he is punished at the threshold (of God).

Pause.

O my heart, drop second love!
Within thee Hari dwells, by the service of the Guru thou wilt obtain comfort.
(2). True is the speech, true is the word (of the Guru), when (one) loves the truth.
Having removed egotism and wrath, the name of Hari dwells in (his) heart.
If with a pure heart the name is meditated upon, he obtains the gate of salvation.
(3). In egotism the world (=people) passes away, having died it is born (again), it comes and goes.
The fleshly-minded do not know the word (of the Guru), they will depart having lost their honour.
By whom the name is obtained by the service of the Guru, he remains absorbed in the True one.
(4). (By whom) the Guru is obtained by minding the word, he removes from within his own self.
Daily he performs devotion, his thoughts are always directed on the True one.
O Nānak! when the name, the highest good, dwells in (his) heart, he is easily absorbed (in God).

Sirī Rāg; mahalā III.

XX. LIII.

(1). Those men, who have not served the true Guru, are afflicted in the four periods (of the world).
The Supreme Spirit which is in their house (=body) is not known (by them), they are ruined by conceit and selfishness.
Begging from those who are cursed by the true Guru, they are consumed in the world.
The true word (of the Guru), which is putting all things right, is not received (by them).

Pause.

O my heart, behold always Hari in (thy) presence!
He takes away the pain of birth and death, in the word (of the Guru) he is contained brimful.
(2). Those who praise the True one are true, the true name is their support.
They do true work, they love the True one.
What the true Lord is doing, none is erasing.
The fleshly-minded do not obtain (his) palace, the false ones are ruined by falsehood.
(3). Practising selfishness the world has died, without the Guru there is deep darkness.
By the infatuation of the Māyā the comfort-giving donor is forgotten.
If it serves the true Guru, then it is saved, if it keep the True one in the breast.
By mercy Hari is obtained and by reflection on the true word.
(4). Having served the true Guru, (his) mind is pure by abandoning the passion of egotism.
Having given up his own self, he dies whilst living by meditating on the word of the Guru.
The hurried avocations (of life) are stopped, love to the True one has set in.
The faces of those who are immersed in the True one, are bright at that true court.

(5). By whom the true Guru, the Supreme Spirit, is not minded, whose love is not attached to the word (of the Guru).

As much bathing and liberality as he may practise, he is wretched by second love.

If Hari bestow his own mercy (on him), then he will give himself to the love of the name.

O Nānak! remember thou the name by infinite love to the Guru!

Sirī Rāg; mahalā III.

XXI. LIV.

(1). Whom shall I serve? what silent repetition shall I perform? I will go and ask the true Guru.

The decision of the true Guru I will obey, having removed from within my own self.

By this service and attendance the name comes and dwells in the heart.

From the name comfort is obtained, from the true word splendour.[1]

Pause.

O my heart, wake daily, thinking of Hari!

Protect thy own field, the crane will fall on thy field.

(2). The heart's desires (of him) are fulfilled who remains brimful in the word (of the Guru).

He who performs devotion in fear and love day and night, sees always Hari in his presence.

His heart is always immersed in the true word, error has gone far from his body.

The pure Lord, who is true and profound in qualities, is obtained by him.

(3). Those who have waked are saved, those who have fallen asleep are plundered.

Who has not known the true word has passed his (time) (like) a dream.

As the guest of an empty house goes as he has come.

The life of the fleshly-minded one has passed uselessly, what face will he show when having gone (to the threshold)?

(4). Everything is he himself, (but) in egotism he cannot be described.

If he is known from the word of the Guru, he removes the pain of egotism from within.

I cling to the feet of those who serve their own true Guru.

I, Nānak, sacrifice myself for those who are true at the true gate.

Sirī Rāg; mahalā III.

XXII. LV.

(1). If the time is considered, at which time shall devotion be made?

Those who are daily immersed in the name have true knowledge of the True one.

If but a little the beloved be forgotten, what devotion is (then) made?

If soul and body is cool (happy) with the True one, no breath goes in vain.[2]

Pause.

O my heart, meditate on the name of Hari!

True devotion is then made, when Hari comes and dwells in the heart.

(2). Having sown the seed of the true name, the field is easily cultivated.

The field springs up abundantly and the heart is readily satiated.

The word of the Guru is nectar, by the drinking of which thirst ceases.

(If) this mind be true and immersed in truth, it remains absorbed in the True one.

[1] ਸੁਹਾਇ = ਸੁਹਾਈ; it is shortened for the sake of the rhyme.

[2] *i.e.* Without remembering Hari.

(3). He is telling, seeing, and speaking,[1] (who) is continually absorbed in the word (of the Guru).
(His) voice is sounding in the four periods (of the world), proclaiming the perfectly True one.
(His) egotism and selfishness are stopped, (who) is united by the True one.
They have the palace (of Hari) in their presence who direct their constant thoughts on the True one.
(4). By his (merciful) look the name is meditated upon, without destiny it cannot be obtained.
By a perfect destiny he obtains the assembly of the pious, with whom the true Guru falls in.
By being daily immersed in the name, the pain of the world departs from within.
O Nānak! by means of the word (of the Guru) union is (effected), (who) praises,[2] he is absorbed in the name.

Sirī Rāg; mahalā III.

XXIII. LVI.

(1). His own love he has put in them who reflect on the word of the Guru.
With the assembly of the pious they remain always united, remembering the qualities of the True one.
He has cleared away the dirt of duality (in those) who have put Hari in their breast.
True is (their) speech, truth in (their) heart, they love the True one.[3]

Pause.

O my heart, (thou art) filled with the dirt of egotism!
Hari is pure and always beautiful, by means of the word (of the Guru) he is adorning.
(2). Those are united by the Lord himself whose heart is fascinated by the true word.
By being daily immersed in the name, light is absorbed in the luminous (Hari).
By the (inward) light tbe Lord is known, without the true Guru understanding is not obtained.
To whom it has been decreed beforehand, with them the true Guru has fallen in.
(3). Without the name the whole (world) is distressed, by second love it is lost.
Without it it does not live twenty-four minutes, in pain the night is passed.
He who is led astray by error is blind, again and again he comes and goes.
(If) the Lord bestow his own look (of mercy), he himself unites (with himself).
(4). He hears and sees all things, how shall it be denied?[4]
They commit sin on sin (and) are consumed by sin, and cause (others) to be consumed.
That Lord does not come into their sight, the fleshly-minded do not obtain understanding.
Whom he makes seeing, he sees; O Nānak! the disciple obtains (understanding).

Sirī Rāg; mahalā III.

XXIV. LVII.

(1). Without the Guru sickness is not broken, the pain of egotism does not depart.
In whose heart he dwells by the favour of the Guru, he remains absorbed in the name.
By the word of the Guru Hari is obtained, without the word he is led astray in error.

Pause.

O my heart, dwell in thy own house!
Praise thou the name of Rām, there will not be again coming and going.

[1] Though no trace of the subject be given, it must be, according to the whole context, the disciple.

[2] *i.e.* The name.

[3] Some MSS. read ਪਿਆਰੁ, which, however, is against the rhyme; the right reading is ਪਿਆਰਿ, the Abl. sing., by, on account of love with (=to) Hari.

[4] The lithographed copy reads ਮੁਕਰਿ ਪਇਆ ਜਾਇ, but the MSS. read correctly ਪਾਇਆ; ਮੁਕਰਿ ਪਾਇਆ ਜਾਇ is the passive: how shall it be denied?

(2). Hari is the only donor, there is none other.

He dwells in the heart of him who praises him by the word (of the Guru), comfort is easily obtained (by him).

He sees all within his look, to whom he pleases, he gives.

(3). Egotism is all calculation, in calculation are not the nine comforts.

Those who practise works of poison[1] are absorbed in very poison.

Without the name they get no place, in the city of Yama they suffer pain.

(4). Soul and body, all is his, even he sustains them.

By whom (the truth) is understood by the favour of the Guru, he obtains the gate of salvation.

O Nānak! praise thou the name (of him who has) no end nor limit!

Sirī Rāg; mahalā III.

XXV. LVIII.

(1). They have always joy and comfort whose support the true name is.

By the favour of the Guru truth is obtained, the remover of pain.

He always, always sings the qualities of the True one, who has love to the true name.

Having bestowed his own mercy, he has given him a storehouse (full of) devotion.

Pause.

O my heart, sing the qualities of him who is always happy!

The true words of Hari are obtained by him, who remains absorbed with Hari.

(2). By true devotion the heart has become red,[2] it is coloured by a natural process.

By the word of the Guru the heart is enchanted, nothing can be said (about it).

The tongue, coloured by the true word (of the Guru), drinks nectar, having the right taste[3] it sings the qualities (of Hari).

This colour is obtained by that disciple on whom he (Hari) bestows mercy and favour.

(3). This world is in uncertainty, sleeping the night is passed.

Some are drawn out (from uncertainty) by his own decree and united by himself (with himself).

He himself dwells in their heart and stops the infatuation of the Māyā.

He himself gives greatness and makes the disciple understand (the truth).

(4). The donor of all is one, the erring he instructs.

Some are ruined by himself, they are attached by him to another (love).

From the instruction of the Guru Hari is obtained, the luminous (Hari) unites light (with himself).

O Nānak! those who are daily steeped in the name are absorbed in the name.

Sirī Rāg; mahalā III.

XXVI. LIX.

(1). By the virtuous the True one is obtained, having given up the passion of thirst.

By the word of the Guru the mind is coloured, the tongue with love and affection.

Without the true Guru he is not obtained by any one; behold, having reflected in thy mind!

From the fleshly-minded the dirt does not go off, as long as he does not love the word of the Guru.

[1] ਬਿਖੁ, poison, anything detestable or wicked.

[2] *i.e.* Filled with love.

[3] ਰਸਿ, *adj.* (Sansk. रसिन्) having the right taste, *i.e.* being enamoured.

Pause.

O my heart, walk according to the will of the true Guru!

If thou dwellest in thine own house and drinkest nectar, thou wilt easily obtain the palace (of Hari).

(2). The vicious (woman) has no virtue, she does not attain to sit in the presence.

The fleshly-minded does not know the word, from the vicious the Lord is far.

By whom the True one has been known, they are fully steeped in truth.

By the word of the Guru their heart is perforated, the Lord himself has met with them in the presence.[1]

(3). By himself they are coloured with dye-stuff, by means of the word (of the Guru) they are united by him.

True colour does not go off, those who are steeped in truth, give themselves to devout meditation.

Having wandered about in the four corners (of the earth) they have become tired, the fleshly-minded do not obtain understanding.

Whom the true Guru unites, he is united, having been absorbed in the true word (of the Guru).

(4). I am tired of making many friends, (that) one should cut off my pain.

Having met with the beloved my pain is cut off, by the word of the Guru union is brought about.

The acquisition of truth is true capital, the knowledge of the True one is true.[2]

Those who are united with the True one are not separated (again), after having become disciples, O Nānak!

Sirī Rāg; mahalā III.

XXVII. LX.

(1). He himself, the creator of the elements,[3] makes creation, having produced (it) himself, he sees (it).

In all the One exists, the invisible cannot be seen.

The Lord himself is merciful, he himself gives understanding.

By means of the instruction of the Guru he always dwells in the heart of those, whose thought is continually absorbed in the True one.

Pause.

O my heart, obey the will of the Guru!

Soul and body, all becomes cool (refreshed), (if) the name comes and dwells in the heart.

(2). By whom the element (of the world) has been made and put down, he takes care (of it).

By the word of the Guru he is known, when he himself looks down (in mercy).

Those men are shining by the word (of the Guru) at that true court (of Hari).

The disciples, who are steeped in the true word, are united by the creator himself.

(3). By means of the instruction of the Guru the True one is to be praised, who has no end nor limit.

He himself dwells in every heart by (his) order, he reflects on the order.

If he be praised by means of the word of the Guru, he destroys egotism[4] from within.

That woman, who is without the name, will weep, being vicious.

[1] *i.e.* The Lord himself has joined them and is in their presence, present with them.

[2] The knowledge (ਸੋਇ, according to the traditional interpretation of the Sikhs) of the True one (=God) is true (real, lasting), all other knowledge is to no purpose.

[3] ਕਾਰਣ ਕਰਤਾ (=ਕਾਰਣ ਕਰਣ), the maker or creator of the elements or rudiments. The elements are evolved from primary matter (प्रधान). This, however, is considered अनादि (without beginning), and therefore as a part of the Supreme Being itself. ਕਾਰਣ ਕਰਤਾ could, however, also be translated by: the maker of the causality = the cause of causes.

[4] *i.e.* Individuality, the consciousness or opinion of individual existence (as separated from the Supreme).

(4). The True one I will praise, to the True one I will cling, by the true name satiety is given.
On virtue I will reflect, virtue I will collect, vice I will wash away.
If he himself unites to union (with himself), there will not be again separation.
I, Nānak, will praise my own Guru, from whom I obtain that Lord.

Sirī Rāg; mahalā III.

XXVIII. LXI.

(1). Hear, hear, O thou careless of work! why walkest thou swinging the arm?
Thou dost not know thy own beloved, how wilt thou show thy face having gone (to the threshold of Hari)?
I hold the foot of those friends who have known their beloved.
(That) I may become like them, whom he unites with the company of the society of the pious.

Pause.

O false handsome woman, thou art ruined by falsehood!
The beloved, the true, beautiful Lord, is obtained by means of reflection (on) the Guru.
(2). The fleshly-minded do not know the beloved, how is the night passed by them?
They are filled with pride, in thirst they burn, they are distressed by second love.
From the heart of those favoured women, who are attached to the word (of the Guru), egotism departs.
They always enjoy[1] their own beloved, in continual happiness (their time) is passed.
(3). She who is without divine knowledge is abandoned by the beloved, the beloved cannot be obtained (by her).
Ignorance is darkness, without seeing the beloved hunger does not cease.
Come, join me, O companion! unite with me the beloved!
If by a perfect destiny the Guru is met with (by any), the beloved is obtained, she is absorbed in the True one.
(4). Those friends are favoured women on whom he looks (in mercy).
(Those) know their own husband (who) put their body and soul before him.
In the house their own bridegroom is obtained (by them) who remove egotism.
O Nānak! beautiful are the favoured women, who perform devotion day by day!

Sirī Rāg; mahalā III.

XXIX. LXII.

(1). Some enjoy their own beloved, to which door shall I go and ask (for him)?
I will serve the true Guru with love (saying): join to me the beloved!
All created beings he sees himself, to some one he is near, from some one far.
She who has known, that her beloved is with her, always retains the beloved in her presence.

Pause.

O handsome woman, walk thou in the love of the Guru!
Daily thou wilt enjoy thy own beloved, being readily absorbed in the True one.
(2). Favoured women steeped in the word (of the Guru), adorned by the true word:
Obtain Hari, their own bridegroom, in (their) house, by infinite love and affection to the Guru.
The bed is beautiful, Hari sports in love, with devotion their storehouses are filled.
That beloved Lord dwells in the heart who gives support to every one.

[1] ਰਾਵਹਿ, literally, they cause their beloved (husband) to dally with them, or to stay with them.

(3). I always sacrifice myself for those who praise their own beloved.
Soul and body I surrender, I give my head, I cling to their feet:
Who have known the One, having done away second love.
O Nānak! (if) by the disciple the name is known, she is absorbed in the True one.

Sirī Rāg; mahalā III.

XXX. LXIII.

(1). O Hari, thou art perfectly true, everything is in thy lap.
In the eighty-four lakhs (of forms of existence) they wander about, longing (for thee), without meeting with the Guru they are in pain.
(If) thou, O liberal Hari! bestowest it, there is always comfort in the body.
By the favour of the Guru I serve thee, O true, deep, and profound one!

Pause.

O my heart, he who is steeped in the name obtains comfort!
By means of the instruction of the Guru the name should be praised, there is none other.
(2). Dharmrāi (*i.e.* Yama) has the order: sit down and decide on true religious merit!
He who by second love is of a wicked mind, is under thy dominion.
Who mutter the qualities of the Supreme Hari, the vessel of virtues, the one Murāri, in their heart:
To them Dharmrāi performs service; blessed is he who is remembering (Hari)!
(3). If the passions of the heart leave the heart, spiritual ignorance and conceit is stopped in the heart.
By whom the Supreme Spirit is known, he is readily absorbed in the name.
Without the true Guru final emancipation is not obtained, the fleshly-minded one wanders about mad.
He does not know the word (of the Guru), he is chattering, in worldly objects he is absorbed.
(4). He himself is everything, there is none other.
As he causes (them) to speak, thus it is spoken, when he himself calls (them).
The speech of the disciple is Brahm, by the word (of the Guru) union is effected.
O Nānak! remember thou the name, by the worship of which comfort is obtained!

Sirī Rāg; mahalā III.

XXXI. LXIV.

(1). In the world filth and (consequent) pain of egotism is obtained, by second love dirt sticks (to men).
The filth of selfishness, though washed, does not go off at all, if (one) bathe at a hundred Tīrthas.
They practise works of many kinds, (but) twofold dirt has stuck to them.
By reading the dirt does not go off, go and ask the sages!

Pause.

O my heart, if one come to the asylum of the Guru, then he will become pure.
The fleshly-minded in saying: Hari, Hari! have become tired, the dirt could not be washed off (by them).
(2). By a dirty heart devotion cannot be made, the name cannot be obtained.
The dirty fleshly-minded have died dirty, they will go, having lost their honour.
If he (Hari) dwell in the heart by the favour of the Guru, the filth of egotism is absorbed.
As in darkness a lamp is lighted, so causes the Guru by (his) divine knowledge ignorance to be dispersed.

(3). "It is done by us," "we shall do it," (saying thus) we are foolish and ignorant.
The (real) actor is forgotten (by us), (our) affection is (turned to) second love.
There is no pain like that of the Māyā, all have become tired wandering about in the world.
From the instruction of the Guru comfort is obtained, having put the true name in the breast.
(4). Whom he[1] unites, he is united, I sacrifice myself for him.
O heart! to them, who are immersed in devotion, the true speech (of the Guru) is their own place.[2]
The heart being coloured the tongue is coloured (also) and sings (then) the true qualities of Hari.
O Nānak! (by whom) the name is not forgotten, he is absorbed in the True one.

Sirī Rāg; mahalā IV.[3]

Ghar I.

I. LXV.

(1). In my soul and body are excessive pangs of separation, how shall the beloved come to my house and meet (with me)?
When I see my own Lord, my pain goes by seeing the Lord.
I will go and ask those friends, in what wise the Lord may come to an interview (with me)?

Pause.

O my true Guru! without thee there is none other.
I, foolish and stupid man, have come to thy asylum, out of mercy join to me that Hari![4]
(2). The true Guru is the giver of the name of Hari, he himself unites that Lord (with men).
From the true Guru the Lord Hari is known, like the Guru there is none other.
I fall on the asylum of the Guru (saying): kindly join to me that Lord!
(3). No one has obtained him (Hari) by the obstinacy of his mind, every one becomes tired making shifts (to obtain him).
If he practise a thousand clevernesses, on an unaltered[5] heart colour does not stick.
By falsehood and hypocrisy he has not been obtained by any one; what he sows, that he will eat.
(4). The hope of all is in thee, O Lord! all creatures are thine, thou (art their) capital.
O Lord! no one is empty of thee, at (thy) gate the disciples (obtain) praise.
Draw out those, who are drowning in the poison, the water of existence! this is the petition of humble Nānak.

Sirī Rāg; mahalā IV.

II. LXVI.

(1). If the name is obtained, the heart is satiated, without the name I shall live in misery.
Would that some disciple, a friend, would meet (with me), that he would show me the Lord, the vessel of virtues!
I will be quartered for him who manifests to me the name!

Pause.

O my beloved! I live, having meditated on the name.
Without the name I cannot live; O my true Guru, make fast (in me) the name!

[1] *i.e.* Hari.

[2] The sense is: they live in the true speech of the Guru, are wholly given to it.

[3] *i.e.* Guru Rāmdās.

[4] It appears that these verses were made by Rāmdās before he himself had succeeded to the Guruship.

[5] ਰੇਗਾ, *adj.* new, fresh, not improved or prepared (by a course of discipline).

(2). The name is a priceless jewel; it is with the perfect, true Guru.

The true Guru, having taken it out, reveals it to those who give themselves to his service.

Blessed and very fortunate are the men, very fortunate the women, who have come and joined the Guru.

(3). With whom the true Guru, the Supreme Spirit, has not met, they are luckless and in the power of death.

They are again and again compelled to wander about in the womb, being made hideous in ordure.

One should not come near to them, in whose heart is wrath, the Čhanḍāl.

(4). The true Guru, the Supreme Spirit, is the pond of immortality, the very fortunate come and bathe therein.

The dirt of their several births goes off, having made fast the pure name (in themselves).

Humble Nānak has obtained the highest station, having directed his devout meditation on the true Guru.

Sirī Rāg; mahalā IV.

III. LXVII.

(1). (His) qualities I will sing, (his) qualities I will spread, (his) qualities I will tell, O my mother!

The disciple who tells (his) qualities, is my friend; having joined (this my) friend, I will sing the qualities of Hari!

A diamond, having met with a diamond, is perforated; in deep red colour I will bathe!

Pause.

O my Gōvind! if I sing (thy) qualities, my heart is satiated.

Within (me) is thirst after the name of Hari, the Guru being pleased procures it (for me).

(2). Colour the heart, O ye very fortunate! the Guru being pleased grants the favour.

The Guru makes fast the name with colour; I sacrifice myself for the true Guru.

Without the true Guru the name of Hari is not obtained, though they do lakhs and crores of (good) works.

(3). Without destiny the true Guru is not found, (though) always sitting near him in (his) house.

Within (whom) is the pain of ignorance and error, in (whom) is a film (over the eyes), they (fem.) have fallen far off (from the Guru).

Without meeting with the true Guru gold is not made (of iron), the fleshly-minded, the iron, is drowned at the side of the boat.

(4). The true Guru is the boat of the name of Hari, in what wise can it be ascended?

He who walks according to the will of the true Guru, comes and sits down in the boat.

Blessed, blessed, very fortunate are those, O Nānak! whom the true Guru unites (with Hari).

Sirī Rāg; mahalā IV.

IV. LXVIII.

(1). I always stand and inquire after the road; if any show me the Lord, to them I go.

I go about following those who have got hold of my beloved, making entreaty, making supplication, (for) I desire to meet the Lord.

Pause.

O my brethren, may any one unite me to union with Hari the Lord!

I have devoted myself to the true Guru, who has shown (to me) Hari the Lord.

(2). Humble I fall down at the side of the perfect, true Guru.

The hope of the humble is the Guru, the Guru, the true Guru, applauds them.

I cannot praise enough the Guru, who makes me meet with Hari the Lord.

(3). Every one is desiring the true Guru, all the world, everybody.

Without destiny an interview (with him) is not obtained; he, whose lot it is not, sits and weeps.

What has pleased to Hari, that has come to pass; what is written from the beginning, no one will blot out.

(4). He himself is the true Guru, Hari himself unites to union with himself.

He himself, having bestowed mercy, will unite, who follow after the Guru, the true Guru.

He himself is in the world the life of the whole world; O Nānak! water is absorbed in water.

Sirī Rāg; mahalā IV.

V. LXIX.

(1). The name is juice of nectar, a very good juice; how is it obtained, that I may drink (this) juice?[1]

Go and ask the favoured women: how has the Lord come and joined you?

These fearless ones say: I, rubbing, rubbing, wash his foot.[2]

Pause.

O brother! having met with the friend, remember the qualities of Hari!

The friend is the true Guru, the Supreme Spirit, he removes (thy) pain by destroying (thy) egotism![3]

(2). The (female) disciples are favoured women, into their heart mercy has fallen.

The word of the true Guru is a jewel; who minds it, drinks the juice of Hari.

Those are known as very fortunate who have drunk the juice of Hari by love to the Guru.

(3). This juice of Hari is in every tree and grass, the luckless do not drink it.

Without the true Guru it does not come to hand,[4] the fleshly-minded are lamenting (at not getting it).

They do not bow before the true Guru, in their heart is the calamity of wrath.

(4). Hari, Hari, Hari himself is the juice, from Hari himself the juice issues.

He himself, having bestowed mercy, will give it, and the disciple will suck the nectar.

When that Hari has taken his dwelling in the heart, O Nānak! the whole body and soul has become green.

Sirī Rāg; mahalā IV.

VI. LXX.

(1). The day rises and sets again, the whole night passes (again).

The time of life decreases, man does not perceive it; continually the mouse gnaws the rope (of life).

Sweet molasses are spread out by the Māyā, the fleshly-minded one, sticking to it like a fly, is consumed and causes (others) to be consumed.[5]

Pause.

O brother! my friend and companion is that Lord.

The fascination of son and wife is poison, at the end no one will be a companion.

[1] The idiomatic expression is ਰਸ ਖਾਉਣਾ, to eat the juice.

[2] ਮਲਿ ਮਲਿ ਧੋਵਾ ਤਿਨ ਪਾਇ, these words are apparently to be referred to the Guru (ਤਿਨ being taken in an honorific sense).

[3] ਹੌ ਮੈ is often to be taken in the sense of the Sansk. अहंकार, the individuality as separated from the Supreme Spirit. The Guru removes the pain by causing the individuality to be re-absorbed into the world-soul.

[4] ਪਲੈ ਨਾ ਪਵੈ, literally, it does not fall into the lap.

[5] ਪਚੈ ਪਚਾਇ may also be translated: he is thoroughly consumed, being taken as an *intensive* verb.

(2). The disciples of the Guru are saved by devout meditation on Hari, uncontaminated they remain in the asylum (of the Guru).

Their departure is always kept in view by them, Hari is taken as their viaticum, they will receive honour.

The disciples are accepted at the threshold, by Hari himself they are received and embraced.

(3). To the disciples the way is manifest, at the gate (of Hari) they are by no means kept back.

They praise the name of Hari, the name is in their heart, they continue devoutly meditating on the name.

Whilst sounds not produced by beating (an instrument) are sounded at the gate, they obtain lustre [1] at the true gate.

(4). Every one applauds the disciples by whom the name is praised.

O Lord! give me their company! (this is) the petition of (this) beggar.

O Nānak! the lot of those disciples is great in whose heart the name is shining.

Sirī Rāg; mahalā V.[2]

Ghar I.

I. LXXI.

(1). How thou art delighted, having seen the ornaments of thy son and wife!

Thou enjoyest thyself, livest in pleasures, art given to innumerable merriments.

Thou givest many orders and art inflexible.

The creator does come into thy mind, (thou art) a blind, ignorant, self-willed man.

Pause.

O my heart! the giver of comfort is that Hari.

By the favour of the Guru he is obtained, by destiny he is acquired.

(2). Thou art covetous of clothes and enjoyment, of the dust of gold and silver.

Excellent horses and elephants are much liked [3] (by thee); indefatigable chariots are made.

(But in spite of all this) thou dost not come into anybody's mind, thou art forgotten by all (thy) relationship (after thy death).

Being led astray by the creator (thou art) impure without the name.

(3). Earning the imprecations (of others) thou collectest wealth.

On what thou art putting thy trust, that does not remain always with thee.

Thou practisest egotism; O selfish one! thou art immersed in the inclination of thy heart.

He who is led astray by that Lord himself has no caste nor fellowship.

(4). He, who has been joined (with Hari) by the true Guru, the Supreme Spirit, is alone my friend.

One is the protector of the people of Hari, what do men weep in selfishness?

What is pleasing to the people of Hari, that he (=Hari) does, at the gate of Hari they are never turned back.

O Nānak! he who is steeped in the love of Hari becomes a light in the whole world.

[1] ਸੋਭਾ ਪਾਉਣਾ, to obtain lustre = to be adorned, to be received with honour.

[2] Guru Arjun. On the whole, his poetry is the most incoherent and the least refined in the Granth and therefore frequently obscure, as little attention is paid by him to a clear grammatical construction.

[3] ਹੈਵਰ = Sansk. हयवर, excellent horse; ਗੈਵਰ, Sindhī गंयरु = Sansk. गजवर (Prākrit first गअवर, thence the Hinduī गयवर, य being a euphonic insertion to avoid the hiatus). The Lahōr lithographed edition reads ਰੰਗੇ, two other MSS. read only ਰੰਗ, which suits the context better; the translator has followed the latter reading.

Sirī Rāg; mahalā V.

II. LXXII.

(1). In (their) heart (is) much wantonness and great merriment; being led astray by the pleasures of the sight:

The umbrella-wearing sovereignties have fallen into doubt[1] (*i.e.* duality).

Pause.

O brother! happiness is obtained in the society of the saints.

To whom it is decreed by that Supreme Spirit, who fixes the destiny, the pain of his uncertainty is blotted out.

(2). As many places and countries there are, so many have (I) wandered through.

The wealthy man and great landowner says (everywhere): "it is mine, it is mine."

(3). He carries out his order, fearless and unflinching he is in his pursuit.

Every one is subjected by him, (but) without the name he is mingled with dust.

(4). Thirty-three crores of servants, Siddhs and Sādhiks,[2] standing at the gate.

Wealth, great dominion—all, O Nānak! has become (=passed) like a dream.

Sirī Rāg; mahalā V.

III. LXXIII.

(1). Having risen early in the morning (the body) is adorned, without understanding (the truth) she is foolish and ignorant.

(If) that Lord has not come into her mind, she will be left in the desert.

Having directed her thought to the true Guru she always, always enjoys pleasure.

Pause.

O man,[3] thou art come (into this world) to gain advantage.

In what bad brawl art thou engaged? (thy) whole night,[4] passing away, is gone,

(2). Cattle and birds jump about, death is not seen (by them).

In that company (*i.e.* like them) is man, who is ensnared in the net of the Māyā.

Those are perceived as emancipated who remember the true name.

(3). The house, that is to be abandoned, has become dear to thy heart.

Whither thou hast to go and to remain, of that thou dost not think.

Those ensnared ones have come out (of the net), who fall down at the feet of the Guru.

(4). No one can protect, no other (can) show (Hari).

Having searched in the four corners (I) have come and fallen on the asylum (of the Guru).

By the true king[5] (=Guru) Nānak the drowning one has been drawn out.

[1] They have fallen into doubt or uncertainty, *i.e.* they no longer know who they are, they do not know their own self.

[2] ਸਿਧ, a man supposed to have acquired miraculous powers (a Jōgī); ਸਾਧਿਕ (साधक), an ascetic, engaged in a course of austerities and observances in order to obtain final emancipation,

[3] ਪ੍ਰਾਣੀ, any living being, but chiefly man (man and woman).

[4] ਰੈਣਿ (रजनी), night, the time of enjoyment = lifetime.

[5] By Arjun the title of ਸਚ ਪਾਤਿਸਾਹ, true king, is applied to the Guru, which afterwards has become the usual address to the Sikh Gurus.

Sirī Rāg; mahalā V.

IV. LXXIV.

(1). The guest of twenty-four or forty-eight minutes is intent on his business.
Being immersed in the business of the Māyā the foolish one does not understand (the truth).
Having risen and departed he repents, he has fallen into the power of the executioner (of Yama).

Pause.

O blind one, thou art seated near the bank (of a river)!
If it be written before, then thou wilt obtain the word of the Guru.
(2). Not the green nor the half-ripe, the ripe (field) he is cutting.
Having taken the sickle he has arrived (on the field), having kept ready the reapers.
When the order of the farmer is given, then the field is reaped and measured.
(3). The first watch (of the night) is gone in business, the second he has slept, in the third nonsense is chattered, in the fourth it has become morning.
He has never come into his mind, by whom soul and body were given.
(4.) (My) soul is devoted and made a sacrifice for the assembly of the holy ones:
From which sagacity has fallen into (my) heart and the Supreme wise Spirit is obtained.
Nānak has seen (thus) the heart-knowing, wise Hari always (dwelling) with him.

Sirī Rāg; mahalā V.

V. LXXV.

(1). All things are forgotten (by me), the One is not forgotten.
Having burnt all (worldly) business, the Guru has given (to me) the relish of the true name.
Having dropped all hopes, I acquire one hope.
Those who have served the true Guru, have obtained a place (in the other world).

Pause.

O my heart, praise the creator!
Having abandoned all clevernesses fall down at the feet of the Guru!
(2). Pain and hunger do not pervade (the body), if the giver of comfort be in the heart.
One is not ruined by any business (or work), if that True one is in the heart.
Whom thou protectest having given thy hand (to him), him no one can kill.
If the comfort-giving Guru be served, he washes off all vices.
(3). (Thy) servant asks the service (of those), (by whom) thy service is performed.
By the assiduity of the assembly of the holy ones I obtain a pleased God.
Everything is subject to the Lord, he himself achieves the action.[1]
I sacrifice myself for the true Guru, who accomplishes all my desires.
(4). One friend is seen (by me), one brother and friend.
The One's are the materials, the One's the manner (of applying them).
If with the One my heart is conciliated, my mind has become immovable.
The True one is (my) eating, the True one (my) clothing, by Nānak the True one is made his support.

[1] There is no real liberty of the created beings, the Lord himself is performing the actions in and through them. ਕਰੇਦ is an alliteration instead of ਕਰੇ, likewise ਪੂਰੇਦ instead of ਪੂਰੇ, to rhyme with ਰੇਦ. Arjun, who pays little attention to a pure rhyme, adds any meaningless syllable to make up the rhyme, so that the final words of a verse are often hardly recognizable.

Sirī Rāg; mahalā V.

VI. LXXVI.

(1). All things are obtained, if the One come to hand.
The boon of human birth is bearing fruit, if one tell the true word.[1]
He obtains the palace (of Hari) from the Guru, on whose forehead it may be written.

Pause.

O my heart, apply thy mind to the One!
Without the One all is trouble, all the fascination of the Māyā is false.
(2). There are lakhs of pleasures and sovereignties, if the true Guru cast a glance (of mercy).
If he gives (me) one moment the name of Hari, my soul and body become cool.
For whom it is decreed before, he has seized the feet of the true Guru.
(3). Fruitful are the forty-eight minutes, fruitful the twenty-four minutes, in which there is love to the True one.
Pain and affliction do not touch him, whose support is the name of Hari.
Whom the Guru, having seized his arm, has drawn out, he has passed across.
(4). That place is beautiful and pure, where the assembly of the saints is.
Entrance obtains he, who has got the perfect Guru.
O Nānak! their house is built there, where there is no death, nor birth, nor old age.

Sirī Rāg; mahalā V.

VII. LXXVII.

(1). He should be meditated upon, O soul, who is king above kings!
O heart, place thy hope on him, in whom every one trusts!
Having given up all cunning fall down at the feet of the Guru!

Pause.

O my heart, with comfort and ease mutter the name!
Meditate the eight watches (of the day) on the Lord, sing continually the qualities of Gōvind!
(2). Fall on the asylum of him, O heart, like whom there is none other!
By the remembrance of whom much comfort is obtained, and no pain whatever arises.
Perform always, always the service of the Lord, he is the true Lord.
(3). In the assembly of the saints thou becomest pure, the noose of Yama is cut off.
Before him, who is the giver of comfort and the remover of fear, offer thy supplication!
On whom the kind one bestows kindness, his business is put right.[2]
(4). More than much he should be praised, whose place is higher than high.
Of him, who is without colours and marks, I cannot tell the value.
O Lord, have compassion on Nānak, give him thy own true name!

Sirī Rāg; mahalā V.

VIII. LXXVIII.

(1). He, who meditates on the name is happy, his face becomes bright.
From the perfect Guru he is obtained, who is manifest in all the worlds.
In the house of the society of the pious dwells that One true.

[1] *i.e.* If one always utter: Hari! Hari! the true Sabd is the name of Hari, the Gur-mantr.

[2] *i.e.* He obtains the object of his coming into this world.

Pause.

O my heart, meditate on the name of Hari, Hari!
The name is always a companion and with (thee), in the other world it will bring (thee) emancipation.
(2). Of what use are the greatnesses of the world?
The amusement of the Māyā is all insipid, at last it passes away and is annihilated.
In whose heart Hari dwells, he is perfect and foremost.
(3). Become the dust of the pious having abandoned thy own self!
Give up all schemes and cunning and cling to the feet of the Guru!
He gets the jewel, on whose forehead the lot may be (written).
(4). He gets it, O brother! to whom the Lord himself gives (it).
He performs the service of the true Guru, the heat of whose egotism is put out.
With Nānak the Guru has met and all his passions have become extinct.

Sirī Rāg; mahalā V.

IX. LXXIX.

(1). One knows the creatures, One is their preserver.
In One I trust in (my) heart, One is the support of my life.
In the asylum of him, who is the Supreme Brahm, the creator, there is always happiness.

Pause.

O my heart, give up all schemes!
Worship the perfect Guru, apply thyself continually to the meditation on the One!
(2). The One is (my) brother, the One (my) friend, the One (my) mother and father.
In the One I trust in my heart, who has given (me) soul and body.
That Lord is not forgotten from (my) heart, who has subjected to himself everything.
(3). In the house is the One, outside is the One, in every place is he himself.
By whom the living creatures are made, him repeat silently the eight watches (day and night)!
Those who are in love with the One have no grief nor affliction.
(4). The Supreme Brahm, the Lord is One, there is no second.
Body and soul, all is his, what is pleasing to him, that is done.
In the perfect Guru he has become complete;[1] O Nānak, repeat thou silently that True one!

Sirī Rāg; mahalā V.

X. LXXX.

(1). Those who have applied their mind to the true Guru, are perfect and foremost.
To whom he himself is merciful, in their mind divine knowledge springs up.
To whom it is written on the forehead, they obtained the name of Hari.

Pause.

O my heart, meditate on the One name!
All comforts spring up, thou wilt go dressed (in a robe of honour) to the threshold.
(2). The fear of birth and death is gone by the love and worship of Gōpāl.[2]
He himself preserves (those, who) are pure by the society of the holy ones.
The dirt of birth and death is cleared away, having seen the sight of the Guru they are happy.

[1] The sense is: In the perfect Guru the Supreme is completely contained, present.

[2] A name of Krishṇa, identified with the Supreme.

(3). In every place is contained that Supreme Brahm, the Lord.
The donor of all is the One, there is no second.
In his asylum emancipation is obtained; what one desires, that comes to pass.
(4). In whose heart the Supreme Brahm dwells, they are perfect and foremost.
Their pure lustre has become manifest in the world.
Nānak is a sacrifice for those who have meditated on my Lord.

Sirī Rāg; mahalā V.

XI. LXXXI.

(1). Having met with the true Guru all pain is gone, the comfort of Hari has come and settled in the heart.

Within (them) light is manifested (who) direct (their) thoughts on the One.

Having joined the holy ones the face is bright, they (*i.e.* the disciples) obtain what is written before (for them).

Those who sing continually the qualities of Gōvind, are pure by the true name.

Pause.

O my heart, by the word of the Guru comfort is obtained!
The service of the perfect Guru is by no means fruitless.
(2). The desires of the heart are fulfilled, the treasure of the name is obtained.
The creator, the knower of the heart, is known[1] as always indwelling.

By the favour of the Guru the face is bright, having repeated the name (and practised) liberality (and) ablution.

Lust, wrath, covetousness have become extinct, all pride is abandoned.[2]
(3). The gain of the name is obtained, all the business is completed.
By the Lord, having bestowed mercy, he is united (with himself), his own name is given to him.
His coming and going has been stopped, he himself (*i.e.* Hari) has become kind (to him).
The true palace and house (*i.e.* of Hari) is obtained (by him), (who) has known[3] the word of the Guru.
(4). The devotees he protects having bestowed his own mercy (on them).
In this and that world the faces of them are bright who remember the qualities of the True one.
Remembering (his) qualities the eight watches (=day and night) they are steeped in infinite love.
Nānak is always a sacrifice for the Supreme Brahm, the ocean of happiness.

Sirī Rāg; mahalā V.

XII. LXXXII.

(1). If the perfect, true Guru be met with, the treasure of the word (=name) is obtained.
If the Lord bestow his own mercy, the immortal name is silently repeated.
The pain of birth and death is cut off, meditation is easily brought about.

Pause.

O my heart, fall on the asylum of the Lord!
Without Hari there is none other, meditate on the One name!
(2). His value cannot be told, he is an unfathomable ocean of qualities.

[1] ਪਛਾਣੁ = ਪਛਾਣਾ, on account of the rhyme.
[2] All this is the fruit of the service of the Guru.
[3] *i.e.* Who has received as true.

O very fortunate, join the society (of the holy ones), believe in the true word (of the Guru)!
Serve the ocean of happiness, who is king above kings!
(3). My trust is the lotus of the foot (of Hari), there is no other place.
My hold is on thee, O Supreme Brahm! by thy power I remain (abide).
O Lord! thou art the trust of the humble, into thy society I enter.
(4). Hari should be silently repeated, Gōvind should be worshipped the eight watches!
(By whom) soul, life, body, property are preserved, (by whom) mercifully life is protected.
O Nānak! all pains are removed by him, the Lord, the Supreme Brahm, is forgiving (or: giving).

Sirī Rāg; mahalā V.

XIII. LXXXIII.

(1). Who has fallen in love with that True one, he does not die nor come (again) after having gone.
Though separated, he is not separated (from him, who) is continually contained in all.
The pain and trouble of the humble he (Hari) is breaking on account of his good disposition towards (his) worshipper.
The wonderfully formed, the unstained (Supreme) has been united (to me) by the Guru, O mother!

Pause.

O brother, make that Lord thy friend!
Away with the fascination and friendship of the Māyā! no happy one is seen.
(2). He is wise, bountiful, well-disposed, pure, of an infinite form (or beauty).
A friend, a helper, very great, high, great, infinite.
He is not known as young (or) old, his court is immovable.
What is asked (from him), that is obtained, he is the support of the helpless.[1]
(3). Looking upon whom the sins are taken away and tranquillity is made in soul and body.
If with one mind the One be meditated upon, the error of the mind ceases.
He is the abode of virtues, always young, whose bountifulness is (all-) filling.
Always, always he should be worshipped, day and night he should not be forgotten!
(4). For whom it was written before, their friend is Gōvind.
Body, soul and property, all I offer (to those, by whom) this whole life is devoted (to him).
He always sees and hears in the presence, in everybody Brahm is contained.
(Even) the ungrateful[2] he cherishes; the Lord, O Nānak! is always giving.

Sirī Rāg; mahalā V.

XIV. LXXXIV.

(1). By the Lord, by whom soul, body and property have been given, they are easily (naturally) taken care of and preserved.
Having made all the constituent parts (of the body), infinite light has been put within it (by him).[3]
Always, always the Lord should be remembered, put and keep him within thy breast!

[1] ਨਿਧਾਰਾ = ਨਿਧਰਾਂ; Arjun lengthens or shortens the syllables, not only at the end of the verse (for the sake of the rhyme), but also in the midst of the line, just as he pleases.

[2] ਅਕਿਰਤਘਣ, ungrateful. It is somewhat doubtful if it is to be derived from कृतघ्न or from अकृतघ्न. In the first case the initial ਅ would be wrong, in the second the assimilation of घ्न to ghaṇ is without analogy.

[3] ਕਲਾ is here identical with ਧਾਤੁ, a constituent part of the body, of which seven are enumerated: blood, marrow, fat, flesh, bones, medullary substance, semen. The ਜੋਤਿ ਅਪਾਰ, the infinite light, is the ਆਤਮਾ, or the individual spirit which has directly emanated from the Supreme Spirit.

Pause.

O my heart, there is none other without Hari!
Remain always in the asylum of the Lord, no pain will enter thee.
(2). Jewels, choice things, rubies, gold, silver are dust.
Mother, father, son, relative, all kinsmen are false.
By whom he was made, him he does not know, the fleshly-minded one is an impure beast.
(3). Who is inside and outside diffused, him he considers as being far away.
Thirst (worldly covetousness) has seized him, he is absorbed in it, in his heart is cruel egotism.
The boat's load[1] of them, who are destitute of devotion and the name, comes and goes.
(4). Be merciful, O Lord creator, and preserve the creatures!
Without the Lord there is no protector, very formidable has Yama become.
Nānak does not forget (thy) name, O Hari, bestow (on me) thy own mercy!

Sirī Rāg; mahalā V.

XV. LXXXV.

(1). My body and property, my kingdom and beauty, my country,
(My) many sons and wives, many amusements and clothes:
Are, if the name of Hari do not dwell in (my) heart, of no use nor account.

Pause.

O my heart, meditate on the name of Hari, Hari!
Keeping always company with the holy ones direct thy mind to the feet of the Guru!
(2). The treasure of the name is meditated upon (by him), upon (whose) forehead the lot may be (written).
All the works (of him) are adjusted, (who) clings to the feet of the Guru.
The sickness of egotism (and his) error is cut off, he does not come nor will he go (again into other wombs).
(3). Keep thou company with the holy ones (and thus) bathe at the sixty-eight Tīrthas![2]
Life, soul, body become fresh (thereby), this is true relish.
Here (in this world) greatnesses will accrue to thee and at the threshold thou wilt obtain a place.
(4). The Lord himself does and causes to be done (everything), all is in his hand.
He himself having killed vivifies, within and without he is with (every one).
Nānak has taken refuge with the Lord, who is the Lord of all bodies.

Sirī Rāg; mahalā V.

XVI. LXXXVI.

(1). I have fallen[3] on the asylum of my Lord, the Guru has been merciful.
By the instruction of the Guru all my troubles have become extinct.
My heart has clung to the name of Rām, by the sight of the nectar I am happy.

Pause.

O my heart, the service of the true Guru is the best.
If the Lord bestow his own mercy (on me), I do not forget him one moment from my heart.

[1] ਪੂਰ, *s.m.* the party taken over in one boat's trip.

[2] The sense is: if thou keep company with the pious, it is as much as if thou wouldst bathe at the sixty-eight Tīrthas.

[3] ਪਏ; no subject is mentioned, but it must be, according to the whole context, ਹਮ, we = I.

(2). The qualities of Gōvind should continually be sung, who is the extinguisher of vices.

Without the name of Hari comfort is not obtained, I have seen a great many things.[1]

Those who were given to his praises, have easily crossed the water of existence.

(3). (It is equal to) a Tīrtha, fasting, lakhs of abstinences, if the dust of the holy ones be obtained.

From whom will (one) hide himself, as he (=Hari) always sees in the presence?

In every place my Lord is contained brimful.

(4). True is (his) kingdom, true his order, true is the place of the True one.

True power he has applied, by the True one the world has been created.

I, Nānak, am always a sacrifice for him, by whom the true name is silently repeated.

Sirī Rāg; mahalā V.

XVII. LXXXVII.

(1). Who with effort is silently repeating Hari, he is very fortunate and acquires wealth.

He who remembers Hari in the society of the saints, cuts off the dirt of (all his) births.

Pause.

O my heart, go on repeating the name of Hari!

Enjoy the fruits desired by the heart, all grief and anguish ceases.

(2). By whose agency the body is sustained, that Lord is seen as being with (=indwelling).

In the water, the earth, on the surface of the earth he is present,[2] the Lord beholds his own sight.

(3). Soul and body have become pure, love to the True one has sprung up.

By whom the feet of the Supreme Brahm are worshipped, they have performed all silent repetitions and austerities.

(4). A gem, jewel, ruby, nectar is the name of Hari.

Comfort, ease, joy, relish; humble Nānak sings the qualities of Hari.

Sirī Rāg; mahalā V.

XVIII. LXXXVIII.

(1). That is a Shāstr, that is a magic spell,[3] by means of which the name of Hari is muttered.

By (that) placeless one a place has been obtained, (to whom) by the Guru the wealth of the lotus of the foot is given.

(That is) true capital, (that is) true abstinence, if (one) sing the eight watches the qualities (of Hari).

With whom the Lord has met bestowing his mercy (upon him), he does not die, nor does he come and go (again).

Pause.

O my heart, worship always Hari with one mind!

He is contained within everybody, he is always a helper with (thee).

(2). How shall I count the amount of comforts, when I remember Gōvind?

They have been satiated who have tasted it, that relish knows (their) soul (only).

The Lord dwells in the heart of him who is associated with the saints, the beloved is bestowing (his) favour (on him).

He, who has served his own Lord, is king and chief of men.

[1] The sense is: I have seen a great deal and can speak from experience.

[2] ਪੂਰਿਆ, literally: filled in, *i.e.* completely diffused, so that no place is empty of him.

[3] ਸਉਣੁ, Sansk. शकुन, a magic spell or hymn, sung to obtain favourable events.

(3). At (every) opportunity (I) delight in the glory and qualities of Hari, in which (are contained[1]) crores of ablutions and bathings.

(If) the tongue utters the reports of the qualities (of Hari), no alms will come up to it.

Having bestowed a favourable look he dwells in soul and body, the merciful Supreme Spirit, the kind one.

Soul, body and wealth are his, I am always, always a sacrifice (for him).

(4). Who is united by the creator (with himself), he, being united, is never separated (from him).

The fetters of his servants are cut asunder by the true creator.

The erring one is put by him into the (right) way not considering his virtues and vices.

Nānak has gone to the asylum of him, who is the support of all bodies.

Sirī Rāg; mahalā V.

XIX. LXXXIX.

(1). If by the tongue the True one be remembered, soul and body become pure.

(Though there be) mother, father and numerous relatives, without him there is none other.

If he bestow his own favour, he is not forgotten a minute.

Pause.

O my heart, serve the True one as long as there is (any) breath!

Without the True one all is falsehood, at the end it is annihilated.

(2). My Lord is pure, without him I cannot abide.

In my heart and body is very great hunger, may some one bring and unite (him with me), O mother!

In the four corners (of the earth) (a place) has been sought (by me), without the bridegroom there is no other place.

(3). Make supplication before him, who is uniting the creator (with men)!

The true Guru is the giver of the name (of him) whose storeroom is full.

Always, always he should be praised, (who has) no end nor limit!

(4). The preserver should be praised, whose actions are many!

Always, always he should be worshipped! this is the greatest wisdom.

In soul and body it is sweet to him, on whose forehead (this) destiny is (written), O Nānak!

Sirī Rāg; mahalā V.

XX. XC.

(1). O brother, join the saints, remember the true name!

Store up provisions for the soul! (that will be) with (thee) here and there.

From the perfect Guru he (=Hari) is obtained, having bestowed his own favourable look.

By destiny he obtains (him), to whom he is merciful.

Pause.

O my heart, there is no one like the Guru!

No other place is seen, the Guru (alone) unites that True one (with thee).

(2). All things he has got, who has gone and seen the Guru.

Whose mind is fixed on the feet of the Guru, they are very fortunate, O mother!

The Guru is bountiful, the Guru is powerful, the Guru is contained in all.

The Guru is the Lord, the Supreme Brahm, the sinking ones the Guru causes to swim.[2]

[1] The sense is: which is equal to crores of ablutions.

[2] The Guru, as an avatār, is identified with the Supreme Being.

(3). By what mouth is the Guru praised, who is the powerful (=efficient) cause of causes?[1]
Those foreheads remained immovable, on which the Guru put his hand.
The nectar of the name, which the Guru gave to drink, is a suitable food against birth and death.
(By whom) the Guru, the Lord, the destroyer of fear, has been served, (his) pain has gone off.
(4). The true Guru is deep and profound, the ocean of comfort, sin-removing.
Who has served his own Guru, on him the club of the messenger of Yama does not fall.
I have searched and seen the whole world (and found that) nothing can be compared with the Guru.
The treasure of the name was given (to me) by the true Guru, in the heart of Nānak is (therefore) the pith of happiness.

Sirī Rāg; mahalā V.

XXI. XCI.

(1). Having considered it sweet I ate it, (but) a bitter taste sprang up (after).
Brothers, friends, good friends were made (by me), (I) was occupied with talking about worldly subjects.
(But all) passes quickly,[2] without the name it is insipid.

Pause.

O my heart, stick to the service of the true Guru!
What is visible, that is annihilated, give up the opinion of thy (own) mind!
(2). Like a dog, who has become mad, runs in the ten directions.
(So) a greedy creature does not know what is eatable and not eatable, it eats all.
Being immersed in the intoxication of lust and wrath, it falls again and again into the womb.
(3). By the Māyā a net is spread out having made a bait within it.
By greediness the bird is caught and cannot get out, O mother!
It does not know him by whom it is made, again and again it comes and goes.
(4). This world is fascinated in many ways and in many manners.
Whom he preserves, he is preserved (abides), the infinite Supreme Spirit is powerful.
The people of Hari are saved by their constant meditation on Hari, Nānak is always a sacrifice (for them).

Sirī Rāg; mahalā V.

Ghar II.

XXII. XCII.

(1). The cowherd has come to the cowhouse,[3] what ostentation has he to make?
The time has arrived, it must be gone, take thou care of thy household things!

Pause.

O my heart, sing the qualities of Hari, serve the true Guru in love!
Why art thou conceited of a trifle?

[1] ਕਰਣ ਕਾਰਣ may be translated in different ways. The expression is also found in Tulsī Dās Rāmāyaṇ, where it is explained by: महत्तत्वादि के कारण, the efficient causes of the Mahat, etc. (see Wilson's Vish. Pur. p. 14). ਕਰਣ ਕਾਰਣ ਸਮਰਥ may therefore be translated by: who is able to make the primary elements or substances (कारण). But it is perhaps more simple to take it = ਕਰਣਾਂ ਕਾ ਕਾਰਣ, he is the (efficient) cause of causes, and the whole expression, ਕਰਣ ਕਾਰਣ ਸਮਰਥ, might be translated by: he is the powerful (efficient) cause of causes.

[2] Literally: In going delay is not made.

[3] ਗੋਇਲ, cow-house, a hut built on pasture ground, thence the adjective or *s.m.* ਗੋਇਲੀ, the cowherd, who belongs to the ਗੋਇਲ. The word is obsolete in Hindī now, but still in use in Marāṭhī (गोवळ).

(2). Like the guest of a night thou wilt rise and depart at dawn.

Why art thou enamoured with thy household? all is (like) a flower-garden.

(3). Why sayest thou: "mine, mine"? desire that Lord, who has given it!

By any means thou must rise and go, thou wilt go leaving behind lakhs and crores (of rupees).

(4). Whilst wandering in the eighty-four lakhs (of forms of existence) thou hast obtained the hard-to-be-acquired human birth.

O Nānak, remember thou the name! that day (of departure) has come near to thee.

Sirī Rāg; mahalā V.

XXIII. XCIII.

(1). So long thou livest comfortably, as thy companion is with (thee).

When thy companion has risen and gone, thou art mingled with dust, O woman!

Pause.

(If) in (thy) heart indifference to the world has been effected, (if there be) a desire to see the sight (of the Guru).

Blessed is that thy state!

(2). As long as thy beloved (husband) dwells in the house, all say: yes, yes!

When thy beloved will rise and go, then none will ask a word about thee.

(3). Serve in thy father's house thy bridegroom and thou wilt dwell in comfort in thy father-in-law's house.[1]

Having joined the Guru learn wisdom and good conduct, (then) pain will never befall thee.

(4). All must go to their father-in-law's house, all are bringing their wives home.

O Nānak, blessed are the favoured women, who have love to their bridegroom!

Sirī Rāg; mahalā V.

Ghar VI.

XXIV. XCIV.

(1). He alone is the (primary) cause of causes, by whom the form (of every thing) is made.

Meditate on him, O my heart, who is the support of all!

Pause.

Meditate in thy heart on the feet of the Guru!

Giving up all cunning fix thy thoughts on the true word (of the Guru)!

(2). Pain, trouble and fear do not befall him, in whose heart the mantr (initiatory word) of the Guru is.

(Though) one make crores of efforts, no one has crossed without the Guru.

(3). Having seen the sight (of the Guru) he (the disciple) subdues his mind, all his sins go off.

I am a sacrifice for them, who fall down at the feet of the Guru.

(4). The true name of Hari dwells in a heart associated with the saints.

Those are very fortunate, O Nānak, in whose heart this is the case!

Sirī Rāg; mahalā V.

XXV. XCV.

(1). Collect the wealth of Hari, worship the true Guru, give up all passions!

By whom thou wast made, having kept in mind that Hari thou wilt be saved.

[1] This is a simile often used in the Granth. The sense is: if thou servest God in this present world (thy father's house), thou wilt live in happiness hereafter (in thy father-in-law's house = the next world).

Pause.

Recite silently, O heart, the One, infinite name!
The support of the heart is he, by whom life, soul and body were given.
(2). In lust, wrath and conceit the world is immersed, O mother!
Fall on the asylum of the saints, cling to the feet (of the Guru)! pain and darkness are done away.
(3). He practises truth, contentment and mercy: these are the best works.
He gives up his own self and becomes the dust of all, to whom the Lord, the shapeless, gives it.
(4). What is seen, all that art Thou, (thy) expansion is spread out.
Nānak says: by the Guru (my) error has been cut off, I consider (now) all as Brahm.

Sirī Rāg; mahalā V.

XXVI. XCVI.

(1). In bad and good actions the whole world is (engaged).
Free from both is the devotee; some rare one is knowing.[1]

Pause.

The Lord is contained in all (things). What shall I say (and) hear?
Thou, O Lord, art the great Supreme Spirit, the wise!
(2). He who is in pride and conceit, is no worshipper.
Of unbiassed regard for truth, O saints, is one amongst a crore.
(3). Telling and causing to be told is a false renown.[2]
By telling a story some rare disciple is emancipated.
(4). The state of him, who is everywhere present,[3] does not come into sight.
He has obtained (this) gift, O Nānak! who is the dust of the saints.

Sirī Rāg; mahalā V.

Ghar VII.

XXVII. XCVII.

(1). On account of my trust in thee indulgent treatment has been shown to me.
The child errs and makes mistakes, thou, O Hari, art father and mother!

Pause.

Telling and causing to be told (legends) is easy, (but) what is pleasing to thee is difficult.
(2). I put my trust in thee, I know, thy own self is I.
In all and without all art thou, O father! who art not in need of anything.
(3). O father, I do not know what word is conformable to thee!
He who is free from bonds, O saints, keeps affection for me!
(4). The Lord has become merciful, coming and going has been stopped.
Having met with the Guru, the Supreme Brahm was known by Nānak.

[1] *Some rare one is knowing*, supply: the fact, that good and bad actions are not existing for the devotee, who sees in all Brahm.

[2] By telling or narrating stories or legends of the gods, making others tell them, emancipation is not obtained. The recital of the legends of the gods is considered very meritorious.

[3] ਅਵਿਗਤਿ, *adj.* (Sansk. अविगत) literally: not disappeared, not gone = present (everywhere), व्यापक. The explanation (in the Panjābī Dictionary): free from the ordinary conditions of human life, is gratuitous.

Sirī Rāg; mahalā V.

Ghar I.

XXVIII. XCVIII.

1. Having joined the saints death has been cut off.
The true Lord has settled in (my) heart, the Lord has become merciful.
The perfect, true Guru has been met with (and) all troubles have become extinct.

Pause.

O my true Guru, I am a sacrifice for thee!
I devote myself for thy sight, having been pleased thou hast given me the nectar-name.
(2). Those are wise men, who have served thee in love.
Final emancipation is obtained (following) after those, in whose heart the treasure of the name is.
There is no donor like the Guru, who has given the gift of the soul.[1]
(3). Those have become acceptable, (with) whom the Guru has met by (their) good destiny.[2]
Those who are in love with the True one, get a place to sit in his court.
In the hand of the creator are honours; they obtain what is written before (for them).
(4). True is the creator, true the maker; true is the Lord, true his support.
The perfectly True[3] one is praised (by him), whose intelligence and discrimination is true.
He is contained in all unintermittingly; Nānak lives by reciting silently the One.

Sirī Rāg; mahalā V.

XXIX. XCIX.

(1). The Guru, the Supreme Lord, should be worshipped, loving him in heart and body!
The true Guru is the donor of the creatures, he gives support to every one.
The words of the true Guru should be done, this is true consideration.
Without being attached to the society of the saints all the fascination of the Māyā is (but) ashes.

Pause.

O my friend, remember the name of Hari, Hari!
(If) connexion with the saints dwell in the heart, the toil is accomplished.[4]
(2). The Guru is infinitely powerful, the very fortunate get an interview with him.
The Guru is inapprehensible, pure, like the Guru there is none other.
The Guru is the creator, the Guru the maker, the disciple has true information (regarding him).
Without the Guru there is nothing, what the Guru wishes to do, that is done.
(3). The Guru is the Tīrtha, the Guru is the Coral-tree,[5] the Guru is the accomplisher of the desires (of men).
The Guru is the donor, having given the name of Hari he saves the whole world.
The Guru is powerful, the Guru is formless (or the formless Supreme Being), high, inaccessible, infinite.
The greatness of the Guru is incomprehensible, what will the narrator say?

[1] ਆਤਮਦਾਨੁ must here be taken as a Tatpurusha, the gift of the soul, *i.e.* the gift, by which the soul may be saved.

[2] ਸੁਭਾਇ, Abl. of ਸੁਭਾਉ, from सुभाग, good lot or destiny. This seems to be the simplest explanation, the meaning "naturally" not fitting so well the context.

[3] ਸਚੋਸਚੁ, literally: truer than true = perfectly true.

[4] The sense is: man's toil is accomplished, or over.

[5] ਪਾਰਜਾਤੁ, Sansk. पारिजात, the Coral-tree, one of the five trees of heaven.

(4). As many fruits as are desired in the heart, so many are with the Guru.

The (fruits) written before are to be obtained (by him), (to whom) he gives the capital of the true name.

He who has come to the asylum of the true Guru, will not again be destroyed.

O Hari, mayst thou never be forgotten by Nānak! this life, body and breath are thine.

Sirī Rāg; mahalā V.

XXX. C.

(1). Hear, O saints, O brother! final emancipation (is obtained) by the true name.

The feet of the Guru should be embraced,[1] the name of Hari is the Tīrtha.

In the next world (such a one) is received at the threshold, the placeless one obtains a place.

Pause.

O brother, true is the service of the true Guru!

From the Guru, being pleased, the (all-) filling, the invisible and indivisible[2] is obtained.

(2). (I am) devoted to the true Guru, who has given (me) the true name.

Daily I praise the True one, the qualities of the True one I sing.

The True one I eat, the True one I put on (as clothes), true is the name of the True one.

(3). May he not be forgotten at any breath (or) morsel, the Guru himself is the fruit-yielding body (or person).

Like the Guru none is seen, recite him (silently) day and night!

If he bestow a favourable look, then is obtained the true name, the vessel of (all) qualities.

(4). The Guru, the Supreme Lord, is One, he is contained in all.

To whom it was decreed before, they meditate on the name.

O Nānak! who has resorted to the asylum of the Guru, does not die nor does he come (again) having gone.

Ōm! By the favour of the true Guru!

SIRĪ RĀG.

Mahalā I.; *Ghar* I.

(*Asṭpadīs.*)[3]

I.

(1). Speaking, speaking (my) heart is proclaiming (his qualities), as, as it is known (to my heart), so it proclaims (them).

He, who is proclaimed, how great is he, in which place is he?[4]

As many as are telling (his qualities), all having told (them) continue meditating (upon them).

[1] ਸਰੇਵਣਾ (srēvaṇā), (Sansk. आश्रयण), *v.a.* To embrace, to hold fast, to resort to.

[2] ਅਭੇਵ = ਅਭੇਦ, having no difference (from the universe), the identity of the Supreme and of the universe.

[3] The ਅਸਟਪਦੀ does not always contain the exact number of eight verses, but sometimes one more or less.

[4] The whole verse is obscure and the sense can only be arrived at by conjecture.

Pause.

O father, he (Hari) is invisible, inaccessible, infinite!

True is the preserver, of a pure name, of a pure place.[1]

(2). It is not known how much thy command is, no one knows to write it down.

If a hundred poets be assembled, not a moment they cause to arrive (at it), though they weep.

His value has been obtained (found out) by no one, all tell it by hearsay.

(3). Pīrs, prophets, Sāliks, Ṣādiqs and martyrs.[2]

Shēkhs, Mullās, Darvēshes: a great blessing has come upon them, who continually read (his) salutation.[3]

(4). Without asking (any body) he makes, without asking he pulls down, without asking he gives and takes.

His own power he himself knows, he himself produces the (primary) causes.

He, looking on, sees all; to whom he pleases, he gives.

(5). The name of (his) place is not known nor how great his name is.

How great is that place, where my king dwells?

None can arrive there, to whom shall I go to ask?

(6). Castes and no-castes do not please (him),[4] if he makes one great.

In the hand of the great one are the greatnesses (=honours), to whom he pleases, he gives.

By his own order he adorns (a man), not a moment he delays.

(7). Every one recites much (his qualities) in the thought of taking much (from him).

What a great donor shall he be called? his gifts are not counted.[5]

O Nānak! there is no deficiency coming forth, thy store-rooms are from age to age.

Mahalā I.

II.

(1). All are the female friends of the beloved (=husband), all adorn themselves.

They are come to make an estimate (of their respective virtues): a bastard scarlet dress is not the right state.

By hypocrisy the affection of the husband is not obtained, counterfeit overgilding is miserable.

Pause.

O Hari, thus the woman lays hold of the beloved!

The favoured women, who please thee, thou adornest in thy own mercy.

[1] The explanation of the words ਪਾਕੀ ਨਾਈ ਪਾਕ ਥਾਇ by the Sikh commentary: ਪਵਿਤ੍ਰਾਂ ਤੇ ਪਵਿਤ੍ਰ is a mere guess and only shows that the Sikhs themselves no longer understand their Granth.

[2] ਸਾਲਕ = سَالِکْ, literally, a traveller, the first stage in Sūfism, a devotee; ਸਾਦਕ = صَادِق, *adj.* True, sincere; ਸੁਹਦੇ, a plural of the plural شُهَدَا (from شَهِید), martyrs. ਸੁਹਦੇ ਅਉਰ ਸਹੀਦ, literally: martyrs and martyr, a mere tautology, to fill up the verse, as Nānak apparently did not understand that ਸੁਹਦਾ was the plural of شَهِید. The same is the case with the following ਸੇਖ ਮਸਾਇਕ, مَشَائِخ being likewise the plural of شَیخ.

[3] The whole verse is very obscure and the Sikhs are totally at a loss how to explain it. ਦਰਿ ਰਸੀਦ must apparently be taken as one word (Pers. دَر رَسِیدن, to arrive, to happen) and joined with ਤਿਨ ਕਉ ਬਰਕਤਿ ਅਗਲੀ ਦਰਿ ਰਸੀਦ, to them a great blessing has arrived. As in the whole sentence a number of Arabic-Persian words are jumbled together, we need not be surprised if also a Persian verb is employed. Such a jumbling of foreign (and frequently not at all understood) words is considered a great feat of learning. It does not come into consideration if even the rhyme be broken thereby (ਰਸੀਦ—ਦਰੂਦ).

[4] ਵਰਨਾਵਰਨ, castes and no-castes, *i.e.* he has no regard to any castes, if he wishes to make one great.

[5] ਦੇਕੈ ਰਹਿਆ ਸੁਮਾਰ, literally: having given, the amount, estimate is stopped, *i.e.* he never counts how much he gives.

(2). The body and heart of her, who is adorned with the word of the Guru, is with her beloved (husband).

Having joined both hands she stands and looks out, she utters a true petition.

She is steeped in red (colour), dwells in true fear, she is steeped in love, in the true colour.

(3). Servant and slave of the beloved she is called, who minds the name.

True love does not break, if he unite to true union (with himself).

I am always a sacrifice for her, who is imbued with the word (of the Guru) and whose heart is perforated (by it).

(4). That woman will not sit down as a widow, who is absorbed in the true Guru.

Her beloved is delightful, young, true, he does not die nor go.

He always sports with the beloved woman, true is his favourable look and goodwill (towards her).

(5). Truth is laid out (by her) as her wealth,[1] the ornament of her dress is love.

Having applied the paint of sandal-dust, the tenth gate[2] is made her palace.

Her lamp is lighted by the word (of the Guru), her necklace on her breast is the name of Rām.

(6). She is beautiful amongst women, on whose forehead is the jewel of love.

Her beauty and wisdom is charming by the infinite love of the True one.

Without her beloved she knows no man, on account of her love and affection to the true Guru.

(7). O thou, who hast fallen asleep in the dark night, how will the night be passed without thy friend?

(Thy) bosom burns, (thy) body is set on fire, (thy) heart, O woman, is consumed by fire!

When the woman is not enjoyed by the husband, her youth passes to no purpose.

(8). On the bed (is) the husbaud, the wife has fallen asleep (and) obtains (therefore) no understanding.

I have fallen asleep, my beloved is waking, to whom shall I go and ask?

She who is united (with her Lord) by the true Guru, abides in fear; love, O Nānak! is her companion.

Sirī Rāg; mahalā I.

III.

(1). Thou thyself art the qualities, thou thyself recitest (them), thou thyself having heard (them) reflectest.

Thou thyself art the jewel, thou (thyself) examinest (it), thou thyself art its infinite price.

Thou art true honour and greatness, thou thyself art bestowing (it).

Pause.

O Hari, thou art the creator! As it pleases thee, so keep me!

May thy name, O Hari, be obtained as rule of conduct!

(2). Thou thyself art the pure diamond, thou thyself are the majīṭh[3] colour.

Thou thyself art the bright pearl, thou thyself art the mediator of the devotees.

By the word of the Guru (thou art) praising (thyself), in every body (thou art) visible and invisible.

(3). Thou thyself art the ocean and the boat, thou thyself art the near and further shore (of it).[4]

Thou knowest the true way, by means of the word (of the Guru) thou art ferrying over (the water of existence).

[1] ਪਜੀ ਪਨ; ਪਜੀ, amount (of weight), ਪਜੀ ਪਨ, amount of wealth.

[2] ਦਸਵਾਂ ਦੁਆਰ, the tenth gate, said to be in the crown of the head (the so-called ब्रह्मरंध्र, the aperture of Brahma). The Jōgīs pretend to keep the breath fast in the tenth gate and to drink thus the nectar of immortality, by union with Brahm, which is brought about there.

[3] ਮਜੀਠ, *s.f.* the root of a vine, from which a genuine red colour is extracted (ਮਜੀਠਾ, coloured with majīṭh, genuine red, in contradistinction to ਸੂਹਾ, ungenuine red).

[4] ਪਾਰੁ ਅਪਾਰੁ = Sansk. पारापार (= पारावार), the near and further bauk or shore.

The fear of the fearless[1] is known, without the Guru there is darkness.

(4). Thou, O creator, art seen as firm, all the other (creatures) come and go.

Thou alone art pure, the other (creatures) are bound and fall into dullness.

Those who are preserved by the Guru, are saved, who fix their meditation on the True one.

(5). Hari is known from the word (of the Guru) by him, who is attached to the true discourse of the Guru.

To his body dirt does not stick, who has a habitation in the house of the True one.

If he bestow a favourable look, the True one is obtained, without the name what can he do?

(6). Those, who have known the True one, are happy in the four ages.

Having extinguished the thirst of egotism, they put firmly the True one in their breast.

(By them) the gain of the One name is obtained in the world having made the Guru the object of their reflection.

(7). (By whom) true goods are laden, he has always gain, true is his stock.

In the true court he will sit, whose devotion and supplication is true.

With honour his account will be settled, the name of Rām is making (him) manifest.

(8). He (=Hari) is called higher than high, he cannot be seen by any one.

Where I see, there art thou alone, by the true Guru thou art shown.

(Thy) all-pervading light is easily known by Nānak.

Sirī Rāg; mahalā I.

IV.

(1). The fish did not know the net, the saltish pond is bottomless.

Why did the very clever and beautiful (fish) confide (in it)?[2]

On account of its (own) action it was caught, death does not recede from its head.

Pause.

O brother, know thus death (impending) on thy (own) head!

As the fish, so man falls unawares into the net.

(2). The whole world is fettered by death, without the Guru death does not recede (from them).

Those who are attached to the True one, are saved having abandoned the anomalous state of duality.

I am a sacrifice for those, who are true (=accepted as true) at the true gate.

(3). Like a hawk is the birds' net in the hand of the huntsman.

Those who are preserved by the Guru, are rescued, the others are caught with the bait.

Without the name they are picked out and thrown down, no one is a companion with them (at the time of death).

(4). Truer than true he is called, true is the place of the True one.

By whom the True one is minded, in their heart is true meditation.

Those disciples are known as pure in heart and face, who have divine knowledge.

(5). Offer before the true Guru the prayer: join to me the friend!

The sweetheart being met with, happiness is obtained, the messengers of Yama have died having eaten poison.

If I abide within the name, the name comes and dwells in (my) heart.

[1] ਨਿਡਰਿਆ ਡਰੁ, the fear of the fearless; the sense of the words is: the fear of those, who do not fear thee, is known. Though they are apparently fearless, they are at the end afraid: for without the Guru and his word all is darkness. But ਨਿਡਰਿਆ ਡਰੁ might also be translated by: *thou art known as fearless* (Nānak using such compounds as: ਅਕਲ ਕਲਾ, free from parts), ਨਿਡਰਿਆ standing for ਨਿਡਰਾ = ਨਿਡਰ.

[2] *i.e.* in the net; why did it confidently go into the net?

(6). Without the Guru there is darkness, without the word (initiatory mantr) (one) does not obtain understanding.

By the instruction of the Guru light is made, if (one) continually meditate on the True one.

There death does not enter, light is absorbed in the luminous (Supreme Being).

(7). Thou art the sweetheart, thou art wise, thou thyself art uniting (men with thyself).

By the word (of the Guru) thou art praised, who hast no end nor limit.

There death does not arrive, where the boundless word of the Guru is.

(8). By (his) order all are produced, by (his) order they do their work.

By his order they are in the power of death, by his order they are absorbed in the True one.

O Nānak! what is pleasing to him, that is done, nothing is in the power of these creatures.

Sirī Rāg; mahalā I.

V.

(1). He who is of an impure body, is of an impure heart, his tongue (also) becomes impure.

He who is of a false mouth, speaks falsehood, how shall he become pure?

Without the word (of the Guru) (his) heart is not cleansed,[1] from the true one truth is obtained.

Pause.

O fair lady! what comfort has she, who is destitute of virtues?

Joined with thy beloved thou wilt enjoy pleasure, happiness is in the love to the true word (of the Guru).

(2). If the beloved (husband) goes abroad, the woman, separated from her husband, is in grief.

As a fish in little water makes pitiful moaning.[2]

If it is pleasing to the beloved, comfort is obtained (by her), when he himself bestows a favourable look.

(3). I will praise my own beloved with my friends and companions.

By the beauty of (his) body my heart is enchanted, having seen (him) I am imbued with love.

Being adorned with the word (of the Guru) (I am) beautiful, (my) beloved enjoys (me) with favour.

(4). A fascinating woman is of no use, if false and vicious.

She has no comfort in her father's nor in her father-in-law's house, she burns in a false passion.

Her coming and going is annoyance, she is forgotten and abandoned by her husband.

(5). The wife of the beloved is bright (happy), she, who is abandoned, what relish has she?

She is of no use to the beloved (husband), who speaks a great deal of nonsense.

At the gate and house she is not admitted, who has abandoned herself to another pleasure.

(6). The Paṇḍit reads books, (but) does not understand the subject under consideration.

He gives instructions to others—(on his part) a money business.

In a false story the world wanders about, to remain in the word (of the Guru) is the best.

(7). Many Paṇḍits and astrologers reflect on the Vēdas.

In discussion and opposition, in praise and discussion is (their) coming and going.

Without the Guru (their) destiny will not be loosened, they tell, hear and deliver explanations.

(8). All are called virtuous, I have no virtue whatever.

Hari is the bridegroom of the woman that is pleasing (to him), to me that Lord pleases.

O Nānak! if by the word (of the Guru) union is effected, there is no more separation.

[1] ਘਿਨੁ ਅਤ ਮਘਰ ਨ ਭਾਂਜੀਐ. The words are inverted and must thus be placed to get any sense out of them: ਘਿਨੁ ਮਘਰ ਅਤ ਨ ਭਾਂਜੀਐ. ਅਤ or ਅਤਿ = अभ्यंतर, heart, mind. Another reading is: ਘਿਨ ਮਤ ਮਘਰ, very likely instead of: ਘਿਨੁ ਮੁਤ ਮਘਰ. But the text is apparently corrupt here.

[2] ਕਰਣ ਪਲਾਵ = ਕਰੁਣ ਪਲਾਵ, pitiful moaning.

Sirī Rāg; mahalā I.

VI.

(1). If silent repetition (of the Vēdas, etc.), austerity and abstinence be practised, if at a Tīrtha (one's) residence be made.

Religious merit, alms, good actions, what are they to him without the True one?

What he sows, that he will reap, without virtue birth is destruction.

Pause.

O fair lady, the slave of virtue obtains comfort!

She is perfect who, having abandoned vice, is absorbed by the instruction of the Guru.

(2). Without a trading-stock the trafficker looks about in the four corners (of the earth).

He does not comprehend his own capital stock, that the thing remains in his (own) household.[1]

Without goods his pain is very great, the false (world) is ruined by falsehood.

(3). Who tries the jewel (of the name) reflecting (upon it), his gain is day and night new.[2]

He obtains the thing in his own house, he goes having accomplished his business.

Make traffic with the traffickers, O disciple, reflecting on Brahm!

(4). He (Brahm) is obtained in the society of the saints, if he, who is uniting, unite (the disciple with himself).

Within whom the boundless light (of Brahm) is, he, being united, is not separated (again from him).

He remains in the true seat of the True one, (who has) love and affection to the True one.

(5). By whom their own self is known, (they have) in their (own) house,[3] in their own palace, the palace (of Hari).

The True one falls into the lap of those who are in love with the True one.

That Lord, who is true and of a true name, is known as (being present) in the three worlds.

(6). That woman is quite happy, who has known that her beloved is with her.

The woman is called to the palace, (where) she enjoys (her) beloved with pleasure.

She is a true and good-favoured woman, who is fascinated by the beloved with his qualities.

(7). Wandering about, wandering about I ascend a sand-hill, having ascended a sand-hill I go to a mountain.

Though I wander about in the forest, I do not get understanding without the Guru.

If I wander about, having strayed from the name, again and again I shall come and go.

(8). Go and ask the travellers, who, having become servants (of God), have departed.

(If) they know their own king, they are not repulsed at the gate of the palace.

O Nānak! the One is contained (everywhere), there is no other.

Sirī Rāg; mahalā I.

VII.

(1). From the Guru the Pure one is known, whose body is pure.

In whose heart the Pure and True one dwells, he knows the sweet friend.[4]

Easily[5] abundant comfort (accrues) to him, the arrow of Yama does not touch him.

[1] The sense is: he does not know that the Supreme is within him.

[2] *i.e.* He has a new gain day and night.

[3] ਘਰੁ is here = body; in their own house = within themselves.

[4] ਅਤਪੀਰ instead of ਅਤਿਪਿਰੁ, the sweet friend (Sansk. अभिप्रिय), the final short syllable being lengthened for the sake of the rhyme. The explanation of the Sikh Granthīs, that ਅਤਪੀਰ means *the pain of the heart,* gives no sense and does not suit the context.

[5] ਸਹਜੇ ਤੇ may also be translated: from the innate (Hari); see Asṭp. xxiii., note.

Pause.

O brother, (on him) is no filth, who bathes in pure water.

Thou (O Hari) alone (art) pure, all the other (creation) is defiled with filth.

(2). The palace of Hari has been made beautiful by the creator.[1]

The light of the lamp of the sun and moon is incomparable, in the three worlds is boundless light.

In the shop, the city, the fort, the cells, is the trade and traffic of the True one.

(3). The collyrium of divine knowledge breaks the fear (of him) (who) sees the light of him, who is without collyrium (*i.e.* of the Supreme).[2]

The hidden and manifest (things), all are known (by him), who keeps his mind steady.

If such a true Guru (who keeps his mind steady, etc.) be met with, he easily unites (with the Supreme).

(4). A scratch is made with the touchstone, he carefully examines the good ones.

The counterfeited do not obtain a place, the genuine ones he puts into the treasury.

Remove hope and anxiety! thus (thy) filth will be absorbed.

(5). Every one desires comfort, no one desires pain.

Comfort (has) abundant pain (following), (but) the fleshly-minded one (has) no understanding (of this).

If comfort and pain be considered as the same, comfort is obtained from the secret of the word (of the Guru).

(6). If the Vēda be read with a loud voice, the speech of Brahm (and) Vyāsa:

The Munis, worshippers and devotees are imbued with love to the name, the vessel of virtues.[3]

Those, who are in love with the True one, have overcome; I shall always be a sacrifice for them.

(7). In the four periods (of the world) those are dirty and filled with filth, in whose mouth is not the name.

The face of those, who are destitute of devotion and love (to the name), is black, they lose their honour.

Those, who have forgotten the name, weep being ruined by vice.

(8). By searching and searching he is found, he meets with him who fears him and unites (him with himself).

He dwells in the house (=body) of him who knows his own self, the thirst of (his) egotism ceases (then).

O Nānak! those are pure and bright, who are in love with the name of Hari.

Sirī Rāg; mahalā I.

VIII.

(1). Hear, O misled and foolish heart, cling to the feet of the Guru!

Silently recite and meditate on the name of Hari! Yama is (then) afraid and pain flees.

Great is the pain of the ill-favoured woman, how shall her happy state (of wifehood) remain firm?

Pause.

O brother! I have no other place!

My wealth is the treasure of the name, I sacrifice myself for the Guru, by whom it is given.

(2). (By means of) the instruction of the Guru honour is (obtained), praise be to him! in his society is union (with God).

[1] ਹਰਿ ਦਾ ਮੰਦਰ, the palace of Hari is the Universe, which is illuminated by the lamp of the sun and moon. ਹਾਟ, shop = heart; ਪਟਣ, city = body; ਗੜ੍ਹ, fort = the crown of the head containing the tenth gate (ਦਸਵਾਂ ਦੁਆਰ); ਕੋਠੜੀ, the seventy-two cells or compartments of the human body.

[2] ਨਿਰੰਜਨ; God is without collyrium, *i.e.* without any spot or darkness. ਭਾਇ, *s.f.* light, splendour.

[3] ਗੁਣ ਤਾਸੁ may here also be translated by: and its qualities.

Without him I do not live twenty-five minutes, without the name I die.

May by me, the blind one, the name be not forgotten! if I remain steady (in it), I shall go to the house (of Hari).

(3). That disciple (finds) no place (in Hari's palace), whose Guru is blind.

Without the true Guru the name is not obtained, without the name what relish is there?

He comes and goes repenting, (he is) like a crow in an empty house.

(4). Without the name there is pain in the body, like a wall made of soil impregnated with saltpetre (it crumbles down).

As long as the True one is not in the mind, so long the palace (of Hari) is not obtained.

By him the house (of Hari) is obtained, who is imbued with the word (of the Guru), he is continually in the state of emancipation from individual existence.

(5). I ask my own Guru, having asked the Guru I do the work (enjoined by him).

If I praise (Hari) by means of the word (of the Guru), he dwells in (my) heart, the pain of egotism (or individual existence) is consumed.

Union (with the Supreme) is naturally effected, the true (disciple) has union with the True one.

(6). Those who are imbued with the word (of the Guru) are pure, having abandoned lust, wrath and conceit.

They praise always, always the name, they keep Hari in their breast.

How should he be forgotten from the heart, who is the support of all creatures?

(7). He who dies by means of the word (of the Guru), has (really) died, he will not die again another time.

From the word (of the Guru) Hari is obtained (by him), who has love to the name.

Without the word the world strays about, it dies and is born again and again.

(8). Every one praises his own self, a high-flown (speech)[1] is made (in self-commendation).

Without the Guru one's own self is not known, what is done by speaking and hearing?[2]

O Nānak! if by means of the word (=instruction of the Guru) (one's own self) be known, then no one will practise deceit.

Sirī Rāg; mahalā I.

IX.

(1). If, without (having) the beloved (husband), the woman be adorned, her youth is useless and wretched.

She does not enjoy in comfort her bed, without the beloved her ornament is useless.

The ill-fated woman has much pain, the Lord of the bed is not in the house.[3]

Pause.

O heart, mutter the name of Rām, then comfort will arise!

Without the Guru the love (of the husband) is not obtained, by the word (of the Guru) it accrues and pleasure springs up.

(2). By the service of the Guru comfort is obtained; if Hari be the bridegroom, there is easily decoration.

The beloved enjoys the bed of the true (woman), whose love and affection is deep.

[1] ਵਡਹੁ ਵਡੇਰੀ; supply: ਗਲ or ਘਾਤ, a higher than high (word or speech) is made.

[2] ਕਹੇ ਸੁਣੇ ਕਿਆ ਹੋਇ; the sense of these words is: what is the good of saying that he has known his own self, or of hearing that such a one has known his own self?

[3] This simile is used by Nānak all through the Granth *ad nauseam*.

She is recognized as a disciple, who is united (with Hari) by the Guru (on account of her) virtuous conduct.[1]

(3). Meet with (thy) true husband, O fascinating woman, charmed by (thy) beloved enjoy thyself!

Heart and body is delighted in the True one, whose value cannot be told.

(If) Hari (be thy) husband, (thou art) a favoured woman in the house; he is pure, of a true name.

(4). If in the mind the mind die, then the woman will enjoy the beloved.

A necklace of pearls in one thread is joined together on her neck.[2]

In the assembly of the saints comfort springs up, the name is the support of the (female) disciple.

(5). In a moment (man) is born, in a moment he is consumed, in a moment he comes, in a moment he goes.

If he know the word (of the Guru, *i.e.* the name) and remain (in it), death will not persecute him.

The unequalled Lord cannot be compared (with any thing), from a story (that is told) he cannot be obtained.

(6). The traders and traffickers are come, having written down their wages.

If they do the work of the True one, profit accrues to them by his favour.

The true trading-stock is obtained from the Guru, he has not a bit of covetousness.

(7). The disciple he will weigh accurately, true is his balance and weight.

Hope and desire is charming (him), by the Guru it is stopped, true is (his) word.

He himself will weigh accurately, full is the weight of the Perfect.

(8). By the telling of legends (final) emancipation is not obtained, nor by reading loads of books.

Purity of the body is not obtained without devotion and love to Hari.

O Nānak! him, by whom the name is not forgotten, the Guru, the creator, unites (with himself).

Sirī Rāg; mahalā I.

X.

(1). If the true, perfect Guru be met with, the jewel of reflection is obtained.

If the heart be given to one's own Guru, the love of all is obtained.

The boon of final emancipation is obtained, that is blotting out vices.

Pause.

O brother, without the Guru divine knowledge is not acquired!

Go and ask one of the Brahmās, Nāradas and Vēd-Vyāsas![3]

(2). He, who is known by application to divine knowledge and meditation, is called inexpressible.

(If) a tree is fruitful and green, its shade becomes large.

Rubies, jewels, gems, are in the store-room of the Guru.

(3). From the store-room of the Guru is obtained the love to the pure name.

The true, boundless stock of goods is collected by a full destiny.

He is a giver of comfort, a remover of pain, the true Guru is destroying the demons.

[1] ਗੁਣਚਾਰੁ = ਗੁਣ ਅਚਾਰੁ, virtuous conduct. The case or grammatical connexion is utterly neglected by Nānak, and the translation can only be made according to conjecture.

[2] As a sign of her ਸੁਹਾਗ, or happy state of wifehood.

[3] ਨਾਰਦ, the son of Brahmā, and one of the ten original Rishis. He delighted in exciting quarrels (hence ਨਾਰਦ = an embroiler). He is said to be the inventor of the Vīṇā or lyre, of a code of laws, and of the Nāradīya Purāṇa. ਬਿਆਸ = व्यास, the supposed compiler of the Vēdas. Twenty-eight Vyāsas are mentioned, who are incarnations of Nārāyaṇa (or Brahmā), and descend to earth from time to time to promulgate the Vēdas.

(4). The water of existence is difficult and terrible, there is no shore nor limit of it.

There is no boat nor buoy, nor is there a pole (to work the boat with) or a boatsman for it.

There is a boat (consisting) of the fear of the true Guru, by a favourable look he ferries across.

(5). If but a little (only) the beloved be forgotten, pain sets in and happiness departs.

May the tongue be burned with firebrands, that does not mutter the delightful name!

When (his) body is destroyed, his pain is very great, when Yama seizes (him), he repents.

(6). Saying "mine, mine," they are gone, body, wealth, wife, is not with (them).

Without the name wealth is useless, he[1] is gone astray on the road.

The true Lord is served by the disciple, (whose) story (description) is inexpressible.

(7). He (=man) comes (into the world), having gone, he is caused to wander about (in transmigration), his lot having fallen he follows his occupation.[2]

How shall that, which is written before, be blotted out? the destiny is written after the pleasure (of the Supreme).

Without the name of Hari there is no (final) emancipation, by the instruction of the Guru he finds union (with the Supreme).

(8). Without him I have nobody, whose my soul and life is.

May egotism and selfishness be consumed, may covetousness and conceit be burnt!

O Nānak! if the word of (the Guru) be reflected upon, the abode of virtues (or of all qualities = the Supreme) is obtained.

Sirī Rāg; mahalā I.

XI.

(1). O my heart, entertain such a love with Hari, as the lotuses with the water!

Though they be knocked down by the waves, yet they expand in love.

Having received their life in the water, they must die without water.

Pause.

O my heart, how wilt thou be released without love (to Hari)?

He who is contained within the disciple, bestows on him a storehouse (full) of devotion.

(2). O my heart, entertain such a love with Hari, as the fish with the water!

As it is very great, so is its joy great, in its mind and body is tranquillity.

Without water it does not live twenty-four minutes, it considers the Lord very dear.

(3). O my heart, entertain such a love with Hari, as the Chātrik[3] with the cloud!

The tanks are full, the deserts are green, not a drop (more) falls, what is that?

What accrues by destiny, that is obtained, he gives to him, on whose head the destiny has fallen.

(4). O my heart, entertain such a love with Hari, as the water has with milk!

[1] We should expect here "they," but the change from either number to the other is very frequent, as it may suit the rhyme.

[2] ਪਇਐ ਕਿਰਤਿ ਕਮਾਇ, an expression which is frequently met with in the Granth, but which the Sikhs are no longer able to explain. ਪਇਐ is the Formative (here Locative) of ਪਇਆ, fallen, used absolutely: after having fallen (पतिते), *i.e.* his lot (ਕਿਰਤੁ). In the Granth it is a frequent expression: ਕਿਰਤੁ ਪਇਆ, the lot has fallen = to reap one's (evil) deserts. It may therefore be translated: after having met with his deserts, after being punished, he (being born again in human shape) does his avocation (assigned to him by the caste, in which he is born). ਕਿਰਤਿ is also the Locative of ਕਿਰਤੁ, *m.* destiny, the whole construction being used in the sense of the Latin Ablative absolute.

[3] ਚਾਤ੍ਰਿਕ (Sansk. चातक), the Cuculus melano-lucus. It is said, that he only drinks from clouds and that he is therefore always eagerly expectant of rain.

It endures itself the boiling, but does not allow the milk to be consumed.

He (= Hari) himself having united the separated (from him), gives (them) true greatness.

(5). O my heart, entertain such a love with Hari, as the Chakvī[1] with the sun!

Not a moment she falls into sleep, she thinks that the far (sun) is present.

The fleshly-minded does not get any understanding, the disciple (considers him as) always (being) in (his) presence.

(6). The fleshly-minded make calculation, (but) what the creator does, that comes to pass.

His value is not obtained, though every one search (for it).

(If) by the instruction of the Guru it be given, then it is obtained; he who meets with the True one, finds comfort.

(7). True love does not break, if that true Guru falls in (with the disciple).

If the blessing of divine knowledge be obtained, the knowledge of the three worlds accrues (thereby).

The pure name is not forgotten, if he take (=repeat) the qualities (of Hari).

(8). Having played those little birds are gone, which are picking up food on the surface of the tank.

In twenty-four (or) in forty-eight minutes one must go; the play (lasts) to-day (or) to-morrow.

Whom thou unitest (with thyself), he is united, having gone he treads on the true arena.[2]

(9). Without the Guru love (to God) does not spring up, the filth of egotism does not go off.

By whom his own self is known as the "Sō ham,"[3] he believes in the secret of the word (of the Guru).

If by the disciple his own self be known, what else shall he do or cause to be done?

(10). What of those, who have been united, shall be united? he (Hari) believes[4] in (them, who) are united by the word (of the Guru).

The fleshly-minded one gets no understanding, being separated (from the Supreme) he is struck in the face.

O Nānak! there is only One palace (of Hari), there is no other place.

Sirī Rāg; mahalā I.

XII.

(1). The self-willed (ungodly) woman goes astray and is led astray, having gone astray she finds no place (of rest).

Without the Guru no one points out (the way), blind she comes and goes.

The blessing of divine knowledge is lost (by her), deceived and ruined she goes.

Pause.

O father, the Māyā deludes into error!

The ill-fated woman, deluded by error, is not taken to the bosom of the beloved.

(2). Erring she wanders about in foreign countries, deluded she goes and abandons her house.

Erring she ascends a mountain and a sand-hill, in error she agitates her mind.

[1] ਚਕਵੀ (Sansk. चक्रवाकी), the Brāhmanī goose or duck. It is said, that the male and female bird separate at night-fall and are anxiously expecting the re-appearance of the sun to be reunited. They are therefore said to be in love with the sun.

[2] ਪਿੜੁ (Sindhī), a level piece of ground, on which sports are made; ਪਿੜੁ ਮਲਣਾ, to tread on the arena, to sport. The play down here is transitory, the true play will come hereafter, when united to the Supreme.

[3] ਸੋਹੰ (= सोऽहम्), literally: he is I, absolute identification of the individual existence with the Supreme. The Absolute becomes conscious only in the human spirit. The tenor of the instruction of the Guru is here perfectly lucid, and Sikhism is in no way differing from the common Hindū pantheism.

[4] ਸਬਦਿ ਮਿਲੈ ਪਤੀਆਇ: these words are, as usual, only a hint, by themselves they are quite unintelligible. They should be thus construed: ਜੋ ਸਬਦਿ ਮਿਲੈ ਤਿਨਾ ਉਪਰਿ ਪਤੀਆਇ, who are united by means of the word of the Guru, in them he (Hari) confides, places his full trust in them.

How shall she, who is separated (from the Supreme) from the beginning, be united? ruined by pride she will lament.

(3). Those separated ones the Guru will unite, who have their joy in Hari and love the name.
Those have easily true great splendour, who rely for support on the qualities and the name of Hari.
As it pleases thee, so keep me, without thee what Lord have I?

(4). By reading and reading letters one is led astray, in (faqīr-) dresses there is much pride.
What does he, who has bathed at a Tīrtha, (if) in (his) heart be the filth of conceit?
Without the Guru, by whom shall the heart, the King and Sultān, be admonished?

(5). (If) the boon of love (to Hari) be obtained, the disciple will reflect on truth.
That woman has parted with her own self, (whose) ornament is in the word of the Guru.
In her (own) house that beloved is obtained by infinite love to the Guru.

(6). By the service of the Guru the heart becomes pure and happy,
In (whose) heart the word of the Guru is settled, she removes from within egotism.
When the boon of the name is obtained, there is always (new) profit acquired in the heart.

(7). If it accrue by destiny, then it (the name) is obtained, by thyself it cannot be taken.
Cling always to the feet of the Guru, remove from within thy own self!
The True one falls into the lap of those who are in love with the True one.

(8). Every one is subject to error, unerring is the Guru, the creator.
By the teaching of the Guru the mind is instructed, love (to Hari) springs up in it.
(By whom) the name is not forgotten, (him) the inexhaustible word (of the Guru) unites (with the Supreme).

Sirī Rāg; mahalā I.

XIII.

(1). The thirst after the Māyā (illusive world) is deluding (men), sons, relations, house and wife.
By wealth and youth the world is deceived, by greediness, covetousness and selfishness.
In consequence of the deceit of spiritual darkness I have died, this prevails in the world.

Pause.

O my beloved, I have none other without thee!
Without thee none other is pleasing to me, (if) thou art pleasing (to any one), happiness is obtained.

(2). The name I will praise with pleasure, from the word of the Guru contentment (is obtained).
What is seen, that will go off, false is the infatuation (of the world), do not look (at it)!
The travelling caravan has come, (but) behold, it is continually going along.

(3). Many tell a story, (but) without the Guru understanding (of truth) is not found.
If the greatness of the name accrue (to any one), he is steeped in the True one and obtains honour.
Those who please thee, are good, there is no false nor genuine one (by himself).

(4). In the asylum of the Guru final emancipation is obtained; the trading-stock of the fleshly-minded is false.
The eight metals[1] of a king, (which) are malleated (into money), are inscribed with a word.
He himself is the examiner who tries them; the right ones are put into the treasury.

(5). Thy value does not become known, all has been seen by me and carefully examined.[2]
By telling it does not come to hand; he who abides in the True one, obtains honour.
According to the instruction of the Guru Thou art to be praised, another value (of thine) cannot be told.

[1] The eight metals are: gold, silver, copper, tin, lead, brass, iron, steel.

[2] ਸਭਿ ਡਿਠੀ ਠੋਕਿ ਵਜਾਇ. ਠੋਕਿ ਵਜਾਇ, having struck and sounded. This refers to the habit of striking on earthenware and sounding it (before buying it), to see if it be sound = to examine carefully.

(6). In which body the name is not approved of, in that body is the contention of egotism.

Without the Guru divine knowledge is not obtained, the enjoyment of the visible world is duality.

Without (praising) the qualities (of Hari) it is of no use, the relish of the Māyā is insipid.

(7). In hope they are born, in hope they enjoy the pleasures (of this life).

Bound in hope they are marched off, ruined (robbed) they are struck in the face.

He who is bound by vice, is beaten, who follows the instruction of the Guru, is saved by the name.

(8). Thou alone art in all places, as it pleases thee, so keep me!

In (whose) heart the True one dwells by means of the instruction of the Guru, he has a good name, honour and reputation.

By whom the disease of egotism (individuality) is removed by means of the true word (of the Guru), he perceives the True one.

(9). In the sky and in the nether region, in the three worlds thou art present.

Thou thyself art the devotee and the object of his love, thou thyself art united (with him) and unitest him (with thyself).

May the name not be forgotten by Nānak! as it pleases thee, so thou fillest (all places).

Sirī Rāg; mahalā I.

XIV.

(1). By the name of Rām my heart is perforated, what other reflection shall I make?

By attention to the word (of the Guru) comfort arises, love to the Lord is the pith of happiness.

As it pleases thee, so keep me! the name of Hari is my support.

Pause.

O my heart, true is the will of the Lord!

Meditate on him who has created and adorned body and soul!

(2). (If my) body be thrown into the fire as an offering, having cut it (to pieces of) one ratī and weighed it.

If I make body and soul the fuel, daily burning (them) in the fire.

It does not come up to the name of Hari, though I perform lakhs of crores of works.

(3). (If my) body be cut into halves, having ordered the saw[1] to be placed upon my head.

(If my) body be melted in the Himālaya (snow-mountain), yet the disease will not leave my mind.

It does not come up to the name of Hari; every (place) I have seen and carefully examined.

(4). Though I give (in charity) castles of gold and present many excellent horses and elephants.

(Though) I give land and many cows, yet (there is) pride and conceit within (me).

By the name of Rām my heart is pierced,[2] the Guru has given (me) the true gift.

(5). Many are the opinions of the mind, many the reflections on the Vēda.

Many are the fetters of the soul, (but) the disciple has the gate of salvation.

On the side of truth is every one, (but) above it is good conduct.[3]

(6). Every one is called high, none is seen low.

One reason (leading thought) is in the created vessel (=man), One light is in the three worlds.

[1] ਕਰਵਤੁ (Sansk. करपत्र), a kind of large saw, but without teeth, as formerly suspended at Benares, by which the body was cut into two halves (lengthwise).

[2] The sense of घेपला, to pierce, is: to have a lively, never intermitting remembrance of a thing, to have a constant pricking.

[3] The sense of these words is: every one wants to know truth, but a good religious conduct is better than this research after truth.

If it accrue by destiny, then the True one is obtained, the original gift none erases.

(7). (If) a holy man meet with holy men, contentment dwells (in him) on account of his love to the Guru.

If the inexpressible tale be reflected upon, he is absorbed in the true Guru.

Having drunk nectar he is contented, dressed (in a dress of honour) he will go to the court (of Hari).

(8). In every body sounds the kingurī[1] daily by the natural property of the word.

Some rare one gets understanding, (but) the disciple informs his heart.

O Nānak! by whom the word is not forgotten, he is rescued (from material existence), having performed the word (of the Guru).

Sirī Rāg; mahalā I.

XV.

(1). Painted and white is the aspect of the mansions, beautiful are the doors.

According to the pleasure of the heart they were erected, in second love and affection.[2]

If the inside is empty and without love (of God), the body tumbles down (and becomes) a heap of ashes.

Pause.

O brother, (thy) body and property will not go with thee (after death).

The name of Rām is a pure property, the Guru bestows that Lord as a present.

(2). The name of Rām is a pure property, which the Giver gives.

In the future world no question will be asked from him, whose companion the Guru, the creator is.

(If) he himself release, emancipation is obtained, he himself is bestowing the gift.

(3). The fleshly-minded one considers his own daughters and sons as a chance.

Having seen women, he is delighted, (but) the joy he has, is grief.

The disciple enjoys, by the delightful word (of the Guru), day and night the juice of Hari.

(4). (His) reason goes (if) his wealth is going, the worshipper of the Śakti is continually wandering about.[3]

Seeking it outside one is ruined, the thing is in the house, in one's own place.

The fleshly-minded one is robbed by egotism, into the disciple's lap (the thing) falls.

(5). O thou vicious worshipper of the Śakti, know thy own origin!

The body (consists) of blood and semen, near the fire[4] life (is infused into it).

The body is in the power of the breath, on the forehead is the sign of the True one.[5]

(6). Long life is desired (by every one), no one wishes to die.

The life of that disciple is called happiness, in whom that (Hari) is indwelling.

Upon what does he, who is void of the name, count, who has not the sight of Hari, the Guru?

(7). As one is led astray by night in a dream, as long as sleep lasts.

So are the creatures in the power of the female snake,[6] within them is the duality of egotism (*i.e.* individuality).

If instruction by the Guru is given, it is reflected, that this world is (but) a dream (has no real existence).

[1] A sort of a lute, containing only two wires.

[2] Or: in love and affection for duality.

[3] ਡੋਲਿ ਡੋਲਾਇ = ਡੋਲਿ ਡੋਲੈ.

[4] The fire is the fire of the womb.

[5] ਸਚੁ ਨੀਸਾਣੁ = ਸਚ ਦਾ ਨੀਸਾਣੁ, the sign of the True one is on the forehead written already in the womb; *i.e.* man's destiny is allotted to him already in the womb.

[6] The ਸਰਪਨਿ is identical with the Māyā.

(8). Fire dies if water be poured (upon it), as a child by the milk of the mother (is satiated).

Without water no lotus is produced, without water the fish dies.

O Nānak! if the disciple obtains the juice of Hari, he lives and sings the qualities (=praises) of Hari.

Sirī Rāg; mahalā I.

XVI.

(1). Having seen a terrible mountain in my father's house I became afraid.

High and difficult is the mountain, there is no staircase (leading up) to it.[1]

By the disciple he (*i.e.* Hari) is known (as being) within; being united (with Hari) by the Guru, I am saved (*i.e.* I have crossed).

Pause.

O brother, the difficult water of existence frightens (me).

(If) the perfect and true Guru fall in with one, being friendly disposed (to him),[2] the Guru brings him across (by) the name of Hari.

(2). Though I make preparations for departure (and) know, that I am going.

Who has come will depart (again), immortal is that Guru, the creator.

Yet (I am) praising the True one, (I have) love to the True one.[3]

(3). Beautiful mansions and palaces, thousands of solidly-built forts.

Elephants, horses, saddles, armies in boundless lakhs:

Are gone with no one; wearing away they have died being sapless (unsolid).

(4). If gold and silver be collected, wealth is a net of anxieties.

If one cry out for justice (or help) in the whole world, without the name death is upon his head.

When the body falls down, the soul will sport,[4] what will be the state of the evil-doer?

(5). Having seen his sons and wives the Lord of the bed is delighted.

Perfume is applied (by him), he adorns his dress and figure.

Dust is mingled with dust, he departs leaving his family behind.

(6). He may be called a chief, a King, a Rājā, a Rāu[5] or Khān.

He may be called a Chaudharī,[6] a Rāu, he may burn in haughtiness.

The fleshly-minded one, by whom the name is forgotten, is (like) a reed burnt in a jungle-fire.

(7). He, who has come into the world, will go having practised egotism.

The whole world is a chamber of lamp-black,[7] body, mind and trunk (are or become) ashes.

Those are pure who are preserved by the Guru, by the word (of the Guru) their fire is extinguished.

(8). O Nānak! it is crossed (=salvation is obtained) by the true name (of him who is) king above kings.

By me the name is not forgotten, the jewel of the name of Hari is my trust.

The fleshly-minded are consumed in the water of existence and die, the disciples cross the bottomless (water).

[1] ਤਿਤੁ ਤਾਸੁ; the second is superfluous and only added to make up the rhyme.

[2] ਰਸਿ must here be taken as Part. p. conj. of ਰਸਲਾ, to become well-disposed.

[3] The words ਸਚੇ ਥਾਨਿ ਪਿਆਰੁ, of which the Sikh Granthīs could give me no explanation, must be constructed thus: ਸਚੇ ਥਾਨਿ ਪਿਆਰੁ ਮੈਂ ਨੂੰ ਹੈ, I have love to the True one. ਥਾਨਿ is here simply postposition (= स्थाने), Hindī ताईं, to, for.

[4] ਜੀਉ ਖੇਲਸੀ, the soul will sport (*i.e.* in transmigration).

[5] There is some difference between rājā and rāu, the latter signifying a *chieftain*.

[6] ਚਉਧਰੀ, the head man of a village or trade.

[7] ਕਾਜਲ ਕੋਠੜੀ, a chamber of lamp-black, by entering which one is sullied = a place of defilement.

Sirī Rāg; mahalā I.

XVII.

Ghar II.

(1). Having fixed (thy) residence remain in the house; why is there continually the apprehension of going?

This is considered a residence, when people remain stationary.

Pause.

How is there a (firm) residence in the world?

Practising righteousness bind thou up good works as viaticum, apply thyself continually to the name!

(2). The Jōgī practising his sitting-postures[1] sits down, the Mullā sits down in (his) place (or house).

The Paṇḍit explains books, the Siddh[2] sits down in a temple.

(3). The Gods, the Siddhs, the Gaṇas,[3] the Gandharvas, the Munis, the Shēkhs, Pīrs, chiefs:

Are departed to the threshold (of God), and others also will go (there).

(4). Sultāns, Khāns, Kings, nobles are gone, having departed (from the world).

In twenty-four minutes (or) in forty-eight minutes it must be gone; O heart, understand it, thou also wilt arrive there!

(5). If he (the Supreme) be described in words, some rare one will understand it.

Nānak tells this supplication (=says): he is in the water, in the earth and on the surface of the earth.

(6). Allāh is invisible, inapproachable, powerful, creator, merciful.

All the world is coming and going, only the residence of the Merciful one is firm.

(7). He is called stationary, on whose head there is no destiny.

Heaven and earth will pass away, he alone (will remain) stationary.

(8). Day and sun will pass away, night and moon will pass away, lakhs of stars will be destroyed.[4]

He alone is stationary; O Nānak, call him the True one![5]

SIRĪ RĀG; MAHALĀ III.

Ghar I.

Asṭpadīs.

By the favour of the true Guru!

I. XVIII.

(1). If he (the Guru) bestow mercy on the disciple, devotion is made, without the Guru devotion cannot be made.

[1] The Jōgīs have eighty-four sitting-postures.

[2] The Siddh, an ascetic, who is said to have acquired superhuman powers. In the following verse the Siddhs are a sort of demi-gods, inhabiting, with the inferior deities and Munis, the region between the sun and earth.—See Vishṇu Purāṇa, ed. Wilson, p. 227.

[3] The Gaṇas (Sansk. गण) are troops of inferior deities attendant on Shiva and under the superintendence of Gaṇēsh.

[4] ਪਲੋਇ, from ਪਲੋਣਾ or ਪਲੋਵਣਾ, to be destroyed, from the Sansk. प्रलय.

[5] ਬੁਗੋਇ is Persian بگوی, call, say! The insertion of a Persian word or phrase is considered very elegant by the Sikhs.

He himself unites (the disciple with himself), if he (the disciple) understand (the truth), then he will become pure.

Hari is true, true is (his) word, by the word (of the Guru) union is brought about.

Pause.

O brother, why hast thou come into the world void of devotion?

The service of the perfect Guru is not performed (by thee), uselessly (thy) human birth is wasted.

(2). Hari himself is the life of the world, the donor, he himself, having bestowed (the gift), unites.

What are these helpless creatures? what can one say or tell?

He himself gives greatness to the disciple, he himself makes (him) perform worship.

(3). Having seen (his) family he is charmed with fascination, when departing, it does not go with (him).

Who serves the true Guru, obtains the abode of (all) qualities, his value is not ascertained.

My friend is the Lord Hari, he will be a companion (also) at the end.

(4). In the father's family[1] the life of the world is the donor; by the fleshly-minded one (his) honour[2] is lost.

Without the true Guru no one knows the road, the blind one (has) no place whatever.

In whose heart Hari, the giver of comfort, is not dwelling, he will regret it at the end, when he is gone.

(5). In the father's family the life of the world is the donor; by the instruction of the Guru he is caused to dwell in the heart.

Daily, day and night, (such a one) performs devotion, the infatuation of his egotism (individuality) is stopped.

He becomes such as the person is, with whom he is in love; the true ones are absorbed in the True one.

(6). When he himself (=Hari) bestows a favourable look, he (=the disciple) conceives love (to him), having reflected on the words of the Guru.

By the service of the true Guru tranquillity springs up, having extinguished the thirst of egotism.

Hari, the giver of favours, always dwells in the heart (of him, by whom) the True one is put and kept in his breast.

(7). My Lord is always pure, by a pure heart he is obtained.

In whose heart the treasure of the name of Hari dwells, all the pain of his egotism (individuality) ceases.

By the true Guru the word (=the name of Hari) is proclaimed, I am always a sacrifice for him.

(8). One may say (so) in his own heart and mind, (but) without the Guru "self" does not go.

Hari is propitious to (his) devotees, the giver of comfort, if he bestow mercy, he dwells in the heart.

O Nānak! the Lord himself gives beauty and reflection, he gives greatness to his disciple.

Sirī Rāg; mahalā III.

II. XIX.

(1). Who are practising works of egotism, on them the punishment of Yama falls.

Those are saved who serve the true Guru, being occupied in their thoughts with Hari.

Pause.

O my heart, meditate on the name, directing thy face towards the Guru!

To them it is originally and before by the creator decreed, who by means of the instruction of the Guru are absorbed in the name.

[1] *i.e.* Whilst living in one's father's house = in this world.

[2] The honour of the human birth.

(2). Without the true Guru faith does not come, love to the name does not arrive.

Not (even) in a dream they obtain comfort, absorbed in pain they sleep.

(3). Though it may be said: Hari, Hari! though he may be much desired, the destiny cannot be effaced.

Those devotees have become acceptable at the gate, by whom the will of Hari has been obeyed with love.

(4). The Guru makes the word firm with colour, without mercy it cannot be taken.

If a hundred nectars be sprinkled, yet the Dhāu[1] will bear a poisonous fruit.

(5). Those people are true and pure, who have love to the true Guru.

They are performing the will of the true Guru, having given up the poison and passion of egotism.

(6). From the obstinacy of the mind one is not liberated by any contrivance, go and search the Smriti and the Shāstras!

Those who have joined the assembly of the holy ones, are saved by performing the word of the Guru.

(7). The name of Hari is a treasure, which has no end nor limit.

Those disciples are lustrous, on whom the creator bestows mercy.

(8). O Nānak, the donor is One, there is no other!

By the favour of the Guru he (Hari) is obtained, by destiny he is acquired.

Sirī Rāg; mahalā III.

III. XX.

(1). There is a beautiful bird on a tree, he picks up (as food) truth by love to the Guru.

He drinks the juice of Hari, he remains at his ease, he does not fly, nor come nor go.

In his own house he has obtained a dwelling, in the name of Hari, Hari he is absorbed.

Pause.

O my heart, do the work of the Guru!

If thou walkest according to the will of the Guru, thou wilt daily be steeped in the name of Hari.

(2). There are beautiful birds on a tree, they fly and go to the four quarters (of the earth).

As much as they may fly, their pains are great, they always burn and lament.

Without the Guru the palace (of Hari) does not become known, nor is the fruit of immortality found.

(3). (In) the disciple Brahm is verdant with true, natural ease.

The three branches[2] are removed (by him) having directed his thoughts on the One word (=name).

Hari alone is (or has) the fruit of immortality, he himself gives it to eat.

(4). The fleshly-minded are oppressed with heat and dried up, they have neither fruit nor shade.

One should not sit near them, they have neither house nor village.

They are cut down and continually burnt, they have neither the word (of the Guru) nor the name (of Hari).

(5). According to his order they do works, when the lot has fallen they wander about.

According to his order they see the sight (of the Guru), where he sends them, thither they go.

By his order Hari, Hari dwells in (their) heart, by his order they are absorbed in the True one.

(6). The helpless do not know his order, the fools wander about being led astray.

In the obstinacy of their mind they are doing (religious) works, continually, continually they become wretched.

No rest comes into their heart, nor do they conceive love to the True one.

[1] ਧਾਉ, *s.m.* (Sansk. धातकी) the *Grislea tomentosa*, a poisonous shrub.

[2] The three branches are the three qualities ਸਤੋ, ਰਜੋ, ਤਮੋ.

(7). The faces of the disciples are beautiful by their love and affection to the Guru.

By true devotion they are attached to the True one, at the gate of the True one they are (found) true.

They have become acceptable (themselves) and save all their family (also).

(8). All do their works (in) his sight, outside his sight no one (is doing a work).

As the True one is looking upon one, such he is.

O Nānak, from the name (come) greatnesses,[1] by destiny they are acquired!

Sirī Rāg; mahalā III.

IV. XXI.

(1). The disciples meditate on the name, the fleshly-minded get no understanding.

The faces of the disciples are always bright, Hari comes and dwells in (their) heart.

Quite easily comfort is obtained (by them), easily they remain absorbed (in Hari).

Pause.

O brother, become the slave of the slaves!

The service of the Guru is attachment to the Guru, some rare one obtains it.

(2). There is always the happy state of wifehood of that favoured woman, who walks in the love of the true Guru.

The immovable beloved is always obtained (by her), he does not die nor go.

Being united by the word (of the Guru) she is not separated, she is absorbed in the bosom of the beloved.

(3). The pure and exceedingly bright Hari cannot be obtained without the Guru.

One reads the Vēdas (but) does not understand (them), by (faqīr-) dresses and error he is led astray.

By the instruction of the Guru Hari is always obtained, the tongue is absorbed in the juice of Hari.

(4). By the innate nature of the instruction of the Guru the infatuation of the Māyā is brought to an end.

Without the word (of the Guru) the world goes about in pain, the fleshly-minded she (the Māyā) has eaten up.

He who by the word (of the Guru) meditates on the name, is absorbed in the True one by means of the word.

(5). The ascetics (Siddhs) wander about being led astray by the Māyā, by the natural property (of the Māyā in them) deep meditation (so as to identify themselves with the Supreme) is not made (by them).

In the three worlds she (=the Māyā) is contained, excessively she is clinging (to them).

Without the Guru final emancipation is not obtained, nor does the duality of the Māyā cease.

(6). What is called Māyā? What works does the Māyā practise?

By pain and happiness this soul is bound, it practises the works of egotism (individuality).

Without the word (of the Guru) the error does not cease, egotism (individuality) does not depart from within.

(7). Without love devotion is not possible, without the word (of the Guru) it is not acceptable (with Hari).

If by the word egotism (individuality) be annihilated, the error of the Māyā will cease.

The boon of the name is obtained by the disciple with natural ease.

(8). Without the Guru the qualities (of Hari) are not known, without the qualities (of Hari being known) devotion cannot be made.

In (whose) heart Hari, the propitious to the devotees, has taken his abode, he has naturally found that Lord.

O Nānak! Hari is praised by means of the word (of the Guru) (by him, who) obtains (him) by destiny.

[1] Or: in the name are.

Sirī Rāg; mahalā III.

V. XXII.

(1). The infatuation of the Māyā is made by my Lord, he himself leads astray in error.

The fleshly-minded one practises (religious) works, (but) does not understand (the truth), uselessly he wastes his human birth.

The word of the Guru is the light in this world, by destiny it comes and dwells in the heart.

Pause.

O my heart, repeat silently the name, and comfort will be obtained.

If the true Guru be praised, naturally that Lord will be found.

(2). (His) error is gone, (his) fear has fled, who applies his thoughts to the feet of Hari.

If the word (of the Guru) be performed by the disciple, Hari comes and dwells in (his) heart.

To the true house and palace (of Hari) he is admitted, death cannot eat him.

(3). Nāmā (was) a calico-printer and Kabīr[1] a weaver, (but) from the perfect Guru they obtained salvation.

The sons of Brahmā know the word, they parted (therefore) with egotism (individuality) and family.[2]

Gods and Naras sing their praise, no one effaces it, O brother!

(4). The son of the Daitya[3] does not at all read (with his preceptor) the duties, religious observances and abstinences (prescribed by the Shāstras) (and yet) he knows no duality.

Having met with the true Guru he became pure, daily he praises the name.

The One he recites, the One name he meditates upon, he knows no other.

(5). The six (philosophical) systems, the Jōgīs and Sanyāsīs[4] are led astray in error without the Guru.

If they serve the true Guru, then they obtain the station (degree) of salvation, Hari dwells in (their) heart.

If (their) thought is fixed on the true word (of the Guru), coming and going is stopped.

(6). The Panḍit reading and reading explains an argumentation, without the Guru he is led astray in error.

[1] Nāmā or Nāmdēv, a famous devotee, who is considered the first Marāṭhī writer (Molesworth, Marāṭhī Dictionary, Introd. p. xxv), is said to have been a contemporary of Kabīr (about 1480 A.D.). Kabīr, the weaver, a Musalmān by birth (as borne out by the Granth and the testimony of Ravidās) and disciple of Rāmānand, lived partly at Magar and partly at Benares under the reign of Sikandar Shāh Lōdī (1488—1512). Portions of the writings of both are incorporated in the Granth, especially of Kabīr, who comes in for a considerable share in every Rāg, and who is to be considered as the author of the whole reformatory movement going on in India during the Middle Ages. Nānak and the following Sikh Gurūs have iudorsed the tenets of Kabīr and made them their own.

[2] *The sons of Brahmā*; the mind-born sons of Brahmā, who are called Sanatkumāra, Sananda, Sanaka and Sanātana (with sometimes a fifth, Ribhu, added). They are said to have declined to create progeny and to have ever remained boys (Kumāra), pure and innocent. The "sabd" means here the initiatory mantr (sō ham), implying identity with the Supreme; they refused therefore to enter duality by procreation.

[3] ਦੈਤ ਪੁਤ, the son of the Daitya (Hiraṇyakaśipu) Prahlād, whose story is told in the Vishṇu Purāṇa. His preceptor did not teach him the name of Vishṇu, but Vishṇu himself (who is here to be understood by the ਸਤਿ ਗੁਰੁ), the instructor of the whole world. His father is said to have made different attempts on the life of his son, but to have signally failed; at last Hiraṇyakaśipu was torn in pieces by Vishṇu in the Avatār of the Narsinha (man-lion) issuing from a pillar of the hall. This story is frequently mentioned in the Granth.

[4] ਸੰਨਿਆਸੀ (सन्यासी), one who has cast off all worldly desires and possessions, a religious mendicant (now different from the fourth order of Brāhmans). The Sanyāsīs are generally followers of Shiva, the Bairāgīs of Vishṇu.

The round of the eighty-four lakhs (of forms of existence) is allotted (to him), without the word (instruction of the Guru) he does not obtain salvation.

When he reflects on the name, then he obtains salvation, when the true Guru unites (him) to union (with Hari).

(7). In the assembly of the holy ones the name of Hari is produced, where the true Guru is naturally met with.

Soul and body I offer up, my own self I remove, I walk in faith in the true Guru.

I am always a sacrifice for my own Guru, who fixes my mind on Hari.

(8). He is a Brāhmaṇ who knows Brahm, who is in love with Hari.

The Lord, who dwells near in the heart of all, is known by some rare disciple.

O Nānak! the name, (by means of which) greatness is obtained, is known from the word of the Guru.

Sirī Rāg; mahalā III.

VI. XXIII.

(1). The whole world seeks composure,[1] (but) without the Guru it cannot be obtained.

The Panḍits and astrologers, reading and reading (treatises), have become tired, by (faqīr-) dresses and error they are led astray.

By meeting with the Guru composure is obtained, if he (*i.e.* Hari) bestow his own mercy and good pleasure.

Pause.

O brother, without the Guru composure does not accrue.

From the word (of the Guru) alone composure springs up, that true Hari is obtained (from it).

(2). What is sung in composure is acceptable, without composure the recital (of the Purāṇs, etc.) is useless.

Easily devotion is produced by composure, out of natural love and abandonment of the world.

From composure comfort and tranquillity are obtained, without composure life is useless.

(3). By composure (the disciple) always, always praises (Hari), easily giving himself to deep meditation.

By composure he utters the qualities (of Hari), he performs devotion directing his thoughts (on Hari).

By the word (of the Guru) Hari dwells in his heart, his tongue eats the juice of Hari.

(4). By composure death is driven away, if (one) fall on the asylum of the True one.

By composure the name of Hari dwells in (his) heart, he does true work.

Those are very fortunate who have obtained it, they remain easily absorbed (in Hari).

(5). In the Māyā composure is not produced, the Māyā is in duality.

The fleshly-minded are doing (the prescribed) works, (but) they burn continually in egotism.

Birth and death do not cease, again and again they come and go.

(6). In the three qualities composure is not obtained, the three qualities lead astray in error.

It may be read, it may be pondered, what shall be said (by him), when he goes astray from the beginning?

In the fourth stage is composure,[2] it falls into the lap of the disciple.

[1] The whole Astpadī is a play with the meaning of ਸਹਜੁ, ਸਹਜਾ. It signifies here (as a substantive m.), according to the whole context: "*composure, ease of mind.*" In Sindhī it is still used in this sense (सहजु), but no longer in modern Hindī. ਸਹਜ is also used as adjective, "*innate,*" *natural*, and as adverb (ਸਹਜੇ), *naturally, easily.*

[2] In the fourth stage the individual spirit identifies itself completely with the Supreme Spirit.

(7). The name of him that is without attributes (=the Supreme) is a treasure, by composure sagacity (of mind) is obtained.[1]

By the virtuous it is praised, true is the story of the True one.

Those who are gone astray he (Hari) will unite (with himself) by composure, by the word (of the Guru) union is brought about.

(8). Without composure every one is blind, the infatuation of the Māyā is darkness.

By composure sagacity is obtained from the true inexhaustible word (of the Guru).

He himself, the perfect Guru, the creator unites (him).

(9). By composure the invisible one is known, the fearless, the luminous, the formless.

He alone is the donor of all creatures, the luminous is uniting (with himself) that which is luminous.

By the perfect word (of the Guru) he is praised, who has no end nor limit.

(10). The wealth of those endowed with divine knowledge is the name, naturally (=readily) they traffic (with it).

Daily they take as profit the name of Hari, the store-rooms (of whom) are inexhaustible and filled.

O Nānak! no deficiency befalls them, they are given by the giver.

Sirī Rāg; mahalā III.

VII. XXIV.

(1). After the true Guru is found, no wandering (in transmigration) takes place, the pain of birth and death ceases.

From the perfect word all knowledge is obtained, he (the disciple) remains absorbed in the name of Hari.

Pause.

O my heart, fix thy mind on the true Guru!

He himself, (whose) name is pure and always fresh, will come and dwell in the heart.

(2). O Hari, keep me in thy asylum! As thou keepest me, so I remain.

The disciple, who whilst living dies by means of the word (of the Guru), crosses the water of existence.

(3). By a great destiny the name is obtained, by the word approved by the Guru he (=the disciple) obtains honour.

In whose heart the Lord, the creator himself dwells, he remains easily absorbed (in Hari).

(4). To some fleshly-minded the word (of the Guru) is not pleasing, bound in fetters they are caused to wander about (in transmigration).

Again and again they come having passed through the eighty-four lakhs (of forms of existence), uselessly their human birth is lost.

(5). In the heart of the devotees is joy, by the true word they are steeped in the love (of Hari).

Daily they sing (his) qualities, they are always pure (and) are easily absorbed in the name.

(6). The disciples speak a speech of nectar, they recognize all (the world) as the Supreme Spirit.

The One they serve, the One they worship, the disciples recite the inexpressible one.

(7). If the true Lord be served, he comes and dwells in the heart of the disciples.

Those who are always in love with the True one, he unites (with himself) out of his own mercy.

(8). He himself does (everything) and causes it to be done, he himself awakens some who have fallen asleep.

He himself unites to union (with himself) (those), O Nānak! (who) are absorbed in the word (of the Guru).

[1] By ਸਹਜੇ (abl.), composure, ਸੋਝੀ, brightness of intellect or sagacity of mind, is obtained.

Sirī Rāg; mahalā III.

VIII. XXV.

(1). By serving the true Guru soul and body have become pure and holy.
He always gets joy and comfort in his heart, who has joined the deep and profound (Hari).
He who sits in the true assembly, his mind is composed by the true name.

Pause.

O my heart, fearlessly serve the true Guru!
By serving the true Guru, Hari dwells in the heart, not a bit of filth clings to it.
(2). From the true word honour springs up, true is the name of the True one.
I shall become a sacrifice for those who, having extinguished their egotism (individuality), have known it.
The fleshly-minded do not know the True one, they have nowhere a place or spot.
(3). The True one (I) eat, the True one (I) put on, in the True one is my abode.
(I) praise always the True one, in the True one is (my) dwelling.
All is recognized (by me) as the Supreme Spirit, by means of the instruction of the Guru (my) abode is in (my) own house.
(4). (Who) sees the True one, who speaks the True one, (his) body and soul become true.
True is (his) evidence, true his instruction, the story of the True one is true.
By whom the True one is forgotten, they go in pain and weep.
(5). By whom the true Guru is not served, for what have they come into the world?
Being bound they are beaten at the gate of Yama, he does not hear (=listen to) their screams and cries.
Uselessly their human birth is lost, they die and are born repeatedly.
(6). Having seen this world burning (I)[1] have fled to the asylum of the true Guru.
By the true Guru the True one is made firm (in me), (I) always remain in true continence.
The true Guru is the true boat, by (his) word (I) cross the water of existence.
(7). In the eighty-four lakhs (of forms of existence) they continually wander about, (but) without the true Guru final emancipation is not found.
The Paṇḍits and silent ascetics reading and reading have become tired, by duality they have lost their honour.
By the true Guru the word (=the name) is proclaimed, without the True one there is no other.
(8). Those who are applied by the True one, cling to the True one, and do always true (good) work.
They have obtained a dwelling in their own house[2] and remain in the true palace.
O Nānak! devotees are always happy, they are always in love with the true name.

Sirī Rāg; mahalā V.

I. XXVI.

(1). Whom a very great difficulty befalls, to him none gives an entrance.
If his enemies are lying in wait for him, even his relatives keep aloof from him.
Every asylum is broken down, every protector fails.
(But) if he remember the Supreme Brahm, no hot wind will touch him.

Pause.

The Lord is the strength of the weak.
He neither comes nor goes, he is always firm; from the word of the Guru the True one is known.

[1] No subject whatever is pointed out, it can only be guessed at.

[2] The sense is: they do not seek the Supreme outside, but they find him in their own heart, which is his palace, where he dwells.

(2). If one be weak, naked, in the pain of hunger.

If no money fall into his lap, if no one encourage him.

If no one do his aim and object,[1] if there be no business whatever (for him).

If he remember the Supreme Brahm, his satiety will be immovable.

(3). Who has much anxiety, whose body much sickness pervades.

Who is surrounded by a household and family, who has sometimes joy and sometimes grief.

Who wanders about in the four corners of the earth, who sits not down nor sleeps for twenty minutes.

If he remember the Supreme Brahm, his body and soul will be refreshed.

(4). He may be subdued by lust, wrath and spiritual blindness; he may be a miser, given to greediness.[2]

He may have committed the four sins and crimes,[3] he may have perpetrated an atrocious murder.

He may never have caught with his ear any book, song, poetry.

If he remember the Supreme Brahm, he is saved by the remembrance of a moment.

(5). He may go through the Shāstras, Smriti, the four Vēdas from memory.

The great ascetic may practise austerities, the Jogī may go to a Tīrtha.

He may (practise) twofold more than the six duties,[4] performing worship he may bathe.

If he has no love to the Supreme Brāhm, he will surely go to hell.

(6). (If he have) dominion, property, chieftainships, an abundance of enjoyment of (sensual) pleasures.

(If he have) delightful and beautiful gardens, if his order go unflinching.

(If he have) merriments and shows of many kinds, if he have adhered continually to his pleasure.

If he has not remembered the Supreme Brahm, he has gone into the womb of a snake.

(7). He may be very rich and of virtuous conduct, his comeliness and manners may be spotless.

He may be in love with mother, father, son, brothers, friend.

He may be addressed by the whole quiver-bearing army in homage:[5] Sir, Sir!

If he has not remembered the Supreme Brahm, he is seized and thrown into the lowest hell.[6]

(8). In his body there may be no sickness nor any defect, no pain nor grief whatever.

Death may not come into his mind, day and night he may enjoy himself.

He may have made all his own, he may not have got anxiety in his heart.

[1] ਸੁਆਰਥ and ਸੁਆਉ are synonymous; the latter stands for स्वाद = ਸੁਆਉ (in Prakrit dissolved already into सुआओ). The word सुआउ is also used in the same sense in Sindhī.

[2] ਲੋਭਿ ਪਿਆਰੁ; ਪਿਆਰੁ stands here (for the sake of the rhyme) for ਪਿਆਰਾ, attached to, given to (= प्रिय), constructed with the locative (ਲੋਭਿ), as in Sanskrit.

[3] The four sins are now said to be: the killing of a girl, the killing of a cow, the killing of a Brahman, and cohabitation with one's Guru's wife. Formerly five heinous sins were enumerated: (1) killing a Brahman, (2) stealing gold, (3) drinking liquors (सुरापानं), (4) intercourse with the wife of one's Guru, (5) associating with any one guilty of such crimes.

[4] The six duties, as far as they are binding on the Khatrī, are mentioned already, p. 17, note. The six duties of the Brahman are: (1) अध्ययन (reading of the sacred texts), (2) अध्यापन (teaching the same), (3) यजन (sacrificing), (4) याजन (procuring or vicariously conducting sacrifice), (5) दान (almsgiving), (6) प्रतिग्रह (accepting donations).

[5] ਤਰਕਸ ਬੰਦ ਬੰਦ must be thus divided: ਤਰਕਸ ਬੰਦ = ترکش بَند wearing a quiver, the other ਬੰਦ is = वन्दना to worship, to do homage, and is the participle past conjunctive: having done homage.

[6] ਰਸਾਤਲ is originally one of the seven divisions of Pātāla (see Vishṇu Purāṇa, p. 204); but in the modern Hindī it denotes the lowest of the seven divisions, and is identical with ਨਰਕ.

If the Supreme Brahm he has not remembered, he falls (has fallen) into the power of the servant of Yama.

(9). On whom the Supreme Brahm bestows mercy, he obtains the society of the holy ones.
As, as he (Brahm) is magnified, so, so love with Hari (is increased).
He himself is the Lord of both boundaries,[1] there is no other place.
From the true Guru, if he be pleased, the true name is obtained, O Nānak!

Sirī Rāg; mahalā V.

Ghar V.

II. XXVII.

Pause.

I do not know what things please (him).
O heart, seek the way!
(1). He who is given to meditation, makes meditation;
He who has divine knowledge, acquires divine knowledge.
By whom is the Lord known?
(2). The Bhagautī[2] remains in his practice.
The Jōgī says: (I am) emancipated.
The ascetic is absorbed in his austerity.
(3). The silent devotee keeps silence, the Sanyāsī is given to chastity.
The stoic is absorbed in indifference (to the world).
The devotee bows down in (different) manners.
The Paṇḍit reads with a loud voice the Vēda.
The householder is fulfilling his duties in his household.
(4). The Ik-sabdī and Avadhūt is (given) to mimicry.
The Kāpaṛī is given to show (sport).
Some bathe at a Tīrtha.[3]
(5). (Some) who go without food and are fasting, are touchable (*i.e.* mingling with people).
Some hide themselves and do not give an interview.
Some are wise in their own mind.
(6). No one says: he is wanting.[4]
All say: he is obtained (by me).
Whom he (Hari) unites (with himself), he is a devotee.
(7). Giving up all contrivances and shifts:
I will fall on the asylum (of the Guru).
Nānak flees to the foot of the Guru.

---

[1] ਦੁਹਾਂ ਸਿਰਿਆਂ ਖਸਮੁ, the Lord of both ends or boundaries, *i.e.* of this and that world, or of the whole universe.

[2] The Bhagautī is a faqīr, who imitates the dress, dance, etc., of Krishṇa; ਜੁਗਤਾ, given to the practice, performance (of the ਰਾਸ, etc.).

[3] The Ik-sabdī is the same as the Alokh-nāmī, who only uses the word Alakh (Brahmā). The Avadhūt is a naked faqīr; both are said to be given to mimicry. The Kāpaṛī is a faqīr who makes pilgrimage to Hinglaj; they carry a red flag, sell rosaries, etc., and also give public shows (ਰਉਤਾ = कौतुक). ਜਾਗੁਤਾ = Sansk. जाग्रत, wakeful, attentive to, given to.

[4] ਘਾਟਿ, he (*i.e.* God) is wanting, or not found.

Ōm! By the favour of the true Guru!

SIRĪ RĀG; *mahalā* I.[1]

Ghar III.

I.

(1). Amongst Jōgīs thou art a Jōgī, amongst sensual men thou art sensual.
Thy end cannot be obtained; in heaven, on earth, in the nether region art thou!

Pause.

I devote myself, I devote myself, I am a sacrifice to thy name.
(2). Thou hast created the world, thou hast put the created beings into (their) occupation.[2]
Thou seest thy own work, by the omnipotence thou lettest fall the dice.[3]
(3). Thou art manifest and known in the world (the expansion).
The whole (world) longs for (thy) name.
Without the true Guru (thou art) not obtained, the whole (world) is in the net of the illusive Māyā, O Lord!
(4). One should offer himself a sacrifice to the true Guru!
By meeting with whom perfect salvation is obtained.
What the Gods, Naras, the Munis are longing for, that is taught by the true Guru, Sir![4]
(5). Now is the society of the good known:
Where the One name is praised.
The One name is the commandment (of God), O Nānak! by the true Guru it is taught, Sir!
(6). This world is led astray in error.
By thyself it is ruined.
Anguish has seized those ill-fated women, whose lot thou art not, O Lord!
(7). What are the signs of the ill-fated women?
Having strayed away from their husband, they wander about wretched.
Dirty are the clothes of those fascinating women, in pain the night is passed (by them), O Lord!
(8). What work is done by the lucky women?
They have obtained the fruit decreed for them before.
Casting upon them thy own favourable look, thou thyself unitest them (with thyself), O Lord!
(9). Whom (thou hast) caused to obey (thy) order:
Within them (thou hast) planted the word (of the Guru).
Those lucky women are (thy) intimate friends, who have love with (thee) the husband, O Lord!
(10). Who are pleased with the divine decree: from their heart error is removed.
O Nānak, such a one is known as the true Guru, who unites every one, Sir!
(11). By meeting with the true Guru those have obtained the fruit (of their former good actions):
Who have cleared away from within egotism (individuality).

[1] In the best MSS. of the Granth the following two pieces are numbered by themselves, and not among the Astpadīs, to which they do not belong. No title is given to either piece; we head them therefore by the first words.

[2] ਸਿਰੇ = ਸਿਰਜੇ, the created beings; ਧੰਧੇ ਸਿਰਿ ਲਾਉਣਾ, to put into (upon) their occupation, to assign to every created being its peculiar work.

[3] ਪਾਸਾ ਢਾਲਣਾ, to let fall or pour out the dice, *i.e.* to assign the lot to every creature.

[4] ਜੀਉ may be translated by "Lord" or "Sir" (or brother). In the following verses ਜੀਉ is partly applied to God, partly redundant (applied to a brother = ਭਾਈ).

The pain of (their) foolishness[1] is cut off, destiny has come and settled on their forehead, Sir!

(12). Thy words are nectar.

In the heart of (thy) devotees they are deeply fixed.

By keeping up worship in the heart, comfort (is obtained);[2] (on whom) thou bestowest a favourable look, (him) thou savest, O Lord!

(13). The true Guru, being met with, is known.

By the meeting with whom the name is praised.

Without the true Guru it is not obtained; the whole (world), doing (religious) works, has become tired,[3] O Lord!

(14). I have devoted myself to the true Guru.

Who has put me, who was led astray by error, into the (right) way.

If he bestows his own favourable look, he himself unites (with himself), Sir!

(15). Thou art contained in all.

By that creator his own self is hidden.

O Nānak, he has become manifest to that disciple, to whom the creator has communicated his light, Sir!

(16). By the Lord himself he is cherished.

Who has given and made soul and body.

He preserves the honour of his own servant, putting both hands on his forehead, Sir!

(17). All abstinences and cunnings have come to an end.

My Lord knows everything.

His glory is laid out manifest, all the world cries: victory! Sir!

(18). My virtues (and) vices he has not taken into account.

The Lord has remembered his practice.[4]

Taking me to his neck he has preserved (me), no hot wind touches (me), Sir!

(19). In my heart and body the Lord is meditated upon.

The fruit desired by my heart I have obtained.

Thou art Lord above a king and emperor, Nānak lives reciting silently (thy) name, O Lord!

(20). Thou thyself hast created thyself.

Thou hast made another sport (= the world) and shown it.

In all is the perfectly True one; whom he pleases, him he lets know (the truth), Sir!

(21). (Where) he is obtained by the favour of the Guru.

There the infatuation of the Māyā is brought to an end.

He himself, out of his own mercy, absorbs (with himself), Sir!

(22). (Thou art) the Gōpīs, the river, the cowherd.

Thou thyself hast removed the kine.

By (thy) order the vessels are made, thou thyself having broken (them) makest (them again),[5] O Lord!

(23). Who have fixed their mind on the true Guru.

[1] The ਦੁਰਮਤਿ, or foolishness, consists in considering oneself different from the Supreme.

[2] The words ਸੁਖ ਸੇਵਾ ਅੰਦਰਿ ਰਖਿਐ must be thus constructed: ਸੇਵਾ ਅੰਦਰਿ ਰਖਿਐ ਸੁਖ (ਹੁੰਦਾ ਹੈ).

[3] Has become tired, knocked up. The sense is: all their (religious) works have been of no use, the name was not obtained by their works.

[4] The sense is: the Lord has remembered that it is his practice ever to forgive.

[5] ਆਪੇ ਭੰਨਿ ਸਵਾਰਿ ਜੀਉ may also be translated: thou thyself, having prepared (or adorned them), breakest (them).

They have brought duality to an end.
A pure light is in those men, they are gone, having adorned their human birth, Sir!
(24.) (Thou art) always, always (doing) good works.
I (am saying) (thy) praises night and day.
(Thou art) giving gifts without being asked; Nānak says: remember the True one, Sir!

Sirī Rāg; mahalā V.

I.

Pause.

Having fallen at his feet I will conciliate him, Sir!
By the true Guru, the Supreme Spirit, (I am) united, like him there is none other, Sir!
(1). The Lord[1] (is) my dear friend.
(He is) sweeter (to me) than mother and father.
(Sweeter than) sister, brother and all friends; like thee there is none other, O Lord!
(2). By thy order Sāvaṇ[2] has come.
I have applied the plough of truth.
I commenced to sow the name in hope; O Hari, having made it grow, bestow heaps of corn, O Lord!
(3). I, having met with the Guru, know the One.
I do not know any other word in my mind.
By Hari I was put into one work; as it pleases (thee), so accomplish it, O Lord!
(4). O brethren, enjoy yourselves and eat!
I have been invested by the Guru in the court with the mantle.
I have become the master of the village; the five partners were brought bound, Sirs![3]
(5). I have come to thy protection.
The five are the labourers of my fields.
No one lifts up his shoulder and is remiss, O Nānak! by hard labour the village is cultivated, Sir!
(6). I sacrifice and devote myself (to thee).
Continually I am meditating on thee.
The desolate heap of ruins is built up, I am a sacrifice to thee, O Lord!
(7). I am always meditating on the beloved Hari.
I obtain the fruit, I desire in my heart.
All my works are adjusted by him, the hunger of my heart is taken away by him, Sir!
(8). All (worldly) occupation is given up by me.
I serve the true Lord.
The name of Hari, the receptacle of the nine treasures, I have taken and bound in my lap, Sir!
(9). I have obtained the comfort of comforts.
The Guru has fixed the word in my heart.

[1] ਗੋਸਾਈ (=गोस्वामी), an epithet of Krishṇa, the Lord of cows. Arjun was a great worshipper of Krishṇa: he was his इष्टदेव (the God whom he had specially chosen for his worship); his tomb at Lahore is still covered with paintings exhibiting the feats of Krishṇa.

[2] Sāvaṇ = July-August (the rainy month in the Panjāb).

[3] The master of the village, the master of the heart. The five partners are explained by: ਕਾਮ, ਕ੍ਰੋਧ, ਲੋਭ, ਮੋਹ, ਅਹੰਕਾਰ.

By the true Guru, the Supreme Spirit, it was shown (to me), having put his hand on my forehead, Sir!

(10). I have built a true Dharmsālā.

I obtain the instruction of the Guru, having searched (for it).

I wash the feet (of the Guru), I swing the Pankhā, bowing and bowing to him I cling to his feet, Sir!

(11). Having heard (his) words (I) came to the Guru.

The name, alms-giving, bathing was enjoined (by the Guru).

The whole world was saved, O Nānak, having ascended the true boat, Sir!

(12). The whole creation serves (him) day and night, Sir!

Give ear and hear my supplication,[1] Sir!

I have seen and accurately examined all: he himself, being pleased, has released (saved) it (the creation), Sir!

(13). Now the order of the kind (Hari) has been given.

No one is troubling the other.

All (the world) has settled in happiness, this rule of mildness has set in, Sir!

(14). Softly and lightly nectar is raining.

I speak, what I am caused to speak by the Lord.

I have put much trust in thee, thou thyself wilt accept me, O Lord!

(15). The hunger of thy devotees is always thy own.

O Hari, (thou art) fulfilling my desires!

Give me a sight of thee, O giver of comfort, take and put me to thy neck, O Lord!

(16). Like thee none other is found.

Thou art in the earth, the heavens and in the nether regions.

Thou art contained in every place; Nānak (says): thou art the true support of (thy) devotees, O Lord!

(17). I am the brave combatant of the Lord.

Having met with the Guru the back-part of my turban stands high up.

All the (world) has been assembled for the wrestling; God himself, being seated, looks on, Sir!

(18). The mouths of the drums and kettledrums sound.

The wrestlers have descended and take their rounds.

Five young men were killed (by me); the Guru, rejoicing, tapped me, Sir!

(19). All have come together.

They will go home, having changed the road.[2]

The disciples are gone, having got the advantage, the fleshly-minded are gone, having lost their capital, Sir!

(20). Thou art without colours and signs.

Thou, O Hari, art seen present and manifest.

Having heard, having heard, they are meditating on thee; thy devotees are attached to thee, O ocean of qualities!

(21). I am constantly the servant of the Deity.

The Guru has cut my rope.

I shall not again dance in wrestling. Nānak has sought and found the fit time, Sir!

---

[1] *i.e.* my word.

[2] ਵਾਟ ਵਟਾਇਆ = ਵਾਟ ਵਟਾਇ; final $\bar{a}$ is an alliteration, for the sake of the rhyme.

Ōm! By the favour of the true Guru!

SIRĪ RĀG; PAHARĒ.[1]

Mahalā I.

Ghar I.

I.

(1). In the first watch of the night, O friend merchant, he (= man) has fallen into the womb[2] by order (of God).

He performs within austerity, the face being turned upwards, O friend merchant, and supplication to the Lord.

He makes supplication to the Lord, being given to meditation and devout absorption, the face being directed upwards.

Without decency (= naked) he has come into the Kali-yug, and will go again naked.

As the pen (of God) has flown (= written) on the forehead, such (a lot) the creatures will obtain.

Nānak says: in the first watch man has fallen into the womb.[3]

(2) In the second watch of the night, O friend merchant, meditation has been forgotten.

From hand to hand he is fondly passed,[4] O friend merchant, as Kān (= Krishṇa) in the house of Jasudā.[5]

The child is fondly passed (danced) from hand to hand, the mother says:

My son! know, O my thoughtless foolish heart, at the end nothing will be thine.

Thou doest not know him, by whom creation was made; form (= conceive) in thy mind divine knowledge!

Nānak says: in the second watch meditation is forgotten by man.

(3). In the third watch of the night, O friend merchant, his mind is intent on wealth and youth.

He does not remember the name of Hari, O friend merchant, by which the bound one is released.

Man does not remember the name of Hari, he is confused and (engaged) with the Māyā.

He is enamoured of property, drunk by youth, uselessly his human birth is lost.

He has not carried on traffic with religion, he has done no (good) works, O friend!

Nānak says: in the third watch the thought of man (is directed) towards wealth and youth.

(4). In the fourth watch of the night, O friend merchant, the reaper has come (and reaped) the field.

When he is seized and marched off by Yama, no one has undergone a change of mind.[6]

No one has undergone a change of mind, when he is seized and marched off by Yama.

A false weeping is made round about him, in a moment he has become a stranger.

That thing he has obtained, on which he had bestowed his affection.

Nānak says: in the fourth watch the field of man is reaped by the reaper.

[1] The following pieces bear the superscription "paharē," *watches*, for reasons apparent from the contents. These verses are addressed to a vaṇjārā mitr, which the Sikhs take for a proper name, but it is perhaps more simple to take it for an appellative.

[2] ਗਰਭਾਸਿ, Loc. of ਗਰਭਾਸ = गर्भाशय, uterus.

[3] The Hindūs fancy that the fœtus in the womb is meditating on Brahm.

[4] Literally: he is caused to dance.

[5] ਜਸੁਦਾ, the wife of Nanda, in whose house Krishṇa was brought up.

[6] ਫੇਰੁ = ਫੇਰ, a changed state, change of mind; man dies as he lived.

Sirī Rāg; mahalā I.

II.

(1). In the first watch of the night, O friend merchant, the child is of a thoughtless mind.

It drinks milk, it is caused to play, O friend merchant, mother and father are in love with their son.

Mother and father have great love to their son, all are under the infatuation of the Māyā.

By copulation[1] (of the parents) he came (into the world), he has earned his deeds, he does the work, which he has to do.

Without the name of Rām final emancipation is not obtained, he is drowned in the love of duality.

Nānak says: man will be released (=saved) in the first watch by keeping Hari in his mind.

(2). In the second watch of the night, O friend merchant, (his) mind is filled with full youth.[2]

Day and night he is given to lust, O friend merchant, the blind one has not the name in his mind.

The name of Rām is not in his heart, he considers other (things) as sweet pleasures.

(Who have) no divine knowledge, no meditation, virtue nor continence; they are false and, being born, they will die (again).

Not by a Tīrtha, nor fasting, nor purity and abstinence, nor good works, religious practices and worship.[3]

O Nānak, by love and devotion salvation (is obtained), by another (work) duality is diffused (in the mind).[4]

(3). In the third watch of the night, O friend merchant, the geese have come and alighted on the pond.[5]

Youth decreases, old age gets the upper hand, O friend merchant, life diminishes, the days go.

At the end thou wilt repent, O blind one, when thou art seized and carried off by Yama.

Thou hast made all thy own, in a moment it has become the property of another.

Wisdom is abandoned (by thee), cunning is gone, having practised vices thou wilt repent.

Nānak says: O man, in the third watch remember the Lord, directing (thy) thoughts (on him)!

(4). In the fourth watch of the night, O friend merchant, he (man) has become old, (his) body emaciated.

Blind in his eyes he does not see, O friend merchant, with his ears he does not hear a word.

He is blind in his eyes, his tongue has no taste, his power and strength have come to a stand-still.

There are no virtues in him, how should he obtain comfort, the fleshly-minded one is coming and going.

The straw has ripened, being emaciated it breaks and is destroyed; having come he goes, what is his trust?

Nānak says: O man, in the fourth watch become acquainted with the word proceeding from the mouth of the Guru!

(5). The end of those breaths has come, O friend merchant, a burning fever is on the shoulder.

Not a bit of virtue is contained (in them), having collected vices they will take them (with themselves).

[1] But ਸੰਜੋਗਿ may also be translated by: "destiny," "fate."

[2] ਮੈ is here adjective (Sansk. मय, replete, full of); his mind is filled (=intoxicated) with full youth.

[3] Supply: salvation is obtained. There is no verb nor subject in these verses, and the translation can only be made according to conjecture, as not even any case-relation is pointed out.

[4] The words ਦੁਬਿਧਾ ਵਿਆਪੈ ਦੂਜਾ might also be translated: the other (he who is given to the practices) duality permeates.

[5] The sense of this allusion is: the hairs of men have become white, the geese being white. ਸਰ, pond, lake = body.

He who goes having collected virtues will not be struck in the face, he will not be born (and) die (again).

Yama with the net of death will not be able to overpower him; by love, devotion and fear (of God) he is saved.

With honour he goes (to the threshold of Hari), he is easily absorbed, all pains he removes.

Nānak says: a man (who has become) a disciple, will be emancipated, from the True one he will receive honour.

Sirī Rāg; mahalā IV.[1]

I. III.

(1). In the first watch of the night, O friend merchant, he (man) is placed in the belly by Hari.

He meditates on Hari, he utters Hari, O friend merchant, he remembers the name of Hari, Hari.

He silently mutters the name of Hari, Hari, he adores (him), muttering in the fire (of the womb) Hari, he lives.

He is born into the world, he is applied to the mouth (*i.e.* kissed), father and mother have become happy.

Think of him, O man, whose property thou art, reflecting in thy heart on the word proceeding from the mouth of the Guru.

Nānak says: in the first watch man silently mutters Hari, (who) bestows mercy (on him).

(2). In the second watch of the night, O friend merchant, (his) mind is bent on duality.

Mother and father, pressing him to their cheek, nourish him, O friend merchant, saying: mine, mine (thou art).

Mother and father always press him to their cheek, they think in their heart:

Having got (from us food) he will (again) feed (us).

Him, who gives, he does not know, the fool clings to the gift.

Some one, who becomes a disciple, reflects, he reflects in his mind on Hari, directing his thoughts on him.

Nānak says: in the second watch, O man, this one death will never devour.

(3). In the third watch of the night, O friend merchant, his mind is occupied with care and trouble.

Of wealth he thinks, wealth he collects, O friend merchant, the name of Hari, Hari he does not remember.

The name of Hari, Hari, Hari he does never remember, who at the end becomes a companion.

This wealth and prosperity is a false illusion, having given it up at the end and having gone, he repents.

Whom the Guru in mercy unites (with Hari), he remembers the name of Hari, Hari.

Nānak says: in the third watch, O man, that one, having gone, is united with Hari.

(4). In the fourth watch of the night, O friend merchant, Hari has brought on the time of departure.

Serve with (thy) hand the perfect true Guru, O friend merchant, all the night is gone and passed.

Serve Hari,—not a moment make any delay,—whereby thou wilt for ever become firm (not subject to transmigration).

In union with Hari thou wilt ever enjoy pleasures, the pain of birth and death thou wilt remove.

[1] The following Gurus had apparently the writings of Nānak before them; hence these imitations, which usually add very few ideas.

Do not make in thy thought a difference between the Guru (and) the true Guru, the Lord, meeting with whom (*i.e.* the Guru) the worship of Hari becomes pleasant.

Nānak says: O man, in the fourth watch the night of the devotees is fruitful.

Sirī Rāg; mahalā V.

I. IV.

(1). In the first watch of the night, O friend merchant, he (Hari) puts (him) into the belly.[1]

In ten months he is made a man, O friend merchant, after some delay he earns (his former) works.

The time is passed, the (former) works are earned, as it is originally written, so he has received.

Mother, father, brother, son, wife—amongst them he is placed by the Lord.

He himself (*i.e.* the Lord) causes him to do bad and good works, in the power of this creature is nothing.

Nānak says: in the first watch man is put into the womb.

(2). In the second watch of the night, O friend merchant, he gives way to the freaks of full youth.

Bad and good he does not know, O friend merchant, his mind is intoxicated with egotism.

Bad and good thou doest not know, O man, the journey further on (to the other world) is difficult!

The perfect true Guru was never served (by thee), on (thy) head the executioners of Yama are standing.

When Dharm-Rāe (= Yama) will seize (thee), what answer wilt thou make, O fool?

Nānak says: in the second watch man gives way to the freaks of full youth.

(3). In the third watch of the night, O friend merchant, he collects poison and blind ignorance.

He clings to son and wife in infatuation, O friend merchant, within he is tossed about by emotions.

Man is tossed about within by emotions (desires), that Lord does not come into his mind.

With the assembly of the holy ones he has not associated, in many wombs he will (therefore) suffer pain.

The creator is forgotten (by him), not a moment he has meditated on the Lord.

Nānak says: in the third watch (of the night) poison and blind ignorance he collects.

(4). In the fourth watch of the night, O friend merchant, that day has come near.

Remember thou, O friend merchant, the name communicated by the Guru, it will be thy companion to the court (of Hari)!

Remember the name given by the Guru, O man, at the end it will be thy companion!

This is an illusion, the Māyā will not go with thee, she has made a false friendship (with thee).

The whole night is passed; serve the true Guru and the darkness will become light.

Nānak says: O man, in the fourth watch that day has come near!

(5). The decree of Gōvind has come, O friend merchant, they have risen and gone and their work with them.

Not a bit of delay they (*i.e.* the messengers of Yama) give, O friend merchant, firm hands are laid upon them.

The decree has come, they are marched off, the fleshly-minded are always distressed.

Those, who have served the perfect, true Guru, are always happy at the threshold (of Hari).

The body is the ground (soil) of works in (this present) world, what they sow, they are eating.

Nānak says: the devotees obtain honour at the court (of Hari), the fleshly-minded are always wandering about (in transmigration).[2]

---

[1] ਪਾਇਤਾ may be the participle present (from ਪਾਉਣਾ) or the past part. = Sansk. पातित.

[2] ਭਵਾਤਿ, for the sake of the rhyme = ਭਵਤੇ (ਭਉਂਦੇ).

SIRĪ RĀG.

Mahalā IV.; *Ghar* II.

ČHANT.[1]

I.

(1). How shall the ignorant girl see the sight of Hari in her father's house?

If Hari, Hari bestow his own mercy (upon her), she learns from the mouth of the Guru the work of her father-in-law's house.

Of her father-in-law's house she learns the work from the mouth of the Guru, meditating always on Hari, Hari.

Amongst her friends she goes about happy, at the threshold of Hari she swings leisurely her arm.

The account, as much as Dharm-Rāe (Yama) has to ask (from her), she clears away by muttering the name of Hari, Hari.

The ignorant girl, (having become) a disciple, sees the sight of Hari in her father's house.[2]

(2). The wedding has taken place, O my father, from the mouth of the Guru Hari is obtained.

Ignorance and darkness are cut off, by the Guru divine knowledge is kindled bright.

By the Guru divine knowledge is kindled, darkness is extinguished, Hari, the choice jewel, is obtained.

The disease of egotism is gone, pain has ceased, self is consumed by means of the instruction of the Guru.

The timeless being is obtained as husband, the imperishable, who never dies nor goes.

The wedding has taken place, O my father, from the mouth of the Guru Hari has been obtained.

(3). Hari is true, true, O my father! having met with the people of Hari the marriage-procession is beautiful.

Muttering Hari in her father's family she (the girl) is happy, in her father-in-law's family she is quite shining.

In her father-in-law's family she is quite shining, who has remembered the name in her father's family.

The human birth of those, whose mind is turned to the Guru, is bearing all fruits; having won (the game) the dice is thrown down (by them).[3]

Having met with the holy people of Hari (their) work is adorned (excellent), the joyful man is obtained as husband.

Hari is true, true, O my father! having met with the people of Hari the marriage-procession is beautiful.

(4). The Lord Hari, O my father, Hari gives me the dowry-gift.

Hari gives clothes, Hari gives splendour, by which (my) work is adorned.

By the worship of Hari, Hari (my) work is easy, he caused the Guru, the true Guru to give (me) the gift.

[1] ਛੰਤ (= छन्द), a peculiar kind of verse, consisting of six hemistichs (occasionally also of less); five such verses form a whole.

[2] This (rather poor) simile is used very frequently in the Granth. The girl is the disciple, her father's house implies this present world, her father-in-law's house is the next world, to which she is transferred by marriage (*i.e.* death).

[3] ਪਾਸਾ ਢਾਲਿਆ, the dice are thrown down, in token that the game is over.

In the world and universe[1] the splendour of Hari is spread; this gift, though coveted,[2] is not apportioned.

The other gifts, which the fleshly-minded have and exhibit, are falsehood, conceit, glass and plaiting.

The Lord Hari, O my father, Hari gives me the dowry-gift.

(5). Hari is lovely, lovely, O my father! having met with her beloved the woman is an increasing vine.

Hari is from age of ages, from age of ages, the generation[3] of the Guru is always going on.

From age to age the generation of the true Guru goes on, by which the name coming from the mouth of the Guru, is meditated upon.

Hari, the Supreme Spirit, is never annihilated nor does he pass away, he gives continually and becomes (even) more abundant.

O Nānak, the saints, the saints (and Hari) are One; muttering the name of Hari, Hari (the girl) is shining.

Hari is lovely, lovely, O my father; being united with her beloved the woman is an increasing vine.

Sirī Rāg; mahalā V.

ČHANT.

Ōm! by the favour of the true Guru!

I. II.

(1). O dear heart, O friend, remember the name of Gōvind!

O dear heart, O friend, Hari goes through with thee.

Hari is a companion; no one, who meditates on (his) name, goes uselessly.[4]

The fruits he desires in his heart he obtains, having directed his mind on the lotus of the foot (of Hari).

In water and earth he is fully diffused, the Banvārī[5] sees in everybody.

Nānak gives (this) instruction: O dear heart, burn (thy) error in the assembly of the holy ones!

(2). O dear heart, O friend, without Hari the expansions (= worlds) are a falsehood.

O dear heart, O friend, an ocean of poison are the worlds.

Make the lotus of the foot of the creator the boat, and the pain of doubt will not enter (thee).

(With whom) the perfect Guru meets, he is very fortunate, the eight watches the Lord is known (to him).

In the beginning, in the beginning of the Yug is the Lord; O worshipper, to (his) devotees (his) name is a support.

Nānak gives (this) instruction: O dear heart, without Hari the expansions are a falsehood.

(3). O dear heart, O friend, lade the cheap cargo of Hari![6]

O dear heart, O friend, knock[7] at the immovable door of Hari!

[1] ਵਰਤੰਡ is a corruption from ਵਰਭੰਡ (= ब्रह्मांड), the egg of Brahmā or universe.

[2] ਨ ਰਲੈ ਰਲਾਇਆ, it is not apportioned (or met with), though caused to be apportioned, *i.e.* though some one cause it to be apportioned to himself, try to get it.

[3] ਪੀੜ੍ਹੀ, or generation of the Guru, are his disciples.

[4] *i.e.* Without having accomplished his purpose.

[5] ਬਨਵਾਰੀ, an epithet of Krishṇa, having a garland of wild flowers (Sansk. वनमालिन्).

[6] ਖੇਪ ਲਦਣੀ, to lade an assortment of goods and go about trafficking with them.

[7] ਮਲੀ, lengthened for the sake of the rhyme = ਮਲਿ.

He who serves the gate of Hari, the invisible and impenetrable, has obtained an immovable seat.
He is not subject to birth and death, he is not coming and going, the pain of his doubt is effaced.
The paper of Čitragupt is torn in pieces, the messengers of Yama cannot do anything against him.
Nānak gives (this) instruction: O dear heart, lade the cheap cargo of Hari!
(4). O dear heart, O friend, dwell in the company of the holy ones!
O dear heart, O friend, muttering the name (thou wilt be) conspicuous.
Remembering the Lord (thou art) living in happiness, all (thy) wish is fulfilled.
By former works the husband of Lakshmī (=Vishṇu) is obtained; Hari meets with the long-time separated.
Inside and outside, everywhere he is contained, faith springs (therefore) up in the mind.
Nānak gives (this) instruction: O dear heart, dwell in the company of the holy ones!
(5). O dear heart, O friend, by love and attachment to Hari the mind is absorbed.
O dear heart, O friend, the fish, having met with the water of Hari, lives.
Having drunk Hari they are satiated, nectar is poured out, all comforts are showered down on the heart.
The husband of Lakshmī is obtained, songs of congratulation are sung, (their) desire is fulfilled, the true Guru is pleased.
They are absorbed in (his) skirt, the nine treasures are obtained, the name and all his property the Lord has given them.
Nānak has given (this) instruction to the saints: by love and attachment to Hari the mind is absorbed.

SIRĪ RĀG KĒ ČHANT; MAHALĀ V.

Ōm! By the favour of the true Guru!

I. III.

Ḍakhaṇā.[1]

(1). How shall I see in my heart the sight of my beloved?
O Nānak, in the asylum of the saints the support of life is to be obtained.

Čhant.

Love with the lotus of the foot (of Hari) is the custom of the saints, he comes into their heart, Sir!
Another love is perverse impropriety, it is not pleasing to the servants (of Hari), Sir!
It is not pleasing to (his) servants, without (his) sight how should they have patience one moment?
Void of the name body and soul are decayed, as a fish dies without water.
Join me, O my beloved, O support of my life! having joined the saints I will sing thy qualities!
O Lord of Nānak, bestow a favour, that in heart and body I may be absorbed in (thy) bosom!

Ḍakhaṇā.

(2). He is shining in every place, no other is seen.
The shutters (of the tenth gate) are opened by meeting with the true Guru, O Nānak!

Čhant.

Thy words are quite incomparable; (thy) word, the support of the saints, should be reflected upon, Sir!

[1] डखणा is a peculiar kind of verse, consisting of two hemistichs. The following piece is a mixture of Ḍakhaṇās and Čhants.

Who remembers (thee) at every breath and morsel, his faith (thou art) making full, how shouldst thou be forgotten from (=by) the mind?

How shouldst thou be forgotten from the mind, (who art) not removed a moment, O my life, the abode of qualities!

Thou givest the fruits the heart is desiring, O Lord, thou rememberest the request (desire) of the creatures.

O Lord of the helpless, (who art) with all! who mutters (thy name), (by him) his birth is not lost in the play!

(This is) the prayer of Nānak to the Lord: in mercy make me cross the water of existence![1]

Ḍakhaṇā.

(3). (Who is) bathing[2] in the dust and ashes of the saints, (to him) the Lord becomes merciful.
All things are obtained (by him), O Nānak, the wealth and property of Hari.

Čhant.

Beautiful is (thy) house, O Lord, the rest[3] of (thy) devotees, in hope (on thee) they live, Sir!

In heart and body they are immersed (in devotion), they are remembering the name of the Lord, the nectar of Hari they are drinking, Sir!

The nectar of Hari they are drinking, they are becoming firm for ever, the water of sensual pleasures is considered insipid (by them).

(To whom) thou, O Gōpāl, my Lord, hast become merciful, they have appreciated the treasure (in) the society of the saints.

In all ways they have much comfort and joy, the jewel of the beloved Hari they are sowing up within their heart.

The support of life is not forgotten a moment, muttering, muttering (the name) they live, O Nānak![4]

Ḍakhaṇā.

(4). Whom thou hast made thy own, with them thou art united.
Thou thyself art in thyself, that praise, (says) Nānak, thou thyself hast heard.

Čhant.

Thou, O Gōvind, applying the trick of love and gratifying me, hast enchanted my heart, Sir!

Clinging to (thy) unfathomable neck I have become illustrious by the favour of the saints, Sir!

Clinging to the neck of Hari I have become illustrious, all vices are overcome, the characteristics of devotion have come into my power.

On (my) heart all comforts are showered, Gōvind is pleased, all birth and death is done away.

By (my) friends a song of congratulation is sung, (my) wish is accomplished, there is not again a motion of the Māyā.[5]

My hands are seized, (says) Nānak, by the beloved Lord, I am not influenced by the ocean of the world.

[1] ਤਾਰੀਐ, literally: may he (*i.e.* Nānak) be caused to cross, brought over the waters of existence!

[2] ਮਜਨੁ (मज्जन) must here be taken as an adjective.

[3] Or: resting-place.

[4] O Nānak = says Nānak.

[5] ਮਾਇਆ ਹੋਰਿਆ = ਮਾਇਆ ਦਾ ਹੋਰਾ, a motion of the Māyā (in my heart) = I am not any more affected by the Māyā. But there is another reading, which better suits the context, viz.: ਮੋਹਿਆ, I am not again deluded by the Māyā.

Ḍakhaṇā.

(5). The name of the Lord is priceless, its value no one knows.

On whose forehead the lot is, those, (says) Nānak, enjoy the pleasure of Hari.

Čhant.

Those, who utter (the name), are pure, all who hear it are happy, by those, who write it, their family is saved, Sir!

Who have the society of the saints and love to the name of Hari, they meditate on Brahm, Sir!

Brahm is meditated upon (by them), their human birth is adorned (and) by the Lord his mercy is made full.

The hands (of those) are seized (by Hari), who have praised Hari, they do not run into a womb nor do they die.

Those, who meet with the true, merciful and kind Guru, are flourishing, lust, anger and covetousness is destroyed.

The inexpressible Lord cannot be described; Nānak sacrifices and devotes himself (to him).

SIRĪ RĀG; MAHALĀ IV.

VAṆJĀRĀ.[1]

Ōm! The true name! By the favour of the Guru!

(1). Hari, Hari is the highest name, by whom every one has been created, Sir!

Hari cherishes all creatures, in everybody he is contained.

That Hari should always be meditated upon! without him there is none other.

Those, who direct their mind to the infatuation of the Māyā, go off leaving her behind and will weep in pain.

By humble Nānak the name is meditated upon: Hari will be a companion at the end.

Pause.

I have none other without Hari.

The asylum of Hari, the Guru, should be obtained, O friend merchant! by a great destiny it is laid hold of.

(2). Without the saints, no one, O brother! has obtained the name of Hari.

Those who practise works in egotism are like the son of a whore without a name.

The lineage of the father is then brought about, if the Guru, being pleased, bestow his favour.

By (that) very fortunate one[2] the Guru is obtained, who has put his love day and night on Hari.

Humble Nānak (says): Brahm is known (by him, who) practises the work of praising Hari.

Pause.

In (my) heart a longing after Hari has sprung up.

By the perfect Guru the name is made firm, the name of Hari, Hari the Lord, is obtained (by me).

(3). As long as there is a breath in youth, meditate on the name!

At the time of departure Hari will go with (thee), Hari will at the end release (thee).

[1] Vaṇjārā is the name of a peculiar kind of verse, very likely taken from the circumstance that these verses are addressed to the *friend merchant.*

[2] वडभागी, very fortunate; literally: he whose destiny is great, very auspicious.

I am a sacrifice for those, into whose heart Hari has come and settled (there).

Who have not kept the name of Hari, Hari in their mind, they are gone at the end with remorse.

On whose forehead it was written in the beginning by Hari, the Lord, (says) humble Nānak, they meditate on the name.

Pause.

O heart, bestow love on Hari, Hari!

By the very fortunate one the Guru is obtained, by the word of the Guru he will pass over.

(4). Hari himself is producing (everything), Hari himself gives and takes.

Hari himself leads astray in error, Hari himself gives wisdom.

Those disciples, in whose heart he is manifest, are some rare ones.

I am a sacrifice for those who have obtained Hari from the instruction of the Guru.

Humble Nānak (says): the lotus (=heart) (of them) is opened, in whose heart Hari, Hari has settled.

Pause.

Mutter in (thy) heart: Hari, Hari!

Flee and fall on the asylum of Hari, the Guru, O beloved! he takes away all sins and pains.

(5). Who is contained (diffused) in everybody, how shall he dwell in the heart, in what manner is he obtained?

If the Guru, the perfect, true Guru be met with, Hari comes and dwells in the heart and mind.

To me the name is refuge and support, from the name of Hari (comes) knowledge of salvation.[1]

My trust is in the name of Hari, Hari, in the name of Hari is my caste-fellowship.[2]

Humble Nānak has meditated on the name, he is steeped in love, in love and affection to Hari.

Pause.

Meditate on Hari, Hari the Lord is true.

From the words of the Guru the Lord Hari is known, the whole creation is from Hari the Lord.

(6). To whom it has been written (=decreed) before, they have come and joined the Guru.

In servantship,[3] O friend merchant, the name of Hari, Hari the Guru, is shining forth.

Blessed, blessed is the traffic of the traders, who have laden the goods and stock of Hari!

The faces of the disciples are bright at the gate (of Hari), having come they are placed at the side of Hari.

Humble Nānak (says): those have obtained the Guru, with whom he himself, the abode of qualities, has been pleased.[4]

Pause.

Meditate on Hari at (every) breath and morsel!

Love is produced in the heart of those disciples, whose prayer is (for) the name of Hari.

---

[1] ਗਤਿ ਮਤਿ, ਗਤਿ signifying here salvation (final emancipation).

[2] ਜਤਿ ਪਤਿ, caste-fellowship. ਜਤਿ = ਜਾਤਿ, caste, and ਪਤਿ = patti (from the Sansk. पंक्ति, row, line, which is also frequently assimilated to ਪਾਂਤਿ pānti, or, with elision of the nasal, to pāt, fem.). The derivation which Molesworth assigns in his Marāṭhī Dictionary to पात (see under जात पात) is therefore a mistake; for पात, falling, is always *masculine*.

[3] ਸੇਵਕ ਭਾਇ, in servantship, *i.e.* in the state of being a servant or worshipper.

[4] ਤਾਸਿ = ਤਾਸੁ, on account of the rhyme, ਤਾਸੁ being *masculine*.

Ōm! By the favour of the true Guru!

SIRĪ RĀG, VĀR; MAHALĀ IV.

With Slōks.[1]

I.

Slōk I.; *mahalā* III.

Amongst the Rāgs is the Srī Rāg; if (one) bestow love on the True one:
Hari, the True one always dwells in his heart, whose wisdom is immovable and boundless.[2]
The priceless jewel is obtained (by him, who) reflects on the word (instruction) of the Guru.
His tongue is true, his heart is true, true is his body and form.
Nānak (says): by serving the true Guru there is always true traffic (made).

Slōk II.; *mahalā* III.

Other pangs of separation are all deception,[3] as long as there is no love to the Lord.
This (human) mind is deluded by the Māyā, there is no (proper) seeing nor hearing.
Without the sight of the husband love is not produced, what will the blind do?
O Nānak, by whom the eyes are taken, that True one gives (them again).

Pauṛī.

Hari alone is the creator, there is only, only the court of Hari (as refuge).
The order of Hari alone is (executed), keep the One Hari in thy mind!
Without that Hari there is no one, who removes fear, error and dread.
Praise that Hari, who keeps thee abroad and at home.
To whom Hari becomes merciful, he, muttering: Hari! crosses the difficult existence.

II.

Slōk I.; *mahalā* I.

They are the gifts of the Lord; what will prevail with him?[4]
Some, being awake, do not obtain them, some, having fallen asleep, he raises.

Slōk II.; *mahalā* I.

Sincerity and contentment is the viaticum of the sincere ones, patience that of the angels.
I shall obtain a sight of the Perfect one, (but) there is no place for the foolish.

Pauṛī.

Thou thyself, having created all creation, hast put it into its (several) work.[5]
Thou thyself, seeing thy own greatness, art happy.

[1] Vār is in the Granth a peculiar kind of poetical composition, every piece consisting of two or three Slōks and one Pauṛī. In one Vār are often Slōks and Pauṛī belonging to different authors, so that the whole is an eclectic, artificial collection.

[2] This refers to Hari.

[3] ਪਾਤੁ, *s.f.* deception, shortened from ਪਾਤੁਰ (= धूर्त्तता)? But it seems better to derive ਪਾਤੁ (as *s.m.*) from धावितं, running, worldly activity = प्रवृत्ति. In the same sense ਪਾਦਤੁ is also used in the Granth.

[4] ਕਿਆ ਚਲੈ ਤਿਸੁ ਨਾਲਿ, literally: what goes with him? Who can say anything to him, or compel him to give anything?

[5] The sense is: thou hast created every creature and assigned to them their several occupations.

O Hari, without thee there is nothing, thou art the true Lord.
Thou thyself art existing in all places.
Meditate on that Hari, O ye saints, who gives final emancipation.

III.

Slōk I.; *mahalā* I.

Castes are (but) raillery and names are (but) raillery.
Upon all living creatures is one shade (of ignorance).
If one call himself good:
O Nānak, it will then be known afterwards,[1] when he obtains honour in the account.

Slōk II.; *mahalā* II.

After death it is gone to the presence of that beloved, with whom there was love (in this world).
Life in (this) world is a misery, after that (comes the right) life.

Paurī.

By thyself the earth is made, moon and sun are two lamps (in it).
Fourteen shops[2] are made by thee, (in which) traffic is carried on.[3]
To some Hari gives profit, who have become disciples.
Those death does not enter, who have drunk the true nectars.
They are themselves emancipated (from existence) with their family, and after them the whole world is released.

IV.

Slōk I.; *mahalā* I.

Having exerted his power He has taken a form of appearance.[4]
He who reflects on (that) time, becomes (his) servant.
(His) power is (visible), (his) value (man) does not obtain (find out).
When he obtains (his) value, it cannot be told.
(One) may reflect on the law.[5]
Without understanding (the truth) how shall he cross over?
(Who) practises sincerity and bows down (to him), he accomplishes (his) heart's purpose.
Wherever I see, there He is present.

Slōk II.; *mahalā* III.

By the Guru's natural disposition (or favour) the bridegroom is obtained, (who) is neither near nor far.
O Nānak, the true Guru is then met with, when the heart remains in his presence.

[1] ਪਰੁ = उपरांत्, after, afterwards.

[2] ਦਸ ਚਾਰਿ ਹਟੁ, fourteen shops = fourteen worlds, seven above and seven below.

[3] ਕਰੀਦੇ = ਕਰੀਐ, on account of the rhyme (ਦੀਦੇ); similarly ਛੁਟੀਦੇ = ਛੁਟੀਐ.

[4] It is more suitable to the context to take ਵਸਿਆ for the Sansk. p. p. वसित, dressed in, having taken a form of appearance; the subject is the Supreme (not man).

[5] ਸਰੈ ਸਰੀਅਤਿ (genitive dependent on ਬੀਚਾਰੁ) = ਸਰਾ = شَرع and ਸਰੀਅਤਿ = شَرِيعت, the Muhammadan law; in Panjābī ਸਰਾ is *feminine*, in Hindūstānī *masc.*

Pauṛī.

In the seven insular continents, the seven oceans, the nine regions (of the earth), the four Vēdss, the eighteen Purāṇas:

In all, thou, O Hari, art abiding, in all (thy) decree, O Hari, is (working).

All creatures are meditating on thee, O Hari, holding the bow in hand!

I am a sacrifice for those disciples, who adore Hari.

Thou thyself art abiding (everywhere), doing strange[1] wonders.

V.

Slōk I.; *mahalā* III.

Why is pen and inkstand called for? Write in (thy) heart!

If thou always remainest in the love of the Lord, (thy) love will never break down.

Pen and inkstand will pass away, and what is written will pass away with (them).

O Nānak, that love to the bridegroom will not pass away, which from the beginning the True one has instilled (into the heart).

Slōk II.; *mahalā* III.

What is visible (comes into sight), does not go with, let one ascertain[2] and see it.

By the true Guru the True one is made fast (established in him, who) directs his thoughts continually to the True one.

O Nānak, from the word (of the Guru) the True one is (known),[3] by destiny he falls into the lap.

Pauṛī.

Thou, O Hari, alone art inside and outside, thou knowest the secret (of the heart).

What is done, that Hari is knowing, O my heart, keep Hari in mind!

He is afraid, who commits sin, the righteous one is happy.

Thou art true, thou thyself art justice, why should the true one be afraid?[4]

O Nānak, those, who have known the True one, are united with the True one.

VI.

Slōk I.; *mahalā* III.

May the pen be burnt, the ink in the inkstands, may the paper also be burnt!

May the writer be consumed, by whom other love (or duality) is written.

O Nānak, what is originally written, must be earned, anything else cannot be done.

Slōk II.; *mahalā* III.

Other reading is falsehood, other speaking is falsehood,[5] love to the Māyā (is falsehood).

O Nānak, without the name no one becomes firm, reading and reading (anything else but the name) he becomes wretched.

[1] ਵਿਡਾਣਾ Adj. strange, wonderful (Sansk. विडम्बन).

[2] ਵਿਉਪਾਇ having measured it through, = having ascertained it, from ਵਿਉਪਾਉਣਾ = विमपाना (Sansk. विमापन).

[3] The words: ਸਬਦੀ ਸਚੁ ਹੈ could also be translated: in the word (of the Guru) is the True one.

[4] ਕੇਤੁ = ਕਿਤੁ what for? why?

[5] The sense is: reading and uttering anything but the *name* of Hari is falsehood = useless.

Pauṛī.

Great is the greatness of Hari, the praising of Hari, Hari (is great).[1]
Great is the greatness of Hari, who judges on religious actions.
Great is the greatness of Hari, whose is the fruit of the creatures.[2]
Great is the greatness of Hari, who does not hear the words of the slanderer.
Great is the greatness of Hari, who is giving gifts without being asked.[3]

VII.

Slōk I.; *mahalā* III.

Practising egotism (*i.e.* saying I, I) the whole (creation or world) has died; with no one (goes) his wealth.
By second love (or duality) pain is received, the whole (world) is overpowered by death.
O Nānak, the disciples are saved by remembering the true name.

Slōk II.; *mahalā* I.

In words we are good, in conduct bad.
In the heart we are impure and black, outside we (are) white.
Let us emulate those, O sisters, who, standing serve the gate (of Hari)!
(Who) are in love with (their) Lord, they enjoy pleasures in comfort.
Whilst there is strength (in us) shall we remain powerless and wretched?
O Nānak, (our) human birth is successful, if we join their company.

Pauṛī.

Thou thyself art the water, thou thyself art the fish, thou thyself art the net.
Thou thyself art moving about the net, thou thyself art therein the sebāl.[4]
Thou thyself art the lotus uncontaminated in water a hundred cubits deep.[5]
Thou thyself art procuring final emancipation, having sported one moment (or) twenty-five minutes.[6]
O Hari, without thee there is nothing; having seen (this) from the word of the Guru (I am) happy.

VIII.

Slōk I.; *mahalā* III.

She who does not know the order (of Hari), weeps (= will weep) much.
She who is alarmed in her heart, does not sleep.
The woman, that walks after the will of her Lord:

[1] It might also be translated: Hari is praising Hari, ਕੀਰਤਨੁ being taken as a verbal adjective.

[2] *i.e.* who is awarding retribution to the creatures, according to their works.

[3] Literally: unasked for is the gift of God (read: ਦੇਵ ਦਾ).

[4] ਸੇਬਾਲੁ, Sansk. शैवाल, name of an aquatic plant, the root of which is esculent. It is used as a bait for fish, as it appears.

[5] The Sikh Granthīs explain ਸੈਹਥਾ by *water* and ਗੁਲਾਲੁ as an adjective signifying *deep*. But we cannot detect any etymology for either meaning. ਸੈਹਥਾ is apparently an adjective signifying: *containing a hundred cubits* (ਹਥ); ਗੁਲਾਲੁ is very likely the Sansk. कीलाल *water*. This explanation would suit very well the context.

[6] The form of existence, a creature goes through, before its absorption into the Supreme (ਮੁਕਤਿ), is called the *sport, frolics* of Hari. Hari has his sport in or with the creature.

Is called with honour to the court and palace.
O Nānak, by destiny this wisdom is obtained.
By the favour of the Guru she is absorbed in the True one.

Slōk II.

O fleshly-minded one, destitute of the name, be not led astray, having seen the colour of the saffron-flower!
Its colour (lasts) only a few days, its value is nothing.
The fools and blockheads, who cling to another (but Hari), are consumed and die.
Having fallen like worms into ordure, they are again and again consumed.
O Nānak, those, who are attached to the name, are joyful by the natural good disposition of the Guru.
From the devotees the colour does not go off, easily they remain absorbed.

Pauṛī.

The whole creation is produced by thee, by thyself the daily bread is prepared.
Some eat practising fraud and deceit, falsehood and lies are emitted from their mouth.
What is pleasing to thee, that thou dost, by thyself they are applied to that work.
Some he has instructed [1] in truth, to them he has given inexhaustible store-rooms.
Who eat, thinking of Hari, to them it is profitable, the hand of the thoughtless (= who do not think of him) is beaten.

IX.

Slōk I.; *mahalā* III.

Reading and reading the Paṇḍit explains the Vēda, (but) the infatuation of the Māyā lulls him to sleep.
By reason of second love (duality) the name of Hari is forgotten, the foolish heart incurs punishment.
He never thinks of him, who has given soul and body, who prepares and gives the daily bread.
The noose of Yama is not cut off (his) neck, again and again he comes and goes.
The blind fleshly-minded one does not see anything, he earns what is written before (for him).
By a full (perfect) destiny the true Guru is found, the comfort-giving name comes and dwells in the heart.
Comfort he (*i.e.* the disciple) enjoys, comfort he puts on (as clothes), in comfort, comfort he passes his time.
May not that name be forgotten by Nānak [2] from his mind, by which he obtains lustre at the true gate!

Slōk II.; *mahalā* III.

By serving the true Guru comfort is obtained, the true name, the vessel of (all) qualities.
(Who) has known his own self by the instruction of the Guru, (to him) the name of Rāma is manifest.
He is acquiring the perfectly True one, greatness is with the great.
Soul and body, all is his; offer praise and supplication (to him)!
Who is praising him by the true word (of the Guru), he dwells in full comfort.

[1] The subject is here changed at once; he is = Hari.

[2] Nānak might also be taken as Vocative, and then the translation would be: may not (by the disciple) that name be forgotten, etc.!

(Though) in the heart be silent repetition (of the Vēdas, etc.), austerity and continence, he has lived in misery without the name (of Hari).

From the instruction of the Guru the name is obtained, the fleshly-minded one is ruined by spiritual blindness.

As it pleases thee, so keep me! Nānak is thy slave.

Pauṛī.

Every one is thine, thou art every one's, thou art the capital stock of all.

All are begging from thee, continually making supplication.

To whom thou givest, he obtains everything; from some thou art far, to some (thou art) near.

Without thee there is no place, from which (anything) might be asked; may some one ascertain this in his mind!

All are praising thee, at (thy) gate thou makest manifest the disciples.

X.

Slōk I.; *mahalā* III.

The Panḍit, reading and reading cries aloud, (but in him is) the infatuation of the Māyā and love (to her).

In his heart he does not know Brahm, in his mind he is foolish and ignorant.

In duality (other love) he instructs the world, he does not understand the (right) consideration.[1]

Uselessly his human birth is wasted, having died he is born again and again.

Slōk II.; *mahalā* III.

By whom the true Guru is served, by them the name is obtained; (who) reflects, he comprehends (this).

Tranquillity and comfort always dwell in the mind, crying and screaming ceases.

(Whose) own self consumes itself, (his) heart becomes pure, (if) he reflect on the words of the Guru.

O Nānak, those are emancipated, who are attached to the word (of the Guru), on account of (their) love to Hari.

Pauṛī.

The service of Hari is fruitful, the disciple he (= Hari) receives.

To whom Hari is pleasing, with him the Guru falls in, he meditates on the name of Hari.

From the word of the Guru Hari is obtained, Hari brings him (= the disciple) across.

By the obstinacy of his mind no one has obtained him, go and ask the Vēdas!

O Nānak, he performs the service of Hari, whom Hari puts into (it).[2]

XI.

Slōk I.; *mahalā* III.

O Nānak, he is a hero and great warrior, who has destroyed from within wicked egotism.

The disciple, praising the name, has adorned his human birth.

He himself has always become emancipated and all his family (too) is saved (by him).

They obtain honour at the true gate, (to whom) the name is dear.

[1] The sense is: he does not know nor comprehend that there is (properly) no duality.

[2] ਜਿਸ ਲਏ ਹਰਿ ਲਾਇ; ਲਾਇ ਲਏ, he puts into it, *i.e.* the service; ਲਾਇ is part. p. conj. of ਲਾਉਣਾ.

The fleshly-minded one dies in egotism, his death is spoiled.[1]
In all his (= Hari's) order is current, what will the helpless creature do?
Clinging to another the Lord is forgotten (by him) from his own self (= mind).
O Nānak, without the name all is pain, comfort is forgotten!

Slōk II.; *mahalā* III.

(In whom) by the perfect Guru the name is made firm, from their heart doubt is removed.

The name of Rāma, the praise of Hari is sung (by them), light is made and the road is shown (to them).

Having destroyed egotism devout meditation on the One has sprung up, in (their) heart the name is fixed.

The disciple of the Guru Yama cannot overpower, he is absorbed in the true name.

In all the creator himself is abiding, who pleases (to him), he is put into (his) name.

If humble Nānak takes the name, then he lives, without the name he dies in a moment.[2]

Paurī.

Who is admitted to the court of Hari, is admitted to all courts.

Where he goes, there he is honoured, by seeing his face every sinner is saved.

Within him is the treasure of the name, by the name he is much exalted.[3]

The name should be worshipped, the name should be minded, by the name all sins are removed.

By whom the name is meditated upon with one mind and one thought, they remain firm in the world.

XII.

Slōk I.; *mahalā* III.

The self-deity[4] is worshipped by the innate good disposition of the Guru.

When the spirit becomes conscious of the Spirit (within),[5] then intimacy (intercourse) in the house (= body) takes place (between the two).

The spirit becomes immovable and does naturally not shake by faith in the Guru.

Without the Guru composure does not come,[6] the filth of covetousness does not depart from within.

In (whose) heart the name of Hari dwells one moment, he bathes at all the sixty-eight Tīrthas.[7]

Filth does not stick to the true one, dirt sticks (to man) by duality.

(The dirt) though washed off, does not go off, if he bathe at the sixty-eight Tīrthas.

The fleshly-minded one does (religious) works out of egotism and earns (from them) all sorts of pains.

O Nānak, the dirty (= sinful) one becomes then bright, when he is absorbed in the true Guru.

[1] ਮਰਣੁ ਵਿਗਾੜਿਆ his dying or death is spoiled, damaged; the sense is: by his death he is not absorbed into the Supreme, and his death is therefore not fruitful to him, but a damage.

[2] ਮਰਿ ਜਾਇਆ on account of the rhyme (ਲਾਇਆ), instead of ਮਰਿ ਜਾਇ or ਜਾਏ.

[3] ਪਰਵਰਿਆ on account of the rhyme: ਪਰਵਰ or ਪਰਵਰਾ (Sansk. प्रवर) much exalted; foremost.

[4] ਆਤਮਾ ਦੇਉ, God, who is identical with ਆਤਮਾ, the spirit or soul of man.

[5] The sense is: when the spirit gets knowledge of the spirit (= the Supreme Spirit), *i.e.* when man becomes conscious that he himself is the Supreme Spirit.

[6] ਸਹਜੁ, as explained on p. 94 note 1, composure, ease of mind, which is not acquired without the instruction of the Guru.

[7] *i.e.* it is equal to bathing at all the sixty-eight Tīrthas.

Slōk II.; *mahalā* III.

If the fleshly-minded men are admonished, will they ever take it to heart?

The fleshly-minded one though united is not united (with the Supreme),[1] he walks as his lot has fallen.

Contemplative devotion and (worldly) activity are the two ways (of men),[2] according to the order (of Hari) they (*i.e.* men) do (their) work.

The disciple destroys his own mind, applying the touchstone of the word (of the Guru) (to it).

Even with (his) mind he has a quarrel, even with his mind he holds a Pančāyat, even in his mind he is reconciled.

What his heart desires, that he obtains by his love to the true word (of the Guru).

The nectar of the name is always enjoyed (by him), the disciple does (good) works.

He who fights with others but his (own) mind, will go, having wasted his human birth.

The fleshly-minded one is defeated by the obstinacy of his mind, he works falsehood and lies.

He who overcomes his mind by the favour of the Guru, applies devout meditation on Hari.

O Nānak, the follower of the Guru works truth, the fleshly-minded one comes and goes.

Pauṛī.

Hear, O holy men of Hari, O brother, the word of Hari, the true Guru!

On whose face and forehead (this) destiny may be from the beginning, that man receives it and keeps it in his heart.

The nectar-like word of Hari is the best and highest, from the word of the Guru it is easily tasted.

By that light is made, the darkness is extinguished, as by the sun the night is dispersed.[3]

The unseen, the imperceptible, the invisible, the spotless (Supreme) is seen by the eyes of the disciple.

XIII.

Slōk I.; *mahalā* III.

Those who serve their own Guru, bring their head into account.[4]

Having removed from within their own self, they continually apply deep meditation on the True one.

Who have not served the true Guru, they have uselessly wasted their human birth.

O Nānak, what is pleasing to him (*i.e.* Hari), that he does, nothing can be said.

Slōk II.; *mahalā* III.

The (human) mind is encircled by passions and does the work of (its) passions.

The ignorant, who worship in second love (or duality), are punished at the threshold (of Hari).

Though the self-deity be worshipped, without the true Guru understanding is not obtained.[5]

Silent recitation, austerity, continence—(this) is the will of the true Guru, by destiny they fall into the lap.

O Nānak, (though) they perform service (to him and make) reflection—he who pleases Hari, is accepted.

[1] The sense is: though one attempt to unite him with the Supreme, he is not united, he does not blend with.

[2] ਲਿਵ (=लय) contemplation, meditation (without any regard to the prescribed works) and ਧਾਤੁ *s.m.* (=धावितं) busy, stirring or running, worldly, active life, corresponding to निवृत्ति and प्रवृत्ति respectively.

[3] ਕਿਰਾਖੀ, on account of the rhyme (ਚਾਖੀ)=ਕਿਰਖੀ.

[4] ਲੇਖੈ ਲਾਉਣਾ to bring into account, *i.e.* before Hari, to make worthy, acceptable.

[5] ਪਾਇ=ਪਏ or ਪਵੇ.

Pauṛī.

Mutter the name of Hari, Hari, O my heart, by which always, day and night, comfort is brought about.

Mutter the name of Hari, Hari, O my heart, by the remembrance of which all sins and vices go off.[1]

Mutter the name of Hari, Hari, O my heart, by which poverty and all pain of hunger cease.

Mutter the name of Hari, O my heart, the disciples show (bestow) their love with (their) mouth.

On which mouth the lot is written from the beginning by the true Hari, by that mouth he (Hari) causes the name to be recited.

XIV.

Slōk I.; *mahalā* III.

Who have not served the true Guru nor reflected on the word (of the Guru).

Into (their) heart divine knowledge has not come, they are corpses in the world.

The round of the eighty-four lakhs (of forms of existence) is allotted to them, they die and are born (again) and become wretched.

He does service to the true Guru, whom he (Hari) himself causes to do so.

In the true Guru is the treasure of the name, by destiny it is obtained.

Who are attached to the true word of the Guru, by them always true meditation is made.

O Nānak, whom he unites (with himself), he is not separated (again), he is easily absorbed (in him).

Slōk II.; *mahalā* III.

He is a worshipper of Bhagavān, who knows Bhagavān.

(Who) by the favour of the Guru knows his own self.

(Who) restrains (his) running (mind) and brings (it) into one house.

(Who) whilst living dies and praises the name.

Such a worshipper of Bhagavān will become very great.

O Nānak, he is (or will be) absorbed in the True one.

Slōk III.; *mahalā* III.

He is called a Bhagautī, (but) in his heart is hypocrisy.

By hypocrisy he never obtains the Supreme Brahm.

Who calumniates another, heaps up filth within (himself).

Though he wash off the dirt on the outside, the defilement of the mind does not go off.

He disputes with the society of the saints.

Day by day he is afflicted and absorbed in second love (=duality).

He does not remember the name of Hari, (but) does much work.

What is written before, that cannot be effaced.

O Nānak, without the true Guru being served he does not obtain final emancipation.

Pauṛī.

By whom the true Guru is meditated upon, they do not sleep in distress (fretting).[2]

By whom the true Guru is meditated upon, they are fully satiated.

[1] ਲਹਾਤੀ = ਲਹਤੇ; similarly the following ਲਹਿ ਜਾਤੀ = ਲਹਿ ਜਾਤੇ, ਲਗਾਤੀ = ਲਗਾਤੇ, ਜਪਾਤੀ = ਜਪਾਤੇ (honorific plural, referred to Hari). When the first rhyme (ਗਾਤੀ) is once put down, the following final nouns are often violently pressed into it, though they become thereby quite disfigured and unintelligible.

[2] The words ਸੇਝੜਿਨਸਵਾਹੀ must thus be divided: ਸੇ ਝੜਿ ਨ ਸਵਾਹੀ; ਸਵਾਹੀ = ਸਵਹਿ (rhyming with the following ਅਘਾਹੀ), they do not sleep in distress or fretting; ਝੜਨਾ, *v.n.* to be distressed, to fret, Sindhī झड़णु or झढ़णु. It would lead me too far, to refute all the false interpretations of the Sikh Granthīs, which they put on this passage.

By whom the true Guru is meditated upon, they are not afraid of Yama.
To whom Hari has become merciful, they fall down at the feet of the true Guru.
Their faces are bright here and there, dressed (in a dress of honour) they go to the court of Hari.

XV.

Slōk I.; *mahalā* II.

The head, that does not bow down to the Lord, should be thrown down.
The chest, in which there are no pangs of love (to Hari), burn that!

Slōk II.; *mahalā* V.

From the beginning, O Nānak, I have gone astray; again and again I was born and died.
Mistaking it for musk, I fell into a stinking puddle.

Pauṛī.

The name of that Hari should be meditated upon, O my heart, who executes his order above all.

The name of that Hari should be silently recited, O my heart, who at the end-time releases (from individual existence).

The name of that Hari should be silently recited, O my heart, who removes the thirst of the heart and all hunger.

Those disciples are very fortunate, by whom the name is silently repeated; all their wicked slanderers fall down at their feet.

O Nānak, adore the name! by the name all are brought before thee and caused to bow down (to thee)!

XVI.

Slōk I.; *mahalā* III.

The ugly, ill-tempered (woman), of a false and lying heart, makes disguises.
She does not walk after the will of her husband, the ignorant (woman) commands.
She who walks after the will of the Guru, is putting a stop to all pains.
What is written, cannot be effaced, what is written from the beginning by the creator.
She entrusts soul and body to her husband, (who) puts her affection on the word (of the Guru).
Without the name he (Hari) is not obtained by any one, see and reflect in (thy) heart!
Nānak (says): She is beautiful and endowed with graces, who is enjoyed by the creator.

Slōk II.; *mahalā* III.

The infatuation of the Māyā is darkness, neither this nor that side of it (= the world) is seen.

The fleshly-minded are ignorant and fall into great pain, they are drowned, having forgotten the name of Hari.

Having risen early they do much work, (but their) affection is in duality.
Those who serve their own Guru, cross the water of existence.
O Nānak, the disciples are absorbed in the True one, by keeping the true name in their breast.

Pauṛī.

Hari is omnipresent in water, earth and on the surface of the earth, there is none other.
Hari himself being seated administers justice, all false ones he beats and casts out.[1]

[1] ਕਢੋਇ, for the sake of the rhyme (ਕੋਇ), instead of ਕਢੈ.

To the true (righteous) he gives greatness (honour), by Hari equity is practised.
All praise Hari, by whom the poor and helpless are protected.
The righteous are applauded by him and the sinners punished.

XVII.

Slōk I.; *mahalā* III.

The self-willed, dirty woman has evil-boding qualities and is a bad woman.
She has given up her own beloved (= husband) in her house and is in love with another man.
Her thirst never ceases, she cries out for water.
O Nānak, without the name she is deformed and ugly and abandoned by (her) husband.

Slōk II.; *mahalā* III.

She who is attached to the word (of the Guru), is a happy, married woman by (her) love and affection to the Guru.
Her own husband she always delights by true love and affection.
She is a very beautiful, handsome and graceful woman.
O Nānak, by the name she is a happy married woman and united (with himself) by him, who is uniting.

Pauṛī.

O Hari, all praise thee, by whom the ensnared are loosened.
O Hari, all bow down to thee, by whom they are preserved from sin.
O Hari, thou art the hope of the lowly, thou, O Hari, art stronger than the strong!
The proud are beaten and caused to bow down by Hari, the foolish self-willed (men) are subjected (by him).
Hari gives greatness to the devotees, to the poor and helpless.

XVIII.

Slōk I.

Who walks after the will of the true Guru, his greatness will be great.
In whose heart the high name of Hari dwells, him nobody can annihilate.
On whom he bestows his own mercy, he obtains it (the name) by destiny.
Nānak (says): the causality is in the power of the creator; some disciple comprehends (the truth).

Slōk II.

O Nānak, by whom the name of Hari is adored, they are daily (engaged) in a continual meditation on Hari.
The Māyā is the servant of the Lord, (therefore) she does work before them.[2]
By the perfect (every thing)[3] is made perfect, by his order he is settling (it).
Those who have comprehended (this) by the favour of the Guru, have obtained the gate of salvation.
The fleshly-minded do not know his order, the executioners of Yama (therefore) kill (them).
All disciples, who adore him (Hari), cross the water of existence, the world.
All their vices are blotted out by virtues, the Guru himself is pardoning (them).

[1] ਕੀਉਇ=ਕੀਉ, for the sake of the rhyme.

[2] ਤਿਨ ਅਗੈ ਕਮਾਵੈ ਕਾਰ, she (the Māyā) does work (= is doing service) in the presence of the disciples or devotees; the Māyā must be their servant.

[3] There is no hint whatever to be gathered from the context to what ਪੂਰਾ ਕਰਿ ਛੋਡਿਆ is to be referred.

Pauṛī.

Hari has a thorough knowledge of his devotees, Hari knows everything.
Like Hari none is knowing, Hari reflects on the religious merit (of men).
Why should grief and anxiety be entertained, as he is not striking in injustice?
True is the Lord, true is his justice, the sinful man he is taking away.
O ye devotees, join your hands and praise him! the devotees he is saving.

XIX.

Slōk I.; *mahalā* III.

I will continually join my own beloved, I will put him in my breast and keep (him) in my heart.

I will always, always praise that Lord, by love and affection to the Guru.

Nānak (says): On whom he bestows a favourable look, her he unites (with himself), that is a happy married woman.

Slōk II.; *mahalā* III.

By the service of the Guru Hari is obtained (by them), on whom he bestows his favourable look.

(By whom) the name of Hari is mediated upon, they have become Gods from men.[1]

Having destroyed their egotism (individuality) they are united by him (with himself), by the word of the Guru they are saved.

O Nānak, they are easily absorbed by him, (if) Hari bestow his own mercy (on them).

Pauṛī.

Hari has shown his greatness, causing his own worship to be made.

He himself makes apprehension (ascertainment) of himself, he himself has set up (his) service.

To his worshippers he gives joy, he has seated them firm in (his) house.

He does not give a firm standing to the sinners, gathering them he marches them off to the horrible hell.

Hari bestows love on his worshippers, siding with them he saves them.

XX.

Slōk I.; *mahalā* III.

Evil-mindedness is a Ḍūmnī,[2] cruelty a butcher's wife, she who is occupied with the censure of others is a sweeper's wife, she who is overcome by wrath is a Čanḍāl's wife.

What is effected by the drawing of lines,[3] when (these) four are sitting with (thee)?

Truth and abstinence is the (right) drawing of lines, bathing is, if one silently repeaṭ the name.

O Nānak, in the other world he (will be) the highest, who does not give way[4] to sins.

[1] From being men they become Gods, deities. The meditation on the name of Hari turns men into Gods.

[2] ਡੂਮਣੀ, the wife or female of the Ḍūm caste (Muhammadan drummers or musicians), noted for their wickedness and depravity.

[3] ਕਾਰੀ ਕਢੀ ਕਿਆ ਥੀਐ, literally: What is done by lines being drawn? ਕਾਰ *s.f.* a line (a furrow, Sansk. कर्ष्, Paṣ̌tō کر); the Hindūs draw lines round their cooking place, to keep off defilement.

[4] The Sikh Granthīs explain ਪੰਰਿ by *wish, desire*, but this is only a guess. It is identical with ਪੰਧੀ, which is also found in the Granth (Mārū, Vār II., Slōk II.).

Slōk II.; *mahalā* I.

What is the goose, what is the white heron, on which he looks in mercy?
Who pleases him, O Nānak, him he transforms from a crow into a goose.

Pauṛī.

The work, that one wishes to do, should be told to Hari.
He settles the business by the true words of the true Guru.
In the society of the saints is the treasure, nectar is tasted (there).
By the fear-destroying and kind (Lord) (the honour) of his servant is preserved.
O Nānak, (who) sings the qualities of Hari, (by him) the invisible Lord is seen.

XXI.

Slōk I.; *mahalā* III.

Soul and body is his, to every one he gives support.
Nānak (says): by the disciple the liberal donor is always, always served.
I am a sacrifice for them, by whom the formless Hari is meditated upon.
Their faces are always bright, the whole world pays them reverence.

Slōk II.; *mahalā* III.

By meeting with the true Guru deflection (from one's former ways) is effected, all the nine treasures (that man now) enjoys.

The eighteen prosperities[1] follow (him), he dwells in his own house, in his own place.

The sounds not beaten (by human hands) are always sounding,[2] being absorbed in divine contemplation[3] he deeply meditates on Hari.

Nānak (says): attachment to Hari dwells in the heart of them, on whose forehead it is written from the beginning.

Pauṛī.

I am a musician[4] of Hari, the Lord and master, I have come to the gate of Hari.
Hari has heard within (the house) the cry, he has put the musician to his mouth.[5]
Hari, having called the musician has asked (him): for what purpose hast thou come?
"Give continually a gift, O merciful Lord, the name of Hari is meditated upon (by me)."
The liberal Hari has caused (me) to repeat silently the name of Hari, he caused Nānak to be dressed (with a dress of honour).

[1] Else eight Siddhis are enumerated, but in the Granth their number is swelled to *eighteen*.

[2] The ਅਨਹਦ ਧੁਨੀ or unbeaten sounds, are said to sound in the dasvā̃ duār as a sign, that the personality is merged in the Supreme, by hearing continually these supernatural sounds (Ōm! Ōm!).

[3] ਉਨਮਨਿ, adj., having lost the consciousness of individual existence and being merged in the Supreme or in divine contemplation. The ਉਨਮਨੀ (*s.f.*) is the fifth of the modes of human existence, viz.: जागृति, स्वप्न, सुषुप्ति, तुरीयं, उन्मनी. In Boehtlingk's and Roth's Sansk. Dictionary this signification of उन्मनस् is quite overlooked.

[4] ਢਾਢੀ, a class of Musalmāns, who are musicians and beggars in one person.

[5] ਮੁਖਿ ਲਾਉਲਾ to apply to the mouth, to kiss, to caress.

Om! By the favour of the true Guru!

I. SIRĪ RĀG. KABĪR.[1]

To be sung after the tune: "Ek suān."[2]

I.

The mother thinks, that her son is getting big (growing).
She does not know so much, that day by day his life-time is getting less.
Saying: "mine," "mine" (thou art), she fondles him excessively, Yam Rāu looking on laughs.

Pause.

Thus the world is misled by thee in error!
How shall it understand, when it is deluded by the Māyā?

II.

Kabīr says: give up the pleasure of the world, in this society (thou) must certainly die!
Mutter him, who is omnipresent, O man, (it is) the word of another life,[3] in this wise wilt thou cross the ocean of the world.

III.

When it is pleasing to him, then faith springs up.
Error and mistake depart from within.
Understanding and knowledge (of the Supreme Being) are produced, the mind is wakeful.
By the favour of the Guru deep meditation settles in the heart.

Pause II.

In this society (thou wilt) not die.
If thou knowest his order, thou wilt be united with the Lord.

II. SIRĪ RĀG. TRILŌČAN.[4]

I.

There is a very great infatuation of the Māyā in (thy) mind, O man, old age and the fear of death are forgotten (by thee).

Having seen (thy) family thou expandest, like a lotus, thou lookest on another's wife, O hypocritical man!

[1] Kabīr (see p. 93, note 1), one of the most important reformers of mediaeval India, and at the same time one of the oldest Hinduī writers, is quoted at the end of nearly every Rāg, as well as other famous Bhagats, as a witness for the truth of the teaching of the Sikh Gurus. By profession he was a *weaver*, to which he frequently alludes. He was a pantheist, who equally ridiculed the idolatry of the Paṇḍit and the bigotry of the Mullā. There is still a sect in India, bearing his name (which is by no means fictitious), the so-called Kabīr-panthīs. — I have been so fortunate as to collect nearly all the works of Kabīr, which are still current in India, though some of them appear to be spurious.

[2] *cf.* Sirī Rāg, Sabd 29.

[3] ਅਨਤ ਜੀਵਨ might also be translated: life not sinking or declining (अ + नत); otherwise ਅਨਤ is the formative of ਅਨ, other.

[4] Trilōčan is said to have been a Brāhmaṇ; who he was, and where he lived, is not known. He is not mentioned by Garcin de Tassy in his Histoire de la Littérature Hindoui et Hindoustāni. But as far as may be judged from the use of the word ਬੀਠਲੁ, he was from the Dakhaṇ, where this God was worshipped.

Pause.

A messenger has come from the side of Yama.
Before him I cannot abide.
Is there some, some friend, who will come and say:
Join me, O my Bīṭhal,[1] take (thy) arm and sling it round (me)!
Join me, O my dear, release me!

II.

By many, many enjoyments and passions (lusts) he is forgotten (by thee), O man, on the ocean of the world thou hast become immortal (in thy eyes).

Carried away by the Māyā (illusion) thou dost not remember (him), thy human birth is lost (by thee), O lazy man!

III.

On a difficult, terrible road thou must go, O man, whither sun and moon do not penetrate.
The infatuation of the Māyā is then forgotten (by thee), when thou hast left behind[2] the world.

IV.

To-day he has become manifest in my mind, Dharm-Rāu (Yama) has been seen.
His strong arms break in pieces (men), before him I cannot abide.

V.

If one gives me instruction, then Narāyaṇ is contained (diffused) in tree and grass.
O Sir, thou thyself knowest every thing!
Trilōčan says: he is contained (everywhere).

III. SIRĪ RĀG. THE BHAGAT KABĪR.

I.

One is wonderful, hear, O Paṇḍit; now nothing can be said.

By whom the Gods, Naras (centaurs), Gaṇas and Gandharvas are deluded, (by whom) a rope is applied to the three worlds.[3]

Pause.

The Kingurī of Rām, the king, sounds without being struck.
By his favourable look deep meditation springs up (in the heart) by (its) sound.

[1] ਬੀਠਲ, Sansk. विट्ठल, said to be an incarnation of Krishṇa and much worshipped in पंढरपूर (in the Dakhaṇ), which city he is believed to have visited. Nāmdēv was also a worshipper of ਬੀਠਲ. The Sikhs no longer know what is meant by the word ਬੀਠਲ, and proffer all sorts of guesses about it.

[2] ਤਜੀਅਲੇ is a Marāthī form (त्यजिलें), another proof that Trilōčan was from the Dakhaṇ.

[3] ਮੇਖੁਲੀ *s.f.*, a rope, by which cattle are fastened together. God has bound the three worlds with a rope and leads them as he pleases. (Sansk. मेखल a girdle.)

II.

The furnace is the skull,[1] (under) the horns and funnels[2] a pot of gold is placed.

Into this (pot) a very pure stream oozes, the juice is caused to drop on the organ of taste (= the tongue).[3]

III.

The one incomparable thing, that is made, (is this, that) the breath is made the cup.[4]

In the three worlds is the Jōgī alone; say, who is (their) king?

IV.

By such divine knowledge the Supreme Spirit has become manifest.

Kabīr says: I am steeped in (his) colour (= identified with him).

All the other world is led astray in error; (my) mind is intoxicated by the elixir of Rām.

IV. SIRĪ RĀG. THE SPEECH OF THE BHAGAT BEṆĪ.[5]

To be sung after the tune: "PAHARIĀ KAI."

Ōm! By the favour of the true Guru!

I.

O man, when thou wast in the circle of the womb, thou wast given to meditation and contemplative absorption with the head upwards.

In the mortal body (= womb) (is) no pride of rank, day and night (there is) one thorough absence of ignorance.

Remember those days, the trouble and great pain, now (thy) thought is excessively expanded.

Having left the womb, thou hast come into the region of death, thou hast forgotten from thy mind Hari, the divine male.

[1] ਭਾਠੀ, *s.f.* = ਭਠੀ, a furnace, kiln. ਗਗਨੁ, literally: the sky, the vaulted firmament; thence metaphorically, the skull = the tenth gate (in the skull), where the nectar is distilled, according to the language of the Jōgīs.

[2] ਸਿੰਙਿਆ, ਚੁੰਙਿਆ, Gen. Plur. from ਸਿੰਙਾ and ਚੁੰਙਾ. ਸਿੰਙਾ signifies in the language of the Jōgīs the ਇੜਾ (*s.m.*), one of the channels of the vital breath. The ਇੜਾ is said to be the passage on the *right* side, proceeding from the os coccygis (the lower back bone) and passing through the नाभिचक्र or umbilical region and through the right upper nostril to the head; the ਚੁੰਙਾ (Hindī चोंगा) or funnel is the channel of the vital breath on the *left* side (usually called ਪਿੰਗੁਲਾ); the supposed channel between the two, leading to the middle part of the head, is called ਸੁਖਮਨਾ *s.f.* (ਸੁਖਮਨੁ), Sansk. सुषुम्ना. We shall often meet with these expressions in the Granth.

[3] ਰਸਨੁ *s.m.* The organ of taste (Sansk. रसनं, neuter) = tongue, on which the juice is dropped, to be thence put into the pot of gold, which is said to be the heart.

[4] The breath is made the cup; the sense is: by means of the breath the Supreme is enjoyed, the Jōgī being united with him by shutting up the breath in the dasvā̃ duār. The Jōgī alone is thereby in the three worlds (penetrating them as united with the vital spirit) and their king in reality.

[5] Nothing is known about this Bhagat.

Pause.

Thou wilt again repent (of it), O fool! into what folly and error hast thou fallen?

Remember Rām and thou wilt not go to the city of Yama, do not[1] go about without having been accomplished!

II.

The child is given to the thought of pastime and enjoyment, every moment it is replete with spiritual ignorance.

Mistaking (it) for sugarcane-juice, thinking (it to be) nectar, poison is tasted (by the child), then the five passions[2] (have become) manifest.

Having abandoned silent repetition, austerity, continence, virtue and wisdom, the name of Rām is not worshipped (by it).

Lust has sprung up, its mind is bent on death, the Sakti (= Māyā) has come and bound it round its neck.[3]

III.

In the young man is heat, he looks at the face of another's wife, going and retreating (= right and wrong) he does not know.

Intoxicated in lust, the great poison, he is led astray, sin and religious merit he does not know.

Having seen a son and prosperity this (human) heart becomes proud, Rām is dropped from the mind.

His mind weighs the property of another, who is dying, then being defeated, his human birth is ruined (spoiled).

IV.

White is the hair, whiter than a flower, the voice is (weak like) that of the seven nether regions.

The eye becomes weary, intellect (and) strength flee, then lust falls into the churning-pot.[4]

By hot worldly pursuits (his) mind was confused,[5] in the rainy season[6] the lotus of the (= his) body became withered.

Having given up in the region of death (= this present world) the word of the inherent[7] (Hari) (or sound of Hari), he repents there afterwards.

V.

Having seen (his) body dried up[8] a noise arises, he makes calculation (of the rest of his life), but does not understand (it).

[1] ਜਨੁ = not (ne); ਅਨਰਾਧਾ = अराद्ध (अ + राद्ध).

[2] The five ਸੰਤਾਪ or passions are: ਕਾਮ, ਕ੍ਰੋਧ, ਲੋਭ, ਮੋਹ, ਅਹੰਕਾਰ.

[3] ਗਲਿ ਬਧਿਆ; the sense is: the Māyā has laid a rope round the child's or young man's neck.

[4] ਕਾਮੁ ਪਵਸਿ ਮਾਂਧਾਣੀ; ਮਾਂਧਾਣੀ on account of the rhyme = ਮਾਂਧਣੀ, *s.f.* churning-pot (Sansk. मन्थनी); lust falls into the churning-pot, an idiomatic expression for: to be utterly at a loss.

[5] ਭਈ = ਭਵੀ, from ਭਵਣਾ (भ्रम) to be confused.

[6] ਪਾਵਸਿ, Locative of ਪਾਵਸੁ (प्रावृष्), in the rainy season, when the lotus should flourish and be verdant. The sense is: he has lost his good opportunity.

[7] ਅਵਗਤਿ = अ + विगत, inherent (व्यापक); the word or sound of Hari, who is inherent (in man).

[8] ਨਿਕੁਟੀ, dried up (from ਨਿਕੁਟਣਾ, *v.n.* to be dried up). The Sikhs merely start conjectures about these passages, but do not understand any of them.

He covets to live a quarter[1] (of his life longer) (though) his eye does not see any thing.

The strength[2] (of his body) is exhausted, the soul, the bird has flown off, it is (no longer) happy in the courtyard of the house (= body).

Bēṇī says: hear, ye devotees, who has obtained final emancipation when dying?

V. SIRĪ RĀG. RAVIDĀS.[3]

I.

Thou art I, I am thou, of what kind is the difference?
Like gold (and) the bracelet (made of it), like water and a wave.

Pause.

But if I would not commit sins, O endless!
How would be thy name "purifier of the sinner"?

II.

Thou, who art the Lord, art acquainted with the secrets of the heart.
From the Lord the servant is known, from the servant the Lord.

III.

(My) body adores (thee), give me discernment!
May somebody instruct Ravidās, who is of the same mass[4] (as the Supreme)!

[1] पर = Sansk. पद्, a *quarter*, or a *step, pace*.

[2] तेज्, the energy or strength of the body.

[3] Ravidās (in the Bhakta Mālā called Raidās, see Price, Hindī and Hindūstānī collections, vol. i. p. 124) was a Čamār (चमार) or leather-dresser, and lived at Benāres, not long after Kabīr, whom he mentions. He was one of the twelve disciples of Rāmānand (like Kabīr, who is the second in the number), who himself was a disciple of Rāmānuj.

[4] मभरल, *adj.*, being of the same mass or lump, as the Supreme, or a fellow mortal; the word may be applied either way.

RĀGU MĀǰHU.

Čaupadās; Ghar I.

Mahalā IV.

Ōm! The true name is the creator, the Spirit without fear, without enmity, of timeless form, unproduced from the womb.[1] By the favour of the Guru!

I.

(1). The name of Hari, Hari, to my mind Hari is pleasing.

By the very fortunate the name of Hari is meditated upon.

From the perfect Guru the fruit[2] of the name of Hari is obtained, some rare one walks according to the instruction of the Guru, O dear!

(2). As provisions (viaticum) I have taken Hari, Hari and bound it up in (my) lap.

My dear friend[3] goes always with me.

By the perfect Guru the name of Hari is made firm in me; Hari is immovable, the wealth of (this) Hari is in (his) lap, O dear!

(3). Hari is (my) sweetheart, (my) beloved, (my) king.

If some one bring and unite (him with me), my life is vivified (revived).

I cannot exist without having seen my beloved, my water (= tears) flows and goes on flowing, O dear!

(4). The true Guru is my friend and companion from youth up.

I cannot exist without having seen him, O my mother.

O Hari, bestow mercy (on me)! join (to me) the Guru! humble Nānak (says): the wealth of Hari is in (his) lap, O dear!

Māǰh; mahalā IV.

II.

(1). The destroyer of Madhu[4] is the life of my soul and body.

I do not know any other but Hari.

Would that some friend and pious man would meet (with me) by a lucky destiny, and show me my beloved Lord Hari, O dear!

(2). I, soul and body, will seek (him), inquiring (myself) and causing (others) to inquire.[5]

How may the beloved sweetheart be met with, O my mother?

Having joined the society of the pious I will inquire after him, in their society the Lord Hari dwells, O dear!

(3). My dearly beloved is the true Guru, he is (my) preserver.

I am a poor child, cherish thou me!

My mother and father is the Guru, the true Guru, the perfect Guru; the lotus having fallen in with water opens, O dear!

[1] ਅਜੂਨੀਸੈਭੰ as one word = अयोनिसंभव, not being produced from the womb.

[2] ਸਿਧਿ, the fruit of the adoration or repetition of the name of Hari.

[3] ਪਰਾਣਸਖਾਈ, a companion of one's life = dear friend.

[4] ਮਧੁਸੂਦਨ (मधुसूदन), destroyer of the Daitya Madhu, an epithet of Vishṇu or Krishṇa.

[5] ਭਲਾਈ = ਭਾਲਾਇ, causal of ਭਾਲਣਾ, to inquire.

(4). I find no sleep without having seen the Guru.

In my soul and body is pain, the Guru causes me pangs of absence.[1]

O Hari, Hari, bestow mercy on me, join to me the Guru! humble Nānak (says): having met with the Guru I am happy, O dear!

Māȷ̌h; mahalā IV.

III.

(1). (If) the qualities (= excellences) of Hari be read, (if) the qualities of Hari be enumerated.

(If) the recital of the name of Hari, Hari be continually heard.

Joining the assembly of the pious (and) singing the qualities of Hari the water of the world, which is difficult to pass, is crossed, O dear!

(2). Come, my friend, we will join Hari!

(Who) gives me a message of love from my beloved.

(Who) shows me Hari, the divine male Hari, he is my friend, my companion, my beloved brother, O dear!

(3). My pain Hari, the perfect Guru, knows.

I cannot exist without praising (his) name.

May a medicine and mantr be given me by the perfect Guru, that by the name of Hari, Hari I may be saved, O dear!

(4). I, poor Čātrik, am in the asylum of the true Guru.

May I obtain a drop of the name of Hari, Hari in my mouth!

Hari is the ocean, we are the fish of the water; humble Nānak (says): without water I die, O dear!

Māȷ̌h; mahalā IV.

IV.

(1). O ye holy people of Hari, O my brother, join me!

Show me my Lord Hari, I am hungry (after him).

Make full my faith in the life of the world, the donor! having met with Hari my heart becomes happy by his sight, Sir!

(2). Having met with the assembly of the pious I will speak the word of Hari.

The story (or recital) of Hari, Hari is pleasing to my mind.

Hari, Hari is nectar, Hari is pleasing to (= in my) mind; having met with the true Guru (this) nectar is drunk, Sir!

(3). He, whose destiny is great, obtains the society of Hari.

The luckless one wandering about is struck in the face.

Without destiny the society of the pious is not obtained, without (their) society he is covered over with dirt, Sir!

(4). Come and join me, O beloved world-soul!

Out of mercy put the name of Hari, Hari into my heart!

By the instruction of the Guru the name is sweet and heart-pleasing; humble Nānak (says): by the name my mind becomes happy, Sir!

Māȷ̌h; mahalā IV.

V.

(1). The knowledge of Hari, the Guru, the taste of Hari, Hari is obtained (by me).

(My) heart is stained in the colour of Hari, the juice of Hari was given it to drink (by him).

[1] ਬਿਰਹੁ, anguish or pangs caused by separation from the beloved.

The name of Hari, Hari, the speech of Hari, Hari is in (my) mouth, by the juice of Hari (my) heart is dozing, Sir!

(2). Come, O saint, take me to thy neck.[1]

Let me hear the story of my beloved!

O saint of Hari, join me! I give my heart (to him) who is telling (me) the word of the Guru (=God) with (from) his mouth.

(3). The very fortunate saint of Hari is united (with Hari).

From the perfect Guru the juice of Hari is obtained in the mouth.

By the luckless the true Guru is not obtained, the fleshly-minded one is continually falling into the womb as embryo, Sir!

(4). By the merciful Lord himself mercy is bestowed.

All the filth of egotism and sensual pleasures is cleared away (by him).

Nānak (says): in the shop[2] of the body the disciples are carrying on the traffic of Hari, Sir!

Māǰh; mahalā IV.

VI.

(1). I will meditate on the excellences of Gōvind, on the name of Hari.

Having joined the society (of the pious) I will fix the name in my heart.

The Lord Hari is an incomprehensible, unattainable Lord, having joined the true Guru Hari is tasted,[3] Sir!

(2). Blessed, blessed are the people of Hari, by whom the Lord Hari is known.

Having gone I will inquire after the people of Hari.

I will rub their feet, having rubbed, rubbed (them) I will wash (them); having met with the people of Hari the juice of Hari is drunk, Sir!

(3). By the true Guru, the donor, the name is fixed (in the heart).

By the very fortunate the sight of the Guru is obtained.

Nectar-juice, true nectar is (his) speech, from the perfect Guru (this) nectar is taken, Sir!

(4). By the society of the pious Hari, the true (Universal) Spirit is joined (with man).

Having joined the society of the pious the name of Hari is meditated upon.

Nānak (says): (by whom) the story of Hari is heard and told with (his) mouth, he believes in the name by the instruction of the Guru, Sir!

Māǰh; mahalā IV.

VII.

(1). Come, O sister! join me, O beloved!

Who shows me my beloved, to him I devote myself.

Having joined the society of the pious, Hari, my sweetheart is obtained, to the gratuitous service of the true Guru I devote myself, O dear!

(2). Wherever I see, there is the Lord.

Thou art contained in every body, O thou near and dear one!

By the perfect Guru Hari is shown as being with (every one), I am always devoted to the gratuitous service of the Guru, O dear!

[1] ਮੈ ਗਲਿ ਮੇਲਾਈਐ = ਮੈ ਨੂੰ ਗਲਿ ਮੇਲਾਈਐ, passive construction, literally: may it be joined me = may I be joined to, etc.

[2] ਹਟ-ਪਟਣ is to be taken as one word, *shop* (literally: a city-shop).

[3] ਕੀਚੈ, generally ਕੀਜੈ, a Sindhī form of the Passive = ਕਰੀਦਾ ਹੈ, *is made*.

(3). There is one breath, all the earth is one (and the same), all the light is one (and the same) in all.

In all there is one (and the same) light,[1] (but) individually distinct,[2] it does not mingle, though one try to mingle it.

By the favour of the Guru the one (light) is perceived, I am devoted to the gratuitous service of the true Guru, O dear!

(4). Humble Nānak (says): he (*i.e.* the Guru) speaks words of nectar.

They are dear and pleasing to the mind of the disciples of the Guru.

The true Guru, the perfect Guru gives instruction, the true Guru is beneficent, O dear!

Mājh; mahalā V.

Čaupadās; Ghar I.

I. VIII.

(1). My heart is longing for the sight of the Guru.[3]

It laments like a Čātrik.

The thirst does not leave it, it gets no rest without the sight of the beloved saint, O dear Sir!

Pause.

I sacrifice myself, O dear, I sacrifice myself for the sight of the Guru, the beloved saint, O dear Sir!

(2). Thy face is beautiful, Sir, comfortable is the voice of thy speech!

A long time has passed, since I have seen the bow-holder.[4]

Blessed is the country, where thou dwellest, O my sweetheart, my friend, my Murāri, Sir!

Pause.

I sacrifice myself, I sacrifice myself for the Guru, my sweetheart, my friend, my Murāri, O Sir!

(3). If thou art not met with for twenty-four minutes, then it is to me the Kalī-yug.

Now when shall I meet with thee, O beloved Lord?

To me the night does not pass, I get no sleep without having seen the Gur-darbār,[5] Sir!

Pause.

I sacrifice myself, Sir, I sacrifice myself, Sir, for this true Gur-darbār!

(4). It has been (my good) lot, the pious one is united by the Guru (with himself).

The immortal Lord I have obtained in (my) house.

I will serve (thee), that I may not be separated (from thee) a single moment; humble Nānak is thy slave, Sir![6]

[1] ਜੋਤਿ, light, the heavenly principle of life in the creatures.

[2] The individuality of the soul is thereby asserted.

[3] The following verses are said to be a letter of Arjun to his father, Rāmdās, when living at Lahore, where he had been sent on account of family dissensions. He succeeded his father in the Guruship in 1581.

[4] The word ਸਾਰਿੰਗਪਾਣੀ is properly an epithet of Vishṇu, like Murāri (the enemy of the Daitya Mura), but applied here to his father; rather a gross flattery.

[5] The Gur-darbār (the Guru's court) is the temple at Amritsar, which was built by Rāmdās. Amritsar was formerly therefore called Rāmdāspur, the city of Rāmdās.

[6] This verse is said to have been uttered by Arjun after having been recalled by his father. If this tradition of the Sikhs be true, it would appear that the sons of the Gurus also called themselves Nānak, even before their accession to the Guruship.

Pause.

I sacrifice myself, Sir, I sacrifice myself, humble Nānak is thy slave, Sir!

Rāgu Mājh; mahalā V.

II. IX.

(1). That season is beautiful, in which I remember thee.
That work is easy, which is thy setting on.[1]
That heart feels easy, in which heart thou art indwelling, O donor of all!
(2). Thou, O Lord, art (our) companionship, our father.
Thine are the nine treasures, inexhaustible is thy storeroom.
To whom thou givest, he becomes satiated, he is thy worshipper, O Lord!
(3). Every one puts his hope in thee.
In every body thou art indwelling.
All are (thy) associates, thou art always their support, thou art not seen outside of any one, Sir![2]
(4). Thou thyself procurest final emancipation to the disciple.
Thou thyself causest the self-willed to wander about in birth (transmigration).
Thy slave Nānak is a sacrifice for thee, all is thy play, O Dasāhar.[3]

III. X.

(1). (If) the unbeaten (sound) sounds, (I am) easily happy.
By the sabd[4] I am happy and always delighted.
Easily I practise deep meditation (on thee) in the cavern,[5] O Lord, (who) hast made (thy) seat high!
(2). Having wandered and turned about, (I) have come to my own house.
(The fruit), that was desired (by me), I obtained.
I am fully satiated; by the saint, the Guru, (thou) O Lord, the fearless Supreme Spirit, wast shown (to me).
(3). Thou thyself art the king, thou thyself the people.
Thou thyself art free from all worldly concerns (and enjoyments), thou thyself art enjoying thyself.
Thou thyself sittest on the throne as true judge, all cries and calls[6] (for justice) have ceased, O Lord!
(4). As I have seen (him), so I have described (him).
He has got a taste (of him), who has obtained (his) secret.
Light is mingled with the fountain of light,[7] comfort is obtained (thereby); humble Nānak (says): thou alone, O Lord, art spread out (in the creatures)!

[1] ਘਾਲਿ, *s.f.* putting on; setting a-going. The sense is: which thou settest a-going.

[2] The sense is: none is empty of thee, thou art not outside of any one, but in every one.

[3] ਦਸਾਹਰ is the Sansk. दशार्ह, an appellative of Krishṇa; the Sikh Granthīs explain it by ਦਿਸਟਾ (is appearing), but this is a mere guess.

[4] The ਸਬਦ signifies here sound, *i.e.* the sound not produced by beating, but by coercion of the breath in the dasvā̃ duār, where the sound Ōm! is said to be heard.

[5] The ਗੁਫਾ or cavern is here = the body.

[6] ਪੁਕਾਰਿਆ = ਪੁਕਾਰਾਂ.

[7] Literally: the luminous one, in whom the light (the principle of life) is contained.

Māȷ̌h; mahalā V.

IV. XI.

(1). In which house the wedding-ornament[1] is adjusted by the beloved (= husband).

In that house, O friend, a song of congratulation is sung.

Joy and amusement are in that house; that woman is shining, who is adorned by her beloved, O dear!

(2). She is virtuous, she is very fortunate.

Blessed with sons, and endowed with an amiable disposition, a happy married wife.

That woman is beautiful, skilful and clever, who is attached to her husband, O dear!

(3). She is of virtuous conduct, she is foremost.[2]

All ornaments suit well that intelligent one.

She is of a (good) family, she has brothers,[3] who is adorned with the love of her husband, O dear!

(4). The greatness of her cannot be told.

Who is joined by her husband and taken to his bosom.

Her married state is firm; humble Nānak (says): by the love of her unattainable and inapprehensible husband she is united (with him),[4] O dear!

Māȷ̌h; mahalā V.

V. XII.

(1). Searching and searching I desire his sight.

I enter every uneven ground[5] and every forest (searching for him).

Hari is without qualities and endowed with all qualities: is there any one, O dear, who will bring and join to me my Hari, O dear?

(2). In going through the six Shāstras,[6] in knowing them by heart.

In worship, in (applying) the Tilak, in bathing at a Tīrtha.

In the practice of purity,[7] in the eighty-four ascetic postures[8] tranquillity is not obtained, O dear!

(3). Many years silent repetitions and austerities are practised (by the Jōgī).

Innumerable[9] strolls are made on the earth.

Not one moment comes tranquillity into (his) heart, again and again the Jōgī rises and runs about, O dear!

[1] ਸੋਹਾਗ (सौभाग्य), a wedding-ornament, especially the string, with a bit of gold strung on it, which the bridegroom puts round the neck of the bride and which she wears till widowed.

[2] ਪਰਧਾਨੇ=ਪਰਧਾਨਿ, *adj.* fem.; similarly ਗਿਆਨੇ instead of ਗਿਆਨਿ.

[3] ਸਭਰਾਈ, *adj.* having brothers (ਸ + ਭਰਾਉ), *i.e.* to defend her or take care of her.

[4] ਸਾਧਾਰੀ, from ਸਾਧਾਰਣਾ (=ਸਾਂਧਾਰਣਾ), the causal of ਸਾਧਣਾ (=ਸਾਂਧਣਾ, the Anusvār being usually dropped in the Granth), *to unite.* It might also be the causal of ਸਾਧਣਾ, and could then be translated by: she is accomplished.

[5] ਭਾਤਿ is the Loc. sing. of ਭਾਤੁ, uneven, broken ground, where a man may hide himself.

[6] The six Shāstras are: the Sānkhya, Nyāya, Mīmānsā, Yōga, Vēdānta, Vaišēṣika.

[7] ਨਿਵਲੀ or ਨਿਉਲੀ ਕਰਮ; ਨਿਵਲੀ=निर्मली (by transition of *m* to *v*), *s.f.* purity. This is a peculiar practice of the Jōgīs prior to restraining the breath and falling then into a death-like sleep or torpidity. The Jōgīs are said to purify first their bodies by drinking milk; they swallow then a piece of cotton cloth, drawing it out at the anus, thus cleansing the stomach and the bowels from all impurities.—Relata refero.

[8] This is another practice of the Jōgīs.

[9] ਭਰਮਾਤਾ, Sansk. भ्रमात्र, *n.* a certain large number, corresponding to ਅਨਿਕ ਬਰਖ.

(4). Bestowing mercy (on me) he (Hari) has joined to me the saint (= Guru).
My heart and body became refreshed, I obtained comfort.
The eternal Lord has taken his dwelling in (my) body, Nānak sings (now) the happiness (imparted by) Hari, O dear!

Māȷ̌h; mahalā V.

VI. XIII.

(1). The Supreme Brahm, the infinite God:
The unattainable, inapprehensible, invisible, impenetrable:
The cherisher of the poor, Gōpāl, Gōvind, Hari, meditate upon him in (thy) body, O disciple!
(2). The disciple of the Guru the destroyer of (the Daitya) Madhu[1] saves.
Krishṇa, the enemy of Mura, is the companion of the disciple.
The merciful Damōdar[2] is obtained by the disciple, not by any other votary,[3] O dear!
(3). Kēsav[4] does not eat and is without enmity.
Whose feet crores of men worship.
In which disciple's heart that Hari, Hari is, he alone is (his) worshipper, O dear!
(4). Efficacious is the sight of the endless and boundless one.
He is very powerful, always a donor.
The disciple, by whom (his) name is silently repeated, is saved; Nānak (says): salvation is known by few, O dear!

Māȷ̌h; mahalā V.

VII. XIV.

(1). What thou sayest, must be done, what thou givest, must be taken.
The poor and helpless trust in thee.
Thou, thou art everything, O my beloved, I sacrifice myself to thy power, O Lord!
(2). By (his) decree is the wayless wilderness, by (his) decree is the way.
By (his) decree the disciple sings[5] the qualities of Hari.
By (his) decree (man) wanders about in many wombs; all is in his pleasure, O dear!
(3). No one is foolish, no one is clever.
In everything thy decree is current.
O unattainable, inapprehensible, endless, unfathomable one! thy value cannot be told, O Lord!
(4). Give me the dust of (thy) saints, O beloved!
I have come and fallen down at thy gate, O Hari!
Seeing thy sight my heart is satiated; I am longing to meet (with thee), O Lord!

Māȷ̌h; mahalā V.

VIII. XV.

(1). There is pain, when thou art forgotten.
Hunger seizes (him), he runs about in many ways.

[1] An epithet of Vishṇu or Krishṇa.

[2] ਦਮੋਦਰ, Sansk. दामोदर (दाम + उदर), having a rope round his belly (alluding to an event in Krishṇa's childhood); an epithet of Krishṇa.

[3] ਭਾਤੀ = ਭਾਤਿ = Sansk. भक्त, votary (otherwise ਭਗਤਿ), or *way, manner.*

[4] ਕੇਸਵ, Sansk. केशव, having long hair, an epithet of Krishṇa.

[5] ਗਾਵਾਜਾ, corrupted, on account of the rhyme, instead of ਗਾਵਹਿ; ਗਾਵਾਜਾ itself is meaningless, but that does not matter with Arjun, if only the rhyme be kept up.

To whom thou, O cherisher of the poor, givest the remembrance of (thy) name, he is always happy.

(2). My true Guru is very powerful.

If I remember him in my heart, all pain is gone.

The disease of anxiety, the pain of egotism is departed, thou thyself cherishest me, O Lord!

(3). Like a child I ask everything.

Thou art giving, O Lord, and there is no deficiency of pleasures.

Falling at thy feet I conciliate thee much, O Gōpal, who art compassionate to the poor.

(4). I devote myself for the true, perfect Guru.

By whom all my fetters are cut asunder.

Into whose heart thou givest (thy) name, they are made pure;[1] Nānak is happy in (thy) love, O Lord!

Māǰh; mahalā V.

IX. XVI.

(1). O dear Gōpāl, O merciful and mirthful one!

O deep and profound, O endless Gōvind!

O high, unfathomable, endless Lord! remembering, remembering thee, I live, O Lord!

(2). O remover of pain, O inestimable treasure!

O thou fearless, free from enmity, unfathomable, unweighable one!

O timeless form, not produced from a womb, remembering thee in my mind I become refreshed, O Lord!

(3). Thou art always my companion in every circumstance, O Gōpāl!

Thou art cherishing the high and the low.

The elixir of (thy) name is satiating my heart, I drink the nectar proceeding from the mouth of the Guru, O Lord!

(4). In pain and in comfort I meditate on thee, O beloved!

This good disposition of mind I have obtained from the Guru.

Thou art the support of Nānak, O Lord, by all means I shall pass over (the ocean of the world), O Lord![2]

Māǰh; mahalā V.

X. XVII.

(1). Blessed is that time, in which I have met with the true Guru!

Fruitful is (thy) sight, seeing (thee) with my eyes I am saved.

Blessed are the forty-eight minutes, the seconds and moments and the twenty-four minutes, blessed is that conjunction, O Lord!

(2). By exerting myself (my) mind has become pure.

Walking in the way of Hari every error has been done away.

The treasure of the name was proclaimed to me by the true Guru, all diseases were extinguished, O Lord!

(3). Inside and outside is thy word.

Thou thyself hast told it, thou thyself hast explained it.

The Guru has said: in all there is One (alone), One (alone), there will be no other, O Lord!

[1] Arjun frequently gives no hint as to the subject and all must be found out by conjecture.

[2] The words ਪਾਰਿਪਰੀਵਾ ਜੀਉ must thus be divided: ਪਾਰਿ ਪਰੀ ਵਾ ਜੀਉ; ਵਾ is an interjection, the same as ਮੈ.

(4). Nectar-juice (I have) drunk from Hari, the Guru.
Hari has become (my) clothing, the name (of Hari) my food.
In the name is (my) pleasure, in the name (my) delight and sports, the name is made by Nānak the object of his enjoyments, O Lord!

Mājh; mahalā V.

XI. XVIII.

(1). From all saints I ask one thing.
I make supplication, I give up conceit.
I devote, I devote myself a hundred thousand times: give me the dust of the saints, O Lord!
(2). Thou art the donor, thou art the Supreme Spirit, the disposer of the destiny.
Thou art powerful, always bestowing comforts.
Every one gets from thee his sustenance,[1] bring to an end our drought,[2] O Lord!
(3). By thy sight the house is purified.
The difficult fort of the soul is thereby overcome (conquered).
Thou art the donor, thou art the Supreme Spirit, the disposer of destiny, like thee there is no other hero, O Lord!
(4). The dust of the saints is applied to my face.
Evil-mindedness is extinguished, wickedness of thought has (no longer) a share (in me).
I dwell continually in the house of truth, I sing the excellences (of Hari); Nānak (says): falsehoods have been done away, O Lord!

Mājh; mahalā V.

XII. XIX.

(1). May not such a great donor (like thee) be forgotten (by me)!
Bestowing mercy (on them) thou art attached to (thy) devotees.
That I may day and night meditate on thee, give me this gift, O Lord!
(2). With the blind earth (= body) reflection is joined (by thee).
All is given (by thee): good places (abodes).
Joy, pastime, shows, exhibitions; what is pleasing to thee, that is done, O Lord!
(3). Whose the gift is, (from him) all must be taken.
The nectar (consisting of) thirty-six drugs, victuals and food.
An easy couch, cool breath; naturally thou art making sports and merriments, O Lord!
(4). May that wisdom be given to me, by which thou wilt not be forgotten!
May that mind be given to me, by which I may meditate on thee!
That I may sing thy praises at every breath; the shelter of Nānak are the feet of the Guru, O Lord!

Mājh; mahalā V.

XIII. XX.

(1). To praise thy excellences is thy order and pleasure.
That is (divine) knowledge and meditation, which pleases thee.
That is silent repetition (of thy name), which is pleasing to thee, O Lord; by thy decree (divine) knowledge (becomes) full, O Lord!

[1] ਵਰਸਾਉਣਾ, *v. caus.* to get perquisites, allowances of food, formed from the Sansk. वर्षण, literally: to cause to be rained (gifts, etc.).

[2] ਔਸਰੁ, Sindhī औसरु, drought, Sansk. अवर्ष, want of rain and thence scarcity of food. ਪੂਰਾ ਕਰਣਾ, to make full = to bring to an end.

(2). He sings thy nectar-name:
Who is pleasing to thy mind, O Lord!
Thou art the saints' and the saints are thine, the heart of the saints is won over by thee, O Lord!
(3). Thou art cherishing the saints.
The saints play with thee, O Gōpāl!
Thy saints are very dear to thee, thou art the life of the saints, O Lord!
(4). My heart is a sacrifice for those saints:
By whom thou art known; who are pleasing to thy mind:
In their society comfort is always obtained; by the juice of Hari Nānak is perfectly satiated, O Lord!

Māǰh; mahalā V.

XIV. XXI.

(1). Thou art the ocean, we are thy fish.
Thy name is the drop, we are the Čātriks overcome by thirst.
After thee we long, after thee we thirst, our mind is absorbed in thee, O Lord!
(2). As a child is satiated having drunk milk.
As a poor man is comforted having seen wealth.
(As) a thirsty man drinking water is refreshed: so this (my) mind is happy with Hari, O Lord!
(3). As a lamp is shining in darkness.
As one, who is looking out for her husband, full of desire:
Becomes joyful, when meeting with the beloved; so my heart is mirthful in the love of Hari, O Lord!
(4). The saints have put me into the way of Hari.
By the merciful holy man (= Guru) I have been familiarized with Hari.
Hari is ours, we are the slaves of Hari; the true word (= the name) is given to Nānak by the Guru, O Lord!

Māǰh; mahalā V.

XV. XXII.

(1). (Thy) nectar-name is always pure.
(Thou art) the giver of comfort and the remover of pain, O Hari!
I have tasted and seen all other relishes, the juice of Hari is sweeter than all to my mind, O Lord!
(2). Whoever drinks it, he becomes satiated.
He becomes immortal, who obtains the juice of the name.
The treasure of the name he obtains, in whose heart the word of the Guru is settled, O Lord!
(3). Who has obtained the juice of Hari, he is fully satiated.
Who has obtained the relish of Hari, he is (no longer) agitated.
He obtains the name of Hari, Hari, on whose forehead the destiny[1] (is written), O Lord!
(4). Hari has come into the hand of one man (= the Guru), (from whom) many are benefited.
Many, who cling to him, are emancipated.
The treasure of the name is obtained by the disciple; Nānak says: by some rare ones it is seen, O Lord!

Māǰh; mahalā V.

XVI. XXIII.

(1). Treasure, perfection and prosperity (art thou), O my Hari, Hari, Hari!
The boon of life (art thou), O deep and profound one!

[1] ਭਾਗੀਠਾ is a fanciful word (instead of ਭਾਗ), manufactured to rhyme with the following ਡੀਠਾ.

Lakhs and crores of pleasures and merriments he enjoys, who has clung to the feet of the Guru, O Lord!

(2). Seeing (thy) sight (we) have become purified.
All (our) brothers and friends have been saved.
Unattainable, inapprehensible is my Lord; by the mercy of the Guru I meditate on the True one, O Lord!

(3). For whom all created beings look out.
(Thy) sight some rare lucky one obtains.
High, boundless, imperceptible is (thy) place; that (thy) mansion the Guru shows, O Lord!

(4). Deep and profound is thy nectar-name.
In whose heart (thy) dwelling is, he has become emancipated.
By the Guru all his fetters are cut asunder; humble Nānak (says): easily he is absorbed (in thee), O Lord!

Mājh; mahalā V.

XVII. XXIV.

(1). By the mercy of the Lord I meditate on Hari, Hari.
By the mercy of the Lord I sing a song of joy.
In rising, sitting, sleeping, waking, Hari should be meditated upon through the whole life, O dear!

(2). The medicine of the name was given me by the saint (= the Guru).
My sins were cut off, I became pure.
Joy sprang up, all pain went off, all troubles were effaced, O dear!

(3). Whose side my beloved takes:
He becomes emancipated from the ocean of the world.
Who has known the Guru as true, why should he be afraid, O dear!

(4). Since I obtain the society of the holy ones.
The calamity of egotism[1] is gone by meeting with the Guru.
At every breath Nānak sings (the praises) of Hari; by the true Guru a screen is put over me, O dear!

Mājh; mahalā V.

XVIII. XXV.

(1). He (the Lord) is thoroughly[2] in love with his servant.
The Lord, the giver of comfort, cherishes his servant.
(He brings) water, (swings) the fan, grinds (corn for him), even the Lord is in subserviency to his servant,[3] O dear!

(2). By the Lord he (the servant) is put into his service, after his fetter is cut off.
The order of the Lord has been pleasant to the mind of (his) servant.
He does that, which pleases to the Lord; within (in his heart) he is a servant, outwardly he is a Lord, O dear!

(3). Thou art a wise Lord, thou knowest all rules.
The servants of the Lord enjoy the pleasures of Hari.

[1] ਹਉ, egotism=individuality, considering oneself as distinct from the Supreme.

[2] ਓਤਿ ਪੋਤਿ, *adv.* literally: lengthwise and crosswise (like a texture), Sansk. ओतप्रोत.

[3] ਸੇਵਕ ਕੈ ਠਾਕੁਰਹੀ ਕਾ ਆਹਰੁ; ਆਹਰੁ, *s.m.* (आहर) bringing on, fetching (things) on the part of the Lord; ਸੇਵਕ ਕੈ supply: ਹਥਿ, into the hand of the servant.

Whatever is the Lord's, that is his servant's, the servant is manifest by connexion with his master, O dear!

(4). Who has been dressed (with a dress of honour) by his own Lord:
He is not called again to render account.
Nānak is a sacrifice for that servant, he is a deep and profound jewel, O dear!

Mǎjh; mahalā V.

XIX. XXVI.

(1). All is in the house (= body), not outside (of it).
Who seeks outside, he is led astray by error.
Who has found it inside by the favour of the Guru, he is inside and outside happy, O dear!

(2). A stream of nectar is softly raining down.
The heart drinks it, the word (of the Guru) is heard and reflected upon.
Day and night he (*i.e.* the disciple) indulges in joy and sport, continually he amuses himself with Hari, O dear.

(3). He, who had been separated through his (various) births, is united (with Hari).
By the mercy of the holy one (= the Guru) the dried-up one has become green.
He gets a good conscience, he meditates on the name, having become a disciple he is united (with the Supreme), O dear.

(4). As a wave of water is absorbed (again) in water.
So light is united (blended) with the luminous (Supreme).
Nānak says: the shutters of error[1] are cut down, there will not be (made) again a wandering about,[2] O dear!

Mǎjh; mahalā V.

XX. XXVII.

(1). I am a sacrifice for that (ear), by which thou art heard.
I am a sacrifice for that tongue, by which thou art uttered.
I devote, I devote myself to the gratuitous service of him, who adores thee in soul and body, O Lord!

(2). I will wash the feet of him, who walks in thy way.
With my eye I will see that merciful man.
I give my heart to that friend of mine, who, having met with the Guru, has obtained that Lord, O dear!

(3). They are very fortunate, by whom thou art known.
In the midst of all they are uncontaminated and free from worldly concerns.
In the society of the holy ones the water of existence is crossed by them, all the intoxicated ones are subjected[3] by them, O dear!

(4). My heart has fallen on their asylum,
Having given up (every other) expectation, infatuation and darkness.
May the gift of the name of that unattainable, infathomable Lord be given to Nānak, O dear!

[1] ਭ੍ਰਮ ਕਿਵਾੜ, the shutters of error (by which error was confined to the house) are cut down.

[2] ਜਉਲਾ is very likely the Persian جولان, wandering, straying about, which very well agrees with ਭਰਮ.

[3] ਦੂਤ = Sansk. द्यूत, p.p. of दिव्, drunk, intoxicated. The ਸਗਲ ਦੂਤ are: ਕਾਮ, ਕ੍ਰੋਧ, ਲੋਭ, ਮੋਹ, ਅਹੰਕਾਰ. The Sikh Granthīs explain ਦੂਤ by *wicked, an enemy*, which is a mere guess, as ਦੂਤ cannot be derived from दुष्ट. ਦੂਤ, however, may also be derived from दूद, *causing pain* (final *d* being changed to *t*, which is frequently the case).

Mǡjh; mahalā V.

XXI. XXVIII.

(1). Thou art the tree, thy branch has blossomed.[1]
From (being) large[2] thou hast become small (minute).
Thou art the ocean, thou art the foam, the bubble, without thee none other is found, O Lord!
(2). Thou art the thread, thou art also the beads (thereof).
Thou art the knot, thou art the middle (connecting) gem on its head.[3]
In the beginning, middle and end (art thou) that Lord, none other is shown, O Lord!
(3). Thou art without qualities and endowed with all qualities, the giver of comfort.
Thou art perfectly composed,[4] sensual and given to pleasure.
Thou thyself knowest thy own actions, thou art taken care of by thyself, O Lord!
(4). Thou art the master, thou thyself art also the servant.
Thou art hidden, thou thyself, O Lord, art (also) manifest.
Nānak, (thy) slave sings always thy praises; look a little down on me in mercy, O Lord!

Mǡjh; mahalā V.

XXII. XXIX.

(1). Fruitful is that speech, by which the praises of the name (are uttered).
Some rare one has known it by the favour of the Guru.
Blessed is that time, in which there is the song of Hari (and its) hearing:[5] these are approved of, O dear!
(2). Those eyes are a standard, by whom the sight (of Hari) is seen.
Those hands are good, by whom the glory of Hari is written.
Those feet are beautiful, which walk in the way of Hari; I am a sacrifice for those, in whose society he (Hari) is known, O dear!
(3). Hear, my sweetheart, my beloved friend!
In the society of the holy ones he (Hari) saves in a moment.
He cuts off the sins, the mind becomes pure, coming and going is effaced, O dear!
(4). Having joined both hands supplication should be made:
"May in mercy the sinking stone be taken!"[6]
The Lord has become merciful to Nānak and the Lord has become pleasant to the mind of Nānak, O dear!

Mǡjh; mahalā V.

XXIII. XXX.

(1). A word of nectar is thy word, O Hari, Hari!
Having heard, having heard it, my final emancipation is effected (thereby).

[1] The sense is: Thou art the tree, the branch and flower.

[2] ਅਸਥੂਲੀ is the Abl. Sing. (Sansk. स्थूल).

[3] ਮੇਰੁ, *s.m.* The large middle gem of a necklace, in which the two ends meet. ਸਿਰਿ, Loc., on its (the necklace's) head.

[4] ਨਿਰਘਾਲੁ, dead to all passions and agitations.

[5] ਗਾਵਣੁ, *s.m.* a song (Sansk. गायच); the singing and hearing of the praises of Hari are accepted or approved of, a standard, authority (ਪਰਵਾਣ = Sansk. प्रमाण).

[6] The sense is: May I, who am sinking like a stone, be taken out of the water (of existence).

The burning is extinguished, my mind becomes cool after having obtained the sight of the true Guru, O dear!

(2). Comfort has set in, pain has fled far away.
By the tongue of the saints the name of Hari is praised.
Water and land is filled with water, the ponds are quite full, no one goes in vain, O dear![1]
(3). That creator has bestowed his mercy.
All the living creatures are cherished.
He is kind, merciful and compassionate, all are fully satiated (by him), O dear!
(4). Forest, grass, the three worlds are made green by him.
In a moment this was done by the creator.
Turning his face towards the Guru Nānak adores him, who fulfils the desire of the heart, O dear!

Mājh; mahalā V.

XXIV. XXXI.

(1). Thou art my father, thou art my mother.
Thou art my cousin, thou art my brother.
Thou art my protector in all places, then what fear and grief (is to me), O Lord!
(2). By thy mercy I have known thee.
Thou art my support, thou art my trust.
Without thee there is none other; all is thy play and (thy) arena, O Lord!
(3). All the living creatures are made by thee.
Where, where it pleased (thee), there, there they were placed.
Whatever is made, is thine, nothing is ours, O Lord!
(4). Having meditated on the name I have obtained great comfort.
Having sung the excellences of Hari my mind has become refreshed.
The perfect Guru has congratulated me: thou, O Nānak, hast overcome the world![2]

Mājh; mahalā V.

XXV. XXXII.

(1). Thou, O Lord, art the support of (my) soul, life and mind.
(Thy) worshipper lives by singing (thy) boundless excellences.
(Thou art) the repository of excellences, nectar is the name of Hari, having meditated, meditated on Hari I have obtained comfort, O Lord!
(2). Thou espousest the desire (of him), who comes to thy house.[3]
In the society of the holy ones thou effacest birth and death.
(His) wish and purpose become fulfilled; by the Guru, falling in with (him), thou art shown, O Lord!
(3). (Thou art) unattainable, inapprehensible, no measure (of thine) is known.
The devotees, ascetics and wise meditate (on thee).
Egotism (individuality) is effaced, error has ceased, by the Guru thou art manifested (as being) even in the heart.

[1] These verses apparently refer to a full rainy season. Water and land, *i.e.* rivers, lakes, etc., and the dry ground. No one goes in vain, *i.e.* every one obtains his object, is satisfied.

[2] ਬਿਖਾੜਾ, for the sake of the rhyme, corrupted from ਬਿਖਿਅੜਾ, subst. dim. of ਬਿਖਿਆ.

[3] It must be read: ਜੇ ਘਰਿ ਤੇ ਆਵੈ; ਤੇ is here "thy," and not postposition. If simply ਘਰ ਤੇ be read (as most MSS. do), the verse becomes unintelligible.

(4). (Thou art) the repository of joy, blessing and welfare.
Comfort and easiness is the praising of the name of Hari.
Be merciful, O Lord, thy own name has come into the house of Nānak, O Lord!

Mājh; mahalā V.

XXVI. XXXIII.

(1). Having heard, having heard the information about thee I live.
Thou art (my) beloved Lord, very mighty.
Thy works even thou knowest, I rely on thy support, O Gōpāl!
(2). Singing thy praises (my) heart becomes green (= revived).
Hearing (thy) story I drop all dirt (= sins).
Falling in with the society of the pious and saints I always silently repeat (thy name), O merciful Lord!
(3). I remember my own Lord at every breath.
This method I keep in my heart by the favour of the Guru.
By thy mercy light is made (in my heart), out of kindness thou cherishest all, O Lord!
(4). True, true, true is that Lord.
Always, always, always thou thyself existest.
Thy works are manifest, O beloved! having seen them Nānak has become happy, O Lord!

Mājh; mahalā V.

XXVII. XXXIV.

(1). By (his) order rains have commenced to fall.
O dear friend, having joined the saints let us silently repeat the name!
Coolness, quietness, rest, comfort is obtained, the Lord himself has bestowed coolness, O dear!
(2). Every thing is abundantly produced (by him).
Out of mercy all are satiated by the Lord.
Bestow a gift, O my donor, all living creatures are satiated[1] (by thee), O Lord!
(3). True is the Lord, of a true name.
By the favour of the Guru I always meditate on him.
He cuts off the fear of birth and death, spiritual ignorance, grief and troubles are extinct, O dear!
(4). At every breath Nānak praises him.
By the remembrance of (his) name all nooses are cut off.
The hope (of him) is fulfilled in a moment, who mutters the praises of Hari, Hari, Hari, O dear!

Mājh; mahalā V.

XXVIII. XXXV.

(1). Come, O pious sweetheart, O beloved friend!
Having met together we will sing the praises of the unattainable and boundless one!
Those, who sing and hear (them), are all emancipated; he should be meditated upon, by whom we are made, O dear!
(2). The sins of all the (various) births (forms of existence) go off.
The fruits, which are desired by (thy) heart, thou wilt obtain:
Having remembered the Lord, that true Lord, (by whom) to every one the daily bread is given, O dear!

[1] ध्रापणा, *v.n.* To be satiated, from the Sansk. तृप् (तर्प्), "*t*" being changed to "*d*" and aspirated at the same time by the influence of *r* (Sindhī ढ्रापणु, *dh* having passed to the *cerebral* row at the same time)

(3). By him, who mutters the name, all comforts are obtained.
All fear is destroyed, if Hari, Hari be meditated upon.
By whom he is served, he is passing over, all his works are done, O dear!
(4). I have come and fallen on thy asylum.
As it is pleasing to thee, so unite (me with thee)!
Out of mercy, O Lord, apply me to thy adoration, that Nānak may drink true nectar, O Lord!

Mājh; mahalā V.

XXIX. XXXVI.

(1). Gōvind, the Lord, has become merciful.
The cloud rains in all places.
He is compassionate to the poor and always merciful, coolness is bestowed by the creator, O dear!
(2). He cherishes his own creatures:
As a mother takes care of her child.
He removes pain, the Lord is the ocean of comfort, he gives food to all, O dear!
(3). In water and land is omnipresent the kind one.
I make myself always a sacrifice and oblation (for him).
Always, night and day, I meditate on him, who in a moment saves all, O dear!
(4). All are protected by the Lord himself.
All sorrows and troubles are gone off.
Muttering the name (my) heart and body (become) fresh (revived), (if) the Lord look favourably on Nānak, O dear!

Mājh; mahalā V.

XXX. XXXVII.

(1). Where the name of (my) beloved Lord is muttered:
Those places are golden upper-storied houses.
Where the name of my Gōvind is not muttered, those cities become desolate, O dear!
(2). Who eating dry bread remembers Hari:
(On him) Hari looks in mercy inside and outside.
Who, having eaten and eaten, commits wicked deeds,[1] him consider an offspring of poison, O dear!
(3). Who shows no affection for the saints:
Who commits misdeeds with the Sākats (the worshippers of the Sakti):
By (that) ignorant man his (human) body, so difficult to be obtained, is thrown away, his own root is uprooted by himself, O dear!
(4). O thou compassionate to the poor, (I flee) to thy asylum!
Thou art to me the ocean of comfort, O Guru Gōpāl!
Bestow mercy (on me), that Nānak may sing (thy) praises; keep my honour, O Lord!

Mājh; mahalā V.

XXXI. XXXVIII.

(1). The feet of the Lord are contained in my heart.
All the troubles of the Kali-yug have fled afar.
Tranquillity, ease, understanding, contemplation have sprung up, with the holy ones is (my) dwelling, O Lord!

[1] ਬਦ ਫੈਲੀ is not adjective, but the Format. Plur. (instead of ਬਦ ਫੈਲਾਂ ਨੂੰ).

(2). Love has sprung up (in me) and does not break by any means.
Hari is within and without (me) brimful.
Remembering, remembering, remembering (thee) I sing (thy) praises, the noose of Yama is cut off (by thee), O Lord!
(3). Nectar rains (by) the voice[1] not produced by beating.
In heart and body tranquillity is diffused.
Thy servants are perfectly satiated, the true Guru has comforted them, O Lord!
(4). Whose it was, he has obtained the fruit (of his former works).
By the Lord he is in mercy united with (himself).
(His) coming and going is stopped; Nānak (says): the desire of the very fortunate one (thou art) fulfilling, O Lord!

Māȷ̌h; mahalā V.

XXXII. XXXIX.

(1). Rain has fallen, by the Lord it was poured down.
All living creatures are allowed to dwell in comfort.
The troubles are gone, comfort has set in, the true name of Hari, Hari, I will remember, O Lord!
(2). Whose they were, by him they were cherished.
The Supreme Brahm has become (their) protector.
By my Lord (their) supplication was heard, (their) calamity was brought to an end (by thee), O Lord!
(3). To all creatures he is giving.
By the favour of the Guru he has looked down in mercy.
In water, land and on the face of the earth all have been satiated; I will wash the feet of the holy one (= the Guru), O Lord!
(4). The desire of the heart he is bringing about.
I always, always sacrifice myself (for him).
By the destroyer of pain a gift was given to Nānak; thou gratifiest[2] those, who are imbued with love (to thee), O Lord!

Māȷ̌h; mahalā V.

XXXIII. XL.

(1). (My) heart and body are thine, my wealth also is thine.
Thou art my master, owner and Lord.
Life and body are all thy stock, thine is the strength, O Gōpāl!
(2). Thou art always, always the giver of comfort.
Bowing, bowing I fall down at thy feet.
I do work (for thee), if I please thee (and) when thou givest it to me, O merciful Lord!
(3). O Lord, thou art my credit,[3] thou art my deposit.
What thou givest, that comfort I enjoy.
Where thou puttest (me), there is paradise, thou art the cherisher of all, O Lord!

[1] ਬਾਣੀ *s.f.* voice or sound, not produced by beating (or playing) a musical instrument, but taking its rise in the dasvā̃ duār.

[2] ਰਜਾਣੀ (the causal of ਰਜਣਾ), 2nd pers. sing. pres., instead of ਰਜਾਣਿ, which is more common in the Granth.

[3] ਲਹਣਾ, *s.m.* Literally: what is to be taken or obtained from (ਤੇ) somebody, one's dues, credit. ਗਹਣਾ *s.m.* deposit, pledge (Sansk. ग्रहण), which one is to receive back.

(4). Remembering, remembering (thee) Nānak has obtained comfort.
The eight watches he sang thy praises.
All his desires were fulfilled, he will never be afflicted, O Lord!

Māǰh; mahalā V.

XXXIV. XLI.

(1). By the Supreme Brahm, the Lord, a cloud (containing rain) was sent.
On water, land, on the face of the earth, on the ten regions he made it rain.
Tranquillity (of mind) has sprung up, all thirst is quenched, in all places joy is spread, O dear!
(2). The giver of comfort, the remover of pain (is he).
He himself bestows gifts on all living creatures.
He himself cherishes his own creatures; falling at his feet I will conciliate (him), O dear!
(3). By falling on whose asylum salvation is obtained:
The name of (that) Hari should at every breath be meditated upon!
Without him there is no other Lord, all places are his, O dear!
(4). Thou art my trust, O Lord, even thou.
Thou art the true Lord, weighty with excellences.
Nānak, (thy) slave, says (this) supplication: the eight watches I meditate on thee, O Lord!

Māǰh; mahalā V.

XXXV. XLII.

(1). All comforts have sprung up, the Lord is pleased.
The feet of the perfect Guru are dwelling in (my) heart.
Understanding, deep meditation springs up; (in whose) heart is absorbedness of mind, he knows that sentiment, O dear!
(2). Unattainable, inapprehensible is my Lord.
In every body he dwells near.
The donor of the living beings is always distinct;[1] some rare one knows his own self, O dear!
(3). This is the sign of being united with the Lord:
(If) in his heart he knows (only) one true order (command).
He is easily content and always satisfied, his joy is in the will of the Lord, O dear!
(4). By the Lord, the giver, (his) hand was given (to me).
All the diseases of birth and death are done away.
Nānak is made by the Lord his own slave, by the praise of Hari he enjoys pleasure, O dear!

Māǰh; mahalā V.

XXXVI. XLIII.

(1). Gōpāl, the Lord, has bestowed mercy (on me).
The feet of the Guru dwell in (my) heart.
That creator has espoused (me) as his own, the tabernacle of pain is pulled down (by him), O dear!
(2). In (my) heart and body is settled that True one.
Not any difficult place is seen.
The messengers (of Yama), (my) enemies have become (my) friends, the one Lord is praised (by me), O dear!

[1] The sense is: the Supreme abides in every body, but distinct from it, not mixed up with it. Some rare one knows that the Supreme abides in his own self (or body) and yet is distinct from it.

(3). Whatever he does, that (he does) himself (alone).

By (human) wisdom and cleverness nothing is produced.[1]

He himself assists his own saints, by the Lord (their) error and mistake are taken away, O dear!

(4). The lotus of the foot is the support of (his) people.

(All) the eight watches (their) occupation is with the name of Rām.

In comfort and joy they sing the praises of Gōvind, the Lord; all (his saints) are taken care of (by him), O dear!

Mājh; mahalā V.

XXXVII. XLIV.

(1). That is a true house, in which the True one is meditated upon.

That heart is happy, in which the praises of Hari are sung.

That country is beautiful, in which dwell the people of Hari, (who are) a sacrifice to the gratuitous service of the true name, O dear!

(2). The greatness (and) value (of) the True one is not obtained[2] (by man).

(His) power and works cannot be told.

Thy people live, meditating, meditating (upon thee), the true word (of the Guru) is this heart's trust, O Lord!

(3). The praising of the True one is obtained by a great destiny.

By the favour of the Guru the praises of Hari are sung.

Those who are imbued with love to thee, please thee, (whose) aim is the true name, O Lord!

(4). Nobody knows the end of the True one.

In every place is that True one.

O Nānak! the True one should always be meditated upon, (who is) acquainted with the heart and knowing (all), O dear!

Mājh; mahalā V.

XXXVIII. XLV.

(1). (That) night is beautiful, (that) day is pleasant:

(In which) there is a meeting with the saints in muttering the nectar-name.

Where the ghaṛī, the muhūrta, the pal[3] pass in remembrance (of the name), there life is fruitful, O dear!

(2). By remembrance of the name all sins are taken off.

Inside and outside is the Lord Hari with (them).

Fear and error are removed by the perfect Guru, he (*i.e.* Hari) is seen in all places, O dear!

(3). The Lord is powerful, great, high, boundless.

His store-rooms are filled with the name (containing) the nine treasures.

At the beginning, at the end, in the midst is that Lord; do not compare (him)[4] with another, O dear!

(4). O my compassionate to the poor, bestow mercy (on me)!

The beggar asks the dust of the pious.

Give the gift, (which) Nānak thy servant asks, that I may always, always meditate (on thee), O Lord!

[1] ਜਾਪੈ, Sindhī ॼापणु, to be produced. Arjun uses many words which are preserved in Sindhī only.

[2] *i.e.* Found out or apprehended.

[3] The ghaṛī is, as pointed out already, twenty-four minutes, the muhūrta forty-eight minutes, and the pal the sixtieth part of a ghaṛī (घटिका).

[4] ਦੂਜੈ ਲਵੈ ਨ ਲਾਈ. ਲਵੈ, near to, is originally the Formative (Locative) of ਲਵਾ = Sansk. लय, clinging to, sticking to, contact with; literally: do not bring (him) in contact with another, *i.e.* do not compare him with another.

Mǎjh; mahalā V.

XXXIX. XLVI.

(1). Here (=in this world) thou art, onwards (=in the other world) thou thyself art.
All living creatures are fashioned by thee.
Without thee there is none other; O creator, thou art my refuge and support, O Lord!
(2). (My) tongue lives by muttering, muttering (the name of) the Lord,
The Supreme Brahm, the Lord, who is acquainted with the heart.
By whom he is served, he obtains comfort, he does not lose his human birth in the play,[1] O dear!
(3). That servant of thine, who has obtained the medicine of the name,
Has removed the sickness of his several births.
Sing the praise of Hari day and night! this is a fruitful work, O dear!
(4). Looking down in mercy his servant is accomplished (by him).
Within every body the Supreme Brahm is worshipped.
Without the One there is none other; Bābā Nānak (says): this (contains) all wisdom, O dear!

Mǎjh; mahalā V.

XL. XLVII.

(1). My heart and body are attached to (my) beloved Rām.
All my property shall be devoted and given (to him).
The eight watches the praises of Gōvind shall be sung, may he not be forgotten one breath, O dear!
(2). He is my sweetheart, my beloved friend.
In the society of the pious the name of Rām is reflected upon (by me).
In the society of the pious the ocean is crossed, the noose of Yama is cut off, O dear!
(3). The four objects[2] (are to be obtained) by the service of Hari.
The tree of paradise[3] (is obtained) by muttering the invisible and indivisible one.
Lust, wrath, (all) sins are cut off by the Guru, the desire is fulfilled, O dear!
(4). Which man's destiny has become full:[4]
He falls in with the bow-holder (Vishṇu) in the society of the pious.
Nānak (says): in whose heart the name dwells, his married state (or) retiredness from the world is approved, O dear!

Mǎjh; mahalā V.

XLI. XLVIII.

(1). By remembrance of the name comfort is obtained in the heart.
Out of mercy it (*i.e.* the name) is manifested to (his) devotees.
Having joined the saints Hari, Hari is silently repeated (by them), the diseases of sloth are extinct, O dear!
(2). In whose house the nine treasures of Hari are, O brother!
(Know): to him they accrue, whose gain (they are) from a former birth:

[1] The ਜੂਆ, *s.m.* dice-gambling, is the world, where life is won or lost.

[2] The four objects of human pursuit are: धर्म, virtue; काम, love; अर्थ, wealth; मोच, final emancipation. They are usually called चतुर्वर्ग.

[3] ਪਾਰਜਾਤ (पारिजात), one of the five trees of a paradise, from which every wish may be obtained.

[4] ਭਾਗ ਪੂਰਨ ਭਏ, whose lots have become full, *i.e.* who has met with his full deserts, who has reaped the full fruit of his former works.

(His) divine knowledge and meditation the Lord is making full; the Lord is able to do all things, O dear!

(3). In a moment he establishes and removes (again).

He himself is for himself, he himself is the expansion (of the universe).[1]

He who gives life to the world is not contaminated,[2] by seeing his sight separations cease,[3] O dear!

(4). Putting it into the hem of his garment he causes the whole creation to cross (=he saves it).

He himself causes his own name to be muttered.

The Guru is the boat, by his mercy he obtains it, (says) Nānak, who from the beginning has union with him, O dear!

Mājh; mahalā V.

XLII. XLIX.

(1). He is the cause (causality), who himself causes to be done (all things).

That is a good place, where he puts down.

He is clever, he is famous, to whom the command (of the Lord) is sweet, O dear!

(2). The whole (creation) is strung (by him) in one thread.[4]

Whom he (himself) applies (to them), he clings to his feet.

Whose lotus (heart), being raised upwards has opened, he sees him, who is free from all contamination,[5] O dear!

(3). Thy greatness even thou knowest.

Thou thyself knowest thy own self.

I am a sacrifice for thy saints, by whom lust, wrath and covetousness are ground down, O Lord!

(4). Thou art without enmity, thy saints are without spot.

Seeing whom all sins[6] go off.

Nānak lives meditating, meditating (on thee), (his) error is destroyed, his fear ground down, O Lord!

Mājh; mahalā V.

XLIII. L.

(1). If one asks a false petition:

His death is not put off for twenty-four minutes.

He, who always serves the Supreme Brahm, he, having met with the Guru, is to be called immovable.

(2). In whose heart love and attachment (to Hari) have sprung up:

He sings day by day his praises, and is continually awake.

The Lord, having seized his arm, unites him (with himself), on whose forehead the allotment (is written).

[1] ਇਕੰਤੀ, existing for himself or by himself, separate from the world and at the same time being the ਪਸਾਰਾ, the expansion of the world. Or in philosophic language: he is transcendental and immanent.

[2] ਲੇਪ, contamination by contact with the world; the Supreme is the जगजीवन, the life of the world, but not mixed up with the world and thereby contaminated.

[3] The sense is: though the Supreme is not mixed up with the world so as to be identical with the world (gross Pantheism), yet those who have got a sight of him (have known him) know, that they are not separated from him.

[4] The sense is: the Supreme is the thread, on which all is strung (as beads).

[5] ਸਰਬ ਨਿਰੰਜਨੁ, free from all contamination (by contact with the world), or free from all darkness.

[6] ਕਲਮਲ is the same as ਕਿਲਵਿਖ (किल्बिष), sin.

(3). The lotus of the foot (of Hari) dwells in the heart of (his) devotees.

Without the Lord all are wretched.

(Who) continually desire the dust of the saints, (to them) the name of the True one is a pledge.

(4). In rising and sitting down Hari, Hari should be sung (=praised).

By whose remembrance an immovable boon is obtained.

O Lord, become merciful to Nānak! what thou doest, (I) endure.

RĀG MĀJH. ASṬPADĪS.

Mahalā I.; *Ghar* I.

Ōm! By the favour of the true Guru!

I.

(1). By the word (of the Guru) he (*i.e.* Hari) imbues with love (to him), by his order he prepares[1] (the disciples).

He calls (them) to the true court and palace.

O my true Lord, compassionate to the poor, in (thee) the True one my heart is believing!

Pause.

I am a sacrifice, O Lord, I am a sacrifice, for the beautiful word (of the Guru)![2]

(Thy) nectar-name is always giving comfort, by the instruction of the Guru thou art establishing it in (my) heart!

(2). No one is mine nor am I any one's.

My true Lord is in the three worlds.

Given to egotism many[3] people depart, having practised vices they regret it (afterwards).

(3). Who knows his order, he praises the excellences of Hari.

By the work of the Guru he meditates on the name.

At the gate (of Hari) account (is taken) from all, he is let off, who is shining by the true name.

(4). The self-willed one goes astray and gets no place (with Hari).

Being bound he is struck in his face at the gate of Yama.

Without the name no one is a companion with (him); the emancipated ones are meditating on the name.

(5). To the false Sākat the True one is not pleasing.

Bound by duality he comes and goes.

The written destiny no one effaces; the disciple he (*i.e.* Hari) causes to be emancipated.

(6). In her father's house her beloved was not known (by her).

Separated (from him) by falsehood she weeps with sighs.

Wretched (robbed) by vices she does not obtain the palace (of Hari); forgiveness for vices must be procured by virtues.

(7). By whom in her father's house the beloved is known:

[1] ਸਵਾਏ = ਸਵਾਰੇ, he prepares, he accomplishes the disciples by uniting them to himself, by final emancipation.

[2] ਸਬਦਿ ਸਹਾਵਣਿਆ might also be translated: by the word I am shining, lustrous.

[3] ਘਣੇਰੀ, supply ਸ੍ਰਿਸਟਿ.

That (female) disciple understands (the truth), on the true Being (Deity) she reflects.
Her coming and going are brought to a stop, she is absorbed in the true name.
(8). The disciple comprehends (him, who) is called inexpressible.
To the true one the true Lord is pleasing.
Nānak says a true word: who is united with the True one, he sings his praises.

Mājh; mahalā III.; *Ghar* I.

I. II.

(1). (Whose) destiny it is, (him) the true Guru unites (with Hari).

He applies his mind to the service (of Hari), to the remembrance (of the name of Hari), and to the word (of the Guru).

Having continually destroyed his egotism, comfort is obtained (by him), the infatuation of the Māyā has ceased.[1]

Pause.

I am devoted, Lord, I am devoted, I am a sacrifice (to them, who are) devoted to the true Guru.

By the doctrine of the Guru light has been made (in their) heart, day by day (they are) singing the praises of Hari.

(2). If he search (his) body and heart, then he obtains the name.
He keeps back busy stirring[2] and checks it.
Day by day he sings the word of the Guru, easily he is making adoration (to Hari).
(3). Within this body is an incalculable thing.
If from the mouth of the Guru the True one be obtained, then it is seen.

There are nine gates (to the body), in the tenth[3] he is emancipated and causes the unbeaten sound to be sounded.

(4). True is the Lord, of a true name.
Who by the favour of the Guru causes him to dwell in (his) heart:

He remains day by day and continually imbued with his love, and obtains acuteness of mind at the true gate.

(5). Who has not got knowledge of sin and religious merit:
She clings to duality and is led astray by error.
Blind by ignorance she does not know the way, again and again she comes and goes.
(6). From the service of the Guru comfort is always obtained.
"I," "I," "mine," is stopped.

By the discourse of the Guru darkness is blotted out, the shutters, hard like adamant, he (the Guru) is opening.

(7). Having destroyed egotism (individuality) he (Hari) is established in the mind.
The mind is always directed on the feet of the Guru.
By the mercy of the Guru heart and body are pure, (it is) meditating on the pure name.
(8). Life and death (rest) all with thee.
On whom thou bestowest (thy favour), to him thou givest greatness.
Nānak (says): Meditate thou always on the name, thou art (thus) adjusting[4] (thy) birth and death.

[1] ਚੁਕਾਵਲਿਆ, the last three syllables, ਵਲਿਆ, are a mere alliteration, without any meaning, as the whole cannot be taken here as verbal adjective.

[2] ਧਾਵਤੁ *s.m.*, Sansk. धावितं, busy stirring, running after the things of this world (the same as प्रवृत्ति).

[3] He who concentrates the vital air or breath in the tenth gate (from which the soul takes its flight from the body) is already emancipated and hears there the Ōm.

[4] The sense is: thou art putting a stop to.

Mājh; mahalā III.

II. III.

(1). My Lord is spotless, unattainable, boundless.

Without scales he weighs the world.

Who becomes a disciple, he comprehends (him), having recited (his) qualities he is absorbed in him, who is endowed with (all) qualities.

Pause.

I am devoted, I am devoted (to them), O Lord, who make the name of Hari dwell in (their) heart.

Those who stick to the True one are daily awake, at the true gate they obtain lustre.

(2). He himself hears and he himself sees.

On whom he bestows a favourable look, that man is of account.

Whom he himself applies to (himself), he is applied, the disciple is acquiring the True one.

(3). Whom he himself leads astray, where will he obtain a (helping) hand?

What is written before, that cannot be effaced.

With whom the true Guru has met, they are very fortunate, on account of (their) perfect destiny he is uniting (them with Hari).

(4). In her father's house the woman was daily asleep.

She is forgotten by her beloved (husband), on account of her vice she is sent away.

Daily and continually she goes about lamenting, without her beloved she gets no sleep.

(5). Who has known in her father's house the giver of comfort:

She, having destroyed egotism, has recognized him from the word (of the Guru).

(Her) bed is pleasant, her beloved she always enjoys, she is making true love (to him).

(6). Eighty-four lakhs of living beings have been produced.

On whom he (Hari) bestows a glance of favour, him he makes fall in with the Guru.

He cuts off his sins, his servant is always pure, at the true gate he is shining (lustrous) by the name.

(7). If he asks account, by whom is it given?

There is no happiness also the second and third (time).

The true Lord himself pardons, he himself having pardoned is uniting (them with himself).

(8). He himself does (everything) and causes it to be done (by others).

By the word of the perfect Guru he causes (people) to be united (with himself).[1]

Nānak (says): (who) obtains the greatness of the name, (him) he himself is uniting to union (with himself).

Mājh; mahalā III.

III. IV.

(1). He himself, the only One, goes about concealed.[2]

When (by) the disciple he is seen, then this (human) mind is changed.

Having abandoned (worldly) thirst he obtains ease and comfort, the One is established (by him) in his heart.

Pause.

I am devoted, I am devoted (to them), O Lord, (who are) applying (their) mind to the only One.

By the doctrine of the Guru (their) mind has come to the house of the (only) One,[3] (who is) colouring (them) with true colour.[4]

[1] The primary cause of union with Hari is he himself and the instrumental cause the Guru.

[2] The sense is: the Absolute Being is underlying everything, but not visibly.

[3] The sense of ਘਰਿ ਆਉਣਾ, to come to the house of any one, is: to become intimately connected.

[4] Colouring with true colour = steeping or imbuing with true love.

(2). This world is gone astray, by thyself it is led astray.
Having forgotten the One it has become attached to another.
Daily and continually it goes about, being led astray by error, without the name it suffers pain.
(3). Who are in love with the disposer of the destiny:
They are known in the four ages by the service of the Guru (= God).
To whom he himself gives greatness, he is absorbed in the name of Hari.
(4). On account of the spiritual blindness caused by the Māyā he[1] does not think of Hari.
Being bound he (Hari) makes him suffer pain in the city of Yama.
He is blind and deaf and sees nothing; (this) self-willed (man) is consumed on account of his sin.
(5). Who, being imbued with one love, apply deep meditation on thyself:
They are agreeable to thy mind by their love and devotion.
Who always serve the true Guru, the giver of comfort, all their wishes thou thyself art fulfilling.
(6). O Hari, (I am) always in thy asylum!
Thou thyself pardonest and givest greatness.
Death does not come near him, who is meditating on the name of Hari, Hari.
(7). Who are day by day steeped in the love[2] of Hari:
They are united by my Lord, united to union (with himself).
The true ones are continually in thy asylum, thou thyself art teaching them the truth (or: the True one).
(8). By whom the True one is known, they are absorbed in the True one.
They sing the excellences of Hari, they praise the True one.
Nānak (says): (those who are) attached to the name, (are) Bairāgīs, in their own house they apply themselves to deep meditation.

Mājh; mahalā III.

IV. V.

(1). Who dies by the word (instruction of the Guru), he, being dead, is born (again, anew).
Death does not press him down, pain does not torment him.
Light, being blended with the Luminous (Supreme Being), is absorbed (in him), the mind, having heard (the word of the Guru), is absorbed in the True one.

Pause.

I am devoted, I am devoted, O Lord, (to them, who) from the name of Hari obtain lustre.
Serving the true Guru (their) mind is applied to the True one, by the doctrine of the Guru they are easily absorbed.
(2). (Her) body is raw and wears raw clothing.
Clinging to another (but God) she does not attain the palace (of Hari).
Day by day, quickly, and day and night she goes about, without the beloved she incurs much pain.
(3). Body and caste do not go onward (to the other world).
Where account is asked, there she is set free, who acquires the True one.
Those, who serve the true Guru, are blessed here and there, they are absorbed in the name.
(4). Who with fear and faith shows love (to him):
She attains by the favour of the Guru the palace and house (of Hari).
Daily and always, by day and night, he (Hari) dallies (with her), he is applying (to her) colour of majīṭh.[3]

[1] The subject is ਮਨਮੁਖ.

[2] ਭਾਏ = ਭਾਇ ਰਾਤੇ, steeped in love.

[3] ਮਜੀਠੈ ਰੰਗੁ, colour or dye made from majīṭh (*s.f.*), a red dye, that does not go off. The sense is: he steeps her in true love.

(5). The beloved is always abiding with all.

By the favour of the Guru he casts some glance of favour.

My Lord is far higher than high, bestowing mercy he himself is uniting (with himself).

(6). By the infatuation of the Māyā the world has fallen asleep.

From whom the sleep[1] (comes), he awakes (it), by the instruction of the Guru he is imparting[2] sagacity of mind (to the world).

(7). Who drinks nectar,[3] he removes (his) error.

By the favour of the Guru he obtains final emancipation.

Who is given to devotion is always a Bairāgī; who destroys his own self, (him) he (Hari) is uniting (with himself).[4]

(8). He himself produces (the creatures) and puts (them) into their occupation.

To the eighty-four lakhs of (living creatures) he himself gives their daily bread.

Nānak (says): those, who meditate on the name, are attached to the True one; what is pleasing to him, that work he causes to be done.

Mājh; mahalā III.

V. VI.

(1). Within (the body) a diamond and a ruby are made (by Hari).

By the word of the Guru he (Hari) causes examination (of it) to be made.

In (whose) lap the True one is (and who) praise the True one, (to them) the True one is applying the touchstone.

Pause.

I am devoted, O Lord, I am devoted (to them, who) fix the word of the Guru in (their) hearts.

In the instruction[5] of the Guru he, who is void of all darkness, is obtained (by them); the Luminous one is blending light (with himself).

(2). Within the body is a large outlay (of things).

The pure name is very unattainable and boundless.

He, who becomes a disciple, obtains it; he himself (Hari) bestows and procures it.

(3). My Lord makes fast the True one (in me).

By the favour of the Guru he applies (my) mind to the True one.

He who is truer than true, exists in all places, the true ones are absorbed in the True one.

(4). Fearless and true is my beloved (Lord).

Sins and vices he is cutting off.

(By whom) he is reflected upon in love and affection, him he is causing to be made firm in (his) fear, love and attachment.

(5). Thy worship is true, if it is pleasing to (thee), the True one.

[1] ਸੁਤਾ is here subst. m. sleep (सुप्त).

[2] ਪਾਉਲਾ (ਪਾਵਲਿਆ) implies the same subject as ਜਾਗਾਏ, it must therefore be causal of ਪਵਲਾ (पतन), to fall, to be allotted.

[3] ਅਪਿਉ, *s.m.* nectar (from अमृत, *m* being changed to *v* and thence to *p*, and *t* being elided).

[4] But it is perhaps better to retain the same subject for the whole sentence and to translate: he who destroys his own self, is obtaining (ਮਿਲਾਵਲਿਆ) it (*i.e.* the ਭਗਤਿ). As no subject is indicated, it is difficult to say which is meant.

[5] ਅੰਜਨੁ, literally: collyrium for the eyes; fig., the instruction of the Guru, considered as a means to sharpen the (spiritual) eyes. There is a play of words between ਅੰਜਨੁ and ਨਿਰੰਜਨੁ, which cannot be rendered in English.

Thou thyself givest (it) and dost not repent (of it).

(Thou art) the only donor of all living creatures; having destroyed by the word (of the Guru) (thou art) vivifying (again).

(6). O Hari, without thee I have not any one!

O Hari, thee I serve and thee I praise!

Do thyself unite (me with thyself), O true Lord! by a perfect destiny thou art obtained.

(7). I have none other like thee.

By thy favourable look the body is prospering.

Who day by day remembers and keeps (thee) in mind, (him) thou protectest, O Hari! the disciple is easily absorbed (in thee).

(8). Like thee I have none other.

By thyself (creation) is made, by thyself destroyed.

Thou thyself art forming and breaking (again); Nānak is shining (= becomes lustrous) by the name.

Mājh; mahalā III.

VI. VII.

(1). Everybody he himself is enjoying.

The unattainable, boundless one is present invisibly.

(By whom) my Lord Hari is meditated upon by means of the word of the Guru, he is easily absorbed in the True one.

Pause.

I am devoted, O Lord, I am devoted (to them, who are) fixing the word of the Guru in (their) heart.

(When) the word is understood, then they fight with (their) mind, having destroyed (their worldly) desires they are absorbed (in the Supreme).

(2). The five drunken ones[1] rob the world.

The blind self-willed man takes no notice nor care (of it).

He who becomes a disciple, watches his own house, the five drunken ones he consumes (destroys) by means of the word (of the Guru).

(3). Some disciples are always steeped in true colour (love).

Easily they serve the Lord, being daily intoxicated (in his love).

Having met with their beloved they sing the praises of the True one and obtain lustre at the gate of Hari.

(4). First by the One his own self was produced.

Secondly duality,[2] (and thirdly) the threefold Māyā.

The fourth step is the high (step) of the disciple,[3] (in which) he is acquiring the perfectly True one.

(5). He is quite true, who is pleasing to the True one.

By whom the True one is known, he is easily absorbed (in him).

It is the work (business) of the disciple that he serve the True one, (and) in the True one he is (then) absorbed.

[1] ਦੂਤ, see p. 142, note 3.

[2] ਦੁਬਿਧਾ, duality; by creation the subject (God) became object. First the subtle elements were produced, and thence the Māyā, the illusive world. Whatever is created, is pervaded by the three Guṇas (Satō, Rajō, Tamō). In the first elementary creation the three Guṇas were in equipoise, but in the grosser creation the Guṇas are distributed unequally.

[3] ਚਉਥੀ ਪਉੜੀ, the fourth step or state (Sansk. तुरीयं), that of complete abstraction from without and absorption in the Deity, so that the consciousness of individuality is lost.

(6). Without the True one there is none other.

The world, clinging to another one, is wasted and dead.

He, who becomes a disciple, knows the (only) One, serving the (only) One he obtains comfort.

(7). All living creatures are in thy asylum.

Thou thyself, putting (them) down, seest all the rough and perfect chess-figures.

Day by day thou thyself causest the work to be done (by them), thou thyself unitest to union (with thyself).

(8). Thou thyself joinest (them to thee) and seest (them) in (thy) presence.

In all thou thyself art brimful.

Nānak (says): he himself abides (in them); the disciple gets brightness of intellect.

Mäǰh; mahalā III.

VII. VIII.

(1). The nectar-speech of the Guru is sweet.

Some rare disciple has tasted and seen it.

In (his) heart there is light, he drinks the great juice (of Hari), at the true gate he lifts up (his) voice.[1]

Pause.

I am devoted, O Lord, I am devoted (to them, who) apply (their) mind to the feet of the Guru.

The true Guru is a pond of nectar; (whose) mind is true, (his) filth he (*i.e.* the Guru) is removing by means of the name!

(2). No one has obtained (found out) thy end, O True one!

By the favour of the Guru some rare one has applied his thoughts (to thee).

He never can praise thee enough, to whom thou impartest a hunger after the true name.

(3). The One is seen (by him) and none other.

By the favour of the Guru nectar is drunk (by him).

By the word (instruction) of the Guru his thirst is quenched, naturally he is entering comfort.

(4). Who gives up the jewel-thing (*i.e.* the name), like a straw:

Is a blind fleshly-minded man, that clings to another love (duality).

What he sows, that fruit he obtains, not (even) in a dream he gets comfort.

(5). On whom he (*i.e.* Hari) bestows his own mercy, that man obtains it.

(Who) fixes the word of the Guru in his mind:

He remains day by day always in the fear (of Hari), and having destroyed (other) fear he is removing his error.

(6). (Whose) error is removed, he obtains always comfort.

By the favour of the Guru the highest step (*i.e.* final emancipation) is attained.

His heart is pure, his speech is pure, he is naturally singing the praises of Hari.

(7). He (*i.e.* the Panḍit) explains the Smriti, Shāstras and the Vēda.

(But) being led astray by error he does not know the truth (the Deity).

Without serving the true Guru he does not obtain comfort, he is earning pain upon pain.

(8). He himself does (everything), to whom will one say anything?

One should go tell, if a mistake be made (by him).

Nānak (says): he himself does and causes to be done (everything); who praises (the name), is absorbed in the name.

[1] Literally: he sounds his voice, *i.e.* he makes himself heard.

Māǰh; mahalā III.

VIII. IX.

(1). He himself colours with natural ease.
By the word of the Guru Hari applies the colour.
Mind, body and tongue are steeped in deep red colour, by fear and faith the colour is applied.

Pause.

I am devoted, O Lord, I am devoted (to them, who) cause to dwell the Fearless one in (their) mind.

(By whom) by the mercy of the Guru the fearless Hari is meditated upon, (them) he makes cross the water of existence, the baneful thing, by means of the word (of the Guru).

(2). The stupid self-willed man practises cunning.
(Though) bathed and washed he is not accepted.[1]
As he has come, so he will go, having committed vices he is regretting (it afterwards).

(3). To the blind self-willed man nothing is known.
Hari, (by whom) death has been decreed, he does not comprehend.
The self-willed one does (religious) work, but does not obtain (him, *i.e.* Hari), without the name he throws away his life.

(4). To take the word (of the Guru) as true[2] is the chief thing.
From the perfect Guru the gate of salvation is obtained.
Day by day he lets his voice be heard in the sabd,[3] those who are attached to the True one, he is colouring with dye.[4]

(5). The tongue is steeped in the juice of Hari and joyful.
Mind and body are easily captivated.
Easily the dearly beloved is obtained; easily, easily[5] he (Hari) is uniting (them with himself).

(6). In whose heart is love (to Hari), he sings (his) praises.
By means of the word of the Guru he easily enters comfort.
I am always a sacrifice to the gratuitous service of those who apply their mind to the service of the Guru.

(7). The true one believes in the perfectly True one.
By the favour of the Guru his heart is filled with love (to him).
Sitting in his own place he sings the praises of Hari; he himself, having taken him as True, is winning him (*i.e.* Hari) over.

(8). On whom he (Hari) looks in favour, he obtains (him).
By the favour of the Guru his egotism (individuality) ceases.
Nānak (says): in whose heart the name dwells, he obtains lustre at the true gate.

[1] ਪਾਈ, on account of the rhyme = ਪਵੈ or ਪਏ.

[2] ਸਚੁਕਰਣੀ, *s.f.* verification, taking as true.

[3] ਘਾਲੀ ਸਬਦਿ ਸੁਣਾਏ, he, *i.e.* the Guru, lets his voice be heard in the sabd, *i.e.* instructing in the sabd. The sabd is the Gur-mantr, the secret word or verse communicated by the Guru to a disciple, by means of which the disciple becomes initiated. The purport of the sabd is the *name* (of Hari).

[4] *i.e.* The Guru is imbuing them with love to Hari.

[5] The words ਸਹਜੇ ਸਹਜਿ ਮਿਲਾਵਣਿਆ may also be translated: he (or they) is easily united (ਮਿਲਾਉ verbal adjective) with the Innate or self-existing Supreme. ਸਹਜੁ as adjective signifies *innate*; in Tulsī Dās' Rāmāyaṇ it is also explained by स्वाभाविक, self-existing (as if ਸਹਜੁ had sprung from स्वज).

Mǎǐh; mahalā III.

IX. X.

(1). By serving the true Guru great grandeur (is obtained).
Hari comes and dwells in the heart unawares.
Hari is a fruitful tree; by whom the nectar (of Hari) is drunk, his thirst he (*i.e.* Hari) is quenching.

Pause.

I am devoted, O Lord, I am devoted (to them, who) unite (me) with the company of the society of the pious.
Hari himself unites with the society of the pious (those, who) by the word of the Guru are singing the praises of Hari.
(2). That servant of the true Guru becomes lustrous by the word (of the Guru):
Who fixes the name of Hari in his heart.
The filth (of whose) egotism the pure Hari clears away, he obtains lustre at the true gate.
(3). Without the Guru the name cannot be obtained.
The Siddhs and Sādhiks continually lament.
Without serving the Guru comfort does not spring up; by a full destiny the Guru is obtained.
(4). The mind is a looking-glass (of steel), (which) some (rare) disciple sees.
Rust does not settle on it, when he dries up egotism.
He sounds the sound not produced (by an instrument), the pure voice, by means of the word (of the Guru) he is absorbed (in the Supreme).
(5). Without the true Guru nothing can be seen.
(To whom) by the Guru out of mercy his own self is shown:
He himself remains united with himself, he is easily absorbed in the Innate (Supreme).[1]
(6). He who becomes a disciple, absorbs his mind in the One.
The error of duality he consumes by the word (instruction) of the Guru.
Who within (his) body makes traffic and trade, he obtains the treasure of the true name.
(7). The chief work of the disciple is the praise of Hari.
The disciple obtains (thereby) the gate of salvation.
(Who) sings day by day, steeped in love, the praises (of Hari), him he (*i.e.* Hari) is calling into (his) palace.
(8). The true Guru, the donor is met with, when caused to meet (by Hari).
By dint of a perfect destiny the word (of the Guru) is caused to dwell in the heart.
Nānak (says): Who obtains the greatness of the name, he is singing the praises of the true Hari.

Mǎǐh; mahalā III.

X. XI.

(1). If he (*i.e.* the disciple) part with his own self, then he obtains all.
By the word of the Guru he applies true absorption of mind.
Truth he buys, truth he collects, a traffic of truth he is carrying on.

Pause.

I am devoted, O Lord, I am devoted (to them, who) are day by day singing the praises of Hari.
I am thine, thou art my Lord, by means of the word (of the Guru) thou art giving greatness.

[1] The sense is: the Guru shows, that man's spirit is an emanation of the Supreme Spirit, and therefore in essence identical with it. He, who knows that the Supreme Spirit is innate in himself, remains united with himself, *i.e.* he does not seek the Supreme outside of himself, but considers himself as identical with him (ਸੋ ਹੈ, I am He).

(2). All the season and time is pleasant:
In which the True one is approved by my heart.
By serving the True one true greatness (is obtained), by the mercy of the Guru I obtain the True one.
(3). The food of faith he obtains from the gratified true Guru.
Inclination to other things ceases, when he causes inclination to Hari to dwell in his heart.
True contentment, understanding, comfort he obtains from the word of the perfect Guru.
(4). Who do not serve the true Guru, they are foolish, blind and ignorant men.
Wandering about, whence will they obtain the gate of final emancipation?
Having died and died they are born again, again they come and are struck in (their) face at the gate of Yama.
(5). If they know the flavour of the word (of the Guru), then they knew their own self.
They praise the pure sound (= name) by the word (of the Guru).
Serving the True one they always obtain comfort, the nine treasures of the name they are causing to dwell in (their) heart.
(6). That place is beautiful, which is pleasing to the mind of Hari.
Sitting in the assembly of the pious the praises of Hari are sung (by them).
Day by day they praise the true Hari, they emit the spotless sound (= the name).
(7). The stock (in trade) of the fleshly-minded is false (not genuine), false are the things laid out (by them).
Falsehood they earn and a burthen of pain oppresses them.
Led astray by error they wander about day and night, having died they are born (again), they lose their life.
(8). The true Lord is very dear to me.
In the word of the perfect Guru is my support.
Nānak (says): by the name he obtains greatness, who is considering pain and pleasure as the same.

Mǡjh; mahalā III.

XI. XII.

(1). Thine are the mines (= genera), (thine) the species.[1]
Without the name the whole (creation) is led astray in error.
From the service of the Guru the name of Hari is obtained, without the true Guru no one is obtaining it.

Pause.

I am devoted, O Lord, I am devoted (to those, who) apply their mind to Hari.
The true Hari is obtained by attachment to the Guru, (who) is easily causing him (*i.e.* Hari) to dwell in the heart.
(2). If he (*i.e.* the disciple) serve the true Guru, then he obtains everything.
He obtains such a fruit as he is desiring.
The true Guru is the giver of all things, by a perfect destiny he is obtained.[2]
(3). This (human) mind is dirty and does not meditate on the One.

[1] ਖਾਣੀ, *s.f. Plur.* the four mines; ਬਾਣਿ, *s.f.* species, kind (Sansk. ਵਰ੍ਣ, from which a substantive fem. ਵਾਣੀ is formed, which is now in Sindhī-Hindī commonly written ਬਾਨ or ਵਾਣ). The sense is: by thee all living creatures are created.

[2] ਪੂਰੈ ਭਾਗਿ ਮਿਲਾਵਣਿਆ may be translated either: by a perfect destiny he (*i.e.* the Guru) is obtained (ਮਿਲਾਵਣਿਆ = ਮਿਲਾਉ, *verb. adj.*, ṇiā being then an alliteration), or ਮਿਲਾਵਣਿਆ may be taken as gerundive and translated: he must be acquired. The sense is the same either way.

Inside much filthiness is accumulated by dint of another love (duality).

At the bank (of a river), at a Tīrtha, in a foreign country the selfish man wanders about and accumulates other additional filth of egotism.

(4). If he serve the true Guru, then his filth goes off.

He dies whilst living and applies his mind to Hari.

Hari is spotless and true, no filth sticks to him; who clings to the True one, his filth he (Hari) is taking away.

(5). Without the Guru there is deep (blind) darkness.

He who has no divine knowledge is blind, stark blind.

The worms of ordure are working up ordure, and are again destroyed in ordure.[1]

(6). Who serves the emancipated ones becomes (himself) emancipated.

Egotism and selfishness he removes by means of the word (of the Guru).

Who serves daily Hari in truth, obtains by a perfect (good) lot the Guru.

(7). He himself bestows the gift, that he unites to union (with himself).

From the perfect Guru he (*i.e.* the disciple) gets the treasure of the name.

By the true name the mind always (becomes) true, by serving the True one he is removing his pain.

(8). Consider him (*i.e.* Hari) as being always in (thy) presence, do not consider him as being far away!

Learn from the word of the Guru, that Hari (is present) within (thee)!

Nānak (says): from the name greatness is obtained, from the perfect Guru (thou art) obtaining it (*i.e.* the name).

Māǰh; mahalā III.

XII. XIII.

(1). Who are true here, they are true (also) in the other world.

A true heart is absorbed in the true word (of the Guru).

The True one it serves, the True one it acquires, from the True one it gets comfort[2] (with the Supreme).

Pause.

I am devoted, O Lord, I am devoted (to them, who) cause the true name to dwell in their heart.

The true ones serve (him) and are absorbed in the True one, they are singing the praises of the True one.

(2). The Paṇḍit reads (but) does not obtain a relish (from it).

By another love (duality) the Māyā leads his mind astray.

By the spiritual blindness caused by the Māyā all his intellect is lost, having practised vices he is regretting (it afterwards).

(3). If the true Guru be met with, then he gets the truth (the Deity).

The name of Hari he fixes in his mind.

He dies by the word (of the Guru), he subdues his own mind and is (thus) obtaining the gate of final emancipation.

[1] ਪਚਾਵਲਿਆ, alliteration instead of ਪਚਾਉ, *s.m.* destruction; (their) destruction is in —. Or ਪਚਾਵਲਿਆ is alliteration instead of ਪਚਾਉ, a verbal adjective formed from ਪਚਲਾ, being consumed; the latter is more suitable and borne out by other similar forms (ਮਿਲਾਵਲਿਆ).

[2] ਸਚੁ, *s.m.* comfort, joy, as used in Tulsī Dās' Rāmāyaṇa. The Sansk. सख्यं = सह्य = सच, written also ਸਚਿ (but always *s.m.*), signifies: *friendship*, *intimacy*, and differs from ਸਚੁ, the etymology of which is uncertain.

(4). He cuts off sins, he removes his wrath.

The word of the Guru he puts into his breast.

Those, who are attached to the True one, are always Bairāgīs, having destroyed egotism (individuality) they are in union (with the Supreme).

(5). Within (the body) the jewel (*i.e.* the Supreme) is found, if procured (by the Guru).

Threefold is the will (of man), threefold the Māyā.[1]

Having read and read the Paṇḍits and silent ascetics have become tired, they obtain no knowledge of the fourth state (of the soul).

(6). He himself (*i.e.* Hari) colours and applies the colour.[2]

Those men are dyed, who are coloured by the word of the Guru.

(On whom) the boundless colour of Hari is put, they, having the right taste of Hari, are singing his excellences.

(7). The disciple has prosperity and success, true control (of his passions) and intelligence.

The disciple has divine knowledge, by the name he becomes emancipated.

The disciple's work is, (that) he acquire the True one, the true ones are absorbed in the True one.

(8). The disciple establishes, and having established he removes (again).[3]

The disciple is caste and brotherhood,[4] all is he himself.

Nānak (says): the disciple meditates on the name, by praising (it) he is absorbed in the name.

Māǰh; mahalā III.

XIII. XIV.

(1). Creation and destruction are made by the word (of the Guru).

Even by the word creation (production) is again made.

In all the disciple himself exists, the true disciple, having produced, is again absorbing (what is produced).[5]

Pause.

I am devoted, O Lord, I am devoted (to them, who) make the perfect Guru dwell in their heart.

Quieted by the Guru they perform worship day and night, reciting the qualities (of Hari) they are absorbed in the abode of (all) qualities.

(2). The disciple is earth, the disciple is water.

The disciple is wind and fire, he sports assuming supernatural forms.[6]

Who is destitute of the Guru, he, having died and died, is born again; those who are destitute of the Guru, come and go again.

(3). By that creator one sport is made.

Everything is put (by him) in the (human) body.

[1] ਤ੍ਰਿਬਿਧਿ, threefold, *i.e.* affected by the three Guṇas.

[2] To colour, to dye, etc., in a figurative sense: to impart one's own essence or nature, as a cloth by being dyed is changed.

[3] As to the meaning of these words compare XIV. (1).

[4] ਪਤਿ, the same as ਪਾਤਿ, from the Sansk. पंक्ति, row, line, fellowship.

[5] The Guru, and in him the disciple, is perfectly identified with the Supreme, even ਉਤਪਤਿ and ਪਰਲਉ are ascribed to him.

[6] ਵਿਡਾਣੀ = Sansk. विडम्बिन्, *mb* being changed first to *m* (*mm*), thence to *ṇ* (the preceding vowel being lengthened according to Prākrit rule).

By the secret of the word (of the Guru)[1] some one obtains the palace (of Hari), the palace-servants[2] he calls to (his) palace.

(4). True is the wholesale merchant, true his retail-dealers.

The True one they buy out of infinite love to the Guru.

The True one they purchase, the True one they acquire, from the True one they earn comfort.[3]

(5). Without capital how shall he obtain anything?

The fleshly-minded one wanders about in the whole world.

Without the capital (of the name) all go off empty, having gone empty they are incurring pain.

(6). Some purchase the True one from the dear word of the Guru.

They are saved themselves and save all their families.

Having come (to the threshold of Hari) they are approved of, having met with their beloved they obtain happiness.

(7). Within is the thing (*i.e.* the Supreme), the fool seeks it outside.

The self-willed are blind and wander about without restraint.

Where the thing is, from thence no one gets it, the self-willed are going astray[4] in error.

(8). He himself gives and calls by the word (of the Guru).

The palace-servant obtains easy comfort in the palace.

Nānak (says): from the name greatness is obtained; he himself (*i.e.* Hari) having heard, heard (the word of the Guru) is meditating (on it).

Māǐh; mahalā III.

XIV. XV.

(1). By the true Guru his true instruction is proclaimed.

Think on Hari, at the end he will be (thy) companion!

Hari, the unattainable, the inapprehensible, the masterless, the unproduced from the womb, thou obtainest by faith in the true Guru.

Pause.

I am devoted, O Lord, I am devoted (to them, who) part with (their) own self.

If they part with their own self, then they obtain Hari, they are easily absorbed with Hari.

(2). The work, that is written before, is performed.

By serving the true Guru comfort is always obtained.

Without (divine) allotment the Guru is not obtained, by the word (of the Guru) he (Hari) is uniting to union (with himself).

(3). The disciple remains uncontaminated in the world.

His trust is in the Guru, the name is his support.

If one oppresses the disciple, what is it to him? he himself (*i.e.* the oppressor) is wasting away and subjected to pain.

(4). The fleshly-minded are blind and have no understanding.

The world is a butcher killing itself.

By slandering and slandering it lifts up a great burthen, without wages it conveys the burthen.

(5). This world is an inclosed garden-bed, my Lord the gardener.

[1] ਸਬਦਿ ਭੇਦਿ. ਭੇਦੁ signifies here secret, mystery.

[2] ਮਹਲਾ, *s.m.* a palace-servant (otherwise eunuch).

[3] ਸਚੁ signifies here: joy, comfort, happiness.

[4] ਭੁਲਾਵਣਿਆ, verbal adjective ਭੁਲਾਉ, changed to ਭੁਲਾਵਣਿਆ for the sake of the rhyme.

He always takes care (of it), no one is empty (destitute of his care).

As the smell is, that it gets, so it is, the indwelling (soul) is to be known (from) the smell.

(6). The fleshly-minded are sick in the world.

The giver of comfort, the unattainable, the boundless one, is forgotten (by them).

In pain they continually wander about lamenting, without the Guru they get no composure.

(7). By whom the rules[1] are made, he knows them.

As he himself makes (them), he knows (them to be made) by his order.

As he puts (the rule) inside, so it is, he himself is (also) putting (it) outside.

(8). Without that True one I have none other.

Whom he attaches (to himself), he becomes pure.

Nānak (says): the name dwells within the body; to whom he gives it, he obtains it.

Mājh; mahalā III.

XV. XVI.

(1). (Who) causes to dwell in his heart the nectar-name:

He removes egotism, "mine" and all pain.

Who always praises the nectar-speech, he obtains the free gift[2] of the nectar.

Pause.

I am devoted, O Lord, I am devoted (to them, who) fix the nectar-speech in (their) heart.

(Who) fix the nectar-speech in (their) heart, they (are) meditating on the nectar-name.

(2). He always utters from (his) mouth the nectar-speech.

The nectar he always looks and glances at with (his) eyes.

The nectar-story he always tells day and night and proclaims it to others.

(3). Being steeped in nectar-dye he applies deep meditation.

The nectar he obtains by the favour of the Guru.

(His) tongue speaks day and night nectar, in mind and body he is drinking[3] nectar.

(4). That he (*i.e.* Hari) does, what is not in (anybody's) thought.

(His) order no one can efface.

By (his) order the nectar-speech exists, by (his) order he causes the nectar to be drunk.

(5). Wonderful are the works of Hari, the creator.

This (human) mind, which is going astray, he is turning back (to himself).

He applies the mind to the nectar-speech, he is proclaiming the nectar by means of the word (of the Guru).

(6). The bad and good (men) are created by thyself.

By thyself all people are tried.

The good ones, after having tried them, thou puttest into (thy) treasury, the bad ones thou art leading astray in error.

(7). How shall I see (thee), how shall I praise (thee)?

By the favour of the Guru I praise (thee), by means of the word (of the Guru).

In thy (divine) decree dwells nectar, by thy decree thou art giving nectar to drink.

(8). The word (of the Guru) is nectar, the speech of Hari is nectar.

[1] ਬਿਧਿ (*m.*) may also be translated by: act, deed, *arrangement*. The sense is: he himself is ordering or arranging everything inside and outside.

[2] ਅਭ੍ਰਿਤ ਅਭ੍ਰਿਤ. ਅਭ੍ਰਿਤ signifies also: a free gift that is not asked for; this seems to suit the context.

[3] ਪੀਆਵਲਿਆ, here verbal adjective, instead of ਪੀਆਉ, drinking.

By the service of the true Guru it (*i.e.* the speech) is fixed in the heart.

Nānak (says): the nectar-name is always giving comfort; having drunk nectar all one's hunger is ceasing.

Mājh; mahalā III.

XVI. XVII.

(1). Nectar rains with natural ease (*i.e.* without any human effort).

Some rare disciple obtains it.

Having drunk nectar he is always satiated; he (*i.e.* Hari) bestowing mercy (on him) is quenching his thirst.

Pause.

I am devoted, O Lord, I am devoted to the disciple, who is drinking nectar.

His tongue, having tasted the juice, remains always steeped in love, naturally it is singing the praises of Hari.

(2). By the favour of the Guru some one obtains understanding (of truth).

Having extinguished duality he applies devout meditation on the One.

If he (*i.e.* Hari) bestow a favourable look (on him), then he (the disciple) sings the praises of Hari, by a favourable look (from the part of Hari) he is absorbed in the True one.

(3). Upon all is thy look, O Lord!

Upon some little, upon some much.

Without thee nothing comes to pass; the disciple gets acuteness of mind.

(4). By the disciple the truth (*i.e.* the Supreme) is reflected upon.

Thy store-rooms are filled with nectar.

Without the service of the true Guru no one obtains (it), from the mercy of the Guru he obtains (it).

(5). The man, who serves the true Guru, gets lustre.

By the nectar-name he fascinates heart and mind.

Whose mind and body are imbued with the nectar-word, he is easily proclaiming the nectar.

(6). The fleshly-minded are led astray and wasted by another love (duality).

They do not take the name, they die, having eaten poison.

Daily and always is (their) dwelling in ordure, without the service (of the Guru) they are wasting their life.

(7). He drinks nectar, to whom he himself is giving it to drink.

By the favour of the Guru he easily applies devout meditation.

He himself (*i.e.* Hari) remains brimful in all, by the doctrine of the Guru he is coming into sight.

(8). He himself is that pure one.

By whom (creation) was made, by the same it is destroyed.

Nānak (says): keep thou always in mind the name, easily thou wilt be absorbed in the True one!

Mājh; mahalā III.

XVII. XVIII.

(1). They apply themselves to the True one, who please thee.

They always serve the True one with natural ease.

Who praise the True one by means of the true word (of the Guru), them he is uniting to true union (with himself).

Pause.

I am devoted, O Lord, I am devoted (to those, who) are praising the True one.

Who meditate on the True one, they are imbued with love to the True one, the true ones are absorbed in the True one.

(2). Wherever I see, in all places is the True one.

By the favour of the Guru he dwells in the heart.

The body (becomes) true, the tongue is steeped[1] in the True one, having heard the True one they are speaking (of him) and praising (him).

(3). Having destroyed (worldly) desire she[2] is absorbed in the True one.

This mind has seen, that all (the creation) is coming and going.

By the service of the true Guru the mind is always immovable, it gets a dwelling in its own house.[3]

(4). By the word of the Guru he (*i.e.* the Supreme) is shown (as dwelling) in the heart.

The infatuation of the Māyā[4] is burnt by the word (of the Guru).

Having seen the perfectly True one (in his own heart) he praises (him), by the word of the Guru he is getting the True one.

(5). Those, who are imbued with love to the True one, apply true meditation (on him).

Who praise the name of Hari, they have got a great destiny.

By the true word (of the Guru) he himself (*i.e.* Hari) unites (them), who are singing the praises of the True one in the company of the pious.

(6). An estimation is read, if (a thing) be estimable (calculable).

He is unattainable, inapprehensible; by means of the word (of the Guru) knowledge (of him) is obtained (by those):

(Who) daily praise (him) by the true word; none other gets an estimation (of him).

(7). Having read and read they have become tired, no composure has come (to them).

(Worldly) thirst consumes (them), they have no knowledge.

Poison they purchase, they are thirsty after infatuation, the baneful thing, speaking falsehood they are eating poison.

(8). By the favour of the Guru the One is known.

Having destroyed duality (their) mind is absorbed in the True one.

Nānak (says): in (whose) mind the One name abides, he obtains (the True one) by the favour of the Guru.

Mājh; mahalā III.

XVIII. XIX.

(1). The colours and forms, (that) exist, are all thine.

Having died and died (men) are born (again), many turns (in transmigration) are allotted (to them).

Thou alone art immovable, unattainable, boundless, by the doctrine of the Guru (thou art) conveying understanding (as regards thyself).

Pause.

I am devoted, O Lord, I am devoted (to them, who) fix the name of Rām in (their) mind.

He has not any form, mark or colour, he, by means of the instruction of the Guru, is himself instructing.

(2). (In) all is one light, if one know it.

By the service of the true Guru it becomes manifest.

(Though) concealed, it is manifest in all places, the luminous (Supreme) is blending light (with himself).

[1] ਰਾਤਾ, steeped in = imbued with love to.

[2] ਸਮਾਣੀ; no subject is hinted at, very likely ਸ੍ਰਿਸਟਿ, creation, people, is to be supplied, as in the second line.

[3] The sense is: the mind, being instructed by the Guru (by serving him), wanders no longer about, but dwells in its own house (=body), where it finds the (innate) Supreme. Compare the following verse.

[4] ਮਾਇਆ ਮੋਹੁ, the spiritual darkness or infatuation caused by the Māyā, *i.e. the duality*, by which man considers himself (erroneously) different from the Supreme.

(3). In the fire of (worldly) thirst the world burns.
There is much greediness, conceit and selfishness (in it).
Having died and died it is born (again), it loses its honour, it throws uselessly away (its human) birth.
(4). The word of the Guru some rare one comprehends.
If he destroy his own self, then the three worlds become known (to him).
If he dies, there will not be again death for him,[1] he is easily absorbed in the True one.
(5). He does not again apply his thoughts to the Māyā.
He always remains absorbed in the word of the Guru.
The True one he praises; within every body the perfectly True one is emitting radiance.
(6). The True one he praises (as being) always in his presence.
In the word of the Guru he remains brimful.
By the favour of the Guru the True one comes into sight, from the True one he is obtaining comfort.
(7). The True one is contained within the mind.
The True one is always immovable, he does not come nor go.
The mind, that clings to the True one, is pure, by the doctrine of the Guru it is absorbed in the True one.
(8). The True one he praises, none other:
By whose service comfort is always obtained.
Nānak (says): those, who are attached to the name, are reflecting; the perfectly True one they are acquiring.

Māǰh; mahalā III.

XIX. XX.

(1). Pure is the word, pure the sound.
Pure the light, that is contained in all.
Who is praising the pure word of Hari, (becomes) pure by muttering Hari, he is removing his filth (=sins).

Pause.

I am devoted, O Lord, I am devoted (to him, who) is causing the giver of comfort to dwell in (his) mind.

Who is praising the pure Hari by the word of the Guru, he, having heard the word, is extinguishing his thirst.

(2). Into (whose) mind the pure name comes and dwells:
(His) mind and body (become) pure, he removes the spiritual blindness of the Māyā.
He always sings the praises of the Pure and True one, he is sounding the pure sound (=the name).
(3). The pure nectar is obtained from the Guru.
From (whose) heart his own self has died away, in him is no infatuation of the Māyā.
Pure is his (divine) knowledge, very pure his meditation, the pure word he causes to dwell in his heart.
(4). Who serves the Pure one, he becomes pure.
The filth of egotism he washes away by the word of the Guru.
The pure and unbeaten sound and voice sounds (in him), at the true gate he gets lustre.
(5). From the Pure one all become pure.
A pure heart Hari strings (like a pearl) by the word (of the Guru).
Those are very fortunate, who are given to the pure name, by the pure name they are lustrous.
(6). He is pure, who is radiant by the word (of the Guru).
By the pure name he fascinates his mind and body.

[1] The sense is: he will not be again subject to another birth and consequent death.

On account of the true name no dirt ever sticks (to him), (his) face is bright, he enjoys comfort.[1]

(7). (His) heart is filthy by another love.

(His) cooking-place is filthy (and) in a filthy place.

Having eaten filthy (food) he increases again his filthiness; the fleshly-minded one incurs pain by (his) filthiness.

(8). The filthy and the pure ones, all are made by his order.

Those are pure, who are pleasing to the true Hari.

Nānak (says): in (whose) heart the name dwells, (that) disciple is clearing away his filthiness.

Mājh; mahalā III.

XX. XXI.

(1). Gōvind is bright, bright are (his) devotees.[2]

My mind, temper and desire are pure.

Who is bright in the heart, his face is always brilliant, the very bright name he is meditating upon.

Pause.

I am devoted, O Lord, I am devoted (to him, who) is singing the praises of Gōvind.

(Who) recites day and night Gōvind, Gōvind, (who) proclaims the praises of Gōvind by the word (of the Guru).

(2). (Who) sings (=praises) with natural ease to Gōvind:

He is bright by the fear of the Guru, the filth of his egotism goes away.

He remains always in joy and performs adoration day and night, having heard he sings the praises of Gōvind.

(3). His heart dances (out of joy), he makes firm his devotion.

By the word of the Guru he reconciles his mind with the mind.[3]

He keeps true time (in music),[4] he puts a stop to the infatuation of the Māyā, according to the word (of the Guru) he is dancing.

(4). He cries aloud, he throws down (his) body.

On account of the infatuation of the Māyā he is overcome by death.

The infatuation of the Māyā makes this mind dance; in (whose) heart is deceit, he is incurring pain.

(5). When he himself (*i.e.* Hari) causes the disciple to perform devotion:

His body and mind are easily imbued with love (to Hari).

The word (of Hari) is told (by him), by means of the word (of the Guru) he proclaims (it); the disciple he (*i.e.* Hari) is approving (on account of his) devotion (to Hari).

(6). Being surrounded by a circle[5] on account of the Māyā he dances, by another love (duality) he is incurring pain.

In whose heart love (to Hari) springs up, he (becomes) emancipated.

[1] ਸਚੁ ਵਗਾਵਲਿਆ. ਸਚੁ signifies here *joy, comfort*; cf. p. 162, note 2. ਵਗਾਵਲਿਆ is a new formation of a verbal adjective, ਵਗਾਉ (see my Sindhī Grammar, p. 52, 9), which, by alliteration, is changed to the (in itself meaningless) form ਵਗਾਵਲਿਆ.

[2] ਹੰਸੁ *s.m.* a devotee or ascetic.

[3] The mind was before going astray by duality, it is now reconciled (united) with itself. Cf. p. 170, note 1.

[4] ਤਾਲ ਪੂਰੇ may also signify: he plays the cymbal; see v. 6.

[5] ਪਿੜ ਬੰਧਿ, having bound round (himself) a halo = being surrounded by a halo, like the moon. The sense is: on account of the Māyā (illusion) he has become dim-sighted, so that he is no more able to look upon things as they are in reality, he is ensnared in the error of duality.

(7). His senses (are) in (his) power, he is endowed with true control (of his passions).

By means of the word of the Guru he always meditates on Hari; this devotee is pleasing to Hari.

(8). By the disciple devotion is made (all) the four ages (to Hari).

By devotion to another no one obtains (him, *i.e.* Hari).

Nānak (says): the name is obtained by attachment to the Guru, by him who applies his mind to the feet of the Guru.

Mājh; mahalā III.

XXI. XXII.

(1). (Who) serves the True one, (who) praises the True one:

He has never (any) pain on account of the true name.

Those, who serve the giver of comfort, obtain comfort, by the doctrine of the Guru they are causing him to dwell in (their) heart.

Pause.

I am devoted, O Lord, I am devoted (to them, who) with natural ease practise deep meditation.

Those, who serve Hari, are always lustrous; by beauty and sagacious knowledge they are brilliant.

(2). Every one is called a devotee.

Those are devotees, who are acceptable to thy mind.

They praise thee by the true word (of the Guru), imbued with love (to thee) they perform adoration.

(3). Every one is thine, O true Hari!

If he meet with a disciple, then his wandering about ceases.

When he is pleasing to thee, thou imbuest him with love to the name, thou thyself causest him to mutter the name.

(4). By the doctrine of the Guru Hari is established in the heart.

Joy and grief, all spiritual blindness is parted with.

Devout meditation is made on the One, he is always fixing the name of Hari in (his) mind.

(5). The devotees are always imbued with love and affection to thee.

The name, (containing) the nine treasures, has come and settled in their heart.

By a full destiny the true Guru is obtained (by them), by means of the word (of the Guru) (thou art) uniting (them) to union (with thyself).

(6). Thou art always merciful and bestowing comfort.

Thou thyself unitest (him who) is known (by thee) as a disciple.

Thou thyself givest the greatness of the name; those, who are attached to the name, obtain comfort.

(7). The true ones are continually praising thee.

By the disciple none other is known (but thou).

His mind remains absorbed with the One, by (his) mind being won over he meets with (his) mind.[1]

(8). He, who becomes a disciple, praises

The true Lord, who is without concern.

Nānak (says): (in whose) heart the name dwells, (him) Hari is uniting by means of the word of the Guru.

Mājh; mahalā III.

XXII. XXIII.

(1). Thy devotees are shining in (thy) true court.

By means of the word of the Guru they are adorned by the name.

[1] ਮਨਿ ਮੰਨਿਐ ਮਨਹਿ ਮਿਲਾਵਣਿਆ. ਮਿਲਾਉ governs the Dative (ਮਨਹਿ); by the mind being reconciled, won over to the Supreme, from whom it was separated by duality, duality in the mind ceases.

Always, day and night, they remain in joy, reciting the qualities (of Hari) they are absorbed in the abode of qualities.

Pause.

I am devoted, O Lord, I am devoted (to those, who) hear and fix the name in (their) heart.

Hari, the true, the highest, is uniting (them to himself), having destroyed (their) egotism.

(2). Hari is true, of a true name.

By the favour of the Guru he unites some one.

Those, who are united with him by means of the word of the Guru, are not separated (again), they are easily absorbed in the True one.

(3). Without thee nothing is done.

Thou having made seest and knowest (all).

The creator himself does and causes to be done (everything), by means of the doctrine of the Guru he himself is uniting.

(4). A virtuous woman obtains Hari:

(Who) makes her ornament out of fear and love (to Hari).

By serving the true Guru she is always a (happy) married woman, by means of the true instruction (of the Guru) she is absorbed.

(5). Those, who forget the word (of the Guru), (get) no place nor spot.

They are led astray by error (and are) like a crow in an empty house.

This and the other world, both are lost by them, in pain they pass their time.

(6). In writing and writing[1] paper and ink is lost.

By second love (duality) no one obtains comfort.

Falsehood they write and falsehood they earn, those who apply their thoughts to falsehood, are consumed.

(7). The disciples, who write the consideration of the perfectly True one:

They are true and obtain the gate of salvation.

True is (their) paper, pen and inkstand, writing the True one they are absorbed in the True one.

(8). Thy Lord, being seated within (the heart), sees (it).

Who obtains him by the favour of the Guru, that man is of account.

Nānak (says): from the name greatness is obtained, from the perfect Guru he gets it (*i.e.* the name).

Mājh; mahalā III.

XXIII. XXIV.

(1). The manifestation (explication) of the Supreme Spirit is made by the Guru.

(To whom) the filth of egotism sticks, he clears it away by means of the word of the Guru.

(His) mind (becomes) pure, he is daily engaged in devotion, performing devotion he obtains Hari.

Pause.

I am devoted, O Lord, I am devoted (to them, who) themselves perform devotion and cause others to perform devotion.

To those devotees reverence should always be paid, who day by day sing the praises of Hari.

(2). The creator himself is the causality and causes (everything) to be done.

Whom he pleases, he applies to the work.

In consequence of a perfect destiny the service of the Guru is made; by the service of the Guru he obtains comfort.

[1] Supply from the following lines the word "*falsehood*" (कूड़).

(3). Having died, having died he lives and obtains then everything.

By the favour of the Guru he makes Hari dwell in (his) mind.

He is always emancipated (from matter) and makes Hari dwell in (his) mind, easily he is absorbed in the Innate[1] (Supreme).

(4). (Though) he perform many (religious) works, he does not obtain final emancipation.

He wanders about in foreign countries and is ruined by second love (duality).

Uselessly his (human) birth is lost by the deceitful one, without the word (of the Guru) he is incurring pain.

(5). Who checks busy activity and keeps it back:

He obtains by the favour of the Guru the highest step.

The true Guru himself unites (him) to union (with Hari), being united with the beloved he obtains comfort.

(6). Some are given to falsehood and obtain spurious fruits.

By second love they uselessly waste their life.

They are drowned themselves and all their families are drowned (by them), having spoken falsehood they are eating poison.

(7). Some (rare) disciple sees in this (human) body the mind:[2]

When he soaks up by love and devotion his individuality.

The Siddhs and Sādhiks and silent ascetics continue in deep meditation, yet even in their body the mind is not becoming visible.

(8). That creator himself causes (everything) to be done.

What can another do, what is done by a creature?

Nānak (says): To whom he gives the name, he takes it; he causes the name to dwell in (man's) mind.

Mājh; mahalā III.

XXIV. XXV.

(1). In this cavern (=body) is an inexhaustible treasure.

In it (*i.e.* the body) dwells the invisible, boundless Hari.

He himself is hidden, he himself is manifest, by the word of the Guru he is doing away the individuality (of man).

Pause.

I am devoted, O Lord, I am devoted (to them, who) cause the nectar-name to dwell in (their) mind.

The nectar-name is a great sweet juice, out of the doctrine of the Guru they are drinking nectar.

(2). Having destroyed egotism (individuality) the adamant shutters are opened (by the Guru).

The priceless name is obtained by the favour of the Guru.

Without the word (instruction of the Guru) no one gets the name, by the mercy of the Guru he makes it dwell in (his) mind.

(3). (By whom) the (divine) knowledge of the Guru as a true collyrium is put upon (his) eyes:

In (his) heart there is light, ignorance and darkness are dispersed.

Light is blended with the Luminous (the fountain of light), his heart is won over (conciliated to the Supreme), at the gate of Hari he obtains lustre.

(4). If he go to seek (*i.e.* the name) outside his body:

He does not get the name, he incurs much forced labour and pain.

[1] Or: the self-existing.

[2] ਮਨ, here comprehensively, *the inner man, the intelligent power*, as being light from light.

To the blind fleshly-minded man it (*i.e.* the thing) does not become visible, having returned to his house (= body)[1] the disciple gets the thing (*i.e.* the Supreme).

(5). By the favour of the Guru he obtains the true Hari.

He sees (him) in (his) heart and body, the filth of (his) egotism goes off.

Sitting in his own place he always sings the excellences of Hari, by means of the true word (of the Guru) he is absorbed (in Hari).

(6). He obstructs the nine gates[2] (of the body), he keeps back the running (mind).

He gets his dwelling in the tenth (gate), as in his own house.

There the unbeaten sound is sounded day and night, by the doctrine of the Guru he is hearing[3] the sound.

(7). Without the word (instruction of the Guru) there is darkness in the heart.

He receives the nine (sentiments) and the seven (elementary substances of the body),[4] the revolution (in transmigration) does not cease.

In the hand of the true Guru is the key, by another the door is not opened, the Guru makes (the disciple) meet with a perfect lot.

(8). Thou art hidden and manifest in all places.

Being united by the favour of the Guru acuteness of mind is obtained.

Nānak (says): Praise thou always the name! the disciple makes it dwell in (his) mind.

Mājh; mahalā III.

XXV. XXVI.

(1). The disciple is united (with Hari), he himself unites (him).

Death does not overcome (him), pain does not afflict (him).

Having destroyed egotism (individuality) he breaks all bonds, the disciple is lustrous by the word (of the Guru).

Pause.

I am devoted, O Lord, I am devoted (to them, who) are lustrous by the name of Hari, Hari.

The disciple sings, the disciple dances, he applies his mind to Hari.

(2). The disciple is approved of, he may live (or) die.

(His) life is not consumed, (if) he knows the word (of the Guru).

The disciple does not die, nor does death devour (him), the disciple is absorbed in the True one.

(3). The disciple obtains lustre at the gate of Hari.

The disciple puts away from within his own self (= individuality).

He himself crosses and causes all his families to cross, the disciple is adjusting (his) life.[5]

(4). Pain never befalls the body of the disciple.

The disciple's pain, caused by egotism (individuality), ceases.

The mind of the disciple is pure, filth does not again stick to it; the disciple is easily absorbed.

[1] The reading of many manuscripts: ਘਿਰਿ, is wrong, ਘਰਿ must be read in its stead.

[2] The reading of many manuscripts (and of the lithographed copies): ਦਰਿ, is wrong, ਦਰ must be read, as borne out by the best manuscripts.

[3] ਸੁਣਾਵਣਿਆ is = ਸੁਣਾਉ, verbal adjective: *hearing*. The sense of this verse is; By abstraction from without and restraining the vital breath in the tenth gate the sound not produced by beating (a musical instrument) is heard, *i.e.* Ōm, indicative of the mental absorption in the Supreme.

[4] ਨਵ ਸਤੁ. ਨਵ is to be referred to the nine ਰਸ or sentiments of the ਮਨ, ਸਤੁ to the seven constituent elements of the body.

[5] *i.e.* He gains the object of his life.

(5). The disciple obtains the greatness of the name.

The disciple sings the praises (of Hari) and gets lustre (thereby).

He remains always in joy day and night, the disciple is performing the word (= order of the Guru).

(6). The disciple is daily in love with the word (of the Guru).

In the four periods (of the world) it is known by the disciple.

The disciple sings the praises (of Hari), he is always pure, by means of the word (of the Guru) he is performing devotion.

(7). Without the Guru there is utter darkness.

Seized by death they make shrieks.

They are daily sick, worms of ordure and are incurring pain in ordure.

(8). The disciple himself does and causes to be done (everything).

(For) he himself (=Hari) has come and settled in the heart of the disciple.

Nānak (says): by the name greatness is obtained, from the perfect Guru he (*i.e.* the disciple) obtains it (*i.e.* the name).

Māȷ̌h; mahalā III.

XXVI. XXVII.

(1). There is one and the same light (=vital power) in the bodies.

The true, perfect Guru shows (this) by his instruction.

By (Hari) himself the difference[1] is made within the body, he himself (also) is making the harmony.

Pause.

I am devoted, O Lord, I am devoted (to them, who) sing the praises of the true Hari.

Without the Guru no one obtains understanding (of truth), the disciple is absorbed naturally.

(2). Thou thyself art brilliant, thou thyself fascinatest the world.

Thou thyself stringest the world by a glance.[2]

Thou thyself givest pain and joy, O creator, the disciple is seeing Hari.

(3). The creator himself does and causes to be done (everything).

He himself makes the word (of the Guru) dwell in the mind.

From the instruction (of the Guru) the nectar-sound (= the name) springs up, the disciple tells and proclaims it.

(4). Thou thyself (art) the creator, thou thyself (art) the enjoyer.

(His) bonds are broken, he is always free (from matter):

He himself is always free, he himself is true, (who) is apprehending the inapprehensible one.

(5). Thou thyself (art) the Māyā, thou thyself the shade (caused by the Māyā).

Thou thyself the spiritual blindness, (by whom) the world was created.

Thou thyself (art) the giver of the excellences,[3] thou thyself singest the excellences, thou thyself tellest and proclaimest (them).

(6). Thou thyself doest and thou thyself causest to be done (everything).

Thou thyself establishest and thou thyself disestablishest.

Without thee nothing is done, thou thyself art putting (the creatures) into (their) work.

(7). Thou thyself killest and thou thyself vivifiest.

[1] Difference = duality.

[2] Thou overlookest the world with one glance.

[3] The sense is: he puts his own praise into the mouth of the devotee, and he himself is also the devotee who sings it

Thou thyself unitest (them)[1] and causest (them) to be united (with thee).

From (thy) service comfort is always obtained, the disciple is easily absorbed (in thee).

(8). Thou thyself art higher than high.

To whom thou showest thyself, that one sees (thee).

Nānak (says): in (whose) heart the name dwells, he himself, having seen (him), is showing (him to others).

Mājh; mahalā III.

XXVII. XXVIII.

(1). My Lord is brimfully contained in all places.

By the favour of the Guru I obtain him even in (my own) house (=body).

I always cling (to him), with one mind I meditate (on him); the disciple is absorbed in the True one.

Pause.

I am devoted, O Lord, I am devoted (to them, who) make the world-soul dwell in (their) mind.

Hari is the world-soul, fearless, bountiful; by means of the doctrine of the Guru they are easily absorbed (in him).

(2). In the house (=body) is the earth, the heaven and the nether region.

Even in the house is the young beloved always.

The giver of comfort remains always in joy, by means of the instruction of the Guru he is easily blending (with the disciples).

(3). In (whose) body is: "I, I," "mine" (=individuality):

(His) turn of birth and death does not cease.

Who becomes a disciple, he destroys his egotism (=individuality), he is meditating on the perfectly True one.

(4). Within the body is (religious) demerit and (religious) merit, two brothers.

By both, having met, a creation (of their own) is produced.

Who, having destroyed both, comes into the One house,[2] he is easily absorbed by means of the doctrine of the Guru.

(5). In the house (=intellectual personality) is darkness on account of another love (=duality).

(In whom) light is made, he gives up "I, I," "mine" (=individuality).

(To whom) the comfort-giving word (of the Guru) is known, he is day by day meditating on the name.

(6). Within (the person) light is displayed and spread out.

By the testimony of the Guru darkness is dispelled.

The Lotus (=heart) is opening, comfort is always obtained, the Luminous one (=fountain of light) is blending light (with himself).[3]

(7). Within is the palace (of Hari), with jewels are filled the store-rooms.

The disciple obtains the boundless name.

The disciple purchases and is always trafficking, he obtains always the gain of the name.

(8). He himself keeps the thing (=the name), he himself gives (it).

Some, some disciples purchase it.

Nānak (says): On whom he looks favourably, he obtains it, bestowing his mercy (on him) he dwells in (his) heart.

[1] The first ਮੇਲਣਾ signifies: *to unite*, and ਮਿਲਾਉਣਾ, to cause to be united in union (ਮੇਲਿ Loc.).

[2] ਇਕਤੁ ਘਰਿ, Locative, dependent on ਆਵੈ. The One house is the One personality, freed from the Māyā, and recognizing its identity with the Supreme. Such a personality *demerit* or *merit* does not affect any longer, they are cleared away by knowing the all-pervading world-soul and by absorption in it.

[3] *i.e.* The fountain of light (=the Supreme) is re-absorbing the (infused) light.

Mājh; mahalā III.

XXVIII. XXIX.

(1). Hari himself unites (those) and makes (them) do service:

(Whose) second love (=duality) ceases by means of the word of the Guru.

Hari is pure (and) always giving (his) qualities (to praise), he himself (also) is absorbing (them) in the qualities of Hari.

Pause.

I am devoted, O Lord, I am devoted (to them, who) are making the perfectly True one dwell in (their) heart.

The true name is always pure, by the word of the Guru it dwells in the mind.

(2). The Guru himself is bountiful, disposing the destiny.

(His) servants serve (him), by the disciples Hari is known.

By the nectar-name (his) people are always lustrous, from the instruction of the Guru they obtain the juice (=nectar) of Hari.

(3). In the cavern (=body) is a beautiful place.

By the perfect Guru the error of egotism (individuality) is stopped.

Day by day they praise the name, they are imbued with love (to it), by the mercy of the Guru they obtain it.

(4). By means of the word of the Guru they reflect on this cavern (=body):

Within (whom) the pure name of Murāri dwells.

They sing the praises of Hari, they become lustrous by the word (of the Guru), having met with (their) beloved, they obtain comfort.

(5). Yama is a receiver of customs; on second love he levies an impost.

He punishes him, who has missed the name.

He takes account of twenty-four minutes (ghaṛīs) and of forty-eight minutes, from a Ratī he is drawing out the weight of a Māsā.[1]

(6). Who does not think of her beloved in her father's house:

She, robbed by second love, weeps (with) lamentations.

She is quite unadorned, deformed and bearing ill-boding marks, not in a dream she obtains her beloved.

(7). (By whom) in her father's house the beloved is made to dwell in her heart:

(To her) he is shown (as being) in (her) presence by the perfect Guru.

By (that) woman the beloved is kept fast, she puts (him) to her neck, by means of the word (of the Guru) she enjoys the beloved, her bed is beautiful.

(8). He himself gives (and) calls.

His own name he makes dwell in the heart.

Nānak (says): the greatness of the name accrues (to them, who) daily always sing (his) praises.

Mājh; mahalā III.

XXIX. XXX.

(1). (Their) life is excellent, (who) dwell in their own place:

(Who) serve the true Guru and lead a retired life in their house.

They remain in the love of Hari, they are always imbued with love (to Hari), by the relish of Hari (their) mind is satiated.

[1] A Māsā is equal to eight (or five) Ratīs.

Pause.

I am devoted, O Lord, I am devoted (to them, who) having read and understood (the name) make it dwell in their heart.

The disciples read and praise the name of Hari and are obtaining lustre at the true gate.

(2). Hari is contained (everywhere) inapprehensibly and impenetrably.

By no contrivance can he be obtained.

If he (*i.e.* Hari) bestow his mercy, then the true Guru meets (with one), by his favourable look he is uniting to union (with himself).

(3). Who reads in second love (=duality), does not understand.

On account of the threefold Māyā he is tossed about.

The threefold bond breaks by means of the word of the Guru, by the word of the Guru he (*i.e.* Hari) is procuring final emancipation.

(4). This (human) volatile mind does not come into (one's) power.

It clings to duality and runs in the ten directions (of the earth).

It is a worm of poison, it is steeped in poison and in poison it is consumed.

(5). "I, I," he says, his own self he causes to be brought forth.[1]

He does many (religious) works, but is not at all accepted.

Without thee nothing is done; (on whom) thou bestowest (thy favour), he is lustrous by the word (of the Guru).

(6). He is born and consumed, (but) Hari he does not comprehend.

Daily he wanders about in second love.

The life of the self-willed one is lost uselessly, at the end, when he is gone, he is regretting it.

(7). The beloved (=husband) is in a foreign country, (and) she (=his wife) is decorating (herself).

The blind self-willed woman does such works.

In this world she (gets) no beauty, in that world no entrance, she is uselessly wasting her lifetime.

(8). The name of Hari is known by some rare one.

From the word of the perfect Guru it is apprehended.

Day by day he performs devotion, day and night he easily obtains comfort.

(9). In all abides that (only) One.

Some rare disciple understands (this).

Nānak (says): The people, who are attached to the name, are lustrous, he himself (*i.e.* Hari) is uniting them out of mercy.

Mājh; mahalā III.

XXX. XXXI.

(1). The fleshly-minded one reads and is called a Paṇḍit.

By second love he incurs great pain.

Intoxicated by worldly affairs he sees nothing, again and again he comes into the womb.

Pause.

I am devoted, O Lord, I am devoted (to them, who), having destroyed their egotism (individuality), are united (with Hari).

On account of (their) service of the Guru Hari takes his abode in (their) heart, they are easily drinking the juice of Hari.

(2). They read the Vēda, (but) the taste of Hari has not come (to them).

They explain a discourse, (but) are blinded by the Māyā.

[1] ਜਣਾਉਣਾ, v. caus. To cause to be brought forth; to deliver (said of a midwife). The sense is: he everywhere puts in his own self.

There is always ignorance and darkness in the intoxicated ones, (but) the disciple understands and is praising Hari.

(3). (By whom) the ineffable one is related, he is lustrous by the word.

By the instruction of the Guru he likes[1] in (his) mind the True one.

The perfectly True one abides (with him) day and night, (and) the mind takes delight[2] in the True one.

(4). Those who are attached to the True one, the True one likes.

He himself gives (to them) and does not repent of it.

From the word of the Guru the True one is always known, being united with the True one they obtain comfort.

(5). The filth of falsehood and unrighteousness does not stick to them.

By the favour of the Guru they wake daily.

The pure name dwells within (their) heart, the Luminous one is blending light (with himself).

(6). They read in the three qualities,[3] the truth of Hari they do not know.

Having strayed away from the root (=first cause) they do not apprehend the word of the Guru.

They are overspread with spiritual blindness, nothing is (clearly) seen; from the word of the Guru they obtain Hari.

(7). They read aloud the Vēda, (blinded by) the threefold Māyā.

The fleshly-minded do not understand (them) on account of second love (=duality).

(Blinded by) the three qualities they read, the One Hari they do not know, without comprehending (him) they incur pain.

(8). When it is pleasing to him, then he himself unites (with himself).

By means of the word of the Guru he puts a stop to doubt and pain.

Nānak (says): the greatness of the name is true, by minding the name they obtain comfort.

Mājh; mahalā III.

XXXI. XXXII.

(1). He himself is without any qualities and endowed with all qualities.

Who apprehends the truth (=the Supreme), he becomes a Paṇḍit.

He himself crosses and makes all his families cross, who makes the name of Hari dwell in his mind.

Pause.

I am devoted, O Lord, I am devoted (to them, who), having tasted the juice of Hari, are getting its flavour.

Those people are pure, who taste the juice of Hari, they are meditating on the pure name.

(2). They are exempt from the obligation of (religious) works,[4] who meditate on the word (of the Guru).

In (their) heart is the truth, by divine knowledge they destroy egotism.

[1] ਭਾਉਣਾ is also active, to consider, to like, to incline to.

[2] We have in the manuscripts two readings—(*a*) ਸਚਿ ਰੰਗਾਵਣਿਆ, and (*b*) ਸਚੁ ਰੰਗਾਵਣਿਆ. In the first case ਰੰਗਾਵਣਿਆ (=ਰੰਗਾਉ) is the verbal adjective of ਰੰਗਣਾ, *v.n.*, taking delight in; in the latter ਰੰਗਾਵਣਿਆ (=ਰੰਗਾਵਣਾ) is the verbal adjective of ਰੰਗਾਉਣਾ, colouring, imbuing with love. According to the context the first reading is preferable.

[3] ਤ੍ਰੈਗੁਣ, Sansk. त्रैगुण्य, the aggregate of the three qualities, the same as the following ਤ੍ਰਿਬਿਧਿ ਮਾਇਆ, the Māyā containing the three qualities. It is opposed here to ਤਤੁ (तत्त्व) *truth*.

[4] ਨਿਹਕਰਮੀ (Sansk. निष्कर्म), free from the obligation of religious works (by meditation on the name).

They obtain the boon of the name, the nine treasures; having effaced the three qualities they are absorbed (in the Supreme).

(3). Who says: "I, I," does not become exempt from works.

By the favour of the Guru he puts away egotism.

Within him is discrimination,[1] he always meditates on his own self, by means of the word of the Guru he is singing the praises (of Hari).

(4). Hari is the lake, the ocean, pure is the intelligence (about him).

The saints always pick (it) up, it is obtained from the mouth of the Guru.

They always bathe (in the ocean = Hari) day and night, the filth of egotism (= individuality) they remove.

(5). The devotees are pure by dint of love and affection (to Hari).

They dwell in the pond of Hari, having destroyed egotism.

Day and night they have love to the true word (of the Guru), in the pond of Hari they get (their) dwelling.

(6). The fleshly-minded one is always a filthy heron, the filth of egotism he applies (to himself).

He makes ablution, but (his) filth does not go.

(Who) dies whilst living and reflects on the word of the Guru, he is removing the filth of his egotism.

(7). The jewel and exquisite thing is obtained from (one's own) house.

By the perfect and true Guru the word is proclaimed.

By the favour of the Guru darkness is blotted out, he himself[2] is recognizing the light in (his) body.

(8). He himself produces and he himself sees.

Who serves the true Guru, that man is of account.

Nānak (says): the name dwells in the body (creature),[3] by the mercy of the Guru (one) is obtaining it.

Māȷ̌h; mahalā III.

XXXII. XXXIII.

(1). The whole world is under the infatuation of the Māyā.

The three qualities[4] are seen as beguiled by the Māyā.

By the favour of the Guru some rare one comprehends (the truth), and is applying deep meditation in the fourth state.

Pause.

I am devoted, O Lord, I am devoted (to them, who) consume the infatuation of the Māyā by means of the word (of the Guru).

Who burn the infatuation of the Māyā and direct their thoughts on Hari, they obtain lustre at the gate and palace of Hari.

(2). The root (origin) of the goddesses and gods is the Māyā.

By whom (*i.e.* Māyā) the Smriti and Shāstras are produced.

Lust and wrath are spread out in the world, coming and going (people) incur pain.

(3). In this (world) one jewel of divine knowledge is put down.

By the favour of the Guru it is made to dwell in the heart.

[1] घिघेर (विवेक), the power of discriminating Brahm, the invisible spirit, from the visible (but unreal) objects, reality from unreality.

[2] *i.e.* The disciple.

[3] धट, body, vessel; any created thing or creature.

[4] There are two readings in the MSS.: त्रैगुल and त्रैगुली; if त्रैगुली be read, the translation must be: the creatures endowed with the three qualities (*i.e.* everything created).

Who practises chastity, truthfulness and true control of his senses, he is meditating on the name by means of the perfect Guru.

(4). In her father's house the woman is led astray by error.

She has clung to another and repents (of it) again (afterwards).

This and that world, both are lost, not in a dream she obtains comfort.

(5). (If) in her father's house the woman keeps in mind her beloved:

She sees (him as being) with (her) by the favour of the Guru.

She remains naturally imbued with love to (her) beloved, by means of the word (of the Guru) she makes love (to him).

(6). Their life is fruitful, who have obtained the true Guru.

Other love is consumed (by them) by means of the word of the Guru.

The One abides in (their) heart, having joined the society of the pious they are singing the attributes of Hari.

(7). Who does not serve the true Guru, for what has he come (into the world)?

His life is a misery, his human birth is uselessly thrown away.

The name does not come into the mind of the fleshly-minded one, without the name he is incurring much pain.

(8). By whom creation is made, he knows (with certainty).

He himself unites (him), (who) knows (him) by means of the word (of the Guru).

Nānak (says): the name is obtained by those people, on whose forehead (this) destiny was written[1] from the beginning.

MĀȊH; MAHALĀ IV.

I. XXXIV.

(1). He himself is the primeval, boundless male (=Supreme Being).

He himself establishes, and having established disestablishes (again).

In all exists that One; the disciple obtains lustre.

Pause.

I am devoted, O Lord, I am devoted (to them, who) are meditating on the name of the Formless one.

He has no form nor sign (and is yet) seen in everybody (=in everything created), the disciple is apprehending the inapprehensible one.

(2). Thou art kind and merciful, that Lord.

Without thee there is none other.

If the Guru bestow his favour, he gives the name; who praises (the name), he is absorbed in the name.

(3). Thou thyself art the true creator.

Thy store-rooms are filled with devotion.[2]

The disciple gets the name, his heart is thereby imbued with love, naturally he is applying deep meditation (on the name).

(4). Day by day I sing thy attributes, O Lord!

Thee I praise, O my beloved!

Without thee I do not want any one else, by the favour of the Guru thou art to be obtained.[3]

[1] ਲਿਖਾਵਲਿਆ = ਲਿਖਾ or ਲਿਖਿਆ, the syllable ਵਲਿਆ being a meaningless alliteration.

[2] The sense of this expression, "thy store-rooms are filled with devotion or adoration," is; all devotion is bestowed by thee from thy inexhaustible treasury.

[3] ਪਾਵਲਿਆ is here gerundive.

(5). The measure of the unattainable and inapprehensible one is not obtained.

If thou bestowest thy own mercy, then thou unitest (with thyself).

By means of the word of the perfect Guru thou art meditated upon; who obeys the word (of the Guru), is obtaining comfort.

(6). The tongue of a virtuous woman sings the attributes (of Hari).

(Who) praises the name, she is pleasing to the True one.

The (female) disciple remains always imbued with love (to Hari), having met with the True one she is obtaining lustre.

(7). The fleshly-minded one does (religious) works out of egotism.

In the gambling (for) life all the play is lost (by her).

Within (her) is greediness and great darkness, again and again she is coming and going.

(8). The creator himself gives greatness (to those):

To whom he decreed it from the beginning.

Nānak (says): who gets the name, the fear-destroying, he obtains comfort from the word of the Guru.

MĀJH; MAHALĀ V.

Ghar I.

I. XXXV.

(1). Within (the mind) the inapprehensible one cannot be apprehended.

Having taken the jewel of the name he has concealed it.

The unattainable, inapprehensible one, who is higher than all, is apprehended[1] from the word of the Guru.

Pause.

I am devoted, O Lord, I am devoted (to them, who) in the Kali-(yug) proclaim the name.

The saints are beloved and supported by the True one, by a great lot they obtain (his) sight.

(2). For whom (*i.e.* in whose search) the Sâdhiks and Siddhs wander about:

(On whom) the Brahmās and Indras meditate in (their) heart:

(Whom) the thirty-three crores (of gods) search for, him they praise in their heart, having met with the Guru.

(3). The eight watches the wind mutters thee.

The earth is the servant and runner of (thy) feet.

In the (four) mines and (their) species, in all thou art indwelling, in the mind of all thou art the sentient principle.[2]

(4). The true Lord is known to the disciple.

From the word of the perfect Guru he is known.

By whom he is drunk, they are satiated, the true ones are filled with the True one.

(5). In his house is comfort, he is happy.

He always indulges in joy, pastime and play.

He is wealthy, he is a great merchant, who fixes his mind on the feet of the Guru.

(6). First the daily bread is prepared by thee.

Then the living creatures are produced by thee.

[1] ਲਖਾਵਣਿਆ is here simply = ਲਖਾ or ਲਖਿਆ.

[2] ਭਾਵਨਾ, *s.f.* forming in the mind, conception, feeling (Sansk. भावना), or taken as adjective: *forming, acting*.

Like thee there is no donor, no other Lord, (thou art) not bringing any one in contact (with thyself).

(7). With whom thou art pleased, he meditates on thee.

He performs the advice of the holy people.

He himself crosses and makes all his families cross; at the threshold he is not repulsed.[1]

(8). Thou (art) great, (thou art) higher than high.

Thou art endless, thou art infinitely extended.[2]

I sacrifice myself for thee, Nānak is the slave (of thy) slaves.[3]

Mājh; mahalā V.

II. XXXVI.

(1). Who is free (liberated), who is bound?

Who is endowed with (divine) knowledge, who is the teacher (of it)?[4]

Who is householder, who is living lonely? who attains (his) value, Sir?

(2). In what wise is (one) bound, in what wise set free?

In what wise is coming and going stopped?

Who is doing (religious) works, who is abstaining from works? who orders and is (himself) ordered,[5] Sir?

(3). Who is happy, who is afflicted?

Who is turning his face towards, who is turning it away?

In what wise is meeting (union) effected, in what wise separation? who makes this manner manifest, Sir?

(4). What is that letter, by which (worldly) activity is stopped?

What is the instruction, by means of which (one) bears equally pain and pleasure?

What is the manner of life, by which (one) meditates on the Supreme Brahm? in what manner may (one) sing (his) praise, Sir?

(5). The disciple is free, the disciple is bound (to Hari).

The disciple is endowed with (divine) knowledge, the disciple is teaching.

The disciple, as householder (or) living lonely, is blessed, the disciple attains (his, *i.e.* Hari's) value, Sir!

(6). By egotism one is bound, the disciple is set free.

The coming and going of the disciple is stopped.

The disciple is doing (religious) works,[6] the disciple is abstaining from works, the disciple acts by his (own) natural disposition, Sir!

(7). The disciple is happy, the self-willed one is afflicted.

The disciple is turning his face towards (the Guru), the self-willed one is turning it away (from him).

The disciple is united (with Hari), the self-willed one is separated, the disciple makes (this) manner manifest, Sir!

[1] ਪਾਵਣਿਆ (= ਪਾਵਣਾ) is here verbal adjective = *obtaining*.

[2] ਮੁਚਾ, Sansk. मूर्छित, extended, enlarged.

[3] ਦਾਸ ਦਸਾਵਣਿਆ, a corruption instead of ਦਾਸ ਦਾਸਾਂ (ਦਾ).

[4] ਗਿਆਨੀ only signifies: *endowed with knowledge*, though we should rather expect here (for the sake of contrast) ਜਗਿਜਾਸੀ (जिज्ञासु), seeking after knowledge. ਬਕਤਾ (वक्ता), speaking; *master, teacher*. The construction is ਮੁਕਤਾ ਸੋ ਕਉਣ ਹੈ, etc.

[5] ਕਹੈ ਕਹਾਏ, he orders and is (himself) ordered, *i.e.* he acts for himself spontaneously, as explained in v. 6.

[6] ਕਰਮ = ਕਰਮਾ, *adj.* working, doing religious works, final *ā* being dropped, though the word-becomes thus confounded with the substantive ਕਰਮ, work.

(8). From the mouth of the Guru (comes) the letter, by which (worldly) activity is stopped.

From the mouth of the Guru (comes) the instruction, (by means of which) (one) bears equally pain and pleasure.

It is the walk (conduct) of the disciple, by which (one) meditates on the Supreme Brahm.

It is the disciple, who sings the praise (of Hari), Sir!

(9). All, that is made, is made by himself.

He himself does and causes to be done and to be established.

From the One has come forth the innumerable, in the One it is absorbed, Sir!

Mājh; mahalā V.

III. XXXVII.

(1). The Lord is undecayable (eternal), then what anxiety is there?

Hari is the Lord, (his) servant is therefore quite happy.

(Thou art) the hope of (my) soul and life, thou (art) the giver of comfort, that comfort (which) thou preparest, (I am) obtaining.

Pause.

I am devoted, O Lord, I am devoted (to thee, who art) acting in the mind and body of the disciple.

Thou art my rock, thou art my screen; who clings to thee, (him thou art) not sending away.[1]

(2). To whom thy work is sweet:

That man sees in every (created) body the Supreme Brahm.

In every place even Thou, even Thou, the only One, art existing.

(3). All desires thou art granting.

With devotion and love (thy) store-rooms are filled.

Who are protected by thee in mercy, they, by a perfect destiny, are absorbed (in thee).

(4). From the hell[2] thou pullest out.

Thou bestowest mercy and lookest favourably on thy servant.

He sings (then) the attributes of the all-filling and undecayable one; in telling and hearing (them) there is no end.

(5). Here (in this world) and there (in that world) thou art the protector.

In the womb of the mother thou art the preserver.

The fire of the Māyā does not affect them, who steeped in (thy) love are singing (thy) attributes.

(6). How shall I tell and remember thy qualities?

Within my mind and body I look on thee.

Thou art my friend, my sweetheart; O Lord, without thee I do not know any one else.

(7). To whom thou, O Lord, hast become a helper:

Him no hot wind touches.

Thou, O Lord, art asylum and giving comfort; the society of the pious is muttering and proclaiming (thee).

(8). Thou art high, unfathomable, boundless, inestimable.

Thou art the true Lord, (I am) thy servant and slave.

Thou art the king, true is (thy) sovereignty, Nānak is devoted, devoted (to thee).

[1] ਲਵੈ, from ਲਵਣਾ, *v.n.* (from the Sansk. लय or लयन) to cling to; ਲਾਵਣਾ, to send off, causal of ਲਵਣਾ. The Sikhs do not know what to make of these words.

[2] ਅੰਧਕੂਪ, literally: a well, whose mouth is closed; but also name of a hell.

MĀJH; MAHALĀ V.

Ghar II.

IV. XXXVIII.

Pause.

(1). Continually, continually the deity should be remembered.
By no means it should be forgotten from the mind.
From the society of the saints (that) is obtained,
By means of which one must not go on the road of Yama.
Take as viaticum the name of Hari and no reproach will befall thy family, Sir!
(2). Who are remembering the Lord:
They are not thrown into hell.
No hot wind touches (them), into whose heart he has come and settled (there), Sir!
(3). They are beautiful and lustrous:
Who are sitting[1] in the society of the pious.
By whom the wealth of Hari is collected, they are profound (and) boundless, Sir!
(4). (By whom) the nectar (and) elixir of Hari is drunk:
By seeing the face of (that) man one lives (it is lived).
Having adjusted all (thy) business, worship continually the feet of the Guru, Sir!
(5). Who by Hari is made his own:
To him the Lord is known.
He is a hero, he is foremost, on whose forehead the lot (is written), Sir!
(6). Who (fem.) in (her) heart is immersed (in) the Lord:
She is enjoying kingly (grand) enjoyments.
(By whom) no wicked (thing) is done, she crosses, having applied herself to true work, O dear!
(7). (By whom) the creator is made to dwell in (her) heart:
She obtains the fruit of (her) life.
(If) Hari, the husband is liked in (thy) heart, thy (happy) married state is lasting, O dear!
(8). The immovable thing is obtained (by him):
(Who) is in the asylum of the fear-destroying (Hari).
Nānak (says): putting (him) into the hem (of his garment) he is brought across by him (*i.e.* Hari), endless births are overcome, Sir!

Ōm! By the favour of the true Guru!

MĀJH; MAHALĀ V.

Ghar III.

V. XXXIX.

Pause.

(Who) continually mutters Hari, in (his) mind is calmness.
(1). By remembering, remembering the Gurdēv (his) fears are effaced and removed.
(2). (Who) comes to the asylum of the Supreme Brahm, why should he pine with grief?
(3). By worshipping the feet of the saints and pious all wishes are fulfilled.

[1] ਜਿਨ ਬੈਹਲੇ = ਜਿਨ ਦਾ ਬੈਹਲਾ, ē being added for the sake of the rhyme.

(4). In every body abides the One, in water, land and on the face of the earth, he is fully contained.

(5). (By whom) the remover of sins is worshipped, (he is) pure by the dust of the saints.

(6). All release (emancipation) (is made) by the Lord himself, by muttering Hari calmness (coldness) is effected.

(7). By the creator inquiry (examination)[1] is made, the wicked died having become powerless.[2]

Nānak (says): who is attached to the true name, he always sees Hari in his presence.

BĀRAH MĀHĀ.[3]

Mājh; mahalā V.

Ghar IV.

Ōm! By the favour of the true Guru!

(1). Be merciful, O Rām, and unite (with thyself) those, who were separated (from thee) by (their former) works and deeds.

In the four quarters, in the ten directions (of the earth) (we) erred about, being worn out (we) have come to the protection of the Lord.

A cow without milk is of no use whatever.

Without water vegetables[4] are withering, nothing[5] is produced.

If there be no meeting with Hari, the sweetheart, how shall rest be obtained?

In what house Hari, the beloved (husband), is not present, that town (and) village is a furnace.

All ornaments, all betel-leaf juices with the body are but poor (ornaments).

She who is destitute of the Lord, the beloved (husband), is (without) friend and sweetheart all (her) lifetime.[6]

The prayer of Nānak is: be merciful and give (thy) name!

O Lord Hari, join (me) with the Lord, whose dwelling-place is immovable.

(2). If Gōvind be adored in the (month) Čēt,[7] great joy is produced.

By meeting with the holy people he is obtained, by the tongue (his) name is uttered.

Who have obtained their own Lord, they come into his account.

Who live one moment without him, the life of (those) men is useless.

In water, land and on the face of the earth he is present throughout, he is contained in the trees.

Into whose mind that Lord does not come, how much shall I count his pain?

By whom that Lord is taken possession of, their lot is propitiated.[8]

(My) heart is longing for the sight of Hari, Nānak (has) thirst in (his) mind.

That Lord unites (him with himself) in (the month of) Čēt, who clings to (his) feet.

[1] ਤਪਾਵਸੋ, *s.m.* inquiry, corrupted from تفحص.

[2] ਮੂਠੇ, *p.p.* मूर्त, from the Sansk. मूर्छ्, weak, powerless.

[3] *The twelve months.*

[4] ਸਾਖ, *s.f.*, Sansk. शाक.

[5] ਦਾਮ, thing, from द्रव्य = davva = dāv = dām (*v* being changed to *m*).

[6] ਜਾਮ, contracted from जन्म, lifetime. ਵਿਹੂਣੀਆ must be repeated after ਮੀਤ ਸਜਣ, otherwise no sense is to be got out of this verse.

[7] ਚੇਤ (चैत्र) is the first month of the civil year, commencing about the middle of March.

[8] ਮਣਾ = ਮਨਾ (*v.n.*), on account of the rhyme (ਜਣਾ).

(3). How shall in (the month of) Vaisākh[1] the women, separated (from their husbands), be patient, whose love is cut off?

Having forgotten Hari, the sweetheart, the husband, it (*i.e.* the world) has clung to the deceit of the Māyā.

Son, wife, property (do not go) with (man), that Hari (alone is) imperishable.

Adhering, adhering (to) a false business the whole (world) is dead (by) spiritual blindness.

Without the name of the One Hari it (*i.e.* the world) is robbed on the way onwards (to the other world).

Having forgotten the Deity (man) is ruined; without the Lord there is none other.

Who cling to the feet of the beloved, their reputation is pure.

(This) is the prayer of Nānak to the Lord: O Lord, join (me), let me obtain thee!

Then Vaisākh becomes beautiful, when the saints meet with that Hari.

(4). In (the month of) Jēṭh[2] union with Hari should be desired, before whom all bow.

(Who) clings to the skirt of Hari, the sweetheart, (him) he does not hand over bound to any one.

Rubies and pearls are the name of the Lord, they cannot be stolen.

(With) Nārāyaṇ are (all) the pleasures, which are grateful to the mind.

What Hari wishes, that he does, that very thing the creatures do.

Who are made by the Lord his own, they are called happy.

Who, being taken as his own, are united (with him), how should they be separated (from him) and weep?

(By whom) the society of the pious is obtained, they, O Nānak, enjoy pleasures.

O Lord Hari, (the month of) Jĕ̄ṭh is delightful to him, on whose forehead (this) lot (is written).

(5). (The month of) Āsāṛ[3] becomes hot to him, with whom Hari is not.

Having forsaken the life of the world, the divine male, the hope of man:

He is ruined by duality, on his neck has fallen the noose of Yama.

What he sows, that he reaps, what is written on his forehead.

The night is passed, it (*i.e.* the world) is repenting, it has risen and gone off hopeless.

With whom the pious fall in, they are liberated at the threshold.

O Lord, bestow thy own mercy! (I am) thirsting after thy sight.

O Lord, without thee there is none other! this is the prayer (=word) of Nānak.

(The month of) Āsāṛ becomes agreeable to him, in whose heart the feet of Hari dwell.

(6). In (the month of) Sāvaṇ[4] (that) woman is excellent (who) has love to the lotus of the foot (of Hari).

(Whose) mind and body is imbued with love to the True one, (her) support is the One name.

The pleasure of the world is false, all, that is seen, is ashes.

A drop of the nectar of Hari is delightful, who joins the saints, he (or she) is drinking it.

Wood and grass has become green from the Lord, the boundless divine male is powerful.

(My) heart is longing to be united with Hari; by destiny he is bestowing it.

By whom the Lord has been obtained, to those (female) companions I am always devoted.

Nānak (says): O Hari, bestow mercy! by means of the word of the Guru (thou art) accomplishing (me).

(The month of) Sāvaṇ is pleasant[5] to them, on (whose) breast is the necklace of the name of Hari.

[1] Sansk. वैशाख. [2] Sansk. ज्येष्ठ. [3] Sansk. आषाढ. [4] Sansk. श्रावण.

[5] Most MSS. (and also the lithographed copy of Lahore) read: मुगागली, but this is senseless, मुगाद्दली must be read, though the gender (fem.) is wrong, माद्दल being masc. But as it should rhyme with राभली (मुगाद्दली), it is used here in spite of its being a grammatical blunder.

(7). Those women are led astray by error in (the month of) Bhādū,[1] who have bestowed love on another (than Hari).

(Though) a Lakh of ornaments be made (by them), they are of no use.

In what day the body will be destroyed, at that time they will call it a corpse.

Having seized (man) they march (him) off, the messengers of Yama make no difference with any one.

They stand, having abandoned (him) in a moment, whom he had loved (in his lifetime).

(His) hand is twisted, (his) body trembles, from being black he has become white.

What he sows, that he will reap, the field of his (own) works.

Nānak has fled to the asylum of the Lord, the Lord is giving (him) (his) feet as a boat (to cross over).

They are not thrown into hell in (the month of) Bhādū, who keep fast (their) love to the Guru.

(8). In (the month of) Asun[2] love (to Hari) springs up,[3] how will a meeting with Hari take place?[4]

In (my) mind (and) body is great thirst after an interview (with Hari); O mother, may some one bring and join (him) to me!

I will cling to the feet of (those) saints, who are assistants of (my) love.

How shall happiness be obtained without the Lord? there is no other place.

By whom the relish of (his) love is tasted, they remain fully satiated.

Having given up their own self they offer up the prayer: O Lord, apply (us) to (thy) skirt!

Who is admitted to a meeting by Hari, the husband, she cannot be separated (from him) in any way.

Without the Lord there is no other; Nānak is in the asylum of Hari.

In (the month of) Asū they are dwelling in comfort, (on) whom is the kindness (of) Hari, the king.

(9). Who do (religious) works in (the month of) Katik,[5] they are not deserving any blame.

Who have strayed away from the Lord, into them all diseases enter.

Who have turned their face away from Rām, they lose their life.[6]

In a moment all the enjoyments of the Māyā have become bitter.

No one can make mediation, where shall he weep?

Nothing can be done, the event (=what is to happen) is written from the beginning.

By a great destiny (lot) my Lord is obtained, then all separations cease.

O Lord, preserve Nānak! O my Lord, release the prisoner!

(If) in (the month of) Katik the pious people be joined, all sorrows become extinct.

(10). In (the month of) Manghar[7] those are beautiful, who are seated with Hari, (their) beloved.

How shall I describe the beauty of those, who are united by the Lord (with himself)?

The body and mind of (those) companions, who are with the pious, has flourished with Rām.

Those, who are without the holy people, remain solitary.

Their pain never ceases, they have fallen into the power of Yama.

By whom their own Lord is laid hold of, they are always seen standing.

Gems, jewels, rubies are with Hari, he is setting (them) on them.

Nānak desires the dust of those who have fallen on the asylum and the gate of the Lord.

Who adore the Lord in the (month of) Manghar, they are not born again.

[1] Sansk. भाद्र.

[2] Sansk. आश्विन. In Gurmukhī ਅਸੁਨ and ਅਸੂ are in use.

[3] ਉਮਾਹੜਾ, *s.m.* dim. (of ਉਮਾਹਾ, Pers. اماس) literally: the rising (of love, etc.).

[4] Literally: how, having gone, will it be met (with) Hari?

[5] Sansk. कार्त्तिक.

[6] ਜਨਮ ਵਿਜੋਗ, loss of birth or life, *i.e.* their life goes for nothing, is uselessly wasted.

[7] In Sansk. मार्गशिर or मार्गशीर्ष; in Sindhī also: मंघिरु (Paṣ̌tō مگر).

(11). In (the month of) Pōkh[1] cold does not affect (her), (who) has clung to the neck of Hari, (her) Lord.

(Her) mind is perforated by the lotus of the foot (of Hari), (there is in her) a desire for an interview (with Hari).

(Her) shelter is Gōvind Gōpāl, the king, she serves (her) Lord.[2]

The world cannot affect (her), having met (with) the pious she sings the excellences (of Hari).

From whom she was produced, (with) him she is united; (by) true love she is absorbed (in him).

By the Supreme Brahm she is taken by the hand and absorbed (in him), she is not again separated (from him).

I am devoted a hundred thousand times (to her, whose) sweetheart is Hari, the unattainable, the unfathomable one.

I fall on the protection (of those), (says) Nānak, (who have) fallen down at the gate of Nārāyaṇ.

(The month of) Pōkh is pleasant (to her, she has) all comforts, on whom the fearless (Hari) bestows (them).

(12). In (the month of) Māgh[3] make ablution and bathing with the dust of the saints!

Having heard the name of Hari meditate (on it), give alms to all!

The filth of the business of life goes off, pride will leave the heart.

(Thou) art not deluded by lust; covetousness, the dog, becomes extinct.

The world praises those who walk in the true way.

All the religious merit of the sixty-eight Tīrthas (is nothing), mercy to the creatures is approved of.

To whom he gives it out of mercy, he is a wise man.

Nānak is a sacrifice for them, who have obtained their own Lord.

They are accounted as pure in (the month of) Māgh, to whom the perfect Guru is kind.

(13). In (the month of) Phalguṇ[4] (she is) acquiring joy, (to whom) Hari, (her) sweetheart, comes and is manifest.[5]

The saints are the companions of Rām, in mercy they are united (by him with himself).

(Her) bed is beautiful, (she enjoys) all comforts, now there is no (longer) a place for pain.

(Her) wish is accomplished, (she is) very fortunate, she has got her husband, Hari, the king.

Having joined her companions she sings a song of congratulation, she intunes a song of Gōvind.

Like Hari none other is seen; do not compare any one with him!

This and that world are adjusted by him, he gives an immovable place.

(Who) is preserved by him from the ocean of the world, he does not run about again in births.

The tongue is one, many are the excellences (of Hari); he crosses, (says) Nānak, who falls down at the feet (of Hari).

In (the month of) Phalguṇ he should continually be praised, who has not a bit of covetousness!

(14). By whom the name is meditated upon, their works are accomplished.

(By whom) Hari, the perfect Guru, is adored, they are standing[6] at the true threshold.

The foot of Hari is the repository of all comforts, (by means of it one) crosses the water of the world.

Devotion with love those have obtained, who do not burn in worldly pursuits.

Falsehoods are gone, duality has fled, they are filled with the (all)-filling True one.

Who are serving the Supreme Brahm, the Lord, they keep in (their) heart the One.

Months, days, muhūrtas (forty-eight minutes) are good (to him), on whom he looks favourably.

Nānak asks the gift of meeting with Hari, O Hari, bestow mercy (on me)!

[1] Sansk. पौष. [2] ਸੇਵਾ—ਲਾਹੁ = ਲਾਏ. [3] Sansk. माघ. [4] Sansk. फाल्गुन.

[5] This verse may also thus be translated: In Phalguṇ there is acquisition (ਉਪਾਰਜਨਾ taken as *s.f.*) of joy, Hari, the sweetheart, comes and is manifest. [6] ਖਗ = ਖੜਾ.

MĀJH; MAHALĀ V.

DIN RAIṆI.

Ōm! By the favour of the true Guru!

(1). I serve my own true Guru, I remember Hari all the days and nights.
Having given up my own self, I fall on (his) asylum, with (my) mouth I speak sweet words.
Unite (with me) the sweetheart and companion, separated (from me) through many births, O Hari!
The creatures, that are separated from Hari, do not dwell in comfort, O sister!
Without Hari, the beloved, no rest is obtained, I have searched and seen all ways (=possibilities).
I am separated by my own deed, not any one is to be blamed.
Mercifully, O Lord, preserve me! nobody else does (this) work.[1]
O Hari, without thee (I am) mingled with dust, where shall a word be said?
(This is) the prayer of Nānak: may I see Hari, the sweetheart, with (my) eyes!
(2). The petitions of the creatures he hears, Hari is the powerful, boundless (divine) male.
In death and life (I) adore (him), (who is) the support of all.
In (my) father-in-law's and in (my) father's house (I belong to) that beloved (husband) whose retinue is great.
(He is) high, unattainable, of unfathomable wisdom, without any end (and) limit.
That is service, (which) will please him, (if one) become the dust of the saints.
God is a kind protector of the poor, saving the fallen ones.
(From) the beginning, (from) the beginning of the Yug, he is protecting (them), true is the name of the creator.
(His) value nobody knows, nobody is weighing (him).
In heart and body he dwells continually, (says) Nānak, (of whom) no estimate (can be made).
Who (are) serving day (and) night the Lord, to them (I am) always devoted.
(3). The saints always, always adore the donor of all:
By whom soul and body are created, who in mercy has given life.[2]
By means of the word of the Guru (his) pure mantr is worshipped and muttered.
(His) value cannot be told, the Lord is endless.
In whose heart Nārāyaṇ dwells, he is called a saint.[3]
The desires of the creatures are fulfilled, (if) the Lord, the sweetheart, be found.
Nānak lives by muttering Hari, all sins (he is) destroying.
The creature, that does not forget (him) day and night, becomes flourishing.
(4). All the contentions the Lord is bringing to an end, to me, the humble, (he is giving) a place.
I grasp the shelter of Hari, muttering in (my) heart continually (his) name I live.
O Lord, bestow thy own mercy (on me), (that) I may repose in the dust of (thy) servants!
As thou keepest (me), so I remain, what thou givest, that I put on and eat.
O Lord, produce (in me) that effort, (that), having joined the pious, I may sing (thy) praises!
No other place is seen, where shall I go to cry?
(Thou art) destroying ignorance, removing darkness, O high, unattainable and unmeasurable one![4]
May (my) separated mind be united with Hari! this is the aim of Nānak.
All welfare (I obtain) in that day, (in which) I touch the feet of Hari, the Guru.

[1] ਰੁਲੇਲ = ਰੁਲੇ, ਲ being merely an alliteration.
[2] ਜਿੰਦ, *s.f.* life as the sentient principle or motivity.
[3] ਭਗਵੰਤ, the Supreme God, but also applied to a saint or devotee.
[4] ਅਮਾਉ = ਅਮਾਪ, without measure.

RĀG MĀJH, VĀR I.

Mahalā I.

To be suug after the tune: Mal Kamurīd and Čandraharā, the Sōhīs.[1]

Ōm! the true name is the creator, the divine male.

By the favour of the Guru!

I.

Slōk I.; *mahalā* I.

The Guru is the donor, the house (of the) Guru (is a house of) coolness (=refreshment), the Guru is the lamp in the three worlds.

The boon of immortality, O Nānak, happiness is obtained by the mind being won over (or conciliated with him).

Slōk II.; *mahalā* I.

In (his) first affection[2] he sticks to the milk of (his mother's) teat.
In the second (he gets) knowledge of mother (and) father.
In the third (of) brother, brother's wife (and) sister.
In the fourth affection sporting springs up.
In the fifth (there is) running after eating and drinking.
In the sixth he inquires after the caste of women.
In the seventh a household is set up (by him).
In the eighth wrath is indulged in, (the cause of) the destruction of the body.
In the ninth (his hairs become) white, heavy (his) breathing.
In the tenth he is burnt and becomes ashes.
Gone are those songs,[3] cries and sighs.
The soul has flown away having inquired after the road.
He has come, gone (and) died—a (mere) name!
Afterwards he calls (to) the platter the crows.[4]
Nānak (says): the affection of the fleshly-minded one is blind.
Without the Guru the world is drowned.

Slōk III.; *mahalā* I.

(Up to) ten (years goes) childhood, (with) twenty (years there is) sporting (amorous dalliance), (being a man) of thirty he is called beautiful.

(Being) a man of forty he is in full strength, (being) a man of fifty (his) foot becomes weak, with sixty old age comes on.

(Being) a man of seventy he is weak in understanding, (being) a man of eighty he is no more able to do work.

With ninety he is sitting on a couch, being feeble he does not at all know (anything).

I have searched and sought and seen, (says) Nānak, (that) the world is a house of smoke.

[1] ਸੋਹੀ, name of a tribe of Jaṭs.

[2] ਪਿਆਰੁ, affection, love; ten kinds of affections of men are mentioned, though they are not applicable to all states, the whole description being too artificial and therefore unnatural.

[3] There are many readings: ਸਿਗੀਤ, ਸਗੀਤ, ਸਿੰਗੀਤ; it is best to read ਸਿ (= ਸੇ) ਗੀਤ or ਸੰਗੀਤ; the reading ਸਿੰਗੀਤ gives no sense.

[4] The sense is: when the shraddhā is over, in which the nearest relation has offered a platter (made of leaves and filled with ਪਿਣ੍ਡ or rice-balls), he calls the crows to eat up the offering.

Pauṛī.

Thou art the creator, the unattainable divine male, by thyself creation is produced.
Manifold (is thy) production, of many, many kinds and sorts.
Thou knowest (it), by whom they are produced, all is thy sport.
Some come, some go off, without the name they die.[1]
The disciples are deeply tinged with colour, they are steeped in colour, in the colour of Hari.
Serve that true pure Spirit, Hari, the divine male, the ordainer (of all things)!
Thou thyself, thyself art wise, the great, great divine male.[2]
Who in heart and mind are meditating on thee, O my True one, to them I am devoted.

II.

Slōk I.; *mahalā* I.

The body is created (by him), having put the soul (into it) (and) preserved, having made harmony (between body and soul).
With his eyes he (= man) sees, with (his) tongue he speaks, with (his) ears he hears.
With (his) feet he walks, with (his) hands he is working, what is given (to him) he puts on and eats.
By whom creation is made, him he does not know, the blind one does blind (works).
When (the vessel of the body) is broken, then it becomes shards, the form cannot (again) be shaped.
Nānak (says): without the Guru the Lord is not (obtained), without the Lord (one) does not get across.

Slōk II.; *mahalā* II.

"From the part of the donor good things are given," this the fleshly-minded one knows.
His intelligence, wisdom and cleverness, how shall it be told and described?
Who, sitting within, does the work, he is known in the four corners (of the earth).
Who performs religious works, he gets the name of a religious man, by committing sins he is known as a sinner.
Thou thyself, O creator, doest all (this) sport, how shall another be mentioned (and) described (as a religious man or a sinner)?
As long as thy light (is in him), so long he is enlightened, in (him) thou speakest; without the luminous (Supreme Being) can any one do anything? show (that), O clever one![3]
Nānak (says): to the disciple it has become manifest, that Hari alone is clever and wise.

Pauṛī.

Thou thyself, having produced the world, didst put it into (several) occupations.
Having placed on it the deception of spiritual blindness thou thyself didst put it away (from thee).
Within (it) is the fire of (worldly) thirst, the hungry and thirsty are not satiated.
This world is in doubt (duality), having died it is born (again), it is coming and going.

[1] ਮਰਿ ਜਾਤੀ = ਜਾਤੇ; similarly ਵਿਪਾਤੀ = ਵਿਪਾਤੇ, on account of the rhyme.

[2] In ਵਡਾਤੀ, ਤੀ is probably a meaningless alliteration; whenever the Sikhs cannot find a rhyme, they add a meaningless syllable to make it up. But ਵਡਾਤੀ might possibly be the participle present from ਵਡਿਆਉਲਾ, (I am) praising (thee), the great divine male, only that in this case no subject is hinted at.

[3] ਸਿਆਣੀਐ on account of the rhyme, instead of ਸਿਆਣੀਏ; similarly the following ਸੁਜਾਣੀਐ instead of ਸੁਜਾਣੁ.

Without the true Guru the spiritual blindness is not broken, all become tired having done works (for the sake of their emancipation).

By means of the instruction of the Guru the name is meditated upon, he (= man or the disciple) is filled with comfort, when it is pleasing to thee.

He saves his own family, blessed is the mother, who gave birth (to him)!

His beauty and intelligence is brilliant, who has applied his thoughts on Hari.

III.

Slōk I.; *mahalā* II.

(Who is) seeing without eyes, hearing without ears,

Walking without feet, working without hands,

Speaking without tongue and thus dying, whilst living:

(He), (says) Nānak, having known the order (of the Lord), is then united (with) the Lord.

Slōk II.; *mahalā* II.

Who is crippled in the legs, lame in his hands and blind, how shall he run and cling to the neck (of the beloved)?

Make feet of fear, hands of faith, eyes of understanding!

Nānak says: thus, O clever one! a meeting (with) the sweetheart is brought about.

Pauṛī.

Always, always thou art the (only) One, by thee another sport is made.

Having produced egotism, pride and covetousness thou didst put (them) into the creatures.

As it is pleasing to thee, so thou keepest (them), all do what thou causest them to do.

On some thou bestowest (this) gift and unitest (them with thee), by thee they are applied to the instruction of the Guru.

Some stand and serve thee, without the name nothing else pleases (them).

Others are employed in work, some are applied to true work.

(Some have) sons, wife, family, some remain uncontaminated (by such ties), who please thee.

Those (these latter ones) are inside and outside pure, they are absorbed in the true name.

IV.

Slōk I.; *mahalā* I.

(If) I make a cavern in a mountain of gold or in water, under the earth.

Or in the earth or in the sky, (if) I remain (the feet turned) upwards and the head downwards.

(If) I put on (my) body abundant clothes and wash (them) always, putting (them) off.[1]

(If) I read aloud the white, red, yellow and black Vēdas.[2]

(If), having become filthy I carry about filth (on my body): (all this is) folly and unsoundness of mind.

Emancipated[3] I become by the name, says Nānāk, having reflected on the word of the Guru.

[1] ਕਾਢਿ, part. p. conj. from ਕਾਢਣਾ (= Hindūst. کاڑھنا) to put off.

[2] These are unusual appellations of the four Vēdas. As no further hint is given, it is difficult to say, if these appellations are to be applied to the usual order of the Vēdas (Rik, Yajur, Sāma, Atharva), or not.

[3] ਨਾਹਉ, literally: not I, released from individuality (in German: ein nicht-ich).

Slōk II.; *mahalā* I.

Having washed his clothes he himself washes his body and practises continence.

The dirt sticking to his heart he does not know, from the outside he washes (himself).

The blind one, being led astray, has fallen into the net of Yama.

Another's thing (property) he considers as his own and earns pain in egotism.

Nānak (says): the egotism (individuality) of the disciple is broken, he meditates on the name of Hari, Hari.

The name he mutters, the name he worships, by the name he enters happiness.

Pauṛī.

There is conjunction of the body (with) the soul, (they are) joined in union.

By him separation is made, by whom it is produced.[1]

The fool is given to enjoyments, (but) all (is) pain.

From pleasure diseases arise by committing sin.

From joy, grief (arises), (man) is consumed (by the Supreme) having brought on separation (of the soul from the body).

The fool, making an estimate (of his meritorious actions) raises a quarrel.[2]

From the hand of the true Guru (comes) the settlement, (by him) the quarrel is brought to an end.

What the creator does, that will take place, what is done (moved) (against or without him), does not succeed.

V.

Slōk I.; *mahalā* I.

He speaks falsehood (and) eats carrion.

He goes to teach others.

He himself is ruined (and those who are) with (him), he ruins (also).

Nānak (says): as such a guide he becomes known.

Slōk II.; *mahalā* IV.

In whose heart the True one is, he praises with his mouth the true name (and) the True one.

He himself is walking in the way of Hari and puts others into the way of Hari.

If there would be a Tīrtha of fire, then the filth would go off, by bathing in a puddle he makes himself even more dirty.

The Tīrtha is the perfect, true Guru; who meditates daily on the name of Hari, Hari:

He himself is released (from material existence) with his family, and giving the name of Hari, Hari, he rescues the whole creation.

Humble Nānak is devoted to him, who himself mutters (the name) and causes others to mutter (it).

Pauṛī.

Some gather up tuberous roots and eat them, (their) dwelling is in the forest.

Some having put on flesh-coloured clothes wander about as Jōgīs in renunciation of the world.

(But) within there is much worldly thirst and desire for clothing and food.

Uselessly they waste their life, (they are) neither householders nor living solitary.

Death does not recede from (their) head, threefold is (their) desire.[3]

[1] This sentence is general, without special application.

[2] He quarrels with God, as if being treated unjustly.

[3] *i.e.* कायिक, corporeal, वाचिक, oral and मानसिक, mental.

By means of the instruction of the Guru death does not come near, as he (*i.e.* Yama) is the servant of the servants (of Hari).

(In whose) heart is the true word (of the Guru) and the True one, he is in (his own) house living solitary.

Nānak (says): who serve their own true Guru, they are free from desires.

VI.

Slōk I.; *mahalā* I.

If cloth is stained by blood, the dress becomes defiled.

How shall the mind of them (become) pure, who drink the blood of men?

Nānak (says): take the name of God with a pure heart and mouth!

Other (things) are (only) false shows[1] of the world, (which) practises false works.

Slōk II.; *mahalā* I.

When I am not (anything), what shall I say? (when) I am nothing, what may I become?

The story (of) the creature (and) the creator (efficient cause) is told (by me), what has become defiled, I wash quickly.

I do not understand myself (anything) and teach the people, such a guide I become.

Nānak (says): (who) being blind shows the way, he ruins every one (who is) with (him).

Having gone onwards (to the other world) he is robbed and struck in the face, as such a guide he becomes known.

Pauṛī.

(Though) thou be reflected upon all the months, seasons, ghaṛīs (twenty-four minutes) and muhūrtas (forty-eight minutes):

No one has obtained thee by means of celebration, O true, incomprehensible, boundless one!

That learned man is called a fool, who (is given to) covetousness, greediness and egotism.

The name is read, the name is comprehended, reflection is made by means of the instruction of the Guru.

By the instruction of the Guru the wealth of the name is acquired, with devotion the store-rooms are filled.

(By whom) the pure name is minded, he is (accepted as) true at the true gate.

Whose the soul and body is, (his) inward light is boundless.

Thou alone art the true wholesale-merchant, (all) the other world is (thy) retail-dealer.

VII.

Slōk I.; *mahalā* I.

(Make) kindness the mosque, sincerity the prayer-carpet, rectitude (equity) the lawful (food) (according to the) Kurāṇ.[2]

Modesty circumcision, good conduct fasting, (thus) thou becomest a Musalmān.

(Good) works the Ka'abah, the true Pīr (Guru) the Kalimah, kindness the prayer.

(Make) that the rosary, which will please him; Nānak (says): he preserves thy honour.

[1] रिदाजा, Arab. دِيباجه, preface (to a book), generally written in highly ornamental language and embellished with gilding and decorations; a false show or pageantry!

[2] So, as the words stand, they give no sense, as no grammatical relation of any kind is indicated, the whole verse being only a cumulus of words, as so often.

Shlōk II.; *mahalā* I.

O Nānak, a forbidden thing is (to) that one the swine, to that one the cow.
The Guru (and) Pīr then gives his assent (to him), when he does not eat carrion.
By means of (mere) words one does not go to paradise, he is emancipated by acquiring the True one.
(Though) he put spices into the forbidden food, it does not become lawful (thereby).
Nānak (says): by false words falsehood falls into his lap.

Slōk III.; *mahalā* I.

Five prayers, five times, five names (in) the five.[1]
The first (is) truth, the second "lawful," the third alms (in the name of) God.
The fourth (is) a right intention (and) mind, the fifth praise (and) laud.
Having uttered the spell[2] of the Kalimah he is called a Musalmān.
Nānak (says): As many as are false (Muhammadans), they fall (from) one falsehood into another.

Pauṛī.

Some are trafficking with exquisite gems, some are dealing in glass.
(From) the true Guru, being pleased, treasuries of gems are obtained within (the heart).
Without the Guru no one has obtained (them), the blind and false ones, having barked (like dogs), have died.
The fleshly-minded are consumed by duality and die, they do not understand the investigation (of truth).
Without the One (Supreme Being) there is none other, before whom shall they cry?
Some, being poor, always bark, the treasuries[3] of some are filled.
Without the name there is no other wealth, all the other objects are ashes.
Nānak (says): he himself causes to be done (and) does (everything), he himself by (his) order is arranging (everything).

VIII.

Slōk I.; *mahalā* I.

To be called a Musalmān is difficult, when (one) becomes it, then he may be called a Musalmān.
Before all,[4] having approved of religion, he gives away (his) property (to) the saints.[5]
Having become firm[6] in the way of religion he puts a stop to the gyration of death and life.
He obeys the will of the Lord on his head, he minds the creator, he parts with his own self.
Then, (says) Nānak, having become kindly affected towards all living creatures he is indeed called a Musalmān.

[1] No verb is given nor any logical relation indicated.

[2] ਕਰਣੀ signifies also incantation, spell. The Kalimah (كَلِمَه) is used by the Muhammadans as a sort of magical spell.

[3] ਤੁਜਾਰਾ, *s.m.* Explained by treasury; its etymology is obscure (perhaps derived from تِجَارَت).

[4] ਅਵਲਿ, ਅਉਲਿ can hardly be translated in any other way, as ਅਉਲਿ cannot be taken for ਅਉਲੀਆਂ ਦਾ.

[5] ਮਸਕਲਮਾਨਾ; the Sikhs do not know what to make of this word; at any rate it is a barbarous composition, from مِصْقَل, a polishing instrument and ਮਾਨ = ਵਾਨ, having a polishing instrument = saints, who are polishing the heart of men, cleansing it from rust.

[6] ਮੁਸਲਿਮੁ = مُسَلَّم, firm, sound, secure.

Slōk II.; *mahalā* IV.

Having removed lust, wrath, falsehood, calumny, having given up the Māyā (=illusive world) he puts a stop to egotism.

If, having given up lust and women, he abandons spiritual blindness, then he obtains in the darkness him who is free from all darkness (=the Supreme).

Having given up pride and conceit, love to son (and) wife, having given up (worldly) thirst (and) desire he makes deep meditation on Rām.

Nānak (says): in (whose) heart the True one dwells, he is absorbed, by means of the true word (of the Guru) in the name of Hari.

Paurī.

Kings, subjects, chieftains, none will remain, oh!
Shops, bāzārs will tumble down by (his) order, oh!
Solid, beautiful gates, the fool considers as his own.
Store-rooms filled with wealth (are) empty in one moment.
Horses, chariots, camels, impetuous elephants.
Gardens, property, household goods, whose own are they?
Tents, bedsteads, tapes, tent-walls, satin (whose own are they?).
Nānak (says): the true donor (of all these things) is known[1] from (his) power.

IX.

Slōk I.; *mahalā* I.

(Though) rivers of sour milk be made, (though) springs of milk and ghī gush forth.
(Though) the whole earth become sugar, (that) (my) soul always could enjoy itself.
(Though) the mountains become gold (and) silver, studded with diamonds and rubies.
Yet (I would) praise thee, the desire of praising (thee) would not cease.

Slōk II.; *mahalā* I.

(If) the fruit of the eighteen loads[2] (of trees and plants) should be had, (if) their taste should be exquisite.[3]

(If) both moon (and) sun should be stopped in their course, (and if) (my) place should become immovable.

Yet (I) would praise thee, the desire of praising (thee) would not cease.

Slōk III.; *mahalā* I.

Though pain should be inflicted (on my) body by an inauspicious planet (or) by the two (Rāhus).[4]

[1] ਸਨਾਖਤੁ, Pers. شناخته, known. All sorts of words are jumbled together in this verse.

[2] ਭਾਰ ਅਠਾਰਹ, the eighteen loads (supply: वनस्पति, tree, plant in general). It is said, that if of every tree or plant one leaf should be taken, they would make up eighteen loads.—A comprehensive term for all the trees and plants on earth.

[3] The word ਗਰੁੜਾ is quite unknown to the Sikh Granthīs; but it is apparently the Sindhī गारूड़ो, dissolving, melting. The taste (of the fruit) is melting, *i.e.* the fruit is so delicate in flavour that it melts in the mouth.

[4] ਦੁਇ ਰਾਹੁ, the two Rāhus, *i.e.* Rāhu and Kētu. ਰਾਹੁ is said to have been a दैत्य, with the tail of a dragon, whose head was severed by Vishṇu. Both head and tail retained their separate existence. The head was made in the planetary system the eighth and the tail the ninth planet, called केतु.

(Though) the blood-drinking Rājās[1] should be put on (my) head and my state should appear thus.
Yet (I would) praise thee, the desire of praising (thee) would not cease.

Slōk IV.; *mahalā* I.

(If) fire (and) cold should be my clothing, (if) wind should be (my) food.
(If) all the fascinating women of heaven, (says) Nānak, should become my wives.[2]
Yet (I would) praise thee, the desire of praising (thee) would not cease.

Pauṛī.

The evil-doer is a goblin, (as) he does not know the Lord.
He is called mad, who does not know his own self.
Bad strife is in the world, by contention it is consumed.
Without the name it is labouring under disease (and) error.
Who considers both ways as one (and the same),[3] he will be accomplished.
Who talks infidelity, he, having fallen by (his) infidelity (into hell), will burn.
All the world is contained in the true Lord.
At (his) gate and court he is accepted, who parts with his own self.

X.

Slōk I.; *mahalā* I.

He lives, in whose heart That one dwells.
Nānak (says): none other lives (in reality).
If he lives (without him), (his) honour is gone.
All is unlawful, whatever he eats.
(His) pleasure (is) in dominion, (his) pleasure (is) in wealth, steeped in pleasure he dances naked.
Nānak (says): deceived and robbed he goes.
Without the name he loses, when being gone, (his) honour.

Slōk II.; *mahalā* I.

What is the good of eating and dressing:
When that True one does not dwell in the heart?
What are fruits, ghī, sweet molasses, what flour, what meat?
What clothes, what a comfortable bed, (on which) the sport of enjoyment is made?
What are armies, what the attendance of mace-bearers,[4] (what) the dwelling in great show (and) in palaces?
Nānak (says): without the true name all things pass away.

[1] No hint whatever is given as to who the blood-drinking Rājās are.

[2] ਸਤੇ ਜਾਉ. The Sikh Granthīs are utterly at a loss how to explain these words. But ਜਾਉ is apparently the Sansk. जाया, wife, Sindhī जोइ.

[3] *i.e.* Hindūism and Islām.

[4] ਨੈਬ is traditionally explained by "*mace-bearer.*" ਖਵਾਸੀ *s.f.* (from خَوَاص, domestic servants, pages or valets), attendance (on the body). The following word, of which I could get no explanation from the Granthīs, I would derive from ਆਫ (or ਆਫਾ), *s.m.* great show or display; this word is now only found in Marāṭhī, but it suits the context very well.

Pauṛī.

What is in the hand of the pilgrim, (if) the truth be investigated?
Poison is in his hand, he dies, if he tastes it.
The dominion of the True one is known through all ages.
(Who) minds (his) order, he is a chieftain at (his) gate (and in) his court.
By the Lord a work is ordered, (man) is sent (to do it).
(Under) beat of drum the decision (of the Lord) is proclaimed by means of the word (of the Guru)
Some have mounted, some stand in readiness.[1]
By some the loads are bound, some are in a running haste.

XI.

Slōk I.; *mahalā* I.

When (the field) is ripe, then it is cut, what remains within the inclosure, is the straw.
Like hemp it is bruised, the corn is taken, after the straw is shaken.
Having joined the two millstones of the mill they sit down to grind (the corn).
Those (grains), which remained at the door (= mouth of the mill), were spared.
Nānak (says): I saw a wonderful thing.

Slōk II.; *mahalā* I.

Behold, what is sweet (*i.e.* the sugar-cane), that is cut down, cut down and bruised it is bound by the leg.
Having placed it within the rollers,[2] they punish it squeezing it well.
Its juice and marrow is put into an iron pan, it is heated and laments.
Also the sediment (thereof) is taken care of, fire is kindled (thereby).
Nānak (says): (on account of its being) sweet it is ill-treated; come and behold it, O people!

Pauṛī.

Some do not think of death, (they have) much hope[3] (of living longer).
Having died and died they are continually born (again); it is not in the power of any body.[4]
In their own mind and thoughts they say: (we are) good.
The fleshly-minded are continually observed by Yama, the King.
The fleshly-minded are untrue to their salt, they are ungrateful.
Being bound they will make salām, (to whom) the Lord had not been pleasing (during their life-time).
(By whom) the True one is found, (in whose) mouth (is) the name, (to them) the Lord will be pleasing.
They will make salām at (his) throne, what is written (for them) they will obtain.

XII.

Slōk I.; *mahalā* I.

What does[5] deep (water) to a fish, what the ether to a bird?
What does cold to a stone, what the married state to a eunuch?

[1] ਸਾਖਤੀ *s.f.* a barbarous word (like ਤਾਖਤੀ), readiness (from سَاختن).
[2] ਘੁੰਣ *s.m.* The roller of a sugar-mill (now ਵੇਲਣ).
[3] ਘਣੇਰਿਆ = ਘਣੇਰੀ, on account of the rhyme.
[4] ਕਿਸੈ ਨ ਕੇਰਿਆ = ਕਿਸੈ ਨ ਕੇ (*i.e.* ਹਥਿ), it is not in the hand of any one = they cannot help it.
[5] *i.e.* what affects?

Though sandal-wood preparations be applied to a dog, yet he runs after the bitch.
(Though) a deaf man be instructed and the Smriti be read (to him, he will not hear).
(Though) a blind man be put into the light and fifty lamps be lighted (to him, he will not see).
(Though) gold be put (before) a herd of cattle, it selects and eats grass.
(Though) iron be put on the anvil and crumble to pieces, it does not become cotton-flakes.
Nānak (says): (though one) tell these peculiarities (to) a fool, it is always lost.

Slōk II.; *mahalā* I.

(If) bell-metal, gold (and) iron break:
By means of fire the blacksmith joins (them) together.[1]
(If) the husband falls out with (his) wife,
By (their) sons reconciliation is effected in the world.
(If) the Rājā asks (anything), he is appeased (satisfied) by giving.
The hungry one is appeased, when he eats.
Drought is appeased (by) the swelling (of) the rivers (by) rain.
A bond (of friendship) (is made) (by) affection and sweet words.
The Vēdas are reconciled, if one speaks the truth.
The dead are appeased, if goodness and honesty be done.
In this bond the world goes on.[2]
The fool is appeased by a slap on his mouth.
Nānak expresses this thought:
By praising (God) a tie (of friendship) is made at the court (of God).

Pauṛī.

He himself having created the Māyā,[3] he himself reflects (on her).
Some are false (counterfeit), some are genuine (coins), he himself is trying (them).
The genuine ones are put into the treasury, the false ones are struck off (from the account) and thrown out.
The false ones are thrown down at the true court, before whom will they cry (for justice)?
(Those who) run after the true Guru, (do) the best work.
The true Guru makes genuine (coins) from false ones, by means of his word he is accomplishing (them).
At the true threshold they are accepted on account of (their) love and affection to the Guru.
How can one make an estimate of those, who are pardoned by the creator himself?

XIII.

Slōk I.; *mahalā* I.

Under the earth (are) also the Pīrs and Shēkhs and Rājās of the world.
(And) more kings go, O God!
Thou alone, Thou alone (art abiding).[4]

[1] The sense of the whole Slōk depends on ਗੰਢੁ, which signifies a *tie*, a *bond*, but must be variously rendered by *reconciliation*, *appeasement*, etc., to make it intelligible.

[2] The sense is: by such bonds the world is connected.

[3] ਕੁਦਰਤਿ in the sense of ਸਕਤਿ, Sakti, the Māyā, the illusive world.

[4] The idiom is half Persian and quite barbarous. ਮੇਰਵਦਿ = مي روَند, as Nānak was apparently not aware of the singular and plural in Persian. ਅਫਜੂ = Pers. أفزون, more.

Slōk II.; *mahalā* I.

Not the Gods, Titans and Centaurs (are anything).
Not the Siddhs, Sādhiks on earth.
Is there any other ?[1]
Thou alone, Thou alone (art existing).

Slōk III.; *mahalā* I.

Not the gift-bestowing men (are anything).
Not the seven (regions) under the earth.
Is there any other ?
Thou alone, Thou alone (art existing).

Slōk IV.; *mahalā* I.

Not (is) the disk of sun (and) moon (anything).
Not the seven insular continents, not water.
(Not) fire[2] (and) wind; none is stable.
Thou alone, Thou alone (art abiding).

Slōk V.; *mahalā* I.

The daily bread is not in anybody's power.[3]
Our hope[4] is the One (Supreme Being).
Is there any other ?
Thou alone, Thou alone (art our hope).

Slōk VI.; *mahalā* I.

Birds have no gold in their purse.[5]
The tree is hoping for water.
Who is giving it ?
Thou alone, Thou alone.

Slōk VII.; *mahalā* I.

Nānak (says): what is written on the forehead, that
None can efface.
According to his will[6] he puts down and takes away.
Thou alone, Thou alone (art abiding).

Pauṛī.

True is thy order, by the disciple it is known.

The True one is apprehended (by him), having parted with his own self by means of the instruction of the Guru.

[1] ਅਸਤਿ = Pers. أست ; ਏਕ ਦਿਗਰਿ = يک ديگر. The sentence can only be taken as interrogatory = there is none other.

[2] ਅੰਨ *s.f.* fire, another assimilation from अग्नि.

[3] ਦਸਤ ਆ Pers. دَست آ (but not in use in Persian itself, being rather a barbarous composition after the analogy of دست رَس) coming to hand, used substantively (like دَست رَس) in the sense of "power," "ability." ਵਸੇ = ਵਿਸੇ, altered on account of the rhyme.

[4] ਆਸਵਸੇ = ਆਸਵਾਸ, hope, comfort.

[5] ਗਿਰਾਹੁ, Pers. گِرَہ, a knot in the end of a shawl or cloth, in which money is bound up.

[6] ਰਜਾ, propensity, will.

True is thy court, by means of the word[1] (of the Guru) it is pointed out.
Having reflected on the true word (of the Guru) he is absorbed in the True one.
The self-willed one is always given to falsehood, by error he is led astray.
His dwelling is amongst ordure, no relish is known by him.
Without the name he incurs distress, he is coming and going.
Nānak (says): he himself examines accurately, by whom the false and genuine one is recognized.

XIV.

Slōk I.; *mahalā* I.

Lions, falcons, hawks, kites,[2] these he makes to eat grass.
Those who eat grass, them he makes to eat flesh; these ways he makes (them) go.
In the rivers he makes appear hillocks, in the deserts he makes unfathomable (pools).
He establishes worms and gives them royalty, armies he turns into ashes.
As many creatures as live, their breath he takes away and vivifies them (again), then what is it with (him)?[3]
Nānak (says): as it is pleasing to the True one, so he gives the morsels.

Slōk II.; *mahalā* I.

Some are living on flesh, some eat grass.
To some the food consisting of thirty-six (ingredients) is allotted.[4]
Some (live) in dust (and) eat dust.
Some are counting (their) breath, counting (their) breath.
Some take the name of the Formless one for their support.
(By his) gifts they live, no one dies (of hunger).
Nānak (says): they go, being robbed, in whose heart He is not.

Paurī.

The work of the perfect Guru is done according to destiny.
Who has parted with his own self by means of the instruction of the Guru, (by him) the name is meditated upon.
Who sticks to another work, (by him) his life is lost (wasted).
Without the name all is poison, (whatever) is put on (and) eaten.
By praising the true word (=name) one is absorbed in the True one.
Without serving the true Guru there is no dwelling in comfort, again and again one comes.
The world is a false capital, falsehood is earned (from it).
Nānak (says): by praising the fully True one (one) goes with honour (to the threshold of the Supreme).

XV.

Slōk I.; *mahalā* I.

(When) it is pleasing to thee, then they play and sing, (when) it is pleasing to thee, then they bathe (in) water.

[1] Some MSS. (and the lithographed copy of Lahore) read ਸਬਦੁ ਨੀਸਾਣਿਆ, but this is wrong; the right reading is ਸਬਦਿ ਨੀਸਾਣਿਆ.

[2] ਚਰਗ and ਕੁਹੀ are different species of hawks.

[3] ਤਾ ਕਿਆ ਸਾਹ, what is it with (him)? *i.e.* what does it matter with him? ਸਾਹ = ਸਾਥ, postposition.

[4] ਛਤੀਹ ਅਮ੍ਰਿਤ, food, consisting of thirty-six ingredients = delicate food. ਪਾਹਿ is here = ਪਵੈ, to fall to one's lot.

When it is pleasing to thee, then they exercise superhuman powers,[1] they let hear the sound of the conch.

When it is pleasing to thee, then they read the book (Qurān), they are called Mullās and Shēkhs.

When it is pleasing to thee, then they become Rājās and acquire many enjoyments.

When it is pleasing to thee, then they swing the sword and cut off head and neck.

When it is pleasing to thee, then they go abroad, and having heard (many) words they return to their homes.

When it is pleasing to thee, thou imbuest (them) with love to the name; who please thee, them thou likest.

Nānak utters one supplication (= word): all the others earn falsehood.

Slōk II.; *mahalā* I.

When thou art great, all is greatness,[2] by the good one good (things) are done.

When thou art true (= real), then every one is true, not any one is false.[3]

Telling, seeing, speaking, going, living, dying, running:

He, having issued an order, keeps under his order; Nānak (says): he himself is true.

Pauṛī.

By serving the true Guru (one becomes) confident, his error is put a stop to.

The work, that the true Guru enjoins (to him), is performed.

(If) the true Guru becomes kind (to him), then the name is meditated upon.

The gain of devotion, which is the best, is obtained by the disciple.

By the self-willed one falsehood (and) darkness (are obtained) (and) falsehood is practised.

Having gone to the gate of the True one the true one is comforted.[4]

He is called to the true palace by the True one.

Nānak (says): the true one is always given to truth and is absorbed in the True one.

XVI.

Slōk I.; *mahalā* I.

The Kali-yug is (like) a large knife, the Rājās are the butchers, religion, having made itself wings, has flown away.

There is (now) the new-moon's night, it is not seen, where the moon (of) truth has risen.

Searching about I became bewildered.

In darkness there is no way (seen).

Being given to egotism in (my) heart I weep in pains.

Nānak says: in what manner shall salvation be effected?

Slōk II.; *mahalā* III.

(In) the Kali-yug the praise (of Hari) is the manifest light in the world.

Some (rare) disciple passes across (the water of existence).

[1] घिङुत (Sansk. विभूति), superhuman power, supposed to be acquired by austere worship to Shiva and his wife Durgā. They are eight: अणिमा, extreme minuteness (invisibility); लघिमा, extreme lightness; गरिमा, extreme weight; प्राप्ति, power of obtaining everything; प्राकाम्य, fulfilment of every desire; महिमा, largeness of size (ad libitum); ईशिता, power over nature.

[2] The sense is: everything is a sign of thy greatness.

[3] कूड़ा, of a false, illusive existence, not real.

[4] चढाउिला, caus. of चढला, to cause to be quieted or comforted (Sansk. चप्). It is here not the causal form of चढला, to say (Sansk. जप्).

On whom he (*i.e.* Hari) looks in mercy, to him he gives (the praise).
Nānak (says): the disciple takes that gem.

Pauṛī.

Between devotees and worldly people a union is never brought about.
The creator himself is unerring, he does not err, though one try to mislead him.
(Those) devotees are united by himself (with himself), by whom the perfectly True one has been acquired.
(Those) worldly people are ruined by himself, who, continually speaking falsehood, have eaten poison.
They have no idea of departure, the poison of lust and wrath is increased (by them).
(Those) devotees perform service (to Hari), by whom the name is daily meditated upon,
Having become the slaves of (those) slaves, by whom their own self[1] is parted from within.
Their faces are bright at the gate of the Lord, by means of the true word (of the Guru) they have become lustrous.

XVII.

Slōk I.; *mahalā* I.

At dawn by whom he is praised and meditated upon with one mind:
They are perfect wholesale dealers; having fought (their struggle) they have died at the right time.
In the second (watch) (there are) many ways, many schemes of the mind are laid out.
Many have fallen into bottomless water, they dive and do not get out.
In the third (watch) (there is) a morsel in the mouth, hunger and thirst both are barking.
What is eaten (becomes) ashes, yet (there is) friendship with eating.
In the fourth (watch) drowsiness has come on, having closed the eyes he (*i.e.* man) goes about in his dream.[2]
Having risen (in the morning) dispute is also made by him; (thus) a circle of a hundred years is made by him.
If at every, every time, in the eight (watches) the fear (of God) be entertained:
(Then), (says) Nānak, the Lord dwells in the heart, true bathing is made (in it).

Slōk II.; *mahalā* II.

Those are perfect wholesale merchants, by whom the all-present one is obtained.
They remain unconcerned (all) the eight (watches = the whole day) in the same state of mind.
He, who is unfathomable in appearance (and) form, is obtained by (some) rare one.
By a perfect destiny the perfect Guru (is obtained), whose word is perfect.
Nānak (says): (if) he makes (it) full, the weight is not diminished.

Pauṛī.

When thou art, then what are others? by me the True one is proclaimed.
By her, who is robbed by (worldly) business, the thief, the palace (of Hari) is not obtained.
By this hard mind the service (of Hari) is discarded.
In whose body the True one is not found, that is broken and shaped (again).[3]
How shall it be weighed with a full weight and balance?
No one says: (I am) little, in egotism people go on.

[1] The reading ਆਪਿ, as found in some MSS., is wrong, ਆਪੁ, the substantive, must be read. In the more modern MSS. the copyists no longer know how to make the proper difference between ਆਪੁ and ਆਪਿ.

[2] ਪਵਾਰ, *s.m.* dream.

[3] The sense is: that creature is compelled to enter new bodies.

The good ones are examined and picked out at the gate (of Hari).
The ware is found in one shop[1] by means of the perfect Guru.

XVIII.

Slōk I.; *mahalā* II.

(Who) removes the eight, (who) destroys the eight, (who) destroys the nine (of) the body:[2]

In him (is) the name, containing the nine treasures, the One deep in qualities (= the Supreme Being) he finds.

By them, whose lot it is, he is praised, says Nānak, having made (to themselves) a Guru (or) Pīr.[3]

In the fourth watch of the dawn (of day) the desire (after Hari) of the intelligent ones springs up.[4]

They have friendship with those oceans,[5] in their heart and mouth is the true name.

There nectar is distributed, (according to) one's destiny favour is bestowed.

The body, the gold, is closely examined, its colour comes fully out (on the touchstone).[6]

If the glance of the banker be favourable, it (*i.e.* the body) is not again thrown into the heat (to be melted).

Who removes the seven (temperaments),[7] he is true and good, he sits with the learned.

There demerit and merit are reflected upon, the capital of falsehood sinks down.

There the false ones (like spurious coins) are thrown down, the good ones are applauded.

Talking (*i.e.* remonstrating against this process) is superfluous (= useless), O Nānak, pain and pleasure (rest) with the Lord.

Slōk II.; *mahalā* II.[8]

The breath (wind) is the Guru, water the father, the great earth the mother.

Day and night, the two are the male and female nurses, the whole world sports.

In the presence (of God) Dharm (rājā = Yama) reads the good and bad actions (of the creatures).

By their own works some are near and some far off (from God).

By whom the name is meditated upon, they are gone, having done their work.

Nānak (says): they are bright in their face; how many other people are released (from existence) in their company!

[1] ਸਉਦਾ, ware, or else ਵਥੁ, the thing, *i.e.* the name or the absolute being. ਹਟ, the shop, *i.e.* the heart.

[2] ਅਠੀ, the eight; what eight? perhaps the अष्टभाव or eight affections of the body, the eight members of the body (अष्टांग), and the nine (द्वार) outlets of the body. ਪਹਰੀ = प्रहारी, removing (*adj.*).

[3] *i.e.* having chosen for themselves a Guru (or) Pīr.

[4] The sense is: early, at the dawn of day, the intelligent ones, who have found the Supreme within their body, are filled with desire to praise him.

[5] ਤਿਨਾ ਦਰੀਆਵਾ ਸਿਉ ਦੋਸਤੀ, friendship with those oceans, *i.e.* friendship, love to Hari, the ocean. The plural is honorific or to be explained in the pantheistic sense of the Granth.

[6] ਵੰਨੀ, the colour of gold on the touchstone, by which its quality is indicated. ਚੜ੍ਹਾਉ is a verbal adj., rising it rises, *i.e.* it comes fully out.

[7] ਸਤੀ ਪਹਰੀ, removing the seven; what seven? perhaps the सप्तप्रकृति or seven tempers (of the mind). The whole verse is nearly unintelligible, as only a few hints are thrown out and the whole is purposely made as obscure as possible. Of such sentences a translation cannot properly be made, but only a conjecture. The Sikh Granthīs themselves could give me no explanation whatever.

[8] This Slōk is here (as in all MSS. I have compared) ascribed to Guru Angad, whereas it is verbatim repeated from the Japjī, where it is the concluding Slōk. In the Japjī there is nowhere any indication that the Slōk does not belong to Nānak, but it is very probable that this addition was made by Guru Angad, and that for certain reasons he is not mentioned there as the author of the Slōk.

Pauṛī.

True enjoyment (is) faith, by the true Guru it is pointed out.
(Who) believes in the True one, he is happy in the True one.
In the true fort and village, in his own house he dwells.
By means of the pleased Guru he is happy in the love of the name.
By falsehood one cannot go to the court of the True one.
By a totally false explanation (= doctrine) that palace (of Hari) is lost.
By attention to the true word (of the Guru) one is not repulsed (at the gate of Hari).
Who has heard and comprehended the true explanation (of truth), is called to the palace (of Hari).

XIX.

Slōk I.; *mahalā* I.

(If) I put on (as clothes) fire, (if) I make (my) house in the snow, (if) I make iron my food.

(If), having turned all pains into water I drink (them), (if) I urge and drive on the earth.

(If) I put on the scales the sky and weigh it, (and if) I then put a ṭank[1] on (the scales, to weigh it thereby).

(If) I be so much enlarged, (that) I may not be contained (anywhere), (if) I drive on every one with a nose-ring.

(If) there would be so much power in (my) mind, that I do, and that, having ordered, I cause to be done (everything).—

As great as the Lord is, so great are his gifts, in giving he does as he pleases.

Nānak (says): on whom he casts a favourable look, (he obtains) greatness by the true name.[2]

Slōk II.; *mahalā* II.

The mouth is not satiated with speaking, the ear is not satiated with hearing.

The eyes are not satiated with seeing, they are continually discerning the qualities (of things).

The hunger of the hungry one does not cease, by (mere) words the hunger does not leave off.

Nānak (says): the hungry one is then satiated, when, having uttered the excellences (of Hari), he is absorbed in the abode of (all) qualities (= the Supreme).

Pauṛī.

Without the True one all is falsehood, falsehood is acquired.
Without the True one he, who is given to falsehood, is bound and marched off.
Without the True one the body is ashes and mingled with ashes.
Without the True one all is (but) hunger, what is put on and eaten.
Without the True one, by means of falsehood, the court (of Hari) is not obtained.
(By him who) sticks to false covetousness the palace (of Hari) is missed.
The whole world is deceived, in deception it comes and goes.[3]
The thirst and fire in the body are extinguished by the word (of the Guru).

[1] ਟੰਕ, a weight, equal to four māsās.

[2] The apodosis in this verse is not clear. Nānak rambles about in his thoughts and a clear logical construction (quite abstracted from grammar) is never to be expected. The sense, however, appears to be this: whatever man's feats may be, he never can reach the Lord, whose all gifts are.

[3] ਆਈਐ ਜਾਈਐ, literally: it is come and gone.

XX.

Slōk I.; *mahalā* I.

Nānak (says): the Guru is the tree (of) contentment, religion (virtue) is (its) blossom, divine knowledge (its) fruit.

(The tree) is abounding in succulence (and) always green, by (religious) works (and) meditation (its fruit) ripens.

(The wise one) is eating the flavours of the sirup,[1] the gift descends on the head (of) the wise one.

Slōk II.; *mahalā* II.

(There is) a tree of gold, (its) leaves are red corals, (its) blossoms jewels and rubies.
Fruits of gems are found on it, who eats (them) with his mouth, he is happy in (his) heart and mind.
Nānak (says): (whose) destiny it may be, on (his) face (and) forehead (this) lot is written.
The sixty-eight Tīrthas (are) at the feet of the Guru.
The excellent (men) always worship (the feet of the Guru).
Laughter, desire, covetousness, wrath, are four streams of fire.
Those who fall (into them), are burnt; O Nānak, it is crossed over by sticking to (religious) works.

Pauṛī.

Die whilst living! having destroyed (one's own self) one will not regret it.
This world is false (unreal), who are apprised of it?
Without bestowing love on the True one it has run after (worldly) business.
Death is a bad thing; destruction and death (hang) over the head of the world.
By the order (of Hari) the executioner (of Yama) (stands) on the head (of every one) and lies in wait.
(If) he himself (*i.e.* Hari) gives (his) love, he is made to dwell in the heart.
(If) not forty-eight minutes, not a minute procrastination be made, he is obtained.
(Who) by the favour of the Guru comprehends (the truth), he is absorbed in the True one.

XXI.

Slōk I.; *mahalā* I.

The Tummī and Tummā is poison, the fruit of the Akk, Dhatūrā and Nimm (is poison).[2]
It abides in that self-willed man, into whose mind Thou dost not come.
Nānak (says): the enmity of (those) is told (before Yama), who walk without (doing) religious works.

Slōk II.; *mahalā* I.

The mind of the bird is in conformity with (its) destiny, now it is high, now low.
Now it is on a sandal-tree, now on the bough of an Akk-tree, now in high love.
Nānak (says): by the order (of God) it is moved about, the course (of) the Lord is applied (to it).

Pauṛī.

Many give explanations, having given (them) they go.
They give explanations of the Vēda, (but) its end (object) they do not obtain.
By reading (the Vēda) they do not obtain (its) secret, by comprehending (the truth) they do.

[1] ਪਤਿ *s.f.* sirup or melted sugar; the flavour of the fruits, when ripened, is compared to a sirup in sweetness.

[2] The ਤੁੰਮੀ is a smaller kind of the ਤੁੰਮਾ; in Gurmukhī it signifies a very bitter fruit, a colocynth (not as in Sanskrit, a long white gourd). The ਅਕ (Sansk. अर्क) is the gigantic swallow-wort; the ਧਤੂਰਾ (धत्तूर), the thorn-apple; the ਨਿੰਮੁ (Sansk. निम्ब), Azadirachta Indica, a tree bearing bitter fruits.

Is there in any dress of the six (philosophical) systems an absorption in the True one?[1]
The true (divine) male is inapprehensible, by means of the word (of the Guru) he becomes manifest (bright).
He who minds the incomprehensible name, obtains the threshold (of Hari).
The musician, who sings salutation to the creator:
He, (says) Nānak, causes (him) to dwell continually in his mind.

XXII.

Slōk I.; *mahalā* II.

Having become a conjuror he sticks to scorpions and snakes.
With his own hands he himself applies to himself a faggot.
(If) it has been from the beginning the order of the Lord, he eats excessively flames of fire.[2]
The fleshly-minded one quarrels with the disciple, he is drowned according to justice and equity.
He himself is the Lord of both sides (= worlds), he sees, having ascertained (everything).[3]
Nānak (says): thus it is known, that everything is under his order.[4]

Slōk II.; *mahalā* II.

O Nānak, (if one) examines himself, then he is a wise examiner.
(If) he understands the sickness and the (proper) medicine (for it), then he is an intelligent physician.
(Who) makes no transaction (on) the road, (as) he knows (that he is) a guest.
(Who) speaks, knowing the root (ground), (who) inflicts destruction (on) the destructive one.
(Who) does not walk in covetousness, (who) remains in the True one, he is chosen[5] and approved of.
Who directs an arrow towards the sky, how shall it arrive (there)?
Further on that (sky) is inapproachable, (with) a bumping sound it comes (to him, who) discharges (it).[6]

Paurī.

The women, (who have) love (to) the divine male[7] (and) are adorned with love:
Perform devotion day and night, they remain (in it and) are not prevented (stopped).
(Their) dwelling is in the palaces (of Hari), by the word (of the Guru) they are accomplished.
Those helpless (women) utter a true petition.
They are graceful at the side of the Lord, by (his) order they have departed.

[1] The whole sentence must needs be taken as interrogative; ਸਮਾਵਣੁ is translated here as a verbal noun, which seems to suit the context best.

[2] ਪਰ, *s.f.* flame of fire.

[3] ਵਿਉਪਾਉਣਾ (from ਵਿ + ਮਪਾਉਣਾ = Sansk. वि + मा) has two meanings: to measure through (to ascertain) or to determine, to fix.

[4] The whole Slōk is made against a certain juggler and conjuror.

[5] ਵਿਸਟੁ, *p.p.* of the Sansk. verb वृष्, to choose. The Sikh Granthīs explain it by "mediator," which is, however, a secondary signification (= the chosen of God).

[6] The words: ਵਾਹੇ ਦੜ ਜਾਲੁ are, as they stand, quite unintelligible and a barbarous diction. I have translated them according to surmise. ਜਾਲੁ is here very probably the verbal adjective: going. ਦੜੁ, *s.f.* a bumping sound. But ਵਾਹੇਦੜੁ (as one word) may also be taken as participle present. The translation would then run thus: it (*i.e.* the ਘਾਲੁ) is going (ਜਾਲੁ) (to) the discharger (ਵਾਹੇਦੜੁ).

[7] The words of the text: ਨਾਰੀ ਪੁਰਖ ਪਿਆਰੁ, literally: "the women, the divine male, love," may be translated in any way, as there is absolutely no sign nor hint of any grammatical or logical coherence.

They address (this) petition (to their) female friends: mind (him), O ye beloved!
Without the name there is woe in the house, wretched that life.
By the word (of the Guru) we were accomplished, nectar (was) drunk (by us).

XXIII.

Slōk I.; *mahalā* I.

The desert is not satiated by rain, the fire (of) hunger does not cease.
The Rājā is not satiated by dominion, are dried-up oceans (ever) filled?
Nānak (says): how much is the inquiry after the true name!

Slōk II.; *mahalā* II.

There is no fruit of that (human) birth,[1] so long as one does not know Brahm.
The ocean of the world some one crosses by the favour of the Guru.
The cause of causes is powerful, says Nānak, having reflected.
Causality is in the power of the creator, by whom the skilful machinery (of the world) is put down.

Pauṛī.

At the court of the Lord the musician dwells.
By praising the true Lord the lotus (of his heart) has opened.
Having obtained the omnipresent Lord his heart has become happy.
The enemies are kicked out and beaten, the virtuous ones have got the ascendancy.
Who serve the real and true Guru, (to them) the true word is shown.
Having reflected on the true word (of the Guru) death is destroyed (by them).
The musician rehearses the inexpressible (Supreme Being), by the word (of the Guru) he is accomplished.
Nānak (says): the beloved Hari, who is deep in qualities, is met with.

XXIV.

Slōk I.; *mahalā* I.

From sins sins spring up, if they commit (sins), they fall into sins.
By washing they (*i.e.* the sins) do not go off, though they wash them a hundred (times).
Nānak (says): (if) he (*i.e.* Hari) pardon (them), then they are forgiven, otherwise they follow (them).[2]

Slōk II.; *mahalā* I.

O Nānak, talking and prating are pains, giving (them) up pleasure should be asked.
Pleasure and pain, both are at the gate; man goes and puts them on (like) clothes.[3]
Where by speaking loss is suffered, there silence is the best thing.

[1] There is an attempt on the part of Angad to write Sanskrit. ਤਸਿ ਜਨਮਸਿ is apparently the genitive, as shown by the following ਸਾਗਰੰ ਸੰਸਾਰਸਿ, the ocean of the world. It appears that he has considered ਨਿਹਫਲੰ as a substantive, *fruitlessness* (though it is an adjective) and that ਤਸਿ ਜਨਮਸਿ stands for ਤਸ੍ਯ ਜਨਮਸ੍ਯ, though the Sansk. genitive of जन्म is जन्मनः. That such an attempt at Sanskrit-writing is made, the whole context shows.

[2] ਪਾਹੀ, *adv.* near, from behind (Sindhī पाही); ਪਾਹਿ = ਪਹੈ.

[3] The sense of the words ਦੁਇ ਦਰਿ is: both are at the gate = within reach. Man puts pleasure and pain on as he puts on a cloth, *i.e.* according to his liking.

Pauṛī.

Having looked about in the four corners (of the earth) (my) inside was searched (by me).

By the true, inapprehensible divine male, having created, it is looked down (in mercy).

To him, who has gone astray in the desert, the way is shown by the Guru.

The true Guru is the vehicle of the True one, the True one is held up (by him).

The gem (*i.e.* the Supreme) is obtained in (one's own) house (= personality), the lamp is lighted (therein).

(Who) praise (him) by means of the true word (of the Guru), (they are) happy, truth is kindled (in them).

The fearless one, who is given to pride, is annihilated.

The world, having strayed away from the name, wanders about as a goblin.

XXV.

Slōk I.; *mahalā* III.

In fear (man) is born, in fear also he dies, fear is in his heart.

Nānak (says): if he dies in the fear (of God), he has come into the world happy.

Slōk II.; *mahalā* III.

Without fear he lives, many, many pleasures he enjoys.

Nānak (says): if he dies without fear, he rises and goes with a black face.

Pauṛī.

(If) the true Guru become merciful, then (one's) wish is fulfilled.

(If) the true Guru become merciful, one never grieves.

(If) the true Guru become merciful, pains are not known.

(If) the true Guru become merciful, then the pleasure of Hari is enjoyed.

(If) the true Guru become merciful, then what is the fear of Yama?

(If) the true Guru become merciful, there is always happiness in the body.

(If) the true Guru become merciful, the nine treasures are obtained.

(If) the true Guru become merciful, then one is absorbed in the True one.

XXVI.

Slōk I.; *mahalā* I.[1]

They pluck their head,[2] they drink washings,[3] they ask the leavings of meals and eat them.

Having laid bare the excrements[4] they put them into their mouths, having seen raw[5] water they are afraid.

Like sheep they pluck their head, their hands are filled with ashes.

With mother, father and business they part, their families weep (after them) with lamentations.

[1] This whole Slōk is directed against the Jainas, who are now called in the Panjāb ਸਰਾਉਗੀ; see Sikhā̃ dē rāj̆ dī vithiā, p. 162.

[2] This is their initiatory rite.

[3] ਮਲਵਾਣੀ, now called ਪੇਲਪਾਲ, water used already in vessels. The Jainas drink no fresh water, but either boiled water or washings (from the pots).

[4] ਫਦੀਹਤਿ, *s.f.*, Arabic فضيحت (properly: disgrace).

[5] ਭੜਾਸਣਾ, *v.n.*, *p.p.* ਭੜਾਸਾ, here used in the sense of ਕਚਾ ਪਾਣੀ, natural water, not cooked, but warmed or heated by the sun.

(They offer) no rice-balls nor platter, nor funeral ceremonies, to the dead they do not put down a lamp anywhere.

They are not admitted to the sixty-eight Tīrthas, the Brahman eats no food (from their hands).

They remain always dirty day and night, to their forehead (they do not apply) Tilaks (marks).

They sit down, having always put the shroud of death (over their body), they hide themselves and do not go to a court.

On their loins (they carry) their cups, in their hands a (white) brush (of wool),[1] (thus, having cleansed the place) they go forwards and backwards.

They are neither Jōgīs nor Jangams,[2] nor are they Kāzīs or Mullās.

Ruined by the deity they go about distressed, cursed goes the herd about.

He kills and vivifies the living beings, none other preserves (them).

Alms and ablutions are abandoned, ashes are put on the head of the plucked one (*i.e.* the Jaina).

In the water gems are produced, the (mountain) Mēru was made the churning-staff (by the gods).

The sixty-eight Tīrthas (were) established by the Dēvī, at the festivals the praise (of the gods) is sung.

By him (*i.e.* the Jaina) neither a musical instrument is played (in honour of the gods) nor worship (performed), (whereas) the wise ones always bow down (in worship).

Who whilst living dies, he is saved, when water is put on (his) head.

Nānak (says): the head-plucked ones are devils, to them nothing is pleasing.

After it has rained, joy springs up, the frugal economy of the creatures has come to an end.[3]

After it has rained, there is corn, sugar-cane and cotton (produced), every one gets his sheet.[4]

After it has rained, (the kine, etc.) browse the grass, the woman constantly churns the pleasant thick milk.

By means of that ghī burnt-offering, sacrifice and worship being always made, the business (of man) is prospering.[5]

The Guru is the ocean, all the rivers are disciples, by bathing in which greatness is (obtained).

Nānak (says): if the head-plucked ones do not bathe (in it), seven spits[6] (on them!), dust on their head!

Slōk II.; *mahalā* II.

What can the cold do to the fire, what the night to the sun?

What darkness to the moon, what is the nature of wind and water?

What can the things do to the earth, in which everything is produced?

Nānak (says): then the honour (of a thing) is known, when he (*i.e.* God) protects (its) honour.

Pauṛī.

Thou, O true Lord, art always happy.

Thou art the true court, the others are coming and going.

Who asks the true gift, he is like thee.

[1] The ਫੁਮਣ is a sort of broom, made of white wool, with which the Jainas cleanse the place before and after them, lest they by inadvertence destroy a living being. This broom they call ਰਜੋਹਣਾ.

[2] ਜੰਗਮ, a mendicant; they worship Shiva and the Linga and hate the Brahman. They wear matted hair and ring a bell when begging.

[3] ਜੁਗਤਿ has here the meaning of "*frugal temperance.*"

[4] ਪਤ੍ਰਾ, *s.m.* a sheet spread out to receive rice, etc., from the cooking vessel. The sense is: every one gets his (full) share of food.

[5] The argument used here is just the same as that advanced in the Bhagavad-Gīta, iii. 10.

[6] ਚਟਾ, *m.* = ਥੁਕ, spit, spitting.

True is thy order, by the word (of the Guru) it is made pleasant.
By minding it divine knowledge and meditation are obtained from thee.
According to (one's former) works the sign[1] is made, it does not go off, though one try to remove it.
Thou art the true donor, thou givest always, as it increases, (the more thou givest).
Nānak asks for that gift, which is pleasing to thee.

XXVII.

Slōk I.; *mahalā* II.

Who has been initiated and instructed (in truth), he, by means of praising (Hari) is absorbed in the True one.

What instruction shall be given to them, whose Gur-dēv Nānak is?

Slōk II.; *mahalā* I.

Whom he himself causes to apprehend (the truth), he apprehends (it).
To whom he himself makes it known, to him becomes known everything.
Having related, related the story he fights (with) the Māyā.[2]
By his order he makes all forms (of existence).
He himself knows all (his) reflections.
Nānak (says): the word is told by himself.
(His) misapprehension ceases, to whom (this) gift is made.

Pauṛī.

I, the unemployed musician, was put (by him) into (his) work.
Many times, by day and night, an order was given (by him to me) from the beginning.
The musician was called by the Lord to the true palace.
With true praises praising (him) he obtained clothing.
The true nectar-name was given (to him) as food.
(By whom) it is eaten, they are satiated and obtain comfort.
(If) he (God) bestows favour (on) the musician, the word (= name) is sounded (by him).
Nānak (says): having praised the True one the Omnipresent was obtained (by me).

[1] ਨੀਸਾਣੁ, the sign, mark, *i.e.* the allotment put down for a creature.

[2] This line seems to refer to him, to whom everything is made known. Relating, what he has heard, he struggles with the Māyā (illusion).

RĀGU GAUṚĪ GUĀRĒRĪ.

Čaupadās (and) Dupadās.

Ōm! The true name is the creator, the divine male without fear, without enmity, of timeless form, unproduced from the womb.
By the favour of the Guru!

I.; *mahalā* I.

(1). The fear (of God) is very heavy, a great weight:
The wisdom of the (human) mind is light,[1] it talks (random) words.
(By whom) the load is put on the head and carried about:
He, by the favourable look (of God) and by destiny reflects on the Guru.

Pause.

Without the fear (of God) none will pass over.
The state (of) the fear (of God) is kept up[2] by means of faith.
(2). Fear is in the body (like) fire, it is kindled with fear.
The state of fear is shaped by means of the word (of the Guru).
Without fear the shaping is but rough.
(If) the mould is blind,[3] the cast is blind.
(3). By the sport of the intellect desire is produced.
By a thousand clevernesses passion does not go down.
Nānak (says): the fleshly-minded talk wind.
Blind is (their) word (= instruction) and senseless prattle.

Gauṛī; mahalā I.

II.

(1). In fear is the house (= heart), in the house is fear, by means of the fear (of God) fear goes.
What is that fear, by which fear subsides?
Without thee there is no other place.
Whatever exists, all is thy pleasure.[4]

Pause.

One would be afraid, if there should be another object of fear.
He is alarmed by fear, (in whom there is) an uproar of the mind.
(2). The soul does neither die nor is drowned, it passes over.
By whom (everything) is done, he does everything.
By (his) order it comes, by (his) order it goes.
In future and past (times)[5] it is absorbed by (his) order.
(3). (Who has) love to Brahm (and) a desire (for) heaven:

[1] Light, *i.e.* not able to bear the weight.

[2] ਗਾਖਿਆ ਸਵਾਰਿ is a compound verb, in which ਸਵਾਰਿ is nearly meaningless.

[3] ਸੰਚਾ, *s.m.* mould, stamp. ਅੰਧਾ = indistinct.

[4] ਸਭ ਤੇਰੀ ਰਜਾਇ, all is thy pleasure, *i.e.* all is produced by thy pleasure (or order).

[5] ਆਗੈ ਪਾਛੈ, literally: before and after, *i.e.* the soul in its past and future births is absorbed (re-absorbed) by his order.

In him is much hunger (after) a sign of direction.[1]
Eating and drinking the fear (of God) (is his) support.
Without eating (it) he dies (and) becomes a fool.
(4). (Is there) any, any, any, any one, whose he (*i.e.* God) is?
Every one (is) thine, thou (belongest) to all.
Whose the living creatures, wealth and property are:
To express a thought (about him) is difficult, (says) Nānak.

Gauṛī; mahalā I.

III.

(1). Make wisdom the mother, contentment the father.
Truth the brother; this is the best.[2]

Pause.

There is a talking (about God), (but) nothing (in reality) can be said (about him).
Thy power and value are not attained.
(2). (Whose) two fathers-in-law, modesty and reflection have become:
He makes (in his) heart (religious) works (his) wife.
The day appointed for the wedding (is) union (with the saints), marriage separation (from the world).[3]
The true and holy ones, (says Nānak), they are fit (relatives).

Gauṛī; mahalā I.

IV.

(1). The union (of) wind, water, fire.
The sport of the fickle, active intellect.
The nine doors and the tenth gate.
Comprehend, O wise one, this thought!

Pause.

He is relating, speaking, hearing.[4]
Who reflects on his own self, he becomes wise.
(2). The body is earth, the wind (breath) speaks (in it).
Comprehend, O wise one, who has died?
The form (= body) has died, egotism is rejected.
He has not died, who is seeing.
(3). For whose sake they go to the bank of a Tīrtha:
(That) exquisite jewel is even in the heart.
The Panḍit, having read and read, discusses an argument,

[1] The Sikhs do not know what to make of these two lines. They explain ਹੰਸੁ by ਹਿੰਸਾ, injury; ਅਸਮਾਨ by ਅਸਮਾਨ ਵਤ (like heaven), ਨੈਸਾਨੁ by ਪ੍ਰਗਟ or ਨਦੀ ਵਤ (like a river), all which explanations give no sense whatever. ਹੰਸੁ is a name for Brahm (the absolute substance); ਨੈ ਸਾਨ we would explain by ਨੈ = नय, guidance, direction, and ਸਾਨ = संज्ञा, sign (in Hindūstānī also سان, as: سان بجھانا, to make one understand by hints). These verses are mere riddles, intended for puzzling.

[2] According to the Janampatrī these words are said to have been addressed to Mardānā, when he asked leave to revisit his family.

[3] We have added the words in parenthesis according to conjecture, as Nānak usually only gives a few hints, which by themselves are more or less unintelligible.

[4] The ਸੋਈ is apparently referring to the Supreme.

(But) does not know the thing that is within.
(4). I have not died, my calamity (only) has died.
He has not died, who remains absorbed (in the Supreme).
Nānak (says): by the Guru Brahm is shown:
(Who) is not seen dying and going.

Gauṛī; mahalā I.

Dakhṇī.

V.

(1). (Who), having heard and heard comprehends (and) minds the name:
To him I always devote myself.
(Whom) thou thyself leadest astray, (he has) no place nor spot.
(Whom) thou instructest (in truth), (him) thou unitest to union (with thyself).

Pause.

(If) the name be obtained, it goes with me.
Without the name the whole (world) is bound by death.
(2). Agriculture (and) trade (are under) the protection of the name.
A bundle of seed (of) sins (and) religious merits (is with men).
Pleasure and passion in the heart are a loss.[1]
Who has forgotten the name, departs with a blemish in his heart.
(3). The instruction of the true Guru is true.
Body (and) mind (become) cool (= tranquil) (by) true knowledge.
By the fullness of water in the moat (there) is sap (in) the lotus.[2]
(Who) are attached to the word (of the Guru), (they are) sweet (like) the juice (of) sugar-cane.
(4). In accordance with (his) order[3] there are ten gates in the fort (= body).
Five dwell in it having met, (in) infinite light.
He himself is weighed, he himself is the retail-dealer.
Nānak (says): by means of the word (of the Guru) he is accomplishing[4] (the disciples).

Gauṛī; mahalā I.

VI.

(1). Is it known, from whence (man) comes?
From what he is produced, in what he is absorbed?
How he is bound, how he gets emancipation?
How he is absorbed (in) the imperishable self-born one?

Pause.

The name is nectar in the heart, the name (is nectar) in the mouth.
(It is) the name (of) Nar-Hari, (by) Nar-Hari (he becomes) free from desire.

[1] ਚੋਟ, a blow, a loss (in trade), a misfortune.

[2] Such lines cannot be translated, as all rests on conjecture, no case nor verb being indicated. ਪਰੀਖ is perhaps ਪਰਿਖਾ, a moat or ditch. The sense would be: if there is plenty of water in a moat, the lotuses are full of sap.

[3] ਸੰਜੋਗੀ (संयोगी) is here (as adjective) used in an adverbial sense: *according to.* It is constructed with the Locative (occasionally also with the Nom.).

[4] The sense of this verse is not easily found out, as no grammatical construction is observed. Who the five are (senses?), is not indicated. The Sikh Granthīs themselves are bewildered about it.

(2). Naturally he comes, naturally he goes.
From the mind[1] he is produced, in the mind he is absorbed.
The disciple is emancipated and not bound.
Reflecting on the word (of the Guru) he is released (from matter) by means of the name of Hari.
(3). The dwelling of many birds is at night (on) a tree.
Comfort is in the heart of the afflicted (birds), (their) delusion is destroyed.
(From) evening (till) dawn they look up to the sky.
(Then) they run to the ten quarters (of the globe), this is written (for them) by destiny.
(4). (Who is) devoted to the name (is like) a framework in a pasture-ground.
The jar of pleasure and passion, the poison, bursts asunder.
The house and shop are without chattels and empty.
The diamant-shutters of the disciple are opened.
(5). The saints are met with (on account of) a former conjunction.[2]
Who rejoice in the True one, they are the perfect people of Hari.
Who offer up soul and body with natural ease:
At their feet Nānak falls down.

Gauṛi; mahalā I.

VII.

(1). Pleasure and passion are contained in the mind.
Directed to the disease of falsehood the mind wakes.
A stock of sin (and) covetousness is collected.
He crosses and makes others (cross),[3] whose mind is attentive to the name.

Pause.

Praise, praise (to thee), O True one, thou art my support!
I am a sinner, thou alone art pure.
(2). Fire (and) water speak (with) a crackling and gushing sound.[4]
The tongue (and) the senses (have) a bad taste.
The sight is diseased, (there is) no fear nor love.
(If) (one) destroys his own self, then he obtains the name.
(3). (Who) dies through the word (of the Guru), has not again to die.
Without having died how should he become perfect?
In illusion and duality the mind is involved.
Firm is (only) Nārāyaṇ, what he does, that is done.

[1] ਮਨ must here be taken in the sense, which the Sānkhya attributes to it. According to this system (which is also received in the Yōga of Patanjali) there are 25 components of all existing things (with the exception of the Supreme Being), viz.: (1) Prakṛiti (undeveloped matter); (2) Buddhi, intelligence; (3) Ahankāra, egotism (individual consciousness); (4-8) Tanmātrāṇi, the five subtile elements; (9-13) Mahābhūtāni, the five grosser elements; (14-18) Indriyāṇi, the five senses of perception; (19-23) Karmēndriyāṇi, the five organs of action; (24) the Manas, the internal organ of perception, the director and ruler of the five senses and organs of action; (25) the ātmā or puruṣha, the individual soul. 2-24 are called "*vyakta,*" *developed matter*, and form the kṣhētra, or body. From the *manas* (as the last) man (puruṣha) is said to be produced.

[2] ਪੂਰਬ ਸੰਜੋਗ, a former conjunction, *i.e.* in a former state of existence.

[3] ਤਰੁ ਤਾਰੀ; ਤਰੁ = ਤਰੈ, he crosses, and ਤਾਰੀ (= Sansk. तारिन्), causing to cross. The Sikh Granthīs explain ਤਾਰੀ by ਬੇੜੀ, boat, "he crosses in a boat;" but this is against etymology and grammar.

[4] ਅਗਨਿ ਪਾਣੀ, the fire and water (*i.e.* in the body), the bodily elements break forth violently; this seems to be the sense according to the context.

(4). I ascend the boat, when (my) turn comes.
Who are repulsed (from) the boat, are beaten at the threshold (of Hari).
The True one I praise, blessed is the gate of the Guru.
In the gate and house[1] of Nānak is he who has always the same form.

Gauṛī; mahalā I.

VIII.

(1). The (drooping) lotus (of the heart) was turned up (again) by reflecting on Brahm.
A stream (of) nectar (is flowing) (in) the tenth gate[2] (of) the skull.
The three worlds are penetrated by Murāri himself.[3]

Pause.

O my heart, let no error be entertained!
The mind being reconciled (with itself) nectar-juice is drunk.
(2). Having overcome birth (regeneration) by dying (my) mind is reconciled.
(I have) died in (my) own self, by the mind (my) mind is known.[4]
(If) (his) favourable look is bestowed, the house is known by the house.[5]
(3). Chastity, virtue, (going to) Tīrthas, control of the passions (are contained) in the name.
(If) I make a great extension (of works), of what use is it?
The divine male Nārāyaṇ is the inward governor.
(4). (If) I would mind another one, I would go to another's house.
(From) whom shall I ask (anything)? there is no place.
Nānak is easily absorbed by means of the instruction of the Guru.

Gauṛī; mahalā I.

IX.

(1). (If) the true Guru be met with, he shows that dying is necessary.
(To whom) the taste (of) dying and ceasing to be is pleasing in his heart:
He, having removed pride, obtains the heavenly city.

Pause.

Death is written (decreed), this (creature) is not remaining.
Who mutters Hari, he is remaining in the asylum of Hari.
(2). (If) the true Guru be met with, then duality flees.
The lotus (of the heart) is opening, the mind clings to Hari, the Lord.
Who dies whilst living, (he gets) in the other world great enjoyment.
(3). By the true Guru being obtained, by virtue and control of the passions (one becomes) pure.
The ladder (= instruction) of the Guru is higher than high.

[1] ਦਰੁ, gate = mouth; ਘਰੁ, house = body, heart. ਏਕੰਕਾਰ (ਇਕਾਕਾਰ), who is always of the same form = the Supreme, who never changes.

[2] ਦਸ ਦੁਆਰਿ is a grammatical blunder, instead of ਦਸਵੇ; but as this did not suit the verse, it was exchanged for ਦਸ, ten.

[3] That is, he is present in the three worlds as the absolute substance.

[4] The sense is: the mind becomes conscious of itself.

[5] ਘਰੁ is the same as kṣhētra, the body or house of the ātmā or puruṣha. The house is known as the seat of the spirit (itself an emanation of the Supreme Spirit). It must not be lost sight of, that (according to note 1, p. 215) ਮਠੁ and ਘਰੁ are here essentially the same, ਮਠੁ being the last of the twenty-three components of the kṣhētra.

By destiny he is obtained (and) the fear of Yama (is then) done away with.
(4). By meeting with the Guru (the disciple) is absorbed in the bosom (of Hari).
Out of mercy the house and palace (of Hari) is shown (by the Guru).
Nānak (says): having destroyed his egotism (individuality) he is united (with Hari).

Gauṛī; mahalā I.

X.

(1). The lot has fallen, none effaces it.
What do I know, what will happen in future?
What has pleased him, that has come to pass.
None other is acting (but he).

Pause.

I do not know (thy) works (nor) how great thy gift is.
Acts and deeds are the nature of thy name.
(2). Thou art such a great donor and giver.
There is no deficiency (of gifts), thy store-room is distributed (to the creatures).[1]
(By whom) conceit is entertained, he is not agreeable (to thee).
Soul and body, all is with thee (= in thy power).
(3). Thou killest and vivifiest, thou pardonest and unitest (with thyself).
As it pleases thee, so thou causest thy name to be muttered.
Thou art wise, clear-sighted and true concerning me.
By means of the instruction of the Guru thou givest (me) confidence (in thee).
(4). In (my) body is filth (= sin), (my) mind is not attached (to thee).
By means of the word of the Guru, by (his) true instruction is known
Thy power and the greatness of (thy) name.
Nānak (says): the devotee is remaining (in thy) asylum.

Gauṛī; mahalā I.

XI.

(1). (Whom) he makes recite the ineffable (Supreme):
(Him) he gives nectar to drink.
Other fears are forgotten, in the name he is absorbed.

Pause.

Why should one be afraid? fear is absorbed in the fear (of God).
By means of the word of the perfect Guru he (the Supreme) is known.
(2). In whose heart is the divine male Rām, a ray of light[2] of Hari:
He is with natural ease united (with him), praise (to him)!
(3). Early in the morning and in the evening the snakes go.
Here and there the fleshly-minded are bound by death.
(4). (In whose) heart Rām is day and night, they are perfect.
Nānak (says): (if) Rām be found, error is removed.

Gauṛī; mahalā I.

XII.

(1). He is born and dies (again), who is fostering the three qualities.
The four Vēdas relate the (different) forms (he is going through).

[1] ਭਗਤਿ is here best taken as part. past (Sansk. भक्त), distributed.
[2] ਰਾਸਿ, very likely = रश्मि, a ray of light, contracted to ਰਾਸਿ.

They give an explanation of the three states.[1]
In the fourth state[2] Hari is known from the true Guru.

Pause.

By devotion to Rām and the service of the Guru he is crossing.
He will not again be born and die.
(2). Every one speaks of the four desirable objects.[3]
The Smriti and the Shāstras are in the mouth of the Paṇḍit.
Without the Guru the reflection on the (four) objects is not obtained.
The boon of final emancipation is obtained by devotion to Hari.
(3). In whose heart that Hari dwells:
(That) disciple obtains devotion (to Hari).
Devotion to Hari (brings in) final emancipation (and) joy.
By means of the instruction of the Guru the highest bliss is obtained.
(4). By whom he (*i.e.* Hari) is obtained, (to him) he has been shown by the Guru, who has seen (him).
Who in desire has become free from (all) desires, he is instructed (in the way of truth).[4]
The Lord of the poor is giving all comforts (to him):
(Whose) mind is attached to the feet of Hari, (says) Nānak.

Gauṛī čētī; mahalā I.

XIII.

(1). "The body is immortal" (thus thinking) this world remains in a pleasant sport.
It practises greediness, covetousness (and) much falsehood, it raises many loads.
Thee, O body, I have seen rolling like dust on the ground.

Pause.

Hear, hear my instruction!
Good works will be stopped, O my soul, there will not come again an opportunity (for doing good works).
(2). I address thee, O my body, hear thou my instruction!
Thou revilest another and desirest what is another's, thou makest a false tale-bearing.
Thou lookest at another's wife, O my soul, thou committest theft and adultery.
The soul has departed, thou art left behind; such a forsaken woman thou hast become.
(3). Thou, O body, art left (behind); what work hast thou done (even) in a dream?
When I stole anything, I considered it as good in my mind.
Here there is no lustre, there no entrance (for me), (my) whole[5] life is lost.

Pause.

I have become very much afflicted, O father Nānak, nobody asks a word about me.
(4). Arabian and Turkish horses, gold, silver, loads of clothes:
Go with nobody, (says) Nānak, they fall off, O fool!
A cup of sugar-candy, fruit, everything was tasted by me, thy name alone is nectar.
(5). (If), laying (deep) the foundation, I raise a wall, the house (will be) a heap of ashes.

[1] The three states are: जागृति (wakefulness), स्वप्न (dream), सुषुप्ति (deep sleep).

[2] The तुरीयावस्था is the state of abstraction from without and absorption in the contemplation of one's own spirit (as identical with the Supreme).

[3] The four desirable objects are: धर्म, काम, अर्थ, मोक्ष.

[4] Man must become असक्त, free from desire or hope of getting any reward for his actions, only intent on the contemplation of Hari.

[5] ਅਹਿਲਾ = Sansk. अखिल, whole.

(If) having collected and collected (a hoard) I do not give (anything) to any one—the blind one thinks, "all is mine."

(If I have) a heap of gold, an upper room (full of) gold—it does not belong to any one.

Pause.

Hear, O foolish, ignorant mind!

(6). His (*i.e.* God's) decree will be executed.

Our banker is a weighty Lord, we are his retail-dealers.

Soul and body, all the capital is his, he himself kills and vivifies.

Gauṛī čētī; mahalā I.

XIV.

(1). The others are five,[1] we are (but) one, O man! how wilt thou protect thy household goods, O mind?

They beat and plunder continually, before whom shall I raise a cry (for assistance), O man?

Pause.

Utter the name of Srī Rām, O mind!

On the way onwards (to the other world) the army of Yama is very hostile.

(2). Having raised a small idol-temple[2] he guards the door (of it), within is seated a woman.[3]

The woman plays continually with nectar, the other five men are robbed at night.

(3). Having pulled down the small idol-temple (*i.e.* the heart) the temple (= body) is plundered (by them), the one woman is seized, O man!

(When) the club of Yama and (his) chain has fallen on the neck (of the person), these five men take to flight.

(4). He desires a fascinating woman, gold, silver, he desires friends and dinners at night.[4]

Nānak (says): who commits sins for their sake will go bound to the city of Yama.

Gauṛī čētī; mahalā I.

XV.[5]

(1). (There is) a (large) earring on thy body, (but) the (right) earring is within, (thy) body should be made the patched quilt.

The five should be made the servants and subjected, O Rāval, this mind should be made the staff!

Pause.

Thou, thou wilt get the skill of the Yōga:

(If) thou wilt apply (thy) mind to the esculent roots (of) the one word (=name), (for) there is none other.

(2). After the head is shaved, a Guru should be obtained, by us the Gangā is made the Guru.

The Lord alone brings across the three worlds, thou dost not think (of him), O blind one!

(3). (If) in ostentation thou wilt apply (thy) mind to (mere) words, (thy) doubt will never go off.

If thou appliest (thy) thoughts to the feet of the One, thou wilt not run about in greediness and covetousness.

Pause.

If thou mutter the Pure (Supreme), (thy) mind will be absorbed (in him).

Why dost thou talk, O Jōgī, much deceit?—

[1] The five are: ਕਾਮ, ਕ੍ਰੋਧ, ਲੋਭ, ਮੋਹ, ਅਹੰਕਾਰ.

[2] ਮੜ੍ਹੋਲੀ *s.f.* a small idol-temple in a temple = the heart.

[3] The ਸਾਧਣਾ, or woman, is here the ਬੁਧਿ, or intellect.

[4] In ਖਾਧਾੜਾ the ੜਾ (as well as in ਬਾਧਾੜਾ) is redundant and a mere alliteration.

[5] These lines are addressed to a Jōgī named Rāval.

(4). The body is mad, the soul ignorant, saying: "mine, mine" (life) is passed.
Nānak (says): the naked (body) is burnt, then afterwards (the people) repent.

Gauṛī čētī; mahalā I.

XVI.

(1). The medicine, charm (and) root (of) the mind (is) the One; if the thought be fixed (on him), O dear!
He is obtained, who is cutting off the sinful works of the several births, O dear!

Pause.

Mind the One Lord, O brother!
In thy three qualities thou art involved in the world, the incomprehensible one cannot be comprehended, O dear!
(2). (Like) sugar-candy the Māyā is sweet in the body, by me and thee a bundle (of it) is lifted up, O dear!
The night is dark, nothing is seen, the mouse cuts the rope (of life) to pieces, O brother!
(3). As much as the fleshly-minded do, so much pain they incur, the disciples obtain greatness.
What is done by him (*i.e.* Hari), that is effected, the destiny cannot be effaced, O dear!
(4). Who are full, them he fills, (so that) they do not want (anything), who are coloured, them he steeps in colour, O dear!
If thou becomest their dust, (says) Nānak, then thou wilt obtain something, O foolish one!

Gauṛī čētī; mahalā I.

XVII.

(1). Whose mother (is she), whose father (is he)? from which place have we come?
Within an orb (of) fire (and) water we are produced, for what work are we made?

Pause.

O my Lord, who knows thy qualities?
My vices cannot be told.
(2). How many trees and shrubs are known (by) us, how many animals are produced?
How many snakes come into the cottages, how many birds are caused to fly about?
(3). He breaks into city-shops and palaces,[1] having committed theft he comes home.
He looks forwards and looks backwards, before thee where will he hide himself?
(4). The shores (of rivers), Tīrthas, the shops in the Bāzārs have been seen by me in the nine regions (of the earth).
Having taken the scales (I) began to weigh (all I have seen); the retail-dealer is even in the heart.
(5). As much as the ocean and sea is filled with water, so many are my vices.
Bestow mercy (on me), have a little compassion (on me), bring across the sinking stones!
(6). (My) soul burns like fire, within the shears move about.
Nānak (says): who knows the order (of God), he (enjoys) comfort day and night.

Gauṛī bairāgaṇi; mahalā I.

XVIII.

(1). The night is passed in sleeping, the day is passed in eating.
(One's) life-time is (precious) like a diamond, it is given away for a cowrie.

[1] ਬਿਜ ਮੰਦਰ = شيش محل, a house or palace hung over with glass (literally: a house of lightening).

Pause.

The name of Rām is not known (by thee).

O fool, thou wilt again rue it afterwards!

(2). Unrighteous property they put into the ground, unrighteous (property) cannot be liked.[1]

Those, who go off (to the other world) liking unrighteous (property), come (again in another birth) having lost the unrighteous (property).

(3). If that would be obtained, which one takes himself, every one would enjoy a good destiny.

The decision is made according to (one's) works, though every one wish it (otherwise).

(4). Nānak (says): by whom the work (of creation) is made, he takes care of it.

The order of the Lord is not known, to some one he gives greatness.

Gauṛī bairāgaṇi; mahalā I.

XIX.

(1). (Though) I become a doe and live in the wood and eat esculent roots:

My bridegroom is met with by the favour of the Guru; I am devoted, devoted (to thee), O Lord!

Pause.

I am the (female) retail-dealer of Rām.

Thy name is my goods and trade, O Lord!

(2). (Though) I become a Kōkil and live on a mango-tree and reflect on (my) natural sound (or voice):

With natural ease my bridegroom is met with, who in appearance and form is boundless.

(3). (Though) I become a fish and live in the water: he, who remembers all creatures,

My bridegroom dwells on this and that side, I shall meet (with him) having stretched out my arm.

(4). (Though) I become a (female) snake and live on the ground: (if) the word (of the Guru) dwell (in me), fear goes.

Nānak (says): they are always happy married women, (in) whom the luminous (Supreme) (is), (in) light they are absorbed.

Gauṛī pūrbī dīpakī; mahalā I.

Ōm! By the favour of the true Guru!

XX.

(1). In what house praise is uttered and the creator reflected upon:

In that house sing a song of praise, remember the creator!

Pause.

Sing thou a song of praise of my fearless (Hari).

I am devoted to that song of praise, by which happiness is always obtained.

(2). Continually the living creatures are taken care of, the giver will see (to them).

The estimation of thy gifts is not found out, what is the valuation of that donor?

(3). The year and day appointed for the wedding is written (fixed); having met apply oil!

Give, O sweetheart, a blessing, by which union with the Lord may be brought about!

(4). To every house this message (is sent), the calls are continually made.

If the caller be remembered, (says) Nānak, those days come.

[1] The Sikhs explain ਅਨਤਾ or ਅਨਤ by ਅਨੰਤ, boundless, endless, which is etymologically inadmissible and gives no sense whatever. We derive ਅਨਤ from the Sansk. अनृत, false, unrighteous.

RĀGU GAUṚĪ; MAHALĀ III.

Čaupadās.

Ōm! By the favour of the true Guru!

Gauṛī guārērī.

I. XXI.

(1). The Guru being met with union (with) Hari is brought about.
He himself unites to union (with himself).
My Lord himself knows all the means.
By his order he unites (with himself) (those, whom) he recognizes by the word (of the Guru).

Pause.

By the fear of the true Guru error and dread go off.
Who is immersed in fear, he is tinged in true colour.
(2). By meeting with the Guru Hari dwells naturally in the heart.
My Lord is weighty, his value (estimation) is not found out.
(Who) praises by means of the word (of the Guru) (him who) has no end nor limit:
Him my Lord pardons, he is pardoning.
(3). By meeting with the Guru all wisdom and intelligence are obtained.
In a pure heart dwells that True one.
By the indwelling of the True one every work (becomes) pure.
The highest work is to reflect on the word (of the Guru).
(4). From the Guru the true service (of Hari) is obtained.
Some disciple becomes acquainted with the name.
The liberal Hari lives, he is giving (to him):
(Who) entertains love to (his) name, (says) Nānak.

Gauṛī guārērī; mahalā III.

II. XXII.

(1). From the Guru some pious person obtains divine knowledge.
From the Guru he gets understanding and is accomplished.
From the Guru (he gets) composure and true reflection.
From the Guru he obtains the gate of final emancipation.

Pause.

By a perfect lot (destiny) the Guru comes and is met with.
By true composure one is absorbed in the True one.
(2). By meeting with the Guru he quenches the fire of thirst.
By means of the Guru tranquillity comes and dwells in the mind.
By means of the Guru he becomes pure, clean and holy.
Through the Guru union (with Hari) is effected by means of the word.
(3). Without the Guru all the (world) is led astray by error.
Without the name it incurs much pain.
He who becomes a disciple, meditates on the name.
By the sight of the True one true honour is obtained.
(4). Who shall be called a donor? he alone is the donor.
If he bestow (his) mercy, union (with him) is brought about by means of the word (of the Guru).

Having met with the beloved the praises of the True one are sung.
Nānak (says): the true ones are absorbed in the True one.

Gauṛī guārērī; mahalā III.

III. XXIII.

(1). That place is true (good), (in which) the mind becomes pure.
In the true one that True one fixes his dwelling.
True (is his) word, it is known through the four ages (of the world).
The True one himself is everything.

Pause.

(Whose) destiny it may be, (him) he unites with the society of the pious.
He sings (then) the qualities of Hari, sitting in his own place.
(2). May this tongue be burnt on account of its duality!
It does not taste the juice of Hari, it talks insipid things.
Without comprehending (the truth) body and mind become insipid.
Without the name (man) is afflicted and, having departed, weeps.
(3). By (what) tongue the juice of Hari is tasted with natural ease:
That is absorbed in the True one by the mercy of the Guru.
Having reflected on the word of the Guru it is steeped in the True one.
It drinks a pure stream of nectar.
(4). Who is absorbed in the name becomes a vessel.
In a reversed vessel nothing sticks.
By the word of the Guru there is in the mind dwelling in the name.[1]
Nānak (says): he is a vessel, a vessel, who has a thirst after the word.

Gauṛī guārērī; mahalā III.

IV. XXIV.

(1). Some continue singing (the praises of Hari), (but) get no relish in their heart.
What they sing in egotism, is useless.
They sing a (true) song, who have love to the name.
(Who) reflect on the true word (and) instruction (of the Guru).

Pause.

They continue singing, who are pleasing to the true Guru.
Their mind and body is steeped in love, by the name they become acceptable.
(2). Some sing, some practise devotion.
They do not obtain the name without love.
Devotion (becomes) true by love to the word of the Guru,
(If) their own beloved is always kept in the breast.
(3). They practise devotion, (but) the fools cause (only) their own self to be brought forth.[2]
Dancing and dancing they jump, (but) incur much grief.
By dancing and jumping devotion is not made.
Who dies by means of the word (of the Guru), that man obtains devotion.
(4). The compassionate to the devotees causes devotion to be made.

[1] The sense is: by means of the word of the Guru man dwells in the name in his mind.

[2] Compare in the following verse: ਵਿਚਹੁ ਆਪੁ ਖੋਇ.

By true devotion one clears away from within his own self.
My Lord is true, he knows every procedure.
Nānak (says): (to whom) he gives the name, he knows it.

Gauṛī guārērī ; mahalā III.

V. XXV.

(1). By killing the mind the busy running about (of the mind) dies.
Without dying how shall (one) get Hari?
Does any one know a medicine, by which the mind may die?
(Whose) mind dies by means of the word (of the Guru), that man has understanding.

Pause.

On whom he bestows greatness:
Into (his) mind Hari comes and dwells (therein) by the favour of the Guru.
(2). (If) the disciple practises (religious) works:
Then he gets an insight into this (human) mind.
The mind is intoxicated in egotism like an elephant.
The Guru is the goad; having killed (the selfish mind) he vivifies (it again).
(3). The indomitable mind (hardly) some one subjects.
If it remains steady, then it becomes pure.[1]
By the disciple this mind is adjusted (brought into subjection).
The diseases (of) egotism are removed from within.
(4). (Who) is kept by him from the beginning, (him) he unites to union (with himself).
He is never separated, by means of the word (of the Guru) he is absorbed.
His own machinery he himself knows.
Nānak (says): the disciple knows the name.

Gauṛī guārērī ; mahalā III.

VI. XXVI.

(1). In egotism the whole world is mad.
By second love and error it is led astray.
It makes many reflections, but itself it does not know.
Carrying daily on business life is passed.

Pause.

Enjoy (in thy) heart Rām, O brother!
The tongue (of) the disciple is made juicy (by) the juices (of) Hari.
(2). By which disciple Rām is recognized in his heart:
He, serving the life of the world, is known in the four periods (of the world).
(By whom), having destroyed his egotism he (*i.e.* Rām) is known:
(On him) the Lord bestows mercy, who is requiting according to one's works.[2]
(3). Those people are true, who are united (with the Supreme) by the word of the Guru.
They keep back their running (mind) and stop it.

[1] The Sikh Granthīs could never tell me what ਅਚਰੁ ਚਰੈ means. But ਚਰਨਾ signifies here (as in Sanskrit), *to remain.* If the mind remains steady, fixed (opposed to ਧਾਵਤੁ, running about), it is purified (by being concentrated on the Supreme).

[2] ਕਰਮ ਬਿਧਾਤਾ, requiting according to one's works, disposer of the destiny of men according to their deserts.

They obtain the nine treasures (of) the name from the Guru.
By the mercy of Hari Hari comes and dwells in (their) mind.
(4). Saying "Rām, Rām," there is joy and tranquillity in the body.
(If) he (*i.e.* Rām) dwell within, the torment of Yama is not inflicted.
He himself is the Lord, he himself the Vazīr (prime minister).
Nānak (says): serve thou always Hari, who is profound in qualities.

Gauṛī guārērī; mahalā III.

VII. XXVII.

(1). How should he be forgotten, whose the life and soul is?
How should he be forgotten, who is contained in all?
By serving whom there is assurance (of) honour at the threshold.

Pause.

I sacrifice myself to the gratuitous service of the name of Hari.
(If) thou art forgotten, I am burnt, I die.
(2). By them thou art forgotten, who are led astray by thyself.
By them thou art forgotten, who are (involved) in duality.
The fleshly-minded, (who are) destitute of divine knowledge, fall into the womb (again).
(3). With whom he is invariably pleased, them the true Guru applies to (his) service.
With whom he is invariably pleased, in their mind he causes Hari to dwell.
By the instruction of the Guru they are absorbed in the name of Hari.
(4). In whose bag is religious merit,[1] they are reflecting on divine knowledge.
In whose bag is religious merit, (by them) egotism is destroyed.
Nānak (says): I sacrifice myself to them, who are attached to the name.

Gauṛī guārērī; mahalā III.

VIII. XXVIII.

(1). Thou art ineffable, how canst thou be described?
In the word of the Guru, (which is) subduing the mind, thou art contained.[2]
Thy qualities are many, their estimation is not found out.

Pause.

Whose the species is,[3] in him it is absorbed (again).
Thy ineffable story is explained by the word of the Guru.
(2). Where the true Guru is, there an assembly of pious men is formed.
Where the true Guru is, (there) naturally the qualities of Hari are praised.
Where the true Guru is, there egotism is burnt by means of the word (of the Guru).
(3). The disciple obtains by his service (of Hari) a place in the palace (of Hari).
The disciple makes the name of Hari dwell in his heart.

[1] ਜਿਨ ਪੋਤੈ ਪੁੰਨੁ, in whose bag is religious merit, *i.e.* those, who in a former birth have accumulated religious merit, get in a following birth this reward, that they meditate on divine knowledge, by means of which they obtain final emancipation.

[2] The words are to be constructed thus: ਗੁਰ ਸਬਦੁ ਮਾਰਣੁ ਮਨ ਜੋ ਹੈ ਤਿਸ ਮਾਹਿ ਸਮਾਹਿ, the word of the Guru, which is subduing the mind, in that (word) thou art contained.

[3] ਜਾਤੀ signifies here "species." From which the species (or genus) has taken its rise, into that it is re-absorbed.

The disciple is by his devotion (to Hari) absorbed in the name of Hari.
(4). The donor himself (*i.e.* Hari) bestows gifts (on him):
Who is imbued with love to the perfect true Guru.
Nānak (says): victory to them who are attached to the name!

Gauṛī guārērī; mahalā III.

IX. XXIX.

(1). From the One are all forms and colours.
Wind, water, fire, all (elements) are bound up (in him).[1]
The Lord sees all the colours (=forms) severally.

Pause.

The One is wonderful, that One (only).
Some rare disciple meditates (on him).
(2). Naturally the Lord goes about in all places.
Somewhere he is concealed, (somewhere) manifest, by the Lord harmony (between himself and the creature) is made.
He himself awakes the sleeping ones.
(3). His estimation is not made by any one.
Every one goes on telling (his) story.
Who is absorbed in the word of the Guru, he comprehends Hari.
(4). Having heard and heard he (*i.e.* Hari) sees (everything), by means of the word of the Guru he unites (with himself).
Great grandeur is attained by the service of the Guru.
Nānak (says): those who are attached to the name, are absorbed in the name of Hari.

Gauṛī guārērī; mahalā III.

X. XXX.

(1). The fleshly mind is asleep by the delusion of the Māyā (and its) love (to her).
The disciple is awake, reflecting on the qualities (of Hari) (and) divine knowledge.
Those people wake, who have love to the name.[2]

Pause.

Easily one wakes and does not sleep:
If one gets knowledge (of the truth) from the perfect Guru.
(2). The bad and inexpert one never comprehends (the truth).
He relates a story (of some god) and struggles with the Māyā.
The blind and bare of divine knowledge is never accomplished (emancipated).
(3). In this (Kali)-yug emancipation (is obtained) by the name of Rām.
Some rare one obtains it by reflection on the word of the Guru.
He himself is saved and he is rescuing (also) all his families.
(4). In this Kali-yug are no (good) works nor religion.
The birth of the Kali-yug takes place in the house of a Čaṇḍāl.
Nānak (says): without the name no final emancipation is obtained.

[1] ਸਹਲੰਗ, an arbitrary formation from the Sansk. सलग्न.
[2] ਪਿਆਰਿ, instead of ਪਿਆਰੁ, on account of the rhyme.

Gauṛī guārērī ; mahalā III.

XI. XXXI.

(1). True is (his) order, true is the King.
(Who) with a true mind are attached to the fearless Hari:
They are absorbed in the true palace (and) in the true name.

Pause.

Hear, O my mind, the word (of the Guru) and reflect (on it)!
Mutter Rām and thou wilt cross the water of existence!
(2). In error it comes, in error it goes.
This world is born in second love (duality).
The fleshly-minded one does not reflect, he comes and goes.
(3). Is (man) gone himself astray or is he led astray by the Lord himself?
This creature (man) is put into a stranger's service.
Great pains are earned (by him), uselessly is his lifetime wasted.
(4). The true Guru, bestowing his mercy, unites (with Hari).
Who reflects on the One name, from his heart he removes error.
Nānak (says): who mutters the name, he obtains the nine treasures of the name.

Gauṛī guārērī ; mahalā III.

XII. XXXII.

(1). Go and ask those disciples, by whom (the name) is meditated upon.
By the service of the Guru the mind becomes confiding.
They are blessed, who acquire the name of Hari.
From the perfect Guru they obtain brightness of intellect.

Pause.

O my brother, mutter the name of Hari, Hari!
The worship of the disciple, the service of Hari is accepted.
(2). (Who) knows his own self, (his) mind becomes pure.
He obtains emancipation whilst living,[1] (from) Hari.
He sings the qualities of Hari, his wisdom becomes very great.
Easily he enters tranquillity.
(3). In second love (duality) he cannot be served.
(Who) is immersed in egotism, eats a very poisonous thing.
By son, family, house, the Māyā, he is fascinated.
The fleshly-minded one is blind, he comes and goes.
(4). (If) that man (= the Guru) gives the name of Hari, Hari:
Daily devotion is made by means of the word of the Guru.
By means of the instruction of the Guru some rare one comprehends (the truth).
Nānak (says): that one is absorbed in the name.

Gauṛī guārērī ; mahalā III.

XIII. XXXIII.

(1). (By whom) the service (of) the Guru is performed continually (the four ages):
(He is) a perfect man, if he practise (religious) works.

[1] ਜੀਵਨਮੁਕਤਿ (जीवन्मुक्ति), a state of emancipation durіng life. The soul is not yet actually separated from the body, but is so virtually, the iufluence of the exterior objects on the soul being destroyed by divine knowledge and contemplation on the One Supreme. This state is also called ਸਾਂਤਿ, or tranquillity.

Inexhaustible is the wealth (of) the name (of) Hari, there is no deficiency (in it).
Here (in this world) there is always happiness, and at the gate (of Hari) lustre is obtained.

Pause.

O my mind, no doubt should be entertained!
By the disciple nectar-juice is drunk (by means of his) service (of the Guru).
(2). Who serve the true Guru, they are great men in the world.
They themselves are saved (and) all their families are emancipated.
Who keep the name of Hari in (their) breast:
They, being attached to the name, cross the water of existence.
(3). (Who) serve the true Guru (and are) always (his) slaves in (their) mind:
After having destroyed egotism the lotus (of their) heart is expanded.
The unbeaten (sound) sounds (in them), they dwell in their own house.
Being attached to the name they are lonely in (their own) house.
(4). Who serve the true Guru, their speech is true.
Continually in devotion they utter the praises (of Hari).
Daily they mutter Hari, the bow-holder.
Nānak (says): those, who are attached to the name, are quite his (Hari's) own and without worldly concerns.

Gauṛī guārērī; mahalā III.

XIV. XXXIV.

(1). The true Guru is met with in accordance with a great destiny.[1]
In (whose) heart is the name, he enjoys continually the relish of Hari.

Pause.

O disciple, meditate on the name!
Having overcome regeneration thou obtainest the gain of the name.
(2). Divine knowledge, meditation, the word of the Guru are sweet.
By the mercy of the Guru some rare one tastes and sees them.
(3). (Though) one practise much the prescribed works:[2]
Without the name they are but woe, woe (and) egotism.
(4). (Who) is bound by the fetter and the noose of the Māyā:
He is released, (says) Nānak, by the Guru's explication (of truth).

Gauṛī bairāgaṇi; mahalā III.

XV. XXXV.

(1). As[3] the cloud is raining on the earth, if[4] there be water on the ground or not.
As water comes forth on the ground (and) without affection[5] (for a particular place) the rain turns about:

[1] The sense is: the true Guru is met with, if one's lot or destiny be great, on account of his meritorious works in a former birth.

[2] ਕਰਮਕਾਂਡ, the section of the Vēdas treating of rites or works; then the prescribed works generally.

[3] ਜੈਸੀ, as; we should expect here also ਜੈਸੇ (adv.), as ਜੈਸੀ has the appearance of being in an adjectival connexion with ਧਰਤੀ, which is not the case.

[4] ਕਿਆ, interrogative particle (properly ਕਿਆ—ਕਿਆ, whether—or); before ਨਾਹੀ the particle ਕਿਆ should be repeated.

[5] ਬਿਨੁ ਪਗਾ; the Sikh Granthīs do not know what to make of this word, as ਪਗ cannot signify here "foot." But ਪਗ or ਪਗਾ is a substantive derived from the verb ਪਗਣਾ, "to be attached to," thence "attachment," "affection to." ਫਿਰਾਹੀ = ਫਿਰਹਿ, lengthened on account of the rhyme. But the whole construction of these two lines is barbarous.

Pause.

O father, remove thou in this manner (thy) error!

Whatever one is doing, that he is, O dear, in such a one he is absorbed.

(2). Having become female and male what works are they doing?

Thou art always of various forms, thy (people) are absorbed in thee.

(3). Erring (from truth) he falls into so many births, when he (*i.e.* Hari) is obtained, then he does no longer err.

Whom the affair concerns, he knows it, if he be absorbed in the word of the Guru.

(4). Even thou proclaimest thy word,[1] thou thyself causest error to be told (taught).

Nānak (says): (if) reality is united with reality, then he does not come again into regeneration.[2]

Gauṛī bairāgaṇi; mahalā III.

XVI. XXXVI.

(1). The whole world is in the power of death, being bound by duality.

The fleshly-minded one, practising works of egotism, incurs pain.

Pause.

O my mind, apply thy thoughts to the feet of the Guru!

The disciples, taking the treasure of the name, are emancipated at the threshold (of Hari).

(2). Wandering about in the eighty-four lakhs (of forms of existence) on account of the obstinacy of (their) mind, they come and go.

The word of the Guru is not known (by them), (therefore) they fall again and again into the womb.

(3). By the disciple his own self is known, the name of Hari (therefore) comes and dwells in (his) mind.

Day by day he is given to devotion, he is easily absorbed in the name of Hari.

(4). (If) the mind die by means of the word (of the Guru), then a clear apprehension (of truth) takes place, the passions of egotism are dropped.

Humble Nānak (says): (by whom) they are obtained by destiny (according to their former works), (to them) are distributed the store-rooms (of) the name (of) Hari.[3]

Gauṛī bairāgaṇi; mahalā III.

XVII. XXXVII.

(1). In one's father's house there are four days (to be spent), by Hari, Hari they are fixed.

(That) female disciple is lustrous, (by whom) the praises (of Hari) are sung.

(Who) remembers the excellences (of Hari) in her father's house, she gets a dwelling in her father-in-law's house.

That female disciple is easily absorbed (in Hari), to whose mind Hari, Hari has been pleasing.

Pause.

The beloved[4] dwells in the father-in-law's and in the father's house; say, in what manner may he be obtained?

[1] What is ਹਹਿ? It cannot be here, according to the context, "thou art," but it is very likely the Sansk. ह्वे (ह्वयति), to call, to proclaim, corresponding to ਕਹਾਹਿ, thou causest to be told.

[2] ਆਹੀ = ਆਹੈ.

[3] The construction of this line is utterly confused and a regular puzzle (for which it is intended), but we do not doubt, that the words must be placed in the order we have translated them.

[4] The ਪਿਰੁ, or beloved, is here the Supreme Being.

The pure (Supreme Being) himself is inapprehensible, by himself union is brought about.

(2). (If) the Lord himself give understanding, the name of Hari is meditated upon.

The very fortunate one[1] meets with the true Guru, from (his) mouth nectar is obtained.

Egotism and duality are destroyed, naturally and easily he is absorbed.

In all he himself, he himself is existing, he himself applies (men) to the name.

(3). By the fleshly-minded he is not obtained on account of their pride, by their ignorance (of divine matters) they are foolish.

They do not perform the service of the true Guru, again and again they rue it.

They must dwell in the belly and womb, in the belly they are melted.

Thus it pleases my creator, the fleshly-minded are led astray (by him).

(4). By my Lord Hari the full destiny (of every man) is from the beginning written on the forehead.

(Who) meditates on the name of Hari, Hari, (with him) the Guru, the hero, meets.

My father and mother are the name of Hari, Hari is my relative and brother.

O Hari, Hari, O Lord, pardon and unite (with thyself) humble, poor Nānak!

Gauṛī bairāgaṇi; mahalā III.

XVIII. XXXVIII.

(1). From the true Guru divine knowledge is obtained, the truth (reality) of Hari is reflected upon.

The dull intellect becomes unfolded by muttering the name of Murāri.

By the spirit the illusion is dispelled,[2] darkness ceases.

On whose forehead it is written from the very beginning, to them the name of Hari is dear.

Pause.

In what manner is Hari obtained, O ye saints, seeing whom I live?

Without Hari I do not live a second, O Guru, join (him to me), (that) I may drink the juice of Hari!

(2). I sing the praises of Hari, I continually hear Hari, Hari is made (my) refuge.

The juice of Hari is obtained from the Guru, my mind and body are absorbed (in him).

Blessed, blessed is the Guru, the true divine male, by whom devotion to Hari is communicated.

From which Guru Hari is obtained, that Guru I buy (for myself).[3]

(3). Hari, the King, is the giver of virtues, we are vicious.

The sinful, sinking stones Hari brings across by means of the instruction of the Guru.

Thou art the giver of virtues and pure, we are without virtues.

O Hari, I have fled to (thy) asylum, preserve (me) the foolish one, save the bewildered one!

(4). By means of the instruction of the Guru ease and joy are always (obtained by him), (by whom) Hari, Hari is meditated upon in (his) mind.

(By whom) the Lord Hari, the beloved, is obtained, he sings in (his) house a song of praise.

Bestow mercy (on me), O Hari, O Lord, (this is my) prayer, by Hari, Hari (I am) quickened!

Humble Nānak asks the dust of those, by whom the true Guru is obtained.

[1] *i.e.* He, whose lot or destiny is great, by the performance of meritorious works in a former birth.

[2] ਸਿਵ is here not the god Shiva, but the Spirit, as distinguished from ਜੀਵ, the individual life. ਸਕਤਿ is taken in the sense of Māyā, the illusion spread over the creatures by the three qualities.

[3] ਕੀਣੀ, I buy, from ਕੀਣਨਾ, to buy, to gain over (Sansk. क्री).

GAUṚĪ GUĀRĒRĪ; MAHALĀ IV.

Čaupadās.

Om! by the favour of the true Guru!

I. XXXIX.

(1). By the Paṇḍit the Shāstras and the Smriti are read.
The Jōgī says: Gōrakh, Gōrakh![1]
I the foolish one mutter: Hari, Hari!

Pause.

I do not know what our state is, O Rām!
Worship Hari, O my mind, and thou art bringing the boat safely across the water of existence.
(2). The Sanyāsī besmears his body with cow-dung ashes.
The Brahmačārī lets go another's wife.
I foolish one, O Hari, desire thee.
(3). The Khatrī does works and obtains the fame of a hero.
The Sūdra and Vaisya follow (their own) disposition.
Me, the foolish one, the name of Hari rescues.
(4). All is thy creation, thou thyself art contained in it.
To the disciple, (says) Nānak, thou givest greatness.
By me, the blind one, Hari is made my refuge.

Gauṛī guārērī; mahalā IV.

II. XL.

(1). A story without attributes is the story of Hari.[2]
Worship (him) having joined the assembly of the pious people!
Cross[3] the water of existence having heard the ineffable story about Hari!

Pause.

O Gōvind, join (me) with the assembly of the pious!
(That) (my) tongue may sing the juice of Hari, the qualities of Rām.
(2). Who meditate on (thy) name, O Hari, Hari!
Make me, O Rām, the slave of those (thy) slaves!
The service of thy people is the highest work.
(3). The man who lets (me) hear the story about Hari, Hari:
That man is pleasing to my heart and mind.
He whose lot is great, obtains the dust (of) the feet (of such a) man.
(4). Friendship and intimacy with the saints
Is obtained (by them), to whom it has been decreed from the beginning.
These men, (says) Nānak, are absorbed in the name.

[1] ਗੋਰਖ (गोरख), the name of the famous Hindū reformer.
[2] ਨਿਰਗੁਣ ਕਥਾ, a story without attributes, *i.e.* the attributes or qualities of Hari, cannot be described.
[3] ਤਰੁ, cross (Imper.) = and thou wilt cross.

Gauṛī guārērī; mahalā IV.

III. XLI.

(1). The mother is delighted, (if) her son eats.
The fish is delighted by bathing in the water.
The true Guru is delighted,[1] (if) he receives a disciple into his favour.[2]

Pause.

O Hari, join to me those dear people of Hari,
By meeting with whom[3] my pains depart.
(2). As a cow shows affection having met with her calf.
As a woman is delighted, when her beloved (husband) comes home:
(So) the people of Hari are delighted, when they sing the praise of Hari.
(3). The peacock lives in delight, (if) (there be) a stream of water.
The king (lives) in delight, having seen a profusion of wealth.
The people of Hari (live) in delight, (when) they mutter the Formless one.
(4). Man is greatly delighted,[4] (if) he acquires wealth and property.
The disciple is delighted, (if) he be pressed to the neck of the Guru.[5]
Humble Nānak is delighted, (if) he may lick the feet of the pious.

Gauṛī guārērī; mahalā IV.

IV. XLII.

(1). The beggar is delighted, (if) a Lord gives (him) alms.
The hungry one becomes delighted, (if) he may eat food.
The disciple is delighted by meeting with the Guru, (thereby) he is satiated.

Pause.

O Hari, give (me) an interview, O Hari, I long after thee!
Bestow mercy (on me) and fulfil my desire!
(2). The Čakvī is delighted, (when) the sun shines into her face.
She meets (then) with her beloved and renounces all pains.
The disciple is delighted, (when) he becomes a favourite with the Guru.
(3). The child is delighted (when) it drinks milk with its mouth.
It is happy in its heart, (when) it sees the mother.
The disciple is delighted, (when) the Guru receives (him) into favour.
(4). All other delight is an unsolid delusion of the Māyā.
It passes away and is a false glass and plating.
Humble Nānak (says): delight and satiety is (only) the true Guru.

[1] After ਸਤਿ ਗੁਰ ਪ੍ਰੀਤਿ supply: ਭਈ.

[2] ਮੁਖਿ ਪਾਉਲਾ, to apply to the mouth, *i.e.* to receive (an inferior) into favour, to become familiar with.

[3] ਜਿਨ ਮਿਲਿਆ = ਜਿਨ ਦੇ ਮਿਲਿਆਂ; in the older language it would be ਜਿਨ ਮਿਲਿਐ, by meeting with whom.

[4] ਨਰ ਪ੍ਰਾਣੀ ਪ੍ਰੀਤਿ = ਨਰ ਪ੍ਰਾਣਿ ਪ੍ਰੀਤਿ, the final *i* in ਪ੍ਰਾਣੀ being here lengthened in order to get a long metrical syllable; ਨਰ ਪ੍ਰਾਣੀ ਪ੍ਰੀਤਿ signifies therefore literally: (to) a man it is life's delight.

[5] ਗਲਾਟੇ = ਗਲ, ਆਟੇ is a meaningless alliteration to rhyme with ਘਾਟੇ.

Gauṛī guārērī ; mahalā IV.

V. XLIII.

(1). The service of the true Guru is rendered fruitful:
By meeting with whom the name of Hari, of Hari the Lord, is meditated upon.
By whom Hari is muttered, after them many people are emancipated.

Pause.

O disciple, O my brother, say: Hari!
Saying: Hari! all sins go off.
(2). When the Guru is met with, then the mind is brought into subjection.
The five running (senses) are stopped, Hari is meditated upon.
Day by day the qualities of Hari are sung in the city (=body).
(3). Who put the dust of the feet of the Guru on their mouth:
They abandon falsehoods and meditate devoutly on Hari.
They are bright-faced at the threshold of Hari, O brother!
(4). The service of the Guru is pleasing to Hari himself.
Krishṇa and Balabhadra[1] meditate at the feet of the Guru.
Nānak (says): the disciple Hari himself brings across.

Gauṛī guārērī ; mahalā IV.

VI. XLIV.

(1). Hari himself is the Jōgī and carries a staff (like a Jōgī).
Hari himself, the Banvārī,[2] is contained (in all).
Hari himself practises austerities and is given to deep contemplation.

Pause.

My Rām, who is of this kind, is all-filling.
Hari dwells near and is not far off.
(2). Hari himself is the word, the attention and contemplation is he himself.
Hari himself sees, he himself is expanded.
Hari himself causes (his name) to be muttered, Hari himself mutters it.
(3). Hari himself is the cloud (and) the stream of nectar (=water).
Hari is the nectar, he himself is (also) the drinker (of it).
Hari himself is bringing about final emancipation.
(4). Hari himself is the boat, the buoy and raft.[3]
Hari himself is, by (means of) the instruction of the Guru, salvation.
Hari himself, (says) Nānak, is carrying across.[4]

Gauṛī bairāgaṇi ; mahalā IV.

VII. XLV.

(1). Thou art our wholesale merchant and our Lord, what sort of goods thou givest us, that we take.
We deal in the name of Hari with pleasure, if thou thyself, having become merciful, givest it (to us).

[1] ਬਲਭਦ੍ਰ, name of the elder brother of Krishṇa.
[2] ਬਨਵਾਰੀ = वनमाली, an epithet of Krishṇa, wearing a garland of wild flowers.
[3] ਤਾਰਾ, *s.m.* (=Sansk. तारक, *m.*) boat, raft.
[4] ਪਾਰ ਪਾਵਣਾ, to bring or ferry across; ਪਾਵਣਾ is here the causal of ਪਵਣਾ (to fall).

Pause.

We are the retail-dealers of Rām.

Hari makes (us) carry on traffic, giving us a stock of goods, O dear!

(2). He obtains the gain of the worship of Hari and his wealth, who is pleasing to the mind of Hari, the true wholesale merchant.

(By whom), muttering Hari, the goods of Hari are laden, him Yama, the tax-gatherer, does not approach.

(3). The tradesmen, who carry on another traffic, are absorbed in pain, being tossed about by other (things).

As the traffic is, to which they are applied by Hari, such is the fruit they obtain.

(4). That man carries on the traffic of Hari, Hari, to whom the Lord gives it, having become merciful (towards him).

Humble Nānak (says): (by whom) Hari, the wholesale merchant, is served, (from him) he never takes again an account.

Gauṛī bairāgaṇi; mahalā IV.

VIII. XLVI.

(1). As the mother is nourishing the embryo, in the hope of getting a son,

(Saying): "having become great and having acquired wealth he will give (me), having gone through his enjoyment and pastime:"

So the people of Hari keep love to Hari, (thinking): he himself will give us his hands.

Pause.

O my Rām, O Hari, my Lord, keep me the foolish one!

The greatness of thy servant is greatness to thee!

(2). In (his) palace and house is joy, to (whose) mind the praise of Hari is pleasing.

All juices become sweet to the mouth, when one sings the qualities of Hari.

The people of Hari are the support of their dependents, twenty-one families, (yea) the whole world they save.

(3). Whatever is done, that is done by Hari, it is the greatness of Hari.

O Hari, thine are the creatures, thou art existing (in them), thou art causing (them) to perform worship, O Hari!

Thou lettest them obtain the treasury of devotion, thou thyself art distributing it.

(4). A slave bought in a shop what cleverness has he (in the transaction),

If Hari put him into a sovereignty? a slave (and) grass-cutter he makes utter the name of Hari.

Humble Nānak is the slave of Hari, (this is) the greatness of Hari.

Gauṛī guārērī; mahalā IV.

IX. XLVII.

(1). The husbandman undertakes farming, he takes to it[1] brightening up his spirits.[2]

He yokes on the plough and exerts himself, (thinking): my son and daughter will eat (from the fruits of my labour).

In this way the people of Hari mutter: Hari, Hari! (thinking): Hari will at the end release (us).

Pause.

O my Rām, may my, the foolish one's salvation be effected!

Apply (me) to the service of the Guru, the true Guru, (this is) my desire!

[1] ਲੋਚਣਾ, *v.a.* (Sansk. रुच्, caus. रोचय्) to like, to take to (a thing).

[2] ਜੀਉ ਲਾਉਣਾ, to take courage, to brighten up one's spirits.

(2). The merchant, having taken horses, goes about for the sake of traffic.

He acquires wealth and entertains the desire to increase (still more) the infatuation of the Māyā.[1]

In this way the people of Hari are saying: Hari, Hari! saying: Hari! they obtain comfort.

(3). Poison collects the shopkeeper, (poison) he earns sitting in (his) shop.

Spiritual darkness and falsehood (is in him), (he has) an outlay of falsehood, to falsehood he clings.

In this way the people of Hari collect the wealth of Hari, having taken Hari as their provisions they go.

(4). This infatuation of the Māyā is the family, in second love (there is) a noose (for man).

By means of the instruction of the Guru that man crosses, who is the slave of the slaves (of Hari).

By humble Nānak the name is meditated upon, the disciple is made manifest.[2]

Gauṛī bairāgaṇi; mahalā IV.

X. XLVIII.

(1). Continually, day and night he is given to covetousness, by error he is led astray.

In forced labour the forced labourer turns about, he has put a burden upon his head.

Who performs service to the Guru, him Hari applies to his house-work.

Pause.

O my Rām, break the fetters of the Māyā and apply me to (thy) house-work!

We will continually sing the qualities of Hari, being absorbed in the name of Hari.

(2). All men serve a king and prince on account of the illusive world (money).

He either imprisons or fines (them), or the king dies.

Blessed, blessed and fruitful is the service of the true Guru, by means of which, having muttered the name of Hari, Hari, the comfort of Hari is obtained.

(3). Continually traffic is carried on in divers ways on account of the Māyā.

If it (*i.e.* the traffic) produces gain, then he is happy, if there be loss, then he dies.

Who makes partnership with the Guru in praising (Hari), he gets continually comfort.

(4). As much as there is hunger (after) other relish and pleasure, so much hunger will again befall (one).

On whom Hari himself bestows mercy, he sells his head before (= to) the Guru.

Humble Nānak (says): (who) is satiated by the juice of Hari, (him) no hunger again befalls.

Gauṛī bairāgaṇi; mahalā IV.

XI. XLIX.

(1). In my heart and mind (there is) continually a desire after Hari, how shall I see, O Hari, thy sight?

Who entertains affection (for thee), he knows (thee), in my heart and mind there is much love (to thee), O Hari!

I am a sacrifice to my own Guru, by whom my creator, who was separated from me, has been united (with me).

Pause.

O my Rām, we sinners have fallen on (thy) asylum, on (thy) gate, O Hari!

Believing,[3] that at some time, bestowing thy own mercy (on us), thou wilt unite us the destitute of virtue (with thyself).

[1] The sense is: he desires to increase still more his wealth and in consequence his spiritual blindness.

[2] Or: (to) the disciple (the name) is manifest.

[3] ਮਤੁ, believing that, may be that (= ਹਮਾਗਾ ਮਤੁ ਹੈ).

(2). Our vices are many, many, they are many heaps upon heaps, O Hari, they cannot be counted.

Thou, O Hari, art virtuous, thou, O Hari, art merciful, thou thyself, O Hari, pardonest, (as) it pleases (thee), O Hari!

We sinners are protected by the society of the Guru, (by him) instruction is given (to us), the name of Hari releases (us).

(3). How shall I tell thy qualities, O my true Guru? when we speak of the Guru, then astonishment overtakes (us).

A sinner like me no other protects as we are rescued and protected by the true Guru.

Thou, O Guru, art (my) father, thou, O Guru, art (my) mother, thou, O Guru, art my relative, my companion!

(4). What is our fate, O my true Guru, that fate thou thyself knowest, O Hari!

We are wandering and strolling about, no one is asking a word about us, by the Guru, the true Guru, we poor ones are received into his society.

Blessed, blessed is the Guru of humble Nānak, by meeting with whom all cares and pains have ceased!

Gauṛī bairāgaṇi; mahalā IV.

XII. L.

(1). Gold, women, female buffaloes (my) soul is coveting, sweet is the infatuation of the Māyā.

To house, palace, horse, insipid pleasure (my) mind is attached.

Hari, the Lord, does not come into (my) mind, how shall I be emancipated, O my King Hari?

Pause.

O my Rām, O my Hari, these are low works (of mine)!

Thou art virtuous, O Hari, thou art merciful, out of mercy pardon all my vices!

(2). I have no beauty, nor high birth, nor any good conduct.

What dare we say, who are without virtues, thy name is not muttered (by us).

We sinners are saved in the society of the Guru, it is the meritorious deed of the true Guru.

(3). All, soul, body, mouth, nose is given (by him) and water for sustenance.

The eating of grain, the putting on of clothes is given (by him) and other relishes and enjoyments.[1]

He, by whom they are given, does not come into (my) mind, I consider myself as a beast.

(4). All is thy work, thou art the inward governor.

What shall we helpless creatures do, all is thy sport, O Lord!

Humble Nānak is a shop-bought (slave), O Hari, (I am) the slave (of thy) slaves![2]

Gauṛī bairāgaṇi; mahalā IV.

XIII. LI.

(1). As a mother, having given birth to a son, nourishes him and keeps (him) within her sight,

And inside and outside (of the house) puts a morsel into (his) mouth, thumping him every moment (out of love):

So the true Guru keeps the disciple out of affection and love to Hari.

Pause.

O my Rām, we are ignorant children of Hari, the Lord.

Blessed, blessed is the Guru, the Guru, the true Guru and master, by whom we are instructed concerning Hari and made wise.

[1] ਭੋਗਾਣੀ = ਭੋਗ, āṇī is only a meaningless alliteration.

[2] ਗੁਲਮ ਗੁਲਾਮੀ is a ludicrous corruption instead of ਗੁਲਾਮਾਂ ਦਾ ਗੁਲਾਮ.

(2). As in the sky turns about and flies the white-clothed (bird),[1]
Keeping its mind (thought) behind, in its heart continually remembering its young ones:
So the true Guru, Hari, Hari has an affection for the disciple, the Guru keeps the disciple in his heart.
(3). As the pinchers,[2] thirty (or) thirty-two (in number), preserve within the tongue of flesh and blood:
—Does one think, that the flesh (= the tongue) is in the hand of the pinchers? all is subject to Hari.—
So when men calumniate the saints, Hari protects the honour of his people.
(4). O brother, may not any one think, that anything is in the hand of any one, He does and causes it to be done.
Old age, death, fever, one-sided rheumatism in the face, imprecation, all are in the power of Hari, none (of these evils) can befall (a man), except when put on by Hari.
Meditate continually in (thy) mind and thought on this name of Hari, (says) humble Nānak, which at the end will emancipate (thee).[3]

Gauṛī bairāgaṇi; mahalā IV.

XIV. LII.

(1). By meeting with whom joy springs up in the heart, he is called the true Guru.
The duality of the mind is done away with, the highest station of Hari (= final emancipation) is obtained.

Pause.

My beloved true Guru, how shall he be met with?
I make obeisance every moment, my perfect Guru, how shall he be obtained?
(2). By Hari, out of mercy, my true, perfect Guru is joined (to the pious one).
The wish of the (pious) man is accomplished, having obtained the true, perfect Guru.
(3). Hari makes devotion firm, he hears devotion, if one meet with that true Guru.
No deficiency at all takes place, the acquisition of Hari is continually made solid.
(4). In whose heart there is brightness (of understanding), (he entertains) no second love (= duality).
Nānak (says): he is saved by meeting with that Guru, who makes (him) sing the qualities of Hari.

Gauṛī pūrbī; mahalā IV.

XV. LIII.

(1). By Hari, the merciful Lord, mercy was bestowed (on me), in my mind, body and mouth I speak of Hari.
The colour of the disciple has become very deep, my jacket[4] is steeped in the colour of Hari.

Pause.

I am the female slave of my Lord Hari.
When my mind was reconciled with Hari, the whole world was given away (by me) as a valueless[5] ball.
(2). Make discrimination, O pious brother, search (thy) heart and inquire well!
The form of Hari is all light, Hari dwells near to all, Hari is with (them).
(3). Hari, Hari, the boundless, the inapprehensible divine male, dwells near the whole world.

[1] ਕਪੜੇ ਧਾਮੇ ਵਾਲੀ, *i.e.* the ਕੂੰਜ, or crane.
[2] The ਕਾਤੀ, or pinchers, are the teeth.
[3] ਲਏ ਛਡਾਇਆ = ਛਡਾਇ ਲਏ.
[4] ਚੋਲੀ, jacket, figuratively = heart, mind.
[5] ਅਮੋਲੀ = ਅਮੋਲ, must here be taken in the sense of: without value = valueless.

Hari is made manifest by the perfect Guru, (my) head is (therefore) sold to the Guru.

(4). O Hari, inside and outside of the creatures art thou! I have come to thy asylum, thou art the great, great divine male.

Humble Nānak sings day by day the excellences of Hari, having met with the true Guru, the Guru, the mediator.

Gauṛī pūrbī; mahalā IV.

XVI. LIV.

(1). O Lord, O boundless life of the world, O Lord of the Universe, O divine male, the arranger (of all things)!

On which road thou sendest us, O Lord, on that road do we go.

Pause.

O Rām, my mind is in love with Hari!

Having joined the society of the pious the relish of Rām is obtained (by me), in the delightful name of Hari I am absorbed.

(2). The name of Hari, Hari, Hari, Hari, is a medicine in (this) world, the name of Hari, Hari, Hari, is true.

All their sins and faults are done away with, who by means of the instruction of the Guru eat the juice of Hari.

(3). On whose forehead he writes the decree from the beginning, they are bathing in the pond of contentment, the Guru.

All their filth of foolishness is gone off, who are imbued with love to the name of Rām.

(4). O Rām, thou thyself, thou thyself art the Lord and master, like thee there is no other donor.

(If) humble Nānak takes (thy) name, then he lives; Hari is muttered by the mercy of Hari.

Gauṛī pūrbī; mahalā IV.

XVII. LV.

(1). Bestow mercy (on me), O life of the world, O donor! my mind is absorbed with Hari.

By the true Guru the exceedingly pure word is communicated (to me), muttering Hari, Hari, Hari, my heart brightens up.

Pause.

O Rām, my heart and body are pierced by the true Hari!

By the mouth of which the whole world is devoured, (from that death) we are saved, O Hari, by the word of the true Guru.

(2). Those, who have no love to Hari, are Sākats, fools and ignorant men.

On them birth and death press very heavily, having died and died they are consumed in ordure.

(3). Thou art merciful, cherishing in (thy) asylum, may a gift be given to me, O Hari, I am beseeching (thee)!

May I be made the slave (of) the slave (of) Hari, my mind dances and takes delight (in it).[1]

(4). The Lord himself is the great wholesale merchant, we are his retail-dealers.

My mind, body, life, all is thy stock, the wholesale merchant of humble Nānak is the Lord.

Gauṛī pūrbī; mahalā IV.

XVIII. LVI.

(1). Thou art merciful, removing all pains, give ear and hear one petition (of mine)!

Through whom, thou, O Lord Hari, art known, join to me that true Guru, my life!

[1] ਨਿਰਤਿ = Sansk. निरति, delight; ਰਹਿ ਨਾਚੇ = ਰਹਿ ਨਾਚ, ē being merely an alliteration.

Pause.

O Rām, by me the true Guru is minded as the Supreme Brahm.

I am foolish, stupid, of an erring mind, by means of the word of the Guru, the true Guru Hari is known by me.

(2). As many flavours and tastes as were seen by me, they are all distasteful insipidities.

The name of Hari is nectar juice, having met with the true Guru the sweet juice of sugar-cane[1] was tasted (by me).

(3). With whom the Guru, the true Guru, has not met, they are foolish and mad Sākats.

Their works are put down as mean from the beginning, (though) having seen the lamp (of truth) they are consumed by spiritual blindness.

(4). Whom thou unitest (with thyself), O Hari, bestowing mercy (upon them), they are applied (by thee), O Hari, to the service of Hari.

Humble Nānak (says): muttering Hari, Hari, Hari they are manifest, by the instruction, by the instruction of the Guru they are absorbed in the name.

Gauṛī pūrbī; mahalā IV.

XIX. LVII.

(1). O my mind, that Lord is always near (to thee), say, whereto should one flee from Hari?

Hari himself, the true Lord, pardons, (if) Hari himself releases, then one is emancipated.

Pause.

O my mind, mutter Hari, Hari! Hari should be muttered in the mind!

Flee to the asylum of the true Guru, O my mind, following the Guru, the true Guru one is emancipated.

(2). O my mind, serve that Lord, who is the giver of all comforts, by serving whom one dwells in his own house.

O disciple, go and obtain thy own house! the sandal-dust of the praise of Hari should be rubbed in and impressed on the memory!

(3). O my mind, the praise of Hari, Hari, Hari, Hari, Hari is the highest (thing), having made the acquisition of Hari one rejoices in his mind.

(If) Hari, Hari himself, out of mercy bestows it, then the nectar-juice of Hari is tasted.

(4). O my mind, who cling to any other than the name (of Hari), they are Sākats and are pressed down by Yama.

Those are Sākats and thieves, by whom the name is forgotten, O heart, one should not go near them!

(5). O my mind, serve the inapprehensible, pure, divine male Hari, by serving whom the account is brought to an end.

Humble Nānak (says): who are made full by Hari, the Lord, (their) weight does not diminish a Māsā for one moment.[2]

Gauṛī pūrbī; mahalā IV.

XX. LVIII.

(1). My life is in thy power, O Lord, my soul and body are all thine.

Bestow mercy (on me), O Hari, and show (me) (thy) sight, in my heart there is great desire (for thee).

[1] ਗਾਨੇ = ਗੰਨੇ; ਗੰਨਾ, sugar-cane.

[2] The sense is: they remain full (fully united with the Supreme Being) and no more subjected to transmigration.

Pause.

In my heart and body there is a desire of meeting with Hari.

By the compassionate Guru, by the Guru some mercy was shown (to me), Hari, my Lord[1] came and joined (me).

(2). The procedure, which is going on in my mind and thought, thou knowest, O Hari!

Day by day I mutter (thy) name, (that) I may obtain comfort, in (my) heart there is continually a desire for thee, O Hari!

(3). By the Guru, the true Guru, the way is shown (to me), Hari, my Lord, has come and joined (me).

Daily joy has accrued to the very fortunate one, all the desire of (his) servant is accomplished.

(4). All is in the power of Hari, the Lord of the world, the King of the Universe, the creator.

Humble Nānak has come to (thy) asylum, O Hari, keep the honour of thy servant!

Gauṛī pūrbī; mahalā IV.

XXI. LIX.

(1). This mind does not keep quiet a moment, it is of a versatile disposition, it runs about in the ten, ten directions (of the globe).

(If) by great luck the perfect Guru is obtained, by (whom) the mantra of Hari is given, the mind (becomes) sedate.

Pause.

O Rām, we are called the slaves of the true Guru.

(2). On our forehead a mark is burnt in, we owe much debt to the Guru.[2]

Much assistance and meritorious work is done (by him), (we are) brought across[3] the difficult water of existence (by him).

(3). Who have in their heart no affection to Hari, (by them) false connexions are made.

As paper is dissolved in water, so the fleshly-minded are dissolved in the womb.[4]

(4). We know, (that) we know nothing; as Hari further on keeps us, so we stand.

We are erring and mistaken, O Guru, bestow mercy on us! humble Nānak (says): draw out the bad swimmer![5]

Gauṛī pūrbī; mahalā IV.

XXII. LX.

(1). With lust and wrath the town is much filled; a pious man having come there breaks (them) to pieces.

(If) by a former decree (of God) the Guru be obtained, he establishes in the district devotion to Hari in the heart.

Pause.

Make joining of the palms of the hands to the holy man, it is a great meritorious act!

Make prostration (to him), it is a great meritorious act!

[1] ਪ੍ਰਭੁ ਮੇਰੀ; ਮੇਰੀ is a grammatical blunder (instead of ਮੇਰਾ), but that does not matter, if only the rhyme be kept up thereby (ਕੇਰੀ—ਮੇਰੀ).

[2] ਹਮ ਭਾਰੇ; ਭਾਰਾ is the part. past of ਭਰਿਣਾ (v. intr.), to bear; ਕਰਜ-ਭਰਿਣਾ, to owe a debt. The Sikh Granthīs do not know what to make of it.

[3] ਪਰਾਰੇ (scil. ਹਮ, which is to be supplied here), instead of ਪਰਾਏ, in order to keep up the rhyme with ਭਾਰੇ. ਤਾਰਿ ਪਰਾਉਣਾ, to bring across, to ferry over (ਪਰਾਉਣਾ = ਪਰ੍ਹਾਉਣਾ).

[4] ਗਲਾਰੇ instead of ਗਲਾਏ, for the sake of the rhyme.

[5] ਕਾਰੇ = ਕਾਰਿ, imperative, on account of the preceding imperative ਧਾਰਹੁ.

(2). By the Sākat the taste of the juice of Hari is not known, within him is the thorn of egotism.

As he walks he is pricked (by it), he incurs pain, he suffers death, on (his) head is the club (of Yama).

(3). The people of Hari are absorbed in the name of Hari, Hari, they break the pains of birth and the fear of death.

The imperishable divine male, the Lord, is obtained (by them), in the world and the universe they have much lustre.

(4). We are poor and wretched, O Lord! protect, O Hari, thine own, thou art very great.

The name is the support and prop of humble Nānak, even in the name of Hari is the pith of comfort.[1]

Gauṛī pūrbī; mahalā IV.

XXIII.[2] LXI.

(1). In this fort (= body) is Hari, Rām, the King, (but) the impudent one gets no taste (of him).

(On whom) Hari, who is merciful to the poor, bestows his favour, (by him) Hari is tasted and seen by means of the word of the Guru.

Pause.

The praising of Rām Hari is (made) sweet by meditation on the Guru.

(2). Hari, the Supreme Brahm, is inapproachable, incomprehensible, the true Guru being found acts as mediator.[3]

To whom the words of the Guru are pleasant in (their) mind, to them I come and fall down before them.[4]

(3). The heart of the fleshly-minded one is exceedingly hard, within it is a black venomous snake.[5]

Though much milk may be given to drink to a snake, poison issues (from it), in the twinkling of an eye (the bitten man) swells up.[6]

(4). O Lord Hari, bring and join (to me) the holy Guru, (that), having rubbed (for the bite) as charm the word (of the Guru), I may take it in my mouth.[7]

(To) humble Nānak, the slave and servant of the Guru, the acid (becomes) sweet by clinging to the assembly (of the pious).

Gauṛī pūrbī; mahalā IV.

XXIV. LXII.

(1). For the sake of (obtaining) Hari (my) body is sold (by me) before the perfect Guru.

By the true Guru the name is made firm (in him), (on whose) face and forehead a lucky lot (is written).

Pause.

O beloved, by means of the instruction of the Guru devotion to Hari is stirred up.

[1] ਭੰਡਾਹੇ = ਭੰਡਾ ਹੈ; ਭੰਡਾ = Sansk. मण्ड, pith (= सार).

[2] This verse I laid before the assembled Granthīs at Amritsar, but they could give me no explanation of it whatever.

[3] ਲਾਗਿ = ਲਾਗੈ, acts (as mediator).

[4] ਆਇ ਪੜੀਠਾ, having come, I fall down before them. ਪੜੀਠਾ on account of the rhyme = ਪੜਤਾ.

[5] The words ਕਾਰ ਕਰੀਠਾ are very obscure. I suppose that ਕਰੀਠਾ is corrupted from the Hindī करैत, a very venomous snake. This suits well the context.

[6] ਫੇਲਿ ਫਲੀਠਾ; ਢੇਲਿ = ਢੇਰਿ, in the twinkling of an eye. ਢੇਰੁ occurs in this sense twice more in the Granth. ਫਲੀਠਾ = ਫਲਤਾ, is swelling (*i.e.* the bitten man). The final words are so effectually corrupted in this verse, that we can only translate them by conjecture.

[7] ਲੀਠਾ = ਲੀ, I may take, ਠਾ being a meaningless alliteration.

(2). Sporting in everybody Rām, the king, is contained (therein), by means of the word of the Guru devotion to the Gurū (Rām) is stirred up.

I cut off mind and body, and give (them) to the Guru, (for) my error and fear are dispersed by the word of the Guru.

(3). Having brought a lamp he kindles it in darkness, by the knowledge (communicated by) the Guru devotion to the Gurū (God) is raised.

Ignorance and darkness are totally destroyed, in the house (= one's own body) the thing (= the Supreme Being) is obtained, the mind becomes awake.

(4). The Sākats are killers, depending on the Māyā, Yama begins to look out for them.

They have not sold their head before the true Guru, the luckless ones come and go.

(5). Hear our supplication, O Lord, we ask for the protection of Hari the Lord.

The honour and reputation of humble Nānak is the Guru, (my) head is sold before the true Guru.

Gauṛī pūrbī; mahalā IV.

XXV. LXIII.

(1). We are selfish, of a selfish and foolish mind, by meeting with the Guru (our) own self is done away.

The disease of egotism goes off, comfort is obtained, blessed, blessed is the Guru, Hari the king!

Pause.

O dear, by the word of the Guru Hari is obtained.

(2). In my heart is affection to Rām, the king, by the Guru the way and path are shown.

My soul and body, all is (put) before the true Guru, by whom the separated Hari is applied to (my) neck.

(3). In my heart a desire arose to see (him, *i.e.* Hari), the Guru showed him (as being present) with my heart.

Tranquillity and joy have sprung up in my mind, my own self is (therefore) sold before the Guru.

(4). Many sins and wicked deeds were done by us, becoming a thief and committing wickedness I stole.

Now, says Nānak, we have come to (thy) asylum, keep my honour, O Hari, Hari is liked (by me).

Gauṛī pūrbī; mahalā IV.

XXVI. LXIV.

(1). By reason of the instruction of the Guru the unbeaten sound sounds, by means of the instruction of the Guru (my) mind sings (the praises of Hari).

By him, whose lot is great, the sight of the Guru is obtained, blessed, blessed is he, who directs his thoughts devoutly on the Guru!

Pause.

The disciple Hari applies to deep meditation (on the Guru).

(2). My Lord is the perfect, true Guru, my mind does the work (enjoined by) the Guru.

We, rubbing and rubbing, wash the feet of the Guru, who lets (us) hear the story of Hari, Hari.

(3). In (my) heart is, through the instruction of the Guru, the elixir of Rām, (my) tongue sings the qualities of Hari.

(My) mind, being pleasantly, pleasantly engaged,[1] is satiated with the juice of Hari, it will not again bring on hunger.

[1] ਰਸਕਿ is the part. past conjunctive of ਰਸਕਣਾ, *v.n.* to be pleasantly engaged in an occupation, to be in a happy situation.

(4). (Though) one make many, many contrivances, he will not obtain the name without the mercy (of Hari).

On humble Nānak Hari has bestowed mercy, through the instruction of the Guru he makes firm the name in (my) mind.

Gauṛī mājh; mahalā IV.

XXVII. LXV.

(1). O disciple, O dear friend, mutter the name! (this is thy) work.
Understanding (is) the mother, understanding the life (of him), (in whose) mouth the name of Rām is.
Contentment (is his) father, having made the unborn divine male (his) Guru.
He, whose lot is great, is united (with) Rām.
(2). The Guru, the divine male of magic power is obtained (by me), I enjoy pleasures, O dear!
Being steeped in the colour of Hari the Guru (I am) always without worldly concerns, O dear!
(My) lot is great, having met with the clever and all-wise one, O dear!
My heart and body are steeped in the colour of Hari.
(3). Come, ye saints, we will together mutter the name!
The taking always of the name in the assembly (of the pious) is a gain, O dear!
By serving the saints nectar is obtained in the mouth, O dear!
By a former destiny, written from the beginning, it is obtained.
(4). In Sāvaṇ rain (falls), with nectar the world is overspread, O dear!
My mind has raised a cry (like a peacock), the word (of the Guru) is obtained in (my) mouth.
The nectar of Hari has rained, Hari, the king, is obtained, O dear!
Humble Nānak is steeped in the love (of Hari).[1]

Gauṛī mājh; mahalā IV.

XXVIII. LXVI.

(1). Come, O friend, O dear lady, we will utter the praises (of Hari)!
Joining the pious people, we will enjoy pleasures and amusements, O dear!
By the Guru the lamp of spiritual knowledge is always kindled in the mind, O dear!
Bowing and bowing (we are) united with the pleased Hari, O dear!
(2). In my mind and body love has sprung up to Hari, the beloved, O dear!
May he join me with (my) friend, the true Guru, the mediator, O dear!
I give my heart to the saints, who join to me my Lord, O dear!
I sacrifice myself always to the gratuitous service of Hari, O dear!

(3). Dwell, O my beloved, dwell, O my Gōvind, O Hari, bestowing mercy (on me) dwell (in my) mind, O Lord!

The fruit, desired by my mind, is obtained, O my Gōvind, having seen the perfect Guru I am delighted, O Lord!

The name of Hari is obtained, (I am) a happy married woman, O my Gōvind, daily (there is) joy and merriment, O Lord!

Hari is obtained by (me) the very fortunate one, O my Gōvind, continually getting gain I am happy in (my) mind, O Lord!

(4). Hari himself produces, Hari himself sees, Hari himself applies to the work, O dear!
Some eat, there is no deficiency of the gifts (of Hari), some get (only) a handful, O dear!
Some are kings and sit on a throne being always comfortable, some must beg alms, O dear!
In all only (thy) word is current, O my Gōvind; humble Nānak meditates on (thy) name, O Lord!

[1] ਰਤੰਨਾ = ਰਤਾ.

Gauṛī mā̃jh; mahalā IV.

XXIX. LXVII.

(1). In my mind, in my mind, O my Gōvind, in my mind I am imbued with love to Hari, O dear!

Hari, (my) joy (= husband) is not perceived as being near, O my Gōvind, the perfect Guru causes the inapprehensible one to be apprehended, O dear!

(When) the name of Hari, Hari is made manifest, O my Gōvind, all the pains of poverty go off, O dear!

The step of Hari, which is the highest, is obtained, O my Gōvind, the very fortunate one is absorbed in the name, O dear!

(2). With (her) eyes, O my beloved, with (her) eyes, O my Gōvind, by whom is Hari, the Lord, seen with (her) eyes, O dear?

My heart and body are very sad,[1] O my Gōvind, without Hari, the woman is withering away, O dear!

Joining the pious people, O my Gōvind, my Lord Hari, my sweetheart and companion was obtained (by me), O dear!

Hari, the life of the universe, has come and joined me, O my Gōvind, the night is spent by me (now) in happiness, O dear!

(3). O pious man, join to me my Lord Hari, (my) sweetheart, in my heart and body hunger (after him) is excited (by thee), O dear!

I cannot exist without seeing my beloved, thou hast roused within me the pangs of separation from Hari, O dear!

Hari, the king, is my beloved sweetheart, (if) the Guru join (him to me), my heart is vivified, O dear!

In my mind and body (there is) full desire (after thee), O my Gōvind, (when) Hari is met with, (there are) congratulations in the heart, O dear!

(4). I am devoted, O my Gōvind, I am devoted, O my beloved, I am always devoted to thy gratuitous service, O dear!

In my heart and body is love to the beloved, O my Gōvind! O Hari, keep our store, O dear!

Join (to me) the true Guru, the mediator, O my Gōvind, (that) he guiding (the right way) may unite Hari with me, O dear!

If thou bestowest mercy, the name of Hari is obtained, O my Gōvind, humble Nānak is in thy asylum, O dear!

Gauṛī mā̃jh; mahalā IV.

XXX. LXVIII.

(1). He is wonderful, O my Gōvind, he is wonderful, O my beloved, Hari my Lord is wonderful, O dear!

Hari himself is producing Krishṇa, O my Gōvind, by Hari himself the Gōpī (Rādhā) is sought, O dear!

Hari himself is enjoying everybody, O my Gōvind, Hari himself is given to sensual pleasures and enjoying himself, O dear!

Hari is very wise and does not err, O my Gōvind, he himself is the true Guru, endowed with magic power, O dear!

(2). He himself is producing the universe, O my Gōvind, Hari himself sports in many ways, O dear!

Some he lets enjoy pleasures, O my Gōvind, some wander about naked and disgraced,[2] O dear!

He himself is producing the world, O my Gōvind, Hari gives gifts to every one who asks, O dear!

[1] ਘੈਰਾਗਲਾ, *v.n.* to be sad, to weep.

[2] ਨੰਗ ਨੰਗੀ, Pers. ننگی ننگین, disgraced by shame.

The name is the support of the devotees, O my Gōvind, the good story about Hari, Hari they ask, O dear!

(3). Hari himself causes devotion to be made, O my Gōvind, the devotees of Hari have full desire (after Hari) in their heart, O dear!

He himself is existing in water and land, O my Gōvind, he is contained (everywhere), he is not far away, O dear!

Hari himself is inside and outside, O my Gōvind, Hari himself is omnipresent, O dear!

Hari, the vivifying principle, is spread out, O my Gōvind, Hari himself sees in the presence, O dear!

(4). Hari is within the sound of the breath, O my Gōvind, as Hari himself produces a sound, so it is sounded, O dear!

The hidden treasure of the name of Hari is within (the heart), O my Gōvind, by the word of the Guru Hari the Lord becomes known, O dear!

He himself causes (men) to flee to his asylum, O my Gōvind! Hari keeps the honour of (his) devotees, O dear!

He, whose lot is great, is united (with) the assembly (of the pious), O my Gōvind! the perfection (= emancipation) of humble Nānak is effected[1] by the name, O dear!

Gauṛī mǎjh; mahalā IV.

XXXI. LXIX.

(1). I (have a desire after) the name of Hari, I am suffering the pangs of separation from Hari, O dear!
May my Lord Hari, my friend be met with, (that) I may obtain comfort, O dear!
Having seen the Lord Hari, I live, O dear mother!
My friend is the name, (my) brother is Hari, O dear!
(2). Sing, O pious (man), the qualities of my Lord Hari, O dear!
Mutter, O disciple, the name, thy lot (will be) great, O dear!
The name of Hari, Hari, O dear, of my beloved[2] Hari, O dear!
Will not again make (thee) wander through the waters of existence, O dear!
(3). How shall I see Hari? in my heart and body there is a longing (for him), O dear!
Join Hari (to me), O pious man, in my heart (there is) love to him, O dear!
By the word of the Guru is obtained the beloved Hari, the King, O dear!
O very fortunate one, mutter the name, O dear!
(4). In my heart and body is a great desire after Gōvind, the Lord, O dear!
O holy man, join (to me) Hari, Gōvind, the Lord, O dear!
By the instruction of the true Guru the name is always made manifest, O dear!
Humble Nānak (says): the desire in the heart is (thus) accomplished, O dear!

Gauṛī mǎjh; mahalā IV.

XXXII. LXX.

(1). My desire[3] is the name, if it be obtained, then I live, O dear!
In (my) heart (there is) nectar, by the instruction of the Guru I get Hari, O dear!
My heart is imbued with love to Hari, the juice of Hari I drink always, O dear!

[1] ਕਾਜੈ = ਕਰਜੈ, passive, is made or effected (generally ਕੀਜੈ).

[2] ਪ੍ਰਾਣ, life; anything dearly beloved.

[3] ਬਿਰਹੀ, *s.f.* entreaty, desire (cf. ਬਿਰਥਾ = प्रार्था = प्रार्थना), the termination *ā* being changed to *ī*, which is freqnently the case.

Hari is obtained in my heart, I live, O dear!
(2). In my heart and body there is love, the arrow of Hari has pierced it, O dear!
My beloved friend is Hari, the all-wise spirit, O dear!
Join (to me), O holy man, the Guru Hari, the clever and wise, O dear!
I am a sacrifice to the gratuitous service of the name of Hari, O dear!
(3). I inquire after Hari, Hari, my sweetheart, Hari, my friend, O dear!
Show to me, O ye holy men, Hari, I inquire after the traces of Hari, O dear!
If the true Guru, being pleased, shows Hari (to me), then I obtain (him), O dear!
Praising Hari I am absorbed in the name, O dear!
(4). I suffer the pain of love, the pangs of separation from Hari, O dear!
O Guru, complete (my) faith, (that) I may obtain nectar in my mouth, O dear!
O Hari, become merciful, (that) I may meditate on the name of Hari, O dear!
Humble Nānak (says): (that) I may obtain the juice of Hari, O dear!

RĀGU GAUṚĪ GUĀRĒRĪ; MAHALĀ V.

Čaupadās.

Ōm! by the favour of the true Guru!

I. LXXI.

Pause.

How is happiness brought about, O my brother?
How is Hari Rām obtained as a helper?
(1). (There is) no happiness in the house, (if) mine (be) all the Māyā.
(If) high (and) beautiful palaces be roofed in (by me).
By false covetousness (one's) lifetime is lost.
(2). Having seen elephants and horses he is happy.
Armies, mace-bearers and domestic servants are collected (by him).
On (his) neck is the rope and noose of selfishness.
(3). He may exercise dominion in all the ten quarters (of the earth).
He may enjoy many pleasures and women.
As in a dream the king becomes a beggar.[1]
(4). (There is) one happiness, (which) the true Guru has shown to me.
Whatever Hari does, that is pleasing to the devotees of Hari.
Humble Nānak (says): having destroyed (their) egotism they are absorbed (in Hari).

Pause.

In this wise happiness is brought about, O my brother!
Thus Hari Rām is obtained as a helper.

Gauṛī guārērī; mahalā V.

II. LXXII.

(1). How should one be given to doubt, who should be of slight faith?
When he (*i.e.* Hari) is contained in water, earth and on the surface of the earth.
The disciples are saved, the self-willed lose their honour.

[1] The sense is: he becomes a beggar suddenly, as in a dream.

Pause.

Whom the merciful Rām himself protects:
To him none other can come near.
(2). In all exists the One infinite.
Sleep thou therefore in comfort and be without care!
He knows everything that is happening.
(3). The fleshly-minded die, who have another thirst (than that after Hari).
In many wombs they wander about, (as) it was written from the beginning by destiny.
What they sow, such things they will eat.[1]
(4). Having seen (his) sight happiness has sprung up in my mind.
All has come into my sight as manifestation of Brahm.
Humble Nānak has a full desire after Hari.

Gauṛī guārērī; mahalā V.

III. LXXIII.

(1). In some births thou didst become a worm (and) moth.
In some births an elephant, fish (and) deer.
In some births (thou) didst become a bird (and) snake.
In some births a horse and an ox, that is yoked on.

Pause.

Be united with the Lord of the Universe, this is the time of being united (with him)!
After a long time this (human) body[2] was obtained (by thee).
(2). In some births (thou wast) made a rock and mountain.
In some births thou fellest off as an unripe fruit from the womb.
In some births thou wast produced as a potherb.
In the eighty-four lakhs (of forms of existence) thou wast caused to wander about.
(3). A birth is (now) obtained (by thee) with the pious.
Perform worship, adore Hari, Hari, by means of the instruction of the Guru!
Give up pride and false conceit!
(If) thou diest whilst living, (thou art) approved at the threshold (of Hari).
(4). Whatever is done, that will be done by Thee.
There is none other capable of doing (anything).
Then one is united (with thee), when thou unitest (him with thee).
Nānak says: sing the qualities of Hari, Hari!

Gauṛī guārērī; mahalā V.

IV. LXXIV.

(1). In the field of works[3] sow the name!
Thy work will be completed.[4]

[1] ਖਾਸਾ, on account of the rhyme, instead of ਖਾਸਿ.

[2] Only in the human body the soul can work out its final emancipation.

[3] ਕਰਮ ਭੂਮਿ is this present world.

[4] The sense is: thou will get thereby final emancipation and become freed from the necessity of re-generation.

Thou wilt get the fruit (of thy works), the fear of Yama will be effaced:
(If) thou singest continually the qualities and the praise of Hari.

Pause.

Put the name of Hari, Hari into thy breast:
(And) thou wilt quickly accomplish thy work!
(2). If thou becomest attentive to thy Lord:
Thou wilt obtain honour at the threshold.
Give up all, all contrivance and dexterity!
Cling to the feet of the pious people!
(3). In whose hand all the creatures are:
He is never separated, he is with all.
Give up shifts and seize his asylum!
In a moment thy release will be effected.
(4). Consider him always as (being) near!
Mind the order of the Lord as true!
Blot out, by means of the word of the Guru, thy own self!
Nānak (says): mutter the name of Hari, Hari!

Gauṛī guārērī; mahalā V.

V. LXXV.

(1). The word of the Guru is always imperishable.
By the word of the Guru the noose of Yama is cut asunder.
The word of the Guru is with the creatures.
By the word of the Guru they are imbued with love to Rām.

Pause.

What is given by the Guru, that is useful to the heart.
Mind that, which is done by the holy one (= Guru) as true!
(2). The word of the Guru is immovable and not to be broken.
By the word of the Guru doubt is cut off and duality.
The word of the Guru does not pass away in any way.
Sing by means of the word of the Guru the qualities of Hari!
(3). The word of the Guru is with the creatures.
The word of the Guru is the friend of the friendless one.
For the sake of the word of the Guru he does not fall into hell.
By the word of the Guru (his) tongue enjoys nectar.
(4). The word of the Guru is manifest in the world.
By the word of the Guru (one) sustains no loss.
(To whom) he himself (*i.e.* Hari) is merciful:
(To him), says Nānak, is the true Guru always compassionate.

Gauṛī guārērī; mahalā V.

VI. LXXVI.

(1). Who makes a gem out of (a clod of) earth;
Who with effort preserves in the womb;
Who gives lustre and greatness:
On that Lord I meditate the eight watches (of the day).

Pause.

O my sweetheart,[1] may I obtain the dust of the pious people!
Joining the Guru I will meditate on my Lord!
(2). Who makes of a fool an eloquent man,
Who makes of a stupid an intelligent man,
By whose favour I obtain the nine treasures:
That Lord is not forgotten from my mind.
(3). Who gives a place to the homeless,
Who gives honour to the honourless,
Who fulfils every desire:
(Him) I remember day and night at (every) breath and morsel.
(4). By whose favour the rope of the Māyā is cut.
By the favour of the Guru the acid poison (becomes) nectar.
Nānak says: by this (man) nothing (is done).
I praise the preserver.

Gauṛī guārērī; mahalā V.

VII. LXXVII.

(1). In his asylum there is no fear (nor) grief.
Without him nothing will happen.
I give up dexterity, force, contrivance and passions.
He is preserving (the honour)[2] of his servant.

Pause.

Mutter, O my heart, with pleasure: Rām, Rām!
In the house (and) outside (of it) he is always with thee.
(2). Establish him firmly in thy mind,
(And) thou wilt taste the nectar-juice, the word of the Guru.
Say, of what use are the other efforts?
He himself, bestowing his mercy, keeps (thy) honour.
(3). Say, what is man, what is his power?
All the uproar of the Māyā is but false (= vain).
The Lord causes the work to be done.
He is the inward governor of all the bodies.
(4). Of all comforts the true comfort is this:
Take to heart the instruction of the Guru!
Who is given to contemplation on the name of Rām:
He, says Nānak, is blessed and endowed with a great lot.

Gauṛī guārērī; mahalā V.

VIII. LXXVIII.

(1). By hearing the story about Hari filth is taken off.
(Men) easily[3] become much purified.

[1] ਰਮਈਆ signifies also (like रमण, to which it corresponds) "sweetheart," "husband."
[2] ਦਾਸ ਅਪਨੇ ਕੀ, supply: ਲਜ, honour.
[3] ਸੁਖ ਸੈਲ, used adverbially; "easily," "without difficulty." ਸੈਲ = Sansk. शैथिल्य.

By reason of a great lot (destiny) the society of the pious is obtained.
Love to the Supreme Brahm springs up.

Pause.

The (pious) man, muttering the name of Hari, Hari, is saved.
By the Guru he is brought over the sea of fire.
(2). By praising Hari (his) mind becomes sedate (cool).
The sins of (his different) births are gone off.
The receptacle of all (things) he perceives in his mind.
Now why should he go to seek (it elsewhere)?
(3). When his Lord has become merciful,
The labour of the worshipper has come to an end.
The fetters of (his) servant are cut
By remembering, remembering, remembering the abode of (all) qualities.
(4). The One is in the mind, the One is in every spot.
He abides brimful in every place.
By the perfect Guru every doubt is removed.
By remembering Hari, (says) Nānak, comfort is obtained.

Gauṛī guārērī; mahalā V.

IX. LXXIX.

(1). Those who die before, repose afterwards.
Those, who are spared, they, having girded up their loins, are standing.[1]
The business, to which they cling,
By that duality is made firm, in that they are absorbed.

Pause.

That time (of death) does not at all come into their mind.
They cling to that which passes away.
(2). By desire the body of the fool is bound.
He clings to lust, wrath and love.
On his head is standing Dharm-Rāi (= Yama).
He eats poison considering it a sweet thing.
(3). I bind, I subdue enmity.
Who will put his foot into our ground?
I am a Paṇḍit, I am clever and knowing.
Another does not comprehend the creator.
(4). His own state and mind[2] he himself knows.
What can one say, how can one describe (it)?
Into whatever (business or condition) he puts (a man), there he must remain,
(Though) every one is asking for his own welfare.
(5). Everything is thine, thou art the creator.
There is no end nor limit (of thee).
May to (thy) servant (this) gift be given:
(That) Nānak may never forget (thy) name.

[1] ਉਘਰੇ, who are spared, *i.e.* who spare their life and do not die (by means of contemplation). ਖਰੇ, they are standing, *i.e.* they are engaged in work, must work on (in contradistinction to ਪਰੇ, they repose).

[2] ਗਿਤਿ ਭਿਤਿ is the same as ਗਤਿ ਭਤਿ, one's secret mind or thought.

Gauṛī guārērī ; mahalā V.

X. LXXX.

(1). By many efforts emancipation is not brought about.
(Not) by much dexterity (nor) by great force.
By reason of the pure worship of Hari
Splendour and dignity[1] (are obtained) at the threshold (of the Lord).

Pause.

O my mind, seize the shelter of the name of Hari!
No hot blast of wind will touch thee.
(2). As a boat (preserves) in the ocean of fear.
(As) a lamp lightens up darkness.
(As by) fire the cold season, by laughing pain (is removed):
(So) by muttering the name happiness is brought about in the mind.
(3). The thirst of thy mind will leave off.
All thy desires will be fulfilled.
Thy mind will not vacillate,
Having muttered the nectar-name, O dear disciple!
(4). The medicine of the name that man obtains:
To whom he himself (*i.e.* Hari) causes it to be given out of mercy.
In whose heart the name of Hari, Hari dwells:
His pain and trouble flee away, (says) Nānak.

Gauṛī guārērī ; mahalā V.

XI. LXXXI.

(1). By collecting much wealth (my) mind was not satiated.
Having seen many forms (I was) not assured (of them).
To son and wife my soul clings.
That (wealth) will pass away, these (will be) a heap of ashes.

Pause.

Without the worship of Hari I see (them) lamenting.
Woe to the body, woe to the wealth (of those, who are) in love with the Māyā!
(2). As (when) to a forced labourer money be given,
(And) he be in the house of the Lord (and) that (Lord) undergo[2] toil.
As (when) in a dream he becomes a Rājā and sits down (in state):
When he opens (his) eyes, it is a vain affair.
(3). As a watchman over another's field.
The field is the Lord's (owner's), the watchman goes off.
The watchman vexes himself on account of that field.
Into his hem[3] (= pocket) falls nothing.
(4). Whose the dominion is, even his is (also) the dream (= the Māyā).
By whom the Māyā is given, by him (also) the thirst (after the Māyā) is raised.

[1] ਸੋਤੁ, *s.m.* dignity, rank.
[2] ਉਨ ਦੂਖ ਸਹਾਮਾ ; ਸਹਾਮਾ = ਸਹਾ, ਮਾ being a meaningless alliteration.
[3] ਪਾਲਾ = ਪੱਲਾ, hem of a garment, here = pocket.

He himself annihilates, He himself establishes.
Nānak (makes) supplication before the Lord.

Gauṛī guārērī ; mahalā V.

XII. LXXXII.

(1). The illusive creation of many kinds and sorts was seen (by me).
With the pen wisdom was put down on the paper.
Having become a chief (and) king a (fine) house was seen (by me).
(But) by (all) this my heart was not satiated.

Pause.

Show me that comfort, O holy man!
(By which) my thirst may be quenched and my mind satiated.[1]
(2). Riding on a horse (swift like) the wind, (and) on an elephant.
Perfume of sandal-wood, a bed and a beautiful woman.
The singing of actors and dancers in the arena :
In (all) this my mind receives no satisfaction.
(3). The assembly (round) the throne, the festive procession of (the Rājā's) sedan-chair.
All fruits, beautiful gardens.
Delight in the chase, the kingly sport:
(By all this) my mind is not comforted, (it is) illusion and deceit.
(4). Out of mercy the holy men told me of the True one.
All comfort and joy was obtained (by me) (from) this.
In the assembly of the pious the praise of Hari is sung.
Nānak (says): by him, whose lot is great, he (*i.e.* Hari) is obtained.

Pause.

In whose (house) is the wealth of Hari, he is happy.
By the mercy of the Lord union with the pious (is brought about).

Gauṛī guārērī ; mahalā V.

XIII. LXXXIII.

(1). Man thinks: this body is mine.
Again and again he clings to it.[2]
Son, wife, household are a noose (to him).
(Such men) cannot become the servants of Rām.

Pause.

What is that manner, by which one may sing the excellences of Rām?
What is that method, by which one may cross this Māyā?
(2). What is good, he considers as bad.
(If) one speak the truth, that is (to him) equal to poison.
He does not know victory and defeat.
This is the nature of the Sākat (in) the world.
(3). What is deadly poison, that the fool drinks.
The nectar-name he considers as bitter.

[1] ਤ੍ਰਿਪਤਾਵਹੁ, instead of ਤ੍ਰਿਪਤਾਵੈ, for the sake of the rhyme.
[2] ਲਪਟੇਗਾ = ਲਪਟੇ, ਗਾ being only an alliteration.

He does not go near the assembly of the pious.
He wanders again about in the eighty-four lakhs (of forms of existence).
(4). By one net birds are ensnared.
Glowing with youthful ardour[1] he is given to sensual enjoyments of many kinds.
Nānak (says): to whom he has become merciful:
His nets are cut asunder by the perfect Guru.

Gauṛī guārērī ; mahalā V.

XIV. LXXXIV.

(1). By thy mercy the (right) way is obtained.
By the mercy of the Lord the name is meditated upon.
By the mercy of the Lord the bonds are loosened.
By thy mercy egotism is broken.

Pause.

(Thy) service is done, if thou appliest (one to it).
We can do nothing, O God!
(2). If it is pleasing to thee, then I sing (thy) praise.[2]
If it is pleasing to thee, then I praise the True one.
If it is pleasing to thee, then the true Guru is compassionate.
All comforts, O Lord, (are obtained) by thy mercy.
(3). What is pleasing to thee, that is a true work.
What is pleasing to thee, that is true virtue.
The receptacle of all excellences is with thee.
Thou art the Lord, (thy) servant (is offering up) supplication (to thee).
(4). (My) mind and body become pure by love to Hari.
All comforts I obtain in the society of the saints.
My mind remains attached to thy name.
This is considered by Nānak as happiness.

Gauṛī guārērī ; mahalā V.

XV. LXXXV.

(1). As many other flavours as are tasted by thee:
(By them) not for a moment (thy) thirst is quenched.
If thou tastest the flavour of the juice of Hari:
By tasting (it) thou becomest wonder-struck.

Pause.

O my beloved tongue, drink nectar!
Steeped in this juice thou wilt become satiated.[3]
(2). O tongue, sing thou the excellences of Rām!
Every moment meditate on Hari, Hari, Hari!
Nothing else should be heard nor should one go anywhere else.

[1] ਠਮਿਠਮਿ, part. past conjunctive of ਠਮਿਠਮਲਾ, *v.n.* to be glowing with youthful ardour.
[2] ਘਾਲੀ, *s.f.* reading from the Purāṇs or singing in praise of the Deity.
[3] ਤ੍ਰਿਪਤਾਰੀ = ਤ੍ਰਿਪਤਿ (तृप्त), *adj.* satiated, ārī being a meaningless alliteration.

In the society of the pious he (*i.e.* Hari) is obtained by him, whose lot is great.
(3). O tongue, praise him all the eight watches (of the day)!
The Supreme Brahm, the Lord, is unfathomable.
Here and there (thou wilt) always (be) happy.
Singing the praises of Hari (thou art) priceless, O tongue!
(4). The tree has sprouted, blossoms and fruits are (on) the tree.
Steeped in this juice (of Hari) thou wilt not give it up again.
He brings no (other) juice near his mouth:
(To whom) the Guru has become an assistant, says Nānak.

Gauṛī guārērī; mahalā V.

XVI. LXXXVI.

(1). The mind is made the palace, the body the fence.
Within it is an infinite thing (= the Supreme Being).
Within it the wholesale merchant is heard (saying):
Who is the retail-dealer, on whom there is reliance there?

Pause.

Some (rare) one is a trafficker with the gem of the name.
Who procures it, is feeding on nectar.
(2). Mind and body I offer up as a sacrifice, worship is made (by me).
What is that contrivance, by means of which I may be imbued with love (to Hari)?
I fall down at (his) foot, giving up mine and thine.[1]
Who is that man, who puts (me) into the traffic (of the name of Hari)?
(3). In what wise may I obtain the palace of the wholesale merchant?
What is that manner of life, by reason of which he calls (one) within?
Thou art a great wholesale merchant, who hast crores of retail-dealers.
Who is that donor, who having taken (life) makes (it) enter (again)?
(4). Searching and searching about (our) own house was (at length) obtained.
The true, priceless gem was (then) shown (to us):
When, out of mercy, (we were) united by the wholesale merchant (with himself),
By reason of confidence (faith) in the Guru, says Nānak.

Gauṛī guārērī; mahalā V.

XVII. LXXXVII.

(1). They remain night and day in one (continual) love (of Hari):
(Who) know the Lord (as being) always (present) with them.
The name of the Lord is made (their) occupation.
They are fully satiated by the sight of Hari.

Pause.

(Who) are in love with Hari, they are flourishing in mind and body.
They have fled to the asylum of the perfect Guru.
(2). The lotus-foot (of Hari) is (their) soul's support.

[1] ਮੇਰਾ ਤੇਰਾ, mine and thine, *i.e.* all questions about mine and thine, all earthly goods. ਤੇਰੈ, for the sake of the rhyme, instead of ਤੇਰਾ.

The One they look at obediently.
The One is (their) trade, (with) the One (they are) occupied.
They know no other without the formless one.
(3). They are free from both joy and grief.
They are always free (from contact with the world) and given to devotion.[1]
Who is seen in all and free from all:
On (that) Supreme Brahm they are meditating.
(4). How shall I describe the greatness of the saints ?
(They are) of unfathomable wisdom, I cannot estimate it in any way.
O Supreme Brahm, bestow mercy on me !
May the dust of the saints be given to Nānak !

Gauṛī guārērī ; mahalā V.

XVIII. LXXXVIII.

(1). Thou art my companion, thou art my friend.
Thou art my beloved, with thee (I have) friendship.
Thou art my honour, thou art my jewel.
Without thee I cannot live a moment.

Pause.

Thou art my darling, thou art my life.
Thou art my Lord, thou art my prince.
(2). As thou puttest me down, so I remain.
What thou sayest, that must be done by me.
Wherever I see, there thou art dwelling.
Thy fearless name I mutter with (my) tongue.
(3). Thou art my nine treasures, thou art my treasury.
Thou art my pleasure and delight, the support of my heart.
Thou art my lustre, with thee I am in love.
Thou art my shelter, thou art my support.
(4). Within my mind and body even thou art meditated upon.
Thy secret I obtained from the Guru.
By the true Guru the only One was confirmed (in me).
Nānak, the slave of Hari, relies on Hari, Hari.

Gauṛī guārērī ; mahalā V.

XIX. LXXXIX.

(1). (The Māyā) enters by spreading out joy and grief.
She enters heaven and hell and the avatārs.
She enters the poor one, who is looking out for splendour.[2]
Root-piercing[3] she enters (by) covetousness.

[1] The words must be thus constructed: ਸਦਾ ਅਲਿਪਤ ਹੈ ਅਰੁ ਜੋਗ ਜੁਗਤੇ (योगयुक्त, given to devotion or abstract contemplation).

[2] ਧਨ ਨਿਰਧਨ is to be taken as one word = poor; such (superfluous) compounds are frequent in the Granth. ਪੇਖਿ may be taken as adjective (= Sansk. प्रेक्षिन्), looking out for, or as part. past conjunctive from ਪੇਖਣਾ, having looked out. The sense is the same both ways.

[3] ਮੂਲੁ ਬਿਆਪੀ (Sansk. व्याधिन्), root-piercing, *i.e.* totally destroying.

Pause.

The Māyā enters (men) in many ways.
The saints live in thy protection, O Lord!
(2). She enters him, who is drunk by vain conceit.
She enters him, who is attached to son and wife.
She enters (him who is proud) (about) elephants, horses and things.
She enters him who is drunk in the inebriety of youth and beauty.
(3). She enters the ground, the tabor[1] and the arena.
She enters the assembly, having heard the sound of a song.
She enters the bed, the palace, the ornaments.
The five intoxicated and blind ones[2] she enters.
(4). She enters him, who does works ensnared by selfishness.
She enters the married state, she enters lonely life.
She enters conduct, occupation and caste.
Everything she enters except him, who is steeped in the colour of Hari.
(5). The bonds of the saints are cut asunder by Hari.
How should the Māyā enter them?
Nānak says: who have obtained the dust of the saints:
Near them the Māyā does not come.

Gauṛī guārērī; mahalā V.

XX. XC.

(1). (In) the eyes is sleep (and) the passion of looking at another's wife.
The ears have fallen asleep having heard and reflected on calumny.
The tongue has fallen asleep by greediness and sweet taste.
The mind has fallen asleep, amazed by the Māyā.

Pause.

(If) one remains awake in this house (= body):
He gets his thing unimpaired.
(2). All the companions[3] are intoxicated in their own pleasure.
They have no knowledge of their own house.
The five highwaymen[4] are robbing.
The cheats have fallen on the empty city.
(3). Father and mother cannot protect from them.
Friend and brother cannot protect from them.
They are not stopped by wealth and cleverness.
In the society of the pious these are brought under subjection.
(4). Bestow mercy on me, O thou bow-holder!
The dust of the saints is all (my) treasure.

[1] We divide the words into ਭੂ, ground, and ਮਿਰੰਕ (as ਰੰਕ, poor, gives here no sense); ਮਿਰੰਕ is very likely the same as ਮਿਰਦੰਗ (मृदङ्ग), a tabor or drum, big in the middle and smaller at both ends, used in the ਰੰਗ, or arena (theatre).

[2] *i.e.* ਕਾਮ, ਕ੍ਰੋਧ, etc.

[3] The ਸਹੇਲੀ or companions are here the *senses*.

[4] The ਪੰਚ ਬਟਵਾਰੇ (= ਬਾਟਮਾਰ), or five highwaymen, are ਕਾਮ, ਕ੍ਰੋਧ, ਲੋਭ, ਮੋਹ, ਅਹੰਕਾਰ.

(My) capital (remains) safe with the true Guru.
Nānak wakes in love to the Supreme Brahm.

Pause.

He wakes, to whom the Lord is merciful.
His capital, wealth (and) property (remain) safe.

Gauṛī guārērī ; mahalā V.

XXI. XCI.

(1). In whose power the Khān and Sultān is;
In whose power all the world is;
By whom everything is made:
Without him there is no one.

Pause.

Make thy supplication before thy own true Guru!
He will settle (all) thy affairs.
(2). Whose court is higher than all.
Whose name is the support of all (his) devotees.
All-pervading and omnipresent is the Lord:
Whose splendour is formed in everybody.
(3). Remembering whom the dwelling of pain tumbles down.
Remembering whom Yama does not say anything.
Remembering whom the dried up ones become green.
Remembering whom the sinking stones swim across.
(4). Victory always to the assembly of the saints!
The name of Hari, Hari, is the support of the life of his servants.
Nānak says: he has heard my supplication.
By the favour of the saints I dwell in the name.

Gauṛī guārērī ; mahalā V.

XXII. XCII.

(1). By the sight of the true Guru the fire is extinguished.
By meeting with the true Guru egotism is subdued.
In the society of the true Guru the mind does not vacillate.
The disciple utters the nectar-speech.

Pause.

The whole world is true, when steeped in the True one.
Coolness and tranquillity are (obtained) from the Guru, the Lord is known.
(2). By the favour of the saints he mutters the name.
By the favour of the saints he sings the praise of Hari.
By the favour of the saints all pains are blotted out.
By the favour of the saints he is released from his bonds.
(3). By the mercy of the saints spiritual blindness and error are done away.
Bathing in the dust of the pious is all (his) religion.
When the pious are merciful, Gōvind is compassionate.
Amongst the pious (is) this my soul.

(4). Meditate on the compassionate depository of mercy!
Thou wilt then obtain a seat in the society of the pious.
On me, the destitute of virtues, the Lord has bestowed mercy.
In the society of the pious Nānak has taken the name.

Gauṛī guārērī; mahalā V.

XXIII. XCIII.

(1). In the society of the pious the Lord is muttered (by them):
(To whom) by the Guru the mantra of the name alone is given.
Having given up conceit they have become free from enmity.
The eight watches they adore the feet of the Guru.

Pause.

Now the wicked thought of another is extinguished,
Since the praise of Hari is heard with (their) ears.
(2). The depository of tranquillity, comfort and joy,
The protector protects them at the end.
Pain and trouble, fear and doubt are extinguished.
Coming and going are stopped by his kindness.
(3). He himself beholds, utters and sees everything.
Who is always with (thee), him, O mind, mutter!
By the favour of the saints he was made manifest.
The One, the ocean of virtues, is omnipresent.
(4). Who relates (them)[1] (becomes) pure, (he becomes) cleansed who hears (them).
Who continually sings the excellences of Gōvind.
Nānak says: to whom he becomes merciful:
All that man's toil is brought to an end.

Gauṛī guārērī; mahalā V.

XXIV. XCIV.

(1). Having broken (his) fetters he makes (the disciple) utter Rām.
In (his) mind true meditation springs up.
The troubles are done away, he lives in happiness.
Such a donor the true Guru is called.

Pause.

He is the giver of happiness, who causes to mutter the name.
Bestowing mercy he unites with him (*i.e.* Hari).
(2). To whom he becomes kind, him he himself unites (with himself).
The depository of all (= the Supreme Being) he (*i.e.* the disciple) obtains from the Guru.
Having given up his own self (his) coming and going are effaced.
In the assembly of the pious the Supreme Brahm is known (by him).
(3). To his servants Hari has become merciful.
The support of (his) servants is the One, Gōpāl.
On the One (their) contemplation (is directed), to the One (they havė) love in (their) mind.

[1] *i.e.* the गुण of Gōvind.

All treasures are in the (house) of (his) servants,[1] the name of Hari.
(4). (Who) entertains love to the Supreme Brahm:
(His) work is pure, (his) practice is true.
By the perfect Guru (his) darkness is effaced.
The Lord of Nānak is boundless.[2]

Gauṛī guārērī; mahalā V.

XXV. XCV.

(1). In whose mind he (*i.e.* Hari) dwells, that man crosses over.
By whose destiny (this) may be obtained.[3]
No pain, sickness and fear enter (him):
Who mutters the nectar-name of Hari in (his) heart.

Pause.

That the Supreme Brahm, the Lord, be meditated upon:
This method is obtained from the perfect Guru.
(2). He who causes (every) work to be done, is merciful.
All creatures he is cherishing.
He is unattainable, inapprehensible always and endless.
Remember, O mind, the mantra of the perfect Guru!
(3). By whose worship all treasures (are obtained);
By the adoration of (which) Lord honour is acquired;
Whose service is not left unrequited:
Always, always sing the praises of (that) Hari!
(4). Bestow mercy (on me), O Lord, the inward governor!
(Thou), O Hari, the inapprehensible Lord, art the depository of comfort!
The creatures (flee) to thy asylum.
May (to) Nānak the greatness (of) the name be given!

Gauṛī guārērī; mahalā V.

XXVI. XCVI.

(1). In whose hand is the creation and management[4] of the living beings:
Remember that Lord of the friendless!
If the Lord comes into (thy) mind, all pains leave.
All fear is done away by the name of Hari.

Pause.

Without Hari of what art thou afraid?
Forgetting Hari in what wilt thou find comfort?

[1] ਜਨ ਕੈ, supply ਘਰਿ. ਨਿਧਾਨ must here be taken in the sense of "*treasure.*"

[2] ਅਪਰ ਅਪਾਰ (= अपरंपार, Hindī), boundless, both being identical in meaning, but differently compounded.

[3] The crossing (over the waters of existence = final emancipation) is obtained by destiny (according to one's former works).

[4] ਜੀਅ ਜੁਗਤਿ, a frequent expression in the Granth. ਜੁਗਤਿ (Sansk. युक्ति) signifies *the art or skill of making and the manner of applying* anything (said especially of a machine).

(2). By whom many earths and skies are upheld;
Whose vital energy is manifest in the creatures;
Whose gift no one effaces:
Remembering, remembering (that) Lord thou wilt become fearless.
(3). Remember the eight watches the name of the Lord!
(It is equal to) bathing and ablution in many Tīrthas.
Fall on the asylum of the Supreme Brahm!
Crores of stains (= sins) are blotted out in a moment.
(4). He is a full king, not in want of anything.
The confidence (faith) of the servants of the Lord is true.[1]
The perfect Guru, giving (them) his hand, protects them.
Nānak (says): the Supreme Brahm is powerful.

Gauṛī guārērī; mahalā V.

XXVII. XCVII.

(1). By the favour of the Guru (his) mind clings to the name.
He who had fallen asleep through various births is awakened.
He utters the nectar-speech of the excellences of Lord Hari:[2]
(By whom) the benevolence of the perfect Guru is obtained.[3]

Pause.

By remembering the Lord he obtains all happiness.
In the house and outside (of it) (he gets) all comfort and tranquillity.
(2). He knows (him), by whom he is created.
The Lord himself unites him (with himself) out of mercy.
He takes his arm and makes him his own:
Who is always reiterating the story of Hari.
(3). It is charm, spell and medicaments.[4]
The name of Hari, Hari is the support of the life of the creatures.
True wealth is obtained by love to Hari.
In the society of the pious one crosses (the water of existence), which is difficult to get over.
(4). The followers of the saints and pious dwell in comfort.
The wealth of Hari, which cannot be estimated, is acquired (by them).
Whose lot it is, to him the Guru gives it.
Nānak (says): at random no (wealth of Hari) accrues.[5]

[1] ਸਾਚਾ, true, *i.e.* it is not deceived.

[2] The words of this line must be put thus: ਪ੍ਰਭ ਕੇ ਗੁਣਾਂ ਕੀ ਅੰਮ੍ਰਿਤ ਬਾਣੀ ਉਚਰੈ. There is no grammatical connexion between them and the proper position of the words can only be arrived at by conjecture.

[3] The Sikhs do not know what to make of this verse, as they explain ਪਰਾਣੀ by "man." But here ਪਰਾਣੀ is the part. past of ਪਰਾਉਣਾ (= ਪਾਉਣਾ, from प्रापण), to obtain, a form which is also found in Rāg Āsā, Astpadī, 13, 7.

[4] ਅਉਖਧ ਪੁਨਹਚਾਰੁ; ਅਉਖਧ, drug, medicament; ਪੁਨਹਚਾਰੁ = Sansk. पुनराचार, repeated application (of medicaments); ਅਉਖਧ ਪੁਨਹਚਾਰ is used as a general term for all remedies and operations practised in the medical art (cf. the Sansk. औषधोपचार). The Sikhs have no idea of the signification of ਪੁਨਹਚਾਰ, and guess in all directions; they explain it traditionally by "*expiation*," but without any reason.

[5] ਬਿਰਥਾ signifies here: by chance, at random or accidentally (in contradistinction to ਪਰਾਪਤਿ, lot). ਕੋਇ ਨ ਹੋਇ, supply: ਕੋਇ ਧਨੁ ਖਟਿਓ ਨ ਹੋਇ.

Gauṛī guārērī; mahalā V.

XXVIII. XCVIII.

(1). Then (thy) hand will become pure:
When the clog of the Māyā is done away.
(If) thy tongue sing[1] continually the excellences of Rām:
Thou wilt obtain happiness, O my brother and friend!

Pause.

Write with pen, paper and ink
The name of Rām! (the name of) Hari is nectar-sound.
(2). By this work thy passions (or diseases) go off.
Remembering Rām Yama cannot beat (thee).
The messengers of Dharm-Rāe (= Yama) will not overpower (him):
(Who is) not at all sunk in the infatuation of the Māyā.[2]
(3). He himself is delivered (from existence) and (with him) the world crosses:
(Who) mutters the name of Rām with one mind.[3]
He himself imparts instruction to others:
Into whose heart the name of Rām has entered.
(4). On whose forehead this treasure (is written):
That man mutters the Lord.
(Who) sings the eight watches the praises of Hari, Hari:
To him I devote myself, says Nānak.

GAUṚĪ GUĀRĒRĪ; MAHALĀ V.

Čaupadās; Dupadās.

Ōm! By the favour of the true Guru!

XXIX. XCIX.

(1). What is another's, that (he considers) his own.
What is to be given up, to that his mind is attached.

Pause.

Say, how should union be effected with the Lord?
What is forbidden, for that he has an inclination.
(2). A false word is considered as true.
(If) true (words) be spoken, he does not like it in his mind.[4]
(3). The perverse man goes the road to the left.

[1] ਰਮਣਾ = ਰਵਣਾ (Sansk. रवण), to sing (व being here changed to म).

[2] The order of the words in this line must be: ਮਾਇਆ ਮੋਹਿ ਮਗਨ ਨ ਕਛੂਐ; a grammatical relation is not to be expected, that the reader has to find out for himself.

[3] ਏਕੰਗਾਰ, *adj.* intent in his mind (on Rām only).

[4] The MSS. differ very much in this line. The reading of the lithographed Lahore copy: ਸਤਿ ਹੋਵਨੁ ਮਨੁ ਨ ਲਗੈ ਗਾਤੀ, gives no sense, as the vowels are put wrong. Another MS. reads: ਸਤਿ ਹੋਵਨਿ ਮਨਿ ਨ ਲਗੈ ਗਾਤੀ, which no doubt is the right reading, as the words give a sense at least. ਗਾਤੀ = ਗਤਿ, for the sake of the rhyme.

Having given up the (road) to the right (hand) he chooses the untrodden one.[1]
(4). That Lord is the owner of both extremities (*i.e.* of this and that world).
Whom he unites (with himself), (says) Nānak, he becomes emancipated.

Gauṛī guārērī; mahalā V.

XXX. C.

(1). In the Kalī-yug they have met in union.
So long they enjoy themselves, as his order is (= as he orders them).

Pause.

(Though) she burn (in self-immolation), Rām, (her) friend is not obtained.
Rising according to destiny she becomes a Satī.
(2). (Though) in emulation and obstinacy of mind she burn herself:
She does not obtain the society of (her) beloved, she is caused to wander about in many births.
(3). Who in virtue and continence obeys the order of her beloved:
That woman suffers no pain in (this) world.[2]
(4). Nānak says: who considers the Lord as her beloved:
She is a blessed Satī and accepted at the threshold (of Hari).

Gauṛī guārērī; mahalā V.

XXXI. CI.

Pause.

We are rich and opulent by the true name.
We sing the praises of Hari with natural ease.
(1). When I opened and saw the treasury of (my) father and grandfather:
Then the treasure was put into my heart.
(2). With gems and rubies, the value of which cannot be estimated:
(My) store-rooms are filled, they are inexhaustible and cannot be weighed.
(3). Having met together, O brother, let us eat and spend (the treasures)!
They do not become diminished, they are (rather) increased.
(4). Nānak says: on whose forehead he causes (this) decree to be written:
Him he applies to this treasury.

Gauṛī guārērī; mahalā V.

XXXII. CII.

(1). (Then) people die out of fear, when he is considered as being far off.
Fear ceases, when he is seen as omnipresent.

[1] From the Sikh Granthīs I could get no explanation of this line. The three MSS., which I have at my disposal, read all ਘੁਨਨਾ, *he is weaving*. But this gives no sense whatever. It is also to be noticed, that the rhyme is thus rendered impure (ਚਲਨਾ—ਘੁਨਨਾ), which speaks against ਘੁਨਨਾ. We propose to read ਘਨਨਾ (Sansk. वनन), *he is choosing*. This root is no longer found in Hindī and Panjabī, and therefore very likely ਘਨਨਾ was corrected to the well-known ਘੁਨਨਾ, but in Sindhī वणणु is still in common use. This emendation will make the whole line perfectly clear. ਸੀਧਾ signifies here not "straight," but "right" (opposite to ਖਾਬੀ, left). ਅਪੁਠਾ, untrodden (literally: untouched), is derived from the Sansk. अस्पृष्ट; see my Sindhī Grammar, Introduction, p. xlii. *b*, *β* and p. xliv. *γ*.

[2] The Sikh Granthīs explain ਜਮਾਨੈ = ਜਮ ਦਾ ਦੁਖ (she suffers no pain at the hands of Yama). But ਜਮਾਨੈ may as well be the locative of ਜਮਾਨਾ (زمانہ), time, world, which suits the context better.

Pause.

(I) devote (myself) to my own true Guru.
I do not give him up, he brings me across by any means.
(2). There is pain, sickness and grief, when the name is forgotten.
There is always joy, when I sing[1] the praises of Hari.
(3). None should be called bad (or) good.
Having given up conceit the feet of Hari should be seized!
(4). Nānak says: apply thy mind to the mantra of the Guru!
(And) thou wilt obtain happiness at the true court.

Gauṛī; mahalā V.

XXXIII. CIII.

(1). Whose friend and beloved the Lord[2] is:
Say, what may that man stand in need of?

Pause.

Who has directed his affection on Gōvind:
His pain, trouble and error flee.
(2). Who has tasted the juice of Hari:
He does not stick to another juice.
(3). Whose word has effect at the threshold (of Hari):
To whom should he bring an offering (bowing down) to the ground?
(4). Who belongs to him, whose everything is:
He enjoys always comfort, (says) Nānak.

Gauṛī; mahalā V.

XXXIV. CIV.

(1). Who looks upon pain and pleasure as the same:[3]
How should grief affect him?

Pause.

Tranquillity and happiness (dwell) in (those) saints of Hari:
(Who are) obedient to Hari, Hari the King.
(2). Into whose heart the inconceivable (Supreme Being) comes and dwells (there):
He has no anxiety about anything.
(3). From whose mind error has become extinct:
He has no fear at all of Yama.
(4). Into whose heart the Guru has given the name:
His are all treasures, says Nānak.

Gauṛī; mahalā V.

XXXV. CV.

(1). The place of him, whose form is unattainable, is in the mind.
By the favour of the Guru some rare one has known him.

[1] ਗਾਮੁ = ਗਾਵਉ, I sing; it may also be the third pers. sing. "when one sings."
[2] ਸਮੀਆ = ਸਾਮੀ, Lord (स्वामी).
[3] ਕੈ (= ਕੈਂ), used by Arjun also as a Dative postfix = ਕਉ.

Pause.

The report about composure (of mind) are jars (full) of nectar.[1]
Whose lot it is, he takes and drinks them.
(2). (There is) a sound not produced by beating (an instrument), a pure place.
By its (*i.e.* that sound's) report Gōpāl enchants.
(3). In that (pure place) are many endless courts of tranquillity.
The saints are the companions of the Supreme Brahm.
(4). (Where there is) endless joy and no more grief:
That house the Guru gave to Nānak.

Gauṛī; mahalā V.

XXXVI. CVI.

(1). What is that form of thine, which I should adore?
What is that Yōg, by means of which I should subdue my body?

Pause.

What is (that) excellence, which I should sing in thy praise?
What is that word, by which I may gladden (thee), O Supreme Brahm?
(2). What is that worship of thine, which I should practise?
What is that manner, by which I may cross the water of existence?
(3). What is that austerity, by means of which one may become an ascetic?
What is that name,[2] by means of which one may remove the filth of egotism?
(4). Singing the excellences (of Hari), worship, (the acquisition of) divine knowledge, meditation, all (this) he does,[3] (says) Nānak:
With whom the merciful Guru meets and on whom he bestows mercy.

Pause.

By him are the excellences, by him is the Lord known:
Whose (word) the giver of comfort minds.

Gauṛī; mahalā V.

XXXVII. CVII.

(1). The body, of which thou art proud, is not thy own.
Dominion, property, wealth are not thy own.

Pause.

Why dost thou cling to that which is not thy own?
Thy own (is) the name, (which is) obtained from the true Guru.
(2). Son and wife, O brother, are not thy own.
Not friends and acquaintances, nor father and mother themselves.

[1] ਸਹਜ ਕਥਾ, the story or report about the ਸਹਜ or composure of mind; ਕੇ is misplaced, it should stand after ਅਮ੍ਰਿਤ.

[2] The reading: ਕਵਨ ਸੁਨਾਮੁ, though found in the three MSS. at my disposal, is apparently wrong, we should necessarily expect ਸਨਾਨੁ, bathing, ablution; "what is that bathing, by means of which," etc. The MSS. of later date are often very thoughtlessly written, especially in reference to the vowels, the grammatical importance of which the Sikhs no longer understand.

[3] All the MSS. at my disposal read ਘਾਲ, but this is senseless; ਘਾਲੁ (he does) must be read.

(3). Neither gold, silver and money,
Nor horses and elephants are of use to thee.
(4). Nānak says: who is kindly united (with Hari) by the Guru,
Who has Hari, the king, his is everything.

Gauṛī ; mahalā V.

XXXVIII. CVIII.

(1). The feet of the Guru are on my forehead.
By him all my pains are removed.

Pause.

I am a sacrifice to my own true Guru.
Having known the (Supreme) spirit I mind him with the greatest delight.
(2). Who applies to his face the dust of the feet of the Guru :
By him all egotism[1] is given up.
(3). To whom the word of the Guru has become sweet in his mind:
He has seen in (it) the Supreme Brahm.
(4). The Guru is the giver of comfort, the Guru is the creator.
The Guru, says Nānak, is the support of soul and life.

Gauṛī ; mahalā V.

XXXIX. CIX.

(1). O my heart, praise thou him,
In whose (house) there is no deficiency whatever.

Pause.

O heart, make that beloved Hari thy friend!
The support of life keep always in thy thoughts!
(2). O my heart, serve thou always him,
Who is the primeval spirit, the infinite God.
(3). Put thy hope on him, O heart,
In whom confidence (is placed) from the beginning, the beginning of the Yugs.
(4). The love to whom always becomes happiness :
(Him) Nānak praises, having met (with) the Guru.

Gauṛī ; mahalā V.

XL. CX.

(1). What (our) friend does, that is agreed to by us.
The actions of (our) friend are the reasons of (our) welfare.[2]

Pause.

In my heart and thought I trust in the One,
From whom (every) work proceeds, he is our friend.
(2). Our friend is unconcerned (about anybody).
By the mercy of the Guru he is a friend[3] to me.

[1] ਅਹੰਬੁਧਿ, *s.f.* the consciousness of individual existence.
[2] *i.e.* they tend to our welfare.
[3] ਅਸਨਾਹਾ = Pers. آشنا, friend, acquaintance.

(3). Our friend is the inward governor,
The powerful divine male, the Supreme Brahm, the Lord.
(4). We are thy slaves, (thou art) our Lord.
Honour and greatness, (says) Nānak, are thine, O Lord!

Gauṛī; mahalā V.

XLI. CXI.

(1). To whom thou hast become a powerful advocate:
To him no stain whatever (is applied).

Pause.

O Mādhava, who puts his hope in thee:
To him the world is nothing.
(2). In whose heart the Lord is:
He has no apprehension whatever.
(3). To whom thou, O Lord, hast given firmness (of mind):
Him no pain approaches.
(4). Nānak says: I obtained that Guru,
Who showed to me the Supreme Brahm as omnipresent.

Gauṛī; mahalā V.

XLII. CXII.

(1). By a great lot the human body, which is hard to get, is obtained.
Who do not mutter the name, they are suicides.

Pause.

Having died those (find) no place,[1] by whom Rām is forgotten.
Destitute of Rām of what use is (their) life?
(2). They are eating, drinking, sporting, laughing to a great extent.
Of what use is the embellishment of a corpse?
(3). Who do not hear the praise of the Supreme bliss (= God):
They are born as stupid animals, as quadrupeds and birds.[2]
(4). Nānak says: (in whom) by the Guru the (initiatory) mantra is made firm:
In (his) heart the name alone is contained (and nothing else).

Gauṛī; mahalā V.

XLIII. CXIII.

(1). Who has a mother, who has a father?
All relatives are but nominal and false.

Pause.

Why, O fool, art thou bewildered?
In accordance with (his) order thou hast come.

[1] ਜਾਹੀ = ਜਾਇ, place.

[2] ਤਿਗਰਜੋਨਿ (Sansk. तिर्यग्योनि), here used as adjective: born from the womb of an animal = animal, especially of the lower order. The assimilation of तिर्यग् to ਤਿਗਰ is against all rules and must be considered as a vulgar corruption (Hindī तृजग्).

(2). (There is) one earth, one vital energy (in all).
(There is) one breath (in all), why and for whom (art thou) weeping?[1]
(3). Saying: "mine, mine," thou lamentest.
This soul is not dying.
(4). Nānak says: by the Guru (our) shutters were opened.
(We) became emancipated, all errors were effaced.

Gauṛī; mahalā V.

XLIV. CXIV.

(1). The great, great men, who are seen (in the world):
Them anxiety and sickness penetrates.

Pause.

No one is great (by reason of) the greatness of the Māyā (= wealth).
He is great, who devoutly meditates on Rām.
(2). The land-owner quarrels continually about land.
Having given it up he departs, his thirst not being quenched.
(3). Nānak says: this is the full truth:
Without worshipping Hari there is no emancipation.

Gauṛī; mahalā V.

XLV. CXV.

(1). Perfect is the road, perfect is the ablution.
Everything is perfect, (if) the name (be) in the heart.

Pause.

Perfection abides, when preserved by the perfect one.
The asylum of the Supreme Brahm (accrues) to that man.
(2). Perfect is (his) comfort, perfect (his) contentment.
Perfect (his) austerity, perfect his abstract contemplation.[2]
(3). On the road of Hari the sinner (becomes) purified.
Perfect is (his) splendour, perfect (his) renown.[3]
(4). The creator always dwells in the presence.
Nānak says: my true Guru is perfect.

Gauṛī; mahalā V.

XLVI. CXVI.

(1). By the dust of the saints crores of sins are blotted out.
By the favour of the saints liberation (is obtained) from birth and death.

Pause.

The sight of the saints is perfect ablution.
By the mercy of the saints the name is muttered.

[1] ਕਉਨ ਰੋਤਿ = ਕਿਸ ਨੂੰ ਰੋਤੇ.

[2] ਰਾਜਜੋਗ (राजयोग) signifies, (1) an easy mode of yōg or abstract contemplation, opposed to ਤਪੁ, austerity. (2). The supreme yōg (as practised by a Rājā holding in the world a high position and at the same time practising abstract meditation).

[3] ਲੋਕੀਕ *s.m.* renown, notoriety.

(2). In the society of the saints egotism[1] is effaced.
All is looked upon as having one and the same form.[2]
(3). (If) the saints are favourable, the five[3] are subdued.
The nectar-name is collected in the heart.
(4). Nānak says: whose destiny is perfect:
With him the feet of the pious have fallen in.

Gauṛī; mahalā V.

XLVII. CXVII.

(1). By muttering the excellences of Hari the lotus (of the heart) opens.
By remembering Hari all fear flees.

Pause.

That intellect is perfect, by which one sings the excellences of Hari.
In consequence of a great destiny he obtains the society of the pious.
(2). In the society of the pious the treasure of the name is obtained.
In the society of the pious all affairs are accomplished.
(3). By devotion to Hari (one's) life obtains its object,
(If) by the mercy of the Guru one praise the name.
(4). Nānak says: that man is accepted:
In whose heart the Lord dwells.

Gauṛī; mahalā V.

XLVIII. CXVIII.

(1). Whose heart is attached to the only One:
He forgets (every) thought[4] about other things.

Pause.

Without Gōvind none other is seen.
He is the creator, who causes (every) work to be done.
(2). Who longs for (him)[5] in his heart, who utters with his mouth: Hari, Hari!
That man will not vacillate in any way, neither in this nor that (world).
(3). In whose (house) is the wealth of Hari, he is a true wholesale merchant.
By the perfect Guru faith is imparted (to him).
(4). Hari, the king, the life-giving Supreme Spirit is united (with him).
Nānak says: the highest region[6] is obtained (by him).

Gauṛī; mahalā V.

XLIX. CXIX.

(1). The name is the support of the life of the devotees.
The name is (their) wealth, the name is (their) occupation.

[1] ਅਹੰਕਾਰ, egotism, *i.e.* the idea of individual existence.
[2] *i.e.* all is considered as a form of the Supreme Being.
[3] The five, *i.e.* ਕਾਮ, ਕ੍ਰੋਧ, etc.
[4] ਤਾਤਿ (ਤਾਤ), thought, care about; it is still used in this sense in Sindhī.
[5] ਕਮਾਉਣਾ (Sansk. caus. कामय्), to long for, to love.
[6] ਪਰਮਪਦੁ, the highest region or place = final emancipation.

Pause.

That man obtains the greatness of the name and lustre,
To whom in mercy he himself causes it to be given.
(2). The name is the occasion (place) of the happiness of the devotee.
Who delights in the name, that devotee is accepted.
(3). The name of Hari upholds the (pious) man.
At every breath the pious man remembers the name.
(4). Nānak says: whose lot is perfect:
His mind is attached to the name.

Gauṛī; mahalā V.

L. CXX.

(1). When by the favour of the saints the name of Hari was meditated upon:
From that time the running (unquiet) mind was satiated.

Pause.

By singing the excellences (of Hari) comfort and rest were obtained.
Toil was done away, my calamity was struck down.
(2). Having adored the lotus of the foot of the Lord,
By the remembrance of Hari my anxiety was effaced.
(3). When having given up all (others) I came helpless to the asylum of the One:
Then the high place (of Hari) was easily obtained (by me).
(4). Pain, trouble, error and fear fled.
The creator, says Nānak, took up his abode in my heart.

Gauṛī; mahalā V.

LI. CXXI.

(1). Do service (with thy) hand, (with thy) tongue sing the praises (of Hari)!
(With thy) feet run in the way of the Lord!

Pause.

(This is) the favourable time, (this is) the fit opportunity of remembering (Hari).
By remembering the name thou wilt get safely over (every) fear.[1]
(2). With (thy) eyes behold the sight of the saints!
Regard in (thy) heart the imperishable Lord!
(3). Go to the pious and hear his praise!
He will efface (thy) fear of birth and death.
(4). Put the lotus-foot of the Lord in (thy) breast!
Save (thy human) body, which is hard to get, (from further transmigration)!

Gauṛī; mahalā V.

LII. CXXII.

(1). On whom he bestows his own mercy:
That man utters with his tongue the name.

[1] ਉਤਰੀਆ = ਉਤਰਿੰ, thou wilt get over, on account of the rhyme (ਚੜੀਆ).

Pause.

By forgetting the name the pain of doubt enters (man).
By remembering the name error and fear flee.
(2). Who hears the praise of Hari, who sings the praise of Hari:
That man pain does not approach.
(3). The man who serves Hari is graceful.
The fire of the Māyā does not affect him.
(4). In (his) mind, body and mouth is the name of the merciful Hari.
Nānak (says): other worldly cares are abandoned (by him).

Gauṛī; mahalā V.

LIII. CXXIII.

(1). Giving up cleverness and much dexterity,
I kept fast the perfect Guru.

Pause.

Pains become extinct having sung with pleasure the praises of Hari.
The perfect Guru met (with me), having devoutly meditated (on Hari).
(2). The Guru gave (me) the mantra of the name of Hari.
Cares were effaced, anxiety went off.
(3). Joys sprang up by meeting with the Guru, the merciful.
Bestowing his mercy (on me) the nooses of Yama were cut asunder (by him).
(4). Nānak says: (who) has obtained the perfect Guru:
Him the Māyā does not again overspread.

Gauṛī; mahalā V.

LIV. CXXIV.

(1). (Thou wast) preserved by the perfect Guru himself.
The fleshly-minded ones distress overtook.

Pause.

O my friend, mutter the Guru, the Guru!
Thy face will become bright at the court (of Hari).
(2). Make the feet of the Guru dwell in thy heart!
(Thy) pain, enemies and misfortune he will destroy.
(3). (If) the word of the Guru (be) with thee as a companion:
All creatures become kind (to thee), O brother!
(4). When the perfect Guru bestowed his mercy (on me):
I became fully satisfied,[1] says Nānak.

Gauṛī; mahalā V.

LV. CXXV.

(1). Many relishes he enjoys like an ox.
The thief is bound by the rope of spiritual blindness.

Pause.

(Man) is a lifeless body if destitute of the society of the pious.
He is coming and going, by the pain of the womb he is consumed.

[1] ਪੂਰੀ, *s.f.* fulness, satisfied state.

(2). Many beautiful clothes are put on (by him).
(But they are like) a scare-crow in a field, (by which) (birds) are frightened away.[1]
(3). All other bodies are of (some) use.
(But) the human (body) is of no use, which does not mutter the name.
(4). Nānak says: to whom he became merciful:
He, having joined the society of the pious, adores Gōpāl.

Gauṛī; mahalā V.

LVI. CXXVI.

(1). In the Kali-yug troubles are removed by the word of the Guru.
Coming and going is put a stop to, all comforts (are obtained).

Pause.

Fear is extinct, the fearless Hari is meditated upon.
In the society of the pious the excellences of Hari are sung.
(2). Who have put the lotus-feet in their heart:
They are brought over the sea of fire by the Guru.
(3). Those, who were continually drowning, are drawn out by the perfect Guru.
Those, who were broken through various births, are refitted again.
(4). Nānak says: I am devoted to that Guru,
By meeting with whom my salvation was effected.

Gauṛī; mahalā V.

LVII. CXXVII.

(1). In the society of the pious fall on his asylum!
Place (thy) heart and body before him!

Pause.

Drink the nectar-name, O my brother!
Remembering, remembering (it) all heat (of passions) is extinguished.
(2). Giving up conceit put a stop to birth and death!
Pay reverence to the feet of the servants of Hari!
(3). At every breath think of the Lord in (thy) mind!
Collect that wealth, which goes with (thee)!
(4). To him it accrues, on whose forehead the lot (is written).
Nānak says: cling to his feet!

Gauṛī; mahalā V.

LVIII. CXXVIII.

(1). The dry ones are made green in a moment.
Having got the sight of the nectar they are vivified.

Pause.

The afflictions are cut off by the perfect Guru, the God.
On his worshipper his own worship is bestowed.

[1] The words are very obscure and without a free rendering unintelligible. The literal translation runs: "as by a scare-crow (ਤਰਨਾ, *s.f.*) in a field it is frightened."

(2). Anxiety is effaced, the wish of the heart is accomplished.
By the true Guru, the abode of (all) excellences, mercy is bestowed.
(3). Troubles fled, comforts settled (in the heart).
No delay intervened when they[1] were ordered by the Guru.
(4). Their desire was attained, they met with the perfect Guru.
Nānak (says): those men have borne good fruit.

Gauṛī; mahalā V.

LIX. CXXIX.

(1). The turmoils are passed, tranquillity has set in from the Lord.
Coolness has sprung up, by the Lord (this) gift is given.

Pause.

By the mercy of the Lord they became happy.
Those, who were separated through many births, are united (with the Lord).
(2). By remembering, by remembering the name of the Lord,
The place of all diseases is destroyed.
(3). With natural ease he utters the praise of Hari,
Who remembers the Lord through the eight watches.
(4). Pain and trouble and Yama do not come near (him),
Who sings the praises of Hari, says Nānak.

Gauṛī; mahalā V.

LX. CXXX.

(1). O blessed day, O blessed event,
By which the supreme, unfettered Brahm was met with.

Pause.

I devote myself to that time,
In which my mind mutters the name of Hari.
(2). Fruitful are those forty-eight minutes, fruitful those twenty-four minutes,
In which my tongue utters: Hari, Hari!
(3). Fruitful is that forehead, by means of which I shall pay reverence to the saints.
Pure is that foot, that walks in the way of Hari.
(4). Nānak says: blessed is my destiny,
By reason of which the feet of the pious were met with.

Gauṛī; mahalā V.

LXI. CXXXI.

(1). Keep the word of the Guru in thy mind!
Remembering the name all anxiety departs.

Pause.

Without the Lord there is none other.
He alone kills and preserves.

[1] ਜਾ ਗੁਰਿ ਫੁਰਮਾਏ, when they (*i.e.* the ਸੁਖ, the comforts) were ordered to come.

(2). Put the feet of the Guru in (thy) heart and breast!
The ocean of fire thou wilt cross muttering (the name).
(3). Direct (thy) meditation on the form of the Guru!
Here and there thou wilt obtain honour.
(4). Who having given up every (thing) comes to the asylum of the Guru:
His anxieties are removed, he obtains happiness, (says) Nānak.

Gauṛī; mahalā V.

LXII. CXXXII.

(1). By remembering whom all pain passes off,
(And) the jewel of the name comes and dwells in the mind:

Pause.

Mutter, O my heart, the praise of (that) Gōvind!
The tongue of the pious praises Rām.[1]
(2). Without the One there is none other,
By whose favourable look comfort is always obtained.
(3). Make the One thy friend, acquaintance and companion!
The word "Hari, Hari," write in thy heart!
(4). The Lord is contained everywhere.
Nānak sings the praises of the inward governor.

Gauṛī; mahalā V.

LXIII. CXXXIII.

(1). The whole world is sunk in fear.
He has no fear, whose support is the name.

Pause.

Fear cannot enter thy asylum.
What is pleasing to thee, that (thou art) doing.
(2). There is grief and joy in coming and going.
By that comfort is obtained, what is pleasing to the Lord.
(3). The Māyā enters the great ocean of fire.
They are cool (composed), who obtain the true Guru.
(4). Keep me, O Lord, the preserver!
Nānak says: what (can) the helpless creature do?

Gauṛī; mahalā V.

LXIV. CXXXIV.

(1). By thy mercy the name is muttered.
By thy mercy a place (is obtained) at (thy) threshold.

Pause.

Without thee, O Supreme Brahm, there is none other.
By thy mercy comfort is always obtained.

[1] The words of this line must be constructed thus: ਸਾਧੂ ਜਨ ਕੀ ਰਸਨਾ ਰਾਮ ਵਖਾਣੈ.

(2). (If) thou dwellest in the heart, no pain befalls (it).
By thy mercy suspense and fear flee.
(3). O Supreme Brahm, O boundless Lord!
(Thou art) the inward governor of all bodies.
(4). I offer (this) supplication to my own true Guru:
May the name, the true capital, be given (to me), (says) Nānak.

Gauṛī; mahalā V.

LXV. CXXXV.

(1). Like empty husks without a grain:
So are (those) empty, (whose) mouth is devoid of the name.

Pause.

Mutter the name of Hari, Hari, O man!
Woe to (thy) body void of the name and being another's!
(2). Without the name there is no good lot on the face.
Without the husband there is no happy married state.
(3). Who, having forgotten the name, takes to another enjoyment:
None of his desires will be accomplished.
(4). O Lord, bestow on me thy own mercy and gift,
(That) Nānak may mutter the name day and night.

Gauṛī; mahalā V.

LXVI. CXXXVI.

(1). Thou art powerful, thou art my Lord.
All is from thee, thou art the inward governor.

Pause.

Thou, O supreme, omnipresent Brahm (art) the shelter of thy servants.
In thy asylum are crores of thy servants saved.
(2). All creatures, as many as there are, are thine.
By thy mercy many comforts (are obtained).
(3). Whatever exists, all is thy decree.[1]
Who comprehends (thy) order, he is absorbed in the True one.
(4). O Lord, in mercy bestow (on me) (this) gift,
That Nānak may remember the name (containing) the (nine) treasures.

Gauṛī; mahalā V.

LXVII. CXXXVII.

(1). (That) very fortunate man obtains his sight,
Who devoutly meditates on the name of Rām.

Pause.

In whose heart Hari dwells:
Him no pain (befalls) even in a dream.

[1] *i.e.* exists by thy decree.

(2). All treasures are laid up in (his) people.
In their society sins and pains depart.
(3). The greatness of (his) people cannot be told,
(His) people are absorbed in the Supreme Brahm.
(4). May in mercy my petition be heard, O Lord!
May the dust of (thy) slave be given to Nānak!

Gauṛī; mahalā V.

LXVIII. CXXXVIII.

(1). By remembering Hari thy calamity goes off.
All welfare comes and dwells in thy mind.

Pause.

Adore, O my heart, the one name!
It will be of use to thy soul.
(2). Night and day sing the excellences of the endless one!
The mantra of the perfect Guru is spotless.
(3). Give up shifts, hold fast the One!
Taste the nectar-juice, the great excellent thing!
(4). The difficult ocean (of existence) those people cross:
On whom he bestows a favourable look, says Nānak.

Gauṛī; mahalā V.

LXIX. CXXXIX.

(1). Who put the lotus feet of the Lord in their heart:
They, having met with the perfect true Guru, are saved.

Pause.

Sing the praises of Gōvind, O my brother!
Having met with the pious meditate on the name of Hari!
(2). The (human) body, which is hard to get, becomes approved of.
From the true Guru attention to the name is obtained.
(3). By remembering Hari the perfect degree[1] is attained.
In the society of the pious fear and error are effaced.
(4). Wherever I see, there he (*i.e.* Hari) is contained.
Nānak, the slave, is in the asylum of Hari.

Gauṛī; mahalā V.

LXX. CXL.

(1). I sacrifice myself to the sight of the Guru.
Continually muttering the name of the true Guru I live.

Pause.

O Supreme Brahm, O perfect Gur-dēv!
Bestow mercy (on me), (that) I may apply myself to thy service.

[1] ਪੂਰਨ ਪਦੁ, the perfect degree = final emancipation.

(2). The lotus-feet (of Hari) I put in (my) heart and breast.
(My) heart, body and wealth are the Guru's, who is sustaining (my) life.
(3). (His) life becomes fruitful and approved of:
Who considers the Guru, the Supreme Brahm (as being) near.
(4). The dust of the saints is obtained by the very fortunate.
Nānak (says): by meeting with the Guru devout meditation on Hari is made.

Gauṛī; mahalā V.

LXXI. CXLI.

(1). He does wicked works and shows (outwardly) other ones (*i.e.* good ones).
(But) at the threshold of Rām the thief is bound.

Pause.

Who utters: Rām! he is a devotee of Rām.[1]
In water, earth and on the surface of the earth the One is contained.
(2). In his heart is poison, (but) with his mouth he utters nectar.
In the city of Yama he is bound and struck in his face.
(3). Within the screen (= secretly) he practises many passions.
(But) in a moment he will become manifest in the world.
(4). Who inwardly is delighted with the true name:
To him, (says) Nānak, the ordainer (of all things) is merciful.

Gauṛī; mahalā V.

LXXII. CXLII.

(1). The colour of Rām never goes off (from him):
Whom the perfect Guru instructs.

Pause.

The mind that is steeped in the colour of Hari is true.
The Spirit, the ordainer (of all things), is filling in the red colour.
(2). Who, sitting in the society of the saints, sings his excellences:
His colour does not go off.
(3). Without remembering Hari no happiness is obtained.
All the other relishes of the Māyā are insipid.
(4). Those, who were coloured by the Guru, became happy.
Nānak says: (to whom) the Guru became compassionate.

Gauṛī; mahalā V.

LXXIII. CXLIII.

(1). By remembering the Lord sins flee away,
Happiness, tranquillity and joy settle (in the heart).

Pause.

The people of Rām have faith in Rām.
By muttering the name all anxiety is done away.

[1] ਰਾਮਾਣਾ (ਰਾਮਾਲ਼ਾ), a devotee of Rām, uttering continually: Rām, Rām! They are now known for their impure practices.

(2). In the society of the pious there is no fear nor doubtfulness.[1]
The praises of Gōpāl are sung day and night.
(3). The fetters are broken by the Lord out of mercy.
The protection of the lotus-foot is given to them.
(4). Nānak says: in their mind clear apprehension (of truth) is made.
His servants continually drink (= enjoy) spotless renown.[2]

Gauṛī; mahalā V.

LXXIV. CXLIV.

(1). Whose mind is fixed on the feet of Hari:
His pain, trouble and doubt flee away.

Pause.

Who is dealing in the wealth of Hari, he is perfect.
Whom he (*i.e.* Hari) cherishes, that man is a hero.
(2). To whom the Lord became compassionate:
Those men cling to the feet of the Guru.
(3). (They enjoy) happiness, tranquillity, quiet and joy.
Continually muttering the supreme bliss (= the Lord) they live.
(4). The capital of the name is acquired in the society of the pious.
Nānak says: by the Lord (their) affliction is cut off.

Gauṛī; mahalā V.

LXXV. CXLV.

(1). By remembering Hari all troubles are effaced.
The lotus-feet enter the heart.

Pause.

Utter the name of Rām a hundred thousand times!
Thou wilt drink nectar-juice by love to the Lord.[3]
(2). There is comfort, tranquillity, enjoyment and great happiness.
Continually muttering the supreme bliss (= the Lord) they live.
(3). Lust, wrath, covetousness and passion are removed.
In the society of the pious all blemishes are washed away.
(4). Bestow mercy, O Lord, who art compassionate to the poor!
May to Nānak the dust of the pious be given!

Gauṛī; mahalā V.

LXXVI. CXLVI.

(1). Whose gifts one puts on and eats:
How is indolence towards him becoming, O mother?

[1] ਭਰਾਤੀ = Sansk. भ्रान्ति, final *i* being lengthened on account of the rhyme and medial *n* assimilated to *t*.

[2] ਜਸ (यशस्) signifies in Sanskrit also "*water*," but this meaning is uncommon and does not fit the context.

[3] ਪ੍ਰਭ ਪਿਆਰੀ; ਪਿਆਰੀ cannot be here the feminine of ਪਿਆਰਾ, but must be taken as ablative of ਪਿਆਰੁ, final short *i* being lengthened on account of the rhyme.

Pause.

Who, having forgotten the Lord, sticks to another work:
He gives away a gem for a shell.
(2). Forsaking the Lord he takes to other objects of desire.
Iu paying obeisance to the slave how (shall) lustre (be obtained)?
(3). He enjoys nectar-juice, food and drink.
By whom they are given, him the dog does not know.
(4). Nānak says: we are untrue to our salt (= ungrateful).
Pardon us, O Lord, thou inward governor!

Gauṛī; mahalā V.

LXXVII. CXLVII.

(1). Meditation in the mind (on) the feet of the Lord
Is (equal to) bathing and ablution at all Tīrthas.

Pause.

By remembering Hari every day, O my brother!
The filth of crores of births goes off.
(2). By whom the report about Hari is fixed in his heart:
He gets all the fruits, his mind is desiring.
(3). (His) life and death and birth are approved of:
In whose heart the Lord dwells.
(4). Nānak says: those men are perfect,
Whose lot is the dust of the pious.

Gauṛī; mahalā V.

LXXVIII. CXLVIII.

(1). Who is eating and putting on clothes and denies it:[1]
Him the messenger of Dharm-rāi (Yama) overpowers.

Pause.

Who turns away his face from him, by whom soul and body are given:
He wanders through crores of births and many wombs.
(2). This is the manner of the Sākat:
Whatever he does, all is perverse.
(3). By whom soul and life, mind and body are sustained:
That Lord is forgotten from (his) mind.
(4). Many papers are written (with reference to) the destruction of the passions.[2]
Nānak (says): deliverance (is obtained from) the ocean of mercy and happiness.

Pause.

O Supreme Brahm, (I am) in thy asylum.
(Whose) bonds thou cuttest, he crosses by means of the name of Hari.

[1] ਮੁਕਰਿ ਪਾਇ, denies it, *i.e.* that all is the gift of God.

[2] ਬਧੇ ਬਿਕਾਰ; ਬਧੇ must here be taken as substantive (ਬਧਾ = वध), *destruction.*

Gauṛī; mahalā V.

LXXIX. CXLIX.

(1). According to his own desire he was made (my) friend :
(By whom) all wishes and the post of final emancipation are given.

Pause.

Every one should make such a one his friend :
By whom nobody is disappointed.
(2). According to his own liking he was put into (my) heart:
By whom all pains, troubles and diseases are severed.
(3). (My) tongue became accustomed to say : Rām!
All (my) works are accomplished (thereby).
(4). Many times Nānak is a sacrifice.
The sight of my Gōvind is fruitful.

Gauṛī; mahalā V.

LXXX. CL.

(1). Crores of obstacles are done away in a moment,
(If) in the society of the pious one proclaims the story of Hari, Hari.

Pause.

(Who is) drinking the juice of Rām, (the recital) of whose excellences is nectar:
His hunger is taken away by attending to the feet of Hari.
(2). He has all welfare, comfort, tranquillity and treasures:
In whose heart the Lord dwells.
(3). Medicine, charms and spells are all ashes.
Hold fast the creator in thy heart!
(4). (If) abandoning all doubts the Supreme Brahm is adored :
This is, says Nānak, a virtue that will last for ever.

Gauṛī; mahalā V.

LXXXI. CLI.

(1). (With whom) that Guru meets, bestowing mercy (on him):
Him no disease overtakes and enters.[1]

Pause.

Who is uttering: Rām! crosses the ocean of fear.
In the asylum of (this) hero the papers of Yama are torn to pieces.
(2). By the true Guru the mantra of the name of Hari is given.
By taking this the affairs (of a man) are accomplished.[2]
(3). Recitation (of the name), austerity, control of the senses, perfect greatness (obtains he):
(To whom) the compassionate Guru Hari has become a helper.
(4). Conceit, illusion, error, are removed by the Guru.
He sees the Supreme Brahm spread out (everywhere), (says) Nānak.

[1] ਘਲਿ, past part. conj. from ਘਲਣਾ (*v.a.*), to go round and get before = to overtake.

[2] ਆਸਰ (= Sansk. आश्रय), taking, laying hold of.

Gauṛī ; mahalā V.

LXXXII. CLII.

(1). He is heavily blind by being filled with worldly affairs.
It is painful to him, (if one) remind (him) of the name of Rām!

Pause.

Even thou art greatness to thy servant.
Him, who is sunk in the Māyā, thou marchest off to hell.
(2). Seized by sickness he remembers the name.
(But) he who is intoxicated with poison, (finds) no place nor spot (of rest).
(3). Who is in love with the lotus-feet:
He does not think of other pleasures.
(4). I will continually remember the Lord.
Join Nānak, O Hari, the inward governor!

Gauṛī ; mahalā V.

LXXXIII. CLIII.

(1). The eight watches the highway robbers[1] (were) (my) companions.
They were mercifully removed by the Lord.

Pause.

Such a taste of Hari every one should enjoy.
Every inclination of the mind that Lord is fulfilling.
(2). Over the very hot ocean of the world
The Lord is ferrying in a moment.
(3). The many fetters cannot be broken.
(But) by remembering the name one gets the fruit of final emancipation.
(4). By contrivance and dexterity nothing (is effected) by this one (= by me).
(If) he bestow his mercy (on me), Nānak sings his praises.

Gauṛī ; mahalā V.

LXXXIV. CLIV.

(1). (Who) has obtained as capital the name of Hari:
He passes through the world, all his affairs are accomplished.

Pause.

By him, whose lot is great, the praise of Hari is sung.
O Supreme Brahm, if thou give it, then it is obtained.
(2). Hold fast the feet of Hari in thy heart and breast!
Rising thou wilt pass over the ocean of existence.
(3). Every one should acquire the society of the pious.
(He will) always (enjoy) welfare, pain will not again affect him.
(4). With love and devotion adore the abode of (all) virtues (= God)!
Nānak (says): at (his) threshold honour will be obtained.

[1] The ਬਟਵਾੜੇ or highway robbers are the five: ਕਾਮ, ਕ੍ਰੋਧ, ਲੋਭ, ਮੋਹ, ਅਹੰਕਾਰ.

Gauṛī; mahalā V.

LXXXV. CLV.

(1). In water, earth and on the face of the earth is Hari, the friend, omnipresent.
Doubts are (thereby) done away, his excellences are continually sung.

Pause.

In rising and sleeping Hari is a watchman with (me),
Remembering whom there is no fear[1] of Yama.
(2). The lotus-feet of the Lord are dwelling in (my) heart.
Every pain is (thereby) effaced.
(3). (My) hope, trust and wealth is the One.
In (my) heart I rely on the wholesale merchant.
(4). The very humble and friendless pious people
Are protected by the Lord, holding out his hand to them.

Gauṛī; mahalā V.

LXXXVI. CLVI.

(1). Having made ablution in the name of Hari they (are) pure.
(They get thereby) crores of meritorious deeds done at an eclipse, many fruits (of their good works).[2]

Pause.

If the feet of Hari dwell in the heart:
The blemishes of many births pass away.
(2). As reward for praising Hari in the society of the pious (this) is obtained:
(That) the road of Yama does not come into sight.
(3). (Whose) support Gōvind is in mind, word and deed:
From him the world, the baneful thing, recedes.
(4). Who in mercy is made his own by Hari:
He, (says) Nānak, is muttering (the name), he is muttering Hari.

Gauṛī; mahalā V.

LXXXVII. CLVII.

(1). Fall on (his) asylum! by whom Hari is known:
(Their) mind and body become cool, being attached to the feet of Hari.

Pause.

Who do not settle in their heart the Lord, the destroyer of fear:
They pass in continual alarm through many births.
(2). In whose heart the name of Hari dwells:
All his designs and affairs are accomplished.
(3). In whose power birth, old age and death are:
That powerful (Lord) remember at (every) breath and morsel!

[1] ਡਰੂਆ = ਡਰੁ, *s.m.* fear, on account of the rhyme.

[2] The sense is: bathing in the name of Hari = muttering the name of Hari, is equal to crores of meritorious works done at an eclipse, which bring in many fruits (rewards). At a ਗ੍ਰਹਣ or eclipse it is very meritorious to give alms, etc.

(4). (My) friend, sweetheart and companion is the one Lord.
The name of the Lord is the support of Nānak.

Gauṛī; mahalā V.

LXXXVIII. CLVIII.

(1). Outside (the house) he is kept fast (by me) remembering (him) in (my) heart.
(We) return home taking Gōvind with (us).

Pause.

The name of Hari, Hari (goes) with the saints.
(Their) mind and body are imbued with love to Rām.
(2). By the favour of the Guru the ocean (of existence) is crossed.
All the impurities of the (former) births are removed.
(3). The remembrance of the name of the Lord (brings in) lustre.
The mantra of the perfect Guru is pure.
(4). In (my) heart (there is) attentive regard to the lotus-feet.
Nānak lives by seeing (their) splendour.

Gauṛī; mahalā V.

LXXXIX. CLIX.

(1). Blessed is that place, where the praises of Gōvind are sung.
Welfare and happiness are made to dwell (there) by the Lord himself.

Pause.

Calamity is there, where Hari is not remembered.
Crores of joys are there, where they sing the excellences of Hari.
(2). By forgetting Hari many troubles and diseases (set in).
(Where) the Lord is served, Yama does not come near.
(3). That is a very blessed, immovable place:
Where only the name of the Lord is muttered.
(4). Wherever I go,[1] there my Lord is with (me).
With Nānak the inward governor is united.

Gauṛī; mahalā V.

XC. CLX.

(1). The man that meditates on Gōvind:
Be he learned (or) unlearned, attains the highest state (= final emancipation).

Pause.

Remember Gōpāl in the society of the pious!
Without the name wealth and property are (but) false (= useless).
(2). That man is handsome, clever and intelligent:
By whom the decree of the Lord is heeded.
(3). In the world that (man) is approved of:
Who knows his Lord (as being) in everybody.

[1] ਜਹ ਜਾਈਐ, literally: "wherever it is gone."

(4). Nānak says: whose lot is perfect:
His mind is fixed on the feet of Hari.

* *Gauṛī; mahalā* V.

XCI. CLXI.

Pause.

The Sākat does not keep company with the servant of Hari.
That one is worldly-minded, this one has love to Rām.
(1). Like as one,[1] who rides (only) in his thoughts, dresses out a mare.
Like as a eunuch causes a woman to be brought to him.[2]
(2). (Like as) one, putting a rope on an ox, causes it to be milked.
(Like as) one, being mounted on a cow, runs after a lion.
(3). (Like as) one, taking a jenny-ass[3] and considering her as the cow, that grants all desires, worships her.
(Like as) one runs after traffic without a capital.
(4). Nānak (says): mutter the name of Rām in thy mind!
Remember the Lord Hari, he is (thy) friend.

Gauṛī; mahalā V.

XCII. CLXII.

(1). That is called a pure mind and firm:
Which drinks the elixir of Rām, O brother!

Pause.

By making the feet of Hari (one's) support in the heart:
Release is effected from birth and death.
(2). That body is spotless, from which no sin springs.
By love to Rām it is of pure dignity.
(3). In the society of the pious the passions are extinguished.
Higher than all is this assistance (of the pious).
(4). Who are imbued with love and affection to Gōpāl:
The dust of (those) pious men Nānak asks.

Gauṛī; mahalā V.

XCIII. CLXIII.

(1). In whom such an affection to Gōpāl has sprung up:
Those men of a full great lot are united (with him).

Pause.

As a wife is happy seeing her husband:
So the people of Hari live by remembering the name.

[1] The following lines are meant to show the incongruity of the friendship of the servant of Hari and the Sākat. To make the sense clear, there must be supplied: their company or friendship is as incongruous as if one, etc.

[2] ਪੁਚਾਰਨਾ = ਪੁਚਾਉਣਾ, to cause to arrive, to be brought.

[3] ਗਾਡਰ, *s.f.* here jenny-ass (= ਖੋਤੀ); it may also signify: *sheep*, which does not suit the context here.

(2). As a mother lives seeing (her) son:
So are the people of Hari thoroughly in love with him.
(3). (As) the covetous one is happy seeing wealth (coming in):
(So) the mind of the pious is fixed on the lotus-feet.
(4). May not a bit be forgotten the liberal donor!
The Lord of Nānak is the soul's support.

Gauṛī; mahalā V.

XCIV. CLXIV.

Pause.

Those men, who are accustomed to the elixir of Rām:
Are imbued with love and affection to the lotus-feet.
(1). All other juices appear as ashes.
Without the name the world is devoid of fruit.
(2). From the blind well[1] they are drawn out by himself.
The qualities of Gōpāl are of wonderful majesty.
(3). In tree and grass and in the three worlds Gōpāl is omnipresent.
The creatures are the expansion of Brahm; the merciful is with (them).
(4). Nānak says: this is the best tale,
Which the creator approves of.

Gauṛī; mahalā V.

XCV. CLXV.

Pause.

Continually ablution in the pond of Rām should be made!
Stirring up the great juice the nectar of Hari should be drunk!
(1). The name of Gōvind is a pure water.
Who bathes therein, all (his) affairs are accomplished.
(2). If approval[2] of the saints and conversation with (them) be made:
One clears away the blemishes of crores of births.
(3). (Who) remembers the pious, he is happy.
In his mind and body the highest bliss (= the Supreme) is contained.
(4). To whose lot the treasures of the feet of Hari fall:
To him Nānak, the slave, sacrifices himself.

Gauṛī; mahalā V.

XCVI. CLXVI.

Pause.

Do that by which no dirt will stick to thee!
In the praise of Hari this mind should wake!
(1). Remember the One (and do not entertain) a second love!

[1] ਅੰਧਕੂਪ, a blind well, the mouth of which is covered and into which people fall unawares.

[2] ਤਰ, *s.m.* (Marāṭhī still तह), approval, agreement. But the word is not of Persian origin, it is derived from the same source as the Sindhī ठरु, concord.

In the society of the saints mutter the name alone!
(2). (He performs) religious works, observances, vows, and worship:
Who does not know another besides the Supreme Brahm.
(3). His toil has come to an end:
Whose affection rests with his own Lord.
(4). That Vaishnava (devotee) is boundless (Supreme):
By whom (his) passions are abandoned, says Nānak.

Gauṛī; mahalā V.

XCVII. CLXVII.

(1). Whilst living the fools give (him) up.[1]
Has any one after his death been benefitted (by him)?

Pause.

Remember Gōvind in (thy) heart and body, (this is) written (for thee) from the beginning.
The material world is not of any use (to thee).
(2). Whoever is deceived by the material world:
His thirst will never cease.
(3). The dreadful afflictions, the world, which is hard to cross:
How will he without the name of Rām get through them?
(4). Having joined the pious he accomplishes (= saves) both families:[2]
Who adores the name of Rām, says Nānak.

Gauṛī; mahalā V.

XCVIII. CLXVIII.

(1). (If any one) stroke out his beard against the humble:
That (beard) is burnt in fire by the Supreme Brahm.

Pause.

The creator and administerer of full justice,
He is protecting his own servant.
(2). From the beginning, from the beginning of the ages his majesty is manifest.
The calumniator has died, great distress befalls him.
(3). Who is killed by Him, him none preserves.
Before and after[3] his report is bad.
(4). His own servants he protects, putting them to his neck:
(Who) in the asylum of Hari meditate on the name of Hari, (says) Nānak.

Gauṛī; mahalā V.

XCIX. CLXIX.

(1). By himself their declaration is made false.[4]
Affliction befalls the sinner.

[1] No hint whatever is given what the object of ਛਾਡਿ ਜਾਹਿ is; we suppose, it is Hari or the name. The sense seems to be: whilst living they do not care about Hari and after their death it is too late.

[2] *i.e.* the father's and the mother's family.

[3] ਆਗੈ ਪਾਛੈ, before and after, *i.e.* in the future and in this world.

[4] ਮਹਜਰੁ, Arabic محضر, declaration, deposition. Their declaration is made false = proved to be false.

Pause.

Whose assistant my Gōvind is:
Him Yama does not approach.
(2). Who speaks falsehood at the true court:
(That) blind fool dashes down his head and hands (in token of grief).
(3). Sickness enters them, who commit sin.
The Lord himself sits down administering justice.
(4). By their own work they are bound.[1]
All (their) wealth is gone (lost) with (their) life.
(5). Nānak falls on the asylum and court (of Hari).
My honour is preserved by my creator.

Gauṛī; mahalā V.

C. CLXX.

Pause.

Him he lets acquire the dust of (his) servant, which is sweet to the mind:
(To whom) it is written from the beginning by reason of former works.[2]
(1). Whose mind is deeply imbued with egotism filling the heart:[3]
They (become) pure by cleansing it in the dust of the pious.
(2). (Though) they bathe (their) body in many waters:
The dirt does not go off, they do not (become) pure.
(3). (When) the true Guru, who is always compassionate, has met with (them):
(Then) remembering continually Hari the fear of death is cut off.
(4). Emancipation, joined with enjoyment, is the name of Hari (to him):
(Who) with love and devotion sings his excellences, (says) Nānak.

Gauṛī; mahalā V.

CI. CLXXI.

(1). (Those) servants of Hari (have attained) to the station of life (= emancipation):
To whom their own spirit has become manifest.[4]

Pause.

Having heard the remembrance (= recital) of Hari with thy mind and ears,
Thou wilt obtain happiness at the gate of Hari, O man!
(2). The eight watches Gōpāl should be meditated upon!
Nānak, having seen his sight, is happy.

[1] The sense is: they must eat the fruits of their own works.

[2] *i.e.* works done in a former life.

[3] ਅਹੰਬੁਧਿ must here be taken as two separate words: ਅਹੰ = ਹਉ egotism and ਬੁਧਿ mind, to which the verb ਖਿਪਾਣੀ as predicate is referred.

[4] *i.e.* as the Spirit of the Supreme; who have identified themselves with the Supreme, their spirit being identical with him.

Gauṛī; mahalā V.

CII. CLXXII.

Pause.

Tranquillity has set in, it is obtained from the Guru Gōvind.
Distress and sins are extinct, O my brother!
(1). Praise always the name of Rām with thy tongue!
Diseases become extinct, prosperity sets in.
(2). Reflect on the excellences of the unattainable Supreme Brahm!
In the consociation of the pious salvation is (obtained).
(3). Sing continually the spotless excellences (of Hari)!
Sickness departs, the pious people are saved, O friend!
(4). In mind, word and deed I meditate on my own Lord.
Nānak, thy slave, is in thy asylum.

Gauṛī; mahalā V.

CIII. CLXXIII.

Pause.

The eye was brightened by the Gurdēv.
Doubts departed, (my) worship was made complete.
(1). From the small-pox he was preserved by the sporting (Krishṇa).[1]
The Lord, the Supreme Brahm, bestowed mercy (on him).[2]
(2). Nānak (says): who mutters the name, he lives.
In the society of the pious he drinks the nectar of Hari.

Gauṛī; mahalā V.

CIV. CLXXIV.

(1). Blessed is that forehead, blessed are thy eyes!
Blessed are those devotees, who have love to thee!

Pause.

How should happiness be obtained without the name?
With the tongue the glory of the name of Rām should be told!
(2). One should become a sacrifice for those:
By whom the highest bliss is muttered.[3]

Gauṛī; mahalā V.

CV. CLXXV.

(1). Thou (art my) counsel, thou (art) with (me).
Thou protectest (me), remembering (me) and taking care of (me).

Pause.

Such a helper is Rām in this and the next world.
The honour of his servant he protects, O my brother!

[1] ਬਿਹਾਰੀ, Sansk. विहारिन्, sporting, amusing oneself; an epithet of Krishṇa.

[2] This verse is said to refer to the recovery of the son of Arjun from the small-pox.

[3] ਨਿਰਬਾਣੁ, Sansk. निर्वाण, the highest bliss = ਪਰਮਾਨੰਦ, an epithet of the Supreme.

(2). Onwards he himself is,[1] in whose power this place (= world) is.
The eight watches (my) heart (therefore) mutters Hari.
(3). (With) honour he is approved of, who is intent on the True one.[2]
To whom he himself gives the order.
(4). He himself is the liberal donor, he himself cherishes (him):
(Who) continually takes to heart the name of Rām.

Gauṛī; mahalā V.

CVI. CLXXVI.

(1). The perfect true Guru becomes compassionate (to him):
In (whose) heart Gōpāl always dwells.

Pause.

Who praises Rām, obtains always happiness.
The omnipresent Hari, the King, bestows mercy (on him).
(2). Nānak says: whose lot is perfect:
(To him) the name of Hari, Hari (gives) a firm auspicious state.

Gauṛī; mahalā V.

CVII. CLXXVII.

(1). Having unloosed his Dhōtī[3] he spreads it on the ground.
Like a donkey he appeases his belly.

Pause.

Without (religious) works final emancipation is not obtained.
The boon of final emancipation (is obtained), (if) the name be meditated upon.
(2). He is practising worship, the tilak and ablution.
Having drawn out a knife he takes gifts with his hands.[4]
(3). He reads with his mouth the Vēda, the sweet word,
(But) is killing living creatures, and has no regard for a living being.
(4). Nānak says: on whom he bestows mercy:
(His) heart (is) pure (and) meditates on Brahm.

Gauṛī; mahalā V.

CVIII. CLXXVIII.

Pause.

Sit steadily in your house, O ye beloved people of Hari!
By the true Guru your affairs are adjusted.
(1). The wicked intoxicated ones[5] are killed by the Lord.
The honour of his people is preserved by the creator.

[1] ਆਗੈ ਆਪਿ, onwards he himself is, *i.e.* in the future world God himself is, dwells.

[2] ਸਚੁ ਨੀਸਾਣੁ; ਨੀਸਾਣੁ is here verb = ਨੀਸਾਣੈ; ਨੀਸਾਣਣਾ governs the Accusative or the Locative.

[3] The Dhōtī is a piece of cloth wrapped round the waist, passing between the legs and tucked up behind, supplying the place of our trousers.

[4] He threatens with his drawn knife, if gifts be not given to him.

[5] The ਦੁਸਟ ਦੂਤ are: ਕਾਮ ਕ੍ਰੋਧ, etc.

(2). All emperors and kings are subjected (by him to them):
Who drink the great juice of the nectar-name.
(3). Free from fear adore the Lord!
(Who) joins the society of the pious, (on him) (this) gift is bestowed.
(4). (We) have fallen on the asylum of the Lord, the inward governor.
Nānak has seized the sanctuary of the Lord God.

Gaurī; mahalā V.

CIX. CLXXIX.

(1). Who are imbued with love to Hari do not burn in fire.
Who are imbued with love to Hari, them the Māyā does not deceive.
Who are imbued with love to Hari are not drowned in water.
Who are imbued with love to Hari bear good fruit.

Pause.

All (their) fear is effaced by thy name.
Meeting with the assembly (of the pious) they sing the excellences of Hari, Hari.
(2). All anxiety of him, who is in love with Hari, is extinguished.
He is enraptured with Hari, who has the mantra of the pious.
Who is in love with Hari is not afraid of Yama.
Who is in love with Hari, his wish is fulfilled.
(3). Who is in love with Hari, him pain does not befall.
Who is in love with Hari is daily awake.
Who is in love with Hari dwells easily in his house.
Who is in love with Hari, his doubt and fear flee.
(4). Who is in love with Hari, his wisdom becomes very great.
Who is in love with Hari, his report is spotless.
Nānak says: I devote myself to those:
By whom my Lord is not forgotten.

Gauṛī; mahalā V.

CX. CLXXX.

(1). Who make efforts, (their) minds become sedate.
Who walk on the road (of Hari), all their troubles are gone.
Who mutter the name, in (their) heart joy springs up.
With pleasure the praises of the supreme bliss (= God) are sung.

Pause.

Happiness sets in, welfare enters their house.
Who fall in with the society of the pious, their calamity is gone.
(2). The eyes are purified when seeing (his) sight.
Blessed is the forehead by touching the lotus-feet.
(By) the service of Gōvind this body (becomes) fruitful.
By the favour of the saints the highest place (final emancipation) is obtained.
(3). He himself gives assistance to his people.
Comfort is obtained by clinging to the feet of (his) servants.
(When) their own self is gone, then they are restored to themselves.[1]

[1] ਆਪੁ ਗਇਆ ਤਾ ਆਪਹਿ ਭਏ; the ਆਪੁ is their own individual existence or personality; when this is gone (blotted out), then they become, what they originally are, *i.e.* spirit emanated from the Supreme Spirit.

They fall on the asylum of the depository of mercy.
(4). When one has obtained what he is desiring:
Then why should he go to seek it?
They are firmly established and located on a seat of enjoyment.
By the favour of the Guru they are dwelling in comfort.

Gauṛī; mahalā V.

CXI. CLXXXI.

(1). Crores of immersions and ablutions are made.
Lakhs, Arbs and Kharbs of gifts are given (by him):
In whose mind the name of Hari dwells.[1]

Pause.

All are purified by singing the excellences of Gōpāl.
(Their) sins are blotted out in the asylum of the compassionate pious people.
(2). Much high austerity is practised.
Many gains and desires are obtained (by him):
(Who) with (his) tongue praises the name of Hari, Hari.
(3). The Smriti, Shāstras, and Vedas declare it,
(That) he knows devotion, divine knowledge, perfection, and comfort:
Whose mind, by muttering the name, is reconciled with the Lord.
(4). Of unfathomable wisdom is Hari, unattainable and boundless.
On Nānak, who is muttering the name, (who) reflects on the name in (his) heart,
The Lord bestows mercy.

Gauṛī; mahalā V.

CXII. CLXXXII.

(1). Remembering, remembering and remembering (the name) comfort was obtained (by me).
The lotus-feet (of Hari) are fixed in (my) heart by the Guru.

Pause.

Guru Gōvind, the perfect Supreme Brahm:
Adoring him my mind (became) sedate.
(2). Daily I mutter the name of the Guru, the Guru.
Thereby all my affairs were accomplished.
(3). Having seen (his) sight (my) mind became refreshed.
The blemishes of the different births were wiped away.
(4). Nānak says: of what should one be afraid, O brother!
The honour of his own servant he causes to be preserved.

Gauṛī; mahalā V.

CXIII. CLXXXIII.

(1). His own servant he himself assists.
He cherishes him always like father and mother.

[1] The arithmetical progression is this: **ਲਾਖ** is a hundred thousand; **ਕੋਟਿ** is a hundred Lakhs; **ਅਰਬ** is a hundred **ਕੋਟਿ** (now **ਕਰੋੜ**); **ਖਰਬ** is a hundred **ਅਰਬ**.

Pause.

In the asylum of the Lord every one is saved.
He causes (every) work to be done, he is omnipresent and true.
(2). Now the creator dwells in (my) heart.
Fear is extinct, (my) soul (enjoys) the pith of happiness.
(3). In mercy his own people are protected.
The blemishes of the births are taken away.
(4). The greatness of the Lord cannot be told.
Nānak, his slave, is always in his asylum.

RĀGU GAUṚĪ ČETĪ; MAHALĀ V.

Dupadās.

Ōm! by the favour of the true Guru.

CXIV. CLXXXIV.

Pause.

The power of Rām is perfect, O brother!
From him no one goes away [1] disappointed.
(1). Whatever the servant of Hari thinks of, O mother!
That the creator himself causes to be done.
(2). The honour of the reviler is destroyed by the Lord.
Nānak (says): I will sing the praises of the fearless Hari!

Gauṛī; mahalā V.

CXV. CLXXXV.

Pause.

A hero with a strong arm is Brahm, the ocean of comfort.
Take thou the fingers of her,[2] who is falling into a pit!
(1). In (my) ears there is no hearing, (my) eyes are not beautiful.
Afflicted and a cripple I raise a cry (for help) at (thy) gate.
(2). O friend of the poor, O thou compassionate to the friendless, (thou art) my sweetheart, my friend, my father and mother!
Having seized the lotus-feet (of Hari), I have calmly [3] passed the ocean of fear, (says) Nānak.

RĀGU GAUṚĪ BAIRĀGAṆI; MAHALĀ V.

Ōm! by the favour of the true Guru.

CXVI. CLXXXVI.

Pause.

O Lord God, O my dear friend, abide thou with us, Sir!
(1). Without thee I do not live twenty-four minutes; woe to (my) staying in the world (without thee)!

[1] ਬਿਆਪੈ is also intransitive and signifies here: *to go away.*
[2] The subject is, according to the following lines, in the feminine.
[3] ਸੰਤ signifies also: calm, quiet (in mind).

O thou giver of comfort to my soul and life, every moment I devote myself to thee, O Lord!

(2). Give a support to my hand, O Lord, draw me out from the pit, O Gōpāl!

I, the vicious one, have little wisdom, thou art always compassionate to the poor.

(3). How shall I keep in mind thy comforts, in what manner shall I reflect (on them)?

I enter (thy) asylum, O thou benevolent to thy servant, O high, unattainable and boundless one!

(4). All the (four desirable) objects,[1] the eight perfections (are contained) in the highly delightful name.

To whom thou hast become very kind, O Kēsava, those people sing the praises of Hari.

(5). Thou art (my) mother and father, (my) son and relative, thou (art) the support of my life.

Who in the society of the pious, (says) Nānak, adores (thee), he crosses the difficult world (of existence).

GAUṚĪ BAIRĀGAṆI.

After the tune of the Rahōā-metre.[2]

Mahalā V.

Ōm! By the favour of the true Guru!

CXVII. CLXXXVII.

Pause.

Is there any one, who sings the beloved Rām?
He obtains all welfare and (all) true happiness.
(1). The Bairāgīs wander about, exploring every wood.
Some rare one gives himself to devout meditation on the One.
Who have obtained Hari, their lot is great.
(2). Brahmā and the other (gods), Sanak and the others[3] desire (him).
The Jōgīs, ascetics and Siddhs long for Hari.
Whose good lot it is, he sings the praises of Hari.
(3). By whom the asylum of Hari is not forgotten:
(Those) very fortunate saints Hari unites (with himself).
They are by no means (subject) to birth and death.
(4). Bestow mercy on me and join me, O dearly beloved!
Hear my supplication, O high and boundless Lord!
Nānak is asking the support of (thy) name.

Gauṛī pūrbī; mahalā V.

Ōm! by the favour of the true Guru!

CXVIII. CLXXXVIII.

Pause.

In what manner shall I meet with the Lord of my life, O mother?
(1). I am without beauty, without intelligence and strength, I the stranger have come from afar.

[1] These (four) desirable objects are: ਧਰਮ, ਕਾਮ, ਅਰਥ, ਮੋਖ.

[2] ਰਹੋਆ is said to be a chant or a kind of metre.

[3] These are the four mind-born sons of Brahmā, viz.: Sanatkumāra, Sananda, Sanaka and Sanātana, who declined to create progeny and remained for ever boys. Wilson, Vishṇu Pur. p. 38, note 13.

(2). I have no wealth nor brilliancy of youth; effect thou the union of the friendless one!

(3). Searching and searching about I became a Bairāgaṇi; O Lord, I am wandering about thirsting after thy sight.

(4). By the Lord, who is compassionate and merciful to the poor, my burning heat was quenched, (says) Nānak.

Gauṛī; mahalā V.

CXIX. CLXXXIX.

Pause.

In my heart a desire has sprung up to meet with the Lord.

I cling to (his) feet, I offer up supplication:

May some saint, whose lot is great, meet (with me)!

(1). I offer my mind (to him) as a sacrifice, I put before him my property, all the opinions of my mind I give up.

Who lets me hear the story about the Lord Hari, him I follow day by day, free from worldly passions.

(2). When the sprouts of works done in a former life become manifest, the (pious) men, the delightful Bairāgīs, are met with.

Darkness is cleared away by meeting with Hari; Nānak (says): she, who was asleep through various births, becomes awake.

Gauṛī; mahalā V.

CXX. CXC.

Pause.

Come forth, O bird, remembering the party of Hari![1]

Having met with the pious seize the asylum of the omnipresent Rām, keep this jewel in thy heart!

(1). A well of error is covetousness, a very pungent lotus-juice, a noose of illusion.

Gōvind, the Guru of the world, is cutting it asunder; make his lotus-feet thy dwelling!

(2). Bestow mercy (on me), O beloved Lord Gōvind, O protector of the poor, hear (my) prayer!

Take (my) hands, O Lord of Nānak, soul and body are all thy property.

Gauṛī; mahalā V.

CXXI. CXCI.

Pause.

My mind is thinking about the sight of Hari.

Longing with desire (after him) I think (of him) day and night; is there some saint who will bring him near to me?

(1). I will do service to (his) humble servant, in many ways I will bestow favour on him.

All comforts were weighed (by me) putting them on a pair of scales: without the sight of Hari they are very few.

(2). By the favour of the saints the ocean of (all) excellences is praised, he who was going though various births, is caused to return (to Hari).

He has joy and comfort, who meets with Hari; Nānak (says): his life is soon successful and fruitful.

[1] ਹਰਿ ਪਾਖ, the side, party of Hari = the votaries of Hari.

RĀGU GAUṚĪ PŪRBĪ; MAHALĀ V.

Ōm! by the favour of the true Guru!

CXXII. CXCII.

Pause.

How shall the Lord be met with, my King Rām?

Is there such a saint, a giver of tranquillity and happiness, who will show me the way?

(1). Within the incomprehensible one cannot be apprehended, within (like) a film, egotism is spread out.

In the illusion of the Māyā the whole world is asleep; say, how shall this error pass away?

(2). In one society, in one house they dwell together; there is no word about the creator, O brother![1]

Without the one thing (*i.e.* the name) the five are afflicted; that thing is in an imperceptible place.

(3). Whose the house is, he has put a lock on it, the key (to it) is entrusted to the Guru.

(Though) one may make many contrivances, he does not get it without taking refuge with the true Guru.

(4). Whose bonds are cut by the true Guru, they devoutly meditate on him (in) the society of the pious.

Having joined the pious people a song of joy is sung (by them), there is no (longer) a difference (distinct existence) of Hari (from theirs), (says) Nānak, O brother!

Pause.

(If) one be united with my King Rām, the Lord, in this way:

Tranquillity sets in, error flees in a moment, light, meeting with the fountain of light, is absorbed in it.

Gauṛī; mahalā V.

CXXIII. CXCIII.

Pause.

Such an intimacy (with him) was obtained.

By the compassionate Bīṭhulā[2] mercy was bestowed (on me), he was shown to me by the true Guru.

(1). Wherever I see, there art thou; this assurance has come to me.

To whom shall I make prayer and petition, as Raghu,[3] (my) King is hearing?

(2). (When) doubt is gone off and the bonds are broken by the Guru, then tranquillity and happiness are always obtained.

What he was (before), that he will become again; what is pointed out (to him) as pleasure (or) pain?[4]

(3). The parts and the whole universe stand in the One; the Guru, opening the screen, shows this.

The name, the depository of the nine treasures, is in one place (*i.e.* the heart), then to which place should one go outside (the heart)?[5]

(4). From one (piece of) gold many kinds (of ornaments) are made, many fashions are formed.

Nānak says: error is destroyed by the Guru; thus substance is united with substance.[6]

[1] The reference is to the (five) senses, who do not like to attend to the creator.

[2] ਬੀਠੁਲਾ = विट्ठल, said to be a name of Krishṇa, identified with the Supreme.

[3] ਰਘੁ, an ancestor of Rām; here taken in the sense of a patronymic: a descendant of Raghu = Rām.

[4] ਹੋਤਾ ਸਾ ਸੋਈ, etc., what he was (before) that he will be again, *i.e.* he, as an emanation of the Supreme Spirit, will be again united with it; then there is no longer any pleasure or pain for him, he will be free from all opposites.

[5] ਜਾਇਓ = ਜਾਇ, ō being an alliteration, to rhyme with ਦਿਖਾਇਓ.

[6] The (emanated) individual substance is re-united with the primary substance (the Supreme).

Gauṛī; mahalā V.

CXXIV. CXCIV.

Pause.

The lifetime is diminished, (as) days and nights (pass on).

O heart, having joined the Guru bring thy affairs into order!

(1). I pray thee, hear (me), O my friend! (now) is the time to serve the saints.

Depart, having gained here Hari! in the future world thy dwelling (will be) comfortable.

(2). This world is (subject) to the disease of doubt; he crosses who knows Brahm.

Whom he (Hari) awakens and lets drink the juice of Hari, he knows the tale (= doctrine) about the inexpressible one.

(3). For whose sake thou hast come (into the world), him purchase! by means of the Guru Hari dwells in the heart.

In thy own house and palace (= heart) thou wilt easily obtain happiness, there will not again take place a wandering (in transmigration).

(4). O inward governor, O divine male, the arranger (of all things), make full the faith of (my) heart!

Nānak, (thy) slave asks this happiness: make me the dust of the saints!

Gauṛī; mahalā V.

CXXV. CXCV.

Pause.

Keep me, O my father, my Lord!

I am without virtues, all virtues are thine!

(1). There are five quarrelsome ones (in me),[1] (I), the poor, (am) alone; keep me, O protector!

They cause (me) grief and afflict (me) much, I have (therefore) come to thy asylum.

(2). Cawing I was overcome (by them) in many different ways, they do not let me go in any way.

Having heard one word I espied a sanctuary: in the society of the pious they are destroyed.

(3). Bestowing mercy (on me) the saints met me, from them I obtained courage.

The saints gave me the mantra (of the name), (having become) fearless I did the word of the Guru.

(4). Those very quarrelsome ones were easily overcome by (their) comfortable word.

Nānak says: in (my) heart light was made, the blissful state (of emancipation) was obtained.

Gauṛī; mahalā V.

CXXVI. CXCVI.

Pause.

That imperishable one is King.

The fearless one dwells with thee; whence has come this dread (of thine)?

(1). Sometimes thou art unflinching, sometimes thou art lowly.

Sometimes thou art thyself, sometimes thou art humble.

(2). Sometimes thou art a Paṇḍit and teacher, sometimes thou art silly.[2]

Sometimes thou art taking everything, sometimes thou art taking nothing.

[1] The five quarrelsome ones are ਕਾਮ, ਕ੍ਰੋਧ, etc. ਬਿਖਾਦੀ (विषादिन्) has in Panjābī the sense of "quarrelsome."

[2] ਖਲ (खल) has in the old Hinduī also the sense of *foolish, silly* (else: vile).

(3). What does the helpless image of wood? he who makes it play, knows it.

As that juggler dresses it out, such a decoration it bears.

(4). Many chambers[1] of many kinds were made (by him), he himself became (their) keeper.

In which mansion he put (them) down, in such a one they remain; what can this helpless (creature) do?

(5). By whom everything is made, he knows it, by whom this whole creation is made.

Nānak says: the wisdom of the boundless Lord (is seen) from his own works.

Gauṛī; mahalā V.

CXXVII. CXCVII.

Pause.

Give up, give up, O man, the enjoyments of the world!

Thou clingest to them like cattle that are in the habit of breaking into a sown field.[2]

(1). What thou considerest (as being) of use to thee, that does not go with thee one inch.

Naked thou hast come (into the world), naked thou wilt depart; thou returnest again and art devoured by death.[3]

(2). Having seen the sport of the saffron-flower[4] and being taken up with it,[5] (thy) constant thought (is directed) on those merriments.[6]

The string (of life) is worn away day and night, for (thy) soul thou hast done no work whatever.

(3). Working and working, thus thou hast become old, by (vain) stories thou art overcome, (thy) body is wasted.[7]

As soon as (thou art) enchanted by that fascinating young woman (= the Māyā), the desire for her no (more) diminishes a minute.

(4). (When) the world was shown to me as being in such a condition by the Guru, then I fell on (his) asylum, giving up pride.

The way of the Lord was shown to me by the saint (= the Guru), in Nānak, the slave, the worship and praise of Hari was made firm.

Gauṛī; mahalā V.

CXXVIII. CXCVIII.

Pause.

Who is, without thee,

O my beloved, the support of my life?

(1). The state of the heart even thou knowest, thou art my delightful friend.

All comforts I obtained from thee, O my unfathomable, incomprehensible Lord!

[1] The ਕੋਠਰੀਆਂ (= ਕੋਠੜੀਆਂ) are the chambers and cells of the body, the internal arrangement; the ਮਹਲੁ or mansion, the outward structure.

[2] ਕਿਰਖਾ, *s.m.* a sown field and green. ਹਰਿਆਇਉ (*adj.*), said of cattle that break into fields.

[3] ਗਰਸੂਆ = ग्रस्त, devoured.

[4] ਕੁਸੁੰਭ, the saffron-flower, yielding a bad red dye, that soon wears off, is an image of the world.

[5] ਰਾਚਲਾ, to be taken up with a thing, and ਮਾਚਲਾ, to swell, to be puffed up, joined together in the sense: *to be completely taken up or absorbed in.*

[6] ਹਸੂਆ (here Plural) = ਹਸੁ, laughter, merriment; ਲਉ (= लय), constant thought.

[7] ਖੀਨ ਸੂਆ; ਸੂਆ is here, as in v. 4 (ਗਰਧ ਸੂਆ), merely an alliteration, to make up the rhyme, which he could not find.

(2). I cannot describe all thy appearances, O depository of (all) excellences, O giver of comfort!

The unattainable, inapprehensible, eternal Lord is known from the perfect Guru.

(3). Having cut off our error and fear he made us exclusively his own since (our) egotism was destroyed (by him).

The anxiety about regeneration and death ceased by the interview with the society of the pious.

(4). Washing his feet I will serve the Guru, a hundred thousand times I will devote myself to him.

By whose favour (I) have crossed the water of existence and have met with the beloved, says humble Nānak.[1]

Gauṛī; mahalā V.

CXXIX. CXCIX.

Pause.

Who should gratify thee except thou thyself?

Having seen all thy beauty (I was) enraptured (with it).

(1). In heaven, in the nether region, in the world of death, in all regions (thou), that One, art contained.

Saying: dreadful, dreadful![2] they all join their hands (in supplication), all cry out for help to thee,[3] O Lord of mercy!

(2). Thy name, O Lord, is purifying the sinners, giving comfort, pure and cool.

They have divine knowledge, meditation and greatness, (says) Nānak; the saints converse with thee.

Gauṛī; mahalā V.

CXXX. CC.

Pause.

Join me, O my dearly beloved!

O Lord, thy work has taken effect.

(1). In many regenerations, in many wombs (I) wandered about, again and again I incurred pain.

By thy mercy I have got the human body, give me thy sight, O Hari, (my) King!

(2). That has been done, which pleased him, it is not done by anybody else.

By thy decree I[4] was deluded by error, not being awake I fell asleep.

(3). Hear thou my prayer, O beloved Lord of my life, O compassionate one, O repository of mercy!

Keep me, O my father and Lord, cherish the helpless one!

(4). To whom thou hast shown thy sight, he follows the society of the pious.

Bestow mercy (on me) and give (me) the dust of the saints! this happiness Nānak desires.

Gauṛī; mahalā V.

CXXXI. CCI.

Pause.

I am a sacrifice to him, whose support[5] the name alone is.

(1). How great shall be counted the grandeur of those men, who are imbued with love to the Supreme Brahm?

[1] ਮਿਰੀਆ, for the sake of the rhyme = ਮਿਲਿਆ.

[2] ਸਿਵ ਸਿਵ (repeated) is here an interjection of *abhorrence* or *fright.*

[3] ਤੇਰੀ ਦੋਹੀ, supply: ਕਰਹਿ, they make.

[4] ਮੋਹਿ signifies here *I* (= ਹਉ).

[5] ਅਧਾਰੀ = ਅਧਾਰੁ, for the sake of the rhyme. ਅਧਾਰੀ is otherwise adjective, which is out of question here.

Happiness, tranquillity and joy are with them, no other donor is equal to them.

(2). Those people are come to rescue the world, who are thirsty after (their) sight.

Who falls on their asylum, he is saved, in the society of the saints his desire is fulfilled.

(3). (If) I fall down at their feet, then I live, in the society of the pious (I am) happy.

O Lord, be merciful, (that) my mind may become the dust of (thy) devotees!

(4). Dominion, youth, lifetime, whatever is seen in this world, wastes away.

The treasure of the name is always young and spotless, this wealth of Hari Nānak acquired.

Gauṛī; mahalā V.

CXXXII. CCII.

Pause.

The practice of Jōg I have heard from the Guru.

To me the true Guru has shown it by (his) word (instruction).

(1). The nine regions of the earth are contained in this (human) body; every moment I pay reverence (to it).

Dedication to the Guru (is = signifies) the ring in the ears, the One formless is (thereby) firmly established (in the heart).

(2). (When) the five,[1] having met together, have become slaves and are brought into the power of the One (spirit):

When the ten averse ones[2] (have become) obedient, then the Jōgīs become pure.

(3). Who burns his doubt (or error) and applies (its) ashes (to his body), he beholds the way as one.[3]

That tranquillity and happiness is enjoyed (by him), which is written by the Lord on (his) forehead.

(4). Where there is no fear, there he establishes his seat, (his) little blowing horn is the sound not produced by blowing.[4]

Reflection on the Supreme he keeps as his staff, devotion to the name pleases his mind.

(5). If such a very fortunate Jōgī be met with, he cuts asunder the fetters of the Māyā.

Service and adoration I perform to that person, Nānak licks his feet.

Gauṛī; mahalā V.

CXXXIII. CCIII.

Pause.

Hear the wonderful things of the name! meditating (on them) take them all, O friend!

To whom the medicine of Hari is given by the Guru, his mind (becomes) pure.

(1). Darkness is effaced from that body, (in which) the lamp of the word of the Guru shines brightly.

His net of error is cut asunder, who has faith in the society of the pious.

(2). Take a ferry-boat, the water of existence is deep and difficult, the boat is the society of the pious.

[1] The five are: ਕਾਮ, ਕ੍ਰੋਧ, etc.

[2] ਬੈਰਾਗਨਿ, fem. of ਬੈਰਾਗੀ, which has here its original meaning: *averse, reluctant* (Sansk. विरागिन्). The ten are the *ten* senses, viz.: five ज्ञानेन्द्रिय and five कर्मेन्द्रिय, *i.e.* hearing, feeling, seeing, tasting, and smelling, and the five organs of action: the voice, the hands, the feet, the anus and parts of generation.

[3] The whole is a figure. The sense is: he who clears away his doubt (*i.e.* his duality), will see, that the way is one, whatever may be the outward differences of the sects.

[4] The Jōgīs wear a little blowing horn (ਸਿੰਙੀ), which they sound before eating and drinking and every religious observance, in token of adoration.

The desire of the mind is fulfilled (thereby), the Guru is met with by reason of love to Hari.

(3). The treasury of the name is obtained by dint of devotion, heart and body become fully satiated (by it).

Nānak (says): Hari gives it to him, whom his order appeases.

Gauṛī; mahalā V.

CXXXIV. CCIV.

Pause.

Bestow mercy and compassion on me, O Lord of my life, I, the helpless one (seize) thy asylum, O Lord!

Give me thy hand and protect me in the blind well! I have no cleverness nor contrivance (to extricate myself).

(1). Even thou causest every work to be done, thou art powerful, there is none other.

Thy own secret thought even thou knowest; they are (thy) servants, on whose forehead (this) lot (is written).

(2). Thou, O Lord, art attached to thy own servants, thou hast a thorough connexion with (thy) devotees.

Dear, dear is thy name (to them), they desire (thy) sight, like as those bartavelles (desire) the sight of the moon.[1]

(3). Between Rām and the saints there is no difference whatever; the One is in many people, in Lakhs and Karōṛs.

In whose heart the Lord has become manifest, he daily utters his praise with his tongue.[2]

(4). Thou art powerful, boundless, very high, the giver of comfort, thou, O Lord, art the support of (my) life.[3]

May on Nānak, O Lord, mercy be bestowed, companionship[4] with those saints!

Gauṛī; mahalā V.

CXXXV. CCV.

Pause.

Thou, O Hari, art attached to (thy) saints.

Bring me through, O supreme arranger (of all things), bring me to the end, O donor!

(1). Thy latent power is known by thee, thou art the omnipresent supreme arranger (of all things).

Keep in (thy) asylum (me) the friendless and poor one, effect my salvation![5]

(2). Thy feet are the boat for the sake of crossing the ocean (of existence), thou knowest thy own manner.

Whom in mercy thou keepest with thee, (him) thou bringest across.

(3). Here and there, O Lord, (thou art) mighty, everything is in thy hand.

Give such a treasure to me, thy servant, O Hari, that will go with me!

[1] ਚਕੋਰੀ = ਚਕੋਰ, for the sake of the rhyme. The ਚਕੋਰ, bartavelle or Greek partridge, is said to be in love with the moon.

[2] ਰਵੇਰੀ, spoiled, for the sake of the rhyme, instead of ਰਵੈ or ਰਵਦਾ ਹੈ.

[3] ਅਪੇਰੀ, for the sake of the rhyme = ਅਪਾਰੀ.

[4] ਸੰਗੇਰੀ is a corruption (instead of ਸੰਗੁ), to make up the rhyme.

[5] ਗਾਤੇ, for the sake of the rhyme = ਗਤਿ.

(4). May on (me), the destitute of virtues, favour be bestowed, O Hari! my mind silently repeats (thy) name.

By the favour of the saints Nānak meets with Hari, (his) mind and body become cool and satiated.

Gauṛī; mahalā V.

CXXXVI. CCVI.

Pause.

Easily (I am) absorbed in God.

The true Guru has become a merciful God to me.

(1). Having cut (my) rope he made me his servant (on account of my) service to the saints.

(When) I became a worshipper of the One name, the wonderful (Supreme) was shown to me by the Guru.

(2). All became manifest and clear (to me), by the Guru divine knowledge was unfolded to (my) mind.

The nectar of the name was drunk, (my) heart became satiated, other fear was stopped.

(3). By obeying (his) order all comforts were obtained, the place of pain was removed.[1]

When the Lord God became very favourably disposed (towards me), the all-blissful one was shown (to me).

(4). Nothing is coming, nothing is going, all is made a sport by Hari the king.

Nānak says: unattainable, unattainable is the Lord; the name of Hari is the support of (his) devotees.

Gauṛī; mahalā V.

CXXXVII. CCVII.

Pause.

The sanctuary of the Supreme Brahm, the omnipresent Lord, should be laid hold of, O my mind!

By whom the universe and (its) parts are supported, the name of that Hari should be muttered!

(1). Give up the thoughts of (your own) minds, O ye people of Hari, by understanding (his) order comfort is obtained.

What the Lord does, that consider as good, in pleasure and pain he should be meditated upon!

(2). Crores of sinners are saved by the creator in a moment, without any delay intervening.

The pain and troubles of the poor the Lord is destroying; whom he pleases, him he cherishes, O friends!

(3). The soul and life of all he cherishes like mother and father, he is the ocean of comfort, O friends!

That creator gives without experiencing any deficiency, the ocean remains (always) full, O friends!

(4). The beggar (Nānak) asks for thy name, O Lord; in everybody that (Lord) (is existing), O friends!

Nānak the slave is in his asylum, by whom no one is disappointed, O friends!

RĀGU GAUṚĪ PŪRBĪ; MAHALĀ V.

Ōm! by the favour of the true Guru!

CXXXVIII. CCVIII.

Pause.

Do not forget at any time Hari, Hari in (thy) mind!

Here and there he is the giver of all comforts, all bodies he supports.

[1] The sense is: no more a place for pain was left.

(1). In a moment he cuts off the great troubles (of him, who) repeats his name with (his) tongue.

Coolness, tranquillity and comfort (are obtained) in the asylum of Hari, the burning fire he quenches.

(2). From the cavity of the womb (and) from hell he protects, he brings across the water of existence.

Who worships the lotus-feet in his mind, his fear of Yama he takes away.

(3). The omnipresent Supreme Brahm, the Lord, is high, unattainable and boundless.

Who is singing his excellences and meditating on the ocean of comfort, he does not lose in gambling his life.

(4). In lust, wrath, covetousness and spiritual blindness my mind is absorbed, O thou, who art generous to the vicious!

May in mercy thy own name be given to me! Nānak (will be) always devoted (to thee).

RĀGU GAUṚĪ ČĒTĪ; MAHALĀ V.

Ōm! by the favour of the true Guru!

CXXXIX. CCIX.

Pause.

There is no happiness, O brother, without devotion to Hari.

Thou overcomest regeneration[1] by muttering one moment this priceless jewel (of the name) in the society of the pious.

(1). Having left behind son, wealth, wife, sports,

Enjoyments, many people have departed.

(2). Having left behind horses, elephants, the merriments of dominion:

The fool has gone off naked.

(3). The body, that is blooming with sandal-perfume:

That body is mixed with dust.

(4). Deluded by spiritual blindness he thinks that he (God) is far off.

Nānak says: he is always in the presence.

Gauṛī; mahalā V.

CXL. CCX.

Pause.

Keep in (thy) mind the name of Hari for the sake of crossing the ocean!

The Guru is the boat, that is carrying (thee) across the waves of doubt (of this) world.[2]

(1). The blackness of the Kali-yug is dark.

By the Guru the lamp of divine knowledge is kindled.

(2). Very much poison of worldly objects is laid out.

Those are saved who continually mutter the excellences of Hari.

(3). Who is intoxicated with the Māyā, is gone to sleep.

Who meets with the Guru, his error and fear are done away.

(4). Nānak says: (by whom) the One is meditated upon:

He sees (him) in everybody.

[1] ਜਨਮੁ ਜੀਤਣਾ, to overcome regeneration = to obtain final emancipation.

[2] The construction of this line is very difficult, but no doubt the words cohere, as we have given them in the translation.

Gauṛī ; mahalā V.

CXLI. CCXI.

Pause.

Thou alone art our court (of justice).
Thy service is reliance on the Guru.
(1). By many contrivances it was not obtained.[1]
By the Guru it was brought into servitude.
(2). The five quarrelsome ones were destroyed.
By the mercy of the Guru (their) host was subdued.
(3). Presents (and) wages (are obtained from) the One name.
Happiness, tranquillity, joy and rest.
(4). The servants of the Lord are worthy.
Nānak (says): their faces are bright.

Gauṛī ; mahalā V.

CXLII. CCXII.

Pause.

The shelter of the soul is the name.
The others, who do what they ought not to do,[2] in them is the fear of Yama.
(1). By another effort he is not obtained.
In consequence of a great lot Hari is meditated upon.
(2). (The more) they contemplate (him), the less he (Hari) is known.
Further on (in the other world) they are not regarded a bit.[3]
(3). Who are doing (religious) works in self-conceit:
They are erecting a house of sand in water.
(4). (On whom) the merciful Lord bestows mercy:
He obtains the name, (says) Nānak, in the society of the pious.

Gauṛī ; mahalā V.

CXLIII. CCXIII.

Pause.

I devote myself, I devote myself a hundred thousand times.
The name, yea the name of the Lord, is the support of my soul.
(1). Thou alone causest (every) work to be done.
Even thou art the support of the living creatures.
(2). Thou, O Lord, art the owner of sovereignty and youth.

[1] No subject whatever is mentioned, and from the following verse the ਪੰਚ can hardly be taken up as the subject. We suppose, therefore, that ਮਨ, the mind, may be intended as the subject.

[2] ਕਰਨਕਰਾਵਨੋ can here not be referred to the Supreme, as elsewhere, where it stands for ਕਰਨਕਾਰਨ, *the cause of causes;* it must here be read: kar na karāvanō, *doing what they ought not to do* and *not doing what they ought to do* (literally: doing and not doing) = *perverse*, ਕਰਾਵਨ being an adjective formation = ਕਰਾਊ, *doing*. Similarly in Marāthī: करनकर or करनकरी. The Sikhs do not know what to make of it.

[3] ਆਗੈ ਤਿਲੁ ਨ ਮਾਨੀਐ, these words must refer to those, who contemplate Hari on their own account, without having a ਵਡ ਭਾਗ for it.

Thou art without qualities and endowed with all qualities.
(3). Here and there thou art the protector.
By the mercy of the Guru some one apprehends (thee).
(4). Thou, O Lord, art the inward governor and very wise.
Even thou art the hope and trust of Nānak.

Gauṛī; mahalā V.

CXLIV. CCXIV.

Pause.

Hari, Hari, Hari should be adored.
(Who lives) in the society, in his heart Hari dwells, (his) error, illusion and fear are overcome.
(1). The Vēdas, the Purāṇas, the Smriti tell it.
Every high and lustrous man hears it:
(2). All places are known as being struck with fear.
(But) the servant of Rām is rendered fearless.
(3). They wander about in the eighty-four Lakhs of wombs.
(But) the people of Gōvind are not born (again) nor do they die.
(4). Force, contrivance, dexterity (and) egotism are stopped.
Nānak seized the asylum of the pious people of Hari.

Gauṛī; mahalā V.

CXLV. CCXV.

Pause.

O heart, the praises of the name of Rām should be sung!
Hari should be continually served, at every breath Hari should be meditated upon!
(1). Who is with the saints, in his heart Hari dwells.
Pain and trouble, darkness and error flee (from him).
(2). (By whom) Hari is muttered by the favour of the saints:
That man is not affected by pain.
(3). To whom the Guru gives the mantra of Hari:
He is rescued from the fire of the Māyā.
(4). O Lord, bestow mercy on Nānak!
In my heart and body dwells the name of Hari.

Gauṛī; mahalā V.

CXLVI. CCXVI.

Pause.

(If) with the tongue be muttered the One name:
Here (in this world) much happiness and joy (are obtained), further on (to the other world) it (= the name) goes with (and) is of service to the soul.[1]
(1). If the disease of thy egotism be cut off:

[1] ਜੀਅ ਕੈ ਸੰਗਿ ਕਾਮ, a very obscure construction. The subject is the *name;* it goes with the soul to the other world and is of use there. ਕਾਮ = ਕਾਮਿ ਆਉਂਦਾ ਹੈ, the verb being dropped.

Then thou wilt practise by the favour of the Guru the most excellent devotion.
(2). Who has tasted the juice of Hari:
That man's thirst is quenched.
(3). Who has obtained Hari, the abode of rest:
He does never again run about (in transmigration).
(4). To whom by the Guru the name of Hari, Hari is given:
His fear, (says) Nānak, is gone.

Gauṛī; mahalā V.

CXLVII. CCXVII.

Pause.

Who forgets the name of Hari, he has pain.
Who, joining the assembly of the pious, praise Hari, they are weighty with virtues.
(1). In which disciple's heart there is (true) wisdom:
In his hands are the nine treasures (and) perfection.
(2). Who knows Hari the Lord (and) master:
In his (house) there is no deficiency whatever.
(3). (By whom) the creator is known:
He enjoys all comforts and pleasures.
(4). In whose house the wealth of Hari abides:
From[1] them pain flees, says Nānak.

Gauṛī; mahalā V.

CXLVIII. CCXVIII.

Pause.

(Thy) pride (is) great, (thy) root[2] (origin) (is) this much.
(Tho art) not abiding, as much as (thy) effort (may be).[3]
(1). What is forbidden by the Vēda (and) the saints, to that (thou art) inclined,[4] O friend!
After the manner of hazard-gambling[5] the senses subdue and overcome (thee).
(2). By love to the lotus-feet (of him who is) taking away and supplying all, (I became) disencumbered.[6]
Nānak is rescued; by the society of the pious the abode of mercy was given to me.[7]

[1] ਸੰਗਿ is here the Ablative: from their society = from.

[2] ਮੂਲ, root, origin. The sense is: thou hast no reason to be so proud, thy root or origin is this much (*i.e.* the ਬੀਰਜ or sperma genitale).

[3] ਗਹੁ (= ग्रह) is here substantive: tenacity, effort. Thou must go, in spite of all thy efforts.

[4] ਚਿਤਨੇ = ਚਿਤੁ, nō being merely an alliteration.

[5] ਹਾਰਜੂਆਰ, *s.f.* the vicissitudes of gambling; ਹਾਰਜੂਆਰ ਜੂਆ, gambling with alternate loss and victory = hazard-gambling. ਘਿਧੇ = ਘਿਧਿ.

[6] ਰਿਤਨੇ = ਰਿਤਾ (रिक्त), vacant, disencumbered (from pride, the dominion of the senses, etc.), nō being an alliteration. No subject is hinted at, as usual, but from the following line "*I*" must be supplied.

[7] ਦਿਤਨੇ = ਦਿਤਾ, given. The Sikhs totally misunderstand these lines and could not give me any sensible explanation.

Gauṛī; mahalā V.

CXLIX. CCXIX.

Pause.

I am the slave of the Lord.
The gift of the Lord (is my) food.
(1). Such is my Lord, O friend!
In a moment he prepares (it).
(2). I do works, if I please (my) Lord.
I sing the actions and excellences of (my) Lord.
(3). I fell on the asylum of the Vazīrs[1] of (my) Lord.
Seeing them my mind (became) sedate.
(4). The One is (my) prop, the One (my) support.
Humble Nānak is engaged in the business of (his) Lord.

Gauṛī; mahalā V.

CL. CCXX.

Pause.

Is there such a one, who breaks (his) egotism?
(Who) from this sweet one[2] keeps back his mind?
(1). Man has become destitute of divine knowledge; what is not,[3] that he desires.
The night is dark and black, what is the means, by which dawn of day (may be made)?[4]
(2). Wandering and wandering about he (= man) is worn out with fatigue, in many ways he seeks (it).[5]
Nānak says: (on whom) the mercy of the assembly of the saints is bestowed, he gets the treasure.

Gauṛī; mahalā V.

CLI. CCXXI.

Pause.

O (thou) gem, granting all desires, full of compassion!
(1). O Supreme Brahm, compassionate to the poor, by remembering whom all comforts are obtained!
(2). O timeless Supreme Spirit of unfathomable wisdom!
By hearing (thy) glory crores of sins are blotted out.
(3). O Lord, abode of mercy, bestow mercy (on me).
(That) Nānak may take the name of Hari, Hari!

Gauṛī pūrbī; mahalā V.

CLII. CCXXII.

Pause.

O my mind, in the asylum of the Lord comforts are obtained.
That day passes uselessly, in which he is forgotten, who gives comfort to the soul.

[1] *i.e.* the saints.
[2] ਇਸੁ ਮੀਠੀ ਤੇ, *i.e.* ਮਾਇਆ, the Māyā, which is described as attractive and sweet.
[3] *i.e.* the Māyā, which is not in reality, but only an illusion.
[4] ਭੋਰੈ = ਭੋਰਿ, *s.f.* dawn of day; the verb is left out.
[5] *i.e.* the ਨਿਧਿ, the treasure (= the name).

(1). Thou art come (into this world) as a guest of one night and extendest thy hope (of life) to many ages.

House, palace, property, (whatever) is seen, that is like the shade of a tree.

(2). My body, all my wealth, my garden and all my property pass away.

(If) the Lord, the giver (of them), be forgotten, they become in a moment the property of another.

(3). He puts on (clean) vestments, he makes ablutions, he applies sandal-perfume (to his body).

The fearless, formless (Supreme) is not known (by him), like elephants, which have been bathed.[1]

(4). When he (*i.e.* Hari) becomes merciful (to any), he joins the true Guru (to him), all comforts (are obtained) by the name of Hari.

He becomes released, (his) fetters are opened by the Guru, humble Nānak (says): he sings the excellences of Hari.

Gauṛī pūrbī ; mahalā V.

CLIII. CCXXIII.

Pause.

O my mind, it should always be said : O Guru, Guru, Guru !

The (human) birth, the gem, is made fruitful by the Guru, I sacrifice myself for a meeting (with him).

(1). As many breaths and morsels a man is taking, so many (times) the excellences (of Hari) should be sung.

When one's own true Guru becomes merciful, then this wisdom and understanding are obtained.

(2). O my mind, by taking the name thou art released from the bonds of Yama, all comforts of comforts are obtained (thereby).

Serve the Lord, the true Guru, the donor! the fruit, that is desired by the mind, comes to hand.

(3). The name is friend, acquaintance and son; the creator, O heart, goes with thee.

Serve thy own true Guru, by the Guru it (*i.e.* the name) is put into (thy) lap.[2]

(4). By the Lord, the merciful Guru, mercy was bestowed (on me), all (my) cares were extinguished (thereby).

Nānak obtained happiness, by praising Hari all troubles were done away.

RAGU GAUṚĪ; MAHALĀ V.

Ōm! by the favour of the true Guru!

CLIV. CCXXIV.

Pause.

The thirst of some rare one is quenched.[3]

(1). Crores (of Rupees) they[4] amass, hundred thousand crores, (but) their mind they do not check. For more and more (money) they struggle.

(2). (Though) they have beautiful women of many kinds, (they are) passionate after another's wife. Good and bad are not known (to them).

[1] The sentence is not complete, supply: he sullies himself or wallows in the dust, like elephants which have been bathed.

[2] ਪਾਲੈ = ਪਲੈ (pallai), the border of a garment, in which money is bound up.

[3] ਬੁਝੀਹੇ = ਬੁਝੀਏ.

[4] ਜੋਰੇ—ਹੋਰੇ may also be the singular.

(3). Many (are) the bonds of the Māyā, (by which) he errs and is led astray, the abode of excellences is not praised (by him).

(His) mind struggles in worldly pursuits.

(4). On whom he bestows mercy, O friends, he dies whilst living, in the society of the pious he crosses the Māyā.

Nānak (says): that man is approved at the gate of Hari.

Gauṛī; mahalā V.

CLV. CCXXV.

Pause.

(Thou), O Hari, (art) the essence (pith) of everything.

(1). Sometimes (thou art) abstract meditation, sometimes enjoyment, sometimes divine knowledge, sometimes contemplation.

Sometimes thou holdest a staff.[1]

(2). Sometimes (thou art) silent repetition, sometimes austerity, sometimes worship, a burnt-offering (and) religious observance.

Sometimes thou art moving about.

(3). Sometimes (thou art) the shore, sometimes the water, sometimes reflection on the Vēda.

Nānak (says): (thou art) dear to (thy) devotees.

Gauṛī; mahalā V.

CLVI. CCXXVI.

Pause.

Celebrating (thy) excellences, (this) is my treasure.

(1). Even thou (art my) delight, even thou (my) glory, even thou (my) beauty, even thou (my) splendour.

My hope and support art thou, O Lord!

(2). Even thou (art my) trust, even thou (my) gift, even thou (my) Lord, even thou (my) life.

By the Guru the separated one is united again (with thee).

(3). Thou art in the house, thou art in the wood, thou art in the village, thou art in the desert.

Thou art, (says) Nānak, quite near.

Gauṛī; mahalā V.

CLVII. CCXXVII.

Pause.

(I am) intoxicated, (I am) intoxicated with love to Hari.

(1). He is the beloved, he is (also) the lustful; to the Guru the gift is given (and again) bestowed (by him).

With him my heart is in love.

(2). He is the furnace, he is (also) the besmearing with mud, he is the beloved (and) he is (also) the desire.

In (my) mind he is known (as) happiness.

[1] ਡਾਗੂ ਰੇ; ਰੇ is here an interjection, oh!

(3). Tranquillity, amusement, joy (and) sport (accrued to me), the wanderings (in transmigration) were stopped, union (with the Supreme) was brought about.

Nānak (says): by means of the word of the Guru he was obtained.[1]

RĀGU GAUṚĪ MĀLVĀ; MAHALĀ V.

Ōm! by the favour of the true Guru!

CLVIII. CCXXVIII.

Pause.

Take the name of Hari, O friend, take it!

Before (thee) is a difficult, terrible road.

(1). Serve always the servant of the servants,[2] death is dwelling with thee.

Serve thou the pious, O man, and the net of Yama will be cut off.

(2). Burnt-offerings, sacrifices and pilgrimages to holy watering places are made, but in their heart they are bound by the passion of egotism.

Having enjoyed both hell and heaven they will again and again be born.

(3). In the city of Shiva, in the city of Brahmā and Indra there is no immovable dwelling.[3]

Without the service of Hari there is (no lasting) happiness, O man, the Sākats come and go.

(4). As I was instructed by the Guru, so I have proclaimed it.

Nānak says: hear, O my heart, having praised (Hari) there will be emancipation.

RĀGU GAUṚĪ MĀLĀ; MAHALĀ V.

Ōm! by the favour of the true Guru!

CLIX. CCXXIX.

Pause.

By me, child-like in understanding, happiness was obtained, O friend!

Joy (and) grief, life[4] and death, pain and pleasure are the same in (my) mind, after having met with the Guru.

(1). As long as I meditate and reflect on something, I am full of pain.[5]

(But) when the merciful, perfect Guru is met with, then there is joy and tranquillity.[6]

(2). As many clevernesses and works as I practised, so many fetters fell upon me.

(But) when the holy man (= the Guru) put his hand on my forehead, then we became emancipated.

(3). As long as I was saying: "mine, mine," so long I was encompassed by poison.

When my mind, body and intellect were offered up to the Lord, then we slept in tranquillity.

[1] ਪਰਾਤੇ = Sansk. प्राप्त; the subject is Hari or it may be referred to ਸਹਜ, ਕੇਲ, etc.

[2] ਸੇਵਕ ਸੇਵਕ, the servant of the servants, *i.e.* the Guru, who is otherwise called the ਦਾਸਨ ਦਾਸ, and in the next line the ਸਾਧ (sing.).

[3] The sense is: those, who by reason of their work are transferred to these happy places, must leave them again, after their merits are exhausted.

[4] ਹਾਨਿ ਬਿਰਤੁ. The common meaning of ਹਾਨਿ is *damage, hurt*, etc., which will not suit the context here, as one word is in contraposition to the other; ਹਾਨਿ must therefore be the antithesis of ਬਿਰਤੁ. But we are not able to detect any suitable etymology and must leave it doubtful.

[5] ਦੂਖਨ ਭਰੇ; ਦੂਖਨ is the Format. Plural, ਭਰੇ = ਹਮ ਭਰੇ, we are full of.

[6] ਸਹਜੇ = ਸਹਜੁ, for the sake of the rhyme.

(4). So long as I carried about (my) load, I was mulcted.[1]
When having thrown down the load the perfect Guru met (with me), then Nānak became fearless.[2]

Gauṛī mālā; mahalā V.

CLX. CCXXX.

Pause.

I gave up, I gave up, O dear, (my own) suppositions.

I gave (them) up, I gave (them) up after having met with the Guru.

All comforts, joys, welfare and enjoyments (are obtained) by obeying the command of Gōvind.[3]

(1). Dignity and conceit, both came to an end after having thrown (my) head before the feet of the Guru.

There is prosperity and joy, no calamity nor pain, (when) love to the Lord has sprung up.

(2). The One Lord is the dwelling-place (and) the inhabitant (of it), the pleasure-ground and the spectator (of it).[4]

The saints have become fearless, their apprehension is put down by the all-filling, all-pervading[5] (Supreme).

(3). Whatever is done by the cause of causes,[6] they do not take offence at it in their mind.

In the society of the pious (their) sleeping mind is awakened by the favour of the saints.

(4). Humble Nānak has fallen on thy protection, he has come to (thy) asylum.

(By) love to the name tranquillity and pleasures are enjoyed, pain does not again befall (one).

Gauṛī mālā; mahalā V.

CLXI. CCXXXI.

Pause.

A ruby was obtained, a gem was obtained in (my) mind.

(My) body became cool, (my) mind became cool, by the word of the true Guru I was absorbed (in Hari).

(1). (My) hunger ceased, all (my) thirst was quenched, all anxiety was forgotten.

(When) the perfect Guru placed his hand on (my) forehead, (my) mind was overcome (and) all the world.[7]

(2). (We) are perfectly satiated within (our) heart, we are now set free from staggering.

An inexhaustible treasury was given (us) by the true Guru, there is no deficiency of diamonds and pearls.[8]

(3). Hear, the One is wonderful, O brother! such an understanding is taught by the Guru.

When the Lord, after having removed the screen, is met with, then subservience to others is forgotten.

[1] ਡਾਨੁ ਭਰਨਾ, literally: to pay in a fine.

[2] ਨਿਰਭਏ = ਨਿਰਭਉ, for the sake of the rhyme.

[3] ਆਗਿਓ = ਆਗਿਆ, for the sake of the rhyme.

[4] ਦ੍ਰਿਸਟਾਗਿਓ = ਦ੍ਰਿਸਟਾ (= Sansk. द्रष्टा), giō being a meaningless alliteration.

[5] ਸਰਬਾਗਿਓ = ਸਰਬਗ (सर्वग), for the sake of the rhyme.

[6] ਕਾਰਣੈ ਕਾਰਣੁ = ਕਰਣ ਕਾਰਣੁ, the producer of the cause or cause of causes, the primary cause or principle of whatever is done.

[7] ਸਾਰੀ, instead of ਸਾਰਾ, all, entire.

[8] ਮੁਕਤਾ, pearl, Sansk. मुक्ता.

(4). This wonder cannot be told, he knows it, by whom it is tasted.

Nānak says: the True one is manifested (to him), into (whose) heart the treasure is put by the Guru.

Gauṛī mālā ; mahalā V.

CLXII. CCXXXII.

Pause.

They are saved, who are in the asylum of Rām, the king.

All (other) people are in the circle of the Māyā (and) are falling again and again on the earth.[1]

(1). The great men, having reflected on the Shāstras, the Smriti and the Vēda, have said thus:

"Without adoring Hari there is no salvation, no one obtained happiness."

(2). (If) the wealth of the three worlds be amassed, the impulse of the passions is not extinguished.

How shall one get stability (in rectitude) without devotion to Hari? he is returning (into existence) immediately.[2]

(3). Though he practises many heart-enchanting sports, his lust is not satiated.

It is burning and burning and never extinguished, all (sports) without the name are useless.

(4). Mutter the name of Hari, O my friend, this is the full pith of happiness.

The society of the pious removes regeneration and death, Nānak is the dust of the pious.

Gauṛī mālā ; mahalā V.

CLXIII. CCXXXIII.

Pause.

May any one explain (to me) this arrangement (of the world)?

If he become the creator, he may give information.

(1). By this ignorant one nothing is wrought, not any silent repetition (of the name) nor austerity is practised.

In the ten directions of the globe he makes wander his mind, by doing what work is it bound?

(2). He is the Lord of the mind, body, property and land, I am his and he is mine.

By reason of error and spiritual blindness nothing is understood, these have fallen (like) ropes on the feet.

(3). Then what work can this one[3] undertake, when this one is nothing?

When the One, who is void of all darkness and formless, the Lord himself, is doing everything.[4]

(4). His own works he himself knows, by whom this arrangement (of the world) is made.

Nānak says: he himself is the creator, by the true Guru the error is stopped.

Gauṛī mālā ; mahalā V.

CLXIV. CCXXXIV.

Pause.

Without Hari other works are useless.

(By whom) muttering repetitions, austerities, control of the passions and religious works are practised, they are robbed on this side.[5]

[1] By regeneration.

[2] ਪਹਰੈ ਪਹਰੈ = ਪਹਲੈ ਪਹਲੈ, first of all, immediately.

[3] ਇਹੁ, this one, *i.e.* man.

[4] Human liberty (arbitrium liberum) is totally denied here, as in every pantheistical system.

[5] The sense is: they are stripped of the merits of their works in this world; they do not go with them.

(1). Who are engaged in vows, religious observances and obligations, they do not receive a farthing.[1]
Going on (to the other world) is a different thing, O brother, there they are of no use.
(2). Who bathes at a Tīrtha and is wandering about the earth, does further on not get a place.
There this proceeding is of no use, that world does not believe in it.
(3). Though the four Vēdas be rehearsed from memory, in the other world the palace (of Hari) is not obtained.
If one do not comprehend the one pure name, all is nonsensical talk, (whatever) be prated.
(4). Nānak expresses this result of his reflection,—who does act up to it, is crossing over—
"Serve the Guru and meditate on the name, drop conceit from thy mind!"

Gauṛī; mahalā V.

CLXV. CCXXXV.

Pause.

Mādhava! Hari, Hari, Hari! should be uttered with (one's) mouth.
By us nothing can be done, O Lord, as thou puttest (one) down, so he remains.
(1). What can he do, what is he effecting, what is in the hand of this helpless one?
Where thou puttest (him), there he remains, O our omnipresent Lord!
(2). Bestow mercy (on me), O liberal donor of all, apply (me) to unremitting meditation (on thee)!
This is the prayer of Nānak to Hari: make me mutter thy name!

RĀGU GAUṚĪ MǍJH; MAHALĀ V.

Ōm! by the favour of the true Guru!

CLXVI. CCXXXVI.

(1). Damōdar, the king is merciful to the poor, O dear!
Having made crores of men thou didst apply them to thy service, O Lord!
He is compassionate to (his) devotees, thy affair (or livelihood) is kept up (by him), O dear!
He is omnipresent in all places, O dear!
(2). How shall I see my beloved, what is that work (that I should do), O dear!
(Having become) the slave of the saints I will worship their feet, O dear!
This life I will devote, I will sacrifice myself (to them), O dear!
Bowing and bowing to him[2] I will cling to his feet, O dear!
(3). The Paṇḍit is searching books (and) the Vēda, O dear!
Having become a Bairāgī he is bathing at a Tīrtha, O dear!
He is singing songs[3] and reciting praises, O dear!
I will meditate on the name of the fearless Hari, O dear!
(4). (To whom) my Lord has become merciful, O dear!
(Those) sinners (are made) pure, having clung to the feet of the Guru, O dear!
Having cut off (their) error and fear they are made everybody's friend, O dear!
By the Guru the desire of their heart is fulfilled, O dear!

[1] ਆਢੁ, *s.m.* the eighth part of a pice (now ਅੱਧੀ).
[2] *i.e.* the Guru, the head of the saints.
[3] ਨਾਦ is here used in an adjective sense = ਸ੍ਤੋਤਾ, praising, singing.

(5). Who has obtained the name, he is wealthy, O dear!
Who has meditated on the Lord, (he becomes) lustrous, O dear!
Who (has obtained) the society of the pious, all his actions are good, O dear!
He is easily absorbed, O dear!

Gauṛī mā̃jh; mahalā V.

CLXVII. CCXXXVII.

(1). Come, O my beloved Rām!
Night and day, at every breath I think of thee, O dear!
Give (me) information, O holy one, (that) I may fall at (thy) feet, O dear!
Without thee how shall one be saved, O dear!
(2). In thy society I am happy, O dear!
In (every) tree and grass, in the three worlds (thou), the highest bliss and joy, (art contained).
The bed is beautiful, this mind (of mine) is opening (to thee), O dear!
Having seen (thy) sight this happiness is obtained, O dear!
(3). Washing (thy) feet I will always serve thee, O dear!
Worship, adoration and homage I will offer to thee!
(Having become) the slave of slaves I will mutter (thy) name, O dear!
Supplication I will offer [1] to (thee), the Lord, O dear!
(4). My wish is fulfilled, my mind and body are green (= happy), O dear!
Seeing (thy) sight all (my) pain is taken off, O dear!
Muttering continually the name of Hari, Hari, I have crossed over, O dear!
This imperishable happiness is retained by Nānak, O dear!

Gauṛī mā̃jh; mahalā V.

CLXVIII. CCXXXVIII.

(1). Hear, hear my sweetheart, my friend dear to (my) heart, O dear!
My heart and body are thine, this life also I devote to thee, O dear!
May the Lord, the support of (my) life, not be forgotten (by me), O dear!
I am always in thy asylum, O dear!
(2). May I obtain by the favour of the Guru that Hari, Hari, O dear!
Whom having fonnd my heart lives, O dear brother!
All is the Lord's, (all) places are the Lord's.
I always devote myself to the Lord, O dear!
(3). This treasure he minds attentively, whose lot is great, O dear!
On the one pure name he bestows his devout meditation, O dear!
(By whom) the perfect Guru is obtained, all his troubles are effaced, O dear!
The eight watches the excellences (of Hari) are sung (by him), O dear!
(4). A choice jewel is thy name, O Hari!
Thou art the true wholesale-merchant, thy devotees are (thy) retail-dealers, O dear!
The wealth of Hari is true capital stock and traffic, O dear!
Humble Nānak always devotes himself (to it), O dear!

[1] Literally: *will be said.*

RĀGU GAUṚĪ MǍJH; MAHALĀ V.

Ōm! by the favour of the true Guru!

CLXIX. CCXXXIX.

Pause.

Thou art the object of my high regard, O creator, thou art the object of my high regard.

By thy power I dwell in comfort, the true word (of the Guru) is the object of my attention.

(1). All things are known (by those, who), when having heard, are silent.

Understanding is never obtained by those who are deluded by the Māyā.

(2). The hints and signs, which they give, are seen by their eyes.[1]

He who is foolish and covetous, does not at all hear what is said.

(3). What shall I count one, two (or) four (relishes)? the whole (world) is carried away by one relish (*i.e.* of the Māyā).

Some few delight in the name, (as) some rare place is cultivated.

(4). The devotees are lustrous at the true gate, they are happy day and night.

To those, who are imbued with love to the Lord, humble Nānak always devotes himself.

Gauṛī mǎjh; mahalā V.

CLXX. CCXL.

Pause.

Thy name, O Lord, is clearing away pain, thy name is clearing away pain.

(By whom) it is adored the eight watches, (his) divine knowledge the true Guru is completing.

(1). In which body the Supreme Brahm dwells, that place is beautiful.

The servant of Yama does not approach (him, who) with his tongue sings the excellences of Hari.

(2). The knowledge of (thy) service is not known (to me) nor do I know how to adore (thee).[2]

(I flee to) thy protection, O life of the world, O my unattainable, unfathomable Lord!

(3). (To whom) the Lord has become merciful, (their) grief and afflictions have fled.

No hot wind touches them, who are protected by the true Guru himself.

(4). The Guru is Narāyaṇ, the Guru is God, the Guru is the true creator.

From the Guru being pleased everything is obtained, humble Nānak is always devoted (to him).

Gauṛī mǎjh; mahalā V.

CLXXI. CCXLI.

Pause.

By muttering: Hari, Rām, Rām, Rām, Rām!

(My) affairs were accomplished.

(1). In muttering Rām Gōvind (my) face became pure.

From whom the glory of Hari is heard, he is (my) brother and friend.

(2). In whom (are contained) all things, all fruits and all excellences:

How should (that) Gōvind be forgotten from (one's) mind, by remembering whom pain departs?

(3). By clinging to whose garment's hem one lives and is brought over the water of existence:

[1] Those, who give hints and signs, are the saints. "By their eyes," *i.e.* by the eyes of those, who, when having heard a word of instruction, keep silence and meditate upon it.

[2] ਨਾ ਜਾਪੈ ਆਰਾਧਿ, literally: it is not known to adore, ਜਾਪਣਾ being constructed with the past conjunctive participle, like ਜਾਣਨਾ, the active of it.

Having met with that saint (*i.e.* Guru) salvation is obtained, the face (becomes) bright at the court (of Hari).

(4). The praise of Gōvind, the fountain of life, is the capital of the saints.

Nānak (says): they are saved by muttering the name, at the true gate they are applauded.

Gauṛī mǎjh; mahalā V.

CLXXII. CCXLII.

Pause.

Sing the excellences of the sweet Hari, O dear, sing thou the excellences of the sweet Hari!

By being attached to the True one the placeless one obtains a place.

(1). All other tastes are insipid, body and mind become insipid.

What one does without the Lord, that is wasted, (wasted) is that life.

(2). Having seized the hem of the saint (= Guru) he will cross this world.

If the Supreme Brahm be worshipped, (one's) whole retinue is saved.

(3). He is (my) sweetheart and relative, he is (my) friend, (who) puts the name of Hari into (my) heart.

(Who), having effaced all (my) vices, shows benevolence (to me).

(4). (My) property, treasury, village and house (are in) the repository of the foot of Hari.

Nānak is a beggar at thy gate, O Lord, he asks thee for a gift.

Ōm! by the favour of the true Guru!

RĀGU GAUṚĪ; MAHALĀ IX.[1]

I. CCXLIII.

Pause.

O ye pious people, give up the pride of the heart!

Lust, wrath, the society of the wicked, flee from them day and night!

(1). Who considers both, pleasure and pain, honour and dishonour, as the same,

Who remains aloof from joy and grief, by him the substance of the universe[2] is known.

(2). That one may give up both praise and blame and seek for final emancipation.

This sport, says humble Nānak, is difficult, by some (rare) disciple it is known.

Gauṛī; mahalā IX.

II. CCXLIV.

Pause.

O ye pious, (this) creation is made by Rām.

One considers (him) as perishable,[3] another as eternal, (but) the wonderful one cannot be apprehended.

(1). Man is in the power of lust, wrath and spiritual delusion, the person of Hari is forgotten.

The unreal body is considered as real, like a dream in the night.

(2). What is seen, that all perishes, like the shade of a cloud.

Humble Nānak has known the world as vain, he remained (therefore) in the asylum of Rām.

[1] *i.e.* Guru Tēgh Bahādur, the ninth Sikh Guru, born A.D. 1612 (1621?), executed (at Delhī) 1675.

[2] ਜਗਤਤੁ, the substance of the universe, *i.e.* the supreme or absolute being, constituting the substance of the universe.

[3] ਇਕ ਬਿਨਸੈ ਇਕ ਅਸਥਿਰੁ ਮਾਨੈ, *i.e.* Rām, that he (*i.e.* Rām) perishes, another, that he is firm, eternal.

Gauṛī ; mahalā IX.

III. CCXLV.

Pause.

The praise of Hari does not come into man's mind.

Day and night he remains absorbed in the Māyā, say, how should he sing (his) excellences?

(1). With son, friend, the Māyā, selfishness, thus he fetters his own self.

Having seen this false world he rises and runs after it, as after a mirage.

(2). The cause of devotion (and consequent) final emancipation is the Lord, (but) the fool forgets him.

Humble Nānak (says): among crores some (rare) one attains to the worship of Rām.

Gauṛī ; mahalā IX.

IV. CCXLVI.

Pause.

O ye pious, this mind cannot be seized.

It is fickle, (worldly) thirst dwells in it, therefore it does not remain firm [1] (steady).

(1). In whose body hard wrath is, (by him) all discretion is forgotten.

Every jewel of divine knowledge is taken away (from him), with him nothing abides.

(2). All the Jōgīs have been wearied with their efforts, the skilful have ceased singing (his) excellences.

Humble Nānak (says): when Hari has become merciful, then every affair is accomplished.

Gauṛī ; mahalā IX.

V. CCXLVII.

Pause.

O ye pious, sing the excellences of Gōvind!

You have obtained the priceless human birth, why do ye waste it to no purpose?

(1). Hari is the purifier of the sinners [2] and the friend of the poor, come to his asylum!

By whose remembrance the fear of an elephant [3] is taken away, why do you forget him?

(2). Having given up conceit and the delusion of the Māyā, apply your mind again to the adoration of Rām!

Nānak says: this is the way of final emancipation; having become disciples you will obtain it.

Gauṛī ; mahalā IX.

VI. CCXLVIII.

Pause.

May some one instruct my erring mind, O mother!

(Though) having heard the way of the Vēdas, the Purāṇs (and) the pious, it does not for a moment sing the praises of Hari.

(1). Having obtained a human body, which is hard to get, he spends his life to no purpose.

For the delusion of the Māyā, which is a very intricate forest, he lets spring up a propensity.

[1] ਰਹਾਈ = ਰਹੈ, for the sake of the rhyme.

[2] ਪੁਨੀਤ is here taken in the sense of ਪਾਵਨ, purifying; its usual signification is: *purified*.

[3] ਗਜ ਕੋ ਤ੍ਰਾਸੁ, the fear of an elephant, *i.e.* the fear of being thrown before an elephant, formerly a frequent manner of execution in India.

(2). He entertains no love to the Lord, who is always near inside and outside.
Nānak says: him consider emancipated, in whose body Rām is contained.

Gauṛī; mahalā IX.

VII. CCXLIX.

Pause.

O ye pious, in the asylum of Rām there is rest!
One may read the Vēdas and the Purāṇas, (but) this is virtue, if one remember the name of Hari.
(1). Covetousness, delusion of the Māyā, selfishness and attendance to worldly pursuits:
Joy and grief affect him, in whom that God is not formed.[1]
(2). Heaven and hell, nectar and poison, gold and copper are the same to him:[2]
To whom praise and blame, covetousness, (spiritual) delusion and passion[3] are the same.
(3). Who is not under the obstruction of pain and pleasure, him consider wise!
Nānak says: him consider emancipated, who is a man of this kind.

Gauṛī; mahalā IX.

VIII. CCL.

Pause.

O heart, what has happened to thee, the foolish one?
Day and night life diminishes, and thou dost not know, that thou hast become light (in weight) by covetousness!
(1). The body, beautiful house and women, which thou hast considered thy own:
Of these nothing is thine; see, reflect and think!
(2). Thy life, the jewel, is lost by thee, the way of Gōvind is not known by thee.
Not a moment thou hast become absorbed with his feet, thy life is spent to no purpose.
(3). Nānak says: that man is happy, who sings the excellences of the name of Rām.
All the other world is deluded by the Māyā, it does not obtain the secure place.[4]

Gauṛī; mahalā IX.

IX. CCLI.

Pause.

O thoughtless man, be afraid of sin!
He, who is merciful to the poor, is annihilating all sin, fall thou on his asylum!
(1). Whose excellences the Vēdas and Purāṇas are singing, his name hold fast in thy heart!
The name of Hari is purifying in the world, by continually remembering it take off all sins!
(2). A human body thou wilt not obtain again, make somewhat a scheme for thy final emancipation, O man!
Nānak says: praise him, who is full of compassion, and thou wilt cross the ocean of existence, O man!

[1] It is better here to take ਮੂਰਤਿ as an adjective (= Sansk. मूर्त), *formed, substantial.*

[2] ਤਿਉ = ਤਿਹੁ, to him, referring to ਜਾ ਕੈ (ਮਨਿ), in whose mind = to whom.

[3] ਤੈਸਾ cannot be here a correlative adjective (such), but must be a substantive. It is the Arabic طَيش, passion.

[4] ਨਿਰਭੈ ਪਦੁ, the secure place, from which no more regeneration takes placė.

* RĀGU GAUṚĪ.

Asṭpadīs; mahalā I.

Gauṛī guārērī.

Ōm! the true name is the creator, the supreme spirit.

By the favour of the Guru!

I.

(1). A treasure and perfection is reflection on the spotless name.
(In whom) the all-filling remains full, destroying (his) poison:
His triad is[1] gone off, he is pure within.
The instruction of the Guru became useful in (= to his) soul.

Pause.

In this wise, by uttering Rām, the mind is soothed.
By the word of the Guru, the collyrium of understanding, he (*i.e.* Rām) is known.
(2). (What is) considered as the only happiness, is easily obtained.
By the pure word (of the Guru) error is stopped.
They became red, the false red colour was absorbed.[2]
His favourable look fell (on them) and their poison was stopped.
(3). A return[3] took place, having died whilst living they became awake.
They delighted in the word (of the Guru), their mind was applied to Hari.
Sweet juice they collect, poison is done away and abandoned.
In faith they live, the fear of Yama has fled.
(4). (Worldly) enjoyments, disputes and selfishness are stopped.
The mind is imbued with love to Hari (and to) the order of the boundless one.
The practices of caste and brotherhood[4] are given up.
(His) favourable look has fallen (upon them) and happiness has settled in the soul.
(5). Without thee I see no other friend.
Whom shall I worship, to whom shall I apply my mind?
Whom shall I ask, to whose feet shall I cling?
On whose instruction shall I continue meditating?
(6). The Guru I will worship, to the feet of the Guru I will cling.
I will adore, I will in love attach myself to the name of Hari.
Instruction and initiation (into the mysteries of the Guru) is (my) delight and desire.
According to (his) order I go to my own house.
(7). (My) pride is gone, with pleasure I meditate on my own spirit.
Light has sprung up (in me), in the luminous (Supreme) (I am) absorbed.

[1] ਤ੍ਰਿਕੁਟੀ, the triad, *i.e.* the three qualities.

[2] ਲਾਲ ਭਏ, they became red, *i.e.* tinged with the true colour of the love of God.

[3] The word ਉਲਟ (*f.*), return, nearly corresponds to our "*conversion.*"

[4] ਜਾਤਿ ਰਹੇ ਪਤਿ; ਜਾਤਿ and ਪਤਿ must be taken together; otherwise ਜਾਤਿ ਪਾਤਿ.

What is written, is not effaced; the word (of the Guru is) the sign,[1]
(From which) the creator, the cause of causes, is known.
(8). (I am) not a Paṇḍit, nor clever and wise.
(But nevertheless) I am not erring nor led astray by error.
I do not tell legends (of the Gods), the order (of Hari) is known by me.
Nānak is easily absorbed (in Hari) by the instruction of the Guru.

Gauṛī guārērī; mahalā I.

II.

(1). The mind is the elephant, the body the pleasure-ground.
The Guru is the elephant-goad. (Who) attends to the true word (of the Guru):
He enjoys lustre at the royal gate.

Pause.

By dint of cleverness He[2] cannot be known.
Without (the mind) being subdued how can his estimate be obtained?
(2). In the house is nectar, the thieves[3] take it away.
None denies it.
Who keeps (it from the thieves), to him he himself gives greatness.
(3). Innumerable[4] fires are in one place.
They ceased burning, by the Guru they were extinguished by dint of instruction.
By whom his mind is given over, he sings with pleasure the excellences (of Hari).
(4). As he is in the house, so he is outside.[5]
Sitting (even) in a cave how shall I describe him?
In the sea and on the mountain he is such a fearless one.
(5). Say, who will kill a dead one?
What a fear of any one has he, who is fearless?
By means of the word (of the Guru) he knows the three worlds.
(6). By whom it is said, by him (his) saying is explained.
By whom it is understood, by him it is easily comprehended.
Having seen and reflected (on it) my mind was soothed.
(7). Celebrity, intelligence[6] and final emancipation are in the One name.
In him the Supreme Being is abiding:
Who remains in his own house,[7] in his own place.
(8). How many Munis praise him and show affection to him!
In a pure body and heart think of that True one!
Nānak (says): adore continually Hari!

[1] Most modern MSS. read now ਸਬਦੁ ਨੀਸਾਣਾ, but it is perhaps better to read: ਸਬਦਿ ਨੀਸਾਣਾ, as found in old good MSS.; the translation would then run thus: *in the word* (*of the Guru is*) *the sign*, etc.

[2] He, *i.e.* Hari.

[3] The thieves are the five: ਕਾਮ, ਕ੍ਰੋਧ, etc.

[4] ਨੀਲ ਅਨੀਲ, a fanciful formation. ਨੀਲ = a hundred kharbs.

[5] The subject seems to be Hari, though no hint whatever is given; perhaps the disciple is meant.

[6] ਸੂਰਤਿ here apparently = ਸੁਰਤਿ.

[7] ਨਿਜ ਘਰਿ, in his own house = in his own heart.

Gauṛī guārērī ; mahalā I.

III.

(1). That mind does not die, which is disobedient.[1]
The mind (being) in the power of the inebriated ones (falls) by dint of folly (into) duality.
(If) the mind be reconciled by the Guru, it becomes one (again).

Pause.

Rām, who is devoid of qualities, comes into one's power by means of praising (him).[2]
Who removes his own self, he reflects on him.
(2). (Whose) mind is led astray, many passions are in (his) thoughts.
(Whose) mind is led astray, on (his) head a load comes.
(His) mind is soothed, who is thoroughly intent[3] on Hari.
(3). (Whose) mind is led astray, into (his) house the Māyā comes.
Hindered by lust he does not remain in (his) place.
Adore Hari, O man, causing (thy) tongue to praise him!
(4). Elephants, horses, gold, sons, women
(Cause) much anxiety ; he leaves the arena, having been overcome :
(Who) is playing in a game of dice with raw stones.[4]
(5). By collecting wealth passions are raised.
Joy and grief are standing in the hall.
Happiness is easily (obtained) by muttering in the heart: Murāri!
(6). If he (*i.e.* Hari) bestows a favourable glance (on any one), then he unites (him) to union (with himself).
He (*i.e.* the disciple) accumulates virtues, (his) vices he burns by means of the word (of the Guru).
The disciple obtains the boon of the name.
(7). Without the name all is the abode of pain.
The fleshly-minded one is foolish, the Māyā dwells in (his) mind.
To the disciple divine knowledge is decreed[5] by reason of former works.
(8). The mind is volatile and continually running about.
To the true and pure one filth is not pleasing.
Nānak (says): the disciple sings the excellences of Hari.

Gauṛī guārērī ; mahalā I.

IV.

(1). In saying: "I, I," happiness is not brought about.
The conceptions of the mind are false, He (only) is true.[6]
All are ruined, to whom duality is pleasing.
That one earns, which is written from the beginning.

[1] ਨਕਾਰ is here apparently a new formation, *not acting, disobedient*, as ਨਾਕਾਰੁ, *worthless, bad*, would not suit the context. The whole verse is so obscure, that the sense is only hinted at, not grammatically expressed.

[2] ਗੁਣਹ, the Formative Plur., by praises = by praising him.

[3] ਏਕੰਕਾਰੁ is here adjective (एकाकार), *having one bent of mind, quite intent on.*

[4] ਸਾਰਿ (Sansk. शारि), a stone used in playing Chaupaṛ, etc.

[5] ਲਿਖਿਆਸੁ; the ਸੁ is a mere alliteration.

[6] That is: *really existing.*

Pause.

The world was seen (by me) engaged in such a gambling.
All ask for happiness (and yet) forget the name.
(2). If the invisible world be seen, then he could be described.
Without being seen he is described to no purpose.
By the disciple he is seen with natural ease,
By bestowing adoration and reflection with one devout thought (on him).
(3). (They are) asking for happiness, (yet) their pain increases.
They string a necklace of all passions.[1]
Without the One (they are) false, they do not become emancipated.
Who continually says: "the creator," he sees (him).
(4). He extinguishes the fire of (worldly) thirst by the word (of the Guru),
Duality, doubt, with natural ease:
(Who) by the instruction of the Guru causes the name to dwell in his heart,
(And) sings in true manner the excellences of Hari.
(5). In the body of the disciple is true love (to Hari).
(Who is) without the name, (does not get) his own place.[2]
Who is devoted to the love (of Hari), is most dear (to the) king (Hari).
(If) he bestow his (favourable) glance (on him), then he comprehends the name.
(6). The illusion of the Māyā is all troubles.
The fleshly-minded one is dirty, wicked and ugly.
(If) he serve the true Guru, the troubles cease.
(Who has) the nectar-name, (he has) always happiness.
(7). The disciple comprehends (the True one), bestowing (on him) one (continual) meditation.
He lives in his own house and is absorbed in the True one.
Regeneration and death he stops.
From the perfect Guru he obtains this wisdom.
(8). (If) I would tell (His) story, there would be no end of it.
Having asked the Guru I saw, that there is no other gate.
Pain and pleasure (are allotted) by his decree and pleasure.
Nānak humbly says: devoutly meditate (on him)!

Gauṛī; mahalā I.

V.

(1). "The Māyā is the second,"[3] so thinks the world.
Lust, wrath, selfishness are perdition.

Pause.

Whom shall I call the second? there is none.
In all is that One Supreme.
(2). (She is) the second (to) the foolish one, (who) talks of two.

[1] The sense is: they carry about with themselves all passions.

[2] ਨਿਜ ਠਾਉ, his own place (of rest), *i.e.* final emancipation.

[3] ਦੂਜੀ ਮਾਇਆ, Māyā is the second (next the Supreme). In the mind of the people the Māyā has a reality, though she is only an illusion.

He comes and goes, having died he becomes (again) a second.[1]
(3). The earth and the sky I do not look upon as two.
All people are women and men.
(4). I see the sun and the moon, the bright lamps.
In all is the dearly beloved youth contiguously.[2]
(5). Out of mercy he directed my mind (to the One).
The true Guru gave me the understanding of the One.
(6). The One Supreme is known by the disciple.
Having destroyed duality he has comprehended him by means of the word (of the Guru).
(7). The order of the One is current in all the worlds.
By the One all creation has been made.
(8). Know, that there are two ways,[3] (but) only One Lord.
Learn his order from the word of the Guru.
(9). All forms and colours are in the mind (of him),
Says Nānak, (who is) praising the One.

Gauṛī ; mahalā I.

VI.

(1). If one does works with reference to the Supreme Spirit, he is true.
How does the ignorant one know the secret of final emancipation?

Pause.

Such a Jōgī reflects on union (with the Supreme),
Who, having killed the five, keeps the True one in his breast.
(2). Who makes the True one dwell in his heart:
He gets the price of the practice of Jōg.
(3). In sun, moon, house and garden is the One.
(Whose) work is to praise (him), they are absorbed (in him).
(4). With one word some ask alms.[4]
(Who is) given to divine knowledge and meditation, (in him) the True one wakes.[5]
(5). Who is absorbed in the fear (of God), does not go forth (from his house).
What is the estimate (of him), who continually devotes himself to meditation?
(6). (Whom) he himself unites (with himself), (his) doubt he stops.
By the favour of the Guru he obtains the highest step (= final emancipation).
(7). Service to the Guru and reflection on the word (of the Guru)
Destroy egotism (= individuality): (this is) the best work (one can do).
(8). (Equal to) silent repetition, austerities, control of the senses, reading of the Purāṇas,
Is the reverence of the Boundless one, says Nānak.

[1] These two lines are very defective, the sense is only hinted at. ਦੂਜੀ must apparently be referred to the Māyā. In the eyes of the foolish one (ਦੁਰਮਤਿ) the Māyā is the second, because he believes in duality; therefore he is subject to transmigration and becomes a second (from the Supreme), *i.e.* he is not absorbed in the absolute substance.

[2] ਬਾਲਾ, *youth, young man* (a term of endearment applied to Hari).

[3] Two ways, *i.e.* that of the Hindū religion and that of the Musalmāns.

[4] The Gōsāvīs, when begging, utter the one word ਅਲਖ.

[5] The sense of these lines is: leading the life of mendicity is of no use, the True one is present in him, who is devoted to divine knowledge and meditation.

Gauṛī ; mahalā I.

VII.

(1). Who lay hold of patience, religious observances, good conduct and contentment:
Them sickness does not befall nor the pain of Yama.[1]
They become emancipated (and absorbed into) the Lord, who has no form nor figure.

Pause.

What fear should the Jōgī entertain ?
In every tree, house and outside (of it) is that (Supreme).
(2). The Jōgī, (who is) fearless and meditates on the Supreme,
Who day by day wakes and devoutly reflects on the True one :
That Jōgī is pleasing to my mind.
(3). The net of death he burns by the fire of divine knowledge.[2]
(His) old age and death is gone, (who) removes his egotism.
He himself is saved and saves (also) his forefathers.
(4). Who serves the true Guru, he becomes a Jōgī.
Who remains absorbed in the fear (of the Supreme), he becomes fearless.
As he is, whom he serves, such a one he (himself) becomes.
(5). (Who) praises the Supreme Spirit, who alone is fearless ;[3]
(Who) devotes himself (to him), saying: O Lord of the friendless !
(Who) sings his excellences : he is no more regenerated.
(6). Who knows, that inside and outside is the One ;
Who by means of the word of the Guru comprehends his own self :
He is approved of at the gate (of Hari) on account of the true word (of the Guru).
(7). Who dies by means of the word (of the Guru), he dwells in his own house.
He neither comes nor goes, his desire ceases.
By means of the word of the Guru the lotus (of his heart) is opened.
(8). Whatever is seen, that is in hope and despair.
The poison of lust and wrath (is in them), hunger and thirst.
Nānak (says): some rare ones are met with, who are of mortified passions.

Gauṛī ; mahalā I.

VIII.

(1). (If) such a servant (of Hari) be found, (to him) happiness accrues.
(By whom) pain is forgotten, he obtains that True one.

Pause.

By seeing (his) sight (his) wisdom becomes complete.
The dust of the feet (of Hari) (is equal to) bathing at the sixty-eight (Tīrthas).
(2). The eyes are gladdened by fixed attentive contemplation.
The tongue (is) pure by the juice and essence of Hari.

[1] ਜਮ ਦੋਖ ; ਦੋਖ = ਦੁਖ, for the sake of the rhyme.
[2] ਬ੍ਰਹਮ has here the signification of ਗਿਆਨ.
[3] ਨਾਉ is here verb (ਨਾਉਲਾ = ਨਾਮਲਾ).

(3). By considering as true in the heart and by serving the inapprehensible and impenetrable (Supreme):
The mind is satiated.[1]
(4). Wherever I see, there is the True one.
Without comprehending (him) the ignorant world is disputing.
(5). If the Guru instruct (one), a clear understanding is obtained.
Some rare disciple comprehends (the truth).
(6). Keep (us) in mercy, O protector!
Without comprehending (thee) we become beasts and goblins.
(7). The Guru has said: there is no other.
To whom else shall I look and worship (him)?
(8). The saints are upheld by the Lord, the cause of the three worlds.
Who knows his own self, he reflects on truth.
(9). The True one is in (that) heart, (which is) the abode of true love.
Nānak says: we are his slaves.

Gauṛī; mahalā I.

IX.

(1). Brahmā became proud and did not know (the Supreme).
The calamity of the Vēda befell him, he repented (of his pride).[2]
By whom the Lord is remembered, his mind is soothed.

Pause.

Such a pride is bad in the world.
With whom the Guru meets, his pride he removes.
(2). The king Bali (was) proud of his wealth.
He offers no sacrifices, (on account of his) great power he is unflinching.[3]
The Guru not being asked (by him) he goes to the nether region.[4]
(3). Harīchand[5] gives presents and acquires renown (thereby).
Without the Guru he does not obtain the end of the impenetrable (Supreme).[6]
He himself (*i.e.* the Supreme) leads astray, he himself gives wisdom.
(4). The pride of the evil-minded and wicked Harṇākhas
The Lord Narāyaṇ is smiting down.

[1] ਅਲਖ ਅਭੇਵ must be referred to ਸੇਵਾ, as: ਅਲਖ ਅਭੇਵ ਕੀ ਸੇਵਾ. The order, in which the words are put, offends against all grammatical connexion.

[2] This refers to the story, that the Vēda was stolen from Brahmā whilst sleeping.

[3] ਅਫਾਰੀ, for the sake of the rhyme = ਅਫਾਰ.

[4] This refers to the incarnation of Vishṇu as vāmana or dwarf. Bali, the Daitya, had gained possession of the triple world, and the gods knew not how to recover it. Vishṇu appeared before him in the form of a dwarf, and asked so much land as he could pace in three steps. This request being granted by Bali, Vishṇu extended so much as to step over the two worlds, but left the third, Pātāla, the regions below the earth, to Bali.

[5] Harichandra, the son of Trishanku, known for his unbounded liberality. He is said to have given his country, his wife and son, and finally himself, to Vishvāmitra. See Vishṇu Pur. p. 372, note 9.

[6] ਆਭੇਵੈ = ਅਭੇਵੈ.

He saves Prahlād bestowing mercy on him.[1]
(5). The foolish and thoughtless Rāvaṇa was led astray.
Lankā was taken (from him) with Sītā.
Without love to the true Guru he had become proud.
(6). The thousand-armed Madhu, Kīṭ, Mahikhās,[2]
Harṇākhas he destroyed with (his) nails.
The Daityas, who did not practise devotion (to him), were killed.
(7). Jarāsandh and Kālajamun were killed.[3]
Raktabīju and Kālanēmu were torn in pieces.[4]
The Daityas were destroyed and the saints saved.
(8). The true Guru himself reflects on the word.
By reason of second love the Daityas were destroyed.
The disciples were saved by reason of devotion to the True one.
(9). The old Duryōdhana[5] loses his honour.
(For) Rām, that creator is not known (by him).
He is consumed in pain, who is the (cause of) pain to (other) men.
(10). He is born (again), by whom the word of the Guru is not known.
How should he obtain happiness, who is led astray by error?
Who errs one little bit, he repents (of it) again.
(11). Kans, Kēs and the infamous Čanḍūru.[6]
(By them) Rām was not known, (therefore) their honour was lost.
Without the Lord of the universe none protects.
(12). Without the Guru pride cannot be eradicated.
By the instruction of the Guru virtue (is obtained), by the name of Hari composure of mind.
Nānak (says): who gets the name, he sings the excellences (of Hari).

Gauṛī; mahalā I.

X.

(1). I may put sandal-perfume on my body.
I may put on and wear silk-garments.
What happiness shall I obtain without the name of Hari?

[1] This refers to the story of Hiraṇyakashipu, the king of the Daityas, and his son Prahlāda, which is so often brought forth in the Granth. See Vishṇu Pur. p. 126, sqq.

[2] ਮਧੁ, name of an Asura, always connected with ਕੀਟ, Sansk. कैटभ; both were killed by Vishṇu. ਮਹਿਖਾਸ, Sansk. महिषासुर, however, is said to have been slain by Durgā.

[3] ਜਰਾਸੰਧਿ, Sansk. जरासन्ध, Nom. prop. of a king of Magadha, father-in-law of Kansa, killed by Bhīma. ਕਾਲਜਮੁਨ, Sansk. कालयवन, king of the Yavanas, destroyed by Mučukunda.

[4] ਰਕਤਬੀਜੁ, Sansk. रक्तबीज, Nom. prop. of an Asura. ਕਾਲਨੇਮੁ, Sansk. कालनेमि, Nom. prop. of an Asura, killed by Krishṇa.

[5] Duryōdhana, the eldest of the hundred sons of Dhritarāshtra, who, by persuading his father to banish his cousins, the Pāṇḍavas, from Hastināpura, became the cause of the great war.

[6] Kansa, king of Mathurā and cousin of Dēvakī, the mother of Krishṇa, killed by Krishṇa. Kēs (= Sansk. केश or केशिन्), name of a Daitya, who was sent by Kansa to destroy Krishṇa. He haunted the forest Vrindāvan in the form of a horse to destroy Krishṇa and his brother Balarāma, but was throttled by Krishṇa. ਚੰਡੂਰੁ (or ਚਾਂਡੂਰੁ, as it is also written in some MSS.) is corrupted from the Sansk. चाणूर, Nom. prop. of a wrestler in the service of Kansa and killed by Krishṇa.

Pause.

What shall I put on, in what dress shall I show myself?
What happiness shall I obtain without the Lord of the universe?
(2). (There may be) a ring in my ears, on my neck a necklace of pearls.
A red cushion, flowers and red powder.
What happiness shall I find without the Lord of the universe?
(3). A woman (may be) beautiful, with expressive eyes.
The very lovely (woman) may make stains and ornaments.[1]
Without adoring the Lord of the universe she is continually unhappy.
(4). (Her) gate, house, palace (and) bed (may be) pleasant.
Day and night she may spread out garlands of flowers.
Without Hari the handsome (woman) is aggrieved.
(5). (There may be) horses, elephants, spears, (and) musical instruments.
Armies, mace-bearers, domestic servants (and) slaves.[2]
Without the Lord of the universe (all these are) vain shows.
(6). I may be called a Siddh, I may summon prosperity and success.
I may fasten a crown, royal hat and umbrella on my head.
Without the Lord of the universe how shall I obtain happiness?[3]
(7). I may be called a Khān, King and Ṛājā.
(I may call out): Hollah, Sirrah![4] (all these) are false plaitiugs (=shows).
Without the word of the Guru (my) affair will not be adjusted.
(8). Egotism and selfishness are forgotten by means of the word of the Guru.
By the instruction of the Guru Murāri is known in the heart.
Nānak says: (I am) in thy asylum.

Gauṛī; mahalā I.

XI.

(1). (Who is engaged) in the service of the One, does not know others.
He gives up the bitter troubles of the world.
By love (to God) the True one is obtained (and in) the True one happiness, O friend!

Pause.

(If there be) such a man who is devoted to Rām:
He, by singing the excellences of Hari, is united (with him), having washed away his filth.
(2). Upside down is the lotus (=heart) of the whole world.
The fire of folly consumes the world.
He is saved, who reflects on the word of the Guru.
(3). The black bee, the moth, the elephant and the fish,
The deer die, suffering for their own deeds.
Absorbed in thirst they do not see the reality of things.
(4). Lust, (which is in) the mind of the lover of the fascinating woman,

[1] ਖੋੜ, *s.f.* (Hindī खौड़), stains and other signs, which the Hindūs make on their foreheads, etc., with saffron, etc.

[2] ਪਾਜੇ = ਪਾਜੀ, a slave (mean man), ī being changed to ē for the sake of the rhyme.

[3] ਸਚੁ, *s.m.* happiness.

[4] ਅਬੇ ਤਬੇ, an interjection, addressed to a slave or menial = Sirrah! the verb (ਕਰਾਂ) is left out.

(And) wrath destroy all the passionate ones.
Honour and respect they love, having forgotten the name.
(5). The fleshly-minded one turns his thoughts on another's wife.
On his neck is a rope, he is entangled in worldly business.
The disciple is set free having the excellences of Hari.
(6). As a widow gives (her) body to another:
(So is) he in another's power, (whose) mind (is absorbed) in lust and money.
Without the beloved satiety is never obtained.
(7). Reading continually books he peruses the Smriti.
He reads the Vēda and the Purāṇas, having heard (their) magnificence.
Without being steeped in the love (of Hari) the mind is clean lost.
(8). As the Čātrik has love to and desire for water;
As the fish delights in water:
(So) Nānak, having drunk the juice of Hari, is satiated.

Gauṛī; mahalā I.

XII.

(1). Who dies in obstinacy, does not come into account (before God).
Who puts on (faqīr-) dresses and rubs (his body) much with ashes:
He, having forgotten the name, will regret it.

Pause.

Thou, O Hari, art comfort in (= to) the mind.
Who forgets (thy) name, has to endure the pain of Yama.
(2). Who is delighted with sandal-perfume, aloë-wood, camphor,
(And) the Māyā, he is far from the highest step (= emancipation).
When the name is forgotten, all is quite vain.[1]
(3). (Who has) spears, musical instruments (and) homage on (his) throne:
(Him) excessive desire and lust enter.
Without Hari being implored (there is) no attachment to the name.
(4). By disputing and pride (there is) no union with the Lord.
Who gives his heart, he obtains the delightful name.
In second love (= duality) there is painful ignorance.
(5). Without money (there is) no traffic nor shop.
Without a boat (there is) no road on the sea.
Without the Guru being served (there is) utter want.
(6). Praise, praise to him, who shows the road!
Praise, praise to him, who lets hear the word (of the Guru)!
Praise, praise to him, who unites to union (with Hari)!
(7). Praise, praise to him, whose this life is!
By means of the word of the Guru I churn nectar (and) drink (it).
The greatness of the name thou givest according to (thy) pleasure.
(8). Without the name how shall I live?[2]

[1] ਕੂੜੋਕੂੜਿ = ਕੂੜੋਕੂੜੁ, for the sake of the rhyme.
[2] ਮਾਇਿ, here Pron. absol., I, Sindhī मां, (cf. ਮੈਜਿ), which is also found as Nom. Sing.

Day by day I continue muttering (it), (I am) in thy asylum.
Nānak (says): those, who are attached to the name, receive honour.

Gauṛī; mahalā I.

XIII.

(1). By him, who is given to egotism and wearing a faqīr's (garb), he (=Hari) is not known.
The mind of some rare devoted disciple is reconciled.

Pause.

By practising egotism the True one is not obtained.
(If) egotism depart, the highest step is obtained.
(2). The Rājās, being given to egotism, run much about.
By egotism they are consumed, they are born (again), die and come (again).
(3). (His) egotism is cleared away, (who) reflects on the word of the Guru.
He gives up (his) wavering mind and destroys the five.
(4). In (whose) heart the True one is, into (his) house comes tranquillity.
Having known the king (Hari) he obtains the highest state (=final emancipation).
(5). By taking the Guru as true he removes his doubt.
In which house should the fearless one entertain anxiety?[1]
(6). Practising egotism one must die, what does he obtain?
(With whom) the true Guru meets, he puts a stop to the contention.
(7). As much as there is, all this is nothing.
The disciple, having fallen in with divine knowledge, sings the excellences (of Hari).
(8). Egotism, putting a fetter (on man), turns (him) about (like a captive).
Nānak (says): by devotion to Rām he obtains happiness.

Gauṛī; mahalā I.

XIV.

(1). Brahmā went first to the house of Kāla (death).
He did not obtain the lotus of Brahm in the nether region.
He was not obedient to the command and was led astray by error.

Pause.

What is produced, that is destroyed by death.
We, (by whom) the word of the Guru is reflected upon, are preserved by Hari.
(2). All goddesses and gods are deluded by the Māyā.
Death does not give them up without service (being performed) to the Guru.
He, the inapprehensible and indivisible one, is (alone) imperishable.
(3). The Sultāns, Khāns and Kings do not remain (here).
Having strayed away from the name they must suffer the pain (inflicted by) Yama.
My support is the name; as thou keepest (me), so I remain.
(4). Not a Čaudharī,[2] nor Rājā nor any one has a (firm) place of residence.

[1] ਤਾੜੀ has here the meaning of *solicitude, anxiety* (Sindhī तारि). Otherwise ਤਾੜੀ signifies: absorption of mind in devotion.

[2] ਚਉਧਰੀ, a chief of a small district, now the head man of a trade.

Wholesale merchants die, who amass property and money.
May to me be given the wealth of the nectar-name of Hari!
(5). Subjects, Lords, head men, chieftains,
None is seen ever remaining in the world.
Unflinching death strikes the fleeting ones on the head.
(6). That perfectly True one alone is immovable.
By whom everything is created, by him it is (again) destroyed.
If he be known to the disciple, then honour is obtained.
(7). Kāzīs, Shēkhs, Faqīrs with (religious) garbs
Are called great men, (but) in (their) body is the pain of egotism.
Death does not give them up without the patronage[1] of the true Guru.
(8). The net of death (is) on the tongue and eyes.
In the ears is death, (as) they hear words of poison.
Without the word (of the Guru) they are wretched day and night.
(9). In (his) heart the True one dwells, (who) praises Hari.
Death cannot overcome (him), (who) sings (his) excellences.
Nānak (says): the disciple is absorbed (in him) by means of the word (of the Guru).

Gauṛī; mahalā I.

XV.

(1). They speak truth, (there is) not a bit of falsehood (in them).
The disciples walk according to (his) order and pleasure.
Freed from all passions they remain in the asylum of the True one.

Pause.

Who dwells in the house of the True one, (him) death does not overcome.
The fleshly-minded one in coming and going is subject to the pain of spiritual blindness.
(2). He drinks nectar, who continually utters the inexpressible one.
Sitting in his own house (= heart) he (*i.e.* Hari) is easily obtained (by him).[2]
By him, who is drunk with the juice of Hari, this happiness is told.
(3). By walking according to the instruction of the Guru one becomes immovable and does not vacillate.
By the true instruction of the Guru he easily utters Hari.
He drinks nectar and churns truth.
(4). (By whom) the true Guru is seen (and who) has received the initiation (into truth);
(By whom) mind and body are offered up and who has gone into his own heart:[3]
He, having known[4] his own spirit, obtains salvation.
(5). The best food is the name of the Supreme.
The true Supreme Spirit is infinite light.
Wherever I see, there is the uniform (Supreme).

[1] ਧੀਰਾ, *s.f.* = ਧਿਰਾ, support, patronage.

[2] Some MSS. read: ਸਹਜਿ ਘਰੁ ਲਹੀਐ, which gives no sense; the right reading (as exhibited by one MS.) is: ਸਹਜਿ ਘਰਿ ਲਹੀਐ.

[3] ਅੰਤਰਗਤਿ ਕੀਨੀ, literally: turning to his (own) heart is made (by him), *i.e.* who has returned to his own heart, has found his own inward self.

[4] ਚੀਨੀ, lengthened, for the sake of the rhyme, instead of ਚੀਨਿ.

(6). By considering the One as true he remains independent (of others).[1]
The highest step is obtained (by him) by worshipping the feet of the Guru.
His mind is reconciled with his mind, egotism (= duality) and error have ceased.[2]
(7). Who, who is not saved in this wise?
By the praise of Hari the saints and devotees are saved.
The Lord is obtained by us, we do not seek another.
(8). The invisible one is shown in (his) true palace by the Guru.
(His) palace is immovable and not overshadowed by the Māyā.
By true contentment error is stopped.
(9). In whose heart that True one dwells:
In their society is the disciple.
Nānak (says): by the true name his filth is done away.

Gauṛī; mahalā I.

XVI.

(1). Whose mind is occupied with the delightful name:[3]
His interview (with Hari) is made so as to whisper into his ears.[4]

Pause.

If thou dost not mutter Rām, (it will be) thy misfortune.
Rām, our Lord, is a donor for ages and ages.
(2). Who, according to the instruction of the Guru, mutters Rām, is a perfect man.
In that one's body sounds the musical instrument without being beaten.
(3). The people, who are devoted to Rām and attached to Hari:
They are mercifully preserved by the Lord.
(4). In whose heart that Hari, Hari is:
Touching their sight happiness is obtained.
(5). In all living creatures the One sports.
The conceited self-willed man wanders again about in wombs.
(6). He comprehends (the truth), who obtains the true Guru.
(Who) destroys (his) egotism by means of the word of the Guru, obtains (him, *i.e.* Hari).
(7). How shall one know the connexion of what is below and above?
The disciple gets (this) connexion (and) his mind is reconciled.
(8). May on me, the sinner and vicious man, favour be bestowed!
O Lord, be merciful to me, that Nānak may cross (the water of existence)!

GAUṚĪ BAIRĀGAṆI; MAHALĀ I.

Ōm! by the favour of the true Guru!

XVII.

(1). As the cowherd keeps (his) kine, taking care of them.
(That) day and night he cherishes and protects them, (is) a stream of happiness to himself.

[1] ਨਿਰਾਲਮ, Sansk. निरालम्ब.

[2] Or: the error of egotism has ceased.

[3] Most MSS. read: ਰਾਮਿ ਨਾਮਿ, (with) the delightful name; one MS. reads: ਰਾਮ ਨਾਮਿ, with the name of Rām.

[4] ਉਪਜੰਪਿ, *p.p. conj.* of ਉਪਜੰਪਣਾ (Sansk. उप + जप्), to whisper into one's ears, a sign of intimate familiarity. The Sikh Granthīs explain ਉਪਜੰਪਿ by: *having approached*, which is against the etymology and a mere guess.

Pause.

(So) here and there keep (me), O thou compassionate to the poor!

Who flees to thy asylum, is favourably looked upon (by thee).

(2). Wherever I see, there thou art sporting; keep (me), O protector!

Thou art giving and (at the same time) enjoying, thou, even thou art the support of life.

(3). The lot falls downwards and upwards without reflection on divine knowledge.[1]

Without praising the Lord of the universe darkness is not passing away.

(4). We have seen, that the world is perishing by covetousness and selfishness.

By serving the Guru the Lord is obtained and the true gate of final emancipation.

(5). In (whose) own house is the palace of the infinite (Supreme), he (becomes) infinite (himself).

Without the word (of the Guru) no one (is) firm;[2] (who) comprehends (it), (obtains) happiness.

(6). What has he brought, what does he take away, (when) the net of death ensnares (him)?

(Like) a bucket, that is tightly bound to a rope, (he is) (now) in the sky (= in heaven) (now) in the region below.

(7). (If) by reason of the instruction of the Guru the name be not forgotten, honour is easily obtained.

In (whose) heart is the treasure of the name, his own self (= individuality) is done away, being united (with Hari).

(8). (On whom) the Lord bestows a favourable look, he is absorbed in the repository of (all) virtues.[3]

Nānak (says): the union does not cease (again), he obtains true gain.

Gauṛī; mahalā I.

XVIII.

(1). (If) by the favour of the Guru one comprehend (the truth), then matters come to an issue.

The pure name, that is in every house, is my Lord.

Pause.

Without the word of the Guru one is not emancipated, reflect and look!

If one do Lakhs of (religious) works, without the Guru there is darkness (in him).

(2). Who are blind and without understanding, what shall be said to them?

Without the Guru the road is not known, in which wise shall one get through?

(3). The counterfeit it calls genuine, (because) it has no knowledge of the genuine.

To the blind one it gives the name of examiner; the time of the Kali-yug is wonderful.

(4). The sleeping one it calls awake, the waking one asleep.

The living one it calls dead, for the dead one it is not weeping.

(5). The coming one it calls going, the going one come.

What is another's it calls its own, what is its own, is not considered (as such).

(6). What is sweet, it calls bitter, the bitter it calls sweet.

Who is attached (to it), it calumniates: such things I have seen in the Kali-yug.

(7). It worships the maid-servant (= the Māyā), the Lord is not seen (by it).

Empty water is churned, (but) no butter comes out of it.

(8). (Who) explains this word, he is my Guru.

Nānak (says): (who) knows his own self, he is boundless.

[1] ਗਿਆਨੁ, divine knowledge, the only sure means of effecting final emancipation.

[2] ਥਿਰੁ, firm, *i.e.* no more subject to transmigration.

[3] ਗੁਣ ਅੰਕੁ (Sansk. गुणाङ्क), the place or repository of all qualities or virtues, an epithet of the Supreme.

(9). He himself is all, he himself exists (in all), by himself (all) is led astray.
By the mercy of the Guru it is understood, (that in) all Brahm is contained.

RĀGU GAUṚĪ GUĀRĒṚĪ; MAHALĀ III.

Asṭpadīs.

Ōm! by the favour of the true Guru!

I. XIX.

(1). Impurity[1] of the mind is second love.
Who are led astray and are erring, come and go.

Pause.

The impurity of the self-willed one never goes off,
As long as he does not delight in the word (of the Guru) and in the name of Hari.
(2). All is impurity, whatever has the form of spiritual blindness.
(Such a one) repeatedly dies and is born again.
(3). There is impurity in fire, wind, water.
There is impurity (of) food, as much as one may eat.
(4). By impurity (of) works worship cannot be made.
The mind of him becomes pure, who is attached to the name.
(5). By serving the true Guru impurity goes off.
(Such a one) does not die nor is born again nor doth death eat (him).
(6). Let any one search the Shāstras and the Smriti and see!
Without the name no final emancipation is obtained.
(7). In the four Yugs the name is the highest thing; having reflected on the word (of the Guru),
The disciple will cross over (the water of existence) in the Kali-yug.
(8). (When) the true (disciple) dies, he does not come nor go (again).
Nānak (says): the disciple remains absorbed (in the Supreme).

Gaüṛī; mahalā III.

II. XX.

(1). The disciple (is engaged in) the service (of him, who is) the support of life.
The disciple keeps Hari in his heart and breast.
The disciple (gets) lustre at the true gate.

Pause.

O Panḍit, read Hari and give up passions!
The disciple crosses the water of existence.
(2). From the disciple egotism departs.
No filth sticks to the disciple.
Into the disciple's heart the name comes and dwells (therein).
(3). By the disciple true religious works are done.
The disciple burns egotism and duality.
The disciple being attached to the name obtains happiness.
(4). Who rouses his own mind, he gets understanding.

[1] ਸੂਤਕ, impurity (by reason of the birth of a child in a house).

(Though) one instruct the people, no one hears.
The disciple understands and (lives) always in happiness.
(5). The self-willed one (practises) hypocrisy and much dexterity.
Whatever he does, that is not accepted (with Hari).
He comes and goes and finds no place of rest.
(6). The self-willed one does (religious) works in great conceit.
Like a heron he sits down, always (sunk) in meditation.
When he is seized by Yama, then he repents.
(7). Without serving the true Guru there is no final emancipation obtained.
By the favour of the Guru that Hari is found.
The Guru is the liberal donor of the four ages.
(8). The caste and brotherhood of the disciple is the greatness of the name.
The daughter of the ocean is destroyed and cast off (by him).[1]
Nānak (says): without the name cleverness is in vain.

Gauṛī; mahalā III.

III. XXI.

(1). Read, what is the religious duty of this Yug,[2] O brother?
From the perfect Guru all brightness of intellect is obtained.
Here and further[3] on the name of Hari is a companion.

Pause.

Read Rām and reflect in thy mind!
By the favour of the Guru (thy) filth will go off!
(2). By disputing and opposition he (= Hari) is not obtained.
Mind and body (become) insipid by second love.
By means of the word of the Guru one applies devout meditation on the True one.
(3). The world is dirty by means of selfishness.
Though it bathe continually at a sacred watering place, its egotism does not go off.
Without having fallen in with the Guru Yama renders it wretched.
(4). That is a true man, who destroys (his) egotism.
(Who) by means of the word of the Guru kills the five:
He himself crosses and makes all his family-relations cross.
(5). The Māyā deludes and practises tricks.
The blind fleshly-minded one clings to her.
The disciple keeps aloof (from her) and remains in devout devotion (to Hari).
(6). The hypocritical man assumes many garbs.
In his heart is (worldly) thirst, he wanders about in selfishness.
He does not know his own self, the play is lost (by him).
(7). Having put on clothes he practises shrewdness.
The Māyā leads (him) astray in delusion and excessive error.

[1] ਸਾਇਰ ਕੀ ਪੁਤ੍ਰੀ, the daughter of the ocean (ਸਾਇਰ = सागर) is the Māyā or visible world, as having been raised from the waters by Nārāyaṇa.

[2] The religious duty of the present Kali-yug is to read = to utter the *name.*

[3] The sense is: in this and in the other world.

Without serving the Guru he incurs much pain.
(8). Those who are attached to the name, are always retired from the world.
Within their house they devoutly meditate on the True one.
Nānak (says): Those, who serve the true Guru, are very fortunate.

Gauṛī; mahalā III.

IV. XXII.

(1). The Brahman's chief business is the study of the Vēda.
From it the gods were produced, spiritual illusion and (worldly) thirst.[1]
Who are led astray by the three qualities, do not dwell in their own house.

Pause.

We are preserved by Hari, (by whom) the true Guru is joined (to us).
Day by day the name of Hari is made firm (in us) by dint of devotion.
(2). The word of the Vēda, affected by the three qualities, is an embarrassment.
Having read a sentence, he (*i.e.* the Paṇḍit) explains it, (but) death strikes (him) on the head.
He does not know the truth, he binds together a bundle of straw.
(3). The fleshly-minded are put by spiritual ignorance into a false road.
The name of Hari is forgotten (by them), (though) many (religious) works are performed (by them).
By reason of second love (= duality) they are drowned in the water of existence.
(4). (The Brahman) standing in need of money is called a Paṇḍit.
Being attached to worldly pursuits he incurs much pain.
The rope of Yama is on (his) neck, death continually distresses (him).
(5). Death does not go near the disciple.
Egotism and duality they put away by means of the word (of the Guru).
Being attached to the name they sing the excellences of Hari.
(6). Māyā, the slave-girl, performs service to the devotees.
(If one) cling to (their) feet, he obtains the palace (of Hari).
Being (thus) always pure he is naturally absorbed (in Hari).
(7). Who hear the report about Hari, they appear happy in (this present) Yug.
To them all bow and do daily homage to them.
Naturally they sing the excellences of the True one in (their) heart.
(8). By the perfect true Guru the word is proclaimed.
The three qualities are (thereby) effaced, to the fourth state the mind is applied.[2]
Nānak (says): having destroyed egotism (= individuality) Brahm is found.

Gauṛī; mahalā III.

V. XXIII.

(1). The Brahman reads the Vēda and explains (its) passages.
(But) in his heart is the quality of darkness, he does not know his own self.
Then he will obtain the Lord, (when) he explains the word of the Guru.

[1] A sharp censure of the Vēda and its study. Polytheism is here put down as the result of the study of the Vēda, which is never done by Bābā Nānak himself, who stood quite within the pale of the Hindū Pantheon.

[2] ਚਉਥਾ, the fourth, the same as तुरीया, the fourth state, *i.e.* abstraction from without and absorption in the contemplation of one's own spirit.

Pause.

Serve the Guru and death will not again devour (thee).
The fleshly-minded are devoured (by death) (by reason of) second love.
(2). Sinful men, (having become) disciples, are accomplished.
By the word of the Guru they are easily gratified in their heart.
My Lord is obtained by them, by the word of the Guru they are accomplished.
(3). (Who) are united by the true Guru, they are united by the Lord himself, (with himself).
Who are pleasing to the mind of my true Lord :
They sing with natural ease the excellences of Hari.
(4). Without the true Guru they are led astray by error.
The self-willed are blind and eat always poison.
They suffer the punishment of Yama and incur always pain.
(5). Yama does not overcome (those who are) in the asylum of Hari.
Having destroyed (their) egotism they devoutly meditate on the True one.
Continually they are absorbed in the name of Hari.
(6). Those men, who serve the true Guru, are spotless and pure.
Having reconciled the mind with the mind the whole world is overcome (by them).
In this wise happiness (accrues) to thee, O my friend!
(7). (Who) serves the true Guru, he obtains the fruit (of his life).
(In whose) heart is the name, he removes from within his own self.
The unbeaten tune and sound he produces.
(8). Who, who is not accomplished by the true Guru, O my brother?
Who is accomplished by means of devotion, he obtains lustre at the gate (of Hari).
Nānak (says): in the name of Hari is greatness.

Gauṛī; mahalā III.

VI. XXIV.

(1). (Who) explains the three qualities,[1] (his) error does not cease.
(His) fetters do not break, he does not obtain final emancipation.
The giver of final emancipation is the true Guru in (this present Kali-)yug.

Pause.

A man, (who has become) a disciple, removes his error (of duality).
Naturally contemplation springs up by devoutly meditating on Hari.
(2). In the three qualities is the dominion of death.
One[2] does not think of the name of the creator.
He dies and is born again and again.
(3). (By the instruction of a) blind Guru error does not depart.
Having forsaken the root (= the Supreme) he is given[3] to second love.
He earns poison and is absorbed in poison.
(4). Considering the Māyā as the root (prime cause) the living creatures[4] are led into error.

[1] This refers to the Vēda, which is affected by the three qualities; cf. Asṭp. xxii.

[2] The sense is: a man, in whom the three qualities rule.

[3] *i.e.* the disciple of such a blind Guru.

[4] ਜੰਤ੍ਰ, instead of ਜੰਤੁ, r being occasionally added by way of euphony.

By reason of second love Hari is forgotten (by them).
On whom he bestows a glance of mercy, he obtains the highest step (= final emancipation).
(5). The True one abides[1] inside, the True one abides outside.
The True one is not hidden, though one try to keep him concealed.
He, who is possessed of divine knowledge, comprehends (him) with natural ease.
(6). The disciple is continually absorbed in meditation on the True one.
Egotism and the Māyā (within him) he consumes by means of the word (of the Guru).
My Lord is true (and) unites (him) to union (with himself).
(7). The true Guru is munificent and proclaims the word.
(Who) restrains (his) running mind and checks (it):
He obtains from the perfect Guru brightness of intellect.
(8). He himself is the creator, by whom creation is made and destroyed.
Without him there is no other.
Nānak (says): some (rare) disciple comprehends (him).

Gauṛī; mahalā III.

VII. XXV.

(1). The disciple gets the priceless name.
He saves the name and is absorbed in the name.
The nectar-name he sings continually with his tongue.
On whom he bestows mercy, he obtains the juice of Hari.

Pause.

Mutter day by day the Lord of the universe in (thy) heart!
Thou wilt obtain, O disciple, the highest step (and) final happiness!
(2). (In whose) heart comfort has been diffused:
(That) disciple sings the True one, the abode of (all) qualities.
He becomes always the slave of the slave of slaves.
In (his) house and family he is always indifferent (to the world).
(3). Some disciple, who is emancipated although still abiding in the body,
Obtains the highest category (= final emancipation).
The three qualities are extinguished (in him), he becomes spotless.
Easily that true Lord is obtained (by him).
(4). He has no fondness nor affection for his family,
In whose heart that True one dwells.
The mind of the disciple is closely fixed (on Hari), he becomes steady.
He knows the order and comprehends that True one.
(5). Thou art the creator, I have none other.
Thee I serve, from thee honour is obtained.
If he bestow mercy (on me), I sing that Lord.
The jewel of the name is honour in the whole world.
(6). The praise (of Hari) is sweet to the disciple.
His heart expands, daily devout meditation is made (by him).
The True one is easily obtained by grace.
The true Guru is gotten by a perfect great lot.
(7). Egotism, selfishness, folly (and) pain are destroyed:

[1] ਵਰਤਾਏ = ਵਰਤੈ, for the sake of the (following) rhyme (ਛਪਾਏ).

When in the heart the name of Rām, the abode of (all) qualities, is.
The intellect of the disciple is displayed (and) the praise of the Lord:
When in (his) heart is contained the abode of the feet (of Hari).
(8). To whom he gives the name, that man gets it.
The disciple, (whom) he unites (with himself), removes his own self (*i.e.* his individuality).
(Who) makes the true name dwell in (his) heart:
He is easily absorbed in the True one, (says) Nānak.

Gauṛī; mahalā III.

VIII. XXVI.

(1). By the fear (of Hari) the mind is with natural ease reconciled with the mind.
By the word (of the Guru) the mind is coloured (in love) and applied to devout meditation.
By the favour of the Lord he (*i.e.* the disciple) dwells in his own house.

Pause.

By serving the true Guru conceit departs.
Gōvind, the abode of (all) qualities, is obtained.
(2). Whose mind is of subdued passions, he consumes (his) fear by means of the word (of the Guru).
My spotless Lord is contained in every one.
By the mercy of the Guru he is met with and unites (to himself).
(3). The slave of the slaves of Hari obtains happiness.
My Lord Hari is obtained in this wise.
By the mercy of Hari the praises of Rām are sung.
(4). Woe to that long life, in which no love to the name of Hari is entertained!
Woe to the comfortable bed of the fascinating woman, it is infatuation and affliction!
Their life is fruitful, whose support the name is.
(5). Woe, woe to that house and family, in which there is no love to Hari!
He, he is my friend, who sings the excellences of Hari.
Without the name of Hari I have none other.
(6). From the true Guru I have obtained salvation and honour.
The name of Hari is meditated upon (by me), all (my) pain I efface (thereby).
I am always joyful and meditate devoutly on the name of Hari.
(7). By meeting with the Guru my body has become clean.
Egotism and all thirst and fire (of passions) are extinguished.
Wrath has become extinct, patience is laid hold of.
(8). Hari himself bestows mercy and gives the name.
Some rare disciple takes the jewel (of the name),
(And) sings the excellences of the inapprehensible and impenetrable Hari, (says) Nānak.

Ōm! by the favour of the true Guru!

RĀGU GAUṚĪ BAIRĀGAṆI; MAHALĀ III.

IX. XXVII.

(1). Who turn away their face from the true Guru, they have the appearance of averse and wicked men.

Day by day they are bound and beaten and do not again get an opportunity (of meeting with the Guru).

Pause.

O Hari, Hari, bestow mercy (on me) and keep (me)!

Join (me) to the society of the pious, O Lord Hari! in (my) heart I remember the excellences of Hari.

(2). Those devotees are pleasing to Hari, who, (having become) disciples, walk in (his) love.

(Who), having given up their own self, serve him, who remain (as) dead whilst living.

(3). Whose the body and soul is, his is the dominion.

How should he be forgotten from (one's) mind? Hari should be kept in the heart!

(4). By the acquisition of the name honour is obtained, by heeding the name happiness springs up.

From the true Guru the name is obtained, by destiny that Lord is found.

(5). Who turn away their face from the true Guru, they are straying about and do not remain stable.

Earth and heaven do not suffer them, they fall into ordure and are consumed (therein).

(6). This world is led astray by error, having fallen into the fraud of spiritual delusion.

With whom the true Guru has fallen in, near them the Māyā does not come.

(7). Who serve the true Guru, they are lustrous, they remove the filth of egotism.

Who are attached to the word (of the Guru), they are spotless (and) walk in the love of the true Guru.

(8). O Lord Hari, thou alone art the donor, thou thyself bestowest the gift and unitest (with thyself).

Humble Nānak has come to thy asylum; as it pleases thee, so release (me)!

RĀGU GAUṚĪ PŪRBĪ; MAHALĀ IV.

Karahalē.[1]

Ōm! by the favour of the true Guru!

I. XXVIII.

(1). O quarrelsome[2] mind, roaming abroad! how shall union with and absorption in Hari be effected?[3]

By a full destiny the Guru is obtained, the beloved comes and clings to (one's) neck.

Pause.

O quarrelsome mind, meditate on the true Guru, the supreme spirit!

(2). O quarrelsome mind, (having become) thoughtful meditate on the delightful name of Hari!

Where account is demanded, there Hari himself will release (thee).

(3). O quarrelsome and very pure mind, filth and egotism have come and stuck (to thee).

The friend is present, the beloved is with (thee) in (thy) house, being separated (from him) thou wilt be struck in the face.

(4). O my beloved quarrelsome mind, seek Hari continually in thy heart!

By no contrivance he is obtained, the Guru shows (him) in thy heart.

(5). O my beloved quarrelsome mind, day and night meditate devoutly on Hari!

Having gone to (thy own) house thou wilt find (there) the pleasure-rooms (of Hari), the Guru unites (thee) to union with Hari.

(6). O quarrelsome mind, thou art my friend, give up thy hypocrisy and covetousness!

The hypocritical and covetous one is beaten, Yama fines and punishes (him).

[1] Called so from the first word, with which these Asṭpadīs commence, see the following note.

[2] ਕਰਹਲਾ, Adj.: *quarrelsome, troublesome.*

[3] ਮਾਇ = ਸਮਾਇ, part. past conj. of ਸਮਾਉਣਾ; ਮਾਇ ਮਿਲਣਾ, *to be absorbed and united.*

(7). O my quarrelsome mind, thou art my life, remove the filth of hypocrisy and covetousness!

Hari, the tank of nectar, is supplied to the full by the Guru; having met with the society (of the pious) the filth goes off.

(8). O my dear quarrelsome mind, hear the instruction of the one Guru![1]

This spiritual delusion is laid out by the Māyā, at the end none will go with thee.

(9). O my beloved quarrelsome mind, by whom the viaticum of Hari is taken, he gets honour.

At the threshold of Hari he is dressed (with a dress of honour), by Hari himself he is applied to his neck.

(10). O my quarrelsome mind, do, what is approved by the Guru, (do) the work of a disciple!

Make supplication before the Guru! humble Nānak (says): he will unite (thee with) Hari.

Gauṛī; mahalā IV.

II. XXIX.

(1). O quarrelsome mind, (having become) thoughtful, reflect, see and take care!

The dwellers in the forest have become worn out wandering about in the forest; by means of the instruction of the Guru behold thy friend in (thy) heart!

Pause.

O quarrelsome mind, remember the Guru Gōvind!

(2). O quarrelsome mind, (become) thoughtful! the self-willed is ensnared in a great net.

A man, who becomes a disciple, is emancipated by remembering the name of Hari, Hari.

(3). O my dear quarrelsome mind, in the society of the pious seek the true Guru!

Having joined the society of the pious, Hari should be meditated upon, Hari, Hari will go with thee (to the other world).

(4). O quarrelsome mind, (he is) very fortunate, (on whom) Hari bestows one favourable glance.

(If) he himself release (one), emancipation is obtained by remembering the feet of the true Guru.

(5). O my quarrelsome beloved mind, mind the light that is in thy body!

By the Guru the name, that contains the nine treasures, is shown, by the compassionate Hari (this) gift is bestowed.

(6). O quarrelsome mind, thou art fickle; give up hideous shrewdness!

Mind thou the name of Hari, Hari! Hari will emancipate (thee) at the end.

(7). O quarrelsome mind, thou (wilt be) very fortunate, having minded the Guru of divine knowledge.

The Guru holds the sword of divine knowledge in his hand, Yama is beaten by death.[2]

(8). The hidden treasure is within (thee), O quarrelsome mind, those are led astray by error, who seek it outside (of them).

(With whom) the perfect Guru, the supreme spirit, has met, they have obtained Hari, the sweetheart, within themselves.

(9). O quarrelsome mind, being imbued with love (to Hari), preserve always the love to Hari!

The love to Hari never ceases by holding fast the service of the Guru (and his) word.

(10). O quarrelsome mind, we are the birds, Hari, the timeless divine male, is the tree.

By the disciple, whose lot is great, he is obtained by keeping in mind the name, (says) humble Nānak.

[1] ਸੁਣਾਇ; it is better to take ਸੁਲਾਇ = ਸੁਲਿ, as the translation: "proclaim" does not so well agree with the context.

[2] The sense is: the sword of divine knowledge, which the Guru wields, effects the death of the disciple, thereby Yama loses his right to draw the disciple before his judgment-seat.

RĀGU GAUṚĪ GUĀRĒRĪ; MAHALĀ V.

Asṭpadīs.

Ōm! The true name is the creator, the supreme spirit.

By the favour of the Guru!

I. XXX.

(1). When this one [1] practises conceit in his mind:
Then this one wanders about foolish and estranged (from God).
When this one has become the dust of all:
Then he, who is sporting in everybody, is known by him.

Pause.

The delightful fruit of humility is tranquillity.[2]
By my own true Guru this (humility) is given to me as a present.
(2). When this one considers this one as bad:
Then all make plots against this one.
When this one has stopped "the mine and thine:"
Then these are no (more) enemies with this one.[3]
(3). When by this one it is thought: "it is my own, my own:"
Then this one is under a great difficulty.
When by this one the creator is known:
Then he is not under any subserviency (to another).[4]
(4). When by this one his own spiritual blindness is cherished:
He comes and goes, being always overcome by Yama.
When by him all doubts are extinguished:
(There is) no difference (between him and) the supreme Brahm.
(5). When this one thinks, that there are some differences: [5]
Then there is pain, punishment and affliction.
When this one has comprehended the only One:
Then all becomes manifest to this one (= to him).
(6). When this one runs about greedy after the Māyā:
He is not satiated nor is his thirst quenched.
When he has turned away [6] from her:
Then the Māyā, turning behind him, rises and goes off.
(7). When the true Guru out of mercy has fallen in (with him):
A lamp is kindled in the palace of the heart.

[1] ਇਹੁ, this one = man, rather a contemptible expression.

[2] No case-relation whatever is indicated in this line, it can only be made out by conjecture.

[3] ਵੈਰਾਈ = ਵੈਰੀ, for the sake of the rhyme.

[4] ਤਾਤਾ, for the sake of the rhyme = ਤਾਤਿ.

[5] *i.e.* between him and the Supreme.

[6] ਜਉਲਾ (or ਜਉਲ) is a substantive, signifying: a sweep off, a turn aside (= ਝੋਲ). The Sikh Granthīs explain it by ਜੁਦਾ, *separated*, which comes near the sense, but is only a guess, as usual. ਜਉਲਾ signifies also (from the same original meaning): *deceit*, *evasion*, as in Asṭp. XXXIV. 7, (compare the Marāṭhī झोल and झोला), where they explain it by ਦੁਖ, pain (sic!).

When the right understanding of victory and defeat is made :
Then the value of this house is perceived.
(8). The One is doing and causing to be done everything
Himself by his wisdom, reflection and discrimination.
He is not far off, he is near, with every one.
He is praising the True one, (says) Nānak, (who has) love to Hari.

Gauṛī ; mahalā V.

II. XXXI.

(1). By the service of the Guru (I) was applied to the name.
To him it is given, on whose forehead (this) lot is (written).
In his heart that one (= Hari) is contained :
Whose mind and body become cool and stable.

Pause.

O my mind, make such a praise,
Which will be of use to thee here and there!
(2). Muttering whom fear and calamity depart,
(And) the running mind becomes fixed.
Muttering whom pain does not again befall (thee).
Muttering whom this egotism (= individuality) flees.
(3). Muttering whom the five become subjected.
Muttering whom nectar is amassed in the heart.
Muttering whom this thirst is quenched.
Muttering whom (thou) art approved of at the threshold of Hari.
(4). Muttering whom crores of sins are effaced.
Muttering whom union (with) Hari is effected.[1]
Muttering whom the mind becomes cool (sedate).
Muttering whom (thou) gettest rid of all filth.
(5). Muttering whom the gem of Hari is obtained.
Him he does not give up again, who becomes familiar with Hari.
Muttering whom some residences in paradise (are obtained).
Muttering whom (one) naturally dwells in happiness.
(6). Muttering whom this fire does not affect (thee).
Muttering whom this death is not overpowering (thee).
Muttering whom thy forehead (becomes) spotless.
Muttering whom all pain is taken off.
(7). Muttering whom no difficulty is brought (on thee).
Muttering whom (thou) hearest the unbeaten sound.
Muttering whom (thou hearest) this pure report (that takes place in the tenth gate).
Muttering whom the lotus becomes straight.
(8). By the Guru a favourable look is cast on every one :
Into whose heart Hari gives the mantra (= the name).
Unintermitting praise (of Hari) is made his food by him :
Who has the true, perfect Guru, says Nānak.

[1] माप cannot here be an adjective (pious, साधु), but must be taken = मांपि (= सन्धि), union, though this form is not any longer in use in Hindī.

Gauṛī ; mahalā V.

III. XXXII.

(1). Who keeps the word of the Guru in his heart:
He gives up the society with the five men.[1]
Who subjects and keeps down the ten senses:
In his heart light springs up.

Pause.

Such becomes the firmness of him:
On whom the mercy and kindness of that Lord is.
(2). In whose (mind) friend and enemy is the same:
Whatever his speaking is, it is (all) of divine knowledge.
Whatever his hearing, it is (all) (hearing) the name.
Whatever his looking, it is (all) meditation.
(3). Naturally he is waking, naturally he sleeps.
What naturally happens, that happens.
Naturally indifference (to the world), naturally laughing (is brought about).
Naturally silence, naturally recital (of the name).
(4). Naturally eating, naturally love.
Naturally all hypocrisy is effaced.
Naturally fellowship with the pious takes place.
Naturally the supreme, unrestrained Brahm is met with.
(5). Naturally (he dwells) in (his) house, naturally he is indifferent to worldly cares.
Naturally the duality of (his) body is destroyed.
In whose mind joy has naturally sprung up:
With him the supreme bliss (= Supreme Being) has fallen in.
(6). Naturally the nectar of the name is drunk.
Naturally the soul is made a present (to him).
Whose spirit is naturally delighted in the tale (about Hari):
With him the imperishable one is dwelling.
(7). Naturally he is sitting and firmly fixed.
Naturally the unbeaten sound is sounded (by him).
(To whom) the jingling sound naturally is pleasing:[2]
In his house the supreme Brahm is contained.
(8). To whom (this) destiny has accrued naturally:
(With him) has naturally fallen in the truly pious Guru.
Who has obtained tranquillity of mind, he knows it.
Nānak, the slave, is a sacrifice to him.

Gauṛī ; mahalā V.

IV. XXXIII.

(1). First they left their dwelling in the womb.
(Then) they were connected with son, wife and family.

[1] The five men are: ਕਾਮ, ਕ੍ਰੋਧ, ਲੋਭ, ਮੋਹ, ਅਹੰਕਾਰ, personified here.

[2] ਰੁਣਝੁਣਕਾਰੁ, the jingling sound, which is said to be produced in the dasvā̃ duār (or tenth gate) by deep meditation, and which is taken as a sign of the indwelling of the Supreme.

(They eat) food of many kinds (and put on) many clothes.
At last they will depart helpless.

Pause.

What is the place, that never gives way?
What is the word, by means of which folly is taken away?
(2). In the city of Indra one must die at last.
In the city of Brahmā there is no eternal dwelling.
In the city of Shiva death will take place.
(In whom) the three qualities are contained, he dies and becomes a goblin.
(3). Mountains, trees, earth, sky and stars.
Sun, moon, wind, fire, water.
Day, night, (their) laws and changes.[1]
The Shāstras, the Smriti and the Vēdas will pass away.
(4). Tīrthas, gods, temple, book.
Rosary, frontal mark, purification, pure burnt-offerings.[2]
Dhōtī, prostration, the eating of consecrated food.[3]
The whole world will pass away.
(5). Caste and division, Turk and Hindū.
Cattle, birds, creatures (produced from) many wombs.
The whole expanse (of the universe), (that) is seen spread out.
All forms (of existence) will pass away.
(6). By praise and devotion easily the knowledge of the truth (is obtained).
Perpetual joy and the true, immovable place.
There the society of the pious delights in the excellences (of Hari).
(Where) the city of the fearless (Hari) is, there it always dwells.
(7). There is no fear, error, grief nor anxiety.
Coming and going and death take not place.
There is always joy in (his) inviolate court.
The devotees dwell (there) by the support of praising (Hari).[4]
(8). The supreme Brahm has no end nor limit.
Who can form an opinion about him?
Nānak says: on whom he bestows mercy:
(He gets) the immovable place and crosses in the society of the pious.

Gauṛī; mahalā V.

V. XXXIV.

(1). Who destroys this (duality), he is a hero.
Who destroys this, he is perfect.
Who destroys this, he gets greatness.
Who destroys this, his pain goes off.

[1] ਬਰਤ (Sansk. व्रत) cannot here signify (as usually): *a religious observance*, but must mean: *a law, a fixed rule.* The rules and changes of day and night.

[2] ਹੋਤੀ = ਹੋਤ (= होत्र), burnt-offering.

[3] ਪ੍ਰਸਾਦਨ ਭੋਗ, thus the words must be divided; ਪ੍ਰਸਾਦਨ is the Format. Plur. of ਪ੍ਰਸਾਦ, food, etc., presented to an idol or holy person, to be eaten, thus honoured or blessed, by the worshippers or disciples.

[4] The sense is: praising Hari is their support, which keeps them there.

Pause.

If there is some such one as destroys and removes duality:
He, having destroyed this, practises the most excellent Yōg.
(2). Who destroys this, he has no fear.
Who destroys this, he is absorbed in the name.
Who destroys this, his thirst is quenched.
Who destroys this, he is approved at the threshold (of Hari).
(3). Who destroys this, he is opulent.
Who destroys this, he is honoured.
Who destroys this, he is a man of subdued passions.
Who destroys this, he obtains salvation.
(4). Who destroys this, his coming (into the world) is of account.
Who destroys this, he is immovable (and) rich.
Who destroys this, he is very fortunate.
Who destroys this, he is daily awake.
(5). Who destroys this, he is emancipated whilst being in the body.
Who destroys this, his abstract meditation is spotless.
Who destroys this, he is very well versed in divine knowledge.
Who destroys this, he is naturally given to contemplation.
(6). Without this one being destroyed he is not approved of,
(Though) he practise crores of (religious) works, recitals and austerities.
Without this one being destroyed regeneration is not effaced.
Without this one being destroyed he does not escape from Yama.
(7). Without this one being destroyed no divine knowledge is brought about.
Without this one being beaten impurity is not washed away.
Without this one being destroyed all is filthy.
Without this one being destroyed all is deceit.
(8). To whom the depository of mercy has become merciful:
He has obtained release, (to him) all perfection has accrued.
Whose duality is destroyed by the Guru:
He is reflecting on Brahm, says Nānak.

Gauṛī; mahalā V.

VI. XXXV.

(1). (If) (one) join Hari, every one is (his) friend.
(If) he join Hari, his mind becomes stationary.
(If) he join Hari, anxiety does not enter him.
(If) he join Hari, he is saved.

Pause.

O my mind, join thou Hari!
None other is of use to thee.
(2). The great, great worldly people
Are of no use to thee, O foolish one!
(Though) thou mayst hear, (that) the servant of Hari is of low family:
In his society thou art saved in a moment.
(3). Hearing whose name crores of ablutions (are made).[1]

[1] The sense is: hearing the name of Hari is as much as crores of ablutions.

In the meditation on whom crores of adorations.
Hearing the tale about Hari crores of meritorious actions.
Crores of fruits (= rewards are obtained) (when) knowing from the Guru the method.[1]
(4). Reflect again and again in thy own mind!
By love to the Māyā thou wilt perish.
The imperishable Hari is with thee.[2]
O my mind, be absorbed in love to Rām!
(5). By whose love all hunger ceases.
By whose love the messengers (of Yama) will not overcome (thee).
By whose love thy dignity (will be) great.
By whose love thou wilt become immortal.
(6). On whose servant no punishment (falls).
On whose servant is no fetter.[3]
At whose office no one asks an account:
His service perform especially!
(7). Who does not stand in lack of anything.
The One himself has many kinds (of things).
By whose favourable look thou becomest always happy:
O my mind, perform his service!
(8). No one is clever, no one is foolish (by himself).
No one is weak, no one is a hero (by himself).
To what one is applied, to that he clings.
He is a worshipper, (says) Nānak, whose lot it is.

Gauṛī; mahalā V.

VII. XXXVI.

(1). As without remembering (the name) life is a curse:[4]
So lives the Sākat (in a curse), having forgotten the name.

Pause.

Who lives one moment in remembering (the name):
He becomes always firmly fixed[5] for lakhs of crores of days.
(2). Without remembering (the name) woe to the works that he does![6]
(Like) a crow his occupation and dwelling is in ordure.
(3). Without remembering the name dog's works are done.

[1] The ਬਿਧਿ, method or way of emancipation, which must be learnt from the Guru.

[2] We have translated this line so, as it stands, though it gives no proper sense. We should rather expect: "Hari being with thee thou art or becomest imperishable," though the words, as they stand, will not sanction such a translation. The verses of Arjun are often so dark, that it is nearly impossible to guess what he means.

[3] ਬਾਨ੍ਹ, a new formation from बन्धु, like ਡਾਨ੍ਹ from दण्ड.

[4] ਸਰਪ, very likely = ਸਰਾਪ (= शाप), curse. ਆਰਜਾਰੀ is to be divided into ਆਰਜਾ, *life* and ਰੀ, which is a meaningless alliteration, as it can hardly here be taken for the interjection ਰੀ (fem.).

[5] ਥਿਰੁ, firmly fixed, *i.e.* not subject to transmigration.

[6] ਕਰਾਮ = ਕਰੈ, for the sake of the rhyme.

The Sākat is (like) the son of a whore, nameless.
(4). Without remembering (the name) (he is) like the horns of a ram.[1]
The Sākat speaks falsehood, (his) face is black.
(5). Without remembering (the name) he is like a donkey.
The Sākat, after being filled (sated) in (his) place,[2] blows make him turn about.
(6). Without remembering (the name) he is a mad dog.
On the covetous Sākat a fetter is placed.
(7). Without remembering (the name) he is a suicide.
The Sākat is low, he has no family nor caste.
(8). To whom he has become merciful, him he joins to the assembly of the pious.
Nānak says: by the Guru the world is saved.

Gauṛī; mahalā V.

VIII. XXXVII.

(1). By means of the word of the Guru I have obtained the highest step (= final emancipation).
By the perfect Guru my honour is preserved.

Pause.

By means of the word of the Guru I meditated on the name.
By the favour of the Guru a place[3] was allotted to me.
(2). What I have heard from the word of the Guru I explain (with my) tongue.
By the mercy of the Guru my speech is nectar.
(3). By the word of the Guru my own self (= individuality) is effaced.
By the kindness of the Guru my dignity is great.
(4). By the word of the Guru my doubt is erased.
By means of the word of the Guru all is looked upon as Brahm.
(5). By means of the word of the Guru the supreme Yōg is performed (by me).
In the society of the Guru the whole world crosses.
(6). By means of the word of the Guru my affairs are accomplished.
By the word of the Guru the nine treasures are obtained.
(7). Whosoever puts his hope on my Guru:
From him the noose of Yama is cut off.
(8). By the word of the Guru my destiny became awake.[4]
Nānak (says): the Guru, the supreme Brahm was met with.

Gauṛī; mahalā V.

IX. XXXVIII.

Pause.

That Guru I remember at every breath.
The Guru is my life, the true Guru is my capital (wealth).
(1). Having seen the sight of the Guru I live.

[1] ਛਤਾਗਾ must be divided into ਛਤਾ, ram, and ਗਾ, a meaningless alliteration.

[2] ਘਾਨ ਤਰਿ; it is perhaps better to take here ਤਰਨਾ as intransitive. The sense is: after the Sākat has got his fill here (in this world), he is afterwards turned about in transmigration, like a donkey, by blows.

[3] ਥਾਉ, place, *i.e.* a firm resting-place (opposed to transmigration).

[4] ਜਾਗਿਆ, awake, *i.e.* it took effect, was realized.

Washing and washing the feet of the Guru I drink (the water, wherewith his feet are washed).
(2). I make continually ablution in the dust of the Guru.
The filthiness of egotism of the several births I remove (thereby).
(3). I swing the fan to that Guru,
By whom, having given (me) his hands, (I am) preserved from the great fire.
(4). I carry water to the house of that Guru,
From which Guru I learnt the wisdom of salvation.
(5). In the house of that Guru I always grind (corn),
By whose favour all (my) enemies become friends (to me).
(6). By which Guru life has been given to me:
His own slave (I am), by himself I was bought.
(7). Who himself has bestowed his own love (on me):
To that Guru I continually pay reverence.
(8). The troubles, fear, doubt and pain of the Kali-yug are removed (by him).
Nānak says: my Guru is powerful.

Gauṛī; mahalā V.

X. XXXIX.

Pause.

Join me, O my Gōvind, give (me) thy name!
Woe, woe to (that) love, that is without (thy) name!
(1). Who puts on (clothes) and eats without the name: [1]
He falls like a dog on the impure leavings (of a meal).
(2). Whatever business (is carried on) without the name:
That is as vain as the decoration of a corpse.
(3). Who, forgetting the name, is given to enjoyments:
He gets no comfort (not even) in a dream, in his body is sickness.
(4). Who, abandoning the name, carries on other business:
He perishes, all (his) plaitings [2] are in vain.
(5). Who in his mind entertains no love to the name:
He, though practising crores of (religious) works, goes to hell.
(6). Who does not adore the name of Hari in his mind:
He is bound in the city of Yama like a thief.
(7). (There may be) Lakhs of things and a great profusion.
Without the name they are vain displays.
(8). That man takes the name of Hari,
To whom he gives it in mercy, (says) Nānak.

Gauṛī; mahalā V.

XI. XL.

(1). Who at the beginning, middle and end brings (me) through:
That friend my heart desires.

[1] ਜੂਠਨ is the Format. Plur. of ਜੂਠਿ.
[2] *i.e.* false pretences.

Pause.

The love of Hari goes always with (me),
The compassionate Supreme Spirit, the all-filling, cherishes (me).
(2). He does not perish nor does he give up (any one).
Wherever I look, there he is contained.
(3). He is beautiful, skilful, clever, liberal to the creatures.
The Lord is brother, son, father, mother.
(4). (He is) the support of (my) life and breath, my capital.
(Who) entertains love (to him), (in his heart) he fixes his abode.
(5). The fetter of the Māyā is cut off by Gōpāl.
He made (me) his own, looking (on me) favourably.
(6). By continually remembering (him) all diseases are cut off.
Meditation on his feet is enjoyment of all happiness.
(7). The all-filling Supreme Spirit is continually fresh and young.
Hari is inside and outside with (every one) as protector.
(8). Nānak says: by whom the dignity of Hari is known:
(To that) devotee the whole essence of the name is given.

RĀGU GAUṚĪ; MAHALĀ V.

Ōm! by the favour of the true Guru!

XII. XLI.

(1). Innumerable wander about seeking (him), (but) there is no end nor limit (of him).[1]
They have become devotees, to whom (he is) merciful.[2]

Pause.

I am devoted, I am devoted to Hari.
(2). Having heard of the formidable road I am overcome by much fear.
I espied the sanctuary of the saints, save me!
(3). He is fascinating, red, incomparable, all-supporting.
Bowing repeatedly to the Guru I cling to his feet: show (him to me)!
(4). Many I made my friends, (but) to the One I sacrifice myself.
In none are any virtues, (but) the store-rooms of Hari are full.
(5). In the four quarters (of the globe) the name is muttered and remembered with pleasure.[3]
I come to thy protection, Nānak is a sacrifice (to thee).
(6). The Guru, having stretched out his arms (to me), has drawn me out of the well.
By me infinite regeneration is (thus) overcome, I am not again overcome.
(7). I obtained the depository of all, whose story is ineffable.
At the gate of Hari (I shall be) glorious, I shall swing my arm.[4]
(8). Humble Nānak obtained the priceless, infinite gem.
By service to the Guru the water of existence is crossed, this I publicly proclaim.[5]

[1] ਪਾਰੀਆ = ਪਾਰੁ, the final word being corrupted to ਪਾਰੀਆ, to get two syllables more.

[2] ਕਿਰਪਾਰੀਆ = ਕਿਰਪਾਲ.

[3] ਸਮ੍ਹਾਰੀਆ = ਸਮ੍ਹਾਰਿ = ਸਭਾਲਿ.

[4] ਲੁਡਾਰੀਆ = ਲੁਡਾਰੀ (1st pers. sing.), the causal (ਲੁਡਾਰਨਾ) of ਲੁਡਣਾ. ਬਾਹ ਲੁਡਾਰਨੀ, to swing the arm, is a token of perfect ease and comfort.

[5] ਪੁਕਾਰੀਆ = ਪੁਕਾਰਿ, part. past conjunctive.

GAUṚĪ; MAHALĀ V.

Ōm! by the favour of the true Guru!

XIII. XLII.

Pause.

Take delight in the love to Narāyaṇ, Hari!
Muttering (his name) with thy tongue ask for the One Hari!
(1). Having given up egotism receive the divine knowledge (imparted by) the Guru!
He joins the society (of the pious), (to whom) it is written by destiny from the beginning.
(2). What is seen, that does not go with (any one).
The foolish Sākat clinging (to it) is consumed and dies.
(3). The charming name always remains.
Amongst crores it is obtained by some (rare) disciple.
(4). Paying reverence to the saints of Hari,
Thou obtainest the nine treasures and inestimable happiness.
(5). Behold with (thy) eyes the saints!
Praise in (thy) heart the name, the hidden treasure!
(6). Give up lust, wrath, greediness and illusion!
(And) thou wilt be preserved from both regeneration and death.
(7). Pain and darkness are effaced from (thy) house,
(If) by the Guru divine knowledge is confirmed (in thee) and a lamp kindled.
(8). By whom he (*i.e.* the Guru) is served, he comes across.
Humble Nānak (says): the world, turning its face towards the Guru, is saved.

Gauṛī; mahalā V.

XIV. XLIII.

Pause.

Saying: O Hari, Hari! O Guru! Guru! my doubt went off.
In my heart I obtained all happiness.
(1). When (I was) burning in heat, I was cooled by the Guru, (as by) sandal-wood.
(2). (My) ignorance and darkness were blotted out, by the Guru divine knowledge was kindled (in me).
(3). The deep sea of fire I was carried across, having ascended the boat of the saints.
(4). I have neither (good) works, nor good conduct nor purity; the Lord seized my arm and washed me.
(5). Destroying fear, removing pain, compassionate to his devotees, (this is) the name of Hari.
(6). Friend of the friendless, compassionate to the poor, powerful, refuge of the saints.
(7). (This is) the supplication of (me, who is) devoid of virtues: give (me) (thy) sight, O King Hari!
(8). Nānak (flees) to thy asylum, O Lord! (thy) servant has come to thy gate.

Gauṛī; mahalā V.

XV. XLIV.

(1). Being given to pleasures and to the enjoyment of the world (I am) blind and ignorant.

Pause.

I amass, I acquire (wealth); (thus) my whole life is spent.
(2). I am a hero, I am foremost, no one is equal to me.
(3). Who is youthful, of good conduct[1] and of good family, he becomes proud in his heart.

[1] ਅਚਾਰ = ਅਚਾਰਵੰਤ; the affix ਵੰਤ (as in ਜੋਬਨਵੰਤ) must also be added to ਅਚਾਰ.

(4). By which (matter) the man of child-like understanding is entangled,[1] that is not forgotten at the hour of death.

(5). Brothers, friends, relations, companions, (who remain) behind, to them he entrusts himself.[2]

(6). To which predominant inclination the mind clings, that becomes manifest at the end.

(7). Egotism, practising pure works, is bound by this bond.

(8). O merciful Supreme Spirit, bestow mercy (on me)! Nānak is the slave of slaves.

Ōm! The true name is the creator, the divine male.

By the favour of the Guru!

RĀGU GAUṚĪ PŪRBĪ; ČHANT; MAHALĀ I.

I.

(1). The young woman is distressed by night, O dear, she finds no sleep.
That woman (becomes) feeble, O dear, that is grieving about her beloved (husband).
The woman has become feeble by grieving about her beloved, how shall she see with her eyes?
Ornaments, sweet tastes, fruition of enjoyments, all is vain, it is of no account whatever.
Replete and drunk with youth, dissolved by pride, no milk comes to her breast.
Nānak (says): that woman comes to union (with her beloved),[3] who without the beloved gets no sleep.
(2). The woman is honourless without her beloved Lord.
How shall she obtain happiness without keeping him in her breast?
Without her Lord no family-life is (possible); ask (thy) friends and companions!
Without the name there is no affection nor love, in the True one she dwells happy.
The true friend is joined by contentment in the heart, by the instruction of the Guru the bridegroom is known.
Nānak (says): the woman, that does not give up the name, is naturally absorbed in the name.
(3). Join me, my friend and companion! we will enjoy our beloved!
Having asked the Guru I will write a message of love (to him) by the word (of the Guru), O dear!
The true word is shown by the Guru, the fleshly-minded one repents (for not having attended to it).
(The mind)[4] that is roaming about, remains firm, when the True one is known.
By thinking of the True one (the mind) is always fresh, by love to the word (of the Guru), young.[5]
Nānak (says): by his favourable look true tranquillity (of mind) (is obtained); join me, O friend and companion!
(4). My desire is fulfilled, O dear, my sweetheart has come to my house.
The woman having met with (her) bridegroom sings a song of joy.
She sings (his) excellences (and) a song of joy, by (his) love she is happy, in the heart of the young woman is excessive joy.

[1] The Lahore lithographed copy reads: ਬਾਧ ਬੁਧਿ ਕਾ, another MS. reads: ਬਧ ਬੁਧਿ ਕਾ, which gives no sense. Another MS. reads: ਬਾਲ ਬੁਧਿਕਾ, which must be taken as an adjective (of a new formation): having the understanding of a child. The various readings show, that the Sikhs no longer understand the passage.

[2] ਸੰਧਾਣੀ, for the sake of the rhyme, instead of ਸੰਧਾਣਾ, as the subject is masculine.

[3] ਮਿਲੈ ਮਿਲਾਈ = ਮਿਲਾਇ, Loc. of ਮਿਲਾਉ, to be united to union.

[4] No subject is hinted at, as usual with Nānak, but according to the context ਮਨੁ is very likely to be supplied.

[5] No subject, nor any grammatical relation is indicated in this line, the translation can therefore only be made by conjecture.

The sweetheart is pleased, the wicked ones[1] are absorbed, by muttering the True one the True one is obtained.

Joining her hands that woman makes supplication, who day and night is steeped in love (to her sweetheart).

Nānak (says): the beloved and the woman dally (with each other); my desire is fulfilled.

Gauṛī; Čhant; mahalā I.

II.

(1). Hear, O husband, O Lord, I am alone in the wood!

How shall I be composed without (my) husband, O Lord, that heedest no person?

The woman cannot remain without her Lord, the night (becomes) very troublesome (to her).

She finds no sleep, (for) love pleases (her); hear my supplication!

Without her beloved she thinks of none, (being left) alone she weeps.

Nānak (says): that woman comes to union (with her beloved), who without the beloved suffers pain.

(2). Who shall take her (to himself), who is given up by the beloved?

With love and affection she falls in, O dear, (if) she be inclined to the word (of the Guru).

(If) she be inclined to the word, she obtains honour, the lamp (of the word) brightens up (her) body.

Hear, O friend and companion, she is happy in the True one, (who) remembers the excellences of the True one.

If she is united by the true Guru, then she is enjoyed by the beloved, she is happy by the nectar-speech (of the Guru).

Nānak (says): that woman enjoys her beloved, who is pleasing to his mind.

(3). Who is immersed in the fascinating Māyā, O dear, she is carried away by guileful falsehood.

How shall the rope on (her) neck be opened without the very dear Guru, O dear?

Who in love and affection to Hari reflects on the word, hers he (*i.e.* Hari) becomes.

Meritorious actions, alms, many ablutions, how should they wash away the inward filthiness?

Without the name no one obtains salvation by obstinacy and tenacity in a desert.[2]

Nānak (says): the true house is known by means of the word (of the Guru), how should duality know the palace (of Hari)?

(4). Thy name is true, O Lord, the word (of the Guru) is the true object of reflection.

Thy palace is true, O Lord, (thy) name is true traffic.

The traffic of the name is sweet, by devotion gain is daily (acquired).

Without this (name) no wares are seen,[3] take the name every moment!

Examine the account with a true look, by a perfect destiny it (*i.e.* the name) is obtained.

Nānak (says): the name is a great sweet flavour; from the perfect Guru the True one is obtained.

RĀGU GAUṚĪ PŪRBĪ; ČHANT; MAHALĀ III.

Ōm! the true name is the creator, the divine male.

By the favour of the Guru!

I. III.

(1). That woman makes supplication, O dear, who remembers the excellences of Hari.

Not a moment she can remain, O dear, without the beloved Hari.

Without the beloved Hari she cannot remain, without the Guru the palace (of Hari) is not obtained.

[1] ਦੂਸਟ, the wicked ones, *i.e.* ਕਾਮ, ਕ੍ਰੋਧ, etc.

[2] The sense is: by practising austerities with tenacity in a desert (ਬੇਬਾਣਾ = Pers. بیابان).

[3] The sense is: without this name all other wares or goods are but false.

(If), what the Guru says, that be done, the fire of thirst is quenched.

That Hari is true, without him there is none other, without serving him no comforts are obtained.

Nānak (says): that woman comes to union (with him), whom he himself unites (with himself).

(2). O blessed and delightful night, (in which) she applies her mind to Hari!

(If) she serve the true Guru and bestow love (on him), O dear, he removes from within her own self.

She removes from within her own self, she sings the excellences of Hari, daily she entertains love (to him).

Hear, O my friend and companion, friend of my heart! by the word of the Guru she is absorbed (in Hari).

(If) she recite mentally the excellences of Hari, she is dear to her beloved, (if) she has love to the name.

Nānak (says): that woman is dear to her Lord, (who wears) on her neck (as) necklace the name of Rām.

(3). The woman is solitary, O dear, without her beloved Lord.

By second love she is wretched, O dear, without the word of the Guru she is disfigured.[1]

Who without the beloved word crosses (the ocean), which is hard to cross? by the infatuation of the Māyā she is ruined.

Spoiled by falsehood she is turned off by her beloved; that woman does not obtain the palace (of Hari).

Who is attached to the word of the Guru, is naturally intoxicated (with love), day by day she remains absorbed (in Hari).

Nānak (says): the woman that is always imbued with love (to Hari), Hari himself unites (with himself).

(4). Then union is brought about, if Hari unite (to himself); without Hari who will bring about union?

Without one's own beloved Guru, O dear, who will put a stop to doubt?

The Guru puts a stop to doubt, thus union is brought about, O mother! then that woman obtains happiness.

Without service to the Guru (there is) horrible darkness, without the Guru she does not find the (right) path.

The woman, that is imbued with love (to Hari), is naturally intoxicated by reflecting on the word of the Guru.

Nānak (says): the woman obtains Hari as her husband by love and affection to the Guru.

Gauṛī; mahalā III.

II. IV.

(1). Without (my) beloved (I am) quite wretched, O dear, how shall I live without my beloved, O my mother?

Without the beloved I find no sleep, O dear, the clothes do not fit (my) body.

The clothes fit the body, when they please the beloved, (and) the mind is applied (to him) by the instruction of the Guru.

She is always a happy married woman, who serves the true Guru, and is absorbed in the bosom of the Guru.

(If) the Guru by (his) word unite[2] (her with the beloved), then she enjoys the beloved, in (this world the name (only) is (true) gain.

Nānak (says): (that) woman is dear to the Lord, who mentally recites the excellences of Hari.

(2). That woman enjoys pleasures, O dear, (who is) with her own beloved.

Day and night she is immersed in pleasure, O dear, reflecting on the word of the Guru.

She reflects on the word of the Guru (and) destroys (thereby) her egotism (= individuality); in this wise she is united with her beloved.

[1] ਵਗਾਠ = ਵਗਾਲ, terrible, disfigured.

[2] The Lahore lithographed copy reads: ਮੇਲਾ, which gives no proper sense. The MS. (2483) reads ਮੇਲੇ, which suits well the context.

That is always a happy married woman and in high glee, (who is) attached to the true name.

If she remain united with her own Guru, nectar is received, she destroys and removes her duality.

Nānak (says): the woman, who obtains Hari (as) her husband, forgets all her troubles.

(3). The woman, (that) has strayed away from her beloved by reason of affection and fondness to the Māyā, O dear!

Has stuck to a groundless lie and is ruined by the guileful falsehood (of the Māyā), O dear!

(If) she clear away the falsehood by remembering the instruction of the Guru, she does not lose her life in gambling.

(If) she obey the word of the Guru, she is absorbed in the True one, she destroys from within her egotism (= individuality).

She makes the name of Hari dwell in her heart, this she makes her ornament.

Nānak (says): that woman is naturally absorbed (in the Supreme), whose support the true name is.

(4). Join me, O my beloved, without thee I am quite wretched!

No sleep comes into my eyes, O dear! I loathe food and water.

I do not like water nor food, I die out of grief, how shall happiness be obtained without the beloved?

I offer up supplication before the Guru, if it please the Guru; as one joins (him), so he is united (with him).

The giver of happiness himself unites (with himself), he himself meets (with one) and comes to (his) house.

Nānak (says): (that) is always a happy married woman, (whose) beloved neither dies nor goes away.

Gauṛī; mahalā III.

III. V.

(1). The woman is pierced with love to Hari, O dear! by the natural good disposition of Hari.

She is fascinated by the heart-ravisher, O dear! (her) duality is (therefore) naturally absorbed.

(Her) duality is naturally absorbed, (if) the woman gets (her) bridegroom, by the instruction of the Guru she enjoys pleasure.

This body is filled with falsehood and untruthfulness up to the neck, it practises sin.

(That) disciple is a devotee, in whom tranquillity and meditation spring up, without devotion the filth does not go off.

The woman, that is attached to her beloved, removes from within her own self.

(2). The woman obtains her beloved, O dear! by love and affection to the Guru.

At night she sleeps in comfort, O dear! keeping (him) in her breast.

Keeping (him) in her breast she is united with the beloved, daily she removes her pain.

Within (her) is the palace, (where) the woman enjoys her beloved, reflecting (on him) by means of the instruction of the Guru.

Day and night the nectar of the name is drunk, she destroys and removes (her) duality.

Nānak (says): being united with the True one she is a happy married woman by infinite love to the Guru.

(3). Come, be merciful, O my dearly beloved!

The woman makes supplication, O dear! she is in love with the true word (of the Guru).[1]

She is in love with the true word, she destroys her egotism, (having become) a disciple she adjusts her business.

In every period (of the world) that one alone is true; who reflects on the Guru, comprehends (him, *i.e.* the True one).

[1] ਸੀਂਗਾਰਣਾ, *v.n.* To be in love with (Loc.); cf. the Sansk. शृङ्गारण.

The self-willed one is sunk in lust, afflicted by spiritual blindness, to whom shall she go and cry?

Nānak (says): the self-willed one gets no place (of rest) without the dearly beloved Guru.

(4). The woman is ignorant, foolish and devoid of virtues, O dear! the beloved is unattainable, boundless.

(If) he himself unite (one to himself), union is effected, he himself is pardoning.

The dear husband is pardoning the vices of the woman; in everybody he is contained.

By love, affection, faith and devotion he is obtained, by the true Guru understanding is imparted.

She remains always in joy day and night, (who) daily continues devoutly meditating (on him).

Nānak (says): easily Hari is obtained as husband, that woman gets the nine treasures.

Gaurī; mahalā III.

IV. VI.

(1). The Māyā is a powerful pond, O dear! how shall the hard to cross be got over?

Make the name of Rām the boat, O dear! put within as rower the word (of the Guru).

Who puts the word into (her) as rower, (her) Hari himself ferries over, in this wise the (pond) hard to cross is got over.

The disciple, to whom devotion is allotted, dies whilst living.

In a moment (her) sins are cut off by the name of Rām, (her) body (becomes) pure.

Nānak (says): in the name of Rām is salvation, the slags become gold.

(2). Women and men are sunk in lust, O dear! the precept regarding the name of Rām is not known by them.

Mother, father, son, brother are very dear (to them), O dear! they are drowned without water.

They are drowned without water, (by whom) salvation is not known, (who) run about in the world in egotism.

Every one, that has come (into the world), will go (again), he is saved (who) reflects on the Guru.

(If one) become a disciple (and) praise the name of Rām, he crosses himself and makes (his) family cross.

Nānak (says): in (whose) body the name dwells, he meets with the beloved (Hari) by means of the instruction of the Guru.

(3). Without the name of Rām no one becomes firm, O dear! the world is a play.

He (becomes) firm by true devotion, O dear! (whose) traffic is the name of Rām.

The name of Rām is an unattainable, boundless traffic, (but) by the instruction of the Guru the wealth (of (Rām) is obtained.

Service, reflection, devotion, these are true: one's own self is removed (thereby) from within.

We are devoid of understanding, foolish, silly, blind, by the true Guru we are put into the (right) path.

Nānak (says): the disciple, (who) takes pleasure in the word (of the Guru), sings daily the excellences of Hari.

(4). He himself causes to be done, he himself does (everything), O dear! he himself accomplishes by means of the word.

He himself is the true Guru, he himself is the word, O dear! he himself is adoring love [1] through all ages.

Through all ages he is adoring love, Hari himself accomplishes, he himself applies to his adoration.

[1] ਭਗਤ ਪਿਆਰੇ may be taken either = भक्ति प्रेम (or प्रीति) or = भक्त प्रिय, attached to his devotees; but the first meaning seems to suit better the context. In ਪਿਆਰੇ final ē is only an alliteration.

He himself is wise, he himself is clear-sighted, he himself causes worship to be performed.

He himself is the giver of virtues, he cuts off vices, he causes the name to dwell in the heart.

Nānak is always a sacrifice to the gratuitous service of the True one: he himself does and causes to be done (everything).

Gauṛī; mahalā III.

V. VII.

(1). Serve the Guru, O my friend![1] meditate on the name of Hari!

Do not go far away from thy heart, O friend! sitting in thy house thou wilt obtain Hari.

Sitting in thy house thou wilt obtain Hari by always turning (thy) thoughts (on him) with natural true disposition.

The service of the Guru is quite delightful (to him), whom he himself causes to perform it.

He sows the name, the name springs up, the name he makes dwell in his mind.

Nānak (says): in the true name is greatness: to whom (this) is written before, he gets it.

(2). The name of Hari is sweet, (if) thou tastest it applying thy mind to it, O friend!

Taste with thy tongue the juice of Hari, O dear! giving up other juices and tastes.

Thou wilt always obtain the juice of Hari, when thou pleasest Hari (and) thy tongue delights in the word (of the Guru).

(If) thou meditatest on the name, thou wilt always obtain happiness, if thou continuest devoutly absorbed in the name.

By the name (one) is produced, by the name one perishes, by the name (one) is absorbed in the True one.

Nānak (says): the name is obtained from the instruction of the Guru, he himself (*i.e.* Hari) applies (one) to it.

(3). These (people), having given up (their own) property, go in the service of a stranger to a foreign country, O friend!

From none other is comfort obtained, O friend! by greediness after worldly things they are allured,

By greediness after worldly things they are enticed, by error they are led astray, how should they obtain happiness?

The service of a stranger is very hard, having sold their own self they lose their virtue.

The fetter of the Māyā is not stopped (= ceases),[2] every moment pain distresses (them).

Nānak (says): the pain of the Māyā ceases then, when they apply (their) mind to the word of the Guru.

(4). The self-willed one is foolish and ignorant, O friend! he does not make dwell the word in his mind.

The error (imparted by) the Māyā is blind, O friend! how should he (*i.e.* the self-willed one) find the path of Hari?

How shall he obtain the path without love to the true Guru? the self-willed one takes (only) his own self into account.

The servants of Hari are always happy by applying their mind to the feet of the Guru.

On whom Hari bestows mercy, he always sings the excellences of Hari.

Nānak (says): the jewel of the name is (true) gain in (this) world, the disciple he himself (*i.e.* Hari) instructs.

[1] ਪਿਰਾ ਜੀਉ; ਪਿਰਾ is the Vocat. of ਪਿਰ, dear, beloved, friend.

[2] ਟਿਕਣਾ has here the signification of: *to be stopped, to be checked.*

RĀGU GAUṚĪ; ČHANT; MAHALĀ V.

Ōm! by the favour of the true Guru!

I. VIII.

(1). In my mind a strong passion (of love) has sprung up, O Lord! how shall I see (thee), O liberal Lord?

O Hari, my friend and companion, O Guru, O divine male, O arranger (of all things)!

The supreme spirit, arranging (all things) is alone Shrīdhar;[1] how shall we, who are longing (for thee),[2] meet with thee?

(Our) hand performs service (to thee), (our) head (is laid) on (thy) feet, in the heart of (us), the wretched ones, is a desire to see (thee).

At every breath (thou art remembered), not a moment,[3] a ghaṛī (or) muhūrta thou art forgotten day and night.

Nānak (says): we are thirsty like a Čātrik, how shall union be effected (with thee), O liberal Lord?

(2). One supplication I make, O Lord! hear, O beloved sweetheart!

My heart and body have been fascinated, O Lord, having seen thy actions.

Having seen thy actions I am fascinated; how should the sad woman be of a composed mind?

(Thou art) a virtuous Lord, kind and young, brimful with all virtues.

(It is) not (thy) fault, O beloved, O giver of comfort, I am separated (from thee) by (my own) wickedness.[4]

Nānak prays:[5] Bestow mercy (on me) and come to (my) house, O beloved Lord!

(3). I offer up my heart, I offer up all my body, I offer up all and shall give it.

I offer up my head to that beloved friend, who transmits (my) message to the Lord.

(By whom) in her own place then is offered up (her) head before the Guru, (to her) is shown the Lord (as being) with (her).

In a moment all (her) pain is effaced, what (her) mind desired, is obtained.

Day and night the woman enjoys pleasures, all (her) anxieties are effaced.

Nānak says: the beloved one is met with, as we desired.

(4). In my heart joy has sprung up, O dear! congratulation is sounded.

The dear and beloved one has come to (my) house, all thirst is (now) quenched.

The beloved Gōpāl, the Lord has joined (me), by (my) companions a song of blessing is sung.

(In) all (my) friends and relatives joy has sprung up, the place of the inebriated ones[6] is swept away.

Unbeaten sound the musical instruments in the house, the beloved one is with (me), the bed is spread out.

Nānak says: naturally the beloved, the giver of comfort, remains united (with me).

---

[1] ਸ੍ਰੀਧਰ Sansk. श्रीधर, the bearer of prosperity, an epithet of Vishṇu.

[2] ਉਡੀਣਾ, Sansk. उदीर्ण, p. p. of उत् + ईर्, *risen, roused, longing* (for).

[3] ਪਲੁ, the sixtieth part of a ਘੜੀ (or twenty-four minutes); ਮੂਰਤੁ = मुहूर्त्त, forty-eight minutes (two ghaṛīs). We have put ਪਲੁ first, though in the original it is placed after ਘੜੀ.

[4] ਘੁਰਿਆਰੇ = ਘੁਰਿਆਰੀ, for the sake of the rhyme.

[5] ਬਿਨਵੰਤਿ = विनमति, a Sansk. imitation.

[6] The ਦੂਤ are ਕਾਮ, ਕ੍ਰੋਧ, etc.

Gauṛī ; mahalā V.

II. IX.

(1). O fascinating one![1] high are thy mansions, infinite thy palaces.

O fascinating one! thy gates are beautiful, O Lord! the alms-house of the saints.

Infinite are (thy) alms-houses, O merciful Lord, (where) they always sing (thy) praise!

(Where) the pious and saints are gathered together, there they meditate on thee.

Bestow mercy and compassion, O merciful Lord! be kind to the poor!

Nānak says: (we are) longing after (thy) sight, meeting with (thy) sight is the highest happiness.

(2). O fascinating one! thy words are incomparable, pure (thy) deportment.

O fascinating one! thou alone carest for the creatures, all the others (are) dust.[2]

Thou alone carest (for them), O inapprehensible Lord, by whom the whole machinery (of the universe) is upheld.

By the word of the Guru thou art brought into (one's) power, O primeval divine male, O Banvārī!

Thou thyself departest, thou thyself remainest, by thyself the whole machinery is upheld.

Nānak says: keep (my) honour! all thy servants (flee) to thy asylum.

(3). O fascinating one! on thee the assembly of the pious meditates, (their) meditation (is directed on) (thy) sight.

O fascinating one! Yama does not come near them, who mutter thee at the end.

Death does not touch them, who with one mind meditate (on thee).

Who with heart, word and deed adore thee, they obtain all fruits.

Who are confused by discharging behind and before[3] and silly, they, having seen (thy) sight, (become) well versed in divine knowledge.

Nānak (says): (thy) dominion is immovable, O all-filling supreme spirit, O Lord!

(4). O fascinating one! thou art bearing good fruit; he is accomplished with his retinue.

O fascinating one! he saves his sons, friends, brothers, family.

The world is saved, (their) apprehension of self[4] is removed, by whom thy sight is obtained.

Who have called thee "blessed," near them Yama does not come.

Thy excellences are endless, endless, O true Guru, O divine male, O Murāri!

Nānak says: who lays firmly hold (of thee), he crosses the world.

Gauṛī ; mahalā V.

Slōk.

(Who) purifies innumerable sinners, (to him) (I am) again and again a sacrifice.

Nānak (says): muttering the name of Rām is a fire, (which) is consuming their sins.

Čhant.

III. X.

(1). Mutter, O my mind, Rām, Narāyaṇ, Gōvind, Hari, Mādhava!

Meditate, O my mind, on Murāri, Mukand![5] the pain (and) noose of death is (thereby) cut off.

[1] According to Sikh tradition these verses are said to be addressed to Mōhan, the uncle of Arjun, who withheld the writings of the former Gurus for some time from Arjun. But the verses are apparently addressed to the *Supreme*, as they can hardly refer to a man, except they contain the most abject flattery, which is hardly credible.

[2] ਗਾਲਿ *s.f.* (for the sake of the rhyme ਗਾਲੀ), dust, the same as ਰਵਾਲਿ, from which it is shortened.

[3] ਮਲ ਮੂਤ (Sansk. मलमूत्र), discharging behind and before (as done in consequence of terror, etc.).

[4] ਅਭਿਮਾਨੁ, here in the sense of ਅਹੰਕਾਰੁ, egotism, individuality, apprehension of self as distinct from the Supreme.

[5] ਮੁਕੰਦਾ = Sansk. मुकुन्द, an epithet of Vishṇu.

The lotus-feet of the pain-remover, the asylum of the poor, of Srīdhar, should be adored!

The road of Yama, the difficult ocean of fire is overcome by remembering (him) for a moment.

He is consuming sins, he is rendering pure, day and night adore (him)!

Nānak supplicates: bestow mercy (on me), O Gōpāl, O Gōvind, O Mādhava!

(2). Recite mentally, O my mind, Damōdar, the remover of pain, the destroyer of fear, Hari, the king!

The husband of Srī (= Lakshmī) is merciful, fascinating the mind, kind to his devotees, eminently accomplished.[1]

The all-filling supreme spirit is kind to his devotees, what is desired by the heart, is obtained (from him).

From the blind well of darkness he rescues (him), (by whom) the name is caused to dwell in (his) mind.

By the Gods, the Siddhs, the Gaṇas, the Gandharvas, the Munis, the men, (his) excellences are sung (with) many adorations.

Nānak supplicates: bestow mercy (on me), O supreme Brahm, O King Hari!

(3). Reflect, O mind, on the supreme Brahm, the Lord, by whom the whole machinery (of the universe) is upheld!

The Lord is full of compassion and powerful, in everybody (he is) the support of life.

He bestows breath, intelligence, body and life, he is endless, unattainable, infinite.

The powerful and fascinating one is fit to be an asylum, all sins he destroys.

All (his) diseases, sorrows and sins become extinct, (who is) muttering the name of Murāri.

Nānak supplicates: O powerful one, bestow mercy (on me), (by whom) the whole machinery is upheld!

(4). O my mind, sing the excellences of the eternal and imperishable one, (who is) higher than all and compassionate.

The supporter of the universe alone cherishes, for the sake of giving, all (creatures).

The cherisher (of all) is very compassionate and wise, he bestows mercy on every one.

Death, the plague, covetousness, spiritual blindness, are extinguished (in him), in whose soul the Lord dwells.

(To whom) God is favourable, (his) service is fruitful, (his) affliction is brought to an end.

The desire of him is fulfilled, who is muttering him, who is kind to the poor.

Gauṛī; mahalā V.

IV. XI.

(1). Hear, my friend, join me, we will make efforts, (that) we conciliate Hari, the beloved!

Abandoning pride and performing adoration we will allure (him) by (some) trick with the mantra of the pious (= Guru)!

O friend, if he has come into (one's) power, he does not give (her) up (again); this is a good manner of the Lord.

Nānak says: old age, death and the fear of hell he removes, he renders that creature pure.

(2). Hear, O friend, there is a good petition (= word), this scheme should be matured!

With natural ease the difficulty is stopped, if a song to Gōvind be sung.

The troubles of the Kali-yug are effaced, the doubt is extinguished, the fruit, that is desired, is obtained,

[1] घिठराष्टिभा must here also be an attribute. The Sikhs know nothing about its signification. It very likely corresponds with the Marāṭhī बिरदाईत, *eminently accomplished*, derived from बिरद, fame, reputation, glory.

(If) the name of the supreme Brahm, the all-filling Lord, be meditated upon, (says) Nānak.

(3). I desire and continually enjoy happiness, the Lord grants my desire.

I am thirsting after (his) feet, I am passionate for his sight, I look in every place (for him).

Seeking (him) I find Hari, the assembly of the saints joins the powerful divine male (to me).

Nānak (says): those with whom the sweetheart, the giver of comfort, meets, they are very fortunate, O mother!

(4). O friend, I dwell with my own beloved Lord, my mind and body are familiar with Hari.

Hear, O my companion, (my) sleep is good, my own beloved has joined me.

(My) error is done away, (I have) naturally tranquillity (of mind), the Lord has become manifest, the lotus has opened.

Nānak (says): (who) have obtained as husband the Lord, the inward governor, (their) happy married state does not give way.

Ōm! by the favour of the true Guru!

GAUṚĪ; BĀVANAKHRĪ;[1] MAHALĀ V.

I.

Slōk.

The Gurdēv is (my) mother, the Gurdēv is (my) father, the Gurdēv is (my) master (and) Lord.

The Gurdēv is (my) companion, destroying (my) ignorance, my cousin (and) full brother.

The Guru is a donor, he teaches (me) the name of Hari, the (initiatory) mantra of the Gurdēv is saving.[2]

(From) the Guru (comes) tranquillity and true wisdom, the Gurdēv's body is the mutual philosopher's stone.

The Gurdēv is the Tīrtha, the pond of nectar, the divine knowledge (imparted) by the Guru is (equal to) numberless ablutions.

The Gurdēv is the creator, taking away all sins, the Gurdēv makes the sinners pure.

The Gurdēv is from the beginning, from the beginning of the world, through all ages is the Gurdēv; taking[3] (his) mantra and muttering it I am saved.

O Lord, join me to the society of the Gurdēv! bestow mercy (on me)! I am foolish and sinful, by clinging to whom I may cross (the water of existence).

The Gurdēv, the true Guru, is the supreme Brahm, the Lord; the Gurdēv, says Nānak, I worship (as) Hari.[4]

Slōk.

By himself (everything) is done and caused to be done, he himself is able to do (it).

Nānak (says): he himself is contained (in all), no one has been or will be.

[1] ਬਾਵਨ ਅਖਰੀ, literally: containing the fifty-two letters of the (Sanskrit alphabet), Anusvāra and Visarga being counted also as two letters by the Indian grammarians. The present Gurmukhī alphabet is called the "Paintī," as containing *thirty-five* letters only. In the Bāvanakhrī here following, no regular order of the letters can be discerned.

[2] ਨਿਰੋਧਰ = Sansk. निरुद्धर, rescuing, saving.

[3] ਤਰਿ is here apparently the p. past conj. of ਤਰਣਾ, used here not without an intended double meaning.

[4] The Guru is here quite identified with Hari.

Pauṛī.

Worship to the Ōm (and) the pious true Guru!
In the beginning, midst and end is the formless one.
He himself is devoid of sensation and dwelling in happiness.[1]
He himself is hearing, he himself is praising.
His own self is produced by himself.
He himself is (his own) father, he himself is (his own) mother.
He himself is subtle (atomic), he himself is big.
His sport cannot be seen, (says) Nānak.

Pause.

Bestow mercy (on me), O Lord, who art compassionate to the poor,
(That) my mind may become the dust of thy saints!

II.

Slōk.

The One is formless and endowed with (all) forms, he himself is without qualities and endowed with all qualities.

The One is to be defined as the One, (says) Nānak, (and) the One is (also) manifold.

Pauṛī.

By the large mouth[2] of the Ōm the forms are made.
In one string he is stringing (them all).
In one by one the three qualities are spread out.
From a quality-less one he appears (now) as one endowed with all qualities.
Making all sorts (of forms or creatures) he produced a dissension.
(By) birth and death the infatuation of the mind is increased.
From both kinds[3] he himself is free,
Who has no limit nor bounds, (says) Nānak.

III.

Slōk.

He is the wholesale merchant (and) Lord, true wealth is the capital of Hari.
Nānak (says): (this) true and pure (wealth) is obtained by him, (who) is with the saints.

Pauṛī.

Sasā (S.). True, true, true is he.
None is separate from the true divine male.
He falls on (his) asylum, whom he puts (into it).[4]

[1] The Supreme is ਸੁੰਨ (= Sansk. शून्य) empty, devoid of sensation and at the same time ਸੁਖ ਆਸਨ, living in happiness.

[2] ਗੁਰ ਮੁਖਿ must here be taken as two separate words and ਗੁਰੁ in its original (adjectival) sense of: *large.*

[3] What are the ਦੁਹੂ ਭਾਂਤਿ? It can only be referred to ਜਨਮ ਮਰਨ, the Supreme not being subject to either as formless. Endowed with all forms he is penetrating the universe and all creatures, which are his sport. They perish again, but not his vital energy in them, which called them into existence.

[4] ਪਾਯੰ, ਸੁਨਾਯੰ (in the following line). It is difficult to say, what these corruptedforms are intended for; we have translated them for ਪਾਇ and ਸੁਨਾਇ. Every grammatical connexion is wanting in these lines, and they can only be translated by conjecture.

Remembering, remembering he sings (his) excellences, (whom) he lets hear (them).
Doubt and error do not in any way enter (him).
(To whom) his grandeur is manifest, to him he is known.
He is a pious man, he comes up (to him).
Nānak is always a sacrifice to that man.

IV.

Slōk.

Why are they crying: wealth, wealth! the infatuation of the Māyā is all falsehood.
Without the name all is becoming dust, O Nānak!

Pauṛī.

Dhadhā (Dh.). Thy servants are cleansed from dust.
Blessed are those, whose mind is delighted (with thee).
They do not desire wealth, they do not wish for heaven.
In the love to the very beloved they are absorbed in the dust of the pious ones.
How should worldly affairs occupy them,
Who do not give up the One nor go to any other?
Into whose heart the Lord has given the name:
(Those) pious ones the Lord is filling, (says) Nānak.

V.

Slōk.

By many (faqīr-) garbs and by obstinacy of mind[1] not any divine knowledge and meditation is obtained.

Nānak says: (on whom) mercy is bestowed, he is a devotee endowed with divine knowledge.

Pauṛī.

Ṅaṅa (Ṅ.). Divine knowledge does not (consist) in words of the mouth,
(Nor) in making many arguments[2] (from) (different) kinds of Shāstras.
He is endowed with divine wisdom, in whose (mind) that one is firmly fixed.
By talking and hearing no Yōg (abstract meditation) whatever is made.
He is endowed with divine wisdom, in whose (mind) the order (of the Supreme) remains firm.
Heat and cold, all is the same to him.
That is a disciple endowed with divine knowledge and reflecting on the truth (= the Supreme),
On whom mercy has been bestowed, says Nānak.

VI.

Slōk.

Āvan (A.). They have come into creation (= this world), (but) without comprehending (the truth) they are cattle and oxen.

Nānak (says): that disciple comprehends, on whose forehead (this) lot (is written).

Pauṛī.

They have come for one (purpose) into the world.
(But) their life-time is deluded by the fascinating Māyā.

[1] The ਅਰੁ does not belong to ਙਿਆਨ, but to ਮਨ ਹਠਿ; so as the words stand, they give no sense.

[2] ਜੁਗਤਿ must here be translated by *argument* (ratiocinatio), Sansk. युक्ति.

In the womb they practise austerities with the head turned down and the feet lifted upwards.
They continually remember the Lord at every breath.
Those, who are discharged (from the womb), are entangled.
The giver (of life) is forgotten from their mind.
On whom the Lord bestows mercy:
By him he is not forgotten neither here nor there, (says) Nānak.

VII.

Slōk.

They come by (his) order, they perish by (his) order, no one is sundered from (his) order.
His coming and going are effaced, (says) Nānak, in whose heart that One (= the Supreme) is.

Pauṛī.

These creatures (= men) are undergoing many a formation in the womb.
Sunk in sweet delusion they are ensnared in the womb.
By this Māyā (and) the three qualities they are subdued.
Their infatuation [1] is communicated to everybody.
O friend, tell me some contrivance,
By means of which I may cross this difficult Māyā!
Whom he mercifully joins to the assembly of the saints:
Near him the Māyā (does not come), (says) Nānak.

VIII.

Slōk.

(One's own) works must be earned, prosperous and adverse (circumstances) are made by that Lord himself.
The animals are given to their own interest (and) to selfishness, what do they earn without Hari?

Pauṛī.

He himself alone causes to be done (everything).
By himself demerit and merit are spread out.
In this age to whatsoever he has applied (one):
Even that is obtained, what he causes to be given.
His end no one knows.
Whatever he does, that also takes effect.
From the One (comes) the whole expanse (of the universe).
Nānak (says): he himself is arranging it.

IX.

Slōk.

They are taken up with women and pleasure—a safflower dye,[2] poison and uproar.
Nānak (says): I fall on that asylum, (where) "I and mine" are destroyed.

Pauṛī.

O my mind, with whatever thou art taken up without Hari, by that thou fallest into bonds.
In which manner one never is emancipated, those very (things) the Sākats do.

[1] ਆਪਨ ਮੋਹ, *i.e.* the infatuation of the Māyā and the three qualities.
[2] ਕੁਸੁੰਭ ਰੰਗ, the safflower dye, a false red dye, that soon wears off.

Who, saying "I, I," are fondly engaged in (religious) works, they (get) an unflinching load.
When there is no love to the name, these very works (bring on) a worse state.
They are bound by the rope of Yama (on account of) the enjoyment of the sweet Māyā.
Deluded by error they do not comprehend, (that) that Lord is always with (them).
There is no escape from (giving) account (of one's deeds), (if one's) fear (of God) be raw (and there be) no accurate knowledge (of him).
Whom he makes comprehend (the truth), O Nānak, the intelligence of that disciple (becomes) pure.

X.

Slōk.

Whose fetters are broken, (to him) the society of the pious accrues.
Who are steeped in the colour of the One, (their) colour is deep, (says) Nānak.

Pauṛī.

Rārā (R.). Colour this thy own mind!
Mutter the name of Hari with (thy) tongue!
None will (then) say (to thee) at the threshold: Sirrah![1]
(They will on the contrary say): Come, sit down! pleasant honour they will give (thee).
In those palaces thou wilt obtain a dwelling.
(There will no more be) regeneration (and) death, they will be done away.
On whose forehead (this) destiny is written from the beginning:
In his house the wealth of Hari (will be), (says) Nānak.

XI.

Slōk.

Greediness is a false passion, delusion enters the foolish and blind ones.
They cling to an offensive smell, (says) Nānak, (who) are in the bonds (of) the Māyā.

Pauṛī.

Lalā (L.). Clinging to sensual objects they are given to enjoyments.
Asserting their own self (as distinct from the Supreme) they are always intoxicated with the Māyā.
In this Māyā they are born (and) die.
As (his = God's) order is, so they do.
No one is deficient, no one is full (*i.e.* by himself).
No one is clever, no one is foolish.
To whatever he applies (them), to that they stick.
Nānak (says): the Lord is always distinct.[2]

XII.

Slōk.

The dear Gopāl, Gōvind, the Lord, is deep, profound and unfathomable.
There is no other unconcerned, (says) Nānak.

Pauṛī.

Lalā (L.). No one comes up to him.
He himself is the only One, there will be no other.

[1] ਰੇਰੇ, an interjection expressing some slight: O thou fellow! Sirrah!
[2] ਅਲਿਪਨਾ = ਅਲਿਪਤ (अलिप्त), distinct, not mixed up with the Māyā and not contaminated by her.

He will be, he is and has always been.
His end no one has reached.
In a worm and elephant he is fully contained.
The supreme spirit is known as manifest in all places.
To whom Hari has given his own juice:
That disciple is muttering Hari, Hari with love, (says) Nānak.

XIII.

Slōk.

By whom the taste of one's own spirit is known,[1] they naturally enjoy the pleasure of Hari.
Blessed, blessed, blessed are those men, they are approved of!

Pauṛī.

His coming (into the world) is accounted fruitful,
By whose tongue the praise of Hari, Hari is uttered.
He comes and dwells with the saints.
Day by day he meditates on the name with pleasure.
That man becomes attached to the name,
On whom the mercy and compassion of the creator is.
His coming (into the world) is only one, he does not come again into the womb (afterwards).
Nānak (says): he is absorbed in the sight of Hari.

XIV.

Slōk.

By muttering which joy springs up in the heart and second love is destroyed,
Pain, trouble and thirst are quenched, in (that) name be absorbed, (says) Nānak.

Pauṛī.

Yayā (Y.). Consume folly and duality!
Having given up this thou wilt sleep in comfort and tranquillity.
Yayā (Y.). Go and fall on the asylum of the saints,
By whose support thou wilt cross the water of existence!
Yayā (Y.). He will not be regenerated,
Who takes the One name and strings it into his heart.
Yayā (Y.). His lifetime is not lost (at play), who relies on the perfect Guru.
Nānak (says): he obtains happiness, in whose heart the One is.

XV.

Slōk.

Within the heart and body he dwells, who is a friend here and there.
Who is taught by the perfect Guru, he should always be muttered, (says) Nānak.

Pauṛī.

Daily remember him, who at the end will be an assistant (to thee)!
These worldly goods last four or six days, every one goes and leaves them behind.
(Paternal) uncle, mother, father, son, daughter,

[1] **ਆਤਮ ਰਸੁ**, the taste or flavour of one's own spirit, *i.e.* that true enjoyment is to be found in one's spirit only, where the dwelling of Hari is.

House, wife, nothing is taken with.
Collect such (things), that do not perish.
Thou wilt (then) go with honour to thy house.
(By whom) in the Kali-yug the praise (of Hari) is sung in the society of the pious:
They do not come again, (says) Nānak.

XVI.

Slōk.

Very beautiful, noble and rich is he who knows the four-faced one.[1]
He is called a corpse, O Nānak, who has no love to the Lord.

Pauṛī.

Ṅaṅa (Ṅ.). He becomes learned in the six Shāstras,
Who is practising drawing in the breath, retaining the breath and breathing it forth.[2]
Divine knowledge and meditation (are equal to) ablutions at a Tīrtha,
The giving of a Sōma-sacrifice, pure (and) untouchable.
In whose heart there is no love to the name of Rām:
Whatever is done by him, that is not durable.
Account better than him a Čaṇḍāl,
In whose heart Gōpāl dwells, (says) Nānak.

XVII.

Slōk.

In the four quarters and in the ten directions (of the globe) those wander about, (on whom) is the mark of doing works.[3]
Comfort, pain, final emancipation, regeneration is written by destiny, (says) Nānak.

Pauṛī.

Kakā (K.). He is the cause of causes.
The destiny, that is written (by him), no one effaces.
Nothing takes place twice.
The creator is not making a mistake.
To some he himself shows the path.
Some one wandering about in the wilderness he makes regret it.
His own sport is made by himself.
Whatever is given by him, that is taken (again) away by him, (says) Nānak.

XVIII.

Slōk.

They go on eating, spending and living luxuriously, (but his) store-rooms are not exhausted.
Many innumerable men are muttering Hari, Hari, (says) Nānak.

[1] ਚਤੁਰਭੁਖਿ, having four faces, *i.e.* Brahmā or Vishṇu. But ਚਤੁਰਭੁਖਿਗਿਆਨੀ seems here to stand for ब्रह्मज्ञानी, knowing Brahm as the one real substance.

[2] The पूरक, कुंभक, and रेचक is practised in Jōg and frequently also recommended in the Granth as a means of perfecting abstract meditation and fixing the mind on the Supreme.

[3] The sense is: whose destiny it is to do works.

Pauṛī.

Khakhā (Kh.). There is no deficiency with that powerful one.
What is to be given, that he gives, (wherever) he pleases, there, there he goes.
(Their) expenditure (and) treasury is the wealth of the name, this is the capital of (his) devotees.
In patience, humility, joy and tranquillity they continue muttering his excellences.
They sport and are happy with joy, to whom he becomes merciful.
They are always wealthy and lustrous, the wealth (of whose) house is the name of Rām.
No grief, pain and punishment fall on them, on whom he has bestowed a favourable look.
Nānak (says): who please the Lord, to them fulness[1] is allotted.

XIX.

Slōk.

Calculate and see in thy mind: at last people must depart.
Hope, that is not lasting, is effaced by the disciple, in the name (only) is health, (says) Nānak.

Pauṛī.

Gagā (G.). Utter the excellences of Gōvind at every breath, mutter (them) continually!
What trust is there on (thy) body? make no delay, O friend!
Neither for the child, nor for youth nor for old age is there any restriction.
That time is not known, when the noose of Yama comes and falls (on any one).
Look at the wise, the meditating and clever one, he is not remaining in this place!
Giving up, giving up (everything), all (the world) departs, (but) the fool (still) clings to it.
By the favour of the Guru he continues remembering (the name), on whose forehead (this) lot (is written).
Nānak (says): they have come (into the world) bearing fruit, on whom the affection of the beloved rests.

XX.

Slōk.

All the Shāstras and Vēdas were searched (by me), no one is saying, that there is another (but the Supreme).
Nānak (says): that One alone is at the beginning, at the beginning of the Yugas and is now.

Pauṛī.

Ghaghā (Gh.). Put this into (thy) mind: without Hari there is none other!
No one has been and no one will be, in every one he is contained.
Thou wilt be released, O mind, when thou comest to his asylum.
The essence of the name is in the Kali-yug a medicinal remedy.
Having spent their time many repent (of it).
How should they obtain a firm standing[2] without devotion to Hari?
They, having stirred up the great nectar-juice, drink it,
To whom it is given by Hari, the Guru, (says) Nānak.

XXI.

Slōk.

All the days are counted and passed, the breath is not increasing, it is decreasing (daily) as much as a sesam-seed.
Who desire to live in error and spiritual blindness, they are fools, (says) Nānak.

[1] ਪੂਰੀ, *s.f.* fulness, *i.e.* everything that is desirable.
[2] ਥਿਤਿ, a firm standing (opposed to transmigration).

Pauṛī.

Ṅaṅa (Ṅ.). Death devours him, who is made a Sākat by the Lord.
In many wombs he is born and dies (again), not having known the Supreme Lord.
Divine knowledge and meditation accrue to him,
To whom they are caused to be given by himself out of mercy.
By calculation and reflection no one is emancipated.
An unburnt jar bursts at last.
They live (really), by whom the living (Lord) is muttered.
He has become manifest [1] and is not hidden, (says) Nānak.

XXII.

Slōk.

Reflect in (thy) mind on the lotus-foot! the overturned lotus (of thy heart) is (then) opening.
Gōvind himself becomes manifest by the instruction of the saints, (says) Nānak.

Pauṛī.

Čačā (Č.). (I have) clung to the lotus-foot of the Guru.
Blessed, blessed is that day, auspicious (this) event!
(I) came, having wandered about in the four quarters and in the ten directions (of the globe).
When mercy was bestowed (on me), then (his) sight was obtained.
Light habits and earnest reflections [2] were done away and all duality.
In the society of the pious (my) mind became pure.
Anxiety he forgets by the sight of the One,
On whose eyes the collyrium of divine knowledge (is put), (says) Nānak.

XXIII.

Slōk.

The breast (becomes) cool, the mind comforted, by singing with fondness the excellences of Gōvind.
O Lord, bestow such a mercy (on me), Nānak is (thy) slave of slaves.

Pauṛī.

Čhačhā (Čh.). (We are) thy lads and slaves.
(We are) the water-carriers of the slave of slaves.
Čhačhā (Čh.). (I) am the dust of thy saints.
O Lord, bestow on me thy own mercy!
Having given up cunning and much dexterity,
The saints were firmly fixed in (my) mind.
(That) figure of ashes [3] obtains salvation,
To whom the saints are assistants, (says) Nānak.

XXIV.

Slōk.

(On account of their) power and tyranny they are much puffed up, (but) in their unsolid body is disease.

On account of their conceit they have fallen into bonds; release (= emancipation) (is obtained by) the name.

[1] ਪ੍ਰਗਟ ਭਏ, the Plural apparently referring to the Lord.

[2] ਚਾਰ signifies here, in contradistinction to ਬਿਚਾਰ, light habits or manners.

[3] ਛਾਰੁ ਕੀ ਪੁਤਲੀ, a figure of ashes = man, made of dust.

Pauṛī.

J̌aǰā (J̌.). (When) he thinks, "I am something:"
He is caught, like a parrot by error (is caught) on a reed besmeared with bird-lime.[1]
When he thinks, "I am a devotee and possessed of divine knowledge:"
Further on (= in the other world) he is not a bit minded by the Lórd.
When he thinks, "I am reciting a story (in praise of some god):"
He is wandering about on the earth like a trader.
By whom his own self is destroyed in the society of the pious:
With him Murāri falls in, (says) Nānak.

XXV.

Slōk.

Rising at dawn of day mutter the name, adore it night and day!
Grief will not enter thee, trouble is cleared away, (says) Nānak.

Pauṛī.

J̌haǰhā (J̌h.). Thy grief is effaced
By occupying thyself with the name of Rām.
Grieving and grieving the Sākat dies,
In whose heart there is another love.
Thy sins and vices drop from thy mind,
(If) thou hearest the nectar-tale in the society of the saints.
Lust and wrath, the vile ones, drop off (from him),
On whom the mercy of the Lord is, (says) Nānak.

XXVI.

Slōk.

Make efforts in many ways, thou wilt not be allowed to remain, O friend!
(Whilst) thou remainest living, adore the name of Hari, Hari with love, (says) Nānak.

Pauṛī.

Ńańa (Ń.). Know for sure and certain, that this causality[2] perishes.
(Though) I make calculation, I cannot count how many have risen and gone.
Whatever I see, that is perishing; with whom should fellowship be made?
Know this precept for certain in (thy) mind: false is the appearance of the Māyā.
Who knows (this), he is a saint, he is somewhat[3] removed from error.
Him he (*i.e.* Hari) draws out from the blind well, to whom he becomes very favourable.
In whose hand the power is, he is able to produce the (primary) causes.
Nānak (says): praise him, by whom the conjunction[4] is made!

XXVII.

Slōk.

(His) bonds of regeneration (and) death are broken, (that) pious man obtains happiness by service (to Hari),

[1] The ਨਲਿਨੀ is a reed or bamboo, besmeared with bird-lime, on which birds are caught.
[2] ਹੇਤੁ (हेतु), causality; the causes, that act in this world, will perish or cease.
[3] ਕੀਚਿਤ = Sansk. किञ्चित्, somewhat.
[4] ਸੰਜੋਗ, as in the Sānkhya philosophy: *the incidental conjunction of things.*

(Who) does not forget from his mind the depository of (all) excellences, the King Gōvind, (says) Nānak.

Pauṛī.

(Ṭ.).[1] Perform thou service to the One, none goes away (from him) unsuccessful.

(If) he dwells in (thy) mind, body, mouth and heart, then, whatever thou desirest, that will take place.

The service of (his) palace is given to him, to whom the pious are merciful.
Then thou dwellest in the society of the pious, when he himself becomes kind (to thee).
Many houses have been examined by me: without the name there is no happiness.
The messengers of Yama depart from him who enters the society of the pious.
Again and again I sacrifice myself for the saints,
(By whom) the sins of any time are destroyed.

XXVIII.

Slōk.

They are not stopped at the gate (of Hari), to whom he becomes very propitious.
Whom the Lord has made his own, those people are blessed, blessed, (says) Nānak.

Pauṛī.

Ṭhaṭhā (Ṭh.). (That) mind does not break down,
Which, having forsaken all (things), clings to the One.
By agreeing with the Māyā (people) die.
No happiness accrues to them in any way.
Who dwells in the society of the saints, (to him) tranquillity accrues,
The nectar-name is tasted by him (in) his heart.
Who is pleasing to his own Lord:
That man's mind becomes composed, (says) Nānak.

XXIX.

Slōk.

Prostration and adoration many times (to thee, whose is) all skill and power!
Keep (me) from shaking, O Lord, by giving (thy) hand (to) Nānak!

Pauṛī.

Ḍaḍā (Ḍ.). This is not (thy) dwelling;[2] whose the dwelling is, know him!
Learn the control of that dwelling from the word of the Guru!
For the sake of this dwelling (man) undergoes (much) labour,
Of which not an inch goes with him.
He has the right knowledge of that dwelling,
On whom the glance of the all-filling Lord is.
The immovable and true dwelling is obtained in the society of the pious.
Nānak (says): those men do not shake (any more).

[1] Here no special letter of the alphabet is put down, but it must be ṭ, the first word (ਟਹਲ) commencing with it.

[2] The ਡੇਰਾ or dwelling is the human body.

XXX.

Slōk.

They do not fall, nor is on any a fetter thrown by Dharm Rāe.

Nānak (says): they, who are connected with the pious, are saved by muttering Hari.

Pauṛī.

Ḍhaḍhā (Ḍh.). Why do you wander about searching? search should be made in this mind.

Who dwells with thee, O Lord, why should he wander from forest to forest?

Throw down the little heap[1] in the society of the pious! self-conceit is ugly.

Ye will obtain comfort and dwell in tranquillity, having seen (their) sight (you will be) happy.

A little heap is born, being born it dies, as a fœtus in the womb it suffers pain.

Who being immersed in spiritual blindness continues to cling to it, comes and goes in egotism.

(Formerly) falling and falling (we) have now fallen on the asylum of the pious people.

The nooses of pain were cut asunder, we were absorbed (in the Supreme), (says) Nānak.

XXXI.

Slōk.

Where the pious are, (there) is continually adoration and praising of Gōvind, (says) Nānak.

There is neither "I" nor "thou;" thou wilt not escape, do not come near (them), O messenger (of Yama)![2]

Pauṛī.

Ṇāṇā (Ṇ.). Success is obtained in battle, if one overcome himself.

(Who) dies fighting with his egotism, the duality, he is a hero.[3]

Who, effacing his egotism (= individuality) dies whilst living (according to) the instruction of the perfect Guru:

He overcomes his mind and is united with Hari, he has the appearance of heroism.

He does not consider any (thing) his own, the One is his reliance and support.

Day and night he continues remembering that Lord, the infinite supreme spirit.

He makes this mind the dust (of) all, these works he practises.

He comprehends the order (of God) and obtains always the happiness, that is decreed (for him), (says) Nānak.

XXXII.

Slōk.

Body, mind and property I offer up to him, who joins that Lord to me.

Nānak (says): error and fear is cut off (thereby), the looking out of Yama ceases.

Pauṛī.

Tatā (T.). Make friendship with him, the depository (of all) virtues, the King Gōvind!

Thou wilt obtain the fruits, that are desired by thy mind, thy burning will cease.

(His) fear of the path of Yama is effaced, in whose heart the name dwells.

He obtains salvation, his understanding becomes bright, in the palaces (of Hari) he gets a place.

No burning whatever will take place, when he himself removes the heat.

Nānak (says): he cherishes us, he himself is father and mother.

[1] The ਢੇਰੀ or little heap is here the body.

[2] From the Sikh Granthīs I could not get any explanation of this difficult passage.—ਜਾਈਅਹੁ, literally: may it be gone!

[3] ਭਾਰੂ, very likely corrupted from بهادر.

XXXIII.

Slōk.

Toiling in many ways they have become tired, (there is) no satiety, (their) thirst is not quenched.
The Sākats, continually amassing (wealth), have died, the Māyā (did not go) with them.

Pauṛī.

Thathā (Th.). Nothing is durable ; why do ye stretch out your foot?
You practise many tricks, acts of violence and frauds, the Māyā alone is (your) scheme.
You amass money, you undergo labour, tired you fall down, O ye fools!
(All this) is of no use to your soul at the time of the end.
You obtain a firm standing, (if) you adore Gōvind, if you mind the instruction of the saints.
Entertain always love with the One! this is true love.
Every affair is in the hands of the One, who is the efficient cause of the cause of causes.
To whatever (state or business) he applies (them), to that they stick, (says) Nānak; the creatures (are) helpless.

XXXIV.

Slōk.

(By his) slaves the One is looked at who is giving everything.
They continually remember him at every breath, (his) sight is (their) support, (says) Nānak.

Pauṛī.

Dadā (D.). There is (only) one donor, who is giving to all.
By giving he never experiences any deficiency, innumerable store-rooms (of his) are filled.
The donor is living eternally.
Why, O foolish heart, is he forgotten (by thee)?
It is not any one's fault, O friend!
The fetter of the illusion of the Māyā is made by the Lord.
Whose pain he himself removes:
Those disciples are satiated, (says) Nānak.

XXXV.

Slōk.

Hold and support, O soul, is the One; give thou up other hope!
If the name be meditated upon, (says) Nānak, thy affair will be right.

Pauṛī.

Dhadhā (Dh.). Running activity is then stopped, if (one) take up his abode with the saints.
When he himself in person bestows mercy, then light is made in the heart.
(This) is true wealth, those are true great merchants:
(Who) have the capital of Hari and faith in the name.
Composure, glory and lustre are given to him,
Who hears the name of Hari with his ears.
In whose heart he (*i.e.* Hari) is contained:
That disciple obtains greatness, (says) Nānak.

XXXVI.

Slōk.

Nānak (says): (By whom) the name, the name is muttered, he has pleasure inside and outside.
By the perfect Guru the instruction is given, (that there is) no hell in the society of the pious.

Pauṛī.

Nanā (N.). Those do not fall into hell,
In whose heart and body the name dwells.
The disciples, who are muttering the name, the hidden treasure,
Are not consumed in the Māyā, the baneful thing.
No refusal (at the gate of Hari) is made to him,
To whom the mantra of the name is given by the Guru.
The depositories and treasuries of Hari are filled with nectar.
There sound the musical instruments without being beaten, (says) Nānak.

XXXVII.

Slōk.

(Thy) honour is preserved by the Guru, the supreme Brahm; give up worldly engagements and illusion, the disease!

Nānak (says): he should be adored, who has no end nor limit.

Pauṛī.

Papā (P.). No estimate nor limit (of him) is obtained.
Hari, the king, the purifier of the sinners, is unattainable.
He becomes cleansed from cores of sins,
Who is muttering the nectar-name in the society of the pious.
Deceit, mischievousness, spiritual blindness is blotted out (in him),
Whom the Lord himself protects.
He is king with an umbrella over his head.
There is no other, (says) Nānak.

XXXVIII.

Slōk.

The nooses (of Yama) are cut, transmigrations are effaced, victory is obtained by overcoming the mind.

Nānak (says): from the Guru a firm standing is obtained, wandering about (in transmigration) is for ever done away.

Pauṛī.

Phaphā (Ph.). Wandering and wandering about thou hast come (into this world).
Thou hast obtained in the Kali-yug a (human) body, which is hard to get.
Again this opportunity does not come to hand.
Mutter the name, then the noose (of Yama) is cut off.
There will not be coming and going again and again.
Mutter alone the One, that is (true) muttering.
O Lord creator, bestow mercy (on me)!
Unite the helpless Nānak (with thee)!

XXXIX.

Slōk.

Hear (my) supplication, O supreme Brahm, O Gōpāl, who art merciful to the poor!

Happiness, prosperity and much enjoyment of pleasures (accrue to him, who is) the dust of the pious, (says) Nānak.

Pauṛī.

Babā (B.). Who know Brahm, they are Brāhmans.
They are Vaishnavas, who are disciples (and) of pure practices.
He is a hero, who clears away his own ill conduct.
Him harm will not approach.
He is bound by the fetter of his own egotism,
(And yet) the blind one blames his former deeds.[1]
All talk and cunning is stopped.
Whom he (= Hari) lets know it, he knows it, (says) Nānak.

XL.

Slōk.

(Their) fear he is breaking, (their) sins and pain he is destroying, who adore Hari in (their) mind.
Whose heart dwells with the saints, they do not err, (says) Nānak.

Pauṛī.

Clear away thy own error!
This whole world is (but) a dream.
In error are the Suras, the Dēvīs and Dēvas.
In error are the Siddhs, the ascetics and the Brahmās.
By error the men are deceived.
This Māyā is hard to cross and very difficult.
By whom his error, fear and illusion are cleared away:
That disciple obtains the highest happiness, (says) Nānak.

XLI.

Slōk.

(On account of) the Māyā the mind staggers, it clings to her in many ways.
Whom thou keepest from asking (for her), he delights in the name, (says) Nānak.

Pauṛī.

Mamā (M.). Who is asking, is foolish.
The donor continues giving, he is very wise.
What is given, that (is given) once.
O foolish heart, why art thou crying out?
When thou askest, thou askest for other (things),
From which happiness has not accrued to any one.
If thou ask for anything, then ask for the One,
By whom thou wilt cross over,[2] (says) Nānak.

XLII.

Slōk.

(Their) wisdom is perfect, those are foremost, in whose heart the mantra of the perfect Guru is.
Who have known their own Lord, those are happy, (says) Nānak.

[1] ਆਗਹੁ ਕਉ, literally: what was formerly (done by him, in a former birth). Another MS. (No. 2484) reads: ਆਪ ਕਉ, he blames himself, which seems to be a mistake.

[2] ਪਰਹਿ ਪਰਾਗ; ਪਰਾਗ is here only a corruption for ਪਾਰਿ, over, to the other side, to make up the rhyme.

Pauṛī.

Mamā (M.). By whom the secret is known :
He, meeting with the pious, believes (in it),
Pain and happiness are considered by him as the same.
He is an Avatār-like man[1] free from hell and heaven.
With him, with him the undefiled one
Is the eminent divine male, that is omnipresent in everybody.
(He lives) in enjoyment, he obtains happiness,
(Who) is not defiled by that Māyā, (says) Nānak.

XLIII.

Slōk.

O friend, without the beloved Hari there is no emancipation.
Nānak (says): his bonds are cut asunder, who falls down at the feet of the Guru.

Pauṛī.

Yayā (Y.). (Though) one be making efforts in many ways,
When is he accomplished (= saved) without the One name ?
He, by making efforts, gains emancipation,
(Whose) efforts (are made for) that society of the pious.[2]
This appearance every one assumes.
(But) without muttering it (*i.e.* the name) salvation is not effected.
He is crossing (himself) and able to make (others) cross,
Whom the king, who is void of the (three) qualities, protects.
Whom he himself instructs in heart, word and deed:
His wisdom becomes manifest, (says) Nānak.

XLIV.

Slōk.

Do not be angry with any one, reflect on thy own self!
Remain humble in the world! by his favourable look (thou wilt get) across.

Pauṛī.

Rarā (R.). Becoming the dust of every place,
Thy remaining account is settled, having given up thy individuality.
In battle (and) at the threshold (of Hari) thou wilt then be successful, O brother,
When thou meditatest devoutly on the name of Rām, O disciple!
Losing their power, losing their power the passions subside,
By the exceedingly great word of the perfect Guru.
They are steeped in love and intoxicated by the juice of the name,
To whom Hari the Guru has given (this) gift, (says) Nānak.

[1] ਅਉਤਾਰ, an Avatar = a pious man.

[2] The sense is: who makes efforts to obtain that society of the pious. The passage is very obscure and perplexing.

XLV.

Slōk.

Covetousness is falsehood (= unreality), worldly objects disease; in this (human) body is (their) dwelling.

The disciple drinks the nectar of Hari, Hari and dwells in comfort, (says) Nānak.

Pauṛī.

Lalā (L.). To whom he (Hari) applies medicine :
His pain and ache are cleared away in a moment.
In whose heart the medicine of the name works beneficially :
Him no sickness befalls (even) in a dream.
Hari is the medicine for everybody, O brother!
(But) without the perfect Guru the (right) proceeding is not made.
When by the perfect Guru the restriction (of the passions) is made :
Then no pain is coming on again, (says) Nānak.

XLVI.

Slōk.

Vasudēv is in all, he is not deficient in any place.
Inside and outside he is with (every one), why should one conceal himself? (says) Nānak.

Pauṛī.

Vavā (V.). Enmity should not be made with any one!
Within everybody Brahm is contained.
Vasudēv sports in water and on land.
By the favour of the Guru he is known [1] by some rare one.
Enmity and hostility are effaced from the mind of those disciples,
Who are hearing the praise of Hari.
From caste and mark, from all are those disciples free,
Who say : Hari, Hari! (says) Nānak.

XLVII.

Slōk.

Saying: "I, I" (their life) is passed, the Sākats are foolish and ignorant.
In palpitation they die like thirsty ones, they earn their works, (says) Nānak.

Pauṛī.

Ṛāṛā (Ṛ.). (His) contention is stopped in the society of the pious,
(Who practises) religious works (and) adores the true name.
In whose heart the beautiful [2] (= Hari) dwells :
His (inward) contention is extinguished and destroyed.
The ignorant Sākat is making contention,
In whose heart is the disease of self-apprehension.[3]
The (inward) contention of the disciple is effaced.
In a moment, (says) Nānak, he comprehends (the truth).

[1] ਗਇਆ = Sansk. गत, known.

[2] ਰੂੜਾ (Hindī रूड़ा) signifies: *beautiful*; an epithet of Hari.

[3] ਅਹੰਬੁਧਿ, apprehension of self as distinct from the Supreme. This is called a ਬਿਕਾਰ or disease.

XLVIII.

Slōk.

O mind, seize the protection of the pious, give up contrivances and cunning!
In whose mind dwells complete devotion to the Guru, on (his) forehead a (good) destiny (is written).

Pauṛī.

Sasā (S.): Being worn out (we) have now fallen on (thy) asylum.
The Shāstras, the Smriti, the Vēdas declare it loudly:
—Searching and searching sift thou (also) (this) thought!—
"Without adoring Hari there is no emancipation."
At every breath we are erring.
Thou art powerful, incalculable and boundless.
O merciful one, keep (the honour) of him, who has fallen on (thy) asylum!
We are (thy) children, O Gōpāl, (says) Nānak.

XLIX.

Slōk.

When egotism is extinct, then happiness is obtained, mind and body become free from disease.
Nānak (says): he comes into sight, who is worthy to be praised.

Pauṛī.

Khakhā (Kh.). Standing praise him,
Who in a moment makes brimful that, which is not quite full.
(If) a man is becoming quite humble,
He, being freed from the bonds of matter, mutters daily the Lord.
(If) it pleases the Lord, he gives him happiness.
The supreme Brahm is so unmeasurable,
Innumerable sins he is pardoning in a moment.
Nānak (says): the Lord is always merciful.

L.

Slōk.

I speak truth, hear, O my mind, fall on the asylum of Hari the king!
Give up all contrivance and cunning, (says) Nānak, he will absorb (thee).

Pauṛī.

Sasā (S.). O foolish one, give up cunning!
By skill and command (of men) the Lord is not swayed.
Thou practisest a thousand kinds of cunning,
But not one will go with thee.
Mutter him, him day and night,
O soul, who will go with thee.
Whom he himself applies to the service of the pious:
Him no pain enters, (says) Nānak.

LI.

Slōk.

Hari, Hari should be uttered with the mouth, by his indwelling in the mind happiness is obtained.
Nānak (says): in all he is contained, in every place is he.

Pauṛī.

Behold, in the bodies of all the Lord is fully present.

Continually (men) go and return, the breaker of (this) pain (of transmigration) is the knowledge (imparted by) the Guru.

(Who) is freed from his own self, to him happiness accrues; (in whom) is (no more) his own self, in him is he himself.

The pain of regeneration and death is cut off by the power of the society of the saints.

The merciful one makes firm the name out of benevolence (to them).

To the saints he is kind.

By none other anything is done.

All is done by the Lord, (says) Nānak.

LII.

Slōk.

One never gets free from the account,[1] every moment (we are) erring.

(But) the forgiver is forgiving, (says) Nānak, and brings across.

Pauṛī.

(Man) is untrue to his salt, sinful, estranged (from God), of little understanding.

(By whom) soul, body and comforts are given, him he does not consider as true.

For the sake of profit and the Māyā he goes about searching in the ten directions (of the globe).

The Lord, the liberal donor, he does not let dwell in his mind for a moment.

By covetousness, the false passion, he is deluded, wealth is in his mind.

With lechers, thieves, great revilers he spends his time.

If it pleases thee, then thou pardonest the bad ones with the good.

Nānak (says): if it pleases the supreme Brahm, a stone (even) swims on the water.

LIII.

Slōk.

They eat, drink, sport and laugh, (but) must wander about in many births.

Draw (me) out from the water of existence, O Lord! Nānak relies on thee.

Pauṛī.

Sporting continually they come, (but) incur pain in many wombs.

By meeting with the pious (their) pain is effaced, by means of the word of the true Guru they are absorbed (in the Supreme).

(By whom) meek endurance is laid hold of, the True one is acquired and the nectar-name drunk:

(To them) the mercy of the Lord is insured, joy, happiness and rest.

(Their) trading-trip is successfully accomplished, (they gain) much profit, with honour they come home.

True consolation is given by the Guru; having come they are united with the Lord.

He himself is doing his own work, he himself is before and after.

Nānak (says): he should be praised, who is continually contained in everybody.

[1] The sense is: we have always to account for trespasses.

LIV.

Slōk.

(We) have come to the asylum of the Lord, the depository of mercy, the kind one.

In whose mind the one word "Hari" dwells, he becomes happy.

Pauṛī.

In (= by) a word the three worlds are upheld by the Lord.

Uttering words the Vēdas are reflected upon.

The Shāstras, Smriti and Purāṇas (are) words.

Sounds, recitals (of holy stories), praises (are) words.

Emancipation, devotion, fear, error (are) words.

The performance of actions and pure rites (are) words.

As much as there is seen, (so many) words (there are).

But the supreme Brahm is not couched (in words), says Nānak.

LV.

Slōk.

In (thy) hand is a pen, recondite (is) (thy) writing on the forehead.

Every one is taken up with (thy) incomparable, beautiful (writing).

Thy praise cannot be told with the mouth.

I, having seen (thy) sight, am a sacrifice (to thee), (says) Nānak.

Pauṛī.

O eternal, imperishable supreme Brahm, destroyer of sins!

O omnipresent one, O remover of pain in all, O depository of virtues!

O thou who art with all, O formless one, O support of all who are destitute of virtue!

O Gōvind, O abode of virtues, with whom (there is) always discrimination.

O boundless Hari, Hari, (who) art and wilt be!

O thou, who art always with (thy) saints, the support of the helpless!

O Lord, I am thy slave, I, the void of virtue, have no virtue whatever.

May (thy) name be given as a present to Nānak, (that) I may string it (like pearls) and keep it in my heart!

Slōk.

The Gurdēv[1] is my mother, the Gurdēv is my father, the Gurdēv is the Lord, the supreme Lord.

The Gurdēv is my companion, destroying (my) ignorance, the Gurdēv is my relative and full brother.

The Gurdēv is beautiful, he teaches the name of Hari, the mantra of the Gurdēv is saving.

The Gurdēv is tranquillity, the body of true wisdom, the Gurdēv is the mutual philosopher's stone.

The Gurdēv is the Tīrtha, the pond of nectar, the Gurdēv is infinite ablutions.

The Gurdēv is the creator, the remover of all sins, the Gurdēv is purifying the sinners.

The Gurdēv is at the beginning, at the beginning of the Yuga and through all the Yugas, muttering the mantra of the Gurdēv Hari I am saved.

O Gurdēv, O Lord, join (me) to the society (of the pious), bestow mercy (on me), I am foolish and sinful, clinging to which (society) I shall be saved!

The Gurdēv, the true Guru, is the supreme Brahm, the Lord God, the Gurdēv Hari, (says) Nānak, I worship.

[This Slōk is to be read at the beginning and at the end (of the Bāvanakhṛī).]

[1] The Gurdēv, *i.e.* the (human) Guru is here, as so often in the Granth, completely identified with the supreme Lord.

GAUṚĪ; SUKHMANĪ;[1] MAHALĀ V.

Ōm! by the favour of the true Guru!

I.

Slōk.

Worship to the primeval Guru![2]
Worship to the Guru, who is at the beginning of the Yuga!
Worship to the true Guru!
Worship to the holy Gurdēv!

Astpadī.

(1). Recite (it) mentally, continually reciting it mentally thou obtainest happiness.
The troubles of the Kali-yug thou effacest in (thy) body.
Recite mentally the praise of the all-supporting one,
Muttering the name of the incalculable manifold one.
The Vēdas, the Purāṇas and the Smriti have pronounced the correct words:
(That) the name of Rām is the one (true) word.
In whose heart he dwells one short moment:
His greatness cannot be estimated.
(I) desire one sight of thee.
With (= by) that I am saved, (says) Nānak.

Pause.

In the Sukhmanī is happiness, nectar is the name of Hari.
In the mind of the devotees is tranquillity.
(2). By means of remembering the Lord (man) does not fall into the womb.
By reason of remembering the Lord the pain of Yama is extinguished.
By remembering the Lord he avoids death.
By reason of remembering the Lord the enemy recedes.
Who remembers the Lord, him no harm befalls.
By remembering the Lord he is daily on his guard.
By remembering the Lord fear does not enter him.
By remembering the Lord pain does not afflict him.
The remembrance of the Lord (is made) in the society of the saints.
All treasures (are obtained) (says) Nānak, by attachment to Hari.
(3). By remembering the Lord prosperity and success and the nine treasures (are obtained).
By remembering the Lord divine knowledge, meditation and the comprehension of truth.
By remembering the Lord silent repetition, austerity and worship.
By remembering the Lord duality is extinguished.
By remembering the Lord ablution at a Tīrtha (is made).
By remembering the Lord honour at the threshold (of Hari is obtained).
By remembering the Lord one becomes very virtuous.

[1] ਸੁਖਮਨੀ, (Sansk. सुषुम्ना), the passage of the breath between the ਇੜਾ (the passage on the right side and the ਪਿੰਗੁਲਾ (the passage on the left side), leading to the crown of the head, through which the soul of the wise departs meeting with a ray of the sun, which carries it on to the supreme Brahm.

[2] ਆਦਿ ਗੁਰਏ ਨਮਹ, a mock-Sanskrit (ਗੁਰਏ = गुरवे); similarly: ਦੇਵਏ = देवाय. Such passages are a sure proof that Arjun did not understand Sanskrit.

By remembering the Lord a profitable fruit (is obtained).
Those remember him, whom he himself causes to remember (him).
Nānak (says): to their feet I cling.
(4). The remembering of the Lord is higher than all.
By the remembrance of the Lord many are rescued.
By the remembrance of the Lord thirst is quenched.
By the remembrance of the Lord everything is known.
By the remembrance of the Lord there is no fear of Yama.
By remembering the Lord (one's) desire is fulfilled.
By remembering the Lord the filth of the mind departs.
The nectar-name enters the heart.
The Lord dwells on the tongue of the pious.
Nānak is the slave of slaves of his people.
(5). Who remember the Lord, they are wealthy.
Who remember the Lord, they are honoured.
Who remember the Lord, they are acceptable people.
Who remember the Lord, they are the chief men.
Who remember the Lord, they do not stand in need of anything.
Who remember the Lord, they are the kings of all.
Who remember the Lord, they are dwelling in comfort.
Who remember the Lord, they are always imperishable.
They are occupied with his remembrance, to whom he himself is merciful.
Nānak begs for the dust of his people.
(6). Who remember the Lord, they are beneficent to others.
Who remember the Lord, for them I always sacrifice myself.
Who remember the Lord, they have a beautiful countenance.
Who remember the Lord, (their life) is passed in happiness.
Who remember the Lord, they overcome themselves.
Who remember the Lord, their conduct is spotless.
Who remember the Lord, their joys are many.
Who remember the Lord, they dwell near Hari.
By the mercy of the saints they are daily awake.
By reason of a perfect destiny remembrance (of Hari) (is made).
(7). By remembering the Lord (their) affairs are completed.
By remembering the Lord they never grieve.
By remembering the Lord they sing the excellences of Hari.[1]
By remembering the Lord they are naturally absorbed.
By remembering the Lord (they get) an immovable seat.
By remembering the Lord (their) lotus is opening.
By remembering the Lord a jingling sound, not produced by beating, (is heard).
The remembrance of the Lord, who has no limit nor bound, is happiness.
Those people remember him, on whom the mercy of the Lord is.
Nānak has fallen on the protection of those people.
(8). Remembering Hari the devotees were made manifest.
By sticking to the remembrance of Hari the Vēdas were produced.
By remembering Hari the Siddhs, ascetics and donors were made.

[1] ਹਰਿ ਗੁਨ ਬਾਨੀ, supply: ਕਰਤੇ ਹੈਨ.

By remembering Hari the low ones become known in the four corners (of the earth).
By remembering Hari the whole earth is supported,
Remembering continually Hari, the cause of causes.
By remembering Hari all the forms are made.
In the remembrance of Hari is the formless one himself.
Whom he himself instructs out of mercy:
That disciple obtains the remembrance of Hari, (says) Nānak.

II.

Slōk.

O thou remover of the pain and trouble of the poor, Lord of the friendless in the whole universe!
(I) have come to thy protection, O Lord of Nānak, (I am) with (thee)!

Asṭpadī.

(1). Where no mother, father, son, friend nor brother (will be with thee):
There, O soul, the name (will be) a companion to thee!
Where the very terrible messengers of Yama grind down (people):
There the name only will go with thee.
Where a very great difficulty sets in:
There the name of Hari is rescuing in a moment.
Though one make many repeated practices, he does not cross.
The name of Hari clears away crores of sins.
O my mind, becoming a disciple mutter the name!
Thou wilt obtain many comforts, (says) Nānak.
(2). Though (one) be the king of the whole creation, he is distressed.
He, who is muttering the name of Hari, is happy.
Lakhs and crores of relatives are far off (at the point of death).[1]
He, who is muttering the name of Hari, is saved.
Many pleasures of the Māyā do not quench the thirst.
He, who is muttering the name of Hari, is satiated.
Where this one is going alone:
On that way the delightful name of Hari is with him.
Such a name, O heart, should always be meditated upon!
Nānak (says): the disciple obtains final emancipation.
(3). One is not set free by crores and lakhs of arms.
Who is muttering the name, him it brings across (the waters of existence).
When many obstacles occur and kill (man):
At that time the name of Hari saves.
Who is born in many wombs and dies (again):[2]
He muttering the name finds rest.
(If one be) filthy with egotism and never wash off his dirt:
The name of Hari clears away crores of sins.
Mutter with pleasure such a name, O my mind!
It is obtained, (says) Nānak, in the society of the pious.

[1] The words must be divided thus: ਲਾਖੁ ਕਰੋਰੀ ਬੰਧੁਨ ਪਰੈ. ਪਰੈ = ਪਰੇ at a distance, far off; they keep at a distance, do not go with.

[2] ਮਰਿ ਜਾਮ, a senseless alliteration instead of ਮਰਿ ਜਾਏ.

(4). The Kōs of which way cannot be counted:
On that the name of Hari is a viaticum with (thee).
On which road there is very deep darkness:
(On that) the name of Hari is light with (thee).
On which road thou hast no acquaintance:
The name of Hari is there a friend with thee.
Where there is a very terrible heat and much perspiration:
There the shade of the name of Hari (is) upon thee.
Where thirst, O mind, oppresses thee:
There Hari, Hari rains nectar.
(5). The occupation of the devotees is the name.
In the mind of the saints is tranquillity.
The name of Hari is the shelter of his slave.
By the name of Hari crores of people are saved.
The saints are praising Hari day and night.
The medicine of Hari, Hari the pious are desiring.
The name of Hari is the treasure of the people of Hari.
By the supreme Brahm it is made a present to his people.
In mind and body they are invariably delighted.
Nānak (says): the delight of (his) people is in discrimination.[1]
(6). The name of Hari is to his people the means of salvation.
In the name of Hari his people have satiety and enjoyment.
The name of Hari is the beauty and splendour of his people.
Muttering the name of Hari no discomfiture befalls them.
The name of Hari is the greatness of his people.
By the name of Hari his people obtain lustre.
The name of Hari is to his people the means of enjoyment.
Muttering the name of Hari there is no (more) separation.
The people, who are attached to the service of the name of Hari,
Worship Hari, Hari, the God, (says) Nānak.
(7). Hari is the wealth and treasure of the people of Hari.
The Lord himself gives the wealth of Hari to his people.
Hari is the powerful shelter of the people of Hari.
Besides the majesty of Hari his people know nothing else.
His people are thoroughly steeped in the juice of Hari.
By deep meditation they are of lost sensation,[2] by the juice of Hari they are intoxicated.
The eight watches the people of Hari mutter Hari.
The devotee of Hari is manifest and not concealed.
Devotion to Hari renders many emancipated.
Nānak (says): in the company of his people how many have crossed!
(8). This name of Hari is the Pārijāta-tree (of Paradise).
The Kāmadhēnu is the singing of the excellences of Hari, Hari.
Higher than all is the story about Hari.

[1] ਬਿਬੇਕ (विवेक), in the Vēdānta system: separation or discrimination of the universal spirit from the visible world, reality from illusion.

[2] ਸੁੰਨ = Sansk. शून्य, here in the sense of "benumbed," of lost sensation of self-existence.

Who is hearing his name, his pain and ache pass away.
The greatness of the name dwells in the heart of the saints.
By the power of the saints all sins are extinguished.
The company of the saints is obtained by a very fortunate one.
By means of serving the saints the name is meditated upon.
Nothing else is equal to the name.
Nānak (says): some (rare) man, being attached to the Guru, obtains the name.

III.

Slōk.

Many Shāstras, many Smritis were inspected (by me), searching through all (of them).
(But) they do not come up to the name of Hari, Hari, the name is invaluable, (says) Nānak.

Asṭpadī.

(1). (If) one practise all silent recitations, austerities, knowledge and meditation.
(If one) explain the six (philosophical) Shāstras and the Smritis.
(If one practise) the exercise of the Yōga, religious works and rites.
(If) forsaking all one wander about in the forest.
(If one) make efforts of many kinds.
(If one do) meritorious deeds, (make) burnt-offerings (and give) many jewels as alms.
(If one) cut his body into small pieces and burn it with fire.
(If) one practise fasts and vows of many kinds.
Do not consider it equal to the name of Rām,
If for one time (only) the name be muttered by the disciple, (says) Nānak.
(2). (Though) one wander about in the nine regions of the earth and live long.
(Though) he become a great stoic and austere devotee.
(Though) he throw his life as a burnt-offering into fire.
(Though) he make alms of gold, horses, elephants and land.
(Though) he practise the work of purification [1] and many ablutions.
(Though) he practise very much restraint after the method of the Jainas.
(Though), closing his eyes he let his body be cut to pieces:
Yet the filth of selfishness does not go off.
Nothing is equal to the name of Hari.
Nānak (says): the disciple, muttering the name, obtains salvation.
(3). The lust of the mind does not leave the body at a Tīrtha.
Pride and conceit do not recede (there) from the heart.
(Though) one make purifications day and night:
The filth of the mind does not leave the body.
(Though) one constrain much this (human) spirit:
Worldliness never departs from the mind.
(Though) he wash it with water, (there is) much immorality in the body.
How should a raw wall [2] become pure?
The heart, (in which is) the greatness of the name of Hari, is exalted.
By the name very many sinners are saved, (says) Nānak.
(4). (In spite of) much cunning the fear of Yama enters (man).
Though making many efforts, (his) thirst is not quenched.

[1] About the ਨਿਉਲੀ ਕਰਮ see p. 136, note 7.

[2] ਕਾਚੀ ਭੀਤਿ, a raw wall, built of unburnt bricks.

By many (faqīr's)-garbs the (inward) fire is not extinguished.
By crores of shifts he does not become acceptable at the threshold (of Hari).
He is not emancipated (and goes) upwards and downwards.
By reason of his spiritual blindness he enters the net of the Māyā.
On all other actions (falls) the punishment of Yama.
Without adoring Gōvind (he does not obtain) a bit of honour.
Who is muttering the name of Hari, his pain departs with natural ease, says Nānak.
(5). If one desires the four objects (of human life):
He should stick to the service of the pious people.
If one will remove his own pain :
He should always sing the name of Hari in his heart.
If one desires his own lustre :
He should give up his egotism in the society of the pious.
If one dreads regeneration and death :
He should fall on the asylum of the pious people.
Who has a thirst for the sight of the Lord :
To him Nānak will sacrifice himself.
(6). He is the first man among all men,
Whose egotism is eradicated in the society of the saints.
Who considers himself low :
He is accounted higher than all.
Whose mind becomes the dust of all :
He, lessening and lessening, knows the name of Hari, Hari.
By whom his wicked mind is eradicated from himself :
He looks on the whole creation as a friend.
Who regards pleasure and pain as the same :
He has nothing to do with sinful (or) meritorious actions, (says) Nānak.
(7). To the poor thy name is wealth.
To the homeless thy name is a home.
To the honourless thou, O Lord, art honour.
To all bodies thou givest presents.
Thou, O Lord, art the cause of causes.
Thou art the inward governor of all bodies.
Thy secret thought thou thyself knowest.
Thou, O Lord, art thyself enamoured with thyself.
Thy praise is made by thyself.
Nānak (says): no other knows (thee).
(8). Among all religious practices (this is) the best practice.
Muttering the name of Hari is a spotless work.
Among all religious rites (this is) the highest rite,
(If) in the society of the pious the filth of folly is removed.
Among all efforts (this is) the best effort,
(If one) always mutter in his heart the name of Hari.
Among all words (these are) words of nectar,
(If) one hear and praise with his tongue the glory of Hari.
This is the highest place of all,
In which body the name of Hari dwells.

IV.

Slōk.

O virtueless and ignorant one, remember always that Lord!
By whom thou art made, him keep in thy thought, he will go on with thee, (says) Nānak.

Asṭpadī.

(1). Reflect on the excellences of the sporting (Supreme), O man!
From which root (is he), who is like (him)?[1]
By whom thou art made and adorned.
By whom thou art saved in the fire of the womb.
Who gives thee milk to drink in the state of childhood.
(Who) in full youth (gives thee) enjoyment (of) true happiness.
(When) thou hast become old above thy relations and kinsmen:
He is giving food into (thy) mouth, that thou mayest quietly sit down.
This virtueless one (=I) does not comprehend at all (thy) excellences.
Pardon (me), then Nanak is accomplished.
(2). By whose favour he dwells in comfort on the earth,
(And) laughs with son, brother, friend and wife.
By whose favour he drinks cold water,
(And enjoys) the comfort-giving wind and the invaluable fire.
By whose favour he enjoys all flavours,
(And) all goods are abiding with (him).
By whom hands, feet, ears, eyes and tongue are given:
Forsaking him he is attached to another.
With such vices the blind fool is filled.
Nānak (says): O Lord, draw me out thyself!
(3). Who is preserving (him) at the beginning and at the end:
To him the fool shows no love.
By whose service he obtains the nine treasures:
On him the fool does not direct his mind.
The Lord, who is continually in (his) presence:
Him the blind one considers far off.
By whose service he obtains honour at the threshold:
Him the foolish, ignorant man forgets.
This one is continually going astray.
Nānak (says): the preserver is boundless.
(4). Throwing away the jewel he clings to a Kauṛī (shell).
Giving up the True one he revels in falsehood.
What is forsaking (man), that he considers immovable.
What is (really) being, that he throws far away.
What is forsaking (man), for that he toils.
What is accompanying (him), that he removes.
Sandal-plaster he washes off.
The donkey is in love with ashes.

[1] ਕਵਨ ਦ੍ਰਿਸਟਾਨੋ; the words of this line are somewhat obscure; ਦ੍ਰਿਸਟਾਨੋ is very likely a corruption from the Sansk. दृष्टान्त, *similitude.*

O merciful Lord, draw Nānak out,
Who has fallen into a hideous blind well!
(5). In actions beasts, by birth men,
They go about day and night in the world.
Outside (is a faqīr's) garb, inside the filth of the Māyā, which is not hidden, though they try to hide it.
Outside (they show) divine knowledge, meditation and ablutions.
Inside dwells the greediness of a dog.
Inside (is) a fire, outside (are) ashes on the body.
On whose neck is a stone, how should they cross the bottomless (waters)?
In whose heart the Lord himself dwells:
Those people are easily absorbed (in him), (says) Nānak.
(6). Though having heard (of it), how shall the blind one find the road?
(Who) takes his hand, he brings him to the end (of his way).
How shall the deaf one understand a riddle?
If it is said, that it is night, then he understands "morning."
How shall the dumb one sing the foot of Vishṇu?[1]
Though he make efforts, yet he spoils the tune.
How shall the cripple wander about in a mountain?
He cannot go there.
O creator, full of mercy to the poor, Nānak makes this petition:
By thy mercy he crosses (the waters of existence).
(7). Who is a companion with (him to the end), he does not come into his mind.
Who is (his) enemy, on him he bestows love.
He dwells within a house of sand.
In joy, sport and in the pleasure of the Māyā he delights.
He considers (her) enduring (and puts) faith on her in his mind.
Death does not come into the thought of the fool.
Enmity, opposition, lust, wrath, spiritual blindness,
Falsehood, passion, great greediness, fraud,
Intent on these many births are passed.
Nānak (says): preserve (me), bestowing thy own kindness (on me)!
(8). Thou art the Lord, to thee I pray.
Soul and body, all is thy property.
Thou art mother and father, we are thy children.
In thy mercy are many joys.
No one knows thy end.
Higher than high is the Lord.
All goods are held in thy string.
What is made by thee, that is obedient to thee.
Thy own secret mind thou thyself knowest.
Nānak, thy slave, is always a sacrifice (to thee).

V.

Slōk.

Who, forsaking the Lord, the giver, clings to another:
He never becomes accomplished, without the name his honour goes.

[1] ਬਿਸਨ ਪਦ, literally: the foot of Vishṇu, a song in praise of Vishṇu, in which the beauty of his lotus-foot is set forth.

Astpadī.

(1). These things thou takest and puttest them behind (thyself).
On account of one thing thou throwest away thy faith,
If he do not give the one and also take away the ten.
Say, O fool, what wilt thou do then ?
From whom nothing, nothing can be enforced :
To that Lord worship should be paid!
To whose mind the Lord has become sweet:
In his mind all comforts dwell.
Whom he makes mind his own order :
That man gets all things, (says) Nānak.
(2). The wholesale-merchant gives his own innumerable stock (of goods).
Eating and drinking (man) lives in joy and pleasure.
If the wholesale-merchant takes again something of his deposit :
The ignorant (man) is angry in his mind.
Who himself throws away his own faith :
He will not again attain to faith.
Who puts the thing before him, whose (property) it is,
And (who) minds the order of the Lord with his head :
(Him) he makes fourfold more happy.
The Lord is always merciful, (says) Nānak.
(3). There is much devotedness for the sake of the Māyā.
Know, at last she will pass away.
If one delights in the shade of a tree :
That passes away and he repents in his heart.
Whatever is seen, that is transitory.
Who clings to it, is stark blind.
Who entertains love with a traveller :
Into his hands nothing falls.
O mind, love to the name of Hari is giving comfort.
He himself bestows it (*i.e.* the love) out of mercy, (says) Nānak.
(4). Vanity is all, the body, wealth and family.
Vanity is egotism, selfishness and the Māyā.
Vanity is dominion, youth, wealth and property.
Vanity is lust and hideous wrath.
Vanity are chariots, elephants, horses and clothes.
Vanity delight in the Māyā, seeing whom one laughs.
Vanity is fraud, spiritual blindness and conceit.
Vanity it is, if one be proud of himself.
Durable is worship in the asylum of the pious.
Nānak (says): (one) lives muttering continually the feet of Hari.
(5). Vanity is the ear, that hears slander on other people.
Vanity the hand, that pilfers the property of others.
Vanity the eye, that looks at the beauty of another's wife.
Vanity the tongue, that is enjoying other flavours.
Vanity the foot, that is running to another's deterioration.
Vanity the mind, that excites the greediness of another.

Vanity the body, that is not rendering assistance to another.
Vanity the dwelling, that undergoes change.
All is vanity without comprehending (the truth).
Fruitful is that body, that takes the name of Hari, Hari, (says) Nānak.
(6). Useless is the life of the Sākat.
How shall purity be effected without truth?
Useless is without the name the body of the blind one.
Stench comes out of his mouth.
Uselessly passes (the time) without remembering (Hari) day and night,
As without rain a field is drooping away.
Without remembering Gōvind all works are unprofitable,
As the money of the miser is to no purpose.
Blessed, blessed are those people, in whose heart the name of Hari dwells.
Nānak is a sacrifice to them.
(7). He is continually doing this and that.
(But) in his heart is no love (to God), with his mouth (only) he professes friendship.
(But) the Lord is knowing and all-wise.
Outside (he wears) a garb, (but) is not in love with any one.
He instructs others, (but) does not do it himself.
Coming and going he is regenerated and dies.
In whose heart the Formless one dwells:
By his instruction the world crosses.
Who are pleasing to thee, by them the Lord is known.
Nānak is fleeing to the foot of those men.
(8). Offer prayer to him, the supreme Brahm knows all!
He himself minds his own work.
He himself, he himself, settles (everything).
Some one he makes believe, that he is far off; some one he lets know, that he is near.
Who is free from all shifts and cunning:
He knows all the procedure of the spirit.
Whom he pleases, him he applies to the hem (of his garment).
In every place he is continually contained.
He is a worshipper, on whom he has bestowed mercy.
In every moment he mutters Hari, (says) Nānak.

VI.

Slōk.

Lust, wrath and covetousness, spiritual illusion and egotism pass away.
On him, who has come to the asylum of the Lord, the Gurdēv bestows mercy, (says) Nānak.

Astpadī.

(1). By whose favour thou eatest the nectar-food consisting of thirty-six ingredients:
That Lord keep in thy mind!
By whose favour thou separatest[1] the sweet-smelling substance:
Remembering him thou wilt obtain final emancipation.
By whose favour thou dwellest in comfort in (thy) house:
On him meditate always in thy mind!

[1] ਨਿਲਾਉਣਾ, *v.a.* To separate and spread out (cf. the Marāṭhī: निराविणें), as corn from the husks, etc.

By whose favour thou dwellest in comfort in thy house:
Him remember the eight watches with thy tongue!
By whose favour thou enjoyest pleasures and delights:
He should be meditated upon, (says) Nānak, he is worthy to be meditated upon.
(2). By whose favour thou wearest silk clothes:
Forsaking him whom else dost thou desire?
By whose favour sleep is made in comfort on the bed:
His praise should be sung, O heart, the eight watches!
By whose favour everybody respects thee:
Utter his praise with thy mouth and tongue!
By whose favour thy piety is abiding:
O heart, meditate always on the supreme Brahm alone!
Muttering the name thou wilt obtain honour at the threshold.
With honour thou wilt go to the house (of Hari).
(3). By whose favour the gold-like body (remains) healthy:
Devoutly meditate on that Rām, O friend!
By whose favour thy screen is abiding:
Uttering the praise of (that) Hari, Hari, thou wilt obtain happiness.
By whose favour all thy blemishes are covered:
O heart, fall on the asylum of that Lord!
By whose favour no one comes up to thee:
(That) high Lord remember, O heart, at every breath!
By whose favour the body, so difficult of obtainment, is gotten:
Him worship, (says) Nānak.
(4). By whose favour ornaments are put on:
How should in his remembrance sloth be made, O heart?
By whose favour riding on horses and elephants (is made):
Forget never that Lord, O heart!
By whose favour (thou possessest) gardens, property and wealth:
String and keep (that) Lord in thy heart!
By whom thou art adorned, O heart:
Rising and sitting always meditate on him!
Meditate on him, who alone is inapprehensible!
Here and there he preserves thy (honour), (says) Nānak.
(5). By whose favour thou performest meritorious actions (and givest) many alms:
On him meditate the eight watches, O heart!
By whose favour thou art engaged in religious and secular occupations:
Reflect on that Lord at every breath!
By whose favour thy external appearance is beautiful:
That incomparable Lord remember always!
By whose favour thy caste is good:
That Lord remember always day and night!
By whose favour thy honour abides:
His praise utter by the favour of the Guru, (says) Nānak.
(6). By whose favour thou hearest a sound with thy ears;
By whose favour thou art seeing with amazement;
By whose favour thou speakest nectar with thy tongue;
By whose favour thou art dwelling in comfort and tranquillity;

By whose favour the hand moves;
By whose favour all is fruitful;
By whose favour thou obtainest final emancipation;
By whose favour thou art easily and naturally absorbed:
Forsaking such a Lord to whom else wilt thou cling?
By the favour of the Guru be awake in thy heart! (says) Nānak.
(7). By whose favour thou art manifest in the world:
That Lord forget by no means in thy mind!
By whose favour (thou obtainest) grandeur:
O foolish heart, mutter him!
By whose favour thy affairs are accomplished:
Him, O heart, consider as always being in thy presence!
By whose favour thou obtainest happiness:
O my heart, be in love with him!
By whose favour the salvation of all is effected:
Him mutter, (if) thou makest (any) muttering, (says) Nānak.
(8). He mutters the name, (whom) he himself causes to mutter it.
He sings the excellences of Hari, (whom) he himself causes to sing (them).
By the mercy of the Lord enlightenment (of the understanding) is made.
By the kindness of the Lord the lotus (of the heart) is opening.
In (whose) heart that kindly-disposed Lord is dwelling:
His understanding becomes very great by the mercy of the Lord.
All treasures (are obtained), O Lord, by thy mercy.
No one has got anything from himself.
To whatever thou appliest (them), to that they stick, O Lord Hari!
Nothing is in the hand of these (men), (says) Nānak.

VII.

Slōk.

Unattainable, unfathomable is that supreme Brahm.
Whoever utters (him), he becomes emancipated.
Hear, O friend, humbly says Nānak,
The wonderful story of the pious people!

Astpadī.

(1). In the society of the pious the face becomes bright.
In the society of the pious he (*i.e.* the disciple) removes all (his) filth.
In the society of the pious conceit is effaced.
In the society of the pious is displayed true knowledge.
In the society of the pious he comprehends, that the Lord is near.
In the society of the pious every decision is made.
In the society of the pious he gets the jewel of the name.
In the society of the pious there is effort about the One.
Who can describe the greatness of the pious?
The lustre of the pious is contained in the Lord, (says) Nānak.
(2). In the society of the pious the inapprehensible one is met with.
In the society of the pious he is always happy.
In the society of the pious the five are subdued.

In the society of the pious nectar-juice is enjoyed.
In the society of the pious he becomes the dust of all.
In the society of the pious (there is) a heart-captivating discourse.
In the society of the pious (his mind) does not run anywhere.
In the society of the pious his mind obtains a (firm) standing.
In the society of the pious it is separated from the Māyā.
In the society of the pious the Lord is very propitious, (says) Nānak.
(3). In the society of the pious all enemies (become) friends.
In the society of the pious he gets highly purified.
In the society of the pious (there is) no enmity with any one.
In the society of the pious (there is) no distorted foot.
In the society of the pious (there is) no want.
In the society of the pious he knows the highest bliss (= the Supreme).
In the society of the pious (there is) no burning of egotism.
In the society of the pious he gives up all his own self.
He himself (*i.e.* Hari) knows the greatness of the pious.
Between the pious and the Lord is intimate union, (says) Nānak.
(4). In the society of the pious he does not run about at any time.
In the society of the pious he always obtains happiness.
In the society of the pious he acquires the inapprehensible thing.
In the society of the pious he bears (patiently) the place of exercise (of the senses).[1]
In the society of the pious he dwells (as) in a high place.
In the society of the pious he reaches the palace (of Hari).
In the society of the pious every virtue is confirmed.
In the society of the pious only the supreme Brahm (is meditated upon).
In the society of the pious he acquires the jewel of the name.
Nānak is a sacrifice to the pious.
(5). In the society of the pious he saves his whole family.
In the society of the pious he releases friends, acquaintances and his household (from further transmigration).
In the society of the pious he gets that wealth,
By which every one is profited.
In the society of the pious Dharm-Rāe (= Yama) renders service.
In the society of the pious he (*i.e.* the disciple) acquires the lustre of the Suras and Dēvas.
In the society of the pious sin is fleeing.
In the society of the pious he is singing the excellences of the nectar.
In the society of the pious he is going to all places.
Nānak (says): in the society of the pious (his) life-time is fruitful.
(6). In the society of the pious there is no calamity whatever.
Falling in with (their) sight he (*i.e.* the disciple) becomes happy.
In the society of the pious he takes off his filth.
In the society of the pious he removes hell (from himself).
(Living) in the society of the pious he is happy here and there.
Being separated he is united (again) with Hari in the society of the pious.

[1] ਅਜਰੁ ਸਹੈ. ਅਜਰੁ = Sansk. अजिर, place of exercise of the senses. The sense is: he bears patiently the bustle of the senses in his body, without being affected thereby. The Sikh Granthīs proffer all sorts of surmises about the meaning of ਅਜਰੁ.

The fruit, he wishes, he obtains.
(Living) in the society of the pious he does not depart unprofited.
The supreme Brahm dwells in the heart of the pious.
Nānak (says): he is saved, (if), having heard the pious, he utter (the name).
(7). In the society of the pious hear the name of Hari!
In the society of the pious sing the excellences of Hari!
In the society of the pious he is not forgotten from the mind.
In the society of the pious thou art saved at last.
In the society of the pious the Lord becomes sweet.
In the society of the pious he is seen (as being) in everybody.
In the society of the pious (we) become obedient to his orders.
In the society of the pious our salvation is brought about.
In the society of the pious all diseases are effaced.
Nānak joins the association of the pious.
(8). The greatness of the pious the Vēda does not know.
As much as it hears, so much it describes.
The greatness of the pious is far from the three qualities.
The greatness of the pious remains complete.
There is no end of the splendour of the pious.
The splendour of the pious is always boundless.
The splendour of the pious is higher than high.
The splendour of the pious is greater than great.
The splendour of the pious agrees with the pious.
Nānak (says): between the pious and the Lord there is no difference, O brother!

VIII.

Slōk.

Who is true in his heart, he is true (also) with his mouth.
Without the One he does not see any one else.
Nānak (says): this is the sign of him, who knows Brahm.

Astpadī.

(1). Who knows Brahm, he is always uncontaminated (by the Māyā),
As a lotus in the water is uncontaminated.
Who knows Brahm, he is always without blemish,
As the sun is drying up all.
Who knows Brahm, he looks on all things as the same,
As the wind blows equally on the Rājā and the poor.
Who knows Brahm has one and the same patience (for all),
As the earth, (which) one is digging up and another besmearing with sandal-powder.
This is the quality of him, who knows Brahm.
(It is) like the innate nature of fire, (says) Nānak.
(2). He who knows Brahm is purer than pure,
As filth is not sticking to water.
In the mind of him who knows Brahm, is light,
As the sky is above the earth.
To him, who knows Brahm, friend and enemy are the same.
Who knows Brahm, entertains no egotism.

Who knows Brahm, he is higher than high.
In his own mind he is the lowest of all.
Those people obtain the knowledge of Brahm,
To whom the Lord himself gives it, (says) Nānak.
(3). Who knows Brahm, he is the dust of all.
Who knows Brahm, knows the taste of his own spirit.
Who knows Brahm, is kind to all.
Who knows Brahm, commits no wickedness whatever.
Who knows Brahm, is always looking (on all things) as the same.
The look of him, who knows Brahm, is showering nectar.
Who knows Brahm, is free from bonds.
The practice of him, who knows Brahm, is spotless.
The enjoyment of him, who knows Brahm, is divine knowledge.
The meditation of him, who knows Brahm, is directed on Brahm, (says) Nanak.
(4). The hope of him, who knows Brahm, (is placed) on the One.
He, who knows Brahm, does not perish.
To him, who knows Brahm, humility is a pleasure.
To him, who knows Brahm, benevolence to others is a delight.
He, who knows Brahm, is not engaged in worldly business.
By him, who knows Brahm, the running (mind) is bound.
To him, who knows Brahm, great goodness will accrue.
The reward of him, who knows Brahm, (will be) great.
In the society of him, who knows Brahm, all are saved.
The whole world attends to him, who knows Brahm, (says) Nānak.
(5). He, who knows Brahm, is of the same state (of mind).
With him, who knows Brahm, the Lord dwells.
To him, who knows Brahm, the name is support.
To him, who knows Brahm, the name is retinue.
He, who knows Brahm, is continually awake.
He, who knows Brahm, is giving up his egotism.
In the heart of him, who knows Brahm, is the highest bliss.
In the house of him, who knows Brahm, is always joy.
He, who knows Brahm, is living in happiness and tranquillity.
He, who knows Brahm, does not perish, says Nānak.
(6). He, who knows Brahm, is the outlines[1] of Brahm.
He, who knows Brahm, is in love with the One.
He, who knows Brahm, is free from cares.
The sentiments[2] of him, who knows Brahm, are pure.
He knows Brahm, whom the Lord himself lets know him.
The dignity of him, who knows Brahm, is great.
The sight of him, who knows Brahm, is obtained by the very fortunate one.
To him, who knows Brahm, (people) are a sacrifice.
Him, who knows Brahm, Mahēsvar (= Shiva) seeks.
He, who knows Brahm, is himself the supreme Lord, (says) Nānak.

[1] ਘੇਤ or ਘੇਤਾ *m.*, the form, figure, outlines.
[2] ਮੰਤ = ਮਤ (*m.*), for the sake of the rhyme.

(7). No estimate of him (can be made), who knows Brahm.
All is in the mind of him, who knows Brahm.
Who knows the secret of him, who knows Brahm ?
To him, who knows Brahm, always salutation (should be made).
Not half a letter of him, who knows Brahm, can be told.
He, who knows Brahm, is Lord of all.
Who can describe the value of him, who knows Brahm ?
The state of him, who knows Brahm, the knower of Brahm (only) knows.
There is no end nor limit of him, who knows Brahm.
Nānak is always paying reverence to him, who knows Brahm.
(8). He, who knows Brahm, is the creator of the whole creation.
He, who knows Brahm, lives always and does not die.
He, who knows Brahm, is possessed of emancipation,[1] the donor of the creatures.
He, who knows Brahm, is the (all-)filling Supreme Spirit, the ordainer (of all).
He, who knows Brahm, is the Lord of the helpless.
The hand of him, who knows Brahm, is upon all.
To him, who knows Brahm, all forms belong.
He, who knows Brahm, is himself the formless one.
The splendour of him, who knows Brahm, agrees with the knower of Brahm (only).
He, who knows Brahm, is the Lord of all, (says) Nānak.

IX.

Slōk.

Who keeps the name in his breast :
He beholds in all the Lord.
Who every moment pays reverence to the Lord :
He is untouchable and saves all.

Asṭpadī.

(1). (Who) does not touch with his tongue falsehood;
In (whose) heart is a longing for the sight of the spotless (Supreme);
(Who) does not behold with his eyes the beauty of another's wife;
(Who) does service to the pious and has love to the saints;
(Who) with his ears does not hear the slander of any one;
(Who) considers himself the worst of all;
(Who) by the favour of the Guru removes worldly pursuits;
From (whose) heart the desires of the heart recede;
(Who) has overcome his senses and is free from the five vices :[2]
Among crores such an untouched one is hardly to be found.
(2). He is a Vaishṇava, to whom he is favourably disposed.
Who is separated from the Māyā of Vishṇu;
Who is doing works and is not looking out for future rewards :
The religion of that Vaishṇava is spotless.
Who entertains no desire for any reward;

[1] ਮੁਕਤਿ ਜੁਗਤਿ might also be translated by: *the means of salvation*, if ਜੁਗਤਿ be taken = युक्ति.
[2] The five vices are: ਕਾਮ, ਕ੍ਰੋਧ, ਲੋਭ, ਮੋਹ, ਅਹੰਕਾਰ.

Who in worship and praise alone is absorbed;
Who in heart and body is remembering Gōpāl;
Who is merciful to all;
Who himself is firm and makes others mutter the name:
That Vaishṇava gets final emancipation, (says) Nānak.
(3). He is a Bhagautī,[1] (whose) delight is the worship of the Supreme Being.
Who forsakes the society of all the wicked;
From (whose) mind all error is destroyed;
Who considers and worships all as the Supreme Brahm;
Who in the society of the pious removes the filth of (his) sins:
The understanding of that Bhagautī becomes very high.
Who serves the Supreme Being continually;
Who offers up (his) heart and body out of love to Vishṇu;
Who makes the feet of Hari dwell in (his) heart:
Such a Bhagautī obtains the Supreme Being, (says) Nānak.
(4). He is a Paṇḍit, who enlightens (his own) mind.
Who explores the name of Rām within himself;
Who drinks the essence and juice of the name of Rām:
By the instruction of that Paṇḍit the world lives.
Who makes dwell the story about Hari in his heart:
That Paṇḍit does not come again into a womb.
Who comprehends the root of the Vēda, the Purāṇas and the Smriti;
Who knows, that in the minute the large (objects) (are contained);
Who gives (such an) instruction to the four castes:
To that Paṇḍit always salutation!
(5). The ground-mantra[2] (contains) the knowledge of all.
(If) among the four castes one mutter the name,
Whoever mutters it, his salvation is brought about.
In the society of the pious some (rare) man obtains it.
If in mercy he (*i.e.* Hari) determine in (his) mind,
He makes beasts, goblins, fools and stones cross.
The medicine for all diseases is the name.
The celebration of the Beautiful one (and) the singing of (his) excellences
Is not obtained by any skill nor by any religious practice.
Nānak (says): he obtains it, to whom it is decreed by destiny itself.
(6). In whose heart is the abode of the Supreme Brahm:
He is called a true slave of Rām.
The Supreme Spirit comes into his sight.
By being the slave of slaves[3] he obtains him.
Who always considers Hari as being near him:

[1] ਭਗਉਤੀ, a denomination of Faqīrs, who profess to worship the ਭਗਵਾਨ or Supreme Being.

[2] ਬੀਜਮੰਤ੍ਰ, the mystical letter, which forms the essential part of the mantra of any deity. The ਬੀਜਮੰਤ੍ਰ is here the name of Hari.

[3] ਦਾਸਦਸੰਤਣਭਾਇ, corrupted from ਦਾਸਦਾਸਤਣ, the state of being the slave of slaves (= Sansk. दासदासत्व); to this abstract is again added ਭਾਉ (= भाव), which is quite unnecessary; we find also in the Granth: ਦਾਸਤਭਾਉ, which is quite identical with ਦਾਸਤਣਭਾਉ.

That slave is accepted at the threshold (of Hari).
On his own slave he himself bestows mercy.
To that slave all knowledge accrues.
In the society of all he is retired in his heart.
Such is the practice of the slave of Rām.
(7). To whom the order of the Lord is dear in his heart:
He is called emancipated whilst yet living.
Joy and grief are the same to him.[1]
He is always joyful and not separated (from the Supreme).
Gold and clay are the same to him.
Nectar and bitter poison are the same to him.
Honour and dishonour[2] are the same to him.
The beggar and the king are the same to him.
Who entertains that practice:
That man, (says) Nānak, is emancipated whilst yet living.
(8). All places belong to the Supreme Brahm.
As the house is, into which he puts (men), such is their name.
He himself is able to do and cause to be done (everything).
What pleases the Lord, that will also be done.
He himself being spread out becomes an endless wave.
The (manifold) appearances of the Supreme Brahm cannot be perceived.
As he gives understanding, such is the light.
The Supreme Brahm, the creator, is imperishable.
Always, always he is compassionate.
By continually remembering him Nānak has become happy.

X.

Slōk.

Many people praise (him, who) has no end nor limit.
Nānak (says): an arrangement (creation) has been made by the Lord of many kinds and sorts.

Astpadī.

(1). Many crores are (his) worshippers.
Many crores are engaged in religious practices.
Many crores are dwelling on holy watering-places.
Many crores wander about in woods, having retired from the world.
Many crores are listening to the Vēda.
Many crores are becoming ascetics.
Many crores are meditating upon themselves.
Many crores are poets and reflect on a poem.
Many crores meditate on the (always) new name.
(But) the end of the creator they do not reach, (says) Nānak.

[1] ਤੈਸਾ ਹਰਖੁ ਤੈਸਾ ਉਸੁ ਸੋਗੁ, literally: such is joy, such is grief to him, *i.e.* joy and grief are the same to him.

[2] All the MSS. at my disposal read ਮਾਨੁ—ਅਭਿਮਾਨੁ, but there can hardly be a doubt that ਅਪਮਾਨੁ must be read, as ਅਭਿਮਾਨੁ gives no sense here.

(2). Many crores are selfish.
Many crores are in deep ignorance.
Many crores are hard-hearted misers.
Many crores are skilful,[1] (but) blind in their heart.
Many crores pilfer another's property.
Many crores inflict pain on others.
Many crores toil for the sake of the Māyā.
Many crores wander about in foreign countries.
To whatever (thing) he applies them, to that they stick.
The creator knows the arrangement of the creator, (says) Nānak.
(3). Many crores of Siddhas, ascetics and Jōgīs.
Many crores of Rājās, (who) are given to enjoyments.
Many crores of birds and snakes were created (by him).
Many crores of stones and trees were produced.
Many crores of winds, waters and fires.
Many crores of countries, lands and regions.
Many crores of moons, suns and stars.
Many crores of Dēvas, Dānavas, and umbrella-bearing Indras.
All things he keeps in his own string.
Nānak (says): whomsoever he pleases, him he saves.
(4). Many crores of Rājasa, Tāmasa and Sātvika qualities.
Many crores of Vēdas, Purāṇas, Smritis and Shāstras.
Many crores of gems (and) oceans were made.
Many crores of living beings of various kinds.
Many crores of long-living (beings) were made.
Many crores of gems[2] and kinds of gold were made.
Many crores of Yakshasas, Kinnaras and fiends.
Many crores of goblins, sprites, hogs and deer.
He is near to all and far from all.
Nānak (says): (though) omnipresent he remains distinct himself.
(5). (There are) many crores of inhabitants of the nether-regions.
Many crores of inhabitants in hell and heaven.
Many crores are born, live and die.
Many crores wander about in many wombs.
Many crores are eating at leisure.
Many crores toil along and are wearied out.
Many crores are made rich.
Many crores are anxious for (acquiring) wealth.
Wherever he pleases, there he puts them.
Nānak (says): everything is in the hand of the Lord.
(6). Many crores have become Bairāgīs.
They devoutly meditate on the name of Rām.
Many crores are seeking the Lord.
They obtain in their own heart the Supreme Brahm.
Many crores are thirsting for the sight of the Lord.

[1] ਅਭਿਗ = Sansk. अभिज्ञ, skilful, knowing.

[2] ਗਿਰੀਮੇਰੁ, properly the large middle gem of a necklace, in which both ends meet.

With them meets the imperishable Lord.
Many crores desire the society of the saints.
To them the colour of the Supreme Brahm is applied.
To whom he himself has become very propitious:
Those people are always blessed, blessed, (says) Nānak.
(7). (There are) many crores of quarries and sections.
Many crores of skies and universes.
Many Avatārs have taken place,
(By whom) many skilful contrivances were made.
Many times the expanse (of the world) was spread out.
The Uniform (Supreme) only is always.
Many crores (of worlds) of many kinds were made.
From the Lord they emanated and in the Lord they are absorbed.
His end no one knows.
That Lord himself (only knows it), (says) Nānak.
(8). (There are) many crores of servants of the Supreme Brahm.
In their heart light springs up.
(There are) many crores, who know the truth.
They always behold the One with their eyes.
Many crores drink the juice of the name.
They become immortal and live for ever.
Many crores sing the excellences of the name.
They are absorbed in self-enjoyment, happiness and tranquillity.
Who remember their maker at every breath:
They are dear to the Lord, (says) Nānak.

XI.

Slōk.

The cause of causes is alone the Lord, there is none other.
Nānak is a sacrifice to him; he is in water, land and on the surface of the earth.

Asṭpadī.

(1). The cause of causes is able to create.
What pleases him, that will be done.
In a moment he establishes and disestablishes.
There is no end nor any limit of him.
By his order he upholds the firmament.
By his order (things) are produced and absorbed (again).
By his order is a high (or) low occupation (allotted).
By his order many kinds of colour are (produced).
Having created he beholds his own greatness.
Nānak (says): in all he is contained.
(2). If it please the Lord, man obtains salvation.
If it please the Lord, he makes a stone cross (the waters).
If it please the Lord, he preserves (man) without breath.
If it please the Lord, the qualities of Hari become manifest.[1]

[1] डाधला is here not = भाषण, speaking, but signifies: *to be manifest, to be seen* (= भाखा).

If it please the Lord, he rescues the sinner.
He himself acts, he himself reflects.
He himself is the Lord of both sides (= both worlds).
The inward governor sports and expands.
What pleases him, that work he causes to be done.
Nānak (says): none other comes into sight.
(3). Say, what is done by man?
What pleases Him, that he causes to be done.
If it would be in the hand (= power) of this one (= man), he would take everything.
What pleases to that one, that he does.
The ignorant one clings to the visible objects.
Who is knowing his own self, is saved.
Being led astray by error (man) runs about in the ten directions (of the earth).
In a moment he comes back again (from) the four quarters.
On whom in mercy he (= Hari) bestows his own worship:
Those men fall in with the name, (says) Nānak.
(4). In a moment dominion (is given) to a low worm.
The Supreme Brahm is the cherisher of the humble.
Of whom nothing is seen:
Him he makes manifest at that time in the ten directions (of the earth).
On whom he bestows his own pardon:
From him the Lord of the universe takes no account.
Soul and body, all is his property.
In everybody the light of the Supreme Brahm is fully contained.
By himself his own formation is made.
Nānak lives having seen (his) greatness.
(5). The power of this one is not in this one's hand.[1]
The cause of causes is the Lord of all.
The creature is helpless and must obey.
What pleases to that one, that will be.
Sometime he (*i.e.* man) dwells in a high (or) low (place).
Sometime he is in grief (or) laughs in joy and merriment.
Sometime he is taken up with slander (or) cares.
Sometime he is above in the sky (or) in the nether region.
Sometime he is wise, reflecting on Brahm.
Nānak (says): he himself (*i.e.* Hari) is uniting (them with himself).
(6). Sometime he makes deliberations of many kinds.
Sometime he continues sleeping day and night.
Sometime he is hideous by great wrath.
Sometime he becomes the dust of all.
Sometime he sits down having become a great Rājā.
Sometime he is a beggar, of low attire.
Sometime he falls into disrepute.
Sometime he is called a good man.
As the Lord keeps him, so he remains.
By the favour of the Guru he utters the True one, (says) Nānak.

[1] The sense is: man has no strength of his own.

(7). Sometime, having become a Paṇḍit, he makes explanations.
Sometime, having become a taciturn (ascetic), he meditates.
Sometime he is making ablutions on the bank of a holy watering-place.
Sometime, (having become) a Siddha (= perfect Jōgī) (or) ascetic, there is (divine) knowledge in his mouth.
Sometime he lives having become a worm, elephant (or) moth.
Erratic he wanders about in many wombs.
Like a mimic he shows many appearances.
As it pleases the Lord, so he makes (him) dance.
What pleases to that one, that is done.
Nānak (says): there is none other.
(8). Sometime this one (= man) obtains the society of the pious.
From that place he does not recede again.
In his heart divine knowledge is lighted up.
That place is not destroyed.
His mind and body are coloured in the name throughout.
He always dwells in the society of the Supreme Brahm.
Like water falling into water is settled (therein):
So light is absorbed in the Luminous (Supreme).
Transmigrations are effaced, rest is obtained.
Nānak is always a sacrifice to the Lord.

XII.

Slōk.

Who lives in indigence is happy, having cleared away his own self beneath.
The great selfish men are consumed by pride, (says) Nānak.

Asṭpadī.

(1). In whose heart is the pride of dominion:
He, falling into hell, is becoming a dog.
Who thinks, that he is youthful:
He is becoming a creature living in ordure.
Who calls himself full of (good) works:
He is regenerated and dies and wanders about in many wombs.
Who is proud of his wealth and landed property:
He is a fool, blind and ignorant.
In whose heart he (= Hari) mercifully causes humility to dwell:
He is here (on earth) emancipated and further on (in the other world) he obtains happiness, (says) Nānak.
(2). Who, having become rich, is proud:
Not as much as a blade of grass goes with him.
Who puts much hope on an army of men:
In a moment he will be destroyed.
Who considers himself stronger than all:
In a moment he will become ashes.[1]
The conceited one, who himself does not acknowledge any one,

[1] ਭਸਮੰਤੁ = ਭਸਮ, *antu* being a meaningless alliteration.

Dharm-Rāe (Yama) will render wretched.
Whose pride is effaced by the favour of the Guru:
That man is approved at the threshold, (says) Nānak.
(3). Who does crores of (religious) works, (but) retains his selfishness:
He incurs (only) fatigue; all his (works) are in vain.[1]
Who performs many devout austerities in egotism:
He will again and again come to hell (or) heaven.
Who, though making many efforts, does not eject his own self:[2]
Say, how shall he go to the threshold of Hari?
Who calls himself good:
Near him goodness does not come.
Whose mind becomes the dust of all:
His repute is spotless,[3] (says) Nānak.
(4). As long as (man) thinks, that anything is done by him:
He gets no happiness whatever.
As long as he thinks, that he is doing anything:
So long he is wandering about in wombs.
As long as he considers some one an enemy (or) a friend:
So long his mind is not steady.
As long as in spiritual illusion he is immersed in the Māyā:
So long Dharm-Rāe will inflict punishment on him.
By the mercy of the Lord the fetter is broken.
By the favour of the Guru egotism is done away, (says) Nānak.
(5). (Though) he gain a thousand (Rupees), he rises and runs after a Lakh.
He does not get satiated, he follows up the Māyā.
Though he enjoy many pleasures of the world:
He is not satiated, he wastes away and dies.
Without contentment no one is satisfied.
All (his) works are in vain, (they are) designs of a dream.
By delight in the name all comforts are obtained.
To some very fortunate one it is allotted.
He himself is the cause of causes.
O Nānak, mutter continually: Hari!
(6). The cause of causes is the creator.
In his hand are the order and reflection.
As he looks upon, so it becomes.
He himself, himself is the Lord.
Whatever is made, (that is made) according to his own pleasure.
He is far from all and with all.
He comprehends, sees and makes discrimination.
He himself is One and he himself is many.
He does not die nor perish, he neither comes nor goes.
Nānak (says): he is always contained (in all).

[1] ਬਿਰਥਾਰੇ = ਬਿਰਥਾ, *rē* being a meaningless alliteration.
[2] ਦ੍ਰਵੈ; ਦ੍ਰਵਣਾ = द्रावण, to drive away, to eject.
[3] ਨਿਰਮਲ ਸੋਇ, a pure report, fame.

(7). He himself instructs, he himself understands.
He himself is intimately connected with every one.
By himself his own expansion is made.
Everything is his, he is its producer.
Say, is anything done separate from him?
In every place that one alone is.
His own works he himself is doing.
He makes innumerable amusements and sports.
He himself is in his mind (and) his mind is in himself.[1]
Nānak (says): no estimate of him can be told.
(8). True, true, true is the Lord.
By the favour of the Guru he is described by some (rare) one.
True, true, true (is he, by whom) all is made.
Among crores some rare one knows him.
Splendid, splendid, splendid is thy form,
Excessively beautiful, boundless and incomparable.
Pure, pure, pure is thy voice.
In everybody it is heard with the ears and praised.
Pure, pure, pure and clean
Is (thy) name; he mutters it, who loves it in his heart, (says) Nānak.

XIII.

Slōk.

Who falls on the asylum of the saints, that man will be saved.
By slandering the saints (one) will be regenerated again and again, O Nānak!

Aṣṭpadī.

(1). By afflicting the saints (one's) lifetime is diminished.
By afflicting the saints he does not escape from Yama.
By afflicting the saints all happiness goes.
By afflicting the saints he falls into hell.
By afflicting the saints his mind becomes defiled.
By afflicting the saints he becomes denuded of lustre.
Who strikes[2] the saints, him no one protects.
By afflicting the saints he is degraded from his post.
If the compassionate saints bestow mercy (on him):
The slanderer also crosses in the society of the saints, (says) Nānak.
(2). By afflicting the saints he becomes restless.
By afflicting the saints he chatters like a crow.
By afflicting the saints he falls into the womb of snakes.
By afflicting the saints (he falls into) the womb of creeping animals.
By afflicting the saints he burns in thirst.
By reason of afflicting the saints every one deceives him.

[1] The sense is: the Supreme Being is in and to itself subject and object at the same time.

[2] The MSS. at my disposal all read: ਸੰਤ ਕੇ ਹਤੇ ਕਉ, *him who is struck by the saints;* but this is quite against the context. It should be read: ਹੰਤੇ (हन्ता) instead of ਹਤੇ.

By afflicting the saints all his dignity goes.
By afflicting the saints he (becomes) the lowest of all.
Who is injuring the saints (finds) no place (of rest).
Nānak (says): if it please the saints, he also will obtain salvation.
(3). The slanderer of the saints is a very mischievous person.[1]
The slanderer of the saints does not find a moment's rest.
The slanderer of the saints is a great murderer.
The slanderer of the saints is killed by the Lord.
The slanderer of the saints remains void of satiety.
The slanderer of the saints is afflicted and indigent.
The slanderer of the saints (is oppressed by) all diseases.
The slanderer of the saints is always separated (from the Supreme).
The slander of the saints is the greatest crime.
Nānak (says): if it pleases the saints, he also will obtain emancipation.
(4). Who is injuring the saints is always impure.
Who is injuring the saints is nobody's friend.
Who is injuring the saints incurs punishment.
Who is injuring the saints, him everybody forsakes.
Who is injuring the saints is very selfish.
Who is injuring the saints is always subject to change.[2]
Who is injuring the saints is regenerated and dies.
By afflicting the saints he turns away from (eternal) happiness.
Who is injuring the saints gets no place (of rest).
Nānak (says): if it pleases the saints, they unite (him with the Supreme).
(5). Who is injuring the saints is broken off in the midst of life.
Who is injuring the saints does not come up to any work.
Who is injuring the saints is caused to wander about in the desert.
Who is injuring the saints is thrown into the wilderness.
Who is injuring the saints is inside hollow (empty),
Like the corpse of a dead man without breath.
Who is injuring the saints has no root whatever.
Having sown himself he himself eats it.
Who is injuring the saints has no other protector.
Nānak (says): if it pleases the saints, they save him.
(6). Who is injuring the saints is so in agony,
As a fish without water flutters about.
Who is injuring the saints is hungry and not satiated,
As fire is not satiated with fuel.
Who is injuring the saints is left alone,
As a seedless sesam-stalk is (left) distressed in the field.
Who is injuring the saints is devoid of virtue.
Who is injuring the saints is always talking falsehood.
The deed of the slanderer is falling on himself.
Nānak (says): what pleases to that one (= Hari), that is done.

[1] ਅਤਤਾਈ (Sansk. आततायिन्), literally: wearing a drawn bow, *i.e.* prone to desperate deeds.
[2] ਬਿਕਾਰੀ refers here especially to the changes in transmigration.

(7). Who is injuring the saints, his constitution becomes impaired.
Who is injuring the saints is punished at the threshold (of Hari).
Who is injuring the saints is always caused to pant.
Who is injuring the saints neither dies nor is vivified.
The hope of him, who is injuring the saints, is not fulfilled.
Who is injuring the saints rises and departs hopeless.
By injury to the saints no one is satisfied.
As He pleases, such a one he becomes.
The destiny,[1] that has fallen on one, no one effaces.
Nānak (says): that True one knows it.
(8). All creatures are his, he is the creator.
To him worship be always (paid)!
Praise the Lord day and night!
Meditate on him at every breath and morsel!
All is his work.
As he makes one, such he becomes.
His own sport he himself is executing.
Who else makes reflection?
On whom he bestows mercy, to him he gives his own name.
Those are very fortunate men, (says) Nānak.

XIV.

Slōk.

Give up cunning, O friends, remember Hari, Hari the King!
Put in your heart your hope only on Hari! pain, error and fear go, (says) Nānak.

Astpadī.

(1). Know, all reliance on man is in vain!
The Lord alone is able to give,
By whose gift thou remainest satiated.
Thirst will not again befall (thee).
He alone kills and preserves.
Nothing is in the hands of man.
By comprehending his order thou obtainest happiness.
Stringing His name (like pearls) keep (it) in thy breast!
Remembering, remembering, remembering that Lord,
No harm whatever will befall (thee), (says) Nānak.
(2). Praise in thy heart the Formless one!
O my mind, do (this) true business!
With a pure tongue drink nectar!
Thou wilt always render thy life happy.
Behold with thy eyes the beauty of the Lord!
In the society of the pious all fear[2] passes away.
Go with thy feet on the road of Gōvind!
(Thy) sins are effaced, (if) Hari bc muttered only a little.

[1] ਕਿਰਤੁ, destiny, as the consequence of former works.
[2] ਸੰਗੁ *s.f.* (Sansk. शंका) fear, care.

Do the work of Hari, (hear) with thy ears the story about Hari!
At the threshold of Hari thy head (will be) bright, (says) Nānak.
(3). Those people are very fortunate in the world,
Who continually sing the excellences of Hari.
Who reflect on the name of Rām:
Those are wealthy and rich in the world.
Who with heart, body and mouth utter Hari, the most excellent:
Know, those are continually happy.
Who knows the One, the One, the One:
He has a perfect knowledge of this and that world.
Whose heart is won over to the name:
He knows him, in whom there is no darkness.
(4). Who by the favour of the Guru comprehends his own self:
Know, his thirst is quenched.
Who are uttering the praise of Hari in the society of the pious:
Those people of Hari are free from all sickness.
Who day by day is extolling the praise (of Hari) only:
He, though having a family, is free from worldly concerns.
Who puts his hope on the One:
From him the noose of Yama is cut off.
Who in his heart is hungry after the Supreme Brahm:
Him no pain befalls, (says) Nānak.
(5). Into whose heart and thought Hari comes:
That saint is happy and does not shake.[1]
On whom the Lord bestows his own mercy:
Say, of whom should that worshipper be afraid?
As it was, so it appeared (to him):
In his own work he himself is contained.
Searching and searching he (the disciple) has become successful.
By the favour of the Guru the whole truth was comprehended.
When I behold, everything is the root (= the Supreme).
He is minute and he is large, (says) Nānak.
(6). He (the Supreme) is not born at all nor does he die.
He himself performs his own works.
He is coming and going, visible and invisible.
The whole creation is kept in obedience (by him).
He himself is in all.
He, using many contrivances, establishes and disestablishes.
He is imperishable without any intermission.
He continually upholds the earth and the universe.
Inapprehensible and impenetable is the majesty (of) the Supreme Spirit.
(If) he himself causes (his name) to be muttered, then muttering (of it is made), (says) Nānak.
(7). By whom the Lord is known, they are lustrous.
All the world is saved by their advice.
The worshippers of the Lord are saving all.
The worshippers of the Lord are causing pain to be forgotten.

[1] ਤੁਲਾਵੈਂ = ਤੁਲੈ, on account of the rhyme (ਆਵੈ).

The merciful one himself unites (them with himself).
Muttering the word of the Guru they become happy.
To their service he applies himself,
On whom, as endowed with a great lot, he bestows mercy.
Muttering the name he obtains tranquillity.
Nānak (says): on that man he bestows very high honour.
(8). "Whatever he does, that (is done) according to the pleasure of the Lord.
Continually Hari dwells with (every creature).
What is naturally done, that is done."
(Who knows this), he comprehends the creator.
What the Lord does, is sweet to his people.
As it was, so it is shown (to them):
"From whom (the creatures) have sprung, in him they are absorbed."
He is the abode of happiness, with him they accord.
He himself gives honour to himself.
Nānak (says): know, the Lord and his people are One.

XV.

Slōk.

In every part (of the universe) the Lord is brimful, he is knowing the desire (of the creatures).
By whose remembrance salvation is obtained, to him Nānak is a sacrifice.

Astpadī.

(1). What is broken, Gōpāl is joining together again.
He himself is the cherisher of all creatures.
Who in his heart is caring for all:
From him no one (goes away) unprofited.
O my heart, mutter always Hari!
He himself is the imperishable Lord.
One's own doing will take no effect whatever,
Though one desire it most eagerly.[1]
Without him (*i.e.* Hari) nothing is of any use to thee.
(Thou wilt obtain) salvation by muttering the one name of Hari.
(2). Being beautiful one should not be charmed (by it):
It is the light of the Lord, that shines in all bodies.
Being rich why should one be proud,
As all wealth is the gift of him.
If one be called a very great hero:
Without the will of the Lord where will he run?
If one be a liberal donor:
The foolish one shall know him as the giver.
The disease of whose egotism is broken by the favour of the Guru:
That man is always free from disease, (says) Nānak.
(3). As a post is supporting a house:
So the word of the Guru is supporting the mind.

[1] ਜੇ ਸਉ ਪ੍ਰਾਣੀ ਲੋਚੈ ਕੋਇ, literally: though one desire it with a hundred breaths. ਪ੍ਰਾਣੀ is the Format. Plur.

As a stone being put into a boat crosses (the waters):
So a man is saved by clinging to the feet of the Guru.
As a lamp is lighting up the darkness:
So light (is kindled) in the mind by seeing the sight of the Guru.
As one finds a road in a great wilderness:
So by joining the pious light shines forth.
The dust of those saints I desire.
O Hari, fulfil the desire of Nānak!
(4). O foolish heart, why is lamentation made (by thee)?
What is written before, that is obtained.
Pain and pleasure the Lord is giving.
Giving up others think of him!
Whatever he does, that consider as happiness!
O ignorant one, why dost thou wander about in error?
What thing has come with thee,
(To which) thou stickest with delight (like) a greedy moth?
Mutter the name of Rām in thy heart!
Thou wilt go (then) with honour to (his) house, (says) Nānak.
(5). The goods, for the acquisition of which thou art come (into the world):
The name of Rām is acquired in the house of the saints.
Give up conceit and buy in (thy) mind,
Weigh in thy heart the name of Rām!
Lade a batch of goods and go with the saints!
Having given up other worldly concerns,
Everybody will call (thee) blessed, blessed.
(Thy) face (will be) bright at the threshold of Hari.
This traffic some rare one carries on.
Nānak is always a sacrifice to him.
(6). Washing the feet of the pious drink (the water, in which they were washed)!
Offer up thy life to the pious!
Make ablution in the dust of the pious!
Become a sacrifice to the pious!
The service of the pious is obtained by the very fortunate one.
In the society of the pious the praise of Hari is sung.
From many harms the pious protect.
Who sings the excellences of Hari tastes the nectar-juice.
Who seizes the protection of the saints comes to the gate (of Hari).
He obtains all happiness, (says) Nānak.
(7). The dead one He is vivifying.
To the hungry one he is giving food.
In whose favourable look all treasures are (contained):
He bestows what is apportioned (to man), according to what is written before.
Everything is his, he is able to do (all things).
Besides none other has been nor will be.
O man, mutter him continually day and night!
This is the highest and purest work.
To whom he gives mercifully the name:
That man becomes pure, (says) Nānak.

(8). In whose heart there is faith in the Guru :
Into that man's mind comes Hari, the Lord.
(That) devotee is heard of in the three worlds,
In whose heart the One is.
True is (his) work, true his conduct,
In (whose) heart the True one is, (who) utters the True one with his mouth.
True is (his) look, true his impression,
(That) the True one exists, (that) (his) expansion is true.
Who considers the Supreme Brahm as true :
That man is absorbed in the True one, (says) Nānak.

XVI.

Slōk.

He has no form, nor mark nor colour whatever, the Lord is free from the three qualities.
Him he makes comprehend (this), O Nānak, to whom he is very propitious.

Astpadī.

(1). Keep the eternal Lord in thy heart!
Give up affection to men!
No one at all is far from him.
In all is incessantly that One.
He himself is seeing, he himself is knowing.
He is deep and profound and all-wise.
The supreme Brahm, the Lord Gōvind,
Is the depository of mercy, compassionate and forgiving.
I will fall down at the feet of thy saints!
This desire is in the heart of Nānak.
(2). He is fulfilling the desire of him who is joining his asylum.
What is done (by him), that will take place.
Who takes away and gives in the twinkling of an eye:
His counsel nobody else knows.
In whose (house) are always joyful festive occasions :
In his house all things are heard.
In dominion he is a king, in the Yōga he is a Yōgī (Jōgī).
In austerity he is a great ascetic, in the married state given to enjoyment.
By meditating on whom the devotees obtain happiness :
The end of that Supreme Spirit no one has obtained, (says) Nānak.
(3). Whose sport cannot be estimated:
Entering (his estimate) all the gods were foiled.
What does the son know of the birth of the father?
The whole (creation) he has strung into his string.[1]
To whom he gives wisdom, divine knowledge and meditation :
Those his servants meditate on the name.
Whom he leads astray in the three qualities:

[1] The sense is: he keeps the whole creation, he has made, as in a string and directs it, as he pleases.

He is born and dies, comes and goes again.
The high and low places are his.
As he causes (them) to be born, such they are born,[1] (says) Nānak.
(4). Who has many forms and many appearances:
He makes various disguises, (being himself) unchanging.
An expansion of various kinds is made
By the eternal Lord, who is always the same.
In a moment he makes various proceedings.
He is present in every place.
He has made a structure of various kinds.
His own estimate he himself knows.
All creatures are his, all places are his.
Nānak lives by muttering the name of Hari.
(5). By the name are supported all the creatures.
By the name are supported the regions and the universe.
By the name are supported the Smriti, Vēda and Purāṇas.
By the name are supported hearing, knowledge and meditation.
By the name are supported the sky and the nether region.
By the name are supported all forms.
By the name are supported the (seven) cities and all the worlds.
By the name they are saved, having heard (it) with their ears.
Whom he mercifully applies to his name:
That man obtains salvation in the fourth state,[2] (says) Nānak.
(6). (His) form is true, whose place is true.
The Supreme Spirit alone is true primeval nature (as cause of the material world).
(His) work is true, whose word is true.
The true Supreme Spirit is contained in all.
His works are true, whose creation is true.
True is his root, true his production.
True and perfectly spotless is what he does.
Whom he makes comprehend (this), to him all is good.
The true name of the Lord is giving happiness.
True faith (in it) is obtained from the Guru, (says) Nānak.
(7). True is the word and instruction of the pious.
True are those men, into whose heart it enters.
True is the attachment, if one comprehend (it).
Who is muttering the name, his salvation is brought about.
He himself (*i.e.* Hari) is true, by the True one all is made.
He himself knows his own secret thought.
Whose the creation is, he is the creator.
Another does not understand (it), though he reflect (upon it).
The right knowledge of the creator no creature has.
Nānak (says): what pleases to him, that exists.

[1] ਜਾਨ is here the part. past of ਜਾਉਣਾ, *v.a.*, to bring forth.

[2] ਚਉਥਾ ਪਦ = ਤੁਰੀਆ, the state of abstraction from without and absorption in the contemplation of one's own spirit.

(8). By the wonder of wonders[1] they became astonished.
By whom it is comprehended, he has got a taste of it.
His people are steeped in the colour of the Lord.
By the word of the Guru all things are obtained (by them).
They are the donors and removers of pain,
In whose society the world crosses (the waters of existence).
The servant of his people is very fortunate.
In the society of his people devout meditation is bestowed on the One.
His people sing the excellences and praises of Gōvind.
By the favour of the Guru they obtain their reward, (says) Nānak.

XVII.

Slōk.

At the beginning is the True one, at the beginning of the Yuga is the True one.
The True one is, O Nānak, and will be also.

Asṭpadī.

(1). His foot is true, true who is touching it (in adoration).
His worship is true, true his worshipper.
His sight is true, true who is seeing it.
His name is true, true who is meditating on it.
He himself is true, true every one who has (him).
He himself is the excellences, he himself is praising the excellences.
The word is true, true the Lord, who is telling it.
The hearing is true, true he who hears (his) praise.
To him, who understands, all is true.
Nānak (says): true, true is that Lord.
(2). By whom his own true nature is acknowledged in his heart:
He has comprehended the root of the cause of causes.
Into whose heart faith in the Lord has come:
In his mind the knowledge of the truth is disclosed.
He is allowed to dwell without any fear.
From whom he has sprung, in him he is absorbed.
The thing, that is mixed up with the thing,
Cannot be called separated (from it).
(Who) understanding the (right) discrimination (of Brahm from the objective world) comprehends (it):
He obtains the One Narāyaṇ, (says) Nānak.
(3). The worshipper of the Lord is obedient to him.
The worshipper of the Lord is always adoring him.
In the heart of the worshipper of the Lord is faith.
The practise of the worshipper of the Lord is spotless.
The worshipper knows, that the Lord is with him.
The worshipper of the Lord is in love with the name.
The worshipper the Lord is cherishing.
The Formless one preserves (the honour) of his worshipper.

[1] ਬਿਸਮਨ ਬਿਸਮ, the wonder of wonders = the Supreme.

He is a worshipper, on whom the Lord bestows mercy.
Nānak (says): that worshipper remembers him at every breath.
(4). He himself conceals the faults of his people.
He himself preserves (the honour) of his worshipper throughout.
To his own servant he gives greatness.
His own worshipper he makes mutter the name.
He himself preserves the honour of his worshipper.
No one apprehends his secret thought.
No one comes up to the worshipper of the Lord.
The worshippers of the Lord are higher than high.
Whom the Lord applies to his own worship:
That worshipper becomes manifest in the ten directions (of the globe), (says) Nānak.
(5). Into a little worm he puts ingenuity.
Crores and Lakhs of armies he makes ashes.
Whose breath he himself does not take away:
Him he preserves giving him his hand.
(Though) man be making efforts of many kinds:
His works are in vain.
(If) he kill, none other will protect.
He is the protector of all living beings.
Why, O man, art thou thoughtful?
Mutter the inapprehensible, the wonderful Lord! (says) Nānak.
(6). Without intermission the Lord should be muttered!
Having drunk nectar this mind and body are satiated.
By whom the jewel of the name is obtained:
That disciple does not look upon anything else.
The name is (his) wealth, the name is (his) beauty and delight.
The name is his happiness, the name of Hari (his) companionship.
The people, who are satiated by the juice of the name,
Praise it (in their) mind and body and are absorbed in the name.
In rising, sitting and sleeping
The name is always of use to his people, (says) Nānak.
(7). Utter his praise with (thy) tongue day and night!
By the Lord (this) gift is bestowed on his own people.
Who worship him cheerfully in their heart:
They remain absorbed with their Lord.
He knows, what has been and what will be.
The Lord knows his own order.
Who can describe his greatness?
Not one is able to tell his excellences.
In whose presence the Lord dwells the eight watches:
Those are perfect men, (says) Nānak.
(8). O my heart, seize the protection of those,
Give thy mind and body to those people,
Who have known their own Lord!
Those people are the donors of all things.
In their asylum thou wilt obtain all happiness.
By their sight thou wilt efface all sins.

Give up all other cunning!
Apply thyself to the service of those people!
Thy coming and going will be stopped.
Adore always the feet of those people! (says) Nānak.

XVIII.

Slōk.

By whom the true Supreme Spirit is known, he is called the true Guru.
In his society the disciple is saved, he sings the excellences of Hari, (says) Nānak.

Asṭpadī.

(1). The true Guru is cherishing (his) disciple.
To (his) servant the Guru is always compassionate.
The Guru removes the filth of the foolishness of the disciple.
By means of the words of the Guru he (the disciple) utters the name of Hari.
The true Guru cuts the bonds of the disciple.
The disciple of the Guru recedes from change (of the mind).
The true Guru gives to the disciple the wealth of the name.
The disciple of the Guru is very fortunate.
The true Guru adjusts for the disciple this and that world.
Nānak (says): the true Guru remembers the disciple with his heart.[1]
(2). The servant, who lives in the house of the Guru,
Performs the order of the Guru with his heart.
He does not bring himself forward in any way to notice.
He always meditates in his mind on the name of Hari.
Who sells his heart to the true Guru:
That servant's affairs are all right.
Who is doing service disinterestedly:
He obtains the Lord.
On whom he (= the Lord) bestows his own mercy:
That disciple gets the instruction of the Guru, (says) Nānak.
(3). Who wins over the whole[2] heart of the Guru:
That disciple knows the way to the Lord.
He is the true Guru, in whose heart is the name of Hari.
Many times I am a sacrifice to (that) Guru.
All treasures (are in him), (he is) the donor of the creatures.
The eight watches he is steeped in the colour of the Supreme Brahm.
(His) people are in Brahm and the Supreme Brahm is in (his) people.
In himself alone (there is) no error whatever.
By a thousand dexterities he cannot be acquired.
Nānak (says): such a Guru is obtained by him, whose lot is great.
(4). His (*i.e.* the Guru's) sight is fruitful, who sees him becomes purified.
Who is touching (in adoration) his feet, his walk and practice (become) spotless.
Who is meeting with (him) utters the excellences of Rām.
He goes to the threshold of the Supreme Brahm.

[1] ਜੀਅ ਨਾਲਿ ਸਮਾਰੈ, he remembers him with his heart = he bears him in his heart.
[2] ਬੀਸ ਬਿਸਵੇ, literally: twenty twentieths = the whole.

Hearing (his) words the ears are satiated.
There is contentment in the heart, the soul is assured.
On whom the perfect Guru, whose mantra is unfailing,
Looks with his nectar-glance, he becomes a saint.
(His) excellences (are) endless, an estimate (of them) is not obtained.
Nānak (says): whom he pleases, him he unites (with Hari).
(5). The tongue is one, (his) praises many.
The true all-filling Supreme Spirit
No man reaches by discrimination or by any word.
Unattainable, inapprehensible is the Lord, who enjoys perfect bliss.
He is not eating, without enmity, bestowing happiness.
No one can make an estimate of him.
Many devotees continually serve him.
They remember the lotus-foot in their heart.
(I am) always a sacrifice to my own true Guru,
By whose favour (I am) muttering such a Lord, (says) Nānak.
(6). This juice of Hari some (rare) man obtains.
Who drinks (this) nectar, he becomes immortal.
That man is never destroyed,
In whose heart his (= Hari's) excellences are displayed.
(Who) takes the eight watches the name of Hari:
To that worshipper he gives true instruction.
He does not come into contact with the illusion of the Māyā,
Who keeps in his mind the One Hari.
(To him) in darkness a lamp shines.
Error, illusion and pain are removed from him, (says) Nānak.
(7). In heat coolness is made.
Joy takes place, the troubles are extinct, O brother!
The cares about regeneration and death are effaced
By the full instruction of the pious.
Fear ceases, he (*i.e.* the disciple) dwells in a state of fearlessness.
Every trouble is effaced from the mind.
Whose he was, by him mercy was bestowed (on him),
On account of muttering the name of the Murāri in the society of the pious.
Stability[1] is obtained (by him), wandering and moving about (in transmigration) has ceased,
After having heard the name of Hari with his ears, (says) Nānak.
(8). He himself is without qualities and endowed with all qualities,
By whose ingenuity the whole (creation) is deluded.
By the Lord himself his own deeds are done.
He himself gets his own estimate.
Without Hari there is none other.
In all that One is unintermittingly.
He is thoroughly contained in (every) form and appearance.
(These) explications are made in the society of the pious.
The creation (of the world) is made and upheld by his own skill.
Nānak is many times a sacrifice (to him).

[1] ਥਿਤਿ, stability, as opposed to wandering about in transmigration.

XIX.

Slōk.

Nothing goes with (man) except the worship (of Hari), the whole visible world is (but) ashes.
To acquire the name of Hari, Hari, this is the best wealth, (says) Nānak.

Aṣṭpadī.

(1). Joining the saints make reflection!
Remember the one name, (it is) a support!
Forget all other contrivances, O friend!
Keep the lotus-foot in thy heart and breast!
That powerful Lord is the cause of causes.
Seize firmly the name of Hari, (it is the best) thing!
Acquire this wealth and thou wilt be fortunate!
The counsel of the saints is spotless.
Rely in thy heart on the One!
All thy diseases will be done away, (says) Nānak.
(2). The wealth, for whose sake thou runnest to the four quarters (of the earth),
Thou wilt obtain by the service of Hari.
The happiness, which thou always desirest, O friend,
(Thou wilt obtain) by love to the pious.
The splendour, for whose sake thou dost good works,
(Thou wilt obtain), if thou flee to the asylum of Hari.
By many contrivances (thy) sickness does not cease.
(Thy) sickness is done away by applying the medicine of Hari.
The greatest treasure is the name of Hari.
By muttering it (thou wilt be) approved at the threshold, (says) Nānak.
(3). Instruct thy mind in the name of Hari!
(Thy mind), that is running to the ten directions (of the globe), will come to rest.
No harm whatever will befall him,
In whose heart that Hari dwells.
The Kali-yug is hot, the name of Hari is cool.
Continually remembering it thou wilt obtain happiness.
(Thy) fear is destroyed, thy hope fulfilled.
Who by devoutness and attachment is enlightening himself:
To his house comes the imperishable one and dwells therein.
Nānak (says): (from him) the noose of Yama is cut off.
(4). Who is discussing the truth, he is a true man.
Who is regenerated and dies, is quite an unskilful person.
Coming and going are effaced by serving the Lord,
By giving up one's own self in the asylum of the Gurdēv.
Thus one's life, the jewel, is saved,
By continually remembering Hari, the support of life.
By many contrivances (people) are not emancipated,
(Nor) by reflecting on the Smriti, the Shāstras and the Vēdas.
Perform worship to Hari with thy mind!
And thou wilt obtain the fruit, thou art desiring, (says) Nānak.
(5). Thy wealth will not go with thee.
Why art thou (then) clinging to it, O foolish heart?

Son, friends, family and wife :
Say, which of them wilt thou have for a protector ?
Dominions and merriments and plenty of worldly goods :
Say, what deliverance (comes) from them ?
Horses, elephants and riding on chariots,
Is a vain ostentation, a vain display.
By whom (all these things) were given, him he does not comprehend, (he is) a stranger (to him).
Having forgotten the name he repents (of it), (says) Nānak.
(6). O ignorant one, take thou the instruction of the Guru !
Without worship (of Hari) many clever ones have been drowned.
O friend, worship Hari in thy heart !
Thy intellect will become pure.
Keep the lotus-foot in thy mind !
The sins of (thy) various births will go off.
Mutter thyself, and make others mutter the name !
By continually hearing and uttering (it) thou wilt obtain salvation.
The truly existing of all things [1] is the name of Hari.
Sing his excellences with natural ease ! (says) Nānak.
(7). Singing his excellences thy filth will go off.
The poison of egotism and wickedness departs.
Thou becomest free from cares and wilt dwell in happiness,
Remembering at every breath and morsel the name of Hari.
Give up all cunning, O my heart !
In the society of the pious thou wilt obtain true wealth.
Make it thy business to collect the capital of Hari !
Here (thou wilt have) happiness and at the threshold applause.
He sees in all constantly the One,
On whose forehead (this) destiny (is written), (says) Nānak.
(8). Mutter the One, praise the One !
Remember the One, recite the One in (thy) mind !
Sing the excellences of the One, who is endless !
In heart and body mutter the One Lord !
Hari himself is the only One.
The Lord is brimfully contained (in all).
Many expansions have emanated from the One.
Adoring the One (thy) sins are gone.
In the mind and body the One Lord is sporting.
By the favour of the Guru the One is known, (says) Nānak.

XX.

Slōk.

Wandering and wandering about (I) have come and fallen on thy asylum, O Lord !
O Lord, this is the prayer of Nānak : apply (me) to thy worship !

Astpadī.

(1). The beggar, O Lord, asks a gift.
Mercifully give (me) the name of Hari !

[1] ਸਾਰਭੂਤ = Sansk. सर्वभूत.

I ask for the dust of the pious people.
O Supreme Brahm, fulfil my desire!
Continually I sing the excellences of the Lord.
At every breath I meditate on thee, O Lord!
I entertain love to the lotus-foot.
I worship the Lord continually.
The One is (my) refuge, the One (my) support.
Nānak begs, that he may remember the name of the Lord!
(2). By the favourable glance of the Lord great happiness is obtained.
Some rare one gets the juice of Hari.
Those people are satiated, by whom it is tasted.
They are perfect men and are no more vacillating.
They are entirely filled with love, affection and inclination.
Desire (after Hari) springs up in the society of the pious.
They fall on (his) asylum giving up all others.
In their heart (there is) light, daily devout meditation is made.
By the very fortunate one that Lord is muttered.
Nānak (says): who is attached to the name, obtains comfort.
(3). The desire of the worshipper is fulfilled.
From the true Guru he obtains spotless instruction.
To his servant the Lord becomes merciful.
(His) worshipper is always made exalted.
Cutting (his) bonds (his) servant is made free.
Regeneration and death, pain and error are gone.
His wish is granted, all his desire is fulfilled.
He (Hari) dwells always with him in his presence.
Whose he (= the servant) was, by him he is united (with himself).
Nānak (says): by devotion he is absorbed in the name.
(4). Why should he be forgotten, who does not break (one's) work?[1]
Why should he be forgotten, who is acknowledging one's work?
Why should he be forgotten, by whom everything is given?
Why should he be forgotten, who is the life of the creatures?
Why should he be forgotten, who preserves in the midst of fire?
By the favour of the Guru some rare one apprehends him.
Why should he be forgotten, who draws out from poison?
(Who) reunites him, who had broken away (from him) through various births.
By the perfect Guru this truth is taught.
By Nānak, the servant, his own Lord is meditated upon.
(5). O holy friend, do this work!
Giving up others mutter the name of Hari!
Remembering it continually thou wilt obtain happiness.
Mutter it thyself and make others mutter the name!
By devotion and love the world is crossed.
Without devotion (to Hari) the body will be ashes.

[1] ਘਾਲ ਨ ਭਾਨਣਾ, literally: not to break one's work, *i.e.* not to let pnss unrequited. ਘਾਲ ਭਾਨਣਾ is a Hindī translation of the Sansk. कृतघ्न = unthankful, and the following ਕੀਆ ਜਾਣੈ of the Sansk. कृतज्ञ = thankful.

The depository of all welfare and happiness is the name.
The drowning one gets rest.
All troubles are extinguished.
Nānak (says): mutter the name, the depository of (all) excellences!
(6). Affection, love, inclination and desire spring up (in him),
In (whose) mind and body this very relish is.
Seeing (his) sight with the eyes happiness is obtained.
The mind becomes joyful by washing the feet of the pious.
In the heart and body of the devotees is pleasure.
Some rare one obtains (their) society.
In mercy the one thing is given (to him),
Who mutters by the favour of the Guru the name.
His greatness cannot be told,
Who is contained in all, (says) Nānak.
(7). The Lord is forgiving and merciful to the poor.
Compassionate to the devotees and always kind.
Gōvind Gōpāl is the friend of the friendless,
Making and cherishing all creatures.
The primeval divine male, the cause of causes.
The support of the life of (his) devotees.
Whoever mutters him, he becomes purified.
(Whom) he applies to devoutness, (his) mind is directed (on him).
We are devoid of virtues, low, ignorant.
Nānak (has fled) to thy asylum, O Supreme Spirit, O Lord!
(8). All obtain paradise (and) final emancipation,
By whom the excellences of Hari are sung one moment.
(They get) many royal enjoyments and greatness,
To whose mind the story of the name of Hari is pleasing.
(They have) many enjoyments, clothes and joyful songs,
(Whose) tongue is continually muttering: Hari, Hari!
(Their) practice is virtuous, they have splendour and wealth,
(In whose) heart the mantra of the perfect Guru dwells.
O Lord, let me dwell in the society of the pious!
All happiness (is there) displayed, (says) Nānak.

XXI.

Slōk.

He himself is endowed with all qualities and without any qualities, formless, sunk in objectless, deep meditation.

By himself (all) is created and he himself also is muttering (in adoration).

Asṭpadī.

(1). When this (human) form is no longer seen:
Then demerit and merit whence does it spring?
When by himself objectless, deep meditation[1] is kept up:

[1] सुंन समाधि; सुंन (शून्य), empty, devoid, not directed to any object, as there is not anything, but the supreme, primeval being.

Then with whom do they make enmity and opposition?
When no colour nor mark of man is known:[1]
Then, say, whom does joy and grief fill?
When the Supreme Brahm himself is (man's) own self:
Then where is illusion? who is led astray by error?
His own sport is carried on by himself.
Nānak (says): there is no other creator.
(2). When the Lord alone is the master (of all):
Then say, whom shall I account bound (or) free?
When Hari alone is unattainable, endless:
Then what descent is there to hell (or) heaven?
When the Lord is destitute of qualities by his innate nature:
Then say, in which place is the energy of Shiva?
When he himself applies his own light:[2]
Then who is fearless, who is afraid of any one?
He himself is doing his own works.
Nānak (says): the Lord is unattainable, endless.
(3). When he himself is imperishable, dwelling in happiness:
Then say, where is regeneration and death and destruction?
When the creator, that Lord, is omnipresent:
Then say, who should entertain fear of Yama?
When the Lord alone is not passing and inapprehensible:
Then from whom should Čitragupta ask an account?
When the Lord is free from all darkness, inapprehensible, unfathomable:
Then who are set free, who are bound with fetters?
He himself is wonderful in himself.
Nānak (says): his own form is procured by himself.
(4). When there is the Supreme pure Spirit, the king of men:
Then, say, what is (one) washing in the absence of filth?
When there is he, who is free from all darkness, formless, absorbed in himself:
Then for whom (should there be) regard, of whom (should one be) proud?
When there is only the form of the Lord of the universe:
Then, say, to whom should stick fraud (and) blemish?
When that, which bears the form of light,[3] is re-absorbed in light:
Then who should be hungry, who should be satiated?
The creator is the cause of causes.
Nānak (says): there is no estimate of the creator.
(5). When his own glory is laid out (by) himself with (one):
Then who is his mother, father, friend, son and brother?
When he himself, who is accomplished in every skill, (is in one):
Then what is he gathering (from) the Vēda or the book?[4]

[1] ਇਸ ਕਾ, of this one = man. The sense is: when all human individuality is absorbed.

[2] ਜੋਤਿ, light, as the principle of life in all creatures.

[3] ਜੋਤਿ ਸਰੂਪੀ, bearing or having the form, qualities of (divine) light, *i.e.* the creature is re-absorbed in the fountain of light.

[4] ਕਤੇਬ = كِتاب, the book, *i.e.* the Qur'ān.

When he himself puts his own self into (one's) breast:
What should he reflect on good or ill omens?
When he himself is high, he himself is near:
Then who shall be called Lord, who servant?
(We are) astonished at the wonder of wonders.
Nānak (says): he himself knows his own state.
(6). When the undeceivable, the indivisible, the impenetrable one is contained (in one):
Whom will then the Māyā penetrate?
He himself (gives) order to himself.
The three qualities do not affect (him).
When the One Lord only is (in one):
Then who is free from care, whom does care befall?
When his own assurance of himself (is in one):
Then who speaks, who is the hearer?
He is quite boundless, higher than high.
Nānak (says): he himself comes up to himself.
(7). When by himself the form of the world is created,
And laid out in the three qualities:
Then religious demerit and merit, what is it?
One he makes desire hell and another heaven.
(There is) the useless entanglement and trouble of the Māyā.
(There is) the burden (of) selfishness, spiritual blindness, error and fear.
(There is) pain and pleasure, honour and dishonour,
(Which) are explained in different ways.
(But) he himself makes and beholds his own sport.
(When) the sport is closed, there remains (only) the One, (says) Nānak.
(8). When he himself is not passing away, then (his) devotee (also is not passing away).
When the expansion (of the world) is spread out, (it is done for) the glory of the saints.
He himself is the owner of both sides (=both worlds).
Their beauty is made by him.
He himself makes sports, pleasures and frolics.
He himself is given to enjoyments uninterruptedly.
Whom he pleases, him he applies to his own name.
What he pleases, that play he plays.
No estimate can be made of him, he is unfathomable, unmeasurable, not to be weighed.
Nānak, his slave, speaks, as he makes (him) speak.

XXII.

Slōk.

O Lord of all creatures, thou thyself art existing!
Nānak (says): the One is spread out, where is another to be seen?

Asṭpadī.

(1). He himself speaks and he himself is hearing.
He himself is One and he himself is expansion (= multiplicity).
When it pleases him, he produces a creation.
By his own decree he absorbs it (again).
Without thee nothing whatever is done.
The whole world thou stringest into thy string.

Whom thou, O Lord, instructest thyself:
That man gets the true name.
He looks on all things as the same, who knows the truth.
The whole creation he is overcoming, (says) Nānak.
(2). All creatures are in his hands.
He is merciful to the poor, the friend of the friendless.
Whom he protects, him no one kills.
He is dead, whom he forgets from his mind.
Having given him up where else should one go?
Above all is the One king, in whom there is no darkness.
In whose hand is all the management of the creatures:
Him know (as being) with thee inside and outside!
He is the depository of all excellences, endless and boundless.
Nānak, his slave, is always a sacrifice (to him).
(3). The merciful one is omnipresent.
He is compassionate to all.
He himself knows his own actions.
The inward governor is continually contained (in all).
He cherishes creatures of many kinds.
Whatever is made by him, of that he thinks.
Whom he pleases, him he unites (with himself).
Who worships (him) singing the excellences of Hari,
Who trusting in him in his mind obeys him:
By him the One creator is known (says) Nānak.
(4). Who clings to the One name of Hari:
That man's hope does not remain unfulfilled.
To the servant (of Hari) the service (of Hari) is pleasing.
By understanding (Hari's) order he obtains the highest step.
Nothing higher can be imagined than he,
In whose mind dwells he, who is void of all darkness (= the Supreme).
Breaking their fetters they become friendly to all,
Who day by day worship the feet of the Guru.
In this world they are easy and in the other world happy,
Whom Hari, the Lord himself, unites (with himself), (says) Nānak.
(5). Join the society of the pious and be happy!
Sing the excellences of the Lord, the supreme bliss!
Reflect on the truth of the name of Rām!
Save (thy human) body, which is hard to obtain!
Sing the nectar-words, the excellences of Hari!
The crossing of thy life, this is (thy) object.
Behold the Lord always (as being) near (to thee)!
Thy ignorance will be effaced, thy darkness be extinguished.
Hear (this) instruction and make it dwell in (thy) heart!
And thou wilt obtain the fruits, thy heart desires.
(6). Adjust both, this and that world,
By keeping the name of Rām in thy breast!
The initiation of the perfect Guru is perfect.
In whose heart it dwells, by him the True one is verified (in his own person).

Mutter with devout meditation the name in (thy) heart and body!
Pain, trouble and fear will depart from thy mind.
O trafficker, carry on a true traffic!
Thy batch of goods will get safely to the threshold (of Hari).
Keep in thy heart reliance on the One!
And thou wilt not come nor go again, (says) Nānak.
(7). Away from him whereto will one go?
One is saved by meditating on the preserver.
Who mutters the fearless (Hari), all his fear is effaced.
By the mercy of the Lord man is emancipated.
Whom the Lord protects, he suffers no pain.
In the heart of him, who is muttering the name, happiness springs up.
Anxiety goes, selfishness is effaced.
No one is coming up to that man.
On (whose) head the Guru, the hero, is standing:
His affairs are accomplished, (says) Nānak.
(8). Whose intelligence is perfect, whose glance is nectar:
Seeing his sight the creation is saved.
Whose lotus-feet are incomparable:
His sight is fruitful; beautiful is the form of Hari.
Blessed is (his) service, approved of is (his) servant.
The inward governor, the primeval divine male,
In whose heart he dwells, he becomes exalted.
Death does not come near him.
They become immortal and attain the dignity of immortality,
Who in the society of the pious meditate on Hari, (says) Nānak.

XXIII.

Slōk.

The collyrium of divine knowledge, that is extinguishing ignorance and darkness, is given by the Guru.

(With whom) by the mercy of Hari the saints have met, in (his) mind (there is) light.

Asṭpadī.

(1). In the society of the saints the Lord is seen (as being) within (one).
The name of the Lord becomes sweet.
Everything is in the One vessel,
Which appears under many various forms.
The name of the Lord is nectar (and) the nine treasures.
His place of rest is in the (human) soul.
(Where there is) deep abstract meditation, there the unbeaten sound (is heard).
The wonder and astonishment cannot be told.[1]
By him it is seen, to whom he himself shows it.
Nānak (says): that man gets a right knowledge (of it).
(2). That endless one is inside and outside.
In everybody the Lord is contained:

[1] ਬਿਸਮਾਦ = ਬਿਸਮਾ, *d* being here a meaningless alliteration (not ਬਿਸਮਾਦ, adj., astonished).

In earth, heaven and the nether region.
All the worlds the cherisher is filling.
In tree, grass and mountain is the Supreme Brahm.
As his order is, so it is done.
He is in wind, water, fire.
He is contained in the four quarters and in the ten directions (of the earth).
Without him there is no place.
By the favour of the Guru Nānak obtains happiness.
(3). Behold, in the Vēda, the Purāṇas, the Smriti,
In the moon, sun and stars is the One.
The praise of the Lord every one utters.
He himself is immovable, he never moves to and fro.
Practising all ingenuity he plays his play.
By no estimate he is reached, he is inestimable in qualities.
Whose light is in all (created) light:
(That) Lord is supporting (all) lengthwise and crosswise.
By the favour of the Guru error is destroyed.
This faith has Nānak in him.
(4). What the saints behold, that is all Brahm.
In the view of the saints all is virtue.
What the saints hear, that is a good word.
They are absorbed with the all-pervading Rām.
This is the custom of him, by whom he (Rām) is known.
True are all the words, the pious are uttering.
Whatever happens, that they consider as happiness.
(Because) they know the Lord (as) the cause of causes.
Inside as well as outside he abides.
Nānak (says): all, who have seen (his) sight, are fascinated[1] (thereby).
(5). He himself is true and true is all his work.
From that Lord all the creation has sprung.
If it pleases him, he makes an expansion.
If it pleases him, he is of one form (only).[2]
(His) manifold ingenuity cannot be apprehended.
Whom he pleases, he unites (with himself).
Who can be called near, who far?
He himself is omnipresent.
Whom he lets know his secret mind:
That man he himself makes comprehend (the truth), says Nānak.
(6). In all creatures he himself is abiding.
He himself is seeing all with his eyes.
Whose body the whole (world) is:
He hears himself his own praise.
He has made one sport of coming and going.[3]

[1] ਮੋਹੀ = ਮੋਹੇ, on account of the rhyme (ਓਹੀ).

[2] The sense is: he re-absorbs all into himself.

[3] The sense is: it his sport or pleasure, that creatures come and go.

The Māyā is made obedient (to him).
In the midst of all he remains uncontaminated.
Whatever is to be said, that he says himself.
By (his) order (one) comes, by (his) order (one) goes.
Nānak (says): whom he pleases, him he re-absorbs.
(7). What comes from him, is not bad.
Say, is by anybody else anything done?
He himself is good and his work is very good.
He himself knows what is in his own mind.
He himself is true and all (his) practice is true.
Lengthwise and crosswise he is absorbed with himself.
His secret mind cannot be told.
If there would be somebody else, information would be got.
All that he does, is real.
By the favour of the Guru Nānak knows this.
(8). Who knows (him), to him always happiness accrues.
That Lord himself unites (him with himself).
He is rich, noble and honoured,
Emancipated whilst living, in whose heart the Lord is.
It is good fortune, good fortune, good fortune, that the man has come,
By whose favour the whole world is saved.[1]
This is the object of the coming of (that) man,
(That) in the society of the man the name may come into (one's) mind.
He himself is emancipated and he makes the world (also) emancipated.
To that man reverence (should) always (be made), (says) Nānak.

XXIV.

Slōk.

(By whom) the perfect Lord, whose name is perfect, is adored:
He obtains the perfect one by singing the excellences of the perfect one, (says) Nānak.

Asṭpadī.

(1). Hear the instruction of the perfect Guru!
Behold the Supreme Brahm as being near (thee)!
At every breath remember Gōvind!
The anxiety of (thy) mind will (then) cease.
Give up the transitory wave of hope!
Ask in thy heart for the dust of the saints!
Giving up thy own self make supplication,
(That) in the society of the pious thou mayest cross the ocean of fire!
Fill (thy) store-room with the wealth of Hari!
(Pay) reverence to the perfect Guru! (says) Nānak.
(2). Happiness, welfare, quiet and joy (will accrue to thee),
(If) thou worship the supreme bliss (= the Supreme) in the society of the pious.
Do away with hell and save (thy) soul!
Drink the nectar-juice of the excellences of Gōvind!

[1] Bābā Nānak is here understood.

Think in thy mind of the One Narāyaṇ,
Whose One form has many appearances!
Gōpāl Damōdar is kind to the poor,
Destroying pain and perfectly compassionate.
Remember, remember continually the name!
It is the support of the creatures, (says) Nānak.
(3). The highest Slōks are the words of the pious.
They are priceless rubies and gems.
Who is hearing and doing them, is saved.
He himself crosses and makes also the people cross.
Fruitful is his life, fruitful his society,
In whose heart love to Hari dwells.
All hail! the unbeaten sound resounds (in him).
Hearing, hearing it he is happy: the Lord is manifested (in him).
Gōpāl is manifested in the head of the holy man.
Nānak (says): in his society (people) are saved.
(4). Who hearing of him and being needy of protection come to his asylum:
Them the Lord himself mercifully unites (with himself).
Enmities are extinguished, they become the dust of all.
The nectar-name they take in the society of the pious.
The Gurdēv becomes very propitious to them.
The service of the worshippers is accomplished.
From useless embarrassment and change (of the mind) they are freed.
Having heard the name of Rām they utter it with their tongue.
The Lord bestows favour and mercy (on them).
Nānak (says): our trip is accomplished.
(5). Praise the Lord, O holy friend!
Attentively and exclusively think (of him)!
(In) the Sukhmanī (is) tranquillity; praise the qualities of Gōvind!
In whose mind he dwells, he becomes (his) receptacle.
All his desire becomes fulfilled.
He becomes known as the first man in all the world.
He gets the highest place.
He is not subject again to coming and going.
That man departs, having acquired the wealth of Hari,
To whom it is allotted, (says) Nānak.
(6). Welfare, tranquillity, the nine treasures,
Intelligence, divine knowledge, all perfections are his.
Science, austerity, spiritual devotion, meditation on the Lord,
The best knowledge, the most excellent ablution,
The four desirable objects (of human life), the opening of the lotus (of the heart),
Indifference to all in the midst of all (are his).
He is beautiful, clever, a knower of truth,
Looking on all things as the same, directing his look on the One.
These fruits has he, who with his mouth utters
The name, (says) Guru Nānak, and in his heart hears (these) words.
(7). If one mutter this treasure in his mind:
His salvation is brought about in all the Yugas.

The excellences of Gōvind, meditation on the name and praise (of it),
Are expounded by the Smriti, the Shāstras, the Vēdas and the Purāṇas.
The object of all instruction is solely the name of Hari.
In the mind of the devotee of Gōvind is tranquillity.
Crores of sins are effaced in the society of the pious.
By the mercy of the saints he is rescued from Yama.
On whose forehead (this) destiny is written by the Lord :
Those come to the asylum of the pious, (says) Nānak.
(8). In whose heart it (= the name) dwells and who hears it with affection :
Into his mind the Lord Hari comes.
He removes the pain of regeneration and death.
The body, which is hard to obtain, he saves at once.
Spotless is his lustre, nectar is his speech,
In whose heart the One name is contained.
Pain, disease, fear and error are extinguished.
The name of the pious is pure, (pure are) his works.
His splendour is raised above all,
Who considers it a pleasure[1] to recite this name (of Hari), (says) Nānak.

RĀGU GAUṚĪ; THITĪ;[2] MAHALĀ V.

Ōm! By the favour of the true Guru!

I.

Slōk.

The Lord, the creator, is present throughout in water, earth and on the surface of the earth.
The One, whose form is one, is spread out having become of many kinds, (says) Nānak.

Pauṛī.

On the *first* (lunar day) worship the Lord, whose form is one, meditating on him!
Recite Gōvind, Gōpāl, the Lord, fall on the asylum of Hari the king!
From him (comes) protection, welfare and happiness, by whom everything is made.
In the four corners, in the ten directions (of the earth) I have wandered about: without him there is none other.
The Vēdas, the Purāṇas and the Smriti were heard (by me), I reflect in many ways:
The deliverer of the sinners, the destroyer of fear, the ocean of happiness is the formless one.
He is bountiful and giving enjoyments; with him there is no other place.
What Nānak desires, that he obtains by singing the excellences of Hari.

Pause.

The praise of Gōvind should always be sung!
Joining the society of the pious he should be worshipped, O my friend!

[1] ਸੁਖ ਮਨੀ = ਸੁਖ ਮੰਨਿਆ, on account of the rhyme.
[2] ਥਿਤਿ, *s.f.* a lunar date or day of the lunar period of fifteen days.

II.

Slōk.

Perform worship many times, fall on the asylum of Hari the king!
In the society of the pious error and duality will be cut off and effaced, (says) Nānak.

Pauṛī.

On the *second* (lunar day) remove folly, serve continually the Guru!
Rām, the gem, dwells in (thy) heart and body, O friend, if thou give up lust, wrath and covetousness.
Death is effaced, life is obtained, all distress is annihilated.
Give up thy own self, adore Gōvind, give thyself to love and devotion (to Hari)!
Gain will accrue (to thee), loss will be removed, at the threshold of Hari (thou wilt be) honoured.
If thou collect the wealth of the name of Hari, (thou art) a true and fortunate wholesale merchant.
Rising and sitting adore Hari, being delighted with the pious!
Nānak (says): folly goes off (thus), the Supreme Brahm dwells in (thy) mind.

III.

Slōk.

The three (states) [1] permeate the world, the fourth (state) some (rare) one obtains.
Nānak (says): those saints have become pure, in whose mind that One dwells.

Pauṛī.

On the *third* (day) the fruit of the poison of the three qualities is now and then very high, now and then low.
Wandering much about in hell and heaven death always kills (him again).[2]
In joy, grief and doubt the world (is immersed), in egotism it spends its time.
By whom they have been made, him they do not know, they think of many contrivances (with a view to their salvation).
(His) mental anxiety, difficulty, trouble, passion and inquietude is not broken,
Who does not comprehend the majesty of the Supreme Brahm, the omnipresent Lord.
Being quite immersed in spiritual blindness and error he dwells in the great hell.
O Lord, mercifully protect me, Nānak hopes in thee!

IV.

Slōk.

He is clever, intelligent and skilful, by whom his egotism is abandoned.
(He has) the four (desirable) objects (of human life) and the eight perfections, (who) adores the name of Hari, (says) Nānak.

Pauṛī.

On the *fourth* (day) (by whom) the four Vēdas are heard and investigated and truth reflected upon;
(Who) mutters and remembers the name of Rām, (in which are) all welfare, happiness (and all) treasures:

[1] The three states are: जाग्रत्, स्वप्न and सुषुप्ति; the fourth state is abstraction from without and absorption in the contemplation of one's own spirit (as identical with Brahm).

[2] Whoever is yet subject to the three qualities, though he may afterwards for his good works attain to heaven, is reborn on earth and in the power of death. Who is thrown into hell for his bad works, is reborn on earth, after his punishment is over. Only he is thoroughly emancipated, who on earth has become liberated from the influence of the three qualities.

He prevents hell, removes pain, (his) many troubles are done away.
Death recedes (from him), he is delivered from Yama, by undertaking the praise of Hari.
(His) fear is destroyed, he tastes nectar, he is imbued with love to the formless Hari.
The pain of poverty and impurity is annihilated, the name is (his) support.
Gods, Naras, Munis, men are seeking Gōpāl, the ocean of happiness.
(His) mind is pure, (his) face is bright, (who) becomes the dust of the pious, (says) Nānak.

V.

Slōk.

Five passions dwell in the mind (of him, who) is absorbed with the Māyā.
In the society of the pious he becomes pure, (says) Nānak, by love to the Lord.

Pauṛī.

The *fifth* (day). Those arbitrators are the best, by whom the deceit is known.
There is a great variety of flowers and scents, (but) all is falsehood (unreality) and imposition.
Nothing is known nor understood by it (*i.e.* the world), it makes no reflection whatever.
The world is immersed in ignorance, being deeply engaged in pleasure, worldly attachment and enjoyment.
He is regenerated and dies and wanders about in many wombs, (though) many religious works be done (by him),
(By whom) the creator is not remembered, in (whose) mind (there is) no reflection nor discrimination.
(Who has) a loving attachment to the Lord, he is not a bit contaminated by the Māyā.
Nānak (says): some rare ones are found, who are not enraptured with the world.

VI.

Slōk.

The six Shāstras state, that He is high and has no end nor limit.
The devotees, who are singing his excellences, shine at the gate of the Lord, (says) Nānak.

Pauṛī.

The *sixth* day. The six Shāstras say it and many Smritis tell it:
That the Supreme Brahm is most excellent and high, the end of his excellences Shēsh [1] does not know.
Nārada, the Munis, Shuka [2] and Vyāsa are singing the praise of Gōvind.
They are desirous of (his) juice, they are delighted with Hari, the devotees are enraptured with the Lord.
Infatuation, conceit and error are destroyed, the asylum of the merciful one is obtained (by them).
The lotus-foot dwells in (their) mind and body, having seen (his) sight (they are) happy.
Gain is obtained, loss is taken away by devoutly meditating in the society of the pious.
They acquire the treasury and depository of (all) excellences by meditating on the name, (says) Nānak.

VII.

Slōk.

The assembly of the saints relates the glory of Hari, they utter it with true affection.
Nānak (says): (their) mind becomes content by devoutly applying their thought to the One.

[1] शेष, the thousand-headed serpent king, the couch and canopy of Vishṇu and the upholder of the world, which rests on one of his heads.

[2] शुक, the son of Vyāsa.

Pauṛī.

On the *seventh* day collect the wealth of the name, the treasury (of which) is not exhausted!
In the assembly of the saints he is obtained, (who) has no end nor limit.
Give up thy own self and adore Gōvind, fall on the asylum of Hari, the king!
Thou wilt remove (thy) pain, thou wilt cross the water of existence, thou wilt obtain the fruit desired by (thy) mind.
(If) thou mutter day and night Hari in (thy) mind, (thy) life is fruitful and approved.
Know, that the creator is always inside and outside with thee.
He is a friend, he is a companion and friend, who gives instruction about Hari.
Nānak is a sacrifice to him, who mutters the name of Hari, Hari.

VIII.

Slōk.

(If) the eight watches (his) excellences be sung, (if) the other bores be abandoned:
The servant of Yama cannot overpower (him), Nānak (says): the Lord is merciful.

Pauṛī.

The *eighth* (day). The eight perfections, the nine treasures;
All the (four desirable) objects (of human life), perfect intelligence;
The opening of the lotus (of the heart), continual joy;
Pure conduct, (the giving of) salutary advice;
All virtues, pure ablutions:
Higher and more excellent than all is divine knowledge.
The worship of Hari, Hari (is made) in the society of the perfect Guru.
By muttering the name and by love to Hari one crosses, (says) Nānak.

IX.

Slōk.

Narāyaṇ is not remembered (by him, who is) fascinated by enjoyment and passion.
Nānak (says): by forgetting the name one wanders about in hell and heaven.

Pauṛī.

The *ninth* (day). The nine apertures (of the body) are impure.
Those, who do not mutter the name, act perversely.
They sport with another's wife, they prate slander against the pious.
They do not hear a bit the glory of Hari with their ears.
They steal another's property for the sake of their (own) belly.
Their (burning) fire is not put out, their thirst is not quenched.
Without the service of Hari these fruits are earned.
Nānak (says): by forgetting Hari the unfortunate die and are born (again).

X.

Slōk.

I wandered about searching in the ten directions (of the earth); wherever I see, there is that One (*i.e.* the Supreme).
The mind is brought into one's power, if it be the mercy of the omnipresent one.

Pauṛī.

The *tenth* (day). (By whom) the ten gates (of the body) are brought under subjection :
In (their) heart is contentment, they mutter the name.
(Who) hear with their ears the glory of Hari, Gōpāl :
(Those) pious ones are seeing with their eyes the merciful (Hari).
(Their) tongue sings the praises of the endless one.
In (their) heart they reflect on the omnipresent Lord.
With their hands and feet they perform service to the saints.
Nānak (says) : this control (of the senses) is obtained by the mercy of the Lord.

XI.

Slōk.

The only One should be praised, (but some) rare one knows the relish (of it) !
The excellences of Gōvind are not known, (says) Nānak, every one is astonished (at them).

Pauṛī.

The *eleventh* (day). Behold Hari as being near (thee) !
Subdue (thy) senses and hear the name of Hari !
Contentment is in (thy) mind, (if there be) kindness towards all creatures.
In this wise (thy) religious duty is fulfilled.
If thou keep (thy) running (mind) in one place :
(Thy) heart and body (become) pure in muttering the name of Hari.
In all the Supreme Brahm is present.
Nānak (says) : praise Hari, this is a permanent duty !

XII.

Slōk.

(Their) foolishness is removed, they perform service (to Hari), (with whom) the kind pious people have met.
Nānak (says) : who remain united with the Lord, all their troubles are extinguished.

Pauṛī.

On the *twelfth* day (give) alms, (mutter) the name (and perform) ablutions !
Worship Hari and give up conceit !
Drink the nectar of Hari in the society of the pious !
(Thy) mind will be satiated by praise and love to Hari.
A soft speech renders every one contented.
With the juice of the name of Hari thou nourishest the five elements (=body) and the soul.
From the perfect Guru this assurance is obtained.
Nānak (says) : uttering the name of Rām one does not again fall into a womb.

XIII.

Slōk.

(Who) is comprehended within the three qualities, his affair is not accomplished.
(If) the saviour of the sinners dwells in his heart, he is emancipated (by) the name, (says) Nānak.

Pauṛī.

The *thirteenth* (day). Under three afflictions[1] is the world.
It is coming and going and descends to hell.
The worship of Hari, Hari does not come into its mind.
The Lord, the ocean of comfort, is not praised a moment.
It is bound, now and then having joy and now and then grief.
A long disease is produced[2] by the Māyā.
By making changes (of mind) disquietude is obtained.
In the eyes is drowsiness, it talks (as in) a dream.
This state takes place by forgetting Hari.
Nānak is in the asylum of the Lord, the merciful Supreme Spirit.

XIV.

Slōk.

The four quarters, all the fourteen worlds Rām is pervading.
Nānak (says): no deficiency is seen, his works are everywhere.

Pauṛī.

The *fourteenth* (day). In the four quarters is the Lord himself.
His majesty is filling all the worlds.
In the ten directions the one Lord is contained.
Behold, in earth and sky, in all is the Lord.
In water, earth, wood, mountain and the nether region:
There the merciful Lord abides.
Small and large, all is the Lord.
Nānak (says): the disciple is knowing Brahm.

XV.

Slōk.

(By him) his own self is overcome, (by whom) according to the instruction of the Guru the excellences of Gōvind are sung.

By the favour of the saints fear is effaced, anxiety is extinguished, (says) Nānak.

Pauṛī.

The day of the new moon. They are happy in themselves, (to whom) contentment was given by the Gurdēv.

(Their) mind and body is cool, tranquillity and composure are attained by serving the Lord.

(Their) fetters are broken (and their) many changes (of mind), (their) affairs are fruitful and accomplished.

(Their) folly is swept away, (their) egotism gone off by remembering the name of Hari.

The asylum of the Supreme Brahm is seized, coming and going are effaced.

He is saved himself with his family by uttering the excellences of Gōvind,

(And) by performing service to Hari, (if) the name of the Lord be muttered.

Happiness and tranquillity are obtained from the perfect Guru, (says) Nānak.

[1] The three afflictions are: आध्यात्मिक (psychical or corporeal), आधिभौतिक (physical or material) and आधिदैविक (from the gods or fate).

[2] All the MSS. read: ਆਸਾਧਿ, though the preposition आ is hardly ever found connected with साध् in Sanskrit.

XVI.

Slōk.

The perfect (full) one never vacillates, (who) is made perfect by the Lord himself.
Day by day he increases more, (says) Nānak, and does not decrease.

Pauṛī.

The day of full moon. Full is the Lord alone, the powerful cause of causes.
The Supreme Spirit, whose hand is above all, is merciful to the creatures.
Gōvind, the Guru, whose work takes effect, is the depository of (all) excellences.
The Lord, the inward governor, is wise, inapprehensible and free from all darkness.
The Supreme Brahm, the Lord, is knowing every affair.
To the assistant of the saints and (their) refuge constantly reverence!
(His) inexpressible tale is not comprehended, remember the feet of Hari!
He is saving the sinners, the friend of the friendless.
Nānak is in the asylum of the Lord.

XVII.

Slōk.

(His) pain is extinguished, (his) doubt is gone, (who) has seized the asylum of Hari, the King.
By singing the excellences of Hari he obtains the fruit, his heart desires, (says) Nānak.

Pauṛī.

If one sing, if one hear, if one reflect (on them);
If one teach (them), if one strengthen (them), he is saved.
He cuts off his sins, he becomes pure, the filth of his life goes.
In this and in the other world his face is bright, the Māyā does not affect him.
He is intelligent, he is a Vaishnava, he is endowed with divine knowledge and affluent.
He is a hero, he is of noble family, by whom the Lord is adored.
The Khatrī, the Brahman, the Sūdra, the Vaisya and the Čaṇḍāl are saved by remembering (Hari).
By whom his own Lord is known, his dust is Nānak.

GAUṚĪ; VĀR; MAHALĀ IV.

Ōm! by the favour of the true Guru!

I.

Slōk I.

The true Guru, the Supreme Spirit is merciful, to whom every one is approved.
With one and the same look he beholds (all), from the faith of the heart comes perfection.
In the true Guru is nectar, that highest word of Hari, Hari.
Nānak (says): by mercy Hari is meditated upon, some (rare) disciple obtains (him).

Slōk II.

Egotism and the Māyā, all is poison, in the world (there is) continually loss.
Gain is the wealth of Hari, it is acquired by the disciple by reflecting on the word (of the Guru).
The filth of egotism, the poison, goes off by keeping the nectar of Hari, Hari in the breast.
All the affairs of those disciples are accomplished, on whom he bestows mercy.

Who are personally united (with him), they remain united, being united (with himself) by Hari, the creator.

Pauṛī.

Thou art the true Lord, thou art true, the true, true Lord!
All (the creation) is meditating on thee, all (the creation) clings to thy feet.
Thy praise is beautiful and fine, by whom it is performed, him thou makest pass across.
To the disciples thou art giving (this) fruit,[1] that they are absorbed in the true name.
O my great Lord, great is thy grandeur!

II.

Slōk I.

All other praising and all other speaking, besides the name, is insipidity.
The fleshly-minded praise (their) egotism, their talk is egotism and selfishness.
(But those) who do not praise (him, *i.e.* Hari), they die, they are all consumed (by their) slander.
Humble Nānak (says): the disciples are saved muttering Hari, Hari, the supreme bliss.

Slōk II.

O true Guru, show (me) Hari the Lord, (that) I may meditate on the name of Hari in my mind!
Nānak (says): I will utter with (my) mouth the pure name of Hari, that is removing all pain.

Pauṛī.

Thou thyself art formless and void of all darkness, O King Hari!
By whom thou, the True one, art meditated upon with one mind, all their pain is removed.
Thou hast no partner, who is brought near (to thee) and informed (by thee).
There is no donor like thyself, O pure one, thou art considered as true in my mind.
O my true Lord, O True one, true is (thy) name!

III.

Slōk I.

In (thy) heart is the disease of egotism, by error thou art led astray, O fleshly-minded wicked man!
Nānak (says): remove thy disease by meeting with the true Guru and the pious, good men!

Slōk II.

The heart and body of the disciple are imbued with love to Hari, the depository of (all) excellences.
Humble Nānak (says): him, who flees to the asylum of Hari, he unites (with himself), praise to the Guru!

Pauṛī.

Thou art the creator, the unattainable Supreme Spirit, with whom art thou to be compared?
(If) one would be like thee, it would be told; thou art like thyself (only), (thus) it is read.
Thou alone art existing in all creatures, to the disciple thou art manifest.[2]
Thou art the true Lord of all, thou art higher than all.
What thou doest, that, O True one, will take place, then why should one grieve?

IV.

Slōk I.

I have love to the beloved in heart and body; those who are attached (to the beloved) day and night:
(On them) bestow mercy, O Lord, the true Guru, that they may dwell in comfort! (says) humble Nānak.

[1] The Lahore lithographed copy reads: ਪਾਇਆ, but the MSS. (Nos. 2483 and 2484) read ਪਾਇਰਾ, which we have followed in our translation.

[2] ਪਰਗੜੀਐ, instead of ਪਰਗਟੀਐ, for the sake of the rhyme.

Slōk II.

In whose heart there is love to the beloved, they will shine (at the gate) in proportion as they utter (the name of the beloved).

Nānak (says): Hari himself knows those, who entertain love to the beloved.

Pauṛī.

Thou art the creator, thou thyself art unerring and not subject to (any) mistake.
What thou doest, O True one, that is good, by the word of the Guru thou makest comprehend (this).
Thou art the powerful cause of causes, there is none other.
Thou art the Lord, unattainable and merciful, all meditate on thee.
All creatures are thine and thou art every one's, thou deliverest all.

V.

Slōk I.

Hear, O sweetheart, the message of love, the eyes are attentively fixed (on thee)!

(With whom) by the pleased Guru the sweetheart is joined, they dwell in comfort, (says) humble Nānak.

Slōk II.

The true Guru is bountiful and merciful, whose mercy is everlasting.
The true Guru is inwardly without enmity, that One Brahm he beholds (in) all.
Who entertain enmity with him, who is without enmity, of those no one remains.
The true Guru is seeking the best of all, how should evil come from him?
As one desires a fruit from the true Guru, such a one he gets.
Nānak (says): the creator is knowing all, from whom nothing is hidden.

Pauṛī.

Whom the Lord makes great, him I consider as great.
Whom the Lord pleases, him he pardons, he is acceptable to the Lord.[1]
If one offend him, he is a foolish ignorant man.
Whom the true Guru unites (with himself), he utters (his) excellences and praises (his) qualities.
Nānak (says): he is perfectly true; who comprehends (him), is absorbed in the True one.

VI.

Slōk I.

Hari is true, devoid of all darkness and immortal, without fear, without enmity, without form.
By whom he is muttered with one mind and one thought, their burden of egotism goes off.
By which disciples Hari is adored, victory to those pious people!
If one slander the perfect true Guru, him the whole world curses.
In the true Guru he himself is abiding, Hari himself is protecting him.
Blessed, blessed is he, who is singing the excellences of the Guru, to him (be) constantly reverence!
Nānak is a sacrifice to them, by whom the creator is muttered.

Slōk II.

By himself the earth is created, by himself the sky.
By himself the creatures are produced in it, he himself gives the morsel into (their) mouth.
He himself is abiding (in) all, he himself is the depository of (all) qualities.
Humble Nānak (says): meditate thou on the name, all sins are cut off by it!

[1] ਮਨਿ ਭਾਣੀ = ਮਨਿ ਭਾਣਾ, on account of the rhyme.

Pauṛī.

Thou art the true Lord, the truth, truth is pleasing to the true one.

Who are praising thee as the True one, near them the servant of Yama does not go.

Their faces are bright at the gate, to whose heart the true Hari is pleasing.

The false ones are thrown back; in whose heart is falsehood and hypocrisy, they incur great pain.

The faces of the false ones become black, the false ones become sweepings.

VII.

Slōk I.

The true Guru is the field of religious duties, as one sows on it, such a fruit he gets.

By the disciples of the Guru nectar is sown and Hari gives them the fruit of nectar.

Their faces are bright in this and that world, at the true gate they receive from Hari a dress of honour.

In the heart of some is falsehood, they practise continually falsehood; these, as they sow, such a fruit they will eat.

When the true Guru, the banker,[1] will look closely at them, they will all be disclosed as counterfeit.

They get always such (a fruit) as they intend, they are such as they are sounded by God.[2]

In both worlds the Lord himself abides, working continually he beholds all his proceedings.

Slōk II.

In him, who is directing his mind on the One, the One is abiding, to whom he (the One) attaches himself, he becomes acceptable.

Some one makes many words, (but) in whose house the thing is, he eats it.

Without the true Guru the right knowledge is not obtained, egotism does not depart from within.

The selfish ones suffer the pain of hunger, they stretch out their hand and beg at every house.

Falsehood and deceit do not remain hidden, outward show and plating go off.

For whom it is written before, with him the true Guru, the Lord falls in.

As when iron is brought in contact with the philosopher's stone, so one falling in with the society (of the pious) becomes gold.

O Lord of humble Nānak, thou art the Lord, as it pleases (thee), so thou makest (men) go.

Pauṛī.

By whom Hari is served in (their) heart, them Hari himself unites (with himself).

His qualities are communicated to them, who burn all their vices by means of the word (of the Guru).

(Their) vices are sold for straws, to whom he gives, they obtain true (qualities).

(I am) a sacrifice to my own Guru, who has effaced (my) vices and displayed (in me) virtues.

Great is the grandeur of the great one, the disciple sings (his) praise.

VIII.

Slōk I.

In the true Guru is a great majesty; who daily meditates on the name of Hari, Hari:

He, uttering the name of Hari, Hari (gets) purity and control of the senses, by the name of Hari he is satiated.

The name of Hari (is his) strength, the name of Hari (is his) tribunal, the name of Hari procures his protection.

[1] ਸਰਾਫ = صَرّاف, banker, money-changer.

[2] The sense is: they emit such a sound as God makes them emit, just as a musical instrument gives such a sound as the player desires.

Who intently adores the shape (body) of the Guru, he gets the fruits his heart desires.

Who slanders the true perfect Guru, him the creator will cause to be killed.

That time will not again come into his hand, what he has sown, he will eat himself.

He is carried off to the horrible hell with a black face, as they put a neck-halter on a thief.

If he fall again on the asylum of the true Guru, he is saved, when he meditates on the name of Hari, Hari.

Nānak proclaims the words of Hari, thus he pleases Hari, the creator.

Slōk II.

Who does not mind the order of the perfect Guru, he is self-willed, ignorant and robbed by the Māyā, the poison.

In his heart is falsehood, he is known as practising falsehood, hopeless strifes are put on his neck by God.

He sells many words, but his words please no one.

He wanders about in every house like an ill-fated woman; who comes in contact with him, to him also (his) marks are communicated.

Who becomes a disciple, he remains undefiled, he leaves the side of that one and sits down at the side of the Guru.

Who conceals his own Guru, he is not a good man, O ye saints, by him profit and capital, all is lost.

Nānak lets first hear the Shāstras and the Vēdas.

(But) the word of the perfect Guru comes (stands) above them.

To the disciples of the Guru the grandeur of the perfect Guru pleases, the self-willed do not get this opportunity.

Pauṛī.

The perfectly True one is greater than all, he obtains him, whom the true Guru appoints.

He is the true Guru, who is meditating on the True one, the perfectly True one and the true Guru are One.

He is the true Guru, the divine male, by whom the five intoxicated ones are subdued.

Who without serving the true Guru adore their own self, in them is falsehood, fie upon (them)! (their) faces are dull.

What they speak does not please any one, their faces are black by deviating from the true Guru.

IX.

Slōk I.[1]

The whole field belongs to Hari the Lord, by himself it is cultivated.

Pardoning the disciples he makes germinate (their field), by the self-willed their stock (of seed) is lost.

Every one sows for his own advantage, that field is made to germinate, which is pleasing to Hari.

By the disciples of the Guru the nectar of Hari is sown, the nectar-name of Hari, as fruit they obtain nectar.

Yama, the mouse, is constantly gnawing the field, by Hari the creator he is beaten and ejected.

The field comes forth and germinates, by Hari, who is bestowing heaps of corns, it is caused to germinate.

All their care and anxiety he removes, by whom the true Guru, the divine male, is meditated upon.

Humble Nānak (says): (by whom) the name is adored, he himself is saved and he saves (also) the whole world.

[1] This Slōk is written out by the Sikhs as a charm against mice, and buried in small vessels on the four corners of a field.

Slōk II.

The whole day the fleshly-minded one is absorbed in covetousness (and) other things.
By night he is buried in sleep, all the nine [1] are remiss in sleep.
On the head of the fleshly-minded is the order of (their) wives, they constantly lead them astray.
The men, who are doing what they are told by their wives, are impure, foul and vile.
The man, who is given to lust, is an impure man, he goes along asking his wives.
Who walks according to the bidding of the true Guru, he is a true and good man.
Women and men are all created by himself, the sport of Hari is performed in all.
All thy work is very good, (says) Nānak.

Pauṛī.

Thou art unconcerned (about anything) and bottomless, how should the inestimable one be estimated?
They are very fortunate, who are meditating on thee (and) with whom the true Guru falls in.
The word of the true Guru is true and beautiful, the word of the Guru is brought about.
The others, who in emulation of the true Guru are talking nonsense, are false, by falsehood they are broken down.
Something else is in their heart and something else in their mouth, chattering about the Māyā, the poison, they are dying in grief.

X.

Slōk I.

The service of the true Guru is pure, that man becomes pure, who performs service (to the Guru).
In whose heart is hypocrisy and false change (of mind), they are separated by the True one himself.[2]
The true disciples sit at the side of the true Guru and pass their time.
There, the false ones are not found in any good place.
To whom the word of the true Guru is not pleasing, their faces are dirty, they wander about blasted by God.
In whose heart there is no love to Hari, how long will those fleshly-minded ones be caused to take possession (of bodies) as goblins?
Who meets with the true Guru, he keeps his own mind steady, he himself abides with his own thing.
Humble Nānak (says): some the Guru joins and gives them happiness, some, who are deceitful, are separated by himself.

Slōk II.

In whose heart there is meditation on the name of Hari, their affairs are put right by God.
Their dependence on men ceases, Hari the Lord sits near them and takes their side.
(If) Hari is on (their) side, then every one is on (their) side, all who see (their) sight, applaud (them).
Wholesale merchant and king, all are made by Hari, all come and make supplication to (his) people.
The grandeur of the perfect Guru is great, by serving the great Hari inestimable happiness is obtained.
By the perfect Guru the gift (of) the immovable Hari is given, (though) he always bestows, it increases still more.[3]
A calumniator cannot see (his) greatness, that one is consumed by the creator himself.
Humble Nānak utters the excellences of the creator, he is always protecting his votaries.

[1] The nine are very likely the नवरस, the nine sentiments or passions.

[2] जजभाले; its meaning is unknown.

[3] *i.e.* the store of the gifts of the Guru.

Pauṛī.

Thou art the Lord, unattainable and compassionate, very bountiful and wise.

Like thou no one comes into my sight, thou art clever and pleasing to me.

Love to the family and all that is seen, is passing away, it is coming and going.

Who direct their mind on anything else but the True one, they are given to falsehood, false is their hope.

Nānak (says): meditate thou on the True one, the ignorant are consumed and die without the True one!

XI.

Slōk I.

(If) first true love be not bestowed (on Hari), talking afterwards (of it) is of no use.

The helpless self-willed man wanders about halfway,[1] how shall he obtain happiness by (mere) words?

In whose heart there is no love to the true Guru, he comes in falsehood and departs in falsehood.

If my Lord Hari, the creator, bestow mercy (on him), then the true Guru, the Supreme Brahm, comes into (his) sight.

Then he drinks nectar, (when) the word of the Guru removes all his anxiety, care and error.

He remains always in joy day and night, humble Nānak (says): day by day he sings the excellences of Hari.

Slōk II.

Who is called a disciple of the true Guru, he, rising early, meditates on the name.

He makes efforts early in the morning, he makes ablution, he bathes in the pond of nectar.

According to the instruction of the Guru he makes the Jap[2] of Hari, Hari, and all his sins and faults go off.

Again, when the day rises, he sings the Gur-bānī,[3] in sitting and rising he meditates on the name.

Who at every breath and morsel meditates on my Hari, Hari, he is a disciple of the Guru and pleasing to the Guru.

To whom my Lord is merciful, that disciple of the Guru he lets hear the instruction of the Guru.

Humble Nānak asks for the dust of that disciple of the Guru, who himself mutters and makes others mutter the name.

Pauṛī.

They are a few rare ones, who are meditating on thee, the True one.

Who in heart and mind are adoring the One, their abundance innumerable crores are eating.

All (the world) is meditating on thee, they are accepted, whom thou likest, O Lord!

Who, without serving the true Guru, are eating and dressing themselves, they die, having died they are reborn leprous.

Being present they speak sweetly, outside they emit poison from their mouth; (these) quarrelsome and insincere people are separated by the Lord (from himself).

XII.

Slōk I.

(Whose) tattered blue (or) black quilt is filled with filth and lice, those disaffected ones are driven away.[4]

No one allows (one) to sit near (him) in the world, who has fallen into ordure; the fleshly-minded one comes having the very same filth applied (to himself).

[1] The sense is: halfway between God and the world.

[2] The Jap of Hari (the muttering: Hari, Hari!) as a devotional exercise.

[3] The Gur-bānī is another devotional exercise, consisting of singing the praises of Hari.

[4] The construction of this verse is very intricate; the Sikh Granthīs could not give me any explanation of it. ਵੇਮੁਖਿ or ਵੇਮੁਖ has here a double meaning: *disaffected* (turning away their face from the Guru) and (with the verb ਪਾਉਣਾ) *to turn off* or *drive away* (similarly: ਵੇਮੁਖਿ ਭੇਜਣਾ). The construction is: ਤਿਨਿ ਵੇਮੁਖਾਂ ਨੇ ਵੇਮੁਖਿ ਪਾਇਆ.

Who for censuring and slandering others is sent off, (his) face will be black there also (in the other world); in both (worlds) (the face) of the disaffected ones is black.

"Turn (him) out," (so) it is heard in the whole world, O brother! The disaffected servant is beaten with shoes, being done up he rises and goes home.

Further on he is no more allowed to mix with societies and relatives, his wife and niece bring him again home.

This and the other world, both are lost, in hunger and thirst he always cries.

Blessed, blessed is the Lord, the creator, the Supreme Spirit, who himself causes true justice to be done.

Who slanders the perfect true Guru, he is by the True one killed and consumed.

This word is spoken by him, by whom the whole world is produced.[1]

Slōk II.

Whose master is naked and hungry, whence shall his servant get enough to eat?

The thing, that is in the house of the master, comes into the hands of the servant, whence shall he (the servant) get, what there is not?

That service is difficult, if one, having been served, asks again an account (from the servant).

Nānak (says): serve thou Hari the Guru, whose sight is fruitful, no one will ask again an account (from thee).

Pauṛī.

Nānak (says): the saints reflect (on what) the four Vēdas are saying.

What the devotees utter with their mouth, those words take effect.

It is manifest, spread about and known, all people are hearing it:

The foolish men, who are in enmity with the saints, obtain no happiness.

They desire their virtues, they are burning in selfishness.

What can those helpless ones do, when their own lot is bad?

Who are struck down by that Supreme Brahm, they are destroyed by any one.

The branches of a tree are drying up, that is cut off by the root.

XIII.

Slōk I.

Who in his heart is meditating on Hari the Guru, his grandeur is great.

By the perfect, true Guru, being pleased, it is given, it does not diminish a bit, though one try to diminish it.

The true Lord is on the side of the true Guru, all the people, who chatter (against him), die.

The faces of the slanderers are made black by Hari the creator, by himself (the Guru's honour) is increased.

In proportion as the slanderer slanders (him), it (*i.e.* the Guru's honour) increases continually more.

Humble Nānak (says): by whom Hari is adored, at their feet he places the whole (world).

Slōk II.

Who keeps account[2] with the true Guru, to him all this and that world is lost.

He continually gnashes with his teeth, he emits foam, prating and prating he breaks down.

[1] The verse is said to refer to some Marvāhī Khatrīs, who were sent by some disaffected people to Dillī, to complain of the Guru, and were thus turned out by the king. Under the true Guru he understands himself, who in this and in the following verses pronounces his whole wrath against his backbiters.

[2] ਗਣਤ ਰਖੈ, who keeps account, *i.e.* who closely watches his proceedings, which the Guru did not like by any means.

He makes always schemes for money and wealth, (but) his former property also flies away.

What does he gain, what does he eat, into whose heart the pain of doubt has fallen?

Who entertains enmity with him, who is without enmity, he takes upon his head all the sins of the world.

He gets no entrance neither at the front nor back, in whose heart is calumny and in the mouth a mango.

If he stretches out his hand to gold, it closes upon ashes.

(But) if he come again to the asylum of the Guru, his former vices are pardoned.

Humble Nānak (says): (by whom) daily the name is meditated upon, (his) blemishes and sins go off by the remembrance of Hari.

Pauṛī.

Thou art perfectly true, thou art above all, thou art the supreme authority.

Who are meditating on thee the True one, who serve (thee) the True one, who put (their) hope on (thee) the True one:

In (their) heart is happiness,[1] (their) faces are bright, they speak truth, thy strength, O True one, (is in them).

Those disciples are devotees, by whom he is praised, (whose) flag is the true word (of the Guru).

(I am) always a sacrifice (to them), who are serving the perfectly True one.

XIV.

Slōk I.

Who are smitten by the perfect true Guru himself, they are now smitten by the true Guru.

Though it be much desired to unite them (with the society of the pious), the creator does not allow, that they be united.

They get no entrance into the society of the pious, in the society they are inquired after by the Guru.

If one go and join them now, him the executioner of Yama kills.

The false ones, who were cursed by the Guru Bābā, they were also cursed by the Guru Angad.

The Guru in the third generation reflected: what is in the hand of these helpless ones?

By the Guru, that is anointed in the fourth generation, all slanderers and wicked people are saved.

If some son (of theirs), (becoming) a disciple, serve the true Guru, all his affairs are put right.

He will obtain the fruit, he desires, having got sons, wealth and riches, Hari saves and unites (him with himself).

All treasures are in the true Guru, into whose breast they were put by Hari.

He gets the perfect true Guru, on whose forehead this destiny is written.

Humble Nānak asks for the dust of those, who are the beloved disciples and friends of the Guru.

Slōk II.

To whom he himself gives greatness, at their feet he himself also lays down the world.

Then one would be afraid, if anything would be done by oneself, (but) in all the creator makes go on his own skill.

Behold, O brother, this arena (= the world) belongs to the beloved true Hari, who by his own power makes all bow down (to his saints).

Hari, the Lord protects his own devotees, the faces of the calumniators and wicked people he causes to be blackened.

The greatness of the true Guru increases always more, Hari himself causes constantly praise and devotion to be made.

[1] ਸਚੁ here = ਸੁਖ, happiness.

Mutter day by day the name, O ye disciples of the Guru! Hari the creator himself causes it to be uttered by the mouth.

The faces of the disciples makes bright the beloved Hari, in the whole world he raises the cry: victory to the Guru!

Humble Nānak is the slave of Hari, Hari preserves the honour of the slaves of Hari.

Pauṛī.

Thou thyself art the true Lord, thou art our true wholesale merchant.

Make firm (in us) the true capital of (thy) name, O Lord, we are thy retail-dealers!

(Who) serve the True one, who traffic in the True one, who recite his pure qualities:

Those people, by reason of being (his) servants, are united (with him), by the word of the Guru they are accomplished.

Thou, the true Lord, art inapprehensible, (but) by the word of the Guru thou makest (thyself) known.

XV.

Slōk I.

In whose heart the calumny of another is harboured, he will never do well.

No one heeds what he says, he cries continually standing in a desert.

In whose heart there is backbiting (and who) becomes known as a backbiter, all his clever achievements are lost.

Who always makes untrue backbiting of another, he cannot show his face, it has become black.

In the Kali-yug the body is the field of actions, as one sows, such he will eat.

Justice is not administered by (mere) words; (by whom) poison is eaten, he dies at that very moment.

Behold, O brother, the true justice of the creator! as one acts, so he receives.

To humble Nānak the whole right insight is given, he proclaims the affairs of the gate of Hari.[1]

Slōk II.

Who are separated (from Hari), (when) the Guru is present, they get no entrance at the gate (of Hari).

(If) any go and join those slanderers, (their) faces turn pallid, they are spit in the face.

Who are cursed by the true Guru, they are cursed in the whole world, they are always going about without knowing what to do.

By whom their own Guru is concealed, they wander about sighing.

Their hunger never ceases, they constantly cry out in hunger.

No one hears what they say, they always die gradually.

They cannot see the greatness of the true Guru, they get no place neither in that nor in this world.

Who goes and joins them, who are smitten by the true Guru, (by him) all (his) remaining honour is lost.

Who are cursed by the Guru, they (become) further on leprous; who joins such a one, him he (the Guru) makes take up (his) leprosy.

Hari does not look on those, who apply their mind to another love.

What is decreed by the creator himself, against that there is no remedy.

Humble Nānak (says): adore thou the name, nothing can come up to that!

The majesty of the name is great, and it is constantly more increasing.[2]

[1] The sense is: he proclaims what is going on at the gate of Hari.

[2] ਚੜ੍ਹਾਹੀ is a meaningless corruption (for the sake of the rhyme) instead of ਚੜ੍ਹਾਉ, verbal adjective: *rising;* ਚੜ੍ਹੈ ਚੜ੍ਹਾਉ, *it is going on rising, increasing.*

Slōk III.

Who is appointed (Guru) by the Guru then being, the majesty of that man is great.

To him all the world bows and falls down at his feet, his fame is spread in the world.

To him the (nine) regions and the universe pay reverence; on whose head the perfect Guru places his hand, he (also) becomes perfect.

The majesty of the Guru becomes always greater, no one can come up to him.

Humble Nānak has been appointed (Guru) by Hari the creator himself, that Lord himself protects (his) honour.

Pauṛī.

In the body is a boundless castle, in it are shops also.

The disciple, who carries on traffic, collects the substance of Hari.

The treasure of the name of Hari is purchased, diamonds and red corals.

Who are seeking wealth in another place besides (their) body, they are fools and goblins.

Those foolish ones are turned about in error, like a deer is led astray in brambles.[1]

XVI.

Slōk I.

Who slanders the perfect true Guru, he becomes distressed in the world.

The hell is horrible and a well of pain, he is seized and carried there.

No one hears his cries and screams, in distress he weeps.

He loses all, this and that world, profit and capital, all is wasted.

He is made the ox of an oilman and yoked on by his early rising master.

Hari sees and hears always everything, before him nothing is hidden.

What he sows, that he reaps, as one has sown before (in a former birth).

On whom the Lord bestows his own mercy, he washes the feet of the true Guru.

Following the Guru, the true Guru, he crosses over, as iron with wood.[2]

Humble Nānak (says): meditate thou on the name! muttering Hari happiness is obtained by the name of Hari.

Slōk II.

Those female disciples are very fortunate, happy married women, with whom Hari the king has met.

In their heart light is manifested, they are absorbed in the name, (says) Nānak.

Pauṛī.

This body is all virtue, in which the light of the True one is.

A jewel is hidden and concealed in it, some (rare) disciple and votary draws it out, having searched for it.

When the whole is known (as) the Supreme Being, then the One is contained (everywhere), the One is lengthwise and crosswise.

The One is seen, the One is minded, the One is heard with the ears.

Humble Nānak (says): keep thou in mind the name and thy service is becoming perfectly true!

XVII.

Slōk I.

All relishes are in the heart of those, in whose mind Hari dwells.

Those faces are bright at the threshold of Hari, all go to see them.

[1] ਝਾਲੇ = ਝਲੇ = ਝੁਲੇ.

[2] ਸੰਗੋਇਆ is a meaningless alliteration instead of ਸੰਗਿ.

By whom the name of the fearless one is meditated upon, they have no fear.
The supreme Hari is embraced by them, for whom it has been decreed by himself.
They receive a dress of honour at the gate of Hari, in whose heart Hari dwells.
They themselves cross with all their family, and after them they release the whole world.
O Hari, join to humble Nānak (thy) people! seeing them we live.

Slōk II.

That ground becomes green, on which my true Guru sits.
Those creatures become flourishing, by which my true Guru is seen.
Blessed, blessed is the father, blessed, blessed the family, blessed, blessed the mother, by whom the Guru is born.
Blessed, blessed is the Guru, by whom the name is adored; he himself crosses and he rescues them (also), by whom he is seen.
O Hari, mercifully join to me the true Guru, (that) humble Nānak may wash (his) feet!

Pauṛī.

The true Guru is the perfectly True one and immortal, by whom Hari is kept in (his) breast.
The true Guru is the perfectly True one, the Supreme Spirit,[1] by whom lust and wrath, the baneful thing, is destroyed.
When the perfect true Guru is seen, the mind is subdued within.
(I am) constantly a sacrifice to my own Guru, (I am) devoted (to him).
The disciple is victorious, the self-willed one is overcome.

XVIII.

Slōk I.

With (whom) he (Hari) joins the true Guru out of mercy, (that) disciple will meditate on the name.
Who does that which will please the true Guru, (him) the perfect Guru will let dwell in (his) house.
In whose heart there is meditation on the name, all their fear he (the Guru) will remove.
For whose protection Hari himself stands up, what will all other machinations avail (against them)?
Humble Nānak (says): meditate thou on the name! in this and that world Hari will rescue (thee).

Slōk II.

To the disciples of the Guru the greatness of the true Guru is pleasing.
Hari preserves the honour of the true Guru, it is continually increasing.
In the mind of the true Guru is the supreme Brahm, the supreme Brahm rescues him.
(Whose) strength and tribunal the true Guru is, to them Hari makes bow down the whole (world).
By whom my true Guru is seen and loved, all their sins he removes.
Those faces (will be) bright at the threshold of Hari and much honoured.
Humble Nānak asks the dust of those, who are the disciples of the Guru and my brethren.

Pauṛī.

I utter and praise (his) qualities, true is the greatness of the perfectly True one.
Who praises (him) is true, true is (his) praise, (but) none has got the (right) estimate of the True one.
Who have tasted the juice of the perfectly True one, they remain satiated.
Those are knowing the relish of Hari, as by a dumb one sweetness is eaten (but cannot be told).

[1] The Guru is here, as so often elsewhere, perfectly identified with the Supreme.

From the perfect Guru the fruition of Hari, the Lord, is obtained (and) congratulation is uttered in the heart (in consequence thereof).[1]

XIX.

Slōk I.

Within whom there are flowing sores, they know the pain thereof.

Who know Hari, (they know) the pangs of separation (from him), I am always a sacrifice to them.

Who join to me Hari my sweetheart, for them I roll (my) head on the ground.[2]

Who perform the work of the Guru, to those disciples I am the slave of slaves.[3]

Who are steeped in the deep red colour of Hari, (their) body is filled with love to Hari.

Mercifully join Nānak (to the Guru)! (my) head is sold to the Guru.

Slōk II.

With vices my body is filled, how shall it become pure, O ye saints?

By the disciple virtues are bought, he washes off the filth of egotism.

The True one he purchases with pleasure, the traffic of the True one is carried on (by him).

Loss does not befall him by any means, (to whom) that gain of Hari is pleasing.

Nānak (says): by them the True one is purchased, for whom exactly it is decreed, (that) they should obtain (him).

Pauṛī.

(Who) are praising the True one, (who are) praising the perfectly True one, they are pure men.

In the heart of them, who serve the True one, the True one dwells, the perfectly true Hari is (their) protector.

By whom the True one is adored, they, having departed, are united with the True one.

By whom the perfectly True one is not served, those self-willed fools (become) goblins.

They are talking nonsense like those, who are intoxicated with liquor.

XX.

Slōk I.; *mahalā* III.

In the Gauṛī Rāg she has a good character, (who) keeps (her) husband in (her) mind.

Who makes this her ornament, that she walks according to the will of the true Guru.

The true word (of the Guru) is (her) husband, whom she always enjoys.

As the colour of the boiled Manjīṭh is very deep red, so she gives her soul to the True one.

In very deep colour she is steeped, (her) love is directed on the True one.

Falsehood and deceit do not remain hidden, (though) they put round (themselves) falsehood and deception.

They make false shows of greatness, who entertain love with falsehood.

Nānak (says): he himself (only) is true, he himself beholds (everything).

Slōk II.; *mahalā* IV.

In the society of the saints the praise of Hari is made, in the company of the pious the beloved is met with.

[1] The sense is: who has obtained from the Guru the fruition of Hari, he congratulates himself in his own heart. ਮੇਲਲਾ signifies here: *to receive the fruition of;* ਗੁਰਿ ਪੂਰੈ is the Ablative: *from.*

[2] ਠੇਲੀਆ = ਠੇਲੀ, ā being a meaningless alliteration.

[3] ਗੁਲਮੁ—ਗੋਲੀਆ, a senseless corruption instead of ਗੋਲਿਆਂ ਗੁਲਾਮੁ, the slave of slaves = the lowest slave. For the sake of the rhyme the words are often so disfigured, that they are hardly recognizable.

Those men are blessed men, who give instruction and assistance to others.

They confirm the name of Hari (in others), who proclaim the name of Hari: (for) by the name of Hari the world is saved.

Every one desires to see the Guru, by the nine regions and the universe he is worshipped.

By thyself thy own self is put into the true Guru, by thyself the Guru is adorned.

Thou thyself worshippest and causest the true Guru to be worshipped, O creator!

If one be separated from the true Guru, his face (becomes) black, he is smitten down by Yama.

He gets no entrance neither in the future nor afterwards: (this) is reflected upon in their mind by the disciples of the Guru.

The people, who meet with the true Guru, are saved, by whom the name is remembered in their heart.

Ye, who are disciples and sons of humble Nānak, mutter Hari! Hari is saving you.

Slōk III.; *mahalā* III.

By egotism the world is led astray, by folly, worldly pursuits and passion.

(If) one meet with the true Guru, a look of favour is (cast upon him), but the self-willed one is in stark blindness.

Nānak (says): whom he himself (*i.e.* Hari) joins (to himself), he bestows love on the word (of the Guru).

Pauṛī.

He praises and magnifies the perfectly True one, whose heart is steeped in love (to Hari).

By whom the One is adored with one mind, their wall (=body) is never tattered.

Blessed, blessed are those men and applauded, by whom the true nectar is drunk with their tongue.

To whose mind the perfectly True one is pleasing, they are accepted at the true threshold.

Blessed, blessed is the birth of the lovers of truth, (their) faces (are made) bright, happiness is enjoyed (by them).

XXI.

Slōk I.; *mahalā* IV.

The Sākats go and bow before the Guru, (but) they are insincere and false in their heart.

When the Guru says: rise, O my brother! they sit down being crammed together (like) herons.[1]

In the heart of the disciples of the Guru the true Guru abides, those who are privileged[2] (by God), are selected (by the Guru).

Those insincere (Sākats) hide before and after their face, they do not mingle (with the disciples).

Their food is not there, the rams go and acquire falsehood.

Though the Sākat be fed, yet he necessarily disgorges poison from his mouth.

No fellowship should be made with any Sākat, they are smitten by the creator.

Whose this sport is, he makes and sees it;[3] humble Nānak remembers the name.

Slōk II.

The true Guru is the unattainable Supreme Spirit, by whom Hari is kept in his breast.

No one can come up to the true Guru, on whose side the creator is.

The sword and coat of mail of the true Guru is the worship of Hari, by which death, the plague, is destroyed.

[1] ਬਗੁਲਾੜੇ = ਬਗੁਲੇ, ārī being a meaningless alliteration.

[2] ਲਧੇਵਾੜੇ is explained by the Sikh Granthīs by "spy;" but this is a mere guess. It corresponds to the Sansk. लब्धवर, *one who is privileged* (by God) *on account of his merits*, etc. ਲਧੇਵਾਰਾ stands for ਲਧੇਵਰਾ (or rather ਲਧਵਰ), on account of the rhyme.

[3] The sense is: the whole world is the sport of Hari, he makes it and sees it.

Hari himself is the protector of the true Guru, after the true Guru[1] every one is saved by Hari.

Who excogitates mischief against the perfect true Guru, he is smitten by the creator himself.

He is taken notice of at the threshold of the true Hari, (by whom) the unattainable (Guru) is reflected upon, (says) humble Nānak.

Pauṛī.

By whom the True one is adored whilst being asleep, they utter the True one, when they rise.

Those disciples are scarce in the world, who utter the True one.

I am a sacrifice to those, who day by day utter the True one.

To whose mind and body the True one is pleasing, they go to the true threshold.

Humble Nānak utters the true name, he always worships the perfectly True one.

XXII.

Slōk I.; *mahalā* IV.

What is sleeping, what is waking? those, who are disciples, are acceptable.

By whom at every breath and morsel he (Hari) is not forgotten, they are perfect and most excellent men.

By destiny the true Guru is obtained, (if) day by day meditation be made.

Their society I will hold fast, that I may obtain honour at the threshold,

(Who) in sleeping utter: vāh, vāh! and (who) also in rising say: vāh, vāh![2]

Nānak (says): their faces (are) bright, who, when rising (from sleep), continually remember (him).

Slōk II.; *mahalā* IV.

(If) one's own true Guru be served, the boundless name is obtained.

Those, who are drowning in the water of existence, Hari draws out, the bountiful Hari bestows gifts (upon them).

Blessed, blessed is that wholesale merchant,[3] who deals in the name.

The disciples, the retail-dealers, who come, he ferries across by means of the word.

Humble Nānak (says): on whom mercy is bestowed, they serve the creator.

Pauṛī.

Those men are devotees of the perfectly True one, by whom the perfectly True one is adored.

The disciples, who seek him, find the True one in their heart.

By whom the true Lord is served, they subdue and overcome death, the plague.

The perfectly True one is greater than all, who serve the True one are united with the True one.[4]

Praise to the perfectly True one! serving the perfectly True one they gain their end.

XXIII.

Slōk I.; *mahalā* IV.

The self-willed one is a foolish creature, being destitute of the name he goes astray.

Without the Guru the (human) mind does not become fixed, again and again (man) falls into the womb.

(If) Hari, the Lord, himself become merciful (to one), then the true Guru is met with.

Humble Nānak (says): praise thou the name and the pain of birth and death will go!

[1] After the true Guru, *i.e.* following the true Guru.

[2] Vāh, vāh (supply: *Guru!*).

[3] The ਸਾਹੁ is here the Guru.

[4] ਰਲਾਪਿਆ = ਰਲੇ (or ਰਲਾ), ਪਿਆ being a meaningless alliteration; similarly: ਢਲਾਪਿਆ = ਢਲੇ.

Slōk II.; *mahalā* IV.

I will praise my own Guru in many ways with affection!

Having brought about an intimacy (with the Guru) I keep my mind attached to the true Guru.

Applying my mind to the beloved Hari my tongue cannot get enough in praising (him).

Nānak has a hunger after the name in his heart, having drunk the juice of Hari his heart becomes satiated.

Pauṛī.

The perfectly True one is known (from his) power, by whom day and night is made.

He is true, who is always praising (him), the greatness of the True one is true.

Who is praising (him) is true (and his) praise (also) is true, (but) the estimate of the True one no one has obtained.

When the perfect true Guru is met with, then he (Hari) is present and comes into sight.

By whom the True one is praised, all the hunger of those disciples is done away.

XXIV.

Slōk I.; *mahalā* IV.

Searching my heart and body I found that Lord in seeking.

I obtained the Guru as intercessor, by whom the Lord Hari was joined to me.

Slōk II.; *mahalā* III.

Who is relying on the Māyā is very blind and deaf.

He does not hear the word (of the Guru) and is much wandering about.

To the disciple it is known by devoutly meditating on the word.

Having heard the name of Hari he minds it, and is absorbed in the name of Hari.

What pleases him, that he does being caused to do it.

Nānak (says): the musical instrument emits a sound being caused to sound.

Pauṛī.

Thou, O creator, art knowing everything which is going on within the creatures.

Thou, O creator, art thyself inestimable, (but) the whole world is estimated (by thee).

Whatever exists is made by thee, all is thy work.

Thou alone art existing in every creature, true, O Lord, is thy work.

Who have met with the true Guru, they are united with Hari, there is no confidence (on the part of Hari) on any one else.

XXV.

Slōk I.; *mahalā* IV.

This mind should be kept fast, O disciple, the thought should be directed (on him)!

How should he at any breath and morsel be forgotten, (who) in sitting and rising is always (with thee)?

Anxiety about death and life is gone, this body is in the power of the Lord Hari.

As it pleases (thee), so keep (me), bestow the name on humble Nānak!

Slōk II.; *mahalā* III.

The conceited self-willed man does not know the palace (of Hari), one moment he is before, one moment he is behind.

(Though) he be always called, he does not come to the palace, how shall he be accomplished at the threshold (of Hari)?

Some rare one knows the palace of the true Guru and always joins his hands (in supplication).

(On whom) my Hari bestows his own mercy, (him) he causes to return (to his palace), (says) Nānak.

Pauṛī.

The performance of that service is fruitful, by means of which the mind of the true Guru is won over.

When the mind of the true Guru is won over, then sins and blemishes are destroyed.

The disciples hear with their ears the instruction, that is given by the true Guru.

By whom the will of the true Guru is minded, to them a fourfold colour is applied.

This is only the course of the disciples, that having heard the initiatory mantra of the Guru their hearts are imbued with love.

XXVI.

Slōk I.; *mahalā* III.

Who conceals his own Guru, he gets no place nor spot.

Both, this and that world, are lost, he gets no place at the threshold (of Hari).

That opportunity does not come to hand, that he may again cling to the feet of the true Guru.

He is dropped from the account of the true Guru, in pain he passes his time.

The true Guru, the Supreme Spirit, is without enmity, whom he takes himself, (him) he applies (to his service).

Nānak (says): to whom he shows his sight, them he rescues at the threshold (of Hari).

Slōk II.; *mahalā* III.

The self-willed one is ignorant, foolish and conceited.

In his heart is wrath, in gambling his intelligence is lost.

He is given to falsehood and sins.

What does he hear, what does he speak and tell?

Blind and deaf he falls into a well going astray.

The self-willed one comes and goes blind.

Without joining the true Guru he is not accepted.

Nānak (says): what is written before, that he earns.

Pauṛī.

Whose hearts are hard, they do not sit with the true Guru.

There the True one is abiding, (but) the heart of the false ones is gloomy.

Practising fraud and deceit they are bringing forth false accusations, then they go again and sit with the false ones.

Falsehood does not mingle with the true ones, let one see and ascertain this!

The false ones mingle with the false ones, (whereas) the truthful disciples sit with the true Guru.

XXVII.

Slōk I.; *mahalā* V.

He himself making efforts kills the remaining slanderers.

The assistant of the saints, O Nānak, is everywhere present.

Slōk II.; *mahalā* V.

They are thoroughly gone astray, thoroughly, where will they put their hands?

Even by him they are destroyed, O Nānak, who is the powerful cause of causes.

Pauṛī.

Taking nooses they go at night-time, (but) the Lord knows the creatures.

They look at another's wife, hiding themselves in a place.

They break holes in the wall (of a house) in an uneven place, they enjoy sweet liquor.

(But) they themselves will repent of their own works.
The angel Ajrāīl[1] will press (them like) sesam seed in an oil-press.

XXVIII.

Slōk I.; *mahalā* V.

The servants of the true wholesale merchant are approved of.
Who serve another, O Nānak, those fools are consumed and die.

Slōk II.; *mahalā* V.

The destiny, that has been written by the Lord himself, cannot be effaced.
The name of Rām is wealth and capital, (on that) meditate always, O Nānak!

Pauṛī.

(To whom) Nārāyaṇ has put a stumbling-block, where will he put his foot?
Who is committing countless sins, he tastes continually poison.
Who is calumniating (others) is consumed and dies, he burns in his body.
Who is smitten down by the true Lord, who will protect him?
Nānak has fled to the asylum of him, who is the inapprehensible Supreme Spirit.

XXIX.

Slōk I.; *mahalā* V.

The terrible hell, (in which there are) many tortures, is the place for the ungrateful.
Who are smitten down by that Lord, O Nānak, they, being refused, die.

Slōk II.; *mahalā* V.

All remedies are applied by him (*i.e.* the slanderer), (but) there is no medicine for the slanderer.
(Whom) the Lord himself leads astray, O Nānak, he is consumed and falls (again) into the womb.

Pauṛī; mahalā V.

The perfect true Guru being pleased gives the true inexhaustible wealth of Hari.
All cares are effaced (thereby), the fear of Yama ceases.
Lust, wrath (and all) wickedness are destroyed in the society of the pious.
Who are serving another besides the True one, they will die hip-broken.
On Nānak the Guru has bestowed communion with the name.

XXX.

Slōk I.; *mahalā* IV.

He is not an ascetic, (who) is covetous in his heart, the deceitful one wanders about for the sake of the Māyā.

First, being called, he does not take the alms of the pious one, afterwards repenting, the ascetic comes and places him in the hell of the childless.[2]

All the righteous people begin to laugh, that the ascetic is overcome by greediness and worldly desires.

Where he sees little wealth, there the ascetic does not go near, by keeping his look on much wealth the ascetic loses his sanctity.

O brother, this is no ascetic, he is a heron, thus the pious people think.

[1] ਅਜਰਾਈਲ, (عِزرائِل) the angel of death.

[2] The sense is: the ascetic does not at first take the alms offered by a pious man, afterwards repenting of it he curses him and places him in the hell of the childless (ਪੁਤ, the hell, destined for the childless).

The ascetic, who slanders the pious people, he is smitten down by God on account of this fault, (though) he may be praised by the world.

Behold, by the slander of the great (pious) people all the fruit, which the ascetic had acquired, is gone, destroyed by the ascetic (himself)! [1]

Outside he sits amongst the pious and is called an ascetic.

(But when) he sits inside (the house), he commits sin.

Hari manifests and shows (his) inward sin to the pious.

Dharm-Rāe says to the servants of Yama: seize and put this ascetic there, where the great murderers are!

No one has further any connexion with this ascetic, he is cursed by the true Guru.

What is going on at the gate of Hari, that Nānak tells; he comprehends it, who is fitted for it by God.

Slōk II.; *mahalā* IV.

By the devotion of Hari, Hari is adored; the greatness of Hari,

The praise of Hari the devotees are always singing; the name of Hari is bestowing happiness (on them).

On the devotees of Hari the greatness of the name is always bestowed and it becomes always greater.

The devotees of Hari are placed firmly in (their) houses, he preserves their honour.

Hari will ask account from (their) slanderers, he will punish them severely.

As the slanderers are acting in their own heart, such a fruit they obtain.

What is done within (the heart) will at last become manifest, though one do it sitting within the earth.

Humble Nānak is happy having seen the greatness of Hari.

Pauṛī.

Hari himself is the protector of his devotees, what can the sinner do (against them)?

The foolish conceited man practises conceit, he eats poison and dies.

Few are the days (of life), as a ripe field is cut down.

As the works are, they are practising, such will be their reward.

The Lord of humble Nānak is great, he is the Lord of all.

XXXI.

Slōk I.; *mahalā* IV.

The fleshly-minded one is thoroughly misled, (he lives) in greediness, covetousness, and egotism.

Quarrelling day by day he passes his time, he does not reflect on the word of the Guru.

All their sense and understanding is taken away by the creator, what they talk, is all nonsense.

They are not satisfied with any gift, in their heart is thirst and much ignorance and blindness.

Nānak (says): breaking off connexion with the fleshly-minded is best, who entertain fondness and affection for the Māyā.

Slōk I.; *mahalā* IV.

Who have another love in their heart, with those no friendship should be made by the disciples.

They come and go and are made to wander about (in transmigration), not in a dream they get any happiness.

They practise falsehood and utter falsehood, clinging to falsehood they become stupid.

[1] The readings in this verse differ considerably, as its sense was no longer understood. The MS. (No. 2483) reads: ਨਿੰਦਾ ਕਾ ਦੋਭਖੁ, which gives no sense whatever; the MS. (No. 2484) reads: ਵਡਾ ਪੁਰਖੀ ਕੀ ਨਿੰਦਕਾ ਦੇਖੁ, which is equally senseless. We have translated according to the Lahore lithographed copy, which reads: ਵਡਾਪੁਰਖਾਂ ਕੀ ਨਿੰਦਾ ਕਾ ਦੋਖੁ ਜਿ ਤਪੇ ਨੇ ਫਲ ਲਗਾ; ਕਾ must be joined to ਜਿ = ਜੇ ਕਾ ਫਲੁ ਲਗਾ. But the whole verse is in itself very intricate and clumsy.

Fondness for the Māyā is all pain, in pain they are destroyed, in pain they will weep.

Nānak (says): no union is possible between worldliness and devout meditation, though every one desire it.

Who have got religious merits in their bag, they obtain happiness by the word of the Guru.

Pauṛī; mahalā V.

O Nānak, the saintly Munis state it and the four Vēdas tell it:
(That) the words, which the devotees utter with their mouth, take effect.
They are manifest and known in the world and all people are hearing (them):
The foolish men, who are in enmity with the saints, obtain no happiness.
They desire their virtues, they are burning in selfishness.
What can those helpless people do, when their very lot is bad?
Who are smitten by that Supreme Brahm, they are destroyed by anybody.
Who entertain enmity with him, who is without enmity (= God), they are justly consumed.
Who are cursed by the Saint (= the Guru), they wander about perplexed.
The branches of a tree, that is cut off at the very root, are getting dry.

XXXII.

Slōk I.; *mahalā* V.

By Guru Nānak the name of Hari, who is able to break and to make, was made firm.
O friend, remember thou always the Lord, and thy pain goes off.

Slōk II.; *mahalā* V.

The hungry one knows no modesty, he is shameless and abusive.
Nānak asks for the name; O Hari, grant (me) in mercy devotion (to it)!

Pauṛī.[1]

As the works are, which one is doing, such are the fruits.

Who grind (between their teeth) hot iron, they are bruised in their gullet.

That messenger (of Yama) throws a neck-rope (on them) and marches (them off) (according to their) works.

No hope (of theirs) is fulfilled, (who) are continually taking up another's filth.[2]

The ungrateful ones, who do not acknowledge the work (done to them), are wandering about in (different) wombs.

All (their) firmness is exhausted by him (*i.e.* Hari), (their) support is taken away by him.

(Who) does not let the quarrel drop, he is taken away by the creator.

Whoever are practising conceit, they fall down to the ground.

XXXIII.

Slōk I.; *mahalā* III.

The disciple gets divine knowledge, discrimination and wisdom.
He sings the excellences of Hari in his heart, stringing (them) into a necklace.
He is reflecting on the holy, pure and high (Supreme Being).
Who meets with him, him he brings across (= saves).
(In whose) heart a desire after the name of Hari is contained:

[1] This Pauṛī is extremely intricate and confused, the manuscripts differing also in consequence thereof very much in their readings.

[2] ਪਰਮਲੁ ਚਿਤਨਾ, to take up another's filth = to slander him.

He gets great glory at the gate of Hari, most excellent is (his) speech.
Whichever man hears (it), he becomes happy.
Nānak (says): by joining the Guru the wealth and goods of the name are obtained.

Slōk II.; *mahalā* IV.

No information is obtained about the heart of the true Guru, what pleases the perfect true Guru.

Within the disciples of the Guru the true Guru dwells; who likes the disciples, he comes into the good graces of the Guru.

(Who) do the work, which the true Guru commands, (who) practise that silent repetition (of the name), the service of (those) disciples the True one approves.

Who desires, that work should be done by the disciples of the Guru without the order of the true Guru, him the disciple of the Guru does not approach again.

If one put his life before the Guru, the true Guru, before him the disciples of the Guru do work.

Who comes with deceit and goes with deceit, him the disciple of the Guru does by no means approach.

Nānak proclaims the decision of Brahm: who causes a work to be done (by the disciples) without the mind of the true Guru being won over, that creature will incur great pain.

Pauṛī.

Thou art the true Lord, very great, like thyself thou (only) art great.

Whom thou united (with thyself), he is united with thee, whom thou thyself pardonest, (his) account thou droppest.

Whom thou thyself art uniting (with thyself), he serves the true Guru, his mind becomes firmly fixed.

Thou art the true Lord, thou art true: soul, body, skin, bones, all is thine.

As it pleases thee, so keep (me), O True one! in (my) heart I trust in thee, O great one!

GAUṚĪ KĪ VĀR; MAHALĀ V.

To be sung after the tune of the Vār of Rāe Kamāldī and Mōjdī.

Ōm! by the favour of the true Guru!

I. XXXIV.

Slōk I.; *mahalā* V.

The man, who mutters the name of Hari, Hari, he is approved of.
I am a sacrifice to that man, by whom is adored the Lord, who enjoys perfect bliss.
(His) pain of regeneration and death is cut off, (who) has met with Hari, the all-wise Supreme Spirit.
In the society of the saints he crosses the ocean (of existence), the true one is saved,[1] (says) humble Nānak.

Slōk II.

Rising early, O guest, come to my house!
I wash his feet, who has always in his mind and body love (to Hari).
(Who) hears the name, (who) collects the name, (who) devoutly meditates on the name:
(His) house and property, all become pure, he sings the excellences of Hari.
The name of Hari a very fortunate trafficker obtains, O Nānak!

[1] ਸਚਾ ਤਾਣੁ. It is perhaps better to take here ਤਾਣੁ as p. past. (Sansk. त्राण) = *saved;* but the words might also be translated: "true (is his) salvation," ਤਾਣੁ being taken as substantive.

Pauṛī.

What pleases thee, that is good, true is thy decree.
Thou alone art abiding in all, in all thou art contained.
In every place (thou art) continually contained, (thou art) pervading the creatures.
Who joins the society of the pious, by him thou art obtained, if he mind the will of the True one.
Nānak has fled to the asylum of the Lord, he is continually a sacrifice (to him).

II. XXXV.

Slōk I.; *mahalā* V.

When I remind thee, then mind it: he is the true Lord and master.
Nānak (says): who serves the true Guru and ascends the boat, he crosses the water of existence.

Slōk II.; *mahalā* V.

The fool in his pride puts on clothes of wind.
Nānak (says): they do not go with him, being burnt they become ashes.

Pauṛī.

Those are saved in the world, who are preserved by Himself.
By seeing the face of those, who have tasted the nectar of Hari, one lives.
Lust, wrath, covetousness, spiritual blindness are devoured in the society of the pious.
By the Lord Hari himself, bestowing his own mercy (on them), they are tested.
Nānak (says): his proceedings are not known, none can perceive them.

III. XXXVI.

Slōk I.; *mahalā* V.

Nānak (says): that day is pleasant, in which the Lord comes into (oue's) mind.
On which day the Supreme Brahm is forgotten, cursed is (then even) an agreeable season.

Slōk II.; *mahalā* V.

Nānak entertains friendship with him, in whose hand everything is.
Those are called bad friends, who do not go with (one) one step.

Pauṛī.

The nectar-name is a hidden treasure, come, O brother, and drink it!
By the remembrance of which happiness is obtained and all thirst is quenched.
Serve the Supreme Brahm, the Guru, and no hunger will remain!
All desires are obtained, freedom from death is gotten.
Like thyself thou (only) art; Nānak has fled to the asylum of the Supreme Brahm.

IV. XXXVII.

Slōk I.; *mahalā* V.

I have looked in every spot, no place is vacant (of him).
Nānak (says): they have obtained their object, with whom the true Guru has met.

Slōk II.; *mahalā* V.

As a flash of lightning in the sky, so is the world passing away.
That thing is becoming, (says) Nānak, (if) one is muttering the name of that Lord.

Pauṛī.

No one, having searched the Smriti and all the Shāstras, has found out (his) estimate.
Who falls in with the pious, that man enjoys the pleasure of Hari.

The true name is the creator, the Supreme Spirit, this is a mine of jewels.
On whose forehead this is written, that man remembers Hari.
May the true name be given as viaticum to Nānak, (thy) guest!

V. XXXVIII.

Slōk I.; *mahalā* V.

In (his) heart (is) anxiety, dry (are his) eyes, hunger does not all go off.
O Nānak, without the true name the pain of no one has gone off.

Slōk II.; *mahalā* V.

Those caravāns are plundered, which did not lade the True one.
Nānak (says): those are doing well, by which, joining the Guru, the One is known.

Pauṛī.

Where the pious are sitting, that place is beautiful.
Those serve their own powerful (Lord), all evil is done away.
"The Supreme Brahm is saving the sinners," (thus) the saints and the Vēdas say.
"Compassionate to thy devotees," this is thy practice, that is going on through all ages.
Nānak asks for the One name, that is pleasing to his mind and body.

VI. XXXIX.

Slōk I.

The sparrow chirps at the dawn of day, many waves flow on.
(With their) wonderful form the saints are not enraptured, the delight of Nānak is in the name.

Slōk II.; *mahalā* V.

House and mansion and pleasures are there, where thou comest into (one's) mind.
All the grandeurs of the world, (says) Nānak, are bad friends.

Pauṛī.

The wealth of Hari is true capital, but known by few.
He obtains it, O brothers,[1] to whom the disposer (of all) gives it.
That man is flourishing in heart and body, who is steeped in the colour of Hari.
(By whom) in the society of the pious his excellences are sung, he is devouring all his sins.
Nānak (says): he lives, who has known the One.

VII. XL.

Slōk I.; *mahalā* V.

The fruits are beautiful, which hang at the neck of the Akk-tree.[2]
Parting and separation from the Lord (take place) by the knot of doubt.

Slōk II.

Who are forgetting (him), they die, (but) they cannot by any means die also.
Who turn away from Rām, (they are in agony) like a thief on an impaling stake.

Pauṛī.

I have heard, that the eternal Lord alone is the depository of happiness.
It is said, that Hari is present in water, land, on the surface of the earth and in every creature.

[1] ਭਾਇਰਹੁ, Voc. Plur. (properly a Sindhī Plur. भातर, brothers).
[2] ਖਖੜੀ, *s.f.*, the fruit of the Akk-tree, which is poisonous, but beautiful to look on.

High and low, worms and elephants, all are alike made (by him).
Friends, companions, sons, relations are produced (by him).
Nānak (says): to whom he, being pleased, gives the name, he enjoys the pleasure of Hari.

VIII. XLI.

Slōk I.; *mahalā* V.

Who, minding the mantra (of the Guru), do not forget the name of Hari at every breath and morsel:
Those are blessed, O Nānak, those are perfect saints.

Slōk II.; *mahalā* V.

The eight watches he wanders about in intense pain (caused by) eating.

How shall he be prevented from falling into hell, when the messenger (of God)[1] does not come into his mind?

Pauṛī.

Cling to him, O man, in whose skirt is the name!
Here thou wilt remain happy and further on it (the name) will go with thee.
Build a house of true religion, fix firmly all the posts!
Seize the asylum of Nārāyaṇ! in that and this world he supports (thee).
Nānak (says): by whom the feet of Hari are seized, him he receives at the threshold.

IX. XLII.

Slōk I.; *mahalā* V.

The beggar asks for a gift, give it (me), O beloved!
The beautiful donor is always kept in my mind.
His inestimable store-rooms can by no means be exhausted.
Nānak (says): the word (of the Guru) is inexhaustible, everything is accomplished by it.

Slōk II.; *mahalā* V.

O disciples, by love to the word (of the Guru) regeneration and death are stopped.
Their faces are always bright and happy, (says) Nānak, who are remembering the One.

Pauṛī.

There nectar is distributed, (where one) is happy at the work of Hari.
He is not put into the road of Yama, he is not dying again.
Who has conceived love and affection (for Hari), him he is joining (to himself).
If the pious people are uttering the words (of the Guru), the fountains of nectar flow.
Seeing (their) sight Nānak lives, he holds it fast in his mind.

X. XLIII.

Slōk I.; *mahalā* V.

By serving the true, perfect Guru pain is destroyed.
O Nānak, by adoring the name the business (of human life) is put right.

Slōk II.; *mahalā* V.

By whose remembrance distress goes off, and joy, welfare and rest (come),
O Nānak, (that) Hari should always be muttered, not a moment (his) name should be forgotten!

[1] ਰਸੂਲ, رَسُول, messenger (of God), here = the Guru.

Pauṛī.

How shall I estimate their glory, who have obtained Hari?
Who falls on the asylum of the pious, that bound man is set free.
Who sings the excellences of the Eternal one, he is not rendered miserable in the womb.
(With whom) the Guru meets, he, uttering and comprehending the Supreme Brahm Hari, is satisfied.[1]
Nānak (says): that unattainable, unfathomable Lord Hari is obtained (by him).

XI. XLIV.

Slōk I.; *mahalā* V.

(He) does not do his own business (and) wanders about in the world (like) a whirlwind.[2]
Nānak (says): by forgetting the name what happiness will accrue (to him)?

Slōk II.

The bitterness of poison adheres to the whole world.
Humble Nānak has come to this decision, that the name of Hari (alone) is sweet.

Pauṛī.

This is the sign of the pious one, meeting with whom one crosses.
The servant of Yama does not go near him, he does not die again.
The ocean of existence, the world, the poison, he gets safely through.
He strings together the excellences of Hari, the wealth of Hari is in his heart, he clears away all filth.
Nānak (says): he remains united with the beloved Supreme Brahm, the divine male Hari.

XII. XLV.

Slōk I.; *mahalā* V.

Nānak (says): those are approved of, in whose mind Hari dwells.
Words of little affection are of no use, O friend!

Slōk II.; *mahalā* V.

The Supreme Brahm, the omnipresent, unattainable, wonderful Lord has come into (my) sight.
Nānak has made the name of Rām (his) wealth by the favour of the perfect Guru.

Pauṛī.

Deceit does not avail against the Lord, by greediness and spiritual blindness they are ruined.
(Who) do good works (but) are fallen asleep by the intoxication of the Māyā:
They are again and again made to wander about in the womb, they are thrown into the road of Yama.
They get their own deeds, they are involved[3] in pain.
Nānak (says): by forgetting the name they sink[4] into every evil.

XIII. XLVI.

Slōk I.; *mahalā* V.

In rising, sitting and sleeping that (name) is happiness.
Nānak (says): by praising the name mind and body become tranquil.

[1] ਸਮਧਾ = Sansk. संवृद्ध.
[2] ਅਵ੍ਰਤਾ = Sansk. आवर्त्त, *s.m.* whirlwind.
[3] ਜੁਤਾ = Sansk. युक्त.
[4] ਰੁਤਲਾ *v.n.*, to sink into.

Slōk II.; *mahalā* V.

Who is absorbed in covetousness, wanders always about without gaining at all his end.
With whom the Guru falls in, O Nānak, in his mind (that Hari) dwells.

Pauṛī.

All things are bitter, the name of the True one is sweet.
To those people of Hari it is sweet, who, being pious, taste it.
For whom it is decreed by the Supreme Brahm, in his heart he dwells.
(In whom) the One Supreme Being is contained, (his) second love is cut off.
Nānak joining (his) hands asks for Hari; the Lord, being pleased, gives (this gift to him).

XIV. XLVII.

Slōk I.; *mahalā* V.

That begging is the best, which asks for the One.
Other words, which have not the Lord for their object, are useless, O Nānak!

Slōk II.; *mahalā* V.

A heart pierced with love (and) knowing (God) is rare.
(Whom) the saint (= the Guru) is uniting (with God), (to him) the road (becomes) smooth.

Pauṛī.

Serve him, O soul, who is liberal and bountiful!
All sins are destroyed by remembering Gōvind.
The way of Hari is shown by the pious, (if) the mantra of the Guru be muttered.
All the pleasures of the Māyā are insipid (to him, to whom) Hari is pleasing in (his) mind.
Meditate, O Nānak, on the Lord, by whom life is given!

XV. XLVIII.

Slōk I.; *mahalā* V.

The right time for sowing the true name has come; what one sows, that he will eat.
He gets it (the name), O Nānak, for whom it is decreed.

Slōk II.; *mahalā* V.

He is asking for the only True one, to whom he himself, being pleased, gives (it).
Nānak (asks) for (that) gift of the Lord, by the eating of which the mind is satiated.

Pauṛī.

They acquire profit in the world, whose wealth and capital Hari is.
They do not know another love, their trust is in the True one.
The One immovable is laid hold of (by them), every other thing is passing away.
Who forgets the Supreme Brahm, his breath is useless.
Nānak will be a sacrifice to that man, who keeps him pressed to his neck.

XVI. XLIX.

Slōk I.; *mahalā* V.

The Supreme Brahm has given the order and rain has fallen with natural ease.
Much corn and grain is produced, the earth is filled and abundantly satiated.
(Who) always recites his excellences, the pain of his poverty passes away.
What is written before, that is obtained and found by his order.
O Nānak, meditate on that Lord, by whom thou hast been vivified!

Slōk II.; *mahalā* V.

The One life-giving ground of eternal bliss should be remembered!
There is no other place, in which wise should one become tranquil?
I have seen the whole world, there is no happiness without the name.
Body and property will become ashes, as everybody knows.
Complexion and enjoyment are worthless, what will the creature do?
Whom he himself leads astray, he does not know the trick.
Who are imbued with love to the blissful (Supreme), they sing the True one.
Nānak (says): those, who are at the gate of thy asylum, please thee.

Pauṛī.

Regeneration and death do not happen to them, who cling to the skirt of Hari.
They become approved of whilst living, who are intent on the praise of Hari.
Who have obtained the society of the pious, they are very fortunate.
Woe to the life, in which the name is forgotten! raw threads break.
Nānak (says): the dust of the pious is purifying (equally to) Lakhs and Crores of Prāgs.[1]

XVII. L.

Slōk I.; *mahalā* V.

(Like) the golden earth, studded with gems of grass, (is) a man, (in whose) mind the love of Hari dwells.[2]
All his affairs become easy, (says) Nānak, (if) the Guru, the true Guru, is pleased.

Slōk II.; *mahalā* V.

(The Ill or kite) is wandering about in the ten directions, (on) water, mountain and forest.
Where a corpse is seen, there the Ill goes and sits down (on it).

Pauṛī.

Who desires the fruit of all comfort, he should acquire the True one.
He should see the Supreme Brahm (as being) near him, he should meditate on the One name
Having become the dust of all he is united with Hari.
If he give no pain to any creature, he will go with honour to the house (of Hari).
Nānak proclaims the Supreme Spirit, that is purifying the sinners.

XVIII. LI.

Slōk I.; *mahalā* V.

The One, whom I have made my friend, is versed in every ingenuity.
My life is sacrificed to Hari, (my) heart and body are his property.

Slōk II.; *mahalā* V.

If thou seizest (my) hand, O beloved, I will not give thee up by any means.
Those, who give up Hari, are wicked men, they fall into the pain of hell.

[1] Sansk. **प्रयाग**, the modern Ilahābād, at the confluence of the Ganges and Jamnā with the supposed (subterraneous) addition of the Sarasvatī; thence called also **त्रिवेणी**.

[2] **This verse is a masterpiece of confusion, it can only be translated by conjecture, as so many more, no attention being paid by the author to grammatical order or clearness.**

Pauṛī.

What Hari does, in whose house are all treasures, that takes effect.
The saints live by continually muttering (him), they wash off the filth of (their) sins.
In whose heart the lotus-footed one dwells, his difficulty he clears away.
With whom the perfect Guru meets, he does not die nor is he regenerated nor does he weep.
Nānak is very thirsty after the sight of the Lord, may he in mercy grant it (to me)!

XIX. LII.

Slōk I.; mahalā V.

O foolish woman, let go thy doubt! by love thy beloved and thou are one.
Wherever thou goest, there he is present.

Slōk II.; mahalā V.

(In) the sport of the battle-field[1] they mount horses and seize the stocks of the guns.
(Whose) mind (is) with the geese, he delights (in) the flight of a cock.

Pauṛī.

Who (with his) tongue utters (and with his) ears hears Hari, he is saved, O friend!
Those hands are pure, which with faith write the praise of Hari.
Ablution at the sixty-eight Tīrthas and all the meritorious actions are done by them.
They are rescued from the ocean of the world, the fort of sensuality is conquered.
Nānak (says): them he applies to his skirt and saves, by whom God is served, O friend!

XX. LIII.

Slōk I.; mahalā V.

That business is a bad profit, (in which) the One does not come into one's mind.
Nānak (says): those bodies burst, by whom the Lord is forgotten.

Slōk II.

From a goblin they are made a Dēvtā by that creator.
All disciples are saved by him, by the Lord (their) affairs are adjusted.
The false calumniators are thrown down by him in (his) court.
The Lord of Nānak is great, he himself prepares and arranges (everything).

Pauṛī.

The Lord is endless and has no bounds whatever, all is his doing.
The Lord is unattainable, inapprehensible, the trust of the creatures.
Giving his hand (to them) he cherishes (them), filling and supporting (is his) doing.
He himself is kind and forgiving; (who) mutters the True one, is crossing.
What pleases thee, that is good; Nānak, (thy) slave, (is in thy) asylum.

XXI. LIV.

Slōk I.; mahalā V.

To him no hunger whatever remains, who has that Lord.
Nānak (says): every one is saved, who clings to his feet.

[1] ਖੁਡੀ *s.f.* (Khuḍḍī) the battle-field, arena.

Slōk II.; *mahalā* V.

Nānak (says): (whose) patron the Lord is, he has no hunger by any means.

Pauṛī.

(Whose) heart is imbued with love to Gōvind, he acquires true enjoyment.

Who entertains affection for the name of Hari, he has elephants and horses.

(Who) in meditating (on Hari) does not draw back (his) face, he has dominion, wealth and much pleasure.

The musician is begging at the gate of the Lord, he never gives up (his) gate.

Nānak has in his heart and body this desire, he continually longs for the Lord.

RĀGU GAUṚĪ; THE SAYINGS OF THE DEVOTEES.

Ōm! The true name is the creator, the Supreme Spirit.

By the favour of the Guru!

GAUṚĪ GUĀRĒRĪ; ČAUPADĀS OF KABĪR.

I.

Pause.

I, who was burning, have now obtained the water of Rām.
By the water of Rām my burning body has been extinguished.
(1). (Though) one go to the forest in order to subdue (his) mind:
Without the water (of Rām) that Lord is not obtained.
(2). The fire, by which gods and men are burnt:
(From that) the burning people are saved by the water of Rām.
(3). The ocean of existence is in the ocean of happiness (= God).
(Though) people go on drinking, (yet) the water is not exhausted.
(4). Kabīr says: adore the bow-holder (= Vishṇu)!
By the water of Rām my thirst is quenched.

II.

Pause.

O Mādhava, (my) thirst for water does not cease!
(In drinking) the water the fire increases still more.
(1). Thou art the ocean, I am the fish of the water.
I dwell in the water, without the water I am done for.
(2). Thou art the cage, I am thy parrot.
Yama, the cat, what can he do unto me?
(3). Thou art the tree, I am the bird.
The unlucky one does not get thy sight.
(4). Thou art the Guru, I am thy new disciple (= apprentice).
Kabīr says: join me at the time of the end!

III.

(1). When he (the Supreme) is considered by me as the only One:
Then why are the people annoyed by it?

Pause.

I am without honour, my honour is lost.
May not any one fall into my track!
(2). We are tardy, tardy in the mind.
We have no partnership nor fellowship with any one.
(3). Honour and dishonour,—we do not care for it.
Then you will know, when the plaiting[1] is laid open.
(4). Kabīr says: the honour (of) Hari[2] is real.
Give up all and adore only Rām!

IV.

(1). If by wandering about naked union (with Hari) be obtained:
Then every deer of the forest will become emancipated.

Pause.

What are the naked, what are those with skins,[3]
When they do not know the Supreme?
(2). If by shaving the head perfection is obtained:
The sheep is emancipated, no one is lost.
(3). If by retaining the semen virile one cross, O brother!
Why should then not the eunuch obtain salvation?
(4). Kabīr says: hear, O man and brother!
Without the name of Rām no one has obtained salvation.

V.

(1). Who perform ablution in the evening and at dawn:
They become like frogs in the water.

Pause.

If there is no love to the name of Rām:
They go all to the house of Dharm-Rāe.
(2). Who are absorbed in many ways in the love of the body:
They get no mercy, not even in a dream.
(3). The four Vēdas and the very clever ones say:
(That) the pious obtain happiness in the ocean of the Kali-yug.
(4). Kabīr says: why is much done?
Giving up all (other) juices the great juice should be drunk!

VI.

(1). What is muttering, what austerity, what vows and worship (to him),
In whose heart there is another love?

Pause.

(2). Remove greediness and the way of the world!
Remove lust, wrath and egotism!

[1] ਪਾਜ, plaiting = false show or imposition.

[2] The honour, that Hari bestows.

[3] The sense is: what is the difference between them?

(3). Those who are practising works are bound by egotism.
Falling in with a stone they worship it.
(4). Kabīr says: by performing devotion he is obtained.
By sincere love they are united with King Raghu (= Rām).
O people, the mind should be applied to the Mādhava!
By cleverness the four-armed (Vishṇu) is not obtained.

VII.

(1). Whilst dwelling in the womb there is no clan nor caste.
From the seed of Brahm the whole creation (is made).

Pause.

Say, O Paṇḍit, when were the Brāhmans made?
By saying: (I am) a Brāhman, (thy) life (and) religion are lost.
(2). If thou art a Brāhman born from a Brāhman woman:
Why hast thou not come in another way?
(3). Whose art thou, O Brāhman, whose am I, the Sūdra?
Whose blood am I, whose milk art thou?
(4). Kabīr says: who reflects on Brahm:
He is called a Brāhman by me.

VIII.

(1). In darkness no one will ever sleep in comfort.
The king and the poor, both will meet and weep.

Pause.

If you will not utter with (your) tongue Rām:
In being born and destroyed you will continue weeping.
(2). As the shade of a tree is seen (passing away):
So life passes; say, whose is (then) the Māyā?
(3). The soul, that is contained in the creatures,
Does any one know its secret (or has he) any knowledge[1] of it when it is dead?
(4). The goose is (on) the pond, death (in) the body.[2]
O Kabīr, drink the elixir of Rām!

IX.

(1). Production is of light and light is of production.[3]
To that adhere crystal,[4] fruits and pearls.

Pause.

What is that house, which is called fearless?
When fear goes off, one remains fearless.

[1] ਕਰ *s.f.* Intelligence, information (Sindhī कार *s.f.*).

[2] ਹੰਸਾ ਸਰਵਰ, the goose (is on) the pond, *i.e.* the hair has become white.

[3] The sense of the verse: ਜੋਤਿ ਕੀ ਜਾਤਿ ਜਾਤਿ ਕੀ ਜੋਤਿ is apparently: everything produced (ਜਾਤਿ) owes its origin to the divine light (or vital energy) and *vice versâ*: there would be no light without production, the one is dependent on the other, one cannot be separated from the other.

[4] The sense of ਕੰਚੂਆ is not quite certain; we have translated it by *crystal* (= ਕਾਂਚ or ਕਚ). The whole verse is obscure in its relation to what precedes.

(2). At the bank (of a river) and at a Tīrtha the mind (of him) is not re-assured,
(Who) is clinging to light ways.
(3). Religious demerit and merit, both are the same.
The philosopher's stone is in thy own house, give (therefore) up other methods!
(4). Kabīr says: in the name, which is destitute of the (three) qualities, there is no wrath.
Remain in intimate intercourse with this Lord!

X.

(1). Is the measure of the Yōjanas (and their) amount known?
In the very heart paradise is contained.

Pause.

I do not know where paradise is!
Every one says, know, know, it is there!
(2). By telling and being told (by others) it (the mind) will not be re-assured.
Then the mind becomes tranquil, when egotism will depart.
(3). As long as there is in the mind a longing for paradise:
So long it will not settle down at the feet (of Hari).
(4). Kabīr says: why is this said?
In the society of the pious is paradise.

XI.

(1). Thou art produced and born and being born thou art absorbed (again).
Whilst looking on with (thy) eyes this world passes away.

Pause.

Doest thou not die out of shame, that thou sayest: (this is) my house?
At the time of the end nothing is thine.
(2). By many efforts the body is nourished.
At the time of death it is burnt on fire.
(3). The body which (thou art) rubbing with sandal-perfume:
That body is burnt with wood.
(4). Kabīr says: hear, O clever one!
(Thy) beauty will pass away, the whole world sees (this).

XII.

(1). Others have died, what grief is made about it?
Then (grief) is made, when one oneself becomes emaciated.

Pause.

I do not die, the world (in me) will die.
Now the vivifier has met with me.
(2). In this body sweet scent is exhaled,
(But) by its delight the supreme bliss is forgotten.
(3). There is one well and five water-drawers.
The rope is broken, (with which) the captivators of the intellect draw (water).[1]

[1] The words: ਭਰੈ ਮਤਿਹਾਰੀ, are very brief and obscure; ਭਰਨਾ (*i.e.* ਪਾਨੀ) to draw water; ਮਤਿਹਾਰੀ, taken as one word, captivators of the intellect, obscuring the right understanding (of things).

(4). Kabīr says: who is holding and considering (all) as One:
(For him exists) neither well nor water-drawers.

XIII.

(1). As fixed and movable (things), as worms and moths:
In many and various ways we have been born.

Pause.

Many such houses have been inhabited (by us),
Till we have returned to the womb of Rām.
(2). (Now and then we have been) Jōgīs, sages of subdued passions, ascetics, abstaining from all sexual commerce.
Now and then Rājās and sovereigns, now and then beggars.
(3). The Sākats die, all the saints live.
They drink with their tongue the elixir of Rām.
(4). Kabīr says: O Lord, bestow mercy (on me)!
We have become tired, may (now) the full (happiness) be given!

XIV.

Gauṛī Kabīr-jī, with which is intermixed the fifth mahalā.[1]

Pause. (*Mahalā* V.)

Such a wonderful thing Kabīr has seen.
He churns water, mistaking it for curdled milk.
(1). The green young blade of corn the donkey grazes.
Rising continually it laughs, brays and dies.
(2). The intoxicated buffalo goes along restlessly.
Jumping about, it grazes and goes utterly to ruin.
(3). Kabīr says: the sport has become manifest.
The sheep always sucks the lamb.
(4). By uttering Rām wisdom comes forth.
Kabīr says: (from) the Guru the right knowledge is obtained.

Pančpadās.

XV.

(1). As a fish that leaves the water and is outside of it:
(So I was) in a former birth, (when) destitute of austerity.

Pause.

Say, O Rām, what is now my state?
Benāres is left (by me) and my intellect has become little.
(2). (My) whole life is lost in Shivpurī (= Benāres).
At the time of death I have risen and come to Maghar.
(3). Many years I have practised austerities at Kāsī.

[1] With this fourteenth verse a line of Arjun (Pause) is mixed up, which is carefully noted down. The remark itself contains a sharp censure of Kabīr.

Death has come on in the dwellings of Maghar.[1]
(4). Kāsī and Maghar I consider as the same.
How shall I come across by slight devotion?
(5). The Guru, the elephant, says: everybody knows Shiva.[2]
(But) Kabīr dies uttering: Srī Rām!

XVI.

(1). The body, (which) they rub with sandal-perfume:
That body is burnt with wood.

Pause.

What is the greatness of this body and wealth?
It falls on the ground and does not go to that side.
(2). Who sleeps at night and is given to lust in day-time:
He does not take the name of Hari one moment.
(3). In (whose) hand is a rope (and who) eats betel-leaf with his mouth:
(That) thief is tightly bound at the time of death.
(4). Who by means of the instruction of the Guru sings ardently the excellences of Hari:
He obtains happiness by uttering: Rām, Rām!
(5). (In whom) he mercifully makes firm the name:
(In him) Hari makes dwell the scent and perfume of Hari.
(6). Kabīr says: be thoughtful, O blind one!
True is Rām, false is every worldly occupation.

Verses consisting of three and four lines severally.

XVII.

(1). From the restraint of the passions pleasures[3] have been made on the contrary.
The pain is gone, happiness and tranquillity are enjoyed.
The enemies have on the contrary become friends.
The Sākats have on the contrary become virtuous men in their mind.

Pause.

Now all is considered by me as happiness.
Tranquillity set in, when Gōvind was known (by me).
(2). Crores of troubles were (in my) body.
(Now) on the contrary meditation is made (by me) with comfort and ease.
(Who) himself knows his own self.
(Him) no sickness enters nor the three classes of affliction.[4]
(3). Now (my) mind on the contrary has become eternal.
Then it (*i.e.* the mind) is known, when one dies whilst living.
Kabīr says: he is absorbed with comfort and ease:
(Who) himself is not afraid nor frightens others.

[1] Kabīr lived first at Kāsī (Benāres), and removed in his old age to the town of Magbar (ਮਗਹਰ), where he died, and where his tomb is still visited by Hindūs and Musalmāns.

[2] The sense of this line is somewhat obscure; it seems to be: everybody knows Shiva to be the Supreme Being, acknowledges him as such.

[3] ਰਾਮ must here (according to the context) signify: *pleasure, delight.*

[4] See p. 429, note 1.

XVIII.

(1). When the body is dead, to which house does the soul go,
(Which) is attached to the passed, unbeaten sound?
By whom Rām is known, he knows it,
As the mind of the dumb one is pleased by sugar.

Pause.

Such divine knowledge Krishṇa communicates.
O mind, keep firm the breath in the Sukhmanī-artery!
(2). Make him (thy) Guru, who is not to be made again (Guru)!
Utter that word, which is not to be uttered again!
Take up that meditation, which is not to be taken up again!
Die in such a way, that thou must not die again!
(3). Let the Gangā and Jamnā meet in the inverse direction!
Bathe without the confluence of the water in (thy) heart!
(Consider) the desires as the same! this is thy business.
(4). Water, fire, wind, earth, ether
Are remaining so (as they are); remain thou with Hari!
Kabīr says: meditate thou on the Supreme!
Go to his house, that thou come not again!

XIX.

(1). For gold he is not obtained.
Rām is obtained for the price of the heart.

Pause.

Now that Rām is considered by me as my own,
My heart is comforted with natural ease.
(2). Brahmā, though always speaking (of him), did not get his end.
(But) Rām comes to the house of his devotee, who is sitting (there in rest).
(3). Kabīr says: I have given up my fickle mind.
Devotion to Rām alone is my lot.

XX.

(1). Death, by which the whole world is frightened,
That death is lighted up by the word of the Guru.

Pause.

How should I die now? my heart is comforted by death.
Those die, who do not know Rām.
(2). Every one says: we must die, we must die.
Who dies in tranquillity (of mind), he becomes immortal.
(3). Kabīr says: joy has sprung up in (my) mind.
Doubt is gone, the highest joy remains (with me).

XXI.

(1). There is not a place anywhere; with whom shall I connect the root?
Searching in (my) body I find no place.

Pause.

He knows the pain, whom it has befallen.
The arrows of the worship of Rām are very sharp.
(2). With one love I look on all women.
What do I know, who is beloved by the husband?
(3). Kabīr says: on whose forehead the lot (is written):
She obtains at every watch the affection of her husband.

XXII.

(1). Who has a Lord like Hari, O brother!
(Him) I go to call emancipated and eternal.

Pause.

Now I say: O Rām, I trust in thee!
What have I then to bow down to any one?
(2). Hari, on whom the load of the three worlds is,
Why should he not cherish (me)?
(3). Kabīr says: I reflect on him with one mind.
What can one do, when (his) mother gives (him) poison?

XXIII.

(1). How shall a woman become chaste without chastity? [1]
See and reflect in thy heart, O Paṇḍit!

Pause.

How shall love increase without affection?
As long as there is enjoyment (of the world), so long there is no love (of God).
(2). Who considers in his heart the great merchant (= God) as untrue:
She does not meet with the sweetheart (even) in a dream.
(3). Who entrusts to him body, heart, property and house:
She is a happy married woman, says Kabīr.

XXIV.

(1). The whole world is immersed in sensuality.
With (all her) dependents she is drowned (in) sensuality.

Pause.

O man, why is the boat destroyed and sunk?
By being torn away from Hari and united with the world.
(2). Gods and men are burnt, fire seizes them.
The water is near, but the cattle do not drink in wading through it.
(3). By continually remembering (Hari) water issues.
That water is pure, says Kabīr.

XXV.

(1). In which family the son is not reflecting on divine knowledge:
Why has not his mother (rather) become a widow?

[1] This line may also be translated: how shall a woman become a Satī without burning herself with her husband?

Pause.

Who does not perform worship to Rām :
Why has that sinful man not died when being born ?
(2). Many abortions have taken place, why is he preserved,
Who with stumpy arms lives in the world ?[1]
(3). Kabīr says : such as are beautiful and well-formed :
They are hump-backed and ugly without the name.

XXVI.

(1). Who take the name of the Lord :
For those men I always sacrifice myself.

Pause.

He is pure, who sings the excellences of the pure Hari.
That man is pleasing to my mind, O brother !
(2). In whose heart Rām remains brimful :
Of their lotus-foot we are the dust.
(3). By caste a weaver and patient of mind,
Utters Kabīr with natural ease the excellences (of Rām).

XXVII.

(1). (My) head is the distillery, my spirit still oozes.
Having collected the sugar-cane,[2] my body has become the wood.

Pause.

He is naturally called drunk,
Who is drinking the juice of Rām and meditating on divine knowledge.
(2). When the wife of the distiller naturally comes and joins (them) :
They become daily intoxicated with joy.
(3). (When) the knowing mind is applied (to) the Supreme :
Then the Fearless one is obtained, says Kabīr.

XXVIII.

(1). The nature of the mind penetrates the mind.
By subduing the mind what perfection is established ?

Pause.

Who is that Muni, that subdues his mind ?
Having subdued his mind, say, whom does he save ?
(2). Every one says (so) in his mind.
(But) without subduing the mind devotion is not made.
(3). Kabīr says : who knows the secret :
He is, like Madhusūdhana,[3] the god of the three worlds.

[1] ਘੁਡ = ਘੁਟ (ਬੁਟ੍ਟਾ) stumpy ; ਘੁਡ ਭੁਜ ਰੂਪ, Bahuvrīhi, *formed with stumpy arms.*

[2] ਮਹਾਰਸ, here substantive, sugar-cane, from which spirits are distilled.

[3] ਮਧੁਸੂਦਨ, the destroyer of the Daitya Madhu, an epithet of Vishṇu (and thence of Krishṇa).

XXIX.

(1). The stars, that are seen in the sky,
By which painter have they been painted?

Pause.

Say, O Paṇḍit, with what is the sky connected?
Who understands it, is a very fortunate, intelligent man.
(2). The sun and the moon they call lights.
In all is spread out the diffusion of Brahm.
(3). Kabīr says: he will know (it),
In whose heart is Rām (and in whose) mouth (also) there is Rām.

XXX.

(1). The daughter of the Vēda is the Smriti, O brother!
She has come with a chain and a rope.

Pause.

She has built herself her own city.
By the snare of spiritual blindness the arrow of death is kept ready.
(2). Though cut off it is not cut off, it does not break (scil. the rope).
It becomes a serpent, that devours the world.
(3). We see, by whom the whole world is plundered.
Kabīr says: saying: Rām! I have escaped.

XXXI.

Pause.

Thou shouldst ride on thy own reflection!
Thou shouldst put (thy) foot into the stirrup of tranquillity (of mind)!
(1). Apply the nose-string, put on the bridle,
(And) all decoration, and make (it) run about in the sky!
(2). Go on, I will take thee to paradise.
If thou draw back, I will strike thee with the whip of love.
(3). Kabīr says: those are good riders,
Who keep aloof from the Vēda and the Qur'ān.

XXXII.

(1). By which mouth the five nectareous substances [1] were eaten:
To that mouth I saw fire-brands applied.

Pause.

O my King Rām, cut off my one pain!
I am burnt by fire and by dwelling in the womb.
(2). The body is destroyed in many kinds and ways.
Some burn (it), some bury it in the earth.
(3). Kabīr says: O Hari, show (me thy) feet!
Behind (me) is Yama, why do you not drive (him) away?

[1] The ਪੰਚ ਅਮ੍ਰਿਤੁ or five nectareous substances are: पय milk, दधि curds, घृत clarified butter, मधु honey, शर्करा sugar.

XXXIII.

(1). He himself is fire, he himself is wind.
When the Lord burns (one), who will protect (him)?

Pause.

(Who) is muttering Rām, (his) body is not burnt at all.
(In whose) mind the name of Rām is, he remains absorbed (in Rām).
(2). Why should it (=the body) burn, why should it be injured?
The trickish bow-holder (=Vishṇu) (only) plays.
(3). Kabīr says: utter two words![1]
They will become the Lord, who will keep (thee).

XXXIV.

(1). I have not applied my mind either to abstract devotion (Yōga) or meditation.
Without indifference to the world I shall not get rid of the Māyā.

Pause.

What will become of my life,
When the name of Rām is not (my) support?
(2). Kabīr says: (though) I seek in heaven,
I see none other equal to Rām.

XXXV.

(1). On which head (thou art) arranging and fastening a turban:
That head the bill of the crow will dress.

Pause.

Why (art thou) proud of this body and wealth?
Why is not the name of Rām made firm (by thee)?
(2). Kabīr says: hear, O my heart!
Even this will be thy state.

GAUṚĪ GUARĒRĪ OF KABĪR.

Ōm! By the favour of the true Guru!

Asṭpadī.

XXXVI.

(1). (Who are) asking for pleasure, (them) pain befalls (in the other world).
That pleasure is not desired by us (nor) does it please (us).

Pause.

(If there be) still attention to the world and a longing for pleasure:
How will the indwelling of King Rām be effected?

[1] The two words are: Rām, Rām!

(2). By this pleasure Shiva and Brahmā are frightened.
(But) that pleasure is considered by us as the true one.[1]
(3). Sanaka and the other (mind-born sons of Brahmā), the Muni Nārada and Shēsh(-nāga):
These also did not see the mind in (their) body.
(4). Let one seek this mind, O brother!
When the body is dissolved, where is the mind absorbed?
(5). By the favour of the Guru, Jayadēva and Nāmā (= Nāmadēva)
Have by love of devotion known (it).
(6). This mind is not subject to coming (or) going.
Whose error is gone, he knows the True one.
(7). This mind has no form nor mark whatever.
By the order (of God) it has sprung into existence; by comprehending (this) order it is re-absorbed (again into the Supreme).
(8). If one knows the secret of this mind:
Being absorbed in this mind he becomes easily God.
(9). The soul (or life) is One and all bodies (are therefore One).
Kabīr remains in connexion with this mind.

XXXVII.

Pause.

Who are day and night intent on the one name:
How many of them have become perfected by applying devotion!
(1). The ascetics, Siddhs and all the Munis have been unsuccessful.
The one name is the wishing-tree, (that) brings (men) across.
(2). Who gains Hari, he is not put to shame.
Kabīr says: the name of Rām is known (by him).

Gauṛī and Sōraṭhi.

XXXVIII.

Pause.

O shameless creature, thou art without shame!
Abandoning Hari why goest thou to any (other's house)?
(1). Whose Lord is high:
That man it does not become to go to another's house.
(2). That Lord is (everywhere) brimful (= omnipresent).
He is always with (thee), Hari is not far off.
(3). Whose lotus-feet are an asylum:
Say, O man, why doest thou not go to his house?
(4). Of whom every one speaks:
He is powerful, (my) own Lord is bountiful.
(5). Kabīr says: he is perfect in the world,
In whose heart there is none other (but the Lord).

[1] The sense of these obscure lines is: the pleasure of knowing or finding out "the mind (ਮਨੁ)" was given up by Shiva and Brahmā in despair, they were frightened by the boundless depth of the mind. But Kabīr asserts, that this is true pleasure or happiness. The mind, the intelligent power, is an emanation from the Supreme, the *scintilla animae divinae* and the conjunctive link of the creature with the absolute substance.

XXXIX.

(1). Say, who is son? who is father and paternal uncle?[1]
Who dies, who causes agony?

Pause.

Hari, the deceiver, has practised deceit on the world.
In separation from Hari how shall I live, O my mother?
(2). Say, who is a man or[2] who is a woman?
Reflect on this truth in thy body!
(3). Kabīr says: my mind is reconciled with the deceiver.
The deceit is gone, the deceiver is known (by me).

XL.

Pause.

Now that King Rām has become my helper:
Birth and death are cut off, I have obtained final emancipation.
(1). I have been joined to the society of the pious.
I have been rescued from the five attackers.
The nectar-name I mutter (now) with (my) tongue.
I have been made his own slave with a price (being paid for me).
(2). The true Guru has afforded (me) assistance.
I have been drawn out from the way of the world.
Love to the lotus-feet has sprung up (in me).
Gōvind dwells continually in my mind.
(3). The burning coals of the Māyā are extinguished.
In (my) heart is contentment, the name (is my) support.
In water and on land the Lord is omnipresent.
Wherever I see, there he is near and dear.
(4). His own worship is established by himself.
What is written before, that is obtained, O my brother!
On whom he bestows mercy, his accoutrement is complete.
The Lord of Kabīr is cherishing the poor.

XLI.

(1). There is impurity in water, impurity on land, impurity arises by birth.
There is impurity by one being born, there is also impurity by one having died, there is impurity by people being destroyed.

Pause.

Say, O Paṇḍit, who is pure?
Attend, O my friend, to such knowledge!
(2). In the eyes is impurity, in the speech is impurity, in the ears impurity takes place.
In rising and sitting impurity clings (to man), impurity falls into the food.
(3). The way of ensnaring every one knows, but some rare one the way of getting rid (of it).
Kabīr says: who reflect in their heart on Rām, in them no impurity takes place.

[1] ਕਉਨ ਕੋ; beware of the artful use of ਕੋ! after ਕਉਨ it signifies here: say! (contracted from ਕਹੋ); otherwise it is used = ਕਉਨ; ਕਾਕੋ is = ਕਾਕਾ, a paternal uncle. These lines are very perplexing.

[2] ਕਉਨ ਕੀ. ਕੀ is here not the sign of the Genitive, but a conjunction = *or*.

XLII.

Pause.

Settle (this) one dispute, O Rām!
If thou art more beautiful[1] than thy people?
(1). Is this (human) mind great[2] or (he), with whom the mind is conciliated?
Is Rām great or he, (by whom) Rām is known?
(2). Is Brahmā great or he, by whom he is produced?
Is the Vēda great or he, from whom it has come?
(3). Kabīr says: I have become dispirited.
Is the Tīrtha great or the servant of Hari?

Rāgu Gauṛī čētī.

XLIII.

Pause.

See, O brother, a storm of divine knowledge has come!
All the matted shutters, made by the Māyā, are blown away, they do not remain (any longer).
(1). The two posts of double-mindedness are pulled down, the ridge-pole of spiritual blindness is broken.
The roof of (worldly) thirst has fallen on the ground, the vessel of folly has burst.
(2). By the water, that is falling after the storm, the large pitcher[3] is wetted.
Kabīr says: light has arisen in (my) mind, when the rise of the sun was known.

Gauṛī čētī.

Ōm! by the favour of the true Guru!

XLIV.

(1). They do neither hear the praise of Hari nor do they sing the excellences of Hari.
With words only they pull down the heaven.

Pause.

What shall be said to such people?
Who are made destitute of devotion, of them one should always remain afraid.
(2). They themselves do not give a handful of water.
They censure him, by whom the Gangā is brought (down).
(3). Sitting and rising they walk in perverseness.
They themselves are lost and ruin also others.
(4). They know nothing else but wicked talk.
The order of Brahmā even they do not obey.
(5). They themselves are lost and ruin others also.
Having applied fire to (their) mansion they sleep in it.
(6). They laugh at others and are themselves one-eyed.
Seeing them Kabīr is ashamed.

[1] ਕਾਮ is here adjective: lovely, beautiful (Sansk. कम्र); it also occurs already in Tulsī Dās' Rāmāyaṇ.
[2] Here of course used in the sense of a comparative.
[3] ਗਾਜਨੁ = ਗੰਜਨੁ (Hindī), a large pitcher.

RĀGU GAUṚĪ; BAIRĀGAṆI OF KABĪR.

Ōm! By the favour of the true Guru!

I. XLV.

(1). Some one does not obey his living father, (but) when he has died, he causes a Shrādh to be performed for him.

Say, how shall the helpless defunct fathers also obtain (the offering)? the crow and the dog eat it.

Pause.

Would that some one would show me welfare!

Saying: welfare, welfare! the world passes away, how should welfare be obtained?

(2). Having made a Dēvī (or) Dēva of earth, thou sacrificest before them an animal (a he-goat).

Such are called thy forefathers, what is called their own, they do not take.

(3). An animate being they slaughter and worship (therewith) a lifeless thing, which proves a calamity at the end.

The salvation by the name of Rām is not known (by them), the worldly people are sunk in fear.

(4). They worship Dēvīs and Dēvas and vacillate about, (but) the Supreme Brahm is not known (by them).

Kabīr says: the Omnipresent one[1] is not thought of, they cling to the outward objects of the senses.

II. XLVI.

(1). Who, whilst living, goes on dying, he lives again, in this wise he is absorbed in the Vacuum.

If one remains in the darkness[2] exempt from darkness, he is not thrown again into the water of existence.

Pause.

O my dear, such milk should be churned!

Keep steady the mind by means of the instruction of the Guru! in this wise nectar is drunk.

(2). By the arrow of the Guru the Kali-yug, hard like a diamond, is pierced, the station of light is displayed.

The darkness of the Sakti (Māyā), the rope of error is cut off, perpetual welfare dwells in the house.

(3). By him, (though) the bow is strung without an arrow, this world is pierced, O brother!

The wind swings the paper-kite in the ten directions, (but) he keeps his attention on the string (by which it is fastened).

(4). The mind sunk into contemplation (of the Supreme) is absorbed in the Vacuum, the folly of duality has fled.

Kabīr says: the Fearless one alone is seen, (if) deep meditation is applied to the name of Rām.

Gauṛī Bairāgaṇi; Tripadās.

III. XLVII.

(1). (Whose) breath is returning (through) the six (mystical) spheres[3] (of the human body), (whose) thought is intent on the Vacuum:

He neither comes nor goes, he neither dies nor lives; seek for him, O Bairāgī!

[1] ਅਕੁਲੁ = Sansk. आकुल = पूरन, the brimful or omnipresent one, an epithet of the Supreme.

[2] The ਅੰਜਨ, collyrium or figuratively darkness, designates here the Māyā.

[3] ਚਕ੍ਰੁ ਖਟੁ ਭੇਦੇ = ਖਟਚਕ੍ਰੁ ਭੇਦੇ (Plur. Format.), the six mystical spheres of the human body, according to the doctrine of the Jōgīs. The six spheres are: 1) आधारचक्र, the pelvis; 2) लिंगचक्र, the external organs of generation; 3) नाभिचक्र, the sphere of the navel; 4) हृत्चक्र, the sphere of the heart; 5) कंठचक्र, the

Pause.

O my mind, the mind, that turns back (from the world), is absorbed (in the Supreme).

By the favour of the Guru understanding is produced in the perverse one (*i.e.* mind), otherwise it would be estranged (from the Supreme).

(2). He is near and far, far and also near, as he is considered by them.

The sherbet, that is made by means of sugar-candy, is known by them, by whom it is drunk.

(3). To whom shall thy story, which does not contain any qualities (of thine), be told? is there any such discriminating one?

Kabīr says: by whom the match is applied, by them the flash is seen as such.

IV. XLVIII.

(1). In him (the Supreme) there is no fire and ocean, no sunshine and no shade, in him is neither production nor destruction.

Neither life nor death, neither pain nor pleasure pervades him, there is empty, abstracted meditation (in him), both[1] (therefore) are not in him.

Pause.

The story of the self-existing[2] one is inexpressible and wonderful.

He cannot be weighed, he is neither consumed nor increased,[3] there is neither lightness nor heaviness in him.

(2). Below and above, both are not in him, neither night nor day are in him.

(There is) no water, no wind and fire (are in him), the true Guru brings about absorption in him.

(3). He remains constantly unattainable and inapprehensible, (but) he is obtained by the favour of the Guru.

Kabīr says: I am a sacrifice to my own Guru, (by whom) I remain in connexion with the society of the pious.

V. XLIX.

(1). Religious demerit and merit are the oxen, he buys, the breath is manifested as the capital.

(Worldly) thirst is the filled sack in the heart; in this wise the venture of goods is bought.

Pause.

Such a Lord is my Rām,

(That) the whole world has been made (by him) a trafficker.

(2). Lust and wrath are made the two receivers of customs, the whim of the mind is the highway-robber.

The five elements, having met, determine the fine (*i.e.* death) and the venture of goods is (thus) brought across.

(3). Kabīr says: hear, O ye saints, now there such a thing happened:

Ascending a pass one ox became exhausted; he is gone and the sack scattered!

sphere of the throat and neck; 6) मूर्धचक्र, the sphere of the head, having at its crown the ब्रह्मरंध्र, or vent-hole of Brahm, through which the soul escapes. Through these six spheres the Jōgīs pretend to draw the breath up and to become thus absorbed in Brahm, whilst living.

[1] ਦੋਉ, either adjective, both, *i.e.* life and death, pleasure and pain, or as substantive: duality.

[2] ਸਹਜ signifies here: self-existing; in this sense the word occurs also in the Rāmāyaṇa of Tulsī Dās.

[3] ਘਾਟਿ = ضائع, consumed; ਭਰਤਿ signifies also in Hindī: much, abundant; here = increased (in contradistinction to ਘਾਟਿ).

Gauṛī; Pañcpadā.

VI. L.

(1). In the house of one's father's family there are four days, one must go to one's father-in-law.
The blind people do not know (this), they are foolish and ignorant.

Pause.

Why does the constable seize and bind the woman?
Persons have come to the house, those, who bring home the wife, have come.
(2). Which rope is let down into the well, that is seen?
The rope with the jug is broken and fallen down, the water-drawing woman rises and goes.
(3). The Lord, becoming compassionate, bestows mercy and accomplishes his own work.
Then she is known as a happy married woman, (when) she reflects on the word of the Guru.
(4). Every one goes about being bound by her former works, see and reflect (on this)!
What shall be said to her, what shall the helpless one do?
(5). Having become hopeless she rises and goes, not having brought about steadiness in her mind.
Cling continually to the feet of Hari, flee to his asylum, O Kabīr!

VII. LI.

(1). The Jōgī says: the Jōg is good and sweet, there is nothing else, O brother!
The plundered and shorn ones (= Jainas) and the Ek-sabdīs [1] say: we have obtained perfection.

Pause.

Without Hari they are led astray by error and are blind.
To whom I go to get rid of my own self, they are bound by many nooses.
(2). From whom things have sprung, in that very one they are absorbed: this rule is forgotten at that very time.
The Paṇḍits, virtuous, heroes and bountiful ones say: we are great.
(3). Whom he informs, he comprehends, without comprehending how should one [2] remain steady?
If one meet with the true Guru, darkness ceases, in this wise the ruby is obtained.
(4). Give up all changes to the left and right! by making firm the foot of Hari (in oneself) one remains steady.
Kabīr says: (if) a dumb person eats molasses, what can he say (about it) when being asked?

RĀGU GAUṚĪ PURBĪ OF KABĪR.

Ōm! by the favour of the true Guru!

I. LII.

(1). Where something was, there is nothing, the five elements are not there.
(If) the right and left and the middle channel (of the vital breath) be stopped, where will the vices go?

Pause.

The thread is broken, the sky (= the soul) has passed away, where is thy speaking (soul) absorbed?
This doubt seizes me daily and no one clears it up for me.
(2). Whose body the universe is, he is not in it, the creator is not in it.

[1] ਏਕ ਸਬਦੀ, an order of mendicants, who only vociferate: ਅਲਖ; they are also called Gōsāvīs.

[2] Or supply from the following line "darkness" as subject, and translate ਠਹੀਐ by: how should it be stopped?

Who is putting (the things) together, he is always aloof (from them), in what can he be said (to be contained)?

(3). Being joined together it is joined, it does not break though being broken off, till it becomes annihilated (by the Supreme).

What for a master, what for a servant? who goes (to the house) of any one?

(4). Kabīr says: where he (= Hari) dwells, there devout meditation is made day and night.

His secret that very man knows, he then is always imperishable.

II. LIII.

(1). The Vēda and the Smriti are the two earrings, true knowledge the patched quilt outside.

Dwelling in an empty cave is (my) sitting free from any design, (this is my) religion.

Pause.

O my king, I am a Bairāgī and Jōgī.

When dying, I am not grieved nor am I separated (from thee).

(2). In the world and universe is (my) little horn, my bag is the whole world, (that is) living on ashes.

Clapping of hands is made, which is returned every minute,[1] if it ceases, it is spread (further).

(3). The mind and breath are made the drinking-gourd, the fiddle is constantly prepared.

The string has become firm, it does not break, unbeaten the fiddle sounds.

(4). Hearing (its sound) (my) mind has become delighted, it is absorbed in the omnipresent one, it does not (any more) vacillate.

Kabīr says: that one is not subject again to birth, the Bairāgī having played (his part), is gone (for ever).

III. LIV.

(1). Nine yards, ten yards, twenty-one yards one body is stretched out.

Seven threads, nine sections, seventy-two woofs are moreover added (to it).[2]

Pause.

(The woman) goes to get it (= the semen) woven (in) a month.

When the house[3] is given up, the weaver goes.

(2). It is not measured by yards, it is not weighed by weight, the baking means is two Seers and a half.[4]

If it (= the fœtus) does not get the baking means quickly, it quarrels and laments in the house (= the womb).

(3). The sitting of the days,[5] the opposition of the husband, how has this time come?

The platters are left,[6] the body gets wet, the weaver goes in disgust.

[1] ਤ੍ਰਿਪਲ, the space of three palas, one pala being the sixtieth part of a ਘੜੀ, or twenty-four minutes.

[2] These lines are extremely difficult, and I could get no explanation whatever from the Sikh Granthīs. I have translated therefore according to conjecture. ਪੁਰੀ is here apparently = body, which meaning it has already in Sanskrit. It is uncertain, what measure is here understood by ਗਜ, as the relative size of the human body is apparently hinted at. In the second line the seven threads seem to imply the seven chief arteries, the nine sections (ਖੰਡ) the different divisions of the body, the seventy-two woofs the seventy-two small veins of the body, (according to Hindū anatomy).

[3] ਘਰ signifies here: wife. The act of conception seems to be hinted at.

[4] ਪਾਚਨੁ the baking or ripening means (of the fœtus), the quantity of food taken for this purpose.

[5] ਦਿਨ ਕੀ ਬੈਠ, the sitting of the days, very likely the lying-in of the woman.

[6] ਛੂਟੇ ਕੂੰਡੇ, the platters are left; ਕੂੰਡਾ refers probably to the vessels, in which the fœtus is enveloped.

(4). The shuttle is empty, no thread issues or it remains entangled.
Giving up (further) prostration she remains here helpless, (this) says Kabīr in admonition.

IV. LV.

(1). There is one light throughout, is it so or not?
In whose heart the name is not produced, that man bursts and dies.

Pause.

(Thou art) dark blue and beautiful, O sweetheart!
My heart clings to thee!
(2). If a pious man is met with, perfection is obtained, (be) this either abstract meditation or enjoyment.
Both objects together are produced by connexion with the name of Rām.
(3). The people think, that this is a song, (but) this is indeed reflection on Brahm,
As (at) Kāsī instruction is given to man at the time of death.
(4). (If) one sing and hear attentively the name of Hari:
There is no doubt, says Kabīr, that he will obtain salvation at the end.

V. LVI.

(1). As many as are making efforts, they are drowned, the ocean of existence is not crossed (by them).
(Though) they be performing works and many abstinences, (their) mind is burnt by egotism.

Pause.

Why is the Lord, the giver of breath and food, forgotten from the mind?
The human birth, the priceless diamond and ruby, is thrown away for a shell.
(2). By reason of error thirst and hunger befall (them, who) do not reflect (on him) in their heart.
(By) arrogant pride they are carried away, (who) do not keep the word of the Guru in (their) mind.
(3). (Who are) incited by the enjoyment of the senses, which are greedy for pleasure, they, taking the juice of liquor, (become) vicious.
(Who) by the lot of (their former) works are joined to the saints, they are saved (like) iron (with) wood.
(4). Wandering and running about in wombs and births we have become weary, undergoing pain we are now worn out.
Kabīr says: meeting with the delicious Guru (we are) saved by love and devotion.

VI. LVII.

(1). It is (only) the figure of a female elephant, O mad mind, the Lord of the world has made a trick.
By the desire of lust the elephant falls into the power (of man), O mad mind, he suffers the goad on his head.

Pause.

Escape from the objects of senses, delight in Hari, understand (this), O mad mind!
Having become fearless thou dost not worship Hari, O mad mind, the boat of Hari is not seized (by thee)!
(2). The monkey has stretched out his hand and taken a handful of grain, O mad mind!
He is perplexed how to get loose, O mad mind! he dances (now) at the door of every house.
(3). As by a lime-twig the parrot is caught, O mad mind!—this is the occupation of the Māyā.
As the colour of the saffron-flower is, O mad mind! so the world is spread out.
(4). For the sake of bathing there are many Tīrthas, O foolish mind! for the sake of worshipping there are many gods.
Kabīr says: no emancipation (is obtained by it), emancipation is in the service of Hari.

VII. LVIII.

(1). Fire does not burn it, the wind does not carry it away, no thief comes near it.

Collect the wealth of the name of Rām, that wealth does not go in any way!

Pause.

Our wealth is the Mādhava Gōvind, who is supporting the earth, this is called the best wealth.

The happiness, that is found in the service of the Lord Gōvind, that happiness is not obtained in dominion.

(2). Searching for this wealth Shiva, Sanaka and the others became Udāsīs.

In (whose) mind Vishṇu, (on whose) tongue Nārāyaṇ is, (on him) the noose of Yama does not fall.

(3). By the Guru his own wealth of divine knowledge and devotion is given (to him, whose) mind is applied to his excellent instruction.

To the burning one water (is given), the running mind is stopped, the fetter of error and fear is gone.

(4). Kabīr says: O thou intoxicated with lust, see and reflect in thy heart!

In thy house are Lakhs and Crores of horses and elephants, in my house is only the enemy of Mura (=Vishṇu).

VIII. LIX.

(1). As by the hand of a greedy monkey a handful of gram is not given up (and he gets caught thereby):

(So) all the works, which are done out of greediness, fall again back on the house.

Pause.

Without devotion life goes to no purpose.

Without worshipping the Lord in the society of the pious, happiness[1] remains in none.

(2). As no one is smelling the flower that is blooming in the desert:

So is he, who is wandering about in many wombs, again and again struck down by death.

(3). This wealth, youth, son and wife, which are given for looking at:

Who clings to them, he is carried away by his senses.

(4). The time (to pass over) is five, the body is a mansion of grass, in the four quarters (of the earth) (this) show is made.

Kabīr says: for the sake of crossing the ocean of fear I have seized the protection of the true Guru.

Gaurī čētī.

IX. LX.

(1). The water is dirty, the earth white.

Of this earth an image is made up.

Pause.

I am nothing, nor is anything mine.

Body, property, all relishes are thine, O Gōvind!

(2). In this earth breath is contained.

Applying a false trick it is moved about.

(3). By some (a fortune[2]) of five Lakhs is amassed.

At the time of the end the water-pot is broken.

(4). Kabīr says: one foundation is raised.

In a moment the conceited man passes away.

[1] ਸਚੁ is here = ਸੁਖ, happiness.

[2] ਲਾਖ ਪਾਂਚ ਕੀ, supply ਆਇਆ.

X. LXI.

(1). O (my) heart, mutter Rām in such a way,
As Dhrū and Prahlād muttered Hari.

Pause.

O thou compassionate to the poor, I trust in thee!
All my family I have put into the boat.
(2). When it pleases him, he makes (me) obey his order.
He brings this boat across.
(3). By the favour of the Guru such wisdom is contained (in me).
Error is gone, there is no more coming and going.
(4). Kabīr says: adore the bow-holder!
On this and that side he alone is bountiful (to) all.

XI. LXII.

(1). When having abandoned the womb he (man) has come into the world:
(Then) as soon as he breathes, the Lord is forgotten (by him).

Pause.

O my heart, sing the excellences of Hari!
(2). When he was practising austerities in the womb with the head downwards,
He was remaining in the fire of the belly.
(3). Having wandered through the eighty-four Lakhs of wombs he has come (into the world).
Now having gone out (of the body) he has no spot nor place.
(4). Kabīr says: adore thou the bow-holder!
When coming, (man) is seen, when going, he is not known.

Gauṛī pūrbī.

XII. LXIII.

(1). Dwelling in heaven should not be desired nor should dwelling in hell be dreaded.
What is to be, that will be, no desire should be made in the heart.

Pause.

The excellences of the sweetheart should be sung,
From whom the highest treasure is obtained.
(2). What is muttering, what austerity and control of the passions, what vows, what ablutions,
As long as the right, loving worship[1] of the Lord is not known?
(3). Seeing prosperity, one should not be joyful, seeing misfortune, one should not weep.
As prosperity is, so is misfortune; what is arranged by destiny, that happens.
(4). Those worshippers are excellent (by their) worship, in whose heart the enemy of Mura dwells.

XIII. LXIV.

(1). O heart, do not put on thyself any burden!
(As) the bird has its dwelling on a tree, so (fleeting) is this world.

Pause.

He drinks the juice of Rām, O dear!
Who has forgotten all other juices.

[1] ਭਾਉਭਗਤਿ, a Tatpurusha, *worship out of love* (not fear, etc.).

(2). Others have died, why should one weep, when oneself does not remain stable?
What is produced, will be annihilated, passing away it weeps in pain.
(3). From what (a being) is produced, with that it is in love, drinking (the breast) it begins to squeeze it (out of love).
Kabīr says: in (my) mind Rām is reflected upon, remembering (him) love (springs up to him).

XIV. LXV.

(1). The woman looks at the road, her eyes are filled with sighs.
Her breast is not divided (= vacillating), her foot does not move, she is longing for the sight of Hari.

Pause.

Do not fly up, O black crow![1]
Speedily a meeting will take place with my beloved Rām.
(2). Kabīr says: for the sake of (eternal) life Hari is worshipped (by me).
(My) only support is the name of Nārāyaṇ, Rām is uttered by (my) tongue.

XV. LXVI.

(1). Round about is the dense Tulsī-shrub in the village of Benāres,[2] O dear!
Having seen his form the shepherdess was enraptured: "do not leave me, come, do not go, O dear!"

Pause.

My mind clings to thy feet, O bow-holder!
He meets (with thee), who is very fortunate.
(2). Vindrāvan is enchanting (my) heart, thou, O Krishṇa, who art grazing the cows, art ravishing (my) heart!
Whose Lord thou art, O bow-holder, to him I, Kabīr, bow, O dear!

Gauṛī pūrbī.

XVI. LXVII.

(1). Many garbs have been put on, dwelling in the forest is made.
What is effected by deceiving men and gods, what, (if) the wise man be drowned in water?

Pause.

O my heart, I know, I shall go.
Comprehend him, who is not going, O ignorant one!
Wherever I see, I do not see (thee) again with (me), (thou art) clinging to the Māyā.
(2). The wise and meditating people are giving much instruction, (that) this whole world is a deception.
Kabīr says: without the name of Rām this world is blind by the Māyā.

XVII. LXVIII.

(1). O my mind, come forth and dance (on) this pathway of the Māyā!
The hero is not afraid of the face of any one in battle, or does the Satī collect the vessels?

Pause.

O mad mind, give up (these) unsteady things!
(If) thou now suffer patiently and die, perfection is obtained, the tree of perfection[3] is laid hold of.

[1] The flying up of a black crow is an evil omen.

[2] Benāres is here a village near Mathurā, where Krishṇa lived.

[3] ਸਿਧਉਗਾ, Sansk. सिद्धवट, the tree, that grants सिद्धि; ਸਿਧਉਗਾ stands therefore for ਸਿਧਉਨ੍ਨਾ.

(2). By lust and wrath people are absorbed in the Māyā, in this wise the world is ruined.
Kabīr says: I do not give up the king Rām, who is higher than all.

XVIII. LXIX.

(1). Thy order is on (my) head, I do not again make (any) reflections.
Thou art the ocean, thou art the elephant (to cross it), from thee (comes) salvation.

Pause.

The servant chooses service,
May the Lord be angry (with him) or treat (him) kindly.
(2). Thy name is my support, as the flower will grow out of the lotus-stalk.
Kabīr says: (I am) the slave of (thy) house, vivify or kill me, as it pleases (thee)!

XIX. LXX.

(1). Wandering about in the womb of the eighty-four Lakhs of creatures Nand became much worn out, O dear!

On account of his devotion (Krishṇa) entered upon an incarnation, great became the lot of the helpless (Nand), O dear!

Pause.

You, who are saying, he is the son of Nand, (tell me), whose son is that Nand?
(When) earth and heaven were not in the ten directions, where was this Nand?
(2). He does not fall into trouble, he does not come into a womb, whose name is the Supreme.
The master of Kabīr is such a Lord, who has neither mother nor father.

XX. LXXI.

Pause.

Slander, slander me, O people, slander me!
Slander is very pleasant to the people.
Slander (is my) father, slander (is my) mother.[1]
(1). If one is slandered, he goes to paradise.
The blessing of the name is settled in (his) mind.
When he, who is of a pure heart, is slandered:
The slanderer washes then my clothes.
(2). Who slanders me, he is my friend.
My thought is in the slanderer.
He is a slanderer, who stops the slander.
The slanderer seeks my life.
(3). Slander against me I like and love.
Slander effects my salvation.
To humble Kabīr slander is the best.
The slanderer is drowned, I cross over.

XXI. LXXII.

Pause.

O king Rām, thou art such a fearless one!
O king Rām, (thou art) the saviour of the saved ones!

[1] It is hard to say, how these words are to be translated, as there is no grammatical relation between them. It is perhaps best to take here ਨਿੰਦਾ as *object of slander*.

(1). When I was, thou (wast) not.

Now art thou and I am not.

Now I and thou have become one, my mind is assured seeing One (only).

(2). When there was volition[1] (in me), what was the strength? now there is no clash[2] between volition and strength.

Kabīr says: my volition is taken away, the volition is changed and perfection obtained.

XXII. LXXIII.

(1). Digging six holes a house is made and an incomparable thing put into it.

Creating the breath, key and lock is put (on it), no delay is made by the creator.

Pause.

Now, O brother, remain wakeful in (thy) mind!

Becoming careless thy lifetime is lost, the thief plunders the house and goes off.

(2). Five watchmen remain at the gate, there is no confidence in them.

Beware, remain attentive in thy mind and thou wilt obtain light and brightness!

(3). The woman, who seeing the nine houses[3] is led astray, does not obtain the incomparable thing.

Kabīr says: the nine houses are plundered, in the tenth[4] (house) the truth is contained.

XXIII. LXXIV.

Pause.

O mother, I do not know any other.[5]

Whose excellences Shiva, Sanak and the others sing, in him dwells my life.

(1). In (my) heart is light and divine knowledge imparted by the Guru, in the orb of the sky (= the head) meditation.

The diseases of sensuality, the bonds of fear are broken, the mind is in its own house, happiness is known.

(2). With affection and love it knows and obeys the One, no other Lord is in the mind.

With sandal-perfume the mind is fumigated, egotism is abandoned and depressed.

(3). Who sings and meditates on the glory of the Lord, his place is the Lord.

In his mind dwells a great lot, on whose head (this is) the chief occupation.[6]

(4). Having cut off the Māyā salvation and tranquillity are manifested, in the only One (I am) absorbed.

Kabīr says: by meeting with the Guru great happiness (is obtained), the straying mind remains reconciled (with the Supreme).

RĀGU GAUṚĪ PŪRBĪ; BĀVANAKHRĪ OF KABĪR.

Ōm! by the favour of the true Guru!

(1). In the three worlds are the fifty-two letters, everything (is contained) in these.

These letters will pass away, those letters are not in these.

(2). Where there is speech, there is the sound of letters.

Where there is no speech, there is no stay for the mind.

[1] ਬੁਧਿ must here be taken in the sense of *volition*, the will and design of the intellectual power.

[2] Properly: sourness.

[3] The nine houses are the nine outlets of the human body.

[4] The tenth house is the dasvā̃ duār, said to be on the crown of the head.

[5] ਆਨਾਨ = ਆਨਾ other (ਨਾ being an alliteration).

[6] ਮਥਾਨਾਨਾ = ਮਥਾ, ਨਾਨਾ being a meaningless alliteration.

In speech and absence of speech is that One.
Such as[1] he is, no one perceives him.
(3). If I obtain the Unattainable one, what shall I say? (and if) I say, what is the benefit (of it)?
Is he contained in the seed of a globule, whose expansion the worlds are?
(4). (If) I obtain the Unattainable one, the difference[2] is abolished, (his) secret is somewhat obtained.
The unbroken and indivisible one is obtained, by separation (from whom my) mind was upset and pierced.
(5). (By) the Turk he is known (from) worship,[3] (by) the Hindū (from) the Vēda and Purāṇas.
In order to inform the mind divine knowledge should be read to some extent.
(6). The holy syllable Ōm is known (to be) in the beginning.
(Who) writes and effaces (it), he has no honour.
If one comprehend the holy syllable Ōm,
He having comprehended it is not effacing (it again).
(7). *Kakā.* A ray of light is put into the lotus.
The moonshine does not come into a covered box.
And though I put into it the juice of flowers:
To whom shall I tell and make understand the inexpressible story?
(8). *Khakhā.* Into this cavity (=body) the mind has come.
Without leaving the hole it runs in the ten directions.
Having known the Lord it remains patient.
Then it settles down quietly, when it obtains the imperishable place.
(9). *Gagā.* (From) the word of the Guru he (the Supreme) is known (by him),
(Who) does not put another word (into) his ears.
He ceases travelling about in the air, he does not go anywhere.
He seizes the unseizable one and having seized (him) he ceases soaring in the skies.
(10). *Ghaghā.* In everybody he dwells.
When the body bursts, he never becomes diminished.
When he has obtained a landing-place in a body:
Why does he run to an inaccessible place, giving up that body?
(11). *Ṅaṅā.* Restrain love, remove anxiety!
Do not run away from what thou hast not seen, this is the highest wisdom.
(12). *Čačā.* A (well)-made picture is of high price.
Leave the picture and think of the painter!
Variously coloured is this immense (world).[4]
Leaving the picture keep the painter (in thy) thoughts!
(13). *Čhačhā.* This is the snare of the king.
Why does he not remain satisfied, why does he not give up desire?
O my mind, I admonish thee every moment:
Cast out (thy own self)! why causest thou thyself to be bound?
(14). *J̌aǰā.* If one causes his body to be burned whilst living:
He, burning (his) youth, obtains salvation.

[1] ਜਸ—ਤਸ = ਜੈਸਾ—ਤੈਸਾ.

[2] The difference between him and me.

[3] ਤਰੀਕਤ (طریقت), the second step in Sūfism. The first is شریعت, the law, the outward rites; the second طریقت, worship of God in the mind; the third معرفت, knowledge (ਗਿਆਨ); the fourth حقیقت, certainty, *i.e.* pantheistic union with the Supreme.

[4] ਅਵਝੇਗਾ = ਅਵਝੜ Adj., immense, huge (Marāṭhī). In Sindhī अवझड़ु signifies: labyrinth (Gurmukhī ਔਝੜ).

When he goes on being burned and consumed in this way:
Then, having gone, he attains to light and brightness.
(15). *Jhajhā.* (Who) does not know how to apply his mind and to understand (the truth):[1]
He remains boggling and is not approved of.
Being bewildered (myself) how shall I make others comprehend (it)?
By making disputes I raise even disputes.
(16). *Ñaṅā.* Why should one go far away giving up him, who remains near in the heart?
For whose sake the world is searched through, he is obtained near.
(17). *Ṭaṭā.* A difficult pass is in the heart.
Having opened the door why does he not go into the palace?
Having seen the immovable one I do not move to any other place.
(If my) heart continues clinging (to him), I obtain intimacy (with him).
(18). *Ṭhaṭhā.* This one is far, the cheat near.
At last, at last (my) mind was made sedate.
By which cheat the whole world is cheated (and) devoured:
That cheat was cheated (by me), (my) mind came to a place (of rest).
(19). *Ḍaḍā.* If fear (of God) springs up, fear goes.
Then fear is absorbed in the fear (of God).
If (his) fear (of God) subside,[2] fear sticks again (to him).
(Who) has become fearless (of God), (in his) breast fear is produced, he flees.
(20). *Ḍhaḍha.* (He is) near, whom else does he seek?
In searching about (one's) life is wasted.
When searching about he ascends the Sumēru:[3]
He is obtained in the fort, by whom the fort is made.[4]
(21). *Ṇaṇā.* A man that enters battle makes a close fight.[5]
He does not stoop nor vacillate.
One may account his life happy.
He kills the One and gives up many.
(22). *Tatā.* The impassable (ocean) cannot be crossed.
The body is contained in the three worlds.
When the three worlds are contained in the body:
Then the substance is united (with the absolute) substance, the True one is obtained.
(23). *Thathā.* The bottom of the bottomless one is not obtained.
That one is bottomless, this one (= the human mind) is not kept steady.
In a small place and spot he commences.
Without posts he supports the palace.
(24). *Dadā.* What thou seest, that is passing away.
Whom thou dost not see, on him continue to reflect!
When in the tenth gate the key is given:
Then the sight of the Merciful one is obtained.

[1] ਉਰਝਣਾ *v.n.* to apply the mind; ਸੁਰਝਣਾ *v.a.* to understand, to comprehend.

[2] ਡਰੁ ਡਰੈ; ਡਰਨਾ is to be taken here in its original meaning: *to burst, to break* = to subside (Sansk. दरण).

[3] ਸੁਮੇਰੁ is here the crown of the head, where the tenth gate is.

[4] The ਗੜ੍ਹ or fort is the human body.

[5] ਨੇਹੀ (= ਨੇਹਿ), originally: cohesiveness = close fight.

(25). *Dhadhā.* Below and above there is a settlement.
In the nether and upper regions there is dwelling.
Having given up what is below, when one has come to what is above:
Then, what is above, is united with what is below, happiness is obtained.[1]
(26). *Nanā.* Night and day (I am) looking at a place.
(My) eyes looking (at it) have become red.
When looking on and looking on I reach the place:
Then the look is blended with the look.
(27). *Papā.* The boundless one is not obtained.
(Who) enters into intimacy with the highest light:
He subdues his five senses.
Religious demerit and merit, both he discards.
(28). *Phaphā.* A fruit is produced without blossoms.
If one behold a mouthful of that fruit,
He does not fall into duality, he reflects on the mouthful.
A mouthful of that fruit rends all bodies.[2]
(29). *Babā.* A drop is mixed with a drop.
A drop cannot be separated from a drop.
(Who) becomes a servant, takes up service.
Who becomes a prisoner, gets knowledge of the prison.
(30). *Bhabhā.* The difference is united with the difference.
Now fear is broken and confidence is come.
Who (was considered as being outside), he is (now) known (as being) inside.
The separated king is recognized (as one and the same with me).
(31). *Mamā.* (By whom) the root is seized, he reconciles (his) mind.
(Who) becomes acquainted with (these) secrets, he knows (his) mind.
May no one keep back (his) mind from meeting (with its root)!
By being immersed (in him) he obtains that True one.
(32). *Mamā.* The matter is with (one's) mind; by subduing the mind perfection is obtained.
Kabīr says: from the mind the mind does not obtain any desire.
(33). This mind is the Shakti, this mind is Shiva.
This mind is the life of the five elements.
If one taking this mind remain absorbed in divine contemplation:
Then he relates the things of the three worlds.
(34). *Yayā.* If one knows (the truth), he destroys folly, having subdued (his) body, he sings.
A hero engaged in battle does not flee, fame stimulates (him).
(35). *Rarā.* (Worldly) relish is considered as insipid.
What is insipid is known as relish.
Who gives up this (worldly) relish, he gets that (divine) relish.
(By whom) that (divine) relish is tasted, (to him) this (worldly) relish does not please.
(36). *Lalā.* (If one) apply (his) mind in such a way to devout meditation:
He, not going anywhere else, obtains the highest truth.

[1] Verses of this kind, being destitute of all grammatical connexion, cannot be properly translated; we can only give a conjecture. The verse tends to pantheistical union of the finite with the infinite being.

[2] It is difficult to say what is meant by these strange allegories. The fruit produced without blossoms seems to signify *the Absolute*.

And if he bestow devout meditation on it with love,
He obtains the unattainable one, and having obtained (him) he is absorbed in (his) feet.
(37). *Vavā.* Remember again and again Vishṇu !
Who remembers Vishṇu is not overcome.
Who is a sacrifice to Vishṇu and sings his praise (in his) body:
He is united (with) Vishṇu and obtains him, who of all (alone) is true.
(38). *Vavā.* (Who) is known by him, (who) knows him, this one is.
When this and that one meet together, then no one knows (them), they being united.
(39). *Sasā.* Examine and consider that as good!
Hold firm the word of familiar intercourse with the heart!
If love to familiar intercourse with the heart springs up (in any one):
In him is fully present the king of the three worlds.
(40). *Khakhā.* If one diligently search (for him)—
Who searches (for him), he is not again born—
If searching and comprehending he reflect (on him):
Then he is crossing the water of existence without delay.
(41). *Sasā.* That one adorns the bed of the bridegroom.
That one removes the doubt of the female friend.
Having given up little pleasure the highest pleasure is obtained.
Then this one is called wife, that one husband.
(42). *Hahā.* That he is existing, is not known.
When he is, then the mind is comforted.
When one apprehends, that he is indeed:
Then that one is that, this one is not.
(43). Absorbed in thought all the people wander about.
On his account much grief affects (them).
When they direct their thoughts on the husband of Lakshmī:
Grief is effaced, they obtain all comforts.
(44). *Khakhā.* How many are gone drooping and wasting away!
(Though) drooping and wasting away, they do not think (of him) till now.
If the world now, having known (him), go on to conciliate (him):
It obtains (him) firmly, from whom it was separated.
(45). Fifty-two letters are joined together (by me),
(But I am) not able to know one letter.
Kabīr tells the word of the True one.
Who becomes a Paṇḍit, he remains fearless.
The profession of the Paṇḍit is for the sake of the people.
Who is skilled in divine knowledge, he is reflecting on truth.
In whose heart such an understanding is:
He will know it, says Kabīr.

Ōm ! by the favour of the true Guru !

RĀGU GAUṚĪ; THE THITĪS OF KABĪR.

Slōk.

There are fifteen lunar dates and seven week-days.
Kabīr says : (of him who has) no limit,
If the ascetics and perfect devotees obtain the secret :
They are themselves the creator, themselves God.

Thitīs.

(1). On *the day of new moon* remove hope (desire) !
Remember Rām, the inward governor !
Obtain the gate of salvation whilst living !
The word of the Fearless one is the very essence of truth.

Pause.

(Who are) filled with love to the lotus-foot of Gōvind :
They by the favour of the saints become pure in their mind, they wake day by day in the praise of Hari.
(2). On the *first* (lunar) day reflect on the beloved !
In the body sports the bodiless and boundless one.
The pain of death never devours (him),
Who is absorbed in the primeval divine male.
(3). *Second* (lunar) day. Thou knowest, that two are (in) the body.
The Māyā and Brahm sport with all.
That one neither increases nor decreases.
The bodiless and undefiled one is of one and the same state.
(4). *Third* (lunar) day. (Who) grinds and subdues the three (qualities) :
He obtains the root of joy, the highest place.
In the society of the saints confidence springs up.
Outside and inside there is always light.
(5). *Fourth* (lunar) day. Seize the fickle mind.
Never sit together with lust and wrath !
In water and land is he himself.
He himself mutters the recitals of his own name.
(6). The *fifth* (lunar) day. The five elements are spread out.
Gold and women are the occupation of the world.
If one drink with love the nectar-juice :
The pain of old age and death will not again befall him.
(7). The *sixth* (lunar) day. In the six spheres (of the body)[1] and in the six directions (of the world) (the mind) runs about.
Without intimacy (with the Supreme Spirit) it does not remain steady.
(Who) having effaced duality lays hold of patience :
He does not undergo the sharp pain of works.
(8). The *seventh* (lunar) day. Take (this) word as true !
Take the Supreme Spirit as real !

[1] About the ਖਟ ਚਕ੍ਰ see p. 472, note 3.

Doubt is dissolved, pain is effaced.
In the vacant pond[1] thou wilt obtain happiness.
(9). The *eighth* (lunar) day. The body consists of eight substances.[2]
In that ignoble one is the great treasure of the king.
Divine knowledge, obtainable from the Guru, shows the secret.
The infrangible and indivisible (Supreme) is turned over (= disclosed).
(10). The *ninth* (lunar) day. Subdue the nine gates!
Bind down the wandering desire!
(If) all greediness and fondness be forgotten:
Thou wilt live for ever and eat the fruit of immortality.
(11). The *tenth* (lunar) day. In the ten directions joy springs up.
Doubt is dissolved, Gōvind is met with.
The incomparable substance is consisting of light.
It is pure, there is no filth (in it), neither shade nor sunshine.
(12). The *eleventh* (lunar) day. (If one) run in one direction:
He does not fall again into the pain of the womb.
(His) body becomes cool and pure.
Whom they are showing (as being) far away, him he obtains near (in his heart).
(13). The *twelfth* (lunar) day. Twelve suns rise.
Unbeaten sound day and night the musical instruments.
The beloved of the three worlds is seen.
Wonderful! from a created soul he has become the Supreme Soul.[3]
(14). The *thirteenth* (lunar) day. Expound the thirteen holy Shāstras!
Below and above consider (all) as the same!
There is neither low nor high, neither honour nor dishonour.
In all things Rām is contained.
(15). The *fourteenth* (lunar) day. He is in the fourteen worlds.
In every hair dwells the enemy of Mura.
Keep up meditation on true contentment!
The story of the knowledge of Brahm should be told!
(16). On *the day of full moon* the moon is full in the sky.
The digit (of the moon) is spread out, (there is) naturally light.
In the beginning, end and middle he exists, O brother!
Kabīr sports in the ocean of happiness.

[1] ਸੁੰਨਿ ਸਰੋਵਰਿ in the vacant pond = the Supreme, which is described by ਸੁੰਨ, the vacuum.

[2] Seven substances of the body are usually enumerated.

[3] ਜੀਉ (जीव) as distinguished from शिव, designates the created or rather emanated soul (individual life); ਸੀਉ (= शिव) is on the contrary the universal, supreme soul, the actuating principle in animated beings.

Ōm! by the favour of the true Guru!

RĀGU GAUṚĪ; THE VĀRS OF KABĪR.[1]

Pause.

Sing continually the excellences of Hari!
Get that secret of Hari, which is to be expounded by the Guru!
(1). Who on *Sunday* commences devotion:
He is stopping in the mansion of the body (his) desires.
If day and night the melody goes on uninterruptedly:
The flute sounds in tranquillity without being sounded.
(2). On *Monday* nectar flows (from) the moon.
Who is quickly tasting it removes all poison.
If the speech be stopped in the gate (= mouth):
Then the intoxicating mind is drinking.
(3). On *Tuesday* acquire knowledge![2]
(That) thou mayest know the proceeding of the five thieves.
Do not leave the house and go forth!
Otherwise the king will be much displeased.
(4). On *Wednesday* wisdom diffuses light.
In the lotus of the heart is the dwelling of Hari.
Who having met (with) the Guru considers the two[3] equal to One:
He, having erected (the lotus of the heart) (from) the mud, puts (it) straight.
(5). On *Thursday* let the world go!
Comprehend the three Gods in One!
Three rivers are in that triad.
(If thou) wash away day and night (thy) filth, thou bathest (in them).
(6). Who on *Friday* overcomes thirst,[4] he ascends to this vow:
That he daily struggles himself with himself.
If all the five (senses), which are very watchful (for an opportunity of action), he watch:
No second sight (= duality) ever enters (him).
(7). If on *Saturday* he keeps firm
That torch of light in (his) body:
Outside and inside light is diffused.
All works are then set aside (by him).
(8). As long as in the body is another command:
So long the sweetheart is not obtained in the palace.
(When) love is bestowed on the sporting Rām:
Then the body (becomes) pure, says Kabīr.

[1] ਵਾਰ *m.* Week-day.

[2] ਮਾਹੀਤਿ *s.f.* knowledge, conversancy (with a branch of knowledge); Arab. مَاهِيت (quality, essence of a thing).

[3] ਦੋਊ, the two, *i.e.* God and the creature (thou and I).

[4] ਤਸ = ਤਿਸ (fem.) thirst, worldly desires.

RĀGU GAUṚĪ ČĒTĪ.

The Speech of Nāmdēv.

Ōm! by the favour of the true Guru!

Pause.

By God stones are caused to swim.

How should not men by the order of Rām cross?

(1). Seizing the raft the whore, the hump-backed woman without beauty, the hunter[1] and Ajāmal were brought across (= saved).

The man, who struck the feet (of Krishṇa), became emancipated.

I am a sacrifice (to) the man, (who) utters: Ram!

(2). To the son of the slave-girl, the humble Bidar,[2] to Sudāmā and Ugrasēna kingdoms were given.

Who were without muttering, without austerity, without family, without works, they were saved, O Lord of Nāmā!

RĀGU GAUṚĪ; VERSES OF RAVIDĀS.

Gauṛī guārērī.

Ōm! the true name is the creator, the Supreme Spirit.

By the favour of the Guru!

I.

(1). My company is day and night low.

My work perverseness, my birth vile.

Pause.

O Lord Rām, life of the creatures! do not forget me, I am thy servant!

(2). Remove my calamity, bestow affection (on thy) servant!

I do not let go (thy) feet, (though my) body be consumed.

(3). Ravidās says: I fall on thy protection.

Join quickly (thy) servant, do not delay!

II.

(1). Bēgampur[3] is the name of (my) city.

Pain and anguish are not in that place.

Nor anxiety nor tribute on property.

No fear and no sin, no dread and decline.

Pause.

Now I have got a good country.

There is always happiness, O my brother!

[1] The name of the hunter was Jarā (old age).

[2] Vidura, the son of Vyāsa and of a female servant (Wilson, Vish. Pur. p. 459). Sudāmā, a poor Brāhman, enriched by Krishṇa. Ugrasēna was placed on the throne by Krishṇa (Wilson, Vish. Pur. p. 560).

[3] ਬੇਗਮਪੁਰਾ, Literally: a city without grief (بي غم).

(2). Stable and always enduring is (my) dominion.
There is no second nor third there, there is only One.[1]
It is always cultivated and famous.
There the rich and happy dwell.
(3). As it pleases (them), so they walk about.
The confidant of the palace no one stops.
Ravidās says: the tanner is free.[2]
Who is my fellow-citizen, he is my friend.

Ōm! by the favour of the true Guru!

Gauṛī bairāgaṇi; Ravidās.

I. III.

(1). Very inaccessible is the mountain, I have one vicious bullock.
I address one supplication to my sweetheart: O Murāri, keep my capital-stock!

Pause.

(I am) some retail-dealer of Rām, my venture of goods is laden, O dear!
(2). I am a retail-dealer of Rām, I naturally carry on traffic.
I have laden the wealth of the name of Rām, the world has laden poison.
(3). O receiver of customs, write down anything you please!
The punishment of Yama does not fall on me, I have given up all worldly cares.
(4). As the colour of the safflower is, so is this world.
The colour of my sweetheart is of Majīth, says Ravidās, the tanner.

Gauṛī pūrbī; Ravidās.

Ōm! by the favour of the true Guru!

I. IV.

(1). As a well is filled with frogs, which have no knowledge of other countries:
So my mind is fascinated by the world, it has no knowledge of this and that side (= world).

Pause.

O Lord of all the worlds, show me one moment thy sight, O dear!
(2). My intellect has become impure, (so that) thy state cannot be apprehended (by me), O Mādhava!
Bestow mercy (on me), (that) my error may cease; instruct me and give me a good intellect!
(3). The most excellent Jōgī does not reach (them), thy qualities are beyond telling.
On account of love and devotion (to thee) Ravidās, the tanner, tells (them).

Gauṛī bairāgaṇi.

Ōm! by the favour of the true Guru!

I. V.

(1). In the Satya Yug (was) truth, the Trētā (was) offering sacrifices, in the Dvāpar (was) the performance of worship.
In the three ages three (practices) were established, in the Kali-yug the name (of Hari) alone is support.

[1] ਦੋਮ (دُوُم) *i.e.* duality; ਸੇਮ (سِيُم) *i.e.* the three qualities.
[2] Ravidās was a ਚਮਾਰ or tanner.

Pause.

How shall I get to the other side, O dear?

No one instructs and tells me, by what coming and going may vanish?

(2). Religious duties (of) many kinds are described, (but) the creator is seen in all the worlds.

Which are those works, by which one may become emancipated, by practising which all perfections may be obtained?

(3). Outside one may be washed with water, (but) in his heart are manifold vices.

In what wise may he become pure, (whose) practice is after the manner of a clean elephant?[1]

(4). Good and bad actions must be weighed, (but) there is doubt when one hears the Vēda and the Purāṇas.

Doubt always dwells in the heart, who puts away (his) conceit?

(5). As the night passes before the light of the sun—(this) the whole world is knowing—

(So), mind, copper is turned into gold without delay, (if) it come into contact with the philosopher's stone.

(6). He meets with the Guru, the most excellent philosopher's stone, on (whose) forehead it is written by destiny.

(If) a mind absorbed in divine contemplation meet (with) the mind, the diamond shutters are opened.

(7). (Whose) mind is intent on devotion and performing worship, cutting off the bonds of error and vices:

He is happy (in his) mind (and) united (with the Supreme), reflecting only on the excellences of him, who is without qualities.

(8). Many efforts (of) repression were made (by me), (but though) put aside the noose of error does not recede.

Devotion out of love does not spring up, Ravidās is sad about that.

[1] The elephant, when washed, wallows again in the dust.

Ōm! The true name is the creator, the Supreme Spirit, without fear, without enmity, of a timeless form, unproduced from a womb.

By the favour of the Guru!

RĀGU ĀSĀ.

Mahalā I.; *Ghar* I.

Sō dar.[1]

What is that thy gate, what that house, where sitting thou supportest all?

Thy musical instruments (and) sounds are many, (yea) innumerable, how many are thy musicians?

How many are called thy Rāgs with the Rāgiṇīs, how many (are) thy singers?

To thee sing the wind, water, fire, Dharm-rājā sings (to thee) at (thy) gate.

To thee sing the recording-angels, (who) know how to write (and who) writing down reflect on moral actions.

To thee sing Īsar (Shiva), Brahmā, the Dēvī, (who) display lustre being always adorned by thee.

To thee sing the Indras sitting on Indra's throne with the gods, who are at (his) gate.

To thee sing the perfect ascetics in their deep meditations, to thee sing the pious reflecting (on thee).

To thee sing the ascetics of subdued passions, the chaste (women), the contented ones, to thee sing the hardy heroes.

To thee sing the Paṇḍits, (who) read, the great abstinent ascetics with the gods (sing) continually.

To thee sing the fascinating women, (who) fascinate the mind of those in heaven, earth and in the nether region.

To thee sing all the gems, produced by thee, with the sixty-eight Tīrthas.

To thee sing the heroes very powerful in battle, to thee sing the four sources (of production).

To thee sing the regions, orbs and universe, which are made, kept and supported by thee.

They sing to thee, who please thee; thy devotees, who have a taste (of thee), are attached (to thee).

It does not come into my mind, how many others sing to thee, what can Nānak judge?

He, he is always the true Lord, true, of a true name.

He is and will be and will not be destroyed, by whom the creation was made.

By whom the Māyā of various sorts and kinds was produced.

Having made (it) he beholds (it), his own work is as his greatness.

What pleases him, that he will do, his order cannot be overturned.

He is the king, Lord of kings, Nānak (says): the order (of) the Lord remains (firm).

Āsā; mahalā IV.

I. II.

(1). He is the Supreme Being, Hari is the Supreme Being, Hari is quite unattainable, boundless.

All meditate, all meditate on thee, O Hari, O true creator!

All creatures are thine, sir, thou art the donor of the creatures!

Meditate on Hari, O ye saints, who causes all pain to be forgotten.

Hari himself is the Lord, Hari himself is the servant, what is the helpless creature, (says) Nānak.

(2). Thou art in every body, in all thou, O Hari, the one Supreme Spirit, art continuously contained.

Some are munificent, some are beggars, all are thy wonderful frolics.

Thou thyself art the giver, thou thyself the enjoyer, without thee I do not know another.

Thou, O Supreme Brahm, art endless, endless, how can I describe thy qualities?

Who serve, who serve thee, their sacrifice is humble Nānak.

[1] See p. 14.

(3). Who meditate on thee, who meditate on thee, O Hari, those people live comfortably in the world.

They are emancipated, they are emancipated, who meditate on thee, O Hari, the noose of Yama on them is broken.

Who meditate on the fearless one, who meditate on the fearless Hari, all their fear will go.

Who serve, who serve my Hari, they will be absorbed into the form of Hari.

They are happy, they are happy, who meditate on Hari, humble Nānak will be a sacrifice to them.

(4). Thy store-rooms are filled with devotion to thee, with devotion to thee, O endless, endless one!

Thy devotees, thy devotees praise thee, O Hari, who art many, many (and) endless![1]

They perform many, many adorations to thee, O Hari, they practise austerities and mutter (thee), O endless one!

They read many, many Smritis and Shāstras of thine, they are performing religious ceremonies (and) the six (prescribed) works.

Those devotees, those devotees are excellent, (says) humble Nānak, who are pleasing to my Lord Hari.

(5). Thou art the primeval divine male, the boundless creator, there is none other like thee.

Thou art for ages the One, (thou art) always, always the One, thou art that immovable creator.

What pleases to thyself, that exists, what thou doest thyself, that takes place.

By thyself the whole creation is produced, by thyself all (the world) is created and destroyed (again).

Humble Nānak sings the excellences of the creator, who is knowing all.

Ōm! by the favour of the true Guru!

RĀGU ĀSĀ; MAHALĀ I.

Čaupadās; Ghar II.

I.

(1). Every one calls (thee) great, having heard (it from others).
(For) has it been seen, how great (thou art)?
(Thy) estimate cannot be obtained nor told.
Those, who are telling (it), remain absorbed in thee.

Pause.

O my great Lord, deep and profound, weighty with excellences!
No one knows, how great thy garb is.
(2). Though all intelligent ones meet and take it into consideration;
(Though) all valuers meet and make an estimate (of it);
The wise and meditative ones, the Gurus of the Gurus: alas![2]
Not a bit can thy greatness be told.
(3). All virtues, all austerities, all good actions,
The greatnesses of the perfect men—
Without thee no one has obtained perfection.
By destiny it accrues (and is then) not prevented.
(4). What is the helpless speaker?
Thy store-rooms are filled with praises.

[1] Hari becomes by expansion many and endless.

[2] ਗੁਰਗੁਰ ਹਾਈ, the great of the great; or: the Gurus of the Gurus, alas! the interjection ਹਾਈ (ਹਾਇ) belongs properly to the following line. But ਗੁਰਗੁਰਹਾਈ may also be taken = ਗੁਰਗੁਰਹ (ਗੁਰਹ the Format. Plur. of ਗੁਰ), āī being then a meaningless alliteration.

To whom thou givest (them), what can he do?
Nānak (says): the True one is arranging (all).

II.

(1). (If) I utter (the name), I live, if I forget (it), I die.
It is difficult to utter the true name.
Who has hunger after the true name:
The pain of his hunger departs having eaten.

Pause.

How should he be forgotten, O my mother?
True is the Lord, of a true name.
(2). The greatness of the true name
Having uttered a little they became tired, (its) estimate was not reached.
Though all having met, set to utter it:
It does not increase nor decrease.
(3). He does not die nor does grief befall (him).
He goes on giving, (his) enjoyment does not cease (at the same time).
This is his (inherent) property (and) none other.
Nor has been any (other) nor will be.
(4). As great as thou art thyself, so great is thy gift,
(Thou), by whom day and night is made.
Who forget the Lord, they are of low birth.
Nānak (says): without the Lord (they are) low caste people.[1]

III.

(1). If a beggar at the gate raises a cry, the Lord hears it in (his) palace.
Whether (thou give him) assurance (or) push him away, thou alone givest greatness.

Pause.

Thou acknowledgest the light (that is in him) and dost not ask after (his) caste.
(For) in the other world there is no caste.
(2). Thou thyself causest to be done, thou thyself dost (all things), thou thyself puttest taunts into the mind (of man).
When thou art the creator and maker:
What is (then) dependence (on others), what the world?
(3). Thou thyself producest and givest.
Thou thyself causest the folly of the mind.
If thou comest and dwellest in the mind by the favour of the Guru:
The pain (of) darkness departs from within.
(4). The true one thou lovest thyself.
To the others thou dost not give the truth.
If thou give and unfold it to any one:
Him thou dost not interrogate[2] in the other world, (says) Nānak.

IV.

(1). The brass-plates and cymbals (are) the volitions of the heart.
The drum (is) the world, the instrument (of which) sounds.

[1] ਸਨਾਤਿ *s.f.* Arab. صِناعت, profession, trade; here in the sense of *low caste, mean profession.*
[2] *i.e.* take or ask account from him.

Nārada[1] dances—(this is) the love of the Kali-yug.
Where shall the abstinent and chaste set their foot?

Pause.

Nānak is a sacrifice to the name.
The world is blind, know thou the Lord!
(2). (If) a disciple turn to the Guru and eat;
(If) out of love for food he come and dwell in (his) house;
Though he be living and eating a hundred years:
That day is the best, (in which) he gets acquainted with the Lord.
(3). By having an interview mercy is not obtained.
Without taking and giving none remains.
The king administers justice (on him who) is in (his) power.[2]
For the order of God no one cares.
(4). He has the shape and name of a man, (says) Nānak.
(But) in actions he is a dog, (being) at the gate (by) order.
(If) by the favour of the Guru he knows, (that he is) a guest:
Then he obtains some honour at the threshold (of God).

V.

(1). As much as the sound is, so much is the hearing of the sound, as much as the form is, (so much) is thy body.
Thou thyself art the tongue, thou thyself the flavour,[3] there is no other, I say, O mother!

Pause.

My Lord is the only one, the only one, O brother, the only one.
(2). He himself destroys, he himself sets loose, he himself takes and gives.
He himself sees, he himself expands, he himself beholds (it).
(3). Whatever was to be done, that he has done, nothing else can be done.
As it is, such it is called, all is thy greatness.
(4). (In) the Kali-yug the Māyā is selling liquors, the intoxicated mind keeps on drinking (her) sweet liquor.
He himself (the Supreme) makes forms of many kinds, so says helpless Nānak.

VI.

(1). Wisdom is music, love the tambourine,
(By which) always joy and pleasure are produced in the mind.
This is devotion, this is austerity.
Dance in this wise, keeping (thy) foot (in proper time)!

Pause.

(These are) full chimes, (if one) know the praise (of the Lord).
Is other dancing a pleasure in the mind?[4]
(2). Truth (and) contentment (are) the two cymbals, (that) sound.
Music of the feet, (if one be) always happy.

[1] Nārada, figuratively for an embroiler.

[2] It is nearly impossible to say, what the meaning of ਹਥਿ ਹੋਇ is; literally it signifies: it is in hand or in (one's) power; but as no grammatical relation or connexion is hinted at, it can only be translated by conjecture.

[3] ਬਸਨਾ here = ਵਾਸਨਾ, properly *scent*, but also misused for *flavour*, *taste*.

[4] This line, if it is not to stultify itself, is to be taken in an interrogatory sense.

The sound (of) melody, (if there be) no second love.
Dance in this wise, keeping (thy) foot (in proper time)!
(3). Turning round (in dancing) is, (if) fear (of God) be in the mind and heart,
Continually in sitting down and rising.
Lying down on the reclining place (is, if) one knows, (that his) body is ashes.
In this wise dance, keeping (thy) foot (in proper time)!
(4). (He is) a disciple, (who) aims at initiation into the assembly.
(He is) a disciple of the Guru, (who is) hearing the true name,
(And) uttering it continually, (says) Nānak.
Dance in this wise, keeping (thy) foot (in proper time)!

VII.

(1). Having produced the wind, the whole earth is supported (by him), bonds were assigned to water and fire.

The ten-headed head (of) the blind one was cut off, by killing Rāvaṇa[1] what great thing was done?

Pause.

How can thy greatness be told?
Thou remainest full in all, sunk in thoughts.

(2). Producing the creatures he subdues (them) by (his) skill;[2] by putting a nose-ring into the nose of Kālī[3] what great thing was done?

Whose husband art thou, who is called (thy) wife? in all thou art present uninterruptedly.

(3). Brahmā, the giver of blessings, went wailing with (his) wife to investigate creation.

But he did not find out its end; by perforating Kans what great thing was done?

(4). Gems were produced and put down, milk was churned, the others were led astray to think, that it was done by them.[4]

Nāuak says: how should the hidden one be hidden, (who) distributes (his gifts) to every one?

VIII.

(1). By practising works a vine is spread out, the name of Rām becomes its fruit.

He (Rām) has no sign nor mark, the unbeaten sound sounds, (that) is produced by the Supreme.[5]

Pause.

If one expound and know (it):
He drinks nectar.

(2). By whom it is drunk, they have become intoxicated, (their) bonds (and) nooses break.

Light is absorbed in the Luminous one; (who) is within it, gives up the the profits of the Māyā.

(3). Thy luminous form is seen (in) all, all the worlds (and) the Māyā is thine.

In beautiful form (thou art) sitting aloof (from the created things), thou lookest on, being spread out within (them).

[1] Rāvaṇa, sovereign of Lankā (Ceylon) and prince of the Rākshasas, is said to have had ten heads; he was killed by Rāma (or Rāmačandra).

[2] ਹਥਿ ਕੀਨੀ, supply: ਸ੍ਰਿਸਟਿ the creation.

[3] ਕਾਲੀ (Sansk. कालीय) *s.m.*, the serpent that infested the Yamunā and was overcome by Krishṇa (see Wilson's Vish. Purāṇa, p. 512 *sqq.*).

[4] This refers to the churning of the ocean by the Gods and Daityas for getting the Ambrosia.

[5] The sense is: the Supreme is not perceptible by any outward signs or forms, he is only known by an unbeaten (= not produced by beating) sound, that pervades the universe.

(4). The Jōgī produces the sound of the lute, (but) he (the Supreme) is of infinite sight (and) form.
That sweetheart is in the unbeaten sound, Nānak being attached (to him) pronounces (this) thought.

IX.

(1). The words of (thy) excellences (are) a burden (on my) head.
(I am) melted (by these) words, O creator![1]
Eating, drinking and laughing is in vain,
As long as thou dost not come into (my) mind.

Pause.

What is thy concern, what is done?
In every birth something has been taken (and) is taken.[2]
(2). The intellect of (my) mind is intoxicated, (my) throat is intoxicated.
Whatever is spoken, all is error and mistake.
With what face shall prayer be made?
Religious demerit and merit, both are as witnesses with (me).
(3). As thou makest one, such he is.
Without thee there is no other.
As thou givest intellect, so one receives.
As it pleases thyself, so thou makest one walk.
(4). (In this) gem-like Rāg (with its) retinue of Rāgiṇīs,
In this is produced the pith of nectar.
Nānak (says): this is the wealth and property of the creator.
If one comprehends (it), he reflects (on it).

X.

(1). Bestowing mercy (when) he has come to his own house:
Then the female companions, having met, arrange the work.
Joy springs up in the mind seeing the sport.
The bridegroom is come in order to marry.

Pause.

Sing, sing, O woman, reflect on discrimination!
The world-soul, the husband, has come to our house.
(2). If our marriage has been brought about by means of the Guru, he is then known, when the bridegroom is met with.
The word is noised out in the three worlds; self is gone and the mind is reconciled.
(3). He himself arranges his own work, by others the work is not done.
In which work truth, contentment, mercy and piety is, that some (rare) disciple understands.
(4). Nānak says: the beloved of all is that One.
On whom he bestows a glance of favour, she becomes a happy married woman.

XI.

(1). House and forest are naturally the same.
Foolishness departs, (when) praise (of God) is made in the house.
(In whose) mouth is the true Pauṛī, the true name:
He serving the true Guru gets his own place.

[1] These lines are extremely confused; I have translated according to conjecture, as there is no grammatical connexion or relation whatever.

[2] The sense of these words is quite obscure.

Pause.

O mind, consider the six (philosophical) systems as rubbish!
In all is the Lord, who is full of light.
(2). (Who is) excessively greedy, puts on many garbs.
(But) the world is pain, (that) takes away happiness from the body.
Lust and wrath within take away (one's) wealth.
One is saved by the name, having given up duality.
(3). Praising and magnifying (God) (is) tranquillity and joy.
(My) friend and relative is the love of Gōvind.
He himself does (everything), he himself is bestowing (everything).
(My) body and mind are with Hari, further on (in the next world) there is life (to me).
(4). Falsehood and vice are great pain (to) the body.
Garbs and castes appear all as ashes.
What is produced, that comes and goes.
O Nānak, firm is the name (and) will (of God).

XII.

(1). There is one pond, (in which is) an incomparable lotus.
It always opens (its) sweet scent and beauty.
The bright pearl the goose picks up.
All parts are a portion of the Lord of the universe.

Pause.

What is seen, that is produced and (again) annihilated.
Without water no lotus is seen in a pond.
(2). Some rare one comprehends and gets (this) secret.
The Vēda always says, that there are three branches (= three gods).[1]
In the sound the knowledge of the drop is contained.[2]
Who serves the true Guru obtains the highest step.
(3). (Who is) steeped in (thy) colour, (is) emancipated, (him thou art) delighting.
(Thou art) always making (him) happy in the king of kings.
Whom thou keepest bestowing (thy) mercy (on him):
(Him) thou makest cross in a boat (like) a sinking stone.
(4). (By whom) the light, (that is) in the three worlds, is known in the three worlds:
(By him) a return (to himself) is made, (his) house is brought into (his) house.
Who day and night perform worship with deep devotion:
To their feet Nānak clings.

XIII.

(1). By the true instruction of the Guru dispute is removed.
By much cunning dust sticks (to one).
The filth that sticks (to one), is done away by the true name.
By the favour of the Guru he continues in devout devotion.

Pause.

(My) prayer is present before the Lord.
Pain and pleasure are with the true creator, the Lord.

[1] The Hindū Triad, Brahmā, Vishṇu, Shiva.

[2] These words are utterly confused; we can only guess what they mean. The ਨਾਦ, the sound or proclamation, seems to hint at the instruction of the Guru, as gathered from the following line. The ਬਿੰਦੁ, th drop, is the Supreme, from whom all emanates as from a drop.

(2). Who practises falsehood, he comes and goes.
By saying and telling no advantage is obtained.
What is seen, if one gets no understanding?
Without the name no satiety enters the mind.
(3). Who are born, they are subject to sickness.
They are afflicted by the pain of egotism and the Māyā.
Those people are preserved, who are kept by the Lord.
By serving the true Guru they drink nectar-juice.
(4). Who checks his wandering mind, he tastes nectar.
By serving the true Guru he utters the nectar-word (= the name).
By the true word he gets emancipation and salvation.
Nānak (says): he removes from within his own self.

XIV.

(1). What is done by him, that becomes true (real).
The nectar-name is given by the true Guru.
(In whose) heart is the name, (in his) mind there is no disappointment.
He keeps day by day communion with the beloved.

Pause.

O Hari, keep (me) in thy asylum!
By the favour of the Guru the juice of Hari is obtained, the blessing and the nine treasures of the name are obtained.
(2). (Whose) actions (are) true (and who has) the true name:
To him I am always a sacrifice.
Who are steeped in Hari, those people are excellent.
Their society is the highest treasure.
(3). Blessed is the woman, who has got Hari for her husband.
Being in love with Hari she reflects on the word (of the Guru).
She herself crosses and brings her companions and family across.
Serving the true Guru she reflects on truth.
(4). Our caste and fellowship are the true name.
Works, continence, truth, love.
(To whom) he gives, (says) Nānak, (from him) no account is taken.
He alone effaces duality.[1]

XV.

(1). Some come, some go, having come.
Some, who are attached to Hari, remain absorbed (in him).
Some find no place on earth (and in) the sky.
They are disregardful of (religious) actions, who do not meditate on the name of Hari.

Pause.

From the perfect Guru the knowledge of salvation is obtained.
This world is like poison; Hari ferries across the great water of existence by means of the word of the Guru.
(2). Whom the Lord himself unites (with himself):
Them death cannot push on.

[1] This last line is missing in MS. No. 2484.

The beloved disciples remain pure,
Like the lotuses on the water (remain) aloof (from the water).
(3). Say, who shall be called bad (or) good?
Brahm is seen (in all), by the disciple the True one is obtained.
(Who) relates the inexpressible one (and) reflects on the instruction of the Guru:
He joining the society of the Guru gains the other side.
(4). The Shāstras, Vēdas and Smritis of many kinds (he has read);
Bathing (at) the sixty-eight (Tīrthas he has made), (in whose) heart the love of Hari is.[1]
The disciple is spotless, no filth sticks (to him).
Nānak (says): in (whose) heart the name is, their lot is great.

XVI.

(1). Bowing and bowing I cling to the foot of my Guru, the Supreme was seen (by me).
Who is reflecting, in (his) heart Hari is contained, having seen (him) in (his) heart, he reflects (on him).

Pause.

Say: Rām brings about salvation.
By the favour of the Guru Hari, the gem, is obtained, ignorance is effaced, light is produced.

(2). The woman sports, (her) fetters do not break, in (her) heart are egotism and error, (which) do not depart.

(If) she meet with the true Guru, then egotism is broken, then she may fall into some account.[2]

(3). The name of Hari is very dear to (his) devotees, they keep the ocean of happiness in (their) breast.

The life of the world, the donor, is compassionate to (his) devotees, Hari saves (them) by means of the instruction of the Guru.

(4). (Who) fights with (his) mind, he obtains the Lord, (his) desire is absorbed in the mind.

Nānak (says): (if) the world-soul bestows mercy (on him), it bestows devout devotion (on the Supreme) with natural ease.

XVII.

(1). To whom does he tell it, whom does he let hear (it), whom does he let know (it), (that) he may understand (it)?

Whom does he make read (it), (that), reading and pondering, he may comprehend (it) (and) remain delighted with the word of the true Guru?

Pause.

Such a one delights (in) the instruction of the Guru (in his) body.
Worship Hari, O my mind, the deep and profound one!
(2). Who are devoted in love to Hari, the endless wave:
(They are) daily pure, the excellences of Hari (are) with (them).
Useless is the birth (life) of the Sākat in the world.
The devotee of Rām remains aloof (from him).
(3). Pure is the body (of him, by whom) the excellences of Hari are sung.
Having known himself, he continues in devout meditation.
Being in love with the primeval, boundless, infinite diamond,
The ruby, my mind, has become sedate.
(4). Who recite, recite the legends (of the gods), they have died.
That Lord is not far off, thou art the Lord.

[1] These lines are so confused, that they can only be translated by conjecture. ਹੇਰ is likely = ਹਿਰ, heart.
[2] ਪਾਈ = ਪਏ, for the sake of the rhyme.

I saw, that the whole word is overshadowed by the Māyā.
Nānak (says): by means of the instruction of the Guru the name is meditated upon.

XVIII.

(1). Some one is a beggar (and) eats alms.
Another is engaged in sensual pleasures.
Some one has honour, another dishonour.
Having pulled down (some one) raises (a building), (another) continues in meditation.
No one is greater than thou.
Whom shall I point out, that is good?

Pause.

Thy name is my support.
Thou, the maker and creator, (art) bountiful.
(2). I do not get (the right) road, I go winding about.
(I do not get) a place for sitting down at the threshold.
(I am) blind in mind, a prisoner of the Māyā.
(My) body is continually wasted and consumed.
I am very desirous of eating and living.
In thy account (is every) breath (and) morsel (I take).
(3). Give a lamp to him, who is blind by day and night!
Sinking in the water of existence he is in anxiety.
Who tells, hears and minds the name:
To him I make myself a sacrifice.
Nānak utters this one petition (= word):
Soul and body is all with thee.
(4). When thou givest (it), then I mutter thy name,
(By which) a place for sitting at (thy) threshold is obtained.
When it pleases thee, then folly departs.
The gem of divine knowledge comes and dwells in the mind.
(If) thou bestowest (on one) a favourable glance, then the Guru is met with.
Nānak says: he crosses the water of existence.

Panǒpadē.

XIX.

(1). A cow without milk, a bird without wings, sprouts without water, are useless.
What is a Sultān, to whom no reverence is paid? dark is the chamber, (in which) thy name is not.

Pause.

Art thou forgotten, when much pain sets in?
When pain sets in, thou art not forgotten.
(2). Blind in the eyes, no taste on the tongue, the wind not being heard in the ears,
He walks on foot being led on,[1] (this is) the fruit, that (man) gets without serving (God).
(3). The words (of the Guru) are the trees; (if one) sprinkle love (on) the good soil (of) the garden:
All (trees) bear fruit; how will one obtain the one name without works?
(4). As many creatures as there are, they are all thine, without service (to thee) no one obtains a reward.
Pain and pleasure (are distributed according) to thy decree, without the name life does not remain.
(5). One must die in one's mind, what is living longer? when I live, I am not absorbed in contemplation.
Nānak says: thou vivifiest the creatures; whom thou likest, him thou keepest.

[1] ਪਜੁਤਾ, Sansk. प्रयुक्त, carried, led on.

XX.

(1). (My) body is Brahmā, the mind (my) Dhōtī.
Divine knowledge the sacred cord, meditation the leaves of Kusa-grass.
Hari I praise, I ask for the praise of the name.
By the favour of the Guru I am absorbed in Brahm.

Pause.

O Paṇḍit, such is (true) reflection on Brahm.
By the name (one becomes) pure, by the name learned, by the name clever conduct (is acquired).
(2). Outwardly (keep) the sacred cord, as long as there is light with (thee).
The (right) Dhōtī and Ṭikā is, (if) thou remember the name.
Here and there it will go with (thee).
Do not seek other works besides the name!
(3). Burn the worship and love of the Māyā!
Look at the One, do not seek for another!
He knows the truth in the tenth gate of the head:
Who utters Hari at the tip of his tongue, reflecting (on him).
(4). Love of enjoyment, error and fear flee.
(If) the watchman watch, the thief does not set on.
The (right) religious mark on the forehead (is, if one) know the One Lord.
Discrimination (is, if one) understand, that Brahm is within (himself).
(5). By religious practices he cannot be overcome.
Who practises reading, does not get an estimate (of him).
By the eighteen (Purāṇas) and the four (Vēdas) (his) secret is not obtained.
Nānak (says): by the true Guru Brahm is pointed out.

XXI.

(1). (Who) is (his) servant and slave, that man is a devotee.
(Who) becomes a disciple, he is the slave of the Lord.
By whom (creation) is made, by him it is again destroyed.
Without him there is no other.

Pause.

Reflect on the true name by means of the word of the Guru!
The disciples are true at the true court.
(2). A true petition, a true prayer
The Lord hears in (his) palace, praise be (to him)!
(Whom) he calls to the true throne:
(To him) he gives greatness; what he does, that takes place.
(3). Thine is the power, thou art the tribunal.
The word of the Guru is the true sign (for guidance).
Who minds (his) order becomes manifest.
Under the true sign (or flag) he is not repulsed.
(4). The Paṇḍit reads and expounds the Vēda.
He does not know the secret of the thing within.
Without the Guru right knowledge and understanding are not obtained.
(He is) true, (in whom) that Lord is contained.
(5). What shall I say and sing (thy) praises?
Thou thyself knowest (it), assuming the forms of all.

Nānak (says): there is One gate and royal hall.
The true disciple is living there.

XXII.

(1). Like a raw jug the ailing body is produced and destroyed and suffers pain.

How shall this world, the ocean, which is hard to cross, be crossed? without Hari, the Guru, I do not get across.

Pause.

Without thee there is no other, O my beloved, without thee there is no other, O Hari!

In all colours and forms art thou; on whom thou bestowest a glance of favour, him thou pardonest.

(2). (My) mother-in-law is wicked, she does not let me dwell in the house, the wicked one does not let me meet with (my) beloved.

I embrace the feet of (my) companion and friend, Hari, the Guru, bestowed a glance of favour (on me) out of mercy.

(3). Reflecting on myself and subduing (my) mind I saw, that there is no other friend like thee.

As thou keepest (one), so he remains, the pain and pleasure, thou givest, that accrues (to him).

(4). Hope and desire, both are ruining (me), (by) the three qualities I have been made despondent.

The fourth state[1] is obtained by the disciple, (who) has got the protection of the assembly of the saints.

(5). (He has) all divine knowledge and meditation, all mutterings and austerities, (in) whose heart Hari, the inapprehensible and indivisible one, is.

Nanāk (says): (whose) mind is attached to the name, he gets easily by means of the instruction of the Guru the service (of Hari).

Pančpadē.

XXIII.

(1). Affection for (thy) family, affection for all works.
Give up affection! all (this) is useless.

Pause.

Give up affection and (consequent) error, O brother!
In (whose) heart the true name is, he delights (in his) body.
(2). Who has obtained the nine treasures of the name:
That mother is not distressed, if (her) son weeps.
(3). In this spiritual blindness the world is drowned.
Some (rare) disciple gets across.
(4). In this spiritual blindness one falls again into the womb.
Who clings to spiritual blindness goes to the city of Yama.
(5). (Who) takes the initiation of the Guru, practises muttering and austerities.
(Who) breaks away from the name, does not become acceptable.
(6). (When) he bestows a glance of favour (on any one), then this spiritual blindness departs.
Nānak remains absorbed with Hari.

XXIV.

(1). The True, inapprehensible, boundless one does himself (everything).
I am a sinner, thou art the pardoner.

Pause.

All that pleases thee, is done.
What is done out of obstinacy of mind, that thou destroyest at the end.

[1] ਤੁਰੀਆਵਸਥਾ, *s.f.* the fourth state, that of abstraction from without and absorption in the contemplation of one's own spirit (as identical with the Supreme).

(2). The mind of the self-willed one is sunk in falsehood.
Without remembering Hari it is distressed by sin.
(3). Having given up folly acquire some profit!
What is produced, that (is produced) from the inapprehensible, indivisible one.
(4). Such is our companion and helper.
Hari the Guru is obtained, (our) devotion is strengthened.
(5). The whole (world) is sleeping and suffers loss.
To the mind of Nānak the name of Rām is pleasing.

XXV.

(1). (When one) is meditating on science, then he is rendering services to others.
When he is subduing the five (senses), then he is dwelling at a Tīrtha.

Pause.

The toe-bells sound, if (my) mind be applied (to devotion).
Then what will Yama do to me further on (= in the other world)?
(2). When one has laid aside (all) hope, then he is a Sanyāsī.
When one is given to chastity, then he is enjoying his body.
(3). Who is reflecting on kindness, is naked-bodied.
He dies himself and does not kill others.
(4). Thou art One, (but) hast many other garbs.
Nānak does not know thy marvels.

XXVI.

(1). I am defiled, not (having practised) one (virtue); practising virtues I will wash away (my filth).
My bridegroom wakes, I sleep the whole night long.

Pause.

How shall I thus become dear to my husband?
My bridegroom wakes, I sleep the whole night long.
(2). Longing (for him) I come to the bed,
(That) in future I please (my) bridegroom, why should I not please (him)?

Pause.

What do I know, what will happen, O mother!
Without the sight of Hari I cannot live.
(3). I have not tasted love, my thirst is not quenched.
That youth is gone and the woman repents.

Pause.

Till now I wake in expectation and desire.
I have become dejected, I remain hopeless.
(4). (If) she adorn herself by doing away egotism:
Then the woman sports with her husband on the bed.

Pause.

Then, (says) Nānak, she will please the mind of her husband.
Having given up greatness she will be absorbed in her husband.

XXVII.

(1). In her father's house the woman (is) very ignorant.
I had no knowledge of that bridegroom.

Pause.

My bridegroom is One, there is no other.
If he bestow a favourable look, then union is brought about.
(2). In her father-in-law's house the True one is known by the woman.
With natural ease her beloved is recognized (by her).
(3). By the favour of the Guru such wisdom is obtained.
Then the woman is pleasing to the mind of her husband.
(4). Nānak says: if she adorns herself with fear and love:
Then she always sports with her husband on the bed.

XXVIII.

(1). There is not any one's son nor any one's mother.
By false affection and error (the world) is misled.

Pause.

O my Lord, I am thy creature.
When thou givest it (to me), then I mutter thy name.
(2). One may weep (on account of) many vices.
When it pleases him, he pardons (him).
(3). By the favour of the Guru foolishness is done away.
Where I see, there is that One.
(4). Nānak says: if one gets such an understanding:
Then he is absorbed in the perfectly True one.

Dupadē.

XXIX.

(1). In that pond his dwellings are made, (by whom) water and fire are produced.
I am fascinated by the lotus,[1] (but) the foot does not go there.
I saw, that (people) were drowned in it.

Pause.

O foolish mind, why dost thou not think of the One?
By forgetting Hari thy virtues are consumed.
(2). I am not chaste nor learned, foolish and stupid I was born.
Nānak says: (I flee) to the asylum of those, by whom thou art not forgotten.

XXX.

(1). There are six houses, six Gurus, six (methods of) instruction.[2]
The Guru of the Gurus is One, the garbs many.

Pause.

In which house the creator is praised:
That house hold fast, greatness (will accrue) to thee.
(2). Of seconds, minutes, ghaṛīs, watches, (lunar) days, week-days, a month is made up.
The sun is One, the seasons many.
Nānak says: how many are the garbs of the creator!

[1] The literal translation is: (there is) fascination of the lotus = I am fascinated, attracted by it. The explanation of this passage, as given on p. 18 (III.), is different, though grammatically correct. The sense is apparently: the Supreme dwells in a place (pond), where the foot of man cannot go: he is ਅਗਮ ਅਗੋਚਰ.

[2] The six Darshanas or philosophical systems.

Ōm! By the favour of the true Guru!

ĀSĀ; GHAR III.; MAHALĀ I.

I. XXXI.

(1). (Thou mayst have) Lakhs of armies, Lakhs of musical instruments and spears, Lakhs may rise and make salutation (to thee).

Thou mayst have a sway over Lakhs, Lakhs may rise and pay (thee) reverence.

When thou dost not come into account before the Lord, all (thy) works are fruitless.

Pause.

Without the name of Hari the world is but labour.

If the foolish (world) be ever so much admonished, yet it remains totally blind.

(2). Lakhs may be acquired, Lakhs collected, Lakhs may be eaten, Lakhs may come and go.

When thou dost not come into account before the Lord, where will (thy) soul wander about?

(3). Lakhs of Shāstras they may teach, Lakhs of Purāṇas the Paṇḍits may read.

When they do not come into account before the Lord, they are all rejected.

(4). From the true name honour is produced, the name of the creator (is obtained) by destiny.

In (whose) heart it dwells day and night, he by his favourable look (gets) across, (says) Nānak.

II. XXXII.

(1). My lamp is the One name, pain is thrown into it as oil.

By that light that (pain) is soaked up, falling in with Yama has ceased.

Pause.

O people, may not any one fall into wrangling!

Having collected a Lakh of reels of cotton one little bit sets fire to it.

(2). My platter with the oblation (to the deceased ancestors) is Kēshava, my funeral obsequies, (I perform), the true name of the creator.

Here and there, in future and past (time), this is my support.

(3). He bathes in the Gangā at Benāres, (who) praises thee, O Supreme Spirit!

True bathing is then made, when day and night love towards thee is entertained.

(4). Some are dwelling in heaven, some under the earth;[1] the Brāhman having twisted the rice-ball eats it.[2]

Nānak (says): the rice-ball of pardon is never exhausted.

ĀSĀ; GHAR IV.; MAHALĀ I.

Ōm! By the favour of the true Guru!

I. XXXIII.

(1). For the sake of visiting idols pain and hunger are undergone at a Tīrtha.

The Jōgī and ascetic are continuing in their practice, having put on reddish-yellow garbs they wander about.

Pause.

On thy account, O Lord, they are imbued with love.

Thy names are many, thy forms endless, it cannot be told, how many thy qualities are.

[1] ਲੋਕੀ (लोकिन्) dwelling in heaven; ਛਮਿਛਰੀ is the Sansk. चमाचर, dwelling in or under the earth; both adjectives refer to the manes of the deceased ancestors.

[2] After having offered it to the manes; usually these rice-balls are left on the ground.

(2). Having forsaken house, palace, elephants, horses, they went to a foreign country.

The Pīrs, prophets, devotees and sincere ones gave up the world and became acceptable.

(3). Relishes, tranquillity, comfort and pleasure were given up (by them), laying aside their clothes they put on skins.

In pain and suffering (they stand) at thy gate, being in love with thy name they became Darvīshes.

(4). A skin, an earthen cup, a staff, a little wallet (is taken), a tuft of hair, a (sacred string), a Dhōtī is made (by me):

Thou art the Lord, I am thy mimic; Nānak says: of what kind is (my) caste?

ĀSĀ; GHAR V.; MAHALĀ I.

Ōm! By the favour of the true Guru!

I. XXXIV.

(1). Within (my) mind dwell the five (passions) concealed.

They do not remain steady, they wander about like those who are indifferent (to the world).

Pause.

My mind does not remain steady with the merciful one.

Being greedy, deceitful, sinful, hypocritical, it clings excessively to the Māyā.

(2). A wreath of flowers I will put as necklace on my neck.

When (my) beloved will be met with, then I will adorn myself.

(3). We are five companions,[1] (who have) One husband.

The tree is transplanted,[2] life is going.

(4). We five companions having met, weep.

The breath is separated, and we give account, says Nānak.

ĀSĀ; GHAR VI.; MAHALĀ I.

Ōm! By the favour of the true Guru!

I. XXXV.

(1). If the mind be the pearls and jewels, if the breath be the stringholder;

If the woman put on her body the decoration of patience, then, being dear to (her) beloved, she enjoys him.

Pause.

By the very excellent sweetheart the woman is fascinated.

Thy excellences are not in others.

(2). (If) she make Hari, Hari (her) necklace and put it (on her) breast, (if) she take Damōdar (as her) tooth-powder.

(If) she make the creator her wrist-ornament and put it on, (if) she apply (her) thoughts in this wise.

(3). (If) she put on Madhu-sūdana (the subduer of Madhu) as her finger-ring, if she take the Lord as her cloth.

(If) she patch patience (on her forehead) as her Dhaṛī,[3] (if) she apply the husband of Lakshmī as collyrium (to her eyes).

[1] The five companions are the five senses.

[2] ਪੇਡਿ *s.f.* a tree especially for transplantation. The death of man is compared to the transplantation of a tree.

[3] ਧੜੀ is in the Panjāb a line of red lead painted on the forehead.

(4). (If) she light a lamp in the mansion of her mind and make her body the bed:
Then he enjoys her, says Nānak, when the King of divine knowledge comes to (her) bed.

II. XXXVI.

(1). What is created, that does what it is caused to do; what can be said to it, O brother?
What must be done, that it does; what cleverness has the creature?

Pause.

Thy order is good; who pleases thee:
To him accrues greatness, (says) Nānak, he is absorbed in the true name.
(2). The destiny is fixed, the order is written, no order is again given.
As it is written, so it falls, no one can efface it.
(3). If one talk much at the threshold, he gets the name of a low person.
The chess-figure, that is not well arranged in the chess-play, is beaten.
(4). No one is read, learned, wise, no one foolish and bad.
Within which servants he causes (his) praise to be made, they are called servants.

III. XXXVII.

(1). (If) the word of the Guru is in (my) mind, (if) I wear patience as ear-ring and patched quilt.
(If) I consider as good, whatever he (God) does, I get easily the treasure of the Yōga.

Pause.

(Whose) soul is continually intent (on the Supreme), O brother, he is a Jōgī.
(Who) is intent on the most excellent essence (= the Supreme):
He obtains the nectar-name of the Supreme, he is enjoying this relish of divine knowledge.
(2). I sit in a sitting posture at Benāres,[1] (if) I give up designs and disputes.
(My) horn is the word of the Guru, its sound is always beautiful, day and night it produces a (continuing) sound.
(3). (My) bowl is reflection (on) divine knowledge, intelligence (my) staff, what is existing (my) ashes.[2]
The praise of Hari my prayer, (living as) a disciple my ascetic life.[3]
(4). In all is the (divine) light; our appellation is of various and many kinds.
Nānak says: hear, O Bharthari,[4] (he is) a Jōgī, (whose) thoughts are continually directed on the Supreme Brahm.

IV. XXXVIII.

(1). Make divine knowledge the molasses, meditation the flowers of the Dhāvā-tree, good actions the bark of the Kīkar-tree and put (them into it)!
The world the distilling pot, love the plastering! from this juice nectar is caused to ooze out.

Pause.

O brother, (who) is drunk in (his) mind (and) drinks the juice of the name, he is easily absorbed in love.

[1] ਸਿਵਨਗਰੀ, the city of Shiva = Benāres.
[2] ਬਿਭੂਤਿ, ashes rubbed on the body by devotees. The sense is: whatever exists, I consider as ashes.
[3] ਗੁਰਮੁਖਿ ਪੰਥ ਅਤੀਤ, literally: (my) ascetic way of life is facing the Guru.
[4] Bharthari is the name of a Jōgī, with whom Nānak is said to have had a discussion. (See Janam-Sākhī, Lahore edition, Sākhī 44.)

Day and night devout meditation (with) love is made (and) entertained, the unbeaten sound is laid hold of (by him).

(2). A full and true cup he makes easily drink him, on whom he bestows a glance.

Who is a dealer in nectar, what should he entertain love for mean liquor?

(3). The discourse of the Guru is a nectar-speech, who drinks it becomes acceptable.

(Who is) very fond of the sight of the gate (of God), he becomes emancipated, what shall he do in paradise?

(4). Who is fond of (his) praises, is always indifferent to the world, he does not lose his life in gambling.

Nānak says: hear, O Bharthari! the Jōgī is intoxicated by a stream of nectar!

V. XXXIX.

(1). Khorasān rendered assistance (and) Hindustān was frightened.[1]

I myself do not blame (thee), O creator, who hast made the Mugal the angel of death and raised him.

Such a great slaughter took place, no compassion was shown to the weeping ones.

Pause.

O creator, thou art the same to all.

If the powerful one kills the powerful, no anger arises in (my) mind.

(2). If the powerful lion falls on a herd of cattle and kills (them), this is the bravery of the Lord.

Having spoiled the jewel they were destroyed; no one takes any notice of dead dogs.

Thou thyself joinest and separatest, thou thyself seest thy own greatness.

(3). If one assumes a great name and enjoys (all) pleasures, he likes in (his) mind:

—A worm comes into the sight of the Lord (and) as many[2] as pick up grains—

He having died repeatedly lives (= is born again); then he will get something, (says) Nānak, (if) he praise the name.

RĀGU ĀSĀ; GHAR II.; MAHALĀ III.

Ōm! By the favour of the true Guru!

I. XL.

(1). The very fortunate one obtains a sight[3] of Hari

By true love to the word of the Guru.

Six (philosophical) systems are current.

(But) the system of the Guru is profound and boundless.

Pause.

By the system of the Guru emancipation and salvation are brought about.

That True one himself dwells in the mind (of the disciple).

(2). By the doctrine[4] of the Guru the world is saved,

If one bestow affectionate love (on it).

[1] This refers to the sack and destruction of Sayyid-pur by Bābar.

[2] Supply: birds.

[3] ਦਰਸਨ, sight, is here = knowledge, clear insight.

[4] ਦਰਸਨ might here also be translated by: "sight of the Guru."

Affectionate love some rare one bestows (on it).
By the doctrine of the Guru happiness is always produced.
(3). In the doctrine of the Guru is the gate of salvation.
(Who) serves the true Guru is the support of (his) family.
Who are without the Guru get by no means salvation.
Ruined by vice they are struck (at the gate of Yama).
(4). By the word of the Guru happiness and tranquillity (are produced) in the body.
(Who becomes) a disciple, him no pain touches.
Yama, the death, does not come near him.
Nānak (says): the disciple is absorbed in the True one.

II. XLI.

(1). (Who) has died by means of the word (of the Guru), he removes from within his own self.
(Who) serves the true Guru, he has not a bit of covetousness.
The fearless and munificent (Supreme one) is always in (his) mind.
The true word (of the Guru) some (rare) one obtains by destiny.

Pause.

Collect (his) excellences,[1] vice will go from within!
By means of the word of the perfect Guru thou wilt be absorbed.
(2). Who is discerning (his) excellences, he knows his excellences.
He praises the name by means of the nectar-word (of the Guru).
By the true word he becomes pure.
By praise the name is obtained.
(3). (His) inestimable qualities cannot be obtained.
(Who) is pure in (his) mind, he is absorbed (in him) by means of the true word (of the Guru).
Those are very fortunate, by whom the name is meditated upon.
He, who is always bestowing favours, is made to dwell in (their) mind.
(4). Who remember (his) excellences, to them I become a sacrifice.
(Those are) true at the true gate, (who) sing (his) excellences.
He himself gives (them) with natural ease.
Nānak (says): the estimate (of them) cannot be told.

III. XLII.

(1). In the true Guru is a great dignity.
Those, who have been separated a long time (from Hari), he unites to union (with him).
He himself (*i.e.* Hari) unites (them, whom the Guru) unites to union (with him).[2]
His own estimate (only) he himself reaches.

Pause.

In which wise is the estimate of Hari made?
Hari is boundless, unattainable, inapprehensible, by means of the word of the Guru some man falls in (with him).
(2). Some (rare) disciple knows his estimate.
By (some) rare one (his estimate) is obtained according to destiny.

[1] The sense is: collect them in thy mind = remember them.

[2] The Guru is the instrument of Hari, through whom Hari himself is bringing about union with himself.

High is (his) word, (he himself) is high.
Some disciple praises (him) by means of the word (of the Guru).
(3). Without the name there is pain and ailment in the body.
When the true Guru is met with, the pain recedes.
Without meeting with the Guru he suffers pain.
Much punishment is inflicted on the self-willed one.
(4). The name of Hari is sweet and very tasteful.
He goes on drinking it, whom he lets drink it.
By the mercy of the Guru he gets the juice of Hari.
Nānak (says): those who are attached to the name, obtain salvation.

IV. XLIII.

(1). My Lord is true, deep and profound.
Who serves him, (in his) body is happiness and tranquillity.
(Who) are naturally attached to the (word of the Guru):
To their feet we always cling.

Pause.

Who are coloured in their mind by applying the colour of Hari:
Their pain of birth and death is done away, they naturally come together at the threshold of Hari.
(2). Who tastes the word (of the Guru), he gets true relish.
He fixes the name of Hari in his mind.
Hari, the Lord, is always omnipresent.
He himself is near, he himself is far off.
(3). Every one tells a story and chatters away.
(On whom) he himself bestows (it), him he unites (with himself).
By telling and relating (stories)[1] he cannot be obtained.
By the favour of the Guru he comes and dwells in the heart.
(4). The disciples clear away from within their own self.
Being steeped in the colour of Hari they put an end to their spiritual blindness.
Reflecting on the word (of the Guru) (they are) very pure.
Nānak (says): by the name he (Hari) is accomplishing (them).

V. XLIV.

(1). Who gives himself to another love incurs pain.
Without the word (of the Guru) life is wasted to no purpose.
Who serves the true Guru, gets true knowledge.
He clings by no means to another love.

Pause.

Who cling to the root (of all things), those people are acceptable.
Day by day they mutter the name of Rām (in their) heart, by means of the word of the Guru they know the One Hari.
(2). Who clings to the branch (= the creature), becomes unfruitful.
On blind works a blind punishment (is inflicted).
The self-willed one is blind and gets no place (of rest).
Being a worm of ordure he is consumed in ordure.

[1] This refers to the reading of the Purāṇas.

(3). By the service of the Guru (one) obtains always happiness.
Joining the society of the pious he sings the excellences of Hari.
(If), praising the name, he reflect (on it):
He is himself saved and becomes the saviour of his family.
(4). The word of the Guru makes (the disciple) dwell in the name.
Nānak (says): by the word (of the Guru) he obtains the palace (and) house (of Hari).
By the instruction of the Guru he bathes in the true pond, in the water of Hari.
Foolishness, filth and all sins are removed.

VI. XLV.

(1). The self-willed one dies and death ruins (him).
By second love he kills himself.
By continually saying: "mine, mine" he is ruined.
He does not know himself, he is asleep in error.

Pause.

He indeed is dead, who dies by means of the word (of the Guru).

Praise and blame are shown to be the same by the Guru; having made profit in this world by muttering Hari, he departs.

(2). Who is destitute of the name, is dissolved in the womb.
His life is useless, who is attached to duality.
All who are destitute of the name, burn in pain.
By the true, perfect Guru understanding is communicated.
(3). (Whose) mind is unsteady, he gets many blows.
Having departed hence he finds no place.
(Becoming) a fœtus (in) the womb (he gets) a dwelling of ordure.
In that house the self-willed one makes his abode.
(4). I become always a sacrifice to my own true Guru.
The disciple, who is endowed with (divine) light, he unites with the light.
His (the disciple's) speech is pure, he dwells in his own house.
Nānak (says): who destroys egotism, is always indifferent (to the world).

VII. XLVI.

(1). The slave, (who) has laid aside his own caste;
(Who) has offered body and soul, (is) in the asylum of the true Guru.
(In whose) heart the name is, (his) dignity is great.
The beloved Lord becomes always (his) companion.

Pause.

That slave dies whilst living.

He considers, both grief and joy, as the same, and is saved by the favour of the Guru, by means of the word (of the Guru).

(2). The doing of (religious) works is commanded throughout.
(But) without the word (of the Guru) none becomes acceptable.
By offering praises (to Hari) (one) makes dwell the name (in oneself).
(Hari) himself gives it without any delay.
(3). The self-willed world is led astray by error.
Without capital it makes a false traffic.

Without capital it does not receive wares.
The self-willed one is going astray and loses his life.
(4). Who serves the true Guru, he becomes (his) slave.
He becomes the highest of the highest caste people.
The ladder of the Guru is the highest of all.
Nānak (says): by the name greatness is obtained.

VIII. XLVII.

(1). The self-willed (woman) is false and practises falsehood.
She never obtains the palace of the Lord.
Who clings to another, her he leads astray.
Being bound by selfishness she comes and goes.

Pause.

Do not look at the desire and decoration of the ill-fated woman!

(Who) directs (his) mind on (his) son, wife, wealth (and) the Māyā, (in him is) falsehood, spiritual blindness, deceit (and) vice.

(2). She is always a happy married woman, who is pleasing to the Lord.
(Who) makes the words of the Guru (her) ornament:
(Her) bed is delightful, day by day she enjoys Hari.
Meeting with her beloved she always obtains happiness.
(3). She is a true happy married woman, who has love to the True one.
(Who) always keeps her beloved in her breast:
She sees (him) near her and always in (her) presence.
My Lord is present in all.
(4). Caste and beauty do not go with her to the other world.
One will become such, as are the works he practises.
(Who) becomes the highest by means of the word (of the Guru):
He is absorbed in the True one, (says) Nānak.

IX. XLVIII.

(1). A man who is naturally given to devotion:
He is absorbed in the True one by true fear of the Guru.
Without the perfect Guru devotion cannot be made.
The self-willed ones weep having lost their honour.

Pause.

O my mind, mutter Hari always meditating (on him)!
Always, day and night joy will spring up, thou wilt get the fruit, thou desirest.
(2). From the perfect Guru he obtains the Perfect one.
The word (of the Guru) makes dwell the true name in (his) heart.
(His) heart becomes pure, he bathes in the pond of nectar.
Being always pure he is absorbed in the True one.
(3). Hari, the Lord, he sees always in (his) presence.
By the favour of the Guru he (Hari) remains brimful (in him).
Wherever I go, there I see him.
Without the Guru there is no other donor.
(4). The Guru is the ocean, the full store-house.
The best gems, infinite jewels (are in it).

Out of favour the Guru is giving (them).
The liberal donor bestows (them), (says) Nānak.

X. XLIX.

(1). The Guru is the ocean, the true Guru is that True one.
By a perfect destiny the service of the Guru is obtained.
He comprehends (this), whom he himself makes to comprehend (it).
Out of favour the Guru makes him do service.

Pause.

By the gem of (divine) knowledge all right knowledge is effected.
By the favour of the Guru he (the disciple) extinguishes (his) ignorance, he wakes day by day and sees that True one.
(2). Spiritual blindness and conceit he consumes by the word of the Guru.
From the perfect Guru he obtains brightness of intellect.
He learns by the word of the Guru, (that) the palace (of Hari) is within (himself).
Coming and going are stopped, (he becomes) steady and is absorbed in the name.
(3). The world undergoes regeneration and death.
The self-willed one is thoughtless, spiritual blindness and darkness are contained (in him).
He slanders others and practises much falsehood.
Being a worm of ordure he is absorbed in ordure.
(4). (Who) joins the assembly of the pious gets all true knowledge.
The word of the Guru renders the worship of Hari firm.
Who minds (his) order gets always happiness.
Nānak (says): he is absorbed in the True one.

XI. L.

Pančpadē.

(1). Who dies by the word (of the Guru), he has always joy.
He meets with the true Guru, the Guru Gōvind.
He does not die again nor come after having gone.
By means of the true Guru he is absorbed in the True one.

Pause.

For whom the name is decreed by destiny itself:
They always meditate day by day on the name, by the perfect Guru (their) devotion (is rendered) excellent.
(2). Whom Hari the Lord unites (with himself):
Their mysterious procedure cannot be told.
By the perfect true Guru greatness is given them.
(They obtain) the highest step, they are absorbed in the name of Hari.
(3). Whatever he does, that (he does) himself.
In one Gharī he establishes and disestablishes.
In telling a story and reciting it,
Though one spend a hundred (years), he does not accept (of him).
(4). Who are possessed of religious merits, with them he makes the Guru meet.
The true word, the word of the Guru he lets them hear.
Where the word (of the Guru) dwells, thence pain departs.
By means of the gem of (divine) knowledge they are easily absorbed in the True one.

(5). No other wealth is so great as the name.
On whom he bestows it, he is true.
Who by means of the perfect word (of the Guru) make dwell it in (their) mind:
They, being attached to the name, obtain happiness, (says) Nānak.

XII. LI.

(1). One may dance and beat many musical instruments:
This (human) mind is blind and deaf, whom shall he let hear it?
Within is greediness, error, fire and wind.
No lamp burns (nor) is true knowledge obtained.

Pause.

In the heart of the devoted disciple light springs up.
(Who) knows his own self, he is united with the Lord.
(2). The disciple (in) dancing conceives love to Hari.
He keeps time in music (and), removes from within his own self.
He himself knows, (that) my Lord is true.
By means of the word of the Guru he learns, (that) Brahm is within (himself).
(3). Within the devoted disciple is love and affection (to Hari).
He naturally reflects on the word of the Guru.
The disciple, that is attached and deeply meditating (on Hari), is true.
By sham-devotion pain is incurred (in) dancing.
(4). This devoted man dies whilst living.
By the favour of the Guru he crosses the water of existence.
By attachment to the word of the Guru he becomes acceptable.
Hari himself comes and dwells in his mind.
(5). Hari, becoming merciful, makes the true Guru meet (with them),
(Who) in continual devotion direct (their) thoughts on Hari.
Who are given to devotion, their report (reputation) is true.
Nānak (says): who are attached to the name, (they obtain) happiness.

GHAR VIII.; KĀFĪ;[1] MAHALĀ III.

Ōm! By the favour of the true Guru!

XIII. LII.

(1). By the decree of Hari the true Guru is met with, true knowledge is obtained (from him).
In (whose heart) Hari dwells by the favour of the Guru, he comprehends (the truth).

Pause.

I have one munificent bridegroom, there is no other.
(If) he dwell in (my) mind by the kindness of the Guru, then there is always happiness.
(2). In this Yuga is the name of the fearless Hari (the means of salvation), it is obtained by meditating on the Guru.
Without the name the self-willed one is in the power of Yama, he is blind and foolish.
(3). (If) a man according to the will of Hari render service (to him), he comprehends that True one.
(If) according to the will of Hari praise be offered, comfort is obtained by obeying the will (of Hari).

[1] काफी is a musical term, denoting a particular kind of melody.

(4). By the decree of Hari (thou hast) obtained the blessing of a (human) birth, (thy) intelligence has become very high.

Nānak (says): praise the name, O disciple, (thy) salvation is effected (thereby)!

ĀSĀ; MAHALĀ IV.; GHAR II.

Ōm! By the favour of the true Guru!

I. LIII.

Pause.

Thou art the true creator, my Lord.
What pleases thee, that will take place, what thou givest, that I obtain.
(1). All is thine, thou art meditated upon by all.
On whom thou bestowest mercy, he gets the jewel of the name.
The disciple obtains it, the self-willed one loses it.
Thou thyself separatest, thou thyself unitest (with thyself).
(2). Thou art the ocean, all is in thee.
Without thee there is none other.
All the creatures are thy sport.
They are separated, having been united (with thee), the separated ones (thou) unitest (again) to union (with thee).[1]
(3). Whom thou lettest know (them), that man knows (them).
He always tells and praises the excellences of Hari.
By whom Hari is served, he obtains happiness.
He is easily absorbed in the name of Hari.
(4). Thou thyself art the creator, all is thy doing.
Without thee there is none other.
(Whom) thou createst and lookest upon (in mercy), he knows (thee).
Humble Nānak (says): (to) the disciple (thou) art manifest.

Ōm! by the favour of the true Guru!

RĀGU ĀSĀ; GHAR II.; MAHALĀ IV.

II. LIV.

(1). Some one puts (his) confidence on a friend, son, brother.
Some one puts (his) confidence in (his) family, kinsman (and) son-in-law.
Some one puts (his) confidence in his chief, head man (and) master.
Our confidence is placed in Hari.

Pause.

My confidence is placed in Hari, my refuge is Hari.
Without Hari I have no other assistance nor reliance, I sing the many (and) innumerable excellences of Hari.
(2). In whom (people) place (their) confidence, they depart.
Having placed a false confidence (in any one), they repent of it.

[1] Sentences of this kind can only be translated according to conjecture, as every grammatical relation is missing. द्विन्नेगि must here be adjective (= द्विन्नेगी) and मन्नेगी is the Locative = मन्नेगि (and not adjective). Everything is applied to render the meaning as obscure as possible.

They do not remain firm, they practise falsehood in (their) mind.
I have placed my confidence in Hari, whom no one equals in power.
(3). All these are gangs (bodies of men), (in whom) is spreading the spiritual darkness of the Māyā.
The foolish ones fight for the sake of the Māyā.
They are born and die, the play is lost in the dice-play.
Our confidence (is placed in) Hari, who adjusts all, this and that world.
(4). In the Kali-yug (there are) gangs (of robbers), the five thieves cause quarrels.
Lust, wrath, covetousness, spiritual blindness, conceit they increase.
On whom he (Hari) bestows mercy, him he joins to the society of the pious.
Our confidence (is placed) in Hari, by whom all these gangs are driven away.
(5). Second love is falsehood; (who) sits (among) the band falls[1] (into it).
He guesses at the faults of others (and) increases his own conceit.
Such things, as he sows, he will eat.
Humble Nānak's confidence is (in) Hari, (thereby) the religious merit (of) the whole creation is surpassed.[2]

III. LV.

(1). Having heard (of it) repeatedly the nectar pleases (my) heart and mind.
(By means of) the word of the Guru the inapprehensible Hari was made known (to me).

Pause.

O disciple and sister, hear the name!
The One is contained in the heart; utter with (thy) mouth the nectar-words of the Guru!
(2). In my heart and body is love and great desire.
The true Guru, the divine male, is obtained by a great destiny.
(3). (Who) wanders about in another love, in the Māyā, the poison:
He is luckless and does not get the true Guru.
(4). The nectar-juice of Hari Hari himself gives (me) to drink.
From the perfect Guru Nānak has obtained Hari.

IV. LVI.

(1). In my heart and body is love, the name is my support.
The name I mutter, the name is the pith of happiness.

Pause.

Mutter the name, O my sweetheart and friend!
Without the name I have none other; in consequence of a great destiny the disciple is getting Hari.
(2). Without the name I cannot live.[3]
In consequence of a great destiny the disciple obtains Hari.
(3). Who is destitute of the name, has a black face, O mother!
Woe, woe to the life without the name!
(4). (On whom) Hari bestows a great, great lot, he obtains him.[4]
Nānak (says): by the disciple the name is kept fast.

[1] ਪਾਵੈ very likely = ਪਵੈ.
[2] The translation is, as so often, a conjecture, there being no grammatical relation.
[3] Literally: it cannot be lived.
[4] Literally: Hari is obtained having bestowed a great lot.

V. LVII.

(1). I sing (his) excellences, I utter (his) excellences (with my) voice.

(Having become) a disciple I tell and praise the excellences of Hari.

Pause.

Muttering continually the name joy has sprung up in (my) mind.

By the true, true, true Guru the name is made firm (in me), the excellences of the highest bliss (= the Supreme) are sung (by me) with love.

(2). The people of Hari sing the excellences of Hari (in the) world.

By a great destiny they obtain Hari, who is unconnected (with anything).

(3). Who are destitute of (his) excellences,[1] they are carrying about the filth of the Māyā.

Without (singing) his excellences the selfish are born (again and) die.

(4). In the body, (as) in a pond, (his) excellences are made manifest.

Nānak (says): the disciple churns (the pond) and extracts the essence.

VI. LVIII.

(1). The name I hear, the name is pleasing to (my) mind.

By a great destiny the disciple obtains Hari.

Pause.

Mutter the name, O disciple, (it is) light!

Without the name I have no other support; the name is uttered (by me) at every breath and morsel.

(2). The name I hear with attention, it is pleasing to my mind.

Who lets (me) hear the name, he is my friend and companion.

(3). Who are destitute of the name, they go as fools (and) naked.

They are gradually consumed and die having seen poison, (like) a moth.

(4). He himself establishes and having established, disestablishes again.

Nānak (says): Hari himself gives (his) name.

VII. LIX.

(1). By the disciple the vine of Hari, Hari is cultivated.

Savoury and tasty fruits of Hari are produced (from it).

Pause.

Mutter the name of Hari, Hari, (who is) of endless waves!

(Who) by the instruction of the Guru is continually muttering the name and praising it, he subdues the servant of Yama, the (fierce) snake.

(2). Hari, Hari caused devotion to be put in the Guru.

The Guru being pleased gives (it to) the disciple, O my brother!

(3). (Who) practises works of selfishness, he does not in any way know the sacred precepts,

As an elephant, who has bathed, sprinkles (again) dust on his head.

(4). If (one's) lot becomes great (and) very high:

He mutters the name, (says) Nānak, in the True one (he becomes) pure.

VIII. LX.

(1). (I have) a hunger in (my) mind after the name of Hari, Hari.

By hearing the name (my) mind is satiated, O my brother!

[1] The sense is apparently: who are not singing his excellences.

Pause.

Mutter the name, O my fellow-disciple and friend!

Mutter the name! for by the name thou wilt get happiness; keep the name in (thy) mind (and) thought by means of the instruction of the Guru!

(2). (If) I hear the name, the name, (my) mind is happy.

I am happy having got the advantage of the name by the instruction of the Guru.

(3). Without the name (I am) leprous, blind (by) infatuation.

All the works, that I have done, are useless, they are pain and trouble.

(4). (Who) mutters the praise of Hari, Hari, Hari, his lot is great.

Nānak (says): by the instruction of the Guru he devoutly meditates on the name.

Ōm! By the favour of the true Guru!

RĀGU ĀSĀ; GHAR VI.; MAHALĀ IV.

IX. LXI.

(1). Taking the chord into (thy) hand thou strikest (it), O Jōgī, (thy) hollow flute sounds.

Utter the excellences of Hari according to the instruction of the Guru, O Jōgī, this (my) mind is imbued with love to Hari!

Pause.

O Jōgī, give (me) advice and instruction (regarding) Hari!

Through all ages Hari alone exists, before him I (make) salutation.

(2). (Thou) singest (different) kinds of Rāgs, thou talkest much, (but) this mind is engaged in play.

The oxen, which thou puttest (to) the well for watering the ground, have risen and gone, having grazed the creepers.

(3). Sow in the city of the body the works (of) Hari! Hari germinates, the field (becomes) green.

The mind (becomes) steady, (if) thou put on the mind (as) bullock, (if) thou sprinkle Hari (as water), (thou art) overcoming (thy mind) by means of the instruction of the Guru.

(4). The Jōgī and Jangam, all the creation is thine, I am the disciple of that instruction, which thou givest.

O Lord of humble Nānak, (thou art) the inward governor, O Hari, keep (my) mind in steady equilibrium!

X. LXII.

(1). Sometime one beats the chime of the toe-bells, sometime one plays the rebeck.

There is a moment's delay between coming and going, I remember so long the name.

Pause.

In my mind such a devotion has been produced.

I cannot exist one moment without Hari, like as a fish dies without water.

(2). Sometime one brings together five (or) seven (female) singers, sometime one intonates a Rāg.

In bringing (them) together and selecting (them) a moment and minute passes, so long my heart sings the excellences of Rām.

(3). Sometime one dances and stretches out the foot, sometime one stretches out the hand.

In stretching out hand and foot a moment's delay takes place, so long my heart remembers Rām.

(4). Sometime one confides in people, by confiding in people honour (with Hari) is not obtained.

Humble Nānak (says): meditate always in thy heart on Hari, then every one says: victory (to thee)!

XI. LXIII.

(1). Join the society of the pious! having joined the society of the pious people of Hari sing the excellences of Hari!

Divine knowledge, the gem (and) light is (thereby) kindled in the heart, darkness departs.

Pause.

O people of Hari, dance meditating on Hari, Hari!

(If) such pious people fall in (with me), O my brother, I wash the feet of (these) people.

(2). Mutter the name of Hari, O my mind, meditating devoutly day by day on Hari!

The fruit, that thou desirest, thou wilt obtain, no hunger will again befall (thee).

(3). (Thou) thyself, O Hari, (art) the boundless creator, what thou thyself sayest, O Hari, that thou causest (one) to say.

(Those) pious people are good, (who) please thee, whose honour thou approvest.

(4). Nānak is not satiated in telling Hari's excellences, in proportion as he recites them, he obtains happiness.

Hari has given (him) his own stores of devotion; (who) is discerning (his) excellences, goes and deals (in them).

Ōm! by the favour of the true Guru!

RĀGU ĀSĀ; GHAR VIII.; KĀFĪ; MAHALĀ IV.

XII. LXIV.

(1). Death comes by all means, (then) it is wept (out of) selfishness.

O disciple, meditate on the name, thou wilt become firm (thereby)!

Pause.

Praise to the perfect Guru, (from whom I) have learnt that I must go!

The profit of the name is the best, by means of the word (of the Guru) (I am) absorbed (in Hari).

(2). The days, which were written before, have come, O mother!

Departure (takes place) to-day or to-morrow, it is ordered so by any means.

(3). Useless is the life of them, who have forgotten the name.

This mind being intent on playing is defeated.

(4). In life and death they have comforts, who have obtained the Guru.

Nānak (says): the true ones are absorbed in the True one.

XIII. LXV.

(1). (Who), having obtained the blessing of (human) birth, meditate on the name:

They, comprehending (the truth) by the favour of the Guru, are absorbed in the True one.

Pause.

For whom exactly (this) destiny is written, they acquire the name.

At the true gate (they are taken as) true (and) called to the palace (of Hari).

(2). (That) disciple obtains in (his) heart the treasure of the name,

(Who) day by day meditating on the name sings the excellences of Hari.

(3). The thing (is) within, by many (efforts) it is not obtained by the self-willed one.

(Who) is proud in egotism, he is ruined by himself.

(4). Nānak (says): he himself is ruined by himself.

In (whose) mind there is light by means of the instruction of the Guru, he obtains the True one.

RĀGU ĀSĀ VARĪ; GHAR XVI. OR II.; MAHALĀ IV. SUDHANG.[1]

By the favour of the true Guru!

XIV. LXVI.

Pause.

I praise day by day the name of Hari.

The true Guru showed me the name of Hari, without Hari I cannot remain one moment.

(1). I hear and remember the praise of Hari, without Hari I cannot remain one moment.

As a goose cannot remain without the pond, how should the people of Hari live without the service of Hari?

(2). Some show affection keeping another love in their heart, some show affection (keeping) spiritual darkness and contempt (in their heart).

The people of Hari entertain love for Hari (and) the state of final emancipation; Nānak (says): (they are) remembering Hari, Hari the Lord.

Asā varī; mahalā IV.

XV. LXVII.

Pause.

O mother, show me my beloved Rām!

I cannot remain one moment without Hari, as a camel delights in creepers.[2]

(1). My mind has become impassioned for the sight of Hari the friend.

As a black bee cannot live without the lotus, so I cannot live without Hari.

(2). Keep me in thy asylum, O beloved Lord of the universe, fulfil my desire, O Lord Hari!

Joy springs up in the heart of humble Nānak, (if) Hari shows (him) his sight for a moment.

RĀGU ĀSĀ; GHAR II.; MAHALĀ V.

Ōm! by the favour of the true Guru!

I. LXVIII.

(1). Who bestows love (on the Māyā),[3] he is again devoured (by her).

Who settles (her) comfortably (in his heart), to him much fear is shown.

Having seen brothers, friends and family she disputes.

To me she has been subjected by the favour of the Guru.

Pause.

Having seen such a (state of things) they were bewildered.

The ascetics, the Siddhs, the gods and men, all were deceived by fraud without the pious (Guru).

(2). Some wander about as Udāsīs (stoics), them lust pervades.

Some are householders and collect (wealth), theirs she does not become of her own accord.

Some are called faithful, them she troubles much.

We are preserved by Hari, clinging to the foot of the true Guru.

[1] सुघंग signifies: graceful, well-formed. This predicate seems rather to refer to the whole verse, than to the melody, to which this verse is to be sung.

[2] The comparison is put the wrong way; we should expect here a negative statement.

[3] No subject is hinted at, but very likely the word Māyā is to be supplied.

(3). The ascetics, who are practising austerities, are led astray.
All the Paṇḍits are beguiled by covetousness.
By the infatuation of the three qualities the sky is deluded.
We are preserved by the true Guru who gives us his hand.
(4). She becomes the slave of those, who are endowed with (divine) knowledge.
Joining her hands in supplication she performs service (to them).
What thou commandest, that work is done (by her).
Humble Nānak (says): she does not come near the disciple.[1]

II. LXIX.

(1). By her beloved (the woman) is separated from her mother-in-law.
Her husband's younger brother's wife and her husband's elder brother's wife have died out of pain and distress.
Obsequiousness towards the elder brother (of the husband) has ceased.
By her clever and wise beloved she is protected.

Pause.

Hear, O people, I have got a taste of love.
The wicked men are killed, the enemies destroyed, the true Guru has given me the name of Hari.
(2). In the first (state) is given up attachment to egotism.
In the second is given up the custom of the people.
(In the third), having given up the three qualities, the enemies (become) like friends.
In the fourth, having met (with) the pious, (his) excellences are known.
(3). Easily dwelling is (then) made in a cave.
The unbeaten (sound) of him, whose form is light, is sounded.
There is great joy in reflecting on the word of the Guru.
Being attached to her beloved the woman is a blessed married wife.
(4). Humble Nānak pronounces (his) investigation on Brahm.
Who hears and does (it), he passes across.
He is not born (again) nor dies, he neither comes nor goes.
He remains absorbed with Hari.

III. LXX.

(1). A woman attached to her own (people), of amiable disposition,
Incomparable in beauty, perfect in conduct:
In which house (such a one) dwells, that house is lustrous.
Some rare man, (having become) a disciple, gets (such a one).

Pause.

Having met with the Guru I have obtained a virtuous woman.
With reference to worship (and) work she is excellent.
(2). As long as she dwells with her father:
So long (her) beloved wanders about very dejected.
By rendering service the true man (= Guru) is conciliated.
She is brought by the Guru to the house, then all happiness is obtained.
(3). She has the twenty-two auspicious qualities, true is her offspring (and) son.
She is obedient, clever and beautiful.

[1] ਆਵਦਾ = ਆਵਈ, for the sake of the rhyme.

She fulfils the wish (of) the mind (of her) husband and Lord.
All the wives of the younger and elder brother are satisfied.
(4). In the whole family she is the best.
She gives advice to the younger and elder brother (of her husband).
Blessed is that house, in which she appears.
Humble Nānak (says): in happiness the time is passed (there).

IV. LXXI.

(1). If I give advice, she does not let it ripen.
Near virtue and continence she is standing[1] (to prevent them).
She puts on many garbs and shows many forms.
She does not let (me) dwell in the house, she makes (me) wander about separate (from it).

Pause.

She is the mistress of the house (and) does not let (me) dwell in the house.
(If) I make efforts, I am entangled (in them).[2]
(2). Being sent by himself she has come as a ruler.
The nine regions and all countries are overcome (by her).
At the border (of a river) and holy watering-place she does not allow the Yōga and renunciation of the world.[3]
Studying the Smriti and the Vēda they become (therefore) tired.
(3). Wherever I sit, there she sits with (me).
The strong one enters all houses.
I have fallen on the asylum of the vile one, I do not get a place where to remain.
Say, O friend, to whom shall I go?
(4). Having heard (his) instruction I came to the true Guru.
The Guru taught (me) the mantra of the name of Hari, Hari.
I dwell (now) in my own house singing the excellences of the endless (Hari).
I have met with the Lord, (says) Nānak, and become free from care.

Pause.

The house is mine, she is the mistress.
She is the ruler, (but) by the Guru we were made courtiers (of Hari).

V. LXXII.

(1). The advice (of) the first is, that I should set a going (= read) the leaves (of the Vēda).
The advice (of) the second is, that I should summon (to me) two men.
The advice (of) the third is, that I should make some contrivance.
Having given up everything I have meditated on thee, O Lord!

Pause.

(I have) great joy, freedom from care and tranquillity.
(My) enemies have died and I have obtained happiness.

[1] ਖਲੋਈ from ਖਲੋਣਾ to stand. The subject is here apparently the Māyā.

[2] ਪਰੇਵੈ = ਪਰਾਂ or ਪਰੈਂ (ਪੜਨਾ, to fall), for the sake of the rhyme.

[3] The sense is: she knows even to hinder the practice of the Yōga (abstract contemplation) and the abandonment of the world.

(2). The true Guru gave me instruction.
Soul and body, all belongs to Hari, (to him) I shall give (it).
Whatever I do, he is my strength.
Thou art my refuge, thou art (my) court.
(3). Having abandoned thee, to whose protection should one go?
There is none other like thine.
To whom does thy servant owe obsequiousness?
The Sākat wanders astray in the desert.
(4). Thy greatness cannot be told.
Whomever thou protectest, taking him to thy neck—
—Nānak, (thy) slave, is in thy asylum—
(His) honour is preserved by the Lord, congratulation is made (to him).

VI. LXXIII.

(1). For the sake of traffic (I) passed through a foreign country.
(I) heard of an incomparable thing and procured it.
Binding the stock of (his) excellences into the hem of my garment I brought it.
Having seen the gem this (= my) mind clung to it.

Pause.

The retail-dealers of the wholesale merchant came to (his) gate.
Issue (to us) wares and let us traffic (with them)!
(2). By the wholesale merchant (I) was sent to (his) wholesale merchant (= the Guru).
Priceless is the jewel, priceless the stock of goods.
The well-disposed mediator (= broker) I obtained for a friend.
I got wares (and) my mind (became) immovable.
(3). There is no fear of a thief, nor of wind or water.
Easily the purchase (is effected), easily it is taken away.[1]
By acquiring the True one no pain is incurred.
In perfect safety I have brought (him) home.
(4). Profit is obtained and rejoicing is made.
Blessed be the perfect wholesale merchant, who is bestowing (his goods).
This traffic is obtained by some rare disciple.
Nānak brought (home) a fruitful[2] batch of goods.

VII. LXXIV.

(1). My virtues (or) vices he does not at all take into consideration.
He does not look at my form, colour and decoration.
My discretion and conduct are by no means scrutinized by him.
Seizing my arm the beloved one brought me to the bed.

Pause.

Hear, O friend, my beloved rendered me assistance.
Putting his hand on my head he protected me, making me his own; what do these ignorant people know (of it)?

[1] ਵਿਹਾਝੀ is subst. fem. and so likewise ਲੈ ਜਾਣੀ must be taken as a substant. fem. Literally: the buying and taking away (are) easily (effected).

[2] ਸਫਲਾ Adj. = सफला fruitful.

(2). My happy wifehood is now excellent.
My husband is met with, all pain is overcome.
In my courtyard is the splendour (of) the moon.
Day and night I rejoice with my beloved.
(3). My clothes are of deep red colour.
All ornaments, splendour (and) flowers (are on my) neck.
By the beloved a look was cast (on me), I obtained all treasures.
Obsequiousness to the wicked enemies ceased.
(4). She is always happy, she always enjoys pleasures.
The nine treasures of the name are in (her) house, she is satisfied.
Nānak says: when she is ornamented by her beloved:
She is lastingly a happy married wife (and) with her husband.

VIII. LXXV.

(1). Having offered a gift they perform worship.
He[1] is taking and giving (them), they deny it:
To which gate thou wilt have to go, O Brāhmaṇ!
At that gate thou wilt repent.

Pause.

Such Brāhmaṇs are drowned, O brother!
Without cause they excogitate wickedness.
(2). In (his) heart is greediness, he wanders about (like) mad.
He calumniates (other people) and puts a load on (his) head (thereby).
Being carried away by the Māyā he does not think.
Being led astray he wanders about in many ways.
(3). Outwardly he puts on many garbs.
Inside has alighted the giddiness of sensual objects.[2]
He teaches others and does himself not understand it.
Such a Brāhmaṇ will not be saved in any way.
(4). O foolish Brāhmaṇ, remember the Lord!
He is seeing and hearing (and) with thee.
Nānak says: if it be (thy) lot,
Give up pride and cling to the feet of the Guru!

IX. LXXVI.

(1). Pain and sickness have left (my) body, (my) mind (has) become pure by singing the excellences of Hari.

I rejoice, having met with the pious, now my mind does not wander anywhere.

Pause.

My heart is quenched by the word of the Guru, O mother!
Anxious inquietude and all doubt is extinct, the cooling Guru is obtained with natural ease.
(2). (My) running (mind) is stopped, the only One is comprehended, it dwells now in an immovable place.
Seeing the sight of thy saints, who are saving the world, it remains satiated.

[1] The subject is here very likely *God*, though not expressed in any way.
[2] ਘੇਰੇ = ਘੇਰਿ *s.f.* giddiness; the turning round (as in a whirlpool).

(3). The sins of (my) life have fallen behind me, the feet of the immovable saint (= the Guru) are now seized (by me).

With natural inclination sings (my) mind a song of congratulation, now death will not devour it again.

(4). The powerful cause of causes is giving me comfort, my king Hari, Hari.

Muttering thy name Nānak lives, thou art with me throughout and my assistant.

X. LXXVII.

Pause.

The slanderer cries aloud and laments.

The Supreme Brahm, the Lord is forgotten (by him), the slanderer earns (therefore) his own doing.

(1). If one become his companion (or) take him with oneself,

He takes up an impossible, immense serpent's load, the slanderer consumes (him) with fire.

(2). Who passes (at) the gate of the Lord, he speaks and lets hear (of it).

His devotees have always joy, singing the praise of Hari they are happy.[1]

XI. LXXVIII.

(1). Though I put on all ornaments:
Yet my mind does not confide (in them).
Though I apply many perfumes to my body :
I do not get a bit of that happiness.
In my mind I entertain such a desire.
Seeing my beloved I live, O my mother.

Pause.

O mother, what shall I do? this (my) mind is not steady.
Love to the dearly beloved one carries (it) away.
(2). Clothes, ornaments, many exquisite pleasures:
They also are of no account whatever, as I know.
Honour, splendour, reverence and greatness (are of no use).
(Nor if) the whole world (be) obedient (to me).[2]
(Though) my house be so beautiful (and) red.[3]
If I please the Lord, then I am always happy.
(3). Delicacies and foods of many kinds.
Abundant pleasures and shows.
Dominion, property and much sway:
(By all these) the mind is not satiated, thirst will not go.
Without meeting (with the beloved) these days are passed.
(If) the Lord is met with, then it obtains all happiness.
(4). Searching and searching about this intelligence was heard (by me):
"Without the society of the pious no one has crossed over."
He gets the true Guru, on whose forehead (this) lot (is written).
His desire is fulfilled, his mind is satiated.
When the Lord is met with, then desire ceases.
Nānak (says): he is obtained in the mind and body.

[1] घिगमाटै = घिगमै, for the sake of the rhyme.

[2] This very likely is the sense, though scarcely hinted at; the literal meaning is only: "the whole world obedient," to whom?

[3] Here apparently must be supplied again: it is of no use.

XII. LXXIX.

Pančpadē.

(1). First thy caste is good.
Secondly thy society is respected.
Thirdly thy place (house) is beautiful.
(But she is) deformed, (in whose) heart (there is) conceit.

Pause.

O fascinating, beautiful, wise and clever (woman)!
Though art roving in excessive pride and infatuation!
(2). Very clean is thy kitchen.
(Thou) makest ablution, worship (and) a red mark (on thy forehead).
(Thou art) dissolved in pride (and) speakest wisdom with (thy) mouth.
All (thy) learning is thrown away, greediness is a dog.
(3). Thou puttest on (fine) clothes and art given to enjoyments.
Thou keepest up a virtuous course of life and art respected amongst the people.
(Thou appliest) plenty of perfumes and scents.
(But thy) companion (= heart) is perfidious: wrath is a Čaṇḍāl.
(4). In thy other form of existence (thou wilt be) a water-carrier.
On this earth (thou enjoyest) a chieftainship.
Thou hast gold, silver and wealth.
Thy work is spoiled by (thy) disposition.
(5). On whom the merciful look of Hari, the king, rests:
She is liberated from the prison (of existence).
By which, joining the society of the pious, the juice of Hari is obtained:
That body is fruitful, says Nānak.

Pause.

All graces, all comforts accrue to a happy married woman.
Thou art very beautiful and clever.

XIII. LXXX.

(1). What is seen living, that must at last die.
Who becomes dead, he will remain immovable.

Pause.

Who die whilst living, they, being dead, live.
They put the medicine of the name of Hari into their mouth, by means of the word of the Guru they drink nectar-juice.
(2). (As) a raw earthen jar is destroyed, (so) he is destroyed.
Whose triad[1] leaves him, he gets a dwelling in his own house.
(3). Who ascends high, he falls down into the nether region.
Who falls on the earth, him death does not touch.
(4). Who are wandering about, they get nothing.
They (become) immovable, who do the word of the Guru.
(5). Soul and body, all is the property of Hari.
Nānak (says): who meet with the Guru, they become exalted.

[1] *i.e.* the three qualities.

XIV. LXXXI.

(1). Thy body is made by Brahmā.
Know it for certain, it will become dust.

Pause.

Remember the root (of all), O thoughtless, ignorant man!
Why art thou proud of this much?[1]
(2). (Thou art) daily a guest of three Seers (= six pounds, *i.e.* of food).
The other things are a deposit with thee.
(3). Ordure, bones and blood are wrapped up in a skin.
On this thou art conceited?
(4). If thou comprehendest the One thing, then thou becomest pure.
Without comprehending it thou art always impure.
(5). Nānak says: (I am) a sacrifice to the Guru,
From whom Hari, the wise Supreme Spirit, is obtained.

XV. LXXXII.

Čaupadē.

(1). One Ghaṛī (= 24 minutes) is to me daily (like) many days.
My mind does not remain (steady), how shall I meet with my beloved?

Pause.

One moment is to me (like) a day, it never passes.
I have much longing after (his) sight; is there such a saint, who may join to me my beloved?
(2). The four watches (are to me) like the four ages (of the world).
When it has become night, I do not know its end.
(3). The five enemies, having met, have separated (me) from my beloved.
Wandering and wandering about I weep wringing my hands.
(4). To humble Nānak the sight of Hari was shown.
Having known himself he obtained the highest bliss.

XVI. LXXXIII.

(1). In the service of Hari is the highest treasure.
The service of Hari (is the uttering of) the nectar-name (with) the mouth.

Pause.

Hari is my companion and my friend.
In pain and pleasure I remember him, he is present.
What can the helpless Yama frighten me?
(2). Hari is my refuge, Hari is my salvation.
Hari is my friend, the council in my heart.
(3). Hari is my capital, Hari is my trust.
(Having become) a disciple I acquire wealth, Hari is my banker.
(4). From the mercy of the Guru this wisdom comes.
Humble Nānak is absorbed in the bosom of Hari.

[1] ਇਤਨੇ ਕਉ, of this much, *i.e.* of this thy body, that will become dust.

XVII. LXXXIV.

(1). If the Lord becomes merciful (to me), then I apply this mind (to him).
Serving the true Guru I obtain all fruits.

Pause.

Why will (my) heart weep? my true Guru is perfect.
He gives (me) what I desire, he is the depository of all happiness, he is brimful of the pond of nectar.
(2). His lotus-feet are kept within (my) heart.
(His) sight is manifested, the beloved Rām is met with.
(3). The five companions (= the five senses) having met sing a song of congratulation.
The sound of the voice not produced (by men) is made to sound.
(4). The Guru of Nānak is pleased, Hari the king is met with.
Easily the night is passed in happiness.

XVIII. LXXXV.

(1). Hari bestowing (his) mercy has become manifest.
By falling in with the true Guru wealth is obtained.

Pause.

Such a wealth of Hari should be collected, O brother!
(Which) fire does not consume, (which) does not sink in water, (which) does not leave (thee) nor go anywhere.
(2). It does not diminish, it is not exhausted.
In eating and spending (it) the mind remains satiated.
(3). He is a true wholesale merchant, in whose house the wealth of Hari is collected.
By this wealth the whole world is benefited.
(4). He obtains the wealth of Hari, to whom it is due by a former decree (of God).
Humble Nānak is seizing at the end the name.

XIX. LXXXVI.

(1). As a husbandman sows (his) field:
(So) is (his) harvest indifferent (or) good, O man!

Pause.

What is born, know, that that dies (again).
The devotee of Gōvind (alone) becomes stable.
(2). After the day is passed, night will fall in.
When the night is gone, it becomes again morning.
(3). (Whom) the Māyā deludes, they remain unlucky.
By the favour of the Guru some rare one wakes.
(4). Nānak says: I sing (his) excellences day and night.
(My) face (becomes thereby) bright, pure (my) mind.

XX. LXXXVII.

(1). All the nine treasures are deposited with thee.
Thou art fulfilling the wishes, thou protectest at the end.

Pause.

If thou art my beloved, what hunger have I?
When thou dwellest in (my) heart, no pain affects (me).

(2). What thou doest, that is right.
O true Lord, true is thy order.
(3). When it pleases thee, then I sing the excellences of Hari.
In thy house there is always, always justice.
(4). O true Lord, inapprehensible and inscrutable!
Nānak applies himself to (thy) service, being applied (by thee).

XXI. LXXXVIII.

(1). He is near the creatures and always with (them).
(His) power is active in (every) form and colour.

Pause.

(If) he acts, he does not grieve nor does (his) mind weep.
He is imperishable, undying, incomprehensible, our Lord is always safe.
(2). To whom does thy slave owe obsequiousness?
Whose order has he to mind, O Lord?
(3). The slave, that has been made free by the Lord,
On whom is that slave dependent?
(4). (He is) independent and without concern.
O slave Nānak, say: vāh Guru!

XXII. LXXXIX.

(1). Giving up the juice of Hari he is inebriated with a mean juice.
The thing is in (his) house and he is going out (for it).

Pause.

The story of the true nectar cannot be heard.
Raising disputes he clings to a false idle chat.
(2). (He takes) the wages of the Lord (and renders) service to another.
With such qualities man is covered over.
(3). He hides himself from him, who is always with him.
What is of no use, that he asks again and again.
(4). Nānak says: the Lord is merciful to the poor.
As it pleases him, so he cherishes them.

XXIII. XC.

(1). The name of Hari is life and wealth.
Here and there it is of use.

Pause.

Without the name of Hari every other thing is but little.
My mind is satiated by the sight of Hari.
(2). A storehouse of devotion, a ruby is the word of the Guru.
Singing, hearing and doing it (I am) happy.
(3). (My) mind clings to the lotus-foot.[1]
By the true Guru being pleased (with me) it was made a present (to me).

[1] ਮਾਨੁ here = ਮੰਨੁ (= ਮਨੁ) mind, heart, for the sake of the rhyme.

(4). The Guru initiated Nānak.
The imperishable Lord is (now) known (by me as being present) in every creature.

XXIV. XCI.

(1). Brimful is the stream of (his) joy and sport.
His own work is adjusted by himself.

Pause.

The means of the perfect Lord are perfect,
The stream of whose splendour remains brimful.
(2). The report of whose name, the treasure, is spotless,
He himself is the creator, there is none other.
(3). All the creatures are in his hand.
The Lord is continually sporting with every one.
(4). The Guru is perfect, a perfect work is made (by him).
Nānak (says): to (his) devotee greatness is given.

XXV. XCII.

(1). By the word of the Guru I fashion this (my) mind.
I collect the wealth of Hari, (which is) the sight of the Guru.

Pause.

O highest wisdom, come into my heart!
(That) I may meditate on and sing the excellences of Gōvind, (his) name is exceedingly dear to me.
(2). By the true name (I am) perfectly satiated.
The dust of the saints (is equal to) bathing at the sixty-eight (Tīrthas).
(3). In all I know the One creator.
Having joined the society of the pious (I obtain) understanding and discrimination.
(4). (I am) the slave of all, having given up conceit.
(This) present the Guru has given to Nānak.

XXVI. XCIII.

(1). Understanding has become bright, wisdom perfect.
Folly is thereby extinguished and removed.

Pause.

Such an instruction of the Guru was obtained,
(That) he, who was drowning in the terrible blind well, came out, O my brother.
(2). Great and bottomless is the ocean of fire.
The Guru is the boat, that ferries across (this) ocean.
(3). Hard to cross, dark and difficult is this Māyā.
By the perfect Guru a clear way is shown.
(4). (I am not possessed) of any muttering, austerity and contrivance.
O Guru, Nānak has fled to thy asylum!

XXVII. XCIV.

Tipadē.[1]

(1). Who is drinking the juice of Hari is always attached (to him).
(By drinking) other juices one sinks down in a moment.

[1] Tipadē, consisting of three verses severally.

Who is intoxicated with the juice of Hari has always joy in his heart.
With other juices care is mixed up.

Pause.

Who drinks the juice of Hari is sufficiently drunk and intoxicated.
All other juices are mean.
(2). The estimate of the juice of Hari cannot be told.
The juice of Hari is to be found in the shop of the pious.
It is not obtained for any Lakhs or Crores (of money).
To whom it is allotted, to him they give it.
(3). Nānak having tasted it became astonished.
Nānak got (this) relish from the Guru.
Here and there it does not leave (one) in any way.
Nānak is much longing after the juice of Hari.

XXVIII. XCV.

(1). (If) thou extinguish lust, wrath, greediness, spiritual blindness, the stream of thy folly ceases.
(If) having become humble thou perform service, thou wilt become dear to the mind of (thy) beloved.

Pause.

Hear, O beautiful woman, the word of the pious, (which is) saving (thee).

Thy pain, hunger and doubt are effaced (thereby), thou wilt obtain happiness in the Sukhmani channel (of the vital breath).

(2). Having washed (his) feet render service to the Guru, being purified in (thy) spirit do away with the thirst after poison!

(If) thou become the lowest slave of (his) slaves, then thou wilt obtain lustre at the gate of Hari.

(3). Even this is the right course of conduct, even this the (proper) occupation; if thou obey (this) order, thy devotion will be effected.

Who performs this advice, (says) Nānak, he will cross the water of existence.

XXIX. XCVI.

Dupadē.

(1). A human body has been obtained (by thee).
This is (now) thy time to be united with Gōvind.
Other works are of no use whatever to thee.
Join the society of the pious, adore the name only!

Pause.

Cling to the apparatus for crossing the water of existence!
In the love of the Māyā thy life is passing to no purpose.
(2). Muttering, austerity, continence and virtue are not practised (by me).
No service (is rendered to) the pious, (nor) is Hari the king known.
Nānak says: we are of mean works.
Preserve the honour of him, who has fallen on thy asylum!

XXX. XCVII.

(1). Without thee I have none other, thou art in my mind.
Thou art my friend and companion, my Lord, why should (my) soul be afraid?

Pause.

Thou art my refuge, thou art my hope.
In sitting, rising, sleeping, walking, at every breath and morsel mayst thou not be forgotten !
(2). Keep, keep (me) in thy asylum, O Lord, the ocean of fire is frightful!
O true Guru, O thou, who art giving comfort to Nānak, we are thy little ones![1]

XXXI. XCVIII.

Pause.

The people of Hari are rescued by the Lord.
My mind is reconciled with my beloved, my heat has died having eaten poison.
(1). No heat and cold in any way affect me, singing the excellences of the name of Rām.
The drawing of the sorcerer[2] does not in any way hit (me), the lotus-foot is (my) asylum.
(2). By the favour of the saints he (= Hari) has become merciful, he himself has become (my) helper.
Nānak sings continually the depository of (all) excellences (and) effaces (thereby) his doubt (and) pain.

XXXII. XCIX.

(1). (When) the medicine of the name of Hari is eaten:
Happiness is obtained, the occasion for pain is done away.

Pause.

The heat is gone by the word of the perfect Guru.
Joy has set in, all cares are effaced.
(2). All creatures obtain happiness,
(By whom) the Supreme Brahm is meditated upon, (says) Nānak.

XXXIII. C.

(1). That time has come, which he is not desiring.
Without the order (of the Lord) how shall he understand the teaching?

Pause.

(By whom) cold and hot flesh is eaten:
He is not young, he is old, O brother!
(2). Nānak, the slave, is in the asylum of the pious.
By the favour of the Guru he crosses the world of existence.

XXXIV. CI.

(1). There is continually light in (my) spirit.
In the society of the pious (my) dwelling is the feet of Hari.

[1] ਬਾਲਗੁਪਾਲ, literally: the children cowherds, the playfellows of Krishṇa; thence: children, little ones.

[2] There is a great variety of readings in the MSS. regarding the first three words of this line, as the sense of them was apparently no longer understood; the Sikh Granthīs at least could give no clue to their meaning. The Lahore lithographed copy reads: ਡਾਰੀ ਰੇ ਚਿਤਿ—ਲਾਗੈ, which gives no sense. The MS. No. 2483 reads: ਡਾਰੀ ਰੇ ਚਿਤੁ and No. 2484 reads: ਡਾਰੀ ਰੀ ਚਿਤੁ. ਡਾਰੀ signifies: *sorcerer* (the masc. of the common ਡਾਰਿਣ or ਡਾਰਣ); ਚਿਤੁ we take = ਚਿਤ੍ਰ, painting, drawing (of figures, for the sake of witchcraft), so that the right reading is that of MS. No. 2483, viz.: ਡਾਰੀ ਰੇ ਚਿਤੁ—ਲਾਗੈ, according to which we have translated.

Pause.

Mutter continually the name of Rām, O my mind!

Thou wilt always obtain coolness, tranquillity and happiness, all thy sins will go off, O mind!

(2). Nānak says: whose destiny is perfect:

He meets with the true Guru, the Supreme Brahm.

(Thirty-four [verses] of the second Ghar.)

XXXV. CII.

Pause.

Whose Lord Hari is, whose friend the Lord is:

(Her) pain is gone, she is not again afflicted.

(1). Bestowing mercy (on her) he joins (her) to (his) feet.

In comfort, tranquillity and joy she is happy.

(2). Singing the excellences (of Hari) in the society of the pious she (becomes) incomparable.

By remembering Hari she becomes inestimable, (says) Nānak.

XXXVI. CIII.

(1). (By whom) these sporting ones, lust, wrath, the Māyā, pride and envy, are all overcome in the play:

He brings virtue, contentment, mercy, morality and truth into his house.

Pause.

Birth and death cease, all burthens (are removed).

Joining the society (of the pious) his mind (becomes) pure, by the perfect Guru he is in one moment brought across.

(2). (His) mind remains the dust of all, all appear (to him) as beloved friends.

In all my Lord is contained, he is giving gifts (to) all creatures, remembering (them).

(3). He himself alone, the One is alone in the whole expansion (of the universe).

By continually muttering (him) all become pious people, by meditating on the One name many are saved.

(4). Deep, profound and endless is the Lord, he has no end nor limit whatever.

By thy mercy Nānak sings (thy) excellences, meditating and meditating he adores the Lord.

XXXVII. CIV.

(1). Thou art endless, not passing away, inapprehensible, all this (universe) is thy form.

What cleverness shall we creatures practise, when all is in thee?

Pause.

O my true Guru, protect thy own child, assuming an incarnation![1]

Give (me) wisdom, (that) I may always sing (thy) excellences, O my unattainable, boundless Lord!

(2). As in the womb of the mother that creature is preserved, taking the name as (its) support:

(So) he is happy, who at every breath remembers (the name), fire[2] does not touch (him).

(3). Remove the love to another's property, to another's wife, to slandering others!

Serve the lotus-foot in thy heart by the support of the perfect Guru!

[1] ਲੀਲਾ *s.f.* sport, play, stands here for ਲੀਲਾਵਤਾਰੁ, a descent of sport = an incarnation of Vishṇu.

[2] ਅਗਨਾਰਿ = ਅਗਨ, āri being a meaningless alliteration.

(4). House, mansion, palace, whatever is seen, nothing (goes) with (thee).
As long as thou livest in the time of the Kali-yug, remember the name, (says) humble Nānak.

ĀSĀ; GHAR III.; MAHALĀ V.

Ōm! By the favour of the true Guru!

I. XXXVIII. CV.

(1). Dominion, property, youth, house, splendour, beautiful youth;
Much wealth, elephants and horses, rubies, the price (of which is) Lakhs (of Rupees):[1]
(All these) are further on (= in the other world) at the gate (of Hari) of no use, the proud one departs leaving (them) behind.

Pause.

Why is the mind applied (to anything) but the One?
In rising and sitting, in sleeping and waking, continually Hari should be meditated upon!
(2). (Whose) courts are very wonderful and beautiful, (who) has acquired high praises in battle;[2]
Who boasts with his mouth: I will kill, bind (and) set free!
(When) the order of the Supreme Brahm has come, he departs giving up (all) in one day.
(3). He does many works and contrivances, (but) the creator he does not know.
He gives instruction (to others), but he himself does not do the truth, the word (of the Guru) he does not recognize.
He has come naked and will go naked, as an elephant shakes off the dust.
(4). Hear, O my pious friend: all this expansion is false!
Saying: "mine, mine" they are drowned, the ignorant people are consumed and die.
Nānak, having met with the Guru, meditates on the name, by the true name he is saved.

RĀG ĀSĀ; GHAR V.; MAHALĀ V.

Ōm! By the favour of the true Guru!

I. XXXIX. CVI.

(1). That whole world is in error,
(Being) blind by (worldly) occupations; some (rare) man of Hari wakes.
(2). (Their) life is absorbed (in) love to the very fascinating and beloved (Māyā).
Some rare one forsakes (her).
(3). The incomparable lotus-foot of Hari is the mantra of the saints.
Some (rare) pious man clings (to it).
(4). Nānak wakes in the society of the pious out of love to divine knowledge.
On him, whose lot is great, mercy (is bestowed).

[1] ਬੈਆਣੀ, corrupted for the sake of the rhyme instead of ਬੈਆਣਾ (Pers. Arab. بیعانه, earnest money = price, cost).

[2] ਪਵਾੜਾ *s.m.* a panegyrical kind of poetry, in which the bravery of heroes, etc., is extolled; thence praises, panegyrics generally.

Ōm! By the favour of the true Guru!

RĀGU ĀSĀ; GHAR VI.; MAHALĀ V.

I. XL. CVII.

(1). Who pleases thee, he is accepted, even that is the happiness and tranquillity (of) the mind.
The powerful cause of causes is boundless, there is no other, O friend!

Pause.

The people delight in singing thy excellences.
The advice, counsel and cleverness of (thy) people is what thou dost and causest (them) to do.
(2). Nectar is thy name, O beloved, in the society of the pious (its) juice is obtained.
Those people become satiated (and) full (of it), (by whom) Hari, the depository of happiness, is sung.
(3). Who is in thy protection, O Lord, he has no care.
On whom thy kindness is bestowed, they are good wholesale merchants, O Lord!
(4). All error, spiritual blindness and mischievousness are gone off since the sight (of Hari) was obtained.
Nānak has made the true name his occupation, in love to the name of Hari he is sunk.

II. XLI. CVIII.

(1). Who washes another's filth,[1] he (through) several births, obtains his own doing (= deserts).
Here (he finds) no comfort (and there) at the threshold (no) entrance, having gone to the city of Yama he is tormented.

Pause.

By the slanderer his whole life is lost.
(Here) he cannot reach anything, further on (in the other world) he gets no place.
(2). (When) the lot of the helpless slanderer has fallen, what will that poor man do?
He is ruined there, where no one protects (him), to whom shall he raise his voice?
(3). No salvation (accrues to) the slanderer in any way, thus it pleases the Lord.
Who calumniates the pious, by him no tranquillity[2] (and) happiness are enjoyed.
(4). The pious are relying on thee, O Lord, thou art the assistant of the pious.
Nānak says: the pious are preserved by Hari, the slanderers are swept away (by him).

III. XLII. CIX.

(1). (Who) washes his outside (white), heart and mind (being) filthy, he loses both his places.
Here he is sunk in lust, wrath and spiritual blindness, in the other world he will sob and weep.

Pause.

The way of worshipping Gōvind is different!
The hillock is beaten, (but) the snake does not die, the snake[3] does not hear the name.
(2). The practice of the Māyā is given up, (and yet) he does not know the essence of devotion.
He gives himself to speculation on the Vēda and the Shāstras, (and yet) he does not become acquainted with truth.[4]

[1] The sense is: to wash the filthy clothes of another, *i.e.* to criticize his actions.

[2] ਸੰਤ is here = ਸਾਂਤਿ *s.f.*

[3] ਡੋਰਾ (Hindī डोंरा, Sansk. डुण्डुभ), a kind of snake (a lizard without feet). The sense of these two lines is: the way of adoring Gōvind is different from the practice of the people, who only touch the outside (the hillock, in which the snake is hidden) without killing the snake itself (selfishness).

[4] ਤਤੁ ਜੋਗੁ = ਤਤੁ ਕਉ, ਜੋਗੁ being here used as a postposition.

(3). As a false rupee is discovered, when it comes into the sight of the money-changer:
(So) the inward governor knows everything; what is hidden from him?
(4). The groundless (= false) man is destroyed in a moment by (his) falsehood, hypocrisy and deceit.
True, true, true he is called by Nānak, (who) in his own heart perceives and remembers (Hari).

IV. XLIII. CX.

(1). (Who) is making efforts, (his) mind becomes pure, he dances having removed his own self.
(Who) is collected in (his) mind, he keeps the five persons[1] in subjection.

Pause.

Thy people dance and sing thy excellences.
The rebeck, tambourine, cymbal and string of toe-bells emit a sound, (though) unbeaten.
(2). (Who) first instructs his own mind and afterwards gladdens others.
(Who) mutters the name of Rām in his heart and with his mouth lets all (men) hear (it).
(3). (Who) with his hand washes the feet of the pious, (who) applies the dust of the saints to his body.
(Who) offers up his heart and body and puts (them) before the Guru, he obtains the true thing.
(4). Whoever hears and beholds with faith, the pain of his birth and death goes off.
Such a dance removes hell; Nānak (says): the disciple wakes.

V. XLIV. CXI.

(1). A low Čanḍāl woman becomes a Brāhmaṇī, from a Shūdra woman (one) becomes the best, O dear!
The insatiable thirst of hell and heaven is quenched and devoured, O dear!

Pause.

The cat of the house is taught something else, seeing the mouse it is frightened, O dear!
The lion is given into the power of the goat by the Guru, (the goat) is set by him on the dog.
(2). Without posts the roof is supported, by the houseless a house is obtained.
Without a setter the setting (of jewels) is made, a wonderful (precious) stone is set, O dear!
(3). The complainer is not reaching his object by means of complaint, by silence a decision is obtained, O dear!
She who is sitting in wealth on a carpet takes a corpse and runs to show it to the eyes.
(4). That ignorant one says: I know; he, who is knowing, (says): I do not investigate (it) minutely, O dear!
Nānak says: (to whom) the Guru has given nectar to drink, he delighting (in it) is made happy.

VI. XLV. CXII.

(1). Cutting (my) bonds (my) vices are forgotten (by him), his own greatness is remembered (by him).
He became kind (to me) like a mother and father, like a child (I was) cherished (by him).

Pause.

The disciples of the Guru are preserved by Gōpāl, the Guru.
They are drawn out (by him) from the great water of existence bestowing his glance (of favour on them).
(2). By remembering whom one escapes from Yama and gets happiness here and there:
(Him) mutter at (every) breath and morsel with (thy) tongue, continually (his) excellences should be sung!

[1] The five persons are ਕਾਮ, ਕ੍ਰੋਧ, etc.

(3). By devotion with love the highest step is obtained, in the society of the saints pain is extinguished.

(Such a one) is neither consumed nor does he go, no fear whatever enters (him), the spotless property of Hari he takes possession of.

(4). At the time of the end the Lord becomes (my) assistant, here and there he is (my) protector.

He is the friend of (my) life, (my) beloved, my wealth; Nānak is always a sacrifice (to him).

VII. XLVI. CXIII.

(1). When thou art (my) Lord, what fear (should I entertain)? without thee whom should I praise?

(When I have) thee alone, then I have everything, without thee I have none other.

Pause.

O father, I have seen, that the world is poison.

Keep me, O my Lord, thy name is my support!

(2). Thou knowest all the pain of the mind, to whom else should it be told?

Without the name the whole world is mad; (if) the name is obtained, happiness is acquired.

(3). What shall be said, to whom shall it be told? what is to be said, that is with (thee), O Lord!

Everything is thy work, my hope is continually (put) in thee.

(4). If thou givest greatness, it is thy greatness, here and there I meditate on thee.

O Lord of Nānak, who art always giving happiness, thy one name is my salvation.

VIII. XLVII. CXIV.

(1). Nectar is thy name, O Lord, this great juice is drunk by (thy) people.

The burdens of fear of repeated birth have ceased, sin is extinct, error is gone.[1]

Pause.

Seeing (thy) sight I live.

Having heard thy words, O true Guru, my mind and body have become tranquil.

(2). By thy mercy the society of the pious was obtained (by me), this work was done by thyself.

Thy feet, O Lord, were firmly seized (by me) and the poison was (thus) easily destroyed.

(3). Thy name, O Lord, is the depository of happiness, this imperishable mantra I obtained.

By the Guru it was given to me out of mercy, my heat, pain and enmity departed.

(4). Blessed is he, who has obtained a human body, whom the Lord has taken to union with himself.

Blessed is that Kali-yuga, (where) in the society of the pious the praise (of Hari) is sung! Nānak says): the name (is) the support (of my) heart.

IX. XLVIII. CXV.

(1). He (the Supreme) has been before everything,[2] what other knowledge does one have?

His own erring and misled child the Supreme Brahm, the Lord, pardons.

Pause.

My true Guru is always merciful, he protects me, the poor one.

(My) sickness is cut off (by him), great happiness is obtained (by me), the nectar-name of Hari is put into (my) mouth (by him).

(2). (My) many sins are taken away, (my) bonds are cut, (I) have become emancipated.

From the very horrible blind well (I) am drawn out by the Guru seizing (my) arm.

[1] ਵੀਓ, p.p. of ਵਞਣਾ to go (Sindhī विञो).

[2] The words ought to be put in the following order: ਆਗੈਹੀ ਸਭੁ ਕਿਛੁ ਤੇ.

(3). (I) have become fearless, all fear is effaced, (I) am protected by the protector.
Such is thy gift, O my Lord, all (my) affairs are adjusted (by thee).
(4). The depository of (all) qualities, the Lord, I have acquired in (my) heart.
Nānak has fallen on (his) asylum and is happy.

X. XLIX. CXVI.

(1). (When) thou art forgotten, then every one (becomes) an enemy (to me).
(When) thou comest into (my) thought, then (every one does) service (to me).
No one else is known (besides thee), O true, inapprehensible and inscrutable one!

Pause.

(When) thou comest into (my) thought, then (thou art) always merciful (to me), what (can) by the helpless people (be done)?
Say, who should be called bad (or) good? all are thy creatures!
(2). I rely on thee, thou art (my) support, thou keepest (me) giving (me) thy hand.
On whom thy mercy is, that man no calamity whatever devours.
(3). That is happiness, that is greatness, which is pleasing, O Lord, to (thy) mind.
Thou art wise, thou art always kind, (if) the name be obtained, I enjoy pleasure.
(4). Before thee is my prayer: soul and body is all thine.
Nānak says: all is thy greatness, nobody knows my name.

XI. L. CXVII.

(1). (If) the Lord, the inward governor, bestows mercy, Hari is obtained in the society of the pious.
(If) he, having opened the shutters, shows (his) sight, one is not subject again to regeneration.

Pause.

Meet with the beloved Lord and thou wilt remove all thy pain, O dear!
Cross in the society of him, by whom the Supreme Brahm is adored in (his) heart!
(2). (Who) wanders about in a great desert and in an ocean of fire, (who is) living in joy and grief:
(His) mind becomes pure having met with the true Guru, by muttering the immortal Hari with (his) tongue.
(3). (By whom) his body and all his wealth is set up (as the object of his thoughts), he is bound (by) a soft fetter.
By the favour of the Guru (his) births are cut off, (by whom) the name of Hari is adored.
(4). They are kept by the Lord, the preserver, who are pleasing to their own Lord.
Soul and body is all thine, O donor! Nānak is always a sacrifice (to thee).

XII. LI. CXVIII.

Pause.

(Thou hast) escaped from spiritual blindness (and) dull sleep, what favour was bestowed (on thee), O dear?
The very fascinating (Māyā) does not affect thee, how is thy sloth gone, O dear?
(1). Lust, wrath and egotism are hard, who has escaped (from them) by means of continence, O dear?
The excellent men, Dēvas and Asuras, are subject to the three qualities, the whole world is robbed (by them), O dear!
(2). The fire of a burning forest consumes much grass, some green shrub is saved, O dear!
Such a powerful one I cannot describe, nothing like him can be told, O dear.

(3). In the chamber of lamp-black (I have not become) black, a spotless colour was applied, O dear! The great mantra of the Guru dwelled in (my) heart, the wonderful name was heard (by me), O dear!

(4). Bestowing mercy (on me) the Lord is looking (on me) with a glance of favour, he applied me to his own foot.

By devotion (with) love I obtained happiness, O Nānak, I entered the society of the pious.

Ōm! by the favour of the true Guru!

RĀGU ĀSĀ; GHAR VII.; MAHALĀ V.

I. LII. CXIX.

(1). Red short breeches shine on thy body.
Thou art pleasing (to thy) sweetheart, his mind is captivated (by thee).

Pause.

By whom is thy redness made?
By what colour hast thou become red?
(2). Thou art beautiful, thou (enjoyest) a good fortune.
In thy house is the sweetheart, in thy house is good luck.
(3). Thou art virtuous, thou art the most excellent.
Thou art pleasing to the beloved, thou art very intelligent.
(4). (Thou) art pleasing to the beloved, therefore (thou art) of red colour.
Nānak says: by (his) favourable look (thou art) exalted.

Pause.

Hear, O my (female) friend, this is the way of (my) passing the time.
The Lord himself is adorning (me).

II. LIII. CXX.

(1). When (my) troubles are intense, they are receding,
Now that I have been advised, (that he is) in (my) presence.

Pause.

Submissiveness has ceased, O friend and companion!
My error is gone, by the Guru (I am) united with (my) beloved.[1]
(2). I am brought near and placed on the bed by the beloved.
I am released from paying submissiveness (to others).
(3). In my house there is light by means of the word (of the Guru).
In joy my Lord is joking (with me).
(4). On my forehead a good lot (is written), (my) beloved has come to my house.
A firm happy wifehood (I have) obtained, O humble Nānak!

III. LIV. CXXI.

(1). My mind is applied to the true name.
(But outwardly) I jest and talk with the people.[2]

[1] ਮੇਠੀ = ਮੇਲ਼ੀ, (I am) united; the subject must be gathered from the context.

[2] ਠਾਠਾ = ਠੰਠਾ, joke, jest; ਘਾਗ = वाच्, talk, speech.

Pause.

Outwardly good terms with all are kept up.
(But inwardly) I remain uncontaminated like a lotus in the water.
(2). By word of mouth I am conversing with all.
(But) my own soul I keep with the Lord.
(3). Much ecstasy also comes into sight.
This mind is the dust of the feet of all.
(4). Humble Nānak has obtained the perfect Guru.
The One is shown (to him as being) inside and outside.

IV. LV. CXXII.

(1). The girl[1] is obtaining pleasures in youth.
(But) without the name she is mingled with dust.

Pause.

In her ear is an ear-ring, (fine) clothes are put on.
(Her) bed is comfortable, in (her) mind she is proud.
(2). Beneath (her) an elephant, above (her) an umbrella of gold.
(But) without devotion to Hari she is buried in the earth.
(3). (One may have) many beautiful women.
(But) without love to Hari every taste is insipid.
(4). The Māyā is deceitful, diseases are spread out (by her).[2]
Nānak is in the asylum of the Lord, the kind Supreme Spirit.

V. LVI. CXXIII.

(1). There is a garden, (in which) many trees are planted.
The nectar-name is produced on them as fruit.

Pause.

O wise one, make such a contemplation,
By which the state of final emancipation may be obtained!
Round about are ponds of poison, in the midst (of that garden) is nectar, O brother!
(2). There is one gardener, who waters (the trees).
He takes care of the branches every morning.[3]
(3). Every tree is brought and firmly planted.
Every one blossoms, not one is fruitless.
(4). Who obtains the nectar-fruit of the name from the Guru:
He crosses the Māyā, (says) Nānak, the slave.

VI. LVII. CXXIV.

(1). Royal sports are made by thy name.
The Yōga (deep meditation) is made by singing thy praise.

[1] ਬਲੀਆ = ਬਾਲੀ, girl. The words in these verses are exceedingly disfigured, as the author took no pains to choose suitable words.

[2] ਬਿਖਲੀਆ = ਬਿਖਰੇ (from ਬਿਖਰਨਾ, to be spread out).

[3] The Lahore lithographed copy reads ਪਾਤਪਤ, the MSS. No. 2484: ਪਤਿਪਾਤਿ, No. 2483: ਪਾਤਪਾਤ; the first two readings are wrong, as they give no sense, the last, ਪਾਤਿਪਾਤ, is = Sansk. प्रातः प्रातः, every morning, which suits well the context.

Pause.

All comforts are brought about in thy shelter.
The curtains of error are opened by the true Guru.
(2). By comprehending the order (of Hari) pleasures are enjoyed.
In the service of the true Guru (there is) great emancipation.
(3). By whom thou art known, he is in his married state of mortified passions and accepted.
Who is attached to the name, he is emancipated.
(4). Who has obtained the treasure of the name :
His treasury is full, says Nānak.

VII. LVIII. CXXV.

(1). (If) I go to a Tīrtha, (I see that) they are practising egotism (there).
(If) I ask the Paṇḍits, they are attached to the Māyā.

Pause.

Show me that place, O friend!
Where there is continually the praise of Hari (goiog on).
(2). By reflection on the Shāstras and Vēdas, on merit and demerit :
There is again and again descent to hell (and ascent to) heaven.
(3). In the married state there is care, dejection and selfishness.
Works bring trouble to the soul.
(4). By the mercy of the Lord the mind becomes subjected.
Nānak (says): (who becomes) a disciple, by him the Māyā is crossed.

Pause.

In the society of the pious the praise of Hari is sung.
This place is obtained from the Guru.

VIII. LIX. CXXVI.

(1). In the house is happiness, outside (of it) also is happiness.
By remembering Hari all troubles are destroyed.

Pause.

(There are) all comforts (enjoyed), when thou comest into (one's) thought.
That man mutters (thy) name, who pleases thee.
(2). Body and mind become cool by muttering thy name.
Who is muttering Hari, Hari, the tent of his pain tumbles down.
(3). Who comprehends the order, he is accepted,
Whose mark is the true word (of the Guru).
(4). By the perfect Guru the name of Hari is made fast (in me).
Nānak (says): I have obtained happiness in (my) mind.

IX. LX. CXXVII.

(1). Wherever thou sendest (me), there I go.
The happiness, thou givest, that I obtain.

Pause.

(I am) always (thy) slave, O Lord Gōvind!
By thy mercy I am fully satiated.

(2). What thou givest, that I put on and eat.
By thy favour, O Lord, I get on comfortably.
(3). In my mind and body I meditate on thee.
No one I compare with thee.
(4). Nānak says: continually I thus meditate.
(My) salvation is effected by clinging to the feet of the pious.

X. LXI. CXXVIII.

(1). In rising, sitting and sleeping he should be meditated upon!
In going on the road Hari, Hari should be sung!

Pause.

With the ear the nectar-story should be heard!
By whom it is heard, in (his) mind joy springs up, all the pain and disease of (his) mind go off.
(2). (If) in every work, on the road, in the places of resort he be muttered:
The nectar of Hari is drunk by the favour of the Guru.
(3). (By whom) day and night the praise of Hari is sung:
That man is not put into the road of (= to) Yama.
(4). By whom he (Hari) is not forgotten the eight watches:
By clinging to his feet salvation is obtained, (says) Nānak.

XI. LXII. CXXIX.

(1). By remembering whom thou dwellest in comfort;
Happiness is enjoyed and pain is effaced:

Pause.

Be joyful (and) sing the excellences of (that) Lord!
Conciliate continually thy own true Guru!
(2). Do the true word of the true Guru!
Being firmly seated in (thy) house thou wilt obtain thy Lord.
(3). (If) the ill conduct of another thou dost not keep in (thy) mind:
Pain (will) not (befall thee), O brother and friend!
(4). (To whom) by the Guru the mantra of Hari is given:
He knows day by day this happiness, (says) Nānak.

XII. LXIII. CXXX.

(1). Whom, being low, nobody knows:
Him, when muttering the name, the four corners (of the earth) mind.

Pause.

I ask for thy sight, give it me, O beloved!
Who is not saved by thy service?
(2). Near whom nobody goes:
His feet the whole creation rubs and washes.
(3). The man, who is not of any use:
His name is muttered by the favour of the saints.
(4). When (my) sleeping mind becomes wakeful in the society of the pious:
Then the Lord becomes sweet to Nānak.

XIII. LXIV. CXXXI.

(1). The only One I behold with (my) eyes.
Continually I remember the name of Hari.

Pause.

I sing the excellences of Rām, Rām, Rām.
By the majesty of the saints I meditate on the name of Hari, Hari in the society of the pious, O dear!
(2). In whose string everything is strung:
He is contained in every creature.
(3). He is making production and destruction in a moment.
He himself, who is without qualities, remains distinct (from all).
(4). The inward governor is the cause of causes.
The Lord of Nānak is enjoying happiness.

XIV. LXV. CXXXII.

(1). (Who) were made to wander about in crores of births:
They won a (human) body, hard to acquire, (and) are not overcome.

Pause.

Sins are destroyed, pain and trouble are removed.
They become purified by the dust of the saints.
(2). The saints of the Lord, (who are) able to save (others),
Meet with him, for whom exactly union (with them is written).
(3). In (his) mind (is) joy, (to whom) the Guru has given (his) mantra.
(His) thirst is quenched, (his) mind becomes immovable.
(4). The name is the (best) thing, the nine treasures and (all) perfections.
Nānak (says): from the Guru understanding is obtained.

XV. LXVI. CXXXIII.

(1). Thirst is effaced, ignorance and darkness.
By the service of the pious many sins are cut off.

Pause.

Happiness, tranquillity and much joy
Are obtained by the service of the Guru; (his) mind (becomes) pure, (by whom) the name of Hari, Hari, Hari, Hari is heard.
(2). The foolish presumption of the mind is destroyed.
The will of the Lord becomes sweet.
(3). The feet of the perfect Guru are seized.
The sins of crores of births go off.
(4). This jewel of birth becomes fruitful (to him),
(On whom) the Lord bestows mercy, says Nānak.

XVI. LXVII. CXXXIV.

(1). My own true Guru I remember continually.
The feet of the Guru I brush with (my) hair.

Pause.

Wake, O my wakeful mind!
Without Hari no one is of use (to thee), false is the fascination (of the Māyā), false the expansion (of the world)!

(2). Bestow (thy) love on the word of the Guru!
(If) the Guru become merciful (to thee), (thy) pain goes.
(3). Without the Guru there is no other place.
The Guru is bountiful, the Guru gives the name.
(4). The Guru himself is the Supreme Brahm, the Lord.
Mutter, O Nānak, the Guru the eight watches!

XVII. LXVIII. CXXXV.

(1). He himself is the tree (and) the spread out branches (of it).
He himself keeps his own field.

Pause.

Wherever I see, there is that One.
In every creature is that one himself.
(2). He himself is the sun and the expansion of (his) rays.
He is hidden, he is the appearance.
(3). One may fix (his) name as having all qualities and as having none.
Both (names) meeting together are united (in him).
(4). Nānak says: by the Guru error and fear are put aside.
The blissful (Supreme) is seen[1] by every eye.

XVIII. LXIX. CXXXVI.

(1). I do not know any contrivance and dexterity.
Day and night I praise thy name.

Pause.

I am vicious and have not any virtue.
That Lord is doing and causing to be done (everything).
(2). I am foolish, doltish, ignorant and thoughtless.
I am longing in my mind after thy name.
(3). Muttering, austerities, continence and works I do not practise.
The name of the Lord I adore in (my) mind.
(4). I do not know anything, little is my understanding.
Nānak says: (I am) in thy asylum, O Lord!

XIX. LXX. CXXXVII.

(1). Hari, Hari, these two words are (my) rosary.
Muttering and muttering (them) he became merciful (to me) the poor one.

Pause.

I make supplication to my own true Guru:
Mercifully keep (me) in (thy) asylum, give me the muttering of Hari, Hari!
(2). (Who) keeps the rosary of Hari in his heart:
He removes the pain of regeneration and death.
(3). Who keeps (him) in (his) heart and utters with (his) mouth: Hari, Hari!
That man does not vacillate in any way neither here nor there.
(4). Nānak says: who is imbued with love to the name:
With him the rosary of Hari goes (to the other world).

[1] ਅਲੋਇਆ = आलोकित, seen, beheld.

XX. LXXI. CXXXVIII.

(1). (Who) becomes his, whose everything is:
That man no contamination whatever enters.

Pause.

The servant of Hari is always emancipated.
Whatever he does, that is good; the practice of the slave of the pious people is exceedingly pure.
(2). Who, having forsaken all, has come to the asylum of Hari:
How should the Māyā enter that man?
(3). In whose mind the treasure of the name is:
He has no care not even in a dream.
(4). Nānak says: (by whom) the true Guru is obtained:
All (his) error and infatuation are extinguished.

XXI. LXXII. CXXXIX.

(1). When my Lord has become kindly disposed (to me):
Then, say, how should pain and error (be) near (me)?

Pause.

Having heard, having heard the report about thee I live.
Save me, who am destitute of virtues!
(2). Pain is effaced, care is forgotten.
Fruit is obtained by muttering the mantra of the true Guru.
(3). He is true, he is true.
Remembering and remembering string and keep (him) in thy bosom!
(4). Nānak says: what work has he (to do),
In whose mind the name of Hari dwells?

XXII. LXXIII. CXL.

(1). By lust, wrath and egotism (people) are ruined.
By remembering Hari the people of Hari are set free.

Pause.

Those are drunk in the intoxication of the Māyā.
The devotees are waking and given to the remembrance of Hari.
(2). By reason of spiritual blindness and error one is made to wander about in many wombs.
The devotee is stationary, (by whom) the feet of Hari are meditated on.
(3). (I am) shutting up the blind well (of) my house.
The saints are emancipated, who comprehend, (that) Hari is near (them).
(4). Nānak says: who is in the asylum of the Lord:
He gets here happiness and in the other world salvation.

XXIII. LXXIV. CXLI.

(1). Thou art my wave, I am thy fish.
Thou art my Lord, I am at thy gate.

Pause.

Thou art my creator, I am thy servant.
I have seized (thy) asylum, O Lord, weighty with excellences!

(2). Thou art my life, thou (art) my support.
Having seen thee the lotus (of my heart) opens.
(3). Thou art my salvation and honour, my ground for assurance.
Thou art powerful, I am saved by thee.
(4). May I daily mutter the name, the depository of (all) excellences!
This prayer Nānak (offers) to the Lord!

XXIV. LXXV. CXLII.

(1). He who is weeping, practises falsehood.
Another, (though) laughing, is grieving.

Pause.

Some one dies, in the house of another (there is) singing.
Some one weeps, another laughing and laughing is conducting the bride.[1]
(2). From childhood (one) has grown old.
Having arrived (at old age) he is not emancipated and repents again.
(3). The world passes on in the three qualities.
Again and again there is descent to hell (and ascent to) heaven.
(4). Nānak says: who is attached (to) the name:
His life is fruitful and accepted.

XXV. LXXVI. CXLIII.

(1). (I) kept on sleeping (and) the news of the Lord was not known (by me).
(When) it became morning, (I) repented again.

Pause.

By love to the beloved one I have naturally joy in my mind, O dear!
I am longing to meet with the Lord, why should I therefore be slothful, O dear?
(2). Nectar was brought forth into (my) hand.
(I) slipt and it was thrown on the ground.
(3). With desire, spiritual blindness and egotism (I am) laden.
It is not the fault of the Lord, the creator.
(4). In the society of the pious error and darkness are effaced.
O Nānak, I am united by the creator (with himself).

XXVI. LXXVII. CXLIV.

(1). (I am) longing after the lotus-foot, O beloved!
The servants of Yama have fled helpless (away from me).

Pause.

It is thy mercy, (that) thou comest into (my) thought.
By remembering the name all diseases are destroyed.
(2). Thou givest much pain to others.
(But) thy people (pain) cannot reach.

[1] ਪਾਂਢਣ *s.m.* the person who conducts the bride from or to the house of her father or father-in-law; a paronymph.

(3). A thirst after thy sight has sprung up in (my) mind.
Tranquillity, joy (and) love dwell (in me).
(4). May the prayer of Nānak be heard!
May only the name be given into my heart!

XXVII. LXXVIII. CXLV.

(1). (My) mind is satiated, (my) troubles are effaced.
(My) own Lord became merciful (to me).

Pause.

By the favour of the saints goodness was done (to me).
In whose house everything is, that all-filling, fearless Lord was met with.
(2). The name was established (in me) (by) the merciful saint.
(My) very dreadful hunger was put out.
(3). By my own Lord the gift was given (to me).
(My) burning heat was quenched, tranquillity was produced in (my) mind.
(4). (My) searching about ceased, (my) mind entered tranquillity.
Nānak obtained the treasury of the name.

XXVIII. LXXIX. CXLVI.

(1). Who are on intimate terms with the Lord:
They remain fully satiated with food.

Pause.

The devotees of the Lord have not little.
They are eating, spending and extravagant in giving.
(2). Whose master the unattainable Lord is:
Say, how much can people do (against him)?
(3). In whose service the eighteen supernatural powers are:
By his moment's glance (on one) they cling to (one's) feet.
(4). On whom thou bestowest mercy, O my Lord!
He has no want, says Nānak.

XXIX. LXXX. CXLVII.

(1). When I meditate on my own true Guru:
Then I obtain great comfort in my mind.

Pause.

Calculation is effaced, doubt is extinct.
The people, who are attached to the name, become saints.[1]
(2). When my own Lord is in my thoughts:
Then fear is effaced, O my friend!
(3). When I seize thy protection, O Lord:
Then my desire is fulfilled.
(4). Having seen thy proceedings my mind was comforted.
Nānak, (thy) slave, trusts in thee.

[1] ਭਗਵੰਤਾ, a devotee, saint.

XXX. LXXXI. CXLVIII.

(1). Day by day the mouse gnaws the rope,
Whilst falling into the well (man) eats sweetmeats.

Pause.

In considering and reflecting the night is passed.
Whilst thinking of the many pleasures of the Māyā the bow-holder (Vishṇu) is never remembered.
(2). (Considering) the shade of a tree immovable he built a house.
Death, throwing[1] (over him) the noose of the Māyā, made ready the arrow.
(3). The shore of sand, the surface (of which) the waves inundate:
That place the fool laid hold of, considering it immovable.
(4). In the society of the pious Hari the king is muttered (by me).
Nānak lives singing the excellences of Hari.

XXXI. LXXXII. CXLIX.

(1). In his society thou (fem.) art sporting.
In his society we are in union with thee.
In his society every one desires thee.
Without him nobody looks (at thee).

Pause.

That loving one where is he contained?
Without him thou art distressed, O dear!
(2). In his society thou art the mistress in the house.
In his society thou wilt become manifest.
In his society thou art kept blooming.
Without him thou art given up to wretchedness.
(3). In his society thou hast honour and greatness.
In his society the world is thy relative.
In his society all thy arrangement is made.
Without him thou wilt become dust.
(4). That loving one neither dies nor goes.
Bound by (his) order (man) does works.
Having joined he separates and establishes (again), (says) Nānak.
He himself knows his own power.

XXXII. LXXXIII. CL.

(1). Neither is he dying nor are we afraid.
Neither is he destroyed nor are we distressed.
Neither is he poor nor are we hungry.
Neither has he pain nor have we pain.

Pause.

There is no other who is killing.
He is our life, (who) is giving life (to us).
(2). Neither is a fetter on him nor are we bound.
Neither has he toils nor have we toils.

[1] ਕੈ here = ਕਰਿ; the words must thus be constructed, if they are to give any sense: ਕਾਲ ਨੇ ਸਕਤਿ ਕੀ ਫਾਸਿ ਕਰਿ ਸਰੁ ਸਾਧਿਆ.

Neither has he filth nor have we filth.
(When) he has joy, then we have always pastime.
(3). Neither is in him reflection nor have we reflection.
Neither is on him (any) daubing nor is on us (any) smearing.
Neither has he hunger nor have we thirst.
When he is pure, then we are asking (for it).
(4). We are nothing, that one alone is (all).
Before and after that One alone is.
Nānak (says): by the Guru the waves of error are put out.
We and he, having met, have become of one colour.

XXXIII. LXXXIV. CLI.

(1). In many ways service is rendered (by me).
Soul, life and property are offered up (to the Guru).
(I fetch) water, I swing the fan (to him), giving up conceit.
Many times I become a sacrifice (to him).

Pause.

She is a happy married woman, who is pleasing to the Lord.
With her I will meet, O my mother!
(2). (I am) the water-carrier of his lowest bond-maids.
(I am) their dust, (my) soul dwells with (them).
(If) the lot (be written) on my forehead, then I obtain (their) society.
The Lord mingles with his own colour.
(3). Muttering, austerity and all religious observances I render (to him).
Works and all burnt offerings I make (to him).
Giving up pride and spiritual ignorance I become (their) dust.
In their society I see the Lord (with my) eyes.
(4). Every moment I adore him.
Day and night I practise this service.
Gōpāl Gōvind became merciful (to me).
In the society of the pious he is pardoning, (says) Nānak.

XXXIV. LXXXV. CLII.

(1). By love to the Lord happiness is always obtained.
By love to the Lord no pain is incurred.
Love to the Lord clears away the filth of egotism.
By love to the Lord one becomes always pure.

Pause.

Hear, O friend, such love and affection
Is the support of (every) life and everybody.
(2). By love to the Lord all treasures are obtained.
By love to the Lord the spotless name (dwells) in the heart.
By love to the Lord (one is) always lustrous.
By love to the Lord all care is effaced.
(3). By love to the Lord (one) crosses this water of existence.
By love to the Lord (one) is not afraid of Yama.

The love of the Lord saves all.
The love of the Lord goes with (one to the other world).
(4). By oneself no one meets (with him), he goes astray.
To whom he is merciful, him he joins to the society of the pious.
Nānak says: (I am) a sacrifice to thee.
In the asylum of the saints I am saved by thee, O Lord!

XXXV. LXXXVI. CLIII.

(1). Having become a king he exercises dominion.
Practising oppression wealth is brought on himself.
Accumulating and accumulating a bag (of money) is made (by him).
(But) the Lord taking it away from him gave it to another.

Pause.

A raw jug, in (which) there is water,
Being proud of that very (water) tumbles down.
(2). He became fearless, he became free from all restraint.
The creator, (who is) with (him), did not come into (his) mind.
Armies were assembled, preparation (for war) was made.
(When) the breath left (him), he became ashes.
(3). High (were) his mansions and palaces and (many) his queens.
Heart-pleasing elephants and horses were collected (by him).
Great (was) the retinue of (his) sons and daughters.
By spiritual blindness he was consumed and the blind one died.
(4). By whom it is produced, by him it is destroyed.
Pleasures and enjoyments are like a dream.
He is emancipated, he has dominion and wealth,
To whom the Lord is merciful, (says) the slave Nānak.

XXXVI. LXXXVII. CLIV.

(1). (When) with this one (*i.e.* the Māyā) close friendship is made:
It increases still more, when union is brought about.
When she has clung to (one's) neck, she no more lets go.
Who clings to the feet of the true Guru, he is set free.

Pause.

She, who is fascinating the world, we have discarded.
He, who is without qualities, was obtained and we congratulated (ourselves).
(2). Such a beautiful one fascinates the mind.
On the road, pass, house and in every wood she looks out.
To mind and body she clings becoming sweet (to them).
By the favour of the Guru I saw, that she is false.
(3). Her forerunners are great cheats.
She leaves neither father nor mother.
Her own associates are bound by her.
By the favour of the Guru I overcame all.
(4). Now joy has sprung up in my mind.
Fear has ceased, all frauds are broken.

Nānak says: when the true Guru was obtained (by me):
My whole house was set up comfortably.

XXXVII. LXXXVIII. CLV.

(1). (All) the eight watches they consider (him as being) near (them).
The doing of the Lord is sweet to them.
The One name is the support of the saints.
They are always the ashes of the feet of all.

Pause.

Hear the manner of life of the saints, O brother!
Their greatness cannot be told.
(2). Whose occupation is the name alone:
(Their) rest is the praising of the joyful (Supreme).
To whom friend and enemy are the same:
(They) do not know any other besides their own Lord.
(3). Crores and crores of sins they are cutting off.
They are removing pain and bestowing life.
They are heroes and champions, true to their promise.
The helpless Lakshmī (= Māyā) is deceived by the saints.
(4). Their society desire the Suras and Dēvas,
(Whose) sight is efficacious, whose service is fruitful.
Having joined the hands Nānak makes (this) supplication:
"May to me the service of the saints be given by the depository of (all) excellences!"

XXXVIII. LXXXIX. CLVI.

(1). All comforts (are contained) in muttering the One name.
All duties (are done) by singing the excellences of Hari.
Very pure is the society of the pious.
With whom they fall in, in him love to the Lord springs up.

Pause.

By the favour of the Guru he obtains joy.
In whose mind light is produced by remembering (Hari), the greatness of his salvation cannot be told.
(2). Vows, religious observances, ablutions and worship (are performed) by him,
The Vēdas, Purāṇas and the Smriti are heard by him,
Whose place is the very pure and spotless
Society of the saints, where the name of Hari, Hari is.
(3). That man is manifest in all the world,
(Who is) the dust of the feet of them, who are purifying the sinners.
With whom Hari, Hari the king has met:
The greatness of his salvation cannot be told.
(4). Joining (my) hands I will meditate the eight watches,
(That) I may obtain the sight of those pious ones.
Join me, the poor one, (with them)!
Nānak has come and fallen on (thy) asylum.

XXXIX. XC. CLVII.

(1). (Who is) bathing the eight watches in (holy) water:
To this wise one fruition always accrues.
He does not give up any one to no purpose.
Again and again we will cling to his feet!

Pause.

The Shāligrām is our object of service.
Worship, adoration and obeisance (we render to) the god.
(2). Whose bell is heard in the four corners (of the earth);
Whose dwelling is always in paradise;
Whose fly-flapper is swinging above all:
His incense is always rising.
(3). Whose covered box is in every creature, O dear!
(Who) is unintermittingly with all pious people.
Ārtī and praise (is offered to this) ever rejoicing one.
(His) greatness is beautiful and always endless.
(4). To whom it is allotted, he will obtain it.
That one has come to the asylum of the feet of the saints.
Into (his) hand has come the Shāligrām of Hari.
Nānak says: by the Guru (this) gift is given (to him).

XL. XCI. CLVIII.

Pančpadē.

(1). On which road the female water-carrier is robbed:
That road is far from the saints.

Pause.

By the true, perfect Guru the true (road) is told (them).
In the lane[1] of thy name they are emancipated, the road of Yama remains far (from them).
(2). On which landing-place (there is) the greediness of the collector of customs:
That road remains far from (thy) people.
(3). In which whirlpool[2] many crowded caravāns are:
(There) the pious are with the Supreme Brahm.
(4). The recording angels are writing the account of all.
(But) on the devotees they do not cast a glance.
(5). Nānak says: who has the true, perfect Guru:
In his (house) the musical instruments sound without being beaten.

XLI. XCII. CLIX.

(1). In the society of the saints the name is taught,
(Which) is fulfilling all desires and wishes.
Thirst is quenched, by the praise of Hari (I am) satiated.
Continually muttering the bow-holder I live.

Pause.

I have fallen on the asylum of the cause of causes.
By the favour of the Guru I obtained my innate house, darkness was effaced, the moon rose.

[1] ਘੀਘੀ *s.f.* a lane (= गली).
[2] ਆਵਟਾ, *s.m.* whirlpool (= Sansk. आवर्त्त).

(2). With rubies and gems the store-rooms are filled.
There is no deficiency by muttering the Formless one.
If any man drink the nectar-word (of the Guru):
He obtains the highest salvation, (says) Nānak.

ĀSĀ; GHAR VII.; MAHALĀ V.

XLII. XCIII. CLX.

Dupadā.

(1). (If) I always meditate on the name of Hari in my heart:
I make cross all my companions and associates.

Pause.

The Guru, (who) is always with me:
Him I remember continually (and) keep in my mind.
(2). Thy doing is sweet to me.
Nānak asks for the name of Hari, the greatest boon.

XLIII. XCIV. CLXI.

(1). In the society of the pious the world is saved.
The name of Hari is support to the mind.

Pause.

The lotus-foot of the beloved Gur-dēv
The saints worship, (being) dear to Hari by (their) love (to the Guru).
(2). On whose forehead the lot is written:
His good fortune is firm, says Nānak.

XLIV. XCV. CLXII.

(1). (To me) the order of the beloved is sweet.
By (my) husband the rival wife of the house is dismissed.
By the beloved the favoured wife is adorned.
The heat of my mind is taken away.

Pause.

Goodness accrues (to her, by whom) the word of the beloved is obeyed.
The happiness and tranquillity of this house are known.
(2). I am the bond-maid, the servant of the beloved.
He is imperishable, unattainable, boundless.
I take the fan and swing it to the beloved.
The five enemies, the mischief-makers, run away.
(3). I am not of (noble) family nor am I beautiful.
What do I know, how I became pleasing to my beloved?
I, the destitute, poor and humble one,
Was taken by the beloved and made his queen.
(4). When my beloved sweetheart became intimate (with me):
(I obtained) happiness and tranquillity, blessed is my wifehood.
Nānak says: he is fulfilling my desire.
By the true Guru (I am) united (with) the Lord, the depository of (all) excellences.

XLV. XCVI. CLXIII.

(1). On her forehead is the triad (=the three qualities), her look is cruel.
She speaks harshly, she is of rude tongue.
She is always hungry, the beloved one she believes to be far off.

Pause.

One woman of this kind has been produced by Rām.
By her the whole world is devoured, we are preserved by the Guru, O my brother!
(2). Practising deceit the whole world is overpowered (by her).
Brahmā, Vishṇu and Mahādēv are deluded (by her).
The disciples, who cling to the name, are purified (from her).
(3). Practising repeatedly vows and religious observances they became tired.
They wander about to every shore and holy watering place of the earth.
Those are saved, who are in the asylum of the true Guru.
(4). By the infatuation of the Māyā the whole world is bound.
The foolish man is consumed by egotism.
We are preserved by the Guru seizing (our) arm, (says) Nānak.

XLVI. XCVII. CLXIV.

(1). All pains (are incurred) when the Lord is forgotten.
Here and there (such a) man is of no use.

Pause.

The saints are satiated by meditating on Hari, Hari.
Mercifully they are applied to thy own name; (they have) all comforts, (on whom) is thy pleasure, O Lord!
(2). Who considers him far away, who is with him:
That man is dying, being continually grieved.
(3). Who does not think of him, by whom everything is given:
His days and nights pass in great bitterness.
(4). Nānak says: who remembers the One Lord:
He obtains salvation in the shelter of the perfect Guru.

XLVII. XCVIII. CLXV.

(1). Who is muttering the name, all his mind and body is flourishing.
All his sins and faults are taken away.

Pause.

That day is good, O my brother!
(In which) singing the excellences of Hari emancipation is obtained.
(2). (By whom) the feet of the pious are worshipped:
(His) troubles are effaced and enmity from (his) mind.
(3). Having met with the perfect Guru the quarrel is stopped.
All the five enemies are brought into subjection.
(4). In whose mind the name of Hari dwells:
For him Nānak is a sacrifice.

XLVIII. XCIX. CLXVI.

(1). Sing thou, O singer!
(Him who is) the support of the life of soul and body!
By whose service thou obtainest all comforts.
Do not go again to any other!

Pause.

The ever-rejoicing, happy Lord, the depository of (all) excellences, should continually be muttered!
(I am) a sacrifice to that beloved saint, by whose favour the Lord is made to dwell in (my) mind.
(2). Whose gift is not exhausted;
Who is quite naturally contained (in) all;
Whose donation no one effaces:
That True one should be made to dwell in the mind!
(3). In whose house all things are fully contained:
The servants of (that) Lord are not grieving from pain.
(By whom) his asylum is laid hold of, he obtains the fearless state (= emancipation).
At every breath that depository of excellences should be sung!
(4). He is not far, wherever one may go.
If he bestows a favourable look, then Hari, Hari is obtained.
I make supplication to the perfect Guru.
Nānak asks for the wealth and capital of Hari.

XLIX. C. CLXVII.

(1). First the pain of the body was effaced.
(Then) happiness was imparted to (my) whole mind.
In mercy the Guru gave (me) the name.
I sacrifice myself for that true Guru.

Pause.

I obtained the perfect Guru, O my brother!
Disease, grief and all pain were destroyed in the asylum of the true Guru.
(2). The feet of the Guru I made dwell in (my) heart.
All the fruits were obtained, which my mind was desiring.
The fire (in me) was quenched, all became tranquillity.
Out of mercy the Guru bestowed (this) gift (on me).
(3). To the placeless one the Guru gave a place.
To the honourless one the Guru gave honour.
Cutting (my) bonds he made (me) his servant and protected (me).
(My) tongue tasted (his) nectar-speech.
(4). By a great lot the feet of the Guru were worshipped.
Forsaking all, the asylum of the Lord was obtained.
To whom the Guru has become kind, (says) Nānak:
That man is always exalted.

L. CI. CLXVIII.

(1). The true Guru was sent by the True one.
A son[1] was produced by copulation.

[1] ਚਿਰੁਜੀਵਨੁ, a term for a son. These verses refer apparently to Bābā Nānak.

He came and dwelt in the womb.
In the heart of the mother (there was) much joy.

Pause.

A son was conceived, a devotee of Gōvind.
What was written by (the Supreme) himself, became manifest amongst all.
(2). By (his) order the child was born after ten months.
Grief was effaced, great joy was produced.
The female friends sing the word of the Guru (in) joy.
(Which) pleases to the mind of the true Lord.
(3). The progeny increased, many generations went on.
The lustre of religion was established by Hari.
What is desired by the heart, is given by the true Guru.
People became free from anxiety, the One was devoutly meditated upon.
(4). As a child puts much trust in his father:
(So) I speak,[1] being caused to speak, according to the pleasure of the Guru.
(His) word is not hidden nor concealed.
Guru Nānak is pleased, (by him) it is bestowed (on me).

LI. CII. CLXIX.

(1). The Guru gave (me) his hand (and) kept (me).
The glory of (his) servant became (thus) manifest.

Pause.

The Guru, Guru I mutter, the Guru, Guru I meditate upon.
The supplication of (my) heart is offered to the Guru.
(2). (We) have fallen on the asylum of the true Gur-dēv.
The service of (his) servant became (thus) accomplished.
(3). Soul, body, youth (and) life he preserves.
Nānak says: (I am) a sacrifice to the Guru!

ĀSĀ; GHAR VIII.; KĀFĪ; MAHALĀ V.

Ōm! by the favour of the true Guru!

I. CIII. CLXX.

(1). I am the bought slave of my true Lord.
Soul and body, all is his, everything is thine.

Pause.

The honour of the honourless one art thou, O Lord, I trust in thee!
Another support, without that of the True one, I consider as unsolid.
(2). Thy order is boundless, no one can reach (its) end.
With whom the perfect Guru falls in, he walks according to (thy) pleasure.
(3). Cleverness and cunning are of no use whatever.
What the pleased Lord gives, that happiness is obtained.

[1] ਬੋਲੈ must here be taken as 1st Pers. Sing.

(4). If Lakhs of works be practised, no bond is (thereby) effected (on him),

(By whom) the name is made his support (and by whom) other business is given up, (says) humble Nānak.

II. CIV. CLXXI.

(1). Every pleasure was sought (by me), none is so great as that of Hari.
From the Guru being pleased that true Lord is obtained.

Pause.

I am continually a sacrifice to my own Guru.
May this gift be given (to me), that I do not forget a moment (or) second the name!
(2). He is a true wealthy man, in whose heart the wealth of Hari is.
He escapes from the great net (of the Māyā), in whom the word of the Guru (dwells) incessantly.
(3). How shall I tell the greatness of the Guru? the discrimination of the Guru is the pond of truth.
He is from the beginning, from the beginning of the Yugas, through all the Yugas, the perfect Lord.
(4). The name I meditate upon continually, in Hari, Hari (my) mind delights.
(My) soul, life and property are with the Guru, (says) Nānak.

III. CV. CLXXII.

(1). (If) the incomprehensible, boundless Lord dwells a little in (my) mind:
All my pain, trouble and disease, O mother, are destroyed.

Pause.

I become a sacrifice to my own Lord.
In my mind and body great joy is produced by muttering (him).
(2). For a moment I heard a word about that true Lord.
Comforts upon comforts I obtained, O mother, (which) I cannot estimate.
(3). (My) eyes (were) looking (at him), having seen (him) I became enamoured (of him).
I, the vicious one, was applied by himself to the hem of his garment.
(4). From the Vēda, the book (Qur'ān), from the whole world he is conspicuous.[1]
The King of Nānak is openly seen.

IV. CVI. CLXXIII.

(1). Lakhs of devotees adore (thee) muttering: O dear, O dear one!
By what contrivance shall I, the vicious, sensual one, obtain (thee)?

Pause.

I rely on thee, O Gōvind, Gōpāl, O merciful Lord!
Thou art the Lord of all, thine is all the creation!
(2). (Thou art) always a companion, the saints behold (thee) always in (their) presence.
Those who are destitute of the name die in grief.
(3). (To whom) the lowest service is pleasing, their wandering about (= transmigration) is effaced.
What is the condition of them, by whom the name is forgotten?
(4). As cattle, that are breaking into fields, so is the whole world.
Nānak (says): O Lord, cut thou thyself (my) bonds and unite (me with thee)!

[1] ਬਾਹਰਾ is here better derived from the Arab.-Hindūst. بَاهِر, *manifest, conspicuous,* which suits well the context, whereas ਬਾਹਰਾ in the sense of: "separate," "distinct from," is out of place here.

V. CVII. CLXXIV.

(1). Having forgotten all things meditate (on) the One!
Drop false conceit, offer up (thy) mind and body!

Pause.

Praise thou the eight watches the creator!
I live by thy gifts, bestow mercy on me!
(2). Do that work, by which (thy) face (will become) bright!
He clings to the True one, to whom thou givest it, O God!
(3). Erect that house, which is not at all tumbling down!
Make the One dwell in thy mind, who never dies!
(4). To them Rām is dear, who are pleasing to the Lord.
By the favour of the Guru the Ineffable one is praised by Nānak.

VI. CVIII. CLXXV.

(1). What sort of men are those, who do not forget the name?
They by no means admit (any) difference,[1] they are like the Lord.

Pause.

(His) mind and body become happy, (who) has met with thee.
Happiness is obtained by the favour of (thy) people, all pain is effaced.
(2). As many people as (are in) the world their dust, they are saved.
In whose mind he himself dwells, they are perfect devotees.
(3). Whom he himself acknowledges, he is acknowledged.
The approved man is manifest and known in all places.
(4). Day and night I adore and remember (thee) at every breath.
Fulfil the desire of Nānak, O true king!

VII. CIX. CLXXVI.

(1). That Lord of ours is fully contained in every place.
There is One Lord, (on whose) head is an umbrella, there is none other.

Pause.

As it pleases thee, so keep (me), O (my) preserver!
Without thee none other is beheld (with) my sight.
(2). The Lord himself cherishes, (who is) pervading[2] everybody.
In whose mind he dwells himself, by him he is not forgotten.
(3). Whatever he does, that is his own pleasure.
In every Yuga he is known as the assistant of (his) devotees.
(4). By muttering continually the name of Hari one is never grieved.
Nānak is longing after (his) sight; may (his) desire be fulfilled!

VIII. CX. CLXXVII.

(1). What sleepest thou forgetting the name, O careless and inattentive one!
How many go speedily away on this river (of life)!

[1] Any difference, *i.e.* between themselves and the Supreme.

[2] ਸਾਰੀਐ = ਸਾਰੀ, Arab.-Hind. سَارِي, pervading, *ai* being a meaningless alliteration.

Pause.

Ascending the boat of the feet of Hari thou wilt cross, O mind!
Sing the eight watches (his) excellences in the society of the pious!
(2). Thou enjoyest many enjoyments, (but) without the name (they are) empty.
Without worship of Hari thou diest repeatedly and weepest.
(3). Clothes (and) food (thou art enjoying), perfumes thou art powdering and rubbing on (thy) body.
Without remembering (Hari) (thy) body (becomes) ashes, at last (thou) must go.
(4). Some rare one sees, that the world is very troublesome.
He is emancipated in the asylum of Hari, (for whom this) destiny is written, (says) Nānak.

IX. CXI. CLXXVIII.

(1). No one (goes) with any one, why should one be proud?
(Whose) support the One name is, he crosses the water of existence.

Pause.

I, the poor one, rely on thee, the True one, O my true, perfect Guru!
Seeing thy sight my mind becomes tranquil.
(2). Dominion and wealth are (but) trouble, account them as useless!
The praise of Hari is (true) support, this is imperishable wealth.
(3). As many as are the pleasures of the Māyā, so many are the regrets.
The name, the depository of happiness, is sung by the disciple.
(4). The true depository of (all) excellences art thou, O deep and profound Lord!
Nānak (entertains) in his heart hope and reliance on the Lord.

X. CXII. CLXXIX.

(1). By whose remembrance pain passes away and tranquillity and happiness are obtained:
(That) Hari should be day and night meditated upon with joined hands.

Pause.

The Lord of Nānak is he, whose every one is.
In all that True one is fully contained.
(2). Who inside and outside is a companion (with thee) through divine knowledge:
Adore him, O mind, all thy disease will pass away!
(3). The boundless preserver preserves in the midst of fire.
The name of Hari is coolness, by remembering (it) the heat goes off.
(4). He has much happiness, tranquillity and joy, (who is) the dust of (his) people, (says) Nānak.
All (his) affairs are accomplished, (with whom) the perfect Guru has met.

XI. CXIII. CLXXX.

(1). Gōvind, the depository of (all) excellences, is known by the disciple.
(If) he become merciful and kind, the pleasure of Hari is enjoyed.

Pause.

Come, let us join the saints, (by whom) the story about Hari is told!
Let us daily remember the name and let us not be ashamed of (his) people!
(2). By continually mutteriug the name I live, great joy is produced (thereby).
Spiritual delusion is false, the world is false and perishable.
(3). Some rare one directs his love to the lotus-foot (of Hari).
Blessed and charming is the face (of him), by whom Hari is meditated upon.

(4). Regeneration and death, the pain of death is effaced by remembering (the name).
Nānak (has) that happiness, which is pleasing to the Lord.

XII. CXIV. CLXXXI.

(1). Come, O friend, having met we will enjoy all pleasures!
Let us mutter the nectar-name of Hari, Hari! having met let us remove (our) sins!

Pause.

On account of reflection on the truth and the holy people an alarming danger does not approach.
All the thieves are destroyed, the disciples wake.
(2). Wisdom and humility take as viaticum, burn the poison of egotism!
True is the shop, perfect the traffic, trade in the wares of the names!
(3). By whom soul, body and property are offered up, they are men of credit.
Who please their own Lord, they are always amusing themselves.
(4). Who are drinking the liquor of folly, they are infected with mad poison.
Who are fond of the elixir of Rām, they are given to a true intoxicating drug, (says) Nānak.

XIII. CXV. CLXXXII.

(1). Effort is made (when) caused to be made, work is set agoing.
By muttering continually the name (I) live, by the Guru the mantra is made fast (in me).

Pause.

Let us fall at the feet of the true Guru, by whom error is destroyed!
By the Lord in his own mercy truth is established.
(2). Seizing (our) hands we were made his own, by the order and pleasure of the True one.
The gift, that was given by the Lord, is full of greatness.
(3). Continually (his) excellences are sung (by me) muttering the name of the enemy of Mura.
(My) vow is accomplished, by the true Guru, the Lord, mercy was bestowed (on me).
(4). The wealth (and) excellences of the name I sing, the perfect Guru gives (me) the profit (of it).
The holy people are retail-dealers, O Nānak, the Lord is an incalculable wholesale merchant.

XIV. CXVI. CLXXXIII.

(1). Whose Lord art thou, O Lord, his lot is great.
He is comfortable and always happy, all his error and fear have passed away.

Pause.

We are the servants of Gōvind, my Lord is profound.
Who is making and causing every arrangement to be made, he is our true Guru.
(2). Who has none other (besides himself), he should be feared.
By service to the Guru (his) palace is reached, the world hard to cross, is crossed.
(3). By thy favourable glance happiness is obtained, a secret treasure in the mind.
To whom thou hast become merciful, that servant is approved of.
(4). Nectar-juice is the praise of Hari, some rare one drinks it.
As wages the One name is obtained, (says) Nānak, by continually muttering it in the heart (one) lives.

XV. CXVII. CLXXXIV.

(1). That Lord is higher than all, whose bond-maid I am.
All is called his, (be it) little (or) much.

Pause.

My life and wealth are acknowledged as the Lord's (property).
By whose name (I become) bright, his bond-maid I am accounted.
(2). (Thou art) without concern and filled with joy, (thy) name is a ruby and diamond.
She is always filled and satiated with happiness, whose Lord thou art.
(3). O friend and companion, hold fast the thought of fellowship (with the saints)!
Serve the pious with love, then thou wilt obtain the treasures of Hari.
(4). (All are saying): (we are) the servants of the Lord, all are saying: he is mine.
Whom he adorns, O Nānak, she dwells in happiness.

XVI. CXVIII. CLXXXV.

(1). Learn, O dear, this conduct, that thou mayst become the slave of the saints!
The highest virtue of all virtues is: do not behold thy husband (as being) far away, O dear!

Pause.

Dye this thy own mind, O beautiful one, in the name of Hari (as) in Majīṭh!
Giving up cleverness and cunning consider Gōpāl (as being) with (thee), O dear!
(2). Make this (thy) ornament, that what the husband says, be agreed to.
Eat this betel-nut, that love to another be forgotten.
(3). Having made the word of the Guru thy lamp spread out this bed of truth, O dear!
Remain with joined hands the eight watches, then Hari the king meets (with thee), O dear!
(4). She has wisdom and all ornaments, she is of boundless beauty, O dear!
She is a happy married wife, O Nānak, who is pleasing to the creator, O dear!

XVII. CXIX. CLXXXVI.

(1). So long there is falling and moving from side to side, as long as the errors of the mind (remain).
(Our) errors are cut off by our own Guru and we obtained rest.

Pause.

Those are eating poison,[1] culpable and driven away from the Guru.
We have now become rid of them and those have become rid of us.
(2). From the time, that (one) is thinking: "(this is) mine, (this) thine," he is bound.
(When) by the Guru (this) ignorance is cut off, then the snares are loosened.
(3). As long as (one) is not comprehending the order (of Hari), so long he is pained.
When having met with the Guru he becomes acquainted with the order, then he is happy.
(4). No one is an enemy, no one blamable and wicked.
(Who) is employed in the service of the Guru, (he is) a servant of the Lord, (says) Nānak.

XVIII. CXX. CLXXXVII.

(1). Happiness, tranquillity, great joy are the singing and praising of Hari.
The demons[2] are removed, the true Guru gives his own name.

[1] ਬਿਖਾਰੀ here perhaps better translated by: *eating poison* (Sansk. विषादिन्).

[2] ਗਰਹ (ग्रह), a kind of demons, who exercise a bad influence on man; an imp.

Pause.

I am a sacrifice to my own Guru, I am always a sacrifice (to him).

I devote myself for the Guru, meeting with whom (I have) true pleasure.

(2). Ill omens stick to him, into whose mind (Hari) does not come.

Him Yama does not approach, who is pleasing to the Lord Hari.

(3). As many religious merits, alms, mutterings and austerities (there may be), above all is the name.

Who mutters Hari, Hari (with) his tongue, his works are accomplished.

(4). All fear is extinct, infatuation is gone, no other (besides Hari) is seen.

O Nānak, (who) are preserved by the Supreme Brahm, (them) no pain again befalls.

ĀSĀ; GHAR IX.; MAHALĀ V.

Ōm! By the favour of the true Guru!

I. CXXI. CLXXXVIII.

(1). (If) I continually keep (him) in mind, I obtain all comforts; shall I please (him) further on or shall I not please (him)?

The One is bountiful to all, shall I as a beggar go to another one?

Pause.

(If) I beg (from) another, I put (him) to shame.

The One Lord is king of kings, whom shall I compare (with him)?

(2). (Though) I rise and sit down, yet I cannot remain, I seek continually (his) sight.

Brahmā and the others, Sanaka and the others (viz.): Sanaka, Sanandana, Sanātana and Sanatkumāra, to them the palace (of the Supreme) is hard to reach.

(3). The unattainable one, of unfathomable wisdom, (who is) beyond calculation, I cannot reach.

I aim at the asylum of the true divine male, on the true Guru, the divine male, I meditate.

(4). The Lord became kind (and) merciful (to me), (my) bond (and) neck-halter were cut (by him).

Nānak says: when the society of the pious is obtained (by me), I am no more subject to birth.

II. CXXII. CLXXXIX.

(1). Inside I sing, outside I sing, waking early I sing.

A viaticum to go with (to the other world) is given to him, who is occupied with the name of Gōvind.

Pause.

Other (things) I forget, I forget.

The gift of the name is given (to me) by the perfect Guru, this (name) is my support.

(2). In pain I sing, in pleasure also I sing, on the way and road I remember (it).

The name was firmly fixed by the Guru in (my) mind, my thirst was quenched.

(3). By day I sing, by night also I sing, at every breath I sing (with my) tongue.

In the society of the pious faith springs up, whilst living and dying Hari is with (me).

(4). Give this gift to humble Nānak, O Lord, that I may get the dust of the saints and keep it in (my) breast!

(That with my) ears (I may hear) the story (about thee), (with my) eyes behold (thy) sight, (that I may put my) forehead (to) the feet of the Guru!

ĀSĀ; GHAR X.; MAHALĀ V.

Ōm! by the favour of the true Guru!

I. CXXIII. CXC.

(1). Whom thou considerest abiding, he is a guest of twenty (days).

Son, wife, house, all furniture, all friends are false.

Pause.

O my mind! why criest thou: alas! alas!

Look upon (all these) as on the city of Harićandaurī![1] take up the worshipping of Rām alone, (this is) advantage.

(2). As clothes put on the body go to pieces (after) two, four days.

How much soever it may be run upon a wall, at last its end comes.

(3). As a layer of rock-salt, (which is) put (into) a pot of water, melts:

(So), when the order of the Supreme Brahm will come, they will rise and go in forty-eight minutes (or) in a second.

(4). O mind, by destiny thou goest, by destiny thou sittest down, by destiny thou art taking breath.

Praising always Hari, (says) Nānak, thou art saved in the protection of the feet of the true Guru.

II. CXXIV. CXCI.

(1). The incomplete thing became complete, the wicked enemies (became) friends.

In darkness the gem became manifest, the sullied intelligence (became) clean.

Pause.

When the mercy of Gōvind was bestowed:

Happiness and prosperity, the fruits of the name of Hari, were obtained, (by me) the true Guru is met with.

(2). I, the poor one, whom nobody was knowing, am (now) manifest in the whole world.

I, who was not allowed to sit with any one, (my) feet now all worship.

(3). I, who was going about and seeking for cowries,[2] the whole thirst of (my) mind was quenched.

I, who was not hearing one word, got coolness in the society of the pious.

(4). Who will with one tongue describe (his) qualities? (they are) unattainable, unattainable, unattainable.

Make (me) the lowest of (thy) slaves! humble Nānak is in the asylum of Hari.

III. CXXV. CXCII.

(1). O fool, for (thy) profit thou art very slow, to (thy) loss thou runnest with haste.

The cheap goods thou dost not take, being bound by demerits (thou becomest) dust.

Pause.

O true Guru, my longing is after thee!

Thy name is: purifier of the sinners; O Supreme Brahm, this is my refuge.

[1] हरिश्चन्द्र, the son of Triśanku, said to be elevated to Svarga with his subjects for his unbounded liberality. Being seduced by Nārada to boast of his merits, he was precipitated again from heaven. His repentance of his pride arrested his downward descent, and he and his train paused in mid-air. The city of Hariśćandra is believed to be at times still visible in the skies, and the word (Gurmukhī ਹਰਿਚੰਦਉਰੀ) has thence received the signification of "a mirage." See Wilson, Vish. Purāna, p. 382, note 9.

[2] ਮਾਰ, properly = the eighth part of a pice.

(2). Thou hearest foul talk and stickest to it, in taking the name thou art lazy.

Thou art very fond of censure, the contrary (thing) is understood (by thee).

(3). Another's property, another's body, another's wife, censure—what is uneatable thou eatest (like) a mad (dog).

For true virtue thou hast no liking, hearing the truth thou art made angry.

(4). The Lord is kind to the poor and merciful, the asylum of the devotees is the name of Hari.

Nānak has come to (thy) asylum, O Lord, preserve thy own honour!

IV. CXXVI. CXCIII.

(1). They cling to falsehood,[1] entertaining affection for the Māyā they are bound.

Whose (their) life is, he does not come into their thought, by egotism they have become blind.

Pause.

O mind, why dost thou not, (becoming) indifferent (to the world), adore (him)?

Thou art dwelling in an unsolid chamber, with all is the disease of poison.

(2). Saying: "mine, mine" day and night is passed, every moment life[2] passes away.

They are attached to (this) false, stinking business (of the world) as to a sweet flavour.

(3). Lust, wrath, covetousness and infatuation—to this enjoyment the senses cling.

By the divine male, the arranger (of all), they are again and again made to wander about in births.[3]

(4). When he, who is breaking the pain of the poor, has become merciful, then having met with the Guru all comforts are obtained.

Nānak says: (if) I meditate (on him) day and night, every difficulty is overcome and removed.

Pause.

(By whom) this divine male, the arranger (of all) is muttered, O brother!

(To him) the destroyer of the pain of the poor (becomes) merciful, the pain of birth and death is done away.

V. CXXVII. CXCIV.

(1). On account of the lust and pleasure of a moment one incurs the pain of a crore of days.

(If one) enjoys pleasures for twenty-four (or) forty-eight minutes, he repents (of it) again and again.

Pause.

O blind one, remember Hari, Hari, the king!

That thy day has come near.

(2). If by mistake thou lookest for one moment at the Akk and Nīm tree, thou wilt die.

As companionship is with a venomous snake, even so is this wife of another.

(3). On account of an enemy (thou art) committing sins, (but) the thing (= the Supreme) remains disregarded (by thee).

(Thou art) a companion with them, (who) leave (thee), (thou art) a friend with (that which) goes to ruin.

(4). The whole world is subject to this law, he is saved, who has the perfect Guru.

Nānak says: the ocean of existence is crossed (by them), whose bodies have been purified.

[1] The Lahore lithographed copy and MS. No. 2484 read: ਮਿਥਿਆ ਸੰਗਿ ਸੰਗਿ ਲਪਟਾਏ, but MS. No. 2483 reads: ਮਿਥਿਆ ਰੰਗਿ ਸੰਗਿ, the literal translation of which is: delighting in falsehood they cling to it.

[2] ਅਰਜਾਪੇ; ਪੇ is a meaningless alliteration.

[3] In ਜਨਮਾਪੇ the ਪੇ is again a meaningless alliteration.

VI. CXXVIII. CXCV.

Dupadē.

(1). What is done secretly, that is seen by thee, the silly, foolish people deny it.
Receiving (the fruit of) their (own) doings they are bound, afterwards they repent again (of it).

Pause.

By my Lord every procedure is known before.
From him who is carried away by doubt, thou concealest thyself, afterwards the creature is listened to.[1]
(2). To whatever they are applied (by thee), to that they stick, what can any man do?
Pardon me, O Supreme Brahm, O Lord, Nānak is always a sacrifice to thee.

VII. CXXIX. CXCVI.

(1). The honour of thy own servant thou thyself keepest, thou thyself makest (him) mutter (thy) name.
Wherever the work of (thy) servant is, there he runs, having risen.

Pause.

To (his) servant he shows, (that) he is near (him).
Whatever the servant says to the Lord, that comes to pass instantly.
(2). I am a sacrifice to that servant, who pleases his Lord.
Having heard the report about him (my) mind became happy, Nānak comes to worship him.

ĀSĀ; GHAR XI.; MAHALĀ V.

Ōm! By the favour of the true Guru!

I. CXXX. CXCVII.

(1). The rope-dancer exhibits disguises in many ways; as he is, such (am I), O dear.
(I) wandered about in many wombs in error and never have entered happiness, O dear!

Pause.

The virtuous saints are my friends, without Hari (I am) continually overcome, O dear!
Having fallen in with the society of the pious the excellences of Hari are sung (by me), regeneration, the (great) thing, is overcome, O dear!
(2). Say, in which wise shall the Māyā with the three qualities, which was made by Brahm, be crossed?
The bottomless, hard whirlpool is crossed by means of the word of the Guru.
(3). Searching and searching I reflected, this truth was known by Nānak, O dear!
By remembering the name, the invaluable treasure, (my) mind, the ruby, believed (in it).

II. CXXXI. CXCVIII.

Dupadē.

(1). By the favour of the Guru he (Hari) dwells in my mind, what I ask, I obtain, O dear!
By delighting in the name this (my) mind is satiated, I do not run again anywhere, O dear!

Pause.

My Lord is higher than all, day and night I praise him.
In a moment he establishes and disestablishes, of him I make thee afraid, O dear!

[1] ਜੀਅ ਕੀ ਮਾਨੀ *i.e.* ਜੀਅ ਕੀ ਬਾਤ ਮਾਨੀ, the word of the creature is minded (by thee).

(2). When I behold my own Lord and master, I do not think in my mind of other friends.

Nānak, the slave, is dressed by the Lord himself (with a dress of honour), having effaced error and fear in a moment.[1]

III. CXXXII. CXCIX.

(1). The four castes and those who are pommelling the public, on the palm of whose hands the six philosophical systems are:

The beautiful, the clever, the handsome, the intelligent are deluded and deceived by the five,[2] O dear!

Pause.

Is there such a strong man as to meet and beat the five heroes and champions?

By whom the five are beaten and cut to pieces, he is a perfect man in this Kali-yuga, O dear!

(2). A very great tribe, that does not flee, a strong and obstinate army

Is destroyed by that man, says Nānak, (who is) in the shelter[3] of the society of the pious.

IV. CXXXIII. CC.

The highest good of the soul is the story about Hari, all other enjoyments are insipid, O dear!

(1). The Munis, acquainted with the six (philosophical systems) calculate much (in their) thought, and nothing is fixed (by them).[4]

(2). The pure, infinite, comfortable antidote[5] against poison is matured in the society of the pious, (says) Nānak.

V. CXXXIV. CCI.

Pause.

My beloved is the nectar-holding (word).

By the Guru it is not removed one moment from (my) mind, O dear!

(1). (His) sight and touch are rendering (me) happy (and) joyful, I delight continually in the creator, O dear!

(2). By uttering one moment Hari, knowable by the Guru, there is no punishment of Yama; Hari is in the bosom of Nānak, Hari is in (his) breast.

VI. CXXXV. CCII.

Pause.

In the society of the pious there is goodness.

(1). (Every) watch, forty-eight minutes and moment they are continually singing Gōvind, Gōvind they praise.

(2). In going, sitting, sleeping the praise of Hari (is) in (their) mind and body, they hang (on his) feet.

(3). I am light, thou art heavy, O Lord! Nānak knows (thy) asylum.

[1] ਖਿਨਾਵਉ = ਖਿਨ *s.f.* (Sindhī खिण) moment, āvau being a meaningless alliteration.

[2] The five are: ਕਾਮ etc. ਛਲੀ = ਛਲੇ, for the sake of the rhyme.

[3] ਝਲੀਣੇ = ਝਲੇ ਣੇ; ਝਲਾ *s.m.* shelter, support (Sindhī झलो).

[4] In ਲਾਈਰੀਣੇ the last two syllables ਰੀਣੇ are a meaningless alliteration.

[5] ਬਿਖਾਰੀ *s.f.* A thorny plant, used as an antidote against poison (Sansk. विषारि, but in Hindī fem.). The Sikh Granthīs explain ਬਿਖਾਰੀ as an adjective, signifying: *uncontaminated!* A groundless conjecture, as in so many other cases.

ĀSĀ; GHAR XII.; MAHALĀ V.

Ōm! By the favour of the true Guru!

I. CXXXVI. CCIII.

(1). Giving up all cunning worship the formless Supreme Brahm!
Without the One true name all appears as dust.

Pause.

That Lord is known (as being) always with (every one).
By the favour of the Guru the One is comprehended by love to Hari.
(2). The protection of the One is powerful, there is no other place (for protection).
The water of the great world is crossed by singing always the excellences of Hari.
(3). Birth and death are removed, no pain is incurred in the city of Yama.
The treasure of the name he obtains, on whom that Lord bestows mercy.
(4). The One is stay and support, the One only is of use to the weak.
Nānak (says): joining the society of the pious he should be muttered, without Hari there is none other.

II. CXXXVII. CCIV.

(1). Soul, mind, body, life, all pleasures and enjoyments are given by the Lord.
He is the friend of the poor, bountiful to the creatures, an asylum for protection.[1]

Pause.

O my mind, meditate on the name of Hari, Hari!
In this and that world he is a companion with (thee), apply thy devotion to the One!
(2). The people meditate on the Vēda and the Shāstras for the sake of crossing the world (of existence).
Above many works and religious ceremonies is the practice of the name.
(3). Lust, wrath, egotism are destroyed, (if one) meet with the true Gurdēv.
(In whom) he makes firm the name and attachment to Hari, (his) service of the Lord is good.
(4). O merciful one, (I flee) to the asylum of thy feet, thou art the hope of the poor.
Thou art the support of (my) life, thou, O Lord, art the protection of Nānak!

III. CXXXVIII. CCV.

(1). Rolling about great pain is incurred without the society of the pious.
Acquire the gain of Gōvind, the juice of Hari! the Supreme Brahm is unchangeable.

Pause.

The name of Hari should continually be muttered!
At every breath meditate on that Lord, give up other love!
(2). That Lord is the powerful cause of causes, he himself is the giver of life.
Giving up all cunning mutter the Lord the eight watches!
(3). He is friend, companion, assistant and associate (to thee), he is high, unattainable, boundless.
Make (his) lotus-foot dwell in (thy) heart! (he is) the support of (thy) life.
(4). Bestow mercy (on me), O Supreme Brahm, (that) I may sing (thy) excellences (and thy) praise!
Nānak lives by muttering (thy) name, (in which) are all comforts (and) great dignity.

[1] ਜੋਗੁ is postposition = ਕਉ.

IV. CXXXIX. CCVI.

(1). Seeing the society of the pious I make efforts, (if) the Lord causes (me) to make (them).
He applies (to me) the colour of the name of Hari, Hari, the Lord himself colours (me).

Pause.

In my mind I mutter[1] the name of Rām.
Mercifully dwell in my heart, become thou thyself (my) companion!
(2). Having heard thy name, O beloved Lord, I desire to see (thee).
Bestow mercy on thy worm, even this is (my) wish and desire.
(3). (My) body and property are thine, thou art my Lord, nothing is in my power.
As thou keepest me, so I remain, what thou givest, I eat.
(4). Thou cuttest off the sins of (my) several births, (I am) bathing in the dust of the people of Hari.
By love and devotion error and fear are annihilated, Hari is always in the presence of Nānak.

V. CXL. CCVII.

(1). Unattainable, incomprehensible is thy form, he attains to it, on whose forehead (this) lot (is written).
(On whom) by the kind Lord himself mercy is bestowed, (to him) by the true Guru the name of Hari is given.

Pause.

The Kali-yug is saved by the Gurdēv.
Who were perplexed and confounded by discharging behind and before (through terror), they all applied themselves to thy service.
(2). Thou thyself art the creator, the upholder of the whole creation, in all thou art contained.
Dharm-rājā became astonished, the whole (creation) came and fell down at (thy) feet.
(3). (There is) the Satya, Trētā and Dvāpar Yuga, (but) the highest among the Yugas the Kali-yuga is called.
Who assents[2] (to the words of the Guru), he is assented to, no one is seized in any place.
(4). O Hari, thou dost, what thy devotees ask for, this is thy glory.
Joining his hands Nānak asks for (this) gift: O Hari, give (me) the sight of thy saints!

ĀSĀ; GHAR XIII.; MAHALĀ V.

Ōm! by the favour of the true Guru!

I. CXLI. CCVIII.

Pause.

O true Guru, by thy words the vicious are saved!
(1). The very dejected, wicked and censorious (become) purified in (thy) society.
(2). (Who were) wandering about in (several) births, (who were) falling into hell, their families are saved (by them).
(3). (Whom) nobody knows, (whom) nobody minds, they are manifest at the gate of Hari.
(4). What glory, what greatness shall I give (to thee)? Nānak is every moment a sacrifice to thee.

[1] ਜਾਪਿ instead of ਜਾਪੀ, for the sake of the rhyme.
[2] ਅਙਿਕਰੁ, assent, consent; Sindhī अंङिकार (fem.).

II. CXLII. CCIX.

Pause.

(Those) remain fools:

(1). (Who) are intoxicated with love to (their) family (and) enjoyment of sensual gifts; laying hold of falsehood they are tied down (by it).

(2). Plans, designs, the joy and delight of a dream are called true by the self-willed.

(3). The secret of the nectar-name, the boon, (that is) with (him), he does not find out a bit.

(4). Bestowing (his) mercy (we) were put (by him) into the society of the pious; Nānak is (in their) asylum.

III. CXLIII. CCX.

Tipadē.

Pause.

That is the love to the beloved.

(1). Gold, rubies, elephants, pearls, rubies, not, not, not.

(2). Not dominion, not fortune, not command, not enjoyment:

Nothing, nothing I desire.

(3). By worshipping the asylums of the feet of the saints [1]

I obtain the highest comfort.

Nānak (says): (my) burning is removed, the friend of (my) affection is met with.

IV. CXLIV. CCXI.

Pause.

By the Guru (thou wast) shown (to my) eyes.

(1). In this and that world, in everybody art thou, thou, O fascinating one!

(2). (Thou) alone, O beautiful one, (art) the cause of causes, the upholder of the earth!

(3). (I am) a sacrifice to the adoring touch and sight of the saints.

Nānak is sleeping in comfort.

V. CXLV. CCXII.

Pause.

The name of Hari, Hari is priceless.

He is naturally happy.

(1). He is a companion with (me), he does not give (me) up, he is unfathomable and inestimable.

(2). The beloved is (my) brother, (my) father and mother, the refuge of (his) devotees.

(3). The invisible one is shown, he is obtained from the Guru, this one is the embodiment of Hari.

VI. CXLVI. CCXIII.

Pause.

He accomplishes his devotion,

(To whom) the Lord has come.

(1). (Whose) aim the blessing of the name is, he makes the feet (of Hari) dwell in (his) heart.

(2). This one is emancipated, this one is devoted, (who) holds fast the society of the saints.

(3). (If) I meditate on the name, I become easily absorbed.

Nānak sings the excellences of Hari.

[1] The whole line is one aggregate of words without any grammatical relation; the translation can therefore be only a guess.

VII. CXLVII. CCXIV.

Pause.

The feet of the Lord are beautiful.

By the saints of Hari they are obtained.

(1). Their own self is parted with, worship is performed (by them), the excellences (of Hari) are sung (by them) with delight.

(2). They long after the One, they are thirsting after (his) sight, no other pleases (them).

(3). (Bestow) thy mercy (on me)! what is the helpless creature

Nānak is a sacrifice (to thee).

VIII. CXLVIII. CCXV.

Pause.

Remember the One in (thy) mind!

(1). Meditate on the name, fix it in (thy) heart, without him there is none other!

(2). Come to the asylum of the Lord, all fruits are obtained (there), all pain departs.

(3). The divine male, the arranger (of all), is bountiful to the creatures, in every creature he is.

IX. CXLIX. CCXVI.

Pause.

Who is forgetting Hari, he dies.

(1). Who meditates on the name, obtains all fruits, that man becomes happy.

(2). (If one) practise works of egotism, (though) he be called a king, he is bound (by them) (like) a parrot by error (is caught) by a twig smeared with quick-lime.

(3). Nānak says: with whom the true Guru has met, that man becomes immovable.

ĀSĀ; GHAR XIV.; MAHALĀ V.

Ōm! By the favour of the true Guru!

I. CL. CCXVII.

Pause.

That love is (always) new.

It clings continually to (its) own beloved.

(1). Who is pleasing to the Lord, is not born again.

He is absorbed in devotion and love to Hari, in affection to Hari.

(2). May this mind be given (to me), (that) union with the Lord may be brought about!

Bestow thy own mercy (on me), that Nānak may obtain the name!

II. CLI. CCXVIII.

Pause.

Join (me), O beloved Rām, without thee nobody remains sedate.

(1). (Though) one do many works (according to) the Smriti and the Shāstras:

Yet without thy sight, O Lord, there is no happiness.

(2). Practising vows, religious observances and control of the senses they have become tired; Nānak (is in) the asylum of the pious, with (whom) the Lord dwells.

ĀSĀ; GHAR XV.; PAṚTĀL;[1] MAHALĀ V.

By the favour of the true Guru!

I. CLII. CCXIX.

(1). (Who) is sunk in vice and asleep in intoxication gets no understanding.

When he is seized by the hair by Yama and marched off, then he is ruined.[2]

Pause.

(Who) are given to covetousness of sensual objects, the poison, they, being deprived (of their) wealth, distress (their) mind.

Being intoxicated with arrogance and pride, the godless do not know (that there will come upon them) destruction in a moment.

(2). The Vēdas, Shāstras and (holy) men cry, but the deaf man does not hear.

Having utterly lost the play he becomes bankrupt (and then) the fool repents in his mind.

(3). All fines are paid (by him) in the wrong way and are not taken account of in the court.

The work, by means of which he remains under protection, he does not do.

(4). When the world was shown to me as such by the Guru, I sang the praise of the One.

Having given up (all other) hope and cunning Nānak came to (his) asylum.

II. CLIII. CCXX.

Pause.

By the occupation with the name of Gōvind

The pious and saints are conciliated, the Beloved one is obtained, (his) excellences are sung and the five sounds and musical instruments played.

(1). He (*i.e.* the Guru) bestows mercy (on me), he goes and shows (me) the bridegroom, now I am in love with Gōvind.

Serving the saint with love he applies (to me) the colour of (my) beloved Lord.

(2). The Guru makes fast divine knowledge in (my) mind, he makes (me) rejoice, (that) the bridegroom neither comes nor goes, he puts (this) treasure into (my) mind.

I have given up all the desire of (my) mind.

It has been a long, long time, much desire has affected (my) mind.

Show me the sight of Hari, show it to me!

Poor Nānak has come to (thy) asylum, take (me) to (thy) neck!

III. CLIV. CCXXI.

Pause.

O that some one would demolish the troublesome pit!

That he would keep (me) away from hope, desire, deception, illusion and error!

(1). May lust, wrath, covetousness and pride, may (all) these diseases leave (me)!

(2). In the society of the saints I will delight in the name and sing the excellences of Gōvind.

Day by day I will meditate on the Lord.

Error and fear I will overcome and efface.

Nānak recovers the treasure of the name.

[1] ਪੜਤਾਲ (*s.f.*), a certain mode in music.

[2] ਖਪਿ ਜਾਣਾ, to be ruined. MS. No. 2483 reads ਪਛੁਤਾਵੈ, he repents.

IV. CLV. CCXXII.

Pause.

Abandon lust, wrath and covetousness!

O (my) mind, remember the name of Gōvind!

The adoration of Hari is a fruitful work.

(1). Give up pride, illusion, vice, (they are) false, mutter: Rām, Rām, Rām!

O my mind, stick to the feet of the saints!

(2). Wake and remember the feet of the Lord Gōpāl, (who is) merciful to the poor, purifying the sinners, of the Supreme Brahm, Hari!

Adore him, O Nānak, (and thy) lot (is) perfect.

V. CLVI. CCXXIII.

Pause.

Joy (and) grief, weeping and gladness are shown as a play.

(1). One moment there is fear, one moment (one is) fearless, in another moment one rises and runs away.

One moment there is relish, one moment there is enjoyment, in another moment (one) gives it up.

(2). One moment there is abstract devotion, austerities and much worship, in another moment there is doubt.

(On whom) one moment there is mercy in the society of the pious, O Nānak, (to him) is applied the colour of Hari.

ĀSĀ; MAHALĀ V.; GHAR XVII.; ĀSĀVARĪ.

Ōm! by the favour of the true Guru!

I. CLVII. CCXXIV.

Pause.

I say: O Gōvind, Govind!

Hari, Hari is dear to (my) mind.

What the Guru says, I keep in (my) mind.

I break it away from others and make it return (to Hari).

Thus the darling I have obtained, O (female) friend!

(1). There is fascination by the lotus in the pond.[1]

(But) the foot does not go there, I am worn out.

I do not remain bewildered and confused.

I make efforts being intent on one object.

(Being) in the asylum of (his) feet I get out, O friend!

(2). I am firm, firm in (my) mind.

Forest and house are the same (to me).

Within (me) is (my) One beloved.

Outside I view (him) as many.[2]

I practise the Rāja-yōga.

In the world I am not of the world, O friend, says Nānak.

[1] The sense is: I am fascinated by the lotus in the pond. There is an allusion to, or rather a paraphrase of Āsā, Sabd. 29 (1).

[2] The sense is: the Supreme has many outward forms.

II. CLVIII. CCXXV.

Pause.

One desire I entertain.
(My) meditation is continually (directed) on the Guru.
Firm is the mantra and knowledge of the saints (in me).
I worship the feet of the Guru.
Then union is brought about, (if) the Guru incline (to thee) in mercy, O my mind.
(1). The support of another breaks down.[1]
He is contained in every place.
The fear of Yama subsides.
The tree is planted in (its) place.
Then all obsequiousness (to others) ceases.
(2). On whose forehead (this) (is written) as his due:
He crosses the fire of existence.[2]
In his own house he gets a (firm) place.
He delights in Hari (and) enjoys (him).
His hunger has ceased.
Nānak (says): he is naturally absorbed (in Hari), O (my) mind!

III. CLIX. CCXXVI.

Pause.

On Hari, Hari, Hari I reflect.
With natural contemplation he is muttered.
The tongue of the pious utters (him).
The way of emancipation is heard.
By the very pure it is obtained, O my mind!
(1). The (holy) men (and) Munis seek (him),
(Who is) the Lord and owner of all.
In the Kali-yuga, in the world it is difficult to find him,
Who is destroying pain.
The Lord is fulfilling the desires of the low, O (my) mind!
(2). O mind, he should be adored,
(Who is) invisible and impenetrable!
Make friendship with him,
(Who) does not perish, nor go nor die!
From the Guru he is known,
(Says) Nānak, who is my heart's content, O my mind!

IV. CLX. CCXXVII.

Pause.

Lay hold of the refuge of the One!
Utter the word of the Guru!
Perform the order of the True one!
Seek the treasure in thy mind!
And thou wilt enter into happiness, O my mind!

1 ਭਗਾ *m.* support, prop. Nihã̄ is a meaningless alliteration, as in many other rhymes of these lines.

2 ਭੈ is here = ਭਉ (भव).

(1). Who dies whilst living:
He crosses (the ocean of existence), which is hard to cross.
Who becomes the dust of all:
Him I call fearless.
(His) anxieties are effaced
By the instruction of the saints, O my mind!
(2). Whose happiness the name is:
That man pain never approaches.
Who hears the praise of Hari, Hari:
Everybody minds him.
He has become fruitful,
(Says) Nānak, who has become acceptable to the Lord, O my mind!

V. CLXI. CCXXVIII.

Pause.

If meeting together the praise of Hari be sung,
The highest step (= emancipation) is obtained.
Who is pierced with love to him:
He has all perfections.
Day by day he wakes.
Nānak (says): he is very fortunate, O my mind!
(1). (If) the feet of the saints be washed,
Folly is removed.
Become the dust of the saints!
No pain whatever will afflict (thee)!
Fall on the asylum of the saints!
Thou wilt never be born (any more) nor die.
Those become immovable,
By whom Hari, Hari is muttered, O my mind!
(2). (My) sweetheart and friend art thou.
Strengthen to me the name!
Without him there is none other.
Adore him in (thy) mind!
May he not be forgotten a moment!
Without him how shall (one) get on?
I am a sacrifice to the Guru.
Nānak mutters the name, O my mind!

VI. CLXII. CCXXIX.

Pause.

Thou art the cause of causes.
None other is known by me.
What thou dost, that takes place.
In ease and comfort they sleep.
Composure is given to the mind (of them),
Who have fallen down at the gate of the Lord, O my mind!

(1). By associating with the pious
Control of the senses (becomes) perfect.
When one's own self is given up:
Then (all) afflictions are effaced.
Mercy is bestowed (on them).
The Banvārī is preserving (their) honour, O my mind!
(2). This should be considered as happiness.
What Hari does, should be minded.
No one is unhappy,
Who becomes the dust of the saints.
Whom he himself protects:
He tastes the nectar of Hari, O my mind!
(3). Who has got no one:
His is that Lord.
Who comprehends (his) inner mind:
To him everything is known.
Save the sinner!
This is the prayer of Nānak, O my mind!

VII. CLXIII. CCXXX.

Ik tukā.

Pause.

Those strangers
Are hearing the message.
(1). To whom they are attached:
All (those) they leave behind.
Those become like a dream,
By whom the name of Hari is taken.
(2). Who forsaking Hari cling to another:
They are born (again) and, having died, are ruined.
By whom Hari, Hari is obtained:
They remain alive.
To whom he (Hari) becomes merciful:
He is a devotee, (says) Nānak.

RĀGU ĀSĀ; MAHALĀ IX.

Ōm! by the favour of the true Guru!

I. CCXXXI.

Pause.

To whom shall I tell the pain of (my) mind?

(I am) devoured by greediness, I am running about in the ten directions (of the earth), I long for wealth.

(1). For the sake of pleasure I undergo much pain, I am serving every man.

At every door I am strolling about like a dog, I have no concern about the worship of Rām.

(2). The human birth (I have got), (I am) wasting to no purpose, I am not ashamed at the laughter of the people.

Why is Nānak not singing the praise of Hari? it destroys the bad thoughts of the body.

RĀGU ĀSĀ; GHAR II.; MAHALĀ I.; ASṬPADĪĀ.

Ōm! by the favour of the true Guru!

I.

(1). Descending he bathes in a pond hard of access.
He neither speaks nor talks, he sings the excellences of Hari.
(Like) water in the atmosphere he is absorbed in the Insentient (Supreme).
Stirring the juice of truth he gets the great juice (of nectar).

Pause.

Hear such divine knowledge, O my mind!
Being omnipresent he upholds all places.
(2). Vows of truth and religious observances do not afflict death.[1]
By means of the word of the true Guru (one) consumes his wrath.
By dwelling in the tenth gate he applies profound meditation.
By the touch of the philosopher's stone he obtains the highest step.
(3). For the sake of the happiness[2] of (his) mind he churns truth.
In a brimful pond he does not wash off his dirt.
As he is, to whom he is attached, such he becomes.
What the creator himself does, that takes place.
(4). The cool snow of the Guru extinguishes the fire (of passions).
(His) service increases intelligence and (superhuman) power.
Bestowing[3] (his) sight he comes easily to (one's) house,
(And) makes (one) utter the pure word (and) sound.
(5). Within (the heart) is divine knowledge (and) the essence of the great juice (= nectar).
Reflecting on the Guru (is equal to) bathing at a Tīrtha.
Within is the place of worship of the enemy of Mura.
The Luminous one is mingling light (with himself).
(6). (Their) mind is delighted in the love of the One.
The pious are absorbed in the king.
They act (according to) the pleasure of the Lord.
The eternal Lord cannot be apprehended.
(7). It is produced in water and is far from the water.[4]
In water the light remains brimful.
Near to whom, far from whom shall I call (him)?
I sing the depository of (all) excellences, seeing (him) in (my) presence.
(8). Inside and outside there is none other.
What pleases him, that takes also place.
Hear, O Bharthari,[5] Nānak expresses (this) thought:
The pure name is my support.

[1] *i.e.* are not able to remove death.

[2] ਸਚੁ is here very likely = ਸੁਖ, happiness.

[3] ਆਪਿ is here part. past conj. from ਆਪਣਾ = Sansk. अर्पण, to bestow.

[4] *i.e.* the reflection of light.

[5] ਭਰਥਰਿ, name of a Jōgī, with whom Nānak is said to have had different discussions.

II.

(1). All mutterings, all austerities, all cleverness (are of no use).
(He) wanders about in the desert, no way is found.
Without comprehending (the truth) no one is accepted.
On a head destitute of the name (there are) dark spots.

Pause.

True is the Lord, the world is subject to destruction.
(That) man is emancipated, (who is) a disciple (and) slave (of the Guru).
(2). The world is bound by spiritual illusion and by much longing.
By the instruction of the Guru some (become) indifferent (to the world).
In (whose) heart the lotus of the name is opened:
They have no fear of Yama.
(3). The world is overcome by women, by the love of fascinating women.
Clinging to son and wife it forgets the name.
Life is wasted to no purpose, the play is lost.
By serving the true Guru (one's) work is accomplished.
(4). Outside he utters egotism and makes (others) enter it.
Inside he is emancipated and never implicates himself.
The infatuation (caused by) the Māyā he consumes by the word of the Guru.
He always meditates in his heart on the pure name.
(5). (Who) keeps and checks (his) running (mind):
(Him) he (*i.e.* the Guru) unites with the society of the disciples (according to his) destiny.
Without the Guru he is led astray, he comes and goes.
(On whom) he (the Guru) bestows a favourable look, (him) he unites to close connexion (with himself).
(6). (If) I speak of the beautiful (Supreme), he cannot be described.
If I relate the Inexpressible, I cannot get any estimate of him.
All pain is thine, (all) happiness (is allotted according to thy) will.
All pain is effaced by the true name.
(7). A musical instrument without a hand, beating time in music without a foot.[1]
If he comprehend the word (of the Guru), then he is truly exalted.
In (whose) heart is the True one, he has all happiness.
(On whom) he casts a favourable look, (him) the preserver preserves.
(8). The three worlds are known (to him), (who) clears away his own self.
(Who) comprehends the word (of the Guru), he is absorbed in the True one.
(Who) with one continual devotion reflects on the word (of the Guru):
Blessed is (that) mindful man, (says) Nānak.

III.

(1). The destinies are innumerable; write (them severally and) mind (them)!
Praise the heart-pleasing True one with attention!
Reading continually the stories (about him) keep (them) in mind![2]
The destinies are innumerable, he who is free from destiny,[3] is boundless.

[1] No grammatical relation of any kind is pointed out.
[2] ਭਾਰੁ here = ਭਾਲੁ, to keep in mind.
[3] ਅਲੇਖੁ, exempt from destiny = the Supreme.

Pause.

Such True one consider thou as the only One!
Recognize birth and death (as his) order!
(2). By the infatuation of the Māyā (and) by death the world is bound.
Who is bound is emancipated by remembering the name.
The Guru is the giver of happiness, do not seek another one!
Here and there he goes on with thee.
(3). (If one) die by means of the word (of the Guru), then he applies his devout meditation to the One.
(If) he remains immovable, he puts a stop to his wandering.
He (becomes) emancipated whilst living, (if) he make the name dwell in his mind.
(If) he becomes a disciple, he is absorbed in the True one.
(4). By whom the earth, the firmament and the sky are made;
By whom all is established and again disestablished:
He himself is unintermittingly in all.
He does not ask any one, he himself bestows.
(5). Thou art the full ocean, the ruby, the diamond.
Thou art pure, true, profound in qualities.
He enjoys happiness, (who) meets with the Guru, the Pīr.
One is the Lord, one his Vazīr.
(6). The world is led captive; (those are) free, (by whom) egotism is destroyed.
In the world the wise and well-conducted one is rare.
In the world the reflecting Paṇḍit is rare.
Without having fallen in with the true Guru every one wanders about in egotism.
(7). The world is afflicted, some few people are happy.
The world is diseased (by its) inclination for sensual pleasures (and) weeps.[1]
The world is produced and destroyed having lost (its) honour.
Who becomes a disciple, he comprehends the truth.
(8). The dear in price, immense in weight,
The unflinching, guileless instruction of the Guru hold thou fast!
By love he is met with, the work of fear pleases (him).
Humble Nānak expresses (his) thought.

IV.

(1). One dies and five weep together.
(His) egotism departs, (who) washes away his dirt by means of the word (of the Guru).
By understanding and knowledge tranquillity is produced in the house.
Without comprehending (the truth) he loses all his honour.

Pause.

Who dies, who are those, that weep?
The cause of causes is pleased with all.[2]
(2). Does any one weep in pain for the dead?
He weeps, who suffers pain.

[1] This line is rather obscure; ਭੋਗੀ ਗੁਣ we translate by: the inherent quality or disposition for pleasure. No grammatical relation, as usual, the sense must therefore be guessed at.

[2] ਤੇਹੀ=तोषी (in Sindhī already तोङ्ग = तोष).

Whom it has befallen, he knows the Lord.
What the creator himself does, that takes place.
(3). (Who is) dying whilst living, saves (others and is himself) saved.
Victory (to thee), O Lord of the world, in (thy) asylum is emancipation!
I am a sacrifice to the feet of the true Guru!
The Guru is the boat, by (means of his) word I am crossing the world of existence.[1]
(4). He himself is fearless and an unintermitting light.
Without the name there is impurity and defilement in the world.
(If) folly be extinguished, what for are they weeping?
Without attention to devotion they are born and die.
(5). A true friend weeps for a dead (friend).
The three qualities weep continually.
Having removed pain and pleasure (I am) naturally of a sedate mind.
Body and soul I entrust to the beloved Krishṇa.
(6). In (whose) mind is the One, many innumerable,
Many countless works (he does).[2]
Without fear and devotion (one's) life is useless.
(Who) sings the excellences of Hari, falls in with the highest object (of human life = emancipation).
(7). He himself dies, he himself also kills.
He himself produces and having established disestablishes (again).
Creation is produced (by thee), thou art by nature luminous.
By reflection on the word (of the Guru) there is uniou (with thee), no doubt.
(8). There is impurity (in) fire, in the food, (which) the world eats.
There is impurity in water, (and) even in all places.
Nānak (says): there is impurity, (when one) is born and dies.
By the favour of the Guru the juice of Hari is drunk.

V.

(1). Who reflects on his own self, he assays the diamond.
By one favourable glance the perfect Guru ferries across.
Who minds the Guru in his mind, his mind becomes tranquil.

Pause.

Such a wholesale merchant carries on banking business.
(On whom his) true glance is, he crosses by devotion to the One.
(2). The name of the Supreme is the best capital stock.
Who is attached to the pure and true one, he is a pedlar.
(By) the praise of the Guru, the creator, tranquillity (is produced in) the house.
(3). (Who) by means of the word (of the Guru) consumes (his) hope and desire;
(Who) utters Rām Nārāyaṇ and causes (him) to be uttered:
He obtains from the Guru the road to (Hari's) palace and house.

[1] ਭੈ is here = भव (= bha-a = bha-y-a = bhai).

[2] These two lines contain no verb nor any grammatical relation; they are little more than a jingling of words, the final rhyme being twice ਅਸੰਖ. The sense seems to be: "If the One is in the mind, this is equal to many innumerable works."

(4). (His) body is of gold, of incomparable light.
All is the form of the God of the three worlds.
That true and inexhaustible wealth is in my lap.
(5). In the five (elements), in the three (qualities), in the nine (regions), in the four (ages or Vēdas?) he is contained.
Earth and heaven he upholds by (his) skill.
He is going out and quickly returning.
(6). (Who) is a fool, (to his) eyes he does not appear.
(Whose) tongue is given to relishes, he does not comprehend what is said.
Being intoxicated with poison he struggles with the world.
(7). In the highest society he becomes the highest,
Who runs after virtue and washes away vices.
Without serving the Guru tranquillity is not found.
(8). The name is a diamond, a jewel, a ruby.
(Whose) mind is a pearl, his property it is.
Nānak (says): who essays (it), he is happy (by its) sight.

VI.

(1). The disciple's heart's desire is divine knowledge and meditation.
The disciple belongs to the palace and is acquainted with the palace.
The attention of the disciple (is directed to) the word (of the Guru) (as his) banner.

Pause.

Such, (who are) reflecting with love and devotion,
Are disciples, (to them) the name of Murāri (is) true.
(2). Day and night he is pure and happy in (his) place.
He alone has the knowledge of the three worlds.
From the true Guru he knows the order (of Hari).
(3). True is his gladness, he has no grief.
The nectar of the very sweet divine knowledge he enjoys.
The five [1] are absorbed, the whole world (becomes) happy.
(4). In all is (thy) light, every one is thine.
That one himself joins and separates.
What the creator himself does, that takes place.
(5). Having pulled down he raises up, by (his) order it is absorbed.
By (his) order that exists, which pleases him.
Without the Guru no one obtains the Perfect one.
(6). In young and old—there is no mindfulness in man.
In full youth he is immersed in conceit.
Without the name what will he get at the end?
(7). From whom food and wealth come, he is not easily known.
He (= man) is led astray by error and repents afterwards.
On his neck is a noose, he is completely mad.
(8). When I saw the world drowning, I fled in terror.
Who are preserved by the true Guru, they are very fortunate.
Nānak clings to the feet of the Guru.

[1] The five, *i.e.* ਕਾਮ, etc.

VII.

(1). They sing (sacred) songs, (but) in (their) mind is iniquity.
They recite Rāgs and are called learned.[1]
Without the name there is falsehood and iniquity in (their) mind.

Pause.

Whither dost thou go, O mind? remain in (thy) house!
The disciple is satiated by the name of Rām; seeking about thou wilt easily find Hari.
(2). Lust, wrath and spiritual delusion are in the mind (and) body.
Greediness and egotism is pain.
How shall the mind become tranquil without the name of Rām?
(3). Who is bathing in the heart, he knows the True one.
The disciple knows the state of his heart.
Without the true word (of the Guru) he does not become acquainted with the palace (of Hari).
(4). Into the Formless one the forms are re-absorbed.
Who abides in him, who is free from parts and perfectly true:
That man is not subject (any more) to regeneration.
(5). Where the name is found, thither I go.
By the favour of the Guru I do works.
I am fond of the name and sing the excellences of Hari.
(6). By the service of the Guru I know my own self.
The comfort-giving nectar-name dwells (in me).
Daily (I am) attached to the word (of the Guru) and the name.
(7). (If) my Lord applies one (to himself), then he is applied.
He destroys (his) egotism by means of the word (of the Guru) and wakes.
Here and there (he enjoys) always happiness.
(8). The fickle mind does not know Brahmā.
The filthy self-willed man does not recognize the word (of the Guru).
The disciple is pure and praises the name.
(9). O Hari, before (thee) I offer my prayer:
May (my) dwelling be in the society of the pious!
Sins and troubles are cut off (by) the light of the name of Hari.
(10). By reflection and religious conduct he (Hari) is obtained.[2]
From the word of the true Guru the One is known.
The mind of Nānak is attached to the name of Rām.

VIII.

(1). The mind is (like) an elephant, the Sākats are mad.
Breaking down the forest they are confounded by the infatuation of the Māyā.
They go here and there being pressed down by death.
The disciple seeking about finds the house (of Hari) (in) himself.

Pause.

Without the word of the Guru the mind (gets) no place (of rest).
Remember the very pure name of Rām, give up other (things), egotism is bitter.

[1] ਚੀਤੇ, on account of the rhyme = ਚੇਤੇ.

[2] ਪਰਾਤਾ = Sansk. प्राप्त, obtained.

(2). This mind is foolish, say, how will it (firmly) remain?
Without understanding (the truth) it will bear the pain of Yama.
(If) he himself pardons, he procures the true Guru.
He destroys death, the plague, the True one upholds (him).
(3). This mind is doing works, this mind is performing religious duties.
This mind is produced from the five elements.
This foolish mind is a greedy Sākat.
The disciple mutters the name, (his) mind is beautiful.
(4). The mind of the disciple has information of the places.[1]
The disciple has accurate knowledge[2] of the three worlds.
This mind is given to contemplation and enjoyments, it performs austerities.
The Lord Hari himself knows the disciple.
(5). The mind (of the disciple) is indifferent to the world and abandoning egotism.
To everybody desire and duality stick.
The disciple (however) tastes the elixir of Rām.
In (his) house (and) hall Hari protects (his) honour.
(6). This mind (of the disciple) is a king, a hero in battle.
This mind (of the disciple) is fearless by the name.
The five (vices) are subdued and brought into (his) power.
Having consumed egotism they are put (by him) in one place.
(7). By the disciple other affections and tastes are abandoned.
This mind of the disciple is intent on devotion.
Having heard the sound not produced by beating he reflects (on it) and minds it.
Having known himself he becomes formless.
(8). Spotless is the report about this mind at (every) gate and house.
The devotion (and) love of the disciple are noised about.
Day and night (he performs) the praise of Hari by the favour of the Guru.
In everybody is that Lord, who is at the beginning, before (all) ages.
(9). This mind is intoxicated with the elixir of Rām.
All the elixir is known by the disciple.
The cause of devotion is the dwelling at the feet of the Guru.
Nānak is the slave of slaves of the people of Hari.

IX.

(1). The body is destroyed, whose (property) is wealth called?
Without the Guru by whom is the name of Rām obtained?
The wealth of the name of Rām is a companion with (him),
(Who) day and night applies deep devotion to the pure Hari.

Pause.

What is ours without the name of Rām?
Considering pleasure and pain alike I do not give up the name, he himself bestows and procures (it).
(2). Gold and women are the aim of the fool.
He clings to duality and the name is forgotten (by him).
On whom thou bestowest the name, causing (him) to mutter it:
(Him) the angel (of death) cannot touch singing (thy) excellences.

[1] मेटी = मेटि, intelligence.

[2] मेश्री, accurate knowledge (Sindhī सोझी).

(3). Hari is the bountiful Guru, Rām Gōpāl.
As it pleases (thee), so keep me, O merciful one!
(I am) a disciple, Rām is pleasing to my mind.
(My) diseases are effaced, (my) pain is stopped.
(4). There is no other medicine, no charm nor spell.
The remembrance of Hari, Hari, is destroying sins.
Thou thyself leadest astray by making forget the name.
Thou thyself keepest by bestowing mercy.
(5). Disease, error, difference and duality are in the mind.
Without the Guru (one) goes astray and mutters another muttering.
By the interview with the Guru he sees the primeval divine male.
Without the word of the Guru he afflicts his life.
(6). Having seen the wonderful one they remain amazed.
In everybody, in gods and men there is naturally (his) deep meditation.
(His) stream remains brimful in the mind.
There is none other equal to thee.
(7). Who (entertain) devotion (and) a desire (for Hari), (in whose) mouth the name is:
In the society of (those) saints and devotees is Rām.
(Their) fetters are broken, easily meditation (is performed by them).
The disciples are emancipated by the knowledge of Hari, the Guru.
(8). The affliction of the angel of Yama does not touch him,
Who wakes in devout meditation on the name of Rām.
He is kind to (his) devotees, Hari is with his devotees.
Nānak (says): they are emancipated by love to Hari.

X.

Iktukī.

(1). Who serves the Guru, he knows the Lord.
(His) pain is effaced, who recognizes the True one by means of the word (of the Guru).

Pause.

Mutter Rām, O my beloved friend!
By serving the true Guru thou wilt see the Lord with (thy) eyes.
(2). A fetter is mother and father in the world.
A fetter is son, daughter and woman.
(3). A fetter are works and egotism.
A fetter is son and wife (and) duality in the mind.
(4). A fetter is husbandry, which the cultivator carries on.
He bears the fire of egotism (and) the Rājā asks gifts.
(5). A fetter is thoughtless traffic.
(One) does not become satiated, the love of the Māyā is (rather) increasing.
(6). It is a fetter, that the wholesale merchant collect perishable wealth.
Without devotion to Hari he is not accepted.
(7). A fetter is the Vēda, dispute and pride.
By a fetter (one) is destroyed, spiritual blindness (is) a disease.
(8). Nānak is in the asylum of the name.
Those, who are preserved by the true Guru, are not fettered.

RĀGU ĀSĀ; MAHALĀ I.; ASṬPADĪĀ; GHAR III.

Ōm! by the favour of the true Guru!

XI.

(1). On which the hair-plaits[1] are beautifully arranged, putting red lead on the dividing lines:
Those heads are sheared by scissors, dust comes on (their) neck.
(Who) were within palaces, they do not now meet to sit in the presence (of their husbands).[2]

Pause.

Salutation, O father, salutation!
O primeval divine male, thy end is not obtained, thou goest on making disguises and seest them.
(2). Since they have been married, they shine at the side of their bridegrooms.
They were raised on swings, broken teeth were repaired.
From above water is sprinkled, fans glitter at (their) side.
(3). One Lakh they obtain when seated, one Lakh they obtain when standing.
The kernels of cocoa-nuts and dates they are eating, they enjoy their bed.
On their neck fetters are (now) placed, (their) pearl-strings[3] are broken.
(4). (Their) wealth and youth, both became (their) enemies, by whom they were entertained with love.
To the messengers (of Yama) the order was given; they marched (them) off, destroying (their) honour.
If it pleases him, then he gives honour; if it pleases him, then he inflicts punishment.
(5). If forethought would be made, why would punishment be met with?
(But) the great merchants had discarded the remembrance (of God) in merriment, shows and pleasure.
The word of Bābar went round: no boy[4] shall eat bread!
(6). The time of some is lost, the worship of others is useless.
Without a Čaukā how shall the Hindū women make their Tilak after having bathed?
Rām was never remembered by them, now on their calling God is not found.
(7). Some come to their house, others having met together ask for comfort.
The fate of some is this, that they sit down and weep in pain.
What is pleasing to him, that is done, Nānak (says): what is man?

XII.

(1). Where is that sport (and) stable of horses, where (are) the large drums (and) clarions?
Where are those sword-belts (and) chariots, where those red cloaks?
Where (are) those mirror-rings (and) fair faces? here they are not seen.

Pause.

This world is thine, thou art the Lord.
In twenty-four minutes thou dost establish and disestablish, thou dividest gold (as) thou pleasest.

[1] ਪਟੀ (paṭṭī), a woman's hair combed smoothly towards the two sides and divided by a line in the middle. This line is called ਮਾਂਗ (f.).

[2] These verses are an allusion to the sack of Eminābād by Bābar, the luxury of the women of that city being censured therein.

[3] ਮੋਤਸਰੀ s.f. A wire of gold or silver, on which pearls are strung, worn round the neck of women.

[4] ਕੁਇਰੁ (= कुमार) a boy, a youngster (unmarried).

(2). Where are those houses, gates, open halls and palaces, where those beautiful mansions?
Where that comfortable bed of the fascinating woman, seeing whom no sleep comes on.
Where are those betel-leaf selling women? they have become ashes, O mother!
(3). On account of this gold many people are destroyed, many are lost by this gold.
Without sin it is not acquired and it does not go with those, who have died.
Whom the creator himself feeds, he is happy (and) obtains prosperity.
(4). Crores of Pīrs tried to stop (him), when the Mīr (Bābar) was heard rushing on.
The palaces and glittering mansions were burnt (by him), the young men were cut to pieces and thrown about.
No Mugal became blind, by no one a miracle[1] was wrought.
(5). A battle took place between the Mugals and Paṭhāns, the sword was swung in the fight.
Those discharged the matchlocks, these provoked the elephants (to a charge).
Whose scrip is torn at the threshold (of God), they must die, O brother!
(6). Some (were) Hindū women and (some) Turk women, (some) the women of Bhaṭs and of Thākurs.
The robes of some were torn from head to foot, the dwelling of some was the burning place.
Whose well-dressed husbands did not come home, how was the night passed by them?
(7). The creator himself does and causes to be done (everything), to whom shall (anything) be said?
Pain and pleasure come by thy decree, to whom shall one go and weep?
He who is giving orders, delights in his order being executed; Nānak (says): what is written, that is obtained.

ĀSĀ KĀFĪ; MAHALĀ I.; GHAR VIII.; ASṬPADIĀ.

Ōm! by the favour of the true Guru!

XIII.[2]

(1). Like a cowherd in a cattle-shed, in such a state is the world.
Men practise vanity, they found households.

Pause.

Wake, wake, ye sleepers, the trafficker is gone!
(2). Continually houses would be built, if they could remain (in the world).
The body falls down, the soul will depart; if one knows this, (it is well).
(3). Why do you cry: alas! alas! that one[3] is and will be.
You will weep for that one, who may weep for you?
(4). Ye do a perplexing affair, O brethren, ye practise vanity.
That one does not hear in any way, you let hear the people (only).
(5). By whom he was put to sleep, O Nānak, he awakens him.
If he comprehends his own house, no sleep befalls him.
(6). Who, on departing, has taken with (him) some wealth:
Having seen his wealth collect it, reflecting comprehend you (too the truth)!

[1] ਪਰਚਾ is here explained traditionally by *miracle*. Its etymology is not known (provided it have this meaning, which would very well suit the context). The Pīrs promised to blind the Mugals, but failed signally.

[2] This Asṭpadī is sung by the Sikhs after the death of a man.

[3] That one (ਸੋਈ), *i.e.* the dead one.

(7). Carry on traffic, that you gain your object, lest you repent!
Abandon vices and practise virtues, in this way you will acquire truth.
(8). Make such farming, that you sow the seed of truth on the soil of duty.
Then you are known as traffickers, (if) you carry off gain.
(9). If it be (one's) destiny, the true Guru is met with (and) he understands the instruction (of the Guru).
He praises the name, he hears the name, with the name is his occupation.
(10). As gain, so is loss; (thus) the way (of the world) is going on.
What is pleasing to him, O Nānak, that is greatness.

XIV.

(1). The four corners (of the earth) were searched (by me), no one is mine.
If it pleases thee, O Lord, thou art mine and I am thine.

Pause.

No gate also pleases (me), to whom [1] shall I make salām?
Thou, O Lord, art alone mine, (thy) true name is in (my) mouth.
(2). The Siddhs have in view supernatural powers, the Pīrs ask for increase and perfection.
May by me the one name not be forgotten, the instruction of the true Guru!
(3). The Jōgī and the sensual Kāpaṛī what for do they wander about in other countries?
The word of the Guru they do not know, the essence of truth is in every place.
(4). The Paṇḍits and astrologers read continually the Purāṇas.
They do not know, that the thing is within, that in the heart Brahm is hidden.
(5). Some ascetics practise austerities in the forest, they dwell continually at a holy watering place.
Affected by the principle of darkness they do not know their own self, why do they wander about in retirement from the world?
(6). Some with great effort check their virile powers and are called chaste.
Without the word of the Guru they are not emancipated, in error they come and go.
(7). Some are householders and servants of the ascetics and attached to the instruction of the Guru.
(Who are given to) the name, alms-giving and bathing (and whose) attachment to Hari is firm, they wake.
(8). (By whom) from the Guru the gate and house (of Hari) are learned, he, having gone (to the other world) recognizes it.
Nānak (says): (by whom) the name is not forgotten, he is pleasing to the mind of the True one.

XV.

(1). Consuming the desire of the mind (I) cross the water of existence easily.[2]
Thou art the first before all ages and merciful, O Lord, (I am) in thy asylum.

Pause.

Thou art munificent, I am a beggar, may the sight of Hari be given (to me)!
(If) by the disciple the name be meditated upon, the mansion of the mind flourishes.
(2). (If) false greediness be given up, he gets acquainted with the True one.
(If) he enter into the word of the Guru, he knows the highest object.

[1] ਕੈ is the Formative of ਕਵਣ = ਕੈ ਕਉ, to whom?
[2] ਸਚਿ is here = ਸੁਖਿ.

(3). This (human) mind is a greedy Rājā and is becoming more greedy.
By the disciple greediness is removed, there is intimacy with Hari.
(4). (If) seed be sown on a sterile field, how shall one get a gain (from it)?
The self-willed man does not delight in the True one, he buries one falsehood in another.
(5). Give up greediness, O ye blind ones, in greediness there is great pain.
(If) the true Lord dwells in the mind, the poison of egotism is destroyed.
(6). Give up duality, it is a bad road, (on which) thou wilt be robbed.
Day and night the name should be praised in the asylum of the true Guru!
(7). The self-willed man is a stone and rock, woe to his life, it is insipid!
Though it may be kept long in the water, it is dry within.
(8). The name of Hari is a treasure, it is given by the perfect Guru.
Nānak (says): (by whom) the name is not forgotten, he churns and drinks nectar.

XVI.

(1). Going on the travellers have departed.
The world is pushing on (its) business, the True one is not pleasing (to it).

Pause.

What do they wander about, what is sought? it is shown by the word of the Guru.
(By whom) selfishness and illusion are abandoned, he comes to his own house.
(2). The truthful man is united with the True one, by falsehood he is not obtained.
By fixing one's thoughts on the True one, one does not come again.
(3). Why do you weep for the dead ones? you do not know how to weep.
Weep by praising the True one and you will recognize (his) order.
(4). By the (supreme) ruler the wages are set down, this should be known.
Who receives the gain in the hem of his garment, he recognizes (his) order.
(5). By the decree of the (supreme) ruler (one) goes dressed (with a dress of honour) to the threshold.
By the order of the Lord (there is likewise) beating on the head and imprisonment.[1]
(6). (This is) gain, (that) true equity be fixed in the mind.
Who has received what is written (for him), removes pride.
(7). The self-willed (woman) is beaten on the head, by disputing she is ruined.
By deceit the false one is robbed, she is bound and marched off.
(8). Who makes the Lord dwell in the heart, will not repent afterwards.
He is pardoning the sins (of her), who does the word (of the Guru).
(9). Nānak asks for the service of a true disciple.
Without thee none other is seen with my eyes.

XVII.

(1). What shall I go and search in the jungle, in my house is a green forest.
By means of the true word (of the Guru) he (Hari) comes quickly to (my) house and dwells (therein).

Pause.

Wherever I see, there is he, no other is known.
By doing the work of the Guru (his) palace is recognized.

[1] ਭਾਣੀਐ = ਭਾਣੇ; constr. ਹੁਕਮੀ ਦੇ ਭਾਣੇ. In the second line ਰਹਾਣੀਐ (= ਰਹਾਣੀ) must be joined with ਹੁਕਮੇਹੀ, by the order of the Lord. The words are much misplaced and corrupted for the sake of making up a rhyme.

(2). (If) the True one himself unites (one with himself), then he is pleasing to the mind.
Who walks always according to (his) pleasure, he is absorbed in (his) bosom.
(3). In (whose) mind the true Lord dwells, he is happy in his mind.
He himself gives greatness, there is no lack in his giving.
(4). By a service (consisting in saying): O thou! how should one get the threshold (of Hari)?
Who ascends a boat of stone, him it drowns with the loaded state.
(5). One's own mind should be sold, the head should be given with it.
By the disciple the thing[1] is recognized, having searched his own house.
(6). Birth and death are said to be made by that creator.
Who, having removed their own self, are dying, they do not die again.
(7). That work must be done, which is ordered by himself.
Some (rare) one, who gives his mind to the true Guru and meets (with him), gets (his = Hari's) estimate.
(8). That Lord is examining the gems, he gets (their true) estimate.
Nānak (says): (in whose) mind the Lord dwells, (he has) true greatness.

XVIII.

(1). By whom the name is forgotten, they are led astray by the error of duality.
Who, giving up the root, cling to the branches, what do they obtain (but) ashes?

Pause.

How should one be emancipated without the name? would that some one would know this!
If one become a disciple, then he is emancipated, the self-willed one loses his honour.
(2). By whom the One is served, their intelligence is perfect, O brother!
The pious are in the asylum of Hari, who is first and before (all) ages.
(3). My Lord is One, there is no other, O brother!
From (his) mercy happiness is obtained by discussion on the True one.
(4). Without the Guru he is obtained by no one, how much soever one may talk (about it).
He himself shows the way, he (himself) confirms true devotion.
(5). Though the self-willed man be admonished, yet he goes astray.
Without the name of Hari he will not be emancipated, having died he enters hell.
(6). (Who) does not take the name of Hari, is born (again) and dies and is made to wander about (in transmigration).
Without serving the Guru he does not get his (= Hari's) estimate.
(7). As one is caused (by Hari) to render service (to the Guru), so also (he is caused to do) works.
He himself does it (in reality), to whom shall (anything) be said? (if one) see (this), (he gets) greatness.[2]
(8). He renders service to the Guru, whom he himself causes to render (it).
Nānak (says): by giving the head (to the Guru) one gets emancipation, at the threshold he receives honour.

XIX.

(1). Well known is the Lord and master, well known is the word of the Guru.
By reason of a great destiny the true Guru is met with, and the step of final emancipation obtained (in consequence).

[1] ਵਸਤੁ the thing = the absolute substance, the Supreme.

[2] The literal meaning of ਵੇਖੈ ਵਡਿਆਈ is: he sees greatness. But there is hardly any sense in such a translation; we have translated therefore according to conjecture, following the hint thrown out in the following verse.

Pause.

I am thy slave of slaves,[1] I am thy orphan.

As thou keepest me, so I remain, in my mouth is the name.

(2). (I have) a great longing after (his) sight, (his) decree I like in (my) mind.

In the hand of my Lord is greatness, by his decree honour is obtained.

(3). The True one should not be considered (as being) far away, he is within.

Wherever I see, there he is contained; who can get an estimate (of him)?

(4). He himself does (everything), he himself takes away; who sees (this), (to him accrues) greatness.

By becoming a disciple it is seen, thus an estimate (of him) is obtained.

(5). He obtains gain whilst living, who does the work of the Guru.

(If) it be written (for him) before, then he gets the true Guru.

(6). The self-willed man continually (suffers) loss, he is wandering about.

The self-willed one is blind and does not think (of Hari), how shall he obtain (his) sight?

(7). Then (one) is known as being aroused from sleep, (if) he meditate on the True one.

Those who meet with the Guru, become philosophers' stones, the Luminous one is blending (with himself) light.

(8). Day and night he remains aloof (from the world), the work fixed from the beginning must be done.

Nānak (says): those, who are happy in the name, are attached to the feet of Hari.

XX.

(1). How much talk is made! I do not know its end.

Thou alone art the support of me, the helpless one, (thou art) my strong protection!

Pause.

It is the petition[2] of Nānak: by the true name (I am) happy.

(My) own self is gone, right knowledge is obtained, by the word of the Guru (I am) united (with Hari).

(2). (If) the pride of egotism be removed, (true) reflection is obtained.

The mind becomes pleased with the Lord, the True one gives support (to it).

(3). (If one be) day and night happy in the name, that is true service.

Him no calamity befalls, (who) walks according to (his) order and will.

(4). Who walks according to (his) order and will, he is received into the treasury (of Hari).

The spurious ones find no place, they are mixed with the false ones.

(5). Continually the genuine (metal) should be taken care of, true traffic should be carried on.

The spurious ones do not come into his sight, they are taken and burnt with fire.

(6). By whom his (own) spirit is known, he is the supreme spirit.

(If) there is one tree of nectar, (its) fruit (also) becomes nectar.

(7). Who taste the nectar fruit, they are satiated by the True one.

They have no error nor difference (from the Supreme), they make (their) tongue utter Hari.

(8). According to his order (thou hast) come (into the world), walk always after (his) pleasure!

The vicious one (gets) virtue, (and) Nānak obtains true greatness.

[1] ਓਲਗੀ (written in another MS. ਓਲ੍ਰਗੀ, ōlragī) is traditionally explained by the Sikhs: 'a slave.' But this meaning is very doubtful. The word occurs here and Āsā Ravidās II. (2) (there ਓਲਗ), and no etymology can be assigned for it. It may be the Turkish اولق ūlaq, a runner, courier.

[2] *i.e.* Nānak says.

XXI.

(1). (My) mind is attached to the name of Hari, the True one is praised (by me).
What can people do (to me), when I please thee?

Pause.

As long as there is life (and) breath (in me), the True one is meditated upon.
By singing the excellences of Hari profit is obtained, happiness is received.
(2). True is thy work, give it (to me), O merciful one!
I live by praising thee, thou art my prop and support.
(3). (I am) a servant at (thy) gate, (I am thy) doorkeeper, (my) pain thou knowest.
By thy worship (I am) perplexed, thou removest (my) pain.
(4). The disciple will consider the threshold and name (of Hari) (as being) in (his) presence.
The true and approved (disciple) will know the word (of the Guru) in (proper) time.
(5). Practise truth, contentment and love, use the name of Hari as viaticum!
Drop from (thy) mind vice and he gives (thee) true happiness.
(6). True is the love to the True one, (that) is fixed on the True one.
He himself administers justice (to him), who pleases him.
(7). True is the gift of the True one, he is merciful (and) gives.
Him I serve day and night, (whose) name is priceless.
(8). Thou art the highest, I am called thy low servant.
Nānak (says): (if) he bestow a favourable look, the True one is found (even) by strangers.

XXII.

(1). How are coming and going stopped, how will union (with Hari) be brought about?
Great is the pain of birth and death, there is always doubt (and) duality.

Pause.

What is life without the name? away with cunning!
Who does not serve the true, pious Guru, (to him) the worship of Hari is not pleasing.
(2). Coming and going are then stopped, when the perfect Guru is obtained.
(To whom) he gives the wealth (and) capital of the name of Rām, (his) false error is destroyed.
(3). To the saints (the name) accrues; blessed, blessed is he, who sings the glory (of Hari)!
The primeval divine male, the boundless Hari, the disciple obtains.
(4). By the juggler a sham and play is made in the world.
Every moment a play is seen, it passes (again) away without delay.
(5). In false pride (the world) is playing the Čaupaṛ-play of egotism.
The whole world is overcome, he wins, who reflects on the word of the Guru.
(6). As a staff in the hand of the blind one, so is the name of Hari to me.
The name of Hari, Rām, is a support, day and night it upholds (me).
(7). As thou keepest me, so I remain, the name of Hari is my support.
At the end (thou art) obtained as companion, (thy) people (are) emancipated at (thy) gate.
(8). The pain of birth and death is effaced by muttering the name of Murāri.
Nānak (says): (by whom) the name is not forgotten, (him) the perfect Guru brings across.

ĀSĀ; MAHALĀ III.; ASṬPADĪĀ; GHAR II.

Ōm! by the favour of the true Guru!

I. XXIII.

(1). Thine is the ocean of the Shāstras, the Vēdas and the Smriti, the Gangā is contained in (thy) foot.

(Thy) wisdom holds fast the root of the three branches, thou art assuming all forms.

Pause.

His feet humble Nānak mutters, he utters a nectar speech.

(2). Thirty-three crores (of gods) are thy servants, affluence (and) life (thou art) upholding.

His forms cannot be conceived, what can I say and reflect?

(3). The three qualities are thine, in the four ages are thy mines.

(If) it be one's destiny, then the highest step (of emancipation) is obtained, one tells the inexpressible story (of Hari).

(4). Thou art the creator, every creature is thine, what can any living being do?

On whom thou bestowest thy own favourable look, he is absorbed in the True one.

(5). Every one is taking thy name, as many as are coming and going.

If (one) be pleasing to thee, then, (becoming) a disciple, he comprehends (the truth), the other, (being) self-willed, wanders about as a silly man.

(6). The four Vēdas were given to Brahmā; going on reading (the Paṇḍit) reflects (on them).

The helpless man does not comprehend (his) order, he is (consequently) frequenting hell and heaven.

(7). Rājās of the several (succeeding) ages were made, they sing (to him), having made their descent (on earth).

These also have not reached his end, what can I say and reflect?

(8). Thou art true, all thy work is true, (if) thou give (it me), I praise the True one.

Whom thou makest comprehend thy own true (name), he is easily absorbed in (thy) name.

II. XXIV.

(1). By the true Guru my doubt is removed.

The pure name of Hari is made to dwell in (my) mind.

Knowing the word (of the Guru) happiness is always obtained.

Pause.

Hear, O my mind, the knowledge of the Supreme Being!

The donor knows every affair, by the disciple the treasure of the name is obtained.

(2). Who meets with the true Guru, obtains greatness.

By whom the fire of egotism and (worldly) desire is quenched:

He is easily intoxicated by singing the excellences of Hari.

(3). Without the perfect Guru no one is knowing (the truth).

By the infatuation of the Māyā and by duality he is affected with greediness.

The disciple gets the name (and) the word of Hari.

(4). The service of the Guru is the highest of all austerities.

(If) Hari dwells in the mind, he makes forget all pain.

At the true gate the truthful one is seen (with honour).

(5). From the service of the Guru the right knowledge of the three worlds is obtained.

Who knows his own self, he obtains Hari.

By means of the true word (of the Guru) the palace (of Hari) is reached.

(6). By the service of the Guru he (*i.e.* the disciple) saves his whole family.
The pure name he keeps in his breast.
True is (his) glory at the true gate.
(7). They have a great lot, who are applied by the Guru (to his own) service.
Day by day they hold firm worship and the true name.
By the name are saved all (their) families.
(8). Nānak delivers true instruction:
Keep the name of Hari in (thy) breast!
Who is attached to the worship of Hari, (gets) the gate of salvation.

III. XXV.

(1). Every one entertains hope upon hope.
Who understands the order (of Hari), becomes free from hope.
In hope many people have fallen asleep.
He wakes, whom he awakens.

Pause.

By the true Guru the name is given to understand, without the name hunger does not go.
By the name the fire of thirst is quenched, the name is given to him, (on whom his) pleasure is.
(2). In the Kali-yug (fame accrues to him who) knows the word (of the Guru).
By this worship (is effected) and egotism ceases.
By serving the true Guru one becomes approved.
By whom hope is entertained, he suffers loss.
(3). What shall be given to him, who lets hear the word?
Who mercifully makes the name dwell in the mind.
This head should be given after having removed one's own self.
Who comprehends the order (of Hari), obtains always happiness.
(4). He himself does and causes to be done (everything).
He himself makes the name dwell (in) the disciple.
He himself leads astray, he himself puts into the (right) way.
By the true word he reabsorbs into the True one.
(5). The true word (of the Guru) is the true speech.
By the disciple it is continually uttered and praised.
The self-willed one is led astray by infatuation and error.
Without the name all wander about mad.
(6). In the three worlds the One is contained.
The fool reading on entertains another love.
He performs many (religious) works, (which are) all pain.
By serving the true Guru happiness is always obtained.
(7). Reflecting on the word (of the Guru) is sweet nectar.
He enjoys it day by day having subdued (his) egotism.
He is naturally in joy, (on whom) he bestows grace.
Who are attached to the name, are always in true love.
(8). Hari should be muttered and read by reflecting on the word of the Guru!
Hari should be muttered and read having subdued one's egotism!
Hari should be muttered with affection and true love!
Nānak (says): keep the name in (thy) breast by means of the instruction of the Guru!

RĀG ĀSĀ; MAHALĀ III.; ASṬPADĪĀ; GHAR VIII.; KĀFĪ.

Ōm! By the favour of the true Guru!

IV. XXVI.

(1). By the Guru tranquillity is produced, by whom the fire of thirst is quenched.
From the Guru the name is obtained, great (is his) greatness.

Pause.

Think of the One name, O my brother!
Seeing the world burning we have fled and fallen on the asylum (of Hari).
(2). From the Guru divine knowledge springs and the reflection on the great truth.
From the Guru goods and chattels are obtained, with worship (his) store-rooms are filled.
(3). By the disciple the name is meditated upon, he comprehends the instruction.
The disciple (is given) to worship and praise, in his heart is the boundless word (of the Guru).
(4). Happiness springs up (in) the disciple, he never (incurs) pain.
By the disciple egotism is destroyed, (his) mind becomes pure.
(5). By meeting with the true Guru self departs, the knowledge of the three worlds is obtained.
A pure light is spread out, by the Luminous one light is blended (with himself).
(6). (Who) is instructed by the perfect Guru, his understanding becomes very high.
(His) heart becomes cool and tranquil, by the name happiness is produced.
(7). The perfect, true Guru is then met with, when he (Hari) bestows a favourable look.
All blemishes and sins are cut off, no pain nor calamity arises again.
(8). In his own hand is greatness, he gives (it to him, whom) he applies to the name.
Nānak (says): in whose mind dwells the treasure of the name, he obtains greatness.

V. XXVII.

(1). Having heard make (him) dwell in (thy) mind, he himself comes and joins (thee), O my brother!
Day by day perform true worship, direct thy thoughts on the True one!

Pause.

Meditate thou on the One name, thou wilt obtain happiness, O my brother!
Egotism and duality remove, (thy) greatness (will be) great.
(2). This worship the excellent men and Munis are desiring, (but) without the true Guru it cannot be obtained.
The Paṇḍits and astrologers are reading, (but) they get no understanding.
(3). By himself everything is preserved, nothing can be said.
What he himself gives, that is obtained, by the Guru comprehension (of the truth) is communicated.
(4). All living creatures are his and he belongs to all of them.
Who shall be called bad? if there would be another.[1]
(5). Only one order is current, there is only one government.
He himself makes (them) wander about, in (whose) heart is the vice of covetousness.
(6). Some are made by himself disciples, they comprehend the instruction (of the Guru).
Devotion is also bestowed on them by him, (which) is in (his) store-rooms.
(7). The wise ones have all the truth, they have true knowledge.
Though led astray by some one they do not go astray, they know the True one.

[1] The sense is: if there would be another (besides the One Supreme), then one could be called bad. But as the Supreme is in all, all are his creatures, they are all the same.

(8). In the house (= the body) the five (senses) are dwelling and reflecting.

Nānak (says): without the true Guru they are not brought into subjection, by the name egotism is destroyed.

VI. XXVIII.

(1). In the house is the whole thing, outside (of it) is nothing.

By the favour of the Guru it is obtained, he draws out the falsity, (that is) within.

Pause.

From the true Guru Hari is obtained, O brother!

(That) the treasure of the name is within (the heart), this is shown by the perfect true Guru.

(2). Who is duly appreciating Hari, he takes and obtains the gem of reflection.

(Who) opens (his) heart, he sees by a supernatural sight, (that) the store-rooms (of Hari) are opened.

(3). Within are many apartments, (where) the soul dwells.

The fruit desired by (his) mind he will obtain, there will no more be wandering about (in transmigration).

(4). By the assayer the thing is taken care of, from the Guru information is obtained.

The boon of the name is priceless, some (rare) disciple obtains it.

(5). Who searches the outside, what does he get? the thing is in the house, O brother!

Being led astray by error the whole world wanders about, by the self-willed one his honour is lost.

(6). Giving up his own house the false one goes to another's house.

Like a thief he is seized, without the name he is beaten.

(7). Who know their own house, they are happy, O brother!

Within it Brahm is recognized (owing to) the greatness of the Guru.

(8). He himself bestows gifts, to whom shall (anything) be said? he himself makes understand (the truth).

O Nānak, meditate thou on the name, at the true gate thou wilt obtain glory.

VII. XXIX.

(1). The knowing one's own self is a sweet taste, O brother!

By tasting the juice of Hari they become emancipated, to whom the True one is pleasing.

Pause.

Hari is pure; (his) pure dwelling is in a pure mind.

(By whom) he is praised (by means of) the instruction of the Guru, he is indifferent to the word in the midst of the world.

(2). Without the word (of the Guru) one's own self is not known, the whole (world) is blind, O brother!

By the instruction of the Guru light (is made) in the heart, the name is a companion at the end.

(3). In the name they live, in the name they abide.

In (their) heart is the name, in (their) mouth is the name, (their) reflection is on the name (and) the word (of the Guru).

(4). By hearing the name, by minding the name greatness (accrues) by the name.

(Who) praises the name continually, he reaches the palace (of Hari) by means of the name.

(5). By means of the name light (is produced) in the heart, by the name splendour is obtained.

By the name happiness is produced, in the name (is) a refuge.

(6). Without the name no one is accepted, by the self-willed (their) honour is lost.

They are bound and beaten in the city of Yama, their life is wasted to no purpose.

(7). All render service to the name, (but) the disciple he makes to comprehend the name.

Even the name, the name should be minded, in the name is greatness!

(8). To whom he gives it, he gets it, by the instruction of the Guru he (Hari) makes comprehend the name.

Nānak (says): everything is in the power of the name, by reason of a perfect lot some one gets it.

VIII. XXX.

(1). The ill-favoured women do not reach the palace, they do not know the relish of the beloved one.

They speak insipid things, they do not bow down, another love is (their) pleasure.

Pause.

How shall this mind be brought into subjection?

By the favour of the Guru it is stopped, by attention to divine knowledge it returns home.

(2). The favoured woman is adorned by himself, bestowing (his) love and affection (on her).

Walking according to the will of the true Guru she is easily decorated by the name.

(3). She always enjoys her own beloved, true is (her) bed by love.

She is charmed by the love of her beloved, meeting with her beloved she gets happiness.

(4). Boundless knowledge is (her) ornament, the woman is decorated (thereby).

She is stout and beautiful by love and affection to her beloved.

(5). On the favoured women love is bestowed by the true, invisible and boundless (Supreme).

They serve their own Guru with true love and affection.

(6). By the favoured woman decoration is made, a necklace of virtues is on her neck.

The exquisite scent[1] of love she is rubbing on her body, within (her) is the gem of reflection.

(7). Who are attached to the worship (of Hari), they are the highest, caste and fellowship come from the word (of the Guru).

Without the name every one is of low caste, he becomes a worm of ordure.

(8). Saying: "I, I," the whole (world) wanders about, without the word (of the Guru) egotism does not depart.

Nānak (says): who are attached to the name, their egotism departs, they are absorbed in the True one.

IX. XXXI.

(1). Who are attached to the True one, they are pure, (their) report is always true.

Here they are known in every house, further on they become manifest in every age.

Pause.

O silly, gay mind, apply thou true colour!

If the well-known word (of the Guru) enter deeply, this colour does not go off nor disappear.

(2). We are low, dirty and excessively conceited, by another love (we are) useless.

By meeting with the Guru, the philosopher's stone, we became gold, pure, infinite light.

(3). Without the Guru no one is coloured, by meeting with the Guru colour is applied.

Who are steeped in the fear and love of the Guru, they by means of praising (Hari) are absorbed in the True one.

(4). Without fear love does not spring up nor does the mind become pure.

Those who are doing works without fear, are false, they get no place (of rest).

(5). Whom he himself colours, he will receive the die, he joins (him) to the society of the pious.

From the perfect Guru the society of the pious springs up in an easy and true manner.

(6). Without the society (of the pious) all remain such as cattle and oxen (are).

By whom they were made, him they do not know, without the name all are thieves.

[1] ਪਿਰਮਲੁ = परिमल, exquisite scent, loosely taken for sandal-wood.

(7). Some buy virtues and sell (their) vices by the natural good disposition of the Guru.

From the service of the Guru the name is obtained, it comes and dwells in (their) heart.

(8). The donor of all is the One, having created (them) he puts (them) into (their) work.

Nānak (says): they are applied by him to the name, by means of the word (of the Guru) they are united (with him).

X. XXXII.

(1). The whole (world) is desiring the name; on whom he bestows mercy, he gets it.

Without the name all is pain, he (gets) happiness, in whose mind he makes dwell (the name).

Pause.

Thou art boundless (and) gracious, (I am in) thy asylum.

From the perfect Guru the greatness of the name is obtained.

(2). Inside and outside is the One, (by whom) a manifold creation is produced.

(According to his) order he makes (them) do works, who may be called (his) second, O brother?

(3). Understanding aud not understanding is made by thee, this is thy sovereignty.

Some thou pardonest and unitest (with thyself), some, who are false, thou beatest at (thy) threshold and kickest them out.

(4). Some are thoroughly pure and clean, they are applied by thee to the name.

From the service of the Guru happiness springs up, by the true word (of the Guru) they are made to comprehend (the truth).

(5). Some are of bad conduct, filthy, infected with poison, he himself makes (them) stray away from the name.

They have neither perfection nor understanding nor control of the passions, they wander about being puffed up.

(6). On whom he bestows his own merciful look, him he applies to faith (in himself).

Who is coercing (his) mind by truth and contentment, (him) he lets hear the pure word (of the Guru).

(7). By reading an estimation one does not arrive (at a true estimate), by telling and reciting (stories) one does not get the end (of him).

From the Guru the (true) estimate (of him) is obtained, by means of the true word (of the Guru) true knowledge (of him) is acquired.

(8). Examine thou this mind (and) body by reflecting on the word of the Guru!

Nānak (says): in this body is the treasure of the name, it is obtained by infinite love to the Guru.

XI. XXXIII.

(1). Those favoured women are attached to the True one, whom he adorns with the word of the Guru.

Even in the house that beloved one is obtained, by reflecting on the true word.

Pause.

By (her) virtues pardon is procured for the vices (of her), (by whom) devout meditation is bestowed on Hari.

Hari is obtained (by her) as husband, the woman is united (with him) by the Guru.

(2). Some do not know, that their beloved one is in (their) presence, he leads them astray by the error of duality.

How should the ill-favoured women obtain (him)? in pain the night is passed (by them).

(3). In whose mind the True one dwells, they practise true work.

Daily they serve (him) with ease, they are absorbed in the True one.

(4). The ill-favoured women are led astray by error, they speak falsehood (and) eat poison.

They do not know their own beloved, their bed is empty (and) they incur pain.

(5). The true Lord is one, may not (any one) lead his mind astray by error!

Who serves him after having asked the Guru, she makes the True and Pure one dwell in (her) mind.

(6). By the favoured woman is (her) beloved one always obtained after having removed egotism and her own self.

She is day by day occupied with her beloved, true is (her) bed, she obtains happiness.

(7). Saying: "mine, mine," they are gone without having put anything into (their) lap.

The ill-favoured woman (does) not (reach) the palace (of Hari), at the end she departs with regret.

(8). That my beloved is One; direct thy devout meditation on the One!

Nānak (says): if the woman desires happiness, let her make the name of Hari dwell in (her) mind!

XII. XXXIV.

(1). Whom he makes taste nectar, they naturally get the relish of it.

The True one is without concern, he has not a bit of covetousness.

Pause.

True nectar is raining, it falls into the mouth of the disciples.

The mind is (thereby) always flourishing, it sings naturally the excellences of Hari.

(2). The self-willed are always ill-favoured women; standing at the gate they lament,

Who have not got the enjoyment of (their) beloved; they do what is written at the beginning.

(3). The disciple sows (truth) and truth springs up, the true name is (her) occupation.

Whom he has here put into gain, (to her) he gives (his) store-rooms of devotion.

(4). The disciple is always a favoured woman by being ornamented with fear and devotion.

Daily she enjoys her own beloved, the True one she keeps in her breast.

(5). By whom their own beloved is enjoyed, for them I sacrifice myself.

They always remain with their beloved, they remove from within their own self.

(6). (Their) mind and body are cool, (their) faces bright by the love and affection to their beloved.

Their bed is comfortable, they enjoy their beloved having extinguished the thirst of egotism.

(7). Out of mercy he has come to the house (by reason of their) infinite love to the Guru.

The favoured women obtained for their only husband the enemy of Mura.

(8). For all sins pardon is procured by him, they are united by him who is uniting (them).

Nānak (says): (this) word is told (to them), who, having heard (it), conceive love (to it).

XIII. XXXV.

(1). From the true Guru excellence is produced, when that Lord procures him (*i.e.* the Guru).

Easily the name is (then) meditated upon, divine knowledge becomes manifest.

Pause.

O mind, do not think, that Hari is far off, behold (him) always in thy presence!

He is always hearing, he is always seeing, by the word (of the Guru he is perceived as being) omnipresent.

(2). He is meditated upon with one mind by those disciples, by whom their own self is known.

They always enjoy their own beloved, by the true name happiness is obtained.

(3). O mind, none is thine, see, having reflected on the word (of the Guru)!

Flee to the asylum of Hari, thou wilt obtain the gate of salvation!

(4). (If the truth) be heard by means of the word (of the Guru), if it be comprehended by means of the word, (one) bestows devout meditation on the True one.

By means of the word egotism is destroyed, he (= the disciple) obtains happiness in the true palace.

(5). In this age (of the world) is the glory of the name (manifest), without the name glory is not to be obtained.

The glory of this Māyā lasts for four days, it passes away without delay.

(6). By whom the name is forgotten, they are dead (and) will die.

The flavour and taste of Hari they do not get, they are absorbed in ordure.

(7). Some are pardoned by himself and united (with himself), day by day he applies (them) to the name.

The True one they gain, in the True one they remain, in the perfectly True one they are absorbed.

(8). Without the word (of the Guru) one neither hears nor sees, the world is deaf and blind and goes astray.

Without the name it will incur pain, the name is obtained by his pleasure.

(9). By whom their mind is applied to the word (of the Guru), those people (become) pure and approved of.

Nānak (says): the name is never forgotten by them, they go to the true gate.

XIV. XXXVI.

(1). By the word (of the Guru) (those) devotees are taught, whose speech is true.

Their own self departed from within, the name is minded (by them), union with the True one is brought about.

Pause.

The name of Hari, Hari is the honour of (his) people.

Their life is fruitful, everybody pays regard to them.

(2). Egotism, excessive passion (and) conceit is the nature (of man).

(If one) die by means of the word (of the Guru), then (this) nature goes, light is blended with the luminous Supreme Lord.

(3). The perfect true Guru has met (with us), our life (has become) fruitful.

The nine treasures of the name are obtained, the store-rooms (of which are) full and inexhaustible.

(4). (Those) retail-dealers of this stock of goods come, who have love to the name.

Who become disciples, they get (this) property, in their heart the word (of the Guru) is reflected upon.

(5). The conceited self-willed people do not know the excellence of devotion.

Even by himself they are ruined, the dice-play is lost (by them).

(6). Without love (to Hari) devotion does not take place, nor is pleasure obtained in the body.

The boon of love is obtained by attachment to the Guru and composure of the mind.

(7). Whom he makes perform devotion, he does it by reflecting on the word of the Guru.

(If) the one name dwells in the heart, it destroys egotism (and) duality.

(8). The caste and brotherhood of the devotees is the one name, he himself adorns (them).

They are always in his asylum, as it pleases (him), so they do works.

(9). Pure devotion to Allah is learnt from the instruction of the Guru.

Nānak (says): in (his) heart the name dwells, (who) adorns (it) with fear and attachment to the name.

XV. XXXVII.

(1). Who is led astray into a false taste, he incurs pain without the name.

The true Guru, the divine male, does not meet (with him), who imparts true understanding.

Pause.

O my silly mind, taste the juice of Hari and thou wilt get (its) flavour!

Thou art wandering about clinging to a false taste, thou wastest thy life to no purpose.

(2). In this age the disciples (are) pure, who devoutly meditate on the true name.

Without destiny nothing is obtained, what can be said?

(3). (Who) knows his own self, (who) dies by the word (of the Guru), (who) drops change from (his) mind;

(Who) flees to the asylum of the Guru, (him) the pardoner pardons.

(4). Without the name happiness is not obtained nor does pain depart from within.

This world is imbued with the infatuation of the Māyā, by the error of duality it is led astray.

(5). The ill-favoured woman has no knowledge of (her) beloved, how will she adorn herself?

Always, day by day she goes about burning, on (her) bed (her) husband does not dally (with her).

(6). The favoured woman reaches (his) palace having removed from within her own self.

Being adorned by the word of the Guru she is joined by her own bridegroom.

(7). Death is forgotten from his mind, the infatuation of the Māyā (and) darkness (are in him).

The self-willed one having died repeatedly is born again and dies, at the gate of Yama he becomes wretched.

(8). Who are united by himself (with himself), they are united having reflected on the word of the Guru.

Nānak (says): they are absorbed in the name, their faces are bright at that true court.

ĀSĀ; MAHALĀ V.; ASṬPADĪÃ; GHAR II.

Õm! By the favour of the true Guru!

I. XXXVIII.

(1). The five[1] are appeased, the five[2] are irritated.

The five are made to dwell (in the mind), the five are despatched.

Pause.

In this wise the town is peopled, O my brother!

(His) sin is gone, (who) holds firmly the divine knowledge of the Guru.

(2). A fence of true piety is made and given (by the Guru).

The planks (of his fence) are strong, (who) reflects on the divine knowledge of the Guru.

(3). Sow the name in (thy) field, O brother and friend!

Carry on traffic, serve continually the Guru!

(4). All (their) shops are shops of tranquillity, ease and comfort.

The retail-dealers of the wholesale merchant (live in) splendour.

(5). None of the poll-tax gatherers[3] takes a fine or tax (from them),

(On whom) the true Guru has set his own seal.

(6). Having laden the name as (thy) goods go on trafficking!

Having obtained profit (thereby) return to (thy) house, O disciple!

(7). The true Guru is the wholesale merchant, the disciples are (his) retail-dealers.

The name is (their) capital-stock, the True one takes account (from them).

(8). He dwells in this house, who (performs) service to the perfect Guru.

Eternal is the city of God, (says) Nānak.

[1] The five virtues are very differently enumerated; *e.g.* ਸਤੁ (truth = सत्त्व) ਸੰਤੋਖ (contentment), ਸੰਜਮ (control of the passions), ਇਸਨਾਨ (ablution), ਦਾਨ (alms).

[2] These five are = ਕਾਮ, ਕ੍ਰੋਧ, etc.

[3] ਜੇਜੀਆ *s.m.* the collector of the poll-tax (Arab. جِزيَه).

ĀSĀVARĪ; MAHALĀ V.; GHAR III.

Ōm! By the favour of the true Guru!

I. II. XXXIX.

Pause.

My mind has conceived love to Hari.

Muttering Hari, Hari in the society of the pious (it becomes) pure, true (its) practice.

(1). (I am) much longing after (thy) sight, I think (of thee) in many ways.

Bestow a favour (on me), O Supreme Brahm, O Hari, O Murāri, be gracious (to me)!

(2). (My) mind has come from a foreign country and joined the society of the pious.

Who is desiring goods, he gets them by love to the name.

(3). All the pleasures and relishes of the Māyā pass away in a moment.

The devotees are attached to thy name, they enjoy happiness in every place.

(4). The whole world is seen as passing away, immovable is the name of Hari.

Having made friendship with the pious thou wilt obtain an immovable spot.

(5). Friends, sweethearts, sons and relatives, no one is remaining with (thee).

The one name of Rām is accompanying (thee), the Lord is the friend of the poor.

(6). The lotus-feet (of Hari) are the boat, by clinging to that the ocean is crossed.

The perfect, true Guru meets with (him, who) has true love to the Lord.

(7). (This is) the solicitation of thy saints: may he (= God) not be forgotten at any breath and morsel!

Who is pleasing to thee, he is good, by thy decree his affair (is put) right.

(8). The beloved one, the ocean of happiness, is met with, great joy has sprung up.

Nānak says: all pains are effaced, the Lord, the highest bliss, has met (with me).

ĀSĀ; MAHALĀ V.; BIRAHAṚĒ;[1] GHAR IV.

A kind of Čhants.

Ōm! By the favour of the true Guru!

I. III. XL.

(1). The Supreme Brahm, the Lord, is remembered (by me), I sacrifice myself for the sight of the beloved one.

(2). By the remembrance of whom pain is forgotten, how can that beloved one be abandoned?

(3). I sell this (my) body to the saint (= the Guru), that he may make meet (with me) my dearly beloved one.

(4). The pleasures and ornaments of the world are insipid, they are given up (by me), O my mother!

(5). Lust, wrath and covetousness are abandoned (by me) having fallen down at the feet of the beloved true Guru.

(6). Those, who are attached to the beloved Rāṃ, they do not go anywhere else.

(7). Who have tasted the juice of the beloved Hari, they are fully satiated.

(8). By whom the hem of the pious (Guru) is seized, (him) he ferries across the ocean of existence, (says) Nānak.

[1] ਬਿਰਹੜੇ, literally: pangs of love caused by separation from the beloved (dim. of ਬਿਰਹੁ).

II. IV. XLI.

(1). The pain of birth and death is cut off, O beloved, when Hari the king meets (with any one).

(2). Beautiful, clever and very wise is the Lord, my life, show (me thy) sight!

(3). The creatures, which are separated from thee, O beloved, they are born (again) and die having eaten poison.

(4). Whom thou unitest (with thee), he is united, O beloved, to his foot I cling.

(5). The happiness, (that is gained) from seeing thy sight, O beloved, cannot be told with the mouth.

(6). True love does not break, O beloved, it remains for all ages.

(7). What pleases thee, that is good, O beloved, thy pleasure is command.

(8). Nānak (says): those who are imbued with love to Nārāyaṇ, O beloved, are naturally intoxicated.

III. V. XLII.

(1). Every affair thou art knowing, O beloved, to whom shall I say (anything)?

(2). Thou art the donor of all creatures, what thou givest, they put on and eat.

(3). Pleasure and pain (come) by thy order, O beloved, there is no other place.

(4). What thou makest me do, that I do, O beloved, nothing else can be done.

(5). All the days and nights are pleasant, O beloved, when the name of Hari is muttered.

(6). That work must be done, O beloved, (which) destiny causes to be written on (one's) forehead from the beginning.

(7). He himself alone is existing, O beloved, in everybody he is contained.

(8). He draws out from the well of the world, O beloved, Nānak is in the asylum of Hari.

RĀGU ĀSĀ; MAHALĀ I.

THE TABLET (PAṬĪ).

Ōm! By the favour of the true Guru!

(1). By *Sasā* (*s*) (he is meant), by whom creation was made, the Lord of all is the One.

They continually serve (him), who have applied their mind (to him), their coming (into the world) has become fruitful.

Pause.

O mind, O foolish mind, why art thou going astray?

When thou givest account, O brother, then (thou art) helpless.

(2). By *Īvaṛī* (the letter *i*). First is the divine male, he himself is munificent and true.

The disciple, who comprehends these letters, has no writing on his head.[1]

(3). By *Ūṛā* (the letter *u*): his magnifying should be made, whose end cannot be reached.

Who serve (him), they obtain rewards, (those) who acquire the True one.

(4). By *Ṅaṅa* (the letter *ṅ*): if any one comprehend divine knowledge, he is a learned Paṇḍit.

(If one) know, that in all creatures is the One, then no one will say: "I, I."[2]

(5). By *Kakkā* (the letter *k*): when the hair has become white and bright without soap:

The spies of Yama have come (to him, who is) bound with the chain of the Māyā.

(6). By *Khakkhā* (*kh*). Purchase thou the independent king of the world, by whom the means of subsistence are given;

By whose fetter the whole world is bound; by others no order (can be) given.

[1] The sense is: he is not subject to the decrees of destiny.

[2] The sense is: he will discard duality.

(7). By *Gaggā* (*g*). Sing the word (of him), by whom the earth is emitted and dissolved, (when) the drop (of semen) has become proud.

By whom, having shaped vessels, a kiln is made (and by whom) he is made who is putting (them into the kiln).[1]

(8). By *Ghagghā* (*gh*). If he puts the servant into (his) service, he sticks to the word of the Guru.

If he considers bad and good as the same, the Lord is sporting (in him) in this manner.

(9). By *Čačča* (*č*). By whom the four Vēdas were made, the four places of production, the four ages (of the world):

He is through all ages a Jōgī and enjoying the sources of production,[2] he himself has become a learned Paṇḍit.

(10). By *Čhaččha* (*čh*). Darkness exists within all, error is made by thee.

Having brought forth error (the creatures) are led astray by thyself; on whom thy mercy is bestowed, with them the Guru meets.

(11). By *J̌aǰǰā* (*ǰ*). Know, the beggar asks, in the eighty-four Lakhs (of forms of existence) he has wandered about in begging.

The One takes and the One gives, no other one has been heard of.

(12). By *J̌haǰǰhā* (*ǰh*). Why dost thou die in grief, O man? what is to be given, that he is giving.

Giving he looks on, he executes his order, as the daily bread of the creatures is allotted.

(13). By *Ńańā* (*ń*). When I look about with my eyes, there is no other (to be seen).

Only One is contained in all places, One dwells in the mind.

(14). By *Taṭṭā* (*ṭ*). Why art thou carrying on works, O man? in twenty-four or in forty-eight minutes thou must rise and go.

Do not lose thy life in gambling, flee and fall on the asylum of Hari!

(15). By *Ṭaṭṭhā* (*ṭh*). Coolness is abiding in the heart of those, whose mind is directed to the feet of Hari.

Whose mind is applied (to thee), they are saved, by thy favour happiness is obtained (by them).

(16). By *Ḍaḍḍā* (*ḍ*). Why makest thou ostentation, O man?

Whatever is created, that is all passing away.

Resort to his asylum and thou wilt get happiness, he is contained in all continually.

(17). By *Ḍhaḍḍhā* (*ḍh*). Having pulled down he builds up (again) himself, as it pleases him, so he does.

Working on he beholds (it), he sets agoing his order, him he saves, on whom he bestows a favourable look.

(18). By *Ṇāṇa* (*ṇ*). In whose heart he is abiding, he sings the excellences of Hari.

The creator himself is uniting (him with himself), regeneration will no more take place.

(19). By *Tatta* (*t*). Who has become the ferryman across the water of existence, his end is not reached.

There is no boat nor buoy, we shall be drowned, bring us across, O saving king!

(20). By *Thatthā* (*th*). In every place is he, by whom all is created.

What is called error, what delusion? what pleases him, that is good.

(21). By *Daddā* (*d*). I do not blame any one, the blame (is owing to) my own works.

What I have done (in a former birth), that I receive, no blame should be given to other people.

(22). By *Dhaddha* (*dh*). By whom by means of his skill all things are made, by whom colour is made:

His gifts all take, according to their several (former) works (his) order is given.

(23). By *Nannā* (*n*). The Lord always enjoys himself, he is not seen nor recollected.

By words (only) I am a favoured woman, O sister, the beloved one has never met with me.

[1] These two lines are so intricate, that the translation can only be made by conjecture.

[2] ਖਾਣੀ ਭੋਗੀ, literally: enjoying the sources of production = all creatures.

(24). By *Pappā* (*p*). The king, the Supreme Lord, has made the world for the sake of beholding (it). He sees, comprehends and knows everything, inside and outside he is contained.

(25). By *Phapphā* (*ph*). The whole world is caught in a noose, it is bound by the chain of Yama. By the favour of the Guru those men are rescued, who have fled to the asylum of Hari.

(26). By *Babbā* (*b*). He commenced to make a game, the four ages (of the world) were made (by him) a Čaupaṛ[1] play.

All the creatures were made the chessmen, he himself commenced to throw the dice.

(27). By *Bhabbhā* (*bh*). Who seek, they get rewards, to whom by the favour of the Guru fear is imparted.

The self-willed wander about, the fools do not reflect, the turn of the eighty-four Lakhs (of forms of existence) is allotted to them.

(28). By *Mammā* (*m*). Spiritual blindness is death; when death has come, then the subduer of Madhu is thought of.

(When) another is read within the body, then the letter *Mamma* (egotism) is forgotten.

(29). By *Yayyā* (*y*). Regeneration never takes place, if one learn to know the True one.

The disciple praises (him), the disciple comprehends (him), the disciple knows the One.

(30). By *Rārā* (*r*). He is sporting in all, as many creatures as were made by him.

Having produced the creatures he applied them all to (their respective) work; on whom his kindness is bestowed, by them the name is taken.

(31). By *Lallā* (*l*). By whom (the creature) is applied to (its) work (and) the infatuation of the Māyā made sweet:

According to his pleasure the order is given, (that) eating and drinking are to be borne as the same.

(32). By *Vavvā* (*v*). Vāsudēv, the Supreme Lord, by whom for the sake of beholding (it) a disguise was made:

He sees, tastes and knows everything, outside and inside he is contained.

(33). By *Rāṛa* (*ṛ*). Why art thou quarrelling, O man? meditate on him, who is immortal!

Meditate on him, be absorbed in the True one! for him (I am) made a sacrifice.

(34). By *Hāhā* (*h*). There is no other donor (besides him), by whom the creatures are produced and their daily bread is given.

Meditate on the name of Hari, be absorbed in the name of Hari! day by day the name of Hari is taken as gain.

(35). By *Āiṛā* (*ā*). Who himself has produced (the creation), he does whatever is to be done.

He does and causes to be done everything, he knows everything; Nānak, the poet,[2] has spoken in this way.

RĀGU ĀSĀ; MAHALĀ III.; PAṬĪ.[3]

Ōm! by the favour of the true Guru!

(1). O! by *Aṅā* (*a* is meant): the whole world has come; by *Kākhā* (*k, kh*), *Ghaṅā* (*gh, ṅ*), death has taken place.

By *Rīrī* and *Lalī* (*r, l*): sins are committed, by reading vices virtues are forgotten.

Pause.

O mind, why is such an account read by thee?

It rests with thee to give account.

[1] The ਚਉਪੜਿ is a kind of chess.   [2] ਸਾਇਰੁ = شاعِر (Arab.)

[3] In this paṭī (paṭṭī) no proper order of the letters of the alphabet can be detected, they are thrown together in confusion. The whole is a poor imitation of the preceding paṭṭī.

(2). The perfect-bodied one[1] thou dost not remember; by *Nannā* (*n*): neither is the name taken by thee.

By *Čhaččhā* (*čh*): thou art wasting away day and night, O fool, how wilt thou escape being seized by Yama?

(3). By *Babbā* (*b*). Thou dost not understand, O fool, thou art led astray by error, thy life is lost.

Thou makest (them) apply a non-existent name, the burden of others is taken by thee.

(4). By *J̌ajǰā* (*ǰ*). Thy light is taken away, O fool, when going at the end thou wilt repent.

The one word thou dost not know, again and again thou wilt fall into the womb.

(5). What is written on thy head, that read, O Paṇḍit, do not teach others worldly things!

First the noose is placed on the instructor, afterwards (also) on the neck of (his) disciples.

(6). By *Sassā* (*s*). Control of the senses is gone, O fool, the one gift thou hast taken to a bad place.

That is the effigy[2] of (thy) customer, that is thine, by eating this corn thy life is gone.

(7). By *Mammā*. Thy understanding is taken away, O fool, the great disease of egotism has befallen thee.

Within thy soul Brahm is not known, thou hast become needy of the Māyā.

(8). By *Kakkhā* (*kh*). By lust and passion thou art led astray, O fool, clinging to egotism thou hast forgotten Hari.

Thou readest and reflectest, thou criest much, (but) without understanding thou art drowned and diest.

(9). By *Taṭṭā* (*ṭ*). Thou burnest in anger, O fool! By *Ṭhaṭṭhā* (*ṭh*): (thy) place became filthy.

By *Ghagghā* (*gh*): to every house thou wanderest about, O fool! By *Daḍḍā* (*ḍ*): no gift is obtained by thee.

(10). By *Pappā* (*p*). Thou dost not come across, O fool, thou clingest to the world.

By the True one himself thou art ruined, this destiny has fallen on thy head.

(11). By *Bhabbhā* (*bh*). In the water of existence thou wast drowned, O fool, in the Māyā thou becamest immersed.

Who by the favour of the Guru knows the One, he is brought across in twenty-four minutes.

(12). By *Vavvā* (*v*). Thy turn (of dying) has come, O fool, Vāsudēv is forgotten by thee.

This opportunity thou wilt not get again, O fool, (when) thou hast fallen into the power of Yama.

(13). By *J̌haǰǰhā* (*ǰh*). Thou dost never grieve, O fool, hear the instruction of the true Guru, O noseless one!

Without the true Guru there is no other Guru; the name of him, who has no Guru, is bad.

(14). By *Dhaddhā* (*dh*). Keep back thy running (mind), O fool, within thee the treasure is laid.

When thou becomest a disciple, then thou wilt drink the juice of Hari, through all ages thou wilt go on eating (it).

(15). By *Gaggā* (*g*). Put Gōvind into thy mind, O fool, by (mere) words no one has obtained him.

Make the feet of the Guru dwell in thy heart, O fool, thy former sins are all pardoned (thereby).

(16). By *Hāhā* (*h*). Understand the story about Hari, O fool, then there will be always happiness.

As much as the self-willed one reads, so much pain befalls (him), without the true Guru no emancipation is obtained.

(17). By *Rārā* (*r*). Put Rām into thy mind, O fool! in the heart of whom he is contained;

By whom through the favour of the Guru Rām is known, by them Rām, who is without qualities, is comprehended.

(18). Thy end cannot be perceived, O Hari! the inexpressible one cannot be described.

Nānak (says): with whom the true Guru has met, their account is settled.

[1] ਸਿਰਬੰਗਾ = ਸਿਰਬਾਙ੍ਗ, the perfect-bodied, a name of Krishṇa.

[2] ਪੁਤ੍ਰੀ = ਪੁਤਲੀ, the meaning "daughter" will hardly suit the context. But the whole verse, though the single words are plain enough, is obscure.

RĀGU ĀSĀ; MAHALĀ I.; ČHANT; GHAR I.

Ōm! by the favour of the true Guru!

I.

(1). O woman in the prime of youth, my beloved is the delightful Rām!

(To) the woman (who has) great love (and) affection to her beloved, Rām is merciful.[1]

The woman meets with her beloved, if the Lord himself bestow mercy (on her).

(Her) bed is delightful in the society of (her) beloved, the seven ponds are filled with nectar.[2]

Bestow mercy and kindness (on me), O merciful one, that falling in with the true word (of the Guru) I may sing (thy) excellences!

Nānak (says): having seen Hari, her bridegroom, the woman is happy, in (her) mind is joy.

(2). O young and naturally beautiful woman! the one love of Rām (is my) prayer.

To my mind and body Hari is pleasing, I am fond of meeting with the Lord Rām!

(Who) is imbued with love to the Lord, (whose) supplication (is) Hari, she dwells comfortably in the name of Hari.

Then she gets acquainted with virtues, then she knows the Lord, her faults are subdued, (her) vices destroyed.

Without thee I cannot remain a moment, by telling and hearing patience is not brought about.

O Nānak: (who) cries: O beloved, O beloved! (her) mind, having tasted (him) with (her) tongue, becomes happy.

(3). O friend, O companion, my beloved is the trader Rām.

The name of Hari is taken up for sale, of infinite taste and value is Rām.

If the inestimable, true, beloved Lord be approved of in the house, then the young woman is well doing.

Some enjoy pleasures in the society of Hari, I cry standing at the door.

The powerful cause of causes, the bearer of prosperity (= Vishṇu) himself accomplishes (my) affair.

Nānak (says): (on whom his) favourable look is, (she is) blessed and a favoured woman, she keeps the word (of the Guru) (in her) heart.

(4). In my house is true rejoicing, the Lord, the friend Rām, has come.

Imbued with love he enjoys (me), (my) mind is taken away and given (to) Rām.

(My) own mind is given (to him), Hari, the bridegroom, is obtained, as he pleases, so he enjoys (me).

(Whose) body and mind (are put) before the beloved, she obtains by means of the auspicious word (of the Guru) the nectar-fruit in her house.

By intelligence and reading and much cleverness he is not obtained, by reason of love he meets (with them who) are pleasing to his mind.

Nānak (says): the Lord is our friend, we are not of the world.

II.

(1). Unbeaten, unbeaten sounds the jingling sound (in my head), O Rām!

My mind, my mind is attached (to thee), O dearly beloved Rām!

Day by day (my) mind is attached (to thee) and in love (with thee), in the void orbit (my) house is placed.[3]

[1] There are eight words in this line without any grammatical connexion whatever. The translation can therefore only be made by conjecture.

[2] It is difficult to say what is meant by the seven ponds. The Granthīs explain them by: two eyes, two ears, two nostrils, the mouth. But this apparently is only a conjecture.

[3] It is difficult to say what the meaning of this mystic allusion may be.

The primeval divine male, the boundless, the beloved, the inconceivable one is given to understand by the true Guru.

Nārāyaṇ is firmly fixed on (his) seat, reflecting (on him) (my) mind became attached (to him).

Nānak (says): those, who are attached to the name, are Bairāgīs, an unbeaten, jingling sound (is in them).

(2). To that inapproachable, to that inapproachable city, say, O brother, in what manner shall one go?

Performing true continence (and) virtues the word of the Guru should be done, O brother!

(If) the true word be done (and if) one go to his own house, the depository of all excellences is obtained.

In him there are no branches, root, leaves nor boughs, he is the first above all.

Practising muttering, austerities and continence (the world) has become tired, by obstinacy and tenacity he is not obtained.

Nānak (says): the life of the world is easily met with, if by the true Guru understanding be imparted.

(3). The Guru is the ocean, the mine of jewels, in him are many gems, O brother!

Make ablution in the seven oceans (and) thy mind (will become) pure, O my brother!

Thou bathest in pure water, when thou art pleasing to the Lord, thou fallest in (with) the saints by meditation.

Abandon lust, wrath, falsity and the world and put the true name into thy breast!

Egotism, greediness, emotion and covetousness are worn away (thereby), he is obtained who is kind to the poor.

Nānak (says): there is no Tīrtha equal to the Guru, (to) the true Guru Gōpāl.

(4). (If) I look on forest by forest, (if) I look at (every) grass, it is prepared (by thee), O Rām!

The three worlds are made by thee, the whole world, O Rām, is made (by thee)!

All is made by thee, thou art firmly fixed, no one is like thee.

Thou art the donor, all are thy beggars, without thee whom shall I praise?

By thee, O donor, gifts are given without being asked for, the store-rooms are filled with thy worship.

Without the name of Rām emancipation is not brought about, Nānak pronounces (this) thought.

III.

(1). My mind, my mind is attached to Rām, O beloved brother!

The true Lord, the primeval, boundless, divine male I keep in my mind, O brother!

Unattainable, incomprehensible, infinite is the Supreme Brahm, first (of all).

He is from the beginning, before (all) ages, he will also be (for ever), every other ground of assurance is false.

(Who) has no knowledge of the (right) works and duties (of man), how should he get true knowledge concerning emancipation?

Nānak (says): the disciple learns (it) from the word (of the Guru), (if) day and night the name be meditated upon.

(2). My mind, my mind is pleased, the name is (my) companion, O brother!

Egotism, selfishness and the Māyā do not go with (thee), O brother!

Mother, father, brother, son, cleverness, wealth, wife (do) not (go) with (thee).

(By whom) the daughter of the ocean is abandoned (and put) under (his) feet, he reflects (on the Supreme).

By the primeval divine male one achievement is shown, wherever I look, there is he.

Nānak (says): the worship of Hari I do not give up; what naturally happens, that takes place.

(3). My mind, my mind (becomes) pure by keeping in mind the True one, O brother!

Having effaced vices (we) walk in harmony with virtue.

Having abandoned vices I perform (religious) works, at the true gate (I become thereby) true.

The coming and going of that disciple is stopped, by whom truth (the Supreme) is reflected upon.

My friend and all-wise companion art thou, from (thee), the True one, greatness is obtained.

(To) Nānak the gem of the name was manifested, such instruction of the Guru was obtained (by me).

(4). True is the collyrium;[1] having applied the collyrium (I) became attached to the spotless one, O brother!

In (my) mind and body is contained the life of the world, the donor, O brother!

(Who) in his mind is attached to the life of the world, the donor Hari, he naturally meets (with him), being united (by him with himself).

In the assembly of the pious, in the society of the saints happiness is obtained by the merciful glance of the Lord.

The Bairāgīs are filled with attachment to Hari, spiritual darkness and worldly thirst have ceased (in them).

Nānak (says): having destroyed egotism they believed (in him); those servants (of him), who are of mortified passions, are rare.

RĀGU ĀSĀ; MAHALĀ I.; ČHANT; GHAR II.

Ōm! By the favour of the true Guru!

I. IV.

(1). Thou art in all places, where I go, (there art thou), the True creator.

(Thou art) the donor of all, the disposer of (their) destiny, bringing pain into oblivion.

Thou, O Lord, makest forget pain, by whom it is made.

Crores upon crores of sins thou dost away in one Gharī.

With geese (thou art) a goose, with cranes a crane, in everybody thou reflectest, O Lord!

Thou art in all places, where I go, (there art thou), the true creator.

(2). By whom he is meditated upon with one mind, they obtain happiness; those are rare in the world, O dear!

Yama does not go near them, who do the word of the Guru, they are never overcome, O dear!

They are never defeated, who remember the excellences of Hari, Hari, Yama does not go near them.

Their regeneration and death have ceased, who cling to the feet of Hari.

By means of the instruction of the Guru the juice of Hari, the fruit of Hari, is obtained by keeping the name of Hari in (their) breast, O dear!

By whom he is meditated upon with one mind, they obtain happiness; those are rare in the world, O dear!

(3). By whom the world is produced, (by whom) it is applied to its (several) occupations, to him (I am) a sacrifice, O dear!

(If) his service be performed, profit is obtained, at the threshold of Hari honour is obtained, O dear!

At the threshold of Hari that man gets honour, who knows the One divine male.

He obtains the nine treasures, who by means of the instruction of the Guru meditates on Hari, who continues rehearsing the excellences of Hari.

Day and night his name should be taken, Hari is the highest and prime divine male.

By whom the world is produced and applied to (its) work, to him (I am) a sacrifice, O dear!

[1] ਅੰਜਨੁ, collyrium; figuratively the instruction of the Guru. ਅੰਜਨੁ and ਨਿਰੰਜਨੁ contain a play upon words, which caonot well be expressed in English.

(4). Who take the name, they become lustrous, their reward is happiness, who mind (it), they go having won (the play), O dear!

Their reward does not diminish, when it pleases him, though several ages pass on, O dear!

Though several ages pass on, O Lord, their reward does not diminish.

They are not subject to old age nor to death nor do they fall into hell, who meditate on the name of Hari.

Who say: Hari, Hari! they do not dry up nor do they suffer pain, O dear, (says) Nānak.

Who take the name, they become lustrous, their reward is happiness; who mind (it), they go having won (the play), O dear!

ĀSĀ; MAHALĀ I.; ČHANT; GHAR III.

Ōm! By the favour of the true Guru!

I. V.

(1). Hear thou, O black deer, why art thou attached to the gardens?[1]
The fruit of poison is sweet four days, then thou becomest again hot.
Thou becomest again hot and quite intoxicated, without the name thou art in pain.
That[2] gives waves like the ocean, it flashes like lightning.
Without Hari there is no protector and he is forgotten by thee.
Nānak speaks truth: think, O mind! thou wilt die, O black deer!
(2). O black bee wandering about flowers, very heavy is (thy) pain.
I asked my own Guru, reflecting on truth.
Reflecting I asked the true Guru, the black bee is attached to creepers.
When the sun rises, (its) body falls (to the ground), like oil it is heated.
On the way to Yama it is bound and beaten, without the word (of the Guru) it is a goblin.
Nānak speaks truth: think, O mind, thou wilt die, O black bee!
(3). O my soul, the stranger, into what trouble dost thou fall!
In (whose) mind the true Lord dwells, is he ensnared by the net of Yama, O brother?
The fish separated (from the water) weeps in its eyes, the fisherman threw a net over it.
The infatuation of the Māyā is sweet to the world, at the end it is led astray by error.
Applying thy mind to Hari perform worship, drop doubt from thy mind!
Nānak speaks truth: think, O my mind, my soul, the stranger!
(4). A canal separated from the river is (again) united with (it).
Continually (the world) takes in sweet poison, some (rare) Jōgī knows (this).

Some one knows (it) naturally and gets acquainted with Hari, he, by whom the true Guru is thought of.

Without the name of Hari they are led astray by error, the foolish thoughtless people are consumed.

Who are not attached to the name of Hari (and in whose) heart the True one is not, they weep at the end in lamentations.

Nānak speaks truth: he (Hari) unites (with himself) by the true word (of the Guru) those, who were a long time separated (from him).

[1] ਵਾੜੀ *s.f.* An enclosed piece of ground, a garden. ਗਾਭ is here a meaningless alliteration.

[2] It does not appear from the context, to what ਓਹੁ "that" is to be referred.

ĀSĀ; MAHALĀ III.; ČHANT; GHAR I.

Ōm! By the favour of the true Guru!

I. VI.

(1). In our house are true rejoicings, it is adorned by the true word (of the Guru).[1]

The woman has met with her beloved, by the Lord himself she was united (with himself).

By the Lord himself she was united (with himself), the True one was made to dwell in (her) mind, the woman became naturally intoxicated.

She is adorned by the word of the Guru, by truth she is decorated, steeped in love she always enjoys (her beloved).

She removes her own self and obtains Hari her bridegroom, the essence of Hari is made to dwell in her mind.

Nānak says: she is adorned by the word of the Guru, her whole life is (made) fruitful (thereby).

(2). (If) the woman is led astray by the error of duality, she does not get Hari (as her) bridegroom.

(If) the woman has no virtues, she spends her life to no purpose.

The foolish self-willed (woman) wastes her life uselessly, being vicious she grieves.

By serving her own true Guru happiness is always obtained by her, her friend is met with (as being) in her presence.

Seeing her friend she is happy, by the true word she is easily full of love within.

Nānak (says): without the name the woman is led astray by error, having met with her beloved she obtains happiness.

(3). The woman knows, that her beloved is with (her), by the Guru she is united (with him).

Being united (with him) within by means of the word, her burning heat is quenched.

By the word (her) burning heat is quenched, tranquillity comes into her heart, the juice of Hari is easily tasted (by her).

Being united with her own beloved she always enjoys pleasure, in the true word there is good food.[2]

Reading on the Paṇḍits (and) anchorites became tired, by assuming (religious) garbs emancipation is not obtained.

Nānak (says): without devotion (to Hari) the world is mad, by the true word he (= Hari) unites (with himself).

(4). In the heart of that woman joy springs up, (whom) thou, O Hari, unitest with (her) beloved!

That woman is steeped in the love of Hari by the boundless word of the Guru.

By the boundless word she meets with (her) beloved, she always remembers his excellences (and) he dwells in her mind.

Her bed is pleasant, when she is enjoyed by her beloved, meeting with her beloved her vices are destroyed.

In which house the name of Hari is always meditated upon, (in that) are rejoicings through the four ages.

Nānak (says): who is attached to the name, has always joy, by meeting with Hari (all) affairs are adjusted.

[1] ਰਾਮ is here, as in the preceding Čhant, a mere alliteration.

[2] ਸੁਭਾਖਿਆ = सुभक्ष्य, good food.

ĀSĀ; MAHALĀ III.; ČHANT; GHAR II.

Ōm! By the favour of the true Guru!

II. VII.

(1). O my beloved friend, worship thou the bridegroom!
Serve always thy own Guru, (that) thou mayst get the boon of the name!
Worship thou the bridegroom, (that) thou mayst please the beloved bridegroom!
(If) thou do, what pleases thee, thou wilt not be pleasing to the bridegroom.
Worship and love, this is the difficult road, by means of the Guru some one gets (it).
Nānak says: on whom he bestows mercy, he applies his mind to the worship of Hari.
(2). O my recluse mind, practising indifference to the world to whom dost thou exhibit it?
They always are rejoicing in Hari, who sing the excellences of Hari.
Practising indifference to the world abandon hypocrisy, that bridegroom knows everything.
In the water, earth and on the face of the earth there is that One, the disciple knows his order.
By whom the order of Hari is known, he obtains all happiness.
Thus says Nānak: he is a Bairāgī, who day by day devoutly meditates on Hari.
(3). Wherever thou art running about, O mind, there is Hari with thee.
O mind, give up cunning, lay hold of the word of the Guru!
That bridegroom is always with thee, (if) thou remember one moment the name of Hari.
The sins of thy several births are cut off, at the end thou wilt obtain the highest step (of emancipation).
If thou make a tie of friendship with the True one, O disciple, he always will keep (thee) in mind.
Thus says Nānak: wherever thou art running about, O mind, there Hari is always with thee.

(4). By falling in with the true Guru the running (mind) is stopped, it comes and dwells in its own house.

The name it buys, the name it takes, in the name it is absorbed.

By falling in with the true Guru the running mind is stopped, the tenth gate is obtained.

There is the enjoying of nectar, that sound is naturally produced, by which sound the world is stopped (from running about).

In him are always many musical instruments sounding without being beaten, who is absorbed in the True one.

Thus says Nānak: by falling in with the true Guru the running mind is stopped, it comes and dwells in its own house.

(5). O mind, thou art of a luminous form, become acquainted with thy own origin!

O mind, Hari is with thee, enjoy (this) pleasure by means of the instruction of the Guru!

(If) thou become acquainted with (thy) origin, thou wilt know the bridegroom, the right knowledge of death and life is obtained.

(If) by the favour of the Guru thou know the One, another love will not take place.
Tranquillity comes into the mind, congratulation is made, (thou) hast become approved of.
Thus says Nānak: O mind, thou art of a luminous form, become acquainted with thy own origin!
(6). O mind, thou art absorbed in pride, laden with pride thou goest.
Thou art deluded by the fascinating Māyā, again and again she makes (thee) wander about in wombs.
Clinging to pride thou departest, O foolish mind, having gone thou repentest at the end.
The disease of egotism and worldly thirst sticks (to thee), thou wastest thy life to no purpose.
The foolish self-willed (man) does not think, having gone on (to the other world) he repents.
Thus says Nānak; O mind, thou art absorbed in pride, laden with pride thou goest.

(7). O mind, do not be puffed up, that thou art knowing something, O disciple, be humble!
Within (thee) is ignorance (and) egotism, clear away (thy) filth by the true word (of the Guru)!
Be humble before the true Guru, he likely makes thee comprehend in some way thy own self!
The world is burnt by its own egotism, would that thou wouldst remove thy own self!
Do works according to the pleasure of the true Guru, keep to that which is pleasing to the true Guru!
Thus says Nānak: having given up thy own self thou wilt obtain happiness, O mind, remain humble!
(8). Blessed is that time, in which I met with the true Guru, that bridegroom came into my mind!
Great joy and tranquillity were produced, in my mind and body I obtained happiness.
That bridegroom came into my mind, he was made to dwell in (my) mind (by the Guru), all my vices were given to oblivion.
When it pleased him, virtues became manifest (in me), the true Guru himself adorns (me).
Those people have become approved of, by whom the One name is kept fast and another love is stopped.
Thus says Nānak: blessed is that Time, in which I have met with the true Guru, that bridegroom has come into my mind!
(9). Some creatures are gone astray in error, (who) are led astray by that bridegroom himself.
In another love they wander about, they do works of egotism.
By that bridegroom himself they are led astray, they are put into a bad road, nothing is in their power.[1]
Thou, by whom this creation is made, knowest their quitting or non-quitting (the material existence).
Thy order is quite weighty, some (rare) disciple thou makest comprehend it.
Thus says Nānak: what are the helpless creatures, when they are led astray by thee in error?
(10). O my true Lord, true is thy greatness!
Thou art the endless Supreme Brahm, O Lord, thy power cannot be told.
True is thy greatness, in whose mind thou makest dwell it, he always sings thy excellences.
He sings thy excellences, when he pleases thee, when he applies his mind to the True one.
Whom thou thyself unitest (with thee), that disciple is absorbed in thee.
Thus says Nānak: O my true Lord, true is thy greatness!

RĀGU ĀSĀ; ČHANT; MAHALĀ IV.; GHAR I.

Ōm! By the favour of the true Guru!

I. VIII.

(1). Life, life I obtained, the disciple pleases Rām.
The name of Hari, the name of Hari he gives,[2] he makes Rām dwell in my soul.
The name of Hari, Hari, he makes dwell in my soul, every doubt and pain is removed.
The unseen, the incomprehensible (Supreme) is meditated upon by means of the word of the Guru, the pure supreme degree (of emancipation) is obtained.
The musical instruments sound continually with a sound not produced by beating (them), the word of the true Guru is sung.
Nānak (says): by the bountiful Lord the gift is bestowed, light is absorbed in the Luminous one.
(2). The self-willed have died self-willed, saying: mine is the Māyā, O brother!
In a moment he comes, in a moment he goes, (his) mind is applied to the stench of a corpse.[3]

[1] The sense is: they cannot help it. [2] The subject is the Guru.
[3] मड़ा, *m.* a corpse (Maraṭhī still मडें).

(His) mind is applied to the stench of a corpse, it sticks (to that), by which[1] the colour of the safflower is exhibited.

In one moment it goes to the east, in (another) moment to the west, as the wheel is moved about by the potter.

Pain it eats, pain it amasses (and) undergoes, the growth of pain is promoted.

Nānak (says): the difficult (ocean of existence) is easily crossed, when one comes to the asylum of the Guru.

(3). My Lord, Lord, is good, unattainable, unfathomable, O brother!

The capital of Hari, the capital of Hari, I desire, O my true Guru, O great merchant!

The capital of Hari I desire, the name I purchase, (his) excellences I sing, (his) excellences please (me).

Sleep and hunger, all I give up, (that) I may be absorbed in the Vacuum, the Vacuum.

The retail-dealers attached to the One, come and take away the gain of the name of Hari.

Nānak (says): offer up (thy) mind and body before the Guru! on whom it is bestowed, he gets it (scil. the name).

(4). With jewels upon jewels (and) many choice things the ocean is filled, O brother!

Who cling to the word, the word of the Guru, upon their hand it is placed, O brother.

Who cling to the word of the Guru, upon their hand is placed the priceless, boundless jewel.

The priceless name of Hari, Hari is obtained (by them), with thy worship (thy) store-rooms are filled.

Having churned the ocean, the body, we have seen (it), the One incomparable thing was shown (to us).

The Guru is Gōvind, between Gōvind (and) the Guru, (says) Nānak, there is no difference, O brother!

II. IX.

(1). Softly, softly, softly, softly a stream of nectar rains, O brother!

On the disciple, the disciple, is the favourable glance of the beloved Rām, O brother!

The dear name of Rām is saving the world, in the name of Rām is greatness.

In the Kali-yuga is the name of Rām the boat, which ferries across the disciple.

In this and in that world they are happy by the name of Rām, the work of the disciples is accomplished.

Nānak (says): bestowing mercy he gives (this) gift, by the name of Rām he brings (them) across.

(2). The name of Rām, Rām is muttered (by me), pain and sin are destroyed (thereby) and removed, O brother!

By intimacy with the Guru, by intimacy with the Guru, he (Rām) is meditated upon, in my heart Rām is made to dwell, O brother!

Rām abides in the heart, the highest step[2] is obtained, when (one) comes to the asylum of the Guru.

The boat, that was sinking in the vice of covetousness, has (safely) come out, when the true Guru makes firm the name (in one).

The gift of life is bestowed by the perfect Guru, he applies the mind to the name of Rām.

The merciful one himself bestowing mercy gives it (the name); Nānak (is) in the asylum of the Guru.

(3). The word of the name of Rām (was) heard (by me), all (my) affair became accomplished and adjusted, O brother!

In every hair,[3] in every hair I, (having become) a disciple, meditate on Rām, O brother!

[1] ਜਿਉ is here the Ablative Sing. of ਜੋ.

[2] *i.e.* emancipation from material existence.

[3] ਰੋਮ (रोमन्) the small hair of the body.

(Who) meditates on the name of Rām, he becomes pure, he has no form nor figure whatever.

Rām, Rām is contained in (his) heart, all thirst and hunger are removed.

(His) mind and body are cool, all is decorated, by the instruction of the Guru Rām is manifested.

Nānak (says): he himself bestowed (his) favour (on us): we are the slaves of the slaves of the slaves.[1]

(4). By whom the name of Rām, Rām, is forgotten, those foolish self-willed people are unfortunate, O brother!

In their heart infatuation dwells, every moment the Māyā clings (to them), O brother!

The filth of the Māyā sticks (to them), those fools have become unfortunate, to whom the name of Rām is not pleasing.

The conceited practise many works, (but) the name of Hari Rām is suppressed.

Very difficult is the way of Yama, painful and turbid (is) the darkness of infatuation.[2]

Nānak (says): (when) by the disciple the name is meditated upon, he obtains the gate of salvation.

(5). The name of Rām, Rām, of Guru Rām, the disciple knows, O brother!

This mind, which in a moment is roaming about above and in the nether regions, he brings to one house,[3] O brother!

(If) he brings (his) mind to one house, he has all knowledge and thorough understanding, the delightful name of Hari pleases (him).

He preserves the honour of his people, the name of Rām saves and makes cross Prahlād.

Rām, Rām is delightful (and) high, by those, who utter his excellences, no end (of them) is reached.

Nānak (says): having heard the name of Rām (we) became imbued with love (to it), in the name of Rām (we) were absorbed.

(6). In whose heart the name of Rām dwells, their care is all removed, O brother!

All objects, all virtues are obtained, the fruit desired by the mind is obtained, O brother!

The fruit desired by the mind is obtained, the name of Rām is meditated upon, the excellences of the name of Rām are sung.

Folly and stupidity are gone, soundness of mind is produced by applying the mind to the name of Rām.

All (his) life (and) body has become fruitful, to whom the name of Rām has been manifested.

Nānak (says): worship always Hari day and night, O disciple, dwelling in thy own house!

(7). Who have a longing after the name of Rām, they do not apply their mind to another, O brother!

If the whole world would be made gold and given (to them), nothing but the name is pleasing (to them), O brother!

The name of Rām pleases their mind, the highest happiness is obtained (by them), it is a companion with (them) when departing at the end.

The wealth and capital of the name of Rām is collected (by them), (which) neither is sunk in water nor goes off.

The name of Rām is in this period of the world a buoy, Yama, the death, does not go near (them, who utter it).

Nānak (says): by the disciple Rām is known, he himself (*i.e.* Rām) mercifully unites (him with himself).

(8). The name of Rām is known to be true by the disciple, O brother!

(That) worshipper applies himself to the service of the Guru, who offers up his mind and body as a sacrifice (to the Guru), O brother!

[1] *i.e.* we are his most humble slaves.

[2] ਕਾਲੂਖਤ, instead of ਕਲੁਖਿਤ (the first two syllables being anomalously lengthened) = कलुषित, muddy, turbid.

[3] ਇਕਤੁ ਘਰਿ ਆਣੈ, literally: he brings to one house, *i.e.* he makes steadily remain in one house, so that it no longer wanders about.

(His) mind and body are offered up by him, in his heart is much longing, the Guru (and his) servant are united by (mutual) love.

The protector of the poor, the liberal patron of the creatures he obtains from the perfect Guru.

The Guru is the disciple, the disciple is the Guru, (that they are) One, (this) instruction the Guru sets agoing.

Into the heart he gives the mantra of the name of Rām, (says) Nānak, union (with Hari) is naturally (effected thereby).

ĀṢĀ; ČHANT; MAHALĀ IV.; GHAR II.

Ōm! by the favour of the true Guru!

I. III. X.

(1). Hari, Hari is the creator, destroying pain, the name of Hari is purifying the sinners, O dear!

By the service of Hari the highest step is obtained, O brother, Hari, Hari is the most excellent desire, O dear!

Hari is the most excellent desire; (by whom) the name of Hari is muttered, Hari is muttered, he becomes steady.

The pain of birth as well as of death is effaced, he naturally sleeps in comfort.

O Hari, Hari, bestow mercy, (that) the Lord Hari, the Supreme Spirit, may be muttered!

Hari, Hari is the creator, destroying pain, the name of Hari is purifying the sinners, O dear!

(2). The name of Hari is the highest boon in the Kali-yuga.

Hari should be muttered according to the intention of the true Guru, O dear!

By the disciple Hari should be read, by the disciple Hari should be heard! by muttering and hearing Hari pain departs, O dear!

(When) the name of Hari, Hari, is muttered, pain is destroyed, the name of Hari, the highest bliss, is obtained.

By the true Guru divine knowledge is kindled, light (springs up) in the heart, ignorance and darkness are removed.

The name of Hari, Hari, is adored by them, on whose forehead it is written at the beginning.

The name of Hari is the highest boon in the Kali-yuga; Hari should be muttered according to the intention of the true Guru, O dear!

(3). To (whose) mind Hari, Hari, is pleasing, (by him) the highest bliss is obtained, the gain of Hari, the step of emancipation, O dear!

(Who) entertains love to Hari, (to him) the name of Hari is a companion, (his) error has ceased (and) his coming and going, O dear!

(His) coming and going, (his) error (and) fear have fled, the excellences of Hari, Hari, Hari, are sung (by him).

The blemishes and pain of (his) several births are gone off, in the name of Hari, Hari, he is absorbed.

By whom Hari is meditated upon (and) for whom it is written by destiny in the beginning, their life is fruitful and approved of, O dear!

To (whose) mind Hari, Hari is pleasing, (by him) the highest bliss is obtained, the gain of Hari, the step of emancipation, O dear!

(4). To whom Hari has become sweet, those people are foremost, those people of Hari are the most excellent, O dear!

The name of Hari is (their) greatness, the name of Hari is their companion, by the word of the Guru they enjoy the relish of Hari, O dear!

The relish of Hari they enjoy, they are without restraint, by the very fortunate the relish of Hari is obtained.

They are blessed, great, virtuous and perfect men, by whom by means of the instruction of the Guru the name is meditated upon.

Humble Nānak asks for the dust of the feet of the pious, in (whose) heart grief and separation (from Hari) have ceased, O dear!

To whom Hari has become sweet, those people are foremost, those people are the most excellent, O dear!

II. IV. XI.

(1). In the Satya-yuga truth (and) contentment (were) in the bodies (of men), religion and meditation (had) four legs,[1] O dear!

In (their) mind and body they sing Hari, they obtain the highest bliss, Hari is in their heart, the knowledge of the excellences of Hari, O dear!

The knowledge of the excellences (of Hari) (was their) object, Hari, Hari they gained, lustre accrued to the disciples.

Inside and outside (of them) was the One Lord Hari, there (was) no second.

Devout meditation was applied to Hari, the name of Hari (was their) companion, at the threshold of Hari they obtain honour, O dear!

In the Satya-yuga truth (and) contentment (were) in the bodies (of men), religion and meditation (had) four legs, O dear!

(2). The Trētā-yuga came; violence was put into the heart (of men), (yet) they practise chastity, control of the senses and (religious) works, O dear!

The fourth leg dropped off, it remained three-legged, in (their) mind and heart they kindle wrath, O dear!

In (their) mind and heart (there is) wrath, the great poison of the Lōdh-tree,[2] the kings rush on (to the attack), pain is obtained (by them) in the fight.

In their heart the disease of selfishness has taken root, egotism and conceit are increased.

(If) by Hari, Hari, my Lord, mercy is bestowed, the poison goes off by the instruction of the Guru (and) the name of Hari, O dear!

The Trētā-yuga came, violence was put into the heart (of men), (yet) they practise chastity, control of the senses (and religious) works, O dear!

(3). The Dvāpara-yuga came, it was led astray by error, Hari produces the Gōpīs and Krishṇa, O dear!

They are eager in practising austerities, sacrifices (and) meritorious acts they commence, they perform great religious ceremonies and works, O dear!

Ceremonies and works were performed, a second leg was dropped, (religion) remains two-legged, O dear!

Many great battles and fights were made, in their hearts egotism is lingering, O dear!

By him, who is kind to the poor, the pious Guru was procured, by meeting with the true Guru the filth goes off, O dear!

The Dvāpara-yuga came, it was led astray by error, Hari produces the Gopīs and Krishṇa, O dear!

(4). The Kali-yuga was made by Hari, the third leg dropped off, (only) the fourth leg (of religion) is remaining, O dear!

[1] The four legs of religion in the Satya-yuga are said to have been: ਸਤ, truth; ਸੰਤੋਖ, contentment; ਤਪ, austerity, and ਕੀਰਤਿ praise (of Hari).

[2] ਲੋਧੁ Sansk. लोध्र, name of a tree, *Symplocos racemosa*.

The word of the Guru was performed, the medicine of Hari was obtained, by the praise of Hari, Hari grants tranquillity, O dear!

The season of the praise of Hari came, the greatness of the name of Hari, the field of the name of Hari, Hari, was caused to germinate.

In the Kali-yuga the seeds are sown, without the name all profit and capital are lost.

Humble Nānak obtained the perfect Guru, (who) in mind and heart makes (me) comprehend the name, O dear!

The Kali-yuga was made by Hari, the third foot dropped off, (only) the fourth leg (of religion) is remaining, O dear!

III. V. XII.

(1). To (whose) mind the praise of Hari is pleasing, the highest step (= emancipation) is obtained (by him), Hari is made sweet to (his) mind and body, O dear!

The juice of Hari, Hari, is obtained, by the instruction of the Guru Hari is meditated upon (by him), on (whose) forehead at the beginning (this) lot has been fixed.

On (whose) forehead the lot is from the beginning, he has good fortune by the name of Hari, the excellences of the name of Hari are sung by him.

On (his) forehead is a jewel, (by whom) much affection is manifested, by the name of Hari he is adorned.

Light is blended with the Luminous one, the Lord is obtained, having met with the true Guru the mind is satisfied, O dear!

To (whose) mind the praise of Hari is pleasing, the highest step (= emancipation) is obtained (by him), Hari is made sweet to (his) mind and body, O dear!

(2). (By whom) the praise of Hari is sung, (by them) the highest degree is obtained, they are the most excellent and the foremost people, O dear!

Their feet we will embrace, their feet we will wash every moment, to whom Hari has become sweet, O dear!

(By whom) Hari is considered sweet, (by them) the highest bliss is obtained, (their) lot is most excellent, (their) destiny pleasant.[1]

(According to) the instruction of the Guru Hari is sung, the necklace of Hari is put on (their) breast, the name of Hari they keep in (their) bosom.

With unassisted sight they look on all (things) as the same, all is recognized (by them) as the Supreme Spirit, O dear!

The praise of Hari, Hari is sung, the highest step is obtained (by them); those people are the highest and foremost, O dear!

(3). (If) the society of the pious is pleasing to the mind, the tongue is made juicy by Hari, in the society (of the pious) is the juice of Hari, O dear!

Hari, Hari is adored, by the word of the Guru he is manifested, there is no other, O dear!

There is no other; by whom that nectar of Hari is drunk, he knows the affair.

Blessed, blessed is he, (by whom) the perfect Guru, the Lord, is obtained! clinging to the society (of the pious) he becomes acquainted with the name.

The name he serves, the name he adores, without the name there is no other, O dear!

(If) the society of the pious is pleasing to the mind, the tongue is made juicy by Hari, in the society (of the pious) is the juice of Hari, O dear!

[1] ਚਾਰੇ = ਚਾਰੁ, on account of the rhyme.

(4). O Lord Hari, bestow mercy, bring us, the stones, across, draw us out (of the water of existence) by the natural property of the word (of the Guru), Sir!

We stick in the mud of spiritual blindness and are immersed in it, O Lord Hari, cause our arm to be seized!

The Lord caused (our) arm to be seized, the highest wisdom was obtained, (his) people clung to the feet of the Guru.

The name of Hari, Hari, is muttered and adored (by him), on (whose) face and forehead a fortunate lot (is written).

Hari bestowed mercy on humble Nānak, (who) in (his) mind considered Hari, Hari, sweet, O dear!

O Lord Hari, bestow mercy, bring us, the stones, across, draw us out by the natural property of the word (of the Guru), Sir!

IV. VI. XIII.

(1). In (their) mind the name is caused to be muttered, to (whose) mind Hari, Hari is pleasing, in the mind of the devotees there is a longing after Hari, O dear!

Those people who having died live, by them nectar is drunk in (their) mind, love has sprung up by the instruction of the Guru, O dear!

In (their) mind is love to Hari, Hari, (on whom) the Guru bestows favour, being emancipated, although in the body, they obtain happiness.

In life and death they are happy by the name of Hari, in their mind and heart is that Hari.

In their mind Hari, Hari dwells, by the instruction of the Guru Hari is tasted, the juice of Hari, Hari, they drink in gulps, O dear!

In (their) mind the name is caused to be muttered, to (whose) mind Hari, Hari is pleasing, in the mind of the devotees there is a longing after Hari, O dear!

(2). In the world death is not liked, continually their own self is concealed, lest Yama seize and carry them off, O dear!

Hari is inside and outside, Hari is the only Lord, this life cannot be preserved, O dear!

How should the life be preserved, (if) the thing be wanted by Hari? whose the thing is, he takes it away, O dear!

The self-willed men, making pitiful lamentations, are led astray (though) applying all medicines, O dear!

Whose the thing is, (that) Lord takes it, the people of the Lord are saved by doing the word (of the Guru), O dear!

In the world death is not liked, continually their own self is concealed, lest Yama seize and carry them off, O dear!

(3). From the beginning death is written, the disciple is approved of, the (pious) people are saved by meditating on Hari, Hari, O dear!

From Hari splendour is obtained, greatness from the name of Hari, to the threshold of Hari they go dressed in a dress of honour, O dear!

At the threshold of Hari they are dressed (with a dress of honour), by the name of Hari they are perfected, from the name of Hari happiness is obtained.

The pain of birth and death is effaced, in the lovely name of Hari they are absorbed.

The people of Hari and the Lord blend together and become one, the people of Hari (and) the Lord are identical, O dear!

From the beginning death is written, the disciple is approved of, the (pious) people are saved by meditating on Hari, Hari, O dear!

(4). The world is produced and destroyed, it goes on being destroyed, (who) clings to the face of the Guru becomes immovable, O dear!

The Guru makes firm (his) mantra (in the heart), the juice of Hari he gives to taste, extracting the nectar of Hari from the mouth of Hari, O dear!

The nectar-juice of Hari is obtained (from him), the dead one is vivified (thereby), death does not again take place.

(By whom) the name of Hari, the degree of immortality, is obtained, he is absorbed in the name of Hari.

To humble Nānak the name is support and prop, without the name there is none other, O dear!

The world is produced and destroyed, it goes on being destroyed, (who) clings to the face of the Guru becomes immovable, O dear!

V. VII. XIV.

(1). Great is my Gōvind, unattainable, incomprehensible, first, free from (all) spots, formless, O dear!

His state cannot be told, immeasurable is his greatness, my Gōvind is invisible, boundless, O dear!

Gōvind is invisible, boundless, infinite, he knows his own self.

What may be said by this helpless creature, that it may describe thee?

On whom thou bestowest thy own (favourable) glance, that disciple reflects (on thee), Sir!

Great is my Gōvind, unattainable, incomprehensible, first, free from (all) spots, formless, O dear!

(2). Thou art the primeval male, the boundless creator, thy end cannot be reached, Sir!

Thou art in everybody, incessantly in all, in all thou art contained, Sir!

In the heart is the Supreme Brahm, the Lord, his end is not reached.

He has no form nor figure, he is invisible, incomprehensible, (but) to the disciple the inapprehensible one is given to comprehend.

He remains always in joy day and night, he is easily absorbed in the name, O dear!

Thou art the primeval male, the boundless creator, thy end cannot be reached, Sir!

(3). Thou art the true Lord, always imperishable, thou, O Hari, Hari, art the depository of (all) excellences, Sir!

O Hari, Hari, thou only art the Lord, there is no other, thou thyself art the all-wise (divine) male, Sir!

The all-wise (divine) male art thou, the ground (of all), like thee there is no other.

Thine is the word, in all thou abidest, what thou thyself dost, that takes place.

That Hari alone is contained in all, by the disciple the name of Hari is comprehended, O dear!

Thou art the true Lord, always imperishable, thou, O Hari, Hari, art the depository of (all) excellences, sir!

(4). Thou art the creator of all, all is thy greatness, as it pleases thee, so thou settest it agoing, Sir!

As it is pleasing to thyself, so thou settest it agoing, all is absorbed (again) by thy word, Sir!

All is absorbed by thy word, when it pleases thee, in thy word is greatness.

By the disciple wisdom is obtained, his own self is removed, by the word (of the Guru) he is absorbed (in Hari).

Thy word is incomprehensible, by the disciple it is obtained, by the name, says Nānak, he is absorbed, O dear!

Thou art the creator of all, all is thy greatness, as it pleases thee, so thou settest it agoing, Sir!

ĀSĀ; MAHALĀ IV.; ČHANT; GHAR IV.

Ōm! By the favour of the true Guru!

I. VIII. XV.

(1). (My) eyes are wetted with the nectar of Hari, (my) mind is imbued[1] with love (to Hari), O king Rām!

Rām has applied the touch-stone to (my) mind, (it has become) beautiful[2] gold.

(Having become) a disciple (my) mind and body are steeped in deep red colour.

(On) humble Nānak musk was shaken, (my) whole life is blessed, blessed.

(2). By the love-story of Hari (my) mind was killed, by taking sharp spears (and piercing it), O king Rām!

On whom the pain of love has fallen, he knows (my) burning heat.

He is called emancipated whilst in the body, who, having died, lives.

O Hari, join the true Guru to humble Nānak, (that) I may cross the world which is hard to cross!

(3). We foolish, doltish people have come to thy asylum, join (us), O thou Gōvind-like king Rām!

From the perfect Guru Hari is obtained, the worship of Hari alone I ask for.

My mind and body are made happy by the word (of the Guru), muttering the endless wave.[3]

By joining the pious people Hari is obtained, Nānak is with the pious.

(4). O thou, who art kind to the poor, hear (my) supplication! Hari, the Lord, Hari is sung (by me), O king Rām!

I ask for the asylum of the name of Hari; Hari, Hari is put into (my) mouth.

The being compassionate to his devotees, (this is) the custom of Hari, by Hari (their) honour is preserved.

Humble Nānak has come to (his) asylum, by the name of Hari he is brought across.

II. IX. XVI.

(1). By searching Hari, the sweetheart is obtained by the disciple, O king Rām!

In the fort of the golden body Hari, Hari is demonstrated (as being present).

Hari, Hari is a diamond (and) gem, (by which) my mind and body are perforated.

By an original great lot Hari is obtained (by him), O Nānak, (who) is covetous[4] of the juice of (Hari).

(2). Standing always I inquire after the road, (I am) a young woman, O king Rām!

Fixing (my) mind on the name of Hari, Hari, I walk on the road of the Guru Hari.

In my mind and body the name is (my) support, the poison of egotism I burn.

Humble Nānak, having procured the true Guru, has met (with) Hari, the wearer of a garland of wild flowers.

(3). O beloved, come and join me, the disciple, the long separated (from thee), O king Rām!

My mind and body are very passionate (after thee), my eyes are wetted by love to Hari.

Hari the Lord is dear (to) me, show (him to me), O Guru! having met with Hari my mind is comforted.

May I, the foolish one, be applied to the work, to the work of Hari, (says) Nānak.

(4). By the nectar of the Guru my body is flourishing, he sprinkles nectar, O king Rām!

To whose mind the word of the Guru is pleasing, they are intoxicated by the nectar after having eaten (it).

From the pleased Guru Hari is obtained, pushing and pulling have come to an end.

The people of Hari have become Hari, Hari, Nānak (and) Hari are one.

[1] ਰਤੰਨਾ = ਰਤਾ. [2] ਸੋਵਿੰਨਾ = ਸੋਇਨਾ (= Sansk. सुवर्ण), beautiful, having a good colour.

[3] ਅਨਤ ਤਰੰਗ, the endless wave = the Supreme Being.

[4] ਗ੍ਰਧਾ = ਗਿਧਾ (Sansk. गृद्ध), covetous, longing for.

III. X. XVII.

(1). The treasury of the nectar (and) worship of Hari is with the Guru, the true Guru, O king Rām!

The true Guru, the Guru is the true wholesale merchant, he gives to the disciple the stock of Hari.

Blessed, blessed is the retail-dealer (and his) traffic, praise be to the Guru, the wholesale merchant!

Humble Nānak (says): the Guru is obtained by them, on whose forehead it is written from the beginning.

(2). Thou, O Lord, art our true wholesale merchant, the whole world is thy retail-dealer, O king Rām!

All vessels are made by thee, in them is thy substance, O Hari!

What thing thou puttest into the vessel, that comes out, what can any helpless man do?

On humble Nānak was bestowed by Hari the treasury of the worship of Hari.

(3). How shall we spread out thy excellences, O Lord, thou art boundless, O king Rām!

The name of Hari we will praise day and night, this is our hope (and) support.

We foolish people do not know anything, how shall we reach (his) end?

Humble Nānak is the slave of Hari, the water-carrier of the slaves of Hari.

(4). As it pleases thee, so keep (us), we have come to thy asylum, O Lord, O king Rām!

We, going astray, damage (it) day and night, O Hari, cause thou our honour to be preserved!

We are children, thou art (our) Guru (and) father, communicate thou wisdom (to us)!

Humble Nānak is called the slave of Hari, O Hari, cause thou (my) honour to be preserved!

IV. XI. XVIII.

(1). On whose forehead it is written by Hari from the beginning, with them the true Guru met, O king Rām!

(Their) ignorance and darkness are cut off, by the Guru divine knowledge is kindled in (their) heart.

Hari is obtained, the exquisite jewel, he does not go again.

By humble Nānak the name is adored, by adoring (it) Hari was met with.

(2). By whom this name of Hari is not kept in mind, why have those come into the world, O king Rām?

This human birth is difficult to obtain, without the name it passes all to no purpose.

(By whom) now in the time of sowing the name of Hari is not sown, afterwards becoming hungry what will he eat?

The self-willed are subject again to birth, (to) Nānak Hari is pleasing.

(3). O Hari, every one is thine, all are produced by thee, O king Rām!

Nothing at all is in the hand of any one, all go off being marched away (by thee).

Whom thou unitest (with thyself), O beloved, they are united with thee, who please the mind of Hari.

Humble Nānak has met with the true Guru, (who) makes (him) cross by the name of Hari.

(4). Some one sings many kinds of Rāgs, sounds and Vēdas, (but) does not sink into Hari, O king Rām!

In whose heart is the disease of hypocrisy, what is done by them, (though) they weep?

Hari, the creator, knows everything, having produced[1] disease, assistance is given (by him also).

By those disciples, whose heart is pure, the worship of Hari is seized.

V. XII. XIX.

(1). In whose heart there is love to Hari, those people are clever and intelligent, O king Rām!

Though outwardly they make mistakes in their speech, yet they are quite pleasing to Hari.

To the saints of Hari there is no other place, Hari is the hope of the humble.

(To) humble Nānak the name is a tribunal, Hari is (my) powerful protection.

[1] ਸਿਰਿ here = ਸਿਰਜਿ p.p. conj. of ਸਿਰਜਣਾ.

(2). In which place my true Guru sits down, that place is pleasant, O king Rām!

That place is sought by the disciples of the Guru, (its) dust is applied to (their) face.

The service of (those) disciples of the Guru is acceptable, by whom the name of Hari is meditated upon.

By whom the true Guru is worshipped, (says) Nānak, them he causes to perform worship to Hari.

(3). In the mind of the disciples of the Guru there is love to Hari, (love) to the name of Hari, (love) to thee, O Hari, O king Rām!

(If) they serve the perfect true Guru, (their) hunger ceases, (their) egotism[1] goes off.

All the hunger of the disciples of the Guru is gone, after them many others eat.

By humble Nānak the meritorious deed of Hari is sown, the meritorious deed of Hari does not diminish again.

(4). There is congratulation in the heart of (those) disciples, by whom my true Guru is seen, O king Rām!

Any one, who lets them hear the word of the name of Hari, becomes acceptable (sweet) to the mind of the disciples of the Guru.

At the threshold of Hari those disciples of the Guru are dressed (with a dress of honour), with whom my true Guru has been pleased.

Humble Nānak has become Hari, Hari; Hari, Hari has settled in (his) heart!

VI. XIII. XX.

(1). With whom my perfect true Guru has met, in them he makes firm the name of Hari, O king Rām!

All his thirst and hunger cease, who meditates on the name of Hari.

Who are meditating on the name of Hari, Hari, near them Yama does not come.

O Hari, bestow mercy on humble Nānak, (that) he may continually mutter the name of Hari! Hari makes cross (the water) by the name.

(2). The disciples, by whom the name is meditated upon, no calamity befalls again, O king Rām!

By whom the true Guru, the (divine) male, is appeased, them every one worships.

By whom the true, beloved Guru is served, their happiness always remains.

With whom the true Guru has met, (says) Nānak, with them that Hari is united.

(3). In the heart of which disciples there is love (to Hari), them Hari is protecting, O king Rām!

What may one censure them, to whom the name of Hari is dear?

Whose mind is pleased with Hari, (about them) every wicked man talks nonsense.

By humble Nānak the name is meditated upon, Hari is his protector.

(4). Hari has produced devotees through all ages, he has been preserving their honour, O king Rām!

The wicked Haraṇākhas[2] was killed by Hari, Prahlād was saved.

Having turned his back on the conceited calumniators he countenanced Nāmdēv.[3]

By humble Nānak that Hari is served, (who) at the end releases (from bodily existence).

[1] ਮੇਠੀ *s.f.* egotism.

[2] Haraṇākhas = हिरण्यकशिपु, the father of Prahlād. See Wilson, Vishṇu Purāṇa, p. 126 *sqq.*

[3] This refers to the story related in the Bhakta-mālā, that Nāmdēv (who was of low extraction—he is said to have been a calico-printer) was kicked out of the temple of Viṭṭhala at Paṇḍharpur (in the Dekhan) by the officiating priests, whereupon he sang his stanzas outside the temple. On this the gate of the temple, which was to the east, changed to the west, and Viṭṭhala, taking Nāmdēv by the hand, seated him at his side. The priests, on seeing this, became terrified and fell down at the feet of Nāmdēv, soliciting his pardon.

ĀSĀ; MAHALĀ IV.; ČHANT; GHAR V.

Ōm! by the favour of the true Guru!

I. XIV. XXI.

(1). (To) my mind, the stranger, O beloved, come to (my) house!
Join (to me) Hari the Guru, O my beloved, (that) Hari may dwell in (my) house!
Merrily I enjoy pleasures, O my beloved, (if) Hari bestow mercy.
Guru Nānak is pleased, O my beloved, he joins Hari (to me).
(2). I have not tasted love, O my beloved, (though) making love.
In (my) heart thirst is not quenched, O my beloved, (though) I continually hope (for it).
Continually youth passes away, O my beloved, Yama takes away (my) breath.
A fortunate happy wife is she, O my beloved, (who) keeps Hari in (her) breast, (says) Nānak.
(3). My eyes are enamoured with my sweetheart, O my beloved, (as) the Čātrik with the rain-drop.
(My) mind has become sedate, O my beloved, (if) it drinks the drop of Hari.
Love keeps (me) awake in the body, O my beloved, no sleep comes on in any way.
Hari, the sweetheart, I obtained, O my beloved, by devout devotion to Guru Nānak.
(4). The month of Čēt comes on, spring, the pleasant season, O my beloved!
(But) without (my) sweetheart, O my beloved, dust is flying about in the courtyard.
A longing has arisen in (my) heart, O my beloved, both (my) eyes are intent (on the sweetheart).
Seeing Guru Nānak I became happy, O my beloved, as a mother (rejoices in her) son.
(5). The stories and tales about Hari, O my beloved, the true Guru let (me) hear!
I am a sacrifice to the Guru, O my beloved, by whom (I am) united (with) Hari.
Every hope (of mine) was fulfilled by Hari, the fruit, (my) mind desired, I obtained.
Hari is pleased, O my beloved, humble Nānak is absorbed in the name.
(6). Without the love of the beloved Hari I shall not sport.
How shall I get the Guru, clinging to whom I shall see the beloved?
O bountiful Hari, procure (me) the Guru, with the face, the face of the Guru I will meet!
Guru Nānak is obtained (by her), O my beloved, on (whose) forehead (this) writ was from the beginning.

RĀGU ĀSĀ; MAHALĀ V.; ČHANT; GHAR I.

Ōm! by the favour of the true Guru!

I. XXII.

(1). There is joy, great joy, I have seen that Lord, O brother![1]

I have tasted, tasted the sweet juice of Hari, O brother!

The sweet juice of Hari has fallen[2] into my heart, the true Guru has become pleased, tranquillity has sprung up (in me).

(My) house has become flourishing, a song of congratulation is sung, those five wicked ones have fled away.

(We are) filled with composure (by) the nectar-speech, the virtuous saint (= the Guru) is (our) intercessor.

Nānak says: my mind is pleased with Hari, that Lord has been seen with (my) eyes.

[1] ਰਾਮ may be translated either by: brother or Rām. It is only added here for the sake of the rhyme.

[2] ਵੁਠਾ, properly: has rained (from ਵਸਣਾ).

(2). Adorned, adorned are my beautiful gates, O brother!

My guests, my guests are the beloved saints, O brother!

By the beloved saint (my) affairs are accomplished, paying reverence (we) stick to (his) service.

He himself is the bridegroom's attendant, he himself is the bride's attendant, he himself is the Lord, he himself is God.

His own work he himself arranges, he himself upholds it.

Nānak says: the bridegroom is seated in (my) house, adorned are the beautiful gates.

(3). The nine treasures, the nine treasures have come into my house, O brother!

Everything, everything is obtained, (if) I meditate on the name, O brother!

(If) I meditate on the name, Gōvind is easily always (my) companion.

Calculation is effaced, running about is stopped, anxiety never enters (my) mind.

Gōvind thunders (with) an unbeaten musical instrument, a wonderful glory is made.

Nānak says: (when) my beloved is with (me), then I obtain the nine treasures.

(4). Abundant, abundant are my brothers, all (arc) (my) friends, O brother!

Difficult, difficult is the arena, by joining the Guru I became victorious, O brother!

By joining the Guru I became victorious, I said: Hari, Hari! the wall of the fort of error was broken down.

The treasure was obtained, a great treasure, he himself assisted me.

He is very wise, he is foremost, who is made by the Lord his own.

Nānak says: when the Lord is on (my) side, then many are (my) brothers and friends.

II. XXIII.

(1). Inexpressible, inexpressible is the story regarding Hari, it cannot be known at all, O brother!

By the excellent men and Munis it is naturally praised, O brother!

The nectar-speech is naturally praised (by them, by whom) love is entertained to the lotus-foot (of Hari).

By muttering the one incomprehensible Lord, the Supreme Spirit, the fruit, that is desired by the mind, is obtained.

Abandoning pride, infatuation, vice (and) duality, light is absorbed in the Luminous one.

Nānak says: by the favour of the Guru I always enjoy the pleasure of Hari.[1]

(2). The saints of Hari, the saints of Hari are my sweethearts, friends and assistants, O brother!

By the very fortunate, by the very fortunate one the society of the saints is obtained, O brother!

The very fortunate one obtains it, (who) meditates on the name, (his) pain and troubles are removed (thereby).

Who cling to the feet of the Guru, (their) error and fear are broken, by themselves (their) own self is effaced.

(Who) are mercifully united by their Lord (with himself), they are not separated (from him nor) do they go anywhere else.

Nānak says: (I am) thy slave, (I am) always in (thy) asylum, O Hari!

(3). At the gate of Hari, at the gate of Hari shine thy devotees, O beloved Rām!

I sacrifice myself to them, I sacrifice myself to them, I am always a sacrifice to them, O Rām!

I am always a sacrifice (to them), paying reverence (to them), who meeting with the Lord have known him.

In everybody he is contained, the Lord, the Supreme Spirit, the arranger (of all) is omnipresent in all places.

[1] ਹਰਿ ਰੰਗ might also be translated by: every pleasure.

(By whom) the perfect Guru is obtained (and) the name is meditated upon, he does not lose (his) lifetime in gambling.

Nānak says: keep (me) in thy asylum (and) bestow mercy (on me)!

(4). Endless, endless are thy qualities, how many shall I sing, O Rām!

The dust of thy feet, of thy feet, I obtain by dint of a great lot, O Rām!

If ablution be made in the dust of Hari, the filth is removed, the pain of birth and death is taken away.

Inside and outside Hari is always present, the Lord is with (me).

(My) pain is effaced, (there is) welfare (and) praise, I do not fall again into the womb.

Nānak says: in the asylum of the Guru crossing is made, (if) I please my own Lord.

ĀSĀ; MAHALĀ V.; ČHANT; GHAR IV.

Õm! by the favour of the true Guru!

III. XXIV.

(1). By the lotus-foot of Hari (my) mind is perforated, nothing else is sweet (to me), O king Rām!

Having joined the society of the saints, he (Hari) is adored (by me), Hari is seen in everybody, O king Rām!

Hari is seen in everybody, nectar has rained, the pain of birth and death is extinguished.

The depository of (all) excellences is sung, all pain is effaced, the tie of egotism is destroyed.

(My) beloved I do not give up easily, Majǐṭh colour[1] is applied to (my) mind.

Nānak is perforated by the lotus-foot of Hari, nothing else is sweet (to him).

(2). As the fish is enamoured with the water, so (we are) intoxicated with the juice of Rām, O king Rām!

By the perfect Guru instruction is given, the devotees are (thereby) liberated whilst in the body,[2] O king Ram!

(Who are) liberated whilst in the body, they are applied by the Lord himself, the inward governor, to the hem of his garment.

Hari, the choice jewel, is manifest (to them), they do not give up the omnipresent one nor do they go anywhere else.

The Lord is a clever, beautiful, all-wise Lord, his gift is not effaced.

As the fish is enamoured with the water, so is Nānak intoxicated with Hari.

(3). As the Čātrik asks for a drop (of rain), so is Hari the support of (my) life, O king Rām!

He is dearer (to me) than wealth, treasure, son, brother, friend, (yea) than all, O king Rām!

Dearer than all is (to me) the Supreme Spirit, (who is) distinct (from all), his state is not known.

(If) at every breath and morsel he be never forgotten, pleasure is enjoyed by means of the words of the Guru.

The Lord is the Supreme Spirit, the life of the world, the saints are drinking (his) juice, the pain of error and spiritual blindness is destroyed (thereby).

As the Čātrik asks for a drop (of rain), so Hari is dear (to) Nānak.

(4). (We) have met with our Nārāyaṇ, our desire is fulfilled, O king Rām!

The wall of error is pulled down by (our) meeting with the Guru, the hero, O king Rām!

[1] *i.e.* a genuine red dye which does not go off.

[2] ਜੀਵਨਗਤਿ = ਜੀਵਨਮੁਕਤਿ (जीवन्मुक्त), gone, liberated whilst living (in the body).

The all-present Guru is obtained (by them, for whom) before all treasures were written down by him, who is kind to the poor.

At the beginning, in the midst and at the end is that Lord, the beautiful Guru Gōpāl.

(There is) happiness, tranquillity and many joys, the dust of the pious is purifying the sinners.

(We) have met with Hari Nārāyaṇ, O Nānak, (our) desire is fulfilled!

ĀSĀ; MAHALĀ V.; ČHANT; GHAR VI.

Ōm! By the favour of the true Guru!

I. IV. XXV.

Slōk.

To whom the Lord Hari, Hari, has been merciful, (them) he causes to mutter (Hari).

Nānak (says): in those love to Hari has sprung up, (who are) joining the society of the pious.

Čhant.

(1). Like the manner of water and milk is—now that there is no flame (unto) the milk—such affection to Hari, O mind, (have thou)!

Now the black bee is immersed in the scent of the lotuses, not even one moment it goes away.

(So) not one moment the love to Hari turns away, all ornaments (and) relishes are offered up (to it).

By whom pain is heard and the way of Yama is spoken of, he, being in the society of the pious, does not tremble.

By praising the excellences of Gōvind all expiations (and) pains are done away.

Nānak says: (as there is) in the mind of Gōvind Hari[1] voluntarily[2] love to Hari, such an affection to Hari entertain thou, O mind!

(2). As the fish (has love to) the water and is not quiet one moment (without it), such a love (to Hari) entertain thou, O mind!

As the thirst of the Čātrik is, which says every moment: rain a drop, a drop, O beautiful cloud!

(So) love to Hari should be made, this mind should be given (to him), the thoughts should be quite applied to Murāri!

Pride should not be entertained, one should fall on (his) asylum, for his sight (one should become) a sacrifice!

The Guru is favourable (to me), join me, O Lord, (who art) separated (from me), the woman is giving (thee) a true message of love!

Nānak says: O mind! such a love entertain thou, as is voluntarily entertained (in the mind) of the endless Lord with Hari.

(3). The Čakvī is in love with the sun, she ponders with great longing: when will the sun be seen?

The Kōkil is in love with the Mango-tree, it says: O beautiful (tree)!

O mind, (in this wise) love should be entertained (by thee) to Hari!

Love to Hari should be made, conceit should not be entertained, (we) all (are) guests of (but) one night!

Now what for is pleasure entertained (and) infatuation made (thereby)? naked (we) come and go!

The asylum of the pious is firm, at (their) feet one should fall down, then the trick[3] of infatuation will break down!

[1] Gōvind Hari = Krishṇa, the incarnate Hari.

[2] ਛੰਤ here in the sense of: fondness, will, pleasure. ਛੰਤ (= छन्द) stands here adverbially: by his own will (= ਛੰਦ ਤੇ = छन्दस्).

[3] ਜੁਗਤੀਐ = ਜੁਗਤਿ, Sansk. युक्ति, contrivance, trick.

Nānak says: (as there is) voluntarily in the mind of the merciful man (love to Hari), (so) make thou love to Hari (saying): when will the sun be seen?

(4). As a deer, hearing at night with its ears a sound,[1] bounds (towards it), so, O mind, love should be made (to Hari)!

As a young woman is entangled with the corpse of her beloved husband (on the funeral pile), so this mind should be given to the darling (Hari)![2]

(If) the mind be given to the darling, enjoyment is made, all pleasures and merriments are enjoyed.

(My) own beloved is obtained, red colour is made, (my) very old friend is met with.

(When) the Guru has become my friend, then he is seen by me with (my) eyes, like my beloved no other is seen.

Nānak says: as in the mind of the kind and fascinating one[3] the feet of Hari are seized, so, O mind, love should be made (to Hari)!

II. V. XXVI.

Slōk.

Entering deeply and wandering from forest to forest and searching about I did not succeed.

O Nānak, when the pious men met (with me), Hari was obtained in my heart.

Čhant.

(1). Whom innumerable Munis and many ascetics seek.

(Whom) crores of Brahmās adore (and) wise men mutter.

(Whom) with muttering, austerity, continence, religious ceremonies, worship and many purifications (they are) adoring,

Travelling over the earth and bathing at the holy watering places for the sake of meeting with the Pure one.

Men, forests, grass, cattle, birds, all are worshipping thee.

Kind is the beloved Gōvind; Nānak (says): join the society of the pious, salvation is brought about (there)!

(2). Crores of avatārs of Vishṇu (and of) Shivas, wearing matted hair,

Desire thee, O merciful one! in their heart and body is infinite desire.

The boundless, unattainable Gōvind, the Lord is filling all, (he is) the Lord and owner (of all).

The gods, the Siddhas, the Gaṇas, the Gandharvas, the Yakshas, the Kinnaras meditate (on him), telling (his) excellences.

Crores of Indras, many gods are muttering the Lord with exultation.

He is the friend of the friendless (and) merciful, Nānak (says): join the society of the pious, salvation (is there)!

(3). Whom crores of Dēvīs serve (and) Lakshmīs of many kinds.

Whom, being hidden and manifest adore the word, the water, day and night.

(On whom) the stars, the moon and the sun meditate, (whom) the earth and the sky sing.

(On whom) all the places of production, all stages of the voice continually meditate.

Whom the Smriti, the Purāṇas, the four Vēdas, the six Shāstras are muttering:

The purifier of the sinners, he who is kind to the devotees, is met with in the society of the pious, (says) Nānak.

[1] The hunters are said to ensnare the deer by making a certain sound at night-time.

[2] The burning of the Sàtī is here in no way impugned.

[3] According to the preceding verses Krishṇa is here the subject.

(4). As much as[1] is made known by the Lord, so much the tongue utters.

What one serves (him) without knowledge, that much cannot be counted.

The eternal, indeterminable, unfathomable Lord is within all and outside (of all).

All are beggars, the One is bountiful, he is not far off, he is a manifest companion.

He is in the power of (his) devotees, he joins the creatures; by whom is his greatness calculated?

May Nānak obtain this gift (and) honour, (that) he may put (his) head on the feet of the pious!

III. VI. XXVII.

Slōk.

Make efforts, O ye very fortunate, remember Hari, Hari the king!

By whose remembrance all happiness accrues (and) pain, affliction and error depart, (says) Nānak.

Čhant.

(1). In muttering the name of Gōvind no sloth should be made!

By meeting with the pious one does not go to the city of Yama.

Pain, affliction and fear do not befall (him), remembering the name he is always happy.

Adore at every breath Hari, Hari, meditate on that Lord with (thy) mind and mouth!

O merciful, kind, delightful depository of (all) excellences, bestow mercy, (that) service may be made (to thee)!

Nānak answers and utters[2] (this) stanza:[3] in muttering the name of Gōvind may no sloth be made!

(2). The pure name of the Pure one is purifying the sinners.

The knowledge of the Guru is the collyrium, which destroys error and darkness.

The knowledge of the Guru is the (right) collyrium, the pure Lord is present in water, land and on the surface of the earth.

In whose heart he dwells one moment, his anxieties are effaced.

The Lord is of unfathomable knowledge and powerful, breaking the fear of all.

Nānak answers and utters this stanza; the pure name of the Pure one is purifying the sinners.

(3). The sanctuary of the kind and merciful Gōpāl, the depository of kindness, is seized (by me).

Thy feet are my refuge, in thy asylum is perfection.[4]

The feet of Hari are the cause of causes, the Lord Hari, Hari is saving the sinners.

The name brings across the ocean of the world (and) existence, by (its) remembrance many have crossed.

(Who) seek him who at the beginning and end is endless, (let them know, that) the way of salvation is heard of in the society of the saints.

Nānak answers and utters (this) line: the sanctuary of the kind and merciful Gōpāl, the depository of kindness, is seized (by me).

(4). Hari himself has made (this) his practice, (that he is) kind to (his) devotees.

Wherever the saints adore (him), there he is manifested.

By the Lord himself they are reabsorbed, the work of the devotees is easily accomplished.

(There is) joy, every success, great rejoicing (on their part), every pain is forgotten.

[1] ਜੇਤੀ, supply = ਘਾਤਿ (word).

[2] ਪਇਅੰਪੈ is derived from the Sansk. प्रतिजल्प्, to answer, to rejoin; similarly ਜੰਪੈ from जल्प्, the Prākrit form of जल्प् being जप् (cf. Weber, Hālā, 222). The Sikh Granthīs explain ਪਇਅੰਪੈ traditionally by: "he says;" but this is a mere conjecture, as they have no idea of the etymology of this verb; ਜੰਪੈ they usually identify with ਜਪੈ, which gives no sense.

[3] ਚਰਣ signifies here: a stanza, a line of poetry.

[4] ਸਿਧਿ (सिद्धि), perfection (of existence = emancipation).

A wonderful appearance is manifest in the ten regions (of the earth), the One is shown there.

Nānak answers and utters (this) line: Hari himself has made (this) practice, (that he is) kind to (his) devotees.

IV. VII. XXVIII.

(1). Firm is the (happy) married state of the saintly woman, he [1] neither dies nor goes.

In whose house Hari is the Lord (husband), she always enjoys (him).

Imperishable, eternal is that Lord, always young and spotless.

He is not far away, he is present, the Lord is always filling the ten regions.

The Lord of life is known by dint of intelligence and understanding, love to the beloved is pleasing to the beloved.

Nānak expounds (what) he knows from the word of the Guru: firm is the (happy) married state of the saintly woman, he neither dies nor goes.

(2). Whose husband is Rām, she has great joy.

That woman is happy, she is full of splendour (and) adorned.

(She has) honour, greatness, welfare (and) every success, her sweetheart, that Lord, (being) with (her).

All perfections, the nine treasures (are) in her house, there is no want of anything.

(By whom) the sweet speech of the beloved one is heeded, her married state is rendered firm.

Nānak expounds, (what) he knows from the word of the Guru: whose husband is Ram, she has great joy.

(3). Come, O friend, to the saint, apply thyself to (his) service!

Grind corn and wash his feet, give up thy own self!

By abandoning thy own self anguish is put out, thy own self is not (again) subjected to regeneration.[2]

(His) asylum should be seized, he should be obeyed, doing that happiness is obtained.[3]

Do the lowest service, give up sadness, day and night joining thy hands (in prayer) wake!

Nānak expounds (what) he knows from the word of the Guru: come, O friend, to the saint, apply thyself to (his) service!

(4). On whose forehead the lot (is written), he is applied to the service (of the Guru).

His desire is fulfilled, by whom the society of the pious is obtained.

In the society of the pious he is applied to the love of Hari (and) the remembrance of Gōvind.

Error, infatuation, vice, duality, all is abandoned by him.

In his mind tranquillity (as) a natural disposition has settled, (with) joy and exultation the excellences (of Hari) are sung.

Nānak expounds (what) he knows from the word of the Guru: on whose forehead the lot (is written), he is applied to the service (of the Guru).

V. VIII. XXIX.

Slōk.

To those, who are muttering the name of Hari, Hari, Yama, the death, says nothing.

Nānak (says): (their) mind and body become happy, at the end Gōpāl meets (with them).

Čhant.

(1). I will join the society of the saints, save me!

Joining my hands I make supplication: O Hari, Hari, give (me) thy name!

[1] *i.e.* her husband = Hari.

[2] ਜਾਲਾਈਐ = ਜਲਾਈਐ; ਆਪੁ ਜਲਾਉਲਾ literally: to cause to be born one's own self = to subject oneself to regeneration.

[3] These words could also be translated: what he (the Guru) does, that should be received as happiness.

I ask for the name of Hari, I cling to (thy) feet, I will give up conceit by thy mercy!
I do not run anywhere, (that) I may obtain (thy) asylum, O Lord, full of mercy, bestow mercy (on me)!
O powerful, unattainable, boundless and spotless Lord, hear this (my) supplication!
Joining (his) hands Nānak asks for (this) gift: remove (from me) regeneration and death!
(2). (I am) a sinner, without understanding, without virtues, friendless and low.
Roguish, hard, of low extraction, steeped in the mud of spiritual blindness.
In filth, error (and) works of selfishness, death does not come into (my) mind.
Dalliance with (my) wife, rejoicing in the Māyā, ignorance sticks (to me).
Youth declines, old age is increasing, death, (that is) with (me), looks out for (its) day.
Nānak says: thou art my hope, keep (me) the low one in the asylum of the pious!
(3). (We) have wandered about in many births, in very narrow wombs.
(I) cling to that, (in which are) sweet enjoyments (and) sleeping.[1]
In wandering about an incalculable burden fell (on me), (I) ran about in many foreign countries.
Now I hold fast the sanctuary of the Lord Murāri, the name of Hari (gives me) all comforts.
O beloved Lord, O protector, by me nothing is effected nor will be effected.
In comfort, composure and joy Nānak crosses by thy mercy the world.
(4). Those, who hold fast the name, are saved, what anxiety is to the devotees (of Hari)?
In any way hear the glory of Hari with (your) ear!
The wise men having heard (it) with (their) ears obtain the treasure in (their) heart.
Steeped in the love of Hari, the all-arranging Lord, they sing the excellences of Rām.
If the earth (be) the paper, the forest the pen, the wind the writer:
The end of the endless one cannot be obtained; by Nānak the asylum of (his) feet is seized.

VI. IX. XXX.

(1). (By me) the asylum of the Supreme Being, the Lord of men, is seized.
(We) have become fearless, all care (about our) life has vanished.
He is known as mother, father, friend, sweetheart, friend (and) relative.
(I am) taken and applied to (his) bosom, by the Guru (I am) united (with him), his pure glory is expounded (to me) by the saint (= the Guru).
Many are the excellences of the endless one, the estimate of his greatness cannot be told at all.
The Lord is One, the incomprehensible Lord is many, by Nanak (his) sanctuary is seized.
(2). The forest (and) the world are nectar (to him, to whom) he himself has become a companion.
(On whose) breast is the necklace of the name of Rām, (his) days of poison have passed.
Gone is error, infatuation and vice are destroyed, all going into the womb is stopped.
He walks cool in the fire of the world, (who) seizes the hem of the garment of the pious.
Gōvind Gōpāl is merciful and powerful; say, O pious man: victory to Hari!
O Nānak, meditate on the name! in the society of the perfect, pious men, emancipation is obtained.
(3). Wherever I see, there the One is present.
He himself is dwelling in everybody, (but only) by some rare one he is obtained.
In water, land and on the surface of the earth he is fully present, in the worm (as well as in) the elephant he is contained.
He is at the beginning, at the end and in the midst, by the favour of the Guru he is known.
Brahm is expanded, (all is) the sport of Brahm, Gōvind is called the depository of (all) excellences by (his) people.
Remember the Lord, the inward governor, the One Hari, O Nānak, is contained (in all)!

[1] ਸੇਣ = ਸੈਣ sleeping.

(4). Pleasant is the day (and) night, (in which) the remembrance of the name of Hari (is made).
By love to the lotus-foot filth and sins are removed.
Pain, hunger and poverty are destroyed, the way is shown evidently.
By joining the saints and by love to the name the desire of the heart is obtained.
By seeing the sight of Hari (one's) wish is fulfilled, all (one's) families are saved.
Day and night (there is) joy by daily remembering Hari, Hari, (says) Nānak.

ĀSĀ; MAHALĀ V.; ČHANT; GHAR VII.

Ōm! by the favour of the true Guru!

I. X. XXXI.

Slōk.

It is a good thing to reflect on Gōvind and to delight oneself with the spotless pious people.
O Lord, bestow mercy, (that) Nānak may not forget the name for twenty-four minutes!
(1). In a clear night the stars glitter.
The saints, who are dear to my Rām, wake.
Those, who are dear to Rām, wake always, day by day they remember the name.
In (their) heart is meditation on the lotus-foot (of Hari), the Lord is not forgotten one moment.
By giving up conceit, infatuation and vice, the filth of the mind and (its) pain are burnt.
Nānak says: the servants of Hari, the beloved saints wake always.
(2). The apparatus of my bed is got ready.
In (my) heart joy sprang up, I heard, that the Lord is coming.
The Lord joined (me), (I am) enjoying happiness, pleasure, rejoicings and enjoyments were supplied.
He clung to (my) bosom, pain fled, (my) life, mind, body, all flourished.
The desire of (my) heart was obtained by meditating on the Lord, the auspicious day for the union was calculated.
Nānak says: the bearer of prosperity joined (me), all joys and pleasures were made.
(3). Having joined (her) companion she asks: tell (me) the sign of the beloved!
(I am) filled with love and affection (to him), tell (me) something, I do not know (his sign)!
The qualities of the creator are dark, hidden and boundless, the Vēda does not reach (their) end.
In devotion with love meditate on the Lord, sing always the excellences of Hari!
She is filled with the knowledge of all (his) qualities, (who) is pleasing to her own Lord.
Nānak says: she, who is imbued with love and affection (to Hari), is easily absorbed (in him).
(4). With pleasure they commenced to sing songs of joy about Hari.
(Their) friends increased, (their) pain (and their) enemies fled.
(Their) comfort (and) tranquillity became abundant, they rejoiced in the name of Hari, the Lord himself bestowed mercy (on them).
They clung to the feet of Hari, they were always waking, they were united with the Lord, the wearer of the chaplet of wild flowers.
Auspicious days came, easily all treasures were obtained (by them), they are blended[1] with the Lord.
Nānak says: the people of Hari are always comfortably settled[2] in the asylum of the Lord.

[1] पागला (= पगला, pagg-ṇā) to be blended, to be mingled with (Sansk. पृक्त, root पर्च्).
[2] डागला (= डगला, taggṇā), to remain, to be settled comfortably (Sindhī ग़गणु, Marāṭhī तगणें). The etymology is not quite clear.

II. XI. XXXII.

(1). Rise and go, O traveller, what delay hast thou made?

(Thy) time has arrived, by what falsehood art thou enticed?

By falsehood (thou art) enticed, by the fraud of the Māyā thou committest innumerable sins.

(Thy) body, the heap of ashes, is looked out for by Yama, the death, O helpless one, (thou art) overcome!

Abandoning wealth (and) youth thou wilt go off, clothing and food are stopped.

Nānak says: (thy) works go with (thee), what is done, cannot be effaced.

(2). Thou art ensnared like the deer, (that) sees at night the moonshine.

From pleasure pain springs up, sin is always committed.

Sins, that are committed do not leave (thee), they carry (thee) away having thrown a neck-halter (over thee).

Having seen the city of Hariśčhandra (= mirage) (thou art) carried away, falsehood is enjoyed (on thy) bed.

(Thou art) intoxicated with greediness and selfishness, (thou art) absorbed[1] in pride.

Nānak (says): the deer is destroyed by (its) ignorance, coming and going (= transmigration) is not effaced (in the state of ignorance).

(3). By a sweet (thing) the fly is killed, how shall it fly (being caught)?

(When) the elephant has fallen into a pit, how shall swimming be made?

Swimming (across) has become difficult (to him), into (whose) mind the Lord never has come for a moment.

There is no counting of (his) pain (and) punishment, he earns his own doing.

(His) hidden works become manifest, here and there he is wretched.

Nānak (says): without the true Guru the conceited self-willed man is wretched.

(4). The servants of Hari live, clinging to the feet of the Lord.

They are applied to (his) neck by that Lord, who is affording (them) protection.

Strength, understanding, divine knowledge (and) meditation are given by himself, his own name he himself causes (them) to mutter.

He himself is in the society of the pious, he himself causes the world to be crossed.

They are preserved by the preserver, (their) work is always spotless.

Nānak (says): they never go to hell, the saints of Hari are in the asylum of Hari.

III. XII. XXXIII.

(1). Depart, O my slothfulness, (this is) my prayer to Hari!

I will enjoy my own bridegroom, in the society of (my) Lord I am beautiful!

In the society of my beloved, the Lord, I am beautiful, day and night he is enjoyed (by me).

Thinking of him at every breath I live, seeing the Lord the excellences of Hari are sung (by me).

Separation is put to shame, (his) sight is obtained, (his) sight is sprinkling nectar (on me).

O Nānak, my desire is fulfilled, he is found, (whom I was) seeking.

(2). Be destroyed, O my sins! the creator has come to my house.

The burning of the attackers has taken place, Gōvind is manifested.

Gōpāl Gōvind is manifested, the darling is expounded in the society of the pious.

A wonderful thing is seen, nectar has rained, by the favour of the Guru he is known.

Tranquillity has come into (my) mind, congratulation is made, no end (of him) can be obtained.

Nānak says: happiness (and) union are easily made by the Lord himself.

[1] मभाष्टिलु = मभाला, on account of the rhyme.

(3). Hell is not seen by remembering Nārāyaṇ.

Dharm-rājā cries out: victory! (his) messengers take to flight.[1]

(By reason of) piety, patience (and) tranquillity they are happy, in the society of the pious Hari is adored (by them).

By (his) favour they are preserved, infatuation and selfishness, all is abandoned (by them).

They are applied to (his) neck, by the Guru they are united (with him), muttering Gōvind they are satiated.

Nānak says: remember the Lord, (who is) fulfilling every desire!

(4). (By whom) the feet (of Hari), (containing all) the treasures and perfections, are seized, what grief has he?

Everything is in the power (of him), whose that our Lord is.

(His) arms are seized, the name is given (to him), the hand (of Hari) is put on (his) head.

He does not enter the ocean of the world, the nectar-juice of Hari is tasted (by him).

In the society of the pious he delights in the name, in the great battle-field he is victorious.

Nānak says: (who (is) in the asylum of the Lord, he is not again uprooted by Yama.

IV. XIII. XXXIV.

(1). What is done by day and night, that comes on (one's) head.

From whom he is hiding himself, he sees (him, being) with (him).

The creator (being) with (him) sees (him), why should sin be committed?

(If) good works be done, if the name be taken, one will go by no means to hell.

Remember the eight watches the name of Hari, it goes with (thee)!

Adore (him) always in the society of the pious! the sins, thou hast committed, are effaced (thereby), (says) Nānak.

(2). Practising deceit thou fillest (thy) belly, O ignorant fool! Hari, the donor, gives everything.

The Lord is always bountiful and kind, why is he forgotten from (thy) mind?

Join the society of the pious, adore him who is without an associate, all (thy) families will be saved.

The Siddhas, the ascetics, the gods, the Munis, the devotees are relying on the name.

Nānak says: the one Lord, the creator, should always be adored!

(3). Insincerity should not be made, the Lord is examining (men).

Those, who are practising falsehood (and) hypocrisy, are born (again) in the world.

The ocean of the world is crossed by them, by whom the One is meditated upon.

Abandoning lust, wrath and the censure of those, who are unblamable, they come to the asylum of the Lord.

In water (and) on the surface of the earth the high, unattainable, boundless Lord is contained.

Nānak says: he is the prop of his people, the lotus-foot is (their) support.

(4). Behold, (all is) a mirage, nothing is durable.

As many as the appearances of the Māyā are, they do not go with (thee).

Hari is always a companion with (thee), day and night he should be kept in mind!

Without the One Hari there is nothing else, other love (but Hari's) should be burnt!

Consider that One Lord in (thy) mind as friend, youth, wealth, (yea) as all!

Nānak says: by a great lot he is obtained, (who obtains him) enters into happiness (and) tranquillity (of mind).

[1] The sense is: they, who remember Hari, do not see hell. Yama cries out to them: victory (to you)! his messengers flee from them.

ĀSĀ; MAHALĀ V.; ČHANT; GHAR VIII.

Ōm! By the favour of the true Guru!

I. XIV. XXXV.

(1). (In) the error of the Māyā (and) in fear, in the error of the Māyā (and) in fear, alas! in sharp, perverse intoxication, alas! life is passing uselessly!

(In) an impenetrable, terrible forest, (in) an impenetrable, terrible forest, alas! the thieves of the heart are robbing the house, alas! the sun is day by day eating up (the life).

The days are eating up (the life), they are passing without the Lord, join (me), O Lord, O compassionate husband!

Many births and deaths have been gone through, without the society of the beloved one there is no salvation at all.

I am without family, beauty, incense, divine knowledge, without thee what mother have I?

Having joined (my) hands, (says) Nānak, I have come to (thy) asylum, O beloved Lord, O Nar Hari, effect (my) salvation![1]

(2). A fish destitute of water, a fish destitute of water, oh! being separated from it (*i.e.* the water) is wretched in mind and body, oh! how is life getting on without the beloved?

It faces the arrow, it faces the arrow, oh! the deer offers up heart, body and life, oh! it is pierced easily whilst listening.[2]

Love to the beloved has sprung up, join the passionate lover! the body is wretched remaining one moment without him.

The eyelids are not closed, the mind is imbued with love to the beloved, thinking daily of the Lord.

Who are attached to Vishṇu (and) intoxicated with the name, they are putting away fear, error, duality, (yea) all.

Bestow mercy and pity, O kind, all-filling Hari! Nānak is being immersed in (thy) love.

(3). The black bee is humming about, the black bee is humming about, oh! it is intoxicated with the scent of the nectar-juice of the flowers, oh! it is binding itself by (its) love to the lotus.

In the mind of the Čātrik there is thirst, in the mind of the Čātrik there is thirst, oh! in (its) mind there is a longing for a beautiful drop of the cloud, oh! drinking a little[3] its heat passes away.

O consumer of heat, O destroyer of pain, join (me), in (my) heart there is excessive love (to thee)!

Beautiful, clever (and) wise is the Lord, by which tongue is (his) excellency told?

Seize (my) arm, give (me) the name! (on whom thou art) bestowing a favourable look, (his) sins are effaced.

Nānak says: he who is seeing the sight of Hari, the purifier of the sinners, is not in distress.

(4). I think in (my) mind of the Lord, I think in (my) mind of the Lord, oh! keep (me), the friendless one, in thy asylum, oh! join (me) cheerfully, take (my) life!

(My) meditation is (on thy) beautiful body, (my) meditation is (on thy) beautiful body, oh! (my) mind is desirous of the knowledge of Gōpāl, oh! (thou art) preserving the honour of (thy) beggars.

The Lord is fulfilling (their) hope, he is destroying (their) pain, all (their) desire is granted.

Who clings to the neck of Hari, (her) days are happy, having met with (her) Lord, (her) bed is beautiful.

By the Lord a favourable look is bestowed (on her), Murāri is met with, all (her) sins are annihilated.

Nānak says: my desire is fulfilled, the bearer of felicity is met with, the depository of (all) excellences.

[1] गाउ = गति, on account of the rhyme. [2] The deer is said to listen to the melodious voice of the hunter.

[3] ਅਲ = Sansk अल्प.

Ōm! the true name is the creator, the (divine) male without fear, without enmity, of a timeless form, not produced from the womb. By the favour of the Guru!

ĀSĀ; MAHALĀ I.

VĀRS WITH SLŌKS.

(The Slōks also are written by the first mahalā).[1] *(To be sung) after the melody of As Rājā, the handless one.*

I.

Slōk I.; *mahalā* I.

I am a sacrifice to my own Guru daily a hundred times.
By whom out of men gods are made without any delay.

Slōk II.; *mahalā* II.

If a hundred moons rise, if a thousand suns ascend:
In spite of there being so much light, there is terrible darkness without the Guru.

Slōk III.; *mahalā* I.

O Nānak, (who) in their cautious mind do not reflect on the Guru:
They are left like an empty stalk of sesam on a cleared field.[2]
Nānak says: it is left on the field by its owner,[3]
(For though) it flourish, there are ashes in the body of the helpless (stalk).

Pauṛī.

By himself his own self was made, by himself (his) name was contrived.
Sitting down (in repose) he sees (with) pleasure, (what) is made (by) the second power.[4]
Thou thyself art the bountiful creator, being pleased thou givest and bestowest favour.
Thou art knowing all; having given thou takest (again) away the life (from) the body.
Sitting down (quietly) (thou) seest (with) pleasure.

II.

Slōk I.; *mahalā* I.

True are thy regions, true (thy) universes, true are thy worlds, true (thy) forms.
True are thy works (and) all (thy) thoughts.
True is thy order, true (thy) tribunal.
True is thy command, true thy injunction.
True is thy work, true thy sign.
O True one, Lakhs and Crores praise thee.
All (are) by thy true power, all by (thy) true might.
True is thy praise, true thy commendation.
True is thy power, O true king!

[1] The words: "the Slōks also are written by the first mahalā," are not found in better and older manuscripts, and are apparently a later addition, the more so, as also Slōks of the second Guru are mixed up with these Vārs.

[2] An empty stalk of the sesam plant is left standing, when the field is cleared, as being useless.

[3] ਸਉ ਨਾਹ = ਨਾਹ ਸਉ, the postposition ਸਉ (from, by) being placed *before* the noun on account of the rhyme.

[4] The ਦੂਜੀ ਕੁਦਰਤਿ is the Māyā.

Nānak (says): those who meditate on the True one, are true.
Those, who having died are born (again), are altogether unripe.

Slōk II.; *mahalā* I.

Great is the greatness (of him), whose name is great.
Great is the greatness (of him), whose justice is true.
Great is the greatness (of him), whose place is immovable.
Great is the greatness (of him, who) knows the conversation (of men).
Great is the greatness (of him, who) comprehends all the conditions (of men).
Great is the greatness (of him), who gives without being asked.
Great is the greatness (of him), to whom alone (it belongs).
Nānak (says): (his) work cannot be told.
What is done and is to be done, (that is) all (done) according to his will.

Slōk III.; *mahalā* II.

This world is the house of the True one, in it is the dwelling of the True one.
Some he reabsorbs (into himself) by his order, some he destroys by his order.
Some he draws out by his order, some abide in the Māyā.
Though having said thus, it is not known, if it appear true to any one.
Nānak (says): by (that) disciple it is known, to whom he himself makes (it) manifest.

Pauṛī.

Nānak (says): having produced the creatures and written (their) names, (their) duty is assigned (to them by him).

There (in the other world) decision is made by the perfectly True one, the intensely burning ones (in egotism) are picked out and set apart.

The false ones get no place, with a black face they are marched into hell.

Those who are attached to thy name go off having got the victory, those deceitful ones are overcome.

Having written (their) names (their) duty is assigned (to them by him).

III.

Slōk I.; *mahalā* I.

Wonderstruck is the sound, wonderstruck the Vēda.
Wonderstruck the creature, wonderstruck the difference.[1]
Wonderstruck the form, wonderstruck the colour.
Wonderstruck the creatures, that wander about naked.
Wonderstruck the wind, wonderstruck the water.
Wonderstruck the fire, that sports assuming strange forms.
Wonderstruck is the earth, wonderstruck the places of production.
Wonderstruck stick the creatures to a sweet taste.
Wonderstruck is union, wonderstruck separation.
Wonderstruck is hunger, wonderstruck enjoyment.
Wonderstruck is praise, wonderstruck eulogy.
Wonderstruck the wilderness, wonderstruck the road.
Wonderstruck (those who are) near, wonderstruck (those who are) far away.

[1] ਭੇਦ very likely signifies here: the inanimate.

Wonderstruck (he who) sees (him) present (in his) presence.
Having seen (his) craftiness he remains wonderstruck.
Nānak (says): by a full lot he is known.

Slōk II.; *mahalā* I.

(His) power is seen, (his) power is heard, the fear of (his) power is the pith of happiness.

(His) power is in the nether regions (and) in the skies, (by his) power all forms (are made).

(By his) power is the Vēda, the Purāṇas and the Book (= the Qur'ān), (by his) power he is reflecting on everything.

(By his) power eating, drinking and clothing (are given), (by his) power is all pleasure.

(By his) power are (all) kinds, species (and) colours, (by his) power (are) the creatures (and) the world.

(By his) power is goodness, (by his) power badness, (by) his power pride and conceit.

(By his) power is the wind, water, fire, (by his) power the earth and land.

All is (by thy) power, thou art the powerful creator, purer than a pure name.[1]

Nānak sees (his) order within: he is quite unique.[2]

Pauṛī.

Having gone through his enjoyments he becomes ashes, the black bee (= the soul) departs.

He was a great, rich man, (but) is marched (now) off, a chain being thrown over his neck.

Further on (in the other world) the memorial of (his) actions is read, the account (of them) is made up and given (him) to understand.

He gets no place, the ace is given,[3] what is he now heard who is made to weep?

In (his) blind mind he has ruined (his) life.

IV.

Slōk I.; *mahalā* I.

In fear the wind (and) a hundred breezes blow.
In fear flow on a hundred thousand rivers.
In fear fire undergoes forced labour.
In fear the earth is pressed down by a burthen.
In fear the moon wanders about with the head downwards.
In fear is Dharm-rājā (at his) gate.
In fear is the sun, in fear is the moon.
They go crores of Kōs, there is no end (of their wanderings).
In fear are the Siddhas, the Buddhas, the gods and Jōgīs.
In fear are the heavens propped.
In fear are the warriors, the very strong heroes.
In fear come and go boat-loads.[4]
On all fear is written (as their) destiny.
Nānak (says): fearless is the Formless, the One True one.

[1] ਪਾਕੀ ਨਾਈ = ਪਾਕ ਨਾਉ ਤੇ, ਨਾਈ being the Ablative Sing.

[2] ਤਾਕੇ ਤਾਕ, literally: more unique than unique = quite unique (ਤਾਕ = طاق), totally unconnected with anything.

[3] ਪਉ ਦੀਈ, literally: the ace is given, *i.e.* his play is utterly lost, he is thoroughly discomfited.

[4] ਪੂਰ, the party taken over in a boat at one time. It alludes to the birth and death of man, which takes place in fear.

Slōk II.; *mahalā* I.

Nānak (says): fearless is the Formless one, how many other Rāms (have become) dust!
How many are the stories of Kanh (Krishṇa), how many the reflections on the Vēda!
How many beggars dance (and) beat the time (with their hands) in falling and turning!
The market-people having come to the market draw out the market.[1]
The Rājās and Rāṇīs (queens) sing and talk nonsense.[2]
Finger-rings worth Lakhs, necklaces worth Lakhs of two-pice pieces:
On which body they are placed, that body becomes ashes.
Divine knowledge is not sought by (mere) words, the story is hard iron.
(If) it accrue by destiny, then it is obtained, (all) other cleverness and order are (but) poor.

Pauṛī.

If he bestows his own favourable look, then by his favourable look the true Guru is obtained.
When this soul had wandered about in many births, the (true) word was told to it by the true Guru.
Like the true Guru there is no donor, hear (it), all you people, all!
By meeting with the true Guru the True one is obtained (by them), by whom their own self is removed from within.
(It is the Guru), by whom the perfectly True one is given to understand.

V.

Slōk I.; *mahalā* I.

(For) a Ghaṛī (twenty-four minutes) all are Gōpīs, (for) a watch (= three hours) (all are) Kanh Gōpāl.[3]
(Whose) jewels (are) wind, water, fire, (whose) incarnation the moon and the sun.
The whole earth, wealth, property (and) occupation, all (is but) trouble.
Nānak (says): (the world) devoid of divine knowledge goes to ruin, Yama, the death, eats (it) up.

Slōk II.

The disciples make music, the Gurus dance.
They move their feet and turn round their head.
Dust flying up falls on (their) hair.
The people look, laugh and go home.
For the sake of bread they clap (their) hands.
They throw themselves down along the ground.
The Gōpīs sing, the Kanhs sing.
Sītās and Rāmas, the kings, sing.
Fearless is the Formless one, (whose) name is true.
Whose work the whole world is.
(His) servants serve (him) by the rising of (their) destiny.
(By them) the night is passed in pleasure, in whose mind (there is) a longing (after him).
Instruction is learnt by reflecting on the Guru.
By (his) favourable look (and) kindness they are brought across.
Wheels of oil-presses, wheels of mills,

[1] ਬਾਜਾਰੀ, the market-people, *i.e.* public singers and dancers. ਬਾਜਾਰ ਕਢਣਾ, to draw out the market, *i.e.* assemble the people to the spectacle.

[2] The Rājās and Rāṇīs, as exhibited in the street spectacles. Here those singers and dancers are alluded to, who publicly perform the Rās of Krishṇa and entertain the public by gross (and frequently indecent) jests and songs.

[3] The sense is: they personate the Gōpīs and Kanh in dancing the Rās of Krishṇa.

Whirlwinds in the desert, there are many endless ones.
Spinning-tops and churning staves in boundless number.
The birds in wandering about do not take breath.
Machines are raised on a spindle and turned about.
O Nānak, there is no number of those things, which turn about.
Those are turned about according to the rule of (their) composition.
When (one's) destiny has fallen (so), every one dances.
Who are dancing and laughing, they go weeping.
They do not fly up, they do not become perfect.
Dancing and jumping is the delight of the mind.
Nānak (says): in whose mind there is fear (of God), in their mind is love (of God).

Pauṛī.

Thy name is "the Formless one," by taking (thy) name one does not go to hell.
Soul and body, all is his; if he gives, it is eaten, if he speaks, (the food) is destroyed.
If (one) desire to make himself excellent, he is again called low.
If he remove the colour of old age,[1] old age, taking disguise, comes on.
No one remains (here); (what) is filled in, (that) is received.[2]

VI.

Slōk I.

The praise of the Muhammadans (is made by means) of (their) law, continually reading (it) they reflect (on it).

Those are (his) servants, who fall into bondage for the sake of seeing (his) sight.

The Hindūs, who are praising, praise him who is boundless in appearance (and) form.

They bathe at a holy watering place and are offering up much adoration, worship and perfume of aloë-wood.

As many as are Jōgīs, they meditate in a state of lost sensation on the incomprehensible name of the creator.

(Whose) name is Niranjan, the form of his body (they consider as being of) a subtile form.

In the mind of the Satīs contentment is produced by the thought of giving (their lives).

Having given they ask a thousand-fold (more), that the world may adorn (honour them).

More wicked and useless than thieves and adulterers (are) the false ones.

Some depart having eaten up here (their) substance, their work also is scum.

In water and on land there are numerous forms of beings, cities and worlds.

Those who say and know, it is Thou, they also have knowledge of thee.

Nānak (says): the hunger of the devotees is to praise (God), the true name is (their) support.

They always remain in joy day and night, following[3] the virtuous.

Slōk II.; *mahalā* I.

The earth is worked into clay by the pestle,[4] it is made into a potter's lump.

Vessels and bricks are made (out of it), burning (in the kiln) it (*i.e.* the clay) cries out.

[1] ਜਰ ਵਾਲਾ I take = ਜਰਾ and ਵਾਲਾ (= ਵਰ੍ਣ), the colour, appearance of old age.

[2] The sense is: what one does, that he will earn.

[3] ਪਾਛਾੜੁ, on the back, following, instead of ਪਾਛਾੜੈ, for the sake of the rhyme.

[4] We divide the words: ਮੁਸਲ ਮਾਣ ਕੀ, as the reading ਮੁਸਲਮਾਣ (musalmān) would not give any sense. ਮਾਣ is still used in the sense of "clay" in Marāṭhī (*s.f.*), though obsolete in Hindī. This signification will best suit the context. From the Sikh Granthīs I could get no explanation whatever.

Burning on the helpless (clay) weeps, fiery coals fall continually (on it).
Nānak (says): that creator knows (it), by whom the elementary matter was made.

Pauṛī.

Without the true Guru no one has obtained him (*i.e.* the Supreme), without the true Guru no one has obtained him.
He has put his own self into the true Guru, he has manifested and proclaimed (this).
By meeting with the true Guru they are always emancipated, in whom spiritual blindness is put a stop to.
This is the highest reflection, by means of which the mind is applied to the True one.
The life of the world, the donor, is obtained (thereby).

VII.

Slōk I.

In egotism (one) comes, in egotism (one) goes.
In egotism he is born, in egotism he dies.
In egotism it is given, in egotism it is taken.
In egotism it is gained, in egotism it is gone.
In egotism is the truthful and the false one.
In egotism reflection is made (on doing) acts of demerit (or) merit.
In egotism descent to hell (or ascent) to heaven (is made).
In egotism (one) laughs, in egotism (one) weeps.
In egotism (one) is defiled, in egotism (one) washes (himself).
In egotism (one) loses caste and kind.
In egotism is the fool, in egotism the clever one.
He has no knowledge of (the way of) emancipation.
In egotism he is immersed, in egotism he is overshadowed.
The creatures are produced with egotism.
If egotism be understood (as adhering to one), then the gate (of salvation) is seen.
He who is devoid of divine knowledge, wrangles in telling (stories of the gods).
Nānak (says): by the (supreme) ruler the destiny is written.
As he makes it,[1] so is the garb (of every creature).

Slōk II.; *mahalā* II.

In egotism is this (human) nature (immersed), in egotism it works.
This egotism is the fetter, (by reason of which) (man) falls again and again into the womb.
Whence does egotism spring? by which abstinence is it removed?
This egotism is the order (of God), when (one's) lot has fallen, he removes (it).
Egotism is a long sickness, yet there is a medicine for it.
If he (God) bestows his own mercy, then (one) obtains the word of the Guru.
Nānak says: hear, ye people, by means of this abstinence the pain (of egotism) departs.

Pauṛī.

By (those) contented ones service (to God) is rendered, by whom the perfectly True one is meditated upon.
By them (their) foot is not put on wickedness, who practise good works and virtue.

[1] ਵੇਖਣਾ is here not used in the sense of "*seeing*," but of "*working*," "*making*" (Sansk. वेषण), to correspond with ਵੇਖੁ (वेष), dress, garb.

By them the fetters of the world are broken, who consume little grain (and) water.
Thou art the foremost donor, thou givest continually and it increases still more.[1]
From the great ones[2] a great (thing or gift) is obtained.

VIII.

Slōk I.; *mahalā* I.

Of men, of trees, of holy watering places, of shores, of clouds, of fields,
Of continents, worlds, provinces, regions, universes.
Of the (four) places of production: of the egg-born, womb-born, plant-born, sweat-born (creatures):
He knows (their) amount, (as also) of ponds, mountains[3] and creatures, O Nānak!
Nānak (says): having produced the creatures he takes care of all.
The creator, by whom the work is made, must also care for it.
That creator cares for it, by whom the world is made.
Obeisance to him, benediction to him! his tribunal is unbroken.
Nānak (says): without the true name what is the (religious) mark (on the forehead), what the sacred cord?

Slōk II.; *mahalā* I.

Lakhs of good actions, Lakhs of approved meritorious deeds.
Lakhs of austerities at Tīrthas (and of) devout meditations in the desert.
Lakhs of acts of heroism in war, (so that) the life is lost in battle.
Lakhs of attention, knowledge and meditation, (with which) the Purāṇas are read.[4]—
The creator, by whom the work is done, has fixed coming and going.
Nānak (says): the wisdom (of men) is false, the favour (of God) is the true standard.

Pauṛī.

Thou alone art the true Lord, by whom the perfectly True[5] one is manifested.
To whom thou givest (it), he gets the True one, by him the True one is acquired.
By meeting with the true Guru the True one is obtained (by them),
In whose heart the True one is caused to dwell (by the Guru).
The fools do not know the True one, by the self-willed (their) life is lost.
What for did they come into the world?

IX.

Slōk I.; *mahalā* I.

(If) reading and reading a cart be loaded (with it), if reading and reading a caravan be filled (with it).

(If) reading and reading a boat be laden (with it), (if) reading and reading a pit be covered (with it).

(If) it be read as many as there are years, (if) it be read as many as there are months.

[1] *i.e.*: thy bounty.

[2] ਵਡਿਆਈ is the Ablative Plur. (with the affix ī), not the substantive ਵਡਿਆਈ, greatness.

[3] Literally: of Mērus; mountains like Mēru.

[4] The sentence ends with an anakoluthon. The logical connexion appears to be this: all good acts, etc. are of no avail to escape transmigration, which is fixed by the creator, all depends on his favour (ਨਦਰੁ). The sense, as so frequently, can only be guessed at.

[5] ਸਚੁ might here also be translated by *truth*.

(If) it be read as long as life (lasts), (if) it be read as many as there are breaths.
Nānak (says): of account there is (only) one word, the other (things) are egotism and vain prating.

Slōk II.

(As much as) is written and read, so much he is grieved.
(As much as) he has wandered about at many Tīrthas, so much (filth) has stuck to him.
Many garbs are put on, pain is inflicted on the body.
Bear, O creature, thy own doings!
Food is not eaten, sweet taste is discarded.
Much pain is incurred, (as) duality pleased (him).
He does not put on clothes, day and night he groans.
Sunk in silence how should he wake? he has fallen asleep without the Guru.
He is barefooted, his own doing is earned (by him).
Dirt is eaten (by him), ashes are put on (his) head.
By the blind fool his honour is lost.
Without the name nothing becomes acceptable (with God).
He remains in deserts, at shrines, in burning places.
(But) the blind one does not know (the truth), afterwards he repents.[1]
Who meets with the true Guru, he obtains happiness.
He (the Guru) makes the name of Hari dwell in the heart.
Nānak (says): on whom (Hari) bestows a favourable glance, he gets (it).
Free from hope and apprehension he burns his egotism by means of the word (of the Guru).

Pauṛī.

The devotees are pleasing to thy mind, those who are singing (thy) praise, are lustrous at (thy) gate.
Nānak (says): without works (of a former birth) they get no entranee, they are wandering about.
Some do not comprehend their own origin, their own non-existent self they bring into account.
I am (the son) of a begging musician, of low caste, the others are called high-caste people.
I ask for them, who are meditating on thee.

X.

Slōk I.; *mahalā* I.

False is the Rājā, false the subjects, false[2] is the whole world.
False is the palace, false the upper-storied house, false he who is living (therein).
False is gold, false silver, false he who is putting (them) on.
False is the body, false the clothing, false boundless beauty.
False the master, false the mistress, they are consumed to ashes.
On falsehood affection is bestowed and the creator forgotten.
With whom shall friendship be made? the whole world is passing away!
Falsehood is sweet, falsehood is honey, falsehood drowns the boat's load.[3]
Nānak makes (this) supplication: without thee (all is) but falsehood.

Slōk II.; *mahalā* I.

Then the True one is thoroughly[4] known, when the True one is in the heart.
The filth of falsehood goes off, he (*i.e.* the disciple) washes and makes clean (his) body.

[1] ਪਛੁਤਾਲੀ = ਪਛੁਤਾਲਾ, on account of the rhyme.
[2] ਕੂੜੁ properly: falsehood, used in the sense of not really existing or lasting.
[3] ਪੂਰੁ, all those, who are together in a boat.
[4] ਪਰੁ = the Sansk. परम्; the form ਪਰਿ is used in a similar sense (= अति).

Then the True one is thoroughly known, when he entertains love to the True one.

Having heard the name the mind becomes glad, he gets the gate of salvation.

Then the True one is thoroughly known, when he knows (his) soul as united (with the Supreme).

Having put right the earth (of his) body he puts (into it) as seed the creator.

Then the True one is thoroughly known, when he puts up his dwelling at the Tīrtha of his own soul.

Asking the true Guru he remains and dwells there.

Then the True one is thoroughly known, when he takes true instruction,

(When) he knows kindness to the creatures (as his duty) and performs some meritorious acts (and gives) alms.

The True one is the medicine for all, it washes away sins.

Nānak utters (this) supplication (to them), in whose possession the True one is.

Pauṛī.

If as my present the dust of the sole of the feet (of the saints) be obtained, then it will be applied to (my) forehead.

False greediness is given up, directing the mind on one object the incomprehensible one is meditated upon.

Such a fruit is obtained, as the works are that are practised.

If it be written before, then their dust is obtained.

(By reason of) little understanding (their) service is discarded.

XI.

Slōk I.; *mahalā* I.

Friendship prevails in the Kali-yug (between) death (and) falsehood, (between) darkness (and) the goblins.[1]

Sowing the seed they have taken (its) honour, how shall now the Dāl spring up?[2]

If it be the One, then it springs up, it is (now) the season of the seasons.

Nānak (says): without the Pāh there is no adhesiveness of colour to raw cloth.[3]

If fear be put into the kettle, the solution of modesty is put on the body.

Nānak (says): (if one) be steeped in devotion, there is no adhesiveness of falsehood whatever.

Slōk II.; *mahalā* I.

Greediness and sin, the two are a Rājā and his collector of rent, falsehood is the Sirdār.

Lust is the mace-bearer, who is called and asked, sitting down he reflects.

The subjects are blind and devoid of (divine) knowledge, they are corpses filled with fire.

The wise ones dance and play musical instruments, they adorn (their) body.

They make loud conversations, they sing (their) thoughts about the heroes.

Fools and learned men collect (thence) wisdom and argument and have a liking (for it).

The virtuous one will practise virtue, he plays (musical instruments) and asks for the gate of salvation.

He who is called an ascetic, does not know union (with his wife), he sits down having forsaken his family.

Every one is perfect by himself, no one calls himself deficient.

[1] The words of this line are very obscure, I have translated them according to conjecture. The Sikh Granthīs could give no hint whatever. ਸਚਿ, *s.m.* friendship, is found in Hindī.

[2] The meaning of these words is quite obscure.

[3] ਪਾਹ is a substance (alum, etc.) dissolved in water, in which cloth is steeped preparatory to dyeing. Also the process itself. ਸੋਇ signifies: adhesiveness (ਰੰਗ ਕੀ ਸੋਇ).

The warrant of honour is obtained afterwards, then, (says) Nānak, being weighed it is known (what man is worth).

Slōk III.; *mahalā* I.

What is determined upon (by God), that becomes manifest, O Nānak, that True one sees (it).
By all jumpings are made, (but) what the creator does, that takes place.
Further on (*i.e.* in the other world) there is no caste nor power, further on the soul bows down.
Whose honour falls into account (before God), those few are good.

Pauṛī.

To whom thou hast appointed (this) work from the beginning, by them the Lord is meditated upon.
In the power of these creatures there is nothing, by thee alone the world is produced.
Some thou unitest (with thyself), others are ruined by thyself.
By the favour of the Guru he knows (thee), whom thou thyself instructest.
He is naturally absorbed in the True one.

XII.

Slōk I.; *mahalā* I.

Pain has become the medicine for the disease of (worldly) pleasures.
When (there is real) happiness, there is no desire (for worldly pleasures).[1]
Thou art the cause of causes, not I, when I do (anything), it does not take place.

Pause.

I am a sacrifice to those who are obedient to thy power.
Thy end cannot be conceived.

Slōk II.

In production there is light, in the light are the productions,[2] he who is without parts is brimful (everywhere).

Thou art the true Lord, thy praise is beautiful, by whom it is made, he passes across.

Nānak speaks words concerning the creator: whatever is to be done, that he does.

Slōk III.; *mahalā* II.

The word of the Brāhmaṇs is about Yōga (abstract meditation), divine knowledge and the Vēda.

The word of the Khatrīs is a word about heroes, the word of the Sūdras is Prākrit (common parlance).

All words are one word, if one know the secret.
Nānak is his slave; he is the Supreme God.

Slōk IV.; *mahalā* II.

The One Krishṇa is in all gods, the god of the gods is the soul.
The soul is from Bāsudēva (Krishṇa), if one understand the secret.
Nānak is his slave; he is the Supreme God.

Slōk V.; *mahalā* I.

The water remains being bound up in a pot, without water the pot is not made.

The mind, bound by divine knowledge, remains steady, (but) without the Guru divine knowledge is not obtained.

[1] The translation is made according to conjecture; for a literal translation would hardly give any sense.

[2] The sense is: in everything, that is produced, is the divine light = the divine principle of life.

Pauṛī.

The learned man may be a sinner and the illitcrate man a saint, he is not beaten (in the other world).
As one passes his time, such a name is applied (to him).
Such a trick should not be played, by which one will be defeated having gone to the threshold.
On the learned and unlearned reflection is made in the other world.
Who goes in bewilderment, he is beaten in the next world.

XIII.

Slōk I.; *mahalā* I.

O Nānak, of Mēru, the body, there is one chariot and one charioteer.
It is continually turned about, the wise one comprehends this.
In the Satya-yuga the chariot was of contentment, piety was the charioteer before it.
In the Trēta-yuga the chariot was of chastity, force was the charioteer before it.
In the Dvāpara-yuga the chariot was of austerity, truth was the charioteer before it.
In the Kali-yuga the chariot is of fire, falsehood is the charioteer before it.

Slōk II.; *mahalā* I.

The Sāma-(Vēda) says: the white-robed Lord (= Shiva) exists in the True one, he remains in the True one.

Everybody is absorbed in the True one.
The Rig-(Vēda) says: he is (everywhere) brimful.
The name of Rām is the hero among the gods.
By taking (his) name expiation is made.
Then, (says) Nānak, (one) gets the gate of salvation.[1]
In the Yajur-(Vēda it is written): Čandrāvalī[2] was forcibly deceived by Kānh, Krishṇa, the Yādava, wandered about.

He brought the Parijāta-tree and the Gōpīs and amused himself in Vindrāvan.
In the Kali-yuga the Atharva-Vēda appeared, the name of God became Allah.
Blue clothes were put on and worn, the Paṭhāns exercised dominion (in India).
The four Vēdas are true.
They read and reflect on those four.
(If one) performing devotion with love be called low:
Then, (says) Nānak, he gets the gate of salvation.

Pauṛī.

I am a sacrifice to the true Guru, by meeting with whom the Lord is kept in mind.
By whom, by means of (his) instruction, the collyrium of divine knowledge is given, (so that) by these (my) eyes the world is beheld.

Who, giving up the Lord, cling to another, those traffickers are drowned.
The true Guru is the boat, by some rare one he is reflected upon.
By bestowing mercy (on me I) was brought across.

XIV.

Slōk I.; *mahalā* I.

The Simmal-tree is straight,[3] very long and very thick.
Those, who come (to it) in hope, why do they go away (from it) hopeless?

[1] ਮੋਖੰਤਰੁ = ਮੋਖ ਦੁਆਰੁ, अन्तर signifying in Sansk. also: an opening or occasion.
[2] One of the playmates of young Krishṇa.
[3] ਸਰਾਇਰਾ is translated according to conjecture; the real meaning is unknown.

(Its) fruits are insipid, (its) flowers nauseous, (its) leaves are of no use.
(Its) sweetness is deep, O Nānak, (whose) quality is goodness and truth.[1]
Everybody bows to himself, no one bows to another.
Who goes down, if put on a balance and weighed, he is heavy.
That sinner sinks down twice as much, who is a slayer of deer.
What is done by bending down the head (in worship), when one goes off with an impure heart?

Slōk II.; *mahalā* I.

He reads books (and is) rehearsing the Sandhyā.
He worships a stone, (his) meditation (is like that) of a heron.
In (his) mouth is falsehood, (outwardly) is excellent decoration.
He reflects three times (a day) on the Gāyatrī.[2]
(Round his) neck is a rosary, a mark on his forehead.
(He has) two Dhōtīs, clothes of silk.
If he thinks, (that these are) the duties of a Brāhmaṇ:
Certainly all (these) works (are but) dregs.
Nānak says and he thinks right:
Without the true Guru he does not find the (right) way.

Pauṛī.

(His) dress and form are pleasing, having left the world he is going in.[3]
What he has done himself, good and bad, that he is receiving.
Orders are given, as they please (his, *i.e.* Hari's) heart, in a narrow road he must go onwards.
Naked he goes into hell, there a very terrible (thing) is seen.
Having committed vices (in this world) he is (now) repenting.

XV.

Slōk I.; *mahalā* I.

(If) kindness (be) the cotton, contentment the thread, continence the knot, truth the twist:
(If) this be the sacred cord of the creatures, then, O Paṇḍit, put it on!
This does not break, nor does filth stick to it, nor is it burnt nor does it go off.
Blessed is that man, O Nānak, who departs having put on (this) on his neck!
For four Damṛīs (= one Paisā) it (= the jaṇēū) was bought and sitting in a čaukā[4] it was put on.
Instruction was delivered into the ears (of the receiver of the cord), a Brāhmaṇ had become the Guru.
This one died and that one fell off; he went off without a cord.

Slōk II.; *mahalā* I.

Lakhs of thefts, Lakhs of fornications, Lakhs of falsehoods, Lakhs of abuses.
Lakhs of deceits (and) frauds are day and night (current) with the creatures.
The (sacred) thread is spun from cotton, the Brāhmaṇ comes and twists it.
A goat is killed, cooked and eaten, every one says: put it on!

[1] The words, as they stand, are totally unconnected, the sense can therefore only be guessed at. ਨੀਵਾ = Sansk. निम्न, deep.

[2] ਤ੍ਰੈਪਾਲ is traditionally explained by: Gāyatrī.

[3] ਅੰਦਰਿ ਜਾਵਣਾ, literally: to go within or into. Whereto, is not mentioned. The sense is very likely: he goes into the court of Yama.

[4] A place smeared with cow-dung.

When it becomes old, it is thrown away and another is put on again.
Nānak says: the thread does not break, if there be strength in the thread.

Slōk III.; *mahalā* I.

By minding the name honour springs up, praising (God) is the true thread.
The thread, that is obtained within the threshold (of God), does not break, (it is) pure.

Slōk IV.; *mahalā* I.

There is no thread for the senses, no thread for the women.
In the early morning spittle falls always on the beard.
There is no thread for the feet, no thread for the hands.
No thread for the tongue, no thread for the eyes.
He himself goes about without a thread.
He twists threads and puts them on others.
Taking the wages for prostitution he marries.
Drawing (lines on a) paper he shows the road.
Hear and see, O people, this wonder!
He is blind in his heart, (but bears) the name of "very wise."

Pauṛī.

If the Lord become kind and bestow mercy, then he will cause that work to be done.
That servant performs service, whom he will make mind (his) order.
By minding (his) order he becomes approved of, then he will reach the palace of the Lord.
Who does, what pleases the Lord, he will obtain the fruit desired by his heart.
Then dressed (with a dress of honour) he will go to the threshold.

XVI.

Slōk I.; *mahalā* I.

On the cow and the Brāhmaṇ you put a tax, for cow-dung no crossing can be made.
(Thou hast) a Dhōtī, front-mark and rosary, (but) eatest the corn of the barbarians.
Pūjā within thou readest the book (Qur'ān), the restraint (or law) of the Turks, O brother!
Give up hypocrisy!
By taking the name thou wilt cross![1]

Slōk II.; *mahalā* I.

Eating men they make prayer.
Those, who let go the knife, wear a (sacred) thread on (their) neck.
In their house the Brāhmaṇs blow the sound.
To them also this very thing is pleasant.
False is (their) stock, false (their) traffic.
By speaking falsehood they get (their) livelihood.
The dwelling of shame and piety is far away (from them).
Nānak (says): falsehood is (everywhere) brimful.
On (their) forehead is a mark, (round) the waist the tucked-in end of the Dhōtī.
In (their) hand is a knife, the world is a butcher.
Putting on blue clothes (like the Musalmāns) they become approved of.

[1] These words Nānak is said to have spoken to a Hindū, who was the receiver of customs at the bridge of Sultānpur.

Taking the food of the barbarians they worship the Purāṇas.
A goat killed not in the language (of the Hindūs) is eaten (by them).[1]
Nobody is allowed to enter their čaukā.
They make a čaukā and draw their lines round it.
Then the false ones come and sit upon it.
"Lest it be defiled, lest it be defiled this our food!"
(Being of) a loose body they clear (it) away.
(Being of) an impure heart they take a mouthful of water.
Nānak says: if the True one be meditated upon:
Purity is effected, then the True one is obtained.

Pauṛī.

He sees every one within (his) mind and makes (him) go under (his) sight.
He himself gives greatness, he himself causes (all) works to be done.
On the immensely large earth he is applying (every one) to his (particular) work.
If he makes a displeased glance, he turns a Sultān into a grass-cutter,
(Who), when begging at the door, does not get alms.

XVII.

Slōk I.; *mahalā* I.

When a thief robs a house, having robbed the house he gives (offerings out of the plunder) to his ancestors.
In the other world the thing is known, that he makes (thereby) his ancestors thieves.
Let the hands of the broker (*i.e.* the Brāhmaṇ) be cut off, this justice[2] (one) should do.
Nānak (says): in the other world that is obtained, what one acquires, works and gives (here).

Slōk II.; *mahalā* I.

As a woman gets her period (menses) from time to time:
(So) the impure live with an impure face and are continually wretched.
Those are not called pure, who sit down after having washed (their) body.
Pure are those, O Nānak, in whose heart that One dwells.

Pauṛī.

Horses are saddled swift like the wind, a Harem of all colours is arranged.
Having built houses, mansions, upper-storied houses, they sit in them and make displays.
They do things pleasing to their mind, (but) Hari they do not comprehend (and are therefore) lost.
They give order and eat, beholding their houses death is forgotten (by them).
Decay has come on, they are defeated in youth.

XVIII.

Slōk I.; *mahalā* I.

If impurity be minded, impurity takes place in all (things).
In cow-dung and wood are worms produced.
As many as are the grains of corn, no one is without a living being.

[1] ਅਭਾਖਿਆ, is an idiom, that is not the bhākhā (of the Hindūs), *i.e.* slaughtering a goat in the Musalmān way, by saying: bismillah (بِسْمِ ٱللّٰهِ).

[2] ਮੁਸਫੀ = مُنْصِفِي, justice.

First (in) the water are living creatures, by which every (thing) becomes green.
How should impurity be kept off, impurity falls into the food!
Nānak (says): in this wise impurity does not go off, divine knowledge (alone) washes it away.

Slōk II.; *mahalā* I.

The impurity of the mind is covetousness, the impurity of the tongue is falsehood.
The impurity of the eyes is the looking at another's wife, at another's property (and) appearance.
Impurity of the ears (it is), (if one) apply to his ear the tale-bearing, (which one) makes.
The souls of men being bound (by these impurities) go to the city of Yama.

Slōk III.; *mahalā* I.

Every impurity is an error, (that) clings to duality.
Birth and death is the order (of God), by (his) decree (man) comes and goes.
Eating and drinking is pure, the daily food is prepared and given by him.
Nānak (says): no impurity (sticks) to those disciples, by whom (the truth or the True one) is comprehended.

Pauṛī.

The true Guru should be magnified and praised, in whom there is a vast greatness.
(When) they are united with (him, *i.e.* the Guru), (his, *i.e.* God's) favourable look falls (upon them).
When it pleases him (*i.e.* the Guru), then he (God) is caused to dwell in the heart (of the disciple).
Having given the order and having put the hand on the head, he eradicates wickedness from within.
From the pleased king (= Guru) the nine treasures are obtained.

XIX.

Slōk I.; *mahalā* I.

First, (if) he himself be pure and come and sit in a pure (place).
(And if) by a pure one it (*i.e.* the food) be placed before, no one goes having become defiled.
(If) being pure he eat and take to read a Slōk
(And) be called to a dirty place (= the closet), who will find fault with this?
Corn is a god, water is a god, fire is a god (and) salt.
When the fifth, ghee, is put into it, then the food becomes pure.
The body that is covered with sins, that is spit upon.
The mouth, that does not utter the name and eats juices without the name:
That mouth is spit upon, let it thus be known, (says) Nānak.

Slōk II.; *mahalā* I.

In a vessel he is coagulated, from a vessel he is born.[1]
A vessel he asks (in marriage) and marries.
(With) a vessel friendship is made, (with) a vessel he goes his way.
(When) the vessel dies, (another) vessel is sought, with a vessel is his engagement.
How should that be called bad, from which a Rājā is born?
From a vessel a vessel is produced, without a vessel there is nobody.
Nānak (says): without the vessel is (only) that True one.
By whose mouth he is always praised, the favour of his lot is beautiful.
Nānak (says): they will have a bright face at that true court.

[1] ਭੰਡੁ (भाण्ड) a vessel = a woman (compare the use of the Greek σκεῦος).

Pauṛī.

Every one says: (it is my) own; whose it is not, he is singled out.[1]
It is (his) own doing, by himself (also) the account is made up.
As there is no remaining here, why does the world walk about in pride?
No one should be called bad, having read this word it is understood.
With a fool one should not strive.

XX.

Slōk I.; *mahalā* I.

O Nānak, by insipid talk body and mind become insipid.
(Such a one) is called utterly insipid, what exudes from the insipid one is insipid.
(When) the insipid one is called to the threshold, the insipid is spit in the face.
The insipid one is called a fool, he is punished by being beaten with a slipper.[2]

Slōk II.; *mahalā* I.

Inside they are false, outside (they have) a good name in the world, inside (they are full of) deceit.
(Though) they bathe at the sixty-eight Tīrthas, (their) filth does not go off.
Whose silk is within and outside a patched quilt, they are excellent in the world.
They have conceived love to the Lord, reflecting on seeing (him).
In pleasure they laugh, in pleasure they weep, in silence also they go.
They do not care for anybody except the true Lord.
They ask for provisions on the road to the gate (of the Lord), when he gives, then they eat.
There is One tribunal, One pen, between us and thee there is union.
At the gate he (*i.e.* the Lord) takes account, as oil is pressed out by pressure, O Nānak.

Pauṛī.

By himself the instrument is made, by himself the machinery is kept up.
He beholds his own work, he keeps and cares for the unripe and the ripe.
What has come (into the world), that will go (again), every one, that has come, is turned back again (into dissolution).
How should that Lord be forgotten from the mind, whose the creatures and their lives are?
His own work is arranged by himself with his own hands.

XXI.

Slōk I.; *mahalā* II.

What sort of love is this, that clings to another?
Nānak (says): he is described as a lover, who is always absorbed (in the beloved).
(Who) considers the good (only) as good (and who) by the evil becomes abated:
He is not called a lover; he is (a lover), who abides in the divine decree.

Slōk II.; *mahalā* II.

He who makes both, salutation (and an impudent) answer, is thoroughly mistaken.
Nānak (says): both (words) are false, not one (of them) is accepted.

[1] It is difficult to say, to what these words refer, as no hint of the subject is given.

[2] पाला *s.m.* a slipper (Hindī पन्ही, Panj. ਪੰਠਾ). To be beaten with a slipper is considered very disgraceful.

Pauṛī.

That Lord should always be praised, by whose service happiness is obtained.
Why is the time (of life) passed in a bad way, from which one reaps his own doings?
No wickedness should be done at all! (his) eyesight reaches far and sees (everything).
Such a dice should be thrown, by which one may not be defeated with the Lord.

XXII.

Slōk I.; *mahalā* II.

A servant, who does service, (but who) is proud and disputatious,
(And) makes many words, he gets no taste of the Lord.
If he serve, removing his own self, then he gets some honour.
Nānak (says): to what he clings, with that he meets, who clings (to the Lord), he is approved of.

Slōk II.; *mahalā* II.

What is in the soul, that springs up, the word of the mouth (is but) wind.
He sows poison and asks for nectar; behold, (what) justice is this?

Slōk III.; *mahalā* II.

With an ignorant man friendship will never do.
As he knows, so he lives, let one see and ascertain (this)!
The thing is contained within the thing, it is close to the second.
To the Lord no order can be given, a supplication, that is uttered, is agreed to.
By practising falsehood one becomes false, (says) Nānak, by praising (God) one becomes happy.

Slōk IV.; *mahalā* II.

Friendship and great love with an ignorant man comes to a break.
Like a line in water it has no place nor spot (that lasts).

Slōk V.; *mahalā* II.

If an ignorant man do a work, he cannot set it right.
If he do one half well, yet the other (will be) wrong.

Pauṛī.

If a servant do service and walk in the love of (his) Lord:
He gets very great honour and receives double wages also.
If he make rivalry with (his) Lord and entertain enmity within:
He loses his former wages and is beaten with the slipper in his face.
Whose gifts are eaten, to him applause should be given.
Nānak (says): with the Lord no order avails, supplication (only) is availing.

XXIII.

Slōk I.; *mahalā* II.

What gift is that, that is obtained by itself?
Nānak (says): what is obtained, (that is obtained) from the generosity of the pleased Lord.

Slōk II.; *mahalā* II.

What service is that, by which the fear of the Lord is not set agoing?
Nānak (says): he is called a servant, who is absorbed in the Lord.

Pauṛī.

Nānak (says): no end nor bound of that Hari can be known.
He himself causes the formations to be made, he himself again causes them to be destroyed.
On the necks of some are chains, many others mount horses.
He himself does and causes to be done (everything), to whom shall I cry out?
Nānak (says): by whom the instrument (= the body) is made, he also must take care of it.

XXIV.

Slōk I.; *mahalā* I.

By himself the vessels are formed, he himself also fills them.
Into some milk is poured, some are put upon the hearth.
Some sleep on a quilt, some stand erect on (it, as servants).
Them he adorns, O Nānak, on whom he bestows a glance of favour.

Slōk II.; *mahalā* II.

He himself creates, he himself destroys, he himself also preserves.
In that (world) he produces the creatures and beholds (them), establishing and disestablishing (them).
To whom shall be said (anything), O Nānak! he himself is everything.

Pauṛī.

By the great one greatness is made, nothing can be said.
That powerful, bountiful creator prepares the daily bread for the creatures.
That work is to be performed, which is put down from the beginning by him.
Nānak (says): without the One there is no other place.
He does what he pleases.

Ōm! the true name is the creator, the divine male without fear, without enmity, of a timeless shape, not produced from the womb.

By the favour of the Guru!

RĀGU ĀSĀ. THE SPEECH OF THE BHAGATS, OF KABĪR, NĀMDĒV (AND) RAVIDĀS.

ĀSĀ OF SRĪ KABĪR.

I.

(1). Clinging to the foot of the Guru I bow down and ask: why is the soul produced?
To what purpose is the world produced and destroyed? let me know this!

Pause.

O God, bestow mercy on me, put me into that road, where the bond of fear may break!

Clear away the pain of birth and death, the pleasure of works, (that) the soul may be liberated from regeneration!

(2). The noose (and) bond of the Māyā it does not break and in the Vacuum (= Supreme) (my) mind is not hidden.

By (my mind) itself the step of final absorption is not known, in this wise the entrance[1] (into a body) does not cease.

(3). He is not produced in any way, what is produced, he knows who is free from existence (and) non-existence.[2]

When the intelligence (or consciousness) of rising and setting is extinguished in the mind, then it is always naturally absorbed in deep meditation.

(4). As the reflected image will be reunited to the body that casts the reflection, when a water-pot is poured out:

So, (says) Kabīr, when the quality of error is broken, is the mind absorbed in the Vacuum.

II.

(1). Who wear Dhōtīs of three yards and a half and threefold cords;
On whose necks are rosaries and (in whose) hands are white Lōṭās:
Those cheats of Benāres are not called the saints of Hari.

Pause.

Such saints do not please me.
They appropriate to themselves fraudulently[3] the tree with its boughs.
(2). Having scoured the vessels they put them on, having washed the wood they light it.
Digging out the earth they make two fireplaces, (but) eat whole men.
(3). Those sinners go about continually in transgressions, (yet) it is said, that their face is not to be touched.
Continually they wander about in egotism and drown their whole family.
(4). To what one is applied, to that he sticks, such works he does.
Kabīr says: with whom the true Guru meets, he is no more regenerated again.

III.

(1). By my father I have been comforted.
(My) bed is pleasant, nectar is put into my mouth.
How shall I forget that father from (my) mind?
Having gone onwards (to the next world) the play is not lost.

Pause.

My mother has died, I am quite happy.
(Though) I do not put on a quilted garment, I feel no cold.
(2). (I am) a sacrifice to that father, by whom I was begotten.
My fellowship with the five is dissolved.
The five are beaten and put under my feet.
By remembering Hari my body and mind have become happy.
(3). My father is the great Lord.
How shall I go to that father?
When the true Guru meets with (me), then the way is shown.
The father of the world is pleasing to my mind.

[1] ਅਭਿਉ, from the Sansk. अभ्यय, coming on, entrance (into a body).

[2] The words of this line are somewhat obscure; they seem to refer to the Supreme.

[3] ਗਟਕਾਵਣਾ, *v.a.* to appropriate fraudulently; to consume.

(4). I am thy son, thou art my father.
In one place is the dwelling of (us) both.
Kabīr says: by me the One is comprehended.
By the favour of the Guru all has become known to me.

IV.

(1). Into one vessel having filled in sweepings,[1] into one vessel having filled in water,
Round about sit the five Jōgīs, in the midst the nose-cut wife of the younger brother.

Pause.

The nose-cut (woman) (makes) a great jingling and din.
By some discriminating man the din is cut off.
(2). In all is the dwelling of the nose-cut woman,[2] all are killed by the sportswoman.
I am the sister and sister's daughter of all, by whom I am married, his slave (I am).
(3). Our husband is a great discriminating man, he himself is called a saint.
He is standing at our head, no other comes near us.
(4). The nose-cut and ear-cropped (woman) is cut and beaten out.
Kabīr says: the (female) enemy of the saints is dear to the three worlds.

V.

(1). The Jōgīs, ascetics, austere devotees and Sanyāsīs wander about at many Tīrthas.
Those with plucked-out hair, those with the Munj-cord,[3] the silent ones, those who are wearing matted hair, are dying at the end.

Pause.

The Tantras are attended to (by them) and not Rām.
On whose tongue is put the name of Rām, what can Yama[4] do (to him)?
(2). The Shāstras, Vēdas, astrology and many many grammars they know.
They know the Tantras, Mantras and all medicines, (yet) at the end they must die.
(3). (They have) enjoyment of dominion, a (royal) umbrella, a throne and many beautiful women.
Betel, camphor, perfume and sandal, (yet) at the end they must die.
(4). All the Vēdas, Purāṇas and Smritis are searched (by them), (but) in no wise are they spared.
Kabīr says: utter Rām, he extinguishes birth and death!

VI.

(1). The elephant is the Rababī, the ox the timbrel, the crow beats the cymbal.
Having put on short breeches the donkey dances, the (male) buffalo causes worship to be made.

Pause.

The king Rām gets cucumbers and balls of Dāl cooked (in ghee), by some intelligent one they are eaten.

[1] The meaning of ਉਰਕਟ ਕੁਰਕਟ is somewhat doubtful; the traditional explanation of the Sikh Granthīs is *sweepings* (*cf.* the Hindī कुर्कट).

[2] Apparently the Māyā.

[3] ਲੁੰਜਿਤ (लुंचित) with plucked-out hair = the Jainas. ਮੁੰਜਿਤ wearing round the loins a cord made of the fibres of munj, *i.e.* Bairāgīs.

[4] ਜਮਠਾ = ਜਮ, ਠਾ being a meaningless alliteration.

(2). The lion sitting in the house prepares betel-leaves, the mammoth-rat brings the folded up betel-leaves.

In every house the mouse sings songs of rejoicing, the tortoise blows the conch.

(3). The son of the sterile woman is gone to marry, with gold the sheds[1] are decked.

By beauty the beautiful girl is pierced, by the hare the praises of the lion are sung.

(4). Kabīr says: hear, ye saints! by insects a mountain is eaten up.

The tortoise says: I churn live coals. A dark word is pronounced (here).

VII.

(1). One bag (of) seventy-two depositories, to which there is one gate.

The earth of the nine regions: (who) asks (for them), that Jōgī is accomplished in the world.

Pause.

Such a Jōgī obtains the nine treasures.

Taking the Brahm of the bottom he makes it ascend to the sky (*i.e.* the head).

(2). Making divine knowledge (and) meditation (his) patched quilt, the word the needle, he puts the thread into the head (of the needle).

Making the five elements (his) deer-skin he walks in the way of the Guru.

(3). Making compassion (his) crutch,[2] the body a smoking fire, he kindles the fire of sight.

Conceiving love to him in his heart he makes deep meditation in the four ages (= continually).

(4). The whole practice of Jōg is the name of Rām, whose the body and soul is.

Kabīr says: if he bestows mercy, he gives the true sign (of himself).

VIII.

(1). From whence have Hindūs and Turks come? by whom have these ways been started?

Having searched and reflected in (thy) mind tell (me): by whom have paradise and hell been made?

Pause.

O Kāzī, what book is expounded by thee?

All such, as are reading and pondering (on the book), are killed, not one has got the (true) knowledge.

(2). By force (and) love circumcision is made, I shall not agree (to it), O brother!

If God will make me a Turk, I shall be circumcised by himself.

(3). If one will become a Turk by being circumcised, what shall be done with a woman?

As the woman does not give up her half-bodied state, she must therefore remain a Hindū.

(4). Giving up the book (= Qur'ān) adore Rām, O silly one, thou art practising heavy oppression.

Kabīr puts his trust on Rām, the Turks are consumed and defeated.

IX.

(1). As long as there is oil in the lamp and in (its) mouth a wick, so long every (thing) is seen.

(When) the oil is burnt (and) the wick is stopped, the mansion becomes empty.

Pause.

O silly one, nobody protects thee in (thy) house.

Mutter that name of Rām!

[1] ਮੰਡਪ *m.* a shed erected for the performance of a marriage.

[2] ਫਾਹੁੜੀ (Hindī: फावड़ी) a crutch, on which a Jōgī leans.

(2). Whose mother (is she), say, whose father (is he), the wife of which husband (is she)?
The body breaks asunder, no one asks a word, "carry it out, carry it out," is (the word).
(3). The mother sitting near the body weeps, they have taken away the bier, O brother!
Dishevelling her hair the wife weeps, (but) the soul goes alone.
(4). Kabīr says: hear, ye saints! on account of the ocean of existence
Oppression falls on the head of this servant, Yama does not recede (from me), O Lord!

ĀSĀ OF SRĪ KABĪR.

Čaupadē.[1]

Ōm! By the favour of the true Guru!

I. X.

(1). Sanak and Sanand have not reached (his) end.
Reading continually the Vēda Brahmā has wasted his time.

Pause.

Churn the churning of Hari, O my brother!
Churn naturally so, that the essence do not go!
(2). Having made the body the jar churn in (thy) mind!
Into this jar collect the word (of the Guru)!
(3). The churning of Hari is the reflection of the mind.
By the favour of the Guru thou gettest a stream of nectar.
(4). Kabīr says: if the Lord bestow a favourable look:
Clinging to the name of Rām thou passest over to the shore.

II. XI.

(1). The wick is dried up, the oil is exhausted.
The (large) drum does not sound, the actor has fallen asleep.

Pause.

The fire is extinguished, no smoke has issued (from it).
The One is contained (in all), there is no other.
(2). The string is broken, the rabāb does not sound.
By error (one's) own work is spoiled.
(3). There is continual telling and relating (of stories of the gods).
When understanding has set in, then the singing is forgotten.
(4). Kabīr says: who bruise the five:
From them the highest step (of emancipation) is not far.

III. XII.

(1). As many faults as a son may commit:
The mother does not bear them in her mind.

Pause.

O dear, I am thy son!
Why dost thou not break my vice?

[1] Čaupadā, consisting of four verses severally, the Rahāu never being counted as a separate verse.

(2). Though (her son) run away having caused (her) excessive anger,
Yet the mother does not bear it in mind.
(3). My mind has fallen into the house of anxiety.
Without the name how shall I cross over?
(4). Give me always a pure mind (and) body!
Easily, easily Kabīr (then) utters thy excellences.

IV. XIII.

(1). My hajj (pilgrimage) is on the bank of the Gōmtī (river),
Where dwells (my) Pīr wearing a yellow robe.

Pause.

Vāh! vāh! how well is he singing!
The name of Hari is pleasing to my mind!
(2). Nārada (and) Sāradā[1] do service (to him).
At his side sits the Lady Lakshmī (as his) slave.
(3). On his neck is a garland, on his tongue Rām.
Taking his name a thousand (times) I make salutation (to him).
(4). Kabīr says: I sing the excellences of Rām.
Both, Hindūs and Turks, I let know (them).

ĀSĀ OF SRĪ KABĪR; PANČPADĒ.

Ōm! By the favour of the true Guru!

I. XIV.

(1). The female gardener breaks off leaves, in the leaves, in the leaves (there is) life.
The stone, for the sake of which she breaks off the leaves, is lifeless.[2]

Pause.

The female gardener is mistaken therein.
The true Guru is a waking God.
(2). Brahmā is the leaf, Vishṇu the bough, Sankara Dēva the blossom.
If she breaks off in reality the three gods, whose service does she (then) perform?
(3). A stone is shaped by the hammer and formed into an image, giving it a breast and feet.
If this image be true, then it will eat the hammerer.
(4). Cooked rice and grain,[3] pottage and hard sweetmeats
Are enjoyed by the enjoying (priest), in the mouth of this image are ashes.
(5). The female gardener is mistaken, the world is led astray, (but) we are not led astray.
Kabīr says: we are preserved (from error) by Rām, Hari, the king, bestowing mercy (on us).

II. XV.

(1). Twelve years of childhood have passed, twenty years no austerity has been practised.
Thirty years God has not at all been worshipped; he repents when he has become old.

[1] माठर = शारदा, a name of Sarasvatī.

[2] This refers to the stone images of Shiva, on which leaves or flowers are placed.

[3] पजिडि, Sindhī पहति, *s.f.* boiled grain.

Pause.

Saying: "mine, mine," the lifetime is gone.

Having dried up the river, he has sown wheat.

(2). In a dried-up pond he constructs a dyke, in a reaped field his hand makes a fence.

The thief has come and quickly carried off what is mine,[1] bewildered goes the watchman about.

(3). The feet, the head and the hands commence to tremble, from the eyes weak water flows.

From the tongue no right word issues; should he then entertain a longing for virtue?

(4). (If) Hari bestows mercy, then he practises deep meditation, the gain of the name of Hari is obtained.

By the favour of the Guru the wealth of Hari is obtained, going off at the end it goes with (him).

(5). Kabīr says: hear, ye saints: of food and wealth he has not taken a bit with himself.

The summons of the king Gōpāl having come, he has departed abandoning (his) wealth and mansion.

III. XVI.

(1). To some one silk-clothes are given, to some one a bedstead (strung with) tapes.

Some one has no haystack (nor) old quilt, some one has a house of rice-straw.

Pause.

Envy[2] and dispute should not be made (about this), O mind!

Good works should continually be done, O mind!

(2). The potter applies to the one clay, that is kneaded (by him), colours of many kinds.

To some (vessel) he gives a fine writing[3] (like) pearls; to some one he applies black leprosy.

(3). To the miser wealth is given for the sake of keeping it, the fool says: the property is mine.

When the staff of Yama is struck on his head, the matter is decided in a moment.

(4). The people of Hari are the highest devotees, by obeying his order they obtain happiness.

Who takes as true, what pleases him, he makes his order dwell in (his) mind.

(5). Kabīr says: hear, ye saints! (the word): "mine, mine," is false.

Having torn the rag[4] he marches off the dissolute man, the fastened[5] boat is loosened.

IV. XVII.

(1). We are thy poor servants, O God, thy praise pleases (our) mind.

O Allah, thou art from the beginning the Lord of religion, thou dost not command oppression.

Pause.

What the Kāzī says is not agreed to (by God).

(2). He keeps fasts, makes prayers (and utters) the Kalimah, (but) paradise does not accrue (thereby).

Seventy Ka'bās are in the heart, if one know (it).

(3). That is prayer, if one reflect on justice, (that is) the Kalimah, if one know wisdom.

If one spread out (his) prayer-carpet having robbed the five (vices), then he knows religion.

(4). Learn to know the Lord with fear, consider egotism insipid and destroy it in (thy) heart!

If, having informed thy own self, thou knowest others, then thou wilt become a partner of paradise.

[1] ਮੇਰੀ, *i.e.* ਦੇਹਿ, the body; the ਗਾਖਤ is the soul here.

[2] ਅਹਿਰਖ *s.f.* envy, emulation, Sansk. ईर्ष्या.

[3] ਮੁਕਤਾਹਲ = मुक्ताफल, fine writing. ਬਿਅਧਿ, especially here, black leprosy; black dots all over as black leprosy.

[4] ਚਿਰਗਟ *s.m.* rag (Hind. चिरकुट). The subject of: "he marches off," is Yama.

[5] ਤਾਗਰੀ is part. past of ਤਾਗਰਨਾ (Mar. तांगडणें), to fasten to a post.

(5). The clay is one, the dress-wearers are manifold, in that (circumstance) Brahm is recognized.
Kabīr says: having given up paradise (my) mind has become reconciled with hell.

V. XVIII.

(1). Not a drop rains in the city of the sky;[1] where is the sound, that was contained therein?
The perfect devotee,[2] having taken the Supreme Brahm, the Lord Mādhava, has departed.

Pause.

O father, where are those gone, who (were) speaking?
Who were living with men, dancing with intelligence (and) telling stories and tales?
(2). Where is the musician gone to, by whom the mansion was made?
Evidence, sound (and) intelligence are no (longer) produced, all vital energy is taken away.
(3). Thou hast become impaired in (thy) ears, the strength of thy senses is exhausted.
The feet are stopped, the hands have sunk down, no word issues from the mouth.
(4). The five attackers are worn out, all the thieves by their own error.
Worn out is the mind, the elephant, the breast is worn out, those who were the string-holders (managers) are sauntering about.
(5). They have become corpses, the ten bonds are loosened, friends and brothers, all are left behind.
Kabīr says: who meditates on Hari, he is living, his bonds are torn.

VI. XIX.

(1). No one is stronger than the female snake (= the Māyā),
By whom Brahmā, Vishṇu and Mahādēv have been deceived.

Pause.

Alas! alas! the female snake has entered the pure water!
By the favour of the Guru she is seen, by whom the three worlds are bitten.
(2). Why do you say, O brother: the female snake, the female snake is eaten.
By whom the True one is known, by him the female snake is eaten.
(3). Nothing is more empty than the female snake.
(By whom) the female snake is overcome, what will Yama do (to him)?
(4). This female snake has been made by him (*i.e.* God).
What is strength and weakness? it is from him.
(5). (When) she is indwelling (in man), he dwells (in) a body.[3]
By the favour of the Guru Kabīr crosses easily over.

VII. XX.

(1). What for should one let hear the Smriti a dog?
What for should one sing the praises of Hari before a Sākat?

Pause.

(That) Rām, Rām, Rām is contained (in all),
Should by mistake not be told to a Sākat.
(2). What for should one let feed a crow on camphor?
What for should one give milk to drink to a black snake?

[1] Very likely: the head in which the sound is said to be produced.

[2] ਪਰਮਹੰਸ (परमहंस), a devotee of the highest order.

[3] The sense of these obscure words seems to be: as long as the Māyā is dwelling in man, he will be subject to transmigration (dwelling in a body).

(3). By joining the society of the pious discrimination and intelligence spring up.
By the touch of the philosopher's stone the iron (becomes) gold.
(4). The Sākat, the dog, does (everything), being caused to do it.
What is written from the beginning, that work is done.
(5). If one take nectar and besprinkle a Nīm-tree:
Its nature does not leave it, says Kabīr.

VIII. XXI.

(1). (There may be) a fort like that of Lankā, a moat like the ocean—
In the house of that Rāvan no information was received.

Pause.

What shall I ask for, as I cannot make anything durable?
Whilst looking on with (my) eyes the world has passed away.
(2). (There may be) a Lakh of sons, one and twenty-five Lakhs of grandsons—
In the house of that Rāvan there is no lamp nor lamp-wick.
(3). In whose (house) by the moon and the sun the kitchen is heated.
In whose (house) fire washes the clothes.
(4). (Whom) the instruction of the Guru makes dwell in the name of Rām:
He remains firm and does not go anywhere.
(5). Kabīr says: hear, ye people!
Without the name of Rām final emancipation is not effected.

IX. XXII.

(1). First is the son, afterwards the mother.
The Guru clings to the feet of his disciple.

Pause.

Hear one wonderful thing, O brother!
(I) see, that the lion is pasturing the cows.
(2). The fish of the water is delivered of young on a tree.
(I) see, (that) the cat has carried off the dog.
(3). Below is the Rēbaisā, above its root.[1]
To the stem of that stick fruits and blossoms.
(4). Mounting a horse the buffalo goes out to pasture (cattle).
Without the bullock the sack has come to the house.
(5). Kabīr says: who comprehends this verse:
To him, uttering Rām, all is manifest.

ĀSĀ; TRIPADĒ OF SRĪ KABĪR.

I. XXIII.

(1). By whom the body is made from a drop (of semen), (by him) he (*i.e.* man) is preserved in the basin of fire (*i.e.* the belly).

Ten months he is kept in the belly of the mother, (then) the Māyā again sticks to him.

[1] ਰੇਬੈਸਾ (Pers. ریباس), a plant of an acid juice, Rheum palmatum. Some MSS. read ਮੂਲ, which gives no sense; the right reading, as supported by the best MSS., is ਮੂਲ, the root.

Pause.

Why do men cling to covetousness and waste their lifetime, the jewel?
In a former birth no seed has been sown by them on the field of works.
(2). From a child (man) has become old, what was to happen, that has come to pass.
When Yama comes and seizes him by the hair, why does he then weep?
(3). He entertains hope of life, (whilst) Yama watches his breath.
The world is a play, O Kabīr! throw the dice with care!

II. XXIV.

(1). My body and also my mind I make the kusumbhā dye-stuff, the five elements the companions in the marriage procession.
With king Rām I go round (the wedding-fire), (my) soul is steeped in his love.

Pause.

Sing, sing, O bride, a beautiful song of blessing!
King Rām, (my) husband, has come to my house.
(2). In the lotus-navel the altar is erected, the knowledge of Brahm is uttered.
That king Rām is obtained as bridegroom, so great is my lot!
(3). The gods and Munis have come to the spectacle, by the thirty-three crores (of gods) (this matter) is known.
Kabīr says: having married me the (divine) male, the One Lord, is gone.

III. XXV.

(1). I am grieved by the mother-in-law and beloved by the father-in-law, of the name of the elder brother I am afraid, O dear!
(My) friend and companion is (my) negligent sister-in-law, by separation from my husband's younger brother I burn, O dear!

Pause.

My mind has run mad, I have forgotten Rām, in what manner shall I get on, O dear!
Who is dallying (with me) on the bed, him I do not see with my eyes, to whom shall I tell this pain, O dear!
(2). The father quarrels with the children, the mother is always drunk.
When I am in the society of the elder brother, then I am dear to (my) Lord.
(3). Kabīr says: the five (vices) are quarrelling, in quarrelling the lifetime is wasted.
By the false Māyā the whole world is bound, by uttering Rām I have obtained happiness.

IV. XXVI.

(1). In our house the string of the body is continually stretched out, on thy breast is a sacrificial thread.
Thou readest the Vēda and the Gāyatrī, in our heart is Gōvind.

Pause.

On my tongue is Vishṇu, in my eyes Nārāyaṇ, in my heart dwells Gōvind.
When at the gate of Yama he will ask (thee), O fool, what wilt thou say (to) Mukand?[1]
(2). We are the cattle, thou art the cowherd, O Lord, who art our keeper through the several births.
Thou pasturest (us), never bringing (us) to the other side, what a Lord of ours art thou!
(3). Thou art a Brāhmaṇ, I am a weaver of Kāshī (Benāres), understand my (divine) knowledge!
Thou petitionest kings and Rājās, my meditation is with Hari.

[1] ਮੁਕੰਦ = Sansk. मुकुन्द, a name of Vishṇu.

V. XXVII.

(1). The life in the world is like a dream, life is similar to a dream.
Considering it as true we made friendship (with it), abandoning the treasure of virtue.

Pause.

O father, friendship has been made (by me with) the infatuation of the Māyā,
By whom the jewel of divine knowledge has been snatched away (from me).
(2). The moth seeing with its eyes (the light) sticks to it, the brute does not see the fire.
The foolish one does not regard the noose of death, the woman clings to gold.
(3). Reflect and remove (thy) disease, that One is the saviour of those, who are saved.
Kabīr says: such is the life of the world (=the Supreme), there is no other.

VI. XXVIII.

(1). Then (=formerly) I made many forms,[1] now no form is again made (by me).
The thread, string and musical instrument, all are worn out, the name of Rām is sufficient (to me).

Pause.

Now no dancing comes (into my mind).
My mind does not beat drums.
(2). The body of lust and passion is taken and burnt, the jug of thirst has burst.
The breeches of lust have become old, error is gone, all is off!
(3). All beings are considered as one, dispute and contention are stopped.
Kabīr says: I have obtained the all-filling (Supreme), the favours of Rām are bestowed (on me).

VII. XXIX.

(1). He keeps fasts, he appeases Allah, (but) for (his) relish he kills living beings.
He looks on himself, (but) not on others, what for does he prate?

Pause.

O Kāzī, the one Lord is in thee, (he is) thine, dost thou not see (him), having meditated and reflected (on him)?

Thou dost not inform (thyself), O thou mad one in religion! therefore (thy human) birth is of no account.

(2). Thou expoundest the book right, that Allah is no woman (nor) man.

(But) by reading and re-perusing nothing (is effected), O mad one, when there is no information in the heart.

(3). Allah is concealed within everybody, reflect (on him) in thy heart!
In both, Hindūs and Turks, is the One, thus says Kabīr with a loud voice.

VIII. XXX.

(1). Decoration is made for the sake of a meeting.
(But) Hari has not met (me), the life of the world, the Lord.

Pause.

Hari is my beloved, I am the wife of Hari.
Rām is great, I am small and tiny.
(2). The living together of the woman and the beloved,
The meeting on one bed is difficult.

[1] The sense is: formerly I made many garbs or outward appearances.

(3). Blessed is the married woman, who is pleasing to her beloved.
Kabīr says: she is no more subject to regeneration.

ĀSĀ; DUPADĒ OF SRĪ KABĪR.

Om! by the favour of the true Guru!

I. XXXI.

(1). A diamond is piercing a diamond, (thus) a pure [1] mind is naturally reabsorbed (into the Supreme).
Every light is pierced by this diamond, it is obtained in the words of the true Guru.

Pause.

The story about Hari is an unutterable word.
Having become a gander recognize and take the diamond! [2]
(2). Kabīr says: such a diamond is seen, it is contained in the world.
The hidden diamond becomes manifest, when the abstruse things are (clearly) shown.

II. XXXII.

(1). The first (wife was) ugly, of low caste, of ill-boding features, wicked in the house of her father-in-law (and) in her father's house.
The present (wife) is beautiful, intelligent, of auspicious features, easily child-bearing.

Pause.

It was lucky, that my first wife died.
May she, whom I keep now, live through all ages!
(2). Kabīr says: when the little one came, the good fortune of the big one ceased.
Now that the little one is with me, another (husband) is taken by the elder one.

III. XXXIII.

(1). The name of my daughter-in-law (was) Dhanīā (mistress).
Now the name of Rām-janīā [3] is given (to her).

Pause.

By these shaven heads [4] my house is made gloomy.
They have put (my) son to the uttering of Rām!
(2). Kabīr says: hear, O my mother!
By these shaven heads my (low) caste is done away.

I. XXXIV.

Pause.

Remain, remain, O my wife, do not put a cloak (veil over thy face)!
At the time of the end thou wilt not obtain a screen.
(1). Having put on a veil thy (companions or friends) [5] are gone onwards (to the other world).
Do thou not stick to their society (or road)!

[1] ਪਵਨ, here very likely = ਪਾਵਨ, which all MSS. exhibit.

[2] The ਹੰਸ (gander) is said to know the diamonds and to devour them.

[3] ਰਾਮਜਨੀਆ, *i.e.* maid-servant of Rām.

[4] ਮੁੰਡੀ *s.m.* a contemptuous term for a Sanyāsī or Bairāgī, because they shave their heads wholly.

[5] ਤੇਰੀ, thy (people or friends), no substantive being mentioned.

(2). The greatness of putting on a veil is this,
(That) the wife is welcome for ten or five days.
(3). Thy veil is then quite true,
When singing the praises of Hari thou jumpest and dancest.
(4). Kabīr says: the wife is then winning (the game),
When singing the excellences of Hari she passes her lifetime.

II. XXXV.

(1). Better is a saw (put on my neck), than that thou turn away (from me).
Cling to my neck, hear my entreaty!

Pause.

I am a sacrifice (to thee), turn thy face (to me), O beloved!
Why dost thou turn away from me, (why) dost thou beat me?
(2). When thou splittest (my) body (in two), I do not move back my limbs.
Though my body fall (to the ground), I do not break my love.
(3). Between me and thee there is no other.
Thou art (my) dear husband, I am (thy) wife.
(4). Kabīr says: hear, O Lōī![1]
Now no confidence is put in thee.

III. XXXVI.

Pause.

By no one is the secret of the weaver known.
The whole world is stretched out (by him) as a warp.
(1). When thou hearest the Vēda and the Purāṇas:
Then (by me) a warp of such extent is spread out.
(2). Of earth and heaven (my) workshop[2] is made.
Sun and moon, both I make go with (me).
(3). Joining the feet one roll was made, then (my) mind was pleased by the strings.
The weaver knows his own house, Rām is known (as being) in his very heart.
(4). Kabīr says: the workshop is broken up,
(When) the threads are joined with the threads on the border.

IV. XXXVII.

(1). Within his heart is filthiness, though he bathe at a Tīrtha; he will not go to paradise.
By the belief of the people nothing is effected,[3] Rām is not ignorant.

Pause.

Adore Rām, the One God!
The service of the Guru is true bathing.
(2). If by immersion in the water salvation be obtained, (know), the frogs bathe continually.
As the frogs, so are those men; again and again they fall into the womb.

[1] ਲੋਈ is said to have been the name of Kabīr's wife.
[2] ਕਰਗਹ = Persian کارگاه, workshop.
[3] The sense is: the opinion or belief of the people, that they will go to paradise, avails nothing.

(3). If the hard-hearted one die at Benāres, he is not saved (from) hell.
If the saint of Hari die at Hāṛambā, he saves his whole relationship.
(4). (Where there) is no day and night, no Vēda and Shāstra, there dwells the Formless one.
Kabīr says: meditate on that divine male, O foolish world!

ĀSĀ; THE WORD OF SRĪ NĀMDĒV.

Ōm! By the favour of the true Guru!

I.

(1). The One is diffused in the many (and) all-filling, wherever I see, there is he.
By the beautiful mirage of the Māyā (the world) is deluded, some rare one comprehends (the truth).

Pause.

All is Gōvind, all is Gōvind, without Gōvind there is no other.
As in one string there are seven thousand beads, (so) is that Lord lengthwise and crosswise.
(2). A wave of water, froth and bubble do not become separate from the water.
This world is the sport of the Supreme Brahm, playing about he does not become another.
(3). False is error and a dream is desire, the true object is known (from the Guru).
The desire for good works is taught by the Guru, in being awake the mind is reconciled.
(4). Nāmdēv says: look at the arrangement of Hari and reflect in thy heart!
In everybody and contiguous to all is only that One Murāri.

II.

(1). A jar is taken and filled with water, (that) I may bathe the Lord.
Forty-two Lakhs of living beings are produced in the water, to Bīṭhal,[1] O brother,[2] what shall I do?

Pause.

Wherever I go, there Bīṭhal is, O brother!
He is very joyful and always playful.
(2). Flowers are brought, a garland is made up, I perform worship to the Lord.
First the scent is taken away by the black bees, what shall I do to Bīṭhal, O brother?
(3). Milk is brought and Khīr[3] cooked, (that) I may make an offering of eatables to the Lord.
First the milk is defiled by the calf, what shall I do to Bīṭhal, O brother?
(4). Here is Bīṭhal, there is Bīṭhal, without Bīṭhal the world is not.
In every place, says Nāmā, in all thou art fully contained.

III.

(1). My mind is a yard, my tongue a pair of scissors.
Measuring and measuring I cut off the noose of Yama.

Pause.

What shall I do with (my) caste, what shall I do with my brotherhood?
Day and night I mutter the name of Rām.
(2). With dye-stuff I colour, a seam I sew.
Without the name of Rām I do not live twenty-four minutes.

[1] ਬੀਠਲੁ = विट्ठल, Vishṇu, apparently a Prākrit dimin. of the p. part. विष्ट: he who is contained (in all), see my Sindhī Gram. Introd. p. xlii.

[2] ਭੈਲਾ = ਭਾਈਲਾ, an old form of the diminutive (ਲ = ਰ), from ਭਾਈ, brother.

[3] ਖੀਰ, rice boiled in milk.

84

(3). I perform worship, I sing the excellences (of Hari).
Through the eight watches I meditate on my Lord.
(4). The needle is of gold, of silver the thread.
The mind of Nāmā is applied to Hari.

IV.

(1). The snake drops its skin, (but) does not give up (its) poison,
As the heron makes meditation in the water.[1]

Pause.

What for is meditation made and recitation (of the name),
When one's mind is not pure?
(2). (Like) a lion,[2] who knows man to be (his) food:
So the cheat expounds God.
(3). O Lord of Nāmā,[3] give up the contention!
Drink the elixir of Rām, O deceitful one!

V.

(1). Who will know the Supreme Brahm, he will please him.
By (which) devotees Rām is kept in mind, they will stop (keep firmly) their thoughtless mind.

Pause.

O mind, how wilt thou cross over? the ocean of the world is a water of poison.
Having seen the false Māyā thou art led astray, O mind!
(2). In the house of a calico-printer birth was given (to me); by the instruction of the Guru, O brother!
(And) by the favour of the saints Nāmā has met with Hari.

ĀSĀ; THE WORD OF SRĪ RAVIDĀS.

Ōm! By the favour of the true Guru!

I.

(1). The deer, the fish, the black bee, the moth, the elephant are (all) destroyed by one (and the same) fault.
In whom are the five incurable faults, how much hope has he?

Pause.

O Mādhava, affection is entertained for ignorance.
The lamp of discrimination is dirty.
(2). The thoughtless one is produced in the womb of an animal, (he who is) indifferent to religious merit (or) demerit.
The human birth is hard to obtain, in that (human) society (also) he is low.
(3). As far as living creatures are, they are subject to destiny.
At the end they are entangled in the noose of death, (against which) no contrivance avails anything.
(4). Ravidās, the slave of slaves, (says): abandon error, the knowledge of the Guru is the austerity of austerities.
The supreme bliss, that is taking away the fear of (his) devotees, consider as the primary cause!

[1] The comparison is only hinted at and must be supplied from the context. As the snake, etc., so does he; as the heron, etc., so is his meditation.

[2] ਸਿੰਘਰ a lion, ਰ being in Marāṭhī an emphatic affix. [3] These words are addressed to a Brāhmaṇ.

II.

(1). The saints—with thee (their) body (and) soul is coherent.
(By) the knowledge of the true Guru the saints know (thee), O God of gods!

Pause.

May the society of the saints, the flavour of the story of the saints,
The love of the saints be given to me, O God of gods!
(2). The deportment of the saints, the way of the saints (I ask for).
(I am) the slave of slaves (to them).
(3). One thing more I ask, the gem of devotion, that is granting all desires.
Let (me) not be written together with the unholy and sinners!
(4). Ravidās says: who knows (this), he is wise:
(That) between the saints and the endless (Supreme) there is no difference.

III.

(1). Thou art the sandal-tree, we helpless ones are the castor-oil tree, with thee there is perfume.
From a low tree (we) have become a high (tree), (our) bad smell is banished[1] by (thy) good smell.

Pause.

O Mādhava, the society of the saints is in thy asylum!
We are vicious, thou art (our) benefactor!
(2). Thou art twisted silk, white and yellow, we are helpless like worms.
We cling to the society of the pious, O Mādhava, like the bee to honey.
(3). My caste is low, my brotherhood is low, low is my birth.
No worship of king Rām has been made (by me), says Ravidās, the Čamār (tanner).

IV.

(1). What is done,[2] when the body is broken to pieces?
When the love (to thee) goes, then thy people are afraid.

Pause.

(Their) mind is wandering about thy lotus-foot.
Drinking (nectar) the wealth of Rām is obtained (by them).
(2). A mass of fortune and misfortune is the wealth of the Māyā.
Thy people are not immersed in it.
(3). By the rope of love thy people are bound.
Ravidās says: how shall I escape from it?

V.

Pause.

Hari, Hari, Hari, Hari, Hari, Hari, Hari!
Remembering Hari (his) people have got safely through and crossed.
(1). By the name of Hari Kabīr (is) famous.
The papers (= accounts) of several births are cut to pieces.
(2). Nāmdēv gave to the stooping (idol of Hari) milk to drink.
He came no (more) into the perplexity of regeneration in the world.
(3). Humble Ravidās is imbued with love to Rām.
Thus he is not going to hell by the favour of the Guru.

[1] ਨਿਵਾਸਾ, from ਨਿਵਾਸਣਾ = निर्वासन, to banish.
[2] The sense is: it is of no consequence.

VI.

Pause.

How is the idol of clay[1] dancing!

It sees, sees, hears, speaks, it is running about and returning.

(1). When it gets something, then it is proud.

When the Māyā (worldly property) is gone, then it begins to weep.

(2). The mind is longing for pleasures in words and deeds.

When it is extinct, it is absorbed in some place.

(3). Ravidās says: the world is a sport, O brother!

I entertain love to the exhibitor of the sport.

ĀSĀ. THE WORD OF THE BHAGAT DHANNA.[2]

Ōm! By the favour of the true Guru!

I.

Pause.

Wandering and turning about many births have passed, body and mind have not become sedate by wealth.

Covetousness is poison; (man) is greedy for and attached to lust, in (his) mind the Lord, the diamond, is forgotten.

(1). The fruit of poison tastes sweet to the foolish mind, light ways and sober ways are not known (by it).[3]

Love to the excellences (of Hari) is cut off, birth and death of other kinds is again expanded.

(2). In whose heart devotion does not dwell, they quickly fall into the net and noose of Yama.

Fruits of poison are collected and filled into (their) mind, thus the supreme divine male, the Lord, is forgotten from (their) mind.

(3). The entrance into divine knowledge is given (by) the blessed Guru, the mind given to meditation (becomes) of one form (with the Supreme).

By them, who are given to devotion with love, happiness is known, they become fully satiated and emancipated.

(4). Into whose understanding[4] light has entered, (by him) the imperishable Lord is known,

Dhannā has obtained the wealth of him, who is upholding the earth, having met with the saints he is absorbed (in him).

MAHALĀ V. (EPILOGUE OF ARJUN.)

II.

Pause.

With Gōvind, Gōvind, Gōvind the mind of Nāmdēv was taken up.

The calico-printer, who was worth half a Dām, became worth a Lakh (of Rupees).

(1). Kabīr was weaving and stretching; having given it up he became delighted with the feet (of Hari).

The low-caste weaver became profound in virtues.

(2). Ravidās was continually carrying cattle,[5] he gave up the Māyā.

He became manifest in the society of the pious, he obtained the sight of Hari.

[1] ਮਾਟੀ ਕੋ ਪੁਤਰਾ, idol of clay = man.

[2] Dhannā is said to have been a Jaṭ; no particulars about his life are known.

[3] ਚਾਰ ਵਿਚਾਰ, literally: light habits and sober reflection, or as we should say: he does not care for what is right or wrong.

[4] ਸਮਾਉ *m.* (Sindhī ਸਮਾਤ) understanding.

[5] Carrying cattle, *i.e.* carrying the hides of cattle, for he was a ਚਮਾਰ, tanner.

(3). Sainu, the barber, was an idol-maker, he was heard in every house.

The Supreme Brahm dwelled in his heart, he was numbered among the devotees.

(4). Having heard this proceeding the Jaṭ (Dhannā) rose and gave himself to devotion.

The Lord appeared (to him), Dhannā was very fortunate.

III. (BY DHANNĀ.)

Pause.

O mind, why dost thou not keep in mind the merciful Damōdar? thou knowest there is no other.

Though thou runnest about in the universe (and the nine) regions—what the creator does, that takes place.

(1). In the water of the belly of the mother the body is made (and) ten openings (to it).

Giving food he preserves (the body of the embryo) in the fire (of the womb); such is our Lord.

(2). The tortoise is in the water, its offspring is outside (the water), they have no wing nor milk.[1]

Know and see, that the all-filling, heart-ravishing supreme bliss is in (thy) heart!

(3). A worm remains concealed in a stone, it has no way.

Dhannā says: he is (also) filling (it); O my soul, be not afraid!

ĀSĀ; THE WORD OF SHĒKH FARĪD.

Ōm! by the favour of the true Guru!

I.

(1). Who have love (to God) from (their) heart, they are true.

In whose mind is another and in the mouth another, they are called raw.

Pause.

(Who) are steeped in the love of God and who delight in his sight, (they are true).

By whom the name is forgotten, they have become a burden upon the earth.

(2). Who are applied by himself to the hem of his garment, they are (true) Darvēshes of his gate.

Blessed is the mother, who has given birth to them, they are fruitful.

(3). Thou art the preserver, boundless, inconceivable, endless.

By whom the True one has been known, their feet I kiss.

(4). (I flee) to thy asylum, O God, thou art the donor![2]

May the happiness of (thy) service be given to Shēkh Farīd!

II.

(1). Shēkh Farīd says: O dear, for Allah's sake (mind this)!

This body will become vile dust in the house of the grave.

Pause.

To-day there is meeting, O Shēkh Farīd, do not look at the cranes, do not mind (thy) desires!

(2). If I know, that I must die and that there is no returning:

One should not cling to the false world, (but) part with one's own self.

(3). True piety should be spoken, falsehood should not be spoken!

The way, which the Guru shows, that, O disciple, should be gone!

[1] The sense is: though the young ones of the tortoise are left to themselves, yet God is preserving them.

[2] घधमंरगी, a barbarous corruption of घधमंरा (for the sake of the rhyme).

(4). When the fop passes over, the mind of the woman is comforted.
(But after) the gold-like sides are split by the saw.[1]

(5). O Shēkh: no one remains firm in the life (and) in the world.
On the seat, we are seated upon, how many have been sitting and gone off!

(6). In (the month of) Katik (come) the cranes, in Čēt (there is) the burning (of the jungles), in Sāvaṇ there are lightnings.
In the cold season the small arms are beautiful (being laid round) the neck of the beloved.

(7). The passers on are gone having reflected in (their) mind:
In joining together there are six months, in being broken there is (only) one moment.

(8). The earth asks the heaven, O Farīd: where are the boatmen gone to?
The women make reproaches to the men, the soul bears up (with it).

[1] The sense is: as a punishment in hell for adultery.

CONCLUSION OF THE RĀG ASA.

SLŌKS OF THE BHAGAT KABĪR.[1]

Ōm! By the favour of the true Guru!

(1). Kabīr (says): my rosary (is, that) on my tongue is Rām.
(He is) at the beginning, before the Yugas, the comfort and repose of all devotees.
(2). Kabīr (says): every one is laughing at my caste.
(I am) a sacrifice to this caste, by which the creator is muttered.
(3). O Kabīr! why dost thou totter, why dost thou shake thy soul?
Rām is the Lord of all comforts, drink the juice of the name!
(4). O Kabīr! (though) earrings of gold be made and rubies be set upon them:
They look like a burnt reed, in whom the name is not.
(5). Kabīr (says): there is hardly one or another,[2] who whilst living dies.
(Such a one) having become fearless utters the praises (of Rām), where he looks, there is he (*i.e.* Rām).
(6). Kabīr (says): on which day I died, after (that) joy sprang up.
The Lord met with me, Gōvind honours his own companion.
(7). Kabīr (says): "I am the worst of all, every one is good except me."
Who considers himself in this light, he is my friend.
(8). Kabīr (says): she (*i.e.* the Māyā) has come to me, having made different disguises.
I have been preserved by my own Guru, to him salutation has been made (by me).
(9). Kabīr (says): he should be killed, by whose death[3] comfort arises.
Every one says: (I am) good, good, no one considers (himself) bad.
(10). Kabīr (says): (when) the nights become black, black creatures (= thieves) are standing about.
(Who) having taken nooses are running about, those the Lord kills.
(11). Kabīr (says): the sandal-tree is good, it is surrounded by the Ḍhāk and Palās-tree.[4]
Those also become sandal-wood, which dwell near the sandal-tree.
(12). The Bamboo is drowned by (its) greatness; may not any one be drowned thus!
(Though) the Bamboo dwell near the sandal-tree, it does not become fragrant.
(13). Kabīr (says): religion is lost with (the acquisition of) the world, and the world does not go with (any one).
The imprudent man has with his own hands struck the axe into his foot.
(14). Kabīr (says): wherever I wandered about, (there was) a show in every place.
(There was) one lover of Rām, except my love (there was) a wilderness.
(15). Kabīr (says): the huts of the righteous are good, a furnace is the village of the unrighteous.
Fire is applied to that palace, in which there is not the name of Hari.
(16). Kabīr (says): the saints have died, why should weeping be made, that they go to their home?
May the wretched Sākats weep, who are sold at every shop.[5]

[1] These Slōks are added at the end of the Ādi Granth.

[2] ਏਕੁ ਆਧੁ, literally: one and a half = one or another, some few. The old and correct way of writing is ਆਧੁ, as here; in later Hindī (and especially in Urdū) it is also written "ād." It is not derived from ਆਦਿ (ādi) *beginning*, as supposed by some.

[3] ਜਿਹ ਮੂਏ = ਜਿਹ ਕੇ ਮੂਏ, literally: by the being dead of whom = by whose death.

[4] ਢਾਕ, the Butea frondosa, according to Shakespear, but as ਪਲਾਸ (Sansk. पलाश) has the same signification, it is likely, that ਢਾਕ is some different species of it.

[5] *i.e.* who are turned about in transmigration.

(17). Kabīr (says): with the Sākats it is, as with a heap of garlic.
Though one sit in a corner and eat it, it becomes manifest at last.
(18). Kabīr (says): the Māyā is the churning jar, the wind is the churner.
By the saints the butter is eaten, the world drinks the buttermilk.
(19). Kabīr (says): the Māyā is the churning jar, the wind blows with a cold stream.[1]
By whom it is churned, by them (the butter) is eaten, (and they are) churning more.
(20). Kabīr (says): the Māyā is a thief, stealing and stealing things she lays (them) out in (her) shop.
One, O Kabīr, she does not rob, by whom she is utterly dispersed.[2]
(21). Kabīr (says): this is not happiness, that one make many friends.
Who keeps his mind with the One, he always obtains comfort.
(22). Kabīr (says): death, of which the world is afraid, is joy to my mind.
(For) by death the full, perfect joy is obtained.
(23). Having obtained Rām, the chief good, do not open the knot, O Kabīr!
There is no city, no examiner, no purchaser, no price (for it).
(24). Kabīr (says): make friendship with him, whose Lord Rām is!
Paṇḍits, Rājās and Lords, of what use are they?
(25). Kabīr (says): by making friendship with the One other duality goes off,
If one wear long hair or shave (the head) with a rattling noise.
(26). Kabīr (says): the world is a room of lampblack, the blind fall into it.
I shall be a sacrifice to them, who go out of it.
(27). Kabīr (says): this body will go, if thou be able, bring it back!
Those are gone with naked feet, who had Lakhs and Crores.
(28). Kabīr (says): this body will go, apply thyself to any road,
Either by keeping company with the saints or singing the praises of Hari!
(29). Kabīr (says): dying and dying the world has died, though no one has known how to die.
Who dies such a death,[3] he will not have to die again.
(30). Kabīr (says): the human birth is hard to obtain, it does not take place again and again.
Like as ripe fruits of a tree fall to the ground and do not stick again to the branch.
(31). O Kabīr, thou art Kabīr, thy name is Kabīr (= great).
The jewel of Rām is then obtained, when thou first leavest the body.
(32). Kabīr (says): prating should not be made, what thou sayest, that does not take place.
The works, the merciful one is doing, nobody can efface.
(33). Kabīr (says): (before) the touchstone of Rām no false one can stand.
He bears the touchstone of Rām, who, having died, has become alive.
(34). Kabīr (says): they put on glittering clothes, they eat betel-leaf and betel-nut.
(But) without the name of the One Hari they go bound to the city of Yama.
(35). Kabīr (says): the boat is shattered, a thousand holes have been opened in it.
The light ones, the light ones, have crossed over, those, on whom was a burden, were drowned.
(36). Kabīr (says): bones are burnt like wood, hair is burnt like grass.
Having seen this world burning Kabīr became indifferent (to the world).
(37). Kabīr (says): pride should not be entertained; the bones are wrapt in a skin.
Those, who are on horseback, under an umbrella, are buried again in the earth.

[1] ਹਿਵ ਧਾਰ, a cold stream or a stream of snow (ਹਿਵ = हिम, by transition of म into व).
[2] ਬਾਰਹ ਬਾਟ ਕਰਨਾ, literally: to make twelve roads = to disperse widely.
[3] ਐਸੇ ਮਰਨੇ ਜੋ ਮਰੈ, who dies by such a death, scil. as I point at.

(38). Kabīr (says): pride should not be entertained, if one sees that one's dwelling is high.
To-day or to-morrow one must lie on the ground and grass will spring up (upon him).

(39). Kabīr (says): pride should not be entertained, a poor one should not be laughed at!
That boat is as yet on the ocean, what do ye know, what will take place?

(40). Kabīr (says): pride should not be entertainod, having seen, that one's body is beautiful.
To-day or to-morrow thou wilt leave it, as the snake its skin.

(41). Kabīr (says): if (something) is to be plundered, then plunder it, the name of Rām is the (true) booty.
Afterwards you will again repent, (when) the breath will go out.

(42). Kabīr (says): no such a one has been born, who applies fire to his own house.
Who, having burnt all the five boys, meditates on Rām.

(43). If there be any one, who sells his boy, any one, who sells his girl:
He makes partnership with Kabīr, he makes traffic with Hari.

(44). Kabīr (says): this is to be kept in mind, do not hurriedly proceed on the road!
Who enjoy themselves, them the molasses eat up afterwards.[1]

(45). Kabīr (says): I know, that reading is good, (but) better than reading is meditation (yōg).
The attachment to Rām I do not give up, though people revile me.

(46). Kabīr (says): what do the helpless people censure (me), in whose mind there is no divine knowledge?
Kabīr delights in Rām, all other concerns are given up by me.

(47). Kabīr (says): fire is applied to the coat of the stranger[2] on four sides.
The patched quilt is burnt and has become coals, (but) the flame has not reached the thread.[3]

(48). Kabīr (says): the patched quilt has become coals, the skull is not bursting.
The helpless Jōgī has played, on his sitting place ashes have remained.

(49). Kabīr (says): in little water, O fish, a net is laid out by the fisherman.
In this small pond thou wilt not escape, think again of the ocean!

(50). Kabīr (says): the ocean should not be given up, though it be very saltish.
Him, who is searching about in every pool, nobody will call good.

(51). Kabīr (says): the impious have passed away, there is not a trace (of them left).[4]
The poor are practising their humility; what happens, that happens.

(52). Kabīr (says): the bitch of a Vaishnava is good, that of a Sākat bad, O mother!
That one hears continually the glory of the name of Hari, this one goes to believe in sin.

(53). Kabīr (says): the deer is weak (and) this yam is green.
There is a Lākh of hunters of one creature, how long will it be saved?

(54). Kabīr (says): who makes his house on the banks of the Gangā, he drinks pure water.
Without attachment to Hari emancipation is not obtained, thus saying Kabīr wanders about.

(55). The mind of Kabīr has become pure like the water of the Gangā.
Hari follows after him, saying: Kabīr! Kabīr!

(56). Kabīr (says): turmeric is yellow, lime is of a white substance.
Rām (and his) lover then unite, (when) both drop (their) colour.

[1] That is: their enjoyments will become to them the cause of their perdition.

[2] The ਪਰਦੇਸੀ, the stranger, is the soul; the ਘਾਘਰਾ, the coat, the body.

[3] The ਤਾਗਾ or thread is the soul.

[4] ਨਿਗੋਸਾਂਈਆ, adjective formed from ਗੋਸਾਈ, a saint, a person of restricted passions, by means of the prefix *nir-* (*r* being assimilated to the following consonant). ਥਾਂਘੀ, *s.f.* (from ਥਾਂਘਾ), a small mark or trace. The word is no longer used in Hindī, but in Marāṭhī.

(57). Kabīr takes away the yellowness of the turmeric without leaving a sign of the lime.
To that love (I am) a sacrifice, by which caste, colour and family are set aside.
(58). Kabīr (says): the gate of emancipation is narrow, of the tenth part of a mustard-seed.
(My) mind however has become an elephant, how shall it pass through it?
(59). Kabīr (says): if such a true Guru be met with, he, being gratified, bestows favour.
The gate of emancipation (he makes) wide, that (one) may easily come and go.
(60). Kabīr (says): I have neither a thatched roof, nor hut, neither have I a house nor village.
I think, Hari will ask: who art thou? I have neither caste nor name.
(61). Kabīr (says): I wish to die, (if) I die, (then may it be) at the gate of Hari.
Perhaps Hari may ask: who has fallen down at my gate?
(62). Kabīr (says): it is not done by us, nor shall we do it, nor is (my) body able to do it.
What do I know anything? being the creature of Hari Kabīr has become Kabīr.
(63). Kabīr (says): from whose mouth, whilst talking in a dream, the name of Rām comes out:
His foot's shoe the skin of my body is.
(64). Kabīr (says): we are idols of clay, to which the name of man is given.
(We are) guests of four days, in a very great pit of fuel[1] (is our) place.
(65). Kabīr (says): I prepared Henna and applied it, having ground my own self.
By thee no word is asked, (I am) never applied to (thy) foot.[2]
(66). Kabīr (says): at which gate the comers and goers nobody stops:
How should that gate, which is such a gate, be given up?
(67). Kabīr (says): I had been drowned and was again saved by the dash of an advantageous wave.
When I saw the boat shattered, I descended palpitating.
(68). Kabīr (says): devotion is not pleasing to the sinner, the worship of Hari is not agreeable (to him).
The fly abandons the sandal-wood, where a stench is, there it goes.
(69). Kabīr (says): the physician has died, the sick man has died, the whole world has died.
One, O Kabīr, has not died, for whom there is no weeper.
(70). By Kabīr Rām is not meditated upon, a great evil propensity[3] has stuck (to him).
The body is a vessel of wood, it does not come up again.
(71). Kabīr (says): so it has happened, what is pleasing to the mind, that is done.
What fear is there of dying, when the tree of perfection[4] is taken in hand?
(72). Kabīr (says): for the sake of the juice the sugar-cane is sucked, for the sake of virtue one should die weeping.
Vicious men nobody will call good.
(73). Kabīr (says): a jar filled with water will to-day or to-morrow burst.
Who do not keep in mind their own Guru, they will in the half (of life) be robbed and carried off.
(74). Kabīr is the dog of Rām, Mutīā[5] is my name.
On my neck is a rope; where he pulls, thither I go.
(75). Kabīr (says): why do the people show a rosary of wood?
In their heart they do not think of Rām, what for is this rosary?
(76). Kabīr (says): separation, the snake, dwells in (my) mind, it minds no charm whatever.
He who is separated from Rām, does not live, and if he lives, he becomes a fool.

[1] ਤੂੰਪਹਿ is the Locative of ਤੂੰਪਹੁ, a pit of fuel = the funeral pile.

[2] ਲਾਈ ਪਾਇ; the pronoun "I" is omitted. ਲਾਈ is feminine, as the words are put into the mouth of a woman.

[3] ਖੋਰਿ (= ਖੋੜਿ), an evil propensity; a vicious habit.

[4] See p. 479, note 3.

[5] ਮੁਤੀਆ = ਮੁਤਿਆ or ਮੁਤਾ (मुक्त), released, emancipated.

(77). Kabīr (says): the philosopher's stone and sandal-wood have one fragrance.
By coming in contact with it (people) have become most excellent, (like) the scentless iron (and) wood (is made fragrant by contact with sandal-wood).
(78). Kabīr (says): the club of Yama is bad, it cannot be endured.
The holy man alone (= the Guru), who met with me, took me to the hem (of his garment).[1]
(79). Kabīr (says): the physician says: I am excellent, the medicine is in my power.
(But) this thing is indeed Gōpāl's, when he pleases, he takes it away.
(80). Kabīr (says): thy turn is ten days, take and sound (the drum)!
Like meeting in a river-boat it will not come on again.
(81). Kabīr (says): (if) I make the seven oceans ink, if I make the trees (my) pen,
If I make the earth the paper, the glory of Hari cannot be written.
(82). Kabīr is by caste a weaver, what shall he do? in (his) heart dwells Gōpāl.
Kabīr is clinging to the neck of the Sporter,[2] all his troubles cease.
(83). Kabīr (says): there is not such a one, who burns down his mansion.[3]
Who, having slain all his five children, continually meditates on Rām.
(84). Kabīr (says): there is not such a one, who sets on fire this body.
The blind people do not know (the thing), they are crying out: O Kabīr!
(85). Kabīr (says): the Satī cries out being stigmatized[4] (by the fire): hear, O men of the burning ground!
All the people went away; "I and thou" is the business at last.
(86). Kabīr (says): (my) mind has become a bird, flying and flying it goes in the ten directions.
As the society is, with which (a man) falls in, such fruits he eats.
(87). Kabīr (says): the place, (we) were seeking, has been obtained.
That one has again become "thou," whom (or which) (I) called "another."[5]
(88). Kabīr (says): the Bēr-tree,[6] that is near a plantain, dies being killed by bad society.
This one dangles about and that one is torn; do not peep into the society of the Sākats!
(89). Kabīr (says): the load of another lies on his head[7] and he wishes to go his way.
He is not afraid of his load, (but) further on the passage becomes impassable.
(90). Kabīr (says): the singed (and yet) standing wood of the forest cries out:
May I not fall into the power of the blacksmith, that he burn me a second time!
(91). Kabīr (says): in the dying of one two have died, in the dying of two four.
In the dying of four six have died, four males and two females.[8]
(92). Kabīr (says): looking about the world was searched (by me), nowhere a place was obtained.
By whom the name of Hari is not minded, they are led astray anywhere.[9]

[1] ਅੰਚਲਿ ਲਾਉਣਾ, to take or apply one to the hem = to give one protection.

[2] ਰਮਈਆ, the sporter (a noun of agency from ਰਮਣਾ), an attribute of the Supreme. Cf. Gauṛī, Sabd LXII. (2), where the words occur: ਘਟਿ ਘਟਿ ਰਮਈਆ ਰਮਤ ਰਾਮ, in everybody Rām, the sporter, sports (or is contained).

[3] The ਮੰਦਰ or mansion is the body; the five children are ਕਾਮ, ਕ੍ਰੋਧ, etc.

[4] ਚਿਹਚੜ੍ਹਾ, stigmatized; literally: having a risen scar or stigma.

[5] The sense of this line is pantheistical; the object has become the subject again by pantheistical union of the finite with the infinite being, brought about in the mind by the negation of duality.

[6] ਬੇਰਿ is here used as feminine; it is usually masculine.

[7] ਭਾਰ ਸਿਰਿ ਚੜੈ, the load ascends to the head, *i.e.* the load is laid on his head.

[8] The explanation, as given by natives, is: first died a deer (*m.*), then the ਮਿਰਗੀ (the female thereof); then the hunter and his wife; the mirgī was with a young one and the wife of the hunter with child.

[9] ਕਹਾ—ਅਉਰ must be joined, though separated for the sake of the rhyme; ਕਹਾਂ ਅਉਰ or ਅਉਰ ਕਹਾਂ, anywhere.

(93). Kabīr (says): the society of the pious should be joined, at the end it brings (one) through.
Company with the Sākats should not be kept, from which destruction results.

(94). Kabīr (says): by whom he (*i.e.* Hari) is well[1] remembered in the world, he is absorbed (in him) in the world.
By whom the name of Hari is not remembered, they are uselessly[2] born.

(95). Kabīr (says): (one's) hope should be placed on Rām, hope on others is useless.
Those men fall into hell, who are regardless of the name of Hari.

(96). By Kabīr many disciples and friends were made, but no friend of Kēsava.
They were gone to join Hari, (but their) mind stopped in the midst (of the way).

(97). Kabīr (says): what shall the helpless creature[3] do when Rām does not give assistance?
On whichever branch I put my foot, that goes down.

(98). Kabīr (says): in teaching others dust falls into the mouth.
Whilst keeping the capital of others the field of the house is eaten up.

(99). Kabīr (says): I remain in the society of the pious and eat the bran of barley.
May happen what will, with the Sākats I shall not go.

(100). Kabīr (says): in the society of the pious there is day by day a twofold love.
(Though) the Sākat wash the black blanket, it does not become white.

(101). Kabīr (says): the mind is not shaved, why do they shave the hair?
Whatever is done, that is done by the mind, the head is uselessly[4] shaved.

(102). Kabīr (says): Rām is not given up (by me); if body and property go, they may go.
By the Lotus-foot (my) mind is perforated, in the name of Rām I am absorbed.

(103). Kabīr (says): the instrument, which we were playing, (of that) every string is broken.
What shall the helpless instrument do, (if) the player goes?

(104). Kabīr (says): I shave the mother of that Guru, who is not able to clear away error.[5]
He himself is drowned in the four Vēdas, (his) disciples are floated away.

(105). As many sins as are committed, they are kept concealed.
They all become at last manifest, when Dharm-rāi questions (about them).

(106). Kabīr (says): having given up the remembrance of the name of Hari, (his) family was much taken care of (by him).
Engaged in business he passed away,[6] no brother nor relative remained (to him).[7]

(107). Kabīr (says): having given up the remembrance of Hari she goes to rouse the night.[8]
Having become a female snake she is born again (and) eats her own children.

(108). Kabīr (says): having given up the remembrance of Hari the woman keeps the Ahōī(-fast).[9]
Having become a jenny-ass she is born again (and) carries a load of four Mans (maunds).

[1] ਨਿਕੇ used here adverbially (Marāṭhī निकें), from the Arab. نقا pure, clean; pronounced in Hinduī निका.

[2] ਬਾਦਹਿ, adverb (with the emphatic ਹਿ), uselessly (Pers. باد, wind).

[3] ਕਾਰਨੁ, originally the elementary matter = creature.

[4] ਅਜਾਇ used here adverbially: *uselessly, to no purpose.* Its origin is not quite clear; very likely it is the Arabic ضائع (which frequently occurs), with a prosthetic (euphonic) *a*. In Sindhī it is अजायो.

[5] ਜਾ ਤੇ ਭਰਮੁ ਨ ਜਾਇ, literally: by whose instrumentality error does not go = who is not able to clear away error. ਜਾਣਾ, constructed with ਤੇ (= Hindūst. سي), implies possibility.

[6] ਰਹਿ ਜਾਣਾ, *v.n.* to get off, to pass away.

[7] *i.e.* to accompany him to the other world.

[8] ਰਾਤਿ ਜਗਾਵਣੀ, to rouse the night, an expression for practising witchcraft.

[9] ਅਹੋਈ, the Hindū festival held in the month of Katak, two days before the Dīpmālā, observed as a fast-day.

(109). Kabīr (says): (it is) very great cleverness, (if one) mutter Hari in (his) heart.
(It is like) playing on the stake; (if) one falls, there is no place (for him).[1]

(110). Kabīr (says): that mouth is blessed, by which Rām is uttered.
Whose (is) the body, the helpless, (by which) the village will become pure?[2]

(111). Kabīr (says): that family is good, (in) which there is a servant of Hari.
In which family no servant (of Hari) is born, that family is a Dhāk (and) Palās-tree.[3]

(112). Kabīr (says): horses, elephants, a dense cloud of vehicles, a Lākh of banners, (that) wave—
Better than this pleasure is begging, (if) the day pass in remembering Hari.

(113). Kabīr (says): I have wandered about in the whole world having put a tabor on (my) shoulder.
No one is any one's, every (thing) I have closely examined.

(114). On the road pearls are scattered, the blind one comes and goes out (of the world without seeing them).
Without the light of the Lord the world passes (them).

(115). The progeny of Kabīr is drowned; there was born a son Kamāl.[4]
Having given up the remembrance of Hari he has brought wealth to the house.

(116). Kabīr (says): one should go to meet with the saints, no one (else) should be taken with!
The foot should not be drawn back; what further on may happen, may happen.

(117). Kabīr (says): may not Kabīr be bound with the rope, with which the world is bound.
Like powdered salt will the gold-like body go.

(118). Kabīr (says): the gander (= the soul) has flown away, the body is buried, a sign is shown.[5]
He does not yet give up life, there is greediness in (his) eyes.

(119). Kabīr (says): with the eye I look at thee, with the ear I hear thy name.
With the speech I utter thy name, (thy) lotus-foot is in (my) heart.

(120). Kabīr (says): from heaven and hell I am freed by the favour of the true Guru.
I remain in the wave of the lotus-foot at the end and at the beginning.

(121). Kabīr (says): say, how is there a weighing of the wave of the lotus-foot?
For expressing (it) there is no beauty (in me), showing (it) is the best.

(122). Kabīr (says): having seen (it), (to) whom shall I tell (it), nobody believes in (my) word.
Hari is such as he is, singing (his) qualities I remain joyful.

(123). Kabīr (says): as the crane picks up and warns, as it picks up again, and picking up warns
His young ones, (so) is in (thy) mind the affection for the Māyā.

(124). Kabīr (says): the sky is covered with clouds, rain having fallen the tanks and pools are filled.[6]
Who are longing (for rain) like the Čātrik, what is their state?

[1] ਸੁਰੀ ਉਪਰ ਖੇਲਨਾ, literally: (it is) playing on the stake. ਸੂਰੀ = ਸੂਲੀ, a stake, in the shape of a sharp nail, on which the delinquent was placed, so that the stake went through his body lengthway. Jugglers also used to play on such stakes; to them and their sport reference is made here. Their life is lost if they fall when playing on the stake. It is equally dangerous to fall away from Hari. This seems to be the meaning of this obscure verse.

[2] The sense is: if one man in a village turn to Rām and become emancipated, the whole village will be purified for his sake. Compare the following verse.

[3] The wood of these trees is of no value.

[4] We learn thence, that Kabīr's son was Kamāl, who did not tread in the footsteps of his father, but was a worldly man.

[5] ਸੈਨਾਹ, for the sake of the rhyme = ਸੈਨ, *s.f.* a sign, wink.

[6] ਸਰ generally a *walled tank*, ਤਾਲ *an unwalled pond or pool.*

(125). Kabīr (says): when the Čakvī is separated (from its mate) at night, it comes and joins (it) at day-break.

The man, that is separated from Rām, joins him neither by day nor night.

(126). Kabīr (says): thou art separated (from) the ocean,[1] remain in (it), O conch!

(Otherwise) thou wilt make a sigh (at) every temple at the rising of the sun.

(127). Kabīr (says): why art thou given to sleep?[2] wake in fear of pain!

Whose dwelling is in the grave, how can he sleep in comfort?

(128). Kabīr (says): why art thou given to sleep? rise! why art thou not muttering the Murāri?

One day there will be sleeping, stretching out the legs long.

(129). Kabīr (says): why art thou given to sleep? remain seated and wake!

From whom thou art separated, cling to him!

(130). Kabīr (says): the road of the saints should not be left, sticking (to it) go on!

In seeing (them) thou becomest purified, in meeting (with them) the name is muttered.

(131). Kabīr (says): with the Sākat company should not be kept, one should flee far from him!

(If) a black vessel be touched, some stain is received.

(132). Kabīr (says): Rām has not been thought of and old age has (now) arrived.

It clings to the gate of the mansion, what can be taken out (of it)?

(133). Kabīr (says): that action has taken place, which was done by the creator.

Without him there is no second, he alone is the creator.

(134). Kabīr (says): fruits have set on, the mangoes have begun to bear fruit and to ripen.

They reach their owner, when putridity[3] does not eat their inside.

(135). Kabīr (says): having bought an idol he worships it, in the obstinacy of his mind he goes to a Tīrtha.

By emulation and imitation (of others)[4] he is led astray and plunged into error.

(136). Kabīr (says): a stone is made the Lord, the whole world worships it.

Who remains in reliance on this, is drowned in the black stream.

(137). Kabīr (says): the threshold[5] is of paper, works of ink[6] the door.

By a stone[7] the earth is drowned, by the Paṇḍit the road is torn up.

(138). Kabīr (says): what (thou art) doing to-morrow, do now, what (thou art) doing now, (do) at once![8]

Afterwards nothing will be done, when death comes on (thy) head.

(139). Kabīr (says): I saw one such being like washed gumlac.

It appears clever and endowed with many qualities, (but) is without understanding (and) impure.

[1] ਰੈਣਾਇਰੁ, *m.* ocean, from the Sansk. रत्नाकर, jewel-mine, रत्न being assimilated to रन्न, which becomes again रैन, and आकर to आइर by elision of क and change of *a* to *i*.

[2] ਸੁਤਾ ਕਰਣਾ, to be given to sleep (frequentative).

[3] ਕਾਂਬ, a disease, which befalls mangoes, putridity.

[4] ਦੇਖਾਦੇਖੀ *s.f.* emulation (literally: looking at each other mutually); ਸ੍ਵਾਂਗ ਧਰਣਾ, to imitate (ਧਰਿ part. p. conj.).

[5] The meaning of ਓਬਰੀ is not quite sure; the Sikh Granthīs explain it by "house," which is apparently only a guess. In Hindī the word is no more in use, but in Marāṭhī we have still उंबरा, the lower cross-piece of a door-frame; ਓਬਰੀ would be the feminine of this.

[6] ਮਸਕੇ ਕਰਮ, works of ink = letters.

[7] ਪਾਹਨ, a stone, here apparently in the sense of an *idol*.

[8] ਇਤਾਲ = ਇਤਕਾਲ, at this time, at once.

(140). Kabīr (says): Yama does not fetter my intelligence by that death.[1]
By whom this Yama is created, that preserver is muttered (by me).
(141). Kabīr has become musk, the black bees have all become (his) servants.
As the devotion of Kabīr is, so is (his) dwelling in Rām.
(142). Kabīr (says): he has closely fallen on the neck of (his) family, Rām has passed (out of his mind).
(The messengers) of Dharm-rāi have fallen in, there is inside (the house) a clamour.
(143). Kabīr (says): a pig is better than a Sākat, it keeps the village clean.
(When) that helpless Sākat has died, nobody will take his name.
(144). Kabīr (says): adding kauṛī to kauṛī he brings together Lākhs and Crores.
At the time of departure he gets nothing at all, (even his) Langōṭī is plucked away (from him).
(145). Kabīr (says): (if one) has become a Vaishnava, what is done by putting together four rosaries?
Outside gold is apparent, inside gumlac[2] is filled in.
(146). Kabīr (says): become a brickbat of the road, giving up the conceit of the mind!
If one become such a slave, him the Lord joins.
(147). Kabīr (says): (if) one has become a brickbat, what is the good (of it, if) he cause pain to the traveller?
Thy servant is such, as dust on the ground.
(148). Kabīr (says): what is the good of becoming dust, that flies up and sticks to the body?
The people of Hari must be such as all-pervading[3] water.
(149). Kabīr (says): what is the good of becoming water, (as) it becomes cold (or) hot?
The people of Hari must be such, as Hari himself is.
(150). (If there be) a high house, gold, a fascinating woman, (if) on the pinnacle a flag wave.
Better than this is coarse bread, (if one) sing the qualities (of Hari) in the society of the saints.
(151). Kabīr (says): better than the town is the wilderness, where devotion to Hari (is made).
Apart from a lover of Rām the city of Yama (rather) pleases me.[4]
(152). Kabīr (says): between the Gangā and Yamunā there are landing places of silent tranquillity.
There Kabīr has made a cloister; the Munis are seeking the road (to it).
(153). Kabīr (says): as thy tree[5] has sprung up, such it remains to the end.
Of what (use) is the wretched diamond? crores of jewels do not come up to it.
(154). Kabīr (says): one wonderful thing is seen: they sell a diamond in a shop.
Without a trafficker it goes for a cowrie.
(155). Kabīr (says): where divine knowledge is, there is religious practice; where falsehood is, there is wickedness.
Where greediness is, there is death, where patience is, there is he himself.[6]
(156). Kabīr (says): what is the good of giving up the Māyā, when conceit is not given up?
By conceit the best Munis were melted, conceit eats up all.
(157). Kabīr (says): the true, real Guru has met with me, the word, he lets flow, (was) one (or the One).
Clinging to it (I) was levelled with the ground, a hole broke into (my) liver.
(158). Kabīr (says): what shall the true, real Guru do, when there is error among his disciples?
To the blind one the One does not stick, (it is) as if one blows into a bamboo.

[1] ਕਰੈ stands here instead of ਕੜ੍ਹੈ (ਕੜ੍ਹਨਾ, to fetter). ਕਾਰ = ਕਾਲ, for the sake of the rhyme.
[2] ਭੰਗਾਰਾ *m.* gumlac; also a peculiar kind of earth.
[3] ਸਰਬੰਗ = Sansk. सर्वग, Anusvāra being a euphonic interpolation.
[4] ਮੋਰੇ ਭਾਇ = ਮੁਝ ਕਉ ਭਾਏ.
[5] ਪੇਡ ਤੇ, thy tree; here apparently = thy body.
[6] ਆਪਿ, himself, *i.e.* the Supreme.

(159). Kabīr (says): a dense cloud of horses, elephants (and) carriages, the wife of a king:

Her comparison [1] does not come up (to) a female water-carrier of the people of Hari.

(160). Kabīr (says): why is the wife of a king censured, why is honour (attributed) to a female slave of Hari?

That one adorns (her) māng [2] for the sake of sensual pleasure, this one remembers the name of Hari.

(161). Kabīr (says): a post was erected, a stand was made, by the true Guru firmness was established (in me).

By Kabīr a diamond was bought at the shore of the lake Mānasa.[3]

(162). Kabīr (says): Hari is the diamond, the saints are the jewellers, having taken (the diamond) they erect a shop.

When an examiner [4] is obtained, then a sale [5] of diamonds (takes place).

(163). Kabīr (says): if business falls in, Hari is remembered, remember him thus always!

Make (thy) dwelling in Amarāpur! Hari returns the gone wealth.

(164). Kabīr (says): two are well fitted for service, one is the saint, the other is Rām.

Rām, who is the giver of emancipation, the saint, (who) makes mutter the name.

(165). Kabīr (says): on which road the Paṇḍits have gone, on that the baggage-people follow after.

There is one difficult pass of Rām, to that Kabīr is climbing up.

(166). Kabīr has died by the faults of the world, walking in obsequiousness to the family.

Whose family will then be ashamed, when they put (him) down in the burning ground?

(167). Kabīr (says): thou wilt be drowned, O helpless one, by obsequiousness to many people.

What has happened in thy neighbour's (house),[6] know, that (will) also (happen) in thy own.

(168). Kabīr (says): good is coarse bread and grain of different kinds.[7]

(If one) does not make any claim, great is (his) country, great (his) dominion.

(169). Kabīr (says): by making claims burning arises, he who makes no claims remains free from all bonds.

The man, who does not make claims, considers Indra as poor.

(170). Kabīr (says): the pond is filled with water up to [8] the embankment, (but) no one can drink water.

By a great lot thou hast obtained it, fill (thy vessel) and drink thou, O Kabīr!

(171). Kabīr (says): (as) the stars at dawn pass away, so the world passes away.

These two letters [9] do not pass away, them Kabīr has seized.

(172). Kabīr (says): the house is of wood, on the ten sides fire is applied to it.

The Paṇḍits, the Paṇḍits are burnt and have died, the fools have fled and escaped.

(173). Kabīr (says): remove doubt, put aside the paper!

Having investigated the fifty-two letters [10] apply (thy) mind to the feet of Hari!

(174). Kabīr (says): the pious man does not give up (his) piety, though he fall in with crores of impious.

(Though) the sandal-wood tree is surrounded by snakes, it is not giving up its coolness.

[1] ਪਟੰਤਰ, comparison, likeness. In the Rāmāyan of Tulsī Dās the word is written पटतर. Its derivation is not clear.

[2] ਮਾਂਗ, the line, which parts the hair on the head (German *Scheitel*).

[3] ਮਾਨਸਰੋਵਰ = ਮਾਨਸ ਸਰੋਵਰ, one ਸ being dropped here.

[4] ਪਾਰਖੁ, one who examines diamonds as to their value = an inquirer.

[5] ਸਾਟ = ਸਟ (saṭṭ), exchange, sale. The word is still preserved in Sindhī.

[6] ਪਾਰੋਸੀ ਕੈ scil. ਘਰ ਵਿਖੇ, ਘਰ (or Loc. ਘਰਿ), being left out.

[7] ਨਾਜ instead of ਅਨਾਜ.

[8] ਸਮੁਹਾ, adj. (= Sansk. सन्मुख), facing, fronting.

[9] *i.e.* Rām.

[10] The fifty-two letters of the Sanskrit alphabet.

(175). The mind of Kabīr has become cool, the knowledge of Brahm was obtained (by him).
The flame, by which the world is burnt, is for [1] the pious equal to water.
(176). Kabīr (says): no one knows the chess figures of the creator.
Either the Lord himself knows them, or (his) servant, (who) is (his) secretary.
(177). Kabīr (says): it was well that fear subsided, that every side was forgotten.
The hail, having melted, has become water, being poured out it has mingled with the brook.
(178). Kabīr (says): having put together dust a complete body is formed.
It is the puppet of four days, at the end it is (again) dust of dust.
(179). Kabīr (says): (under) the rising of the sun (and) moon all bodies are formed.
Without having been united with the Guru Gōvind they are all turned into dust.
(180). Where the fearless one is, there is no fear, where fear is, there Hari is not.
Kabīr (says), having reflected in (his) mind: hear (this), O ye saints!
(181). Kabīr (says): by whom nothing is known, their (life) passes comfortably in sleep.
The egotism,[2] that is comprehended, (its) extinction [3] is a full calamity.
(182). Kabīr being beaten cried much, in pain he cries (even) more.
(After) a blow had hit the vital part, Kabīr remained (dead) on the spot.
(183). Kabīr (says): the blow of the spear is easy, in being applied it takes away the breath.
(Who) undergoes the blow of the Sabd, of that Guru I am the slave.
(184). Kabīr (says): O Mullā, why ascendest thou the minaret? the Lord is not deaf.
For whose sake thou makest the call, ascertain [4] him even in (thy) heart!
(185). O Shēkh, without patience, why dost thou go on a pilgrimage to the Ka'bah?
Kabīr (says): whose heart is not firm, where is to him God?
(186). Kabīr (says): serve Allah, by whose remembrance pain goes!
In the heart the Lord is manifest, the burning (fire) is extinguished by the name.
(187). Kabīr (says): with violence oppression is made, (though) he calls its name "halāl" (= lawful).
(When) in the office account is asked, what will be (his) state?
(188). Kabīr (says): Khīčarī [5] is a good food, in which there is nectar-like salt.
On account of venison [6] who will have his throat cut?
(189). Kabīr (says): that one, who has clung to the Guru, is then known, (if) spiritual blindness and the burning of the body is effaced.
When he does not burn (in) joy and grief, then he is Hari himself.
(190). There is a difference in saying Rām; in that one [7] (there is) reflection on the One.
That one says Rām, Rām! with fear, that one is a show-maker.[8]
(191). Kabīr (says): Rām, Rām! in saying (so) (there is this) discrimination:
The One is blended with the many, one is contained in the other.

[1] ਜਨ ਕੈ; ਕੈ is here used as a Dative postfix in the sense of ਕਉ. (ਕੈ = Sansk. कृते, contracted to ਕੈ, Sindhī खे).

[2] ਹਮਹੁ, here in the sense of "egotism," "individuality."

[3] ਬੂਝਣਾ is here taken in a double sense; it signifies (trans.): *to comprehend*, and (intrans.): *to be extinguished.*

[4] ਜੋਇਣਾ *v.a.* to see, to behold, to ascertain. Now in Panǰābī ਜੋਹਣਾ jŏh-ṇā.

[5] ਖੀਚਰੀ, *s.f.* (Hindūst. كھچڑی), rice and dāl (a kind of pulse) boiled together.

[6] ਹੇਰਾਰੋਟੀ, literally: bread of hunting = venison.

[7] ਸੋ or ਸੋਈ (here used three times) is employed in the sense of: *one, another, a third one.*

[8] ਕਉਤਕਹਾਰ = कौतुकधार, making a show.

(192). Kabīr (says): in which house the pious are not served, (in that) is no service of Hari.
Those houses are like a burning-ground,[1] goblins dwell in them.
(193). Kabīr has become dumb (and) mad, deaf has become (his) ear.
In (his) feet he has become crippled, he was struck by the arrow of the true Guru.
(194). Kabīr (says): the true Guru is a hero, the one arrow, that was shot by him:
In sticking (to me) I fell on the ground, a hole broke into (my) liver.
(195). Kabīr (says): a pure drop of the sky fell on fallow[2] land.
In this way man, without the society (of the pious), becomes (like) ashes of an oven.
(196). Kabīr (says): a pure drop of the sky was mingled with the ground.
(Though) many clever people take pains, it cannot be taken out.
(197). Kabīr (says): I was going on a pilgrimage to the Ka'bah,[3] onwards the Lord met with me.
The Lord began to quarrel with me: by whom has (this) ever[4] been ordered?
(198). Kabīr (says): how often, alas! alas! is Kabīr gone on a pilgrimage to the Ka'bah!
O Lord! what sin is in me? the Pīr does not tell (me) with (his) mouth.
(199). Kabīr (says): those who violently kill animals, say, that this is lawful.
When God will take out his account-book, what will be (their) state?
(200). Kabīr (says): the practice of violence is oppression, God will call for an answer.
In (his) office account is taken, they will be struck in their face.
(201). Kabīr (says): to give account is easy, when the heart is pure.
In that true tribunal no one will seize the hem of the garment.[5]
(202). Kabīr (says): in the earth and the sky (there is) a distance (as between) two gourds.
The six philosophical systems have fallen into doubt and the eighty-four Siddhas (too).
(203). Kabīr (says): in me there is nothing mine, whatever there is, that is thine.
In entrusting what is thine to thee what remains mine?
(204). Kabīr in saying: "thou, thou" has become "thou," "I" has not remained in me.
When my own self, which is another's,[6] has been effaced, (then) where I look, there (art) "thou."
(205). Kabīr (says): expecting a change the false ones entertain hope.
(But) not one object of (their) desire came to hand, they rose and went hopeless.
(206). Kabīr (says): who remembers Hari, he is happy in the world.
Never here and there he is shaken, whom the creator keeps.
(207). Kabīr (says): from the pain of the oil-press (we) were rescued by the true Guru.
Full, strong faith was (in consequence) manifested (in us).
(208). Kabīr (says): in putting off[7] the day has passed, the interest[8] goes on increasing.
Neither Hari has been worshipped nor has the handwriting been torn; death has (now) come on.

[1] ਮਰਹਟ = ਮਰਘਟ (Sansk. मरघट्ट), burning-ground.

[2] ਬਿਰਾਨ = ਬੇਰਾਨ unemployed = fallow, or useless.

[3] Had Kabīr not originally been a Muhammadan, he surely would not have said anything of this kind.

[4] ਗਾਹਿ = گاهی at any time; ever (Pers.).

[5] ਪਲਾ ਪਕਰਨਾ, to seize the hem of the garment = to ask for pardon or protection.

[6] ਆਪਾ ਪਰਕਾ, *the self of another.* It is the pantheistical doctrine, that the insentient Absolute becomes conscious in man.

[7] ਟਾਲਾਟੋਲਾ *m.* evasion; putting off; now in Hindī (and Hindūstānī) टालमटोला.

[8] ਬਿਆਜੁ, interest paid on a debt; its etymology is unknown.

(209). *Mah.* V. Kabīr is a barking dog, he runs after a carcass.
By destiny[1] I obtained the true Guru, by whom I was released.[2]
(210). *Mah.* V. O Kabīr, the country of the pious thieves trample under foot.
They do not spread over the whole earth,[3] excessive greediness[4] brings them down.
(211). *Mah.* V. O Kabīr, for the sake of the rice they apply the pestle to the husk.
Sitting together with bad companions Dharm-rāe afterwards asks (them).[5]
(212). O Nāmā! (thou art) deluded by the Māyā, says Trilōčan, the friend.
Why printest thou (clothes) darkening (them),[6] and dost not apply (thy) mind (to) Rām?[7]
(213). Nāmā says: O Trilōčan, the name I remember[8] with (my) mouth.
Whilst doing (my) work with hand and foot all my mind is with the spotless one.
(214). *Mah.* V. O Kabīr, no one is ours, and we are not any one's.
By whom this creation is made, in him it is absorbed.
(215). Kabīr (says): the flour is fallen into the mire, nothing has come to hand.
(What) in grinding along was chewed, that went on with them.
(216). Kabīr (says): the mind knows everything and knowingly commits vices.
What is the good of it, if one, with a lamp in the hand, falls into the well?
(217). Kabīr (says): love to the omniscient one has seized (me), the ignorant people keep (me) back.
How shall a breach (of love) with him be made, whose the soul and life are?
(218). Kabīr (says): loving houses and halls why do you adorn[9] and gild them?
The work is three cubits and half, if much, three and three-quarters.
(219). Kabīr (says): what I think, he does not, what is effected by my thought?
Hari executes his own thought, which is not in my thought.
(220). *Mah.* III. He himself will (people) make to entertain solicitude, and he himself also gives freedom from solicitude.
Nānak (says): he should be praised, who takes care of all.
(221). *Mah.* V. O Kabīr, Rām has not been thought of, he has wandered about in greediness.
Committing sins he has died, in a moment the end of life has come.
(222). Kabīr (says): the body is a raw water-jug,[10] a mere raw stuff.
If thou wilt keep (it) firm, worship Rām, otherwise (thy) affair is lost.

[1] ਕਰਮੀ, literally: by works (done in a former birth).

[2] Arjun, the compiler of the Granth, has interpolated here some verses, which partly contain a sharp censure of Kabīr.

[3] ਧਰਤੀ ਭਾਰਿ = ਧਰਤੀ ਭਰ. ਭਰ or ਭਾਰਿ, when affixed to a noun, is used in Hinduī adverbially: "up to," "to the full of," "the whole of" (Sansk. भर or भार).

[4] ਲਾਹੁ *n.* excessive greediness, insatiableness.

[5] The sense is: as the rice has to suffer for being in the companionship of the husk, so those have to suffer at the hands of Yama, who sit in bad company.

[6] ਛਾਇ ਲੈ, part. past conj. from ਛਾਇ (ਛਾਉਣਾ) ਲੈਣਾ.

[7] Though "Mah. V." is not put before this verse, it belongs to Arjun, as well as the following verse, which is likewise not specially ascribed to him.

[8] ਸਮ੍ਹਾਲਿ, here, for the sake of the rhyme, instead of ਸਮ੍ਹਾਲੀ (1st pers. sing.).

[9] ਮਰਹੁ here = ਮੜ੍ਹਨਾ (or ਮੜਨਾ), to coat ornamentally; in the older Hinduī ਰ and ੜ ṛ (or ੜ੍ਹ ṛh) is frequently not distinguished.

[10] ਕਾਰਵੀ *s.f.*, Hindī करूआ, from the Sansk. करक; short *a* is occasionally lengthened before *r*. Instead of Kara-a (by elision of क) we find frequently in old Hinduī the form Karū-ā (*e.g.* ਮਨੂਆ = ਮਨ), *a* being changed to *u* for the sake of euphony and lengthened at the same time, as being accented.

(223). Kabīr (says): O Kēsava, Kēsava! should be called out, it should not be slept, O foolish one!
At some time he will hear the cry of him, who is calling out night and day.

(224). Kabīr (says): the body has become an elephant-forest, the mind an intoxicated elephant.
The goad is the jewel of (divine) knowledge, the driver some rare saint.

(225). Kabīr (says): Rām is the jewel, the mouth the bag,[1] open it before an examiner.
If some purchaser will come on, he will take it for a high price.[2]

(226). Kabīr (says): the name of Rām was not known, the crowd of the family was taken care of.
Even in business he died, no bamb![3] came out (of his mouth).

(227). Kabīr (says): in the twinkling[4] of the eyes, in a moment, a moment (of life) has passed away.
The mind does not give up (its) cares, Yama has come and beaten the kettle-drum (of departure).

(228). Kabīr (says): Rām is like a tree, the Bairāgī like (its) fruit.
The pious man, by whom debate and dispute has been given up, like its shade.

(229). Kabīr (says): sow such a seed, that is bearing fruit during the whole year!
(Whose) shade is cool, (whose) fruits are full, (on which) the birds are playing.

(230). Kabīr (says): the tree is liberal, mercy is (its) fruit, assisting the creatures.
The birds are gone to foreign countries, the tree is bearing good fruits.

(231). Kabīr (says): the society of the pious is good luck, it is written on (one's) forehead.
(If) the boon of emancipation be obtained, (there is) no hindrance nor impassable passage.

(232). Kabīr (says): in one Ghaṛī (= twenty-four minutes), half a Ghaṛī, half of a half Ghaṛī:
The conversations, which are made with devotees, those are a gain.

(233). Kabīr (says): whichever men drink Bhang, (eat fish) and (drink) liquors:
(Though they go) to holy watering places, keep fasts and abstinence, they go to hell.

(234). Kabīr (says): I put (my) eyes down, having taken my sweetheart into (my) heart.
Every relish I enjoy with my beloved, I show (him) to nobody.

(235). The eight watches, (every) hour (my) soul remains in thy contemplation.
Why should I put down my eyes, all bodies I look upon as the beloved.

(236). Hear, O friend! dwells the soul in the beloved or dwells the beloved in the soul?
The soul is the beloved; I do not comprehend, whether in (my) body is the soul or the beloved?

(237). Kabīr (says): the Brāhmaṇ is the Guru of the world, he is not the Guru of the devotees.
Being entangled and toiling in the four Vēdas he has died.

(238). Hari is sugar[5] scattered in sand, it cannot be picked up by the hands.
Kabīr says: the Guru taught me a good (word): having become an ant eat it!

(239). Kabīr (says): if thou hast a longing for the beloved, cut off thy head and make a ball[6] of it!
Playing and playing (with it) bring on ecstacy! whatever happens, may it happen!

[1] ਕੋਥਰੀ *s.f.* (fem. of ਕੋਥਰਾ), a small bag; Sindhī कोथिरी, Mārāṭhī कोथळी.

[2] ਮਹਘਾ adj. dear; Hindī now महंगा (Sansk. महार्घ).

[3] ਬੰਬ, bamb, used here as interjection and therefore constructed as feminine. The word is assimilated from ब्रह्म, the full expression being: ब्रह्म महादेव, Mahādēv is the Brahm (or Supreme Being), as mumbled by the votaries of Shiva. Another assimilation of ब्रह्म is ਬੰਭ, which is also met with in the Granth, and essentially the same as ਬੰਬ.

[4] ਮਟੁਕਾ *m.* the twinkling (of the eyes); *cf.* the Hindī मटकना.

[5] ਖਾਂਡ, coarse brown sugar, is in old Hinduī (as still in Panjābī and Marāṭhī) feminine, in modern Hindī and Hindūstānī it is used as masculine.

[6] ਗੋਇ, Pers. گوی.

(240). Kabīr (says): if thou hast a longing after the beloved one, then sport with a ripe one (*i.e.* the Guru)!

By pressing raw mustard-seed[1] neither an oil-cake is made nor oil.

(241). Searching he wanders about like a blind one, and is not knowing the pious.

Nāmā (= Nāmdēv) says:[2] how shall the Lord be obtained without the devotees?

(242). Who, having given up Hari, that diamond, put their hope on another one:

Those men will go to hell, says truly Ravidās.

(243). Kabīr (says): if thou establishest a household, do good, otherwise renounce the world!

(Who) puts an obstacle in the way of a Bairāgī,[3] his lucklessness is great.

THE SLŌKS OF SHĒKH FARĪD.[4]

Ōm! By the favour of the true Guru!

(1). On which day the young woman[5] is married, (for that) the auspicious days[6] are written down (before).

The husband, who (was) heard of[7] (before only) with the ears, comes and shows (his) face.

In making the bones crack the poor soul[8] is extracted (from the body).

The appointed wedding does not recede, inform (thy) soul[9] (of this)!

O dear young woman,[10] death is the husband, he will take away (thy) life.

Having joined[11] (thy) hands to whose neck wilt thou run and cling?

Thinner than a hair is the bridge Salāt,[12] has (this word) not been heard by thee?[13]

O Farīd, a shrill sound is made to thee:[14] stand, do not let thyself be robbed!

[1] ਸਰਸਉ (from the Sansk. सर्षप, by transition of p into b = v = u), is used here as feminine, though it is masculine in Sansk. In Hindī and Hindūst. (सरसों) it is likewise feminine.

[2] The verse is Kabīr's and Nāmdēv is only quoted in the second half, as in the next following verse Ravidās, whose writings were known to Kabīr, as is proved thereby.

[3] The sense is apparently: who prevents one from becoming a Bairāgī.

[4] Shēkh Farīd was a famous Pīr and a contemporary of Nānak. He was a Sūfī and according to the Janam-sākhī Nānak had a good deal of intercourse with him, as he lived not far from Lahore at a place called ਪਾਕਪਟਨ (near the modern Montgomery station), where also he is buried. Disciples of his are still to be found in the Panjāb, called Shēkh Farīdī faqīrs. The Slōks of Farīd are also of great interest in a linguistic point of view, as they represent the idiom of the Musalmāns of those days.

[5] ਧਨ or ਧਨਿ, in Panjābī, a young woman (Sansk. धनिका); it is frequently used in the Granth.

[6] ਸਾਹਾ, *m.* an auspicious day fixed for a wedding. This word is only used in Panjābī and Sindhī (साहो).

[7] ਸੁਣੀਦਾ, passive participle present, peculiar to the Panjābī.

[8] ਜਿੰਦੁ or ਜਿੰਦੂ, soul, used in Panjābī and Sindhī.

[9] ਜਿੰਦੁ ਕੂੰ; ਕੂੰ, as we see from this and other passages of the Granth, was then the usual Dative-postfix, not ਨੂੰ, as now-a-days.

[10] ਵਹੁਟੀ, from ਵਹੁ (वधू), ਟਾ, fem. ਟੀ, being a *diminutive* affix in Panjābī and Sindhī (see my Sindhī Gram. p. 77).

[11] ਜੋਲਣਾ = ਜੋਰਨਾ = ਜੋੜਨਾ, to join.

[12] ਪੁਰਸਲਾਤ, instead of ਪੁਲਸਰਾਤ, *r* and *l* being constantly interchanged. ਸਰਾਤ = Arab. صِراط, name of the bridge, suspended over the midst of hell.

[13] ਸੁਣੀਆਇ = ਸੁਣੀਆ, fem. *i.e.* ਬਾਤ, word; ਇ is the suffix (= Sindhī इ) of the second person sing. "by thee." See my Sindhī Gram. pp. 225 and 345 sqq.

[14] ਪਵੰਦੀਈ, literally: it falls to thee, ī being here again the pronominal suffix of the 2nd pers. sing.

(2). O Farīd, the life of a Darvēsh of the gate (of God) is difficult; I walk after the manner of the world.

I have bound together and taken up a bag, where shall I go and throw it down?

(3). It is not perceived, it is not seen,[1] the world is a hidden fire.[2]

By my Lord I was healed, otherwise I would also burn.

(4). O Farīd, if I know, that the sesam-seeds[3] are few, I fill the cavity of my joined two palms with care.

If I know, that the bridegroom is young, I show him little honour.

(5). If I know, that the hem of my garment is tearing, I put a firm patch (on it).

Like thee I have no one, I have seen and wandered the whole world through.

(6). O Farīd, if thou art clever in understanding, do not write an account of the evil deeds (of others)!

Lowering thy head to thy own collar look there![4]

(7). O Farīd, who beat thee with their fists, do not beat them again!

Go to thy own house having kissed their feet!

(8). O Farīd, when there is for thee the time of earning (eternal goods), thou art occupied with the world.

Death is contained[5] in the love (of the world), when (all) is full, it is departed.

(9). See, O Farīd, what has happened, the beard has become brown and white.

The future has come near, the past has remained far behind.

(10). See, O Farīd, what has happened, sugar has become poison.

Except my own Lord, to whom shall I tell my pain?

(11). O Farīd, the eyes by seeing have become dim-sighted, by hearing and hearing the ears have become half-deaf.

The mango[6] has been ripening and is gaining[7] more colour.

(12). O Farīd, some one enjoys (him) when being with white hair, by whom he was not enjoyed, when his hair was black.[8]

Having made love with the Lord a new pleasure springs up.

(13). *Mah.* III. O Farīd, the Lord is always in black and white hair, if one remembers him.

That love, which one oneself applies (to him), does not affect (him), though every one desire it.

This love is the cup of the Lord, to whom he pleases, to him he gives it.

(14). O Farīd, by which eye the world is fascinated, that eye I have seen.

The bird, which was not bearing a streak of collyrium, has sat down on the needle.

(15). O Farīd, who is crying, screaming and giving instruction continually,

Is moved about by Satan, where shall he turn his mind?

(16). O Farīd, become Kuša-grass flowing along with the stream![9]

One breaks down, another is trodden under foot.

Then thou art introduced[10] to the gate of the Lord.

[1] ਬੁਝਣਾ, Sindhī बुझणु, to be perceived; ਸੁਝਣਾ, to be seen, Sindhī सुझणु.

[2] ਭਾਹਿ, *s.f.* fire, Sindhī बाहि, Sansk. वह्नि (m.).

[3] ਤਿਲ, sesam-seed. Here the sesam-seeds are meant, which are distributed by the bride at a wedding.

[4] The sense is: look into thy own heart!

[5] ਮਰਗ ਸਵਾਈ = ਸਮਾਈ, *m* and *v* constantly interchanging in Panjābī. ਮਰਗ, death, is feminine.

[6] ਸਾਖ *f.* (Marāṭhī शाख), a well-filled mango bordering on ripeness.

[7] ਕਰੇਂਦਾ, Panjābī, instead of ਕਰੰਦਾ (in Sindhī करींदो) = ਕਰਦਾ.

[8] ਕਾਲੀਂ ਪਉਲੀਂ, Loc. plur. of ਕਾਲਾ and ਪਉਲਾ, black and white hair = in youth and old age.

[9] ਪਵਾਹੀ adj. = Sansk. प्रवाहिन्, flowing or driving with the current.

[10] ਵਾੜੀਅਹਿ, the Panjābī Present passive, as still used.

(17). O Farīd, the dust should not be censured, no one is equal to the dust.
It is under the feet of the living and upon the dead ones.

(18). O Farīd, when there is greediness, what is then love? if there is greediness, love is false.
For how long will time be passed in a hut broken by the rain?

(19). O Farīd, why dost thou wander about in the jungle, the jungle, why dost thou smash the thorns in the forest?
The Lord is dwelling in the heart,[1] what art thou seeking in the jungle?

(20). O Farīd, with these slender legs I have wandered over low grounds and hills.
Now, O Farīd, a small march[2] has become to me[3] (as being) of a hundred kōs.

(21). O Farīd, the nights are long, the sides begin to burn.
Woe to the life of those, who put their hope on another!

(22). O Farīd, if I am turned back, when my friend has come:
My body[4] burns like Majīṭh, upon (it) are coals.

(23). O Farīd, he desires Bijaurī grapes and the Jaṭ plants a Kikkar-tree.
He goes about spinning wool and wishes to put on silk-cloth.

(24). O Farīd, in the lanes is mud, the house is far away, with the beloved (I entertain love).
(If) I go, (my) blanket[5] gets wet, (if) I remain (at home), love breaks asunder.

(25). May get wet and soaked the blanket, O Allah, may rain fall:
(Yet) I will go and meet with those friends, lest love break asunder.

(26). O Farīd, I am in error about (my) turban, lest it become dirty.
(My) foolish mind does not know, that my head also will eat earth.

(27). O Farīd, sugar, coarse sugar, refined sugar,[6] molasses, honey, buffalo-milk:
All sweet things, O Lord, do not come up to thee.

(28). O Farīd, my bread is of wood, my condiment is hunger.
By whom buttered bread is eaten, they will suffer much pain.

(29). Eat bare dry bread and drink cold water!
O Farīd, seeing the buttered bread of others do not tantalize (thy) soul!

(30). Till now she has not slept with (her) husband, (her) body is turned back.
Go and ask the ill-fated woman, how the night is passed by her?

(31). At her father's-in-law she gets no entrance, in her father's house she finds no place.
Her husband does not ask her a single word, (and yet) she is called a happy married woman.[7]

(32). In her father's-in-law and in her father's house she is her beloved's, (her) beloved is inapproachable and bottomless.
Nānak (says): she is a happy married woman, who is pleasing to him, who is without concerns.[8]

(33). (Who) is bathed, washed and adorned, who sleeps and has no care:
O Farīd, she is surrounded[9] with Assafoetida, the fragrance of musk is gone.

[1] ਹਿਆਲੀਆ fem. dimin. of ਹਿੰਅ, heart (instead of ਹਿਅਲੀ or ਹਿਅੜੀ).

[2] ਕੂਜੜਾ, *s.m.* dim. usually written ਕੂਚ (ਕੂਚੜਾ, dim.).

[3] ਥੀਓਮਿ, has become to me (Sindhī थिओमि), *mi* being pronominal suffix of the 1st pers. sing.

[4] ਹੇੜਾ, *m.* properly = flesh; here = body; *cf.* verse 40.

[5] ਕੰਬਲੀ (now ਕੰਮਲੀ), a coarse woollen blanket, which the Panjābīs wear in rainy weather and during the cold season.

[6] ਨਿਵਾਤ, Pers. نَبَات refined sugar.

[7] The following verse gives the solution of this paradoxon.

[8] This verse is not Farīd's, but of a certain Nānak; in none of the manuscripts, however, I have compared, I find the mahállā put down; very likely the verse is Guru Arjun's, the compiler of the Granth.

[9] The words must thus be divided: ਸੁ ਘੇੜੀ; ਘੇੜਨਾ = ਵੇੜ੍ਹਨਾ, to surround.

(34). Youth is passing, I am not afraid, if love to the beloved does not pass.

O Farīd, of what (use) is youth without love? it is faded and gone!

(35). Care is (my) bedstead, pain the coarse twine (of the bedstead), the pangs of separation (my) bedding (and) coverlet.

Behold this my life, O true Lord!

(36). O pangs of separation, O pangs of separation, (thus) it should be said, O pangs of separation, you are (my) king!

O Farīd, in which body no pangs of separation spring up, that body consider as a burning-ground!

(37). O Farīd, these Gandal-stalks[1] of poison are put down overlaid with sugar.

Some, in cooking them, are gone off, some have thrown away the cooked one.

(38). O Farīd, four (watches) are passed in walking about, four are passed in sleeping.

The Lord will ask account: of what use wert thou?

(39). O Farīd, having gone to the gate hast thou seen the gong?

This one is innocently beaten, what (will be) the state of us, the guilty ones?

(40). At every Ghaṛī it is beaten, at every watch it receives punishment.

That (my) body passes, like the gong, in pain the night.

(41). Shēkh Farīd has become old, (his) body begins to shake.

If there should be a life of a hundred years, yet the body will become ashes.

(42). O Farīd, let me not sit at the gate of another, O Lord!

If thou wilt put me so, take my soul out of my body!

(43). On the shoulder an axe, on the head a large earthen vessel, the blacksmith is King[2] in the forest.

O Farīd, I desire my own beloved, thou desirest coals.

(44). O Farīd, some have much flour, some have no salt (even).

Having gone on (to the other world) they will be known, who will be beaten in the face.

(45). With (them) are kettle-drums, umbrellas on the head, pipers[3] and minstrels.[4]

Having gone they are fallen asleep in the cemetery, like the poor[5] they are buried.

(46). O Farīd, though they were erecting houses, halls, upper-storied houses, yet they are gone.

Having made a false traffic they are gone and sunk in the grave.

(47). O Farīd, in a patched quilt there are many pins, in the life there is no one.[6]

At their several turns the Shēkhs have departed.

(48). O Farīd, whilst the two lamps[7] were burning, the angel (of death) came and sat down.

The fort (of the body) was taken, the heart robbed, he went away having extinguished the lamps.

(49). O Farīd, look, what is done to cotton, what has happened to the sesam-seeds!

(What) to the sugar-cane and paper in a pit of burning coals!

This is the punishment for those, who do bad works.

[1] ਗੰਦਲ (*s.f.*), name of a certain plant, apparently poisonous.

[2] ਕੈਸਰੁ = قَیصَر, King, Emperor, (Caesar).

[3] ਭੇਰੀ, a piper, Sansk. भैरिक.

[4] ਸਡੇਰੜ, composed of ਸਡੇ, call, cry, and ਰੜ (= ਰੜ੍ਹ, ਰੜ੍ਹਨਾ, to scream, to cry), literally: uttering a cry or scream, as their singing amounts usually to a screaming.

[5] ਅਤੀਮ, corrupted from یتیم, an orphan, a helpless, poor person. ਅਤੀਮਾ (= ਅਤੀਮਾਂ) is the Gen. Plur., the postposition ਜਿਉ being omitted.

[6] The sense is: life cannot be kept together by means of pins as a patched quilt.

[7] *i.e.* the two eyes.

(50). O Farīd, on the shoulder is the prayer-carpet, on the neck a woollen shirt,[1] in the heart a dagger, molasses in the mouth.

Outward light is seen, in the heart there is dark night.

(51). O Farīd, not a bit of blood issues, if one cut the body.

Those who are in love with the Lord, in their body is no blood.

(52). *Mah.* III. This body is all blood, without blood there is no body.

Who are enamoured with (their) beloved, in that (their) body there is no blood of greediness.

When fear has fallen (on it),[2] the body becomes emaciated, the blood of greediness recedes from within.

As by fire the metal becomes purified, so the fear of Hari removes the filth of folly.

Nānak (says): those bodies are beautiful, which are steeped in the colour of Hari.

(53). O Farīd, seek (that) pond, from which the thing is obtained!

What is the good of seeking a pool? the hand sinks into the mire.

(54). O Farīd, when young I did not enjoy my beloved, having become old I died.[3]

The woman is screaming in the grave: I have not met with thee, O beloved!

(55). O Farīd, the head has become grey,[4] the beard is grey, the mustachoes are grey.

O careless, foolish mind, dost thou (still) enjoy pleasures?

(56). O Farīd, how much fluttering is there in the house! O friend, put away sleep!

The days, that are obtained, are counted,[5] they are fast, fast gone.

(57). O Farīd, houses, halls, upper-storied houses—do not apply thy mind to this!

(When) the dust, that is not to be weighed, has fallen (upon thee), no one will be thy friend.

(58). O Farīd, do not apply (thy) mind to mansion and property, apply it with all efforts[6] to death!

Remember that place, whither thou hast to go!

(59). O Farīd, in which works there is no benefit, those works forget!

Lest thou become ashamed in the court of the Lord.

(60). O Farīd, render service to the Lord, put a stop to the wandering[7] of thy heart!

To Darvēshes the patience[8] of trees is necessary.

(61). O Farīd, black are my clothes, black is my dress.

Full of sins I wander about, the world calls me a Darvēsh.

(62). By hot water (a field) does not sprout, though one immerse (it) in water.

O Farīd, the woman, who is disliked by (her) Lord, goes on grieving.

(63). When she is a girl, there is desire (for marriage), (when) she is married, there are troubles.

O Farīd, she regrets it, that she does not again become a girl.

(64). Geese[9] have come and descended on a pond in saltpetre soil.

They dip their bills (into the water), but do not drink, they burn[10] to fly away.

[1] ਸੂਫ (= صوف), here in the sense of كَفْنِي, a kind of shirt, without sleeves, worn by Faqīrs.

[2] ਡੈ ਪਇਐ, Locative, fear having fallen.

[3] ਮੁਈਆਸੁ, as well as ਮਿਲੀਆਸੁ, is the first person sing. fem. of the preterite (*cf.* the Sindhī मुइआसि); see my Sindhī Gram. p. 289.

[4] ਪਲਿਆ, Sansk. पलित.

[5] ਗਣਵਾ (from ਗਣਨਾ, to count), the participle pass. pres., Sindhī गणिबो; see my Sindhī Gram. p. 220.

[6] ਸਤਾਣੀ is the Ablat. of ਸਤਾਣ (or ਸਤਾਣ = सत्राण, with all efforts, as still used in Marāṭhī).

[7] ਭਰਾਂਦਿ, wandering, straying about, Sansk. भ्रान्ति.

[8] ਜੀਰਾਂਦਿ *s.f.* patience, endurance; the word has become quite obsolete.

[9] ਹੰਝ = ਹੰਸ (हंस), *s* being occasionally changed to *ǰh*. See my Sindhī Gram. Introd. p. xxx.

[10] ਡੰਝ *s.f.* burning, verbal noun of ਡੰਝਣਾ to burn (Sansk. दह्य, passive of दह्), Sindhī (without Anusvāra) ड़झणु.

(65). Geese flying along have fallen on Kōdhrā grain,[1] the people go and drive them away.
The foolish people do not know, that geese do not eat Kōdhrā grain.
(66). Off are gone the birds, by which the low grounds were peopled.
O Farīd, the filled pond also will go, the lonely lotuses are knocked up.
(67). O Farīd, a brick for a pillow, sleeping on the ground, the worm fighting in the flesh:
How many ages have passed, since he has fallen on one side?[2]
(68). O Farīd, the beautiful jar is gone to pieces, broken is the rope of the plough.[3]
In which house is the Angel Ajrāīl[4] a guest to-day?
(69). O Farīd, the beautiful jar is gone to pieces, broken is the rope of the plough.
The friends, who were prostrated on the ground, how shall they come to-day?
(70). O Farīd, O prayerless dog, this is not a good custom.
Thou hast never gone the five times to the mosque.
(71). Rise, O Farīd, make oblation, say prayers in the morning!
The head, that does not bow to the Lord, that head cut off!
(72). The head, that does not bow to the Lord, what should be done to it?
It should be burnt under a large jar instead of fuel![5]
(73). O Farīd, where is thy father and thy mother, by whom thou wast begotten?
They have departed from thee and thou dost not yet believe (it)?
(74). O Farīd, considering the mind as a plain remove the holes and hillocks (therein).
Then thou wilt by no means enter the hell-fire in the other world.
(75). *Mah.* V. O Farīd, the creator is in the creature, the creature dwells in the Lord.
Who shall be called bad, when there is no one without him?
(76). O Farīd, on which day (my) navel-string was cut, if (the midwife) had cut a little (my) throat:
So many troubles would not fall (on me), I would not suffer so much pain.
(77). The grinders (*i.e.* the teeth), the feet, the gems (= eyes) and the ears[6] are gone.
The body emitted a sigh, that these dear friends are gone.
(78). O Farīd, do good to a wicked man, do not let anger roam in (thy) mind!
Sickness will not stick to thy body, everything will fall into (thy) lap.
(79). O Farīd, O guest of half a (lunar) month,[7] the world is a beautiful garden.
(Thy) turn has struck, prepare to go off with the dawn!
(80). O Farīd, musk is distributed in the night, to the sleeping ones no portion[8] is allotted.
Whose eyes are drowsy, whence[9] (should) their meeting (with it come)?
(81). O Farīd, I know, that I am in pain and that the whole world is in pain.
Having risen high up I saw, that in every house there is this fire.

[1] ਕੋਧ੍ਰਾ *m.*, an inferior kind of grain (Paspalum frumentaceum), Sansk. कोद्रव. The *d* is aspirated by the influence of *r*.

[2] *i.e.* in the grave. The subject is not mentioned.

[3] ਨਾਗਰ, a plough, Sansk. लाङ्गल.

[4] Arabic: عِزْرائِيل, the angel of death.

[5] ਬਾਲਣ ਸੰਦੈ ਥਾਇ. ਸੰਦਾ is used in the old Panǰābī instead of the modern ਦਾ (or का), as still in Sindhī; see my Sindhī Gram. p. 129.

[6] ਸੁਣੀਅਰੁ ear, literally: the hearer. The word is now quite obsolete. In its original signification (a hearer) it occurs in the Rāg Vaḍhans, Čhant, Mah. V., Slōk I.

[7] ਪੰਖ, Sansk. पक्ष.

[8] ਭਾਉ, portion = Sansk. भाग.

[9] ਕੁਆਉ, Sindhī कुआउ, whence?

(82). *Mah.* V. O Farīd, the world is delightful, (but) in it is a painful garden.
Those who are cherished by (their) Pīr, them the flame does not touch.
(83). *Mah.* V. O Farīd, life is pleasant in company with a beautiful body.[1]
Some rare ones are found, who are in love with the beloved one.
(84). Do not pull down the bank of a river, thou also must give account!
Whither the will of the Lord (points), thither the river makes (its) wandering.
(85). O Farīd, with pain the day is gone, with gripes the night.
Standing the ferryman cries out: the boat is along the bank![2]
(86). Long, long the river flows underneath the bank.
What can the high bank do to the boat, if the ferryman remains cautious?
(87). O Farīd, in words twenty are good friends, seeking the One I *(fem.)* do not obtain him.
I burn like cinders of cow-dung on account of that my beloved.
(88). O Farīd, this body is always barking, it is continually in some pain.
I put stopples into (my) ears, the wind may (then) blow anywhere.
(89). O Farīd, the dates of the Lord are ripe, rivers of honey flow.
The days of youth,[3] they are to be accounted as (real) life.[4]
(90). O Farīd, the body is dried up, it has become a cage, the crows are pecking away (its) plastering.[5]
Till now the Lord has not been met with, behold the lot of (his) servant!
(91). O crow, (my) cadaver is thoroughly searched through, all (my) flesh is eaten (by thee).
Do not touch these two eyes, I hope to see my beloved (with them)!
(92). O crow, do not gnaw (my) cage (= body), it is inhabited, fly therefore away!
In which cage my bridegroom dwells, from that[6] do not eat the flesh!
(93). O Farīd, the humble grave cries out: O houseless one, come to (my) house!
At last thou must come to my place,[7] do not be afraid of dying!
(94). Whilst these mine eyes were looking on how many people have departed!
O Farīd, to the people their own (turn), to me mine is allotted.
(95). (If) thou adornest thy own self, thou wilt meet with me, in meeting with me there will be happiness.[8]
O Farīd, if thou remainest mine, the whole world is thine.[9]
(96). On a river-bank how long will a tree remain firm?
O Farīd, how long will water be kept in a raw vessel?
(97). O Farīd, they are gone to an empty hall, their dwelling is made beneath (the ground).
Wrestling (their) poor spirits dispute with the graves.
Service (to God) is ordered, O Shēkh! to-day or to-morrow we must start.
(98). O Farīd, he who is bound by death appears like one, who is thrown into the river (or ocean).
In the other world the hell is heated, a howl is heard and a scream rises.

[1] The sense is apparently: in company with a beautiful wife.

[2] ਕਪਰੁ, the (high) bank of a river (Sindhī कपरु); ਵਾਟਿ = ਵਟਿ is postposition: on the side of, along (cf. Sindhī वटि, Marāṭhī वतीं).

[3] We divide the words thus: ਜੋ ਜੋਵੰਞੈ ਡੀਹੜਾ; ਜੋਵੰਞਾ, rather a curious form for ਜੋਬਨ youth (यौवन). ਡੀਹੜਾ, day (dim. of ਡੀਹੁ, Sindhī डींहु, Prak. दिअहो, Sansk. दिवसः).

[4] ਉਮਰ ਹਥ ਪਵੰਨਿ, literally: they fall into the hand of life, *i.e.* are possessed as life.

[5] ਤਲੀ *s.f.* in the sense of plastering, is peculiar to the Panjābī.

[6] ਤਿਦੂ = ਤਿ ਦੂ, ਦੂ being an Ablative affix (Sansk. तस्, Prāk. दो, Panjābī ਦੂੰ).

[7] ਮੈ ਥੈ; ਥੈ is the Locative of ਥਉ, place.

[8] This is the address of God and the following line the answer of Farīd.

[9] The sense is: I do not care then for the whole world.

Some have become very prudent,[1] some wander about careless.

The works, that are done in the world, are witness at the court (of God).

(99). O Farīd, on the bank of a river sits a crane and sports.

Whilst playing hawks have unawares fallen on the goose.[2]

The hawks of the Lord have fallen (on) it, the sports are forgotten.

Those who in their mind (and) thought will not remember (him), they[3] are destroyed by the Lord.

(100). To three maunds and a half the body rises by means of water and grain.

The servant has come into the world entertaining again hope.[4]

When the angel of death will come, breaking all gates:

He is bound before all those beloved brothers.

Behold, the servant is gone on the shoulder of four men.

O Farīd, the works, that are done in the world, they are of use at the threshold (of God).

(101). O Farīd, I am a sacrifice to those birds, whose dwelling is in the jungle.

Gravel they pick up (with their beak), they dwell in the desert, they do not give up the side of the Lord.

(102). O Farīd, the season has returned, the tree is shaken, the leaves are dropping off.

In the four corners I have searched, there is nowhere a firm stay.

(103). O Farīd, having torn in pieces (my) silk petticoat I made a flag of it, a small blanket I put on.[5]

In which dresses the Lord is met with, those dresses I make.

(104). *Mah.* III. Why art thou tearing thy silk petticoat and puttest on a small blanket?

Nānak (says): by sitting in (one's) house the beloved one is met with, if thou direct thy intention right.

(105). *Mah.* IV. O Farīd, those who are proud of their greatness, being aware of (their) wealth and youth:

They are gone devoid of the Lord, like hills (devoid) of rain.

(106). O Farīd, their faces are dreadful, by whom the name is forgotten.

Here they have much pain, in the other world they have neither place nor spot.[6]

(107). O Farīd, thou hast not waked the latter part of the night (nor) hast thou died whilst living.

Though thou hast forgotten the Lord, the Lord has not forgotten thee.

(108). *Mah.* V. O Farīd, the beloved is delightful, great and not in need of anything.

To be in love with the Lord, this is true decoration.

(109). *Mah.* V. O Farīd, considering pain and pleasure as the same drop the change (between them) from thy heart!

Who is pleasing to Allah, he is well off, by him (his) court is obtained.

(110). *Mah.* V. O Farīd, the world sounds as it is sounded, thou also art sounding with it.

That creature does not sound, of which Allah takes care.

(111). *Mah.* V. O Farīd, the heart is attached to this world, the world is of no use.

The post[7] of the Faqīrs is difficult, it is obtained by a full destiny.

[1] ਇਕਨਾ ਨੋ ਸਭ ਸੋਝੀ ਆਈ, literally: to some all prudence has come.

[2] ਬਗਲਾ, crane, and ਹੰਸੁ, goose, have here been taken as synonyms.

[3] The subject is feminine.

[4] ਆਸੂਲੀ *s.f.* hope = ਆਸਾ.

[5] The Faqīrs in India generally erect a flag in front of their dwellings and wear coarse woollen clothes. To this custom the verse alludes.

[6] In some good MSS. this verse is ascribed to Arjun (Mah. V.), whereas the Lahore lithographed copy has no such sign.

[7] ਮਿਸਲ, *s.f.* post, station, Arabic مَثَل.

(112). In the first watch (of the night) there are blossoms, fruits also in the latter part of the night.
These who wake obtain (them), they are a gift from the Lord.
(113). The gifts are the Lord's, what can he be prevailed upon?
Some who wake do not obtain them, some who are sleeping he arouses and gives them to them.
(114). O thou, who art seeking the love of thy husband, in thy body is some vice.
Those who have the name of happy married women, they are not given to idle prating (and) wrangling.
(115). (If) patience in the heart (be) the bow, (and if) this be bent by patience:[1]
The arrow of patience does not miss the creator.
(116). Patience is within the patient ones, thus they burn (their) body.
They become near God, (but their) secret they do not give to any one.
(117). This is the object[2] of patience; if thou, O servant (of God), render it firm.
Increasing thou becomest a sea, decreasing thou dost not become a canal.[3]
(118). O Farīd, the Darvēsh-ship is difficult; (with most) it is the love to buttered bread.
By some few (only) the (true) rite of the Darvēshes is set agoing.
(119). (My) body is heated like an oven, (my) bones burn like fuel.
(If) I am tired in my feet, I move on on my head in the hope, that my beloved may be met with.
(120). *Mah.* V.[4] Do not heat (thy) body like an oven, do not burn (thy) bones like fuel!
What is the good of injuring (thy) head and feet? behold (thy) beloved inside!
(121). I am seeking my sweetheart and my sweetheart is with me.
Nānak (says): the invisible one is not seen, (to) the disciple he (*i.e.* the Guru) shows (him).
(122). Seeing the geese swimming the cranes (also) became desirous (of swimming).
The helpless cranes sank and died, with the head downwards and the feet upwards.
(123). When I knew, that it is a great goose,[5] I keep company with it.
If I knew, that it is a helpless crane, I never associate[6] with it in (my) life.
(124). What is the goose, what is the crane? on which he looks favourably:
If it pleases him, O Nānak, he makes from (that) crow a goose.[7]
(125). The bird is alone on the pond, the nooses (and) entanglements are fifty.
This body is immersed in the waves; O True one, (my) hope is in thee!
(126). What is that word, what that virtue, what that gem (and) mantra?
What that garb, that I may make, by which the beloved one may come into my power?
(127). Bowing is that word, patience the virtue, the tongue the gem and mantra.
Make these three thy garb, O sister, then the beloved one will come into thy power!

[1] The Lahore lithographed copy reads: ਨੀਹਲੇ, which gives no sense. The manuscript reading is ਨੀਹੁਲੇ = ਨਿਹੁੜੇ (*ṇ* and *ṛ* frequently interchanging, as in Sindhī), part. past of ਨਿਹੁੜਨਾ, to be bent, literally: this the bent one of patience = this being bent by patience.

[2] ਸੁਆਉ *n.* object, purpose. In this sense the word frequently occurs in the Granth. But the other meaning: *sweetness, savour,* (from स्वाद) will also suit the context here.

[3] ਵਾਹੜਾ, a canal or a side-branch of the river (Sindhī वाहड़ु).

[4] Some MSS. do not ascribe this verse to the Mah. V., but as it is a reply to the preceding verse, it is very likely, that those manuscripts, which attribute this verse to Guru Arjun, are in the right. In the same way the following verse too must be ascribed to Arjun, though none of the MSS. bears the mark of Mah. V.

[5] ਵਡਹੰਸ, literally: a great goose, *i.e.* a great devotee.

[6] ਅੰਗੁ ਭੇੜਨਾ, to associate, to keep company (ਅੰਗ = the Sanskrit अङ्क, not अङ्ग), literally: to close an embrace.

[7] This verse belongs likewise to Arjun, who is fond of criticizing what he reads, and of making objections to it, though in none of the manuscripts nor in the Lahore lithographed copy it is attributed to the Mah. V.

(128). Who, when there is wisdom (in him), becomes foolish;
Who, when there is power (in him), becomes weak;
Who his unreal self gives away:
Such a one is called a devotee.
(129). Do not say, that one (thing) is distasteful, in all is the true Lord.
Do not grieve the heart of any one, all are invaluable rubies!
(130). All hearts are rubies, to grieve them is by no means good.
If thou art longing after thy beloved, do not grieve the heart of any one!

SAVAĪĒ[1] REFERRING TO THE FIRST MAHALĀ.

(PANEGYRIC OF NĀNAK.)

Ōm! By the favour of the true Guru!

(BY THE BHAṬṬ KALASU.)

I.

With one mind meditate on the divine male, the giver of blessings!
He is always renowned as the support of the saints.
Taking his feet I make them dwell in my heart.
Then I sing the qualities of Nānak, the most excellent Guru.

II.

I sing the qualities of the most excellent Guru, the ocean of comfort, the remover of sin, the pond of the Sabd.[2]

The Jōgīs and Jangams sing the deep ocean of firmness (and) wisdom, reflecting on it.

Indra and the others sing (them), the Bhagat Prahlād and the others, by whom the sweetness of their own spirit was known.

I, the poet Kalasu, sing the glory of Guru Nānak, by whom the Rāg-jōg[3] was performed.

III.

Janak and the others sing (them), the devoted chief Jōgīs, who are at all times[4] full of the love of Hari.

Sanak and the others sing (them), the saints, Siddhas and the others, the holy Munis sing (them), who are without deceit.

His qualities sings Dhōm,[5] whose circle is immovable, by devotion (and) love the juice (of Hari) was known by him.

I, the poet Kalasu, sing the glory of Guru Nānak, by whom the Rāg-jōg was performed.

[1] ਸਵਈਏ (Plur.) or ਸਵਯੇ, verses of a certain kind of Prākrit metre.

[2] ਸਰੇ, for the sake of the rhyme = ਸਰ.

[3] ਰਾਜੁ ਜੋਗ, doing secular business and yet performing abstract meditation.

[4] ਸਰਬ ਕਲਾ, for the sake of the rhyme, instead of ਸਰਬ ਕਾਲ.

[5] ਧੋਮ, Sansk. धौम्य, name of a Riṣhi.

IV.

Kapila[1] with the others sings (them), who is at the beginning, the chief Jōgī, boundless, the best of Avatārs.

Jamadagni sings (them), the Lord (= father) of Parasrām with the axe in the hand, who has sprung from Raghu.

Udhau,[2] Akrūr,[3] Bidr[4] sing (his) qualities, by whom (Plur.) the universal spirit was known.

I, the poet Kalasu, sing the glory of Guru Nānak, by whom the Rāg-jōg was performed.

V.

(His) qualities sing the four castes, the six philosophical systems,

Brahmā and the others remember[5] (his) qualities.

(His) qualities sings Sēs (= Shēṣha-nāga) with the juice of a thousand tongues, at the beginning and at the end being given to deep meditation and contemplation.[6]

(His) qualities sings Mahādēv, the Bairāgī, by whom unintermittingly deep reflection is comprehended.

The poet Kalasu sings the glory of Guru Nānak, by whom the Rāg-jōg was performed.

VI.

The Rāj-jōg was performed (by him), the fearless one dwelt in (his) heart.

The whole creation is saved, taking the name (of Hari) it crosses constantly.

(His) qualities sing Sanak and the others, the first ones (of creation), Janak and the others, up to the ages.

Blessed, blessed is the Guru, blessed (his) birth, profitable[7] (and) good to the world.

In hell (and) in the (heavenly) cities there is the cry of "victory," by (me) the humble poet it is beautifully described.

Guru Nānak (was) delighted in the name of Hari, by him[8] the Rāg-jōg was performed.

VII.

In the Satya-yuga it was performed (by him), Bali was deceived (by him) by becoming a dwarf.[9]

In the Trēta-yuga it was performed, (he was) called Rām of the Raghu family.

In the Dvāpara-yuga Krisan, Murāri, Kans was saved[10] (by him).

To Ugrasēṇ the kingdom was given, security to the devotees.

[1] ਕਪਲ = कपिल, a Muni (traditionally the founder of the Sãkhya philosophical system), who is identified with Vishṇu.

[2] ਉਧਉ = Sansk. उद्धव, nom. prop. of a Yādava, companion of Krishṇa.

[3] ਅਕ੍ਰੂਰ = Sansk. अक्रूर, Krishṇa's paternal uncle.

[4] ਬਿਦਰ = Sansk. विदुर, a companion of Krishṇa.

[5] ਸਿਮਰੰਥਿ, a curious form (a Sanskrit imitation, *anti* being changed, by some mistake or other, to *anthi*).

[6] ਧੵਨਾ, for the sake of the rhyme = ਧੵਨਿ, which in Panjābī and Sindhī signifies also "*contemplation.*"

[7] ਸਕਾਰਥ, Sindhī सक्यार्थों, profitable, advantageous (Sansk. शक्यार्थ).

[8] ਤੈ is here Formative Sing. of ਤੇ.

[9] Nānak is here described as an Avatār and identified with Vishṇu-Krishṇa.

[10] ਕ੍ਰਿਤਾਰਥੁ (कृतार्थ), who has accomplished the object of existence = emancipated.

In the Kali-yuga is Guru Nānak the authority, he is (also) called Angad (and) Amar.[1]

The kingdom of the holy Guru is immovable (and) permanent, by the primeval divine male it is ordered.

VIII.

(His) qualities sings Ravidās, the Bhagat, Jaidēv (and) Trilōčan.

Nāmā, the Bhagat Kabīr sing (them) always, who looked on all things as the same.

The Bhagat Bēṇī sings (his) qualities, who easily enjoys the pleasures of his own spirit.

(Who) without profound meditation on the Yōga and the knowledge of the Guru knows no other Lord.

Sukhdēv,[2] Parīkhat[3] sing (his) qualities, the Rishi Gautama sings (his) glory.

By the poet Kalasu the fame of Guru Nānak is continually afresh spread in the world.

IX.

(His) qualities sing in the nether region the Bhagat Nāga and the other serpents.

Mahādēva sings (his) qualities continually, the Jōgīs, the ascetics, the Jangams.

(His) qualities sings Vyāsa, the Muni, by whom the Vēda (and) the Grammar is reflected upon.

Brahmā utters (his) qualities, by whom the whole creation is arranged by (his) order.

Brahm, (who) is filling (all) the portions of the Universe, is considered (by him)[4] as alike possessed of (all) qualities and devoid of (all) qualities.

Kalasa mutters the glory of Guru Nānak, by whom innate deep meditation was practised.

X.

(His) qualities sing the nine Nāths:[5] blessed is the Guru, who is absorbed in the True one!

Māndhātā[6] sings (his) qualities, who was called a universal monarch.[7]

(His) qualities sings the Rājā Bali, who is dwelling in the seven nether regions.

Bharthari[8] utters (his) qualities, (who was) always remaining with (his) Guru (Gōrakh-nāth).

By Dūrbā,[9] Parūrau[10] and Angara[11] the glory of Guru Nānak is sung.

The poet Kalasu (says): the glory of Guru Nānak is naturally contained in everybody.

[1] ਅਮਰ = ਅਮਰਦਾਸ.

[2] ਸੁਖਦੇਉ, so written in all the manuscripts, I have compared. But it is apparent, that (as the context shows) शुकदेव, the son of Vyāsa, is meant here. See Prēm Sāgar, p. 4, l. 2, below.

[3] ਪਰੀਖਤ = परीचित, the well-known King of Hastināpur, grandson of Arjun, to whom the *Prēm Sāgar* was related.

[4] No subject is mentioned, so that it is doubtful, if the subject is Brahmā or Nānak.

[5] ਨਾਥ, an epithet of a Jōgī; nine chief teachers of the Jōgīs are cuumerated, beginning with Gōrakh-nāth, the founder of the sect.

[6] ਮਾਂਧਾਤਾ = Sansk. मान्धातर्, an old Rājā, the father of the hero Muc̆kund (मुचुकुन्द). See Prēm Sāgar, p. 103, l. 10 *sqq.*

[7] ਚਕ੍ਰਵੈ is traditionally explained as signifying चक्रवर्तिन्, a universal monarch.

[8] ਭਰਥਰੀ (= Sansk. भर्तृहरि), a famous Jōgī, said to have been a disciple of Gōrakh-nāth. He has apparently become a fabulous person, as Kabīr and Nānak are represented as having had conversations with him. If he lived so late as that, he cannot be identified with Bhartrihari, the brother of Vikramāditya.

[9] ਦੂਰਬਾ (= Sansk. दुर्वासस्), name of a Brāhmaṇ, notorious for his sudden wrath.

[10] ਪਰੂਰਉ (= Sansk. पुरूरवस्), name of a Rājā or a being belonging to the intermediate regions.

[11] ਅੰਗਰਾ (= Sansk. अङ्गिरस्), the sire of the Angiras, a kind of higher beings (called sons of the gods).

SAVAĪĒ REFERRING TO THE SECOND MAHALĀ.

* (PANEGYRIC OF ANGAD.)

Ōm! By the favour of the true Guru!

(BY THE BHAṬṬ KALASAHĀR).

I.

Blessed be that divine male, the creator, the maker of the primary elements, who is powerful to create!

Blessed be the true Guru Nānak, who has put his hand on thy head!

When [1] naturally he put (his) hand on (thy) head,

Nectar rained in streams; [2] among the body of the gods and the Munis (thy) fragrance [3] is manifest.[4]

Death, the hateful fellow, is killed, having roared.

The running mind is checked, the five beings [5] are kept in one house, having been pacified.[6]

The world is overcome by the medium of the Guru, in harmony [7] play the chess-mates, the vehicle [8] sunk in deep contemplation holds fast meditation on the Formless one.

Kalasahār utters (his) praise; in the seven continents Lahaṇā is the Guru of the world, having touched Murāri.[9]

II.

Whose sight is a stream of nectar, (that) takes away the sins, darkness and ignorance depart by his sight.

Those who receive the nectar-Sabd, the hard, difficult work, those men are brought across the world of individual existence without difficulty.[10]

Remembering (the name) in the society of the pious they are wakeful, having become humble [11] (they are) always in the highest love.

Kalasahār utters (his) praise; in the seven continents Lahaṇā is the Guru of the world, having touched Murāri.

III.

By thee the name has been established.

The expanse of (thy) renown [12] is spotless, (thou art) the support of the ascetics, the perfect (Jōgīs), the good men (and) of the creatures.

[1] ਤ (shortened from ਤਾ), at the time when.

[2] ਛਜਿ *s.f.* (Sindhī छछि, a flood), stream.

[3] ਬੋਹਿਜ *s.f.* smell, fragrance (from the Persian بُوی).

[4] ਅਗਾਜਣਾ, *v.n.* to be sounded, to be noised about, to be publicly known (from the Persian آغاز sound; *cf.* the Marāṭhī: अगाजणें).

[5] The ਪੰਚ ਭੂਤ are ਕਾਮ, etc.

[6] ਸਮਜਣਾ, the same as ਸਮਝਣਾ, to come to an understanding, to be pacified. Compare the Marāṭhī समजणें.

[7] ਸਮਤ = Sansk. संमति.

[8] ਰਥ (रथ), here apparently used for the *mind.*

[9] *i.e.* Guru Nānak, who is already represented by these Bhaṭṭs as an incarnation of Vishṇu.

[10] ਨਿਰਭਾਰ, a new formation, *without* trouble or difficulty.

[11] ਨਿੰਮਰੀਭੂਤ, taken as one word = the Sansk. नम्रीभूत, *a* easily being interchanged with *i* in Hinduī.

[12] ਜਾਸ = जस, fame, renown.

Thou (art) indeed the Avatār of Rājā Janak, (thy) word is nectar to the world, thou remainest reflecting (in) the world, (like) the lotus (in) the water.[1]

(Thou art) the Kalpa-tree[2] destroying sickness, removing the calamity of the world, to thyself there is one continual threefold[3] meditation.

Kalasahār utters (thy) praise, in the seven continents Lahaṇā is the Guru of the world, having touched Murāri.

IV.

Thou hast indeed received honour from his Highness,[4] (by thee) the authoritative Guru was served, by whom, having subdued the great serpent,[5] deep abstract meditation was made.

(Thy) sight is equal to that of Hari, Hari, (thy) knowledge is comprehensive of the Supreme Spirit, (thou art) knowing the state of him, who is without parts, (thou art) the authoritative Guru.

Whose (thy) sight is, (his) place is immovable, spotless is the place of (his) intellect, he puts on the armour[6] of virtue (and) destroys the Sakti (= Māyā).

Kalasahār utters (thy) praise, in the seven continents Lahaṇā is the Guru of the world, having touched Murāri.

V.

(Thy) sight is removing the darkness of the earth, burning sins, destroying vice.
(Thy) word is a powerful hero, annihilating lust and wrath.
Subduing greediness and infatuation, preserving those who solicit (thy) asylum.
Accumulating love to the Supreme Spirit, nectar-speaking in a beautiful way.[7]
O true Guru, beautiful is the Tilak of the true Guru, who clings to the true (Guru), he crosses over.
The Guru is wandering about in the world having the limbs of a lion,[8] Lahaṇā performs the Rāg-jōg.

(BY THE BHAṬṬ KALU.)

VI.

Thou remainest always in meditation on the undivided one, (thy) senses thou makest move[9] according to (thy) wish.

Like a full tree thou bowest down, thou bearest reproof (and) reflectest on pure (things).

In this wise the real substance was known (by thee), the all-pervading, the invisible, the wonderful one.

By (thy) innate love was collected (by thee) the beautiful (moon-)beams-nectar-speech.

[1] This verse can only be translated according to conjecture, as all case-relations are missing. The verse is only a cumulus of words.

[2] The wishing-tree of Indra's heaven.

[3] ਤ੍ਰਿਧਿਪ, threefold, *i.e.* कायिक, वाचिक, मानसिक, corporeal, oral and mental.

[4] ਹਣਰਥਿ (sic!) = حَضرَت, here respectfully applied to Bābā Nānak.

[5] ਅਜਗਰ, Sansk. अजगर, devouring a goat = a Boa; here the Māyā is intended by it.

[6] ਸਾਨਹੁ, a corruption from سِلاح. The word frequently occurs in the Granth.

[7] ਢਾਲ *s.f.* way, manner. ਢਾਲਨ is the Formative Plural.

[8] ਸੀਹ ਅੰਗਰਉ, taken as Bahuvrīhi, having the limbs of a lion (ਅੰਗਰਾ = ਅੰਗੜਾ, dimin. of ਅੰਗ). The Sikhs explain ਅੰਗਰਉ by ਅੰਗਦ, which is very unlikely.

[9] ਚਾਰਹ, second pers. sing. ਚਾਰਨਾ = ਚਾਲਣਾ (caus. of ਚਲਣਾ), to make it rhyme with the following ਬੀਚਾਰਹ.

Thou didst receive (thy) authority by the medium of the Guru (Nānak), goodness (and) contentment thou didst take (from him).

Hari was touched, says humble Kalu impartially,[1] (his) sight was given to Lahaṇā.

VII.

In (thy) mind thou didst obtain faith, profound comprehension was given (thee) by his Highness.
The poison was destroyed and annihilated from (thy) body, nectar was drunk in (thy) heart.
Joy sprang up in the heart, (that) by the invisible one (his) skill is displayed in (this) Yuga.
The true Guru is naturally delighted in deep meditation, he is continually immersed[2] in it.
(Thou art) generous, able to take away poverty, in seeing (thee) the sins[3] are afraid.
I, Kalu, utter always with joy (and) comfort the glory of Lahaṇā with (my) tongue.

VIII.

The name is (thy) medicine, the name (thy) support, and meditation on the name (is) always (thy) happiness, (thy) flag of the name is beautiful.

Thou art steeped in love with the name, in the Kali-yug thou didst teach[4] the name to gods and men.
Who has received the touch of the name, (his) goodness is manifest (like) the sun in the world.
By having an interview with the Guru bathing at the sixty-eight Tīrthas is made.

IX.

(Thou art) the true Tīrtha, the true bathing and feeding, (thy) love is always true, telling the True one thou art beautiful.

The True one is obtained from the word of the Guru, thou teachest the true name (thy) companions.
Whose continence is true, (whose) fasting is true, (him) the humble poet Kalu praises.
By having an interview with the Guru (one's) life is true (and) accepted.

X.

(Thy) nectar-sight brings on good fortune and takes away all the filth of sins and vices.
Lust, wrath, greediness and infatuation it subdues, all it overcomes.
Happiness always dwells in the mind, it removes pain from the world.
The Guru is the ocean of the nine treasures, he washes away all the blackness of the birth.
That brave[5] Guru should be served day and night with natural ease.
By having an interview with the Guru the pain of birth and death goes off.

[1] ਸਮੁ, adj. impartial, without love or hatred, or: truly (Sansk. सम). ਲਵੈ = ਤਵੈ.

[2] ਸਮਾਣਿ = ਸਮਾਣਾ.

[3] ਕਲਮਲ = Sansk किल्बिष, both *i* having been changed to *a*.

[4] ਬੋਹੈ = Sansk. बोधन, to teach, to instruct in.

[5] ਕਹੁਟਲ. The Sikhs explain this word as signifying: "Ṭalu says." But it is very unlikely that these words are to be divided into ਕਹੁ and ਟਲ, as the last line of this verse coincides verbally with the last line of the two preceding verses, which circumstance points to the same author. ਕਹੁਟਲ on the other hand, if taken as one word, is obscure. It may be compared with the Sindhī कुहटु, *a young strong man*, from which a diminutive is derived by adding the affix ल. The vowels are easily transposed and would not stand in the way of this derivation.

SAVAĪĒ REFERRING TO THE THIRD MAHALĀ.

(PANEGYRIC OF AMARDĀS.)

Ōm! By the favour of the true Guru!

(BY THE BHAṬṬ KALHU OR KALU).

I.

Remember that true divine male, whose name alone is real[1] in the world!

By which the devotees are brought over the water of existence, that foremost name remember!

Delighting in that name Nānak established Lahaṇā, in whom (are) all perfections.

By the poet Kalh the praise of the very intelligent Amardās is spread.

His fame is manifest in the world like the rays of the sun, (like) a branch of the Maulsarī shrub.[2]

In the north and south, in the east and west men mutter: "victory!"

The disciples of the Guru taste the name of Hari, which is bestowing blessings, the Gangā was reverted (by it) and turned to the west.

That name, (which) is bringing the guileless devotees over the world of (individual) existence, became manifest[3] to Guru Amardās.

II.

That name remember the Yakshas and Kinnaras, the ascetics and Siddhas in their deep meditation on Hara.

The Nakshatras and the circle of Dhrū[4] remember (it), Nārada with the others and the excellent Prahlād.

The moon and the sun delight[5] in the name, by which people hard like rocks are saved.

That name, (which) is bringing the guileless devotees over the world of (individual) existence, became manifest to Guru Amardās.

III.

Remembering that name the nine Nāths of spotless emancipation, Sanak and the others were saved.

To which being attached the eighty-four Siddhas and Buddhas (and) Ambarīk[6] crossed the water of existence;

Udhau, Akrūr, Trilōčan, Nāmā, (and by which) in the Kali-yug the guilt of Kabīr was taken away.

That name, (which) is bringing the guileless devotees over the world of (individual) existence, became manifest to Guru Amardās.

IV.

Clinging to that name the thirty-three (crores of gods) meditate (on it), it dwells in the mind of the austere and great ascetics.

[1] ਅਛਲ (from ਅ + ਛਲ), not counterfeited, true, real.

[2] ਮਉਲਸਰਾ, for the sake of the rhyme instead of ਮਉਲਸਰੀ (Hindī मौलसरी), a fragrant shrub.

[3] ਫੁਰਣਾ, *v.n.* to become manifest, to break forth (Sansk. स्फुरण).

[4] ਧ੍ਰੂ, Sansk. ध्रुव, the polar-star.

[5] ਉਲਾਸਣਾ, is intransitive in Hindī (not causal, according to the Sansk. उलासन), *to rejoice in.*

[6] ਅੰਬਰੀਕ, Sansk. अम्बरीष, King of Ayōdhyā (Oude).

Remembering that name the Gangā-born grandfather[1] tasted (in his) mind the nectar of the feet (of Hari).

By that name the society (of the saints) is saved, taking as true the weighty (and) deep instruction of the Guru.

That name, (which) is bringing the guileless devotees over the water of (individual) existence, became manifest to Guru Amardās.

V.

The fame[2] of the name in the world is (like) the rays of the sun, (like) the branches of the tree of paradise.

In the north and south, in the east and west they tell (its) glory.

The birth of him is indeed fruitful, in whose heart the name of Hari dwells.

The divisions of the gods, the Gandharvas, the six philosophical systems rely on it.[3]

Very well known is the son of Tējō,[4] Kalh, joining his hands, meditates on him.

That name, (which) takes the devotees (out of) the water of existence, thou hast obtained, O Guru Amardās!

VI.

On the name meditate the thirty-three (crores) of gods, the ascetics and the perfect (Jōgīs), by the name all the portions of the universe are upheld.

By whom the name is meditated upon he bears equally joy and grief.

The name is the diadem in all, the devotees are meditating on it.

That name, the exquisite thing,[5] was given (to thee), O Guru Amardās, by the creator, having been pleased (with thee).

VII.

(Thou art) the true hero, powerful in virtue, in true love to the society (of the saints), of great, weighty wisdom, inimical[6] to no one.

Whose firmness is quite that of the white bull,[7] (whose) flag is white, woven in paradise.[8]

The saints worship (thee) in love, whose connexion is with the creator.

By serving the true Guru comfort is obtained, by the Guru Amar (= Amardās) union (with the Supreme) is brought about.

VIII.

The name is bathing, the name is eating and enjoying of sweet flavour, the name is always sweet juice and taste, a sweet word in the mouth.

The blessed true Guru is served, by whose favour the way to the inapproachable one is known.

[1] ਗੰਗੇਵ, instead of the Sansk. गाङ्गेय, born from the Gangā. Very likely Bhīṣhma is meant, who is mentioned as the son of Šāntanu and the Gangā and represented as the sire (पितामह) of the Bharatas.

[2] ਕਿਤਿ = Sansk. कीर्त्ति, usually ਕੀਰਤਿ in Hindī.

[3] ਆਸਾਸਲਾ (Sansk. आश्वासन), *v.n.* (not causal as in Sanskrit), to rely on; to be comforted.

[4] Tējō (ਤੇਜੋ) was the name of the father of Amardās.

[5] ਪਰਾਰਥ has in Hindī the signification of an *exquisite thing, a rarity.*

[6] ਨਿਰਵੈਰ is here the abstract noun = Sansk. निर्वैर, the state of being an enemy to no one.

[7] ਧਵਲ, the white bull, which is supposed to bear the earth. See Japu, p. 5, note 3.

[8] ਘੀਲਾ p.p. of ਘੀਲਣਾ (or ਘਿਲਣਾ), to weave; in Hindī usually बुनना.

All the families are saved, the indwelling of the name is obtained.
Fruitful is the birth, says Kalu,[1] the Guru was touched, the manifestation of the immortal one.

IX.

A lotus (is) in (his) hand, at (his) right side is success, which looks straight at (his) face.
Increase dwells at (his) left side, which fascinates the three worlds.[2]
In (his) heart dwells the inexpressible one, that taste is known by him.
With (his) mouth he utters devotion, Guru Amar is steeped in this colour.
On (his) forehead is the sign (of) virtuous actions, Kal, joining his hands, meditated (on it).
(By whom) the Tilak of the Guru, the true Guru, is touched, he obtains all his wishes.

(BY THE BHAṬṬ JĀLAP.)

I. X.

The foot is indeed very[3] fruitful (= blessed), (if) the foot (be) the dust[4] of the shoe[5] of Guru Amar.
The hand is indeed very fruitful, (if) the hand (be) applied to the foot of Guru Amar.
The tongue is indeed very fruitful, (if) by the tongue Guru Amar be uttered.[6]
The eye is indeed very fruitful, (if) by the eye Guru Amar be beheld.
The ear is indeed very fruitful, (if) by the ear Guru Amar be heard.
Fruitful is that mind, in which mind dwells Guru Amardās, the world's own father.
Fruitful is that head, says Jālap, which head continually bows to Guru Amar.

II. XI.

That man has no pain nor hunger, that man is not called poor.
That man no grief befalls, from that man no account[7] is taken.
That man does service, that man offers up[8] a hundred (or) thousand (of Rupees).
That man sits on a carpet, that man establishes and disestablishes.[9]
That man obtains comfort in the world, that one has a fearless state amongst his enemies.
Fruitful is that man, says Jālap, to whom Guru Amardās is very favourable.

[1] Here the name of the poet is written ਕਲ੍ਹ, from which it is evident that both, Kalhu and Kal, are identical.

[2] ਲੋਕਾਂਤਰ cannot here signify *the other world* (Sansk. लोकान्तर), but अन्तर is added pleonastically, as in ਮੋਖਾਂਤਰ, *final emancipation.*

[3] ਤਪਰ is to be divided into ਤ (indeed = ਤਾ) and ਪਰ = अति, very, exceedingly.

[4] ਰਜ *s.f.* dust (Sindhī रई, Hindī रज्, *s.f.* from the Sansk. रजस्).

[5] ਪਵਲ, now ਪੌਲਾ *m.* shoe.

[6] ਭਣਿਜੈ is a regular passive formation, as still used in Sindhī (see my Sindhī Grammar, p. 258 *sqq.*).

[7] ਅੰਤੁ can also signify: *account*, which suits here the context very well.

[8] ਸਮਪਣਾ, to offer up (as presents), from the Sansk. समर्पण.

[9] In ਉਥਪਿ (Sansk. उत्थापन) and ਥਿਥਪਿ (Sansk. विष्ठापन) the long *a* has been shortened, which the poets do *ad libitum.*

III. XII.

By thee the One is read, the One is put in thy mind, the One is recognized.

In (thy) eye, word and mouth is the One, the One is known in both places.[1]

In (thy) dream is the One, in (thy) perception[2] is the One, in the One (thou art) absorbed.

(In) the thirty and the five the One is evinced, (in) the thirty-five he is not consumed.[3]

The One, who (is at the same time) Lākhs, is not perceptible by a mark, verifying him as the One he is described (by thee).

O Guru Amardās, says Jālap, thou desirest the One, the One is minded by thee.

IV. XIII.

Which view Jaidēv took, which view was contained in Nāmā.

Which view (was) in the mind of Trilōčan and acknowledged by the Bhagat Kabīr.

(Which was) the practice of Rukamāngad,[4] (according to that) mutter continually Rām, O brother!

Ammarīk,[5] Prahlād obtained emancipation (in) the asylum of Gōvind.

Thou hast given up greediness, wrath (and) worldly desires, thy view is known by Jalh[6] to be right.

Guru Amardās, thou art (God's) own Bhagat, having seen (thy) sight I obtain final emancipation.

V. XIV.

(If) Guru Amardās be touched, the sins[7] of the earth[8] are destroyed.

(If) Guru Amardās be touched, the perfect Jōgīs and ascetics rejoice (in it).

(If) Guru Amardās be touched, profound meditation is obtained, the falling[9] (into the womb) ceases.

(If) Guru Amardās be touched, fearlessness is obtained, going is stopped.

When a man obtains (his) excellent mantra (of initiation), then he remains united[10] with the One without duality.[11]

O Jālap, so many excellent things are obtained by seeing Guru Amardās.

(BY THE BHAṬṬ KĪRATU.)

I. XV.

"The true name is the creator," this was firmly established by Nānak.

Then Angad Lahaṇā becoming manifest remained in meditation on his (Nānak's) feet.

[1] ਦੁਹੁ ਠਾਂਇਨਿ, Formative Plur., in both places = in both worlds.

[2] ਪਰਤਖਿ, the Locative Sing. of ਪਰਤਖ, Sansk. प्रत्यक्ष *n.* perception of the senses, clear cognizance (in contradistinction to ਸੁਪਨ).

[3] This verse is a puzzle; it is very difficult to say, what is intended by these numbers.

[4] ਰੁਕਮਾਂਗਦ is said to have been a Bhagat (according to the tradition of the Sikh Granthīs), though nothing is known about him. I never found him mentioned elsewhere in the Granth.

[5] ਅੰਮਰੀਕ = ਅੰਬਰੀਕ, see p. 700, note 6.

[6] ਜਲ੍ਹ Jalh is only a shortened pronunciation of ਜਾਲਪ, as his verses are counted in a consecutive number.

[7] ਪਾਤਿਕ, Sansk. पातक.

[8] ਪੁਹਮਿ, *s.f.* the earth, from पृथिवी, *ṛ* being changed to *u* (on account of the labial), थ to *h* and व to *m*, according to the usual laws.

[9] ਪਉ *m.* falling (scil. into the womb, in contradistinction to ਗਉ, the going away, *i.e.* dying).

[10] ਜੁਤਉ = Sansk. युक्त.

[11] ਦੁਗਲ *s.f.* duality (Sansk. द्वैगुण्य).

In his (= Angad's) family is Guru Amardās, the abode of hope, how shall I describe his qualities? I know no end of those qualities, which are inconceivable and unreachable.

A ship is provided[1] by the arranger of all things (= the Supreme), the society of the saints is saving (their respective) families.

O Guru Amardās, says Kīratu, save (me), save (me), (I am in) the asylum of (thy) foot![2]

II. XVI.

Narāyaṇ himself, using his skill, was wrapt up[3] (as Avatār) in the world.
The form of the formless one was made bright in the orb of the world.
Everywhere he is brimful, the Sabd (of the Guru) was lighted by (his) lamp.
The disciples, he (the Guru) collected, he united (them) with the foot of Hari.
Nānak[4] became an Avatār in a pure[5] family, he was with Angad Lahaṇā.
O Guru Amardās, saviour of the saved, in every birth (I am in) the asylum of thy foot!

III. XVII.

Seeing the sight of the Guru muttering, austerity, goodness, contentment (accrue) to the disciples.
Who fall on (his) asylum, they are saved, laying aside the written document of Jampur (= Yamapura).
By devotion out of love he utters the creator, who is brimful in (his) heart.
The Guru is an ocean of jewels, in a moment he brings across the drowning ones.
Nānak became an Avatār in a pure family, he utters the qualities of the creator.
By whom Guru Amardās is served, them the pain of poverty leaves.

IV. XVIII.

In (my) mind I ponder (over it), I utter a petition, but am not even able to tell it.
All my thoughts are with thee, I keep in view the society of the saints.
(If) by thy order a sign is given, I do service to the Lord (*i.e.* to thee).
When the Guru looks (at me) with his auspicious glance, the name (of) the creator (is in my) mouth (like) a fruit.
What the unreachable, inconceivable ground (of all things), the divine male, commands, that I do.
Guru Amardās is the primary cause, as thou keepest me, so I remain.[6]

(BY THE BHAṬṬ BHIKĀ).

I. XIX.

The knowledge of the Guru and (his) meditation unites the substance with the (supreme) substance.
From the true one the True one is known, (if) with one thought (one) apply meditation (on him).
Lust and wrath he subdues, (so that) (the mind) does not run about flying (like) the wind.
He dwells in the region of the Formless one, having comprehended the order (of the Supreme) he gets discrimination.

[1] ਨਿਰਮਜੇ, from ਨਿਰਮਤ, and this again from the Sansk. निर्मित.
[2] ਪਾ here = ਪਾਉ or ਪਾਉਂ, foot.
[3] ਪਰਵ੍ਰਿਜਉ = Sansk. परिवारित, wrapt in, veiled up.
[4] By Nānak Guru Amardās is here understood, not Bābā Nānak.
[5] ਨਿੰਮਲੁ = ਨਿਰਮਲੁ, pure.
[6] A gross, abject flattery, identifying the Guru altogether with the Supreme Being.

In the Kali-yug he knows the form (of) the creator, the divine male, by whom something is done.[1]
That Guru was obtained (by me), says Bhikā, with natural pleasure his sight was given (to me).

II. XX.

I searched for saints, many pious people were seen by me.
Sanyāsīs were inquired after,[2] these Paṇḍits were sweet with their mouth.
One year I wandered about, no one worked a miracle.[3]
The word of the speakers I heard, but their conduct did not at all please me.
Having given up the name of Hari, they stuck to another, how shall I tell their qualities?
The Gurdēv was (at last) found, Bhikā (says): as thou keepest me, so I remain.

(BY THE BHAṬṬ SALH.)

I. XXI.

Having put on the armour of profound meditation thou art mounted on the seat of (divine) knowledge.
The bow of religion is seized by (thy) hand, thou hast fought with the arrow of devotion and virtue.
The fearless and immovable Hari is in (thy) mind, in the Sabd the lance of the Guru is buried.
Lust, wrath, covetousness, infatuation, egotism,[4] the five painful things, are broken.
(Thou art) a good king, O son of Tējō, the Lord of kings, O excellent Nānak.[5]
O Guru Amardās, Salh speaks truth, thus carrying on war thou hast overcome the (hostile) army.

(BY THE BHAṬṬ BHALHAU.)

I. XXII.

The drops of a cloud, the verdure of the earth, the flowers of spring cannot be counted.

No one gets the end of the rays of the sun and moon, of the belly of the ocean, of the waves of the Gangā.

The profound meditation of Rudra does not come up[6] to the (divine) knowledge of the true Guru, (says) the poet Bhalhau.

O Amardās, the Bhalā,[7] thy qualities and thy likeness agree (only) with thee!

[1] The words by themselves are plain enough, but the sense of them is obscure.

[2] ਤਪਸੀਅਹਿ, passive of ਤਪਸਣਾ (= ਤਪਾਸਣਾ), to inquire after.

[3] ਪਰਚਉ *s.m.* traditionally explained by *miracle.*

[4] ਅਪਤੁ (properly pronounced appattu), from the Sansk. आत्मत्व, = ਅਹੰਕਾਰ, egotism. आत्मा is in Prakrit changed to *appā*, and *tva* to *ttu*.

[5] ਨਾਨਕ ਬਰਿ, not to be translated by: *the best of Nānaks*, but simply: *excellent Nānak*, as the Sikhs will have it.

[6] ਜੋਗਾਦੈ; thus the word is now written in all the manuscripts, but it should be divided into ਜੋਗ and ਆਦੈ, as ਜੋਗਾਦੈ gives no sense here, whereas ਜੋਗ ਆਦੈ well suits the construction (with ਕੇ).

[7] ਭਲਾ, a proper noun of a tribe of Khatrīs. Amardās was a Khatrī of the Bhalā clan.

SLŌKS OF MAHALĀ IX. (TĒG BAHĀDUR.)[1]

By the favour of the true Guru!

(1). The praises of Gōvind are not sung, uselessly thou hast been born.
Nānak says: worship Hari, O mind, as the fish (worships) the water.
(2). Why art thou occupied with worldly things and art not a moment retired?
Nānak says: worship Hari, O mind, (then) the noose of Yama will not fall on thee.
(3). Youth is thus gone, the body is overcome by old age.
Nānak says: worship Hari, O mind, life is passing away.
(4). Thou hast become old and dost not perceive, that death has arrived.
Nānak says: O foolish man, why dost thou not worship the Lord?
(5). Wealth, wife, all riches, which thou hast considered as thy own:
Of these nothing goes with (thee), consider this as true, (says) Nānak.
(6). The saviour of the fallen sinners, the remover of fear, Hari, the friend of the friendless:
He should be known, says Nānak, who is always dwelling with thee.
(7). By whom body and wealth were given to thee, him thou hast not loved.
Nānak says: O foolish man, why art thou now roaming about needy?
(8). By whom body, wealth, prosperity, comfort and good houses were given:
Nānak says: hear, O mind, why art thou not remembering that Rām?
(9). The giver of all comfort is Rām, there is no other one at all.
Nānak says: hear, O mind, by remembering him salvation is effected.
(10). By remembering whom salvation is obtained, him worship, O thou friend!
Nānak says: hear, O mind, life is continually decreasing.
(11). From the five elements the body is made, know (this), O clever and wise one!
From what it was produced, into that it is absorbed,[2] (says) Nānak.
(12). Hari, who dwells in everybody, (as) proclaimed by the saints:
Nānak says: him worship, O mind, and thou wilt cross the ocean of existence.
(13). Whom pleasure and pain do not touch, nor greediness, infatuation and conceit:
Nānak says: O mind, he is the image of the Lord.
(14). (For whom there is) no praise nor blame, to whom gold and iron are the same:
Nānak says: hear, O mind, him consider thou as emancipated!
(15). Who has no joy nor grief, to whom enemy and friend is the same:
Nānak says: hear, O mind, him consider thou as emancipated!
(16). Who is not causing fear to any one and who is not afraid nor submissive:[3]
Nānak says: hear, O mind, him call thou wise!
(17). By whom all worldly concerns are given up and who has taken the garb of retirement from the world:
Nānak says: hear, O mind, on his head is (an auspicious) lot.
(18). By whom the Māyā and selfishness are given up and who has become indifferent to all:
Nānak says: hear, O mind, in his heart Brahm is dwelling.

[1] These Slōks are written in pure Hindī, having no admixture of the Panjābī dialect.

[2] ਲੀਨ ਤਾਹਿ ਮੈ ਮਾਨ; ਮਾਨ p.p. = the more usual ਸਮਾਨਾ; literally: in that it is immersed (and) absorbed.

[3] ਮਾਨਿ *s.f.* submissiveness (Sindhī माणि); ਮਾਨਿ ਮਾਨਣੀ, to be submissive.

(19). By which man the "I," "I," is given up and Rām, the creator, is known:
Nānak says: that man is emancipated, know this, O mind, as true!
(20). "Destroyer of fear, remover of folly," is the name of Hari in the Kali-yug.
Who day and night worships (him), says Nānak, his work becomes fruitful.
(21). O tongue, adore the qualities of Gōvind, O ear, hear the name of Hari!
Nānak says: hear, O mind, thou wilt not (then) fall into the house of Yama.
(22). Which man gives up selfishness, greediness, infatuation and conceit:
Nānak says: he himself crosses and saves others.
(23). Like a dream and play consider the world!
In these there is no reality without the Lord, (says) Nānak.
(24). Day and night man roams continually about for the sake of the Māyā.
Amongst Crores, says Nānak, there is some (rare) one, who thinks of Narāyaṇ.
(25). As a bubble is produced from the water and disappears continually:
So is the forming of the world made, hear, O friend, says Nānak.
(26). Man does not think of anything, he is blind by the wine of the Māyā.
Nānak says: without worshipping Hari the noose of Yama falls on him.
(27). If thou desirest comfort, take always the asylum of Rām!
Nānak says: hear, O mind, the body of man is hard to get.
(28). For the sake of the Māyā the foolish, ignorant people run.
Nānak says: without worshipping Hari life is uselessly passed.
(29). Which man worships (him) day and night, him consider as the form of Rām!
Between Hari and the people of Hari there is no difference, Nānak (says): mind (this) as true!
(30). The mind is ensnared in the Māyā, the name of Gōvind is forgotten.
Nānak says: without worshipping Hari of what use is life?
(31). Man does not think of Rām, he is blind by the intoxicating liquor of the Māyā.
Nānak says: without worshipping Hari the noose of Yama falls on him.
(32). In pleasure many have become companions, in pain there is none.
Nānak says: worship Hari, O mind, at the end he is thy help.
(33). In various births (I) have wandered about, the fear of Yama was not effaced.
Nānak says: worship Hari, O mind, and thou wilt get a dwelling free from fear.
(34). I made many efforts, but the conceit of my mind was not effaced.
With folly Nānak is ensnared, save me, O Lord!
(35). Childhood, youth and old age consider as three stations of life!
Nānak says: without worshipping Hari take all as useless!
(36). What was[1] to be done, that thou hast not done, thou hast fallen into the snare of covetousness.
Nānak (says): the time is past, why art thou now weeping, O blind one?
(37). (Thy) mind is wandering about in the Māyā, it does not go out of her, O friend!
Like as the paint of a form does not leave the wall, (says) Nānak.
(38). Man is desiring something else and something quite different has happened.
He was pondering on a roguery and the noose has fallen on his neck, (says) Nānak.
(39). Many efforts were made for the sake of pleasure, for the sake of pain not any one was made.
Nānak says: hear, O mind, what pleases Hari, that takes place.
(40). The world wanders about begging, Rām is giving to every one.
Nānak says: O mind, remember him, thy business becomes (thereby) completed.
(41). Why dost thou entertain false conceit, know, the world is like a dream.
Among these (things) nothing is thine, this asserts Nānak.

[1] ਹੁਤੇ = ਹੋਤੇ (ہوتا.)

(42). Thou art proud of (thy) body, which is destroyed in a moment, O friend!
By which man the praise of Hari is said, by him the world is overcome, (says) Nānak.
(43). In whose heart there is the remembrance of Rām, know, that man is emancipated.
Between that man and Hari there is no difference, mind this as true, (says) Nānak.
(44). In which man's heart there is not devotion to the One Lord:
His body consider like that of a hog (or) dog, (says) Nānak.
(45). As a dog never forsakes the house of his master:
In this wise worship Hari, (says) Nānak, with one mind and thought.
(46). Who (goes to) Tīrthas, (keeps) fasts (and) gives alms and entertains conceit[1] in (his) mind:
To him it is fruitless, (says) Nānak, like the bathing of an elephant.
(47). The head shakes, the foot totters, the eye is without light:
Nānak says: (though) this state has set in, love to Hari is not taken up.
(48). I have accurately beheld the world: no one is any one's.
Nānak (says): firm is (only) devotion to Hari, keep that in (thy) mind!
(49). The formation of the world is all falsehood, know this, O friend!
Nānak says: like a wall of sand it does not remain firm.
(50). Rām is gone, Rāvan is gone, who had a great retinue.
Nānak says: nothing remains firm, the world is like a dream.
(51). Anxiety is entertained about that, which does not take place.
This is the way of the world; Nānak (says): no one remains firm.
(52). What is produced, that will be destroyed (again), next year, to-day or to-morrow.
Nānak (says): sing the praises of Hari, giving up all troubles!

Dōhrā (Distich).[2]

(53). (My) strength is exhausted, fetters have fallen (on me), there is no expedient whatever.
Nānak says: now Hari is my refuge, like an elephant he will become my helper.
(54). All my companions and friends have forsaken me, no one has gone on with me.
Nānak (says): in this calamity (my) trust is the One Ragu-nāth.[3]
(55). The name has remained, the saint[4] has remained, Guru Gōvind has remained.
Nānak (says): in this world by some (rare one) the mantra of the Guru is muttered.
(56). The name of Rām is laid hold of (by me) in (my) breast, to whom no one is equal.
By remembering whom the distress is effaced and thy sight is obtained.

Dōhrā; mahalā X.[5]

Strength is afforded, the fetters are loosened, everything becomes an expedient.
Everything is in thy hand, even thou art thy (own) helper.

[1] ਗੁਮਾਨੁ has also the sense of *conceit, pride* in Panǰābī (Pers. گمان).

[2] These Dōhrās were written by Tēg Bahādur, when in prison at Dillī, to his son Gōvind Singh, who was then at Anandpur. See Sikhā̃ dē rāǰ dī vithiā, p. 51.

[3] ਰਘੁ ਨਾਥ, one of the names of Rāma (the same as रघुपति).

[4] By the ਸਾਧੁ very likely Bābā Nānak is understood.

[5] This is the answer of Gōvind Singh to the preceding Dōhrās, and the only verse of Gōvind Singh that was received into the Ādi Granth.

FINIS.

APPENDIX.

ORIGINAL TEXT OF THE JAPJĪ.

(In the original all words are joined, as in Sanskrit manuscripts, we have separated them for the sake of distinctness.)

ੴ ਸਤਿ ਨਾਮੁ ਕਰਤਾ ਪੁਰਖੁ ਨਿਰਭਉ ਨਿਰਵੈਰੁ ਅਕਾਲ ਮੂਰਤਿ ਅਜੂਨੀ ਸੈਭੰ ਗੁਰ ਪ੍ਰਸਾਦਿ ॥

ਜਪੁ ॥

ਆਦਿ ਸਚੁ ਜੁਗਾਦਿ ਸਚੁ ॥ ਹੈ ਭੀ ਸਚੁ ਨਾਨਕ ਹੋਸੀ ਭੀ ਸਚੁ ॥ ੧

ਸੋਚੈ ਸੋਚਿ ਨ ਹੋਵਈ ਜੇ ਸੋਚੀ ਲਖ ਵਾਰ ॥ ਚੁਪੈ ਚੁਪ ਨ ਹੋਵਈ ਜੇ ਲਾਇ ਰਹਾ ਲਿਵ ਤਾਰ ॥
ਭੁਖਿਆ ਭੁਖ ਨ ਉਤਰੀ ਜੇ ਬੰਨਾ ਪੁਰੀਆ ਭਾਰ ॥
ਸਹਸ ਸਿਆਣਪਾ ਲਖ ਹੋਹਿ ਤ ਇਕ ਨ ਚਲੈ ਨਾਲਿ ॥ ਕਿਵ ਸਚਿਆਰਾ ਹੋਈਐ ਕਿਵ ਕੂੜੈ ਤੁਟੈ ਪਾਲਿ ॥
ਹੁਕਮਿ ਰਜਾਈ ਚਲਣਾ ਨਾਨਕ ਲਿਖਿਆ ਨਾਲਿ ॥ ੧

ਹੁਕਮੀ ਹੋਵਨਿ ਆਕਾਰ ਹੁਕਮੁ ਨ ਕਹਿਆ ਜਾਈ ॥ ਹੁਕਮੀ ਹੋਵਨਿ ਜੀਅ ਹੁਕਮਿ ਮਿਲੈ ਵਡਿਆਈ ॥
ਹੁਕਮੀ ਉਤਮੁ ਨੀਚੁ ਹੁਕਮਿ ਲਿਖਿ ਦੁਖ ਸੁਖ ਪਾਈਅਹਿ ॥ ਇਕਨਾ ਹੁਕਮੀ ਬਖਸੀਸ ਇਕਿ ਹੁਕਮੀ ਸਦਾ ਭਵਾਈਅਹਿ ॥
ਹੁਕਮੈ ਅੰਦਰਿ ਸਭੁ ਕੋ ਬਾਹਰਿ ਹੁਕਮ ਨ ਕੋਇ ॥ ਨਾਨਕ ਹੁਕਮੈ ਜੇ ਬੁਝੈ ਤ ਹਉਮੈ ਕਹੈ ਨ ਕੋਇ ॥ ੨

ਗਾਵੈ ਕੋ ਤਾਣੁ ਹੋਵੈ ਕਿਸੈ ਤਾਣੁ ॥ ਗਾਵੈ ਕੋ ਦਾਤਿ ਜਾਣੈ ਨੀਸਾਣੁ ॥
ਗਾਵੈ ਕੋ ਗੁਣ ਵਡਿਆਈਆ ਚਾਰੁ ॥ ਗਾਵੈ ਕੋ ਵਿਦਿਆ ਵਿਖਮੁ ਵੀਚਾਰੁ ॥
ਗਾਵੈ ਕੋ ਸਾਜਿ ਕਰੇ ਤਨੁ ਖੇਹ ॥ ਗਾਵੈ ਕੋ ਜੀਅ ਲੈ ਫਿਰਿ ਦੇਹ ॥
ਗਾਵੈ ਕੋ ਜਾਪੈ ਦਿਸੈ ਦੂਰਿ ॥ ਗਾਵੈ ਕੋ ਵੇਖੈ ਹਾਦਰਾ ਹਦੂਰਿ ॥
ਕਥਨਾ ਕਥੀ ਨ ਆਵੈ ਤੋਟਿ ॥ ਕਥਿ ਕਥਿ ਕਥੀ ਕੋਟੀ ਕੋਟੀ ਕੋਟਿ ॥
ਦੇਦਾ ਦੇ ਲੈਦੇ ਥਕਿ ਪਾਹਿ ॥ ਜੁਗਾ ਜੁਗੰਤਰਿ ਖਾਹੀ ਖਾਹਿ ॥
ਹੁਕਮੀ ਹੁਕਮੁ ਚਲਾਏ ਰਾਹੁ ॥ ਨਾਨਕ ਵਿਗਸੈ ਵੇਪਰਵਾਹੁ ॥ ੩

ਸਾਚਾ ਸਾਹਿਬੁ ਸਾਚੁ ਨਾਇ ਭਾਖਿਆ ਭਾਉ ਅਪਾਰੁ ॥ ਆਖਹਿ ਮੰਗਹਿ ਦੇਹਿ ਦੇਹਿ ਦਾਤਿ ਕਰੇ ਦਾਤਾਰੁ ॥
ਫੇਰਿ ਕਿ ਅਗੈ ਰਖੀਐ ਜਿਤੁ ਦਿਸੈ ਦਰਬਾਰੁ ॥ ਮੁਹੌ ਕਿ ਬੋਲਣੁ ਬੋਲੀਐ ਜਿਤੁ ਸੁਣਿ ਧਰੇ ਪਿਆਰੁ ॥
ਅਮ੍ਰਿਤ ਵੇਲਾ ਸਚੁ ਨਾਉ ਵਡਿਆਈ ਵੀਚਾਰੁ ॥ ਕਰਮੀ ਆਵੈ ਕਪੜਾ ਨਦਰੀ ਮੋਖੁ ਦੁਆਰੁ ॥
ਨਾਨਕ ਏਵੈ ਜਾਣੀਐ ਸਭੁ ਆਪੇ ਸਚਿਆਰੁ ॥ ੪

ਥਾਪਿਆ ਨ ਜਾਇ ਕੀਤਾ ਨ ਹੋਇ ॥ ਆਪੇ ਆਪਿ ਨਿਰੰਜਨੁ ਸੋਇ ॥
ਜਿਨਿ ਸੇਵਿਆ ਤਿਨਿ ਪਾਇਆ ਮਾਨੁ ॥ ਨਾਨਕ ਗਾਵੀਐ ਗੁਣੀ ਨਿਧਾਨੁ ॥
ਗਾਵੀਐ ਸੁਣੀਐ ਮਨਿ ਰਖੀਐ ਭਾਉ ॥ ਦੁਖੁ ਪਰਹਰਿ ਸੁਖੁ ਘਰਿ ਲੈ ਜਾਇ ॥
ਗੁਰ ਮੁਖਿ ਨਾਦੰ ਗੁਰ ਮੁਖਿ ਵੇਦੰ ਗੁਰਮੁਖਿ ਰਹਿਆ ਸਮਾਈ ॥ ਗੁਰੁ ਈਸਰੁ ਗੁਰੁ ਗੋਰਖੁ ਬਰਮਾ ਗੁਰੁ ਪਾਰਬਤੀ ਮਾਈ ॥

ਜੇ ਹਉ ਜਾਣਾ ਆਖਾ ਨਾਹੀ ਕਹਣਾ ਕਥਨੁ ਨ ਜਾਈ ॥ ਗੁਰਾ ਇਕ ਦੇਹਿ ਬੁਝਾਈ ॥
ਸਭਨਾ ਜੀਆ ਕਾ ਇਕੁ ਦਾਤਾ ਸੋ ਮੈ ਵਿਸਰਿ ਨ ਜਾਈ ॥ ੫

ਤੀਰਥਿ ਨਾਵਾ ਜੇ ਤਿਸੁ ਭਾਵਾ ਵਿਣੁ ਭਾਣੇ ਕਿ ਨਾਇ ਕਰੀ ॥ ਜੇਤੀ ਸਿਰਠਿ ਉਪਾਈ ਵੇਖਾ ਵਿਣੁ ਕਰਮਾ ਕਿ ਮਿਲੈ ਲਈ ॥
ਮਤਿ ਵਿਚਿ ਰਤਨ ਜਵਾਹਰ ਮਾਣਿਕ ਜੇ ਇਕ ਗੁਰ ਕੀ ਸਿਖ ਸੁਣੀ ॥ ਗੁਰਾ ਇਕ ਦੇਹਿ ਬੁਝਾਈ ॥
ਸਭਨਾ ਜੀਆ ਕਾ ਇਕੁ ਦਾਤਾ ਸੋ ਮੈ ਵਿਸਰਿ ਨ ਜਾਈ ॥ ੬

ਜੇ ਜੁਗ ਚਾਰੇ ਆਰਜਾ ਹੋਰ ਦਸੂਣੀ ਹੋਇ ॥ ਨਵਾ ਖੰਡਾ ਵਿਚਿ ਜਾਣੀਐ ਨਾਲਿ ਚਲੈ ਸਭੁ ਕੋਇ ॥
ਚੰਗਾ ਨਾਉ ਰਖਾਇਕੈ ਜਸੁ ਕੀਰਤਿ ਜਗਿ ਲੇਇ ॥ ਜੇ ਤਿਸੁ ਨਦਰਿ ਨ ਆਵਈ ਤ ਵਾਤ ਨ ਪੁਛੈ ਕੇਇ ॥
ਕੀਟਾ ਅੰਦਰਿ ਕੀਟੁ ਕਰਿ ਦੋਸੀ ਦੋਸੁ ਧਰੇ ॥ ਨਾਨਕ ਨਿਰਗੁਣਿ ਗੁਣ ਕਰੇ ਗੁਣਵੰਤਿਆ ਗੁਣ ਦੇ ॥
ਤੇਹਾ ਕੋਇ ਨ ਸੁਝਈ ਜਿ ਤਿਸੁ ਗੁਣ ਕੋਇ ਕਰੇ ॥ ੭

ਸੁਣਿਐ ਸਿਧ ਪੀਰ ਸੁਰਿ ਨਾਥ ॥ ਸੁਣਿਐ ਧਰਤਿ ਧਵਲ ਆਕਾਸ ॥
ਸੁਣਿਐ ਦੀਪ ਲੋਅ ਪਾਤਾਲ ॥ ਸੁਣਿਐ ਪੋਹਿ ਨ ਸਕੈ ਕਾਲ ॥
ਨਾਨਕ ਭਗਤਾ ਸਦਾ ਵਿਗਾਸੁ ॥ ਸੁਣਿਐ ਦੂਖ ਪਾਪ ਕਾ ਨਾਸੁ ॥ ੮

ਸੁਣਿਐ ਈਸਰੁ ਬਰਮਾ ਇੰਦੁ ॥ ਸੁਣਿਐ ਮੁਖਿ ਸਲਾਹਣ ਮੰਦੁ ॥
ਸੁਣਿਐ ਜੋਗ ਜੁਗਤਿ ਤਨਿ ਭੇਦ ॥ ਸੁਣਿਐ ਸਾਸਤ ਸਿਮ੍ਰਿਤਿ ਵੇਦ ॥
ਨਾਨਕ ਭਗਤਾ ਸਦਾ ਵਿਗਾਸੁ ॥ ਸੁਣਿਐ ਦੂਖ ਪਾਪ ਕਾ ਨਾਸੁ ॥ ੯

ਸੁਣਿਐ ਸਤੁ ਸੰਤੋਖੁ ਗਿਆਨੁ ॥ ਸੁਣਿਐ ਅਠਸਠਿ ਕਾ ਇਸਨਾਨੁ ॥
ਸੁਣਿਐ ਪੜਿ ਪੜਿ ਪਾਵਹਿ ਮਾਨੁ ॥ ਸੁਣਿਐ ਲਾਗੈ ਸਹਜਿ ਧਿਆਨੁ ॥
ਨਾਨਕ ਭਗਤਾ ਸਦਾ ਵਿਗਾਸੁ ॥ ਸੁਣਿਐ ਦੂਖ ਪਾਪ ਕਾ ਨਾਸੁ ॥ ੧੦

ਸੁਣਿਐ ਸਰਾ ਗੁਣਾ ਕੇ ਗਾਹੁ ॥ ਸੁਣਿਐ ਸੇਖ ਪੀਰ ਪਾਤਿਸਾਹੁ ॥
ਸੁਣਿਐ ਅੰਧੇ ਪਾਵਹਿ ਰਾਹੁ ॥ ਸੁਣਿਐ ਹਾਥ ਹੋਵੈ ਅਸਗਾਹੁ ॥
ਨਾਨਕ ਭਗਤਾ ਸਦਾ ਵਿਗਾਸੁ ॥ ਸੁਣਿਐ ਦੂਖ ਪਾਪ ਕਾ ਨਾਸੁ ॥ ੧੧

ਮੰਨੇ ਕੀ ਗਤਿ ਕਹੀ ਨ ਜਾਇ ॥ ਜੇ ਕੋ ਕਹੈ ਪਿਛੈ ਪਛੁਤਾਇ ॥
ਕਾਗਦਿ ਕਲਮ ਨ ਲਿਖਣਹਾਰੁ ॥ ਮੰਨੇ ਕਾ ਬਹਿ ਕਰਨਿ ਵੀਚਾਰੁ ॥
ਐਸਾ ਨਾਮੁ ਨਿਰੰਜਨੁ ਹੋਇ ॥ ਜੇ ਕੋ ਮੰਨਿ ਜਾਣੈ ਮਨਿ ਕੋਇ ॥ ੧੨

ਮੰਨੈ ਸੁਰਤਿ ਹੋਵੈ ਮਨਿ ਬੁਧਿ ॥ ਮੰਨੈ ਸਗਲ ਭਵਣ ਕੀ ਸੁਧਿ ॥
ਮੰਨੈ ਮੁਹਿ ਚੋਟਾ ਨਾ ਖਾਇ ॥ ਮੰਨੈ ਜਮ ਕੈ ਸਾਥਿ ਨ ਜਾਇ ॥
ਐਸਾ ਨਾਮੁ ਨਿਰੰਜਨੁ ਹੋਇ ॥ ਜੇ ਕੋ ਮੰਨਿ ਜਾਣੈ ਮਨਿ ਕੋਇ ॥ ੧੩

ਮੰਨੈ ਮਾਰਗਿ ਠਾਕ ਨ ਪਾਇ ॥ ਮੰਨੈ ਪਤਿ ਸਿਉ ਪਰਗਟੁ ਜਾਇ ॥
ਮੰਨੈ ਮਗੁ ਨ ਚਲੈ ਪੰਥੁ ॥ ਮੰਨੈ ਧਰਮ ਸੇਤੀ ਸਨਬੰਧੁ ॥
ਐਸਾ ਨਾਮੁ ਨਿਰੰਜਨੁ ਹੋਇ ॥ ਜੇ ਕੋ ਮੰਨਿ ਜਾਣੈ ਮਨਿ ਕੋਇ ॥ ੧੪

ਮੰਨੈ ਪਾਵਹਿ ਮੋਖ ਦੁਆਰੁ ॥ ਮੰਨੈ ਪਰਵਾਰੈ ਸਾਧਾਰੁ ॥
ਮੰਨੈ ਤਰੈ ਤਾਰੇ ਗੁਰ ਸਿਖ ॥ ਮੰਨੈ ਨਾਨਕ ਭਵਹਿ ਨ ਭਿਖ ॥
ਐਸਾ ਨਾਮੁ ਨਿਰੰਜਨੁ ਹੋਇ ॥ ਜੇ ਕੋ ਮੰਨਿ ਜਾਣੈ ਮਨਿ ਕੋਇ ॥ ੧੫

ਪੰਚ ਪਰਵਾਣ ਪੰਚ ਪਰਧਾਨੁ ॥ ਪੰਚੇ ਪਾਵਹਿ ਦਰਗਹ ਮਾਨੁ ॥
ਪੰਚੇ ਸੋਹਹਿ ਦਰਿ ਰਾਜਾਨੁ ॥ ਪੰਚਾ ਕਾ ਗੁਰੁ ਏਕੁ ਧਿਆਨੁ ॥
ਜੇ ਕੋ ਕਹੈ ਕਰੈ ਵੀਚਾਰੁ ॥ ਕਰਤੈ ਕੈ ਕਰਣੈ ਨਾਹੀ ਸੁਮਾਰੁ ॥
ਧੋਲੁ ਧਰਮੁ ਦਇਆ ਕਾ ਪੂਤੁ ॥ ਸੰਤੋਖੁ ਥਾਪਿ ਰਖਿਆ ਜਿਨਿ ਸੁਤਿ ॥
ਜੇ ਕੋ ਬੁਝੈ ਹੋਵੈ ਸਚਿਆਰੁ ॥ ਧਵਲੈ ਉਪਰਿ ਕੇਤਾ ਭਾਰੁ ॥
ਧਰਤੀ ਹੋਰੁ ਪਰੈ ਹੋਰੁ ਹੋਰੁ ॥ ਤਿਸ ਤੇ ਭਾਰੁ ਤਲੈ ਕਵਣ ਜੋਰੁ ॥
ਜੀਅ ਜਾਤਿ ਰੰਗਾ ਕੇ ਨਾਵ ॥ ਸਭਨਾ ਲਿਖਿਆ ਵੁੜੀ ਕਲਾਮ ॥
ਏਹੁ ਲੇਖਾ ਲਿਖਿ ਜਾਣੈ ਕੋਇ ॥ ਲੇਖਾ ਲਿਖਿਆ ਕੇਤਾ ਹੋਇ ॥
ਕੇਤਾ ਤਾਣੁ ਸੁਆਲਿਹੁ ਰੂਪੁ ॥ ਕੇਤੀ ਦਾਤਿ ਜਾਣੈ ਕਉਣੁ ਕੂਤੁ ॥
ਕੀਤਾ ਪਸਾਉ ਏਕੋ ਕਵਾਉ ॥ ਤਿਸ ਤੇ ਹੋਏ ਲਖ ਦਰੀਆਉ ॥
ਕੁਦਰਤਿ ਕਵਣ ਕਹਾ ਵੀਚਾਰੁ ॥ ਵਾਰਿਆ ਨ ਜਾਵਾ ਏਕ ਵਾਰੁ ॥
ਜੋ ਤੁਧੁ ਭਾਵੈ ਸਾਈ ਭਲੀ ਕਾਰ ॥ ਤੂ ਸਦਾ ਸਲਾਮਤਿ ਨਿਰੰਕਾਰ ॥ ੧੬

ਅਸੰਖ ਜਪ ਅਸੰਖ ਭਾਉ ॥ ਅਸੰਖ ਪੂਜਾ ਅਸੰਖ ਤਪ ਤਾਉ ॥
ਅਸੰਖ ਗਰੰਥ ਮੁਖਿ ਵੇਦ ਪਾਠ ॥ ਅਸੰਖ ਜੋਗ ਮਨਿ ਰਹਹਿ ਉਦਾਸ ॥
ਅਸੰਖ ਭਗਤ ਗੁਣ ਗਿਆਨ ਵੀਚਾਰ ॥ ਅਸੰਖ ਸਤੀ ਅਸੰਖ ਦਾਤਾਰ ॥
ਅਸੰਖ ਸੂਰ ਮੁਹ ਭਖਸਾਰ ॥ ਅਸੰਖ ਮੋਨਿ ਲਿਵ ਲਾਇ ਤਾਰ ॥
ਕੁਦਰਤਿ ਕਵਣ ਕਹਾ ਵੀਚਾਰੁ ॥ ਵਾਰਿਆ ਨ ਜਾਵਾ ਏਕ ਵਾਰੁ ॥
ਜੋ ਤੁਧੁ ਭਾਵੈ ਸਾਈ ਭਲੀ ਕਾਰ ॥ ਤੂ ਸਦਾ ਸਲਾਮਤਿ ਨਿਰੰਕਾਰ ॥ ੧੭

ਅਸੰਖ ਮੂਰਖ ਅੰਧ ਘੋਰ ॥ ਅਸੰਖ ਚੋਰ ਹਰਾਮਖੋਰ ॥
ਅਸੰਖ ਅਮਰ ਕਰਿ ਜਾਹਿ ਜੋਰ ॥ ਅਸੰਖ ਗਲਵਢ ਹਤਿਆ ਕਮਾਹਿ ॥
ਅਸੰਖ ਪਾਪੀ ਪਾਪੁ ਕਰਿ ਜਾਹਿ ॥ ਅਸੰਖ ਕੂੜਿਆਰ ਕੂੜੇ ਫਿਰਾਹਿ ॥
ਅਸੰਖ ਮਲੇਛ ਮਲੁ ਭਖਿ ਖਾਹਿ ॥
ਅਸੰਖ ਨਿੰਦਕ ਸਿਰਿ ਕਰਹਿ ਭਾਰੁ ॥
ਨਾਨਕੁ ਨੀਚੁ ਕਹੈ ਵੀਚਾਰੁ ॥ ਵਾਰਿਆ ਨ ਜਾਵਾ ਏਕ ਵਾਰੁ ॥
ਜੋ ਤੁਧੁ ਭਾਵੈ ਸਾਈ ਭਲੀ ਕਾਰ ॥ ਤੂ ਸਦਾ ਸਲਾਮਤਿ ਨਿਰੰਕਾਰ ॥ ੧੮

ਅਸੰਖ ਨਾਵ ਅਸੰਖ ਥਾਵ ॥ ਅਗੰਮ ਅਗੰਮ ਅਸੰਖ ਲੋਅ ॥
ਅਸੰਖ ਕਹਹਿ ਸਿਰਿ ਭਾਰੁ ਹੋਇ ॥
ਅਖਰੀ ਨਾਮੁ ਅਖਰੀ ਸਾਲਾਹ ॥ ਅਖਰੀ ਗਿਆਨੁ ਗੀਤ ਗੁਣ ਗਾਹ ॥
ਅਖਰੀ ਲਿਖਣੁ ਬੋਲਣੁ ਬਾਣਿ ॥ ਅਖਰਾ ਸਿਰਿ ਸੰਜੋਗੁ ਵਖਾਣਿ ॥
ਜਿਨਿ ਏਹ ਲਿਖੇ ਤਿਸੁ ਸਿਰਿ ਨਾਹਿ ॥ ਜਿਵ ਫੁਰਮਾਏ ਤਿਵ ਤਿਵ ਪਾਹਿ ॥
ਜੇਤਾ ਕੀਤਾ ਤੇਤਾ ਨਾਉ ॥ ਵਿਣੁ ਨਾਵੈ ਨਾਹੀ ਕੋ ਥਾਉ ॥
ਕੁਦਰਤਿ ਕਵਣ ਕਹਾ ਵੀਚਾਰੁ ॥ ਵਾਰਿਆ ਨ ਜਾਵਾ ਏਕ ਵਾਰੁ ॥
ਜੋ ਤੁਧੁ ਭਾਵੈ ਸਾਈ ਭਲੀ ਕਾਰ ॥ ਤੂ ਸਦਾ ਸਲਾਮਤਿ ਨਿਰੰਕਾਰ ॥ ੧੯

ਭਰੀਐ ਹਥੁ ਪੈਰੁ ਤਨੁ ਦੇਹ ॥ ਪਾਣੀ ਧੋਤੈ ਉਤਰਸੁ ਖੇਹ ॥
ਮੂਤ ਪਲੀਤੀ ਕਪੜੁ ਹੋਇ ॥ ਦੇ ਸਾਬੂਣੁ ਲਈਐ ਓਹੁ ਧੋਇ ॥
ਭਰੀਐ ਮਤਿ ਪਾਪਾ ਕੈ ਸੰਗਿ ॥ ਓਹੁ ਧੋਪੈ ਨਾਵੈ ਕੈ ਰੰਗਿ ॥

ਪੁਨੀ ਪਾਪੀ ਆਖਣੁ ਨਾਹਿ ॥ ਕਰਿ ਕਰਿ ਕਰਣਾ ਲਿਖਿ ਲੈ ਜਾਹੁ ॥
ਆਪੇ ਬੀਜਿ ਆਪੇਹੀ ਖਾਹੁ ॥ ਨਾਨਕ ਹੁਕਮੀ ਆਵਹੁ ਜਾਹੁ ॥ ੨੦

ਤੀਰਥੁ ਤਪੁ ਦਇਆ ਦਤੁ ਦਾਨੁ ॥ ਜੇ ਕੋ ਪਾਵੈ ਤਿਲ ਕਾ ਮਾਨੁ ॥
ਸੁਣਿਆ ਮੰਨਿਆ ਮਨਿ ਕੀਤਾ ਭਾਉ ॥ ਅੰਤਰਗਤਿ ਤੀਰਥਿ ਮਲਿ ਨਾਉ ॥
ਸਭਿ ਗੁਣ ਤੇਰੇ ਮੈ ਨਾਹੀ ਕੋਇ ॥ ਵਿਣੁ ਗੁਣ ਕੀਤੇ ਭਗਤਿ ਨ ਹੋਇ ॥
ਸੁਅਸਤਿ ਆਥਿ ਬਾਣੀ ਬਰਮਾਉ ॥ ਸਤਿ ਸੁਹਾਣੁ ਸਦਾ ਮਨਿ ਚਾਉ ॥
ਕਵਣੁ ਸੁ ਵੇਲਾ ਵਖਤੁ ਕਵਣੁ ਕਵਣੁ ਥਿਤਿ ਕਵਣ ਵਾਰੁ ॥ ਕਵਣਿ ਸਿ ਰੁਤੀ ਮਾਹੁ ਕਵਣੁ ਜਿਤੁ ਹੋਆ ਆਕਾਰੁ ॥
ਵੇਲ ਨ ਪਾਈਆ ਪੰਡਤੀ ਜਿ ਹੋਵੈ ਲੇਖੁ ਪੁਰਾਣੁ ॥ ਵਖਤੁ ਨ ਪਾਇਓ ਕਾਦੀਆ ਜਿ ਲਿਖਨਿ ਲੇਖੁ ਕੁਰਾਣੁ ॥
ਥਿਤਿ ਵਾਰੁ ਨ ਜੋਗੀ ਜਾਣੈ ਰੁਤਿ ਮਾਹੁ ਨ ਕੋਈ ॥ ਜਾ ਕਰਤਾ ਸਿਰਠੀ ਕਉ ਸਾਜੇ ਆਪੇ ਜਾਣੈ ਸੋਈ ॥
ਕਿਵਕਰਿ ਆਖਾ ਕਿਵ ਸਾਲਾਹੀ ਕਿਉ ਵਰਨੀ ਕਿਵ ਜਾਣਾ ॥ ਨਾਨਕ ਆਖਣਿ ਸਭੁਕੋ ਆਖੈ ਇਕ ਦੂ ਇਕੁ ਸਿਆਣਾ ॥
ਵਡਾ ਸਾਹਿਬੁ ਵਡੀ ਨਾਈ ਕੀਤਾ ਜਾ ਕਾ ਹੋਵੈ ॥ ਨਾਨਕ ਜੇ ਕੋ ਆਪੌ ਜਾਣੈ ਅਗੈ ਗਇਆ ਨ ਸੋਹੈ ॥ ੨੧

ਪਾਤਾਲਾ ਪਾਤਾਲ ਲਖ ਆਗਾਸਾ ਆਗਾਸ ॥ ਓੜਕ ਓੜਕ ਭਾਲਿ ਥਕੇ ਵੇਦ ਕਹਨਿ ਇਕ ਵਾਤ ॥
ਸਹਸ ਅਠਾਰਹ ਕਹਨਿ ਕਤੇਬਾ ਅਸੁ ਲੁ ਇਕੁ ਧਾਤੁ ॥ ਲੇਖਾ ਹੋਇ ਤ ਲਿਖੀਐ ਲੇਖੈ ਹੋਇ ਵਿਣਾਸੁ ॥
ਨਾਨਕ ਵਡਾ ਆਖੀਐ ਆਪੇ ਜਾਣੈ ਆਪੁ ॥ ੨੨

ਸਾਲਾਹੀ ਸਾਲਾਹ ਏਤੀ ਸੁਰਤਿ ਨ ਪਾਈਆ ॥ ਨਦੀਆ ਅਤੈ ਵਾਹ ਪਵਹਿ ਸਮੁੰਦਿ ਨ ਜਾਣੀਅਹਿ ॥
ਸਮੁੰਦ ਸਾਹ ਸੁਲਤਾਨ ਗਿਰਹਾ ਸੇਤੀ ਮਾਲ ਧਨੁ ॥ ਕੀੜੀ ਤੁਲਿ ਨ ਹੋਵਨੀ ਜੇ ਤਿਸੁ ਮਨਹੁ ਨ ਵੀਸਰਹਿ ॥ ੨੩

ਅੰਤੁ ਨ ਸਿਫਤੀ ਕਹਣਿ ਨ ਅੰਤੁ ॥ ਅੰਤੁ ਨ ਕਰਣੈ ਦੇਣਿ ਨ ਅੰਤੁ ॥
ਅੰਤੁ ਨ ਵੇਖਨਿ ਸੁਣਣਿ ਨ ਅੰਤੁ ॥ ਅੰਤੁ ਨ ਜਾਪੈ ਕਿਆ ਮਨਿ ਮੰਤੁ ॥
ਅੰਤੁ ਨ ਜਾਪੈ ਕੀ ਤਾ ਆਕਾਰੁ ॥ ਅੰਤੁ ਨ ਜਾਪੈ ਪਾਰਾਵਾਰੁ ॥
ਅੰਤੁ ਕਾਰਣਿ ਕੇਤੇ ਬਿਲਲਾਹਿ ॥ ਤਾ ਕੇ ਅੰਤੁ ਨ ਪਾਏ ਜਾਹਿ ॥
ਏਹੁ ਅੰਤੁ ਨ ਜਾਣੈ ਕੋਇ ॥ ਬਹੁਤਾ ਕਹੀਐ ਬਹੁਤਾ ਹੋਇ ॥
ਵਡਾ ਸਾਹਿਬੁ ਊਚਾ ਥਾਉ ॥ ਊਚੇ ਉਪਰਿ ਊਚਾ ਨਾਉ ॥
ਏਵਡੁ ਊਚਾ ਹੋਵੈ ਕੋਇ ॥ ਤਿਸੁ ਊਚੇ ਕਉ ਜਾਣੈ ਸੋਇ ॥
ਜੇਵਡੁ ਆਪਿ ਜਾਣੈ ਆਪਿ ਆਪਿ ॥ ਨਾਨਕ ਨਦਰੀ ਕਰਮੀ ਦਾਤਿ ॥ ੨੪

ਬਹੁਤਾ ਕਰਮੁ ਲਿਖਿਆ ਨਾ ਜਾਇ ॥ ਵਡਾ ਦਾਤਾ ਤਿਲੁ ਨ ਤਮਾਇ ॥
ਕੇਤੇ ਮੰਗਹਿ ਜੋਧ ਅਪਾਰ ॥ ਕੇਤਿਆ ਗਣਤ ਨਹੀ ਵੀਚਾਰ ॥
ਕੇਤੇ ਖਪਿ ਤੁਟਹਿ ਵੇਕਾਰ ॥
ਕੇਤੇ ਲੈਲੈ ਮੁਕਰੁ ਪਾਹਿ ॥ ਕੇਤੇ ਮੂਰਖ ਖਾਹੀ ਖਾਹਿ ॥
ਕੇਤਿਆ ਦੂਖ ਭੂਖ ਸਦ ਮਾਰ ॥ ਏਹਿ ਭਿ ਦਾਤਿ ਤੇਰੀ ਦਾਤਾਰ ॥
ਬੰਦਿ ਖਲਾਸੀ ਭਾਣੈ ਹੋਇ ॥ ਹੋਰੁ ਆਖਿ ਨ ਸਕੈ ਕੋਇ ॥
ਜੇ ਕੋ ਖਾਇ ਕੁਆਖਣਿ ਪਾਇ ॥ ਓਹੁ ਜਾਣੈ ਜੇਤੀਆ ਮੁਹਿ ਖਾਇ ॥
ਆਪੇ ਜਾਣੈ ਆਪੇ ਦੇਇ ॥ ਆਖਹਿ ਸਿ ਭਿ ਕੇਈ ਕੇਇ ॥
ਜਿਸ ਨੋ ਬਖਸੇ ਸਿਫਤਿ ਸਾਲਾਹ ॥ ਨਾਨਕ ਪਾਤਿਸਾਹੀ ਪਾਤਿਸਾਹ ॥ ੨੫

ਅਮੁਲ ਗੁਣ ਅਮੁਲ ਵਾਪਾਰ ॥ ਅਮੁਲ ਵਾਪਾਰੀਏ ਅਮੁਲ ਭੰਡਾਰ ॥
ਅਮੁਲ ਆਵਹਿ ਅਮੁਲ ਲੈ ਜਾਹਿ ॥ ਅਮੁਲ ਭਾਇ ਅਮੁਲ ਸਮਾਹਿ ॥

ਅਮੁਲੁ ਧਰਮੁ ਅਮੁਲੁ ਦੀਬਾਣੁ ॥ ਅਮੁਲੁ ਤੁਲੁ ਅਮੁਲੁ ਪਰਵਾਣੁ ॥
ਅਮੁਲੁ ਬਖਸੀਸ ਅਮੁਲੁ ਨੀਸਾਣੁ ॥ ਅਮੁਲੁ ਕਰਮੁ ਅਮੁਲੁ ਫੁਰਮਾਣੁ ॥
ਅਮੁਲੋ ਅਮੁਲੁ ਆਖਿਆ ਨ ਜਾਇ ॥ ਆਖਿ ਆਖਿ ਰਹੇ ਲਿਵ ਲਾਇ ॥
ਆਖਹਿ ਵੇਦ ਪਾਠ ਪੁਰਾਣ ॥ ਆਖਹਿ ਪੜੇ ਕਰਹਿ ਵਖਿਆਣ ॥
ਆਖਹਿ ਬਰਮੇ ਆਖਹਿ ਇੰਦ ॥ ਆਖਹਿ ਗੋਪੀ ਤੈ ਗੋਵਿੰਦ ॥
ਆਖਹਿ ਈਸਰ ਆਖਹਿ ਸਿਧ ॥ ਆਖਹਿ ਕੇਤੇ ਕੀਤੇ ਬੁਧ ॥
ਆਖਹਿ ਦਾਨਵ ਆਖਹਿ ਦੇਵ ॥ ਆਖਹਿ ਸੁਰਿ ਨਰ ਮੁਨਿ ਜਨ ਸੇਵ ॥
ਕੇਤੇ ਆਖਹਿ ਆਖਣਿ ਪਾਹਿ ॥ ਕੇਤੇ ਕਹਿ ਕਹਿ ਉਠਿ ਉਠਿ ਜਾਹਿ ॥
ਏਤੇ ਕੀਤੇ ਹੋਰਿ ਕਰੇਹਿ ॥ ਤਾ ਆਖਿ ਨ ਸਕਹਿ ਕੇਈ ਕੇਇ ॥
ਜੇਵਡੁ ਭਾਵੈ ਤੇਵਡੁ ਹੋਇ ॥ ਨਾਨਕ ਜਾਣੈ ਸਾਚਾ ਸੋਇ ॥
ਜੇ ਕੋ ਆਖੈ ਬੋਲੁ ਵਿਗਾੜੁ ॥ ਤਾ ਲਿਖੀਐ ਸਿਰਿ ਗਾਵਾਰਾ ਗਾਵਾਰੁ ॥ ੨੬

ਸੋ ਦਰੁ ਕੇਹਾ ਸੋ ਘਰੁ ਕੇਹਾ ਜਿਤੁ ਬਹਿ ਸਰਬ ਸਮਾਲੇ ॥ ਵਾਜੇ ਨਾਦ ਅਨੇਕ ਅਸੰਖਾ ਕੇਤੇ ਵਾਵਣਹਾਰੇ ॥
ਕੇਤੇ ਰਾਗ ਪਰੀ ਸਿਉ ਕਹੀਅਨਿ ਕੇਤੇ ਗਾਵਣਹਾਰੇ ॥ ਗਾਵਹਿ ਤੁਹ ਨੋ ਪਉਣੁ ਪਾਣੀ ਬੈਸੰਤਰੁ ਗਾਵੈ ਰਾਜਾ ਧਰਮੁ ਦੁਆਰੇ ॥
ਗਾਵਹਿ ਚਿਤੁਗੁਪਤੁ ਲਿਖਿ ਜਾਣਹਿ ਲਿਖਿ ਲਿਖਿ ਧਰਮੁ ਵੀਚਾਰੇ ॥ ਗਾਵਹਿ ਈਸਰੁ ਬਰਮਾ ਦੇਵੀ ਸੋਹਨਿ ਸਦਾ ਸਵਾਰੇ ॥
ਗਾਵਹਿ ਇੰਦ ਇਦਾਸਣਿ ਬੈਠੇ ਦੇਵਤਿਆ ਦਰਿ ਨਾਲੇ ॥ ਗਾਵਹਿ ਸਿਧ ਸਮਾਧੀ ਅੰਦਰਿ ਗਾਵਨਿ ਸਾਧ ਵਿਚਾਰੇ ॥
ਗਾਵਨਿ ਜਤੀ ਸਤੀ ਸੰਤੋਖੀ ਗਾਵਹਿ ਵੀਰ ਕਰਾਰੇ ॥ ਗਾਵਨਿ ਪੰਡਿਤ ਪੜਨਿ ਰਖੀਸਰ ਜੁਗ ਜੁਗ ਵੇਦਾ ਨਾਲੇ ॥
ਗਾਵਹਿ ਮੋਹਣੀਆ ਮਨੁ ਮੋਹਨਿ ਸੁਰਗਾ ਮਛ ਪਇਆਲੇ ॥ ਗਾਵਨਿ ਰਤਨ ਉਪਾਏ ਤੇਰੇ ਅਠਸਠਿ ਤੀਰਥ ਨਾਲੇ ॥
ਗਾਵਹਿ ਜੋਧ ਮਹਾਬਲ ਸੂਰਾ ਗਾਵਹਿ ਖਾਣੀ ਚਾਰੇ ॥ ਗਾਵਹਿ ਖੰਡ ਮੰਡਲ ਵਰਭੰਡਾ ਕਰਿਕਰਿ ਰਖੇ ਧਾਰੇ ॥
ਸੇਈ ਤੁਧ ਨੋ ਗਾਵਹਿ ਜੋ ਤੁਧ ਭਾਵਨਿ ਰਤੇ ਤੇਰੇ ਭਗਤ ਰਸਾਲੇ ॥ ਹੋਰਿ ਕੇਤੇ ਗਾਵਨਿ ਸੇ ਮੈ ਚਿਤਿ ਨ ਆਵਨਿ ਨਾਨਕੁ ਕਿਆ ਵੀਚਾਰੇ ॥
ਸੋਈ ਸੋਈ ਸਦਾ ਸਚੁ ਸਾਹਿਬੁ ਸਾਚਾ ਸਾਚੀ ਨਾਈ ॥ ਹੈ ਭੀ ਹੋਸੀ ਜਾਇ ਨ ਜਾਸੀ ਰਚਨਾ ਜਿਨਿ ਰਚਾਈ ॥
ਰੰਗੀ ਰੰਗੀ ਭਾਤੀ ਕਰਿਕਰਿ ਜਿਨਸੀ ਮਾਇਆ ਜਿਨਿ ਉਪਾਈ ॥ ਕਰਿਕਰਿ ਵੇਖੈ ਕੀਤਾ ਆਪਣਾ ਜਿਵ ਤਿਸ ਦੀ ਵਡਿਆਈ ॥
ਜੋ ਤਿਸੁ ਭਾਵੈ ਸੋਈ ਕਰਸੀ ਹੁਕਮੁ ਨ ਕਰਣਾ ਜਾਈ ॥ ਸੋ ਪਾਤਿਸਾਹੁ ਸਾਹਾ ਪਾਤਿ ਸਾਹਿਬੁ ਨਾਨਕ ਰਹਣੁ ਰਜਾਈ ॥ ੨੭

ਮੁੰਦਾ ਸੰਤੋਖੁ ਸਰਮੁ ਪਤੁ ਝੋਲੀ ਧਿਆਨ ਕੀ ਕਰਹਿ ਬਿਭੂਤਿ ॥ ਖਿੰਥਾ ਕਾਲੁ ਕੁਆਰੀ ਕਾਇਆ ਜੁਗਤਿ ਡੰਡਾ ਪਰਤੀਤਿ ॥
ਆਈਪੰਥੀ ਸਗਲ ਜਮਾਤੀ ਮਨਿ ਜੀਤੈ ਜਗੁ ਜੀਤੁ ॥
ਆਦੇਸੁ ਤਿਸੈ ਆਦੇਸੁ ॥ ਆਦਿ ਅਨੀਲੁ ਅਨਾਦਿ ਅਨਾਹਤਿ ਜੁਗੁ ਜੁਗੁ ਏਕੋ ਵੇਸੁ ॥ ੨੮

ਭੁਗਤਿ ਗਿਆਨੁ ਦਇਆ ਭੰਡਾਰਣਿ ਘਟਿ ਘਟਿ ਵਾਜਹਿ ਨਾਦ ॥ ਆਪਿ ਨਾਥੁ ਨਾਥੀ ਸਭ ਜਾ ਕੀ ਰਿਧਿ ਸਿਧਿ ਅਵਰਾ ਸਾਦ ॥
ਸੰਜੋਗੁ ਵਿਜੋਗੁ ਦੁਇ ਕਾਰ ਚਲਾਵਹਿ ਲੇਖੇ ਆਵਹਿ ਭਾਗ ॥
ਆਦੇਸੁ ਤਿਸੈ ਆਦੇਸੁ ॥ ਆਦਿ ਅਨੀਲੁ ਅਨਾਦਿ ਅਨਾਹਤਿ ਜੁਗੁ ਜੁਗੁ ਏਕੋ ਵੇਸੁ ॥ ੨੯

ਏਕਾ ਮਾਈ ਜੁਗਤਿ ਵਿਆਈ ਤਿਨਿ ਚੇਲੇ ਪਰਵਾਣੁ ॥ ਇਕੁ ਸੰਸਾਰੀ ਇਕੁ ਭੰਡਾਰੀ ਇਕੁ ਲਾਏ ਦੀਬਾਣੁ ॥
ਜਿਵ ਤਿਸੁ ਭਾਵੈ ਤਿਵੈ ਚਲਾਵੈ ਜਿਵ ਹੋਵੈ ਫੁਰਮਾਣੁ ॥ ਓਹੁ ਵੇਖੈ ਓਨਾ ਨਦਰਿ ਨ ਆਵੈ ਬਹੁਤਾ ਏਹੁ ਵਿਡਾਣੁ ॥
ਆਦੇਸੁ ਤਿਸੈ ਆਦੇਸੁ ॥ ਆਦਿ ਅਨੀਲੁ ਅਨਾਦਿ ਅਨਾਹਤਿ ਜੁਗੁ ਜੁਗੁ ਏਕੋ ਵੇਸੁ ॥ ੩੦

ਆਸਣੁ ਲੋਇ ਲੋਇ ਭੰਡਾਰ ॥ ਜੋ ਕਿਛੁ ਪਾਇਆ ਸੁ ਏਕਾ ਵਾਰ ॥
ਕਰਿਕਰਿ ਵੇਖੈ ਸਿਰਜਣਹਾਰ ॥ ਨਾਨਕ ਸਚੇ ਕੀ ਸਾਚੀ ਕਾਰ ॥
ਆਦੇਸੁ ਤਿਸੈ ਆਦੇਸੁ ॥ ਆਦਿ ਅਨੀਲੁ ਅਨਾਦਿ ਅਨਾਹਤਿ ਜੁਗੁ ਜੁਗੁ ਏਕੋ ਵੇਸੁ ॥ ੩੧

ਇਕ ਦੂ ਜੀਭੌ ਲਖ ਹੋਹਿ ਲਖ ਹੋਵਹਿ ਲਖ ਵੀਸ ॥ ਲਖੁ ਲਖੁ ਗੇੜਾ ਆਖੀਅਹਿ ਏਕੁ ਨਾਮੁ ਜਗਦੀਸ ॥
ਏਤੁ ਰਾਹਿ ਪਤਿ ਪਵੜੀਆ ਚੜੀਐ ਹੋਇ ਇਕੀਸ ॥ ਸੁਣਿ ਗਲਾ ਆਕਾਸ ਕੀ ਕੀਟਾ ਆਈ ਰੀਸ ॥
ਨਾਨਕ ਨਦਰੀ ਪਾਈਐ ਕੂੜੀ ਕੂੜੈ ਠੀਸ ॥ ੩੨

ਆਖਣਿ ਜੋਰੁ ਚੁਪੈ ਨਹ ਜੋਰੁ ॥ ਜੋਰੁ ਨ ਮੰਗਣਿ ਦੇਣਿ ਨ ਜੋਰੁ ॥
ਜੋਰੁ ਨ ਜੀਵਣਿ ਮਰਣਿ ਨਹ ਜੋਰੁ ॥ ਜੋਰੁ ਨ ਰਾਜਿ ਮਾਲਿ ਮਨਿ ਸੋਰੁ ॥
ਜੋਰੁ ਨ ਸੁਰਤੀ ਗਿਆਨਿ ਵੀਚਾਰਿ ॥ ਜੋਰੁ ਨ ਜੁਗਤੀ ਛੁਟੈ ਸੰਸਾਰੁ ॥
ਜਿਸੁ ਹਥਿ ਜੋਰੁ ਕਰਿ ਵੇਖੈ ਸੋਇ ॥ ਨਾਨਕ ਉਤਮੁ ਨੀਚੁ ਨ ਕੋਇ ॥ ੩੩

ਰਾਤੀ ਰੁਤੀ ਥਿਤੀ ਵਾਰ ॥ ਪਵਣ ਪਾਣੀ ਅਗਨੀ ਪਾਤਾਲ ॥
ਤਿਸੁ ਵਿਚਿ ਧਰਤੀ ਥਾਪਿ ਰਖੀ ਧਰਮਸਾਲ ॥
ਤਿਸੁ ਵਿਚਿ ਜੀਅ ਜੁਗਤਿ ਕੇ ਰੰਗ ॥ ਤਿਨ ਕੇ ਨਾਮ ਅਨੇਕ ਅਨੰਤ ॥
ਕਰਮੀ ਕਰਮੀ ਹੋਇ ਵੀਚਾਰੁ ॥ ਸਚਾ ਆਪਿ ਸਚਾ ਦਰਬਾਰੁ ॥
ਤਿਥੈ ਸੋਹਨਿ ਪੰਚ ਪਰਵਾਣੁ ॥ ਨਦਰੀ ਕਰਮਿ ਪਵੈ ਨੀਸਾਣੁ ॥
ਕਚ ਪਕਾਈ ਓਥੈ ਪਾਇ ॥ ਨਾਨਕ ਗਇਆ ਜਾਪੈ ਜਾਇ ॥ ੩੪

ਧਰਮ ਖੰਡ ਕਾ ਏਹੋ ਧਰਮੁ ॥ ਗਿਆਨ ਖੰਡ ਕਾ ਆਖਹੁ ਕਰਮੁ ॥
ਕੇਤੇ ਪਵਣ ਪਾਣੀ ਵੈਸੰਤਰ ਕੇਤੇ ਕਾਨ ਮਹੇਸ ॥ ਕੇਤੇ ਬਰਮੇ ਘਾੜਤਿ ਘੜੀਅਹਿ ਰੂਪ ਰੰਗ ਕੇ ਵੇਸ ॥
ਕੇਤੀਆ ਕਰਮਭੂਮੀ ਮੇਰ ਕੇਤੇ ਕੇਤੇ ਧੂ ਉਪਦੇਸ ॥ ਕੇਤੇ ਇੰਦ ਚੰਦ ਸੂਰ ਕੇਤੇ ਕੇਤੇ ਮੰਡਲ ਦੇਸ ॥
ਕੇਤੇ ਸਿਧ ਬੁਧ ਨਾਥ ਕੇਤੇ ਕੇਤੇ ਦੇਵੀ ਵੇਸ ॥
ਕੇਤੇ ਦੇਵ ਦਾਨਵ ਮੁਨਿ ਕੇਤੇ ਕੇਤੇ ਰਤਨ ਸਮੁੰਦ ॥ ਕੇਤੀਆ ਖਾਣੀ ਕੇਤੀਆ ਬਾਣੀ ਕੇਤੇ ਪਾਤ ਨਰਿੰਦ ॥
ਕੇਤੀਆ ਸੁਰਤੀ ਸੇਵਕ ਕੇਤੇ ਨਾਨਕ ਅੰਤੁ ਨ ਅੰਤੁ ॥ ੩੫

ਗਿਆਨ ਖੰਡ ਮਹਿ ਗਿਆਨ ਪਰਚੰਡੁ ॥ ਤਿਥੈ ਨਾਦ ਬਿਨੋਦ ਕੋਡ ਅਨੰਦੁ ॥
ਸਰਮ ਖੰਡ ਕੀ ਬਾਣੀ ਰੂਪੁ ॥ ਤਿਥੈ ਘਾੜਤਿ ਘੜੀਐ ਬਹੁਤੁ ਅਨੂਪੁ ॥
ਤਾ ਕੀਆ ਗਲਾ ਕਥੀਆ ਨ ਜਾਹਿ ॥ ਜੇ ਕੋ ਕਹੈ ਪਿਛੈ ਪਛੁਤਾਇ ॥
ਤਿਥੈ ਘੜੀਐ ਸੁਰਤਿ ਮਤਿ ਮਨਿ ਬੁਧਿ ॥ ਤਿਥੈ ਘੜੀਐ ਸੁਰਾ ਸਿਧਾ ਕੀ ਸੁਧਿ ॥ ੩੬

ਕਰਮ ਖੰਡ ਕੀ ਬਾਣੀ ਜੋਰੁ ॥ ਤਿਥੈ ਹੋਰੁ ਨ ਕੋਈ ਹੋਰੁ ॥
ਤਿਥੈ ਜੋਧ ਮਹਾਬਲ ਸੂਰ ॥ ਤਿਨ ਮਹਿ ਰਾਮੁ ਰਹਿਆ ਭਰਪੂਰ ॥
ਤਿਥੈ ਸੀਤੋ ਸੀਤਾ ਮਹਿਮਾ ਮਾਹਿ ॥ ਤਾ ਕੇ ਰੂਪ ਨ ਕਥਨੇ ਜਾਹਿ ॥
ਨ ਓਹਿ ਮਰਹਿ ਨ ਠਾਗੇ ਜਾਹਿ ॥ ਜਿਨ ਕੈ ਰਾਮੁ ਵਸੈ ਮਨ ਮਾਹਿ ॥
ਤਿਥੈ ਭਗਤ ਵਸਹਿ ਕੇ ਲੋਅ ॥ ਕਰਹਿ ਅਨੰਦੁ ਸਚਾ ਮਨਿ ਸੋਇ ॥
ਸਚ ਖੰਡਿ ਵਸੈ ਨਿਰੰਕਾਰ ॥ ਕਰਿਕਰਿ ਵੇਖੈ ਨਦਰਿ ਨਿਹਾਲ ॥

ਤਿਥੈ ਖੰਡ ਮੰਡਲ ਵਰਭੰਡ ॥ ਜੇ ਕੋ ਕਥੈ ਤ ਅੰਤ ਨ ਅੰਤ ॥
ਤਿਥੈ ਲੋਅ ਲੋਅ ਆਕਾਰ ॥ ਜਿਵ ਜਿਵ ਹੁਕਮੁ ਤਿਵੈ ਤਿਵ ਕਾਰ ॥
ਵੇਖੈ ਵਿਗਸੈ ਕਰਿ ਵੀਚਾਰ ॥ ਨਾਨਕ ਕਥਨਾ ਕਰੜਾ ਸਾਰ ॥ ੩੭

ਜਤੁ ਪਾਹਾਰਾ ਧੀਰਜੁ ਸੁਨਿਆਰੁ ॥ ਅਹਰਣਿ ਮਤਿ ਵੇਦੁ ਹਥੀਆਰੁ ॥
ਭਉ ਖਲਾ ਅਗਨਿ ਤਪ ਤਾਉ ॥
ਭਾਂਡਾ ਭਾਉ ਅਮ੍ਰਿਤ ਤਿਤੁ ਢਾਲਿ ॥ ਘੜੀਐ ਸਬਦੁ ਸਚੀ ਟਕਸਾਲ ॥
ਜਿਨ ਕਉ ਨਦਰਿ ਕਰਮੁ ਤਿਨ ਕਾਰ ॥ ਨਾਨਕ ਨਦਰੀ ਨਦਰਿ ਨਿਹਾਲ ॥ ੩੮

ਸਲੋਕੁ

ਪਵਣੁ ਗੁਰੂ ਪਾਣੀ ਪਿਤਾ ਮਾਤਾ ਧਰਤਿ ਮਹਤੁ ॥ ਦਿਵਸੁ ਰਾਤਿ ਦੁਇ ਦਾਈ ਦਾਇਆ ਖੇਲੈ ਸਗਲ ਜਗਤੁ ॥
ਚੰਗਿਆਈਆ ਬੁਰਿਆਈਆ ਵਾਚੈ ਧਰਮੁ ਹਦੂਰਿ ॥ ਕਰਮੀਂ ਆਪੇ ਆਪਣੀ ਕੇ ਨੇੜੈ ਕੇ ਦੂਰਿ ॥
ਜਿਨੀ ਨਾਮੁ ਧਿਆਇਆ ਗਏ ਮਸਕਤਿ ਘਾਲਿ ॥ ਨਾਨਕ ਤੇ ਮੁਖ ਉਜਲੇ ਕੇਤੀ ਛੁਟੀ ਨਾਲਿ ॥ ੧

END OF THE JAPJĪ.

STEPHEN AUSTIN AND SONS, PRINTERS, HERTFORD.

Printed in the USA
CPSIA information can be obtained
at www.ICGtesting.com
CBHW081247170524
8663CB00032B/664

9 789353 898847